Fodor's 2010

ENGLAND

Where to Stay and Eat
for All Budgets

Must-See Sights
and Local Secrets

Ratings You Can Trust

Fodor's Travel Publications   New York, Toronto, London, Sydney, Auckland
www.fodors.com

FODOR'S ENGLAND 2010

Editors: Linda Cabasin (*lead project editor*), Jess Moss

Writers: Robert Andrews, Christi Daugherty, Julius Honnor, Kate Hughes, Jack Jewers, Ellin Stein, Roger Thomas, Christina Valhouli, Alex Wijeratna

Production Editor: Carrie Parker
Maps & Illustrations: David Lindroth, Inc.; Ed Jacobus, *cartographers*; Bob Blake, Rebecca Baer, *map editors*; William Wu, *information graphics*
Design: Fabrizio La Rocca, *creative director*; Guido Caroti, Siobhan O'Hare, *art directors*; Tina Malaney, Chie Ushio, Ann McBride, Jessica Walsh, *designers*; Melanie Marin, *senior picture editor*
Cover Photo: Yellow Dog Productions/The Image Bank/Getty Images
Production Manager: Angela L. McLean

ISBN 978-1-4000-0861-2

ISSN 1558–870X

SPECIAL SALES

This book is available at special discounts for bulk purchases for sales promotions or premiums. Special editions, including personalized covers, excerpts of existing books, and corporate imprints, can be created in large quantities for special needs. For more information, write to Special Markets/Premium Sales, 1745 Broadway, MD 6-2, New York, New York 10019, or e-mail specialmarkets@randomhouse.com.

AN IMPORTANT TIP & AN INVITATION

Although all prices, opening times, and other details in this book are based on information supplied to us at press time, changes occur all the time in the travel world, and Fodor's cannot accept responsibility for facts that become outdated or for inadvertent errors or omissions. So **always confirm information when it matters**, especially if you're making a detour to visit a specific place. Your experiences—positive and negative—matter to us. If we have missed or misstated something, **please write to us.** We follow up on all suggestions. Contact the England editor at editors@fodors.com or c/o Fodor's at 1745 Broadway, New York, NY 10019.

PRINTED IN THE UNITED STATES OF AMERICA

10 9 8 7 6 5 4 3 2 1

Your opinion matters. It matters to us. It matters to your fellow Fodor...
too. And we'd like to hear it. In fact, we need to hear it.

When you share your experiences and opinions, you become an active membe...
Fodor's community. That means we'll not only use your feedback to make our t...
better, but we'll publish your names and comments whenever possible. Through
our guides, look for "Word of Mouth," excerpts of your unvarnished feedback.

Here's how you can help improve Fodor's for all of us.

Tell us when we're right. We rely on local writers to give you an insider's perspective. But our writers and staff editors—who are the best in the business—depend on you. Your positive feedback is a vote to renew our recommendations for the next edition.

Tell us when we're wrong. We're proud that we update most of our guides every year. But we're not perfect. Things change. Hotels cut services. Museums change hours. Charming cafés lose charm. If our writer didn't quite capture the essence of a place, tell us how you'd do it differently. If any of our descriptions are inaccurate or inadequate, we'll incorporate your changes in the next edition and will correct factual errors at fodors.com immediately.

Tell us what to include. You probably have had fantastic travel experiences that aren't yet in Fodor's. Why not share them with a community of like-minded travelers? Maybe you chanced upon a beach or bistro or B&B that you don't want to keep to yourself. Tell us why we should include it. And share your discoveries and experiences with everyone directly at fodors.com. Your input may lead us to add a new listing or highlight a place we cover with a "Highly Recommended" star or with our highest rating, "Fodor's Choice."

Give us your opinion instantly at our feedback center at www.fodors.com/feedback. You may also e-mail editors@fodors.com with the subject line "England Editor." Or send your nominations, comments, and complaints by mail to England Editor, Fodor's, 1745 Broadway, New York, NY 10019.

You and travelers like you are the heart of the Fodor's community. Make our community richer by sharing your experiences. Be a Fodor's correspondent.

Happy traveling!

Tim Jarrell, Publisher

~~TS~~

MAPS

ABOUT THIS BOOK

Our Ratings

Sometimes you find terrific travel experiences and sometimes they just find you. But usually the burden is on you to select the right combination of experiences. That's where our ratings come in.

As travelers we've all discovered a place so wonderful that its worthiness is obvious. And sometimes superlatives don't do that place justice: you just have to be there to know. These sights, properties, and experiences get our highest rating, **Fodor's Choice** indicated by orange stars throughout this book.

Black stars highlight sights and properties we deem **Highly Recommended** places that our writers, editors, and readers praise again and again for consistency and excellence.

There's another category: any place we include in this book is by definition worth your time, unless we say otherwise. And we will.

Disagree with any of our choices? Care to nominate a place or suggest that we rate one more highly? Visit our feedback center at www.fodors.com/feedback.

Budget Well

Hotel and restaurant price categories from £ to ££££ are defined in the opening pages of each chapter. For attractions, we always give standard adult admission fees; reductions are usually available for children, students, and senior citizens. Want to pay with plastic? **AE, DC, MC, V** following restaurant and hotel listings indicate whether American Express, Diners Club, MasterCard, and Visa are accepted.

Restaurants

Unless we state otherwise, restaurants are open for lunch and dinner daily. We mention dress only when there's a specific requirement and reservations only when they're essential or not accepted—it's always best to book ahead.

Hotels

Hotels have private bath, phone, TV, and air-conditioning and operate on the European Plan (aka EP, meaning without meals), unless we specify that they use the Continental Plan (CP, with a continental breakfast), Breakfast Plan (BP, with a full breakfast), or Modified American Plan (MAP, with breakfast and dinner). We always list facilities but not whether you'll be charged an extra fee to use them, so when pricing accommodations, find out what's included.

Many Listings

★	Fodor's Choice
★	Highly recommended
✉	Physical address
✛	Directions
✿	Mailing address
☎	Telephone
🖷	Fax
⊕	On the Web
✉	E-mail
🖾	Admission fee
☉	Open/closed times
Ⓤ	Metro stations
▭	Credit cards

Hotels & Restaurants

🏠	Hotel
⇶	Number of rooms
⚘	Facilities
⦿	Meal plans
✕	Restaurant
⌂	Reservations
⬔	Smoking
🍷	BYOB

Other

ℭ	Family-friendly
⇨	See also
✉	Branch address
☞	Take note

1

Experience England

WORD OF MOUTH

"Quintessential England has little to do with sites or sights. It's an attitude of mind, easily accessible by keeping Radio 4 on, interspersed with Radio 1. By reading ALL the tabloids and keeping up with Coronation Street and East Enders. By going round the Liverpool pubs, just as much as the Ye Olde Innes in the pretty villages."

—flanneruk

WHAT'S WHERE

The following numbers refer to chapters.

2 London. Not only Britain's financial and governmental center but also one of the world's great cities, London has mammoth museums, posh palaces, double-decker buses, and iconic sights such as Big Ben. Intriguing villagelike neighborhoods from Notting Hill to Bloomsbury call out to be explored; when you need a break, pop into a pub or relax in one of the city's sprawling parks.

3 The Southeast. This compact green and pleasant region within day-trip distance of London takes in Canterbury and its cathedral, funky seaside Brighton, the appealing towns of Rye and Lewes, Dover's white cliffs, and castles such as Bodiam, Leeds, and Hever. Noted gardens as different as smaller, romantic Sissinghurst and large-scale Wisley add to the mix.

4 The South. Hampshire, Dorset, and Wiltshire are quintessential English countryside, with gentle hills and green pastures. Explore the stone circles at Stonehenge and Avebury, Winchester (Jane Austen country) and Salisbury, and Lyme Regis and the fossil-rich Jurassic Coast.

5 The West Country. Somerset, Devon, and Cornwall are sunnier and warmer than the rest of the country, with sandy beaches. Cornwall has lush gardens and stunning coast, Bristol is a vibrant city, and Wells and Exeter are pretty towns. Take in the brooding heaths and moors of Exmoor and Dartmoor, too.

6 The Thames Valley. London's commuter belt takes in Windsor, where the Queen spends time. Then there are the spires of Oxford, peaceful river towns such as Henley and Marlow, and stately homes such as over-the-top Blenheim Palace.

7 Shakespeare Country. Stratford-upon-Avon, a leafy, literary, theatrical town 100 mi north of London, is the place to see Shakespeare's birthplace and watch his plays. Warwickshire has gentle landscapes as well as noble Warwick and Kenilworth castles.

8 Bath and the Cotswolds. The grand Georgian town of Bath is one of England's highlights, with its Roman Baths and golden-stone 18th- and 19th-century architecture. Nearby, pretty as a picture, the Cotswolds region is justly famous for its tranquil villages, stone cottages, and gardens.

WHAT'S WHERE

9 The Welsh Borders. This lovely rural area bordering Wales has few real sights except the Industrial Revolution museums of Ironbridge Gorge; it's a good place to relax. Ludlow has half-timber buildings, and medieval Shrewsbury is a fine excursion; Chester draws the tourists. Birmingham offers a modern urban experience.

10 Lancashire and the Peaks. Liverpool rides the Beatles' coattails but, like Manchester, has transformed its warehouses and docks into sleek hotels, restaurants, and shops. Buzzing nightlife and museums are highlights. The Peak District has great walking and stately homes such as Chatsworth and Haddon Hall.

11 The Lake District. A national park, this is a startlingly beautiful area of craggy hills, wild moorland, stone cottages, and glittering silvery lakes. Nature lovers and hikers crowd the area in summer. Among the literary high points are Wordsworth's homes.

12 East Anglia. The biggest lure in this green, flat, low-key region is Cambridge, with its medieval halls of learning. The countryside is dominated by the cathedrals of Ely and Norwich and by time-warp towns such as Lavenham. Coastal spots from Aldeburgh to Wells-next-the-Sea add a salty flavor.

13 Yorkshire. This wilder part of England has great appeal for lovers of the outdoors, but ancient walled York is also a center of attention. To York's west are the moors and dales that inspired the Brontës, and in east Yorkshire the moors collide with the sea at Whitby. Leeds is a reviving urban center worth a look.

14 The Northeast. Travelers can walk in the footsteps of Roman soldiers along Hadrian's Wall in this remote northern region. Bamburgh and Dunstanburgh castles guard the coast; Alnwick Castle has stunning gardens. Durham is a medieval gem, a contrast to modern Newcastle.

15 Wales. Clinging to the western edge of England, Wales is green and ruggedly beautiful, with mountainous inland scenery reaching out to a magnificent coastline. Except for Cardiff and Swansea, this is a rural region, with three national parks. Wales is justly famous for castles, including Conwy and Caernarfon.

ENGLAND PLANNER

When to Go

The English tourist season peaks from mid-April to mid-October, and many historic houses close from October to Easter. During July and August, when most of the British take vacations, accommodations in popular resorts and areas are in high demand and at their most expensive. The winter cultural season in London is lively. Hotel rates are lower then, too. Spring and fall can be good alternatives, as prices are still below high-season rates, and the crowds are thinner.

Generally, the climate in England and Wales is mild. Summer temperatures can reach the 90s, with high humidity. In winter there can be heavy frost, thin snow, thick fog, and rain, rain, rain. Here are average daily maximum and minimum temperatures for two cities.

°F   LONDON   °C

°F   MANCHESTER   °C

Getting Here

You can arrive in England by plane, train, or boat, and there are many places to disembark. Most international flights arrive at either London's Heathrow Airport (LHR) or at Gatwick Airport (LGW). A third, much smaller airport, Stansted (STN), handles mainly European and domestic traffic, as does Luton Airport (LLA). These airports have good train and bus options for getting into London.

Manchester (MAN) in northwest England handles some flights from the United States, as does Birmingham (BHX) in the Midlands. Most people fly into London, but other airports can be useful. *For more details, see Getting Here and Around in Travel Smart England.*

Getting Around

England is not a large country: the entire United Kingdom (including England, Scotland, Wales, and Northern Ireland) is about the size of Oregon, so you're less likely to fly. The country's train and bus systems are extensive and relatively well maintained; for major towns and cities, there is generally no need to rent a car. To see castles and historic houses—which may be far from towns—you may have to rent a car or join a tour. Driving is on the left, and gas (petrol) is expensive at about $7 a gallon.

Train tickets tend to be two to three times more expensive than bus fares, but train journeys are at least twice as fast as bus journeys. *For more details, see Getting Here and Around in Travel Smart England.*

FROM LONDON TO	BY CAR	BY TRAIN
Newquay, Cornwall	5½ hours	5 hours
The Lake District	5½ hours	4 hours
York	4 hours	2–3 hours
Liverpool	4 hours	3 hours
Bath	1½ hours	2½ hours
The Cotswolds	1½ hours	2 hours
Oxford	1½ hours	1 hour

Restaurants: The Basics

What you should eat in England depends on where you are, as food is surprisingly regional. Fresh seafood dominates the coastal areas, but lamb and beef lead the way in the inland regions. Local cuisine is also affected by ethnic communities. Although England is increasingly a foodie country with a good restaurant scene, the strongest food culture is still limited to major cities and a few regions, most notably London and the Southeast.

In the rural north—Cumbria, Yorkshire, and Northumberland—you'll get hearty meals in family-friendly pubs and inns. York and Harrogate have better options, and Leeds has a burgeoning food subscene. Look for local lamb and beef. Birmingham, in the Midlands, is famous for its Indian restaurants serving spicy curries. In Cornwall, Devon, and Dorset, it's all about fresh seafood that is some of the country's best. However, don't overlook Cornish pasties (hand-size meat-and-potato pies), sold everywhere. *For details and a price-category chart, see Eating Out in Travel Smart England.*

Lodging: The Basics

London is in part about sleek, modern hotels, where enormous amounts of money get you relatively small amounts of space. One way to get a good deal is to book a chain—such as Millennium or Premier—online well in advance. Check for off-season deals, too. Budget hotels in London can be so unattractive that it's better to look for a special offer at a better chain.

In major towns, you have more options than in rural areas. Hotels are harder to come by in the countryside, and you may stay in a small bed-and-breakfast in a family's home. Prices may be half or less of what you'll pay in London. Some B&Bs are gorgeous, and many are in handy locations; others are neither, so be careful. B&Bs are popular with British travelers and can be a great way to meet locals.

You might also stay in an old coaching inn from the stagecoach era. There are modern twists on the theme, with chains operating cheap modern hotels with bland pub-restaurants. Some older hotels can be old-fashioned but also less pricey. House and apartment rentals can be a good, sometimes cheaper alternative to hotels. *For details and a price-category chart, see the Lodging Primer in this chapter and Accommodations in Travel Smart England.*

Saving Money

Throughout this book and in the Travel Smart England section, you'll find advice for pinching your pence.

Food can be a big cost, so consider these tactics:

■ Take advantage of free breakfasts if your hotel or B&B offers them. Or grab a croissant at a coffee shop.

■ Many pubs serve lunches for less than £10; most restaurants offer cheap lunch deals.

■ Make one meal a prepared sandwich from a grocery store or sandwich shop.

Lodging can seem expensive, but you can get more for your money:

■ In London, consider staying in a house or apartment.

■ Outside of London, stay in a B&B or small guesthouse.

■ Check the Web sites of major chains for deals, especially in the off-season.

You can save big on sightseeing and getting around:

■ Buy a prepaid Oyster Card in London to save on the Tube and buses.

■ Ask about family tickets at major sights.

■ Get your culture kicks in free national museums.

■ Check out a sightseeing pass such as the Great British Heritage Pass.

■ Purchase a BritRail train pass or regional passes.

MAKING THE MOST OF YOUR POUNDS

The world economic situation has brought challenges, but the exchange rate has benefited travelers to England. Greenbacks can punch above their weight with a few well-chosen strategies, and you can still have a fabulously rich travel experience. Travelers posting on the Travel Talk forums at Fodors.com recommend the following budget-saving tips:

"The Great British Heritage Pass, available from www.visitbritain.com, saved us a ton of money versus buying individual tickets! With a seven-day pass, we saw Blenheim Palace, Warwick Castle, Chatsworth, Haddon Hall, Lacock Abbey, Stourhead, and more." —ElendilPickle

"As with anywhere else, once you get out of the larger centers prices drop, sometimes dramatically. We have found northern England and Wales to be cheaper than southern England, for example. And if you are willing to get off the beaten track, you can find some wonderful pubs, B&Bs, etc." —travel2live2

"U.K. grocery stores have a much larger selection of ready-to-eat items than most stores in the U.S. It's so easy to get a picnic lunch or dinner together for so much less than you'd spend at a restaurant." —jent103

"Lots of university dorms in London offer accommodation at a low price during school breaks (summer and Christmas). Some dorms have ensuite rooms and some even offer breakfast. All the dorms have a shared kitchen." —yk

"Train tickets do not have to be expensive if booked far enough in advance. There are various railcards that can save you money on off-peak travel, too." —RM67

"B&Bs and self-catering are definitely the way to go. My husband and I set ourselves the challenge of finding a B&B for £60 pounds per night for a double. Tops. We normally find 4-star B&Bs for that price—even a few 5 stars. B&Bs are cheaper and smaller than guesthouses as well." —travel2live2

"When booking a cottage, check the agency Web site for 'latest offers' or 'deals.' Sometimes you can get up to 30% off the price. Also, if there are only two of you, ask if you can get a discount. If a cottage has two or three bedrooms, the owners will be happy not to have to do all that linen." —rickmav

"Don't stick to the main streets in touristy areas when you are looking for a quick bite to eat or a sit-down with a cup of coffee. Walk a street or two away from the main area and you'll find places that serve the locals—at much better prices. At lunchtime follow the office workers." —nona1

"Most bus companies offer day passes—usually called Day Rover and often about the cost of a one-way short-distance ticket, but good for unlimited rides within the company's network on the same day. The ticket is sold by the bus driver." —JudyC

"Don't forget that there are plenty of fantastic museums in the U.K. with free entry, anything from the British Museum in London (I could spend a week there) to the Museum of Science and Industry in Manchester and the fantastic railway museum in York." —Maria_H

"I've traveled during the off season and it has its advantages. Things are cheaper, no lines to see attractions, and it's not overrun with the tourist hordes." —ronnie36

ENGLAND LODGING PRIMER

If your England dreams involve staying in a cozy cottage with a tidy garden, here's some good news: you won't have to break the budget. Throughout the country, you'll find stylish lodging options—from good-value hotels and intimate bed-and-breakfasts to chic apartments and historic houses—in all price ranges.

Hotels

England is a popular vacation destination, so be sure to reserve hotel rooms weeks (months for London) in advance. The country has everything from budget chain hotels to luxurious retreats in converted country houses. In many towns and cities you will find old inns that are former coaching inns, which served travelers as they journeyed around the country in horse-drawn carriages and stagecoaches. Tourist Information Centres will reserve rooms, usually for a small fee.

Apartments and House Rentals

For a home base roomy enough for a family and that comes with cooking facilities, consider renting furnished "flats" (the word for apartments in England) or houses. These are popular throughout the country and can save you money, especially if you're traveling with a group, and provide more privacy than a hotel or B&B.

Bed-and-Breakfasts

A special English tradition, and the backbone of budget travel, B&Bs are usually in a family home. Typical prices (outside of London) range from £45 to £100 a night. They vary in style and grace, but these days most have private bathrooms. B&Bs range from the ordinary to the truly elegant. Guesthouses are a slightly larger and sometimes more luxurious version of the same thing.

Tourist Information Centres in cities and towns can help you find and book a B&B even on the day you show up in town. There are also many private services. *For reservation services in London, see the Where to Stay section in Chapter 2.*

Cottages

Cottages and other houses are available for weekly rental in all areas of the country. These vary from quaint older homes to brand-new buildings in scenic surroundings. For families and large groups, they offer the best value-for-money accommodations, but because they are often in isolated locations, a car is vital. Lists of rental properties are available free of charge from VisitBritain. You may find discounts of up to 50% on rentals during the off-season (October through March).

Farmhouses

Farmhouses have become increasingly popular; their special appeal is the rural experience. Consider this option only if you are touring by car, since farmhouses may be in remote locations. Prices are generally reasonable. Ask VisitBritain for the booklet "Stay on a Farm" or contact Farm Stay UK. Regional tourist boards may have information as well.

Historic Buildings

Want to spend your vacation in a Gothic banqueting house, an old lighthouse, or maybe in an apartment at Hampton Court Palace? Several organizations, such as the Landmark Trust, National Trust, English Heritage, and Vivat Trust, have specially adapted historic buildings to rent. Many of these have kitchens.

For a price chart, resources, and information on hotel grading and booking, see Essentials in Travel Smart England.

ENGLAND
TOP ATTRACTIONS

Houses of Parliament and Big Ben

(A) One of the world's most famous sights, the gold-tipped towers of Parliament and the famous clock tower stand at the center of British power, and at the heart of London. The facade is glorious when floodlighted at night. *(See Chapter 2.)*

The Tower of London

(D) The scene of much blood and gore since the 11th century, this extraordinary minicity of 20 towers has sturdy outer walls and a deep, drained moat. The Yeoman Wardens, known as Beefeaters, wear colorful Tudor clothes and give magnificent tours. All this, and the Crown Jewels are here, too. *(See Chapter 2.)*

British Museum

(E) The self-appointed protector of global treasures, this vast and varied museum in London is packed to bursting with antiquities and alluring objects. Among the greatest hits are the Parthenon Marbles, the Rosetta Stone, and Egyptian mummies. *(See Chapter 2.)*

Hampton Court Palace

(B) This Thames-side redbrick palace was built by and for Cardinal Wolsey, Henry VIII's religious adviser. But Henry coveted it, so it became a splendid royal home. Hampton Court, a half hour from London by train, has grand Tudor kitchens, sprawling gardens, and a tricky maze. *(See Chapter 2.)*

Bath

(C) Exquisitely preserved but entertaining, this Georgian town still centers on the hot mineral springs that made it the fashionable spa for the wealthy in the 18th and early 19th centuries. Streets lined with Palladian buildings made of golden limestone, an ancient abbey, tea shops, boutiques, and ruined Roman baths combine to give Bath real character. *(See Chapter 8.)*

Hadrian's Wall

(F) Begun in AD122, the thick stone wall built by the Emperor Hadrian across the rugged far north of the country is a remarkable survivor from Roman Britain, where it protected Roman soldiers from invading tribes. Biking, hiking, and horseback riding are wonderful ways to explore. *(See Chapter 14.)*

Oxford

(G) Dubbed "the city of dreaming spires" for its fairy-tale cityscape formed by the steeples, towers, and domes of hundreds of university buildings and churches, Oxford is an ancient, atmospheric university town. *(See Chapter 6.)*

Coastal Cornwall

(H) The coasts of Cornwall, in England's far southwest corner, are beloved by many (too many, in summer) for different reasons. The more rugged northern coast has cliffs that drop to tiny coves and beaches; ruined, cliff-top Tintagel Castle is here.

The south coast has sandy beaches and resort towns such as Penzance and arty St. Ives. *(See Chapter 5.)*

Cotswold Villages

(I) Marked by rolling hills, green fields, and limestone cottages with prim flower beds, the Cotswolds, 100 mi west of London, make a peaceful getaway. There's little to do in idyllic villages except to stroll and pile clotted cream on your scone, but that's the point. Gardens and stately homes add to the charm. *(See Chapter 8.)*

Lake District

(J) Sprawling across northwest England, this area of 16 major lakes and jagged mountains inspired Romantic poets to write sweeping verse. You can hike the trails or view the mountains from a boat, or seek out the retreats of writers in towns such as Grasmere, Hawkshead, and Coniston. *(See Chapter 11.)*

QUINTESSENTIAL ENGLAND

Pints and Pubs

Pop in for a pint at a pub to encounter what has been the center—literally the "public house"—of English social life for centuries. The basic pub recipe calls for a variety of beers on draft—dark creamy stouts like Guinness; bitter, including brews such as Tetley's and Bass; and lager, the blondest and blandest of the trio—a dartboard, oak paneling, and paisley carpets. Throw in a bunch of young suits in London, a generous dash of undergrads in places such as Oxford or Cambridge, and, in rural areas, a healthy helping of blokes around the television and ladies in the corner sipping their *halves* (half pints) and having a *natter* (gossip). In smaller pubs, listen in and enjoy the banter among the regulars—you may even be privy to the occasional *barney* (harmless argument). Join in if you care to, but remember not to take anything too seriously—a severe breach of pub etiquette. Make your visit soon: the encroachment of gastro-pubs (bar-restaurant hybrids) is just one of the forces challenging traditional pub culture.

Daily Rags

To blend in with the English, stash your street map, slide a folded newspaper under your arm, and head for the nearest park bench or café. Lose yourself in any one of the national dailies for often well-written insight into Britain's worldview. For a dose of tabloid melodrama, choose the *Sun*, Britain's most popular newspaper. The sensational headlines are hard to miss—"Prince's Cheating Scandal" and "Empire Strikes Bark: Dogs Dress Up as Vader"—and you can assume that the topless model on Page 3 has helped rather than hindered the paper's success. The biweekly *Private Eye* offers British wit at its best, specializing in political cartoons, parodies, and satirical reporting.

If you want to get a sense of contemporary England culture, and indulge in some of its pleasures, start by familiarizing yourself with the rituals of daily life. Here are a few highlights—things you can take part in with relative ease.

A Lovely Cuppa

For almost four centuries, the English and tea have been immersed in a love affair passionate enough to survive revolutions, rations, tariffs, and lattes, but also soothing, as whistling kettles across the nation mark moments of quiet comfort in public places and in homes and offices. The ritual known as "afternoon tea" had its beginnings in the early 19th century, in the private chambers of the duchess of Bedford, where she and her "ladies of leisure" indulged in afternoons of pastries and fragrant blends. But you don't need to dress up to lift your pinky to sip the steamy brew. Department stores and tearooms across the nation offer everything from simple tea and biscuits to shockingly overpriced spreads with sandwiches and cakes that would impress even the duchess herself. And if tea is not your cup of tea, don't worry; there's no shame for those who prefer coffee with their scones and clotted cream.

Sports Fever

Whoever says England is not an overtly religious country has not considered the sports mania that has descended here, and not merely because of the 2012 Olympic Games in London. Whether water events (such as Henley, Cowes, and the Head of the River Race) or a land competition (the Grand National steeplechase, the Virgin London Marathon, a good football match), most bring people to the edge of their seats—or more often the living room couch. To partake in the rite, you'll need Pimm's (the drink for swank spectators of the Henley Royal Regatta) or beer (the drink for most everything else). You may experience the exhilaration yourself—which, you'll probably sense, is not for the love of *a* sport, but for the love of *sport* itself.

IF YOU LIKE

Castles and Stately Homes

Exploring the diversity and magnificence of England's castles and stately homes, from Norman towers to Palladian palaces, can occupy most of a blissful vacation. Whether world famous or less visited, owned by royalty, aristocratic families, or the National Trust, each abode has tales to tell about history or domestic life. Castles and houses are spread around the nation (with fewer stately homes in Cornwall and the Lake District), but certain clusters may help your planning. Note that most stately homes are open only from spring through fall. England's southeastern coast is lined with sturdy castles; nearby but inland, around Royal Tunbridge Wells, are treasure houses such as Hever Castle and Knole. West of Salisbury are Wilton House, Stourhead, and Longleat, and the Cotswolds have a rich assortment. England's north has gems from Peak District manors to castles on the remote northeastern coast. London visitors won't miss out, either: Buckingham and Kensington palaces, the Tower of London, and Hampton Court Palace and Windsor Castle lie within easy reach. If your itinerary extends to Wales, look for Edward I's "iron ring" of castles, including Harlech and Conwy.

Blenheim Palace, Thames Valley. This baroque extravaganza is touted as England's only rival to Versailles.

Holkham Hall, East Anglia. A splendid 60-foot-tall marble entryway and salons filled with old masters distinguish this Palladian palace.

Petworth House, the Southeast. One of the National Trust's glories is known for art from J. M. W. Turner.

Charming Villages

Year after year, armies of tourists with images of green meadows, thatched roofs, and colorful flower beds flock to England's countryside, for good reason. Most will find their way to famously adorable towns along the Thames, magical seaside resorts in the West Country, and a smattering of fairy-tale hamlets in the Cotswolds—a hilly area in west-central England renowned for its golden and gray stone cottages. However, torrential tourist traffic has made these once-quintessentially quaint areas a little *too* accessible for some. Steer clear of busy Cotswolds towns such as Broadway in summer (especially on weekends); Winchcombe and Snowshill are more unspoiled options. Choose a weekday to visit the Thames Valley towns, which attract Londoners. To avoid some crowds, consider the pastoral flatlands of East Anglia beyond Cambridge, where historic villages remain relatively undiscovered, or explore the Norfolk coast. The rural Welsh Borders region has tranquil landscapes and towns, or head to Wales, with its mountainside hamlets and sleepy seaside resorts.

Lavenham, East Anglia. This village is full of Tudor buildings, the former houses of wool merchants and weavers.

Ludlow, Welsh Borders. Great restaurants and medieval and Georgian buildings cluster below a castle in this town.

Whitby, Yorkshire. A ruined abbey and a cliff-lined harbor combine with a rich fishing and whaling legacy to enhance this coastal gem.

Glorious Gardens

Despite being cursed with impertinent weather and short summers, English gardeners will gladly grab a gardening tool and attack a misbehaving rose garden for just a few short months of enjoyment. The Tudors were the first to produce gardens that were more than strictly utilitarian, and since then French, Italian, Dutch, and even Japanese ideas have been imported and adapted to suit the national aesthetic. A pilgrimage to a garden is an essential part of any spring or summer trip, whether you visit a large educational garden such as Kew Gardens near London or the West Country's Eden Project; a period gem such as Arts and Crafts Hidcote Manor in the Cotswolds; or gardens that are part of a stately home and as lovely as the house. Green havens thrive all over England, but perhaps the most fertile hunting grounds are in Oxfordshire, Gloucestershire (including the Cotswolds), and Kent (the "Garden of England"). Some of these visions of paradise have limited hours, and most close in winter; they're all worth the trip.

Sissinghurst Castle Garden, Southeast. Vita Sackville-West's masterpiece, set within the remains of a Tudor castle, is busy in summer but also spectacular in autumn.

Stourhead, South. One of the country's most impressive house-and-garden combinations is an artful 18th-century sanctuary with a tranquil lake, colorful shrubs, and grottoes.

Wisley, Southeast. The Royal Horticultural Society's garden splendidly blends the pretty and the practical in its inspirational displays.

Urban Action

London has everything a world capital should have—rich culture and history, thrilling art and theater scenes, world-class restaurants and sensational shopping—along with crowds, traffic, and high prices. It shouldn't be missed, but if you appreciate modern cities, fall out of the tourist trap and spend time in some of England's reviving urban centers, including those in its former industrial heartland, where blossoming multiculturalism has paved the way for a unique vibe. Football (soccer) fans might take in a match in Manchester or Liverpool, two bitter sporting rivals in the Northwest, or join hordes of fans to watch the game at a local pub. Manchester's museums are excellent, and its downtown (rebuilt after a 1996 IRA bombing) is worth a look, as are its famous clubs. Liverpool claims the Beatles sites and the stellar museums of the Albert Dock; it transformed itself for a stint as the European Union's Capital of Culture in 2008. See what's gentrifying in Birmingham, the country's second-largest city and a cultural force in England.

Brighton, Southeast. Bold, bright, and boisterous are the words to describe a seaside charmer that has everything from the dazzling Royal Pavilion to the trendy shops of the Lanes.

Bristol, West Country. With its lively waterfront and homegrown music talent, this youthful city has vibrant nightlife as well as a long history.

Leeds, Yorkshire. Another northern, former industrial city polishing its Victorian buildings, Leeds is known for its shopping arcades and youthful music scene.

Ancient Mysteries

Stone circles as well as ancient stone and earthen forts and mounds offer tantalizing hints about Britain's mysterious prehistoric inhabitants. The country's southwestern landscape, particularly the Salisbury Plain, Dorset, and the eastern side of Cornwall, has a notably rich concentration of these sites, perplexing mysteries that human nature compels us to try to solve. Stonehenge, the stone circle begun 5,000 years ago, stands on the wide Salisbury Plain; crowds detract from the magic, so arrive early or late to appreciate the monument's timeless power. Hypotheses about its purpose range from the scientific (ancient calendar) to the fantastic (a gift from extinct giants). Other relics—chambered tombs and mounds—dot the Avebury area to the north. Equally enigmatic are Maiden Castle, a colossal prehistoric hill fort near Dorchester, and the nearby figure of a giant carved into the hillside overlooking Cerne Abbas. Sometimes the setting of these ancient creations, such as Castlerigg Stone Circle in the Lake District, is awesome as the surviving remains.

Avebury Stone Circles, South. Large and marvelously evocative, these circles surround part of the village of Avebury.

Stanton Drew Circles, West Country. Use your imagination to visualize the vast size of the two avenues of standing stones, three rings, and burial chamber that now lie in a field.

Vale of the White Horse, Thames Valley. The gigantic horse here was actually carved into the chalky hillside around 1750 BC.

Wonderful Walks

England seems to be designed with walking in mind—footpaths wind through the contours of the landscape, and popular routes are well endowed with cozy bed-and-breakfasts and pubs. Your decisions will be what kind of landscape you prefer (coast or countryside, flat or mountainous) and how long a hike you want, though you can often do just part of a long-distance trail such as the Thames Path. Ramble through one of England's national parks (which are sprinkled with towns), and you'll generally find well-maintained trails and handy maps at local tourist information centers. The country's most famous walking spots are in the Lake District, from a short meander to a major mountain trek—but beware of summer congestion. Yorkshire's dales and moors are also popular. Cross the border to Wales, where the Brecon Beacons offer windswept uplands with easy paths, and ferocious peaks in Snowdonia National Park promise challenging hikes. Wherever you hike, always be prepared for storms or fogs.

Borrowdale, Lake District. Have a color-pencil kit handy to capture the beauty of the dramatically verdant valleys and jagged peaks.

Peak District, Lancashire and the Peaks. Its rocky outcrops and vaulting meadows make some people say this is the country's most beautiful national park.

South West Coast Path, West Country. Spectacular is the word for the 630-mi trail that winds from Minehead in Somerset to Poole Harbour in Dorset.

Thrilling Theater

There's no better antidote to an overdose of stately homes and glorious gardens than a face-to-face encounter with another British specialty, the theater. London is the heart and soul of the action: here companies famous and lesser known consistently churn out superb productions, from musicals and monologues to comedies and avant-garde dramas. Be sure to sample theater outside London, wherever you travel. Previews of the capital's productions often take place in Lincoln's Theatre Royal, and the Stephen Joseph Theatre in Yorkshire premieres many of Alan Ayckbourn's plays. Stratford-upon-Avon may be the Bard's hometown, but festivals all over the country celebrate Shakespeare's work—the best are the Ludlow Festival in the Welsh Borders and London's Shakespeare Under the Stars at Regent's Park. Brighton Dome and Windsor's Theatre Royal specialize in pantomime—theatrical entertainment with puppetry, slapstick, and music. Theatrical arts are often a major component of English festivals: see musicals at the Exeter Festival (West Country) and street theater at the Harrogate International Festival (Yorkshire). Try a university production; you may see the next big star.

Minack Theatre, West Country. This open-air theater in coastal Cornwall, near Land's End and Penzance, nuzzles the slope of a sandy cliff.

Royal Shakespeare Company, Shakespeare Country. Seeing any play by the Bard performed in Stratford is a treat.

Yvonne Arnaud Theatre, Guildford, the Southeast. The productions at this theater on an island often travel to London.

Country-House Hotels

In all their luxurious glory, country-house hotels are an essential part of the English landscape, particularly in the southern part of the country. Whether you choose a converted castle, Elizabethan manor, or neoclassical retreat, these are places to indulge yourself and escape, however briefly (most are pricey), most realities of modern life. Some hotels are traditional in style, with flowery fabrics and polished wood furniture; a newer breed juxtaposes modern design with the traditional architecture. At some hotels, spas and sports—and even, alas, meeting facilities—are becoming more elaborate, but service is less stuffy. If you can't spend a night, consider just having dinner; notable chefs are turning up in more hotel kitchens. In the Thames Valley, dress up for dinner at Hartwell House or indulge in French cuisine at Le Manoir aux Quat' Saisons. The West Country's concentration includes Bovey Castle and Gidleigh Park in Dartmoor National Park, and the Cotswolds are prime ground for these retreats. One tip: before you reserve, ask if a wedding party will be using the hotel during your stay; these can take over a smaller establishment.

Cliveden, Thames Valley. Live like Lord Astor for a night (and pay accordingly), taking in his palatial parlors and riverfront gardens.

Miller Howe, Lake District. Stunning views of Windermere, Arts and Crafts touches, and superior service are part of the appeal at this retreat.

Victoria at Holkham, East Anglia. In the shadow of stately Holkham Hall, this Eastern-inspired hideaway provides a colorful seaside escape.

GREAT ITINERARIES

BEST OF ENGLAND: UNFORGETTABLE IMAGES

12 days
London

Day 1. The capital is just the jumping-off point for this trip, so choose a few highlights that grab your interest. If it's the Changing of the Guard at Buckingham Palace, check the time to be sure you catch the pageantry. If Westminster Abbey appeals to your sense of history, arrive as early as you can. Pick a museum (many are free, so you needn't linger if you don't want to), whether it's the National Gallery on Trafalgar Square, the British Museum in Bloomsbury, or a smaller gem like the Queen's Gallery. Stroll Hyde Park or take a boat ride on the Thames before you find a pub or Indian restaurant for dinner. End with a play; the experience of theatergoing may be as interesting as whatever work you see.

Windsor

Day 2. Resplendent with centuries of treasures, Windsor Castle is favored by the Queen, and has been by rulers for centuries. Tour it to appreciate the history and wealth of the monarchy. The State Apartments are open if the Queen is not in residence, and 10 kings and queens are buried in magnificent St. George's Chapel. Time permitting, take a walk in the adjacent Great Park. If you can splurge for a luxurious stay, head up the valley to Cliveden, the Thames Valley's most spectacular hotel.

Logistics: Trains depart from Paddington and Waterloo stations twice hourly and take less than one hour. Green Line buses depart High Street Kensington or Hyde Park Corner.

Salisbury and Stourhead

Day 3. Visible for miles around, Salisbury Cathedral's soaring spire is an unforgettable image of rural England. See the Magna Carta in the cathedral's Chapter House as you explore this marvel of medieval engineering, and walk the town path to get the view John Constable painted. Pay an afternoon visit to Stourhead to experience the finest example of the naturalistic 18th-century landscaping for which England is famous; the grand Palladian mansion here is a bonus.

Logistics: For trains to Salisbury, head back to London's Clapham Junction to catch a train on the Portsmouth line.

Bath and Stonehenge

Day 4. Bath's immaculately preserved, golden-stone Georgian architecture helps you recapture the late 18th century. Take time to stroll; don't miss the Royal Crescent (No. 1 may be open, allowing you to view a period interior), and sip the Pump Room's vile-tasting water as Jane Austen's characters might have. The Roman Baths are an amazing survivor of the ancient empire, complete with curses left by soldiers. Today you can do as the Romans did as you relax in the warm mineral waters at the Thermae Bath Spa. There's plenty to do in Bath (museums, shopping, theater), but you might make an excursion to Stonehenge (by car or tour bus). Go early or late to avoid the worst crowds at Stonehenge, and use your imagination to appreciate this enigma.

Logistics: Trains and buses leave hourly from Salisbury to Bath.

The Cotswolds

Day 5. Antiques-shop in fairy-tale Stow-on-the-Wold and feed the ducks at the brook in Lower Slaughter for a taste of the mellow stone villages and dreamy green landscapes for which the area is beloved. Choose a rainy or off-season day to visit Broadway or risk jams of tourist traffic. Another great experience is a walk on the Cotswold Way or any local path.

Logistics: Drive to make the best of the beautiful scenery. Alternatively, opt for a guided tour bus.

Oxford and Blenheim Palace

Day 6. Join a guided tour of Oxford's glorious quadrangles, chapels, and gardens to get the best access to these centuries-old academic treasures. This leaves time for a jaunt to Blenheim, a unique combination of baroque opulence (inside and out) and gorgeous parkland. For a classic Oxford experience, join students in pub-crawling around Jericho, the hopping nightlife district.

Logistics: Hourly trains depart from Bath for Oxford. Buses frequently depart from Oxford's Gloucester Green for Blenheim Palace.

Stratford-upon-Avon

Day 7. Skip this stop if you don't care about you-know-who. Fans of Shakespeare can see his birthplace and Anne Hathaway's Cottage (walking there is a delight), and then finish with a memorable performance at the Courtyard Theater or wherever the Royal Shakespeare Company is performing as it renovates its main stage for reopening sometime in 2010. Start the day early and be prepared for crowds.

Logistics: From Oxford there are direct trains and more frequent Stagecoach bus service.

Shrewsbury to Chester

Day 8. Head north to see the half-timber buildings of Shrewsbury, one of the best-preserved of England's Tudor towns. Strolling is the best way to experience it. In Chester the architecture is more or less the same (though not always authentic), but the Rows, a series of two-story shops with medieval crypts beneath, and the fine City Walls are sights you can't pass by.

Logistics: For Shrewsbury, change trains at Birmingham. The train ride to Chester is 55 minutes.

The Lake District

Days 9–10. In the area extending north beyond Kendal and Windermere, explore the English lakes on foot. This area is jam-packed with hikers in summer and on weekends, so rent a car to seek out the more isolated routes. Take a cruise on Windermere or Coniston Water, or rent a boat. If you have time for one Wordsworth-linked site, head to Dove Cottage; you can even have afternoon tea there.

Logistics: Train to Liverpool, with a switch in either Windermere or Oxenholme.

York

Day 11. This historic cathedral city is crammed with 15th- and 16th-century buildings, but don't miss magnificent York Minster and the medieval streets of the Shambles. Take in the Castle Museum; have tea at Betty's or unwind at a pub. The energetic can take a walk along the top of the several miles of city walls.

Logistics: By train, switch in Carlisle and Newcastle for the four-hour journey. Buses take twice as long.

Cambridge

Day 12. Spend the afternoon touring King's College Chapel and the Backs—gardens and sprawling meadows—and refining your punting skills on the River Cam. Join the students for a pint at one of the many pubs.

Logistics: For train service, switch at Leeds and again at Peterborough or Stevenage. Trains leave Cambridge for London frequently.

STATELY HOMES AND LANDSCAPES TOUR

11 days

Hampton Court Palace

Day 1. Start your trip royally at this palace a half hour from London by train. It's two treasures in one: a Tudor palace with magnificent baroque additions by Christopher Wren. As you walk through cobbled courtyards, Henry VIII's State Apartments, and the enormous kitchens, you may feel like you've been whisked back to the days of the Tudors and William and Mary. A quiet stroll through the 60 acres of immaculate gardens—the sculpted yews look like green gumdrops—is recommended. Be sure to get lost in the 18th-century maze—if it's open (diligent maintenance leads to occasional closures). It's easy to spend a whole day here, so start early.

Logistics: Tube to Richmond, then Bus R68; or catch the train from Waterloo to Hampton Court Station.

Knole and Ightham Mote

Days 2–3. Clustered around Royal Tunbridge Wells south of London is the highest concentration of stately homes in England, and, as if that weren't enough, the surrounding fields and colorful orchards are often wrapped in clouds of mist, creating a picture-perfect scene. We've picked two very different homes to visit, leaving you plenty of time to tour at a leisurely pace. Knole, Vita Sackville-West's sprawling childhood home, has dark, baroque rooms and a famous set of silver furniture. Ightham Mote, a smaller, moated house, is a vision from the Middle Ages. Its rooms are an ideal guide to style changes from the Tudor to Victorian eras. Spend the eve-

ning at one of the many good restaurants in Royal Tunbridge Wells.

Logistics: Take the Hastings-bound train from London's Charing Cross to Tunbridge Wells, then the bus to Knole. There is no public transportation to Ightham Mote.

Petworth House

Day 4. Priceless paintings by Gainsborough, Reynolds, and Turner (19 by Turner alone) embellish the august rooms of Petworth House, present-day home to Lord and Lady Egremont and one of the National Trust's treasures. Check out Capability Brown's 700-acre deer park or the Victorian kitchens, and for the perfect lunch, peruse the offerings in the winding lanes of Petworth town. Head to Chichester for the evening, along a route passing through the rolling grasslands and deep valleys of the South Downs.

Logistics: Train to Chichester, switching in Redhill, then bus to Petworth.

Wilton House

Day 5. Base yourself in Salisbury for two days, taking time to see the famous cathedral with its tall spire and to walk the town path for the best view of it. Visit neoclassical Wilton House first, where the exquisite Double Cube Room contains a spectacular family portrait by Van Dyck and gilded furniture that accommodated Eisenhower when he contemplated the Normandy invasion here. On your way back make a detour to Stonehenge to view the wide-open Salisbury Plain and ponder the enigmatic stones.

Logistics: Take a train from Chichester, with a switch in Cosham; then bus it to Wilton House.

Stourhead to Longleat House

Day 6. Day-trip west to Stourhead, to experience perhaps the most stunning house-garden combination in the country, and either spend the day here (climb Alfred's Tower for a grand view of the house) or leave some time for nearby Longleat House—a vast, treasure-stuffed Italian Renaissance palace complete with safari park and a devilish maze. If you want to see the safari park, you'll need plenty of time here. Once back in Salisbury, relax in one of New Street's many cafés.

Logistics: Bus to Warminster for Longleat; for Stourhead, take the train to Gillingham from Salisbury.

Blenheim Palace

Day 7. Home of the dukes of Marlborough and birthplace of Winston Churchill, Blenheim Palace uniquely combines exquisitely designed parklands (save time to walk) and one of the most ornate baroque structures in the world. After your visit, have afternoon tea at Blenheim Tea Rooms in the adorable village of Woodstock. Overnight in Oxford; do your own pub crawl.

Logistics: From Salisbury, change at Bath or Basingstoke for Oxford, then catch a bus to Blenheim.

Snowshill Manor and Sudeley Castle

Days 8–9. Here you can take in the idyllic Cotswold landscape, a magical mix of greenery and mellow stone cottages and ancient churches (built with wool-trade money), along with some famous buildings. Spend the first night in Broadway to explore nearby Snowshill Manor—with its delightfully eccentric collection of Tibetan scrolls, Persian lamps, and samurai armor—in the unspoiled village of Snowshill. If you have a car, don't linger in busy Broadway. Instead, head to Chipping Campden, one of the best-preserved Cotswolds villages, which nestles in a secluded valley. Move to another charming town, Winchcombe, on the second day. Take a stroll past honey-color stone cottages and impeccably well-kept gardens. Visit Sudeley Castle, once home to Catherine Parr (Henry VIII's last wife), a Tudor-era palace with romantic gardens (only a few rooms are now open to the public). Another option near Winchcombe is Stanway House, a Jacobean manor owned by Lord Neidpath; hours are limited, but this time-worn home and its gabled gatehouse is typically English.

Logistics: Take a train from Oxford to Moreton-in-Marsh for Broadway, then walk to Snowshill Manor; for Sudeley Castle, take a bus from Broadway to Winchcombe, then walk.

Chatsworth House, Haddon Hall, and Hardwick Hall

Days 10–11. For the final stops, head north, east of Manchester, to a more dramatic landscape. In or near the craggy Peak District, where the gentle slopes of the Pennine Hills begin their ascent to Scotland, are three of England's most renowned historic homes. Base yourself in Bakewell, and spend your first day taking in the art treasures amassed by the dukes of Devonshire at Chatsworth House. The gardens, grounds, shops, and farmyard exhibits make it easy to spend a day here. If you have any time left over, get out of Bakewell and take a walk in the hills of the Peak District National Park (maps are available at the town's tourist information center).

On the second day, devote the morning to the crenellations and boxy roofs of medieval Haddon Hall, a quintessentially English house. Give your afternoon to Hardwick Hall, an Elizabethan stone mansion with a facade that is "more glass than wall"—a truly innovative idea in the 16th century. Its collections of period tapestries and embroideries are remarkable reminders of the splendor of the age.

Logistics: Take a train back to Oxford and then up to Manchester for the connection to Buxton; then catch a bus to Bakewell.

ON THE CALENDAR

England's top seasonal events are listed below, and any one of them could provide the stuff of lasting memories. Tickets for popular sporting events must be obtained months in advance. VisitBritain's Web site, ⊕ *www.visitbritain.com*, also has information about events.

ONGOING Late May–August	**Glyndebourne Opera** presents high-quality (and high-priced) performances in a lovely rural setting; booking opens in April. ✆ *Box 2624, Lewes, East Sussex BN8 5UW* ☎ *01273/815000 information, 01273/813813 box office* ⊕ *www.glyndebourne.com.*
Late May–mid-September	**Regent's Park Open Air Theatre** gives you the chance to see Shakespeare's plays and other works. Performances are usually Monday through Saturday at 8, with matinees on Wednesday, Thursday, and Saturday. ✉ *Inner Circle, London* ☎ *020/7486–2431* ⊕ *www.openairtheatre.org.*
Mid-July–mid-September	**The Proms** is a celebrated series of classical-music concerts that take place largely in London, but a few events are held in cities across the country. ✉ *Royal Albert Hall, Kensington Gore, London* ☎ *020/7589–8212* ⊕ *www.bbc.co.uk/proms.*
WINTER December 31	**New Year's Eve at Trafalgar Square** in London is a huge, freezing, sometimes drunken slosh through the fountains to celebrate the new year. Not organized by any official body, it is held in the ceremonial heart of London under an enormous Christmas tree.
January 1	**New Year's Parade,** an American-style extravaganza rare in these parts, with floats and marching bands flown over from the United States, starts on the south side of Westminster Bridge around noon and finishes in Berkeley Square around 3 PM. No tickets are required. ✉ *London* ⊕ *www.londonparade.co.uk.*
SPRING Mid-March	**Crufts Dog Show** brings together more than 8,000 championship dogs for Britain's top canine event. ✉ *National Exhibition Centre, Birmingham* ☎ *0207/518–1012* ⊕ *www.crufts.org.uk.*
Mid-April	The **Head of the River Boat Race** offers the spectacle of up to 420 eight-man crews dipping their oars in the Thames as they race from Mortlake to Putney. The best view is from Surrey Bank above Chiswick Bridge (Tube to Chiswick); the starting time depends on the tide. The **Oxford versus Cambridge**

	University Boat Race takes place a week or two after the Head of the River Boat Race, in the opposite direction but over the same 4½-mi course, carrying on a tradition going back to 1829. Around a quarter of a million people watch from the banks of the river.
Mid-April	**Virgin London Marathon** runners start in Greenwich and Blackheath at 9–9:30 AM and run via the Docklands, the Tower of London, and Parliament Square to the Mall. ⊕*www.london-marathon.co.uk.*
April 21	The **Queen's Birthday** earns a showy 41-gun salute at Hyde Park in London. In June, Elizabeth II's ceremonial birthday is celebrated by Trooping the Colour.
Mid–late May	The **Chelsea Flower Show,** a prestigious four-day floral extravaganza, covers 22 acres on the Royal Hospital grounds in London's Chelsea neighborhood. Tickets can sell out well in advance of the event. ⊠*Royal Horticultural Society, Royal Hospital Rd., London* ☎*0870/906–3781* ⊕*www.rhs.org.uk/chelsea.*
Late May	The **Hay Festival** in the Welsh border town of Hay-on-Wye gathers authors and readers from all over the world for a weeklong celebration of the town's status as the used-book capital of the world. ⊠*Hay-on-Wye* ☎*01497/821299* ⊕*www.hayfestival.co.uk.*
SUMMER Early June	**Trooping the Colour** is Queen Elizabeth's official birthday show at Horse Guards Parade, Whitehall, London. (Her actual birthday is in April.) Note that on the two previous Saturdays there are Queenless rehearsals—the Colonel's Review and the Major General's Review. *Write for tickets from January 1 to February 28 (enclose SASE or International Reply Coupon):* ⌑*Ticket Office, Headquarters Household Division, Horse Guards, London SW1 2AX* ☎*020/7414–2479.*
Mid-June	**Royal Ascot** is the most glamorous date in British horse racing. Usually held during the third week of June, the four-day event in the Thames Valley is graced by the Queen and other celebrities. Reserve months in advance for tickets. ⊠*Ascot Racecourse, Ascot, Berkshire* ☎*01344/876876* ⊕*www.ascot.co.uk.*
Late June	**Glastonbury Festival,** the biggest musical event in England, sprawls across Somerset farmland, where hundreds of bands (rock, pop, folk, and world music) perform on a half-dozen

	stages for three days and nights. Note: Tickets sell out as soon as they go on sale. ☎0844/412–4626 ⊕*www.glastonbury-festivals.co.uk.*
Late June–early July	**Wimbledon Lawn Tennis Championships** get bigger every year. Applications for the ticket lottery for the two-week tournament are available October through December of the preceding year, but you can also line up early each morning for tickets for that day. ✉*All-England Lawn Tennis & Croquet Club, Church Rd., Wimbledon, London SW19 5AE* ☎020/8946–2244 ⊕*www.wimbledon.org.*
	Royal Henley Regatta attracts premier rowers from around the world on the first weekend in July. High society lines the banks of the Thames during this four-day event. ✉*Henley-on-Thames* ☎01491/572153 ⊕*www.hrr.co.uk.*
Early July	**Hampton Court Palace Flower Show,** a five-day event on the grounds of the palace, nearly rivals the Chelsea Flower Show for glamour. ✉*Hampton Court Palace, East Molesey, Surrey* ☎020/7649–1885 ⊕*www.rhs.org.uk/hamptoncourt.*
Mid-August	The **Reading Music Festival** is second only to Glastonbury in its sheer size and longevity. It takes place in two locations—Leeds and Reading (just outside London)—over a three-day weekend, and attracts more than 100,000 mostly college-age fans to hear mostly loud rock bands. ☎0207/009–3001 ⊕*www.readingfestival.com.*
Late August	**International Beatles Festival** sees hundreds of Beatles tribute bands descend on Liverpool for a week to play to fans. ✉*Liverpool* ☎0151/236–9091 ⊕*www.cavernclub.org.*
	Notting Hill Carnival, one of the liveliest street festivals in London, includes Caribbean foods, reggae music, and street parades. ✉*Notting Hill, London* ☎020/8964–0544 ⊕*www. thenottinghillcarnival.com.*
FALL Mid-October	**Cheltenham Festival of Literature** draws world-renowned authors, actors, and critics to the elegant, Regency-era town for 10 days of events. ☎01242/227979 ⊕*www.cheltenhamfestivals. co.uk.*
November 5	**Guy Fawkes Day** commemorates a foiled 1605 attempt to blow up Parliament. Fireworks shows and bonfires are held all over the country, with the biggest celebrations in Lewes in Sussex.

London

WORD OF MOUTH

"I really, really recommend taking a verger's tour at Westminster Abbey—our guide really made history come alive. If you get to the Abbey when it opens, just sign up for the first tour of the day or you can sign up in advance the previous day."

—azzure

"It was raining when I visited Greenwich, but armed with a sturdy brolly I still enjoyed my visit very much. The surrounding park area is also very beautiful and the town itself charming. Check what the Observatory's and Maritime Museum's winter hours are ahead of time, however."

—Rebecka

Updated by
Christi Daugh-
erty, Jack
Jewers, Ellin
Stein, Christine
Valhouli,
and Alex
Wijeratna

London is an ancient city whose history greets you at every turn; it's also one of the coolest cities in the world. If the city contained only its famous landmarks—the Tower of London, Big Ben, Westminster Abbey, Buckingham Palace—it would still rank as one of the world's top cities. But London is so much more.

To gain a sense of its continuity, stand on Waterloo Bridge at sunset. To the east, the great globe of St. Paul's Cathedral glows golden in the fading sunlight as it has since the 17th century, still majestic amid the modern glass towers. To the west stand the mock-medieval ramparts of Westminster, home to the "Mother of Parliaments," which has met here or hereabouts since the 1250s. Past them both snakes the swift, dark Thames, which flowed past the Roman settlement of Londinium nearly 2,000 years ago.

The city beckons with great museums, royal pageantry, and history-steeped houses. There's no other place like it in its medley of styles, in its mixture of the green loveliness of parks and the modern gleam of neon. Modern-day London largely reflects its medieval layout, a will-fully difficult tangle of streets. Even Londoners, most of whom own a dog-eared copy of an indispensable A–Z street finder, get lost in their own city. But the bewildering street patterns will be a plus for anyone who likes to get lost in atmosphere. London is a walker's city, and will repay every moment you spend exploring on foot.

To penetrate beyond the crust of popular knowledge, you should not only visit St. Paul's Cathedral and the Tower of London, but also set aside some time for random wandering. Walk in the city's backstreets and mews, around Park Lane and Kensington. Pass up Buckingham Palace for Kensington Palace. Take in the National Gallery, but don't forget London's "time machine" museums, such as the 19th-century home of Sir John Soane. Abandon the city's standard-issue chain stores for its wonderful markets.

Today the city's art, style, fashion, and dining scenes make headlines around the world. London's chefs have become superstars. Its fashion designers have conquered Paris, avant-garde artists have caused waves at the august Royal Academy of Arts, the raging after-hours scene is packed with music mavens ready to catch the Next Big Thing, and the theater continues its tradition of radical, shocking productions. And the city is now looking forward to hosting the 2012 Olympics.

Although the outward shapes may alter and the inner spirit may be warmer, the base-rocks of London's character and tradition remain the same. The British bobby is alive and well. The tall, red, double-decker buses (in an updated model) still lumber from stop to stop. Then there's that greatest living link with the past—the Royal Family. Don't let the tag of "typical tourist destination" stop you from enjoying the pageantry of the Windsors: the Changing of the Guard, at

TOP REASONS TO GO

Westminster Abbey: Steeped in history, the pillars of this great vaulted hall stand on the final resting place for the men and women who built Britain.

Buckingham Palace: Not the prettiest royal residence, but a must-see for the glimpse it affords of modern royal life. The Queen's Gallery is next door.

St. Paul's Cathedral: No matter how many times you have been here, the scale and elegance of Sir Christopher Wren's masterpiece take the breath away.

Tower of London: The Tower is London at its majestic, idiosyncratic best. This is the heart of the kingdom, with foundations dating back nine centuries.

British Museum: A visit to the British Museum has hours of eye-catching artifacts from the world's greatest civilizations.

Shakespeare's Globe Theatre: Watching an offering from the Bard in a re-created version of the galleried Tudor theater for which he wrote is a special thrill.

Hampton Court Palace: These buildings won over Henry VIII and became his favorite royal residence. Tudor charm, grand gardens, and a wing designed by Sir Christopher Wren make Hampton Court a great day out.

Tate Modern: A visit here is more of an event than the average museum stop. Tate Modern, housed in a striking 1930s power station, is a hip, immensely successful addition to the London gallery landscape.

National Gallery: Whatever the collective noun is for a set of old masters—a palette? a canvas?—there are enough here to have the most casual art enthusiast cooing with admiration. Enjoy pedestrianized Trafalgar Square on the doorstep.

Buckingham Palace and at Whitehall, is one of the greatest free shows in the world.

The London you discover may include some enthusiastic recommendations from this guide, but be prepared to be taken by surprise. The best that a great city has to offer often comes in unexpected ways. The great 18th-century author Samuel Johnson said that a man who is tired of London is tired of life. Armed with energy and curiosity, you can find, to quote Dr. Johnson again, "in London all that life can afford."

ORIENTATION AND PLANNING

GETTING ORIENTED

London grew from a wooden bridge built over the Thames in the year AD 43 to its current 600 square mi and 7 million souls in haphazard fashion, meandering from its two official centers: Westminster, seat of government and royalty, to the west, and the City, site of finance and commerce, to the east. In this city of urban villages, the neighborhoods continue to evolve. If the city's great parks such as Hyde Park are, in

Lord Chatham's phrase, "the lungs of London," then the River Thames remains its backbone. Here are some key areas to explore.

Westminster and Royal London. This is the place to embrace the "tourist" label. Snap pictures of the mounted Horse Guards, play with the pigeons in Trafalgar Square, and visit stacks of art in the national galleries. It's well worth braving the crowds to wander ancient Westminster Abbey and its historic bounty.

Soho and Covent Garden. More sophisticated than seedy these days, the heart of London puts Theaterland, strip joints, Chinatown, and the trendiest of film studios side by side. Nearby Charing Cross Road is a bibliophile's dream, but steer clear of the hectic hordes in Leicester Square, London's answer to Times Square.

Bloomsbury and Legal London. The literary and left-wing set that made Bloomsbury world famous has left its mark, and the area remains the heart of brainy London. The University of London and the Law Courts are worth a passing glance; stop for a good while in the incomparable British Museum.

The City. London's Wall Street might be the oldest part of the capital, but thanks to futuristic skyscrapers and a sleek Millennium Bridge, it looks like the newest. Fans of ages gone by won't be disappointed, however: head for the dome of St. Paul's Cathedral, the storybook Tower Bridge, and grisly tales from the Tower of London.

The South Bank. Diehard culture vultures could spend a lifetime here. The South Bank Arts Complex—including the Royal National Theatre and Royal Festival Hall, the National Film Theatre, Shakespeare's Globe, the Design Museum, and the Tate Modern—pretty much seals the artistic deal. Or take it all in from high up on the London Eye.

Kensington, Knightsbridge, and Mayfair. The museums are as awe-inspiring as ever. The Science Museum and the Natural History Museum are the most fun for children. Flash your cash at the capital's snazziest department stores, Harrods and Harvey Nichols. You might not have the wallet for London's most prestigious district, but the window-shopping in Mayfair is free.

Up and Down the Thames. The quaint Thameside streets of Greenwich are an excellent rummaging ground for trendy antiques. Throw in some brilliant sights, Christopher Wren architecture, and the Greenwich Meridian Line, and you have a great day out. Other excursions include lovely Kew Gardens and Hampton Court Palace, England's version of Versailles.

LONDON PLANNER

WHEN TO GO

The heaviest tourist season runs mid-April through mid-October, with another peak around Christmas—though the tide never really ebbs. Spring is the time to see the countryside and the royal London parks and gardens at their freshest; fall to enjoy near-ideal exploring conditions. In late summer, be warned: air-conditioning is rarely found in places other than department stores, modern restaurants, hotels, and cinemas in London. Winter can be rather dismal, but all the theaters, concerts, and exhibitions go full speed ahead.

One good time to avoid is the October "half-term" when schools in the capital take a break for a week and nearly all attractions are flooded by children. Arriving at the start of August can be a very busy time, and the weather makes Tube travel a nightmare.

GETTING HERE AND AROUND

ADDRESSES

Central London and its surrounding districts are divided into 32 boroughs—33, counting the City of London. More useful for finding your way around, however, are the subdivisions of London into postal districts. The first one or two letters give the location: N means north, NW means northwest, etc.

AIR TRAVEL

For information about airports and airport transfers, see Getting Here and Around in Travel Smart England.

BUS TRAVEL

Buses, or "coaches," as long-distance services are known here, operate mainly from London's Victoria Coach Station to more than 1,200 major towns and cities. Buses are about half as expensive as the train, but trips take twice as long. *For information, see Getting Here and Around in Travel Smart England.*

In central London, Transport for London (TfL) buses are traditionally bright red double- and single-deckers. Not all buses run the full length of their route at all times, so check with the driver. In central London you must purchase tickets from machines at bus stops along the routes before you board. Bus stops are clearly indicated: the main stops have a red TfL symbol on a white background. When the word REQUEST is written across the sign, you must flag the bus down. Buses are a good way to see the town, but don't take one if you're in a hurry.

A flat-rate fare of £2 applies for all bus fares. If you buy a one-day Travelcard for tube, bus and train, it covers all journeys. You can also get an Oystercard, an electronic smart card that you load with money, which is then deducted each time you use the card on buses or the tube: a single fare is £1 or £1.50. A One-Day Bus Pass for zones one through four is £3.50 (a seven-day pass is £13) but must be bought before boarding from one of the machines at bus stops, most newsagents, or underground stations.

If you're traveling on the tube as well as the bus, consider an off-peak one-day Travelcard (£5.60), which allows unrestricted travel on buses *and* tubes after 9:30 AM and all day on weekends and national holidays. "Peak" travelcards—those for use before 9:30 AM—are more expensive (£7.40). Children under 11 travel free on the tube and buses after 9:30 AM, while children ages 11–15 travel free on buses as long as they order an Oystercard at least four weeks before they travel.

Traveling without a valid ticket makes you liable for an on-the-spot fine (£20), or you can be charged with a criminal offense. For more information, there are Transport for London Travel Information Centres at

the following tube stations: Euston, Liverpool Street, Piccadilly Circus, Victoria, and Heathrow. Most are open in daytime only.

Night Buses can prove helpful when traveling in London from 11 PM to 5 AM—these buses add the prefix "N" to their route numbers. You may have to transfer at one of the Night Bus nexuses: Victoria, Westminster, and either Piccadilly Circus or Trafalgar Square. For safety reasons, avoid sitting alone on the top deck of a Night Bus.

Contact **Transport for London** (☎ *020/7222–1234* ⊕ *www.tfl.gov.uk*).

CAR TRAVEL

The major approach roads to London are six-lane motorways. Motorways (from Heathrow, M4; from Gatwick, M23 to M25, then M3; Stansted, M11) are usually the faster option for getting in and out of town, although rush-hour traffic is horrendous. Stay tuned to local radio stations for updates.

The simple advice about driving in London is: don't. The city never had a central street plan, and the result is a chaotic winding mass, made no easier by the one-way street systems. If you must drive, remember to drive on the left and stick to the speed limit (30 mph on most city streets).

An £8 "congestion charge" is levied on all vehicles entering central London (bounded by the Inner Ring Road; street signs and "C" road markings note the area) on weekdays from 7 AM to 6:30 PM, excluding bank holidays. Pay in advance or on that day until 10 PM if you're entering the central zone. You can pay by phone, mail, or Internet, or at retail outlets (look for signs). There are no tollbooths; cameras monitor the area. The penalty for not paying is stiff: £80. For current information, check ⊕ *www.cclondon.com*.

TAXI TRAVEL

Taxis are expensive, but if you're with several people they can be practical. Hotels and main tourist areas have taxi ranks; you can also hail taxis on the street. If the yellow FOR HIRE sign is lighted on top, the taxi is available. Drivers often cruise at night with their signs unlighted, so if you see an unlighted cab, keep your hand up. Generally fares start at £2.20 and increase by units of 20p (per 125 to 191 yards or 24.5 to 37.6 seconds) after a certain initial distance. Surcharges are added around Christmas and New Year's days. Fares also go up between 10 PM and 6 AM. Tips are extra, usually 10% to 15% per ride. The average cost for a journey within central London is £8.

TRAIN TRAVEL

London has eight major train stations, each serving a different area of the country, all accessible by Underground or bus. Trains are operated by a number of private companies, but National Rail Enquiries acts as a central rail information number. *For further information on train travel, see Getting Here and Around in Travel Smart England.*

Contact **National Rail Enquiries** (☎ *0845/748–4950* ⊕ *www.nationalrail.co.uk*).

UNDERGROUND (TUBE) TRAVEL

London's extensive Underground (tube) system has color-coded routes, clear signs, and extensive connections. Trains run out into the suburbs, and all stations are marked with the London Underground circular symbol. (In Britain, the word "subway" means "pedestrian underpass.") Some lines have branches (Central, District, Northern, Metropolitan, and Piccadilly), so be sure to note which branch is needed for your destination. Electronic platform signs tell you the final stop and route of the next train and how many minutes until it arrives.

London is divided into six concentric zones (ask at Underground ticket booths for a map and booklet, which give details of the ticket options). The more zones your trip crosses, the higher the fare. Most tourist sights are within zone 1, but some are not—Kew Gardens, for example, is in zone 4. If you inadvertently travel into a zone for which you do not have the right ticket, you can purchase an "extension" to your own ticket at the ticket office by the barriers. This usually costs a pound, and merely equalizes your fare. Buy an Oystercard (*see Bus Travel*) for fare reductions; it can be a huge money-saver.

The tube begins running just after 5 AM Monday through Saturday; the last services leave central London between midnight and 12:30 AM. On Sunday, trains start two hours later and finish about an hour earlier. Normally you should not have to wait more than 10 minutes in central areas. Most tube stations are not accessible for people with disabilities. Travelers with disabilities should get the free leaflet "Access to the Underground," which lists the stations that are.

Contact Transport for London (☎ *020/7222–1234* ⊕ *www.tfl.gov.uk*).

DISCOUNTS AND DEALS

All national collections (such as the Natural History Museum, Science Museum, Victoria & Albert Museum) are free, a real bargain for museumgoers. The London Pass, a smart card, offers entry to more than 50 top attractions, such as museums and tours on boats and buses. The charge is £39 for one day, which drops to £15 per day for those with weekly passes. London Pass is available by phone, online, or from the Britain Visitor Centre and Tourist Information Centre branches. *For other discounts, see Sightseeing Passes in Essentials in Travel Smart England.*

Contact London Pass (☎ *0870/242–9988* ⊕ *www.londonpass.com*).

TOUR OPTIONS

BOAT TOURS

Year-round, but more frequently from April to October, boats cruise the Thames, offering a different view of the London skyline. Most leave from Westminster Pier, Charing Cross Pier, and Tower Pier. Downstream routes go to the Tower of London, Greenwich, and the Thames Barrier via Canary Wharf. Upstream destinations include Kew, Richmond, and Hampton Court (mainly in summer). Most of the launches seat between 100 and 250 passengers, have a public-address system, and provide a running commentary on passing points of interest. Depending upon the destination, river trips may last from one to four hours.

A Sail and Rail ticket combines the modern wonders of Canary Wharf by Docklands Light Railway with a trip on the river. Tickets are available year-round from Westminster Pier or DLR stations; ticket holders also get discounted tickets to the London Aquarium in Westminster and the National Maritime Museum in Greenwich.

The tranquil side of London can be found on narrow boats that cruise the city's two canals, the Grand Union and Regent's Canal; most vessels operate on the latter, which runs between Little Venice in the west (nearest Tube: Warwick Avenue on the Bakerloo Line) and Camden Lock (about 200 yards north of Camden Town Tube station). Fares are about £5 for 1½-hour cruises.

Contacts Canal Cruises (☎ 020/7485-4433 ⊕ www.walkersquay.com). **Catamaran Cruisers** (☎ 020/7987-1185 ⊕ www.catamarancruisers.co.uk). **Jason's Trip (canal)** (☎ 020/7286-3428 ⊕ www.jasons.co.uk). **DLR Rail and River Rover** (☎ 020/7363-9700 ⊕ www.tfl.gov.uk). **Thames Cruises** (☎ 020/7930-3373 www.thamescruises.com). **Westminster Passenger Services** (☎ 020/7930-4097). **Westminster Passenger Service (Upriver)** (☎ 020/7930-2062 ⊕ www.wpsa.co.uk).

BUS TOURS

Guided sightseeing tours from the top of double-decker buses, which are open-top in summer, are a good introduction to the city, as they cover all the main central sights. Numerous companies run daily bus tours that depart (usually between 8:30 and 9 AM) from central points. You may board or alight at any of the numerous stops to view the sights, and reboard on the next bus. Tickets can be bought from the driver and are good all day. Prices vary according to the type of tour, although £22 is the benchmark.

Green Line, Evan Evans, and National Express offer day excursions by bus to places within easy reach of London, such as Hampton Court, Oxford, Stratford, and Bath.

Contacts Big Bus Company (☎ 020/7233-9533 ⊕ www.bigbustours. com). **Evan Evans** (☎ 020/7950-1777 ⊕ www.evanevans.co.uk). **Green Line** (☎ 0870/608-7261 ⊕ www.greenline.co.uk). **National Express** (☎ 0870/580-8080 ⊕ www.nationalexpress.com). **Original London Sightseeing Tour** (☎ 020/8877-1722 ⊕ www.theoriginaltour.com).

PRIVATE GUIDES

Black Taxi Tour of London is a personal tour by cab direct from your hotel. The price is per cab, so the fare can be shared among as many as five people. An introductory two-hour tour is £100 by day, £110 by night. You can hire a Blue Badge–accredited guide (trained by the tourist board) for walking or driving tours.

Contacts Black Taxi Tour of London (☎ 020/7935-9363 ⊕ www. blacktaxitours.co.uk). **Blue Badge tour guides** (☎ 020/7403-1115 ⊕ www. blue-badge-guides.com).

WALKING TOURS

One of the best ways to get to know London is on foot. Original London Walks has theme tours devoted to the Beatles, Sherlock Holmes, Dickens, Jack the Ripper—you name it. If horror and mystery are your interest, then the City holds plenty of that, as you may discover on a Blood and Tears tour (not suitable for younger children). Tour Guides provides themed historic walks led by accredited Blue Badge guides. Peruse the leaflets at a London Tourist Information Centre for special-interest walks.

Contacts Blood and Tears Walk (☎020/7625–5155 ⊕www.shockinglondon.com). **Original London Walks** (☎020/7624–3978 ⊕www.walks.com). **Tour Guides/Blue Badge** (☎020/7495–5504 ⊕www.tourguides.co.uk).

VISITOR INFORMATION

The main London Tourist Information Centre is at Victoria Station Forecourt; there are also centers at St. Pancras and Waterloo stations. The Britain and London Visitor Centre, open weekdays 9:30 to 6:30, weekends 10 to 4, provides details about travel, accommodations, and entertainment for the whole of Britain, but you need to visit the center in person. VisitLondon, the city's tourist board, has a helpful Web site with links to other sites; you can also book a hotel on the site.

Information Britain and London Visitor Centre (✉1 Regent St., Piccadilly Circus, St. James's ☎No phone ⊕www.visitbritain.com). **London Tourist Information Centre** (✉Victoria Station Forecourt, Victoria ☎No phone). **VisitLondon** (⊕www.visitlondon.com).

EXPLORING LONDON

Westminster and the City contain many of the grand buildings that have played a central role in British history: the Tower of London and St. Paul's Cathedral, Westminster Abbey and the Houses of Parliament, Buckingham Palace, and the older royal palace of St. James's.

London's *un*official centers multiply and mutate year after year. But life is not lived in monuments, as the patrician patrons of the great Georgian architects understood when they commissioned the city's elegant squares and town houses. Within a few minutes' walk of Buckingham Palace, for instance, lie St. James's and Mayfair, neighboring quarters of elegant town houses built for the nobility during the 17th and early 18th centuries and now notable for shopping opportunities. Westminster Abbey's original vegetable patch (or convent garden), which became the site of London's first square, Covent Garden, is now a popular stop.

Hyde Park and Kensington Gardens, preserved by past kings and queens for their own hunting and relaxation, create a swath of parkland across the city center. A walk across Hyde Park brings you to the museum district of South Kensington, with the Natural History Museum, the Science Museum, and the Victoria & Albert Museum. The South Bank has many cultural highlights: the theaters of the South Bank Centre, the Tate Modern, and the reconstruction of Shakespeare's Globe theater. The London Eye observation wheel here gives stunning city views, or you can walk across the Millennium or Hungerford bridges. Farther downstream is the gorgeous 17th- and 18th-century symmetry of Greenwich, and its maritime attractions.

WESTMINSTER AND ROYAL LONDON

If you have time to visit only one part of London, this is it. Westminster and Royal London might be called "London for Beginners." If you went no farther than these few acres, you would have seen many of the famous sights, from the Houses of Parliament, Big Ben, Westminster Abbey, and Buckingham Palace, to two of the world's greatest art collections, in the National and Tate Britain galleries. You can truly call this area Royal London, since it is bounded by the triangle of streets that make up the route that the Queen usually takes when journeying from Buckingham Palace to Westminster Abbey or to the Houses of Parliament on state occasions. The three points on this royal triangle are Trafalgar Square, Westminster, and Buckingham Palace. Naturally, in an area that regularly sees the pomp and pageantry of royal occasions, the streets are wide and the vistas long. St. James's Park lies at the heart of the triangle, which has a feeling of timeless dignity—flower beds bursting with color, long avenues of trees framing classically proportioned buildings, glimpses of pinnacles and towers over the treetops, the distant *bong!* of Big Ben counting off the hours. This is concentrated sightseeing, so pace yourself. For a large part of the year, much of Royal London is floodlighted at night, adding to the theatricality of the experience.

GETTING HERE Trafalgar Square—easy to access and smack dab in the center of the action—is a good place to start. Take the Tube to Embankment (District and Circle lines) and walk north until you cross the Strand, or alight at Charing Cross (Bakerloo, Jubilee, and Northern lines), where the Northumberland Avenue exit deposits you on the southeast corner of the Square.

PLANNING YOUR TIME You could spend a lifetime absorbing the rich history of this part of London. More practically, try to leave at least two days if you want to dip into the full gamut of attractions without feeling horribly rushed. If Royal London is what you want, make a day of Buckingham Palace or Westminster Abbey, the Queen's Gallery, and the Guards Museum at Wellington Barracks. If you've a more constitutional bent, visit the Houses of Parliament and the Cabinet War Rooms.

Numbers in the margin correspond to numbers on the Westminster and Royal London map.

TOP ATTRACTIONS

❾ Buckingham Palace. Supreme among the symbols of London—indeed of Britain generally and of the Royal Family in particular—Buckingham Palace tops many must-see lists, although the building itself is no masterpiece and has housed the monarch only since Victoria (1819–1901) moved here from Kensington Palace on her accession in 1837. Its great gray bulk sums up the imperious splendor of so much of the city: stately, magnificent, and ponderous. In 1824 the palace was substantially rebuilt by John Nash, that tireless architect, for George IV, that tireless spendthrift. Compared with other great London residences, it is a fairly recent affair: the Portland stone facade dates from 1913, and the interior was renovated and redecorated after World War II bombs damaged it. The palace contains some 600 rooms, including the Ballroom and the Throne Room. The state rooms are where much of the business

Fodor'sChoice ★

GREAT ITINERARIES

London overflows with choices: from exploring local pubs and tearooms to taking in great theater and concerts, it's easy to fill a day. A stroll through a quiet neighborhood or a ride on the Thames may be as satisfying as seeing a world-famous museum. Below are suggestions for different experiences.

CROWNING GLORIES

This regal runaround packs more into a day than most cities can offer in a week. Hit Westminster Abbey early to avoid the crowds, then cut through St. James's Park to catch the Changing of the Guard at 11:20 at Buckingham Palace. Take a quick detour to the Tudor delights of St. James's Palace, before a promenade down the Mall past the Regency glory of Carlton House Terrace and through Admiralty Arch to Trafalgar Square. Choose from the treasures of the National Gallery, the Who's Who of the National Portrait Gallery, or a brass rubbing in the crypt of St. Martin's-in-the-Fields. This leaves a stroll down Whitehall—past Downing Street, Horse Guards Parade, and Banqueting House—to the Houses of Parliament, where you have the option of prebooking a tour, or trying to get in to see a debate. If you have any time or energy left, stroll through Hyde Park to Kensington Palace, childhood home of Queen Victoria, and (for aspiring princesses everywhere) the Royal Dress Collection.

MUSEUM MAGIC

London has one of the finest collections of museums in the world, and many are free. Some resemble hands-on playgrounds that will keep children and adults amused for hours; others take a more classical approach. One of the latter is the British Museum in Bloomsbury, an Aladdin's cave of treasures from across the world. While in the area, pop into the nearby museum of architect Sir John Soane.

Alternatively, South Kensington's "Museum Mile" on Cromwell Road houses a triple-whammy that makes for a substantial day's-worth of diversion: the Victoria & Albert Museum, the Natural History Museum, and the Science Museum.

RETAIL THERAPY

It's not hard to shop till you drop in London's West End. Start with the upscale on New Bond Street, an awesome sweep of expense and elegance. In the afternoon, head to Oxford Street, which encompasses four Tube stations and is unbeatable for mass-market shopping. Run the gauntlet of designers, cheap odds and ends, department stores, and ferocious pedestrians: it's seriously busy.

A more sedate but utterly fashionable experience can be found in Knightsbridge, wandering between Harvey Nichols and Harrods department stores. Head south down Sloane Street to Sloane Square and head out along King's Road, with boutiques galore. To dip into the ever-expanding world of urban chic, try an afternoon in the lively Portobello street market in Notting Hill, where you can pick up remnants of various bygone ages: glassware, furniture, art, and clothes.

2

Westminster and Royal London

KEY

U *Tube Station*

1/4 mi

1/4 km

of royalty is played out—investitures, state banquets, and receptions for the great and good—and these are open to the public while the Royal Family is away during the summer. The royal apartments are in the north wing; when the Queen is in, the royal standard is raised. The **Changing of the Guard**—which, with all the pomp and ceremony monarchists and children adore, remains one of London's best free shows—culminates in front of the palace. Marching to live music, the guards proceed up the Mall from St. James's Palace to Buckingham Palace. Shortly afterward, the replacement guard approaches from Wellington Barracks via Birdcage Walk. Once the old and new guards are in the forecourt, the old guard symbolically hands over the keys to the palace. ■TIP→ Get there by 10:30 AM to grab a spot in the best viewing section at the gate facing the palace, since most of the hoopla takes place behind the railings in the forecourt. ⊠ *Buckingham Palace Rd., St. James's* ☎ *020/7766–7300* ⊕ *www.royalcollection.org.uk* 🎟 *£15.50, includes audio tour, credit-card reservations subject to booking charge* ⊙ *Late July–late Sept., daily 9:45–6, last admission 3:45; confirm dates, which are subject to Queen's mandate. Changing of the Guard Apr.– July, daily 11:30 AM; Aug.–Mar., alternating days only 11:30 AM* ⊟ *AE, MC, V* Ⓤ *Victoria, St. James's Park.*

⓮ ⓒ ★ **Cabinet War Rooms & Churchill Museum.** It was from this small warren of underground rooms—beneath the vast government buildings of the Foreign Office—that Winston Churchill and his team directed troops in World War II. Designed to be bombproof, the whole complex has been preserved almost exactly as it was when the last light was turned off at the end of the war. Every clock shows almost 5 PM, and the furniture, fittings, and paraphernalia of a busy, round-the-clock war office are in situ, down to the colored map pins. An exciting addition to the Cabinet War Rooms is the **Churchill Museum,** which opened in 2005 on the 40th anniversary of his death. Different zones explore his life and achievements—and failures, too—through objects and documents, many of which, such as his personal papers, had never previously been made public. Central to the exhibition is an interactive timeline, with layers of facts, figures, and tales. If you visit in August, there are late-night openings and 1940s-style musical events; call ahead or check the Website for details. ⊠ *Clive Steps, King Charles St., Westminster* ☎ *020/7930–6961* ⊕ *cwr.iwm.org.uk* 🎟 *£12, includes audio tour* ⊙ *Daily 9:30–6; last admission 5* Ⓤ *Westminster.*

⓱ **Horse Guards Parade.** Once the tiltyard of Whitehall Palace, where jousting tournaments were held, the Horse Guards Parade is now notable mainly for the annual Trooping the Colour ceremony, in which the Queen takes the Royal Salute, her official birthday gift, on the second Saturday in June. (Like Paddington Bear, the Queen has two birthdays; her real one is on April 21.) At the Whitehall facade of Horse Guards, the changing of two mounted sentries known as the **mounted guard** provides what may be London's most popular photo opportunity. The ceremony lasts about half an hour and follows a similar idea to the change outside Buckingham Palace, except here the guards are on horses. ⊠ *Whitehall, Westminster* ☎ *020/7930–4832* ⊙ *Queen's mounted guard ceremony Mon.–Sat. 11 AM, Sun. 10 AM* Ⓤ *Westminster.*

12 **Houses of Parliament.** Seat of Great Britain's government, the Houses of Parliament are, arguably, the city's most famous and photogenic sight. Facing them you see, from left to right, Big Ben—keeping watch on the corner—the Houses of Parliament themselves, Westminster Hall (the oldest part of the complex), and the Victoria Tower. The most romantic view of the complex is from the opposite, south side of the river, a vista especially dramatic at

Fodor's Choice
★

> **A VIEW TO REMEMBER**
>
> The most romantic view of the Houses of Parliament is from the opposite (south) side of the river, especially dramatic at night when the spires, pinnacles, and towers are floodlighted green and gold—a fairy-tale vision only missing the presence of Peter Pan and Wendy on their way to Never-Never Land.

night when the spires, pinnacles, and towers of the great building are floodlighted green and gold. After a catastrophic fire in 1834, these buildings arose, designed in glorious, mock-medieval style by two Victorian-era architects, Sir Charles Barry and Augustus Pugin. The Palace of Westminster, as the complex is still properly called, was established by Edward the Confessor in the 11th century. It has served as the seat of English administrative power, on and off, ever since. Now virtually the symbol of London, the 1858 **Clock Tower** designed by Pugin contains the bell known as **Big Ben** that chimes the hour (and the quarters). Weighing a mighty 13 tons, the bell takes its name from Sir Benjamin Hall, the far-from-slim Westminster building works commissioner. At the other end of Parliament is the 336-foot-high **Victoria Tower.** There are two houses, the Lords and the Commons. You can see democracy in action in the Visitors' Galleries—if, that is, you're patient enough to wait in line for hours (the Lords line is shorter) or have applied in advance for the special "line of route" tour for overseas visitors in summer (late July through August and mid-September through early October). Tickets can be prebooked by phone or on the Web site; alternatively, you can take a chance and buy same-day tickets from the ticket office opposite the Houses of Parliament. The time to catch the action is Question Time—when the prime minister defends himself against the attacks of his "right honorable friends" on Wednesday between noon and 2:30 PM. For a special exhibition devoted to the history of Parliament, head to the **Jewel Tower,** across the street from Victoria Tower, on Abingdon Street. Be sure to have your name placed in advance on the waiting list for the twice-weekly tours of the **Lord Chancellor's Residence,** a popular attraction since its renovation. ✉*St. Stephen's Entrance, St. Margaret St., Westminster* ☎*020/7219–4272 Commons information, 020/7219–3107 Lords information, 020/7222–2219 Jewel Tower, 020/7219–2184 Lord Chancellor's Residence, 0870/906–3773 summer tours* ⊕*www.parliament.uk* ✉*Free, £12 summer tours* ☉*Commons Mon. and Tues. 2:30–10:30, Wed. 3–10, Thurs. 11:30–7:30; Lords Mon.–Thurs. 2:30–10; Lord Chancellor's Residence Tues. and Thurs. 10:30–12:30. Closed Easter wk, late July–early Sept., 3 wks for party conference recess mid-Sept.–early Oct., and 3 wks at Christmas* Ⓤ*Westminster.*

QUICK BITES

The Wesley Café (⊠ *Storey's Gate, Westminster* ☎ *020/7222–8010*) is a popular budget haunt for office workers around Westminster, and a good stopping point if you don't want to go farther along Victoria Street in search of food. It's almost opposite Westminster Abbey, in the crypt of Central Hall, a former Methodist church.

❷ **National Gallery.** Jan Van Eyck's *Arnolfini Marriage,* Leonardo da Vinci's *Virgin and Child,* Diego Velázquez's *Rokeby Venus,* John Constable's *Hay Wain . . .* you get the picture. There are approximately 2,200 other paintings in this museum, many of them among the most treasured works of art anywhere. The museum's low, gray, colonnaded, neoclassical facade fills the north side of Trafalgar Square. The gallery's east wing in sleek black and white marble has cafés and improved visitor information, such as boards with a color code for different eras of paintings. The National's collection includes paintings of the early Renaissance—in the modern Sainsbury Wing—the Flemish and Dutch masters, the Spanish school, and the English tradition (notably William Hogarth, Thomas Gainsborough, George Stubbs, and Constable).

Fodor's Choice ★

A good place to begin is one of the computer terminals in the "Art Start" multimedia room in the Sainsbury Wing or the Espresso Bar in the East Wing. The interactive screens give you access to information on all of the museum's holdings; you can choose your favorites, and print out a free personal tour map. In addition to the four mentioned above, the museum's top 10 includes Paolo Uccello's *Battle of San Romano* (children love its knights on horseback), Giovanni Bellini's *Doge Leonardo Loredan* (notice the snail-shell buttons), Sandro Botticelli's *Venus and Mars,* Michelangelo Caravaggio's *Supper at Emmaus* (almost cinematically lit), J. M. W. Turner's *Fighting Téméraire* (one of the artist's greatest sunsets), and Georges Seurat's *Bathers at Asnières.* The museum is too overwhelming to absorb in a single viewing, but the free admission encourages repeat visits. The ultracool National Gallery Café in the East Wing makes a fun stop even if you're not visiting the gallery. ⊠ *Trafalgar Sq., Westminster* ☎ *020/7747–2885* ⊕ *www. nationalgallery.org.uk* ☏ *Free, charge for special exhibitions* ☉ *Daily 10–6, Wed. until 9; 1-hr free guided tour starts at Sainsbury Wing daily at 11:30 and 2:30, and additionally Wed. 6 and 6:30, Sat. 12:30 and 3:30* Ⓤ *Charing Cross, Leicester Sq.*

❸ **National Portrait Gallery.** A suitably idiosyncratic collection that presents a potted history of Britain through its people, past and present, this museum is an essential stop for all history and literature buffs, where you can choose to take in a little, or a lot. Some of the faces are obscure and will be just as unknown to you if you're English, because the portraits outlasted their sitters' fame—not so surprising when the portraitists are such greats as Reynolds, Gainsborough, Lawrence, and Romney. But the annotation is comprehensive, the layout is easy to negotiate—chronological, with the oldest at the top—and there's a separate research center for those who get hooked on particular personages. The spacious, bright galleries are accessible via a state-of-the-art escalator, which lets you view the paintings as you ascend to a sky-lighted space. At the summit, a sleek restaurant, open beyond gallery

Where to See the Royals

The Queen and the Royal Family attend approximately 400 functions a year, and if you want to know what they are doing on any given date, turn to the *Court Circular*, printed in the major London dailies, or check out the Royal Family Web site, ⊕*www.royal.gov.uk*, for the latest pictures and events. Trooping the Colour is usually held on the second Saturday in June, to celebrate the Queen's official birthday. This spectacular parade begins when she leaves Buckingham Palace in her carriage and rides down the Mall to arrive at Horse Guards Parade at 11 exactly. To watch, just line up along the Mall with your binoculars!

Another time you can catch the Queen in all her regalia is when she and the Duke of Edinburgh ride in state to Westminster to open the Houses of Parliament. The famous gilded coach, such an icon of fairy-tale glamour, parades from Buckingham Palace, escorted by the brilliantly uniformed Household Cavalry—on a clear day, it's to be hoped, for this ceremony takes place in late October or early November, depending on the exigencies of Parliament.

But perhaps the most relaxed, least formal time to see the Queen is during Royal Ascot, held at the racetrack near Windsor Castle—a short train ride out of London—usually during the third week of June (Tuesday–Friday). After several races, the Queen invariably walks down to the paddock on a special path, greeting race goers as she proceeds.

hours, will satiate skyline droolers. ⊠*St. Martin's Pl., Covent Garden* ☎*020/7312–2463 recorded information* ⊕*www.npg.org.uk* ✉*Free, charge for special exhibitions* ☉*Mon.–Wed., weekends 10–6, Thurs. and Fri. 10–9* Ⓤ*Charing Cross, Leicester Sq.*

🔟 **The Queen's Gallery.** The former chapel at the south side of Buckingham
★ Palace is now a temple of art and rare and exquisite objects, acquired by kings and queens over the centuries. Although Her Majesty herself is not the personal owner, she has the privilege of holding these works for the nation. Step through the splendid portico (designed by John Simpson) into elegantly restrained, spacious galleries whose walls are hung with some truly great works. An excellent audio guide takes you through the treasures. ■TIP➡ **The E-gallery provides an interactive electronic version of the collection, allowing the user to open lockets, remove a sword from its scabbard, or take apart the tulip vases.** ⊠*Buckingham Palace, Buckingham Palace Rd., St. James's* ☎*020/7766–7301* ⊕*www.royal.gov.uk* ✉*£8 with free audio guide, joint ticket with Royal Mews £13.50* ☉*Daily 10–5:30; last admission 4:30* Ⓤ*Victoria, St. James's Park, Green Park.*

☾ **St. James's Park.** With three palaces at its borders (the Palace of Westminster, the Tudor St. James's Palace, and Buckingham Palace), St. James's Park is acclaimed as the most royal of the royal parks. It's London's smallest, most ornamental park, as well as the oldest; it was acquired by Henry VIII in 1532 for a deer park. One of the best times to stroll the leafy walkways is after dark, with Westminster Abbey and the Houses of Parliament rising above the floodlighted lake. The popular

Inn the Park restaurant is a wood-and-glass pavilion with a turf roof that blends in beautifully with the surrounding landscape; it's a good stopping place for a meal or a snack on a nice day. ✉ *The Mall or Horse Guards approach, or Birdcage Walk, St. James's* ⊕ *www.royalparks. gov.uk* Ⓤ *St. James's Park, Westminster.*

⑱ **Tate Britain.** Although the building is not quite as awe-inspiring as its
★ younger sister the Tate Modern, on the south bank of the Thames, Tate Britain's lovely, bright galleries hold only a fraction of the Modern's crowds, making it a pleasant, hands-on place to explore great British art from 1500 to the present. First opened in 1897, funded by the sugar magnate Sir Henry Tate, the museum includes the Linbury Galleries on the lower floors, which stage temporary exhibitions (they can get busy), while the upper floors show the permanent collection. Each room has a theme and displays key works by major British artists: Van Dyck, Hogarth, and Reynolds rub shoulders with Rossetti, Sickert, Hockney, and Bacon. Not to be missed is the generous selection of Constable landscapes. Other highlights are the many stunning works by J.M.W. Turner, housed in the Clore Gallery. ✉ *Millbank, Westminster* ☎ *020/7887–8888, 020/7887–8008 recorded information* ⊕ *www. tate.org.uk/britain* ✉ *Free, exhibitions £3–£10* ⊙ *Daily 10–5:50, last entry at 5* Ⓤ *Pimlico (signposted 5-min walk).*

❶ **Trafalgar Square.** This is literally the center of London: a plaque on the corner of the Strand and Charing Cross Road marks the spot from which distances on U.K. signposts are measured. It's the home of the **National Gallery** on its north side, and **Nelson's Column** at the heart of the square, flanked by two generals who distinguished themselves in the service of empire in India: **Charles Napier,** conqueror of Sind, and **Henry Havelock,** who recaptured Cawnpore (Kanpur) for the British during the Indian rebellion of 1857. Great events, such as the Christmas Tree lighting ceremony, New Year's Eve, royal weddings, political protests, and sporting triumphs always see the crowds gathering in the city's most famous square. ✉ *Trafalgar Sq., Westminster* Ⓤ *Charing Cross.*

⑬ **Westminster Abbey.** A monument to the nation's rich—and often bloody
Fodor'sChoice and scandalous—history, the abbey rises on the Thames skyline as one
★ of London's most iconic sites. Nearly all of Britain's monarchs have been crowned here since the coronation of William the Conqueror on Christmas Day 1066—and most are buried here, too. The abbey's majestic main nave is packed with memories (and, often, crowds), as it has witnessed many splendid royal events. Other than the mysterious gloom of the vast interior, the first thing that strikes most people is the proliferation of statues, tombs, and commemorative tablets. In parts, the building seems more like a stonemason's yard than a place of worship. But in its latter capacity, this landmark truly comes into its own. Although attending a service is not something to undertake purely for sightseeing reasons, it provides a glimpse of the abbey in its full majesty, with the service accompanied by music from the Westminster choristers and the organ that composer Henry Purcell once played.

The current abbey is a largely 13th- and 14th-century rebuilding of the 11th-century church founded by Edward the Confessor, with one notable addition being the 18th-century twin towers over the west entrance, designed by Sir Christopher Wren and completed by Nicholas Hawksmoor. Entering by the north door to follow the one-way route through the abbey, what you see first on your left are the extravagant 18th-century monuments of statesmen in the north transept, as well as the north-transept chapels. Look up to your right to see the painted-glass rose window, the largest of its kind. At many points

IN A HURRY?

If you're pressed for time, concentrate on these four Westminster Abbey highlights: the Coronation Chair; tombs of Elizabeth I and Mary, Queen of Scots, in the Chapel of Henry VII; Poets' Corner; and Tomb of the Unknown Warrior.

the view of the abbey is crowded by the many statues and screens; to your right is the mostly 19th-century choir screen (part is 13th-century), while to the left is the sacrarium, containing the medieval kings' tombs that screen the **Chapel of St. Edward** (because of its fragility the shrine is closed off, unless you take a tour with the verger—ask at the admission desk when you enter). Continuing to the foot of the Henry VII Chapel steps, you can still see the hot seat of power, the **Coronation Chair,** which has been graced by nearly every royal posterior. Then proceed into one of the architectural glories of Britain, the **Henry VII Chapel** (also known as the Lady Chapel), passing the huge white marble tomb of Elizabeth I, buried with her half-sister, "Bloody" Mary I. The tomb of Mary, Queen of Scots, is here also. All around the chapel are magnificent sculptures of saints, philosophers, and kings, with mermaids and monsters carved on the choir-stall misericords (undersides), and exquisite fan vaulting above (binoculars will help you spot the statues high on the walls)—the last riot of medieval design in England and one of the miracles of Western architecture.

Continue to **Poets' Corner;** in 1400 Geoffrey Chaucer became the first poet to be buried here. There are memorials to William Shakespeare, William Blake, and Charles Dickens (who is also buried here). Outside the west front is an archway into the quiet, green **Dean's Yard** and the entrance to the **Cloisters.** If time allows, visit the **Chapter House,** a stunning octagonal room adorned with 14th-century frescoes, where the King's Council met between 1257 and 1547. The **Abbey Museum** is in the **Undercroft,** which survives from Edward the Confessor's original church. The museum includes effigies made from the death masks and actual clothing of Charles II and Admiral Lord Nelson, among other fascinating relics. Adjoining these rooms, the **Little Cloister** is a quiet haven. Just beyond, the **College Garden,** under cultivation for more than 900 years, is planted with medicinal herbs. As you return to the abbey, look again at the truly awe-inspiring nave. Pause for the **Tomb of the Unknown Warrior,** an anonymous World War I martyr who lies buried here in memory of the soldiers fallen in both world wars.

Arrive early if possible, but be prepared to wait in line to tour the abbey. You can rent an audio guide (£3) or ask the information desk about 90-minute verger-led tours (£4). Photography is not permitted. ✉ *Broad Sanctuary, Westminster* ☎ *020/7222–5152* ⊕ *www.westminster-abbey.*

org ✉*Abbey and museum £10* ⏱ *Abbey Mon., Tues., Thurs., and Fri. 9:30–3:45, Wed. 9:30–6, Sat. 9–1:45 (closes 1 hr after last admission). Museum daily 10:30–4. Cloisters daily 8–6. College Garden Tues.– Thurs. Apr.–Sept. 10–6, Oct.–Mar. 10–4. Separate admission for Chapter House daily 10–4. Abbey closed to visitors during weekday and Sun. services* Ⓤ *Westminster.*

WORTH NOTING

⑯ Banqueting House. This is all that remains today of the Tudor Palace of Whitehall, which was (according to one foreign visitor) "ill-built, and nothing but a heap of houses." James I commissioned Inigo Jones (1573–1652), one of England's great architects, to undertake a grand remodeling. Influenced during a sojourn in Italy by Andrea Palladio's work, Jones brought Palladian sophistication and purity back to London with him. James I's son, Charles I, enhanced the interior by employing the Flemish painter Peter Paul Rubens to glorify his father and the Stuart dynasty in vibrant painted ceiling panels. As it turned out, these allegorical paintings, depicting a wise monarch being received into heaven, were the last thing Charles saw before he was beheaded by Cromwell's Parliamentarians in 1649. ✉ *Whitehall, Westminster* ☎*020/3166–6154/5 or 0844/482–7777* ⊕*www.hrp.org.uk* ✉*£4.50, includes audio guide* ⏱ *Mon.–Sat. 10–5; last admission 4:30. Closed Christmas wk* Ⓤ*Charing Cross, Embankment, Westminster.*

❺ Carlton House Terrace. A glorious example of Regency architect John Nash's genius, Carlton House Terrace was built between 1812 and 1830, under the patronage of George IV (Prince Regent until George III's death in 1820). Today Carlton House Terrace houses the Royal College of Pathologists (No. 2), the Royal Society (No. 6), whose members included Isaac Newton and Charles Darwin, the Turf Club (No. 5), and, at No. 12, the **Institute of Contemporary Arts,** better known as the ICA. ✉*The Mall, St. James's* Ⓤ*Charing Cross.*

❻ Clarence House. The London home of Queen Elizabeth the Queen Mother for nearly 50 years, Clarence House is now the Prince of Wales and the Duchess of Cornwall's residence. The Regency mansion was built by John Nash for the Duke of Clarence, who found living in St. James's Palace quite unsuitable. The rooms have been sensitively preserved as the Queen Mother chose, with the addition of many works of art from the Royal Collection. You'll find it less palace, and more home (for the Prince and his sons William and Harry), with informal family pictures and comfortable sofas. ✉*Clarence House, St. James's Palace, St. James's* ☎*020/7766–7303* ⊕*www.royal.gov.uk* ✉*£7.50* ⏱ *Aug.–mid-Sept.* Ⓤ*Green Park.*

⑮ Downing Street. Looking like an unassuming alley but for the iron gates at both its Whitehall and Horse Guards Road approaches, this is the location of the famous **No. 10,** London's modest version of the White House. Just south of Downing Street, in the middle of Whitehall, you'll see the **Cenotaph,** a stark white monolith designed in 1920 by Edwin Lutyens to commemorate the 1918 armistice. ✉*The Mall, St. James's* Ⓤ*Charing Cross.*

❼ St. James's Palace. With its solitary sentry posted at the gate, this surprisingly small palace of Tudor brick was once a home for many British sovereigns, including the first Elizabeth and Charles I, who spent his last night here before his execution. Today it's the working office of another Charles—the Prince of Wales. The front door actually opens right onto the street, but he always uses a back entrance. ⊠ *Friary Court, St. James's* ⊕ *www.royal.gov.uk* Ⓤ *Green Park.*

❹ St. Martin-in-the-Fields. One of London's best-loved and most welcoming of churches. Expensive and time-consuming refurbishment work has now enhanced the church both inside and out, and the building's array of functions continues unabated. The church is also a haven for music lovers; the internationally known Academy of St. Martin-in-the-Fields was founded here, and a popular program of concerts continues today. The crypt is a hive of lively activity, with a café and bookshop, plus the **London Brass-Rubbing Centre,** where you can make your own life-size souvenir knight, lady, or monarch from replica tomb brasses, with metallic waxes, paper, and instructions provided from about £5; and the **Gallery in the Crypt,** showing contemporary work. ⊠ *Trafalgar Sq., Covent Garden* ☎ *020/7766–1100, 020/7839–8362 evening-concert credit-card bookings* ⊕ *www.stmartin-in-the-fields.org* ⊗ *Mon.–Sat. 8–6, Sun. 11–6* Ⓤ *Charing Cross, Leicester Sq.*

❽ Spencer House. Ancestral abode of the Spencers—Diana, Princess of Wales's family—this great mansion is perhaps the finest example of 18th-century elegance, on a domestic scale, extant in London. Superlatively restored by Lord Rothschild, the house was built in 1766 by Palladian architect John Vardy for the first Earl Spencer, heir to the first Duchess of Marlborough. The gorgeous Doric facade, its pediment adorned with classical statues, makes immediately clear Earl Spencer's passion for the Grand Tour and the classical antiquities of the past. Both the house and garden can be seen by guided tour only in limited numbers, so book in advance. ⊠ *27 St. James's Pl., St. James's* ☎ *020/7499–8620* ⊕ *www.spencerhouse.co.uk* ⊠ *£9* ⊗ *Sept.–Dec. and Feb.–July, Sun. 10:45–4:45; guided tour leaves approx. every 25 mins; tickets on sale Sun. at 10:30. Garden: late May–July, separate charge for tour* Ⓤ *Green Park.*

⓫ Wellington Barracks. These are the headquarters of the Guards Division, the Queen's five regiments of elite foot guards (Grenadier, Coldstream, Scots, Irish, and Welsh) who protect the sovereign. If you want to learn more about the guards, or view every kind of toy model soldier, visit the **Guards Museum;** the entrance is next to the Guards Chapel. ⊠ *Wellington Barracks, Birdcage Walk, Westminster* ☎ *020/7414–3428* ⊕ *www. theguardsmuseum.com* ⊠ *£3* ⊗ *Daily 10–4; last admission 3:30* Ⓤ *St. James's Park.*

SOHO AND COVENT GARDEN

Once a red-light district, the Soho of today delivers more "grown-up" than "adult" entertainment. Its theaters, restaurants, pubs, and clubs merge with the first-run cinemas of Leicester Square and the venerable venues (Royal and English National Operas) of Covent Garden to create the mega-entertainment district known as the West End. During the day Covent Garden's historic piazza is packed with shoppers and sightseers, while Soho reverts to the business side of its lively, late-night scene—ad agencies, media, film distributors, actors, agents, and casting agents all looking for each other.

A quadrilateral bounded by Regent Street, Coventry and Cranbourn streets, Charing Cross Road, and the eastern half of Oxford Street encloses Soho. This appellation, unlike the New York City neighborhood's similar one, is not an abbreviation of anything, but a blast from the past—derived from the shouts of "So-ho!" that royal huntsmen in Whitehall Palace's parklands were once heard to cry. For many years Soho was London's peep show–sex shop–brothel center. Legislation in the mid-1980s granted expensive licenses to a few such establishments and closed down the rest. Today Soho remains the address of wonderful ethnic restaurants, including those of London's Chinatown.

The Covent Garden Market became the Covent Garden Piazza in 1980. It was originally the "convent garden" belonging to the Abbey of St. Peter at Westminster (later Westminster Abbey), and still functions as the center of a neighborhood—one that has always been alluded to as "colorful." After centuries of magnificence and misery, Covent Garden became London's vegetable and flower market in the 19th century. When the produce moved to the Nine Elms Market in Vauxhall in 1974, the glass-covered market halls took on new life with stores and entertainment. Today it bustles with tourists and shoppers.

GETTING HERE   Take any train to the Piccadilly Circus station (on the Piccadilly and Bakerloo lines or Leicester Square and Northern lines for Soho). Get off at Covent Garden on the Piccadilly Line for Covent Garden and Embankment (Bakerloo, Northern, District, and Circle lines) or Charing Cross (Northern, Bakerloo, and main railway lines) for the area south of the Strand.

PLANNING   You can comfortably tour all the sights in Covent Garden in a day. Visit
YOUR TIME   the small but perfect Courtauld Institute Gallery on Monday before 2 PM when it's free. That leaves plenty of time to visit the marketplace, watch the street entertainment, and do a bit of shopping, with energy left over for a night on the town (or "on the tiles," as the British say) in Soho.

Numbers in the margin correspond to numbers on the Soho and Covent Garden map.

TOP ATTRACTIONS

❼ Courtauld Institute Gallery. One of London's most beloved art collections, the Courtauld is to your left as you pass through the archway into the grounds of the beautifully restored, grand 18th-century classical **Somerset House.** Founded in 1931 by the textile magnate Samuel Courtauld to house his remarkable private collection, with artists ranging from Bonnard to van Gogh. A déjà-vu moment with Cézanne, Degas, Seurat, or Monet awaits on every wall (Manet's *Bar at the Folies-Bergère* is the star), with bonus post-Renaissance works thrown in. ⊠*Somerset House, The Strand, Covent Garden* ☎*020/7848–2526* ⊕*www.courtauld.ac.uk* ✉*£5, free Mon. 10–2, except bank holidays* ☉*Daily 10–6; last admission 5:30* Ⓤ*Covent Garden, Holborn, Temple.*

❸ **Covent Garden Piazza.** The 1840 market building around which Covent Garden pivots is known as the Piazza. Inside, the shops are mostly
higher-class clothing chains, plus a couple of cafés and some knickknack
stores that are good for gifts. One particular gem is Benjamin Pollock's
Toyshop at number 44 in the market. Established in the 1880s, it sells
delightful toy theaters. There's the superior **Apple Market** for crafts on
most days, too. If you turn right, you'll reach the indoor **Jubilee Market,**
which, with its stalls of clothing, army-surplus gear, and more crafts
and knickknacks, is disappointingly ordinary. In summer it may seem
that everyone you see around the Piazza (and the crowds are legion)
is a fellow tourist, but there's still plenty of office life in the area. Londoners who shop here tend to head for Neal Street and the area to the
left of the subway entrance rather than the touristy market itself. By
the church in the square, street performers—from global musicians to
jugglers and mimes—play to the crowds, as they have done since the
first English Punch and Judy Show, staged here in the 17th century.
⊠ *Covent Garden* Ⓤ *Covent Garden.*

❻ **Somerset House.** An old royal palace once stood on the site, but it was
★ eventually replaced by this 18th-century building, the work of Sir William Chambers (1726–96), during the reign of George III. It was built
to house government offices, principally those of the Navy. Now, for
the first time in more than 100 years, these gracious rooms are on view,
including the Seamen's Waiting Hall and the Nelson Stair. In addition,
the Navy Commissioners' Barge has returned to dry dock at the Water
Gate. The rooms are on the south side of the building, by the river. The
Courtauld Institute Gallery occupies most of the north building, facing
the busy Strand. In between is the cobbled Italianate courtyard where
Admiral Nelson used to walk, the scene of an ice rink in the winter holiday season as well as summer concerts and other cultural events. ⊠ *The
Strand, Covent Garden* ☎ *020/7845–4600* ⊕ *www.somerset-house.
org.uk* 🖼 *£5, free on Mon. 10–2* ⊙ *Daily 10–6; last admission 5:30*
Ⓤ *Charing Cross.*

WORTH NOTING

❽ **The Adam Houses.** All that remains of what was once a regal riverfront
row of houses on a 3-acre site, connected by arches and streets below
grade, are a few of the structures, but such is their quality that they
are worth a detour off the Strand to see. The work of 18th-century
Scottish architects and interior designers (John, Robert, James, and
William Adam, known collectively as the Adam brothers), the original
development was damaged in the 19th century during the building of
the embankment, and mostly demolished in 1936 to be replaced by an
art deco tower. The original houses still standing are protected, and give
a glimpse of their former grandeur. Nos. 1–4 Robert Street and Nos.
7 and 10 Adam Street are the best. At the **Royal Society of Arts** (⊠ *8
John Adam St.* ☎ *020/7930–5115* ⊕ *www.rsa.org.uk* 🖼 *Free* ⊙ *1st
Sun. of month, 10–1*), you can see a suite of Adam rooms; no reservations are required. ⊠ *The Strand, Covent Garden* Ⓤ *Charing Cross,
Embankment.*

Soho and Covent Garden

KEY

U Tube Station

Adam Houses **8**
Benjamin Franklin House **2**
Courtauld Institute Gallery **7**
Covent Garden Piazza **3**
London's Transport Museum **5**
Leicester Square **1**
Royal Opera House **4**
Somerset House **6**

2 **Benjamin Franklin House.** Opened to the public for the first time in 2006, this architecturally significant 1730 house is the only surviving residence of American statesman, scientist, writer, and inventor Benjamin Franklin, who lived and worked there for 16 years preceding the American Revolution. The restored Georgian town house has been left unfurnished, the better to show off the original features—18th-century paneling, stoves, beams, bricks, and

> **FEELING PECKISH?**
>
> Although they may set out a few tables, the coffee shops and snack bars along the Covent Garden market buildings are better for takeout than for comfortable coffee breaks or lunches. They can be overpriced and of iffy quality. Head for Soho when the munchies strike.

windows. Older children (under 16 admitted free) particularly enjoy the "Historical Experience," an interactive biography of the Founding Father that is offered on the hour from noon to 4. ⊠ *36 Craven St., Covent Garden* ☎ *020/7839–2006, 020/7925–1405 booking line* ⊕ *www.benjaminfranklinhouse.org* 🎫 *£7* ⊗ *Wed.–Sun. 10:30–5.*

1 **Leicester Square.** This square (pronounced "Lester") is showing no sign of its great age. Looking at the neon of the major movie houses, the fast-food outlets (plus a useful Häagen-Dazs café), and the disco entrances, you'd never guess it was laid out around 1630. By the 19th century it was already bustling and disreputable, and now it's usually one of the few places crowded after midnight—with suburban teenagers, backpackers, and London's swelling ranks of the homeless. That said, it's not a threatening place, and the liveliness can be quite cheering. But be on your guard—any place so full of tourists and people a little the worse for wear is bound to attract pickpockets, and Leicester Square certainly does. In the middle is a statue of a sulking Shakespeare, clearly wishing he were somewhere else and perhaps remembering the days when the cinemas were live theaters—burlesque houses, but live all the same. ◼ TIP→ **One landmark worth visiting is TKTS, the Society of London Theatre ticket kiosk, which sells half-price tickets for many of that evening's performances. It's open Monday through Saturday from 10 AM to 7 PM, and Sunday from noon to 3 PM.** ⊠ *Covent Garden* Ⓤ *Leicester Sq.*

5 **London's Transport Museum.** As you watch the crowds gawping at the horse trams, steam locomotives, and trolley buses from the past, you're not sure who's enjoying it more, children or adults. This kid-friendly (under 16 admitted free) museum is filled with impressive poster, photograph, and vehicle collections. ⊠ *Covent Garden Piazza* ☎ *020/7379–6344* ⊕ *www.ltmuseum.co.uk* 🎫 *£8,* ⊗ *Sat.–Thurs. 10–6 (last admission 5:15), Fri. 11–9 (last admission 8:15 PM)* Ⓤ *Leicester Sq., Covent Garden, Holborn, Charing Cross.*

4 **Royal Opera House.** London's premier opera and ballet venue has been given a spectacular overhaul, retains the magic of the grand Victorian theater but is now more accessible. The glass-and-steel Floral Hall is the most wonderful feature; you can wander around and drink in (literally, in the foyer café) the interior during the day. ⊠ *Bow St., Covent Garden* ☎ *020/7240–1200* ⊕ *www.royalopera.org* Ⓤ *Covent Garden.*

BLOOMSBURY AND LEGAL LONDON

The hub of intellectual London, Bloomsbury is anchored by the British Museum and the University of London, which houses—among other institutions—the internationally ranked London School of Economics and the School of Oriental and African Studies. As a result, the streets and cafés around Bloomsbury's Russell Square are often crawling with students and professors engaged in heated conversation, while literary agents and academics surf the shelves of the antiquarian bookstores nearby.

The character of an area of London can change visibly from one street to the next. Nowhere is this so clear as in the contrast between fun-loving Soho and intellectual Bloomsbury, a mere 100 yards to the northeast, or between arty, trendy Covent Garden and—on the other side of Kingsway—sober Holborn (pronounced *hoe*-bun). Bloomsbury is known for its famous flowering of literary-arty bohemia, personified during the first three decades of the 20th century by the clique known as the Bloomsbury Group, including Virginia Woolf, E. M. Forster, Vanessa Bell, and Lytton Strachey. The second, filled with ancient buildings of the legal profession, is more interesting and beautiful than you might suppose. The Great Fire of 1666 razed most of the city but spared the buildings of legal London, and all of Holborn oozes history. Leading landmarks here are the Inns of Court, where the country's top solicitors and barristers have had their chambers for centuries.

GETTING HERE   You can easily get to where you need to be on foot in Bloomsbury, and the Russell Square Tube stop on the Piccadilly Line leaves you right at the corner of Russell Square. The best Tube stops for the Inns of Court are Holborn on the Central and Piccadilly lines or Chancery Lane on the Central Line. Tottenham Court Road on the Northern and Central lines or Russell Square (Piccadilly Line) are best for the British Museum.

PLANNING YOUR TIME   Bloomsbury can be seen in a day, or in half a day, depending on your interests. If you plan to visit the Inns of Court as well as the British Museum, and you'd also like to get a feel for the neighborhood, then you may devote an entire day to this literary and legal enclave, or come back on another day to visit the vast British Museum. Avoid Bloomsbury in mid-September, when the streets around Russell Square are filled with students moving into housing for the upcoming school session. At other times it's a pleasure to wander through the quiet, leafy squares, examining Blue Plaques or relaxing at a street-side café. You can also pick up a "Museum Mile" map, which marks all the museums in this area, and use it to plan your path.

Numbers in the margin correspond to numbers on the Bloomsbury and Legal London map.

TOP ATTRACTIONS

❶ **British Museum.** With a facade like a great temple, this celebrated treasure house, filled with plunder of incalculable value and beauty from around the globe, occupies a ponderous Greco-Victorian building that makes a suitably grand impression. Inside are some of the greatest relics of humankind: the Parthenon Marbles, the Rosetta Stone,

Fodor's Choice ★

Bloomsbury and
Legal London

the Sutton Hoo Treasure—almost everything, it seems, but the Ark of the Covenant. Many sections have been updated, particularly in ethnography, including the impressive **Sainsbury African Galleries.** The focal point is the **Great Court,** a brilliant techno-classical design with a vast glass roof that highlights and reveals the museum's best-kept secret—an inner courtyard. The revered **Reading Room** has a blue-and-gold dome, ancient tomes, and computer screens. If you want to navigate the highlights of the almost 100 galleries, join one of the free **Eyeopener** 50-minute tours by museum guides (details at the information desk).

The collection began in 1753 and grew quickly, thanks to enthusiastic kleptomaniacs during the Napoleonic Wars—most notoriously the seventh earl of Elgin, who acquired the marbles from the Parthenon and Erechtheum in Athens during his term as British ambassador in Constantinople. Here follows a highly edited résumé (in order of encounter) of the British Museum's greatest hits: close to the entrance hall, in Room 4, is the **Rosetta Stone,** found by French soldiers in 1799, and carved in 196 BC with a decree of Ptolemy V in Egyptian hieroglyphics, demotic (a cursive script developed in Egypt), and Greek. This inscription provided the French Egyptologist Jean-François Champollion with the key to deciphering hieroglyphics. Maybe the **Parthenon Marbles** ought to be back in Greece, but since these graceful sculptures are here, make a beeline for them in Room 18, west of the entrance in the Parthenon Galleries. These galleries include the spectacular remains of the Parthenon frieze that girdled the cella of Athena's temple on the Acropolis, carved around 440 BC. Also in the West Wing is one of the Seven Wonders of the Ancient World—in fragment form—in Room 21: the **Mausoleum of Halikarnassos.** The **JP Morgan Chase North American Gallery** (Room 26) has one of the largest collections of native culture outside the North American continent, going back to the earliest hunters 10,000 years ago.

Upstairs are some of the most popular galleries, especially beloved by children: Rooms 62–63, where the **Egyptian mummies** live. Nearby are the glittering 4th-century **Mildenhall Treasure** and the equally splendid 8th-century Anglo-Saxon **Sutton Hoo Treasure** (with a magnificent helmet and jewelry). A more prosaic exhibit is that of Pete Marsh, sentimentally named by the archaeologists who unearthed the **Lindow Man** from a Cheshire peat marsh; poor Pete was ritually slain in the 1st century, probably as a human sacrifice. The **Korean Gallery** (Room 67) delves into the art and archaeology of the country, including precious porcelain and colorful screens. ⊠ *Great Russell St., Bloomsbury*

☎*020/7323–8000* ⊕*www.thebritishmuseum.ac.uk* ✉*Free, donation suggested; tickets for special exhibitions vary in price* ⊘ *Museum Sat.– Wed. 10–5:30, Thurs. and Fri. 10–8:30. Great Court Sun.–Wed. 9–6, Thurs.–Sat. 9* AM*–11* PM Ⓤ*Holborn, Russell Sq., Tottenham Court Rd.*

QUICK BITES

The British Museum's **Gallery Café** gets very crowded but serves a reasonably tasty menu beneath a plaster cast of a part of the Parthenon frieze. It's open daily 10 to 5. The self-service café in the Great Court concourse is open Sunday through Wednesday 9 to 5:30 and Thursday through Saturday 9 to 9.

❹ **Dickens House Museum.** This is the only one of the many London houses Charles Dickens (1812–70) inhabited that's still standing, and it would have had a real claim to his fame in any case because he wrote *Oliver Twist* and *Nicholas Nickleby*. The house looks exactly as it would have in Dickens's day, complete with first editions, letters, and a tall clerk's desk (where the master wrote standing up, often while chatting with visiting friends and relatives). ✉*48 Doughty St., Bloomsbury* ☎*020/7405–2127* ⊕*www.dickensmuseum.com* ✉*£5* ⊘*Mon.–Sat. 10–5, Sun. 11–5; last admission 4:30* Ⓤ*Chancery La., Russell Sq.*

❻ **Lincoln's Inn.** There's plenty to see at one of the oldest, best-preserved, ★ and most comely of the Inns of Court—from the Chancery Lane Tudor brick gatehouse to the wide-open, tree-lined, atmospheric Lincoln's Inn Fields and the 15th-century chapel remodeled by Inigo Jones in 1620. ✉*Chancery La., Bloomsbury* ☎*020/7405–1393* ⊕*www.lincolnsinn. org.uk* ✉ *Free* ⊘*Gardens weekdays 7–7, chapel weekdays noon–2:30; public may also attend Sun. service in chapel at 11:30 during legal terms* Ⓤ*Chancery La.*

❺ **Sir John Soane's Museum.** Sir John (1753–1837), architect of the Bank of ★ England, bequeathed his house to the nation on condition that nothing be changed. He obviously had enormous fun with his home: in the Picture Room, for instance, two of Hogarth's *Rake's Progress* series are among the paintings on panels that swing away to reveal secret gallery pockets with more paintings. Everywhere mirrors and colors play tricks with light and space, and split-level floors worthy of a fairground fun house disorient you. Due to the small size of the museum, limited numbers are allowed entry at any one time, so you may have a short wait outside. ✉*13 Lincoln's Inn Fields, Bloomsbury* ☎*020/7440–4263* ⊕*www.soane.org* ✉*Free, Sat. tour £5* ⊘*Tues.–Sat. 10–5; also 6–9 on 1st Tues. of month* Ⓤ*Holborn.*

WORTH NOTING

❷ **British Library.** Since 1759, the British Library had been housed in the British Museum on Gordon Square. But space ran out long ago. The collection of around 18 million volumes now has a home in state-of-the-art surroundings, and if you're a researcher, it's a wonderful place to work (special passes are required). The library's treasures are on view to the general public: the Magna Carta, a Gutenberg Bible, Jane Austen's writings, Shakespeare's First Folio, and musical manuscripts by Handel and Sir Paul McCartney are on show in the Sir John Ritblat Gallery. ✉*96 Euston Rd., Bloomsbury* ☎*0870/444–1500* ⊕*www.*

bl.uk 📧 *Free, charge for special exhibitions* ⊙ *Mon. and Wed.–Fri. 9:30–6, Tues. 9:30–8, Sat. 9:30–5, Sun. and bank holiday Mon. 11–5* Ⓤ *Euston, King's Cross, St. Pancras International.*

❸ **King's Cross Station.** Known for its 120-foot-tall clock tower, this yellow-
🕙 brick Italianate building with large, arched windows was constructed in 1851–52 as the London terminus for the Great Northern Railway. Harry Potter took the Hogwarts Express to school from the imaginary platform 9¾ (platforms 4 and 5 were the actual shooting site) in the movies based on J. K. Rowling's popular novels. The station has put up a sign for platform 9¾; you can snap a picture there. 📧 *Euston Rd. and York Way, Euston* ☎ *0845/748–4950* Ⓤ *King's Cross.*

❼ **Royal Courts of Justice.** Here is the vast Victorian Gothic pile containing the nation's principal law courts, with 1,000-odd rooms running off 3½ mi of corridor. And here are heard the most important civil law cases—that's everything from divorce to fraud, with libel in between. You can sit in the viewing gallery to watch any trial you like, for a live version of Court TV. Check out the gift shop, where useful items (such as umbrellas) are emblazoned with the royal courts' crest. 📧 *The Strand, Bloomsbury* ☎ *020/7947–6000* ⊕ *www.hmcourts-service.gov. uk* 📧 *Free* ⊙ *Weekdays 9–4:30; during Aug. there are no sittings and public areas close at 2:30* Ⓤ *Temple.*

THE CITY

The City, as opposed to the city, is the capital's fast-beating financial heart. Behind a host of imposing neoclassical facades lie the banks and exchanges whose frantic trade determines the fortunes that underpin London—and the country. But the "Square Mile" is much more than London's Wall Street—the capital's economic engine room also has currency as a religious and political center. St. Paul's Cathedral has looked after Londoners' souls since the seventh century, and the Tower of London—that moat-surrounded royal fortress, prison, and jewel house—has taken care of beheading them. The City's maze of backstreets is also home to a host of old churches, marketplaces, and cozy pubs.

The City extends eastward from Temple Bar to the Tower of London, and north from the Thames to Chiswell Street. The pedestrian-only Millennium Bridge connects the area with the South Bank; it's well worth the walk. Twice the City has been nearly wiped off the face of the earth. The Great Fire of 1666 necessitated a total reconstruction, in which Sir Christopher Wren had a big hand, contributing not only his masterpiece, St. Paul's Cathedral, but 49 additional parish churches. The second wave of destruction was dealt by the German bombers of World War II. The ruins were rebuilt, but slowly, and with no overall plan, leaving the City a patchwork of the old and the new, the interesting and the flagrantly awful. Since a mere 8,000 or so people call it home, the nation's financial center is deserted on weekends, with restaurants shuttered.

GETTING HERE   The City is well served by a concentrated selection of underground stops. St Paul's and Bank, on the Central Line, and Mansion House, Cannon Street, and Monument, on the District and Circle lines, deliver

The City

Dr. Johnson's
House **1**
Guildhall **8**
Monument **11**
Museum of
London **5**
Old Bailey **3**
St. Bride's **2**

St. Mary-le-Bow **7**
St. Paul's
Cathedral **4**
St. Stephen Walbrook ... **6**
Tower Bridge **10**
Tower of London **9**

2

visitors to the heart of the City. Liverpool Street and Aldgate border the City's eastern edge, while Chancery Lane and Farringdon lie to the west. Barbican and Moorgate provide easy access to the theaters and galleries of the Barbican, while Blackfriars, to the south, leads to Ludgate Circus and Fleet Street.

PLANNING
YOUR TIME

The "Square Mile" is as compact as the nickname suggests, with very little distance between points of interest, making it easy to dip into the City for an afternoon stroll. For full immersion in the Tower of London, however, set aside half a day, especially if seeing the Crown Jewels is a priority. Allow an hour minimum each for the Museum of London, St. Paul's Cathedral, and the Tower Bridge. On weekends, without the scurrying suits, the City is nearly deserted, making it hard to find lunch—and yet this is when the major attractions are at their busiest. So if you can manage to come on a weekday, do so.

Numbers in the margin correspond to numbers on the City map.

TOP ATTRACTIONS

Millennium Bridge. Norman Foster and sculptor Anthony Caro designed this strikingly modern, pedestrian-only bridge of aluminum and steel. The bridge connects the City—the St. Paul's Cathedral area—with the Tate Modern art gallery. On the South Bank side the bridge marks the middle of the **Millennium Mile**, a walkway taking in a clutch of popular sights. The views from the bridge are breathtaking, with perhaps the best-ever view of St. Paul's. ✉*Peters Hill to Bankside, The City, South Bank* Ⓤ *Mansion House, Blackfriars, or Southwark.*

⓫ **Monument.** Commemorating the "dreadful visitation" of the Great Fire of 1666, this is the world's tallest isolated stone column. At this writing, extensive renovation work is expected to be completed in late 2008. ✉*Monument St., The City* ☎*020/7626–2717* ⊕*www.cityoflondon. gov.uk* ✉*£2* ☉*Daily 9:30–5:30; last admission 5* Ⓤ*Monument.*

❺ **Museum of London.** If there's one place to get the history of London sorted out, right from 450,000 BC to the present day, it's here—although there's a great deal to sort out: Oliver Cromwell's death mask, Queen Victoria's crinolined gowns, Selfridges' art deco elevators, and the Lord Mayor's coach are just some of the goodies. The museum is currently undergoing modernization work so sections may be off-limits to visitors until the end of 2009. ✉*London Wall, The City* ☎*0870/444–3851* ⊕*www.museumoflondon.org.uk* ✉*Free* ☉*Mon.–Sat. 10–5:50, Sun. noon–5:50; last admission 5:30* Ⓤ*Barbican, St Paul's.*

❷ **St. Bride's.** Appropriately named for anyone contemplating impending nuptials, the distinctively tiered steeple of this Christopher Wren–designed church gave rise to the shape of the traditional wedding cake. One early couple inspired to marry here were the parents of Virginia Dare, the first European child born in colonial America in 1587. ✉*Fleet St., The City* ☎*020/7427–0133* ⊕*www.stbrides.com* ✉*Free* ☉*Weekdays 8–6, Sat. 11–3, Sun. for services only 10–1 and 5–7:30* Ⓤ*Chancery La.*

❼ **St. Mary-le-Bow.** This church is another classic City survivor; various versions have stood on the site since the 11th century. The Bow takes its name from the bow-shaped arches in the Norman crypt. The garden contains a statue of local boy Captain John Smith, who founded Virginia in 1606 and was later captured by Native Americans. ✉ *Cheapside, The City* ☎ *020/7248–5139* ⊕ *www.stmarylebow.co.uk* ⊙ *Mon.–Thurs. 7–6, Fri. 7–4* Ⓤ *Mansion House, St. Paul's.*

QUICK BITES

The Place Below (✉ *Cheapside, The City* ☎ *020/7329–0789*), in St. Mary-le-Bow's crypt, is packed with City workers weekdays at lunchtime. The self-service vegetarian menu includes good soup and quiche. Lunches are served from 10:30 until 2:30, weekdays only. It's open for breakfast from 7:30 AM.

❹ **St. Paul's Cathedral.** The symbolic heart of London, St. Paul's may take your breath away, even more so now that it's been spruced up for its 300th anniversary. The dome—the world's third largest—peeps through the skyline from many an angle around London. The structure is Sir Christopher Wren's masterpiece, completed in 1710 after 35 years of building, and, much later, miraculously spared (mostly) by World War II bombs. Wren's first plan, known as the New Model, did not make it past the drawing board. The second, known as the Great Model, got as far as the 20-foot oak rendering you can see here before it also was rejected. The third was accepted, with the fortunate coda that the architect be allowed to make changes as he saw fit. Without that, there would be no dome, since the approved design had a steeple. When you enter and see the dome from the inside, it may seem smaller than you expected. It *is* smaller, and 60 feet lower than the lead-covered outer dome. Beneath the lantern is Wren's famous epitaph, which his son composed and had set into the pavement, and which reads succinctly: LECTOR, SI MONUMENTUM REQUIRIS, CIRCUMSPICE—"Reader, if you seek his monument, look around you." The epitaph also appears on Wren's memorial in the Crypt. Up 259 spiral steps is the **Whispering Gallery,** an acoustic phenomenon; you whisper something to the wall on one side, and a second later it transmits clearly to the other side, 107 feet away. Ascend to the **Stone Gallery,** which encircles the base of the dome. Farther up (280 feet from ground level) is the small **Golden Gallery,** around the dome's highest point. From both these galleries (if you have a head for heights) you can walk outside for a spectacular panorama of London. The climb up the spiraling steps can be fun for older kids.

The remains of the poet John Donne, who was dean of St. Paul's for his final 10 years (he died in 1631), are in the south choir aisle. The vivacious choir-stall carvings nearby are the work of Grinling Gibbons, as are those on the organ, which Wren designed and Handel played. Behind the high altar is the **American Memorial Chapel,** dedicated in 1958 to the 28,000 GIs stationed in the United Kingdom who lost their lives in World War II. Among the

MUSICAL FRICTION

The organ at St. Paul's, with its cherubs and angels, was not installed without controversy. The mighty instrument proved a tight fit, and the maker, known as Father Schmidt, and Wren nearly came to blows. Wren was reputed to have said he would not adapt his cathedral for a mere "box of whistles."

famous whose remains lie in the **Crypt** are the duke of Wellington and Admiral Lord Nelson. The Crypt also has a gift shop and a café. ✉ *St. Paul's Churchyard, The City* ☎ *020/7236–4128* ⊕ *www.stpauls. co.uk* 🖼 *£10, audio tour £3.50, guided tour £3* ☉ *Cathedral Mon.–Sat. 8:30–4:30; last admission at 4; closed occasionally for special services. Shop and Crypt Café also open Sun. 10:30–5* Ⓤ *St. Paul's.*

2

🔟 **Tower Bridge.** Despite its medieval, fairy-tale appearance, this is a Victorian youngster. Constructed of steel, then clothed in Portland stone, the Horace Jones masterpiece was deliberately styled in the Gothic persuasion to complement the Tower next door. The **Tower Bridge Experience** exhibition is a fun tour inside the structure to discover how one of the world's most famous bridges actually works. One highlight is the glorious view from up high on the covered walkway between the turrets. ☎ *020/7403–3761* ⊕ *www.towerbridge.org.uk* 🖼 *£6* ☉ *Daily 9:30–5:30; last entry at 5* Ⓤ *Tower Hill.*

⑨ **Tower of London.** Nowhere else does London's history come to life so vividly as in this minicity of 20 towers filled with heraldry and treasure, the intimate details of lords and dukes and princes and sovereigns etched in the walls (literally, in some places), and quite a few pints of royal blood spilled on the stones. ■TIP➔ **This is one of Britain's most popular sights—the Crown Jewels are here—and you can avoid lines by buying a ticket in advance on the Web site, by phone, at any tube station, or at an on-site kiosk. Arriving before 11 can also help at busy times.** The visitor center provides an introduction to the Tower. Allow at least three hours for exploring, and take time to stroll along the battlements for a wonderful overview.

The Tower holds the royal gems because it's still one of the royal palaces, although no monarch since Henry VII has called it home. It has also housed the Royal Mint, the Public Records, the Royal Menagerie (which formed the basis of the London Zoo), and the Royal Observatory, although its most renowned and titillating function has been as a jail and place of torture and execution.

A person was mighty privileged to be beheaded in the peace and seclusion of **Tower Green** instead of before the mob at Tower Hill. In fact, only seven people were ever important enough—among them Anne Boleyn and Catherine Howard, wives two and five of Henry VIII's six; Elizabeth I's friend Robert Devereux, earl of Essex; and the nine-day queen, Lady Jane Grey, age 17. The executioner's block and ax, along with the equally famous rack, plus assorted thumbscrews, "iron maidens," and so forth, have been moved to the Royal Armouries in Leeds, Yorkshire.

Free tours depart every half hour or so from the Middle Tower. They are conducted by the 39 Yeoman Warders, better known as Beefeaters—ex-servicemen dressed in resplendent navy-and-red (scarlet-and-gold on special occasions) Tudor outfits. Beefeaters have been guarding the Tower since Henry VII appointed them in 1485. One of them, the Yeoman Ravenmaster, is responsible for making life comfortable for the Tower ravens (six birds plus reserves)—an important duty, because if the ravens were to desert the Tower, goes the legend, the kingdom would fall.

In prime position stands the oldest part of the Tower and the most conspicuous of its buildings, the **White Tower**; the other towers were built in the next few centuries. This central keep was begun in 1078 by William the Conqueror; Henry III (1207–72) had it whitewashed, which is where the name comes from. The spiral staircase is the only way up, and here are the **Royal Armouries**, with a collection of arms and armor. The **Chapel of St. John the Evangelist**, downstairs from the armories, is a pure example of 11th-century Norman style—very rare, very simple, and very beautiful. Across the moat, **Traitors' Gate** lies to the right. Opposite Traitors' Gate is the former Garden Tower, better known since about 1570 as the **Bloody Tower**. Its name comes from one of the most famous unsolved murders in history, the saga of the "little princes in the Tower." In 1483 the uncrowned boy king, Edward V, and his brother Richard were left here by their uncle, Richard of Gloucester, after the death of their father, Edward IV. They were never seen again, Gloucester was crowned Richard III, and in 1674 two little skeletons were found under the stairs to the White Tower. The obvious conclusions have always been drawn—and were, in fact, even before the skeletons were discovered. The **New Armouries** have become a restaurant.

The most famous exhibits are the **Crown Jewels,** in the Jewel House, Waterloo Block. Moving walkways on either side of the jewels hasten progress at the busiest times. You get so close to the fabled gems you feel you could polish them (there are, however, wafers of bullet-proof glass), if your eyes weren't so dazzled by the sparkle of the gems, enhanced with special lighting. Before you see them, you view a short film that includes scenes from Elizabeth's 1953 coronation. Security is tight because the jewels—even though they would be impossible for thieves to sell—are *so* priceless that they're not insured. A brief résumé of the top jewels: finest of all is the Royal Sceptre, containing the earth's largest cut diamond, the 530-carat Star of Africa, also known as Cullinan I. Cullinan II lives on the Imperial State Crown (made for Queen Victoria's coronation in 1838); Elizabeth II wears it annually for the State Opening of Parliament.

The little chapel of **St. Peter ad Vincula** is the second church on the site, and it conceals the remains of some 2,000 people executed at the Tower, Anne Boleyn and Catherine Howard among them.

Evocative **Beauchamp Tower** was built west of Tower Green by Edward I (1272–1307). It was soon designated as a jail for the higher class of miscreant, including Lady Jane Grey, who is thought to have added her Latin graffiti to the many inscriptions carved by prisoners here.

For tickets to the Ceremony of the Keys (locking of main gates, nightly between 9:30 and 10), write well in advance to the Resident Governor and Keeper of the Jewel House (at the Queen's House, address below). Give your name, the date you wish to attend (include alternate dates), and number of people (up to seven) in your party, and enclose a self-addressed, stamped envelope. ✉ *H. M. Tower of London, Tower Hill, The City* ☎ *0844/482–7799 recorded information and advance booking* ⊕ *www.hrp.org.uk* 🎫 *£16* ⊙ *Mar.–Oct., Tues.–Sat. 9–6, Sun. and Mon. 10–6; Nov.–Feb., Tues.–Sat. 9–5, Sun. and Mon. 10–5. Last* *admission 1 hr before closing time; and all internal bldgs. close 30 mins after last admission. Free Yeoman Warder guided tours leave daily from Middle Tower (subject to weather and availability) about every 30 mins until 3:30 Mar.–Oct., 2:30 Nov.–Feb.* Ⓤ *Tower Hill.*

WORTH NOTING

❶ **Dr. Johnson's House.** This is where Samuel Johnson lived between 1748 and 1759, compiling his famous dictionary in the attic as his health deteriorated. Built in 1700, it's the only one of Johnson's residences remaining today, and its elegant Georgian lines make it exactly the kind of place you would expect the Great Bear, as Johnson was nicknamed, to live. It includes two first editions of his *Dictionary of the English Language.* ✉*17 Gough Sq., The City* ☎*020/7353–3745* ⊕*www.drjohnsonshouse. org* ✉*£4.50* ⊗*May–Sept., Mon.–Sat. 11–5:30; Oct.–Apr., Mon.–Sat. 11–5; closed bank holidays* Ⓤ*Blackfriars, Chancery La.*

❽ **Guildhall.** The Corporation of London, which oversees the City, has ceremonially elected and installed its Lord Mayor here for the last 800 years. The Guildhall was built in 1411, and though it failed to avoid either the 1666 or 1940 flames, its core survived. The fabulous Great Hall is a patchwork of coats of arms. To the right of Guildhall Yard is the **Guildhall Art Gallery,** which includes portraits of the great and the good, cityscapes, famous battles, and a slightly cloying Pre-Raphaelite section. The construction of the gallery led to the discovery of London's only Roman amphitheater, which had lain underneath for more than 1,800 years. The 1970s west wing houses the the **Clockmakers' Company Museum,** with more than 600 timepieces. ✉*Gresham St., The City* ☎*020/7606–3030, 020/7332–3700 gallery* ⊕*www.cityoflondon. gov.uk* ✉*Free; gallery and amphitheater £2.50* ⊗*Mon.–Sat. 9:30–5; clockmaker museum Mon.–Sat. 9:30–4:45; gallery Mon.–Sat. 10–5, Sun. noon–4; last admission 4:30 or 3:30* Ⓤ*St. Paul's, Moorgate, Bank, Mansion House.*

OFF THE BEATEN PATH

Jack the Ripper's London. *Cor blimey, guv'nor, Jack the Ripper woz here!* Several organizations offer tours of "Jack's London"—the (still) mean streets of the East End, the working-class neighborhood directly to the east of the City. Here, in 1888, the Whitechapel murders traumatized Victorian London. At the haunting hour, tour groups head out to Bucks Row and other crime scenes. Even with a large group, this can be a spooky experience. **Original London Walks** (☎*020/7624–3978* ⊕*www. walks.com*) has frequent tours leaving at 7:30 PM from the Tower Hill tube stop. The **Blood and Tears Walk** (☎*020/8348—9022* ⊕*www. shockinglondon.com*) goes beyond Jack the Ripper and describes other murderers, as well. Tours depart from the Barbican tube; phone for times.

OFF THE BEATEN PATH

Museum of London Docklands. On a quaint cobbled quayside, this museum is worth a visit for its warehouse building alone. The fascinating story of the old port and the river is told using films, together with interactive displays and reconstructions. ✉*No. 1 Warehouse, West India Quay, Hertsmere Rd., East End* ☎*0870/444–3857* ⊕*www. museumindocklands.org.uk* ✉*£5* ⊗*Daily 10–6; last admission 5:30* Ⓤ*Canary Wharf; DLR: West India Quay.*

❸ Old Bailey. If you're put off by West End theater prices, this is the place to watch the real-life drama of justice in action. The day's hearings are posted on the sign outside, but your best bet is to consult the previous day's tabloid newspapers for an idea of the trials that are making waves. The present-day **Central Criminal Court** is where Newgate Prison stood from the 12th century right until the beginning of the 20th century. The most famous feature of the solid Edwardian building is the 12-foot gilded statue of Justice perched on top; she was intended to mirror the dome of St. Paul's. ⊠*Newgate St., The City* ☎*020/7248–3277 information* ⊕*www.cityoflondon.gov.uk* ⊙*Public Gallery weekdays 10–1 and 2–4:30 (approx.); line forms at Newgate St. entrance or in Warwick St. Passage; closed bank holidays and day after* Ⓤ*St. Paul's.*

❻ St. Stephen Walbrook. This is the parish church many think is Wren's best, by virtue of its practice dome, which predates the one at St. Paul's by some 30 years, and its celestial atmosphere inside. Inside the light, airy church, two sights warrant investigation: Henry Moore's 1987 central marble altar, which sits beneath the dome ("like a lump of Camembert," say critics), and, well, a telephone—an eloquent tribute to that savior of souls, Rector Chad Varah, who in 1953 founded the Samaritans, givers of phone aid to the suicidal, here. ⊠*39 Walbrook St., The City* ☎*020/7626–9000* ⊕*www.ststephenwalbrook.net* ⊙*Weekdays 10–4* Ⓤ*Bank, Cannon St.*

THE SOUTH BANK

Culture, history, sights: the South Bank has it all. Stretching from the Imperial War Museum in the southwest as far as the Design Museum in the east, high-caliber art, music, film, and theater venues sit alongside the likes of an aquarium, historic warships, and Borough Market, a foodie favorite. Pedestrians cross between the north and south banks using the futuristic Hungerford Bridge and the curvaceous Millennium Bridge, as they take in the compelling views of the Thames.

There's an old North London quip about needing a passport to cross the Thames, but times have changed dramatically. The Tate Modern is the star attraction, installed in a 1930s power station, with the eye-catching Millennium Bridge linking its main door across the river to the City. Near the theaters of the South Bank Centre, the London Eye observation wheel gives you a flight over the city. The South Bank of the Thames isn't beautiful, but this area of theaters and museums has Culture with a capital C.

It's fitting that so much of London's artistic life should once again be centered on the South Bank—in the past, Southwark was the location of theaters, taverns, and cockfighting arenas. The Globe Theatre, in which Shakespeare acted and held shares, was one of several here. In truth the Globe was as likely to stage bear-baiting as Shakespeare, but today, at the reconstructed "Wooden O," you can see only the latter. Be sure to take a walk along Bankside, the embankment along the Thames from Southwark to Blackfriars Bridge.

GETTING HERE   For the South Bank use Westminster station on the Jubilee or Northern line, from where you can walk across Westminster Bridge; Embankment on District, Circle, Northern, and Bakerloo lines, where you can walk across Hungerford Bridge; or Waterloo on the Jubilee, Northern, and Bakerloo lines, where it's a five-minute walk to the Royal Festival Hall. In the east, alternatively, use Tower Gateway on the Docklands Light Railway (DLR). London Bridge on the Northern and Jubilee lines is but a five-minute stroll from Borough Market and Southwark Cathedral.

PLANNING YOUR TIME   The South Bank sprawls; block out visiting times based on locations and your interests. The Imperial War Museum demands a couple of hours, with the nearby Museum of Garden History worth an hour. The Tate Modern deserves a whole morning or afternoon to do justice to temporary exhibitions and the permanent collection. The Globe Theatre requires about two hours for the exhibition theater tour and two to three hours for a performance. Finish with drinks or dinner at the Oxo Tower or a stroll west along the riverbank and then across Hungerford Bridge.

Numbers in the margin correspond to numbers on the South Bank map.

TOP ATTRACTIONS

⓫ **Design Museum.** This was the first museum in the world to elevate everyday design and design classics to the status of art by placing them in their social and cultural context. Fashion, creative technology, and architecture are explored with thematic displays from the museum's permanent collection, and temporary exhibitions provide an in-depth focus on such subjects as the work of great designers such as Charles Eames and Isamu Noguchi. ✉*28 Shad Thames, South Bank* ☎*0870/833–9955* ⊕*www.designmuseum.org* ✆*£8.50* ⏱*Daily 10–5:45; last admission 5:15* Ⓤ*London Bridge; DLR: Tower Gateway.*

❶ **Imperial War Museum.** This museum of 20th-century warfare does not glorify bloodshed but attempts to evoke what it was like to live through the two world wars. There's hardware—a Battle of Britain Spitfire, a German V2 rocket—but also an equal amount of war art (John Singer Sargent to Henry Moore) and interactive material. One affecting exhibit, "The Blitz Experience," provides a 10-minute taste of an air raid in a street of acrid smoke, sirens, and searchlights. There's also a Holocaust exhibition. The museum is in an elegantly colonnaded 19th-century building that was once the home of the infamous insane asylum called Bedlam. ✉*Lambeth Rd., South Bank* ☎*020/7416–5320* ⊕*www.iwm.org.uk* ✆*Free (charge for special exhibits)* ⏱*Daily 10–6* Ⓤ*Lambeth North.*

❸ **London Eye.** The London Eye is the largest observation wheel ever built, and in the top 10 tallest structures in London. The 25-minute slow-motion ride inside one of the enclosed passenger capsules is so smooth you'd hardly know you were suspended over the Thames, moving slowly round. On a clear day you can take in a range of up to 25 mi, viewing London's most famous landmarks from a fascinating angle. If you're looking for a special place to celebrate, champagne and canapés can be arranged ahead. ✉*Jubilee Gardens, South Bank* ☎*0870/990–8883* ⊕*www.londoneye.com* ✆*£15* ⏱*June and Sept., daily 10–9; July and Aug., daily 10–9:30; Oct.–May, daily 10–8* Ⓤ*Waterloo.*

The South Bank

Design Museum **11**
Golden Hinde **7**
HMS Belfast **10**
Imperial War
Museum **1**

London Aquarium **2**
London Dungeon **9**
London Eye **3**
OXO Tower **4**

Shakespeare's
Globe Theatre **6**
Southwark Cathedral **8**
Tate Modern **5**

4 **OXO Tower.** The art deco–era Oxo building has graduated from its former incarnations as a power station into a vibrant community of artists' and designers' workshops, a pair of restaurants, as well as five floors of community homes. The biggest draw remains the Oxo Tower Restaurant for a meal or a martini. ⊠ *Barge House St., South Bank* ☎ *020/7401–3610* ⊕ *www.oxotower.co.uk* ⊠ *Free* ⊗ *Studios and shops Tues.–Sun. 11–6* Ⓤ *Blackfriars, Waterloo.*

> **WHEN TO GO**
>
> Avoid going to the Tate Modern on weekends, when visitor numbers are at their greatest. Visit during the week or join the cool crowd on Friday evenings, when it's open until 10.

6 **Shakespeare's Globe Theatre.** A spectacular theater, this is a replica of Shakespeare's open-roof, wood-and-thatch Globe Playhouse (built in 1599 and burned down in 1613), where most of the Bard's great plays premiered. For several decades, American actor and director Sam Wanamaker worked ceaselessly to raise funds for the theater's reconstruction, 200 yards from its original site, with authentic materials and techniques; his dream was realized in 1996. The "pit," or orchestra level, can take 500 standees—or "groundlings," to use the historical term—in front of the high stage, and 1,000 can sit in the covered wooden bays. A repertory season of three or four plays is presented in summer, in daylight—and sometimes rain. Throughout the year you can tour the theater as part of the **Shakespeare's Globe Exhibition,** an adjacent museum that provides background material on the Elizabethan theater and the construction of the modern-day Globe. There's also an exhibition at the Globe's near neighbor, the **Rose Theatre,** at 56 Park Street, which was built even earlier, in 1587. ⊠ *21 New Globe Walk, Bankside, South Bank* ☎ *020/7401–9919 box office, 020/7902–1400 New Shakespeare's Globe Exhibition* ⊕ *www.shakespeares-globe.org* ⊠ *£9 for exhibition and tour* ⊗ *Exhibition daily 10–5, plays May–early Oct.; call for schedule* Ⓤ *Mansion House, then walk across Southwark Bridge; Blackfriars, then walk across Blackfriars Bridge; or Southwark, then walk down to river.*

8 **Southwark Cathedral.** Pronounced "Suth-uck," this is the second-oldest Gothic church in London, after Westminster Abbey, with parts dating back to the 12th century. Although it houses some remarkable memorials, not to mention a program of lunchtime concerts, it's seldom visited. ■TIP→ **The Refectory serves light lunches and tea daily 10–5.** ⊠ *Montague Close, South Bank* ☎ *020/7367–6700* ⊕ *www.southwark.anglican.org* ⊠ *Free, suggested donation £4* ⊗ *Daily 8–6* Ⓤ *London Bridge.*

5 **Tate Modern.** This former power station has glowered on the banks on the Thames since the 1930s, and after a dazzling renovation by Herzog & de Meuron, provides a grand space for a massive collection of international modern art. The vast Turbine Hall is a dramatic entrance point. On permanent display in the galleries are classic works from 1900 to the present day, by Matisse, Picasso, Dalí, Francis Bacon, Andy Warhol, and the most-talked-about upstarts. They are arranged in themes that mix the historic with the contemporary—Landscape, Still Life, and the Nude—on different levels, reached by a moving staircase. This is a good

Fodor's Choice
★

2

museum for kids, who respond to the unusual space as well as the art; there are kids' programs, too. The changing exhibitions, for which there are often long lines, are always the talking point of Londoners who have their fingers on the pulse. ⊠*Bankside, South Bank* ☎*020/7887–8888* ⊕*www.tate.org.uk* ✉*Free* ⊗*Sun.–Thurs. 10–6, Fri. and Sat. 10–10* Ⓤ *Blackfriars, Southwark.*

WORTH NOTING

❼ *Golden Hinde.* Sir Francis Drake circumnavigated the globe in this little galleon, or one just like it. This exact replica made a 23-year round-the-world voyage—much of it spent along U.S. coasts, both Pacific and Atlantic—and has settled here to continue its educational purpose. ⊠*Unit 1 & 2, Pickfords Wharf, Clink St., South Bank* ☎*0870/011–8700* ⊕*www.goldenhinde.org* ✉*£6, £5 for prebooked guided tour* ⊗*Times vary, call ahead* Ⓤ*London Bridge, Mansion House.*

❿ **HMS** *Belfast.* At 613 feet, this is one of the largest and most powerful cruisers the Royal Navy has ever had. It played an important role in the D-Day landings off Normandy, left for the Far East after the war, and has been becalmed here since 1971. ⊠*Morgan's La., Tooley St., South Bank* ☎*020/7940–6300* ⊕*www.iwm.org.uk* ✉*£10.30* ⊗*Mar.–Oct., daily 10–6; Nov.–Feb., daily 10–5; last admission 45 mins before closing* Ⓤ*London Bridge.*

❷ **London Aquarium.** Here's a dark and thrilling glimpse of the waters of the world, focused around a superb three-level aquarium full of sharks and stingrays, among other common and rarer breeds. There are also educational exhibits, hands-on displays, feeding displays, and piscine sights previously unseen on these shores. ⊠*County Hall, Riverside Bldg., Westminster Bridge Rd., South Bank* ☎*020/7967–8000* ⊕*www.londonaquarium.co.uk* ✉*£13.25* ⊗*Daily 10–6; last admission at 5* Ⓤ *Westminster, Waterloo.*

❾ **London Dungeon.** Here's the goriest, grisliest, most gruesome attraction in town, where realistic waxwork people are subjected in graphic detail to all the historical horrors the Tower of London merely tells you about. Tableaux depict famous bloody moments—like Anne Boleyn's decapitation and the martyrdom of St. George—alongside the torture, murder, and ritual slaughter of lesser-known victims, all to a sound track of screaming, wailing, and agonized moaning. ⊠*28–34 Tooley St., South Bank* ☎*0871/360–2049* ⊕*www.thedungeons.com* ✉*£19.95* ⊗*Mid-Apr.–mid-July and mid-Sept.–mid-Nov., daily 10–5:30; mid-July–mid-Sept., daily 10–7:30; mid-Nov.–mid-Apr., daily 10:30–5; phone to confirm times* Ⓤ*London Bridge.*

KENSINGTON, KNIGHTSBRIDGE, AND MAYFAIR

Splendid houses with pillared porches, as well as fascinating museums, stylish squares, and glittering antiques shops, line the streets of this elegant area of the Royal Borough of Kensington. Also here is Kensington Palace (the former home of both Diana, Princess of Wales, and Queen Victoria), which put the district literally on the map back in the 17th century. To Kensington's east is one of the highest concentrations of important artifacts anywhere, the "museum mile" of South Kensington, with the rest of Kensington offering peaceful strolls and a noisy main street. Kensington first became the *Royal* Borough of Kensington (and Chelsea) when William III, who suffered terribly from the Thames mists over Whitehall, decided in 1689 to buy Nottingham House in the rural village of Kensington so that he could breathe more easily. Courtiers and functionaries and society folk soon followed where the crown led, and by the time Queen Anne was on the throne (1702–14), Kensington was overflowing. In a way, it still is, since most of its grand houses have been divided into apartments, or are serving as embassies.

Hyde Park and Kensington Gardens together form by far the biggest of central London's royal parks. It's probably been centuries since any major royal had a casual stroll here, but the parks remain the property of the Crown, and it was the Crown that saved them from being devoured by the city's late-18th-century growth spurt.

Around the borders of Hyde Park are several of London's most beautiful and posh neighborhoods. To the south of the park and a short carriage ride from Buckingham Palace is the splendidly aristocratic enclave of Belgravia. Its white-stucco buildings and grand squares—particularly Belgrave Square—are Regency-era jewels. On the eastern border of Hyde Park is Mayfair, which gives Belgravia a run for its money as London's wealthiest district. Two mansions here allow you to get a peek into the lifestyles of London's rich and famous: Apsley House, the home of the duke of Wellington, and the Wallace Collection, a mansion on Manchester Square stuffed with great art treasures.

GETTING HERE   There's good tube service to these areas. On the Central Line, Marble Arch and Bond Street (also Jubilee Line) take you to the heart of Mayfair; the Hyde Park Corner stop on the Piccadilly line is at the southeast corner of the park, near Apsley House. South Kensington and Gloucester Road on the District, Circle, and Piccadilly lines are convenient stops for the South Kensington museums; Knightsbridge on the Piccadilly line leaves you close to Harrods and many retail temptations.

PLANNING   The best way to approach these neighborhoods is to treat Knights-
YOUR TIME   bridge shopping and the South Kensington museums as separate days out, although the three vast museums may be too much to take in at once. The parks are best in the growing seasons and during fall, when the foliage is turning; the summer roses in Regent's Park are stunning. On Sunday the Hyde Park and Kensington Gardens railings all along the Bayswater Road are hung with mediocre art, which may slow your progress; this is prime perambulation day for locals.

Numbers in the margin correspond to numbers on the Kensington, Knightsbridge, and Mayfair map.

TOP ATTRACTIONS

❼ Apsley House (Wellington Museum). Once popularly known as No. 1, Lon-
★ don, because it was the first and grandest house at the old tollgate from Knightsbridge village, this was long celebrated as the best address in town. Built by Robert Adam and later refaced and extended, it housed the Duke of Wellington from 1817 until his death in 1852. As the Wellington Museum, it has been faithfully restored, down to Wellesley's uniforms, weapons, a fine collection of paintings, and his porcelain

and plate collections acquired as a result of his military successes. His extensive art collection includes Dutch Old Masters, Velázquez, Goya, Rubens, and Correggio. There are portraits of his adversary Napoléon Bonaparte, and a huge, towering statue of a naked Napoléon by Canova in the stairwell. ⊠ *149 Piccadilly, Hyde Park Corner, Mayfair* ☎ *020/7499–5676* ⊕ *www.english-heritage.org.uk* ⊙ *Apr.–Nov., Tues.–Sun. 10–5; Dec.–Mar., Tues.–Sun. 10–4. Also open bank holiday Mon.* ⊠ *£5.30, joint ticket with Wellington Arch £6.90* Ⓤ *Hyde Park Corner.*

❻ Harrods. Just in case you don't notice it, this well-known shopping destination frames its domed terra-cotta Edwardian outline in thousands of white lights each night. Don't miss the extravagant Food Hall, with its stunning art nouveau tiling in the neighborhood of meat and poultry and continuing on in the fishmongers' territory, where its glory is rivaled by displays of the sea produce itself. ⊠ *87–135 Brompton Rd., Knightsbridge* ☎ *020/7730–1234* ⊕ *www.harrods.com* ⊙ *Mon.–Sat. 10–8, Sun. noon–6 (sometimes later during sales times)* Ⓤ *Knightsbridge.*

☾ Hyde Park. Along with the smaller St. James's and Green parks to the east, Hyde Park started as Henry VIII's hunting grounds. Along its south side runs **Rotten Row,** once Henry's royal path to the hunt—the name is a corruption of *route du roi* (route of the king). It's still used by the Household Cavalry, who live at the **Knightsbridge Barracks**—a highrise and a low, ugly, red block to the left. This brigade mounts the guard at the palace, and you can see them leave to perform this duty, in full regalia, at about 10:30, or await the return of the ex-guard about noon. Hyde Park is wonderful for strolling, watching the locals, or just relaxing by the **Serpentine,** the long body of water near its southern border. On the south side of the Serpentine, by the Lido, is the site of the **Diana Princess of Wales Memorial Fountain.** On Sunday, **Speakers' Corner,** in the park near Marble Arch, is an unmissable spectacle of vehement, sometimes comical, and always entertaining orators. ☎ *020/7298–2100* ⊕ *www.royalparks.gov.uk* ⊙ *Daily 5 AM–midnight* Ⓤ *Hyde Park Corner, Lancaster Gate, Marble Arch.*

⓭ Keats House. Here you can see the plum tree under which the young Romantic poet composed "Ode to a Nightingale," many of his original manuscripts, his library, and other possessions he managed to acquire in his short life. At this writing, the Keats House was closed for a major refurbishment; the plans include a full redecoration in the style of Keats's time and new exhibition spaces to display previously unseen objects from the museum's collection. Check the Web site for details. ⊠ *Keats House, Wentworth Pl., Keats Grove, Hampstead* ☎ *020/7435–2062* ⊕ *www.keatshouse.org.uk* Ⓤ *Hampstead; overground Silverlink: Hampstead Heath from Highbury & Islington.*

☾ Kensington Gardens. More formal than neighboring Hyde Park, Kensington Gardens was first laid out as palace grounds. The paved Italian garden at the top of the Long Water, the **Fountains,** is a reminder of this, although **Kensington Palace** itself is the main clue to its royal status, with the early-19th-century Sunken Garden north of it. Nearby is George Frampton's beloved 1912 *Peter Pan,* a bronze of the boy who

Kensington, Knightsbridge, and Mayfair

0 — 1/4 mi

0 — 1/4 km

Regent's Park

Outer Circle

12 · 14

10

11

Rossmore Rd.

Lisson Grove

Broadley St.

Marylebone Rd.

York St.

Crawford St.

Paddington St.

Gloucester Pl.

Baker St.

Marylebone High St.

Weymouth St.

New Cavendish St.

Harley St.

Paddington Station

Praed St.

Eastbourne Ter.

Westbourne Ter.

Sussex Gardens

Edgware Rd.

George St.

Portman Sq.

Manchester Sq.

Wigmore St.

9

James St.

Duke St.

Bishop's Bridge Rd.

Porchester Rd.

Gloucester Ter.

Cleveland Sq.

Craven Hill

Inverness Ter.

Porchester Ter.

Queensway

Lancaster Gate

Gloucester Sq.

MARBLE ARCH **U**

Oxford St.

BOND STREET **U**

Brook St.

Grosvenor Sq.

Grosvenor St.

Park St.

S. Audley St.

Hill St.

Bayswater Rd.

Speaker's Corner

Hyde Park

Park Lane

Park Lane

The Serpentine Road

The Serpentine

Knightsbridge Barracks

7

HYDE PARK CORNER **U**

8

Grosvenor Pl.

The Broad Walk

4

Round Pond

Princess Diana of Wales Memorial Fountain

Kensington Gardens

The Ring

Kensington Palace Gardens

Kensington Rd.

Victoria Rd.

Gloucester Rd.

Queen's Gate Ter.

Queen's Gate

Elvaston Pl.

Cornwall Gdns.

Royal Albert Hall

Prince Consort Rd.

Ayrton Rd.

Imperial Institute Rd.

Exhibition Rd.

Prince's Gdns.

Enismore Gdns.

The Carriage Rd.

Knightsbridge

Raphael St.

KNIGHTSBRIDGE **U**

Montpelier Sq.

Trevor Sq.

Brompton Rd.

6

Basil St.

Hans Rd.

Sloane St.

Lowndes Sq.

Metcombe St.

Belgrave Sq.

West Halkin St.

5

Halkin St.

Chapel St.

Chester St.

Eaton Pl.

Lyall St.

Eaton Sq.

Eaton Row

Grosvenor Cres.

Brompton Sq.

Beauchamp Pl.

Hans Pl.

Pont St.

Cadogan Ln.

Cliveden Pl.

Chester St.

Elizabeth St.

Ebury St.

Bourne St.

Egerton Ter.

Cadogan Sq.

Walton

Milner St.

Draycott Pl.

2

3

1

GLOUCESTER ROAD **U**

Cromwell Rd.

Thurloe Pl.

Thurloe Square Gdns.

SOUTH KENSINGTON **U**

Pelham St.

Old Brompton Rd.

Onslow Gdns.

Onslow Sq.

Fulham Rd.

Sloane Ave.

Draycott Ave.

Kings Rd.

Sloane Sq.

SLOANE SQUARE **U**

Elystan St.

KEY

U Tube Station

---

lived on an island in the Serpentine and never grew up, and whose creator, J.M. Barrie, lived at 100 Bayswater Road, not 500 yards from here. The **Round Pond** is a magnet for model-boat enthusiasts and duck feeders. The fabulous **Princess Diana Memorial Playground** has specially designed structures and areas on the theme of Barrie's Neverland. ☎ *020/7298-2100* ⊕ *www.royalparks.gov.uk* ⊙ *Daily 6 AM–dusk* Ⓤ *Lancaster Gate, Queensway.*

❹ **Kensington Palace.** Not as splendid as Buckingham Palace, or as famous
★ as Hampton Court, Kensington Palace is the most intimate of London's great royal residences. Originally a more modest dwelling called Nottingham House, it was bought in 1689 by King William III, whose acute asthma made it necessary for him to live outside the city (Kensington was, in those days, a small countryside village). He commissioned Wren and Hawksmoor to turn the building into a palace, and royals have been living here in grand style ever since. It was at Kensington Palace that Princess Victoria awoke in 1837, shortly after her 18th birthday, to discover that she had become Queen. In 1997, the world watched as the funeral procession for another former resident, the late Princess Diana, made its way out of the front gates. Today, the Duke and Duchess of Gloucester as well as Prince and Princess Michael of Kent have private apartments here.

On the Garden Floor is the palace's visitor entrance, which takes you into the Red Saloon and Teck Saloon, where the **Royal Ceremonial Dress Collection** displays garments dating to the 18th century. State and occasional dresses, hats, shoes, and gloves from the present Queen's wardrobe are showcased, as are some incredible evening gowns worn by Princess Diana. The State Apartments, especially the King's Apartments, are an imposing statement of regal power. The King's Grand Staircase is the impressive starting point of the tour, with its superb trompe-l'oeil paintings by William Kent, portraying the court of King George I. The Presence Chamber (used for formal receptions), painted with mythical gods in the Italian "grotesque" style, is a red-and-gold assault on the eyes. Roman columns and gilded decor in the Cupola Room, where Princess Victoria was christened, reminded the visitor that being admitted beyond the Presence Room was a mark of immense status.

But despite all this splendor, it is perhaps the gardens that are the true natural gem of this palace. If you visit in spring, the tulips, which were a favorite of Mary's, reign supreme in a riot of color. The Orangery, built for Queen Anne, was the scene of many a royal family party; you can take a cup of tea here, before admiring the Sunken Garden with its fountains and Tudor design that echoes Hampton Court. ✉ *The Broad Walk, Kensington Gardens, Kensington* ☎ *0844/482–7799 advance booking, 0844/482–7777 information* ⊕ *www.hrp.org.uk* 🎫 *£12.00; discounted joint tickets for one other palace, specified at time of purchase, are available* ⊙ *Mar.–Oct., daily 10–6; Nov.–Feb., daily 10–5; last admission 1 hr before closing* Ⓤ *Queensway.*

⓮ **Kenwood House.** This gracious Georgian villa was first built in 1616 and
☾ remodeled by Robert Adam between 1764 and 1779. Adam refaced
★ most of the exterior and added the splendid library, which, with its

curved painted ceiling, rather garish coloring, and gilded detailing, is the sole highlight of the house for decorative arts and interior design buffs. What is unmissable here is the **Iveagh Bequest,** a collection of paintings that the Earl of Iveagh gave the nation in 1927, including a wonderful Rembrandt self-portrait and works by Reynolds, Van Dyck, Hals, Gainsborough, and Turner. Top billing goes to Vermeer's *Guitar Player*. In front of the house, a graceful lawn slopes down to a little lake crossed by a trompe-l'oeil bridge—all in perfect 18th-century upperclass taste. The rest of the grounds are skirted by Hampstead Heath. ■ TIP➜ **In summer the grounds host a series of popular and classical concerts, culminating in fireworks on the last night.** A popular café, the Brew House, is part of the old coach house. ✉ *Hampstead La., Hampstead* ☎ *020/8348–1286* ⊕ *www.english-heritage.org.uk* ✑ *Free* ☉ *House daily except Dec. 24–26 and Jan.1, 11:30–4. Gardens daily dawn–dusk* Ⓤ *Golders Green, then Bus 210.*

❶ Natural History Museum. When you want to heed the call of the wild, explore this fun place. Don't be surprised when the dinos notice you— the fierce, animatronic Tyrannosaurus Rex senses when human prey is near and "responds" in character. Don't miss the ambitious Earth Galleries or the Creepy Crawlies Gallery, which includes a nightmarish, super-enlarged scorpion. In the basement, hands-on activities can be experienced in Investigate, which allows you to do just that, with actual objects, from old bones to bugs. The Darwin Centre showcases the museum's entire collection—all 22 million creatures—from a tiny Seychellian frog to the Komodo dragon lizard. Daily Explore tours leave from the museum's main information desk. ✉ *Cromwell Rd., South Kensington* ☎ *020/7942–5000* ⊕ *www.nhm.ac.uk* ✑ *Free* ☉ *Daily 10–5:50; last admission 5:30* Ⓤ *South Kensington.*

Notting Hill. Centered on the famous Portobello Road market *(see Shopping)*, this district is bordered to the west by Lansdowne Crescent— lined by "the hill's" poshest 19th-century terraced row houses—and to the east by Chepstow Road, with Notting Hill Gate and Westbourne Grove Road marking south and north boundaries. In between, the cool crowd, fashion set, and A- to B-list celebs can be spotted at the chic shops on Westbourne Grove and in the lively bars and cafés on Kensington Park Road. Ⓤ *Notting Hill Gate, Ladbroke Grove.*

Regent's Park. Laid out in 1812 by John Nash for the Prince Regent (hence the name), who was crowned George IV in 1820, the park was designed to re-create the atmosphere of a grand country residence close to the center of town. A walk around the Outer Circle, taking in the white-stucco terraces of grand houses facing the park, including the famous **Cumberland Terrace,** shows that it succeeds magnificently. The Inner Circle has many garden themes, the most impressive being **Queen Mary's Gardens,** a scented riot of roses in summer. From June through August, the **Regent's Park Open-Air Theatre** (☎ *0870/060–1811* ⊕ *www.openairtheatre.org*) mounts Shakespeare productions. The park is north of Mayfair. ☎ *020/7486–7905* ⊕ *www.royalparks.gov. uk* ☉ *5* AM*–dusk* Ⓤ *Baker St., Regent's Park.*

② Science Museum. Hands-on exhibits include the Launch Pad gallery, which demonstrates basic scientific principles (try the plasma ball, where your hands attract "lightning"—if you can get them on it); *Puffing Billy,* the oldest steam locomotive in the world; and the actual *Apollo 10* capsule. The six floors are devoted

WORD OF MOUTH

"We also visited the Natural History Museum for what else but the dinos! I really appreciate that these fantastic museums are all free." —tongsa

to subjects as diverse as the history of flight, space exploration, steam power, medicine, and a sublime exhibition on science in the 18th century. ✉*Exhibition Rd., South Kensington* ☎*0870/870–4868* ⊕*www. sciencemuseum.org.uk* ✉*Free, charge for the cinema shows and special exhibitions* ☉*Daily 10–6* Ⓤ*South Kensington.*

③ Victoria & Albert Museum. Recognizable by the copy of Victoria's Imperial Crown on the lantern above the central cupola, this huge museum showcases the decorative arts of all disciplines, periods, nationalities, and tastes. Prince Albert was responsible for the genesis of this permanent version of the 1851 Great Exhibition, and Victoria laid its foundation stone in her final public London appearance in 1899. The collections of the V&A, as it's always called, are *so* all-encompassing that confusion is a hazard; select a few galleries to focus on. One minute you're gazing on the Jacobean oak, 12-foot-square four-poster Great Bed of Ware (one of the V&A's most prized possessions, given that Shakespeare immortalized it in *Twelfth Night*), and the next, you're in the 20th-century end of the equally celebrated Dress Collection, coveting a Jean Muir frock. The British Galleries provide a social context for British art and design from 1500 to 1900 (from Henry VIII through Victoria), with displays such as George Gilbert Scott's model of the Albert Memorial and the first English fork ever made (1632). The Jameel Gallery of Islamic Art, which opened in 2005, has a fresh display of the museum's collection of Islamic decorative arts. Free one-hour tours whirl you by some of the museum's prized treasures. The shop is the museum in microcosm, and quite the best place to buy art nouveau or arts-and-crafts gifts. ✉*Cromwell Rd., South Kensington* ☎*020/7942–2000* ⊕*www.vam. ac.uk* ✉*Free* ☉*Thurs.–Wed. 10–5:45, Fri. 10–10; free tours daily at 10:30, 11:30, 1:30, and 3:30* Ⓤ *South Kensington.*

⑨ Wallace Collection. Assembled by four generations of Marquesses of Hertford and given to the nation by the widow of Sir Richard Wallace, illegitimate son of the fourth, this collection of art and artifacts is important, exciting, undervisited—and free. As at the Frick Collection in New York, Hertford House itself is part of the show: the fine late-18th-century mansion, built for the Duke of Manchester, contains a basement floor with educational activities, several galleries, and a courtyard covered by a glass roof, with the upscale Wallace Restaurant. ✉*Hertford House, Manchester Sq., Mayfair* ☎*020/7563–9500* ⊕*www.wallacecollection.org* ✉*Free, charge for special exhibitions* ☉*Daily 10–5* Ⓤ*Bond St.*

A TRIP TO ABBEY ROAD

For countless Beatlemaniacs and baby boomers, No. 3 Abbey Road is one of the most beloved spots in London. Here, outside the legendary Abbey Road Studios, is the most famous zebra crossing in the world, immortalized on the Beatles' 1969 *Abbey Road* album. ■TIP➔**It's tempting to try to re-create "the" photo, but be careful: rushing cars make Abbey Road a dangerous intersection.** One of the best—and safer—ways Beatle-lovers can enjoy the history of the group is to take one of the smashing walking tours offered by the **Original London Walks** (☎*020/7624–3978* ⊕*www.walks.com*), including **"The Beatles In-My-Life Walk"** (11:20 AM at the Baker Street Underground on Saturday and Tuesday) and **"The Beatles Magical Mystery Tour"** (Wednesday at 2 PM, Thursday at 11 AM, and Sunday at 10:55 AM at Underground Exit 3, Tottenham Court Road), which cover nostalgic landmark Beatles spots in the city.

WORTH NOTING

Albert Memorial. This gleaming, neo-Gothic shrine to Prince Albert created by George Gilbert Scott epitomizes the Victorian era. Albert's grieving widow, Queen Victoria, had this elaborate confection (including a 14-foot bronze statue of the prince) erected on the spot where his Great Exhibition had stood a decade before his early death, from typhoid, in 1861. ⊠*Kensington Gore, opposite Royal Albert Hall, Hyde Park, Kensington* ⓤ*Knightsbridge.*

❺ Belgrave Square. The square, as well as the streets leading off it, are genuine elite territory and have been since they were built in the mid-1800s. The grand, porticoed mansions were created as town residences for courtiers, conveniently close to the monarch—Buckingham Palace is virtually around the corner.

⓬ London Zoo. The zoo, owned by the Zoological Society of London (a charity), opened in 1828. A recent modernization program has seen several big new attractions open up, with a definite focus on wildlife conservation, education, and the breeding of endangered species. By far the biggest new arrival is Gorilla Kingdom, where you can watch the two resident gorillas—Bobby and Zaire—at close range. Also popular is the Clore Rainforest Lookout, home to tiny primates such as marmosets and golden lion tamarins and a large collection of other rainforest-dwelling creatures. ⊠*Regent's Park* ☎*020/7722–3333* ⊕*www.londonzoo.co.uk* ⊠*From £13* ⊙*Late Oct.–Mar., daily 10–4; Mar.–mid-Oct., daily 10–5:30; last admission 1 hr before closing* ⓤ*Camden Town, then Bus 274.*

⓫ Madame Tussaud's. One of London's busiest sights, this is nothing more and nothing less than the world's premier exhibition of lifelike waxwork models of celebrities. What makes people stand in line to invest in London's most expensive museum ticket? It must be the thrill of photo opportunities with Shakespeare, Simon Cowell, and the Queen—all in a single day. ⊠*Marylebone Rd., Regent's Park* ☎*0870/400–3000 for timed entry tickets* ⊕*www.madame-tussauds.com* ⊠*From £15; prices* *vary, call or check Web site. Combination ticket with the London Eye from £32.50* ⊙ *Weekdays 9:30–5:30, weekends 9–6* Ⓤ *Baker St.*

❿ **Sherlock Holmes Museum.** Outside Baker Street station, by the Marylebone Road exit, is a 9-foot-high bronze statue of the celebrated detective. Keep your eyes peeled, for close by his image, "Holmes" himself, in his familiar deerstalker hat, will escort you to his abode at 221B Baker Street, the address of Arthur Conan Doyle's fictional detective. It's all so realistic, you may actually begin to believe that the fictional "great detective" really lived there. ✉ *221B Baker St., Regent's Park* ☎ *020/7935–1127* ⊕ *www.sherlock-holmes.co.uk* ✍ *£6* ⊙ *Daily 9:30–6* Ⓤ *Baker St.*

❽ **Wellington Arch.** Opposite the Duke of Wellington's mansion, Apsley House, this majestic stone arch surveys the busy traffic rushing around Hyde Park Corner. Designed by Decimus Burton and built in 1828, it was created as a grand entrance to the west side of London and echoes the design of that other landmark gate, Marble Arch. In summer, Wellington Arch is the starting point for English Heritage themed walks. ✉ *Hyde Park Corner, Mayfair* ☎ *020/7930–2726* ⊕ *www.english-heritage.org.uk* ✍ *£3.20* ⊙ *Apr.–Oct., Wed.–Sun. 10–5; Nov.–Mar., Wed.–Sun. 10–4* Ⓤ *Hyde Park Corner.*

UP AND DOWN THE THAMES

Downstream—meaning seaward, or east—from central London, Greenwich has enough riches, especially if the maritime theme is your thing, that you should allow a very full day to see them. Upstream, the royal palaces and grand houses that dot the area were built not as town houses but as country residences with easy access to London by river; Hampton Court Palace is the best and biggest of all.

GREENWICH
8 mi east of central London.

Greenwich makes an ideal day out from central London, thanks to its historic and maritime attractions. Sir Christopher Wren's Royal Naval College and Inigo Jones's Queen's House reach architectural heights; the Old Royal Observatory measured time for the entire planet; and the Greenwich Meridian divides the world in two. You can stand astride it with one foot in either hemisphere. The National Maritime Museum will appeal to seafaring types, and landlubbers can stroll the parkland that surrounds the buildings, the pretty 19th-century houses, and the weekend crafts and antiques markets.

Once, Greenwich was considered remote by Londoners, with only the river as a direct route. With transportation links in the form of the Docklands Light Railway (DLR) and the tube's Jubilee Line, getting here is easy and inexpensive. The quickest route to maritime Greenwich is the tube to Canary Wharf and the Docklands Light Rail to the Greenwich stop. However, river connections to Greenwich make the journey memorable. On the way, the boat glides past famous London sights and the ever-changing Docklands.

2

☺ **National Maritime Museum.** Following a millennial facelift, one of Green-
★ wich's star attractions has been completely updated to make it one of
London's most fun museums. Its glass-covered courtyard of beautifully
grand stone, dominated by a huge revolving propeller from a powerful
frigate, is reminiscent of the British Museum. The collection spans seascape paintings to scientific instruments, interspersed with the heroes of
the waves. A permanent Nelson gallery contains the uniform he wore,
complete with bloodstain, when he met his end in 1805. Allow at least
two hours in this absorbing, adventurous place; if you're in need of
refreshment the museum has a good café with views over Greenwich
Park. ⊠*Romney Rd., Greenwich* ☎*020/8858–4422* ⊕*www.nmm.
ac.uk* ☑*Free* ⊗*Daily 10–5; last admission 30 mins before closing*
Ⓤ*DLR: Greenwich.*

**QUICK
BITES**

For the best pub in Greenwich, head to the **Trafalgar Tavern** (⊠*Park Row*
☎*020/8858-2909* ⊕*www.trafalgartavern.co.uk*), with excellent views of
the Thames. It's a grand place to have a pint and some upscale grub.

Old Royal Naval College. Begun by Christopher Wren in 1694 as a rest
home for ancient mariners, it became instead a school for young ones
in 1873. Behind the college are two buildings you can visit. The **Painted
Hall,** the college's dining hall, derives its name from the baroque murals
of assorted allegorical figures. In the opposite building stands the **College Chapel,** built in a more restrained, neo-Grecian style. ⊠*Old Royal Naval College, King William Walk, Greenwich* ☎*020/8269–4747*
⊕*www.oldroyalnavalcollege.org* ☑*Free, guided tours £4* ⊗*Painted
Hall and Chapel Mon.–Sat. 10–5, Sun. 12:30–5; last admission 4:15;
grounds 8–6* Ⓤ*DLR: Greenwich.*

★ **Ranger's House.** This handsome, early-18th-century villa, which was the
Greenwich Park Ranger's official residence during the 19th century,
is hung with Stuart and Jacobean portraits. But the most interesting
diversion is the Wernher Collection, more than 650 works of art with
a north European flavor, amassed by diamond millionaire Julius Wernher at the turn of the 20th century. ⊠*Chesterfield Walk, Blackheath,
Greenwich* ☎*020/8853–0035* ⊕*www.english-heritage.org.uk* ☑*£5.50*
⊗*Apr.–Sept., Sun.–Wed. 10–5; Oct.–Dec. and Mar., by appointment
only* Ⓤ*DLR: Greenwich; no direct bus access, only to Vanbrugh Hill
(from east) and Blackheath Hill (from west).*

☺ **Royal Observatory.** Founded in 1675 by Charles II, this imposing institu-
★ tion was designed by Christopher Wren for John Flamsteed, the first
Astronomer Royal. The red ball you see on its roof has been there
since 1833. It drops every day at 1 PM, and you can set your watch by
it, as the sailors on the Thames always have. Everyone comes here to
be photographed astride the **Prime Meridian,** a brass line laid on the
cobblestones at zero degrees longitude, one side being the eastern, one
the western, hemisphere. An exhibit on the solution to the problem of
measuring longitude includes John Harrison's famous clocks, H1–H4.
The **Peter Harrison Planetarium** is a welcome new addition; its interactive galleries are great for kids. ⊠*Greenwich Park, Greenwich* ☎*020/
8858–4422* ⊕*www.rog.nmm.ac.uk* ☑*Free, planetarium shows £6*

Apr.–Sept., daily 10–6; Oct.– Mar., daily 10–5; last admission 4:30 Ⓤ *DLR: Greenwich.*

HAMPTON COURT PALACE
20 mi southwest of central London.

⟳ On a loop of the Thames lies **Hampton Court,** one of London's oldest royal palaces and more like a small town in size; you need a day to do it justice. It's actually two palaces in one—a Tudor residence and a late-17th-century baroque one—as well as a renowned garden. The magnifi-

WORD OF MOUTH

"[Hampton Court Palace is] a must-see part of your trip to London. You get to experience the feel of life in the castle more than in other royal palaces. You can take the tour at your own pace and there are all sorts of activities to keep you busy."

—Kim from Tennessee

cent Tudor brick house, with its cobbled courtyards and cavernous kitchens, was begun in 1514 by Cardinal Wolsey, the ambitious lord chancellor (roughly, prime minister) of England and archbishop of York. He wanted it to be the best palace in the land, and succeeded so well that Henry VIII grew envious, whereupon Wolsey gave Hampton Court to the king. Henry moved in during 1525, added a great hall and chapel, and proceeded to live much of his astonishing life here. Later, during the reign of William and Mary, Christopher Wren expanded the palace substantially, adding the graceful baroque south and east fronts that are highlights of the palace. Six themed routes, including Henry VIII's State Apartments and the King William III's Apartments, help you plan your visit; special guides in period costume add to the fun.

The site beside the slow-moving Thames is idyllic, with 60 acres of ornamental gardens, lakes, and ponds, including William III's Privy Garden on the palace's south side. Its parterres, sculpted turf, and clipped yews and hollies brilliantly set off Wren's addition. Other horticultural highlights are Henry VIII's Pond Garden and the enormous conical yews around the Fountain Garden. On the east side of the house, 544 lime trees were replanted in 2004 along the Long Water, a canal built during the time of Charles II. Perhaps best of all is the almost half-mile of paths in the fiendish maze, planted in 1714. ⊠ *East Molesey on A308* ☎ *0870/752–7777* ⊕ *www.hrp.org.uk* 🎫 *Palace, gardens, and maze £13.00, gardens only £4.50, maze only £3.50, park grounds free* ⊙ *State apartments Apr.–Oct., daily 10–6; last admission at 5; Nov.–Mar., daily 10–4:30; grounds daily 7–dusk* Ⓤ *Richmond, then Bus R68; National Rail, South West: Hampton Court Station, 35 min from Waterloo.*

KEW GARDENS
6 mi southwest of central London.

Kew Gardens, or more formally the Royal Botanic Gardens at Kew, is the headquarters of the country's leading botanical institute as well as a spectacular public garden of 300 acres and more than 30,000 species of plants. The highlights of a visit to this UNESCO World Heritage Site are the two great 19th-century greenhouses filled with tropical plants, many of which have been there as long as their housing. The bold glass roofs of the ultramodern Princess of Wales Conservatory shelter no fewer than 10 climatic zones. Two 18th-century royal ladies, Queen Caroline and Princess Augusta, were responsible for the garden's founding. The tube ride to Kew is about 40 minutes, but the gardens are very close to the stop. ⊠*Kew Rd., Kew* ☎*020/8332–5655* ⊕*www.kew. org* ✉*£12.25* ⊙*Gardens Apr.–Oct., weekdays 9:30–6:30, weekends 9:30–7:30; Nov.–Mar., daily 9:30–4:30* Ⓤ *Kew Gardens.*

Kew Palace and Queen Charlotte's Cottage. To this day quietly domestic Kew Palace remains the smallest royal palace in the land. The house and gardens offer a glimpse into the 17th century. Originally known as the Dutch House, it was bought by King George II to provide more room in addition to the White House (another royal residence that used to exist on the grounds) for the extended royal family. In spring there's a romantic haze of bluebells. ⊠*Kew Gardens, Kew* ⊕*www.hrp.org.uk* ✉*£5, in addition to ticket for Kew Gardens* ⊙*Apr.–Sept., Tues.–Sun. 10–5, Mon. 11–5* Ⓤ*Kew Gardens.*

QUICK BITES **Maids of Honour** (⊠*288 Kew Rd. Kew,* ☎*020/8940–2752*), the most traditional of Old English tearooms, is named for the famous tarts invented here and still baked by hand on the premises. Tea is served on Tuesday–Saturday 2:30–5:30. If you want to take some of the lovely cakes and pastries to eat at Kew Gardens or on Kew Green, the shop is open Tuesday–Saturday 9:30–6 and on Monday until 1.

WHERE TO EAT

Use the coordinate (✛B2) at the end of each listing to locate a site on the corresponding map.

London rivals New York, Paris, and Tokyo as one of the best places to eat in the world right now. The sheer diversity of restaurants here is unparalleled. Among the city's 6,700 restaurants are see-and-be-seen hot spots, casual ethnic eateries, innovative gastro-pubs, and shrines to haute cuisine.

Now a leading global finance center, London has seen a wall of money cascade from the City's finance markets and help spark the most fantastic restaurant boom that London has ever seen. To measure London's spectacular culinary rise, note that it was once a common dictum that the British ate to live while the French lived to eat.

Hell's Kitchen star Gordon Ramsay is setting the highest standard at his eponymous place at Royal Hospital Road in Chelsea, and the rest of the much-lauded high-cuisine scene is dominated by world-class masters. Marcus Wareing is making waves at the Berkeley; Hélène Darroze works her magic at the Connaught; Michael Roux Jr. rules the roost at Le Gavroche; and Claude Bosi bosses the show at Hibiscus.

Luckily, London also does a good job of catering to people interested in satisfying their appetites without breaking the bank. For cheap eats, don't miss the city's unofficial dish, the ubiquitous Indian curry. The quality of other international cuisines has improved in recent years, as London has become known for its Japanese, Spanish, Thai, and North

BEST BETS FOR LONDON DINING

Where can I find the best food London has to offer? Fodor's writers and editors have selected their favorite restaurants by price, cuisine, and experience in the lists below. In the first column, the Fodor's Choice properties represent the "best of the best" across price categories. You can also search by neighborhood for excellent eating experiences—just peruse our complete reviews on the following pages.

Fodor'sChoice★

Boxwood Café, ££ p. 98

Giaconda Dining Room, ££ p. 96

Great Queen Street, £££££ p. 96

Hélène Darroze at the Connaught, £££££ p. 99

Hibiscus, £££ p. 100

Marcus Wareing at the Berkeley, £££££ p. 98

Scott's, £££ p. 101

Wild Honey, £££ p. 101

The Wolseley, £££ p. 103

By Price

£

Busabe Eathai, p. 95

Côte, p. 96

Cha Cha Moon, p. 96

Wahaca, p. 97

££

Anchor & Hope, p. 103

Arbutus, p. 94

Giaconda Dining Room, p. 96

£££

Barrafina, p. 95

Hibiscus, p. 100

Scott's, p. 101

St. Alban, p. 102

Wild Honey, p. 101

The Wolseley, p. 103

££££

Boxwood Café, p. 98

J Sheekey, p. 96

Locanda Locatelli, p. 100

£££££

Great Queen Street, p. 96

Hélène Darroze at the Connaught, p. 99

Le Gavroche, p. 100

Marcus Wareing at the Berkeley, p. 98

By Cuisine

MODERN BRITISH

Anchor & Hope, ££–£££ p. 103

Hereford Road, ££ p. 89

Great Queen Street, £££££ p. 96

St. John, £££ p. 94

FRENCH

Galvin Bistrot de Luxe, £££ p. 99

Hélène Darroze at the Connaught, £££££ p. 99

The Capital, £££££ p. 98

Marcus Wareing at the Berkeley, £££££ p. 98

INDIAN

Original Lahore Kebab House, ££ p. 91

Rasoi Vineet Bhatia, ££££ p. 98

Tayyabs, £ p. 94

ITALIAN

Cecconi's, £££ p. 99

L'Anima, £££ p. 91

Locanda Locatelli, ££££ p. 100

River Café, ££££ p. 98

SEAFOOD

Golden Hind, £ p. 99

J Sheekey, £££ p. 96

Scott's, £££ p. 101

Sweetings, £££ p. 94

By Experience

MOST KID-FRIENDLY

Busabe Eathai, £ p. 95

Cha Cha Moon, £ p. 96

Royal China, £££ p. 90

BEST VIEW

Plateau, £££££ p. 91

River Café, ££££ p. 98

Skylon, £££ p. 103

HOT SPOTS

Cecconi's, £££ p. 99

Great Queen Street, £££££ p. 96

Nobu Berkeley Street, ££££–£££££ p. 100

Scott's, £££ p. 101

BEST PRETHEATER EATS

Arbutus, £££ p. 94

Giaconda Dining Room, ££ p. 96

St. Alban, £££ p. 102

Quo Vadis, £££ p. 97

African restaurants. With all of the choices, traditional British food, when you track it down, appears as just one more exotic cuisine in the pantheon. The listings here strike a balance between these extremes and include hip-and-happening places, neighborhood spots, ethnic alternatives, and old favorites.

Two caveats: first, an outright ban on smoking in public places—such as restaurants—was enacted in 2007 and has proved a healthy success. Second, beware of Sunday. Many restaurants are closed, especially in the evening; likewise public holidays. Over the Christmas holiday period, London virtually shuts down—it seems only hotels are prepared to feed travelers. When in doubt, call ahead. It's a good idea to book a table at all times.

PRICES AND SAVING MONEY

London is not an inexpensive city. A modest meal for two can cost £40 (about $60) and the £100-a-head meal is not so taboo. Damage-control strategies include making lunch your main meal—the top places have bargain lunch menus, halving the price of evening à la carte—and ordering a second appetizer instead of an entrée, to which few places object. Note that an appetizer, usually known as a "starter" or "first course," is sometimes called an "entrée," as it is in France, and an entrée in England is dubbed the "main course" or simply "mains."

Indian and other international restaurants have always been a good money-saving bet here. Sandwich shops and chains proliferate. *See Local Chains Worth a Taste box for the best bets.* Seek out fixed-price menus, and watch for hidden extras on the check: cover, bread, or vegetables charged separately, and service. Many restaurants exclude service charges from the menu (which the law obliges them to display outside), then add 10% to 12.5% to the check, or else stamp SERVICE NOT INCLUDED along the bottom, in which case you should add the 10% to 12.5% yourself. Don't pay twice for service.

WHAT IT COSTS IN POUNDS					
	£	££	£££	££££	£££££
AT DINNER	under £10	£10–£16	£17–£23	£24–£32	over £32

Prices are per person for a main course, excluding drinks, service, and V.A.T.

BAYSWATER

££
MODERN BRITISH
✕**Hereford Road.** Bespectacled chef/co-owner Tom Pemberton mans the front-of-house grill at this Bayswater favorite, which specializes in pared-back best-of-British fare. With an accent on well-sourced regional and seasonal ingredients, many dishes are as uncluttered as you'll find. Slide into a stylish booth, and gorge on simple pork and Piccadilli, mussels with cider, or ox cheeks with pickled walnuts. Expect to see the well-heeled Tory-leaning Notting Hill set. ⊠*3 Hereford Rd., Bayswater* ☎ *020/7727–1144* ⊕*www.herefordroad.org* ⌔*Reservations essential* ⊟*AE, MC, V* Ⓤ*Bayswater, Queensway* ⊹*A3.*

£££ ✕**Royal China.** The black-and-gold '70s Biba-style decor is half the fun
CHINESE at this flagship dim sum palace on Queensway. Expect queues and mir-
☺ rored ceilings at this longtime favorite that churns out stacks of dim sum
at a furious pace. Start with dumplings stuffed with pork, squid, duck,
prawns, scallops, or crab, and follow up with spareribs and greens, and
pots of Chinese tea. ⊠*13 Queensway, Bayswater* ☎*020/7221–2535*
⊕*www.royalchinagroup.co.uk* ⊟*AE, MC, V* Ⓤ*Queensway, Bays-*
water ✛*A3.*

CHELSEA

£££££ ✕**Gordon Ramsay at Royal Hospital Road.** Ubiquitous chef Ramsay—of
FRENCH *Hell's Kitchen* fame—whips up a heavenly storm of white beans, lobster, foie gras, and shaved truffles at London's most garlanded restaurant in Chelsea. He's one of Britain's finest chefs, and wins the
highest accolades here with French classics, where tables are booked
months in advance. Splurge on seven courses for £120; dance through
a three-course dinner for £85; or shuffle through a £40 three-course
lunch. ⊠*68 Royal Hospital Rd., Chelsea* ☎*020/7352–4441* ⊕*www.*
gordonramsay.com/royalhospitalroad ⌂*Reservations essential* ⊟*AE,*
DC, MC, V ☉*Closed weekends* Ⓤ*Sloane Sq.* ✛*C6.*

££ ✕**The Pig's Ear.** Heir to the throne Prince William came with friends and
MODERN BRITISH split the bill in the first-floor dining room at this classic gastro-pub off
the King's Road. Elbow in at the crowded ground-floor pub area, or
choose a more formal vibe in the dark wood-paneled salon upstairs.
You'll find creative dishes on a short menu, like pig's ear, Cornish lobster, and braised pork belly, which are all typical, and executed . . . royally. ⊠*35 Old Church St., Chelsea* ☎*020/7352–2908* ⌂*Reservations*
essential ⊟*AE, DC, MC, V* Ⓤ*Sloane Sq.* ✛*B6.*

££ ✕**PJ's Bar & Grill.** Enter PJ's and assume the Polo Joe lifestyle: wooden
AMERICAN floors and stained glass, a slowly revolving propeller from a 1911 Vick-
ers Vimy flying boat, and vintage polo gear galore. The place is packed,
relaxed, and efficient, and the menu, which includes all-American staples like organic steaks, salads, and brownies, pleases all except vegetarians. PJ's opens late, and the bartenders are pros. Weekend brunch
is de rigueur with the wealthy Chelsea set. ⊠*52 Fulham Rd., Chelsea*
☎*020/7581–0025* ⊕*www.pjsbarandgrill.co.uk* ⊟*AE, MC, V* Ⓤ*South*
Kensington ✛*B5.*

£££ ✕**Racine.** There's an upscale buzz at this star of the Brompton Road
BRASSERIE dining scene, not far from the Victoria & Albert museum, Holy Trinity Brompton church, and Harrods department store. This chic French
brasserie excels because it does the simple things well—and doesn't
overcharge. Classics like melted Raclette cheese, roast quail, and duck
with juniper sauce all hit the mark. The £17.50 set lunch or early dinners
(6–7:30 PM) are popular. ⊠*239 Brompton Rd., Chelsea* ☎*020/7584–*
4477 ⊟*AE, MC, V* Ⓤ*South Kensington* ✛*B5.*

£££££ ✕**Tom Aikens.** Wonder chef Tom Aikens trained under French stars Pierre
FRENCH Koffman and Joël Robuchon and excels at his eponymous place in
upmarket Chelsea. Prone to flights of fancy, his food is technically
superb. You'll swoon over his foie gras with Sauternes jelly, pollack
with truffle scrambled eggs, John Dory with couscous, and pear-and-

ginger mousse. There's an expert sommelier to help with the wine. ✉ *43 Elystan St., Kensington* ☎ *020/7584–2003* ⊕ *www.tomaikens.co.uk* ⌒ *Reservations essential* ▭ *AE, MC, V* Ⓤ *South Kensington* ✛ *B5.*

THE CITY

£££   ✕ **L'Anima.** Brilliant Southern Italian cuisine in a love-it-or-loathe-it glass
ITALIAN box of a restaurant characterize the scene at L'Anima. Chef Francesco Mazzei draws inspiration from Sicily, Sardinia, and Calabria, and works the floor, bar, and clear-fronted kitchen like the proud owner that he is. Simple, modern dishes like wild mushroom and black truffle tagliolini are near perfection, as is the baked sea bass—as succulent as you could wish. Dessert puddings, like peach and Amaretto, are *belissimo*, and the wines are mainly Italian. ✉ *1 Snowden St., TheCity* ☎ *020/7422–7000* ⊕ *www.lanima.co.uk* ⌒ *Reservations essential* ▭ *AE, MC, V* ☾ *Closed weekends* Ⓤ *Liverpool St.* ✛ *H2.*

£££   ✕ **Moro.** Up from The City, near Clerkenwell and Sadler's Wells con-
MEDITERRANEAN temporary dance theater, is Exmouth Market, a cluster of cute shops, a few delis, an Italian church, and more fine restaurants like Moro. The menu includes a mélange of Spanish and North African flavors. Spiced meats, Serrano hams, salt cod, and wood-fired and char-grilled offerings are the secret to Moro's success. Grilled lamb with marrow and yogurt stands out. Sidle up to the zinc bar, or squeeze into a tiny table and lean in—it's noisy here. But then again, that's part of the buzz. ✉ *34–36 Exmouth Market, The City* ☎ *020/7833–8336* ⊕ *www.moro.co.uk* ⌒ *Reservations essential* ▭ *AE, DC, MC, V* ☾ *Closed Sun.* Ⓤ *Farringdon* ✛ *F1.*

££   ✕ **Original Lahore Kebab House.** Best budget curries in London is the
PAKISTANI mantra at the Original Lahore Kebab House in run-down Whitechapel. It may be BYOB and no-frills, but the halal Pakistani home-style cooking is cheap and brilliant—popular with Asians and City boys alike. Mutton *tikka*, grilled lamb chops, *tarka daal* lentils, masala fish curry, and *karahi* chicken are all super-spiced and fiery. A £15-a-head meal knocks spots off anything on offer in nearby Brick Lane's so-called "curry mile." ✉ *2 Umberston St., The City* ☎ *020/7481–9737* ⊕ *www.lahore-kebabhouse.com* ▭ *MC, V* ⌒ *BYOB* Ⓤ *Aldgate* ✛ *H3.*

£££££   ✕ **Plateau.** Credit crunch or no, Plateau's a useful venue for a Canary
MODERN FRENCH Wharf business meal. In an all-white space, with tulip-shape chairs and floor-to-ceiling glass windows overlooking Canada Square, Plateau houses a restaurant, rotisserie, two bars, private dining, and outdoor terraces. Food like Cornish mackerel, skate wing and capers, and lamb with sweetbreads are all pricey, but well executed. ✉ *4th Fl., Canada Pl., Canada Sq., The City* ☎ *020/7715–7100* ⊕ *www.plateaurestaurant.co.uk* ⌒ *Reservations essential* ▭ *AE, DC, MC, V* Ⓤ *Canary Wharf* ✛ *H3.*

££–£££   ✕ **Simpson's Tavern.** This historic back-alley City chophouse was founded
BRITISH in 1757 and is as raucous as you like. It draws pinstriped City folk, who love the boardinghouse scene and old-school grub: oxtail stew, steak-and-kidney pie, chump chops, potted shrimp, or "stewed cheese" house special (cheese on toast with Béchamel sauce). Brusque service and shared oak bench stalls are all part of the charm. Note it's open

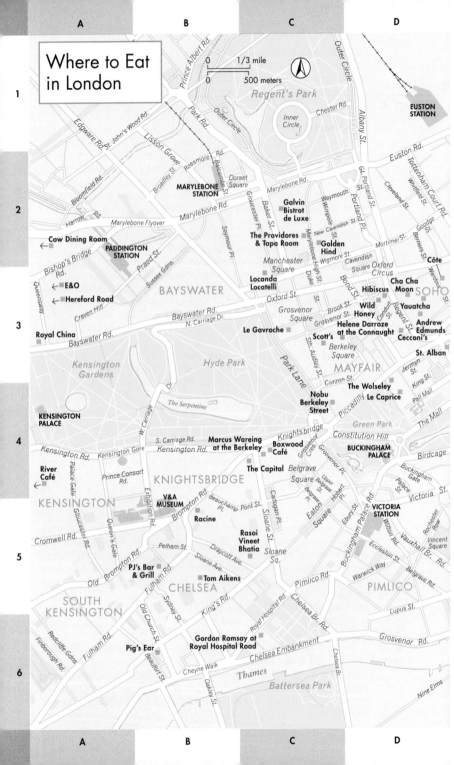

Where to Eat in London

0   1/3 mile
0   500 meters

Regent's Park

Inner Circle

EUSTON STATION

Prince Albert Rd.
Outer Circle
Chester Rd.
Albany St.
Euston Rd.
Tottenham Court Rd.

Edgware Rd.
St. John's Wood Rd.
Lisson Grove
Park Rd.
Outer Circle
Rossmore Rd.
Balcombe Rd.

Bloomfield Rd.
Bradley St.
Dorset Square

MARYLEBONE STATION

Harrow Rd.
Marylebone Flyover
Marylebone Rd.
Marylebone Rd.
Gt. Portland St.
Cleveland St.
Whitfield St.
Goodge St.
Berners St.

Cow Dining Room ←

Bishop's Bridge Rd.
Queensway

PADDINGTON STATION
Praed St.
Sussex Gdns.
Seymour Pl.

Galvin Bistrot de Luxe

Weymouth St.
Wimpole St.
Portland Pl.
Mortimer St.

Côte

E&O ←
Hereford Road ←

BAYSWATER

The Providores & Tapa Room

Golden Hind

New Cavendish St.
Wigmore St.
Cavendish Square

Oxford Circus

Cha Cha Moon

SOHO

Craven Hill
Bayswater Rd.
N. Carriage Dr.

Locanda Locatelli

Manchester Square

Duke St.
Marylebone High St.
Baker St.
Gloucester Pl.

Wardour St.

Royal China

Bayswater Rd.

Le Gavroche

Oxford St.
Grosvenor Square
Brook St.
Grosvenor St.
Bond St.
Regent St.

Hibiscus

Wild Honey

Yauatcha

Andrew Edmunds

Cecconi's

Kensington Gardens

Hyde Park

Scott's

Helene Darroze at the Connaught

Berkeley Square

MAYFAIR

St. Alban

The Serpentine

S. Audley St.
Park Lane
Curzon St.

St. James's St.
Jermyn St.
King St.
Pall Mall

KENSINGTON PALACE

W. Carriage Dr.

Nobu Berkeley Street

The Wolseley

Le Caprice

Piccadilly

Green Park

The Mall

Kensington Rd.
Kensington Gore

S. Carriage Rd.
Kensington Rd.

Marcus Wareing at the Berkeley

Boxwood Café

Knightsbridge
Constitution Hill

BUCKINGHAM PALACE

Birdcage

River Café ←

Prince Consort Rd.
Exhibition Rd.

KNIGHTSBRIDGE

The Capital

Belgrave Square

Sloane St.
Grosvenor Cres.
Grosvenor Pl.

Buckingham Gate
Buckingham Palace Rd.

Victoria St.

Rochester Row

KENSINGTON

Cromwell Rd.
Gloucester Rd.
Queen's Gate

V&A MUSEUM

Racine

Brompton Rd.
Beauchamp Pl.
Pont St.
Cadogan Pl.

Upper Belgrave St.
Lower Belgrave St.
Eaton Square
Hobart Pl.
Ebury St.

VICTORIA STATION

Eccleston St.
Wilton Rd.
Vauxhall Br. Rd.
Vincent Square

SOUTH KENSINGTON

Old Brompton Rd.
PJ's Bar & Grill
Fulham Rd.
Pelham St.
Sloane Ave.
Draycott Ave.

Rasoi Vineet Bhatia

Sloane Sq.

Pimlico Rd.
Warwick Way

PIMLICO

Lupus St.
Belgrave Rd.

Redcliffe Gdns.
Finborough Rd.
Fulham Rd.

Tom Aikens

CHELSEA
King's Rd.

Sydney St.
Old Church St.

Royal Hospital Rd.
Chelsea Br. Rd.

Grosvenor Rd.

Pig's Ear

Gordon Ramsay at Royal Hospital Road

Chelsea Embankment
Cheyne Walk
Oakley St.
Beaufort St.

Thames

Chelsea Br.

Battersea Park

Nine Elms

only for weekday lunch, from noon to 3. ✉ *38½ Cornhill, at Ball Ct., The City* ☎ *020/7626–9985* ⊕ *www.simpsonstavern.co.uk* ⊟ *AE, DC, MC, V* ⊗ *Closed weekends. No dinner* Ⓤ *Bank* ✚ *H3.*

£££ ✕ **St. John.** Fans travel the globe for Fergus Henderson's ultra-British
BRITISH cooking at this stark-white converted smokehouse in Clerkenwell. His chutzpah is galling: one appetizer is pigskin, and others, like ox heart, pig's tongue, gizzard, or pig nose and tail, are marginally less extreme. Dishes from bone marrow and parsley, or chitterlings and dandelion appear stark on the plate but arrive with aplomb. Expect an all-French wine list, plus malmseys and port. Finish with rhubarb trifle and Eccles cakes. ✉ *26 St. John St., Clerkenwell* ☎ *020/7251–0848* ⊕ *www. stjohnrestaurant.co.uk* ⌔ *Reservations essential* ⊟ *AE, DC, MC, V* ⊗ *Closed Sun.* Ⓤ *Farringdon* ✚ *G2.*

£££ ✕ **Sweetings.** Established in 1889, Sweetings is a remnant from the
SEAFOOD old imperial City of London heyday. There are some things Sweetings *doesn't* do: reservations, dinner, coffee, and weekends. It does, however, do seafood. Not far from St. Paul's cathedral, it's patronized by City gents who drink tankards of Black Velvet (Guinness and champagne) and eat potted shrimp, roe on toast, and skate wings with black butter at linen-covered raised counters. The oysters are fresh, and desserts like spotted dick and bread-and-butter pudding are public-school favorites. ✉ *39 Queen Victoria St., The City* ☎ *020/7248–3062* ⌔ *Reservations not accepted* ⊟ *AE, MC, V* ⊗ *Closed weekends. No dinner* Ⓤ *Mansion House* ✚ *G3.*

£ ✕ **Tayyabs.** City finance boys, Asians, and medics from the Royal Lon-
PAKISTANI don Hospital swamp this high-turnover halal Pakistani curry canteen in Whitechapel. Expect queues after dark, and bear in mind it's BYOB, jam-packed, noisy, and mildly chaotic. Nonetheless, prices are dirt cheap and you can gorge for £15 on minced meat shami kebabs, skewed beef seekh kebabs, karahi chicken, or marinated lamb chops. ✉ *83 Fieldgate St., The City* ☎ *020/7247–9543* ⊕ *www.tayyabs.co.uk* ⌔ *Reservations not accepted* ⊟ *AE, MC, V* ⟁ *BYOB* Ⓤ *Aldgate East* ✚ *H3.*

COVENT GARDEN AND SOHO

££ ✕ **Andrew Edmunds.** Rustic food at realistic prices defines this perpetu-
MEDITERRANEAN ally jammed, softly lighted romantic Soho restaurant—though it could be larger and the wooden bench seats more forgiving. Tucked away behind Carnaby Street, it's a favorite with the media crowd that come for daily changing, fixed-price lunch menus. Starters and main courses draw on the taste of Ireland, the Mediterranean, and Middle East. Goose rillettes (£5.50), Roquefort soufflé (£6.50), and swordfish with basil mayonnaise (£14) are all hale and hearty. ✉ *46 Lexington St., Soho* ☎ *020/7437–5708* ⌔ *Reservations essential* ⊟ *MC, V* Ⓤ *Oxford Circus, Piccadilly Circus* ✚ *D3.*

£££ ✕ **Arbutus.** Serious cuisine at midrange prices has established Arbutus
MODERN BRITISH in the winners' enclosure of favorite Soho eateries. The £15.50 three-course lunch or £17.50 pretheater special are bargains of the year. Chef Anthony Demetre might surprise with squid-and-mackerel burger, rabbit and cottage pie, or pollack and tomato jam, and finishes off with apple-and-blackberry charlotte. All wines are offered in third-of-

British Food Decoder

In London, local could mean any global flavor, but for pure Britishness, roast beef and Yorkshire pudding top the list. If you want the best-value traditional Sunday lunch, go to a pub. Gastro-pubs, where Sunday roasts are generally made with top-quality ingredients, are a good bet. The meat is usually served with crisp roast potatoes and carrots, and with Yorkshire pudding, a savory batter baked in the oven until crisp. A rich, dark, meaty gravy is poured on top.

Other tummy liners include shepherd's pie, made with stewed minced lamb and a mashed-potato topping and baked until lightly browned on top; cottage pie is a similar dish, but made with minced beef instead of lamb. Steak-and-kidney pie is a delight when done properly: with chunks of lean beef and ox kidneys, braised with onions and mushrooms in a thick gravy, and topped with a light puff-pastry crust.

Fish-and-chips, usually battered deep-fried cod or haddock, comes with thick chips, or french fries, as we call them in the States. A plough-man's lunch in a pub is crusty bread, a strong-flavored English cheese with bite (cheddar, blue Stilton, crumbly white Cheshire, or smooth red Leicester), and tangy pickles with a side-salad garnish. For a hot, comforting dessert, seek out a sweet bread-and-butter pudding, made from layers of bread and dried currants baked in cream until crisp. And one can't forgo English cream tea, which consists of scones served with jam and clotted cream, and sandwiches made with wafer-thin slices of cucumber—served as an accompaniment to properly brewed tea.

---

a-bottle carafes—a great way to sample new wines. ✉ *63–64 Frith St., Soho* ☎ *020/7734–4545* ⊕ *www.arbutusrestaurant.co.uk* ▤ *AE, MC, V* Ⓤ *Tottenham Court Rd.* ✛ *E3.*

£ ✕ **Baozi Inn.** Mao paraphernalia decorates the walls of this handy Sich-
CHINESE uan café on a busy side street in Chinatown. Baozi steamed buns—pork and onion or shrimp and radish—are house specials (£1.20), and there's dragon wonton broth or Chengdu pork dumplings with chili oil (£5.20). Try "ginger juice" spinach (£4), or "peace and happiness" noodle soup, topped with duck, garlic, and Chinese toon tree shoots (£6.10). Tables are cramped, and service is bang, bang, bang! ✉ *25 Newport Ct., Soho* ☎ *020/7287–6877* ▵ *Reservations not accepted* ▤ *AE, MC, V* Ⓤ *Leicester Sq.* ✛ *E3.*

£££ ✕ **Barrafina.** London's top tapas bar on Frith Street in Soho is modeled
SPANISH on Cal Pep in Barcelona and similarly has only a few (23) raised counter seats. It doesn't take bookings and you're likely to queue, but staff are past masters, and the tapas are supreme. Pick at gambas or chorizo, quail, sardines, and octopus, or classics like Jabugo ham and tortilla. You can check out the scene—or the queue—at the live webcam. ✉ *54 Frith St., Soho* ☎ *020/7813–8016* ⊕ *www.barrafina.co.uk* ▵ *Reservations not accepted* ▤ *AE, MC, V* Ⓤ *Tottenham Court Rd.* ✛ *E3.*

£ ✕ **Busabe Eathai.** It's top Thai nosh for little moolah at this superior
THAI no-bookings canteen in the heart of Soho. Fitted with bench seats and

hardwood tables, it's no less seductive for the communal dining, rapid service, and fast-moving queue out the front. The menu includes noodles, curries, soups, juices, and stir-fries. Try the chicken with shiitake, cuttlefish curry, or vermicelli with prawns, squid, and scallops. ✉ *106–110 Wardour St., Soho* ☎ *020/7255–8686* ⚐ *Reservations not accepted* ▤ *AE, MC, V* Ⓤ *Tottenham Court Rd.* ✛ *E2.*

£ ✕**Cha Cha Moon.** Alan Yau's slump-proof Chinese noodle joint off Carnaby Street charges £3.50 for all mains and sides, so it's no wonder the communal tables are usually crammed like a Hong Kong subway train. It's known to be hit-and-miss, so pick wisely from the long menu and you can score a tasty meal for £15. Spring onion pancakes, chili prawn noodles, and eggplant or duck lo mein with broth are good. ✉ *15–21 Ganton St., Soho* ☎ *020/7297–9800* ⚐ *Reservations not accepted* ▤ *AE, MC, V* Ⓤ *Oxford Circus* ✛ *D3.*

CHINESE

££ ✕**Côte.** Where else can you get a surprisingly good three-course French meal for £11.95? The Côte French brasserie—softly lighted and smoothly decked out with banquettes and Parisian-style round tables—does just the trick, and offers these deals weekdays from noon until 7. With four choices per course, you'll find all your favorites: Bayonne ham, Les Landes chicken, moules marinière, tuna Niçoise, and steak haché. ✉ *124–126 Wardour, Soho* ☎ *020/7287–9280* ⊕ *www.cote-restaurants.co.uk* ▤ *AE, MC, V* Ⓤ *Tottenham Court Rd.* ✛ *D3.*

FRENCH

££ ✕**Giaconda Dining Room.** A real find on Denmark Street's "Tin Pan Alley" (think Bowie, Marley, and the Clash), the Australian-run two-room dining room may seat only 35, but the menu is inspired and the prices are cheap. Chef Paul Merrony sends out starters—pumpkin risotto, crispy pigs' trotters—and a full range of main entrées for a reasonable cost. Try the fish cakes, salmon and fennel, or hearty dishes like poached veal, Italian pork sausage stew, or ham-hock hash with a fried egg on top. Popular puddings such as apricot compote with walnuts and whipped cream come in at a tasty £5. ✉ *9 Denmark St., Soho* ☎ *020/7240–3334* ⊕ *www.giacondadining.com* ⚐ *Reservations essential* ▤ *AE, MC, V* ⊙ *Closed weekends* Ⓤ *Tottenham Court Rd.* ✛ *E3.*

MODERN EUROPEAN
Fodor'sChoice
★

£££££ ✕**Great Queen Street.** Expect crowds and a buzz at Covent Garden's leading gastro-pub that showcases classic British dishes in a burgundy and bare oak-floor-and-table setting. Old-fashioned dishes like pressed tongue, mackerel and gooseberry, and mussels and chips may be revived from a bygone era, but Londoners adore them. Dishes for the whole table—like venison pie or seven-hour shoulder of lamb—are highly convivial. There's little for nonmeat eaters, and no dinner Sunday. ✉ *32 Great Queen St., Covent Garden* ☎ *020/7242–0622* ⚐ *Reservations essential* ▤ *MC, V* ⊙ *No dinner Sun.* Ⓤ *Holborn, Covent Garden* ✛ *E2.*

MODERN BRITISH
Fodor'sChoice
★

£££ ✕**J Sheekey.** Theater and film stars slip in here as an alternative to Scott's, Cipriani, or Nobu Berkeley. Linked with nearby Theaterland, J Sheekey is one of Londoners' favorite West End haunts. It charms with warm wood paneling, showbiz monochromes, alcove tables, and lava-rock bar tops. Opt for caviar, jellied eels, Dover sole, monkfish, or famous Sheekey fish pie. Dine at the mirrored bar for true romance, or enjoy the £24.75 weekend lunch. ✉ *28–32 St. Martin's Ct., Covent*

SEAFOOD

Garden ☎020/7240–2565 ⊕*www.j-sheekey.co.uk* ⊟*AE, DC, MC, V* Ⓤ*Leicester Sq.* ✚*E3.*

££££ ✕**L'Atelier de Joël Robuchon.** Glitterati sit side by side at the counter and
FRENCH graze tapas-style at Joël Robuchon's super-seductive London outpost.
Decked out in plush red and black, counter seating frames the ground-
floor open kitchen, creating a spectacle that is pure culinary theater.
Navigate exquisite French tapas—from frogs' legs and egg cocotte to
scallops and quail with butter and truffle mash. The £85 nine-course
tasting menu is a decadent way to blow the bank. There's also a bar,
and a formal restaurant, La Cuisine, on the first floor. ⊠*13–15 West St.,
Covent Garden* ☎020/7010–8600 ⊕*www.joel-robuchon.com* ⊟*AE,
DC, MC, V* Ⓤ*Leicester Sq.* ✚*E3.*

£££ ✕**Quo Vadis.** Home to Karl Marx in the 1850s, and a renowned Soho
MODERN institution since 1924, the revamped Quo Vadis is back. Awesome
EUROPEAN stained-glass windows bathe the ground-floor dining room in a colorful light as a mixed media/business crowd works its way through a
no-surprises but highly likable Euro brasserie menu. Opt for Piccolo
oysters, razor clams, roast chicken, or grilled turbot from the à la carte
menu, or have a three-course pretheater meal for £19.50. ⊠*26–29
Dean St., Soho* ☎ 020/7437–9585 ⊕*www.quovadissoho.co.uk* ⌁*Reservations essential* ⊟*AE, MC, V* Ⓤ*Tottenham Court Rd.* ✚*E3.*

£££–££££ ✕**Rules.** Come, escape from the 21st century. Opened by Thomas Rule
BRITISH in 1798, London's oldest restaurant has hosted everyone from Charles
Dickens to Laurence Olivier and the current Prince of Wales. This traditional English dining salon has plush red banquettes and lacquered
yellow walls crammed with oil paintings, engravings, and Victorian
cartoons. Try historic British dishes—steak-and-kidney pie or roast beef
and Yorkshire pudding—for a taste of the 18th century. In season, daily
specials include game from the restaurant's High Pennines estate. ⊠*35
Maiden La., Covent Garden* ☎020/7836–5314 ⊕*www.rules.co.uk*
⊟*AE, MC, V* Ⓤ*Covent Garden* ✚*E3.*

££ ✕**Wahaca.** Expect a wait for the fab-value Mexican street food at this
MEXICAN brightly colored Covent Garden favorite. Mud walls and bench seats
make for buzzy basement surroundings, but it's the cheap £3.50–£7
tacos, tostadas, quesadillas, and burritos that pull in the crowds. A
£19.50 spread for two will produce a feast of chorizo quesadillas, tacos,
slaw, and guacamole, but note that bookings aren't taken and that it's
often full by 6:30 PM. ⊠*66 Chandos Pl., Covent Garden* ☎020/7240–
1883 ⊕*www.wahaca.co.uk* ⌁*Reservations not accepted* ⊟*AE, MC,
V* Ⓤ*Charing Cross* ✚*E3.*

££££ ✕**Yauatcha.** It's all-day dim sum at this superbly lighted slinky Soho
CHINESE classic. Well designed by Christian Liaigre—with black granite floors,
aquarium, candles, and a starry ceiling—the food is a match for the
seductive setting. There's wicked dim sum (try prawns or scallops),
crispy duck rolls, silver cod, fancy cocktails, and tea and colorful cakes
in the first-floor tearoom. Note the quick table turns, and ask to dine
in the more romantic basement at night. ⊠*15 Broadwick St., Soho*
☎020/7494–8888 ⊕*www.yauatcha.com* ⌁*Reservations essential*
⊟*AE, MC, V* Ⓤ*Oxford Circus* ✚*D3.*

HAMMERSMITH

££££ ✕ **River Café.** This open-kitchen Italian restaurant sets the standard with
ITALIAN its simple roasts, fresh salads, pastas, and char-grilled meats. Chefs
Rose Gray and Ruth Rogers source ultrafresh, impeccable seasonal
ingredients, so expect squid with rocket and chili, handmade nettle-
and-nutmeg pasta, and wood-roasted Castle Mey beef with fennel and
marjoram (£29)—plus one of London's highest bills. This is in distant
Hammersmith, so if you snag an evening table, remember that you'll
need to book a cab ahead or walk about 10 minutes to the closest
Tube. Note that tables are cleared by 11 PM on weekdays, and 11:20 PM
Friday and Saturday. ⊠*Thames Wharf, Rainville Rd., Hammersmith*
☎*020/7386–4200* ⊕*www.rivercafe.co.uk* ⌕*Reservations essential*
🖃*AE, DC, MC, V* ⓤ*Hammersmith* ✛*A4.*

KNIGHTSBRIDGE

££ ✕ **Boxwood Café.** Attached to the Berkeley and in the Gordon Ram-
MODERN say stable, the Boxwood is the best uptown but relaxed place to dine
EUROPEAN in Knightsbridge, with opulent marble, brown, and greens. The New
☾ York–style restaurant is open late (until midnight Thursday–Saturday)
Fodor'sChoice and set lunch is useful at £28. Favorite dishes range from Orkney
★ scallops to yellowfin tuna, and veal burger to treacle tart. Service is
top-notch, and you'll find a fashionable buzz. ⊠*The Berkeley, Wil-
ton Pl., Knightsbridge* ☎*020/7235–1010* ⊕*www.gordonramsay.com/
boxwoodcafe* ⌕*Reservations essential* 🖃*AE, MC, V* ⓤ*Knightsbridge*
✛*C4.*

££££££ ✕ **The Capital.** The French haute cuisine is sublime at this legendary
FRENCH clublike hotel dining room that has retained a grown-up atmosphere
and formal service since it opened in 1978. Chef Eric Chavot serves
impeccable dishes in chic surroundings. Go for exquisite scallops with
cucumber jelly, frogs' legs with gnocchi, or turbot and ravioli. Desserts
like mint parfait or lemon sorbet are sensational, too. It's two seconds
from Harrods, and the £27.50 set lunch is an absolute bargain. ⊠*22
Basil St., Knightsbridge* ☎*020/7589–5171* ⊕*www.capitalhotel.co.uk*
⌕*Reservations essential* 🖃*AE, DC, MC, V* ⓤ*Knightsbridge* ✛*C4.*

££££££ ✕ **Marcus Wareing at the Berkeley.** Wonder chef Marcus Wareing vies to
MODERN be the best in London at his eponymous restaurant at the Berkeley.
EUROPEAN Opulently designed by David Collins—all clarets, carpet, and burgundy
Fodor'sChoice leather seats—Wareing pulls out all the haute cuisine stops with a suc-
★ cession of world-class dishes. Standouts include roast quail with hispi
cabbage; a fine chunk of Scottish halibut with charred leeks and English
watercress; or Anjou pigeon with cob nuts and amaretti. Warm chocolate moëlleux with banana jelly or orange crème with spiced brioche are
absolutely faultless, and the wine list includes page after page of famous
names. ⊠*The Berkeley, Wilton Place Knightsbridge* ☎*020/7235–1200*
⊕*www.the-berkeley.co.uk* ⌕*Reservations essential* 🖃*AE, MC, V*
☾*Closed Sun. No lunch Sat.* ⓤ*Knightsbridge* ✛*C4.*

££££ ✕ **Rasoi Vineet Bhatia.** Chef-proprietor Vineet Bhatia showcases the finest
INDIAN new Indian cuisine in London at this tony town-house venue off the
King's Road. Super-seductive and decked with Indian silks, prints, masks,

bells, and ornaments, Bhatia pushes the boundaries with signatures like wild mushroom rice with tomato ice cream or grilled lobster dusted with cocoa and sour spices. Don't leave without sampling the warm chocolate samosas. ⊠ *10 Lincoln St., Knightsbridge* ☎ *020/7225–1881* ⊕ *www.vineetbhatia.com* ▤ *AE, DC, MC, V* Ⓤ *Sloane Sq.* ✛ *C5.*

MARYLEBONE AND MAYFAIR

£££

ITALIAN

✕ **Cecconi's.** Enjoy all-day buzz at this fashionable Italian brasserie opposite the Royal Academy on Burlington Gardens. Between Savile Row and New Bond Street, the jet set pitch up for breakfast, brunch, and Italian tapas (*cichetti*) at the bar, and return for something more substantial later on. Ilse Crawford's green-and-brown interior is a stylish background for classics like veal Milanese, Venetian calves' liver, and tiramisu. Note: it's a cool pit stop during a shopping spree. ⊠ *5A Burlington Gardens, Mayfair* ☎ *020/7434–1500* ⊕ *www.cecconis.co.uk* ☖ *Reservations essential* ▤ *AE, DC, MC, V* Ⓤ *Green Park, Piccadilly Circus* ✛ *D3.*

£££

BISTRO

✕ **Galvin Bistrot de Luxe.** The Galvin brothers blaze a trail for the deluxe bistro concept on a no-man's-land stretch of Baker Street. Feted chefs Chris and Jeff forsake Michelin stars and cut loose under the brasserie banner. A more mature crowd enjoys impeccable service in a handsome slate floor and mahogany-paneled salon. There's no finer crab lasagna around, and mains punch above their weight: duck with Lyonnaise salad, daube of beef with Vichy carrots, and calves' liver with Alsace bacon are all a triumph. The £17.50 set lunch or dinner (6–7 PM) is unbeatable. ⊠ *66 Baker St., Marylebone* ☎ *020/7935–4007* ⊕ *www. galvinrestaurants.com* ▤ *AE, MC, V* Ⓤ *Baker St.* ✛ *C2.*

£

SEAFOOD

✕ **Golden Hind.** You'll find some of the best fish-and-chips in London at the Golden Hind, a British chippy run by Greek Cypriots in a 1914 art deco café, off Marylebone High Street. Locals and tourists alike love the calamari, skate wings, and fish cakes, but it's the perfect—and nongreasy—deep-fried or steamed battered cod, plaice, and haddock, the classic Maris Piper chips, and mushy peas that are the big draw. Note it's open noon–3 PM and 6–10 PM weekdays only. ⊠ *73 Marylebone La., Marylebone* ☎ *020/7486–3644* ▤ *AE, MC, V* ⫸ *BYOB* ⊗ *Closed weekends* Ⓤ *Bond St.* ✛ *C2.*

£££££

FRENCH

Fodor'sChoice
★

✕ **Hélène Darroze at the Connaught.** London's crème de la crème flock to Hélène Darroze at the Connaught for exemplary regional French haute cuisine, served in a quintessentially Edwardian wood-paneled hotel dining room. Taking inspiration from Les Landes region in southwest France, Darroze sallies forth with a procession of magical dishes. Caviar d'Acquitaine wows with oyster tartare in a stylish martini glass, topped with black caviar jelly and white haricot bean velouté. Spit-roasted and flambéed grouse is served delightfully pink, with duck foie gras, and mini–Brussels sprouts. To finish, enjoy Madagascar chocolate ganache with raspberry sorbet and galangal crème brûlée. Note that the prices are high: £39 for lunch, and £75 or £95 for the set dinners. ⊠ *The Connaught, Carlos Pl. Mayfair* ☎ *020/3147–7200* ⊕ *www.the-connaught.co.uk* ☖ *Reservations essential. Jacket required* ⊗ *Closed weekends* ▤ *AE, DC, MC, V* Ⓤ *Green Park* ✛ *C3.*

£££ ✕**Hibiscus.** Chef and front-of-house Claude and Claire Bosi excel at one
MODERN FRENCH of London's finest Modern French restaurants, tucked away on Maddox
Fodor'sChoice Street in Mayfair. Wood-paneled and kitted in muted gray and green,
★ gastronomes swoon at the fireworks on the plate. Bosi's effortless cuisine
might impress with Brixham crab-and-almond puree, suckling pig with
Savoy cabbage, or Lyonnaise tripe with pig's ear and cuttlefish. Passion-
fruit mille-feuille (puff pastry) and mango gel is bound to send you
home happy. ⊠*29 Maddox St., Mayfair* ☎ *020/7629–2999* ⊕*www.
hibiscusrestaurant.co.uk* ⌂*Reservations essential* ▤*AE, DC, MC,
V* ☺*No lunch Sat. Closed Sun.* Ⓤ*Oxford Circus, Piccadilly* ⊕*D3.*

£££££ ✕**Le Gavroche.** Michel Roux Jr. thrives at this 40-year-old clubby base-
FRENCH ment haven in Mayfair, which some rate the best formal dining in London. With silver domes and unpriced ladies' menus, Roux's mastery
of classic French cuisine dazzles with signatures like foie gras with
cinnamon-scented crispy duck pancake, langoustine with Hollandaise
sauce, or lamb with flageolets. Desserts, like roast pineapple with white-
pepper ice cream, are delightful, too. Weekday set lunch is a relatively
affordable treat at £48—with a half bottle of wine, water, coffee, and
petits fours. ⊠*43 Upper Brook St., Mayfair* ☎*020/7408–0881* ⊕*www.
le-gavroche.co.uk* ⌂*Reservations essential* ▤*AE, DC, MC, V* ☺*Closed
10 days at Christmas. No lunch weekends* Ⓤ*Marble Arch* ⊕*C3.*

££££ ✕**Locanda Locatelli.** Celebs like Kate Moss and photographer Poppy
ITALIAN de Villeneuve patronize Giorgio Locatelli's glamorous Italian at the
Churchill InterContinental. Warmly designed with beige banquettes,
convex mirrors, and cherrywood dividers, the regional Italian food
is highly accomplished—silky risottos, handmade pastas, gorgeous
grilled fish, subtle desserts. Be bold, and try the calves' kidney or Sicil-
ian prawns with risotto, and lose yourself in the all-Italian wine list. ⊠*8
Seymour St., Mayfair* ☎*020/7935–9088* ⊕*www.locandalocatelli.com*
⌂*Reservations essential* ▤*AE, MC, V* Ⓤ*Marble Arch* ⊕*C3.*

££££–£££££ ✕**Nobu Berkeley Street.** Supermodels, rugby stars, and the Formula One
JAPANESE crowd pay silly money for new-style sashimi with Peruvian flair at this
so-hip-it-hurts Nobu spin-off near Piccadilly. The beautiful people go
bonkers for miso black cod, tuna teriyaki, whitefish sashimi, Wagyu
beef, and stunning bento boxes (£28 or £40). Prices are extreme, but
the people-watching is just so good. ⊠*15 Berkeley St., Mayfair* ☎*020/
7290–9222* ⊕*www.noburestaurants.com* ⌂*Reservations essential*
▤*AE, MC, V* Ⓤ*Green Park* ⊕*C4.*

£££ ✕**The Providores & Tapa Room.** New Zealander Peter Gordon scores high-
ASIAN ly with his Pacific Rim fusion food on Marylebone High Street. Have
a classy meal in the formal restaurant upstairs or try the packed and
more relaxed ground-floor Tapa Room. All sorts of exotica are on the
menu, from tamarind and coconut *laska* (spicy noodle soup) to New
Zealand *kumara* (sweet potato). On Sunday morning you'll find the
whole of Marylebone village reading the Sunday supplements. New
Zealand venison with cassava chips, or Wagyu beef with bone marrow
and Parmesan sauce are typical delights. ⊠*109 Marylebone High St.,
Marylebone* ☎*020/7935–6175* ⊕*www.theprovidores.co.uk* ▤*AE,
MC, V* Ⓤ*Baker St.* ⊕*C2.*

£££ ✗**Scott's.** Scott's is so hot that it's where the A-list go to celebrate.
SEAFOOD Founded in 1851, and recently renovated and reborn as a glamorous
Fodor'sChoice seafood haven and oyster bar, it draws beautiful people who pick at
★ Cumbrae oysters, Red Sea prawns, and Stargazy pie. Standouts like
cod with chorizo and padron peppers are to die for. Prices are high,
but you're dining at the hippest joint in town. ☒*20 Mount St., May-*
fair ☎*020/7495–7309* ⊕*www.scotts-restaurant.com* ⌂*Reservations*
essential ▤*AE, DC, MC, V* Ⓤ*Bond St.* ✛*C3.*

£££ ✗**Wild Honey.** Wild Honey's recession-busting set lunch or early evening
MODERN deals (£16.50–£18.95) are wildly popular. Book ahead at this wood-
EUROPEAN paneled clublike salon, with modern pictures and comfy booths, in
Fodor'sChoice swanky Mayfair. Try the tasty Scottish girolles with snail and parsley,
★ Elwy lamb, panna cotta, or signature warm chocolate soup with milk ice
cream. All 50-odd wines are available in third-of-a-bottle carafes. ☒ *12*
St. George St., Mayfair ☎*020/7758–9160* ⊕*www.wildhoneyrestaurant.*
co.uk ▤*AE, MC* ⊘*No lunch Sun.* Ⓤ*Oxford Circus.* ✛*D3.*

NOTTING HILL

£££ ✗**The Cow Dining Room.** A boho-chic gastro-pub, the Cow comprises
MODERN BRITISH a faux-Dublin '50s backroom saloon bar that serves Fines de Claires
oysters, seafood platters, whelks and winkles, and Dorset crab. Upstairs
the chef whips up Brit specialties like Welsh lamb cutlets, English summer salad, black bream, and sea trout and shrimp. Post-recession ex-
millionaire Notting Hill locals love the house special in the packed bar:
draft Guinness with a pint of prawns and mayonnaise. ☒*89 Westbourne*
Park Rd., Notting Hill ☎*020/7221–0021* ⊕*www.thecowlondon.co.uk*
⌂*Reservations essential* ▤*MC, V* Ⓤ*Westbourne Park* ✛*A2.*

£££ ✗**E&O.** The jet set hang at E&O, one of London's hip scene bars and
ASIAN restaurants on Blenheim Crescent, off Portobello Road. E&O means
"Eastern and Oriental," and the mix of Chinese, Japanese, Vietnamese,
and Thai dishes includes a slew of vegetarian options. Don't skip the
lychee martinis, miso black cod, chili tofu, Thai rare beef, or papaya
salad. ☒*14 Blenheim Crescent, Notting Hill* ☎*020/7229–5454*
⊕*www.rickerrestaurants.com/eando* ⌂*Reservations essential* ▤*AE,*
DC, MC, V Ⓤ*Ladbroke Grove* ✛*A3.*

ST. JAMES'S

£££ ✗**Le Caprice.** Twenty-five-year-old Le Caprice in St. James's commands
MODERN BRITISH the deepest loyalty of any restaurant in London. Why? Because it gets
everything right. It's the celebrity history—think Liz Taylor to Lady
Di—the David Bailey prints, '80s Eva Jiricna interior, perfect service,
and appealing menu that sits somewhere between Euro peasant and
trendy fashion plate. Sit at the counter and enjoy calves' liver with crispy
bacon, red-legged partridge, and Scandinavian iced berries with white
chocolate sauce—all served with an ample dollop of celebrity spotting. ☒*Arlington House, Arlington St., St. James's* ☎*020/7629–2239*
⊕*www.le-caprice.co.uk* ⌂*Reservations essential* ▤*AE, DC, MC, V*
Ⓤ*Green Park* ✛*D4.*

LOCAL CHAINS WORTH A TASTE

When you're on the go or don't have time for a leisurely meal—and Starbucks won't cut it—you might want to try a local chain restaurant or sandwich bar. The ones listed below are well priced and are the best in their category.

Café Rouge: A classic 32-strong French bistro chain that's been around for eons and does great prix-fixe deals—so "uncool" that it's now almost fashionable. ⊕ www.caferouge.co.uk

Carluccio's Caffé: The Carluccio's chain of 20 all-day Italian café/bar/food shops are freshly sourced, family-friendly, and make brilliant pasta and salad stops on a shopping spree. ⊕ www.carluccios.com

Gourmet Burger Kitchen (GBK): This Kiwi-run line of eight burger joints is wholesome and handy, with Aberdeen Angus Scotch beef, lamb, or venison burgers. ⊕ www.gbkinfo.com

Le Pain Quotidien: Try tartine open sandwiches or baguettes and salads at the communal tables. Branches are at Great Marlborough St., W1, and Eurostar's stunning St. Pancras station. ⊕ www.lepainquotidien.co.uk

Pizza Express: Serving classic thin-crust pizzas, Pizza Express is everywhere (there are nearly 100 in London). Soho and Knightsbridge branches have a live jazz program. ⊕ www.pizzaexpress.com

Pret A Manger: London's high-street take-out supremo isn't just for store-made sandwiches: there are wraps, noodles, baguettes, sushi, salads, fruit, juices, and tea cakes, too. ⊕ www.pret.com

Ranoush Juice Bar: Shawarma kebabs are the draw at these mirrored late-night kebab and juice bars (open 8 AM to 3 AM daily). They also serve falafel, meze, and tabbouleh. ⊕ www.maroush.com

Strada: Stop at this 28-strong chain for authentic hand-stretched pizzas baked over a wood fire, plus classic pastas, steaks, and risottos. It's cheap, stylish, and packed. ⊕ www.strada.co.uk

Tootsies: This superior burger joint does yummy grilled burgers, fries, salads, steaks, BLTs, and chicken spreads. It's family-friendly, with a children's meal for £4.95. ⊕ www.tootsiesrestaurants.com

Wagamama: Londoners drain bowls and bowls of noodle soup at this favorite chain of high-tech, high-turnover, high-volume Japanese communal canteens. ⊕ www.wagamama.com

£££ ✕ **St. Alban.** South of Piccadilly, close to Theaterland, and with a stylish
MEDITERRANEAN retro-Modern aesthetic, St. Alban is one of the more fashionable places to dine in town. The '60s-airport lounge interior—gray slate walls, turquoise-and-cerise banquettes, carpets, and Michael Craig-Martin murals—is a winning backdrop for the Mediterranean-inspired menu. Try paella, wood-fired pizza, gilthead bream, or Sardinian fish stew. ✉ 4–12 Regent St., St. James's ☎ 020/7499–8558 ⊕ www.stalban.net ⌂ Reservations essential ☐ AE, DC, MC, V Ⓤ Piccadilly ✛ D3.

£££ ✕**The Wolseley.** All of London enjoys the grand elegance at this Viennese-
AUSTRIAN style grand café on Piccadilly. Framed with black lacquerware, the bras-
Fodor'sChoice serie begins its long decadent days with breakfast at 7 AM and stays
★ opens until midnight. Linger for haggis, kippers, and kedgeree, or
Matjes herrings and Wiener Holstein. For dessert, go for apple strudel
or *kaiserschmarren*—a pancake with stewed fruit. It's known for Vien-
noiserie pastries and sinful afternoon tea. ⊠*160 Piccadilly, St. James's*
☎*020/7499–6996* ⊕*www.thewolseley.com* ⌦*Reservations essential*
⊟*AE, DC, MC, V* Ⓤ*Green Park* ⊕*D4.*

SOUTH BANK

££–£££ ✕**Anchor & Hope.** Great things at friendly prices come from the open
MODERN BRITISH kitchen at this permanently packed, no-reservations, leading gastro-pub
on the Cut in Waterloo: pot-roast duck and chicken *pithivier* (puff pastry pie) are two standouts. It's cramped, informal, and highly original,
and there are great dishes for groups, like slow-roasted leg of lamb.
Expect to share a table, too. ⊠*36 The Cut, South Bank* ☎*020/7928–*
9898 ⌦*Reservations not accepted* ⊟*MC, V* Ⓤ*Waterloo, Southwark*
⊕*F4.*

£££ ✕**Skylon.** Located in the Royal Festival Hall, Skylon is the Southbank
MODERN Centre's destination restaurant/bar/grill. Spacious, attractive, and with
EUROPEAN huge picture windows with spectacular views of the Thames, Skylon
guarantees a classy pre- or post-performance meal in the '50s Festival
Hall. Against a background of dancing and music, concertgoers sip
lush cocktails at the central bar and dine on lamb and harissa at the
grill, or Anjou pigeon, spelt risotto, and sea bass with bok choy in
the restaurant. The food is accomplished, and the setting impressive.
⊠*Southbank Centre, Belvedere Rd., South Bank* ☎*020/7654–7800*
⊕*www.skylonrestaurant.co.uk* ⌦*Reservations essential* ⊟*MC, V*
Ⓤ*Waterloo* ⊕*F4.*

PUBS AND AFTERNOON TEA

PUBS

The city's pubs, public houses, or "locals" dispense beer, good cheer,
and casual grub in settings that range from ancient wood-beam rooms
to ornate Victorian interiors to utilitarian modern rooms. Pubs in
the capital are changing: 90-year-old licensing laws have finally been
modernized, gastro-pub fever is sweeping London, and smoking in all
pubs has been illegal since 2007. At many places, char-grills are being
installed in the kitchen out back, and up front the faded wallpapers
are being replaced by abstract paintings. The best of these luxe pubs
are reviewed above. Some of the following also showcase nouveau pub
grub, but whether you have Moroccan chicken or the usually dismal
ploughman's special, do order a pint. Note that American-style beer is
called "lager" in Britain, whereas the real British brew is "bitter" (usually served warm). Order up your choice in two sizes—pints or half

pints. Some London pubs also sell "real ale," which is less gassy than bitters and, many would argue, has a better flavor.

The list below offers a few pubs selected for central location, historical interest, a pleasant garden, music, or good food, but you might just as happily adopt your own temporary local.

✕**Black Friar.** A step from Blackfriars Tube stop, this spectacular pub has an Arts-and-Crafts interior that is entertainingly, satirically ecclesiastical, with inlaid mother-of-pearl, wood carvings, stained glass, and marble pillars all over the place. In spite of the finely lettered temperance tracts on view just below the reliefs of monks, fairies, and friars, there is a nice group of ales on tap from independent brewers. ⊠*174 Queen Victoria St., The City* ☎*020/7236–5474* Ⓤ*Blackfriars.*

✕**Dove Inn.** Read the list of famous ex-regulars, from Charles II and Nell Gwyn to Ernest Hemingway, as you wait for a beer at this smart, comely, and very popular 16th-century riverside pub by Hammersmith Bridge. After a few pints you can practice your singing skills to the English patriotic song that was composed here, "Rule, Britannia!" If the Dove is too full, stroll upstream along the bank to the Old Ship or the Blue Anchor. ■TIP➡**Please note, you must be 18 to be admitted to this pub.** ⊠*19 Upper Mall, Hammersmith* ☎*020/8748–9474* Ⓤ*Hammersmith.*

✕**Lamb & Flag.** This refreshingly un-gentrified 17th-century pub was once known as the Bucket of Blood because the upstairs room was used as a ring for bare-knuckle boxing. Now it's a friendly—and bloodless—pub, serving food (lunch only) and real ale. It's on the edge of Covent Garden, off Garrick Street. ⊠*33 Rose St., Covent Garden* ☎*020/7497–9504* Ⓤ*Covent Garden.*

✕**Mayflower.** An atmospheric 17th-century riverside inn with exposed beams and a terrace, this is practically the very place from which the Pilgrims set sail for Plymouth Rock. ⊠*117 Rotherhithe St., South Bank* ☎*020/7237–4088* Ⓤ*Rotherhithe.*

★ ✕**Museum Tavern.** Across the street from the British Museum, this friendly and classy Victorian pub makes an ideal resting place after the rigors of the culture trail. Karl Marx unwound here after a hard day in the Library. He could have spent his *Kapital* on any of seven well-kept beers available on tap. ⊠*49 Great Russell St., Bloomsbury* ☎*020/7242–8987* Ⓤ*Tottenham Court Rd.*

★ ✕**Prospect of Whitby.** Named after a ship, this is London's oldest riverside pub, dating from around 1520. Once upon a time it was called the Devil's Tavern because of the lowlife criminals—thieves and smugglers—who congregated here. Ornamented with pewter ware and nautical objects, this much-loved "boozer" is often pointed out from boat trips up the Thames. ⊠*57 Wapping Wall, East End* ☎*020/7481–1095* Ⓤ*Wapping.*

✕**Sherlock Holmes.** This pub used to be known as the Northumberland Arms, and Arthur Conan Doyle popped in regularly for a pint, in the days before old black-and-white Basil Rathbone films played on loop on the pub's television. It figures in *The Hound of the Baskervilles,* and you can see the hound's supposed head and plaster casts of its huge paws among other Holmes "memorabilia" in the bar. Even if you're not a Conan Doyle fan, the beer is excellent. ⊠ *10 Northumberland St., Trafalgar Square* ☎ *020/7930–2644* Ⓤ *Charing Cross.*

✕ **Spaniards Inn.** Ideal as a refueling point when you're on a Hampstead Heath hike, this historic oak-beam pub has a gorgeous garden, scene of the tea party in Dickens's *Pickwick Papers.* Dick Turpin, the highwayman, frequented the inn; you can see his pistols on display. Before Dickens's time, Shelley, Keats, and Byron hung out here as well. It's extremely popular, especially on Sunday, when Londoners roll in. ⊠ *Spaniards Rd., Hampstead* ☎ *020/8731–8406* Ⓤ *Hampstead.*

★ ✕ **White Hart.** This elegant, family-owned pub on Drury Lane is one of the best places to mix with cast and crew of the stage. A female-friendly environment, a cheery skylight above the lounge area, a late license, and above-average pub fare make the White Hart a particularly sociable spot for a drink. ⊠ *191 Drury La., Covent Garden* ☎ *020/7242–2317* Ⓤ *Holborn.*

Fodor'sChoice ✕ **White Horse.** This pub in well-to-do Parson's Green has a superb menu ★ with a beer or wine chosen to match each dish. Open early for weekend brunch, the "Sloaney Pony" (named for its wealthy Sloane Square clientele) is enormously popular and a place to find many a Hugh Grant and Liz Hurley look-alike. In the summer delicious barbecues are rustled up on the patio. The owner is an expert on cask-conditioned ale, with as many as 20 on tap, and there are more than 70 wines. ⊠ *1–3 Parson's Green, Parson's Green* ☎ *020/7736–2115* Ⓤ *Parson's Green.*

✕ **Ye Olde Cheshire Cheese.** Yes, it's a tourist trap, but it's also an extremely historic pub (it dates from 1667, the year after the Great Fire of London), and it deserves a visit for its sawdust-covered floors, low wood-beam ceilings, and the 14th-century crypt of Whitefriars' monastery under the cellar bar. But if you want to see the set of 17th-century pornographic tiles that once adorned the upstairs, go to Blacks Museum. This was the most regular of Dr. Johnson's and Dickens's *many* locals. ⊠ *145 Fleet St., The City* ☎ *020/7353–6170* Ⓤ *Blackfriars.*

AFTERNOON TEA

The English afternoon tea ritual has been quietly brewing among London polite society. Perhaps it's an anti-Starbucks thing, but nevertheless, it is now ever *so* fashionable to take afternoon tea—and preferably in the warm embrace of an established hotel tea salon.

So, what is afternoon tea, exactly? Well, it means real tea (English Breakfast, Ceylon, Indian, or Chinese—and preferably loose leaf) brewed in a china pot, and usually served with china cups and saucers and silver spoons any time between 3 and 5:30 PM daily. In particularly grand places—such as some bigger hotels—there should be elegant finger foods on a three-tier silver tea stand: bread and butter, and crustless cucumber, watercress, and egg sandwiches on the bottom; scones with clotted cream and strawberry preserve in the middle; and rich fruitcake and fancies on top.

Dress is smart casual in posh hotels. Make reservations for all these below.

✕**Brown's Hotel.** This classic Mayfair town-house hotel sets the standard at the English Tea Room, where one of London's best-known afternoon teas is served (£35–£48). ✉*33 Albermarle St., Mayfair* ☎*020/7493–6020* ▭*AE, DC, MC, V* ⊙*Tea weekdays 3–6, weekends 1–6* Ⓤ*Green Park.*

✕**Café at Sotheby's.** What could be better than perusing the famous Mayfair auction house before afternoon tea? It's open from 9:30 AM and tends to book up days in advance. Teas are available from £5.75 to £12.50, including toasted tea cakes, scones, and Welsh rarebit. ✉*Sotheby's, 34 New Bond St., Mayfair* ☎*020/7293–5077* ⚖*Reservations essential* ▭*AE, DC, MC, V* ⊙*Tea weekdays 3–4:45* Ⓤ*Green Park.*

✕**The Dorchester.** Amid a maze of marble and gold leaf, afternoon tea in the Promenade is best taken on comfy sofas and to the sound of the resident pianist. Teas are £31.50, £40.50, or £46 for high tea—with light bites like salmon and Cromer crab. Book well ahead. ✉*53 Park La.* ☎*020/7629–8888* ⚖*Reservations essential* ▭*AE, DC, MC, V* ⊙*Tea daily 2:30 and 4:45* Ⓤ*Hyde Park Corner.*

✕**Fortnum & Mason.** Upstairs at the revamped 300-year-old Queen's grocers, three set teas are ceremoniously served: afternoon tea (sandwiches, scones, and cakes: £32), old-fashioned high tea (the traditional nursery meal, with scrambled eggs and salmon: £34), and champagne tea (£42). ✉*St. James's Restaurant, 4th fl., 181 Piccadilly, St. James's* ☎*020/7734–8040* ▭*AE, DC, MC, V* ⊙*Tea Mon.–Sat. 2–7, Sun. noon–5* Ⓤ*Green Park.*

✕**The Ritz.** At the Ritz tea is served in the impressive Palm Court, with marble tables and Louis XIV chaises complete with musical accompaniment, giving the last morsel of Edwardian London. Afternoon tea is £37 and champagne tea £48. Reserve at least four weeks ahead and remember to wear a jacket and tie. ✉*150 Piccadilly, St. James's* ☎*020/7300–2309* ⚖*Reservations essential* ▭*AE, MC, V* ⊙*Tea daily 11:30, 1:30, 3:30, 5:30, 7:30* Ⓤ*Green Park.*

✕**The Wolsely.** This bustling art deco tea salon was inspired by the grand Viennese cafés. Cream teas are well priced at £9.75 or £19.75; you'll find Vienna opera cake and mini-mousse fancies. ✉*160 Piccadilly, St. James's* ☎*020/7499–6996* ⚖*Reservations essential* ▭*AE, DC, MC, V* ⊙*Tea Mon.–Sat. 3:30–5:30, Sun. 3:30–6:30* Ⓤ*Green Park.*

WHERE TO STAY

Use the coordinate (✛ B2) at the end of each listing to locate a site on the corresponding map.

It's hard to get a bargain on a London hotel. That is simply a fact of travel life, although the economic downturn has brought some deals. London has yet to get the knack of moderately priced hostelries that offer a high level of quality. Some chains are starting to change that— the Premier chain and the Millennium chain both have attractively

BEST BETS FOR LONDON LODGING

Fodor's offers a selective listing of quality lodging experiences at every price range, from the city's best budget motel to its most sophisticated luxury hotel. Here, we've compiled our top. recommendations by price and experience. The very best properties—in other words, those that provide a particularly remarkable experience in their price range—are designated in the listings with the Fodor's Choice logo.

Fodor'sChoice ★

Mandarin Oriental Hyde Park, ££££–£££££ p. 124
One Aldwych, £££££ p. 116
Zetter Rooms, ££££–£££££ p. 115

Best by Price

£

easyHotel, p. 119
The Generator, p. 114

££

B&B Belgravia, p. 123
base2stay, p. 122
The Hoxton, p. 117
Premier Travel Inn County Hall, p. 127

£££

Athenaeum Hotel and Apartments, p. 124
Best Western Premier Shaftesbury Kensington, p. 119
Guesthouse West, p. 110
Millennium Gloucester, p. 122
Number Sixteen, p. 122

££££

The Levin, p. 123
The Portobello, p. 110
The Rookery, p. 118

£££££

Claridge's, p. 125
Covent Garden Hotel, p. 116
The Dorchester, p. 125

Best by Experience

BEST SPAS

One Aldwych, ££££–£££££ p. 116
Claridge's, ££££–£££££ p. 125

BEST HISTORIC HOTELS

Claridge's, ££££–£££££ p. 125
The Dorchester, £££££ p. 125
The Rookery, ££££–£££££ p. 118

BUSINESS TRAVELERS

Brown's, £££££ p. 125
Millennium Gloucester, ££–£££ p. 122
Ramada Hotel and Suites Docklands, ££–£££ p. 118
Zetter Rooms, ££££–£££££ p. 115

BEST CONCIERGE

The Dorchester, £££££ p. 125
Mandarin Oriental Hyde Park, £££££ p. 124

MOST ROMANTIC

Number Sixteen, £££–££££ p. 122
The Rookery, ££££–£££££ p. 118

MOST KID-FRIENDLY

22 Jermyn Street, ££££ p. 124
Premier Travel Inn County Hall, ££ p. 127

designed, pleasant, central hotels that, if booked well in advance, have rooms below £80 a night. At the budget level, ultramodern "pod hotels" are growing in popularity. These are an Asian concept, offering tiny rooms with just the basics—bed, shower, toilet—for low prices. The easyHotel chain has a few of these in town, including at Heathrow.

If you can afford to spend a bit of money, London is the place to do it. Prices can soar into the empyrean, but many of the best hotels are worth it—although even at the top of the market, rooms can be small by American standards. Paying top dollar does not mean you'll get stately English grandeur—some of the more expensive hotels have a sort of neo-Bauhaus minimalism. But that's London for you—always looking for the next new thing.

WHICH NEIGHBORHOOD?

Where you stay can affect your experience. The West End is equivalent to downtown, but there's a big difference between, say, posh Park Lane and bustling, touristy Leicester Square. Hotels in Mayfair and St. James's are central and yet distant in both mileage and sensibility from funky, youthful neighborhoods such as Notting Hill and from major tourist sights such as the Tower of London, St. Paul's Cathedral, and the Kensington museums. On the edges of the West End, Soho and Covent Garden are crammed with eateries and entertainment options. South Kensington, Kensington, Chelsea, and Knightsbridge are patrician and peaceful, which will give you a more homey feeling than anything in the West End; Belgravia is super elegant. From Bloomsbury it's a stroll to the shops and restaurants of Covent Garden, to Theatreland, and to the British Museum; Hampstead and Islington are close enough to explore easily, too. Bayswater is an affordable haven north of Hyde Park. The South Bank, with all its cultural attractions, is an affordable option.

RESERVATIONS

Wherever you decide to stay, do reserve in advance. London is popular, and special events can fill hotels suddenly. If you arrive without a room, the **London Tourist Board Information Centres** at Heathrow, Victoria Station Forecourt, and on Regent's Street can help. The **VisitLondon Accommodation Booking Service** (☎ *020/7932–2020* ⊕ *www.visitlondon. com*) is open weekdays 9 to 6, Saturday 10 to 2; it offers a best-price guarantee.

PRICES AND MONEY-SAVING OPTIONS

London is expensive, and in the £££££ category you can often pay considerably more than £300 per room. Finding a cheap but tolerable double room is a real coup. Look around Russell Square in Bloomsbury, around Victoria and King's Cross stations, on the South Bank, in Bayswater or Earl's Court, or farther out in Shepherd's Bush. Your cheapest option is a pod hotel, a bed-and-breakfast, or a dorm bed in a hostel; but apartments are an increasingly popular choice. *For other suggestions, see Accommodations in Travel Smart England.*

University residence halls offer a cheap alternative during university vacation periods. Whatever the price, *don't* expect a room that's large by American standards. **City University Hall of Residence: Walter Sickert Hall** (✉ *Graham St.* ☎ *020/7040–8822* ⊕ *www.city.ac.uk/ems*) starts at £20 per person year-round, and gives you access to kitchen facilities. **London School of Economics Vacations** (☎020/7955–7575 ⊕*www.lsevacations. co.uk*) starts at £45 for a double without a private bathroom and £53 for a double with one . You can choose from a variety of rooms in their five halls of residence around London. **University College London** (✉*Residence Manager, Campbell House, 5–10 Taviton St.* ☎020/7679–1479 ⊕*www.ucl.ac.uk*) starts at £45 for a double and is open from mid-June to mid-September.

In any event, you should confirm *exactly* what your room costs before checking in. British hotels are obliged by law to display a price chart at the reception desk; study it carefully. In January and February you can often find reduced rates, and large hotels with a business clientele have frequent weekend packages. The usual practice these days in all but the cheaper hotels is for quoted prices to cover room alone; breakfast, whether continental or "full English," costs extra. V.A.T. (Value Added Tax—sales tax) follows the same rule, with the most expensive hotels excluding a hefty 17.5%; middle-of-the-range and budget places include it in the initial quote.

WHAT IT COSTS IN POUNDS					
	£	££	£££	££££	£££££
FOR TWO PEOPLE	under £80	£80–£140	£141–£200	£201–£300	over £300

Prices are for a standard double room in high season, including V.A.T., with no meals or, if indicated, CP (with continental breakfast), BP (Breakfast Plan, with full breakfast), or MAP (Modified American Plan, with breakfast and dinner).

BAYSWATER, NOTTING HILL, AND SHEPHERD'S BUSH

£££–££££ 🏠**Abbey Court.** Sink deep into the Victorian era at this gracious, antiques-laden white mansion on a quiet street off Notting Hill Gate. This place is hardly all eye candy, though, as it strives to meet the needs of business travelers with amenities such as Wi-Fi. A continental breakfast buffet is served in the conservatory. Bathrooms are tiny but modern with Italian marble; some have whirlpool baths. **Pros:** handy location; quiet neighborhood. **Cons:** skimpy breakfasts; tiny bathrooms; expensive Wi-Fi (£10 per day). ✉*20 Pembridge Gardens, Notting Hill* ☎*020/7221–7518* ⊕*www.abbeycourthotel.co.uk* ⇔*19 rooms, 3 suites* ⌂*In-room: no a/c, Wi-Fi. In-hotel: no-smoking rooms* ➡ *MC, V* ⎮◎⎮*CP* Ⓤ*Notting Hill Gate* ⊕*A3.*

£–££ 🏠**Garden Court Hotel.** This small hotel is formed from two 19th-century town houses in a quiet garden square. Each room has a character of its own, some with original Victorian fittings. Note that all the rooms are individually decorated—some are nicer than others. Rooms with toilet and shower cost an extra £30, and a hot breakfast also ups the bill. The little, lush garden is a lovely hideaway when the sun shines. **Pros:** lovely garden; lots of charm; new elevator makes the upper floors more pleasant. **Cons:** not all rooms have private baths; some rooms need updating. ✉*30–31 Kensington Gardens Sq., Bayswater* ☎*020/7229–2553*

⊕*www.gardencourthotel.co.uk* 🗨*12 rooms, 10 with bath* ☖*In-room: no a/c. In-hotel: bar, some pets allowed, no-smoking rooms* ⊟*MC, V* 🍴*BP* Ⓤ*Bayswater, Queensway* ✛*A3.*

£££ 🏠**Guesthouse West.** This hip hotel offers high-class chic at moderate prices. They almost get it right. The minimalist decor and technology—cool black-and-white photos and flat-screen TVs—are stylish. Rooms, however, are truly tiny, and there's no room service. The restaurant is child-friendly and packed with locals, and the bar is a beautiful homage to the 1930s. The hotel's relationship with a local spa and restaurant provides guests with discounts, and there are guaranteed seats for shows at the small Gate Theatre. If you fall deeply in love with the place, you can "buy" a room for £235,000, which gives you "ownership" of it for 52 days of the year. **Pros:** sophisticated decor; lots of gadgets. **Cons:** a bit out of the way; tiny rooms; no room service. ⊠*163–165 Westbourne Grove, Notting Hill* ☎*020/7792–9800* ⊕*www.guesthousewest.com* 🗨*20 rooms* ☖*In-room: DVD, Wi-Fi. In-hotel: restaurant, bar, parking (paid), no-smoking rooms* ⊟*AE, MC, V* Ⓤ*Notting Hill Gate* ✛*A3.*

£££–££££ 🏠**K West.** The proudly edgy K West is hidden away inside a feature-less glass-and-steel building near the Shepherd's Bush Tube stop, just outside Notting Hill. This is a grown-up place popular with business types and young couples, and *not* geared toward families with kids. Suites have two-person baths and drawers with "adult entertainment" supplies. Dark wood, soft suede, and sleek beige walls combine to create a designer look in the bedrooms. And the minimalist style extends to the all-white hotel bar, dubbed the K Lounge, and the hotel restaurant "Kanteen." **Pros:** sleek, modern decor; funky attitude. **Cons:** a bit off the tourist track; not for kids. ⊠*Richmond Way, Shepherd's Bush* ☎*020/7674–1000* ⊕*www.k-west.co.uk* 🗨*216 rooms, 6 suites* ☖*In-room: safe, DVD, Wi-Fi. In-hotel: restaurant, room service, bar, gym, spa, laundry service, parking (paid), no-smoking rooms* ⊟*AE, DC, MC, V* 🍴*CP* Ⓤ*Shepherd's Bush* ✛*A4.*

££–£££ 🏠**Main House.** A brass lion door knocker marks Main House's Victorian front door, typical of Notting Hill. With just four rooms, this hotel offers nothing but a good night's sleep in a Victorian home. Furnished with clean white linens, polished wood floors, modern furniture, and Asian art, it is uncluttered and delightfully spacious. The tiny urban terrace is a great place for stargazing or reading the morning paper. A day rate at the local health club is available, too. **Pros:** unusual option; great location. **Cons:** few rooms mean it books up far in advance; no room service. ⊠*6 Colvile Rd., Notting Hill* ☎*020/7221–9691* ⊕*www.themainhouse.com* 🗨*4 rooms* ☖*In-room: Wi-Fi (some). In-hotel: bicycles, laundry service, parking (paid), no-smoking rooms* ⊟*MC, V* 🍴*CP* Ⓤ*Notting Hill Gate* ✛*A3.*

££££–£££££ 🏠**The Portobello.** One of London's most famous hotels, the little Portobello (formed from two adjoining Victorian houses) is seriously hip and attracts scores of celebrities. It's a quirky place, decorated with utter abandon. In your (small but stylish) room, you're likely to find an assortment of antiques, luxurious fabrics, statues, and bizarre bric-a-brac. Some rooms have balconies and claw-foot bathtubs. Room 16 has an extraordinary Victorian "bathing machine" that actor Johnny

Depp is said to have once filled with champagne for Kate Moss, a former flame. **Pros:** stylish; great for celebrity-spotting; good location. **Cons:** most rooms are quite small; may be too eccentric for some. ⊠*22 Stanley Gardens, Notting Hill* ☎*020/7727–2777* ⊕*www.portobello-hotel.co.uk* ⊅*24 rooms* ⌂*In-room: no a/c (some), safe, refrigerator, Internet. In-hotel: restaurant, room service, bar, no-smoking rooms* ⦿|*CP* ⊟*AE, MC, V* ⊙*Closed 10 days at Christmas* Ⓤ*Notting Hill Gate* ✛*A4.*

££–£££   ⊡**Portobello Gold.** This no-frills B&B in the heart of the Portobello Road antiques area is on the floor above the pub and restaurant of the same name. Flat-screen TVs are mounted on the wall, and the beds take up almost the entire tiny room in the doubles. The best of the bunch is the split-level apartment (£££—sleeps six) with roof terrace, small kitchen, and soothing aquarium. The casual restaurant serves international food and has a great wine list, all at reasonable prices. There's free Wi-Fi in guest rooms as well as an Internet café that charges £1 per half hour. **Pros:** great location; free Internet access in rooms. **Cons:** rooms are tiny; no elevator. ⊠*95–97 Portobello Rd., Notting Hill* ☎*020/7460–4910* ⊕*www.portobellogold.com* ⊅*6 rooms, 1 apartment* ⌂*In-hotel: restaurant, room service, bar, Wi-Fi* ⊟*MC, V* ⦿|*CP* Ⓤ*Notting Hill Gate* ✛*A3.*

££   ⊡**Vancouver Studios.** This little hotel in a heritage-listed Victorian town house is perfect for those wanting a home away from home. All rooms are like efficiency apartments, with mini-kitchens and microwaves, and you can even preorder groceries, which are stocked in your mini-refrigerator upon arrival. Each studio has daily maid service as well as room service. Some rooms have working fireplaces, and one opens onto the leafy, paved garden. **Pros:** more space than a hotel room; unique little apartments. **Cons:** a bit out of the way; a bargain only if several people share the space. ⊠*30 Prince's Sq., Bayswater* ☎*020/7243–1270* ⊕*www.vancouverstudios.co.uk* ⊅*45 studios* ⌂*In-room: no a/c, kitchen, refrigerator, DVD, Wi-Fi. In-hotel: room service, bar, laundry facilities, laundry service, parking (paid)* ⊟*AE, DC, MC, V* Ⓤ*Bayswater, Queensway* ✛*A3.*

BLOOMSBURY, HAMPSTEAD, AND HOLBORN

£   ⊡**Alhambra Hotel.** One of the best bargains in Bloomsbury, this family-run hotel has singles as low as £45 and doubles as low as £55. Rooms are small and the look is dated, but they're definitely good value. Some rooms have a private shower but no toilet (you share one down the hall); others have both. All rooms have a TV, all guests have access to free Wi-Fi, and tea/coffeemakers are available on request. It's not fancy, but it certainly is cheap. **Pros:** low price; great location. **Cons:** decor's a bit old-fashioned; no frills here. ⊠*17–19 Argyle St., Bloomsbury* ☎*020/7837–9575* ⊕*www.alhambrahotel.com* ⊅*52 rooms* ⌂*In-room: no a/c, no phone, Wi-Fi. In-hotel: parking (paid), no-smoking rooms* ⊟*AE, MC, V* ⦿|*BP* Ⓤ*King's Cross* ✛*G1.*

££   ⊡**Arosfa Hotel.** The friendly owners, Mr. and Mrs. Dorta, and an interesting historical tidbit (the property once was the home of pre-Raphaelite painter Sir John Everett Millais) set this B&B apart from the

Where to Stay in London

A   **B**   **C**   **D**

1

Inner Circle
Chester Rd.
Outer Circle
Park Rd.
St. John's Wood Rd.
Lisson Grove
Rossmore Rd.
Clifton Rd.
Bloomfield Rd.
Edgware Rd.
Broadley St.
Sutherland Ave.

2

Marylebone Rd.
Wimpole St.
☐ **22 York Street**
Marylebone High St.
Gloucester Pl.
Baker St.
Seymour St.
Durrants ☐
Manchester Square
Portman Square
Harrow Rd.
Westway A40
Harrow Rd.
Harrow Rd.
Marylebone Flyover
Chepstow Rd.
Seymour Pl.
Duke St.

PADDINGTON STATION
Bishop's Bridge Rd.
Praed St.
Sussex Gdns.
Edgware Rd.
Seymour St.
MAYFAIR
Oxford St.
Gr
☐ **Main House**
Westbourne Grove
☐ **Garden Court Hotel**
BAYSWATER

3

☐ **Guesthouse West**
Craven Hill
Inverness Terr.
Vancouver Studios ☐
Queensway
Portobello Gold ←☐
Bayswater Rd.
N. Carriage Dr.
Abbey Court ☐
Notting Hill Gate
Bayswater Rd.
Hyde Park
The Dorchester ☐
S. Audley St.
Park Lane
☐ **K West**
Kensington Gardens
Di.
←☐ **The Portobello**
The Serpentine

4

KENSINGTON PALACE
W. Carriage Dr.
Mandarin Oriental Hyde Park ☐
Grosvenor Cres.
S. Carriage Rd.
Knightsbridge
The Berkeley ☐
Milestone Hotel & Apartments ☐
Kensington Rd.
Kensington Gore
Kensington Rd.
Victoria Rd.
Palace Gate
The Gore ☐
Prince Consort Rd.
The Levin ☐
Belgrave Square
Upper Belgrave St.
KNIGHTSBRIDGE
Sloane St.
Belgrave Pl.
Cadogan Pl.
Eaton Square

5

KENSINGTON
Gloucester Rd.
Queen's Gate
Exhibition Rd.
V&A MUSEUM
Brompton Rd.
Beauchamp Pl.
Pont St.
easyHotel ☐
Cromwell Rd.
Pelham St.
Sloane Sq.
Best Western Premier Shaftesbury Kensington ←☐
Millennium Gloucester ☐
Brompton Rd.
☐ **Number Sixteen**
Sloane Ave.
Astons Apartments ☐
Old Brompton Rd.
CHELSEA
Pimlico Rd.
base2stay ☐
King's Rd.
Royal Hospital Rd.
Chelsea Br. Rd.

6

SOUTH KENSINGTON
Fulham Rd.
Old Church St.
Sydney St.
Oakley St.
Chelsea Embankment
Ebury St.

| 0 | 1/3 mile |
| 0 | 500 meters |

A   **B**   **C**   **D**

Gower Street hotel pack. Rooms are simple and comfortable in white and pastel shades. Those at the back are far quieter and overlook the hotel's pleasant garden, although even at the front, the double glazing somewhat tames the din of the students from nearby University College London. **Pros:** good location for museums and theaters. **Cons:** price a bit high for what you get; few services. ✉ *83 Gower St., Bloomsbury* ☎*020/7636–2115* ⊕*www.arosfalondon.com* ➪*15 rooms* ⅃*In-room: no a/c, Wi-Fi. In-hotel: bar, no-smoking rooms* ⊟*MC, V* ⦿|*BP* Ⓤ*Goodge St.* ✛*F2.*

££   ▦**The Buckingham.** This Georgian town house near Russell Square is a great bargain for the money. Its spacious, well-designed rooms are all studios and suites. Each has its own tiny kitchenette, giving you an alternative to eating in restaurants every night. All have marble-and-granite bathrooms and plenty of amenities. Staff are friendly, and the location is an easy walk from the British Museum and Covent Garden. **Pros:** great location; small kitchens free you from restaurants. **Cons:** no room service. ✉ *11–13 Bayley St., Bedford Sq., Bloomsbury* ☎*020/7636–2474* ⊕*www.grangehotels.com* ➪*17 rooms* ⅃*In-room: no a/c, Internet. In-hotel: bar, no-smoking rooms* ⊟*MC, V* Ⓤ*Tottenham Court Rd.* ✛*F2.*

££   ▦**Crescent Hotel.** Located on one of Bloomsbury's grand old squares, the Crescent is a friendly, attractive B&B. Rooms are small and simply decorated in cheery colors, and breakfast is big and hearty. Bathrooms are tiny and utilitarian—some have a bath and shower, others only a bath, a few have neither, so if you have a preference, ask when you book. You can use the tennis courts and private gardens in the square—great for picnics on a sunny day. **Pros:** lovely, convenient location; friendly staff. **Cons:** basic decor; no elevator. ✉ *49–50 Cartright Gardens, Bloomsbury* ☎*020/7383–2054* ⊕*www.crescenthoteloflondon. com* ➪*27 rooms, 10 with bath* ⅃*In-room: no a/c, Internet. In hotel: tennis court* ⊟*MC, V* ⦿|*BP* Ⓤ*Russell Sq.* ✛*F1.*

£   ▦**The Generator.** This is where the young, enthusiastic traveler comes to find fellow partyers. It's also the cleverest youth hostel in town. Set in a former police barracks, the Generator has decor that makes the most of the bunk beds and dim lighting. The Internet café provides handy maps and leaflets. The Generator Bar has cheap drinks and a rowdy crowd, and the Fuel Stop cafeteria provides inexpensive meals. There are singles, twins, and dormitory rooms, each with a washbasin, locker, and free bed linens. Prices run from £20 to £35 per person. **Pros:** funky, youthful attitude; great location. **Cons:** bar is crowded and noisy; party atmosphere is not for everyone. ✉ *MacNaghten House, Compton Pl. off 37 Tavistock Pl., Bloomsbury* ☎*020/7388–7666* ⊕*www. generatorhostels.com* ➪*214 beds* ⅃*In-room: no a/c, no phone, no TV. In-hotel: restaurant, bars, Internet terminal, parking (paid), no-smoking rooms* ⊟*MC, V* ⦿|*CP* Ⓤ*Russell Sq.* ✛*F1.*

££   ▦**Harlingford Hotel.** The Harlingford is by far the sleekest and most contemporary of the Cartwright Gardens hotels. Bold color schemes and beautifully tiled bathrooms enliven the family-run place. Bedrooms aren't big, but they're attractive, quiet, and comfortable. Public rooms are similarly small but perfectly appointed. With space for four, the quad rooms are a good choice for traveling families. For those who tire of eggs and sausage every morning, the hotel promises a choice of 20 kinds of cereal. **Pros:** good location; friendly staff; breakfast included. **Cons:** rooms are quite small; bathrooms are tiny. ⊠ *61–63 Cartwright Gardens, Bloomsbury* ☎ *020/7387–1551* ⊕ *www.harlingfordhotel. com* ⇗ *43 rooms* ⌂ *In-room: no a/c, Internet. In-hotel: bar, tennis court* ⊟ *AE, DC, MC, V* ⦿ *BP* Ⓤ *Russell Sq.* ⊹ *F1.*

££££ꞏ ▨**Renaissance Chancery Court.** This landmark structure, built by the Pearl Assurance Company in 1914, houses a beautiful Marriott hotel. So striking is the architecture that the building was featured in the film *Howards End.* The spacious bedrooms are popular with business travelers and the decor has a masculine edge—lots of leather and dark-red fabrics, with new luxurious mattresses. The day spa in the basement is a peaceful cocoon. There's marble everywhere, from the floors in public spaces and the massive staircase to the in-room bathrooms. The restaurant, Pearl, is known for its Modern European cuisine, and the bar, in an old banking hall, has elegant soaring ceilings. **Pros:** gorgeous space; your every need catered to. **Cons:** area is deserted at night and on weekends. ⊠ *252 High Holborn, Holborn* ☎ *020/7829–9888* ⊕ *www. marriott.com* ⇗ *343 rooms, 14 suites* ⌂ *In-room: safe, refrigerator, Internet. In-hotel: restaurant, room service, bar, gym, spa, laundry service, no-smoking rooms* ⊟ *AE, MC, V* Ⓤ *Holborn* ⊹ *G2.*

£ ▨**The Ridgemount.** Mere blocks away from the British Museum and London's West End theaters, this guesthouse has clean and neat rooms at a bargain. The public areas, especially the family-style breakfast room, are rather sweetly cluttered Victorian-style parlors. Rooms are plainly decorated and not all have private bathrooms, but some overlook a leafy garden. **Pros:** good location near the museums. **Cons:** guest-room decor is basic; no customer services; cheapest rooms have shared bathrooms. ⊠ *65 Gower St., Bloomsbury* ☎ *020/7636–1141* ⊕ *www.ridgemounthotel.co.uk* ⇗ *32 rooms, 15 with bath* ⌂ *In-room: no a/c, no phone. In-hotel: no-smoking rooms* ⊟ *MC, V* ⦿ *BP* Ⓤ *Goodge St.* ⊹ *F2.*

£££–£££££ ▨**Zetter Rooms.** By day, nothing but business suits buzz through the area between Holborn and Clerkenwell. By night, though, the ties are loosened and it's all oh-so-trendy. One of London's latest "it" hotels, Zetter reflects both personalities. The dizzying five-story atrium, art deco staircase, and slick European restaurant are your first indications of what to expect at this converted warehouse: a breath of fresh air (and a little space) in London's mostly Victorian hotel scene. Rooms are smoothly done up in soft dove gray and vanilla fabrics, and the views of the city from the higher floors are wonderful. It's all lovely to look at, although its prices have been climbing lately. **Pros:** big rooms; lots of gadgets; free broadband in rooms. **Cons:** recently increased prices mean this place is no longer a bargain; rooms with good views cost more. ⊠ *86–88 Clerkenwell Rd., Holborn* ☎ *020/7324–4444* ⊕ *www. thezetter.com* ⇗ *59 rooms* ⌂ *In-room: safe, refrigerator, DVD, Internet. In-hotel: restaurant, room service, bar, laundry service, no-smoking rooms* ⊟ *AE, MC, V* Ⓤ *Farringdon* ⊹ *H2.*

Fodor's Choice
★

COVENT GARDEN, PICCADILLY, AND SOHO

£££–££££ **Best Western Shaftesbury.** This Best Western chain in the midst of historic London does an admirable job of fitting in, while using as much chrome and frosted glass as anybody could ask for. Complimentary newspapers are scattered about, and bedrooms are ultramodern, with neutral rugs, white walls, dark curtains, and sleek furniture. The price reflects all this effort, so it's not the typical Best Western bargain, but it's pleasant and ideally situated in the heart of theaterland. **Pros:** great location for theaters, shopping, and museums. **Cons:** the price is clearly based on its location, rather than its amenities. ⊠ *65–73 Shaftesbury Ave., Piccadilly* ☎ *020/7871–6000* ⊕ *www.shaftesburyhotel.co.uk* ⤴ *69 rooms* ⟁ *In-room: DVD, Internet. In-hotel: no-smoking rooms* ☐ *AE, MC, V* Ⓤ *Piccadilly Circus* ✛ *F3.*

£££££ **Covent Garden Hotel.** In the midst of boisterous Covent Garden, this hotel is now the London home-away-from-home for a mélange of off-duty celebrities, actors, and style mavens. With painted silks, *style anglais* ottomans, and 19th-century Romantic oils, the public salons are perfect places to decompress over a glass of sherry from the honor bar. Guest rooms are *World of Interiors* stylish, each showcasing matching-but-mixed couture fabrics to stunning effect. For £30, the popular Saturday-night film club includes dinner in the brasserie and a film in the deluxe in-house cinema. **Pros:** great for star-spotting, and movie buffs. **Cons:** you can feel you don't matter if you're not a film star. ⊠ *10 Monmouth St., Covent Garden* ☎ *020/7806–1000, 800/553–6674 in U.S.* ⊕ *www.firmdale.com* ⤴ *55 rooms, 3 suites* ⟁ *In-room: safe, DVD, Wi-Fi. In-hotel: restaurant, room service, gym, spa, laundry service* ☐ *AE, MC, V* Ⓤ *Covent Garden* ✛ *F3.*

££££ **Hazlitt's.** Three connected early-18th-century houses, one of which was the last home of essayist William Hazlitt (1778–1830), make up this charming Soho hotel. It's a disarmingly friendly place, full of personality but devoid of certain modern amenities (as the owners say, "In 1718 there were no elevators, and there still aren't"). Robust antiques are everywhere, most beds are four-posters, and every room has a Victorian claw-foot tub in its bathroom. There are tiny sitting rooms, wooden staircases, and more restaurants within strolling distance than you could visit in a year. **Pros:** great for art and antiques lovers; truly beautiful and relaxed. **Cons:** no in-house restaurant; no elevators. ⊠ *6 Frith St., Soho* ☎ *020/7434–1771* ⊕ *www.hazlittshotel.com* ⤴ *20 rooms, 3 suites* ⟁ *In-room: Wi-Fi. In-hotel: room service, laundry service, parking (paid), some pets allowed, no-smoking rooms* ☐ *AE, DC, MC, V* Ⓤ *Tottenham Court Rd.* ✛ *F3.*

£££££ **One Aldwych.** An understated blend of contemporary and classic results in pure, modern luxury here. Flawlessly designed inside an Edwardian building, One Aldwych is coolly eclectic, with an artsy lobby, feather duvets, Italian linen sheets, and ample elegance. It's the ultimate in 21st-century style, from the free, hotel-wide Wi-Fi, down to the gorgeous swimming pool in the awesome health club. Suites have amenities such as a private gym, a kitchen, and a terrace. Breakfast is made with organic ingredients. The pool at One Aldwych has underwater speakers that play music you can hear only when you dive

Fodor'sChoice
★

in. **Pros:** understated (and underwater) luxury. **Cons:** all this luxury doesn't come cheap. ✉*1 Aldwych, Covent Garden* ☎*020/7300–1000* ⊕*www.onealdwych.co.uk* ☎*93 rooms, 12 suites* ⚲*In-room: safe, kitchen (some), refrigerator, Wi-Fi. In-hotel: 2 restaurants, room service, bars, pool, gym, spa, laundry service, parking (paid), no-smoking rooms* ▤*AE, MC, V* Ⓤ*Charing Cross, Covent Garden* ✛*G3.*

THE CITY AND EAST LONDON

£££££ 🏨 **Andaz.** This swanky, upscale hotel owned by the Hyatt group opened in late 2007 and has been making headlines for its modern, masculine design and unconventional approach. Instead of checking in at a desk, guests sit in a lounge while a staff member with a handheld computer takes their information. Rooms are sparsely decorated with designer furniture, and most important, intensely comfortable beds. Most have white walls, charcoal floors, and ruby-red touches. Rooms have Wi-Fi, MP3 docking stations, and "healthy minibars" stocked with nuts, fruit, and yogurt. The Aurora restaurant is exquisite, with marble floors and modern chandeliers, and the bar is popular with city workers. **Pros:** nice attention to detail; guests can borrow an iPod from the front desk; no standing in line to check in. **Cons:** the price is off the charts; sparse decor is not for all. ✉*40 Liverpool St., East London* ☎*020/7961–1234* ⊕*london.liverpoolstreet.andaz.com* ☎*267 rooms* ⚲*In-room: safe, Wi-Fi. In-hotel: restaurant, room service, bar, gym, laundry service, parking (paid), no-smoking rooms* ▤*MC, V* Ⓤ*Liverpool Street* ✛*H2.*

£–££ 🏨 **The Hoxton.** This trendy, East London hotel sits in the eponymous neighborhood and is designed to reflect the funky galleries and small boutiques for which the area is known. It claims to combine a country-lodge lifestyle with true urban living, and to that end its lobby has both crackling fires and cool cocktails, and the comfortable guest rooms have Frette linen sheets, down comforters, and free Wi-Fi. The design throughout is contemporary—but not so modern as to be absurd. There's still wood furniture and soft carpets. The bar is popular with local office workers, and the Hoxton Grille restaurant combines American steak-house style with French bistro chic. All rooms come with a free healthful breakfast of yogurt and fruit. **Pros:** cool-looking place; every night five rooms in this hotel are priced at £1, but you'll need to join the mailing list. **Cons:** restaurant and bar can be crowded in the evening; area is a bit off the beaten tourist track. ✉*81 Great Eastern St., East London* ☎*020/7550–1000* ⊕*www.hoxtonhotels.com* ☎*205 rooms* ⚲*In-room: safe, Internet, Wi-Fi. In-hotel: restaurant, room service, bar, no-smoking rooms* ▤*AE, MC, V* ⦿*BP* Ⓤ*Old St.* ✛*H1.*

££££–£££££   🏨**Malmaison.** Part of a small chain of well-regarded U.K. boutique hotels, this Clerkenwell address is filled with elegant furnishings, clean lines, and all the electronic extras. Stylish rooms are well decorated in neutral cream and beige, and have huge comfortable beds and CD systems with a library of music on demand, as well as satellite TVs and free broadband. The hotel prides itself on fast, high-quality room service, so breakfast in bed can be a pleasure. The whole package is a business traveler's dream. **Pros:** luxurious rooms; excellent service. **Cons:** neighborhood is off the tourist track; area can be quiet at night. ⊠*18-21 Charterhouse Sq., The City* ☎*020/7012–3700* ⊕*www.malmaison.com* 🛏*95 rooms, 2 suites* ᗧ*In-room: safe, refrigerator, Internet. In-hotel: restaurant, room service, bar, gym, laundry service, no-smoking rooms* ▭*AE, MC, V* |◎|*CP* Ⓤ*Barbican, Farringdon* ✛*H1.*

££–£££   🏨**Ramada Hotel and Suites Docklands.** Built in a dramatic waterfront location, this modern hotel is in the rejuvenated London Docklands in East London. Many rooms have water views, and others have views of the city. Rooms are sleek and modern, geared at business travelers, with Wi-Fi, large desks, data ports, and personal voice mail. The hotel's restaurants and bars are handy, although there's plenty to choose from these days in Docklands. **Pros:** waterfront views; big discounts for weekend bookings. **Cons:** area is very quiet on weekends; about a 20-minute Tube ride to central London. ⊠*ExCel, 2 Festoon Way, Royal Victoria Dock, East London* ☎*0870/111–8779* ⊕*www.ramadadocklands. co.uk* 🛏*224 rooms* ᗧ*In-room: safe, Internet. In-hotel: restaurant, room service, bar, gym, no-smoking rooms* ▭*AE, MC, V* |◎|*BP* Ⓤ*Old St.* ✛*H3.*

££££–£££££   🏨**The Rookery.** This is an extraordinary hotel, where each beautiful double room is decorated with a lavish, theatrical flair and an eye for history. Many have four-poster beds, and each has a claw-foot bathtub, antique carved wooden headboard, and period furnishings, including exquisite salvaged pieces. In the Rook's Nest, the hotel's duplex suite, you can relax in an antique bath in the corner of the bedroom or enjoy a magnificent view of The City's historic buildings. The conservatory, with its small patio garden, is a relaxing place to unwind. Great deals are available here in the winter. **Pros:** beautiful, quirky space; helpful staff. **Cons:** area is quiet at night and busy during the day. ⊠*12 Peter's La., at Cowcross St., The City* ☎*020/7336–0931* ⊕*www.rookeryhotel.com* 🛏*30 rooms, 3 suites* ᗧ*In-room: no a/c, safe, refrigerator, Internet. In-hotel: room service, bar, laundry service, parking (paid), no-smoking rooms* ▭*AE, DC, MC, V* Ⓤ*Farringdon* ✛*H2.*

KENSINGTON AND SOUTH KENSINGTON

££–£££   🏨**Astons Apartments.** Three redbrick Victorian town houses on a quiet residential street hold Astons's comfortable studios and apartments. All are simple and small but well designed with tiny kitchenettes, and the apartments (£££) have marble bathrooms and other extra touches as well. Some sleep families of four; others are barely big enough for two people. The decor has a modern, blond-wood look, and it all makes a nice alternative to normal hotel rooms. **Pros:** kitchenettes free you from restaurant tyranny; rooms are well designed. **Cons:** furnishings look a bit cheap; few customer services. ⊠ *31 Rosary Gardens, South Kensington* ☎ *020/7590–6000, 800/525–2810 in U.S.* ⊛ *www.astons-apartments. com* ⤏ *43 rooms, 12 suites* ⏦ *In-room: no a/c, safe, kitchen, refrigerator, Internet. In-hotel: parking (paid), some pets allowed, no-smoking rooms* ▤ *AE, MC, V* Ⓤ *Gloucester Rd.* ✛ *B6.*

£££ ▦ **Best Western Premier Shaftesbury Kensington.** Just steps from Earl's Court Tube station at the edge of Kensington, this hotel offers a lot for your money. Its look is fresh and relaxing, with cool grays and earth tones in the guest rooms, and firm queen-size beds. Bathrooms are small but handsome, with modern bowl sinks, towel warmers, and big walk-in showers. Staff are friendly and helpful. **Pros:** rates are as low as half price in the off-season and for early bookings; free Wi-Fi. **Cons:** rooms are quite small; reservations do get lost here, so bring your confirmation number. ⊠ *30–33 Hogarth Rd., Kensington* ☎ *020/7370–6831* ⊛ *www.bestwestern.co.uk* ⤏ *133 rooms* ⏦ *In-room: safe, refrigerator, Wi-Fi. In-hotel: restaurant, room service, no-smoking rooms* ▤ *AE, MC, V* ⏣| *BP* Ⓤ *Earl's Court* ✛ *A5.*

£ ▦ **easyHotel.** This budget hotel opened in 2005 as London's first "pod hotel." Crammed into a big white town house are 34 tiny rooms, all with a double bed, private bathroom, and little else. Each is brightly decorated in the trademark orange and white of the easyGroup (which includes the budget airline easyJet). The idea behind the hotel is to provide high-quality basics (bed, sink, shower, and toilet) for little money. The small reception desk can't offer much in terms of service, and if you want your room cleaned while you stay, it's an additional £10 a day. The concept continues to be a huge hit—easyHotel is fully booked months in advance and has opened additional branches at Heathrow Airport, as well as near Victoria and Paddington stations and elsewhere in Kensington. Check the Web site for all locations. **Pros:** amazing price; safe and pleasant space. **Cons:** not for the claustrophobic; everything costs extra, from a TV in your room to fresh towels; no customer services. ⊠ *14 Lexham Gardens, Kensington* ☎ *020/7216–1717* ⊛ *www. easyhotel.com* ⤏ *34 rooms* ⏦ *In-room: no a/c, no phone. In-hotel: no-smoking rooms* ▤ *MC, V* Ⓤ *Gloucester Rd.* ✛ *A5.*

££££–£££££ ▦ **The Gore.** Just down the road from the Albert Hall, this gorgeous, friendly hotel has a luxurious mixture of the comfortable and the extraordinary. The lobby evokes a wealthy estate from centuries past, and upstairs most rooms are spacious and decorated in calming neutral tones with rich fabrics. A handful of rooms are spectacular: one is a Tudor fantasy with minstrel gallery, stained glass, and four-poster bed, another—the "Judy Garland"—is done up in over-the-top Hollywood style. **Pros:** small scale means the staff can lavish attention on you; spacious rooms. **Cons:** price has gone up in recent years, making this only for those with deep pockets. ⊠ *189 Queen's Gate, Kensington* ☎ *020/7584–6601* ⊛ *www.gorehotel.com* ⤏ *50 rooms* ⏦ *In-room: no a/c, safe, refrigerator, Wi-Fi. In-hotel: restaurant, room service, bar, laundry service, no-smoking rooms* ▤ *AE, DC, MC, V* Ⓤ *Gloucester Rd.* ✛ *B5.*

£££££ ▦ **Milestone Hotel & Apartments.** This pair of intricately decorated Victorian town houses overlooking Kensington Palace and Gardens is

RENTALS, B&BS, AND HOME EXCHANGES

APARTMENT RENTALS

For a home base that's roomy enough for a family and that comes with cooking facilities, consider renting furnished "flats" (what apartments are called in Britain). These can save you money, especially if you're traveling with a group. If you're interested in home exchange, but don't feel like sharing, some home-exchange directories list rentals as well. If you want to deal directly with local agents, get a personal recommendation from someone who has used the company; there's no accredited rating system for apartment-rental standards like the one for hotels.

INTERNATIONAL AGENTS

At Home Abroad (⊠ *163 3rd Ave., No. 319, New York, NY* ☎ *212/421–9165* ⊕ *www. athomeabroadinc.com*).

Hideaways International (⊠ *767 Islington St., Portsmouth, NH* ☎ *603/430–4433 or 800/843–4433* ⊕ *www.hideaways.com*), annual membership $195.

Interhome (⊠ *1990 N.E. 163rd St., Suite 110, North Miami Beach, FL* ☎ *305/940–2299 or 800/882–6864* ⊕ *www.interhome.us*).

Vacation Home Rentals Worldwide (⊠ *235 Kensington Ave., Norwood, NJ* ☎ *201/767–9393 or 800/633–3284* ⊕ *www. vhrworld.com*).

Villanet (⊠ *1251 N.W. 116th St., Seattle, WA* ☎ *206/417–3444 or 800/964–1891* ⊕ *www. rentavilla.com*).

Villas International (⊠ *4340 Redwood Hwy., Suite D309, San Rafael, CA* ☎ *415/499–9490 or 800/221–2260* ⊕ *www. villasintl.com*).

LOCAL AGENTS

Acorn Apartments (⊠ *103 Great Russell St.* ☎ *020/7813–3223* ⊕ *www.acorn-apartments.co.uk*) cost from £90.

The Apartment Service (⊠ *5 Francis Grove, Wimbledon* ☎ *020/8944–1444* ⊕ *www. apartmentservice.com*).

At Home in London (⊠ *70 Black Lion La., Hammersmith* ☎ *020/8748–1943* ⊕ *www. athomeinlondon.co.uk* ⊟ *MC, V*)has rooms in private homes in Knightsbridge, Kensington, Mayfair, Chelsea, and West London. Prices average around £75 a night per room, making this a great alternative to budget hotels.

Bulldog Club (⊠ *14 Dewhurst Rd., Kensington* ☎ *020/7371–3202, 877/727–3004 in U.S.* ⊕ *www.bulldogclub.com* ⊟ *AE, MC, V.* ☞ *There's a 2.5% fee for using a credit card; debit cards incur no fees; the full price of the room must be paid in advance. Check their cancellation policies to make sure it will work with your own plans.*) offers delightful little London flats in sought-after Knightsbridge, Kensington, and Chelsea. Most properties are available for about £105 per night. Full English breakfasts as well as other goodies are often provided.

Stay in the properties of Londoners who are temporarily away with **Coach House London Vacation Rentals** (⊠ *2 Tunley Rd., Balham* ☎ *020/8772–1939* ⊕ *www.rentals. chslondon.com* ⊟ *AE, MC, V.* ☞ *Payment by credit card only; 10% deposit required*). Apartments and houses are primarily in Notting Hill, Kensington, and Chelsea, and most cost around £115 per night. The minimum booking of three nights is a bit limiting, though, and you must make a substantial security deposit (usually between £200 and £1,000), which is returned after your stay.

Landmark Trust (☎ *01628/825–925* ⊕ *www.landmarktrust.org.uk*) has London apartments in unusual and historic buildings.

Uptown Reservations (☎ *020/7937–2001* ⊕ *www.uptownres.co.uk*) accepts only themore upscale addresses, and specializes in finding hosted homes or short-term apartments for Americans, often executives of small corporations. Nearly all the 85 homes on its register are in Knightsbridge, Belgravia, Kensington, and Chelsea. Self-catering rentals—ideal for families—start at £550 per week; double rooms start at £105 per night. There's limited information on their Web site, and bookings must be made over the phone. A nonrefundable deposit is required.

Additionally, travelers on Fodors.com recommend these rental services:

"I've used **London Guest Suites** (⊕www.londonguestsuites.com) many times and like them. They have rentals of all lengths. I also just booked a flat at **A Place Like Home** (⊕www.aplacelikehome.co.uk)" —carrybean

"We stayed in 1 Sloane Ave. and were extremely happy and pleased with the apartment and the company **The Apartment**s (⊕www.theapartments.co.uk/)" —jrecm

"Try the biggest rental site in Europe: **Holiday-Rentals from Home Away** (⊕www.holiday-rentals.co.uk)" —travel_tomato

"Check out **VRBO** (⊕ www.vrbo.com), lots of London listings, and **Farnum-Christ** (⊕www.farnum-christ.com/) which is a high-ish end agency with some wonderful flats." —janisj

"I've used **London Connections** (⊕www.londonconnections.com) several times and I've been very pleased." —Tinathread

BED-AND-BREAKFASTS

You can stay in small, homey B&Bs for an up-close-and-personal brush with city life (Arosfa Hotel), or find yourself in what is really a modern guesthouse, where you never meet the owners (B&B Belgravia).

The main benefit of staying in a B&B is that the price is usually cheaper than a hotel room of comparable quality, and you receive more personal service. The limitations may be few in number, but can be off-putting for some: although you can sometimes arrange for daily maid service, there is no restaurant or bar, and no concierge should you have a question.

If you book a room in a privately owned house through an agency, prices start as low as £70 a night, and go up for more central neighborhoods and larger and more luxurious homes. It's a nice option, both for seasoned travelers and for those trying to travel well without busting their budgets. Search the Web and call around to find the place that's right for you.

AGENCIES

Host & Guest Service (⊠ *103 Dawes Rd., Fulham* ☎*020/7385–9922* ⊕*www.host-guest.co.uk* ▭*MC, V* ☞*Full payment in advance*) can find you a room in London as well as the rest of the United Kingdom. It's a great way to find bargains, knowing that all have been vetted by the agency, but the Web site functionality is a bit creaky.

The long-established family-run agency **London B&B** (⊠ *437 J St., Suite 210, San Diego, CA* ☎*800/872–2632* ⊕*www.londonbandb.com* ☞*30% deposit required*) has some truly spectacular—and some more modest—homes in central London. You can check many of them out online, but you still have to call even to find out prices.

HOME EXCHANGES

If you would like to exchange your home for someone else's, join a home-exchange organization, which will send you its updated listings of available exchanges for a year and will include your own listing in at least one of them. It's up to you to make specific arrangements.

For details on home exchange clubs, see Travel Smart England.

an intimate, luxurious alternative to the city's more famous high-end hotels. Great thoughtfulness goes into the hospitality, and everything is possible in this special place. You'll be offered a drink upon arrival and, if you so desire, you can return to a post-theater midnight snack in your room or leave with a picnic basket for the park across the street. Each sumptuous room is full of antiques; many have canopied beds. A favorite is the Ascot Room, which is filled with elegant hats of the kind worn at the famous races. **Pros:** beautiful space; big rooms. **Cons:** service can be a bit stuffy (it seems you're not expected to do anything for yourself). ⊠ *1 Kensington Ct., Kensington* ☎ *020/7917–1000* ⊕ *www. milestonehotel.com* ⊅ *45 rooms, 12 suites, 6 apartments* ⌂ *In-room: safe, kitchen (some), refrigerator, DVD, Wi-Fi. In-hotel: 2 restaurants, room service, bar, gym, laundry service, some pets allowed, no-smoking rooms* ▤ *AE, DC, MC, V* Ⓤ *High Street Kensington* ✛ *A4.*

££–£££   🏨 **Millennium Gloucester.** Recently refurbished in 2007, the hotel has a sleek lobby with polished wood columns, a warming fireplace, and glittering chandeliers. Guest rooms are done in neutral creams and earth tones, and blond-wood desks and leather chairs have a blandly masculine look. The hotel is popular with business travelers, so rooms come equipped with satellite TV and fast broadband connections. Bathrooms are relatively small but have all you need. There are two bars and several restaurants, which means you don't have to go out if you'd prefer to stay in. **Pros:** good deals available if you book in advance. **Cons:** public areas and restaurant can get crowded. ⊠ *4–18 Harrington Gardens, Kensington* ☎ *020/7373–6030* ⊕ *www.millenniumhotels. co.uk/millenniumgloucester* ⊅ *143 rooms* ⌂ *In-room: safe, refrigerator, Wi-Fi. In-hotel: restaurant, room service, no-smoking rooms* ▤ *AE, MC, V* ⑩ *BP* Ⓤ *Gloucester Rd.* ✛ *B5.*

£££–££££   🏨 **Number Sixteen.** In a white-portico row of Victorian houses, close to the South Kensington Tube and a short walk from the Victoria & Albert Museum, Number Sixteen is a lovely luxury guesthouse. Rooms are spacious and have marble- and oak-clad bathrooms. The style is not so much interior-designed as understated—new furniture and modern prints are juxtaposed with weighty oil paintings and antiques. The staff is friendly, so lingering in the drawing rooms is a pleasure, and drinks are served in the leafy garden in summer. **Pros:** just the right level of helpful service; decor is gorgeous. **Cons:** there's no restaurant; very small elevator. ⊠ *16 Sumner Pl., South Kensington* ☎ *020/7589–5232, 800/553–6674 in U.S.* ⊕ *www.firmdale.com* ⊅ *42 rooms* ⌂ *In-room: no a/c (some), safe, refrigerator, Wi-Fi. In-hotel: room service, bar, laundry service* ▤ *AE, MC, V* ⑩ *CP* Ⓤ *South Kensington* ✛ *B5.*

KNIGHTSBRIDGE, CHELSEA, AND BELGRAVIA

££–£££   🏨 **base2stay.** In a creamy white Georgian town house in chic Kensington, this hotel promises a new approach—a near-budget hotel. Prices are just above budget and just below moderate. Rooms are mostly comfortable doubles, but some have bunk beds, for traveling friends or children. Bathrooms are small but well designed. The air-conditioned rooms are not big, but have a stylish, modern look with white walls and bedding, and dark throws and pillows. Tiny kitchenettes give you alternatives

2

to another restaurant meal. Its "arrival base" system allows you to use a room before your check-in time for £15 an hour. **Pros:** attractive rooms; handy mini-kitchens; good location. **Cons:** prices are a bit high for what you get; bathrooms are very tiny. ⊠ *25 Courtfield Gardens, South Kensington* ☎ *020/7244–2255, 800/511–9821 in U.S.* ⊕ *www. base2stay.com* ⤳ *67 rooms* ⚒ *In-room: kitchen, refrigerator, Internet. In-hotel: no-smoking rooms* ⊟ *MC, V* Ⓤ *Earls Court Station* ✛ *A6.*

££ **B&B Belgravia.** This modern guesthouse a short walk from Victoria Station has cool all-white decor—white chairs and walls, white pillars and desks, white linens and towels. It all looks a bit ethereal, which is what they're aiming for. Rooms are small but beds are comfortable, and at least nothing you're wearing will clash. There's a modern, open-plan lounge where a fire crackles away in the winter. It's a good place to grab a cup of tea (always available) and check your e-mail on the free computer. **Pros:** free Wi-Fi; nice extras like free use of a laptop in the hotel lounge; coffee and tea always available. **Cons:** bathrooms are small; no hotel restaurant or bar. ⊠ *64–66 Ebury St., Victoria* ☎ *020/7259–8780* ⊕ *www.bb-belgravia.com* ⤳ *17 rooms* ⚒ *In-room: no a/c, Wi-Fi. In-hotel: Wi-Fi, no-smoking rooms* ⊟ *AE, DC, MC, V* ⦶ *CP* Ⓤ *Knightsbridge* ✛ *E5.*

£££££ **The Berkeley.** The elegant Berkeley is increasingly known for its luxurious, modern approach, which culminates in its splendid penthouse swimming pool. The big bedrooms have either swags of William Morris prints or art deco touches. All have sitting areas and ample luxury, including CD/DVD players, and Floris toiletries in the big marble bathrooms. Dining venues include Marcus Wareing's high-class Pétrus restaurant, Gordon Ramsay's excellent and extremely popular Boxwood Café, the eclectic and sumptuous Blue Bar (popular with celebrities), and the whimsical Caramel Room where morning coffee and decadent doughnuts are served to slim ladies who look as if they've never eaten such a thing in their lives. **Pros:** lavish luxury; attentive service; handy location for shopping. **Cons:** stratospheric prices; you'll need designer clothes to fit in here. ⊠ *Wilton Pl., Belgravia* ☎ *020/7235–6000, 800/637–2869 in U.S.* ⊕ *www.the-berkeley.com* ⤳ *103 rooms, 55 suites* ⚒ *In-room: safe, refrigerator, DVD, Internet. In-hotel: restaurant, room service, bar, pool, gym, spa, laundry service, parking (paid), no-smoking rooms* ⊟ *AE, DC, MC, V* Ⓤ *Knightsbridge* ✛ *D4.*

££££ **The Levin.** This small hotel created by the people behind the Capital Hotel is owned by luxury-loving oenophiles. Expect smooth, duck-egg-blue walls, hyper-modern furnishings, and a champagne bar in every room. Yes, that's right—each room has its own selection of pricey splits of bubbly, along with all the mixings (and directions) for making champagne cocktails. This boutique hotel is so posh it's frequently used in fashion photography shoots. Downstairs, the relaxed Le Metro Bar & Brasserie serves French and English classics (steak frites, sausages and mash) paired with an outstanding wine list. Located next door to Harrods, shopping locations don't get any more prime than this. **Pros:** your own champagne bar; sauntering to Harrods. **Cons:** no elevator; no bargains here. ⊠ *28 Basil St., Knightsbridge* ☎ *020/7589–6286* ⊕ *www.thelevinhotel.co.uk* ⤳ *12 rooms, 1 suite* ⚒ *In-room: DVD, Internet. In-hotel: restaurant, bar, parking (paid)* ⊟ *AE, V* ⦶ *CP* Ⓤ *Knightsbridge* ✛ *C5.*

££££££   🏨**Mandarin Oriental Hyde Park.** Stay here, and the three greats of
Fodor'sChoice   Knightsbridge—Hyde Park, Harrods, and Harvey Nichols—are on your
★   doorstep. Built in 1880, the Mandarin Oriental is one of London's
most elegant hotels. Bedrooms are Victorian but with hidden high-tech
gadgets and luxurious touches like Frette linen duvets, fresh orchids,
and delicate chocolates. Miles of marble were used to fill the grand
entrance. The Park restaurant, glittering Foliage restaurant, and quirky
Mandarin Bar all attract Europe's jet setters. The service here is legendary and there's a butler on every floor, should you, for example, need
a bit of help with the pillow menu. **Pros:** amazing views of Hyde Park;
excellent service. **Cons:** nothing here comes cheap; you must dress for
dinner (and lunch and breakfast). ⊠*66 Knightsbridge, Knightsbridge*
☎*020/7235–2000* ⊕*www.mandarinoriental.com* 📠*177 rooms, 23*
suites ⚲*In-room: safe, refrigerator, DVD (some), Wi-Fi. In-hotel: 2*
restaurants, room service, bar, gym, spa, laundry service, parking (paid),
no-smoking rooms ⊟*AE, DC, MC, V* Ⓤ*Knightsbridge* ✛*D4.*

MAYFAIR, MARYLEBONE, AND ST. JAMES'S

££££   🏨**22 Jermyn Street.** This historic guesthouse is on a fashionable shop-
☾   ping street in Piccadilly near the delightful department store Fortnum
& Mason. Flexible room configurations, including sitting rooms that
convert to bedrooms, mean families have plenty of space. In fact, the
hotel rolls out the red carpet for children, providing anything from high
chairs and coloring books to kiddie-sized bathrobes and personal nan-
nies. For grown-ups, there is access to a nearby gym, complimentary
newspapers, and a shoe shine. **Pros:** great for families; nice extras. **Cons:**
no restaurant or bar. ⊠*22 Jermyn St., St. James's* ☎*020/7734–2353,*
800/682–7808 in U.S. ⊕*www.22jermyn.com* 📠*5 rooms, 13 suites*
⚲*In-room: safe, DVD (some), Wi-Fi. In-hotel: room service, laundry*
service, parking (paid) ⊟*AE, DC, MC, V* Ⓤ*Piccadilly Circus* ✛*F3.*

££   🏨**22 York Street.** This Georgian town house has a cozy, family feel with
polished pine floors and plenty of quilts and antiques. Pride of place
goes to the central, communal dining table where guests share a varied
continental breakfast. A living room with tea/coffeemaker is at your
disposal as well. The homey bedrooms are individually furnished in
charming white and cream tones. Triples and family rooms for four
are available. **Pros:** handy guesthouse in a great location for shoppers.
Cons: price is a bit steep for what is, in the end, a glorified B&B. ⊠*22*
York St., Mayfair ☎*020/7224–2990* ⊕*www.22yorkstreet.co.uk* 📠*10*
rooms ⚲*In-room: no a/c. In-hotel: bar, no-smoking rooms* ⊟*AE, MC,*
V �*◯*|*CP* Ⓤ*Baker St.* ✛*D2.*

£££–££££   🏨**Athenaeum Hotel and Apartments.** This grand hotel overlooking Green
Park offers plenty for the money. Rooms are both comfortable and lavishly decorated, with deeply comfortable Hypnos beds, plasma-screen
television systems, luxurious fabrics, and original contemporary artworks. If you need more space, you can choose one of its apartments
instead. (These occupy a row of Georgian town houses next to the
main hotel buildings, and each has separate living, dining, and sleeping spaces; and tiny, fully equipped kitchenettes.) The spa downstairs is
available only to guests, ensuring you can always get an appointment.

The elegant restaurant serves butter-rich European cuisine, and a full afternoon tea here (£24) is an elegant experience. Breakfasts are luxurious and varied, with endless Continental and cooked options. **Pros:** peaceful park views; handy for Buckingham Palace and Piccadilly; great value for elegant setting. **Cons:** some rooms could use a decor update; bathrooms are almost all small. ⊠ *116 Piccadilly, Mayfair* ☎ *020/7499–3464* ⊕ *www.athenaeumhotel.com* ⇥ *111 rooms, 46 suites and apartments* ⌂ *In-room: safe, kitchen (some), DVD, Wi-Fi. In-hotel: restaurant, room service, bar, spa, no-smoking rooms, gym* ⊟ *AE, MC, V* ⦿ *BP* Ⓤ *Green Park* ⊕ *E4.*

£££££ 🖭 **Brown's.** Founded in 1837 by James Brown, Lord Byron's "gentleman's gentleman," this hotel, made up of 11 Georgian town houses, holds a treasured place in London society. Lounges and dining rooms are chic and contemporary. Everything is done up in cool neutral tones of coffee and cream; all guest rooms have an office space; and marble bathrooms have high-end bath products. No expense has been spared here, and if you stay here, you will not be spared expense either. The staff is exceedingly professional and helpful; nothing is too much trouble for them. **Pros:** elegant space; attentive service. **Cons:** everything costs here. ⊠ *34 Albemarle St., Mayfair* ☎ *020/7493–6020* ⊕ *www. brownshotel.com* ⇥ *88 rooms, 29 suites* ⌂ *In-room: safe, refrigerator, DVD, Internet. In-hotel: 2 restaurants, room service, bar, gym, spa* ⊟ *AE, DC, MC, V* Ⓤ *Green Park* ⊕ *E3.*

££££–£££££ 🖭 **Claridge's.** Stay here, and you're staying at a hotel legend with one of the world's classiest guest lists, founded in 1812. The friendly, liveried staff is not in the least condescending, and the rooms are never less than luxurious. Enjoy a cup of tea in the lounge, or retreat to the stylish bar for cocktails—or, better, to Gordon Ramsay's inimitable restaurant. The bathrooms are spacious (with enormous showerheads), as are the bedrooms (with soothing, modern decor in tones of taupe and cream). The grand staircase and magnificent elevator complete with sofa and driver are equally glamorous. Perhaps Spencer Tracy said it best when he remarked that, when he died, he wanted to go not to heaven, but to Claridge's. **Pros:** serious luxury everywhere—this is an old-money hotel. **Cons:** it's a bit pretentious—the guests in the hotel bar can be almost cartoonishly snobbish. ⊠ *Brook St., St. James's* ☎ *020/7629–8860, 800/637–2869 in U.S.* ⊕ *www.claridges.co.uk* ⇥ *203 rooms* ⌂ *In-room: safe, DVD, Wi-Fi. In-hotel: restaurant, bar, gym, spa, laundry service, parking (paid), no-smoking rooms* ⊟ *AE, DC, MC, V* Ⓤ *Bond St.* ⊕ *E3.*

£££££ 🖭 **The Dorchester.** Few hotels this opulent manage to be as personable. The glamour level is off the scale: 1,500 square yards of gold leaf and 1,100 square yards of marble. Bedrooms (some not as spacious as you might expect) have Irish linen sheets on canopied beds, brocades, velvets, and Italian marble and etched-glass bathrooms with toiletries created by Floris exclusively for the Dorchester. Furnishings throughout are English country-house style, with more than a hint of art deco, in keeping with the original 1930s building. The hotel has embraced modern technology, and employs "e-butlers" to help guests figure out the advanced Web TVs in the rooms. There are three elegant-to-the-point-of-fussy restaurants, including one helmed by Alain Ducasse, which is always making headlines. **Pros:** historic luxury; lovely views of Hyde Park; top-notch star-spotting. **Cons:** traditional look is not to all tastes; prices are high. ✉*Park Lane, Mayfair* ☎*020/7629–8888* ⊕*www.dorchesterhotel.com* ⬦*195 rooms, 55 suites* ⬦*In-room: safe, DVD, Internet. In-hotel: 3 restaurants, bar, gym, spa, laundry service, parking (paid), no-smoking rooms* ▤*AE, DC, MC, V* Ⓤ*Marble Arch, Hyde Park Corner* ⬦*D3.*

££££   ⌂**Durrants.** A stone's throw from Oxford Street and the smaller, posher shops of Marylebone High Street, Durrants sits on a quiet corner not far from the Wallace Collection. It's a tasteful option, with old-English wood paneling, leather armchairs, and patterned carpet. Note: bedrooms at the back of the hotel are smaller than those at the front, but also quieter and air-conditioned. The building has served as a hotel since the late 18th century. **Pros:** comfortable; relaxed base for exploring. **Cons:** not all rooms are air-conditioned; some rooms are quite small. ✉*26–32 George St., Mayfair* ☎*020/7935–8131* ⊕*www.durrantshotel.co.uk* ⬦*87 rooms, 5 suites* ⬦*In-room: no a/c (some), Internet. In-hotel: restaurant, room service, bar, laundry service* ▤*AE, MC, V* Ⓤ*Bond St.* ⬦*D2.*

££££–£££££   ⌂**The Stafford.** This is a rare find: a posh hotel that is equal parts elegance and friendliness. It's hard to check in without meeting the gregarious manager, and his unshakable cheeriness must be infectious, for the staff are also upbeat and helpful. The location is one of the few peaceful spots in the area, down a small lane behind Piccadilly. Its 13 adorable carriage-house rooms are installed in the 18th-century stable block; each individually decorated room has a cobbled mews entrance and gas-fueled fireplace, exposed beams, iPod dock, and CD player. The popular little American Bar has ties, baseball caps, and toy planes hanging from a ceiling modeled, presumably, on New York's 21 Club. **Pros:** great staff; big, luxurious rooms; quiet location. **Cons:** traditional decor is not to all tastes; the bar is tiny. ✉*St. James's Pl., St. James's* ☎*020/7493–0111* ⊕*www.thestaffordhotel.co.uk* ⬦*81 rooms* ⬦*In-room: Internet. In-hotel: restaurant, bar* ▤*AE, DC, MC, V* Ⓤ*Green Park* ⬦*E4.*

SOUTH BANK

£££–££££   ⌂**London Bridge Hotel.** Just steps away from the London Bridge rail and Tube station, this thoroughly modern, stylish hotel is popular with business travelers, but leisure travelers find it just as handy. Most of the South Bank's attractions are within easy walking distance, and it's a short stroll to London Bridge station to catch the Tube. Each diminutive but sleek room is understated and contemporary, with a calming, neutral decor. Three spacious two-bedroom apartments (£££££) come with kitchen, living room, and dining room. **Pros:** great for the arty South Bank; good deals available on its Web site in the off-season. **Cons:** small rooms, even smaller bathrooms. ✉*8–18 London Bridge St., South Bank* ☎*020/7855–2200* ⊕*www.london-bridge-hotel.co.uk* ⬦*138 rooms, 3 apartments* ⬦*In-room: safe, kitchen (some), refrigerator, Internet. In-hotel: restaurant, room service, bar, gym, laundry ser-*

vice, parking (paid), no-smoking rooms ☐*AE, DC, MC, V* Ⓤ*London Bridge* ✠*H3.*

££ 🏠**Premier Travel Inn County Hall.** It might be near the riverfront, but any
Ⓒ view of the Thames from this hotel is blocked by the nearby Marriott.
Still, it's got a handy location near the London Eye, and you get a decent
value here. Rooms are not very big, but they're nicely decorated, and
the staff are helpful. Best of all for families on a budget are the foldout
beds that let you accommodate two kids at no extra charge. *That's* a
bargain. **Pros:** good location for the South Bank; bargains to be had
if you book in advance. **Cons:** denied great views by other buildings
nearby; limited services. ✉*Belvedere Rd., South Bank* ☎*0870/238–
3300* ⊕*www.premiertravelinn.com* ↩*313 rooms* ♿*In-room: no a/c,
Internet. In-hotel: 2 restaurants, bar, parking (paid), no-smoking rooms*
☐*AE, DC, MC, V* Ⓤ*Westminster* ✠*G4.*

££ 🏠**Premier Travel Inn Southwark.** This excellent branch of the Premier
Travel Inn chain is a bit out of the way on the South Bank, but it sits on
a quiet cobbled lane, and is ideally located for visiting the Tate Modern
or the Globe Theatre. Rooms are simply decorated, and all have the
chain's signature 6-foot-wide beds (really two 3-foot-wide beds zipped
together). Ask for a room away from the elevators, which can be a
little noisy. **Pros:** great location for the South Bank; quiet street. **Cons:**
small rooms; limited customer services. ✉*34 Park St., South Bank*
☎*020/7089–2580 or 0870/990–6402* ⊕*www.premiertravelinn.com*
↩*56 rooms* ♿*In-room: Internet. In-hotel: parking (paid), no-smoking
rooms* ☐*AE, DC, MC, V* Ⓤ*London Bridge* ✠*H3.*

WESTMINSTER AND VICTORIA

£££–££££ 🏠 **City Inn Westminster.** In a rather stark steel-and-glass building steps
from the Tate Britain, this member of a small U.K. chain has some
rooms with spectacular views of Big Ben and the London Eye. Extras
like floor-to-ceiling windows and flat-screen TVs complement the contemporary, monochrome guest rooms. Cots, baby baths, Nickelodeon,
special menus, and baby food are all on tap for kids. The restaurant and
bar serve Modern British cooking. **Pros:** amazing views; lots of high-
tech toys. **Cons:** some rooms are starting to look a little worn around
the edges. ✉*30 John Islip St., Westminster* ☎*020/7630–1000* ⊕*www.
cityinn.com* ↩*444 rooms, 16 suites* ♿*In-room: safe, DVD, Internet.
In-hotel: restaurant, room service, bar, gym, laundry service, parking
(paid), no-smoking rooms* ☐*AE, MC, V* Ⓤ*Pimlico* ✠*F5.*

£££–££££ 🏠 **Jolly Hotel St. Ermin's.** The hotel is just a short stroll from Westminster
Abbey, Buckingham Palace, and the Houses of Parliament. An Edward-
ian anomaly in the shadow of modern skyscrapers, it's set on a tiny
cul-de-sac courtyard. The lobby is an extravaganza of Victorian stylings
like cake-frosting stuccowork in shades of baby blue and creamy white.
Sadly, guest rooms are much more ordinary and not likely to be much to
write home about. The hotel's Cloisters restaurant is an ornately carved
19th-century Jacobean-style salon, and one of the most magnificent
rooms in which to dine in London. **Pros:** amazing lobby; great location near Buckingham Palace. **Cons:** rooms are a bit small and plain.
✉*2 Caxton St., Westminster* ☎*020/7222–7888* ⊕*www.jollyhotels.it*

🛏277 rooms, 8 suites ♿In-room: safe (some), refrigerator, Internet. In-hotel: restaurant, room service, bar, laundry service, parking (paid), no-smoking rooms ▭AE, DC, MC, V ⓤSt. James's Park ✛F5.

££ 🏠**Lime Tree Hotel.** On a street filled with budget hotels, the homey Lime Tree stands out for its gracious proprietors, the Davies family, who also act as concierges. The flowery, comfortable rooms include tea/coffeemakers. The triples and quads are suitable for families, but children under five are not allowed. The simple breakfast room covered with notes and gifts from former guests opens onto a garden. **Pros:** friendly and cheap; great location. **Cons:** some rooms are up several flights of stairs, and there's no elevator. ✉135–137 Ebury St., Victoria ☎020/7730–8191 ⊕www.limetreehotel.co.uk 🛏25 rooms ♿In-room: no a/c, safe. In-hotel: Wi-Fi, no kids under 5 ▭MC, V ⦿BP ⓤVictoria ✛E5.

££ 🏠**Windermere Hotel.** This sweet little hotel will not let you forget that it stands on the site of London's first B&B, which opened here in 1881. It's draped in charmingly sunny floral fabrics, which look appropriate on the antique beds. Bathrooms are thoroughly modern, and the attached restaurant, small though it may be, is actually quite good. It's a decent option if you can't get a discount rate at a plusher hotel for the same price. **Pros:** attractive rooms; good location. **Cons:** price is a bit high for what you get; rooms and bathrooms are tiny; there's no elevator. ✉142–144 Warwick Way, Victoria ☎020/7834–4163 ⊕www.windermere-hotel.co.uk 🛏22 rooms ♿In-room: Internet. In-hotel: room service, bar, no-smoking rooms ▭MC, V ⓤVictoria ✛E6.

NIGHTLIFE AND THE ARTS

London is a veritable utopia for excitement junkies, culture fiends, and those who like to party. Most who visit London will be mesmerized by the city's energy, which reveals itself in layers. Whether you prefer a romantic evening at the opera, rhythm and blues with fine French food, the gritty guitar riffs of east London, a pint and gourmet pizza at a local gastro-pub, or swanky cocktails and sushi at London's sexiest lair, the U.K. capital is sure to feed your fancy. Admission prices are not always bargain-basement, but when you consider how much a London hotel room costs, the city's arts and nightlife diversions are a bargain.

NIGHTLIFE

As with nearly all cosmopolitan centers, the pace with which bars and clubs go in and out of fashion is mind-boggling. The phenomenon of absinthe has been replaced by bourbon's bite and the frenzy for the perfect cocktail recipe, and the dreaded velvet rope has been usurped by the doorbell-ringing mystique of members-only drinking clubs. The understated glamour of North London's Primrose Hill, which makes movie stars feel so at ease might be considered dull by the über-trendy clubgoers of London's West End, whereas the price of a pint in Chelsea would be dubbed blasphemous by the musicians and poets of racially diverse Brixton. Meanwhile, some of the city's most talked-about nightlife spots are turning out to be those attached to some of its best restaurants and hotels—no wonder when you consider the increased popularity of London cuisine in international circles.

BARS

Time was, bars were just a stopover in an evening full of fun—perhaps the pub first, then a bar, and then it's off to boogie the night away at the nearest dance club. These days, however, bars have become less pit stops and more destinations in themselves. With the addition of dinner menus, DJs, dance floors, and the still-new later opening hours, people now stay into the wee hours of the morning at many fashionable bars.

American Bar. Festooned with a chin-dropping array of club ties, signed celebrity photographs, sporting mementos, and baseball caps, this sensational hotel cocktail bar has superb martinis. ■TIP➔**Jacket required.** ⊠*Stafford Hotel, 16–18 St. James's Pl., St. James's* ☎*020/7493–0111* ⊙*Weekdays 11:30–11, weekends noon–11* Ⓤ*Green Park.*

★ **The Blue Bar at the Berkeley Hotel.** With low-slung gray-blue walls this hotel bar is ever so slightly sexy. Immaculate service, an excellent cocktail list—try the Sex in the City—and a trendy David Collins design, make this an ideal spot for a secretive tête-à-tête, complete with jazzy music in the background. ⊠*Wilton Pl., Knightsbridge* ☎*020/7235–6000* ⊙*Mon.–Sat. 4 PM–1 AM, Sun. 4–11 PM* Ⓤ*Knightsbridge.*

Cafe des Amis. This relaxed basement wine bar near the Royal Opera House is the perfect pre- or post-theater spot, popular among musicians and performers alike—and a friendly enough place to go on your own. More than 30 wines are served by the glass, along with a good selection of cheeses. Opera buffs will enjoy the performance and production prints on the walls. ⊠*11–14 Hanover Pl., Covent Garden* ☎*020/7379–3444* ⊙*Mon.–Sat. 11:30 AM–1 AM* Ⓤ*Covent Garden.*

Fodor'sChoice **Claridge's Bar.** This elegant Mayfair meeting place remains unpretentious
★ even when it brims with beautiful people. A library of rare champagnes and brandies as well as a delicious choice of traditional and exotic cocktails—try The Flapper or the Black Pearl—will occupy your taste buds. Request a glass of vintage Cristal in the Macanudo Fumoir. ⊠*55 Brook St., Mayfair* ☎*020/7629–8860* ⊙*Mon.–Sat. noon–1 AM, Sun. noon–midnight* Ⓤ*Bond St.*

Fodor'sChoice **Cocoon.** Pan-Asian restaurant Cocoon transforms itself into a sophisti-
★ cated lounge bar (with DJ) Thursday through Saturday until 3 AM. Soft curves give the tastefully modern place a bubbly feel, and contrasting levels of lighting blend intimacy with a vibrant atmosphere. Nibble away on one of chef Ricky Pang's original dishes while you sip on some of London's best cocktails, all with an Asian twist—try the Love & Rockets. ⊠*65 Regent St., St. James's* ☎*020/7494–7600* ⊙*Thurs.–Sat. 11 PM–3 AM* Ⓤ*Piccadilly.*

★ **Crazy Bear.** This sexy basement bar with cowhide stools and croc-skin tables feels like Casablanca in Fitzrovia. As you enter Crazy Bear, a spiral staircase leads to a mirrored parlor over which presides a 1947 Murano chandelier. But don't let the opulence fool you: waitstaff here are warm and welcoming to an all-ages international crowd abuzz with chatter. ✉ *26–28 Whitfield St., Fitzrovia* ☎ *020/7631–0088* ⏱ *Mon.–Wed. noon–midnight, Thurs.–Sat. 6 PM–1 AM* Ⓤ *Goodge St.*

★ **Dogstar.** This popular South London hangout is frequented by local hipsters and counterculture types. The vibe is unpretentious, and the Mexican cuisine is a treat. This "surrealist boudoir" space hosts top-name DJs playing cutting-edge sounds every night (free Monday–Thursday). ✉ *389 Coldharbour La., Brixton* ☎ *020/7733–7515* 🎟 *Free–£5* ⏱ *Mon.–Thurs. 4 PM–2 AM, Fri. and Sat. noon–4 AM, Sun. noon–2 AM* Ⓤ *Brixton.*

Nordic. With shooters called "Husky Poo" and "Danish Bacon Surprise" and crayfish tails and meatballs on the smorgasbord menu, Nordic takes its Scandinavian feel the whole way. This secluded, shabby-chic bar serves many couples cozied up among travel brochures promoting the Viking lands. If you can't decide what to drink, the cocktail roulette wheel on the wall may help. ✉ *25 Newman St., Soho* ☎ *020/7631–3174* ⊕ *www.nordicbar.com* ⏱ *Mon.–Thurs. noon–11 PM, Fri. noon–midnight, Sat. 6 PM–midnight* Ⓤ *Tottenham Court Rd.*

COMEDY

Amused Moose. This Soho basement/retro nightclub is widely considered the best place to see breaking talent as well as household names doing "secret" shows. Ricky Gervais, Eddie Izzard, and Russel Brand are among those who have graced this stage, and every summer a handful of the Edinburgh Fringe comedians preview here. The bar is open late, and there's a DJ and dancing until 5 AM after the show. Tickets are often discounted with a printout from their Web site. ✉ *Moonlighting, 17 Greek St., Soho* ☎ *020/7287–3727* ⊕ *www.amusedmoose.com* 🎟 *£9 and up* ⏱ *Showtimes vary; call for details* Ⓤ *Tottenham Court Rd.*

★ **Comedy Store.** Known as the birthplace of alternative comedy, this is where the United Kingdom's funniest stand-ups have cut their teeth before being launched onto prime-time TV. Comedy Store Players entertain audiences on Wednesday and Sunday; the Cutting Edge team steps in every Tuesday; and on the last Monday of every month the King Gong show (£5) hits the stage, where amateur comedians try their luck. Thursday, Friday, and Saturday have the best stand-up acts. There's a bar with food also available. ■ TIP→ **Tickets can be booked through Ticketmaster or over the phone.** Note that children under 18 are not admitted to this venue. ✉ *1A Oxendon St., Soho* ☎ *0844/847–1728* ⊕ *www.thecomedystore.co.uk* 🎟 *£13–£18* ⏱ *Shows daily 8 PM, with extra shows Fri. and Sat. at midnight* Ⓤ *Piccadilly Circus, Leicester Sq.*

Fodor's Choice ★ **Soho Theatre.** This innovative theater's programs include comedy shows by established acts and up-and-coming comedians. The bar downstairs, Café Lazeez, stays open until 11:30 Sunday through Thursday, and until 1 AM on Friday and Saturday. Check local listings or the Web site for what's on, and book tickets in advance. ✉ *21 Dean St., Soho* ☎ *020/7478–0100* ⊕ *www.sohotheatre.com* 🎟 *£10–£22.50* ⏱ *Mon.–Sat. usually 9:30–11, although show times vary* Ⓤ *Tottenham Court Rd.*

2

DANCE CLUBS

The club scene ranges from mammoth-size playgrounds to more intimate venues where you can actually hear your friends talk. Check the daily listings in *Time Out* for "club nights," which are theme nights that take place the same night every week. Another good way to learn about club nights is by picking up fliers in your favorite bar.

★ **The End.** This intimate club is owned and designed by clubbers for clubbers. Top-name DJs, a state-of-the-art sound system, and minimalist steel-and-glass decor—clubbing doesn't get much better than this. Next door, the **AKA Bar** is a stylish split-level Manhattan-esque cocktail bar with excellent food. ⊠*18 West Central St., Holborn* ☏*020/7419–9199* ⊕*www.endclub.com* ⊡*£4–£16* ☉*Mon. and Wed. 10:30 PM–3 AM, Fri. 10 PM–6 AM, Sat. 10 PM–7 AM. Also some Sun.* Ⓤ*Tottenham Court Rd.*

Fabric. This sprawling subterranean club is now a firm fixture on the London scene. "Fabric Live" hosts drum 'n' bass and hip-hop crews and live acts on Friday; international big-name DJs play slow, sexy bass lines and cutting-edge music on Saturday. Sunday is "Polysexual Night." The devastating sound system and "bodysonic" dance floor ensure that bass riffs vibrate through your entire body. ■TIP➔**Get there early to avoid a lengthy queue, and don't wear a suit.** ⊠*77A Charterhouse St., East End* ☏*020/7336–8898* ⊕*www.fabriclondon.com* ⊡*£13–£16* ☉*Fri. 10 PM–6 AM, Sat. 10 PM–7 AM* Ⓤ*Farringdon.*

★ **KOKO.** This Victorian theater, formerly known as Camden Palace, has seen acts from Charlie Chaplin to Madonna, and genres from punk to rave. Updated with lush reds not unlike a cockney Moulin Rouge, this is still one of London's most stunning venues. Sounds of live indie rock, cabaret, funky house, and club classics keep the big dance floor moving, even when it's not heaving. ⊠*1A Camden High St., Camden Town* ☏*0870/432–5527* ⊕*www.koko.uk.com* ⊡*£3–£20* ☉*Fri. and Sat. 10 PM–4 AM, also some Wed.* Ⓤ*Mornington Crescent.*

Fodor's Choice ★ **Vendome Mayfair.** This recently opened classy club draws a trendy crowd for house music, colorful furnishings, and futuristic designs with '70s retro disco decor. The revolving DJ booth at the center of the club, the Renaissance-like entrance, the individually themed booths, and the faux snakeskin banisters shout out pure decadence. ⊠*85 Piccadilly, Mayfair* ☏*020/7581–8609* ⊕*www.vendomemayfair.com* ⊡*£20* ☉*Wed. and Thurs. 10 PM–3 AM, Fri. and Sat. 10 PM–4 AM.*

ECLECTIC MUSIC

The Borderline. This important small venue has a solid reputation for booking everything from metal to country and beyond. Oasis, Pearl Jam, Blur, Sheryl Crow, PJ Harvey, Ben Harper, Jeff Buckley, and Counting Crows have all played live here. ⊠*Orange Yard off Manette St., Soho* ☏ *020/7734–5547* ⊕*www.meanfiddler.com* ⊡*£6–£25* ☉*Mon.–Sat. 7 PM–3 AM, Sun. 7–10:30* Ⓤ*Tottenham Court Rd.*

Fodor's Choice ★ **Carling Academy Brixton.** This legendary Brixton venue has seen it all—mods and rockers, hippies and punks. Despite a capacity for almost 5,000 people, this refurbished Victorian hall with original art deco fixtures retains a clublike charm; it has plenty of bars and upstairs seating. ⊠*211 Stockwell Rd., Brixton* ☎*020/7771–3000* ⊕*www.brixton-academy.co.uk* ⊠*£10–£30* ⊙*Opening hrs vary* Ⓤ*Brixton.*

★ **Union Chapel.** This beautiful old chapel has excellent acoustics and sublime architecture. The beauty of the space and its impressive multicultural programming have made it one of London's best musical venues, especially for acoustic shows. Performers have included Björk, Beck, and Goldfrapp, though now you're more likely to hear lower-key alternative country, world music, and jazz. ⊠*Compton Terr., Islington* ☎*020/7226–1686* ⊕*www.unionchapel.org.uk* ⊠*Free–£25* ⊙*Opening hrs vary* Ⓤ*Highbury and Islington.*

JAZZ

Dover Street Restaurant & Jazz Bar. Put on your blue-suede shoes and prepare to dance the night away—that is, after you've feasted from the French Mediterranean menu. Fun for dates as well as groups, Dover Street Restaurant has three bars, a DJ, and a stage with the latest live bands performing everything from jazz to soul to R&B, all this encircling linen-covered tables with a friendly staff catering to your every whim. ⊠*8–10 Dover St., Mayfair* ☎*020/7491–7509* ⊕*www.doverst.co.uk* ⊠*Free–£15* ⊙*Mon.–Thurs. noon–3 PM and 5:30 PM–3 AM, Fri. noon–3 PM and 7 PM–3 AM, Sat. 7 PM–3 AM* Ⓤ*Green Park.*

★ **Jazz Café.** A palace of high-tech cool in bohemian Camden—it remains an essential hangout for fans of both the mainstream end of the repertoire and hip-hop, funk, rap, and Latin fusion. Book ahead if you want a prime table overlooking the stage, in the balcony restaurant. ⊠*5 Pkwy., Camden Town* ☎*020/7688–8899 restaurant reservations, 0870/060–3777 standing tickets* ⊕*www.jazzcafe.co.uk* ⊠*£10–£25* ⊙*Daily 7 PM–2 AM* Ⓤ*Camden Town.*

★ **Pizza Express Jazz Club Soho.** One of the capital's most ubiquitous pizza chains also runs a great Soho jazz venue. The dimly lighted restaurant hosts top-quality international jazz acts every night. The Italian-style thin-crust pizzas are good, too, though on the small side. ⊠*10 Dean St., Soho* ☎*020/7439–8722* ⊕*www.pizzaexpresslive.com* ⊠*£10–£25* ⊙*Daily from 11:30 AM for food; music 7:30 PM–11 PM* Ⓤ*Tottenham Court Rd.*

Ronnie Scott's. Since the '60s, this legendary jazz club has attracted big names. It's usually crowded and hot, the food isn't great, and service is slow—but the mood can't be beat, even since the sad departure of its eponymous founder and saxophonist. Reservations are recommended. ⊠*47 Frith St., Soho* ☎*020/7439–0747* ⊕*www.ronniescotts.co.uk* ⊠*£15–£25 nonmembers, £5–£15 members, annual membership £165* ⊙*Mon.–Sat. 6 PM–3 AM, Sun. 6:30 PM–11 PM* Ⓤ*Leicester Sq.*

ROCK

The Astoria. This balconied theater hosts cutting-edge and big-name alternative bands (punk, metal, indie guitar). Shows start early, at 7 PM most nights; the building is often cleared, after gigs, for club events. ⊠*157 Charing Cross Rd., West End* ☎*020/7434–9592* ⊕*www.festivalrepublic.com* ⊠*£8.50–£25* ⊙*Opening hrs vary, depending on concert schedule. Fri.–Sun. 7–11 PM when a show is on; club nights 10 PM–4 AM* Ⓤ*Tottenham Court Rd.*

★ **Barfly Club.** At one of the finest small clubs in the capital, punk, indie guitar bands, and new metal rock attract a nonmainstream crowd. Weekend club nights upstairs host DJs (and live bands) who rock the decks. ✉ 49 *Chalk Farm Rd., Camden Town* ☏ 020/7424–0800 ⊕ *www.barflyclub. com* 🎫 *£5–£8* ⏱ *Mon.–Wed. 7–midnight, Thurs. 7* PM *–2* AM *, Fri. and Sat. 7* PM *–3* AM *, Sun. 7–11* Ⓤ *Camden Town, Chalk Farm.*

Forum. The best medium-to-big-name rock performers consistently play at the 2,000-capacity club. It's a converted 1920 art deco cinema, with a balcony overlooking the dance floor. Consult the Web site for current listings. ✉ *9–17 Highgate Rd., Kentish Town* ☏ 020/7428–4099 ⊕ *www.kentishtownforum.com* 🎫 *£12–£25* ⏱ *Opening hrs vary, depending on concert schedule* Ⓤ *Kentish Town.*

THE ARTS

London's arts scene pushes the boundaries, whether you prefer your art classical or modern, or as a contemporary twist on a time-honored classic. Celebrity divas sing original-language librettos at the Royal Opera House; the Almeida Opera focuses on radical productions of new opera and musical theater. Shakespeare's plays are brought to life at the reconstructed Globe Theatre, and challenging new writing is produced at the Royal Court.

To find out what's showing now, the weekly magazine *Time Out* (£2.99, issued every Tuesday) is invaluable. The *Evening Standard* carries listings, many of which are available online at ⊕ *www.thisislondon.co.uk.* London's widely available free newspapers are also worth checking out, as are many Sunday papers, and the Saturday *Independent, Guardian,* and *Times.* You can pick up the free fortnightly *London Theatre Guide* from hotels and tourist-information centers.

CLASSICAL MUSIC

Whether it's a concert by cellist Yo-Yo Ma or a Mozart requiem by candlelight, it's possible to hear first-rate musicians in world-class venues almost every day of the year. The London Symphony Orchestra is in residence at the Barbican Centre, although other top orchestras—including the Philharmonia and the Royal Philharmonic—also perform here. The Barbican also hosts chamber-music concerts, with celebrated orchestras such as the City of London Sinfonia. Wigmore Hall, a lovely venue for chamber music, is renowned for its song recitals by up-and-coming young singers. The Southbank Centre has an impressive international music season, held in the Queen Elizabeth Hall and the small Purcell Room as well as in the Royal Festival Hall, now completely refurbished. Full houses are rare, so even at the biggest concert halls you should be able to get a ticket for £12. If you can't book in advance, arrive at the hall an hour before the performance for a chance at returns.

■ TIP➡ Lunchtime concerts take place all over the city in smaller concert halls, the big arts-center foyers, and churches; they usually cost less than £5 or are free, and feature string quartets, singers, jazz ensembles, or gospel choirs. St. John's, Smith Square, and St. Martin-in-the-Fields are popular locations. Performances usually begin about 1 PM and last one hour.

A great British tradition since 1895, the **Henry Wood Promenade Concerts** (more commonly known as the "Proms" ⊕*www.bbc.co.uk/proms*) run eight weeks, from July to September, at the Royal Albert Hall. Despite an extraordinary quantity of high-quality concerts, it's renowned for its (atypical) last night: a madly jingoistic display of singing "Land of Hope and Glory," Union Jack–waving, and general madness. Demand for last-night tickets is so high that you must enter a lottery. For regular Proms, tickets run £5–£80, with hundreds of standing tickets for £5 available at the hall on the night of the concert. ■ TIP→**The last night is broadcast in Hyde Park on a jumbo screen, but even here a seat on the grass requires a paid ticket that can set you back around £20.**

Barbican Centre. Home to the London Symphony Orchestra (⊕*www. lso.co.uk*) and frequent host of the English Chamber Orchestra and the BBC Symphony Orchestra, the Barbican has an excellent season of big-name virtuosos. ⊠*Silk St., East End* ☎*020/7638–8891 box office* ⊕*www.barbican.org.uk* Ⓤ*Barbican, Moorgate.*

★ **Royal Albert Hall.** Built in 1871, this splendid iron-and-glass–dome auditorium hosts music programs in a wide range of genres, including top-flight pop artists, as well as being the home of Europe's most democratic music festival, the Proms. The hall is also open daily for daytime guided tours (£6). ⊠*Kensington Gore, Kensington* ☎*020/7589–8212* ⊕*www.royalalberthall.com* Ⓤ*South Kensington.*

St. John's, Smith Square. This baroque church behind Westminster Abbey offers chamber music and organ recitals as well as orchestral concerts September through July. There are occasional lunchtime recitals for £7. ⊠*Smith Sq., Westminster* ☎*020/7222–1061* ⊕*www.sjss.org.uk* Ⓤ*Westminster.*

★ **St. Martin-in-the-Fields.** Popular lunchtime concerts (free but £3.50 donation suggested) are held in this lovely 1726 church, as are regular evening concerts. You can sit in on many rehearsals for free. ■ TIP→**Stop for a snack at the Café in the Crypt.** ⊠*Trafalgar Sq., Covent Garden* ☎*020/ 7766–1100* ⊕*www.stmartin-in-the-fields.org* Ⓤ*Charing Cross.*

Southbank Centre. After a £70 million refurbishment, the Royal Festival Hall reopened in 2007 with large-scale choral and orchestral works in newly improved acoustic surroundings. Both the Philharmonia and the London Philharmonic orchestras are based here. Another £20 million has been spent on the rest of the Southbank Centre, where other venues host smaller-scale music performances; the Queen Elizabeth Hall has chamber orchestras and top-tier soloists, and in the intimate Purcell Room you can listen to chamber music and solo recitals. ⊠*Belvedere Rd., South Bank* ☎*0871/663–2500* ⊕*www.southbankcentre.org.uk* Ⓤ*Waterloo.*

Fodor'sChoice **Wigmore Hall.** Hear chamber music and song recitals in this charming ★ hall with near-perfect acoustics. Don't miss the midmorning Sunday concerts. ⊠*36 Wigmore St., Marylebone* ☎*020/7935–2141* ⊕*www. wigmore-hall.org.uk* Ⓤ*Bond St.*

CONTEMPORARY ART

In the 21st century, the focus of the city's art scene has shifted from the past to the future. Helped by the prominence of the Tate Modern, London's contemporary art scene has never been so high profile. In publicly funded exhibition spaces like the Barbican Gallery, the Hayward Gallery, the Institute of Contemporary Arts, and the Serpentine Gallery, London now has a modern-art environment on a par with Bilbao and New York. Young British Artists (YBAs, though no longer as young as they once were) Damien Hirst, Tracey Emin, and others are firmly planted in the public imagination. The celebrity status of British artists is in part thanks to the annual Turner Prize, which always stirs up controversy in the media during a monthlong display of the work, usually at Tate Britain.

Depending on whom you talk to, the Saatchi Gallery is considered to be either the savior of contemporary art or the wardrobe of the emperor's new clothes. It recently reopened in the former Duke of York's barracks off Chelsea's Kings Road.

The South Bank's Tate Modern may house the giants of modern art, but East London is where the innovative action is. There are dozens of galleries in the fashionable spaces around Old Street, and the truly hip have already moved even farther east, to areas such as Bethnal Green. The Whitechapel Art Gallery and Jay Jopling's influential White Cube in Hoxton Square remain at the epicenter of the new art establishment and continue to show exciting work by emerging British artists.

Barbican Centre. Innovative exhibitions of 20th-century and current art and design are shown in the Barbican Gallery and the **Curve** (✉ *Usually free* ☉ *Mon., Thurs.–Sun. 11–8, Tues. and Wed. 11–6*). Recent highlights have included a retrospective of modernist architect Alvar Aalto and a look at photography and European 20th-century history. ✉ *Silk St., The City* ☎ *020/7638–8891* ⊕ *www.barbican.org.uk* ✉ *Prices vary with exhibition (some free), tickets cheaper if booked online in advance* ☉ *Mon., Thurs.–Sun. 11–8, Tues. and Wed. 11–6* Ⓤ *Barbican.*

★ **Hayward Gallery.** This modern art gallery is a classic example of 1960s Brutalist architecture. It's part of the Southbank Centre and is one of London's major venues for contemporary art exhibitions. ✉ *Belvedere Rd., Southbank Centre, South Bank* ☎ *08703/800–400* ⊕ *www.hayward. org.uk* ✉ *Prices vary with exhibition (some free)* ☉ *Sat.–Thurs. 10–6, Fri. 10–10* Ⓤ *Waterloo.*

Institute of Contemporary Arts. Housed in an elegant John Nash–designed Regency terrace, the ICA's three galleries have changing exhibitions of contemporary visual art. The ICA also programs performance, film, new media, literary talks, and photography. There's an arts bookstore, cafeteria, and bar. ✉ *Nash House, The Mall, St. James's* ☎ *020/7930–3647 or 020/7930–0493* ⊕ *www.ica.org.uk* ✉ *Free* ☉ *Daily noon–7:30, Thurs. noon–9* Ⓤ *Charing Cross.*

Lisson. Owner Nicholas Logsdail represents about 40 blue-chip artists, including minimalist Sol Lewitt and Dan Graham, at arguably the most respected gallery in London. The gallery is most associated with

New Object sculptors like Anish Kapoor and Richard Deacon, many of whom have won the Turner Prize. A branch down the road at 29 Bell Street features work by younger, up-and-coming artists. ⊠*52–54 Bell St., Marylebone* ☎*020/7724–2739* ⊕*www.lissongallery.com* ✉*Free* ⊘*Weekdays 10–6, Sat. 11–5* Ⓤ*Edgware Rd., Marylebone.*

★ **Photographer's Gallery.** Britain's first photography gallery brought world-famous photographers like André Kertesz, Jacques-Henri Lartigue, and Irving Penn to the United Kingdom, and continues to program cutting-edge and provocative photography. The prestigious annual Deutsche Börse Photography Prize is exhibited and awarded here annually. There is a print sales room (closed Monday), a bookstore, and a café. The gallery moves to a striking new Soho building in 2010. Designed by architects O'Donnell + Tuomey, the new site, at 16–18 Ramillies Street, just off Oxford Street, will have a much improved exhibition space. ⊠*5 and 8 Great Newport St., Covent Garden* ☎*020/7831–1772* ⊕*www. photonet.org.uk* ✉*Free* ⊘*Mon.–Wed., Fri., and Sat. 11–6, Thurs. 11–8, Sun. noon–6* Ⓤ*Leicester Sq.*

Royal Academy. Housed in an aristocratic mansion and home to Britain's first art school (founded in 1768), the academy is best known for its blockbuster special exhibitions—like the record-breaking Monet, and the controversial Sensation drawn from the Saatchi collection. The annual Summer Exhibition has been a popular London tradition since 1769. ⊠*Burlington House, Mayfair* ☎*020/7300–8000* ⊕*www. royalacademy.org.uk* ✉*From £8, prices vary with exhibition* ⊘*Daily 10–6, except Fri. 10–10* Ⓤ*Piccadilly Circus.*

Saatchi Gallery. Charles Saatchi's ultramodern gallery devoted to leading contemporary artists reopened in all 70,000 square feet of the Duke of York's HQ building in Chelsea in 2008 complete with a new bookshop and café-bar. ⊠*Duke of York's HQ, Sloane Sq., Chelsea* ☎*020/7823–2332* ⊕*www.saatchi-gallery.co.uk* ✉*Free* Ⓤ*Sloane Sq.*

Serpentine Gallery. Built in 1934 as a tea pavilion in Kensington Gardens, the Serpentine has an international reputation for exhibitions of modern and contemporary art. Man Ray, Henry Moore, Andy Warhol, Bridget Riley, Damien Hirst, and Rachel Whiteread are a few of the artists who have had exhibits here. The annual Summer Pavilion, designed by a different leading architect every year, is always worth catching. ⊠*Kensington Gardens, South Kensington* ☎*020/7402–6075* ⊕*www.serpentinegallery.org* ✉*By donation* ⊘*Daily 10–6* Ⓤ*South Kensington, Knightsbridge.*

★ **Tate Modern.** This converted power station is one of the largest modern-art galleries in the world, so give yourself ample time to take it all in. The permanent collection includes work by all the major 20th-century artists, though only a fraction is shown at any one time. There are also blockbuster touring shows and solo exhibitions of international artists. ■TIP➔**The bar on the top floor has gorgeous views overlooking the Thames and St. Paul's Cathedral.** ⊠*Bankside, South Bank* ☎*020/7887–8888* ⊕*www.tate.org.uk* ✉*Free–£10* ⊘*Sun.–Thurs. 10–6, Fri. and Sat. 10–10* Ⓤ*Southwark.*

★ **Victoria Miro Gallery.** This important commercial gallery has exhibited some of the biggest names on the British contemporary art scene—Chris Ofili, the Chapman brothers, Peter Doig, to name a few. ✉ *16 Wharf Rd., Islington* ☎ *020/7336–8109* ⊕ *www.victoria-miro.com* ✉ *Free* 🕙 *Tues.–Sat. 10–6* Ⓤ *Old St., Angel.*

★ **White Cube.** Jay Joplin's influential gallery is housed in a 1920s light-industrial building on Hoxton Square. Many of its artists are Turner Prize stars—Hirst, Emin, Hume, et al.—and many live in the East End, which supposedly has the highest concentration of artists in Europe. Farther west, White Cube has a second gallery in a striking building in Mason's Yard, St. James's. ✉ *48 Hoxton Sq., Hoxton* ☎ *020/7930–5373* ⊕ *www.whitecube.com* ✉ *Free* 🕙 *Tues.–Sat. 10–6* Ⓤ *Old St.*

★ **Whitechapel Art Gallery.** Established in 1897, this independent East End gallery is one of London's most innovative and consistently interesting. Jeff Wall, Bill Viola, Gary Hume, and Janet Cardiff have exhibited here. In spring 2009 the gallery will complete its expansion into what was previously a library next door; confirm opening hours in advance. ✉ *80–82 Whitechapel High St., Shoreditch* ☎ *020/7522–7888* ⊕ *www. whitechapel.org* ✉ *Free–£8* 🕙 *Wed.–Sun. 11–6* Ⓤ *Aldgate East.*

DANCE

The **English National Ballet** and visiting international companies usually perform at the London Coliseum and at Sadler's Wells. The **Royal Ballet,** world renowned for its classical excellence, as well as innovative contemporary dance from several companies and scores of independent choreographers, can be seen at the Royal Opera House. Encompassing the newly refurbished **Royal Festival Hall,** the Southbank Centre has a seriously good contemporary dance program that hosts top international companies and important U.K. choreographers, as well as multicultural offerings from Japanese Butoh and Indian Kathak to hip-hop. The **Place** and the **Lilian Baylis Theatre** at Sadler's Wells are where you'll find the most daring, cutting-edge performances.

The biggest annual event is **Dance Umbrella** (☎ *0844/412–4312* ⊕ *www. danceumbrella.co.uk*), a seven-week season from September to November that hosts international and British-based artists at various venues across the city.

The following theaters are the key dance venues. Check weekly listings or ⊕ *www.londondance.com* for current performances and fringe venues.

DANCE BOX OFFICES **London Coliseum** (✉ *St. Martin's La., Covent Garden* ☎ *020/7632–8300* Ⓤ *Leicester Sq.*).

The **Place** (✉ *17 Duke's Rd., Bloomsbury* ☎ *020/7121–1000* ⊕ *www. theplace.org.uk* Ⓤ *Euston*).

Fodor'sChoice ★ **Royal Opera House** (✉ *Bow St., Covent Garden* ☎ *020/7304–4000* ⊕ *www.roh.org.uk* Ⓤ *Covent Garden*).

Fodor'sChoice ★ **Sadler's Wells** (✉ *Rosebery Ave., Islington* ☎ *0844/412–4322* ⊕ *www. sadlers-wells.com* Ⓤ *Angel*).

Southbank Centre (✉ *Belvedere Rd., South Bank* ☎ *0871/663–2500* ⊕ *www.southbankcentre.co.uk* Ⓤ *Waterloo, Embankment*).

FILM

There are many lovely movie theaters in London and several that are committed to nonmainstream cinema, notably the National Film Theatre. Most of the major houses, such as the Odeon Leicester Square and the Empire, are in the Leicester Square–Piccadilly Circus area, where tickets average £12. Monday and matinees are often cheaper, at around £6–£10, and there are also fewer crowds.

☾ ★ **BFI Southbank.** With easily the best repertory programming in London, the three cinemas at what was previously known as the National Film Theatre are effectively a national film center run by the British Film Institute. They show more than 1,000 titles each year, favoring arthouse, foreign, silent, overlooked, classic, noir, and short films over Hollywood blockbusters. After a recent rejuvenation and expansion, the center also has a gallery, bookshop, and "mediatheque," where visitors can watch film and television from the National Archive. ■TIP→ **The London Film Festival is based here at BFI Southbank; throughout the year there are minifestivals, seminars, and guest speakers. Members (£35) get priority bookings (useful for special events) and £1 off each screening.** ⊠*Belvedere Rd., South Bank* ☎*020/7633–0274 information, 020/7928–3232 box office* ⊕*www.bfi.org.uk/whatson/bfi_southbank* Ⓤ*Waterloo.*

★ **Curzon Soho.** This comfortable cinema runs an artsy program of mixed repertoire and mainstream films. There are also branches in Mayfair, Bloomsbury, Chelsea, and Richmond. Members (£25) get discounts. ⊠*99 Shaftesbury Ave., Soho* ☎*0871/703–3988* Ⓤ*Piccadilly Circus, Leicester Sq.* ⊠*38 Curzon St., Mayfair* ☎*0871/703–3989* ⊕*www. curzoncinemas.com* Ⓤ*Green Park.*

☾ **The Electric Cinema.** This refurbished Portobello Road art house screens mainstream and international movies. The emphasis is on comfort, with leather sofas, armchairs, footstools, and mini–coffee tables for your popcorn. Saturday matinees for kids are popular. ⊠*191 Portobello Rd., Notting Hill* ☎*020/7908–9696* ⊕*www.electriccinema.co.uk* Ⓤ*Ladbroke Grove, Notting Hill Gate.*

OPERA

The two key players in London's opera scene are the Royal Opera House (which ranks with the Metropolitan Opera House in New York) and the more innovative English National Opera (ENO), which presents English-language productions at the London Coliseum. Only the Theatre Royal, Drury Lane, has a longer theatrical history than the Royal Opera House—the third theater to be built on the site since 1858.

Despite occasional performances by the likes of Björk, the Royal Opera House struggles to shrug off its reputation for elitism and ticket prices that can rise to £190. It is, however, more accessible than it used to be—the cheapest tickets are just £4. Conditions of purchase vary; call for information. Prices for the ENO are generally lower, ranging from around £12 to £80. You can get same-day balcony seats for as little as £5.

Almeida Opera is a festival that often showcases cutting-edge opera. In summer, the increasingly adventurous Opera Holland Park presents the usual chestnuts alongside some obscure works under a newly enlarged canopy in leafy Holland Park.

OPERA BOX OFFICES **Almeida Theatre** (✉*Almeida St., Islington* ☎*020/7359–4404* ⊕*www. almeida.co.uk* Ⓤ*Angel*).

English National Opera (✉*St. Martin's La., Covent Garden* ☎*0871/911– 0200* ⊕*www.eno.org* Ⓤ*Leicester Sq.*).

Opera Holland Park (✉*Holland Park, Kensington High St., Kensington* ☎*0845/230–9769* ⊕*www.operahollandpark.com* Ⓤ*Kensington High St.*).

Fodor'sChoice ★ **Royal Opera House** (✉*Bow St., Covent Garden* ☎*020/7304–4000* ⊕*www.royalopera.org* Ⓤ*Covent Garden*).

THEATER

In London the play really *is* the thing, ranging from a long-running popular musical like *Mamma Mia!*, a groundbreaking reworking of Pinter, imaginative physical theater from an experimental company like *Complicite*, a lavish Disney spectacle, or a small fringe production above a pub. West End glitz and glamour continue to pull in the audiences, and so do the more innovative productions. Only in London will a Tuesday matinee of the Royal Shakespeare Company's *Henry IV* sell out a 1,200-seat theater.

The Royal Shakespeare Company (⊕*www.rsc.org.uk*) and the Royal National Theatre Company (⊕*www.nationaltheatre.org.uk*) often stage contemporary versions of the classics. The Almeida, Battersea Arts Centre (BAC), Donmar Warehouse, Royal Court Theatre, Soho Theatre, and the Old Vic attract famous actors and have excellent reputations for new writing and innovative theatrical approaches. These are the venues where you'll see an original production before it becomes a hit in the West End or on Broadway (and for a fraction of the cost.) From mid-May through mid-September you can see the Bard served up at the open-air reconstruction of Shakespeare's Globe Theatre on the South Bank.

Theatergoing isn't cheap. Tickets less than £10 are a rarity, although designated productions at the National Theatre have seats at this price. At the commercial theaters you should expect to pay from £15 for a seat in the upper balcony to at least £25 for a good one in the stalls (orchestra) or dress circle (mezzanine). However, last-minute returns available on the night may provide some good deals. Tickets may be booked through ticket agents, at individual theater box offices, or over the phone by credit card. Be sure to inquire about any extra fees—prices can vary enormously, but agents are legally obliged to reveal the face value of the ticket if you ask. All the larger hotels offer theater bookings, but they tack on a hefty service charge.

Be very wary of ticket touts (scalpers) and unscrupulous ticket agents outside theaters and working the line at TKTS (a half-price ticket booth)— they try to sell tickets at five times the price of the ticket at legitimate box offices, and you pay a stiff fine if caught buying a scalped ticket.

Ticketmaster (☎*0870/534–4444* ☎*161/385–1420 from outside U.K.* ⊕*www.ticketmaster.co.uk*) sells tickets to a number of different theaters, although they charge a booking fee. You can book tickets in the

United States through **Keith Prowse** (✉ *234 W. 44th St., Suite 1000, New York, NY* ☎ *800/669–8687* ⊕ *www.keithprowse.com*). For discount tickets, **Society of London Theatre** (☎ *020/7557–6700*) operates TKTS, a half-price ticket booth (⊕ *www.tkts.co.uk*) on the southwest corner of Leicester Square, and sells the best available seats to performances at about 25 theaters.

It's open Monday–Saturday 10–7, Sunday noon–3; there's a £2.50 service charge (included in the price). Major credit cards are accepted.

THEATERS

★ **Almeida Theatre.** This Off–West End venue premieres excellent new plays and exciting twists on the classics. Hollywood stars often perform here. ✉ *Almeida St., Islington* ☎ *020/7359–4404* ⊕ *www.almeida.co.uk* Ⓤ *Angel, Highbury, and Islington.*

★ **BAC.** Battersea Arts Centre has a reputation for producing innovative new work. Check out Scratch, a monthly, pay-what-you-can night of low-tech cabaret theater by emerging artists where the audience provides feedback on works-in-progress. Tuesday shows also have pay-what-you-can entry. ✉ *176 Lavender Hill, Battersea* ☎ *020/7223–2223* ⊕ *www.bac.org.uk* Ⓤ *British Rail: Clapham Junction.*

Barbican Centre. Built in 1982, the Barbican Centre puts on a number of performances by British and international theater companies as part of its year-round **B.I.T.E.** (Barbican International Theatre Events), which also features groundbreaking performance, dance, drama, and musical theater. ✉ *Silk St., The City* ☎ *020/7638–8891* ⊕ *www.barbican.org. uk* Ⓤ *Barbican.*

Fodor's Choice **Donmar Warehouse.** Hollywood stars often perform here in diverse and
★ daring new works, bold interpretations of the classics, and small-scale musicals. It works both ways, too—former director Sam Mendes went straight from here to directing *American Beauty.* ✉ *41 Earlham St., Covent Garden* ☎ *0870/060–6624* ⊕ *www.donmarwarehouse.com* Ⓤ *Covent Garden.*

National Theatre. Opened in 1976, the National Theatre has three venues: the 1,120-seat Olivier, the 890-seat Lyttelton, and the 300-seat Cottesloe. Musicals, classics, and new plays are in repertoire. ■ TIP→ **An adventurous ticketing scheme means some performances can be seen for as little as £10.** ✉ *Southbank Centre, Belvedere Rd., South Bank* ☎ *020/7452–3000* ⊕ *www.nationaltheatre.org.uk* ⟴ *Tour £5* ⊙ *Foyer Mon.–Sat. 10 AM–11 PM; 75-min tour backstage up to 6 times daily weekdays, twice on Sat.* Ⓤ *Waterloo.*

The Old Vic. American actor Kevin Spacey is the artistic director of this grand 1818 Victorian theater. Legends of the stage have performed here, including John Gielgud, Vivien Leigh, Peter O'Toole, Richard Burton, Judi Dench, and Laurence Olivier, who called it his favorite theater.

⊠*The Cut, Southwark* ☎*0870/060–6628* ⊕*www.oldvictheatre.com* Ⓤ*Waterloo.*

Fodor'sChoice **Open Air Theatre.** On a warm summer evening, classical theater in the
★ pastoral and royal Regent's Park is hard to beat for magical adventure.
Enjoy a supper before the performance, a bite during the intermis-
sion on the picnic lawn, or drinks in the spacious bar. ⊠*Inner Circle,
Regent's Park* ☎*0844/826–4242* ⊕*www.openairtheatre.org* Ⓤ*Baker
St., Regent's Park.*

★ **Royal Court Theatre.** Britain's undisputed epicenter of new writing, the
RCT is now 50 years old and continues to produce gritty British and
international drama. ■TIP➔**Don't miss the best deal in town–£10 tickets on Monday.** ⊠*Sloane Sq., Chelsea* ☎*020/7565–5000* ⊕*www.
royalcourttheatre.com* Ⓤ*Sloane Sq.*

Fodor'sChoice **Shakespeare's Globe Theatre.** This faithful reconstruction of the open-air
★ playhouse where Shakespeare worked and wrote many of his great-
est plays re-creates the 16th-century theatergoing experience. Standing room in the "pit" right in front of the stage costs £5. The season
runs May through September. ⊠*21 New Globe Walk, Bankside, South
Bank* ☎*020/7401–9919* ⊕*www.shakespeares-globe.org* Ⓤ*Southwark,
Mansion House, walk across Southwark Bridge; London Bridge.*

Soho Theatre. This sleek theater in the heart of Soho is devoted to foster-
ing new writing and is a prolific presenter of work by emerging writers and comedy performance. ⊠*21 Dean St., Soho* ☎*0870/429–6883*
⊕*www.sohotheatre.com* Ⓤ*Tottenham Court Rd.*

↺ **Tricycle Theatre.** The Tricycle is committed to the best in Irish, African-
Caribbean, Asian, and political drama, and the promotion of new plays.
⊠*269 Kilburn High Rd., Kilburn* ☎*020/7328–1000* ⊕*www.tricycle.
co.uk* Ⓤ*Kilburn.*

Young Vic. Ensconced in a new home near Waterloo, big names perform
here alongside young talent, often in daring, innovative productions of
classic plays. ⊠*66 The Cut, Waterloo, South Bank* ☎*020/7928–6363*
⊕*www.youngvic.org* Ⓤ*Waterloo.*

SHOPPING

Napoléon was being scornful when he called Britain a nation of shopkeepers, but Londoners have had the last laugh. The finest empori-
ums are in London, still. You can shop like royalty at Her Majesty's
glove maker, discover an uncommon Toby jug in a Kensington antiques
shop, or find a leather-bound edition of *Wuthering Heights* on Charing
Cross Road. If you have a yen to keep up with the Windsors, head for
stores proclaiming they are "By Appointment" to H. M. the Queen—
or to Prince Philip or the Prince of Wales. The fashion-forward crowd
favors places such as Harvey Nichols or Browns of South Molton Street,
whereas the most ardent fashion victims will shoot to Notting Hill,
London's prime fashion location. If you have limited time, zoom in on
one of the city's grand department stores, such as Harrods, Marks &
Spencer, or Selfridges, where you can find enough booty for your entire
gift list. Below is a brief introduction to the major shopping areas.

THE SPORTS SCENE

London will host the 2012 Olympics, but don't expect to see many city inhabitants practicing their javelin throws in Hyde Park. Sport in the capital comes into its own when it's watched, rather than participated in. You'll most easily witness London's fervent sporting passions in front of a screen in a pub with a pint in hand. And those passions run deep.

CRICKET

★**Lord's** (⊠ *St. John's Wood Rd., St. John's Wood* ☎ *020/7432–1000* ⊕ *www.lords.org* Ⓤ *St. John's Wood*) has been hallowed turf for worshippers of England's summer game since 1811. Tickets are hard to come by: obtain an application form and enter the ballot (lottery) to purchase tickets. Forms are sent out in early December or you can apply online. Test Match tickets cost between £25 and £95. Cheaper county matches (Middlesex plays here) can usually be seen by lining up on match day.

FOOTBALL

Three of London's football (soccer) clubs competing in the **Premier League** and the Football Association's FA Cup are particularly popular, though not always correspondingly successful: **Arsenal** (⊠ *Emirates Stadium, Ashburton Grove, Islington* ☎ *020/7704–4040* ⊕ *www.arsenal.com* Ⓤ *Arsenal*), **Chelsea** (⊠ *Stamford Bridge, Fulham Rd., Fulham* ☎ *0871/984–1905* ⊕ *www.chelseafc.co.uk* Ⓤ *Fulham Broadway*), and **Tottenham Hotspur** ("*Spurs*" ⊠ *White Hart La., 748 High Rd., Tottenham* ☎ *0844/499–5000* ⊕ *www.tottenhamhotspur.com* Ⓤ *National Rail: White Hart La.*). Try to buy tickets in advance, and don't get too carried away by the excitement a vast football crowd can generate.

TENNIS

The **Wimbledon Lawn Tennis Championships** (☎ *020/8946–2244* ⊕ *www.wimbledon.org*), the most prestigious of the four Grand Slam tournaments, is also one of London's most eagerly awaited annual events. There's a lottery system for advance purchse; check the Web site. You can purchase tickets online for the next day's matches throughout the tournament.

Apart from bankrupting yourself, the only problem you may encounter is exhaustion. London is a town of many far-flung shopping areas.
■TIP➔ **Real shophounds plan their excursions with military precision, taking in only one or two shopping districts in a day, with fortifying stops for lunch, tea, and a pint or glass of wine in the pub.**

CAMDEN TOWN   Every kind of alternative style—retro, Goth, New Romantic, New Age, punk, hippie, "Annie Hall"—is catered to in the crafts and vintage-clothing markets spreading out from Camden Town Underground Station.

CHELSEA   Chelsea centers on King's Road, once synonymous with ultrahigh fashion; it still harbors some designer boutiques, plus antiques and home-furnishings stores.

COVENT GARDEN   This neighborhood has chain clothing stores and top designers, stalls selling crafts, and shops selling gifts of every type—bikes, kites, tea, herbs, beads, hats—you name it.

2

FULHAM Newly popular, Fulham is divided into two postal districts, SW6 (farther away from the center of town) and SW10 (which is the closer, beyond Chelsea) on the high-fashion King's Road.

KENSINGTON Kensington's main drag, Kensington High Street, houses some small, classy shops, with a few larger stores at the eastern end. Try Kensington Church Street for expensive antiques, plus a little fashion.

KNIGHTS-BRIDGE Knightsbridge, east of Kensington, has Harrods but also Harvey Nichols, the top clothes stop, and many expensive designers' boutiques along Sloane Street, Walton Street, and Beauchamp Place.

MARYLEBONE Behind Oxford Street lies this quiet backwater, with Marylebone High Street as its main artery. There are restaurants, upscale delis, and designer furniture stores; chic boutiques spill over onto satellite streets.

MAYFAIR In Mayfair are the two Bond streets, Old and New, with desirable dress designers, jewelers, and fine art. South Molton Street has high-price, high-style fashion, and the tailors of Savile Row have worldwide reputations.

NOTTING HILL Go westward from the famous Portobello Road market and explore the Ledbury Road–Westbourne Grove axis, Clarendon Cross, and Kensington Park Road for a mix of antiques and up-to-the-minute must-haves for body and lifestyle. Toward the more bohemian foot of Portobello are Ladbroke Grove and Golborne Road, where, in among the tatty stores, Portuguese cafés, and patisseries, you can bag bargains.

PIMLICO AND VICTORIA Not quite Belgravia, not quite anywhere really, this odd little corner of London, bounded by Lower Sloane Street, Pimlico Road, Ebury Street, and Elizabeth Street, is a center for quirky and individual antiques, home decor, fashion, and food shops.

REGENT STREET At right angles to Oxford Street is Regent Street, with possibly London's most pleasant department store, Liberty, plus Hamleys, the capital's favorite toy store. Shops around once-famous Carnaby Street stock designer youth paraphernalia and 57 varieties of the T-shirt.

ST. JAMES'S Here the English gentleman buys everything but the suit (which is from Savile Row): handmade hats, shirts and shoes, silver shaving kits, and hip flasks. Nothing in this neighborhood is cheap, in any sense.

DEPARTMENT STORES

Browns (⊠ *24–27 South Molton St., Mayfair* ☎ *020/7514–0016* Ⓤ *Bond St.*) caters to the very label-conscious customer in a mini-department store setting. You will find men's and women's fashion from Alexander McQueen and Marni and Chloe, as well as lesser-known designers.

FodorsChoice **Harrods** (⊠ *87–135 Brompton Rd., Knightsbridge* ☎ *020/7730–1234*
★ Ⓤ *Knightsbridge*), one of the world's most famous department stores, can be forgiven its immodest motto, *Omnia, omnibus, ubique* ("everything, for everyone, everywhere"), because it has more than 300 well-stocked departments. If you approach Harrods as a tourist attraction rather than a fashion store, you won't be disappointed: focus on the spectacular food halls, the huge ground-floor perfumery, the marble-clad accessory rooms, and the theme park–like Egyptian Room.

Harvey Nichols (✉*109–125 Knightsbridge, Knightsbridge* ☎*020/7235–5000* Ⓤ*Knightsbridge*) is famed for five floors of ultimate fashion; every label any chic, well-bred London lady covets is here, as well as a home-furnishings department. It's also known for the restaurant, Fifth Floor.

Fodor'sChoice **Liberty** (✉*Regent St., Mayfair* ☎*020/7734–1234* Ⓤ*Oxford Circus*), ★ full of nooks and crannies, is famous principally for its fabulous fabrics. It also carries Eastern and exotic goods, menswear, womenswear, fragrances, soaps, and accessories.

Marks & Spencer (✉*458 Oxford St., Oxford Street* ☎*020/7935–7954* Ⓤ*Marble Arch*) is a major chain that's an integral part of the British way of life—sturdy, practical clothes and good materials. What it *is* renowned for is underwear; the English all buy theirs here. The food department at M&S is consistently superb. (Look for their M&S Simply Food stores all over town.)

★ **Selfridges** (✉*400 Oxford St., Oxford Street* ☎*0870/837–7377* Ⓤ*Bond St.*), huge and hip, is giving Harvey Nicks a run as London's leading fashion department store. It's packed with high-profile, popular designer clothes for everyone in the family. There's a globe-spanning Food Hall on the ground floor, and a ground-floor Wonder Room, which showcases extravagant jewelry and unusual gifts.

SPECIALTY STORES

ANTIQUES

★ **Alfie's Antique Market** (✉*13–25 Church St., Marylebone* ☎*020/7723–6066* ⊙*Closed Sun. and Mon.* Ⓤ*Edgware Rd.*), a huge labyrinth on several floors, has dealers specializing in anything and everything but particularly in vintage clothing, decorative accessories, and furniture. **Antiquarius** (✉*131–145 King's Rd., Chelsea* ☎*020/7823–3900* ⊙*Closed Sun.* Ⓤ*Sloane Sq.*), near Sloane Square, is an indoor antiques market with around 100 stalls selling collectibles, art deco brooches, vintage costume jewelry, old pocket watches, and silver salt cellars. **Grays Antique Market** (✉*58 Davies St., Mayfair* ☎*020/7629–7034* ⊙*Closed Sun.; open Sat. in Dec. only* Ⓤ*Bond St.*) assembles dealers specializing in everything from Sheffield plates to Asian antiquities. Bargains are not impossible, and proper pedigrees are guaranteed. It's closed Saturday (except December) and Sunday. **Hope and Glory** ✉*131A Kensington Church St., Kensington* ☎*020/7727–8424* ⊙*Closed Sun.* Ⓤ*Notting Hill Gate*)is one of the many specialty stores in Kensington with commemorative ceramics from Victoria's reign to the present; there are also affordable lesser pieces. The entrance is on Peel Street.

★ **London Silver Vaults** (✉*53–64 Chancery La., Holborn* ☎*020/7242–3844* ⊙*Closed Sat. after 1, and Sun.* Ⓤ*Chancery La.*) has more than 30 dealers specializing in antique silver and jewelry.

BOOKS, CDS, AND RECORDS

BOOKS Charing Cross Road is London's "booksville," with a couple of dozen antiquarian booksellers and many mainstream bookshops, too. Cecil Court, off Charing Cross Road, is a pedestrian-only lane filled with specialty bookstores (⊕*www.cecilcourt.co.uk*).

Books for Cooks (⊠*4 Blenheim Crescent, Notting Hill* ☎*020/7221– 1992* Ⓤ*Notting Hill Gate*) is hard to resist. Just about every world cuisine is represented on its shelves, along with the complete lineup of celebrity-chef editions.

Fodor'sChoice ★ **Foyles** (⊠*113–119 Charing Cross Rd., Soho* ☎*020/7437–5660* Ⓤ*Tottenham Court Rd.*) is so vast you can find almost anything. Store-within-a-store Ray's Jazz has a cool café, and there's even a piranha tank on the children's floor.

Fodor'sChoice ★ **Hatchards** (⊠*187 Piccadilly, St. James's* ☎*020/7439–9921* Ⓤ*Piccadilly Circus*) has a huge stock and a well-informed staff. **John Sandoe Books, Ltd.** (⊠*10 Blacklands Terr., Chelsea* ☎*020/7589–9473* Ⓤ*Sloane Sq.*) has more than 25,000 titles that fill three dollhouse-size floors of an 18th-century house. **Maggs Brothers Ltd.** (⊠*50 Berkeley Sq., Mayfair* ☎*020/7493–7160* ⊘*Closed weekends* Ⓤ*Green Park*), with a deliciously Dickensian name, is in a Georgian town house in one of Mayfair's elegant squares. Maggs was established in 1853, and is one of the world's oldest and largest rare-book dealers. **Stanfords** (⊠*12–14 Long Acre, Covent Garden* ☎*020/7836–1321* Ⓤ*Covent Garden*) specializes in travel books and maps. **Waterstone's** (⊠*203–206 Piccadilly, St. James's* ☎*020/7851–2400* Ⓤ*Piccadilly Circus*) is part of an admirable chain with long hours and a program of author readings and signings. Their most upscale branch is book buying as hedonistic leisure activity, with five floors, a studio cocktail lounge with a view, and a café in the basement.

CDS AND RECORDS
The place for house, drum 'n' bass, electro, and dubstep, **BM Soho** (⊠*25 D'Arblay St., Soho* ☎*020/7437–0478* ⊘*Closed Sun.* Ⓤ*Oxford Circus*) stocks the hottest club music around. There are some CDs, but this is really a shop for vinyl lovers. **MDC Music & Movies** (⊠*Festival Riverside, Royal Festival Hall, South Bank* ☎*020/7620–0198* Ⓤ*Waterloo*) is a classical music specialist that has branched out into jazz and world music. **Music & Video Exchange** (⊠*38 Notting Hill Gate, Notting Hill* ☎*020/7243–8573* Ⓤ*Notting Hill Gate*) is a convenient destination for seekers of unusual and mainstream chart music as well as classical and pop.

★ **Rough Trade East** ⊠*Dray Walk, Old Truman Brewery, 91 Brick La., East End* ☎*020/7392–7788* Ⓤ*Liverpool St.*is a veteran indie-music specialist that seems to have gotten the formula right—in 2007 it opened this spacious new East End branch that's as much a hangout as a shop, complete with a stage for live gigs, a café, and even free Internet access.

HOME DECOR

Fodor'sChoice ★ **Mint** (⊠*30 Wigmore St., Marylebone* ☎*020/7224–4406* Ⓤ*Bond St.*) stocks an eclectic mix of furniture, art, ceramics, and home accessories. Mint also showcases works by up-and-coming designers and sells plenty of limited edition and one-off pieces.

CHINA AND GLASS
Emma Bridgewater (⊠*81A Marylebone High St., Marylebone* ☎*020/ 7486–6897* Ⓤ*Baker St., Regents Park*) is the home of fun and funky casual plates, mugs, jugs, and breakfast tableware for country-style designer kitchens. **Thomas Goode** (⊠*19 S. Audley St., Mayfair* ☎*020/ 7499–2823* ⊘*Closed Sun.* Ⓤ*Green Park*) stocks lead crystal and

GREAT SPOTS TO SHOP

Portobello Road Market. Whether you are a serious antiques buyer or just want to browse the stalls and people-watch, Portobello Road is London's most dynamic market.

Liberty. In a Tudor-style building, Liberty has an outstanding collection of clothing crafted from its famous prints and furniture, as well as cutting-edge fashion.

Dover Street Market. This concept store is a combination art gallery and department store, and also hosts design retrospectives.

Hamleys. With floor after floor of treasures for every child on your list, this is *the* London toy shop.

Rellik. Celebs love Rellik for its superb collection of vintage clothing, ranging from classic Dior to Vivienne Westwood.

Mint. Fans of contemporary furniture and housewares should head to Mint, which showcases the work of both leading and up-and-coming designers.

formal china, including English Wedgwood and Minton, and is one of the world's top shops for these items.

CLOTHING

Agent Provocateur (⊠*16 Pont St., Knightsbridge* ☎*020/7235–0229* ☺*Open Sun. in Dec. only* Ⓤ*Knightsbridge, Sloane Sq.*) is the place to go for sexy, naughty-but-nice lingerie in gorgeous fabrics and lace. **Aquascutum** (⊠*100 Regent St., Soho* ☎*020/7675–8200* Ⓤ*Piccadilly Circus*) is known for its classic raincoats but also stocks clothing for men and women in classic British style. The men's suits and sweaters are timeless, and the women's collection has become surprisingly funky, offering fresh takes on overcoats and items like tunics and jersey dresses. Up-to-the-minute **b Store** (⊠*24A Savile Row, Mayfair* ☎*020/7734–6846* ☺*Closed Sun.* Ⓤ*Bond St., Oxford Circus*) couldn't be farther away in terms of style from the traditional tailors down the street. Head here for cutting-edge pieces from avant-garde London designers such as Diana Brinks and Ute Ploeir, plus the store's quirky own-label shoes. **Burberry** (⊠*21–23 New Bond St., Mayfair* ☎*020/7968–0000* Ⓤ*Piccadilly Circus*) has gone for a more rock and roll image of late but still evokes English tradition, with mahogany closets and merchandise with the trademark "Burberry Check" tartan—scarves, umbrellas, shortbread tins, and those famous raincoats.

Fodor's Choice ★ **Dover Street Market** (⊠*17–18 Dover St., Mayfair* ☎*020/7518–0680* Ⓤ*Green Park*) isn't just about buying; with its arty displays, it's as fascinating as any gallery. The creation of Comme des Garçons' Rei Kawakubo, it showcases the label's collections alongside other designers such as Lanvin, Alaïa, and exclusive Japanese lines, plus curiosities including antique medical specimens. ■TIP→**An outpost of the Rose Bakery on the top floor makes a handy pit stop.**

James Lock & Co. Ltd. (⊠*6 St. James's St., St. James's* ☎*020/7930–5849* ☺*Closed Sun.* Ⓤ*Green Park, Piccadilly Circus*) is a cozy shop with a full selection of classic and traditional hats. **Margaret Howell** (⊠*34*

Wigmore St., Soho ☎020/7009–9009 ⊘*Closed Sun* Ⓤ*Oxford Circus*) makes quintessentially English clothes that have a nostalgic feel while managing to look contemporary. Howell mixes impeccable British tailoring and traditional fabrics (linen, cashmere, tweed) with relaxed modern cuts. **Nicole Farhi** (✉*158 New Bond St., Mayfair* ☎020/7499–8368 Ⓤ*Bond St.*) makes contemporary yet timeless quality clothes that are standbys in many a working woman's wardrobe; the men's collection is available at a branch in Covent Garden.

Rellik (✉*8 Golborne Rd., Ladbroke Grove* ☎020/8962–0089 Ⓤ*West-bourne Park*) is favored by the likes of Kate Moss and began as a street stall on Portobello Road. Today vintage hunters looking to splurge can find a selection of YSL, Chanel, and Dior, as well as items from lesser-known designers. Prices start at £30 and go up well over £1,000.

Fodor's Choice ★ **Topshop** (✉*214 Oxford St., Soho* ☎020/7636–7700 Ⓤ*Oxford Circus*) is a genuine fashion hot spot with affordable prices. Clothing and accessories are geared to the younger end of the market, and the aim is to copy runway trends as fast as possible—although the store also has its own catwalk line, and a changing array of front-of-the-pack designers create small collections for the in-store Boutique. Topman is the male version of the chain.

MENSWEAR **Bamford & Sons** (✉*31 Sloane Sq., Chelsea* ☎020/7881–8010 Ⓤ*Sloane Sq.*) combines the British heritage of tailoring and fabrics with suave modernity. Dashing city wear, romantically nonchalant country clothes, plus fine leather and cashmere accessories are all available.

★ **Ozwald Boateng** (✉*12A Savile Row, Mayfair* ☎0870/777–1377 ⊘*Closed Sun* Ⓤ*Piccadilly Circus*), pronounced Bwa-teng, is one of the funkiest tailors working on Savile Row. His made-to-measure suits are sought after by rock luminaries for their shock-color linings as well as great classic cuts.

★ **Turnbull & Asser** (✉*71–72 Jermyn St., St. James's* ☎020/7808–3000 ⊘*Closed Sun.* Ⓤ*Piccadilly Circus*) is *the* custom shirtmaker. Alas, the first order must be for a minimum of six shirts, from about £150 each. There are less expensive, still exquisite ready-to-wear shirts, too.

WOMENSWEAR **Browns** (✉*23–27 S. Molton St., Mayfair* ☎020/7514–0000 ⊘*Open*
★ *Sun. in Dec. only* Ⓤ*Bond St.*) was a pioneer designer boutique in the 1970s and continues to talent-spot the newest and best around. You may find the windows showcasing the work of top graduates from this year's student shows or displaying well-established designers such as Marni, Chloé, Juyna Watanabe, Yves Saint Laurent, Dries Van Noten, or Anne Demeulemeester.

Jigsaw (✉*126–127 New Bond St., Mayfair* ☎020/7491–4484 Ⓤ*Bond St.*) wins points for its reasonably priced separates, which don't sacrifice quality for fashion and suit women in their 20s through 40s. **Jimmy Choo** (✉*32 Sloane St., Knightsbridge* ☎020/7823–1051 Ⓤ*Knightsbridge*), the name on every supermodel's and fashion editor's feet, creates exquisite, elegant shoes.

Koh Samui (✉*65–67 Monmouth St., Covent Garden* ☎020/7240–4280 Ⓤ*Covent Garden*) stocks the clothing of about 40 hot young designers. Discover the next fashion wave before *Vogue* gets there. **Rigby &**

Peller (⊠ *2 Hans Rd., Knightsbridge* ☎ *020/7589–9293* ⊘ *Closed Sun.* Ⓤ *Knightsbridge*) is a magnet for those who love luxury lingerie. The quality and service are excellent and much friendlier than you might expect. **Vivienne Westwood** (⊠ *44 Conduit St., Mayfair* ☎ *020/7439–1109* Ⓤ *Bond St.*), one of the top British designers, produces pompadour-punk ball gowns, Lady Hamilton vest coats, and foppish landmark getups that still represent the apex of high-style British couture.

CRAFTS

★ The **Lesley Craze Gallery** (⊠ *33–35A Clerkenwell Green, East End* ☎ *020/7608–0393* ⊘ *Closed Sun.; open Mon. in Nov. and Dec. only* Ⓤ *Farringdon*) carries exquisite jewelry by some 100 young designers from around the world, with a strong British bias, featuring both precious and semiprecious stones. There's also a textiles room showcasing unusual and colorful handmade scarves, bags, and cushions. **OXO Tower** (⊠ *Bargehouse St., South Bank* ☎ *020/7401–2255* ⊘ *Some studios closed Mon. or Sun.* Ⓤ *Southwark*) holds around 30 glass walled workshops that sell excellent handmade goods.

GIFTS

Cath Kidston (⊠ *28–32 Shelton St., Covent Garden* ☎ *020/7836–4803* Ⓤ *Covent Garden*) signature look is bright, girly prints—ginghams, polka dots, and miles and miles of roses—pasted over everything in sight, from ceramics and bed linens to fine china, stationery, and dog beds.

★ **Floris** (⊠ *89 Jermyn St., St. James's* ☎ *020/7930–2885* ⊘ *Closed Sun.* Ⓤ *Piccadilly Circus*) is one of London's most beautiful shops, with 19th-century glass and mahogany showcases filled with beautifully packaged soaps, perfumes, and its famous rose-scented mouthwash, gift possibilities include goose-down powder puffs and cut-glass atomizers.

★ **Fortnum & Mason** (⊠ *181 Piccadilly, St. James's* ☎ *020/7734–8040* Ⓤ *Piccadilly Circus*), the Queen's grocer, is, paradoxically, the most egalitarian of gift stores, with plenty of luxury foods, stamped with the gold BY APPOINTMENT crest, for less than £5. Try the teas, preserves, tins of pâté, or or a box of Duchy Originals oatcakes.

★ **Hamleys** (⊠ *188–196 Regent St., Soho* ☎ *0870/333–2455* Ⓤ *Oxford Circus*) is at the top of every London childs' wish list. A Regent Street institution, the shop has demonstrations, a play area, a café, and every cool toy on the planet.

Penhaligon's (⊠ *41 Wellington St., Covent Garden* ☎ *020/7836–2150* Ⓤ *Covent Garden*), established by William Penhaligon, court barber to Queen Victoria, was perfumer to Lord Rothschild and Winston Churchill.

JEWELRY

Asprey (⊠ *167 New Bond St., Mayfair* ☎ *020/7493–6767* ⊘ *Closed Sun.* Ⓤ *Bond St.*) displays exquisite jewelry and gifts, both antique and modern, in a discreet and very British environment

★ **Butler & Wilson** (⊠ *189 Fulham Rd., Chelsea* ☎ *020/7352–3045* Ⓤ *S. Kensington*) has been marketing the diamanté, colored rhinestones, and crystal look—long before anybody ever heard the word bling. You can also find nostalgic gowns here. There's another branch at 20 South

Molton Street. **Garrard** (⊠*24 Albemarle St., Mayfair* ☎*020/7758–8520* ☺*Closed Sun.* Ⓤ*Bond St.*) sets precious gems in simple, classic settings. Tradition rules, so you can still drop in to pick up a jeweled tiara.

★ **Kabiri** (⊠*37 Marylebone High St., Marylebone* ☎*020/7224–1808* Ⓤ*Baker St., Bond St.)*is a dazzling array of exciting contemporary jewelry by emerging and established designers from around the world is packed into this small shop. There is something to suit most budgets and tastes.

PRINTS

Besides print stores, browse around the gallery shops, such as those at the Tate Britain and Tate Modern. In the open air, try hunting around Waterloo Bridge along the Riverside Walk Market, at St. James's Craft Market at St. James's Church in Piccadilly, and at the Apple Market near the Piazza, Covent Garden.

Grosvenor Prints (⊠*19 Shelton St., Covent Garden* ☎*020/7836–1979* ☺*Closed Sun.* Ⓤ*Covent Garden*) sells antiquarian prints, with an emphasis on London views and architecture as well as sporting and decorative prints

STREET MARKETS

★ **Bermondsey** is the market the dealers frequent for small antiques, which gives you an idea of its scope. The real bargains start going at 4 AM, but there'll be a few left if you arrive later. Take Bus 15 or 25 to Aldgate, then Bus 42 over Tower Bridge to Bermondsey Square; or take the tube to London Bridge and walk. ⊠*Long La. and Bermondsey Sq., South Bank* ☺*Fri. 5 AM–noon* Ⓤ*London Bridge.*

★ **Borough Market,** a foodie's delight, carries whole-grain, organic everything, mainly from Britain but with an international flavor. ⊠*Borough High St., South Bank* ☺*Thurs. 11–5, Fri. noon–6, Sat. 9–4* Ⓤ*London Bridge, Borough.*

The **Camden Markets** area is actually several markets gathered around a pair of locks in the Regent's Canal. The markets on Camden High Street mainly sell cheap T-shirts, secondhand clothes, and tacky pop-culture paraphernalia; it's best to head to Camden Lock and Stable Markets. Though much of the merchandise is youth oriented, the markets have a lively appeal to aging hippies, fashion designers, and anyone with a taste for the bohemian who doesn't mind crowds and a bit of a madhouse scene. ⊠*Camden Town* ☺*Camden Market, Daily. 9–5:30; Camden Lock Market, Stables Market, and Canal Market, Daily 10–6; Electric Market, Sat. (most) 10–5, Sun. 9–5:30* Ⓤ*Camden Town, Chalk Farm.*

Covent Garden has craft stalls, jewelry designers, clothes makers, potters, and other artisans who congregate in the undercover central area known as the Apple Market. The Jubilee Market, toward Southampton Street, is less classy (printed T-shirts and the like), but on Monday the selection of vintage collectibles is worthwhile. This is more of a tourist magnet than other markets, and prices may reflect this. ⊠*The Piazza, Covent Garden* ☺*Daily 9–5* Ⓤ*Covent Garden.*

Fodor'sChoice ★ **Portobello Market,** London's most famous market, still wins the prize for the all-round best. There are 1,500 antiques dealers here, so bargains are still possible. Nearer Notting Hill Gate, prices and quality are highest; the middle is where locals buy fruit and vegetables and hang out in trendy restaurants. Under the Westway elevated highway is a great flea market, and more bric-a-brac and bargains appear as you walk toward Golborne Road. Take Bus 52 or the tube here, and arrive early to beat the crowds. ⊠ *Portobello Rd., Notting Hill* ⊙ *Fruit and vegetables Mon.–Wed. and Fri. 8–5, Thurs. 8–1; antiques Fri. 8–3; food market and antiques Sat. 6–4:30* Ⓤ *Ladbroke Grove, Notting Hill Gate.*

Spitalfields, The covered market (once London's wholesale meat market) is at the center of this area's boho revival. The original building has been restored to its Victorian splendor, and a modern shopping complex that respects its character has been developed around it, with a covered area housing additional stalls. Wares include crafts, retro clothing, handmade rugs, soap, and cakes. And, from Spanish tapas to Thai satays, it's possible to eat your way around the world. ⊠ *Brushfield St., East End* ⊙ *Stalls weekdays 10–4, Sun. 9–5; restaurants weekdays 11–11, Sun. 9–5, retail shops daily 11–7.* Ⓤ *Liverpool St., Aldgate, Aldgate East.*

The Southeast

WORD OF MOUTH

"Dover Castle is massive. It takes much of a day by itself. There is everything from a Roman lighthouse to World War II tunnels. It isn't just a castle on top of a hill; it is a huge complex. Even driving and parking right at the top of the cliff without having to travel up from the town, I have usually spent about 5 hours there."

—janisj

"There's lots to see in Southeast England. If you like history, there's Dover Castle and Fishbourne Roman Palace [near Chichester], Battle and Hastings, cute little Rye, and Bodiam and Leeds castles. A car is best to get around this area."

—Mimar

Updated
by Christi
Daugherty

Once you are away from the highways and commuter tract housing near London, the Southeast—including Surrey, Kent, and Sussex, East and West—reveals some of England's loveliest countryside. Gentle hills and woodlands are punctuated with farms and storybook villages rooted in history, and the area's cathedral cities, including noble Canterbury, wait patiently to be explored. Rivers wind down to a coast that is alternately sweeping chalk cliff and bustling seaside resort.

Where ancient hedgerows have been allowed to stand, this is still a landscape of small-scale features and pleasant hills. Viewed from the air, the tiny fields, neatly hedged, form a patchwork quilt. On the ground, fruit trees and even vineyards flourish in archetypal English landscapes and, often, atypical English sunshine.

Although it is close to London (both Surrey and Kent reach all the way to London's suburbs) and is one of the most densely populated areas of Britain, the Southeast includes Kent, the "Garden of England." Acre upon acre of orchards burst into a mass of pink-and-white blossoms in spring, though even here large-scale modern farming has done much to homogenize the landscape. In the Southeast, too, are ancient Canterbury, site of the mother cathedral of England, and Dover, whose chalky white cliffs and brooding castle have become symbols of Britain. Castles and stately homes, such as Petworth House and Knole, are major draws for travelers.

Famous seaside towns and resorts dot Sussex and Kent, the most famous being that eccentric combination of carnival and culture, Brighton. The busy ports of Newhaven, Folkestone, Dover, and Ramsgate have long been gateways to continental Europe. The Channel Tunnel, linking Britain to France by rail, runs from near Folkestone.

Indeed, because the English Channel is at its narrowest here, a great deal of British history has been forged in the Southeast. The Romans landed in this area and stayed to rule Britain for four centuries. So did the Saxons—Sussex means "the land of the South Saxons." The biggest invasion of them all took place here when William ("the Conqueror") of Normandy defeated the Saxons at a battle near Hastings in 1066, changing the island forever.

TOP REASONS TO GO

Bodiam, Dover, Hever, and Herstmonceux castles: Take your pick: the most evocative castles in a region filled with them dazzle you with their fortitude and fascinate you with their histories.

Brighton: With its nightclubs, sunbathing, and funky, relaxed atmosphere, this is the quintessential English seaside city. From the arcades of Brighton Pier to the fanciful rooms of the Royal Pavilion, there's something for everyone.

Canterbury Cathedral: This massive building, a textbook of medieval architecture, inspires awe with its soaring towers and flagstone corridors. The past seems very near in such places as Trinity Chapel, where ancient stained-glass windows celebrate Thomas à Becket's miracles.

Rye: Wandering the cobbled streets of this medieval town is a pleasure, and rummaging through its antiques stores is an adventure in itself. Reward yourself afterward as the English do, with tea and scones.

Treasure houses: Here is one of England's richest concentrations of historic homes: among the superlatives are Petworth House, with its luminous paintings by Turner; sprawling Knole, with its set of silver furniture; Ightham Mote, with its Tudor chapel; and Chartwell, home of Winston Churchill.

ORIENTATION AND PLANNING

GETTING ORIENTED

For sightseeing purposes, the Southeast can be divided into four sections. The eastern part of the region takes in the cathedral town of Canterbury, as well as the port city of Dover. The next section stretches along the southern coast from the medieval hill town of Rye to picturesque Lewes. A third area reaches from the coastal city of Brighton inward to Chichester and to sprawling Guildford. The fourth section takes in the spa town of Royal Tunbridge Wells and western Kent, where the farmland is dotted with stately homes and castles. Larger towns in the area can be easily reached by train or bus from London for a day trip. To visit most castles, grand country homes, or quiet villages, though, you will need to rent a car or join a tour.

Canterbury to Dover. Dover's distinctive white chalk cliffs plunging hundreds of feet into the sea are just a part of this region's dramatic coastal scenery. Don't miss Canterbury's medieval town center, dominated by its massive cathedral.

Rye to Lewes. Medieval villages dot the hills along this stretch of Sussex coastline. The centerpiece is Rye, a pretty hill town of cobbled streets lined with timbered homes. Lewes, with its crumbling castle, is another gem.

Brighton to Guildford. Funky, lively Brighton perfectly melds Victorian architecture with a modern vibe that includes the best shopping and dining on the coast. Outside of town you'll find beautiful old homes such as Petworth House and even a Roman villa.

Castles and Houses Near Tunbridge Wells. From Anne Boleyn's regal childhood abode at Hever Castle to the medieval manor at Ightham Mote, this area is rich with grand houses. Spend a couple of days exploring them; Tunbridge Wells is a comfortable base.

PLANNING

WHEN TO GO

The counties of Kent, Surrey, and Sussex offer marvelous scenic landscapes, and you'll want to get your fill of the many outdoor attractions. It's best to visit in the spring, summer, or early fall. Many privately owned castles and mansions are open only between April and September or October. Failing that, the great parks surrounding the stately houses are often open all year. If crowds tend to spoil your fun, avoid August, Sunday, and national holidays, particularly in Canterbury and the seaside towns.

PLANNING YOUR TIME

With the exception of Brighton, you can easily see the highlights of most of the towns in less than a day. Brighton has more to offer, and you should allot at least two days to take it all in. Consider basing yourself in one town while exploring a region. For example, you could stay in Brighton and take in Lewes on a day trip. Base yourself in Rye for a couple of days while exploring Winchelsea, Battle, Hastings, and Herstmonceux Castle. Tunbridge Wells is a great place to overnight if you plan on exploring stately homes and castles like Hever and Ightham Mote.

GETTING HERE AND AROUND

AIR TRAVEL

Heathrow is very convenient for Surrey, but Gatwick Airport is a more convenient gateway for Kent. The rail station inside Gatwick has trains to Brighton and other major towns, and you can take a taxi from Heathrow to Guildford for around £40.

BUS TRAVEL

National Express buses serve the region from London's Victoria Coach Station. Trips to Brighton and Canterbury take two hours; to Chichester, about three hours. Megabus runs buses at budget prices from Victoria Coach Station to many of the same destinations as National Express and can be cheaper, although luggage limits are strict.

Bus service between towns can be useful but can often be intermittent. Out in the country, don't expect buses more often than once every half hour or hour. Sometimes trains are a better option; sometimes they're much worse. Traveline is the best central place to call for bus information, and local Tourist Information Centres can help. Because more than one private bus company can operate in a region, it's best to start with Traveline.

The Southeast

ESSEX

LONDON

Around
Tunbridge Wells

Rochester

Broadstairs

Faversham

Great Bookham

Canterbury
see detail
map

Deal

Guildford   Dorking

SURREY

Royal
Tunbridge Wells

KENT

Dover

Canterbury to Dover

WEST
SUSSEX

EAST
SUSSEX

Battle
Winchelsea

Rye

Chichester Arundel

Lewes

Hastings

Brighton
to Guildford

Brighton
see detail
map

Wilmington

Rye to Lewes

0   5 miles

0   5 km

Contacts Megabus (⊕ www.megabus.co.uk). **National Express** (☏ 0871/781–8181 ⊕ www.nationalexpress.com). **Traveline** (☏ 0871/200–2233 ⊕ www. traveline.org.uk).

CAR TRAVEL

Traveling by car is the best way to get to the stately homes and castles in the region. Having a car in Canterbury or Brighton, however, is a nuisance; you'll need to park and walk. Major routes radiating outward from London to the Southeast are, from west to east, M23/A23 to Brighton (52 mi); A21, passing by Royal Tunbridge Wells to Hastings (65 mi); A20/M20 to Folkestone (58 mi); and A2/M2 via Canterbury (56 mi) to Dover (71 mi).

TRAIN TRAVEL

Trains are the fastest and most efficient way to travel to major cities in the region, but they do not stop in many small towns. From London, Southeastern trains serve Sussex and Kent from Victoria and Charing Cross stations, and South West trains travel to Surrey from Waterloo station. Getting to Brighton takes about 1 hour, to Canterbury about 1½ hours, and to Dover almost 2 hours. A Network Railcard costing £21, valid throughout the southern and southeastern regions for a year, entitles you and three companions to one-third off many off-peak fares.

Contacts National Rail Enquiries (☎ *0845/748–4950* ⊕ *www.nationalrail. co.uk*). **Network Railcard** (⊕ *www.railcard.co.uk*).

RESTAURANTS

If you're in a seaside town, look for that great British staple, fish-and-chips. Perhaps "look" isn't the word—just follow your nose. On the coast, seafood, much of it locally caught, is a specialty. Try local smoked fish (haddock and mackerel), or the succulent local oysters. Inland, sample fresh local lamb and beef. In cities such as Brighton and Tunbridge Wells there are numerous restaurants and cafés, but out in the countryside your options will be limited largely to pubs.

HOTELS

All around the coast, resort towns stretch along beaches, their hotels standing cheek by jowl. Of the smaller hotels and guesthouses only a few remain open year-round; most do business only from mid-April to September or October. Some hotels have all-inclusive rates for a week's stay. Prices rise in July and August, when the seaside resorts can get solidly booked, especially Brighton. (On the other hand, hotels may drop rates by up to 40% off season.) Places in Brighton may not take a booking for a single night in summer or on weekends.

WHAT IT COSTS IN POUNDS					
	£	££	£££	££££	£££££
Restaurants	Under £10	£10–£14	£15–£19	£20–£25	over £25
Hotels	Under £70	£70–£120	£121–£160	£161–£220	over £220

Restaurant prices are for a main course at dinner. Hotel prices are for two people in a standard double room in high season, including V.A.T., with no meals or, if indicated, CP (with continental breakfast), BP (Breakfast Plan, with full breakfast), or MAP (Modified American Plan, with breakfast and dinner).

VISITOR INFORMATION

Local Tourist Information Centres in the main towns can help with information and accommodations.

Contacts Southeast England Tourist Board (☎ *023/8062–5400* ⊕ *www. visitsoutheastengland.com*).

CANTERBURY TO DOVER

The cathedral city of Canterbury is an ancient place that has attracted travelers since the 12th century. Its magnificent cathedral, the Mother Church of England, remains a powerful draw. Even in prehistoric times, this part of England was relatively well settled. Saxon settlers, Norman conquerors, and the folk who lived here in late-medieval times all left their mark. From Canterbury there's rewarding wandering to be done in the gentle Kentish countryside between the city and the busy port of Dover. Here the landscape ravishes the eye in spring with apple blossoms, and in the autumn with lush fields ready for harvest. It is a county of orchards, market gardens, and round oasthouses with their tilted, pointed roofs; they were once used for drying hops, but now many are pricey homes.

CANTERBURY

56 mi southeast of London.

Just mention Canterbury, and most people are taken back to memories of high-school English classes and Geoffrey Chaucer's *Canterbury Tales,* about medieval pilgrims making their way to Canterbury Cathedral. Judging from the tales, however, in those days Canterbury was as much a party for people on horses as it was a spiritual center.

The city has been the seat of the Primate of All England, the Archbishop of Canterbury, since Pope Gregory the Great dispatched St. Augustine to convert the heathen hordes of Britain in 597. The height of Canterbury's popularity came in the 12th century, when thousands of pilgrims flocked here to see the shrine of the murdered archbishop St. Thomas à Becket. This southeastern town became one of the most-visited in England, if not Europe. Buildings that served as pilgrims' inns (and that survived World War II bombing of the city) still dominate the streets of Canterbury's center, though it's tourists who flock to this city of about 40,000 people today.

GETTING HERE AND AROUND

The fastest way to reach Canterbury from London is by train. Southeastern trains to Canterbury run every half hour in peak times from London's Charing Cross station. The journey takes around 1½ hours. Canterbury has two centrally located train stations, Canterbury East Station (a 5-minute walk from the cathedral square) and Canterbury West Station (a 10-minute walk from the cathedral).

National Express and Megabus buses bound for Canterbury depart several times a day from London's Victoria Coach Station. Trips to Canterbury take around 2 hours, and drop passengers near the train stations. If you're driving, take the A2/M2 to Canterbury from London (56 mi). Park in one of the signposted parking lots at the edge of the town center.

Canterbury has a small, walkable town center. Although the town has good local bus service, you're unlikely to need it. Most major tourist sites are on one street that changes name three times—beginning as St. George's Street and then becoming High Street and St. Peter's Street.

Canterbury Guild of Guides provides walking guides who have a specialized knowledge of the city and its surrounding area. Tours (£5) are at 2 PM every day between Easter and October, with an additional tour at 11:30 AM from Monday to Saturday during July and August.

TIMING

The town tends to get crowded around religious holidays—particularly Easter weekend—and on other national holiday weekends. If you'd rather avoid the tour buses, try visiting midweek.

ESSENTIALS
Visitor and Tour Information Canterbury (⊠ *12–13 Sun St.* ☎ *01227/378100*
⊕ *www.canterbury.co.uk).* **Canterbury Guild of Guides** (⊠ *Arnett House, Hawks*
La. ☎ *01227/459779* ⊕ *www.canterbury-walks.co.uk).*

EXPLORING

TOP ATTRACTIONS

4 Canterbury Cathedral. The focal point of the city was the first of England's great Norman cathedrals. Nucleus of worldwide Anglicanism, the Cathedral Church of Christ Canterbury (its formal name) is a living textbook of medieval architecture. The building was begun in 1070, demolished, begun anew in 1096, and then systematically expanded over the next three centuries. When the original choir section burned to the ground in 1174, another replaced it, designed in the new Gothic style, with tall, pointed arches. Don't miss the **North Choir aisle**, which holds two windows that show Jesus in the Temple, the three kings asleep, and Lot's wife turned to a pillar of salt. The windows are among the earliest parts of the cathedral, but only 33 of the original 208 survive.

Fodor'sChoice
★

The cathedral was only a century old, and still relatively small, when Thomas à Becket, the archbishop of Canterbury, was murdered here in 1170. Becket, a defender of ecclesiastical interests, had angered his friend Henry II, who was heard to exclaim, "Who will rid me of this troublesome priest?" Thinking they were carrying out the king's wishes, four knights burst in on Becket in one of the side chapels and killed him. Two years later Becket was canonized, and Henry II's subsequent submission to the authority of the church and his penitence helped establish the cathedral as the center of English Christianity.

Becket's tomb, destroyed by Henry VIII in 1538 as part of his campaign to reduce the power of the church and confiscate its treasures, was one of the most extravagant shrines in Christendom. In **Trinity Chapel,** which held the shrine, you can still see a series of 13th-century stained-glass windows illustrating Becket's miracles. So hallowed was this spot that in 1376, Edward, the Black Prince, warrior son of Edward III and a national hero, was buried near it. The actual site of Becket's murder is down a flight of steps just to the left of the nave. In the corner, a second flight of steps leads down to the enormous Norman **undercroft,** or vaulted cellarage, built in the early 12th century. A row of squat pillars whose capitals dance with animals and monsters supports the roof.

If time permits, be sure to explore the **cloisters** and other small monastic buildings to the north of the cathedral. The 12th-century octagonal water tower is still part of the cathedral's water supply. The Norman staircase in the northwest corner of the Green Court dates from 1167 and is a unique example of the domestic architecture of the times. The cathedral is very popular, so arrive early or late in the day to avoid the worst crowds. You can just walk around, or you can buy a guidebook with an overview of the building's history, use an audio guide for the most detail, or take a tour for the personal touch. ⊠ *Cathedral Precincts*
☎ *01227/762862* ⊕ *www.canterbury-cathedral.org* ⊠ *£7.50, free for*
services and ½ hr before closing; £5 for tour, £3.50 for audio guide

⊙ *Easter–Sept., Mon.–Sat. 9–6:30, Sun. 12:30–2:30 and 4:30–5:30; Oct.–Easter, Mon.–Sat. 9–5, Sun. 12:30–2:30. Restricted access during services.*

QUICK BITES

The Custard Tart (⊠ *35A St. Margaret's St.* ☎ *01227/785178*), a short walk from the cathedral, serves freshly made sandwiches, pies, tarts, and cakes. You can take your choice upstairs to the seating area. It's not open for dinner.

❶ Canterbury Roman Museum. Below ground, at the level of the remnants of Roman Canterbury, this museum features colorful mosaic Roman pavement and a hypocaust—the Roman version of central heating. Displays of excavated objects (some of which you can hold in the Touch the Past area) and computer-generated reconstructions of Roman buildings and the marketplace help re-create the past. ⊠ *Butchery La.* ☎ *01227/785575* ⊕ *www.canterbury-museums.co.uk* 💷 *£3.10; £6.40 combined ticket includes Museum of Canterbury and West Gate Museum* ⊙ *June–Oct., Mon.–Sat. 10–5, Sun. 1:30–5; Nov.–May, Mon.–Sat. 10–5; last admission at 4. Closed last wk in Dec.*

❿ Medieval city walls. For an essential Canterbury experience, follow the circuit of the 13th- and 14th-century walls, built on the line of the Roman walls. Those to the east survive intact, towering some 20 feet high and offering a sweeping view of the town. You can access these from a number of places, including Castle Street and Broad Street.

WORTH NOTING

② **Buttermarket.** Mercery Lane, with its medieval-style cottages and massive, overhanging timber roofs, runs off High Street and ends in the tiny Buttermarket, an old dairy market square with a sweet name and a dark past. Before the 16th century it was called "the Bullstake," because animals were tied here and tortured (a popular activity of the time known as "baiting") before they were slaughtered. Today it's surrounded by bars and restaurants.

⑤ **The Canterbury Tales.** It's a kitschy audiovisual (and occasionally olfactory) dramatization of 14th-century English life—touristy but popular. You'll "meet" Chaucer's pilgrims at the Tabard Inn near London and view tableaus illustrating five tales. In the summer, actors in period costume play out scenes from the town's history. ⊠*St. Margaret's St.* ☎*01227/479227* ⊕*www.canterburytales.org.uk* ☉*£7.75* ⊗*Nov.– Feb., daily 10–4:30; Mar.–June, Sept., and Oct., daily 10–5; July and Aug., daily 9:30–5.*

OFF THE BEATEN PATH

Chilham. The village square in the little town of Chilham, 5 mi southwest of Canterbury, is filled with textbook examples of English rural architecture, complete with gabled windows beneath undulating roofs. The church dates from the 14th century. ■TIP→**From this hilltop village, midway between Canterbury and Ashford on the A252 (off the A28), you can walk the last few miles of the traditional Pilgrim's Way back to Canterbury.**

③ **Christchurch Gate.** This immense gate, built in 1517, leads into the cathedral close. As you pass through, look up at the sculpted heads of two young figures: Prince Arthur, elder brother of Henry VIII, and the young Catherine of Aragon, to whom Arthur was betrothed. After Arthur's death, Catherine married Henry. Her failure to produce a male heir after 25 years of marriage led to Henry's decision to divorce her, creating an irrevocable breach with the Roman Catholic Church and altering the course of English history.

⑫ **Dane John Mound.** Just opposite the Canterbury East train station, this was originally part of the city defenses; now it's a park and a good place to unwind. There's a maze here, too.

⑦ **Eastbridge Hospital of St. Thomas.** The 12th-century building (which would now be called a hostel) lodged pilgrims who came to pray at the tomb of Thomas à Becket. It's a tiny place, fascinating in its simplicity. The refectory, the chapel, and the crypt are open to the public. ⊠*25 High St.* ☎*01227/462395* ⊕*www.eastbridgehospital.org.uk* ☉*£1* ⊗*Mon.– Sat. 10–5; last admission at 4:30.*

⑧ **Museum of Canterbury.** The medieval Poor Priests' Hospital is the site of this local museum, where exhibits provide an overview of the city's history and architecture from Roman times to World War II. It's a quirky place that covers everything and everyone associated with the town, including the Blitz, the mysterious death of the 16th-century writer Christopher Marlowe, and the British cartoon characters Bagpuss and Rupert Bear. ⊠*20 Stour St.* ☎*01227/475202* ⊕*www.canterbury-*

museums.co.uk ✉*£3.60; £6.40 combined ticket includes Canterbury Roman Museum and West Gate Museum* ⊙*Jan.–May, Oct.–Dec., Mon.–Sat. 10:30–5; June–Sept., Mon.–Sat. 10:30–5, Sun. 1:30–5; last admission at 4.*

⓫ **St. Augustine's Abbey.** Augustine, England's first Christian missionary, was buried here in 597, at one of the oldest monastic sites in the country. The site remained intact for nearly 1,000 years, until Henry VIII seized the abbey in the 16th century, destroying some of the original buildings and converting others into a royal manor for his fourth wife, Anne of Cleves. A free interactive audio tour vividly puts events into context. ✉*Longport* ☎*01227/767345* ⊕*www.english-heritage.org. uk* ✉*£4.30* ⊙*Apr.–June, Wed.–Sun. 10–5; July and Aug. daily 10–6; Sept.–Mar., Sun. 11–5.*

❻ **Weavers' Houses.** Huguenot weavers who settled here after fleeing from religious persecution in France occupied this lopsided group of 16th-century half-timber buildings. The houses are just past where St. Peter's Street crosses a branch of the River Stour. ✉*St. Peter's St.*

❾ **West Gate Museum.** Only one of the city's seven medieval gatehouses
☾ survives, complete with twin castellated towers; it now contains this museum. Inside are medieval bric-a-brac and armaments used by the city guard, as well as more contemporary weaponry. The building became a jail in the 14th century, and you can view the prison cells. ■ **TIP**➡**Climb to the roof for a panoramic view of the city.** ✉*St. Peter's St.* ☎*01227/789576* ⊕*www.canterbury-museums.co.uk* ✉*£1.30; £6.40 combined ticket includes Canterbury Roman Museum and Museum of Canterbury* ⊙*Mon.–Sat. 11–12:30 and 1:30–3:30; last admission 1 hr before closing.*

WHERE TO EAT

£   ✕**City Fish Bar.** Long lines and lots of satisfied finger-licking attest to
BRITISH   the deserved popularity of this excellent fish-and-chips outlet in the center of town. Everything is freshly fried, the batter crisp and the fish tasty; the fried mushrooms are also surprisingly good. There's no seating, so your fish is wrapped up in paper and you eat it where you want, perhaps in the park. This place closes at 7. ✉*30 St. Margaret's St.* ☎*01227/760873* ▭*No credit cards.*

££   ✕**The Goods Shed.** Next to Canterbury West station, this vaulted wooden
BRITISH   space with exposed stone and brick walls was a storage shed in Victorian times. Now it's a farmers' market with a restaurant that has wooden tables and huge curved windows overlooking the market and a butchers' stall. It offers a foodie's feast of the best Kentish food—from freshly caught fish and smoked meats to local cider and bread baked in-house. The menu varies with the availability of the local produce. ✉*Station Rd. W* ☎*01227/459153* ▭*MC, V* ⊙*Closed Mon. No dinner Sun.*

££££   ✕**Michael Caines.** Canterbury's most-sought-after tables are at Michael
MODERN FRENCH   Caines (named not for the actor, but for the chef with a similar name).
Fodor'sChoice   This light-filled eatery in the trendy Abode Canterbury, with its pine
★   tables, white walls, and cashing country style, packs in the foodies. Modern French cuisine is the main attraction—true aficionados will reserve the chef's table in the kitchen to watch the staff in action.

Try the marinated foie gras with apple jelly, and then move on to the peppercorn-crusted duck breast cassoulet. The seven-course tasting menu (£55) is great for special occasions. There's a glass-enclosed wine room and an adjoining champagne bar, ensuring that the wine is as good as the food. ⊠*High St.* ☎*01227/766266* ⚑*Reservations essential* ☰*AE, DC, MC, V.*

££   ✕**Old Brewery Tavern.** Although it's part of a hotel, this pub has a sepa-
BRITISH   rate entrance leading to a room with polished floors, wooden tables, and whitewashed stone. The menu and kitchen are overseen by top chef Michael Caines, so it's a good place to try his food without paying as much as you would at his flagship restaurant in the hotel (a two-course lunch is £8). The atmosphere is relaxed and casual, except on weekend nights when the music gets turned up for the party crowd. Expect reliably good comfort food—juicy burgers, excellent fish pie, flavorful lamb stew. There are daily specials and a roast on Sunday. The courtyard is perfect for alfresco dining. ⊠*Abode Canterbury, High St.* ☎*01227/826682* ☰*AE, MC, V.*

WHERE TO STAY

££–£££   🏨**Abode Canterbury.** This glossy boutique hotel inside the old city walls brought an up-to-date style to traditional Canterbury. The good-size rooms, modern but not minimal, are classed as Comfortable, Desirable, and Enviable. Enviable rooms have the most space and extras like wood floors, sitting areas, and nibbles. Even Comfortable rooms are nicely designed with soft bedding in neutral colors, although most have no view. Michael Caines is one of the town's top restaurants because of its elegant atmosphere and French-influenced cuisine. The Old Brewery Tavern, an upscale pub, serves less expensive meals, and there's a champagne bar. **Pros:** central location; luxurious handmade beds; great restaurants and bars. **Cons:** one of the priciest hotels in town; bar gets quite crowded. ⊠*High St.* ☎*01227/766266* ⊕*www.abodehotels. co.uk* ⚑*73 rooms* ⚐*In-room: DVD (some) Internet. In-hotel: 2 restaurants, bar, laundry service, parking (paid), no-smoking rooms* ☰*AE, DC, MC, V.*

£–££   🏨**Cathedral Gate Hotel.** Older even than the adjoining cathedral gateway, this hotel was built as a hostelry for pilgrims in 1438. The large beams, sloping floors, and twisting corridors are evidence of its medieval origins; the plainly furnished rooms, however, have been sympathetically modernized, although it's nothing too fancy. You'll pay the lowest price if you're willing to share a bathroom. The bow-window restaurant looks out over the Buttermarket. A full English breakfast costs an extra £7. **Pros:** like stepping back in time; affordable rates. **Cons:** not all rooms have private baths; creaky floors; full breakfast is extra. ⊠*36 Burgate* ☎*01227/464381* ⊕*www.cathgate.co.uk* ⚑*27 rooms, 12 with bath* ⚐*In-room: no a/c. In-hotel: restaurant, bar, some pets allowed* ☰*AE, DC, MC, V* ⦿*CP.*

££   🏨**Ebury Hotel.** Family-run, this hotel earns raves for its laid-back attitude and comfortable rooms. Made up of two big Victorian buildings a 10-minute walk from central Canterbury, it has been sympathetically converted. Rooms are simply decorated but good size (bathrooms can be a bit tiny), and beds are firm. The cozy lounge has a wood-burning fireplace, and the indoor pool is perfect for hot days. The hotel's old-fashioned look is not for everyone, but if you like the kind of inn that has a house Labradoodle, it's perfect. Ask for a room on the lower floors if you have mobility problems. **Pros:** cozy lounge; comfortable rooms. **Cons:** a bit of a walk to the town center; no elevator. ✉*65–67 New Dover Rd.* ☎*01227/768433* ⊕*www.ebury-hotel.co.uk* ↩*15 rooms* ⌂*In-room: no a/c. In-hotel: restaurant, bar, pool* ▤*MC, V* ⦿|*BP.*

££–£££   🖼 **Magnolia House.** This bed-and-breakfast in a Georgian house is charmingly elegant, with a lovely walled garden. Bedrooms have floral motifs and traditional furnishings; one has a four-poster. Evening meals are available from November to February by prior arrangement. The location is a 10-minute walk from the center of town. To get here, follow St. Dunstan's Street until London Road and take a left; it will be three blocks on the right side. **Pros:** adorable house; friendly atmosphere; good dinners. **Cons:** a bit of a walk to the town center; some rooms are smaller than others; no elevator. ✉*36 St. Dunstan's Terr.* ☎*01227/765121* ⊕*www.magnoliahousecanterbury.co.uk* ↩*7 rooms* ⌂*In-room: no a/c, no phone, Wi-Fi. In-hotel: no kids under 12, no-smoking rooms* ▤*AE, DC, MC, V* ⦿|*BP.*

££   🖼**The White House.** Reputed to have been the place in which Queen Victoria's head coachman came to live upon retirement, this handsome Regency building on a quiet road off St. Peter's Street sits between the city center and Canterbury West train station. Guest rooms are decorated in pastel shades, and a few are large enough for four people. **Pros:** historic house; spacious rooms; family-friendly atmosphere. **Cons:** a bit outside the center; no restaurant; no elevator. ✉*6 St. Peter's La.* ☎*01227/761836* ⊕*www.canterburybreaks.co.uk* ↩*9 rooms* ⌂*In-room: no phone. In-hotel: bar, no-smoking rooms* ▤*No credit cards* ⦿|*BP.*

NIGHTLIFE AND THE ARTS

NIGHTLIFE   Canterbury is home to a popular university, and the town's many pubs and bars are busy, often crowded with college-age folks. **Alberry's Wine Bar** (✉*St. Margaret's St.* ☎*01227/452378*), with late-night jazz and hip-hop and a trendy crowd, is the coolest place in town. The **Parrot** (✉*3–9 Church La.* ☎*01227/762355*) is a pub known for its real ales—at least six kinds are available at any time—and its convivial setting in an old wood-beam building. **Thomas Becket** (✉*21 Best La.* ☎*01227/464384*), a traditional English pub, has a fire crackling in the winter, copper pots hanging from the ceiling, and a friendly crowd.

THE ARTS   The two-week-long, mixed-arts **Canterbury Festival** (☎*01227/452853* ⊕*www.canterburyfestival.co.uk*) is held every October. The **Gulbenkian Theatre** (✉*Giles La.* ☎*01227/769075*), outside the town center at the University of Kent, mounts all kinds of plays, particularly experimental works, and is a venue for dance performances, concerts, comedy shows, and films. The **Marlowe** (✉*St. Margaret's St.* ☎*01227/787787*) theater is closed for renovation through 2010, but productions are being staged around town.

Canterbury
to Dover

SHOPPING

Hawkin's Bazaar (✉*34 Burgate* ☎*01227/785809*) carries an exceptional selection of traditional and modern toys and games.

FAVERSHAM

9 mi west of Canterbury.

In Roman times Faversham was a thriving seaport. Today the port is long gone, and all that is left is a waterway at the edge of town known as the Creek. Still, Faversham is a worthwhile stop for those in search of Ye Quaint Olde Englande. The town center, with its Tudor houses grouped around the 1574 guildhall and covered market, looks like a stage set. There are few actual sights here, as such, but it's a lovely place to take a break and have a stroll. You can reserve a tour of the Shepherd Neame brewery, near the heart of town; the visitor center is at 11 Court Street.

ESSENTIALS

Visitor Information Faversham (✉*Fleur de Lis Heritage Centre, 13 Preston St.* ☎*01795/534542* ⊕ *www.faversham.org*).

WHERE TO EAT AND STAY

££££ ✗**Read's.** The glorious food in this elegant "restaurant with rooms"
BRITISH is assuredly British but puts an audacious spin on old favorites. The
★ accent falls firmly on local ingredients, many of which come from the
vegetable garden (in which you are welcome to stroll). After a main
course of Kentish lamb in a fresh herb crust with mini–shepherd's pie,
try the "chocoholics anonymous" dessert. Prices are fixed, with three-
course lunch options at £24 and a three-course dinner costing £52.
Cream linens and tall candlesticks decorate the tables in the cream-
color dining room, where large windows overlook the grounds; there
are also six traditionally decorated Georgian guest rooms. ⊠*Macknade
Manor, Canterbury Rd.* ☎*01795/535344* ▤*AE, DC, MC, V* ⊘*Closed
Sun. and Mon.*

£ 🍴**Sun Inn.** A pretty, clapboard pub dating to the 1400s, this traditional
place still follows the old tradition of hanging up hops in September. Their pleasant, wheaty scent fills the room, a nice accompaniment
to the Kentish ales and lagers of the local Shepherd Neame brewery.
Guest rooms are neatly done in neutral colors and are well priced giv-
en the quality. **Pros:** rooms are sunny and light; comfy beds. **Cons:**
downstairs pub can be a bit noisy. ⊠*10 West St.* ☎*01795/535098*
⊕*www.sunfaversham.co.uk* ⇨*9 rooms* ⌂*In-room: no a/c. In-hotel:
restaurant, bar* ▤*MC, V* ⏐○⏐*BP.*

££ 🍴**White Horse Inn.** Mentioned in Chaucer's *Canterbury Tales,* this
ancient coaching inn outside Faversham on the old London-to-Dover
road retains much of its traditional character. The pale blue guest rooms
have antique furniture. In addition to the friendly bar, there's an excellent restaurant in what used to be a courtroom; you might find shark
steak on the list of mostly classic British daily specials. **Pros:** pretty
decor; great for antiques lovers. **Cons:** bar can be a bit crowded; outside Faversham. ⊠*The Street, Boughton* ☎*01227/751343* ⊕*www.
whitehorsecanterbury.co.uk* ⇨*13 rooms* ⌂*In-room: no a/c. In-hotel:
restaurant, bar* ▤*AE, MC, V* ⏐○⏐*BP.*

BROADSTAIRS

25 mi east of Faversham, 17 mi east of Canterbury.

Like other Victorian seaside towns such as Margate and Ramsgate on
this stretch of coast, Broadstairs was once the playground of vacation-
ing Londoners. Charles Dickens spent many summers here between
1837 and 1851 and wrote glowingly of its bracing freshness. Today
grand 19th-century houses line the waterfront. In the off-season Broadstairs is a peaceful retreat, but day-trippers pack the town in July and
August.

Park your car in one of the town lots, and strike out for the crescent
beach or wander down the residential Victorian streets. Make your
way down to the amusement pier and try your hand in one of the game
arcades. You can grab fish-and-chips to go and eat it on the beach.

ESSENTIALS

Visitor Information Broadstairs (⊠*6B High St.* ☎*01843/583334* ⊕*www.
broadstairs.gov.uk).*

EXPLORING

The cliff overlooking Viking Bay is dominated by a stern structure long known as **Bleak House.** This was one of Dickens's homes, and it was here that he wrote *David Copperfield* and drafted the novel *Bleak House.* A fire tore through the privately owned building in 2006, doing significant damage. Since then the interior has been closed to visitors, though the owners plan to reopen. ⊠ *Fort Rd.* ⊕ *www.bleakhouse.info.*

What is now the **Dickens House Museum** was originally the home of Mary Pearson Strong, on whom Dickens based the character of Betsey Trotwood, David Copperfield's aunt. It's a funny little place, with a reconstruction of Miss Trotwood's room as described by Dickens, a few objects that once belonged to the Dickens family, and prints and photographs commemorating the author's association with Broadstairs. ⊠ *2 Victoria Parade* ☎ *01843/861232 or 01843/863453* ⊕ *www. dickensfellowship.org/DHMB.htm* ⊡ *£3.50* ⊙ *Apr.–Oct., daily 2–5.*

WHERE TO STAY

£–££ ⊡ **Number 68.** Charming accommodations and a friendly atmosphere are the pluses of this sweet Edwardian house a five-minute walk from central Broadstairs. The three guest rooms are individually decorated with unobtrusive themes (French, Seaside, Chinese), and puffy white comforters top the comfortable beds. Breakfasts, made to order, range from the meaty English variety to lighter croissants and fruit. In high season a minimum two-night stay is required, and there is a minimum 50% penalty for any cancellation. **Pros:** attractive rooms; close to the sea; tasty breakfasts. **Cons:** minimum stay required; tough cancellation policy. ⊠ *68 West Cliff Rd.* ☎ *01843/609459* ⊕ *www.number68.co.uk* 🛏 *3 rooms* ⟁ *In-room: no a/c, no phone. In hotel: no kids under 11, no smoking rooms* ⊟ *No credit cards* ⦿ *BP.*

NIGHTLIFE AND THE ARTS

Each June Broadstairs holds a **Dickens Festival** (☎ *01843/865265* ⊕ *www. broadstairsdickensfestival.co.uk*), lasting about a week, with readings, people in Dickensian costume, a Dickensian cricket match, a Victorian bathing party, and vaudeville, among other entertainments.

DEAL

18 mi south of Broadstairs.

The large seaside town of Deal, known for its castle, is famous in history books as the place where Caesar's legions landed in 55 BC, and it was from here that William Penn set sail in 1682 on his first journey to the American colony he founded, Pennsylvania.

EXPLORING

Deal Castle, erected in 1540 and intricately built to the shape of a Tudor rose, is the largest of the coastal defenses constructed by Henry VIII. A moat surrounds its gloomy passages and austere walls. The castle museum has exhibits about prehistoric, Roman, and Saxon Britain. ⊠ *Victoria Rd.* ☎ *01304/372762* ⊕ *www.english-heritage.org.uk* ⊡ *£4.30* ⊙ *Apr.–Sept., daily 10–6.*

Walmer Castle and Gardens, one of Henry VIII's fortifications, was converted in 1708 into a residence for the lord warden. Among the famous lord wardens were William Pitt the Younger; the duke of Wellington, hero of the Battle of Waterloo, who lived here from 1829 until his death here in 1852 (a small museum contains memorabilia); and Sir Winston Churchill. Except for when the lord warden is in residence, the drawing and dining rooms are open to the public, and attractive gardens and a grassy walk fill what was the moat. ⊠ *A258, 1 mi south of Deal* ☎ *01304/364288* ⊕ *www.english-heritage.org.uk* ⊡ *£6.50* ⊗ *Mar., Wed.–Sun. 10–4; Apr.–Sept., daily 10–6; Oct., Wed.–Sun. 10–4.*

> ## HENRY VIII'S CASTLES
>
> Why did Henry VIII rapidly (1539–42) build sturdy forts along the southern coast? After enraging the pope and Europe's Catholic monarchs with his marriages and by seizing control of the wealthy monasteries, he prepared for a possible invasion. It did not come. Today you can bike or walk along the beachfront between Deal and Walmer castles.

DOVER

8 mi south of Deal, 78 mi east of London.

The busy passenger port of Dover has for centuries been Britain's gateway to Europe and is known for the famous White Cliffs. You may find the town itself a bit disappointing; the savage bombardments of World War II and the shortsightedness of postwar developers left the city center an unattractive place. Roman legacies include a lighthouse adjoining a stout Anglo-Saxon church.

GETTING HERE AND AROUND

National Express buses depart from London's Victoria Coach Station for Dover every hour and a half. The journey takes about 2 hours and 40 minutes. Drivers from London take the M20, which makes a straight line south to Dover. The 76-mi journey should take around two hours. Southeastern trains leave London's Charing Cross station every 20 minutes or so for Dover Priory station in Dover. The trip is an hour and 45 minutes.

For the best views of the cliffs, you need a car or taxi; it's a long way to walk.

ESSENTIALS

Visitor Information Dover (⊠ *The Old Town Gaol, Biggin St.* ☎ *01304/205108*).

EXPLORING

★ Plunging hundreds of feet into the sea, Dover's chalk **White Cliffs** are an inspirational site and a symbol of England. They stay white because of the natural process of erosion. Because of this, you must be cautious when walking along the cliffs. Experts recommend staying at least 20 feet from the edge. The best places to see the cliffs are at Samphire Hoe, St. Margaret's Bay, or East Cliff & Warren Country Park. Signs will direct you from the roads to scenic spots. ■ TIP→ **The visitor center at**

Langdon Cliffs on Upper Road introduces you to the area and has 5 mi of walking trails with some spectacular views.

☺ Spectacular and with plenty to explore, **Dover Castle,** towering high
★ above the ramparts of the White Cliffs, was a mighty medieval castle, and it has served as an important strategic center over the centuries, even in World War II. Most of the castle, including the keep, dates to Norman times. It was begun by Henry II in 1181 but incorporates additions from almost every succeeding century. There's a lot to see besides the castle rooms: among the exhibits, many of which will appeal to kids, are the Siege of 1216, the Princess of Wales Regimental Museum, and Castle Fit for a King. ■TIP→**Take time to tour the secret wartime tunnels (timed ticket needed), a medieval and Napoleonic-era system that was used as a World War II command center during the evacuation of Dunkirk in 1940.** ⊠*Castle Rd.* ☏*01304/211067* ⊕*www.english-heritage.org.uk* ☑*£10* ☺*Feb. and Mar., daily 10–4; Apr.–Sept., daily 10–6; Oct., daily 10–5; Nov.–Jan., Thurs.–Mon. 10–4.*

The **Roman Painted House,** believed to have been a hotel, includes some wall paintings, along with the remnants of an ingenious heating system. ⊠*New St.* ☏*01304/203279* ☑*£3.80* ☺*Apr.–Sept., Tues.–Sat. 10–5, Sun. 1–5.*

WHERE TO STAY

£ ⌂**Number One Guest House.** One of the best bargains in the area is this family-run guesthouse. Wallpapers and porcelain collections decorate the cozy corner terrace home built in the early 19th century, and you can even have breakfast in your room. The walled garden has a fine view of the castle. **Pros:** affordable rates; breakfast in bed. **Cons:** rooms are small. ⊠*1 Castle St.* ☏*01304/202007* ⊕*www.number1guesthouse. co.uk* ⌨*4 rooms* ⌂*In-room: no a/c, no phone. In-hotel: parking (paid)* ▤*No credit cards* ◎*BP.*

RYE TO LEWES

From Dover the coast road winds west through Folkestone (a genteel resort, small port, and Channel Tunnel terminal), across Romney Marsh (reclaimed from the sea and famous for its sheep and, at one time, its ruthless smugglers), and on to the delightful medieval town of Rye. The region along the coast is noted for Winchelsea, the history-rich sites of Hastings and Herstmonceux, and the Glyndebourne Opera House festival, based outside Lewes, a town celebrated for its architectural heritage. One of the three steam railroads in the Southeast services part of the area: the Romney, Hythe, and Dymchurch Railway.

RYE

★ *68 mi southeast of London, 34 mi southwest of Dover.*

With cobbled streets and ancient timbered dwellings, Rye is an artist's dream. It was an important port town until the harbor silted up and the waters retreated more than 150 years ago; now the nearest harbor is 2 mi away. The village of Rye begins where the sea once lapped at

Rye to Lewes

its ankles, and winds its way to the top of a low hill that overlooks the Romney Marshes and the old seabed. Virtually every building in the little town center is intriguingly old. Rye is known for its many antiques stores and also for its sheer pleasantness. This place can be easily walked without a map, but if you prefer guidance, the local tourist office has an interesting audio tour of the town as well as maps.

GETTING HERE AND AROUND

If you're driving to Rye, take the M20 to A2070. There's no direct route by train; take a Southeastern train from Charing Cross or Victoria Station to Ashford and change for the Rye train, which runs every hour or so.

ESSENTIALS

Visitor Information Rye (✉ *The Heritage Centre, Strand Quay* 🕾 *01797/ 226696* ⊕ *www.rye-tourism.co.uk*).

EXPLORING

The diminutive **Rye Castle Museum**, below the remains of the castle wall, displays watercolors and examples of Rye pottery, for which the town was famous. ✉ *3 East St.* 🕾 *01797/226728* ⊕ *www.ryemuseum.co.uk* 💷 *£1.90, £2.90 includes Ypres Tower* ⊘ *Apr.–Oct., Thurs.–Mon. 2–5, weekends 10:30–1 and 2–5; last admission 30 mins before closing.*

At the top of the hill at the center of Rye, the **Church of St. Mary the Virgin** is more than 900 years old. A classic English village church, it encompasses a number of architectural styles. The turret clock dates to 1561 and still keeps excellent time. Its huge pendulum swings inside the church nave. ■ TIP➜ **You can climb the tower to see amazing views.** ✉ *Church Sq.* ⊘ *Daily 10–4.*

Mermaid Street is one of the original cobbled streets that heads steeply from the top of the hill to the former harbor. Its name, according to local lore, came from the night a sailor who had sipped a few too many walked down it. He swore he heard a mermaid call him down to the sea. Do take a stroll here to see the many ancient buildings that make it one of the town's most scenic streets.

Down the hill past Church Square, **Ypres Tower** was originally built as part of the town's fortifications (now largely gone) in 1249; it later served as a prison. The stone chambers hold a rather random collection of local items, such as smuggling bric-a-brac and shipbuilding mementos. ⊠ *Gungarden* ☎ *01797/226728* 🖙 *£1.90, £2.90 includes Rye Castle Museum* ⊙ *Apr.–Oct., Thurs.–Mon. 10:30–1 and 2–5; Nov.–Mar., weekends 10:30–3:30; last admission 30 mins before closing.*

Something about **Lamb House,** an early-18th-century dwelling, attracts writers. The novelist Henry James lived here from 1898 to 1916. E. F. Benson, onetime mayor of Rye and author of the witty *Lucia* novels (written in the 1920s and 1930s, with some set in a town based on Rye; worth a read), was a later resident. The ground-floor rooms contain some of James's furniture and personal belongings. ⊠ *West St.* ☎ *01892/890651* ⊕ *www.nationaltrust.org.uk* 🖙 *£3.80* ⊙ *Apr.–Oct., Thurs. and Sat. 2–6; last admission at 5:30.*

Several miles north of Rye, **Tenterden Vineyard** is one of Britain's leading wine producers. The Chapel Down wines have won awards, including one for a sparkling wine. You must join a one-hour guided tour to view the grounds, after which you are free to peruse the herb garden, plant center, shop, and the restaurant, the Grapevine Bistro. ⊠ *Off B2082, Small Hythe* ☎ *01580/763033* ⊕ *www.englishwinesgroup.co.uk* 🖙 *£7 tour* ⊙ *June–Sept., daily 10–5; May and Oct., weekends 10–5.*

WHERE TO EAT AND STAY

£££ ✕**Fish Café.** One of Rye's most popular restaurants occupies a brick
SEAFOOD building that dates to 1907, but the interior has been redone in a sleek, modern style. The ground-floor café has a relaxed atmosphere, and upstairs is a more formal dining room. Most of the seafood here is caught nearby, so it's very fresh. Try modern dishes such as Mediterranean fish stew with tomato and basil, lemon sole with cauliflower purée, or squid-ink risotto. Reservations are recommended for dinner. ⊠ *17 Tower St.* ☎ *08710/756316* 🖃 *DC, MC, V* ⊙ *Closed Mon. Oct.– Apr. No dinner Sun.*

££ ⌂**Jeake's House.** Antiques fill the cozy bedrooms of this rambling 1689 house. The snug, painted-and-paneled parlor has a wood-burning stove for cold days. Breakfast, which might include deviled kidneys or kippers, is served in a galleried room formerly used for Quaker meetings. Rooms are 20% cheaper from November to March. **Pros:** charming atmosphere; delicious breakfasts; winter discounts. **Cons:** Mermaid Street is steep and cobbled; books up far in advance. ⊠ *Mermaid St.* ☎ *01797/222828* ⊕ *www.jeakeshouse.com* 🖘 *11 rooms, 10 with bath* ⌂ *In-room: no a/c. In-hotel: bar, some pets allowed, no kids under 8* 🖃 *MC, V* ⍾⏅*BP.*

££££ ⌂**The Mermaid.** Once the headquarters of a smuggling gang, this classic half-timber inn has been in business for nearly six centuries. Sloping floors, oak beams, low ceilings, and a huge open hearth in the bar testify to its roots in the 15th century (some parts date back to the 12th century). Rooms vary in size; some have nice touches like four-posters. The decor is a bit dated for the price, but the history keeps the crowds coming in. The main restaurant allows you to soak up the period details while choosing from an extensive English menu. **Pros:** the city's most historic hotel; full of period charm; good restaurant. **Cons:** some parts need refurbishment; some rooms are bigger than others; it's allegedly haunted. ✉*Mermaid St.* ☎*01797/223065* ⊕*www.mermaidinn.com* ⇆*31 rooms* ♿*In-room: no a/c. In-hotel: restaurant, bar* ⊟*AE, MC, V* ⲓ⊙|*BP.*

£££ ⬚**White Vine House Hotel.** Occupying a building from the late 1500s (although the cellar is two centuries older), this small guesthouse has a traditional feel. Bedrooms pleasantly mix antiques and reproductions; some have four-poster beds, others have pretty headboards. The lounges are wood paneled and have warming fireplaces. In the downstairs restaurant (no dinner Monday and Tuesday) you can sample excellent British cuisine from local sources, including lamb and Rye bay scallops. Two-night stays are expected on weekends in high season. **Pros:** beautiful building; soothing neutral-tone decor; a fireplace to warm your toes; pampering touches such as organic toiletries. **Cons:** a little too quiet for some; minimum stay on weekends. ✉*24 High St.* ☎*01797/224748* ⊕*www.whitevinehouse.co.uk* ⇆*7 rooms* ♿*In-room: no a/c, no phone, DVD, Wi-Fi. In-hotel: restaurant* ⊟*MC, V* ⲓ⊙|*BP.*

SHOPPING

Rye has great antiques shops, perfect for an afternoon of rummaging, with the biggest cluster at the foot of the hill near the tourist information center. **Black Sheep Antiques** (✉*72 The Mint* ☎*01797/224508*) has a superior selection of antique crystal and silver. **Collectors Corner** (✉*2 Market Rd.* ☎*01797/225796*) sells a good mix of furniture, art, and silver.

David Sharp Pottery (✉*55 The Mint* ☎*01797/222620*) specializes in the ceramic name plaques that are a feature of the town.

WINCHELSEA

2 mi southwest of Rye, 71 mi southeast of London.

Like Rye, Winchelsea perches prettily atop its own small hill amid farmland. Its historic houses, some with clapboards, are surrounded with lush flower gardens. Look for the splendid (though damaged) church built in the 14th century with Caen stone from Normandy. This was once a walled town, and some of the original town gates still stand. Winchelsea was built on a grid system devised in 1283, after the sea destroyed an earlier settlement at the foot of the hill. The sea later receded, leaving the town high and dry.

WHERE TO STAY

££ ⬚**The New Inn.** In the heart of town, this 18th-century hostelry is an excellent place to stop for a pub lunch or a bed for the night. The quiet, refurbished rooms are modest but have deep-pile carpets and pleasant views. A bar serves up juicy roasts and quaffable cask ales, and there's a warming log fire. **Pros:** great views; good restaurant. **Cons:** rooms are a bit small; not many amenities. ✉*German St.* ☎*01797/226252* ⊕*www.thenewinnwinchelsea.co.uk* ⇆*6 rooms* ♿*In-room: no a/c, no phone. In-hotel: restaurant* ⊟*AE, MC, V* ⲓ⊙|*BP.*

HASTINGS

9 mi southwest of Winchelsea, 68 mi southeast of London.

Big and sprawling, this Victorian seaside town will always be associated with the 1066 Norman invasion, when William, duke of Normandy, landed his troops at Pevensey Bay and was met by King Harold's army. A vicious battle ensued. Though it was called the Battle of Hastings, the skirmish actually took place 6 mi away at a town now called, well, Battle. Harold's troops had just successfully fended off the Vikings near York and marched across the country to take on the Normans. Utterly exhausted, Harold never stood a chance, and William became known as William the Conquerer.

In the 19th century Hastings became one of England's many popular resorts. Tall row houses painted in lemony hues cover the cliffs around the deep blue sea, and the views from the hilltops are extraordinary. The old town, east of the amusement pier, offers a glimpse into the city's 16th-century past. It has been through difficult times in recent decades, and the town developed a reputation as a rough place. However, gentrification has encouraged a climb back to respectability. All visitors may notice, though, is that it's a handsome place, and the seafront has all the usual English accoutrements—fish-and-chips shops, candy stores, shops selling junk, miniature golf, and rocky beaches that stretch for miles.

> ## BEACH HUTS
>
> As English as clotted cream, rows of tiny, cheerfully painted, one-room wooden beach huts brighten the shoreline in Sussex (look for them at the edges of Hastings and Brighton) and elsewhere. The huts originated in the Victorian wheeled bathing machines that were rolled into the water so that women could swim modestly behind them. Eventually the wheels came off, and they and similar structures became favored for storage and as a windbreak. Many huts lack electricity or plumbing but are beloved for their adorableness. Some are rented; others are owned, and prices can be high.

ESSENTIALS

Visitor Information Hastings (✉ *Queens Sq., Priory Meadow* ☎ *01424/781111* ✉ *2 The Stade* ☎ *01424/781111* ⊕ *www.visithastings.com*).

EXPLORING

☺ Take the West Hill Cliff Railway from George Street precinct to the atmospheric ruins of the Norman fortress now known as **Hastings Castle,** built by William the Conqueror in 1069. All that remains are fragments of the fortifications, some ancient walls, and a number of gloomy dungeons. Nevertheless, you get an excellent view of the chalky cliffs, the rocky coast, and the town below. The 1066 Story retells the Norman invasion in a film and display aimed largely at kids. ✉ *West Hill* ☎ *01424/781112* ⊕ *www.discoverhastings.co.uk* ✉ *£3.75* ✆ *Easter–Sept., daily 10–5; Oct.–Easter, daily 11–3; last admission 30 mins before closing.*

☼ Waxworks and exhibits recall the history of smuggling at **Smuggler's Adventure,** in a labyrinth of caves and passages a 5- or 10-minute walk above Hastings Castle. You can spend about an hour here. ✉ *St. Clement Caves* ☏ *01424/422964* ⊕ *www.smugglersadventure.co.uk* 💷 *£7* ☉ *Easter–Sept., daily 10–5:30; Oct.–Easter, daily 11–4:30; last admission 30 mins before closing.*

Below the East Cliff in the Stade, tall, black wooden towers called **net shops,** unique to the town, are still used for drying fishermen's nets and for selling fresh seafood.

Carr Taylor Vineyards are well known locally for their traditional methods of bottled fermentation, also known as *Méthode Champenoise.* The store also stocks fruit wines, ranging from strawberry to apricot, and mead—a wine of medieval origin—made following the *very* sweet Carr Taylor recipe with fermented grapes, apple juice, and honey. Take the A21 north from Hastings for 3 mi, turn onto the A28, and follow the signs. ✉ *Westfield, Hastings* ☏ *01424/752501* ⊕ *www.carr-taylor. co.uk* 💷 *Free* ☉ *Daily 10–5; closed last wk of Dec.*

WHERE TO EAT AND STAY

£ ✕ **Blue Dolphin.** The crowds line up all day to make their way into this

SEAFOOD   small fish-and-chips shop just off the seafront, down near the fish shacks. Although the atmosphere is humble, reviewers consistently rank the battered fresh cod and haddock and huge plates of fries as among the best in the country. Everything is steaming fresh, and it's all cheaper if you get it to take out. ✉ *61 High St.* ☏ *01424/425778* ▭ *No credit cards* ☉ *No dinner.*

£ ▦ **Eagle House Hotel.** This guesthouse in St. Leonards, just west of Hastings's city center, is in a large Victorian building with a lovely garden. It's a quirky place with somewhat dated decor, but the guest rooms have Victorian touches. The restaurant uses fresh produce from local farms. **Pros:** quiet neighborhood; historic house. **Cons:** furnishings are a bit worn; service is hit or miss. ✉ *12 Pevensey Rd., St. Leonards* ☏ *01424/430535* ⊕ *www.eaglehousehotel.co.uk* 🛏 *18 rooms* ☖ *In-room: no a/c. In-hotel: restaurant* ▭ *AE, DC, MC, V* ⏹ *BP.*

BATTLE

7 mi northwest of Hastings, 61 mi southeast of London.

Battle is the actual site of the crucial Battle of Hastings, at which, on October 14, 1066, William of Normandy and his army trounced King Harold's Anglo-Saxon army. Today it's a sweet, quiet town, and a favorite of history buffs.

ESSENTIALS

Visitor Information Battle (✉ *High St.* ☏ *01424/773721*).

EXPLORING

The ruins of **Battle Abbey,** the great Benedictine abbey William the Conqueror erected after his victory, still convey the sense of past conflict. A memorial stone marks the high altar, which stood on the spot where Harold II was killed. Despite its historical significance, this abbey was not spared Henry VIII's wrath, and it was largely destroyed during his dissolution of the monasteries. The visitor center shows filmed explanations of the battle and its impact on England, and interactive exhibits engage kids and adults. You can also take the 1-mi-long walk around the edge of the battlefield and see the remains of many of the abbey's buildings. ⊠*High St.* ☎*01424/773792* ⊕*www.english-heritage.org. uk* ☎*£6.70* ☉*Apr.–Sept., daily 10–6; Oct.–Mar., daily 10–4.*

WHERE TO STAY

£ ⬚ **Foxhole Farm.** About 2 mi outside Battle, this pretty wood-and-brick bed-and-breakfast sits in farm country. The owners are a friendly couple, and the house is spacious with sturdy beamed ceilings, colorful bedspreads, a handful of antiques, and lots of homey touches. There's a wood-burning stove for chilly nights, and on sunny days you can sit in the garden and look out over the hills as sheep nibble the grass nearby. In the morning, your eggs come fresh from the henhouse. **Pros:** peaceful views; relaxing atmosphere. **Cons:** outside of town; small, so tends to book up. ⊠*Kane Hythe Rd.* ☎*07801/668669* ⊘*foxholefarm@ kanehythe.orangehome.co.uk* ⊅*3 rooms* ⌂*In-room: no a/c, no phone. In-hotel: no-smoking rooms* ⊟*No credit cards* ⦶*BP.*

££ ⬚ **Little Hemingfold Hotel.** Forty acres of fields and woodlands, including a lake full of trout, provide the main enticement of this early-Victorian farmhouse. Guest rooms, done in simple country style, are bright and serene, and there's a piano in one of the sitting rooms. The fixed-price dinner in the candlelighted restaurant uses homegrown fruit and vegetables; the menu changes daily. The hotel is 2 mi south of Battle off the A2100. **Pros:** peace and quiet; fishing galore; great food. **Cons:** outside of town; not close to the sights. ⊠*Hastings Rd., Telham* ☎*01424/774338* ⊅*12 rooms* ⌂*In-room: no a/c. In-hotel: restaurant, bar, tennis court, some pets allowed, no kids under 7* ☉*Closed Jan.–mid-Feb.* ⊟*AE, MC, V* ⦶*BP.*

HERSTMONCEUX CASTLE

★ *11 mi southwest of Battle, 61 mi southeast of London.*

EXPLORING

A banner waving from one tower and a glassy moat crossed by what was, surely, once a drawbridge—this fairy-tale castle has everything except knights in shining armor. For true castle lovers, **Herstmonceux** is a fabled name. The redbrick structure was originally built by Sir Roger Fiennes (ancestor of actor Ralph Fiennes) in 1444, although it was altered in the Elizabethan age and again early in the 20th century, after it had largely fallen to ruin. Canada's Queen's University owns the castle, so only part of it is open for guided tours once or twice a day (except Saturday). Highlights include the magnificent ballroom, a medieval room, and the stunning Elizabethan-era staircase. When school is not in session, the castle rents out its small, plain guest rooms for £75 per night. ■ TIP➔ **Explore the formal walled garden, lily-covered lakes, and miles of woodland—the perfect place for a picnic on a sunny afternoon.** Try the scones in the castle's tea shop and watch the outside from within. ⊠*Off A271, Hailsham* ☎*01323/834481* ⊕*www.herstmonceux-castle.*

com ✉ *Castle tours £2.50, grounds £6* ⊙ *Mid-Apr.–Oct., daily 10–6; Oct., daily 10–5; last admission 1 hr before closing.*

WHERE TO EAT AND STAY

£££
MODERN FRENCH

✕ **The Sundial.** This 17th-century brick farmhouse is home to a popular modern French restaurant run by chef Vincent Rongier and his wife, Mary. The frequently changing menu lists imaginative choices: foie gras and truffles vie with smoked salmon from the Shetland Isles. The fixed-price options are a good value. ✉ *Gardner St., Herstmonceux* ☎ *01323/832217* ▤ *DC, MC, V* ⊙ *Closed Mon. No dinner Sun.*

££–£££

▥ **Crossways Hotel.** Near the Long Man of Wilmington, this small hotel in a whitewashed house with 2 acres of gardens is under the hills of the South Downs by the river Cuckmere. The interior is decorated in warm, upbeat colors that contrast with the antiques the owners have collected. Convenient for walking, the hotel is also only a 15-minute drive from the Glyndebourne Opera House near Lewes. The cottage here offers more privacy and a kitchen (prices start at £110 for two nights in the off-season). ✉ *Lewes Rd., Polegate* ☎ *01323/482455* 📠 *01273/487811* ⊕ *www.crosswayshotel.co.uk* ↩ *7 rooms, 1 cottage* ⚘ *In-room: no a/c. In hotel: restaurant, no-smoking rooms* ▤ *AE, MC, V* ⚑ *BP.*

EN ROUTE
Wilmington, 9 mi southwest of Herstmonceux Castle on A27, has a famous landmark that people drive for miles to see. High on the downs to the south of the village (signposted off A27), a 226-foot-tall white figure, known as the **Long Man of Wilmington,** is carved into the chalk; he has a staff in each hand. His age is a subject of great debate, but some researchers think he might have originated in Roman times.

LEWES

★ *10 mi northwest of Wilmington, 8 mi northeast of Brighton, 54 mi south of London.*

The town nearest to the celebrated Glyndebourne Opera House, Lewes is so rich in architectural history that the Council for British Archaeology has named it one of the 50 most important English towns. A walk is the best way to appreciate its appealing jumble of building styles and materials—flint, stone, brick, tile—and the secret lanes (called "twittens") behind the castle, with their huge beeches. Here and there are smart antiques shops and secondhand-book dealers. Most of the buildings in the center date to the 18th and 19th centuries.

Something about this town has always attracted rebels. It was once the home of Thomas Paine (1737–1809), whose pamphlet *Common Sense* advocated that the American colonies break with Britain, and was also favored by Virginia Woolf and the Bloomsbury Group, early-20th-century countercultural artistic innovators.

Today Lewes's beauty and proximity to London mean that the counterculture crew can't really afford to live here anymore, but its rebel soul still peeks through, particularly on Guy Fawkes Night (November 5), the anniversary of Fawkes's foiled attempt to blow up the Houses of Parliament in 1605. Flaming tar barrels are rolled down High Street and into the River Ouse; costumed processions fill the streets. The night here is enthusiastically anti-Catholic (Fawkes was a Catholic fanatic), if a bit tongue-in-cheek. Although the pope is burned in effigy, figures from popular culture are also burned, in the spirit of (dark-humored) fun.

GETTING HERE AND AROUND

If you're driving to Lewes from London, take the M23 south. The 57-mile journey takes around an hour and 45 minutes. Southern trains run direct to Lewes from Victoria Station every 30 minutes or so on the Brighton line. It may be faster to take a train to Brighton and change to the regional service for Lewes. There's no easy way to get to Lewes by bus; you need to take a National Express or Megabus to Brighton and change to a regional bus line.

ESSENTIALS

Visitor Information Lewes (⊠ *187 High St.* ☎ *01273/483448* ⊕ *www.lewes. gov.uk*).

EXPLORING

High above the valley of the River Ouse stand the majestic ruins of **Lewes Castle,** begun in 1100 by one of the country's Norman conquerors; it took 300 years to complete. The castle's barbican holds a small museum with archaeology collections, a changing temporary exhibition gallery, and a bookshop. There are panoramic views of the town and countryside. ⊠ *169 High St.* ☎ *01273/486290* ⊕ *www.sussexpast. co.uk* ⊠ *£4.95, £7.70 includes Anne of Cleves House* ⊙ *Tues.–Sat. 10–5:30 or dusk; Sun., Mon., and holidays 11–5:30 or dusk; last admission 30 mins before closing; closed Mon. in Jan.*

The 16th-century **Anne of Cleves House,** a fragile, timber-frame building, holds a notable collection of Sussex ironwork and other items of local interest, such as Sussex pottery. A famous painting of the local Guy Fawkes procession is also here. The house was part of Anne of Cleves's divorce settlement from Henry VIII, but she did not live in it. To get to the house, walk down steep, cobbled Keere Street, past lovely Grange Gardens, to Southover High Street. ⊠ *52 Southover High St.* ☎ *01273/474610* ⊕ *www.sussexpast.co.uk* ⊠ *£3.90, £7.70 includes Lewes Castle* ⊙ *Mar.–Oct., Tues.–Thurs. 10–5, Sun., Mon., and holidays 11–5; Nov.–Feb., weekends 11–5; last admission at 4.*

Of interest to Bloomsbury fans, **Monk's House** was the home of novelist Virginia Woolf and her husband, Leonard Woolf, who purchased it in 1919. Leonard lived here until his death in 1969. Rooms in the small cottage include Virginia's study and her bedroom. Artists Vanessa Bell (Virginia's sister) and Duncan Grant helped decorate the house. ⊠ *C7, off A27, 3 mi south of Lewes, Rodmell* ☎ *01323/870001(c/o Alfriston Clergy House)* ⊕ *www.nationaltrust.org.uk* ⊠ *£3.80* ⊙ *Apr.–Oct., Wed. and Sat. 2–5:30.*

Art and life mixed at **Charleston,** the farmhouse Vanessa Bell—sister of Virginia Woolf—bought in 1916 and decorated with Duncan Grant (who resided here until 1978), fancifully painting the walls, doors, and furniture. The house became a refuge for writers and artists of the Bloomsbury Group and displays ceramics and textiles of the Omega Workshop—in which Bell and Grant participated—and paintings by Picasso and Renoir as well as by Bell and Grant. You view the house on a guided tour (there may be a wait) except on Sunday. ⊠ *Off A27, 7 mi east of Lewes, Firle* ☎*01323/811265* ⊕*www.charleston.org.uk* ⊠*£7.50; gardens only, £3* ⊘ *Apr.–June, Sept., and Oct., Wed.–Sun. 1–5; July and Aug., Wed.–Sat. noon–5, Sun. 1–5.*

WHERE TO EAT AND STAY

£ ✕ **Robson's of Lewes.** Good coffee, fresh produce, and delicious pas-
CAFÉ tries have made this coffee shop very popular with locals. A light-
filled space with wood floors and simple tables creates a pleasant,
casual spot to enjoy a cup of joe with breakfast, a scone, or a light
sandwich or salad lunch. You can also order to go. ⊠*22A High St.*
☎*01273/480654* ⊟*AE, MC, V* ⊘ *No dinner.*

££ ⊞ **Berkeley House.** A smart town house in one of Lewes's Georgian terraces is now a cozy B&B. Rooms are spacious and homey, if somewhat
beige, and full English breakfasts are made using free-range eggs from
a local farmer. **Pros:** warm atmosphere; great breakfast. **Cons:** rooms
are a bit bland; nothing fancy here. ⊠*2 Albion St.* ☎*01273/476057*
⊕*www.berkeleyhousehotel.co.uk* ⇖*3 rooms* ⇘*In-room: no a/c. In-
hotel: no-smoking rooms* ⊟*AE, DC, MC, V* ⏀*BP.*

££££ ⊞ **Horsted Place.** On 1,100 acres, this luxurious Victorian manor-house
hotel is a few minutes' drive from Glyndebourne Opera House. Built
as a private home in 1850 with Gothic Revival elements by Augustus-
Charles Pugin, it was owned by a friend of the Queen's until the 1980s,
and Elizabeth was a regular visitor. Today it is richly furnished in
country-house style and has a magnificent Victorian staircase and a
Gothic library with a secret door that leads to a courtyard. The dining
room, also Gothic, prepares such elegant fare as roasted quail cutlet. Golfers get a special rate at a nearby course. **Pros:** historic building; amazing architecture; lovely gardens. **Cons:** too formal for some;
creaky floors bother light sleepers. ⊠*Little Horsted TN22 5TS* ✛*2½
mi south of Uckfield, 6 mi north of Lewes* ☎*01825/750581* ⊕*www.
horstedplace.co.uk* ⇖*15 rooms, 5 suites* ⇘*In-room: no a/c. In-hotel:
restaurant, tennis court* ⊟*AE, DC, MC, V* ⏀*BP.*

££££ ⊞ **The Shelleys.** A 17th-century building, this hotel on the hilly main
road is a traditional overnight stop for Glyndebourne operagoers. Public rooms are on the grand scale, furnished with antiques; the garden is
a joy. The hotel is known for its old-fashioned but friendly service and
its excellent restaurant. **Pros:** historic atmosphere; excellent French-
influenced cuisine. **Cons:** service a bit spotty; securing a table at the
restaurant can be tough. ⊠*High St.* ☎*01273/472361* ⊕*www.the-
shelleys.co.uk* ⇖*19 rooms* ⇘*In-room: no a/c. In-hotel: restaurant,
bar* ⊟*AE, DC, MC, V* ⏀*BP.*

NIGHTLIFE AND THE ARTS

NIGHTLIFE Lewes has a relatively young population and a nightlife scene to match;
there are also many lovely old pubs. Try the **Brewers' Arms** (⊠*91 High
St.* ☎*01273/475524*), a good pub with a friendly crowd. The **King's
Head** (⊠*9 Southover High St.* ☎*01273/474628*), a traditional pub,
has a good menu with game and fish dishes.

THE ARTS **Glyndebourne Opera House** (⊠*Off A26, Glyndebourne* ✛*Near Lewes*
☎*01273/813813* ⊕*www.glyndebourne.com*) is one of the world's

leading opera venues. Nestled beneath the downs, Glyndebourne combines first-class productions, a state-of-the-art auditorium, and a beautiful setting. Seats are *very* expensive (£25–£140) and often difficult to acquire, but they're worth every penny to aficionados, some of whom wear evening dress and bring a hamper for a picnic in the gardens. The main season runs from mid-May to the end of August. The Glyndebourne Touring Company performs here in October, when seats are cheaper and slightly easier to obtain.

SHOPPING

Antiques shops offer temptation along the busy High Street. Lewes also has plenty of tiny boutiques and independent clothing stores vying for your pounds. **Adamczewski** (✉*88 High St.* ☏*01273/470105*) is a marvelous throwback to the days when everything was made by hand. Its homemade soaps, scents, and even hand-hewn brooms are works of art. **Cliffe Antiques Centre** (✉*47 Cliffe High St.* ☏*01273/473266*), a great place for one-stop antiques shopping, carries a fine mix of vintage English prints, estate jewelry, and art at reasonable prices. Classic bone china and antique glass are the center of attention at **Louis Potts & Co.** (✉*43 Cliffe High St.* ☏*01273/472240*).

BRIGHTON TO GUILDFORD

The self-proclaimed belle of the coast, Brighton is upbeat, funky, and endlessly entertaining. Outside of town the soft green downs of Sussex and Surrey hold stately homes you can visit, including Arundel Castle and Petworth House. Along the way, you'll discover the largest Roman villa in Britain, the bustling city of Guildford, and Chichester, whose cathedral is a poem in stone.

BRIGHTON

9 mi southwest of Lewes, 54 mi south of London.

For more than 200 years, Brighton has been England's most interesting seaside city, and today it is more vibrant, eccentric, and cosmopolitan than ever. A rich cultural mix—Regency architecture, specialty shops, sidewalk cafés, lively arts, and a flourishing gay scene—makes it unique and unpredictable.

It could be said that Brighton owes its fame and fortune to seawater. In 1750 physician Richard Russell published a book recommending seawater treatment for glandular diseases. The fashionable world flocked to Brighton to take Dr. Russell's "cure," and sea bathing became a popular pastime. Few places in the south of England were better for it, since Brighton's broad beach of smooth pebbles stretches as far as the eye can see. It has been popular with sunbathers ever since.

The next windfall for the town was the arrival of the Prince of Wales (later George IV). "Prinny," as he was called, created the Royal Pavilion, a mock-Asian pleasure palace that attracted London society. Visitors followed, triggering a wave of villa-building, and today the elegant terraces of Regency houses are among the town's greatest attractions.

The coming of the railroad set the seal on Brighton's popularity: the *Brighton Belle* brought Londoners to the coast within an hour.

Londoners are still flocking to Brighton. Add them to the many local university students, and you have a trendy, young, laid-back city that does, occasionally, burst at its own seams. Property values have sky-rocketed, but all visitors may notice is the good shopping, excellent restaurants, attractive (if pebbly) beach, and wild nightlife. Brighton is also carving out a name for itself as the place to go if you're looking for hotels with offbeat design and party nights.

GETTING HERE AND AROUND

Brighton-bound National Express and Megabus buses depart from London's Victoria Coach Station. The trip takes about two hours. Southeastern trains leave from London's Victoria and Charing Cross stations every 30 minutes. The journey takes just under an hour, and the trains stop at Gatwick Airport. If you're traveling by car from London, head to Brighton on the M23/A23. The journey should take about 1½ hours.

Brighton (and the adjacent Hove) sprawls in all directions, but the part of interest to travelers is fairly compact. None of the sights is more than a 10-minute walk from the train station. You can pick up a town map at the station. City Sightseeing has a hop-on, hop-off tour bus that leaves Brighton Pier every 20 to 30 minutes. It operates May through mid-September and costs £8.

TIMING

On summer weekends, the town is packed with Londoners looking for a day by the sea. Oceanfront bars can be rowdy, especially on national holidays when concerts and events bring in people. But summer is also when Brighton looks its best, and all the shops, restaurants, and bars are packed with revelers. At other times, the town is much quieter. The Brighton Festival in May fills the town with music and other performances.

ESSENTIALS

Visitor and Tour Information Brighton (✉ *10 Bartholomew Sq.* ☎ *0906/ 7112255* ⊕ *www.visitbrighton.com*). **City Sightseeing** (☎ *01789/294466* ⊕ *www.city-sightseeing.com*)

EXPLORING

TOP ATTRACTIONS

Beach. The foundation of everything in Brighton is its broad beach, which spreads smoothly from one end of town to the other. In the summer sunbathers, swimmers, and hawkers selling ice cream and toys pack the shore; in the winter people stroll at the water's stormy edge, walking their dogs and searching for seashells. The water is bracingly cold, and the beach is covered in a thick blanket of large, smooth pebbles.

■TIP➔**If you plan on swimming, bring a pair of rubber swimming shoes, as the stones are hard on bare feet.**

❶ **Brighton Museum and Art Gallery.** The grounds of the Royal Pavilion contain this museum, whose buildings were designed as a stable block for the prince regent's horses. The museum, looking great after a

£10 million face-lift, has particularly interesting art nouveau and art deco collections. Look out for Salvador Dalí's famous sofa in the shape of Mae West's lips, and pause at the Balcony Café for its bird's-eye view over the 20th-century Art and Design Gallery. ⊠ *Church St.* ☎ *01273/290900* ⊕ *www.brighton. virtualmuseum.info* ⊠ *Free* ☉ *Tues. 10–7, Wed.–Sat. 10–5, Sun. 2–5.*

> **WE DO NOT APPROVE**
>
> When Queen Victoria came to the throne in 1837, she so disapproved of the Royal Pavilion that she stripped it of its furniture and planned to demolish it. Fortunately, the local council bought it from her, and today the palace looks much as it did in its Regency heyday.

⑤ Brighton Pier. Opened in 1899, the pier is an amusement park set above the sea. In the early 20th century it had a music hall and entertainment; today it has carnival rides and game arcades, along with clairvoyants, henna tattoo artists, and greasy food stalls. In the summer it is packed with children by day and teenagers by night. The skeletal shadow of a pier you can see off in the water is all that's left of the old West Pier. Longterm plans call for construction of an observation tower called i360 where that pier once touched the shore. ☎ *01273/609361* ⊕ *www. brightonpier.co.uk* ☉ *Mid-Sept.–June, daily 10 AM–midnight; July–mid-Sept., daily 9 AM–2 AM.*

④ The Lanes. This maze of tiny alleys and passageways was once the home of fishermen and their families. Closed to vehicular traffic, the area's narrow cobbled streets are filled with interesting restaurants, boutiques, and antiques shops. Fish and seafood restaurants line the heart of the Lanes, at Market Street and Market Square. ⊠ *Bordered by West, North, East, and Prince Albert Sts.*

② Royal Pavilion. The city's most remarkable building is this domed and pinnacled fantasy. Planned as a simple seaside villa and built in the fashionable classical style of 1787 by architect Henry Holland, the Pavilion was rebuilt between 1815 and 1822 by John Nash for the prince regent (later George IV), who wanted an exotic, Eastern design with opulent Chinese interiors. Today period furniture and ornaments, some given or lent by the current Royal Family, fill the interior. The two great set pieces are the **Music Room,** styled in the form of a Chinese pavilion, and the **Banqueting Room,** with its enormous flying-dragon "gasolier," or gaslight chandelier, a revolutionary invention in the early 19th century. The gardens, too, have been restored to Regency splendor, following John Nash's naturalistic design of 1826. ■ TIP→ **For an elegant time-out, retire to one of the Pavilion's bedrooms, where a tearoom serves snacks and light meals.** ⊠ *Old Steine* ☎ *01273/290900* ⊕ *www.royalpavilion.org. uk* ⊠ *£9* ☉ *Oct.–Mar., daily 10–5:15; Apr.–Sept., daily 9:30–5:45; last admission 45 mins before closing.*

QUICK BITES

On the street adjacent to the bus stop, and less than a five-minute walk from the Royal Pavilion, the **Mock Turtle** (⊠ *4 Pool Valley* ☎ *01273/ 328380*) is a great old-fashioned, homey café. Alongside a decent selection

of teas and coffees are four types of rarebit, soups, and scones. It's closed
Monday.

❸ Steine. One of the centers of Brighton's action is the Steine (pronounced
steen), a large open area close to the seafront. This was a river mouth
until the Prince of Wales had it drained in 1793.

WORTH NOTING

❻ Sea Life Centre. Near Brighton Pier, this aquarium has many sea-dwelling
⟳ creatures—from sharks to sea horses—in more than 30 marine habitats.
It also has a giant-turtle convalescence center. Allow two hours to see it.
✉ *Marine Parade* ☎ *01273/604234* ⊕ *www.sealifeeurope.com* 🎫 *£10*
🕐 *Apr.–Oct., daily 10–5; Nov.–Mar., daily 10–4.*

❼ Volk's Electric Railway. Built by inventor Magnus Volk in 1883, this was
⟳ the first public electric railroad in Britain. In summer you can take the
1¼-mi trip along Marine Parade. ✉ *Marine Parade* ☎ *01273/292718*
⊕ *www.volkselectricrailway.co.uk* 🎫 *£1.70 one-way, £2.70 round-trip*
🕐 *Apr.–Sept., weekdays 10:30–5, weekends 10:30–6.*

WHERE TO EAT

££ ✕ **Brighton Rock Beach House.** Come here for a tongue-in-cheek take on
AMERICAN   a classic New England–beach bar that could have been lifted whole
off Cape Cod and dropped in central Brighton. The menu is just as

Brighton and the Regent

CLOSE UP

The term "Regency" comes from the last 10 years of the reign of George III (1811–20), who was deemed unfit to rule because of his mental problems. Real power was officially given to the prince of Wales, also known as the prince regent, who became King George IV and ruled until his death in 1830.

Throughout his regency, George spent grand sums indulging his flamboyant tastes in architecture and interior decorating—while failing in affairs of state.

The distinctive architecture of the Royal Pavilion is a prime, if extreme, example of the Regency style, popularized by architect John Nash (1752–1835) in the early part of the 19th century. The style is characterized by a diversity of influences—French, Greek, Italian, Persian, Japanese, Chinese, Roman, Indian—you name it. Nash was George IV's favorite architect, beloved for his interest in Indian and Asian designs and for his neoclassical designs, as evidenced in his plans for Regent's Park and its terraces in London.

American, with Maine crab cakes, New England clam chowder, and irresistible lobster cheesecake. The mood is pure beach: some tables are outside, surrounded by driftwood. (This is Brighton, so there's no sand.) Cool jazz plays as you eat. ⊠*6 Rock Pl.* ☎*01273/601139* 🖃*MC, V.*

£££ ✕**Due South.** Arguably the highest-quality dining option on Brighton's
SEAFOOD seafront, this beachfront place is making waves on the local food scene, drawing young professionals who also appreciate its celebratory atmosphere. Big windows overlook the sea and let in plenty of light. The menu showcases clever, classic seafood dishes, with everything from the fish to the vegetables sourced locally and organically. Or try the char-grilled, free-range sirloin steak with Jersey Royal potatoes and a walnut-and-horseradish sauce. Don't miss the butterscotch cheesecake. ⊠*139 King's Road Arches* ☎*01273/821218* 🖃*AE, MC, V.*

£ ✕**Nia Café.** In the funky North Laine area, Nia has views down Trafal-
CAFÉ gar Street from its outdoor tables. Besides good coffees and leaf teas, excellent café food is available all day, from simple (but freshly made) sandwiches to cod stuffed with wild mushrooms and served with a lemony spinach salad. The decor is basic, but large windows and fresh flowers make it friendly. Nia is near the station, which is handy if you have time to kill before a train or need to reenergize before sightseeing. ⊠*87–88 Trafalgar St.* ☎*01273/671371* 🖃*MC, V.*

££ ✕**Nounou.** Inspired by contemporary Moroccan and French cuisine,
MOROCCAN this polished, romantic restaurant has made headlines in Brighton for its delightful, unique fare. Dishes combine the best French techniques with Moroccan specialties such as tagine of lamb with *merquez* (a spicy lamb sausage) and couscous. Grilled scallops on lemongrass risotto is a great starter. ⊠*120 St. George's Rd.* ☎*01273/682200* 🖃*AE, MC, V* ⊘*Closed Sun. and Mon.*

£££ ✕**Seven Dials.** A former bank houses a restaurant that's undeniably
MODERN BRITISH striking and surprisingly laid-back. Sophisticated modern English cuisine rules the menu, with choices such as roasted rump of lamb given a

new look when served with eggplant caviar and an olive-and-rosemary sauce. It's worth blowing your diet for the desserts. ⊠ *1 Buckingham Pl.* ☎ *01273/885555* ⚑ *Reservations essential* ▭ *AE, MC, V.*

££ ✕ **Terre à Terre.** This inspiring vegetarian restaurant is popular, so come
VEGETARIAN early for a light lunch or a more sophisticated evening meal. The linguine with pumpkin confit and sheep's cheese, the spicy cheese kebabs with smoked almond custard risotto, and an eclectic choice of salads should satisfy most palates. All wines served here are organic, too. ⊠ *71 East St.* ☎ *01273/729051* ▭ *AE, DC, MC, V* ⊘ *Closed Mon.; no lunch Tues. and Wed. in winter.*

WHERE TO STAY

£££–££££ ⊞ **Blanch House.** A theatrical experience as much as a night's rest, this boutique hotel off the seafront sets itself apart with eclectic, clever theme rooms, including a '70s-style Boogie Nights room (with animal-print wallpaper) and elaborate Moroccan and Renaissance rooms. As you'd expect, the bathrooms are stylish and have the latest amenities. The hip cocktail bar (the owner is a former manager of London's Groucho Club) and sleek modern restaurant complete the picture. **Pros:** quirky approach; popular bar; good restaurant. **Cons:** may be far too theatrical for some; restaurant books up fast. ⊠ *17 Atlingworth St.* ☎ *01273/603504* ⊕ *www. blanchhouse.co.uk* ⛱ *9 rooms, 3 suites* ⚐ *In-room: no a/c, Internet. In-hotel: restaurant, bar* ▭ *MC, V* ⛺ *BP.*

££–£££ ⊞ **Brighton Wave.** Sleekly designed, this hotel off the seafront but near the Brighton Pier is all about relaxation. Beds are big and covered in soft, white linens; rooms are painted in restful, pale shades of blue and white; and breakfast is served in bed. The look is minimal without being cold, and service hits just the right note of friendliness and helpfulness. **Pros:** big, comfy beds; soothing decor; breakfast in bed. **Cons:** not a lot of privacy. ⊠ *10 Madeira Pl.* ☎ *01273/676794* ⊕ *www.brightonwave. com* ⛱ *8 rooms* ⚐ *In-room: DVD. In-hotel: Wi-Fi* ▭ *AE, DC, MC, V* ⛺ *BP.*

£££–££££ ⊞ **Drakes.** It's easy to miss the low-key sign for this elegant, modern hotel, tucked away amid the frilly houses on Marine Parade on the seafront. Inside, everything is cool, calm, and sleekly designed. The lobby is dark and sophisticated, and each guest room has its own style, with handmade wallpaper, firm beds covered in luxurious linens, well-designed bathrooms, and art everywhere. Some "feature" rooms have quirky touches, including claw-foot tubs in front of the bedroom windows. Rooms with sea views are more expensive than other rooms. Gingerman, the hotel restaurant, has a huge local following for its modern British cuisine. **Pros:** cool atmosphere; great attention to detail; excellent restaurant. **Cons:** can feel a bit cold; too trendy for some. ⊠ *43–44 Marine Parade* ☎ *01273/696934* ⊕ *www.drakesofbrighton. com* ⛱ *20 rooms* ⚐ *In-room: DVD, Internet. In-hotel: restaurant, bar* ▭ *AE, DC, MC, V.*

£££££ ⊞ **Grand Hotel.** The city's most famous hotel and a Brighton landmark,
★ the Grand sits on the seafront, a huge, creamy Victorian wedding cake of a building dating from 1864. It's both imposing and elegant, with high-ceiling public rooms richly decorated with enormous chandeliers and plenty of marble. Having tea here is a Brighton tradition, and highly

recommended. The spacious bedrooms are traditional in style, with luxurious fabrics and large bathrooms. The Grand is famous in Britain for having survived an IRA bombing attack in 1984 that targeted Prime Minister Margaret Thatcher. **Pros:** as grand as its name; lovely sea views. **Cons:** a bit impersonal; lobby can be crowded with people taking tea. ⊠*King's Rd.* ☎*01273/224300* ⊕*www.grandbrighton. co.uk* ☞*200 rooms, 3 suites* ⚿*In-room: no a/c (some), Internet. In-hotel: restaurant, bar, pool, gym, some pets allowed* ⊟*AE, DC, MC, V* ⦿|*BP.*

££–£££   ▨**Granville Hotel.** Three grand Victorian buildings facing the sea make up this hotel. Guest rooms, heavily decorated with a theme (themed rooms are a Brighton fad), include the pink-and-white Brighton Rock and the art deco Noël Coward rooms. You'll pay the highest price for rooms with sea views. Dadu, the hotel's restaurant, is worth a stop. **Pros:** creative design; friendly staff; rambunctious atmosphere. **Cons:** rooms are a bit too quirky; can get noisy. ⊠*124 King's Rd.* ☎*01273/326302* ⊕*www.granvillehotel.co.uk* ☞*24 rooms* ⚿*In-room: no a/c, Internet. In-hotel: restaurant, bar, some pets allowed, no-smoking rooms* ⊟*AE, DC, MC, V* ⦿|*BP.*

££££   ▨**Hotel du Vin.** In the Lanes area, this outpost of a stylish chain has crisply modern rooms. Pampering touches include Egyptian linens and large "monsoon" showers. The bistro restaurant offers classic fare that makes use of local seafood, and the extensive wine list includes many good values. Even connoisseurs will be satisfied by the wine bar (special events take place throughout the year), and you can have a cigar from the cigar gallery before you play billiards. **Pros:** gorgeous rooms; comfortable beds; excellent eatery. **Cons:** bar can get crowded; restaurant books up fast. ⊠*Ship St.* ☎*01273/718588* ⊕*www.hotelduvin.com* ☞*34 rooms, 3 suites* ⚿*In-room: no a/c, Wi-Fi. In-hotel: restaurant, bar* ⊟*AE, DC, MC, V.*

£££–££££   ▨**Nineteen.** A calm oasis of white, this guesthouse is filled with contemporary art and chic designer accessories. Beds are supported on platforms of glass bricks that filter an ocean-blue light. Massages, yoga sessions, and manicures are pampering amenities, and the basement kitchen stocks snacks for guests. **Pros:** relaxing rooms; innovative design. **Cons:** a bit New Agey. ⊠*19 Broad St.* ☎*01273/675529* ⊕*www.hotelnineteen. co.uk* ☞*8 rooms* ⚿*In-room: no a/c, DVD, Wi-Fi. In-hotel: Wi-Fi, some pets allowed, no-smoking rooms* ⊟*MC, V* ⦿|*BP.*

££–£££   ▨**Pelirocco.** Here the imaginations of designers have been given free rein, and the result is a vicarious romp through pop culture and rock and roll. Rooms have themes: there's the leopard-print pin-up parlor, a boxing ring, and the futuristic Bubble Suite with a plunge bath and mirrored ceiling. It's way over the top, so you'll either love this place or hate it. **Pros:** quirky design; laid-back atmosphere; near the beach. **Cons:** a bit too form-over-function. ⊠*10 Regency Sq.* ☎*01273/327055* ⊕*www.hotelpelirocco.co.uk* ☞*18 rooms, 1 suite* ⚿*In-room: no a/c, Internet. In-hotel: bar, no kids under 12 on weekends, no-smoking rooms* ⊟*AE, MC, V* ⦿|*BP.*

NIGHTLIFE AND THE ARTS

NIGHTLIFE

Brighton is a techno hub, largely because so many DJs have moved here from London. Clubs and bars present live music most nights, and on weekends the entire place can be a bit too raucous for some tastes. There's a large gay scene. The popular **Above Audio** (⊠*10 Marine Parade* ☎*01273/606906*), in an art deco building east of Brighton Pier, has a mix of house and underground music. Specialty nights at the **Funky Buddha Lounge** (⊠*169 King's Road Arches* ☎*01273/725541*) are at the forefront of Brighton's underground, with funk and acid disco blasting out to a fairly sophisticated crowd. Small, friendly, and unfailingly funky, the **Jazz Place** (⊠*10 Ship St.* ☎*01273/328439*) can get a little cramped but makes up for it with cool, jazzy attitude. The **Zap Club** (⊠*189–192 King's Road Arches* ☎*01273/202407*), under the arches right on the beach, is Brighton's most established club, but no longer as trendy as it once was.

THE ARTS

★ The three-week-long **Brighton Festival** (☎*01273/706771* ⊕*www. brighton-festival.org*), one of England's biggest and liveliest arts festivals, takes place every May in venues around town. The more than 600 events include drama, music, dance, and visual arts.

The **Brighton Dome** (⊠*New Rd.* ☎*01273/709709*), just west of the Royal Pavilion, was converted from the prince regent's stables in the 1930s. It includes a theater and a concert hall that stage pantomime (a British theatrical entertainment with songs and dance) and classical and pop concerts. The **Theatre Royal** (⊠*New Rd.* ☎*01273/328488*), close to the Royal Pavilion, has a gem of an auditorium that is a favorite venue for shows on their way to or fresh from London's West End.

The **Cinematheque** (⊠*9–12 Middle St.* ☎*01273/384300*) screens subart-house oddities, obscurities, and rarities. The elegant 1910 **Duke of York's Picture House** (⊠*Preston Circus* ☎*01273/626261*), a 10-minute walk north of the main train station, shows art-house movies.

SHOPPING

The main shopping area to head for is **the Lanes,** especially for antiques or jewelry. It also has clothing boutiques, coffee shops, and pubs. Across North Street from the Lanes lies the **North Laine,** a network of narrow streets full of little stores, less glossy than those in the Lanes, but fun, funky, and exotic.

Colin Page (⊠*36 Duke St.* ☎*01273/325954*), at the western edge of the Lanes, stocks a wealth of antiquarian and secondhand books at all prices. The **Pavilion Shop** (⊠*4–5 Pavilion Bldgs.* ☎*01273/292798*), next door to the Royal Pavilion, carries well-designed toys, trinkets, books, and cards—all with a loose Regency theme—and high-quality fabrics, wallpapers, and ceramics based on material in the Pavilion itself. The old-fashioned **Pecksniff's Bespoke Perfumery** (⊠*45–46 Meeting House La.* ☎*01273/723292*) mixes and matches ingredients to suit your wishes. **Simultane** (⊠*52 Ship St.* ☎*01273/777535*), a boutique near the waterfront, displays women's fashions from its own label—contemporary looks inspired by the styles of the 1940s and '50s—and clothing from other designers.

Brighton
to Guildford

ARUNDEL

23 mi west of Brighton, 60 mi south of London.

The little hilltop town of Arundel is dominated by its great castle, the much-restored home of the dukes of Norfolk for more than 700 years, and an imposing neo-Gothic Roman Catholic cathedral—the duke is Britain's leading Catholic peer. The town itself is full of interesting old buildings and well worth a stroll.

ESSENTIALS

Visitor Information Arundel (✉ *61 High St.* ☎ *01903/882268* ⊕ *www.sussex-by-the-sea.co.uk*).

EXPLORING

Begun in the 11th century, vast **Arundel Castle** remains rich with the history of the Fitzalan and Howard families and with paintings by Van Dyck, Gainsborough, and Reynolds. It suffered destruction during the Civil War and was remodeled during the 18th century and in the Victorian era, when it was reconstructed in the fashionable Gothic style. The keep, rising from its conical mound, is as old as the original castle (you can climb its 130 steps for great views of the River Arun and the area), and the barbican and the Barons' Hall date from the 13th century.

Among the treasures are the rosary beads and prayer book used by Mary, Queen of Scots, in preparing for her execution. Although the castle's ceremonial entrance is at the top of High Street, you enter at the bottom, close to the parking lot. ⊠*Mill Rd.* ☎*01903/882173* ⊕*www. arundelcastle.org* ☑*£15; grounds only, £7* ⊘*Apr.–Oct., Tues.–Sun. noon–5 (grounds open at 10); last admission at 4.*

WHERE TO EAT AND STAY

£

BRITISH

✕ **Black Rabbit.** This renovated 18th-century pub outside Arundel is a find, and you must persevere along Mill Road to find it. Its location by the River Arun, with views of the castle and a bird sanctuary, makes it ideal for a summer lunch. There's a good selection of real ales and an all-day restaurant. ⊠*Mill Rd., Offham* ☎*01903/882828* ▤*DC, MC, V.*

££££–£££££

★

▥ **Amberley Castle.** The lowering of the portcullis every night at midnight is a sure sign that you're in a genuine medieval castle. Across the dry moat, present-day luxury dominates. Antiques and rich drapery furnish the individually designed bedrooms, and many have lattice windows, beamed ceilings, and curtained four-posters. You can dine in either the Queens restaurant, beneath a 12th-century barrel-vaulted ceiling, or amid suits of armor in the Great Room. **Pros:** sleep in a castle, with a moat; putting course for golfers; lovely gardens and grounds. **Cons:** a bit too formal; you have to dress for dinner. ⊠*5 mi north of Arundel, off B2139, Amberley* ☎*01798/831992* ⊕*www.amberleycastle.co.uk* ⇱*20 rooms* ♨*In-room: no a/c, Internet. In-hotel: restaurant, bar, tennis court, no kids under 12* ▤*AE, DC, MC, V* ▢*CP.*

££–£££

▥ **Norfolk Arms Hotel.** Like the cathedral and the castle in Arundel, this 18th-century coaching inn on the main street was built by one of the dukes of Norfolk. Some rooms are small (the hotel dubs them "cozy"), but those in an annex in the courtyard block are larger and more modern. Many are decorated in a frilly style. **Pros:** charming building; historic setting. **Cons:** many rooms are very small; decor is dated. ⊠*22 High St.* ☎*01903/882101* ⊕*www.norfolkarmshotel.com* ⇱*34 rooms* ♨*In-room: no a/c, Wi-Fi. In-hotel: restaurant, bars, Wi-Fi, some pets allowed* ▤*AE, DC, MC, V* ▢*BP.*

NIGHTLIFE AND THE ARTS

The **Arundel Festival** (☎*01903/883690* ⊕*www.arundelfestival.co.uk*) presents drama productions and classical and pop concerts in and around the castle grounds for 10 days in August or September.

CHICHESTER

10 mi west of Arundel, 66 mi southwest of London.

The Romans founded Chichester, the capital city of West Sussex, on the low-lying plains between the wooded South Downs and the sea. The city walls and major streets follow the original Roman plan. This cathedral town, a good base for exploring the area, is a well-respected theatrical hub, with a reputation for attracting good acting talent during its summer repertory season. North of town is Petworth House, a National Trust treasure house.

GETTING HERE AND AROUND

From London, take A3 south and follow exit signs for Chichester. The 67-mile journey takes slightly more than 2 hours; much of it is in on smaller highways. Southern trains run to Chichester every half hour from Victoria station, with a travel time of about 90 minutes. Bus service from London requires a trip to Brighton or Portsmouth and a change to a regional service; the train is faster.

ESSENTIALS

Visitor Information Chichester (⊠ *29A South St.* ☎ *01243/775888* ⊕ *www. chichester.gov.uk*).

EXPLORING

TOP ATTRACTIONS

Chichester Cathedral. Standing on Roman foundations, Norman Chichester Cathedral celebrated its 900th birthday in 2008. Inside, a glass panel reveals Roman mosaics uncovered during restoration. Other treasures are the wonderful Saxon limestone reliefs of the raising of Lazarus and Christ arriving in Bethany, both in the choir area. Among the outstanding contemporary artworks are a stained-glass window by Marc Chagall, a colorful tapestry by John Piper, and a painting by Graham Sutherland. ⊠ *West St.* ☎ *01243/782595* ⊕ *www.chichestercathedral. org.uk* ⊠ *£3 suggested donation* ⊙ *Easter–Sept., daily 7:15–7; Oct.– Easter, daily 7:15–6. Tours Mon.–Sat. at 11:15 and 2:30.*

Fishbourne Roman Palace. In 1960, workers digging a water-main ditch uncovered a Roman wall; so began nine years of archaeological excavation of this site, the remains of the largest, grandest Roman villa in Britain. Intricate mosaics (including Cupid riding a dolphin) and painted walls lavishly decorate what is left of many of the 100 rooms of the palace, built in the 1st century AD, possibly for local chieftain Tiberius Claudius Togidubnus. It's a glimpse of high living, Roman-leader style. You can explore the sophisticated bathing and heating systems, and the only example of a Roman garden in northern Europe. An expansion has added many modern attributes, including a video reconstruction of how the palace might have looked. The site is ½ mi west of Chichester. ⊠ *Salthill Rd., Fishbourne* ☎ *01243/785859* ⊕ *www.sussexpast.co.uk* ⊠ *£7.30* ⊙ *Mar.–July, Sept., and Oct., daily 10–5; Aug., daily 10–6; Nov.–mid-Dec. and Feb., daily 10–4; mid-Dec.–Jan., weekends 10–4.*

Fodor'sChoice   **Petworth House.** One of the National Trust's greatest treasures, Pet-
★   worth is the imposing 17th-century home of Lord and Lady Egremont and holds an outstanding collection of English paintings by Gainsborough, Reynolds, and Van Dyck, as well as 19 oil paintings by the great proponent of Romanticism J. M. W. Turner, who often visited Petworth and immortalized it in luminous drawings. A 13th-century chapel is all that remains of the original manor house. The celebrated landscape architect Capability Brown (1716–83) added a 700-acre deer park. Other highlights include Greek and Roman sculpture and Grinling Gibbons wood carvings, such as those in the spectacular Carved Room. Six rooms in the servants' quarters, among them the old kitchen, are open to the public. A restaurant serves light lunches. You can reach the house off A272 and A283 (parking lots are off the latter);

Petworth house is 13 mi northeast of Chichester and 54 mi south of London. Between 11 and 1 visits are by guided tour only. ⊠*Petworth* ☎*01798/342207* ⊕*www.nationaltrust.org.uk* ⌨*£9.40; gardens only, £4* ☉*House mid-Mar.–early Nov., Sat.–Wed. 11–5; last admission at 4:30. Gardens Mar.–late Oct., Sat.–Wed. 11–6; Nov.–mid-Dec., Wed.–Sat. 10–3:30. Park daily 8–dusk.*

> **A TEMPTING TOWN**
>
> After you visit Petworth House, take time to explore the small town of Petworth, a jewel-studded place with narrow old streets and timbered houses. Temptation awaits, too: this is a center for fine antiques and collectibles, with many excellent shops.

★ **Sculpture at Goodwood.** Twenty acres of woodland provide a backdrop for this collection of contemporary British sculpture specially commissioned by the Hat Hill Sculpture Foundation. A third of the approximately 40 exhibits change annually, and walks through green fields connect the pieces, sited to maximize their effect. It's a stimulating way to spend a nice afternoon. The park is 3 mi north of Chichester, signposted on the right off A286. ⊠*Hat Hill Copse, Goodwood* ☎*01243/538449* ⊕*www.sculpture.org.uk* ⌨*£10* ☉*Easter–Oct., Tues.–Sun. and national holidays 10:30–5.*

WORTH NOTING

Pallant House. Chichester's architecture is mainly Georgian, and its 18th-century stone houses give it a wonderful period appearance. One of the best is Pallant House, built in 1712 as a wine merchant's mansion. At that time its state-of-the-art design showed the latest in complicated brickwork and superb wood carving. Appropriate antiques and porcelains furnish the faithfully restored rooms. The **Pallant House Gallery,** attached to the house, showcases a small but important collection of mainly modern British art. Admission includes entry to the **Hans Fiebusch Studio,** nearby in St. Martin's Square, with an exact recreation of the St. John's Wood (London) studio of this exiled German artist (1898–1998) who was the last member of the so-called degenerate art group. ⊠*9 N. Pallant* ☎*01243/774557* ⊕*www.pallant.org.uk* ⌨*£7.50* ☉*Tues., Wed., Fri., and Sat. 10–5, Thurs. 10–8, Sun. and national holidays 12:30–5.*

☼ **Weald and Downland Open Air Museum.** It's worth a stop in Singleton, a secluded village 5 mi north of Chichester, to see this excellent museum, a sanctuary for historical buildings dating from the 13th to 19th century. Among the 45 structures moved to 50 acres of wooded meadows are a cluster of medieval houses, a water mill, a Tudor market hall, and an ancient blacksmith's shop. ⊠*A286* ☎*01243/811363* ⊕*www.wealddown.co.uk* ⌨*£8.95* ☉*Apr.–Oct., daily 10:30–6; Nov., Dec., and mid-Feb.–Mar., daily 10:30–4; Jan.–mid-Feb., weekends and Wed. 10:30–4:30; last admission 1 hr before closing.*

WHERE TO EAT AND STAY

£££ ✕**Comme Ça.** Its location, about a five-minute walk across the park from
FRENCH the Chichester Festival Theatre, makes this attractively converted pub a pleasant spot for a meal before a performance. Bunches of dried hops,

suspended from the ceiling, and antique children's toys decorate the dining room. The owner, Michel Navet, is French, and his chef produces sophisticated, authentic French dishes such as duck with poached figs and lamb with an herb crust and ratatouille. The fixed-price lunch menu offers two courses for £19. ✉ *67 Broyle Rd.* ☎ *01243/788724* ▤ *AE, DC, MC, V* ⊘ *Closed Mon. No dinner Sun. No lunch Tues.*

£££   ⊞ **Ship Hotel.** Built in 1790, this architecturally interesting hotel near the Chichester Festival Theatre was originally the home of Admiral Sir George Murray, one of Admiral Nelson's right-hand men. Among the outstanding elements are the flying (partially freestanding) staircase and colonnade. The house has been restored to its 18th-century elegance after spending time as a dental clinic and then an antiques shop. Reproduction period furniture fills the guest rooms, which have a simpler design than the grand public areas. Prices rise steeply during the Glorious Goodwood horse race in July. **Pros:** well-restored building; great for architecture buffs; good location. **Cons:** rooms are a little bland; not many amenities. ✉ *North St.* ☎ *01243/778000* ⊕ *www.shiphotelchichester.co.uk* ⬗ *36 rooms* ⬙ *In-room: no a/c, Internet. In-hotel: restaurant, bar, some pets allowed* ▤ *AE, DC, MC, V* ⦶*BP.*

NIGHTLIFE AND THE ARTS

The **Chichester Festival Theatre** (✉ *Oaklands Park* ☎ *01243/781312* ⊕ *www.cft.org.uk*) presents classics and modern plays from May through September and is a venue for touring companies the rest of the year. Built in 1962, it has an international reputation for innovative performances and attracts theatergoers from across the country.

GUILDFORD

22 mi north of Petworth House, 35 mi north of Chichester, 28 mi southwest of London.

Guildford, the largest town in Surrey and the county's capital, is a busy commuter town with a noted theater, but its town center retains a faint 18th-century air. Gabled merchants' houses line the steep, pleasantly provincial High Street, filled with upscale household shops and restaurants. The remains of its old Norman castle are tucked away in a peaceful garden off High Street, and the large clock on the town's old guildhall adds charm. Wisley, a notable garden, is 10 mi away.

ESSENTIALS

Visitor Information Guildford (✉ *14 Tunsgate* ☎ *01483/444333* ⊕ *www.guildford.gov.uk*).

EXPLORING

Displays in the **Guildford Museum,** in the old castle building, include interesting exhibits on local history and archaeology, as well as memorabilia of Charles Dodgson, better known as Lewis Carroll, the author of *Alice in Wonderland.* Dodgson spent his last years in a house on nearby Castle Hill. He was buried in the Mount Cemetery, up the hill on High Street. **Castle Arch,** all that remains of the entrance of the old castle, displays a slot for a portcullis. ✉ *Quarry St.* ☎ *01483/444751* ⊕ *www.guildfordmuseum.co.uk* ▣ *Free* ⊘ *Mon.–Sat. 11–5.*

HIKING IN THE SOUTHEAST

For those who prefer to travel on their own two feet, the Southeast offers long sweeps of open terrain that makes walking a pleasure. Ardent walkers can explore all or part of the **North Downs Way** (153 mi) and the **South Downs Way** (106 mi), following ancient paths along the tops of the downs—the undulating treeless uplands typical of the area. Both trails give you wide views over the countryside.

The North Downs Way follows part of the old Pilgrim's Way to Canterbury that so fascinated Chaucer. The South Downs Way crosses the chalk landscape of Sussex Downs, with parts of the route going through deep woodland. Along the way, charming little villages serve the walkers cool ale in inns that have been doing precisely that for centuries. The 30-mi (north–south) **Downs Link** joins the two routes. Along the Kent coast, the Saxon Shore Way, 143 mi from Gravesend to Rye, passes four Roman forts. Guides to these walks are available from the Southeast England Tourist Board (⊕ *www.visitsoutheastengland.com*); also check the National Trails Web site (⊕ *www.nationaltrail.co.uk*).

Fodor'sChoice ★ In a nation of gardeners and garden goers, **Wisley** is the Royal Horticultural Society's innovative and inspirational 240-acre showpiece. Both an ornamental and scientific center, it claims to have greater horticultural diversity than any other garden in the world. The rock garden and alpine meadow in spring, the flower borders and displays in the central area, and the impressive year-round conservatories are just a few highlights, along with a garden center that sells more than 10,000 types of plants and an impressive bookstore. Near Woking, the garden is 10 mi northeast of Guildford. It's very easy to spend half a day or more here. ⊠ *A3, Woking* ☎ *01483/224234* ⊕ *www.rhs.org.uk/gardens/wisley* ☒ *£8.50* ⊙ *Mar.–Oct., weekdays 10–6, weekends and national holidays 9–6; Nov.–Feb., weekdays 10–4:30, weekends 9–4:30.*

WHERE TO EAT AND STAY

£££
FRENCH
✕ **Café de Paris.** An 18th-century building holds this family-owned French brasserie. The menu focuses on game and fish: try the venison in red-wine sauce, roast sea bass with braised fennel, or the artichoke risotto, but leave enough room for a sorbet. There are specials on the fine blackboard menu, and there's a £12.50 fixed-price menu at lunchtime and for pretheater dining on weekdays. ⊠ *35 Castle St.* ☎ *01483/534896* ▤ *AE, MC, V* ⊙ *Closed Sun.*

£
THAI
✕ **Rumwong.** On the incredibly long menu, the Thai name of each dish appears with a clear English description. Good choices are the fisherman's soup, a spicy mass of delicious saltwater fish in a clear broth, or *yam pla muek,* a hot salad with squid. The restaurant runs an Asian supermarket next door. ⊠ *16–18 London Rd.* ☎ *01483/536092* ▤ *MC, V* ⊙ *Closed Mon.*

££££ ★ ▥ **Angel Posting House and Livery.** Guildford was once famous for its coaching inns, but this 500-year-old hotel is the last of them. The courtyard, where coaches and horses clattered to a stop, opens to the sky, and light lunches are offered here in summer. Individually designed guest rooms have luxurious fabrics, reproductions of antiques, and marble-lined bathrooms; 10 are in a modern annex. There's a salon with a fireplace and minstrels' gallery, and the 13th-century stone-vaulted crypt serves as the backdrop for fine modern British food (£32 for fixed-price menu). **Pros:** historic building; lovely rooms. **Cons:** creaky floors; books up far in advance. ✉ *91 High St.* ☎ *01483/564555* ⊕ *www.angelpostinghouse.com* ➘ *21 rooms* ⚲ *In-room: no a/c, Wi-Fi. In-hotel: restaurant, gym, spa, some pets allowed* ☐ *AE, DC, MC, V.*

££ ⬛ **Old Great Halfpenny.** Surrounded by well-maintained grounds, this 16th-century half-timbered house looks like something out of a picture book. The owners are decorators and gardeners, so the place is impeccably done, from top to bottom. Rooms have comfortable antique beds, and you can have breakfast on the patio in the summertime. **Pros:** beautiful gardens; lovely old building; peace and quiet. **Cons:** a 15-minute drive out of town; small. ✉ *Halfpenny La., St. Martha* ✛ *5 mi north of Guildford* ☎ *01483/567835* ➘ *2 rooms* ⚲ *In-room: no a/c, no phone. In-hotel: Wi-Fi, no smoking rooms* ☐ *No credit cards* ⭐ *CP.*

NIGHTLIFE AND THE ARTS

The **Yvonne Arnaud Theatre** (✉ *Millbrook* ☎ *01483/440000*), a horseshoe-shape building on an island in the River Wey, frequently previews West End productions; it also has a restaurant. The smaller Mill Studio showcases more intimate productions.

CASTLES AND HOUSES NEAR TUNBRIDGE WELLS

England is famous for its magnificent stately homes and castles, but many of them are scattered across the country, presenting a challenge for travelers. Within a 15-mi radius of Tunbridge Wells, however, in that area of hills and hidden dells known as the Weald, lies a wealth of architectural wonder in historic homes, castles, and gardens: Penshurst Place, Hever Castle, Chartwell, Knole, Ightham Mote, Leeds Castle, Sissinghurst Castle Garden, and Bodiam Castle.

ROYAL TUNBRIDGE WELLS

39 mi southeast of London.

Nobody much bothers with the "Royal" anymore, but Tunbridge Wells is no less regal because of it. For whatever reason, this historic bedroom community has been the butt of jokes for years. It's seen as conservative and upper-middle class—and so it is. But that doesn't make the town any less attractive and handy as a base for exploring the region if you are driving.

The city owes its prosperity to the 17th- and 18th-century passion for spas and mineral baths. In 1606 a mineral-water spring was discovered here, drawing legions of royal visitors looking for eternal health. Tunbridge Wells reached its zenith in the mid-18th century, when Richard "Beau" Nash presided over its social life. The buildings at the lower end of High Street are mostly 18th century, but as the street climbs the hill north, changing its name to Mount Pleasant Road, structures become more modern.

GETTING HERE AND AROUND

National Express buses headed to Kent and Tunbridge Wells depart from London's Victoria Coach Station several times a day. The trip takes about 90 minutes. Southeastern trains leave from London's Charing Cross station every 30 minutes. The journey takes just under an hour. If you're traveling by car from London, head here on the A21; travel time is about an hour.

Tunbridge Wells sprawls in all directions, but the historic center is compact and walkable. None of the sights is more than a 10-minute walk from the main train station. You can pick up a town map at the station.

ESSENTIALS

Visitor Information Royal Tunbridge Wells (⊠ *The Old Fish Market, the Pantiles* ☎*01892/515675* ⊕ *www.visittunbridgewells.com).*

EXPLORING

A good place to begin a visit is at the **Pantiles,** a famous promenade with colonnaded shops near the spring on one side of town. Its odd name derives from the Dutch "pan tiles" that originally paved the area. Now bordered on two sides by busy main roads, the Pantiles remains an elegant, tranquil oasis, and the site of the actual well. ■TIP➜**You can still drink the waters when a "dipper" (the traditional water dispenser) is in attendance, from Easter through September.**

The **Church of King Charles the Martyr** (⊠ *Chapel Pl.*), across the road from the Pantiles, dates from 1678, when it was dedicated to Charles I, who had been executed by Parliament in 1649. Its plain exterior belies its splendid interior; take special note of the beautifully plastered baroque ceiling.

OFF THE BEATEN PATH

All Saints Church. This modest 13th-century church holds one of the glories of 20th-century church art. The building is awash with the luminous yellows and blues of 12 windows by Marc Chagall (1887–1985), commissioned as a tribute by the family of a young girl who was drowned in a sailing accident in 1963. The church is 4 mi north of Tunbridge Wells; turn off A26 before Tonbridge and continue a mile or so east along B2017. ⊠ *B2017, Tudeley* ☎*0870/744–1456* ⊡*Free* ⊙*Daily 9–6 or dusk.*

WHERE TO EAT

£££
CHINESE

✕**Gracelands Palace.** Weird and wonderful, this place is a temple to Chinese food and, well, Elvis. Owner Paul Chan is famous in the region for his cabaret of Elvis songs and two- or three-course fixed-price menus of Szechuan and Cantonese fare. Pictures of Chan and Elvis decorate the building; it's packed most nights with cheerful fans. ⊠ *3 Cumberland Walk* ☎*01892/540754* ⊟*AE, MC, V* ⊙*Closed Sun. No lunch Mon.*

£
ASIAN

✕**Himalayan Gurkha Restaurant.** It's not what you might expect to find in the cozy confines of Tunbridge Wells, but the Nepalese cuisine of this friendly spot is popular with locals. Spicy mountain dishes are cooked with care in traditional clay ovens or barbecued on flaming

Around
Tunbridge Wells

0   5 miles
0   5 km

KENT

EAST
SUSSEX

charcoal. Vegetarian options are appealing, too. ⊠*31 Church Rd.*
☎*01892/527834* ▤*MC, V.*

££ ╳**Mount Edgcumbe Restaurant and Bar.** To some degree, the attraction of
FRENCH this creative restaurant above the old town center is the fact that it's
in a candlelighted cave. The fact that it's carved out of the limestone
foundation of the Mount Edgcumbe Hotel means that it's a very nice
cave indeed. Service can be a bit shaky, but the food is quite good: on
the menu are French-inspired European dishes such as pan-seared duck
breast with raspberry jus and roast salmon with olive tapenade. ⊠*The
Common* ☎*01892/526823* ▤*MC, V.*

££££ ╳**Thackeray's House.** Once the home of Victorian novelist William
FRENCH Makepeace Thackeray, this mid-17th-century tile-hung house is now
★ an elegant restaurant known for creative French cuisine. Dishes could
include braised pork cheek with black pudding and clove-and-ginger
jus, or pan-fried sea bream with wild mushrooms. The lunchtime menu
du jour is a good value at £16.50 for two courses. ⊠*85 London Rd.*
☎*01892/511921* ▤*AE, MC, V* ☉*Closed Mon. and last wk in Dec.
No dinner Sun.*

WHERE TO STAY

£££ **Hotel du Vin.** This elegant sandstone house dating from 1762 has been transformed into a chic boutique hotel with polished wood floors and luxurious armchairs and sofas. Oriental rugs give public rooms a warmth that is both intimate and grand, and guest rooms are minimalist modern, with pampering bathrooms. The Burgundy Bar stocks a fine selection of wines from the eponymous region of France. The contemporary menu in the bistro changes daily but is strong on creamy soups and crisp salads. **Pros:** beautifully renovated historic building; luxurious linens. **Cons:** restaurant can get booked up. ⊠ *Crescent Rd. near Mount Pleasant Rd.* ☎ *01892/526455* ⊕ *www.hotelduvin.com* ⤏ *34 rooms* ⌂ *In-room: no a/c, Wi-Fi. In-hotel: restaurant, bars* ⊟ *AE, DC, MC, V.*

> **WORD OF MOUTH**
>
> "Tunbridge Wells might do the trick for you. It's a nice little town, a tad on the twee side but cute for visitors, some interesting history and places to visit in the town, and well-placed for exploring. With children it has the advantage of a large park area in the center. It has a nice historic shopping area." —nona1

££ **Old Parsonage.** A friendly guesthouse, 2 mi south of Tunbridge Wells via A267, stands at the top of a quiet lane beside the village church. Built in 1820, the Georgian manor has lovely antique furniture, a dining room with oak refectory table, and a big conservatory for afternoon tea. Two pubs and a restaurant are a short walk away. **Pros:** laid-back atmosphere; friendly staff; cozy conservatory. **Cons:** no on-site restaurant; outside of town. ⊠ *Church La., Frant* ☎ *01892/750773* ⊕ *www. theoldparsonagehotel.co.uk* ⤏ *3 rooms* ⌂ *In-room: no a/c, no phone. In-hotel: some pets allowed, no kids under 7* ⊟ *MC, V* ⍿ *BP.*

£££–££££ **Spa Hotel.** Carefully chosen traditional furnishings and details help maintain the country-house flavor of this 1766 Georgian mansion, although modern touches like wireless Internet connections in the guest rooms make it convenient. There are superb views from the 15-acre grounds across the town and into the Weald of Kent. Kids can take pony-riding lessons at the stables here. The traditional English fare of the Chandelier Restaurant is popular with locals. **Pros:** lap-of-luxury feel; gorgeous views. **Cons:** very formal atmosphere; can be a bit stuffy. ⊠ *Mount Ephraim* ☎ *01892/520331* ⊕ *www.spahotel.co.uk* ⤏ *69 rooms* ⌂ *In-room: no a/c (some), Wi-Fi. In-hotel: restaurant, bar, tennis court, pool, gym, spa, Wi-Fi, some pets allowed* ⊟ *AE, DC, MC, V.*

PENSHURST PLACE

7 mi northwest of Royal Tunbridge Wells, 33 mi southeast of London.

EXPLORING

★ At the center of the adorable hamlet of Penshurst stands **Penshurst Place,** one of England's finest medieval manor houses, hidden behind tall trees and walls. Although it has a 14th-century hall, Penshurst is mainly Elizabethan and has been the family home of the Sidneys since 1552, giving it particular historical interest. The most famous Sidney is the

Elizabethan poet Sir Philip, author of *Arcadia*. The **Baron's Hall,** topped with a chestnut roof, is the oldest and one of the grandest halls to survive from the early Middle Ages. Family portraits, furniture, tapestries, and armor help tell the story of this house that was first inhabited in 1341 by Sir John de Pulteney, the very wealthy four-time London mayor. The grounds include a toy museum, a gift shop, and the enchanting 11-acre walled Italian Garden, which displays tulips and daffodils in spring, roses in July, and mistletoe during the winter months. The house is off Leicester Square; take time to study the village's late-15th-century half-timber structures adorned with soaring brick chimneys. ⊠ *Off B2188; from Tunbridge Wells, follow A26 and B2176* ☎ *01892/870307* ⊕ *www.penshurstplace.com* ⊠ *£8.50 for house and grounds; grounds only, £7; £12 for tours of house and gardens (call to confirm if tours are available)* ⊙ *Mar., weekends noon–5:30; Apr.–Oct., daily noon–5. Grounds daily 10:30–6. Last admission 30 mins before closing.*

WHERE TO EAT AND STAY

££ ✕ **Spotted Dog.** This pub first opened its doors in 1520 and hardly
BRITISH appears to have changed. Its big inglenook fireplace and heavy beams give it character, the views from the hilltop are lovely, and the good food and friendly crowd make it a pleasure. Cheeses, meats, and beer are locally sourced. The pub is 1.3 mi from Penshurst by the narrow B2188. ⊠ *Smarts Hill* ☎ *01892/870253* ▭ *MC, V.*

££ ▦ **Rose and Crown.** Originally a 16th-century inn, this hotel on the main street in Tonbridge (5 mi east of Penshurst, 5 mi north of Tunbridge Wells) has low-beam ceilings and good Jacobean woodwork in the snug, inviting bar and the restaurant. Guest rooms in the main building are traditionally furnished, whereas rooms in the newer annex are more modern in style. There's a pretty bicycle route from Tonbridge to Penshurst. **Pros:** lovely old building; atmospheric setting. **Cons:** older rooms are quite small; annex rooms have less charm. ⊠ *125 High St., Tonbridge* ☎ *01732/357966* ⊕ *www.rose-andcrownhotel.co.uk* ⇆ *50 rooms* ⌂ *In-room: no a/c. In-hotel: restaurant, bar, laundry service, parking (free)* ▭ *AE, MC, V* ⦿ *BP.*

HEVER CASTLE

3 mi west of Penshurst, 10 mi northwest of Royal Tunbridge Wells, 30 mi southeast of London.

EXPLORING

Fodor'sChoice For some, 13th-century **Hever Castle** fits the stereotype of what a castle
★ should look like: all turrets and battlements, the whole encircled by a water lily–bound moat. For others, it's too squat in structure (and perhaps too renovated). Here, at her childhood home, the unfortunate Anne Boleyn, second wife of Henry VIII and mother of Elizabeth I, was courted and won by Henry. He loved her dearly for a time but had her beheaded in 1536 after she failed to give birth to a son. He then gave Boleyn's home to his fourth wife, Anne of Cleves, as a present. Famous though it was, the castle fell into disrepair in the 19th century. American millionaire William Waldorf Astor acquired Hever in 1903, and the Astor family owned it until 1983. Astor built a Tudor village to

house his staff (it's now a hotel for corporate functions) and created the stunning gardens, which include an excellent yew maze, a water maze, ponds, playgrounds, tea shops, gift shops, plant shops—you get the picture. In summer activities are nonstop here, with jousting, falconry exhibitions, and country fairs, making this one of southern England's most rewarding castles to visit. ⊠ *Off B2026, Hever* ☎ *01732/865224* ⊕ *www.hevercastle.co.uk* ✉ *£12; grounds only, £9.50* ⊘ *Castle Apr.–Oct., daily noon–6; Mar., Wed.–Sun., noon–4; Nov. and Dec., Thurs.–Sun. noon–4. Grounds Apr.–Oct., daily 10:30–6; Mar., Wed.–Sun. 10:30–4; Nov. and Dec., Thurs.–Sun. 10:30–4. Last admission 1 hr before closing.*

CHARTWELL

9 mi north of Hever Castle, 12 mi northwest of Tunbridge Wells, 28 mi southeast of London.

EXPLORING

A grand Victorian mansion with views over the Weald, **Chartwell** was the home of Sir Winston Churchill from 1924 until his death in 1965. Virtually everything has been kept as it was when he lived here, with his pictures, books, photos, and maps. There's even a half-smoked cigar that the World War II prime minister never finished. Churchill was an amateur artist, and his paintings show a different side of the crusty politician. Admission to the house is by timed ticket, which can't be prebooked. The garden may be open year-round, weather permitting. ■ TIP→ **Be sure to explore Chartwell's rose gardens and take one of the country walks.** ⊠ *Off B2026, Westerham* ☎ *01732/866368* ⊕ *www.nationaltrust.org.uk* ✉ *£10.60, garden only £5.30* ⊘ *Mid-Mar.–June and early Sept.–late Oct., Wed.–Sun. 11–5; July–early Sept., Tues.–Sun. 11–5; last admission at 4:15.*

KNOLE

8 mi east of Chartwell, 11 mi north of Royal Tunbridge Wells, 27 mi southeast of London.

EXPLORING

Fodor's Choice
★

The town of Sevenoaks lies in London's commuter belt, a world away from the baronial air of its premier attraction, **Knole,** the grand, beloved home of the Sackville family since the 16th century. Begun in the 15th century and enlarged in 1603 by Thomas Sackville, Knole, with its complex of courtyards and buildings, resembles a small town. You'll need most of an afternoon to explore it thoroughly. The house is noted for its tapestries, embroidered furnishings, and the most famous set of 17th-century silver furniture to survive. Most of the salons are in the pre-baroque mode, rather dark and armorial. The magnificently florid staircase was a novelty in its Elizabethan heyday. Vita Sackville-West grew up at Knole and set her novel *The Edwardians,* a witty account of life among the gilded set, here. Encompassed by a 1,000-acre deer park, the house lies in the center of Sevenoaks, opposite St. Nicholas Church. To get there from Chartwell, drive north to Westerham, then pick up

A25 and head east for 8 mi to A225. ⊠*Off A225* ☎*01732/450608* ⊕*www.nationaltrust.org.uk* ⊠*House £9, gardens £2* ☼*Mar., weekends noon–4; Apr.–June, Sept., and Oct., Wed.–Sun. noon–4; July and Aug., Tues.–Sun. 11–4:30. Gardens Apr.–Sept., Wed. 11–4. Last admission 30 mins before closing.*

IGHTHAM MOTE

7 mi southeast of Knole, 10 mi north of Royal Tunbridge Wells, 31 mi southeast of London.

EXPLORING

★ Finding **Ightham Mote** requires careful navigation, but it's worth the effort to see a vision right out of the Middle Ages. To enter this outstanding example of a small manor house, you cross a stone bridge over one of the dreamiest moats in England. This moat, however, does not relate to the "mote" in the name, which refers to the role of the house as a meeting place, or "moot." Ightham (pronounced *i*-tem) Mote's magical exterior has changed little since the 14th century, but within you'll find that it encompasses styles of several periods, Tudor to Victorian. The Great Hall is an antiquarian's delight, both comfy and grand, and the Tudor chapel, drawing room, and billiards room in the northwest quarter are highlights. To reach the house from Sevenoaks, follow A25 east to A227 (8 mi) and follow the signs. ⊠*Off A227, Ivy Hatch, Sevenoaks* ☎*01732/810378* ⊕*www.nationaltrust.org.uk* ⊠*£9.40* ☼*House Mid-Mar.–Oct., Thurs.–Mon. 11–5; Nov. and Dec., Thurs.–Sun. 11–3. Estate daily all yr, dawn–dusk.*

ROCHESTER

15 mi north of Ightham Mote, 28 mi southeast of London.

Positioned near the confluence of the Thames and the River Medway, this posh town has a history of Roman, Saxon, and Norman occupation, all of which have left architectural remains, including the vast castle at the town center. Novelist Charles Dickens called Rochester home for more than a decade, until his death in 1870. The Charles Dickens Centre in Eastgate House on High Street is closed, though you can still stroll through the garden and see the exterior of the Swiss-style chalet where he wrote. Plans are afoot to reopen the center. Across the river from Rochester is Chatham, with a noted maritime museum and the Dickens World theme park.

ESSENTIALS

Visitor Information Rochester (⊠*95 High St.* ☎*01634/843666* ⊕*www. cometorochester.co.uk*).

EXPLORING

The impressive ruins of **Rochester Castle** are a superb example of Norman military architecture. The keep, built in the 1100s using the old Roman city wall as a foundation, is 125 feet high, the tallest in England. It's been shored up but left without floors, so that from the bottom you can see to the open roof and study the complex structure.

Tips for Visiting Treasure Houses

Throughout the Southeast you can wander through the gorgeous homes of the wealthy and the formerly wealthy. Some are privately owned; hundreds of other homes and castles are owned by the National Trust or English Heritage, organizations that raise part of the money needed to maintain them through entrance fees. Here are some things to keep in mind when you visit:

Houses and castles are unique. What you get for your entrance fee differs enormously. You may be free to wander at will, or you may be organized into groups like prisoners behind enemy lines. Sometimes the exterior of a building may be spectacular, but the interior dull. It's also true that the gardens and grounds may be just as (or more) interesting than the house. Our individual reviews alert you to these instances. You can often pay separately for the house and grounds, so choose your admission ticket accordingly.

Passes may save you money. If you plan to see lots of houses and castles, it might be cheaper to buy a pass, such as Visit Britain's Great British Heritage Pass, or to join an organization such as the National Trust (⇨ Sightseeing Passes in Essentials in Travel Smart England) and thus

get free entry. Check entrance fees against your itinerary to be sure what you will save.

Opening hours are seasonal and change. Hours can change abruptly, so call the day before. Many houses are open only from April to October, and they may have extremely limited hours. In other cases the houses have celebrated parks and gardens that are open much of the year. Consider a trip in shoulder seasons if you can't take the crowds that inevitably pack the most popular houses; or explore lesser-known abodes. You'll still have a great time.

Transportation can be a challenge. If you don't have a car, plan transportation in advance. Some places are tucked deep in the countryside; others are more accessible.

Consider a stay at a property. To get even more up close and personal, you can rent a cottage from the National Trust (⊕ www.nationaltrustcottages. co.uk) or English Heritage (⊕ www. english-heritage.org.uk/holidaycottages). You could stay in the servants' quarters, a lodge, or even a lighthouse. Some privately owned houses have cottages for rent on their estates; their Web sites generally have this information. Also ⇨ See Accommodations in Travel Smart England.

At the shop you can pick up well-researched guides to the building. ⊠ Boley Hill ☎ 01634/402276 ⊕ www.english-heritage.org.uk ⊠ £5 ⊗ Apr.–Sept., daily 10–6; Oct.–Mar., daily 10–4; last admission 30 mins before closing.

In AD 604 Augustine of Canterbury ordained the first English bishop in a small cathedral on the site of **Rochester Cathedral.** The current cathedral, England's second oldest, is a jumble of architectural styles. Much of the original Norman building (1077) remains, including the striking west front, the highly carved portal, and the tympanum above the doorway. Some medieval art survives, including a 13th-century Wheel of Fortune on the choir walls; it's a reminder of how difficult medieval life was. ⊠*Boley Hill* ☎*01634/843366* ⊕*www.rochestercathedral.org* ⊠*£2 donation suggested* ⊙*Mon.–Sat. 7:30–6, Sun. 7:30–5.*

Filling an aluminum-clad hangar, **Dickens World** is a literary theme park. It introduces you to the great author (himself a showman) and his works, and re-creates the sights of Victorian England, including its darker aspects. There's a Victorian school, complete with a fierce headmaster; a haunted house; and a boat ride based on the story of Pip and Magwitch in *Great Expectations*. This curiosity is popular for families with young children. Shuttle buses (£1) run from the Chatham train station. ⊠*Leviathan Way, Chatham* ☎*01634/890421* ⊕*www. dickensworld.co.uk* ⊠*£12.50* ⊙*Daily 10–5:30; last admission at 5.*

The buildings and 47 retired ships at the 80-acre **Historic Dockyard** across the River Medway from Rochester constitute the country's most complete Georgian-to-early-Victorian dockyard. Fans of maritime history could easily spend a day at the exhibits and structures. The dockyard's origins go back to the time of Henry VIII; some 400 ships were built here over the centuries. There's a guided tour of the submarine HMS *Ocelot*, the last warship to be built for the Royal Navy at Chatham. ■TIP➜**Each ticket is good for 12 months, so you don't have to see it all in one visit.** ⊠*Chatham* ☎*01634/823807* ⊕*www.chdt.org.uk* ⊠*£14* ⊙*Mid-Mar.–Oct., daily 10–6 (or dusk if earlier); Nov., Sat. and Sun. 10–4.*

WHERE TO STAY

££ 　**Gordon House Hotel.** Across from the cathedral, this friendly guesthouse in central Rochester is a well-priced option. Rooms are done in creamy colors, and some have Victorian architectural details; most have antiques. You can have a cup of tea and relax in the ground-floor lounge after a busy day of sightseeing. **Pros:** friendly staff; lovely rooms. **Cons:** some rooms are small; bathrooms are a bit old-fashioned. ⊠*91 High St.* ☎*01634/814769* ⊕*www.gordonhousehotel.net* 🛏*12 rooms* ⅃*Inroom: no a/c. In-hotel: restaurant, bar* ⊟*MC, V* ⍨*BP.*

NIGHTLIFE AND THE ARTS

Rochester sponsors a **Dickensian Christmas Festival** (☎*01634/306000*) on the first weekend in December. Thousands of people in period dress participate in reenactments of scenes from the author's novel *A Christmas Carol.* A candlelight procession, mulled wine and roasted chestnuts, and Christmas carols at the cathedral add to the celebration. Another important Dickens festival takes place in Broadstairs (40 mi east).

LEEDS CASTLE

12 mi south of Rochester, 19 mi northwest of Royal Tunbridge Wells, 40 mi southeast of London.

EXPLORING

The bubbling River Medway runs through Maidstone, Kent's county seat, with its backdrop of chalky downs. Nearby, the fairy-tale stronghold of **Leeds Castle** commands two small islands on a peaceful lake. Dating to the 9th century and rebuilt by the Normans in 1119, Leeds (not to be confused with the city in the north of England) became a favorite home of many medieval English queens. Henry VIII liked it so much he had it converted from a fortress into a grand palace. The interior doesn't match the glories of the much-photographed exterior, although there are fine paintings and furniture, plus a curious dog-collar museum. The outside attractions are more impressive and include a maze, a grotto, an aviary of native and exotic birds, and woodland gardens. The castle is 5 mi east of Maidstone. ⊠A20 ☎01622/765400 ⊕*www.leedscastle.org.uk* ☜*£16.50; grounds only, £11* ⊗*Apr.–Oct., daily 10–5; Nov.–Mar., daily 10–3:30.*

SISSINGHURST CASTLE GARDEN

10 mi south of Leeds Castle, 53 mi southeast of London.

GETTING HERE AND AROUND

For those without a car, take a train from London's Charing Cross station and transfer to a bus in Staplehurst. Direct buses operate on Tuesday, Friday, and Sunday between May and August; at other times, take the bus to Sissinghurst village and walk the remaining 1¼ mi. From Leeds Castle, make your way south on B2163 and A274 through Headcorn, and then follow signs.

EXPLORING

Fodor'sChoice ★ One of the most famous gardens in the world, **Sissinghurst Castle Garden** rests deep in the Kentish countryside, unpretentiously beautiful and quintessentially English. The gardens, 10 themed garden "rooms," were laid out in the 1930s around the remains of part of a moated Tudor castle by writer Vita Sackville-West (one of the Sackvilles of Knole; she grew up there) and her husband, the diplomat Harold Nicolson. Climb the tower to see Sackville-West's study and to get wonderful views of the garden and surrounding areas. You can also enter the house to see the library, with its echoes of Knole. ■TIP➔ **Good times to visit the grounds are June and July, when the roses are in bloom. It's also less busy later in the afternoon.** The White Garden, with its white flowers and silver-gray foliage, is a classic, and the herb garden and cottage garden show Sackville-West's knowledge of plants. There are woodland and lake walks, too, making it easy to spend a half-day or more here. Stop by the big tea shop for lunch or a snack; at the time of this writing, the owners were restoring farmland so that they could supply all of the restaurant's vegetables. ⊠*A262, Cranbrook* ☎*01580/710701* ⊕*www. nationaltrust.org.uk* ☜*£8.80* ⊗*Mid-Mar.–Oct., Mon., Tues., and Fri. 11–6:30, weekends 10–6:30; last admission at 6.*

Biddenden Winery and Cider Works, 3½ mi east of Sissinghurst on the A262, cultivates 9 types of grapes on 22 acres, with a focus on the German Ortega, Huxelrebe, Bacchus, and Reichensteiner varieties. There are tours once a month or so; check ahead. It also rents out a loft with a kitchen by the week (from £240 per week in winter to £420 in summer). ⊠*Biddenden* ☎*01580/291726* ⊕*www.biddendenvineyards.com* ☜*Free* ⊗*Mon.–Sat. 10–5, Sun. 11–5; closed Christmas wk and Sun. in Jan. and Feb.*

WHERE TO EAT AND STAY

£   ✗ **Claris's Tea Shop.** Claris's, near Sissinghurst Castle Garden, serves tra-
CAFÉ   ditional English teas in a half-timber room and displays attractive English crafts items. The Cream Tea set includes scones with butter, fresh
cream, preserves, and a pot of tea for £5.20. There's a garden for summer, and a gift shop stocks china and glass. ⊠*1–3 High St., Biddenden*
🖀*01580/291025* ▭*No credit cards* ⊙*Closed Mon. No dinner.*

£–££   🏠 **Bishopsdale Oast.** This converted 18th-century double-kiln oasthouse
(used for drying hops) makes an atmospheric place to stay in tiny Biddenden, near Sissinghurst. The sprawling redbrick house with its tip-
tilty roof has been elegantly renovated, with cream-color walls, dark
furniture, and framed pictures of flowers on the walls. On cold days
a fire burns in the spacious lounge, and on warm, sunny days you
can breakfast outside on the terrace. Bedrooms vary in size: the more
expensive rooms are quite spacious, but cheaper rooms are more of
a squeeze. All are nicely decorated, and many have sweeping views
of a nearby deer park. **Pros:** quiet and restful setting; owner is a chef
so breakfasts are great (dinners can be arranged, too); nice garden.
Cons: some rooms are small; car needed to get around. ⊠ *Biddenden*
🖀*01580/291027* ⊘*www.bishopsdaleoast.co.uk* ⇥*5 rooms* &*In-
room: no a/c, no phone. In hotel: no-smoking rooms* ⑩*BP.*

EN
ROUTE

As you leave Sissinghurst Castle Garden, continue south along A229
through Hawkhurst, a little village that was once the headquarters of
a notorious gang of smugglers. Turn left onto the B2244 and left at the
Curlew pub to arrive in the tiny Sussex village of Bodiam.

BODIAM CASTLE

*9 mi south of Cranbrook (Sissinghurst), 15 mi southeast of Royal Tun-
bridge Wells, 57 mi southeast of London.*

EXPLORING

☼   Immortalized in paintings, postcards, and photographs, the ruins of
★   **Bodiam Castle** rise out of the distance like a piece of medieval legend. Its
turrets, battlements, wooden portcullis, glassy moat, and 2-foot-thick
walls survive, but all that was within them is long gone. Built in 1385
to withstand a threatened French invasion, it was "slighted" (partly
demolished) during the English Civil War of 1642–46 and has been
uninhabited ever since. Still, you can climb the towers to take in sweeping countryside views, and kids can run around in and around the castle.
The castle schedules organized activities for kids during school holidays.
⊠*Off B2244, Bodiam* 🖀*01580/830436* ⊕*www.nationaltrust.org.uk*
⊡*£5.20* ⊙*Mid-Feb.–Oct., daily 10:30–6 or dusk; Nov. and Dec.,
Wed.–Sun. 10:30–4 or dusk; Jan.–mid-Feb., weekends 10:30–4; last
admission 1 hr before closing.*

The South

4

WORD OF MOUTH

"We visited Stonehenge on the Stone Circle Access tour, which lets a limited number of people enter for a one-hour period before (or after) regular visiting hours, and allows visitors to walk in among the stones. After 30 minutes people in our time slot started to leave and by the end of the hour we had Stonehenge to ourselves in the early morning light. Fabulous."

—noe847

"You might consider going to Salisbury and staying the night before. It is a great little city with the cathedral, the Magna Carta, and everything, and close—less than 30 minutes—to Stonehenge."

—laurie_ann

Updated
by Robert
Andrews

Cathedrals, stately homes, stone circles—the South, made up of Hampshire, Dorset, and Wiltshire counties, holds all kinds of attractions, and not a few quiet pleasures. Two important cathedrals, Winchester and Salisbury (pronounced *sawls-bree*), are here, as are stately homes—Longleat, Stourhead, and Wilton House, among them—intriguing market towns, and hundreds of haunting prehistoric remains, two of which, Avebury and Stonehenge, should not be missed.

These are just the tourist-brochure superlatives. Anyone spending time in these parts should rent a bike or a car and set out to discover the back-road villages—*not* found in those brochures. After a drink in the village pub and a look at the cricket game on the village green, stretch out in a field for a nap. Close to London, the green fields of Hampshire divide the cliffs and coves of the West Country from the hustle and bustle of the big city. If you have a coastal destination in mind, you may see this as farmland to rush through, but hit the brakes—there's plenty to see.

One of the area's many historical highlights was when Alfred the Great, teaching religion and letters, made Winchester the capital of 9th-century England and helped lay plans for Britain's first navy, sowing the seeds of the Commonwealth. This well-preserved market town is dominated by its cathedral, an imposing edifice filled with the Gothic tombs of 15th-century bishops. Winchester is a good center from which to visit quiet villages where so many of England's once great personages, from Florence Nightingale to Lord Mountbatten, lived or died. Jane Austen and her works are enduringly popular, and the road to her home at Chawton has become a much-trodden path.

Beyond the gentle, gardenlike landscape of Hampshire, you can explore the somewhat harsher terrain of Salisbury Plain. Two monuments, millennia apart, stand sentinel over the plain. One is the 404-foot-tall stone spire of Salisbury Cathedral, which dominates the entire Salisbury valley and has been immortalized in oil by John Constable. Not far away is the most imposing and dramatic prehistoric structure in Europe: Stonehenge. The many theories about its construction and purpose only add to its mystical attraction.

Other districts have their own pleasures, and many have literary or historical associations. Turn your sights to the Dorset heathland, the countryside explored in the novels of Thomas Hardy. This district is spanned by grass-covered chalk hills—the downs—wooded valleys, and meadows through which course meandering rivers. Facing the sea are Lyme Regis, on the fossil-rich Jurassic Coast, and Cowes, on the Isle of Wight—Queen Victoria's favorite getaway—where colorful flags flutter from sleek yachts.

TOP REASONS TO GO

Salisbury Cathedral: You may be stunned by the sight of one of England's most spectacular cathedrals; try a tour around the roof and spire for a fascinating angle on this must-see monument.

Stonehenge: Despite mixed reports of just how impressive this greatest of all prehistoric stone circles actually is, don't put off a visit. At the right time of day (early or late is best), this mystical ring can still cast a memorable spell against the backdrop of Salisbury Plain.

House and garden at Stourhead: It's the perfect combination. Acres of parkland, landscaped in the 18th century, induce feelings of Arcadian bliss. There are classical temples, a folly, and gorgeous vistas over the lake, as well as a Palladian mansion to explore.

The New Forest: Get away from it all in the South's most extensive wilderness—crisscrossed by myriad trails that are ideal for horseback riding, hiking, and biking.

Historic Dockyard, Portsmouth: Rule, Britannia! Immerse yourself in the country's seafaring history, including an informative and fascinating tour around Nelson's flagship, HMS *Victory*, conducted by naval personnel.

Literary trails: Jane Austen, Thomas Hardy, and John Fowles have all made this part of Britain a happy stomping ground for book buffs, with a concentration of sights in Chawton, Dorchester, and Lyme Regis. The Isle of Wight was particularly popular with Victorian literati, notably Tennyson.

The South has been quietly central to England's history for well over 4,000 years, occupied successively by prehistoric man, the Celts, the Romans, the Saxons, the Normans, and the modern British. History continues to be made here. On D-Day, Allied forces sailed for Normandy from this coast; nearly 40 years later, British forces set out to recover the Falklands.

ORIENTATION AND PLANNING

GETTING ORIENTED

The wide-open, wind-blown inland county of Wiltshire offers a sharp contrast to the tame, sequestered villages of Hampshire and Dorset and the self-important bustle of the ports of Southampton and Portsmouth. You may not want to spend much time in these two cities; instead, spend your nights in the more compelling towns of Salisbury and Winchester.

The obvious draw outside Salisbury is Stonehenge, but you're also within reach of an equally interesting prehistoric monument, Avebury. From there you can swing south to the cultivated woodlands of the New Forest. The southern coast of Dorset is another major area, with a couple of popular vacation resorts, Bournemouth and Weymouth, and a string of ancient sites: Corfe Castle, Maiden Castle, and Cerne

Abbas. Lyme Regis, on the Devon border at the center of the wide arc of Lyme Bay, is a favorite vacation destination in this area. It provides a gateway to the Jurassic Coast, a World Heritage Site that stretches between Swanage in the east and Exmouth in Devon.

Winchester to Southampton. One of the region's most compelling and historically rich towns, Winchester, lies a short distance from the well-heeled villages of New Alresford and Chawton and the great south-coast ports of Portsmouth and Southampton.

Isle of Wight. Osborne House, near Cowes, and Carisbrooke Castle, outside Newport, have much historic interest. The picturesque east-coast resorts of Ryde and Ventnor contrast with the dramatic Needles, the island's most iconic landmark, on the western tip.

Salisbury, Stonehenge, and Salisbury Plain. A tour of Wiltshire kicks off in the cathedral city of Salisbury, close to Wilton and Stonehenge. Farther afield are the market towns of Shaftesbury and Sherborne, and the great estates of Stourhead and Longleat.

New Forest to Lyme Regis. The sparsely populated New Forest stretches between Southampton and Bournemouth. The route west passes Wimborne Minster, dominated by its church, and ruined Corfe Castle. Historic Dorchester and Weymouth lead to Lyme Regis.

PLANNING

WHEN TO GO

Don't plan to visit the cathedrals of Salisbury and Winchester on a Sunday, when your visit will be restricted, or during services, when it won't be appreciated by worshippers. Places such as Stonehenge and Longleat House attract plenty of people at all times; bypass such sights on weekends, public holidays, or school vacations. In summer the coastal resorts of Bournemouth and Weymouth are crowded; it may be difficult to find the accommodations you want. The Isle of Wight gets its fair share of summer visitors, especially during the weeklong Cowes Regatta in late July or early August. Because ferries fill up to capacity, you may have to wait for the next one. The New Forest is most alluring in spring and early summer (for the foaling season) and fall (for the colorful foliage), whereas summer can be busy with walkers and campers. In all seasons, take waterproof boots for the mud and puddles.

PLANNING YOUR TIME

The South has no obvious hub, though many people base themselves in one or both of the cathedral cities of Winchester and Salisbury and make excursions to nearby destinations. The coastal cities of Portsmouth and Southampton have their charms, but neither of these large urban centers is particularly attractive as an overnight stop. Busy Bournemouth, whose major sight is a Victorian-era museum, has quieter areas that are more conducive for staying over.

To escape the bustle, the New Forest, southwest of Southampton, offers space and semi-wilderness. It's easy to take a morning or afternoon break to enjoy the activities it offers, whether on foot, by bike, or on

The South

horseback. The Isle of Wight needs more time, and is worth exploring at leisure over at least a couple of days.

GETTING HERE AND AROUND

BUS TRAVEL

National Express buses at London's Victoria Coach Station on Buckingham Palace Road depart hourly for Bournemouth (2½ hours) and Southampton (2 hours, 40 minutes), and every two hours for Portsmouth (2½ hours) and Winchester (2 hours). There are three buses daily to Salisbury (about 3¼ hours). Bluestar and Stagecoach South operate a comprehensive service in the Portsmouth, Southampton, New Forest, Winchester, and Bournemouth areas. First and Wilts & Dorset serve Salisbury, Bournemouth, and Dorchester, and Southern Vectis covers the Isle of Wight. At this writing, Greyhound was planning to launch a daily bus service between Bulleid Ways, near Victoria Coach Station, and Portsmouth and Southhampton. Visit the Web site for updates.

Wilts & Dorset offers both one-day Dayrider and seven-day Network passes valid on all the company's bus routes. Ask about the Megarider Gold tickets offered by Stagecoach, Rover and Freedom tickets offered by Southern Vectis, and Dayrider tickets offered by Bluestar. Explorer tickets allow you unlimited travel on buses operated by different companies. Contact Traveline for all information on routes and tickets.

Bus Contacts **Bluestar** (☎ *023/8061–8233* ⊕ *www.bluestarbus.co.uk*). **First** (☎ *0870/010–6022* ⊕ *www.firstgroup.com*). **Greyhound** (⊕ *www.greyhounduk. com*). **National Express** (☎ *0871/781–8181* ⊕ *www.nationalexpress.com*). **Southern Vectis** (☎ *01983/827000* ⊕ *www.islandbuses.info*). **Stagecoach South** (☎ *0845/121–0170* ⊕ *www.stagecoachbus.com*). **Traveline** (☎ *0871/ 200–2233* ⊕ *www.traveline.org.uk*). **Wilts (Wiltshire) & Dorset Bus Co.** (☎ *01722/336855* ⊕ *www.wdbus.co.uk*).

CAR TRAVEL

On the whole, the region is easily negotiable using public transportation. But for rural spots, especially the grand country estates, a car is most useful. The well-developed road network includes M3 to Winchester (59 mi from London) and Southampton (77 mi); A3 to Portsmouth (70 mi); and M27 along the coast, from the New Forest and Southampton to Portsmouth. For Salisbury, take M3 to A303, then A30. A35 connects Bournemouth to Dorchester and Lyme Regis, and A350 runs north to Dorset's inland destinations.

TRAIN TRAVEL

South West Trains serves the South from London's Waterloo Station. Travel times average 1 hour to Winchester, 1¼ hours to Southampton, 2 hours to Bournemouth, and 2¾ hours to Weymouth. The trip to Salisbury takes 1½ hours, and Portsmouth about 2 hours.

A yearlong Network card, valid throughout the South and Southeast, entitles you to up to one-third off some train fares (and ferries to the Isle of Wight). It costs £20.

Train Contacts **National Rail Enquiries** (☎ *0845/748–4950* ⊕ *www. nationalrail.co.uk*). **South West Trains** (☎ *0845/748–4950 or 0845/600–0650* ⊕ *www.southwesttrains.co.uk*).

TOURS

The Guild of Registered Tourist Guides maintains a directory of qualified Blue Badge guides who can meet you anywhere in the region for private tours. Local organizations such as Wessexplore can also arrange Blue Badge tours. On the Isle of Wight, Southern Vectis operates open-top bus tours.

Tour Information **Guild of Registered Tourist Guides** (☎ *020/7403–1115* ⊕ *www.blue-badge-guides.com*). **Wessexplore** (☎ *01722/326304* ⊕ *www. dmac.co.uk/wessexplore*).

RESTAURANTS

In summer, and especially on summer weekends, visitors can overrun the restaurants in small villages, so either book a table in advance or be prepared to wait. The more popular or upscale the restaurant, the more critical a reservation is. For local specialties, try fresh-grilled river trout or sea bass poached in brine, or dine like a king on the New Forest's renowned venison. Hampshire is noted for its pig and sheep farming, and you might zero in on pork and lamb dishes on local restaurant menus. The region places a strong accent on seasonal produce, so venison, for example, is best sampled between September and February.

HOTELS

Modern hotel chains are well represented, and in rural areas you can choose between elegant country-house hotels, traditional coaching inns (updated to different degrees), and modest guesthouses. Some seaside hotels do not accept one-night bookings in summer. If you plan to visit Cowes on the Isle of Wight during Cowes Week, the annual yachting jamboree in late July or early August, book well in advance.

WHAT IT COSTS IN POUNDS					
	£	££	£££	££££	£££££
Restaurants	Under £10	£10–£14	£15–£19	£20–£25	over £25
Hotels	Under £70	£70–£120	£121–£160	£161–£220	over £220

Restaurant prices are for a main course at dinner. Hotel prices are for two people in a standard double room in high season, including V.A.T., with no meals or, if indicated, CP (with continental breakfast), BP (Breakfast Plan, with full breakfast), or MAP (Modified American Plan, with breakfast and dinner).

VISITOR INFORMATION

Tourism South East (⊠ *40 Chamberlayne Rd., Eastleigh* ☎ *023/8062–5400* ⊕ *www.visitsoutheastengland.com*).

WINCHESTER TO SOUTHAMPTON

From the cathedral city of Winchester, 70 mi southwest of London, you can meander southward to the coast, stopping at the bustling ports of Southampton and Portsmouth to explore their maritime heritage. From either port you can strike out for the restful shores of the Isle of Wight, vacation home of Queen Victoria and thousands of modern-day Britons.

WINCHESTER

70 mi southwest of London, 12 mi northeast of Southampton.

Winchester is among the most historic of English cities, and as you walk the graceful streets and wander the many gardens, a sense of the past envelops you. Although it is now merely the county seat of Hampshire, for more than four centuries Winchester served as England's capital. Here, in AD 827, Egbert was crowned first king of England, and his successor, Alfred the Great, held court until his death in 899. After the Norman Conquest in 1066, William I ("the Conqueror") had himself crowned in London, but took the precaution of repeating the ceremony in Winchester. William also commissioned the local monastery to produce the Domesday Book, a record of the general census begun in 1085. The city remained the center of ecclesiastical, commercial, and political power until the 13th century, when that power shifted to London. Winchester still preserves some of its past glory even if some fast-food outlets and retail chains have moved onto High Street.

GETTING HERE AND AROUND

On a main train line and on the M3 motorway, Winchester is easily accessible from London. The train station is a short walk from the sights; the bus station is in the center, opposite the tourist office. The one-way streets are notoriously confusing, so find a parking lot as soon as possible. The city center is very walkable, and most of High Street is closed to vehicular traffic.

TIMING

The city is busier than usual during the farmers' market, held on the second and the last Sunday of each month.

ESSENTIALS

Visitor and Tour Information **Winchester** (⊠ *The Guildhall, Broadway* ☎ *01962/840500* ⊕ *www.visitwinchester.co.uk*). **Winchester Tourist Guides** (⊕ *www.winchestertouristguides.com*).

EXPLORING
TOP ATTRACTIONS

7 **City Museum.** Across from the cathedral, the museum interprets Winchester's past through displays of Celtic pottery, Roman mosaics, Saxon jewelry and coins, and reconstructed Victorian shops. ⊠ *The Square* ☎ *01962/863064* ⊠ *Free* ☉ *Apr.–Oct., Mon.–Sat. 10–5, Sun. noon–5; Nov.–Mar., Mon.–Sat. 10–4, Sun. noon–4.*

❷ Close. Nearly enveloping the cathedral, this area contains neat lawns and the Deanery, Dome Alley, and Cheyney Court.

❻ Great Hall. A few blocks west of the cathedral, this hall is all that remains of the city's Norman castle. Here the English Parliament met for the first time in 1246; Sir Walter Raleigh was tried for conspiracy against King James I and condemned to death in 1603 (although he wasn't beheaded until 1618); and Dame Alice Lisle was sentenced to death by the brutal Judge Jeffreys for sheltering fugitives, after Monmouth's Rebellion in 1685. Occupying one corner of the Great Hall is a huge and gaudy sculpture of Queen Victoria, carved by Sir Alfred Gilbert (responsible for *Eros* in Piccadilly Circus) to mark her Golden Jubilee in 1887. But the hall's greatest relic hangs on its west wall: King Arthur's Round Table has places for 24 knights and a portrait of Arthur bearing a remarkable resemblance to King Henry VIII. In fact, the table dates back no farther than the 13th century and was repainted by order of Henry on the occasion of a visit by the Holy Roman Emperor Charles V; the real Arthur was probably a Celtic cavalry general who held off the invading Saxons after the fall of the Roman Empire in the 5th or 6th century. The Tudor monarchs revived the Arthurian legend for political purposes. Take time to wander through Queen Eleanor's Garden—a re-creation of a medieval noblewoman's shady retreat. ⊠ *Castle Hill* ☎ *01962/846476* ✆ *Free* ☉ *Daily 10–5.*

> ### ST. SWITHUN WEATHER
>
> St. Swithun (died AD 862) is interred in Winchester Cathedral, although he requested outdoor burial. Legend says that when his body was transferred inside from the cathedral's churchyard, it rained for 40 days. Since then, folk wisdom says that rain on St. Swithun's Day (July 15) means 40 more days of wet weather. (Elsewhere in England the name is usually spelled "Swithin.") Near St. Swithun's Church at King's Gate, at 8 College Street, is the house where Jane Austen died on July 18, 1817, three days after writing a comic poem about the legend of St. Swithun's Day (copies are usually available in the cathedral).

❸ King's Gate. On St. Swithun Street on the south side of the Close, this structure was built in the 13th century and is one of two gates remaining from the original city wall. **St. Swithun's Church** is built over King's Gate.

❶ ★ Winchester Cathedral. The city's greatest monument, begun in 1079 and consecrated in 1093, presents a sturdy, chunky appearance in keeping with its Norman construction, so that the Gothic lightness within is even more breathtaking. Its tower, transepts, and crypt, and the inside core of the great Perpendicular nave, reveal some of the world's best surviving examples of Norman architecture. Other features, such as the arcades, the presbytery (behind the choir, holding the high altar), and the windows, are Gothic alterations carried out between the 12th and 14th century. Little of the original stained glass has survived, however, thanks to Cromwell's Puritan troops, who ransacked the cathedral in the 17th century during the English Civil War, but you can still see the sumptuously illuminated 12th-century Winchester Bible in the Library and Triforium Gallery.

Among the many well-known people buried in the cathedral are William the Conqueror's son, William II ("Rufus"), mysteriously murdered in the New Forest in 1100; Izaak Walton (1593–1683), author of *The Compleat Angler,* whose memorial window in Silkestede's Chapel was paid for by "the fishermen of England and America"; and Jane Austen, whose grave lies in the north aisle of the nave. Firmly in the 20th century, Antony Gormley's evocative statue *Sound II* (1986) looms in the crypt, as often as not standing in water (as it was designed to do), because of seasonal flooding. You can also explore the bell tower—with views as far as the Isle of Wight in fair weather—and other recesses of the building on a tour. Special services or ceremonies may mean the cathedral is closed to visits, so telephone first to avoid disappointment. ⊠ *The Close, Cathedral Precincts* ☎ *01962/857200* ⊕ *www. winchester-cathedral.org.uk* 🎫 *£5; Library and Triforium Gallery free; bell tower tour £5* ⊘ *Mon.–Sat. 8:30–6, Sun. 12:30–3, longer for services. Library and Triforium Gallery Apr.–Oct., Mon. 2–4, Tues.–Sat. 11–4; Nov., Dec., and Mar., Wed. and Sat. 11–3:30; Jan. and Feb., Sat. 11–3:30. Free tours on the hr Mon.–Sat. 10–3, bell tower tours late May–Aug., Mon., Wed., and Fri. 2:15, Sat. 11:30 and 2:15; Sept.–late May, Wed. 2:15, Sat. 11:30 and 2:15.*

WORTH NOTING

❽ City Mill. This working 18th-century water mill, complete with small island garden, is at the east end of High Street. Part of the premises is a National Trust gift shop open year-round, and part is a hostel. ⊠ *Bridge St.* ☎ *01962/870057* ⊕ *www.nationaltrust.org.uk* 🎫 *£3.50* ⊘ *Mid-July–early Sept., daily 11–5; late Oct.–late Dec., daily 11–4:30; rest of yr Wed.–Sun. 11–5 and daily 11–5 during school vacations.*

❾ St. Giles's Hill. To top off a tour of Winchester, you can climb this hill for a panoramic view of the city. A walk down High Street and Broadway will bring you to the hill.

❺ Westgate. At the top of High Street, this fortified medieval structure was a debtor's prison for 150 years, and now holds a motley assortment of items relating to Tudor and Stuart times. Suits of armor—examples can be tried on—and the opportunity to make brass rubbings make it popular with kids, and you can take in a view of Winchester from the roof. ⊠ *High St.* ☎ *01962/869864* 🎫 *Free* ⊘ *Apr.–Oct., Mon.–Sat. 10–5, Sun. noon–5; Feb. and Mar., Tues.–Sat. 10–4, Sun. noon–4.*

❹ Winchester College. One of England's oldest "public" (i.e., private) schools was founded in 1382 by Bishop William of Wykeham, who has his own chapel in Winchester Cathedral. The school chapel is notable for its delicately vaulted ceiling. Among the buildings still in use is Chamber Court, center of college life for six centuries. Notice the "scholars"— students holding academic scholarships—clad in their traditional gowns. ⊠ *College St.* ☎ *01962/621209* ⊕ *www.winchestercollege.co.uk* 🎫 *£4* ⊘ *1-hr tours Mon., Wed., Fri., and Sat. 10:45, noon, 2:15, and 3:30, Tues. and Thurs. 10:45 and noon, Sun. 2:15 and 3:30* ☞ *Tours may be canceled because of college events: call to check.*

WHERE TO EAT

£££ ✕ **The Bistro at Hotel du Vin.** Classic French and English fare is served with
MODERN BRITISH modern touches in this stylish bistro, converted from a redbrick Georgian town house. Dishes such as fillet of sea trout and braised hock of
ham are complemented by the many eclectic wine selections. In summer,
food is served in the walled garden. The hotel's luxurious rooms (£££)
are richly furnished in crisp modern style, with Oriental rugs enhanc-
ing the polished wooden floors. ⊠ *14 Southgate St.* ☎ *01962/841414*
▤ *AE, DC, MC, V.*

£ ✕ **Cathedral Refectory.** The bold, modern style of this self-service eatery
BRITISH next to the cathedral helps make it a refreshing lunch or snack stop. The
menu ranges from traditional soups and panini to Chicken Provençal,
but do sample the Welsh Rarebit "trencher," a dish dating from medieval times, consisting of thick bread covered in a cheesy topping and
grilled. There are tables outside for fair-weather eating. ⊠ *Inner Close*
☎ *01962/857200* ▤ *MC, V* ⊙ *No dinner.*

£££ ✕ **Chesil Rectory.** The timbered and gabled building may be old English—
MODERN BRITISH 15th or 16th century—but the cuisine is contemporary, mixing classic
recipes with local ingredients. Dishes might include lamb shoulder terrine, followed by beetroot risotto or fish pie. Good-value fixed-price
lunches and early-evening dinners are available. Service and the antique
charm of the surroundings match the quality of the food. ⊠ *1 Chesil St.*
☎ *01962/851555* ▤ *AE, DC, MC, V* ⊙ *Closed Mon. No dinner Sun.*

£ ✕ **The Royal Oak.** Quaff a half pint of draft bitter or dry cider at this lively
BRITISH traditional pub, which claims to be England's oldest bar. The interior
has been modernized, and there's plenty of space to find a comfortable
spot, including a secluded cellar with the remains of a Saxon wall. Bar
meals, including roasts and burgers, are served until 9 PM. ⊠ *Royal Oak*
Passage, off High St. ☎ *01962/842701* ▤ *AE, MC, V.*

WHERE TO STAY

£ ☷ **Enmill Barn.** Surrounded by gardens, this converted barn in peaceful
★ countryside 3 mi west of the center of Winchester makes a good base for
exploring villages and the South Downs. The ground-floor guest rooms
are freshly decorated in neutral tones and filled with personality—not
to mention refrigerators stocked with drinks and nibbles—and breakfast includes fresh fruit and free-range eggs (sometimes fresh duck eggs
are available). The large beamed and galleried sitting room holds a
snooker table. **Pros:** comfortable and spacious rooms; personal service;
top-quality snooker and tennis facilities. **Cons:** guests share one breakfast table; rather remote location. ⊠ *Enmill La., Pitt* ☎ *01962/856740*
⊕ *www.enmill-barn.co.uk* ⇆ *3 rooms* ⌂ *In-room: no a/c, no phone,*
refrigerator, Wi-Fi (some). In-hotel: tennis court, Wi-Fi, no-smoking
rooms ▤ *No credit cards* ⊠ *BP.*

££££–£££££ ☷ **Lainston House.** Dating from 1668, this elegant country-house hotel in
a 63-acre park is discreetly secluded, an obvious attraction for such eminent guests as Margaret Thatcher, who stayed here to write her memoirs.
Inside, cedar and oak paneling and other restored 17th-century details
adorn the public rooms. Bedrooms, many of which are beamed, are
done in warm colors and rich fabrics. Ground-floor suites have access
to the gardens, and a converted stable holds luxury rooms. The hotel

is 2½ mi northwest of Winchester. **Pros:** beautiful setting; attentive staff; large walk-in showers. **Cons:** lower-priced rooms are drab; food can be disappointing. ⊠*Off B3049, Sparsholt* ☎*01962/776088* ⊕*www.lainstonhouse.com* ☞*41 rooms, 9 suites* ⌂*In-room: no a/c (some), Wi-Fi. In-hotel: restaurant, tennis courts, gym, Wi-Fi, some pets allowed* ⊟*AE, DC, MC, V* ⵌ*BP.*

££–£££   ⬚**Winchester Royal.** Formerly a bishop's house and then a convent, this traditional hotel lies within easy reach of the cathedral on a quiet side street. Bedrooms, decorated with floral fabrics and dark wood, surround a large inner garden; rooms in the main building have more period features. You can have a good lunch in the bar or a fuller meal in the Conservatory Restaurant. **Pros:** central location; friendly staff. **Cons:** dated; inattention to detail; restricted parking. ⊠*St. Peter St. near High St.* ☎*01962/840840* ⊕*www.thewinchesterroyalhotel.co.uk* ☞*75 rooms* ⌂*In-room: no a/c. In-hotel: restaurant, bar, Wi-Fi, parking (free), some pets allowed, no-smoking rooms* ⊟*AE, DC, MC, V* ⵌ*BP.*

££   ⬚**Wykeham Arms.** This old place is conveniently central, near the cathedral and the college. Bedrooms at the inn itself are cozy and full of quirky knickknacks, with period touches; those across the road in the St. George annex are slightly larger. The bars, happily cluttered with prints and pewter, make use of old school desks for tables. A good wine list sets off the French and English dishes at the restaurant, which is popular with locals. **Pros:** central location; quirky charm; lively bar. **Cons:** rooms above pub can be noisy; some rooms are small; shabby in places. ⊠*75 Kingsgate St.* ☎*01962/853834* ⊕*www.fullershotels. com* ☞*13 rooms, 1 suite* ⌂*In-room: no a/c, Wi-Fi. In-hotel: restaurant, bars, Wi-Fi, parking (free), no kids under 14, no-smoking rooms* ⊟*AE, MC, V* ⵌ*BP.*

SHOPPING

A complete list of local antiques stores is available from the **Winchester Tourist Information Centre** (⊠*The Guildhall, Broadway* ☎*01962/840500*). **King's Walk**, off Friarsgate, has a number of stalls selling antiques, crafts, gift items, and bric-a-brac. **The Jays' Nest** (⊠*King's Walk* ☎*01962/ 865650*) specializes in jewelry, silver, and china. **Kingsgate Books and Prints** (⊠*Kingsgate Arch, College St.* ☎*01962/864710*) has a selection of secondhand books, maps, and prints. The oldest bookshop in town, **P&G Wells** (⊠*11 College St.* ☎*01962/852016*) has numerous books by

---

OPEN-AIR MARKETS

Local markets provide a unique sense of place. Among the best is Winchester's, held in Middle Brook Street on the second and the last Sunday of each month. It specializes in local produce and goods. Also worth a look are Salisbury's traditional city market (Tuesday and Saturday); Southampton's Bargate Market for bric-a-brac (Friday), arts and crafts (first Saturday of each month), antiques (third Saturday), and local produce (second and fourth Saturday); Dorchester's massive market of more than 500 stalls (Wednesday); and a general country market at Ringwood, near the New Forest (Wednesday).

and about Jane Austen, who took lodgings almost next door in 1817. It also has the region's largest selection of children's books.

NEW ALRESFORD

8 mi northeast of Winchester, by A31 and B3046.

New Alresford (pronounced *awls*-ford) has a village green crossed by a stream and some Georgian houses and antiques shops.

EXPLORING

The village is the starting point of the **Watercress Line,** a 10-mi railroad reserved for steam locomotives that runs to Alton. The line (named for the watercress beds formerly in the area) takes you on a nostalgic tour through reminders of 19th-century England. ⊠ *Railway Station* ☏ *01962/733810* ⊕ *www.watercressline.co.uk* ⊠ *£12* ⊙ *May–Sept., departures most days; Oct., Dec., and Jan.–Apr., weekends and national holidays; call for details.*

CHAWTON

8 mi east of New Alresford.

Jane Austen (1775–1817) lived the last eight years of her life in the village of Chawton; she moved to Winchester only during her final illness. The site has always drawn literary pilgrims, but with the ongoing release of successful films based on her novels, the popularity of the town among visitors has grown enormously.

EXPLORING

★ Here, in an unassuming redbrick house, Austen wrote *Emma, Persuasion,* and *Mansfield Park,* and revised *Sense and Sensibility, Northanger Abbey,* and *Pride and Prejudice.* Now a museum, the rooms of **Jane Austen's House** retain the atmosphere of restricted gentility suitable to the unmarried daughter of a clergyman. In the left-hand parlor, Jane would play her piano every morning, then repair to her mahogany writing desk in the family sitting room—leaving her sister, Cassandra, to do the household chores ("I find composition impossible with my head full of joints of mutton and doses of rhubarb," Jane wrote). In the early 19th century the road near the house was a bustling thoroughfare, and one traveler reported that a window view proved that the Misses Austen were "looking very comfortable at breakfast." Jane was famous for working through interruptions, but one protection against the outside world was the famous door that creaked. She asked that its hinges remain unattended to because they gave her warning that someone was coming. ⊠ *Signed off A31/A32 roundabout* ☏ *01420/83262* ⊕ *www.jane-austens-house-museum.org.uk* ⊠ *£6* ⊙ *Mar.–May and Sept.–Dec., daily 10:30–4:30; June–Aug., daily 10–5; Jan. and Feb., weekends 10:30–4:30; last admission 30 mins before closing.*

4

PORTSMOUTH

24 mi south of Chawton, 77 mi southwest of London.

This largely charmless city was England's naval capital and principal port of departure for centuries. The newly developed Gunwharf Quays and the soaring Spinnaker Tower reflect a recent upturn in the fortunes of this weary old coastal town. Along with these, the main attraction for many travelers is the extraordinary collection of maritime memorabilia, including well-preserved warships from the Napoleonic era. For others, Portsmouth is primarily of interest for the ferries that set off from here to the Isle of Wight and more distant destinations.

GETTING HERE AND AROUND

The M27 motorway from Southampton and the A3 from London take you to Portsmouth. There are also frequent buses and trains that drop you off at the Hard, the main transport terminus. It's near the tourist information center and a few steps from the Historic Dockyard and Gunwharf Quays. Regular passenger ferries cross Portsmouth Harbour from the Hard for Gosport's Submarine Museum. Attractions in Southsea are best reached by car or by buses departing from the Hard.

IN SEARCH OF JANE AUSTEN

A tour of "Jane Austen country" in the South of England and beyond can put you into the world of Austen's novels. Thanks to film adaptations of *Sense and Sensibility, Emma, Persuasion,* and *Pride and Prejudice,* the great author has captured another audience eager to peer into decorous 18th- and early-19th-century society. By visiting one or two main locales—such as Chawton and Winchester—it is possible to imagine hearing the tinkle of teacups raised by the likes of Elinor Dashwood and Mr. Darcy. Serious Janeites will want to retrace her life—starting out in the hamlet of Steventon, southwest of Basingstoke, where she spent her first 25 years, and then moving on to Bath, Southampton, Chawton, and Winchester.

Jane Austen country—a pleasant landscape filled with intimately scaled villages—is a perfectly civilized stage on which her characters organized visits to stately homes and husband-hunting expeditions. Entering that world, you find that its heart is the tiny Hampshire village of Chawton. Here, at a former bailiff's cottage on her brother's estate— now a museum—Austen produced three of her greatest novels. Her daily 6-mi walks often took her to

Chawton Manor—her brother's regal Jacobean mansion, now Chawton House Library, a center for the study of 16th- to 18th-century women's literature (for a consultation, call ☎01420/541010 or see ⊕*www. chawton.org*)—or to nearby Lyards Farm, where her favorite niece, Anna Lefroy (thought to be the model for Emma Woodhouse), came to live in 1815.

Driving southwest from Chawton, take A31 for about 15 mi to Winchester, where you can visit Austen's austere grave within the cathedral; then take in No. 8 College Street, where her battle with Addison's disease ended with her death on July 18, 1817. Heading 110 mi southwest you can visit Lyme Regis, the 18th-century seaside resort on the Devon border where Austen spent the summers of 1804–05. Here, at the Cobb, the stone jetty that juts into Lyme Bay, Louisa Musgrove jumps off the steps known as Granny's Teeth—a turning point in Chapter 12 of *Persuasion.* Northwest of Winchester by some 60 mi is Bath, the elegant setting that served as the backdrop for some of Austen's razor-sharp observations. The Jane Austen Centre explores the relationship between Bath and the writer.

ESSENTIALS

Visitor Information Portsmouth (⊠ *The Hard* ☎*023/9282–6722* ⊕*www. visitportsmouth.co.uk* ⊠ *Clarence Esplanade, Southsea* ☎*023/9282–6722*).

EXPLORING

TOP ATTRACTIONS

☾ **D-Day Museum.** In the absorbing D-Day Museum, in nearby Southsea, an
★ eclectic range of exhibits illustrates the planning and logistics involved in the D-Day landings, as well as the actual invasion on June 6, 1944. The museum's centerpiece is the Overlord Embroidery ("Overlord" was the code name for the invasion), a 272-foot-long embroidered cloth with 34 panels illustrating the history of World War II, from the Battle of Britain in 1940 to D-Day and the first days of the liberation. ⊠ *Clarence*

Esplanade, Southsea ☎*023/9282–7261* ⊕*www.ddaymuseum.co.uk* 🎫*£6* ☉*Apr.–Sept., daily 10–5:30; Oct.–Mar., daily 10–5; last admission 30 mins before closing.*

Fodor'sChoice **Portsmouth Historic Dockyard.** The city's most impressive attraction
★ includes an unrivaled collection of historic ships and the comprehensive Royal Naval Museum (a great place to learn about British naval hero Admiral Lord Horatio Nelson). The dockyard's youngest ship, **HMS Warrior 1860,** was England's first ironclad battleship. Admiral Nelson's flagship, **HMS** *Victory,* has been painstakingly restored to appear as it did at the battle at Trafalgar (1805). You can inspect the cramped gun decks, visit the cabin where Nelson entertained his officers, and stand on the spot where he was mortally wounded by a French sniper. Visits aboard the *Victory* are by guided tour only and may entail a long wait. The *Mary Rose,* former flagship of the Tudor navy, which capsized and sank in the harbor in 1545, was raised in 1982. Described in the 16th century as "the flower of all the ships that ever sailed," the *Mary Rose* is now housed in a special enclosure, where water continuously sprays her timbers to prevent them from drying out and breaking up. Exhibits in the intriguing *Mary Rose* Museum display more than 1,200 artifacts from the ship. The **Royal Naval Museum** has a fine collection of painted figureheads, extensive exhibits about Nelson and the battle of Trafalgar, and galleries of paintings and mementos recalling naval history from King Alfred to the present. **Action Stations,** an interactive attraction, gives you insight into life in the modern Royal Navy and tests your sea legs with tasks such as piloting boats through gales. **Dockyard Apprentice** showcases the skills of the shipbuilders and craftsmen who constructed and maintained the naval vessels, with illustrations of rope making, sail making, caulking, signals, and knots. You should allow the best part of a day to tour all the attractions in the Historic Dockyard. ⊠*Historic Dockyard, Portsmouth Naval Base* ☎*023/9283–9766* ⊕*www.historicdockyard.co.uk* 🎫*£18.50 includes harbor tour; valid for return visits* ☉*Apr.–Oct., daily 10–6; Nov.–Mar., daily 10–5:30; last admission 90 mins before closing.*

QUICK
BITES

After a slog around the Historic Dockyard you can find rest and replenishment, including seafood, at the harborside **Still & West Country House** (⊠*Bath Sq.* ☎*023/9282–1567*), a pub with plenty of outdoor seating. It faces the Spice Island Inn, another pub.

Spinnaker Tower. Newly erected on the lively Gunwharf Quays development of shops and bars, Spinnaker Tower provides a striking visual focus on Portsmouth's skyline. The slender structure, with the form of a mast and billowing sail, rises to a height of 541 feet. An elevator whisks you to three viewing platforms 330 feet high, for thrilling all-around views over the harbor and up to 20 mi beyond. ⊠*Gunwharf Quays* ☎*023/9285–7520* ⊕*www.spinnakertower.co.uk* 🎫*£7* ☉*Sept.–July, daily 10–6; Aug., daily 10–8.*

WORTH NOTING

🕐 **Explosion!** In a former arms depot near Submarine World, Explosion! (the name given to the Museum of Naval Firepower) gathers together munitions, mines, and missiles in relating the history of armaments used at sea. The museum also tells the story of the many locals who manufactured them. Interactive exhibits help you understand what it's like to do nautical things such as walk on a seabed. ⊠*Priddy's Hard, Gosport* ☎*023/9250–5600* ⊕*www.explosion.org.uk* 🎟*£4* ⊘*Weekends 10–4; last admission 1 hr before closing.*

Portchester Castle. Portchester Castle incorporates the walls of a Roman fort built more than 1,600 years ago; these are the most complete set of Roman walls in northern Europe. In the 12th century a Norman castle (now in ruins) was built inside the impressive fortifications. From the keep's central tower you can take in a sweeping view of the harbor and coastline. ⊠*Off A27, near Fareham* ☎*023/9237–8291* ⊕*www. english-heritage.org.uk* 🎟*£4.30* ⊘*Apr.–Sept., daily 10–6; Oct.–Mar., daily 10–4.*

🕐 **Submarine World.** The highlight at Submarine World is the tour of the World War II submarine HMS *Alliance,* from the cramped quarters to the engine room. The museum fills you in on submarine history and lets you view Portsmouth Harbour through a periscope. There are plenty of subs, weapons, and diving paraphernalia around the large site. From Portsmouth Harbour, take the ferry to Gosport and walk along Millennium Promenade past the huge sundial clock. ⊠*Haslar Jetty Rd., Gosport* ☎*023/9252–9217* ⊕*www.rnsubmus.co.uk* 🎟*£8* ⊘*Apr.–Oct., daily 10–5:30; Nov.–Mar., daily 10–4:30; last tour 1 hr before closing.*

WHERE TO EAT AND STAY

£££
SEAFOOD

✕ **Lemon Sole.** Seafood doesn't get much fresher than this. After ordering your appetizer and bread from the waiter, you head over to the amply stocked fish bar to choose your main course, which will be priced by its weight. You also select a cooking method, sauces such as honey and ginger or mushroom and fennel, and side dishes. Ask for the sauce on the side, as it can overpower the dish. Chef's recommendations are chalked up, and you can also order oysters in ice and prawns by the pint. Non-fish-eaters will find meat and vegetarian options. In the evening, dine downstairs in the more intimate and historic ambience of Croft's Wine Cellar, which offers the same menu. ⊠*123 High St.* ☎*023/9281–1303* ▤*AE, MC, V.*

4

£££££ ✕**Montparnasse.** Modern photographs on cinnamon walls add a contem-
MEDITERRANEAN porary touch to this relaxed, semiformal restaurant. The wide-ranging
fixed-price menus (£28.50 and £33.50) may include fillet steak with
Bourguignonne ravioli and baby leeks. ⊠ *103 Palmerston Rd., Southsea*
☎ *023/9281–6754* ▤ *AE, MC, V* ⊗ *Closed Sun. and Mon.*

£ ▦**Sailmaker's Loft.** This low-key bed-and-breakfast in Portsmouth's old
town makes a handy option, not least because it's close to the water
and some rooms have excellent sea views. It's also convenient to many
sights. Rooms are simply decorated but pleasant; two have private bathrooms. Ask for the spacious top-floor room, which has a balcony and
the best view. **Pros:** very convenient for Old Portsmouth; great view
from top room. **Cons:** most rooms are small; many stairs to climb. ⊠ *5
Bath Sq.* ☎ *023/9282–3045* ⊕ *www.sailmakersloft.org.uk* ➷ *4 rooms,
2 with bath* ⚘ *In-room: no a/c, no phone, Wi-Fi. In-hotel: Wi-Fi, parking (free), no-smoking rooms* ▤ *MC, V* ⦿*BP.*

££ ▦**Westfield Hall.** Portsmouth is well supplied with chain offerings, but
this pleasant smaller establishment has personal service and character. It
occupies two converted early-20th-century houses close to the water in
the resort of Southsea. Rooms (seven are on the ground floor) have large
bay windows and are restfully furnished in greens and creams; three
sitting rooms provide a place to relax. **Pros:** reliably clean; hospitable
staff; good breakfast. **Cons:** dated decor; smallish rooms. ⊠ *65 Festing
Rd., off Eastern Parade* ☎ *023/9282–6971* ⊕ *www.whhotel.info* ➷ *26
rooms* ⚘ *In-room: no a/c, Internet, Wi-Fi. In-hotel: restaurant, parking
(free), no-smoking rooms* ▤ *AE, MC, V* ⦿*BP.*

THE OUTDOORS

Queen Elizabeth Country Park, part of an Area of Outstanding Beauty in
the South Downs, has 1,400 acres of chalk hills and shady beeches with
scenic hiking trails. You can climb to the top of Butser Hill (888 feet) to
take in a splendid view of the coast. The park lies 12 mi north of Portsmouth, and 4 mi south of the Georgian market town of Petersfield, in a
wide valley between wooded hills and open downs. The visitor center
has an audiovisual theater, café, and shop. ⊠ *A3* ☎ *023/9259–5040*
⊕ *www3.hants.gov.uk/qecp* ▨ *Free; parking £1, Sun. £1.50* ⊗ *Park
open 24 hrs; visitor center Mar.–Oct., daily 10–5:30; Nov.–Feb., daily
10–4:30. Closed late Dec.–early Jan.*

SOUTHAMPTON

*17 mi northwest of Portsmouth, 24 mi southeast of Salisbury, 69 mi
southwest of London.*

Seafaring Saxons and Romans used Southampton's harbor, Southampton Water, as a commercial trading port for centuries. The city thrived,
becoming one of England's wealthiest. But Plymouth eventually sup-
planted it, and Southampton has been going downhill ever since. Still,
it remains England's leading passenger port, and as the home port of
Henry V's fleet bound for Agincourt, the *Mayflower,* the *Queen Mary,*
and the ill-fated *Titanic,* along with countless other great ocean liners
of the 20th century, Southampton has one of the richest maritime traditions in England. Much of the city center is shoddy, having been hastily

rebuilt after World War II bombing, but bits of the city's history peek out from between modern buildings. The Old Town retains its medieval air, and considerable parts of Southampton's castellated town walls remain. Other attractions include a decent art gallery, extensive parks, and a couple of good museums. The Southampton International Boat Show, a 10-day event in mid-September, draws huge crowds.

GETTING HERE AND AROUND

Located on the M3 motorway from London and Winchester, and on the M27 from Portsmouth, Southampton is also easily accessed by bus or train from these cities. The bus and train stations are a few minutes' walk from the tourist office, and all the main sights can be reached by foot.

ESSENTIALS

Visitor Information Southampton (⊠ *9 Civic Centre Rd.* ☎ *023/8083–3333* ⊕ *www.visit-southampton.co.uk*).

EXPLORING

Incorporated in the town walls are a number of old buildings, including **God's House Tower,** originally a gunpowder factory and now an archaeology museum. Displays focus on the Roman, Saxon, and medieval periods of Southampton's history. ⊠ *Winkle St.* ☎ *023/8063–5904* ⊕ *www. southampton.gov.uk* ⊠ *£1.95* ⊗ *Tues.–Sat. 10–4, Sun. 1–4.*

Mayflower Park and the Pilgrim Fathers' Memorial (⊠ *Western Esplanade*) commemorate the departure of 102 passengers on the North America–bound *Mayflower* from Southampton on August 15, 1620. A plaque also honors the 2 million U.S. troops who left Southampton in World War II.

Incongruously housed in a 14th-century wool warehouse, the **Southampton Maritime Museum** brings together models, mementos, and pieces of furniture from the age of the great clippers and cruise ships, including a wealth of memorabilia relating to the *Titanic*—footage, photos, crew lists, and so on. Boat buffs will relish plenty of vital statistics dealing with the history of commercial shipping. ⊠ *Bugle St.* ☎ *023/8022–3941* ⊕ *www.southampton.gov.uk* ⊠ *£1.95* ⊗ *Tues.–Sat. 10–4, Sun. 1–4.*

WHERE TO EAT AND STAY

£££
BRASSERIE
✕**Oxford Brasserie.** This informal place close to the docks gets lively in the evening, but it's calmer at lunchtime. Fresh fish is always available (the fixed-price menus are a particularly good value), along with Mediterranean fare. The tile floor and cream-color walls hung with paintings are straightforward and not gimmicky. ⊠ *33–34 Oxford St.* ☎ *023/8063–5043* ⊟ *AE, MC, V* ⊗ *Closed Sun.*

£££–££££
⬚**TerraVina Hotel.** This small and select boutique hotel outside town is owned by two of the founders of the esteemed Hotel du Vin group, and the same high standards are evident here. The public areas combine contemporary and period furnishings. Guest rooms—decorated in soothing tones with splashes of emerald green and burnt orange—are spacious and have thoughtful touches like espresso machines. The three ground-floor (and more expensive) rooms have private patios. The California wine country–themed restaurant (£££) boasts an impressive wine cellar

and uses organic ingredients in its Modern British cuisine. The hotel's location on the edge of the New Forest makes it well placed for excursions. **Pros:** large, well-equipped rooms; great restaurant; attentive service. **Cons:** pricey breakfast; a little remote from Southampton. ⊠ *174 Woodlands Rd., Woodlands, Netley Marsh* ☎ *023/8029–3784* ⊕ *www. hotelterravina.co.uk* ⇋ *11 rooms* ⟁ *In-room: no a/c, safe, DVD, Wi-Fi. In-hotel: restaurant, bar, pool, Wi-Fi* ⊟ *AE, MC, V.*

NIGHTLIFE AND THE ARTS

The **Mayflower** (⊠ *Commercial Rd.* ☎ *023/8071–1811*) is among the larger theaters outside London; the Royal Shakespeare Company and Barnum on Ice are among the organizations that have packed the house. The **Nuffield** (⊠ *University Rd.* ☎ *023/8067–1771*), at Southampton University, has a repertory company and also hosts national touring groups.

ISLE OF WIGHT

A slightly tattered, slightly romantic place, this island sometimes gets so crowded it seems that it might sink beneath the weight of the throngs of summer visitors. Its appealingly dusty Victorian look comes courtesy of Queen Victoria, who put the Isle of Wight (pronounced white) on the map by choosing it for the site of Osborne House. She lived here as much as she could, and ultimately she died here. Perhaps understandably, islanders are chauvinistic; like Tennyson, who lived here until tourist harassment drove him away, they resent the crowds of tourists. But every season the day-trippers arrive—thanks to the ferries and hydrofoils that connect the island with Southampton, Portsmouth, Southsea, and Lymington. People come to this 23-mi-long island for its vacation resorts—Ryde, Bembridge, Ventnor, Freshwater (stay away from tacky Sandown and Shanklin)—its rich vegetation, narrow lanes, thatched cottages, curving bays, sandy beaches, and walking paths. The fabulous ocean air, to quote Tennyson, is "worth six pence a pint." All is not sea and sails, however. There is splendid driving to be done in the interior of the island, in such places as Brading Down, Ashley Down, and Mersely Down, and the occasional country house to visit, none more spectacular than Queen Vicky's Osborne House.

GETTING HERE AND AROUND

Wightlink operates a car ferry between the mainland and the Isle of Wight. The crossing takes about 30 minutes from Lymington to Yarmouth, 40 minutes from Portsmouth to Fishbourne. The company also operates catamaran service between Portsmouth and Ryde (20 minutes). Red Funnel runs a car ferry (1 hour) and hydrofoil service (25 minutes) between Southampton and Cowes. Hovertravel runs a hovercraft shuttle between Southsea (Portsmouth) and Ryde (10 minutes). The island is covered by a good network of roads, and you can rely on a regular local bus service.

Southern Vectis, the local bus company, operates open-top tours between March and October. One goes to Osborne House and Carisbrooke Castle, another to Dimbola Lodge, the Needles, and Alum Bay. You can board and disembark at different points for £10.

TIMING
Summer traffic slows things down considerably. Try to avoid Cowes Week in late July or early August and the two major rock festivals that take place in mid-June and mid-September.

ESSENTIALS
Ferry Information **Hovertravel** (☎01983/811000 or 023/9281–1000 ⊕www. hovertravel.co.uk). **Red Funnel** (☎0844/844–9988 ⊕www.redfunnel.co.uk). **Wightlink** (☎0871/376–4342 ⊕www.wightlink.co.uk).

Tour Information **Southern Vectis** (☎01983/827000 ⊕www.islandbuses.info).

4

COWES

7 mi northwest of Ryde.

If you embark from Southampton, your ferry will cross the Solent channel and dock at Cowes, a magic name in the sailing world because of the internationally known Cowes Week yachting festival, held each July or August. Fifty years ago the Cowes Regatta was a supreme event; the world's most famous figures crowded the green lawns of the Royal Yacht Squadron. Although its elegance is a thing of the past, the Cowes Regatta remains an important yachting event. At the north end of High Street, on the Parade, a tablet commemorates the 1633 sailing from Cowes of two ships carrying the first English settlers of the state of Maryland.

ESSENTIALS
Visitor Information **Cowes** (✉Fountain Quay ☎01983/813813 ⊕www. islandbreaks.co.uk).

EXPLORING
Queen Victoria's **Osborne House,** designed by Prince Albert after a villa in the stodgiest Italian Renaissance style, holds enormous interest for anyone drawn to the domestic side of history. After Albert's death in 1861 the queen spent much of her time here, mourning her loss in relative seclusion. In this massive pile, one sees the engineer manqué in Prince Albert and his clever innovations—including a kind of central heating—as well as evidence of Victoria's desperate attempts to give her children a normal but disciplined upbringing. A carriage ride will take you to the Swiss Cottage, a superior version of a playhouse built for the children. The antiques-filled rooms have scarcely been altered since Victoria's death here in 1901. The house and grounds—which can be quite crowded during July and August—were used as a location for the 1998 movie *Mrs. Brown.* ■TIP→ **Ask about guided tours of the house and gardens, available throughout the year.** ✉Off A3021, 1 mi southeast of Cowes ☎01983/200022 ⊕www.english-heritage.org.uk ☑£10.20; grounds only, £8.40 ☉Apr.–Sept., daily 10–6; Oct., daily 10–4; Nov.– Mar., Wed.–Sun. prebooked guided tours only, last tour at 2:30.

WHERE TO STAY

££–£££   ⊡**New Holmwood Hotel.** This Best Western hotel occupies an unrivaled location above the western end of the Esplanade—ideal for watching yachters in the Solent. The three sitting rooms include one with an open fire on winter evenings, and the sun terrace and bijou pool take full advantage of fine weather. Patterned fabrics contrast with plain walls in the guest rooms. **Pros:** good sea views; friendly staff; within walking distance of passenger ferry. **Cons:** some rooms are small and dated; slightly run-down feel. ⊠*Queens Rd., Egypt Point* ☎*01983/292508* ⊕*www.newholmwoodhotel.co.uk* ⇔*28 rooms* ♿*In-room: no a/c, Wi-Fi. In-hotel: restaurant, bar, pool, Wi-Fi, some pets allowed, no-smoking rooms* ⊟*AE, DC, MC, V* ⍟*BP.*

RYDE

7 mi southeast of Cowes.

The town of Ryde has long been one of the Isle of Wight's most popular summer resorts, with several family attractions. After the construction of Ryde Pier in 1814, elegant town houses sprang up along the seafront and on the slopes behind, commanding fine views of the harbor. In addition to its long, sandy beach, Ryde has a large lake (you can rent rowboats and pedal boats) and children's playgrounds. To get here from Cowes, leave on A3021, and then follow the signs on A3054.

ESSENTIALS

Visitor Information Ryde (⊠*81–83 Union St.* ☎*01983/813813* ⊕*www. islandbreaks.co.uk*).

WHERE TO EAT

££££   ✕**Seaview.** A strong maritime flavor defines this restaurant, in the heart
MODERN BRITISH   of a harbor village just outside Ryde. Spilling out into the conservatory,
Fodor's Choice   the dining room has the feel of a contemporary yacht club, and offers
★   a fixed-price menu (£24.95 for three courses), specializing in seafood and fresh island produce. Depending on the season, you might start with the wild mushroom soup and then move on to the panfried brill served with an herb mash. Plainer, less expensive dishes and snacks can be ordered in the two congenial bars, one modern, one traditional. Pale brown tones and luxurious fabrics characterize the chic guest rooms in the adjoining hotel (£££–££££). ⊠*Seaview Hotel, High St., Seaview* ☎*01983/612711* ⊟*AE, DC, MC, V.*

BRADING

3 mi south of Ryde on A3055.

In Brading, St. Mary's Church, dating from Norman times, contains monuments to the local Oglander family, whose ancestor from Normandy served William the Conqueror.

EXPLORING

Next to the Old Town Hall stands the 16th-century rectory, said to ♺ be the oldest dwelling on the island; it now holds **Brading: The Experience,** which includes a wax museum, a chamber of horrors, and a collection of stuffed animals. ⊠*46 High St.* ☎*01983/407286* ⊕*www. bradingtheexperience.co.uk* ☑*£7.25* ⊗*Easter–Oct., daily 10–5, last entry 3:30; call for winter hrs.*

☺ Housed within a striking wooden-walled, glass-roofed building, the remains of the substantial 3rd-century **Brading Roman Villa** include walls, splendid mosaic floors, and a well-preserved heating system. The mosaics, depicting peacocks (symbolizing eternal life), gods, gladiators, sea beasts, and reclining nymphs, are a rare example of this type of floor preserved in situ in a domestic building. There's also a café at the site, 1 mi south of Brading. ⊠*Morton Old Road, off A3055* ☎*01983/406223* ⊕*www. bradingromanvilla.co.uk* ☑*£5* ⊗*Late July–early Sept., daily 9:30–6; early Sept.–late July, daily 9:30–5; last entry 1 hr before closing.*

VENTNOR

11 mi south of Ryde.

The south coast resorts are the sunniest and most sheltered on the Isle of Wight. Handsome Ventnor rises from such a steep slope that the ground floors of some of its houses are level with the roofs of those across the road.

EXPLORING

The **Ventnor Botanic Gardens,** laid out over 22 acres, contain more than 3,500 species of trees, plants, and shrubs. The impressive greenhouse includes banana trees and a waterfall, and a visitor center puts the subtropical and display gardens into context. ⊠*Undercliff Dr.* ☎*01983/855397* ⊕*www.botanic.co.uk* ☑*Free* ⊗*Gardens always open. Visitor Center Mar.–Oct., daily 10–5; Nov.–Feb., weekends 10–4.*

WHERE TO EAT

££££–£££££
MEDITERRANEAN

✕**The Pond Café.** Overlooking a secluded, elongated pond in the hamlet of Bonchurch, a mile north of Ventnor, you can gently unwind in this quiet, understated place. The simply furnished interior is compact and contemporary in style, and there are a few outdoor tables for eating alfresco when the weather permits. Come for a tea or coffee, or tuck in to a full meal. The set-price menus (£14–£19 at lunch, £24–£28 at dinner) include such dishes as local crab salad with Datterino tomatoes, followed by smoked eel or confit duck leg. There are fresh-baked breads and homemade ice creams, among other toothsome desserts. ⊠*Bonchurch Village Rd., Bonchurch* ☎*01983/855666* ▭*MC, V* ⊗*Closed Tues. and Wed. Sept.–May.*

ALUM BAY AND THE NEEDLES

19 mi northwest of Ventnor, 18 mi southwest of Cowes.

At the western tip of the Isle of Wight is the island's most famous natural landmark, the **Needles**, a long line of jagged chalk stacks jutting out of the sea like monstrous teeth, with a lighthouse at the end. It's part of the Needles Pleasure Park, which has mostly child-oriented attractions. Adjacent is **Alum Bay**, accessed from the Needles by chairlift. Here you can catch a good view of the multicolor sand in the cliff strata or take a boat to view the lighthouse.

EXPLORING

Dimbola Lodge was the home of Julia Margaret Cameron (1815–79), the eminent Victorian portrait photographer and friend of Lord Tennyson. A gallery includes more than 60 examples of her work, including striking images of Carlyle, Tennyson, and Browning. There's also a room devoted to the various Isle of Wight rock festivals, most famously the five-day event in 1970 that featured the Who, the Doors, Joni Mitchell, and Jimi Hendrix. On the ground floor you'll find a bookshop and a good café for snacks and full meals. ⊠*Terrace La., Freshwater Bay* ☎*01983/756814* ⊕*www.dimbola.co.uk* ⊠*Gallery £4* ⊙*Mar.–Oct., Tues.–Sun. and national holiday Mon. 10–5; Nov.–Feb., Tues.–Sun. and national holiday Mon. 10–4; open daily during school summer vacation.*

WHERE TO STAY

£££ 🏨 **Farringford Hotel.** For more than 40 years this splendid 18th-century house was the home of the Victorian poet laureate Alfred, Lord Tennyson. Now a gracious hotel on 33 acres of parkland, it also includes self-catering accommodations. Victorian mahogany and rich damask fabrics reign supreme in the bedrooms in the main house, four of which (with a supplementary charge) were the main bedrooms of the Tennyson family. **Pros:** lovely grounds; full of character and history. **Cons:** cottages are disappointing; occasionally poor service. ⊠*Bedbury La., near Alum Bay, Freshwater Bay* ☎*01983/752500* ⊕*www.farringford.co.uk* ➲*14 rooms, 18 suites, 5 apartments, 4 cottage rooms* ৬*In-room: no a/c, Wi-Fi. In-hotel: 2 restaurants, golf course, tennis court, pool, Wi-Fi, some pets allowed* ⊟*AE, DC, MC, V* ◎|*BP.*

CARISBROOKE CASTLE

14 mi east of Alum Bay, 1¼ mi southwest of Newport, 5 mi south of Cowes.

GETTING HERE AND AROUND

The hourly Medina Breezer open-top bus runs to Carisbrooke Castle between late May and late August; catch it at East Cowes or Newport. Otherwise, take Buses 7, 11, or 38 from Newport to Carisbrooke High St., from which it's a 10–15-minute uphill walk to the castle, or take a taxi.

ESSENTIALS

Visitor Information Newport (⊠*The Guildhall, High St.* ☎*01983/813813* ⊕ *www.islandbreaks.co.uk*).

EXPLORING

★ Standing above the village of Carisbrooke, **Carisbrooke Castle** was built by the Normans and enlarged in Elizabethan times. It had its moment of historical glory when King Charles I was imprisoned here during the English Civil War. Note the small window in the north curtain wall through which he tried unsuccessfully to escape. A museum holds items from his incarceration. You can stroll along the battlements and visit the well house, where donkeys draw water from a deep well. The castle is a short distance outside the Isle of Wight's modern-day capital,

Newport. ⊠*Off B3401* ☎*01983/522107* ⊕*www.english-heritage.org.
uk* 🖾*£6.70* ⊘*Apr.–Sept., daily 10–5; Oct.–Mar., daily 10–4.*

SALISBURY, STONEHENGE, AND SALISBURY PLAIN

The roster of famous sights in this area begins in the attractive city of Salisbury, renowned for its glorious cathedral, and then loops west around Salisbury Plain, up to Avebury, and back to Stonehenge. A trio of stately homes reveals the ambitions and wealth of their builders— Wilton House with its Inigo Jones–designed state rooms, Stourhead and its exquisite gardens, and the Italian Renaissance pile of Longleat. Your own transportation is essential to see anything beyond Salisbury.

SALISBURY

24 mi northwest of Southampton, 44 mi southeast of Bristol, 79 mi southwest of London.

The silhouette of Salisbury Cathedral's majestic spire signals your approach to this historic city long before you arrive. Although the cathedral is the principal interest in the town, and the Cathedral Close one of the country's most atmospheric spots (best experienced on a foggy night), Salisbury has much more to see, not least its largely unspoiled— and relatively traffic-free—old center. Here are stone shops and houses that grew up in the shadow of the great church over the centuries. You're never far from any of the three rivers that meet here, or from the bucolic water meadows that stretch out to the west of the cathedral and provide the best views of it.

Salisbury did not become important until the early 13th century, when the seat of the diocese was transferred here from Old Sarum, the original settlement 2 mi to the north, of which only ruins remain. In the 19th century, novelist Anthony Trollope based his tales of ecclesiastical life, notably *Barchester Towers*, on life here, although his fictional city of Barchester is really an amalgam of Salisbury and Winchester. The local tourist office organizes walks—of differing lengths for varying stamina—to lead you to the treasures.

GETTING HERE AND AROUND

Salisbury is on main bus and train routes from London and Southampton; regular buses also connect Salisbury with Winchester. The bus station is centrally located on Endless Street. Trains stop west of the center. After negotiating a ring-road system, drivers will want to park as soon as possible. The largest of the central parking lots is by Salisbury Playhouse. The city center is compact, so you won't need to use local buses for most sights. For Wilton, take Bus 60, 60A, or 61 from Market Square.

TIMING

Market Square hosts general markets every Tuesday and Saturday and farmers' markets on the first and third Wednesday of the month. It is also the venue for other fairs and festivals during the year, notably the one-day Food & Drink Festival in mid-September and the four-day Charter Fair in October. Expect congestion during any of these events. The city gets busy during the arts festival in May and June, when accommodation may be scarce.

The Stonehenge Tour has open-top buses leaving once or twice an hour all year from the train station and the bus station. Tickets cost £11, or £17.50 including admission to Stonehenge. Salisbury City Guides offers tours, departing from the tourist office, every day from April through September and on weekends the rest of the year. The cost is £3.50. Wessexplore has everything from walking tours to trips in luxury cars. There are even helicopter rides over Stonehenge.

ESSENTIALS

Visitor and Tour Information **Salisbury** (✉ *Fish Row off Market Sq.*
☎ *01722/334956* ⊕ *www.visitwiltshire.co.uk/salisbury).* **Salisbury City Guides** (☎ *01722/320349* ⊕ *www.salisburycityguides.co.uk).* **Stonehenge Tour** (☎ *01722/336855* ⊕ *www.thestonehengetour.info).* **Wessexplore** (☎ *01722/326304* ⊕ *www.dmac.co.uk/wessexplore).*

CLOSE UP

Ancient Sites

Prehistoric monuments dot Britain's landscape, silent but tantalizing reminders of civilizations long vanished. Ceremonial stone circles, barrows used for burials, and Iron Age hill forts attract endless speculation about the motives and methods of their ancient builders. The South contains not only 5,000-year-old Stonehenge, one of the great treasures of Britain and, indeed, Europe, but also an abundance of other sites, some of them overlaid with reminders of other eras. At Old Sarum, near Salisbury, the earthwork ramparts of an Iron Age hill fort survive, although Romans and Normans took over the site. The evocative Avebury Stone Circles surround part of a village; nearby is the West Kennett Long Barrow, a chambered tomb. Close to Dorchester, Maiden Castle is a stone-and-earth hill fort with ramparts that enclose 45 acres. If all this fuels your imagination, the shop at Stonehenge sells plenty of books with plenty of theories, and the Salisbury and South Wiltshire Museum in Salisbury and the Alexander Keiller Museum in Avebury provide helpful background. Start by visiting one site, and you may find yourself rerouting your trip to seek out others.

4

EXPLORING
TOP ATTRACTIONS
Cathedral Close. Salisbury's close forms probably the finest backdrop of any British cathedral, with its smooth lawns and splendid examples of architecture from many periods (except modern) creating a harmonious background. Some of the historic houses are open to the public.

❸ Mompesson House. One of Britain's most appealing Queen Anne houses, dating from 1701, sits on the north side of Cathedral Close. There are no treasures per se, but some fine original paneling and plasterwork, as well as a fascinating collection of 18th-century drinking glasses, are highlights. Tea and refreshments are served in a walled garden. ⊠*The Close* ☎*01722/335659* ⊕*www.nationaltrust.org.uk* 💷*£4.70* ☉*Mid-Mar.–Oct., Sat.–Wed. 11–5; last admission 4:30.*

Old Sarum. Massive earthwork ramparts in a bare sweep of Wiltshire countryside are all that remain of the impressive Iron Age hill fort, which was successively taken over by Romans, Saxons, and Normans (who built a castle and cathedral within the earthworks). The site was still fortified in Tudor times, though the population had mostly decamped in the 13th century for the more amenable site of New Sarum, or Salisbury. You can clamber over the huge banks and ditches and take in the bracing views over the chalk downland. ⊠*Off A345, 2 mi north of Salisbury* ☎*01722/335398* ⊕*www.english-heritage.org.uk* 💷*£3.30* ☉*Apr.–June and Sept., daily 10–5; July and Aug., daily 9–6; Oct. and Mar., daily 10–4; Nov.–Jan., daily 11–3; Feb., daily 11–4.*

❷ Salisbury and South Wiltshire Museum. Models and exhibits at the Stonehenge Gallery of this museum arm you with helpful background information for a visit to the famous stones. Also on view are collections of costumes, lace, embroidery, and Wedgwood pottery, all dwarfed by the medieval pageant figure of St. Christopher, a 14-foot-tall giant, and his companion hobbyhorse, Hob Nob. ☒*The King's House, 65 The Close* ☏*01722/332151* ⊕*www.salisburymuseum.org.uk* ☚*£5.45* ⊙*July and Aug., Mon.–Sat. 10–5, Sun. noon–5; Sept.–June, Mon.–Sat. 10–5.*

❶ **Salisbury Cathedral.** Salisbury is dominated by the towering cathedral,

Fodor'sChoice a soaring hymn in stone. It is unique among cathedrals in that it was

★ conceived and built as a whole, in the amazingly short span of 38 years (1220–58). The spire, added in 1320, is the tallest in England and a miraculous feat of medieval engineering—even though the point, 404 feet above the ground, is 2½ feet off vertical. For a fictional, keenly imaginative reconstruction of the drama underlying such an achievement, read William Golding's novel *The Spire.* The excellent model of the cathedral in the north transept, the "arm" of the church to your left as you look toward the altar, shows the building about 20 years into construction, and makes clear the ambition of Salisbury's medieval builders. For all their sophistication, the height and immense weight of the great spire have always posed structural problems. In the late 17th century Sir Christopher Wren was summoned from London to strengthen the spire, and in the mid-19th century Sir George Gilbert Scott, a leading Victorian Gothicist, undertook a major program of restoration. He also initiated a clearing out of the interior and removed some less-than-sympathetic 18th-century alterations. Despite this, the interior seems spartan and a little gloomy, but check out the remarkable lancet windows and sculpted tombs of crusaders and other medieval heroes. The clock in the north aisle—probably the oldest working mechanism in Europe, if not the world—was made in 1386.

▉ TIP➔ **You can join a free 45-minute tour of the church leaving two or more times a day, and there are tours to the roof and spire at least once a day.** The **cloisters** are the largest in England, and the octagonal **Chapter House** contains a marvelous 13th-century frieze showing scenes from the Old Testament. In the Chapter House you can also see one of the four original copies of the **Magna Carta,** the charter of rights the English barons forced King John to accept in 1215; it was sent here for safekeeping in the 13th century. ☒*Cathedral Close* ☏*01722/555120* ⊕*www.salisburycathedral.org.uk* ☚*Cathedral £5 requested donation, tower tour £6.50, Chapter House free* ⊙*Cathedral mid-June–late Aug., Mon.–Sat. 7:15–7:15, Sun. 7:15–6:15; late Aug.–mid-June, daily 7:15–6:15. Chapter House Apr.–mid-June and late Aug.–Oct., Mon.–Sat. 9:30–5:30, Sun. 12:45–5:30; mid-June–late Aug., Mon.–Sat. 9:30–6:45, Sun. 12:45–5:30; Nov.–Mar., Mon.–Sat. 10–4:30, Sun. 12:45–4:30. Access to cathedral restricted during services.*

WORTH NOTING

❹ **High Street Gate.** On the north side of the Cathedral Close is one of the four castellated stone gateways built to separate the close from the rest of the city. Passing through it, you enter into the heart of the modern town.

❽ **Long Bridge.** For a classic view of Salisbury, head to the Long Bridge and the town path. From High Street walk west to Mill Road, which leads you across Queen Elizabeth Gardens. Cross the bridge and continue on the town path through the water meadows along which you can find the very spot where John Constable set down his easel to create that 19th-century icon, *Salisbury Cathedral,* now hung in the Constable Room of London's National Gallery.

QUICK BITES In a lively, central location but away from traffic, **Polly Tearooms** (✉ *8 St. Thomas's Sq.* ☎ *01722/336037*) provides relief from sightseeing fatigue in the form of lemon curd *gâteaux* (cakes), Wiltshire cream teas, and freshly ground coffee.

6 **Market Square.** One of southern England's most popular markets fills this square on Tuesday and Saturday. Permission to hold an annual fair here was granted in 1221, and that right is still exercised for four days every October, when the Charter Fair takes place. A narrow side street links Poultry Cross to Market Square.

9 **Old Mill.** Reached via a 20-minute walk along the town path southwest of the town center, this mill, dating from the 12th century, makes a pleasant destination. It is now a hotel and atmospheric pub. ✉ *Town Path, West Harnham.*

5 **Poultry Cross.** One of Salisbury's best-known landmarks, the hexagonal Poultry Cross is the last remaining of the four original medieval market crosses, and dealers still set up their stalls beside it. ✉ *Silver St.*

7 **St. Thomas's Church.** This church contains a rare medieval doom painting of Judgment Day, the best-preserved and most complete of the few such works left in Britain. Created around 1470 and covering the chancel arch, the scenes of heaven and hell served to instill the fear of damnation into the congregation. ■ TIP→ **It's best seen on a spring or summer evening when the light through the west window illuminates the details.** ✉ *Silver St.* ☎ *01722/322537* ⊕ *www.stthomassalisbury.co.uk* ✑ *Free* ☉ *Apr.–Oct., Mon.–Sat. 9:30–6, Sun. noon–6; Nov.–Mar., Mon.–Sat. 9:30–3:30, Sun. noon–6.*

WHERE TO EAT

££ ╳ **Chapter 69.** Tucked behind the cathedral within the King's Arms Hotel, BRITISH this friendly, relaxed restaurant in a traditional setting is an ideal spot for a light lunch or dinner. The menu lists everything from beer-battered haddock-and-chips to curries and steaks, and there are good-value set-price Sunday lunches. ✉ *9–13 St. John's St.* ☎ *01722/340000* ☐ *AE, MC, V* ☉ *No dinner Sun.*

££ ╳ **Charter 1227.** Casual and friendly but upscale, with regal blue carpets BRITISH and cream leather seats, this second-floor restaurant enjoys a prime position overlooking Market Square. The menu blends traditional English and Mediterranean dishes, such as homemade pastas and slow-braised lamb shank. There are good-value lunches and early-bird dinners. ✉ *7 Ox Row, Market Sq.* ☎ *01722/333118* ☐ *MC, V* ☉ *Closed Sun. No dinner Mon.*

££ ╳ **Haunch of Venison.** This wood-panel tavern opposite the Poultry Cross BRITISH has been going strong for more than six centuries and brims with period details, such as the mummified hand of an 18th-century card player still clutching his cards, found by workmen in 1903. You can fortify yourself with any of 40-odd malt whiskies, and choose between bar food or more substantial meals such as roasted peppered salmon and haunch of venison (naturally). Sit in the bar area or the stylish upstairs restaurant. ⊠*1 Minster St.* ☎*01722/411313* ▤*MC, V* ⊘*No dinner Sun.*

££££ ✕**Howard's House.** If you're after complete tranquillity, head for this early-17th-century house set on 2 acres of grounds in the Nadder Valley. French windows lead from the tidy lawns into the lovely dining room. Sophisticated contemporary fare makes up most of what's on the set-price menus, such as caramelized belly of Wiltshire pork and

BRITISH

★

FOOD AND DRINK FESTIVAL

Salisbury forces you to squeeze a lot in during its one-day Food & Drink Festival (☎01722/332241 ⊕*www.salisburyfestival.co.uk*) in mid-September. There are wine and beer tents, a Waiters' Race, cooking demonstrations, barbecues, and festival menus in the restaurants. The main venue is Market Square.

spiced breast of Gressingham duck with crab wontons. Nine luxuriously furnished guest rooms (££££) may tempt you into forgoing the 10-mi drive back to Salisbury. ⊠*Off B3089, Teffont Evias* ☎*01722/716392* ▤*AE, MC, V.*

££ ✕**Lemon Tree.** It's just a few steps from Cathedral Close and the High Street Gate to this light, airy café and bistro. Hot dishes range from spinach-and-ricotta pancakes to pork fillets panfried with apricots and pine nuts. You can also come here just for morning coffee or afternoon tea. Choose to sit in the conservatory or in the paved garden. ⊠*92 Crane St.* ☎*01722/333471* ▤*AE, MC, V* ⊘*No dinner Sun.*

BRITISH

WHERE TO STAY

££ 🏨**Cricket Field House Hotel.** As the name suggests, this gamekeeper's cottage overlooks a cricket ground, allowing you to puzzle over the intricacies of the game at leisure. Some of the functional rooms are in the main house and others are in the annex. There is no restaurant, but snacks are available with notice. The hotel is on the main A36 road, a mile or so west of Salisbury's center. **Pros:** efficient, helpful management; well-maintained rooms. **Cons:** outside the city center; on a busy road; lacks charm. ⊠*Wilton Rd.* ☎*01722/322595* ⊕*www. cricketfieldhousehotel.co.uk* ⇆*17 rooms* ⌂*In-room: no a/c, no phone, Wi-Fi. In-hotel: Wi-Fi, parking (free), no kids under 14, no-smoking rooms* ▤*MC, V* ⓄⒷⓅ.

££–£££ 🏨**Red Lion Hotel.** A former coaching inn—parts of the building date from 1220—this centrally located hotel in the Best Western consortium makes a good base for exploring the city. It's packed with old clocks and relics from its long past. Rooms are in modern or antique style, with an abundance of drapery and rich red, gold, and blue colors. Room 22 has a restored fireplace dating from the inn's original construction, though the four-poster rooms are more spacious. The Vine restaurant (£££) serves mainly modern British dishes such as poached and grilled chicken breast. It's popular, so reservations are essential. **Pros:** unbeatable location; atmospheric building. **Cons:** no views from the small windows; street noise in some rooms; no parking. ⊠*Milford St.* ☎*01722/323334* ⊕*www.the-redlion.co.uk* ⇆*51 rooms* ⌂*In-*

room: no a/c, Wi-Fi (some). In-hotel: restaurant, bar, Wi-Fi, no-smoking rooms ⊟*AE, DC, MC, V.*

£–££ 🏠**Rokeby Guest House.** Easy to find on the east side of town, this four-story Edwardian B&B has a spick-and-span, traditionally styled interior and a large, landscaped garden with a summerhouse and small gym. Despite its proximity to Salisbury's ring road, it's a peaceful spot, and less than a 15-minute walk from the town center. Bedrooms, with private or ensuite bathrooms, are pleasantly decorated—for more space, book a premier room. In the split-level conservatory, breakfast choices include smoked salmon and pancakes. **Pros:** convenient location; helpful hosts; abundant and tasty breakfasts. **Cons:** not central; some rooms are small. ⊠*3 Wain-a-Long Rd.* ☎*01722/329800* ⊕*www.rokebyguesthouse. co.uk* ⇆*8 rooms* ⚘*In-room: no a/c, no phone, Wi-Fi. In-hotel: Internet terminal, parking (free), no-smoking rooms* ⊟*MC, V* ⦿*BP.*

£ 🏠**Wyndham Park Lodge.** This simple Victorian house in a quiet part of town (off Castle Street) provides an excellent place to rest and a delicious breakfast, as well as a garden. Furnishings are in keeping with the period, with antiques and elegant patterned wallpapers and drapes, and one room has its own patio. **Pros:** hospitable owners; convenient location; good breakfast. **Cons:** decor sometimes too frilly. ⊠*51 Wyndham Rd.* ☎*01722/416517* ⊕*www.wyndhamparklodge.co.uk* ⇆*4 rooms* ⚘*In-room: no a/c, no phone, DVD, Wi-Fi. In-hotel: Internet terminal, Wi-Fi, parking (free), no-smoking rooms* ⊟*MC, V* ⦿*BP.*

NIGHTLIFE AND THE ARTS

★ The **Salisbury International Arts Festival** (⊠*87 Crane St.* ☎*0845/241–9651* ⊕*www.salisburyfestival.co.uk*), held in May and June, has outstanding classical concerts, recitals, plays, and outdoor events. The **Salisbury Playhouse** (⊠*Malthouse La.* ☎*01722/320333*) presents high-caliber drama all year and is the main venue for the Salisbury Arts Festival.

SHOPPING

Ellwood Books (⊠*38 Winchester St.* ☎*01722/322975*) stocks all kinds of secondhand books, including some rare first editions. The **National Trust Shop** (⊠*41 High St.* ☎*01722/331884*) has a range of traditional gifts, from pottery to books, bags, ornaments, and fragrances. **Reeve the Baker** (⊠*2 Butcher Row* ☎*01722/320367*) is a great independent bakery with goodies ranging from lamb pasties to apple dumplings.

SPORTS

Hayball Cyclesport (⊠*26–30 Winchester St.* ☎*01722/411378*) rents bikes for about £10 per day or £65 per week, with a £25 cash deposit.

WILTON

4 mi west of Salisbury.

Five rivers—the Avon, the Bourne, the Nadder, the Wylye, and the Ebble—wind from Salisbury into the rich heart of Wiltshire. Following the valley of the Nadder will lead you to the ancient town of Wilton, from which the county takes its name. A market is held here every Thursday, and the Wilton Carpet Factory Shop draws visitors (Wilton is renowned for its carpets), but the main attraction is Wilton House.

Salisbury and Salisbury Plain

EXPLORING

★ The home of the 17th earl of Pembroke, **Wilton House** would be note-worthy if it contained no more than the magnificent 17th-century state rooms designed by Inigo Jones, Ben Jonson's stage designer and the architect of London's Banqueting House. John Webb rebuilt the house in neoclassical style after fire damaged the original Tudor mansion in 1647. In fine weather the lordly expanse of sweeping lawns that surrounds the house, bisected by the River Avon and dotted with towering oaks and a gracious Palladian bridge, is a quintessential English scene. Wilton House contains the Single Cube Room (built as a perfect 30-foot cube) and one of the most extravagantly beautiful rooms in the history of interior decoration, the aptly named Double Cube Room. The name refers to its proportions (60 feet long by 30 feet wide and 30 feet high), evidence of Jones's classically inspired belief that beauty in architecture derives from harmony and balance. The room's headliner is the spectacular Van Dyck portrait of the Pembroke family. Elsewhere at Wilton House, the art collection includes several other old master paintings, including works by Rembrandt and members of the Brueghel family. ■TIP→ **Be sure to explore the extensive gardens; children will appreciate the large playground.** ⊠ *Wilton* ☎ *01722/746729* ⊕ *www. wiltonhouse.co.uk* 💷 *£13.50; grounds only, £5.50* ⊙ *House Easter weekend and May–Aug., Sun.–Thurs. noon–5, last admission 4:15;*

grounds Easter and Apr.–Aug., daily 11–5:30; Sept., weekends 11–5:30, last admission 4:30.

EN ROUTE

Between Salisbury and Sherborne on the A30, **Shaftesbury** was the model for the town of Shaston in Thomas Hardy's *Jude the Obscure*. Shaftesbury lies on a ridge overlooking Blackmore Vale—you can catch a sweeping view of the surrounding countryside from the top of Gold Hill, a steep, relentlessly picturesque street lined with cottages. It has even appeared in TV commercials.

> ## DOUBLE CUBE ROOM
>
> Adorned with gilded furniture by William Kent, Wilton House's Double Cube was where Eisenhower prepared plans for the Normandy invasion during World War II. It has been used in many films, including *The Madness of King George, Mrs. Brown,* the 2005 version of *Pride and Prejudice,* Emma Thompson's adaptation of *Sense and Sensibility,* and *The Young Victoria.*

4

SHERBORNE

15 mi west of Shaftesbury.

Once granted cathedral status, until deferring to Old Sarum in 1075, this unspoiled market town is awash with medieval buildings honed from the honey-color local stone. The focal point of the winding streets is the abbey church. Also worth visiting here are the ruins of the 12th-century Old Castle and Sherborne Castle with its grounds.

ESSENTIALS

Visitor Information Sherborne (⊠ *3 Tilton Ct., Digby Rd.* ☎ *01935/815341* ⊕ *www.westdorset.com*).

EXPLORING

The glory of **Sherborne Abbey,** a warm, "old gold" stone church, is the delicate and graceful 15th-century fan vaulting that extends the length of the soaring nave and choir. ("I would pit Sherborne's roof against any contemporary work of the Italian Renaissance," enthused Simon Jenkins, in his *England's Thousand Best Churches.*) If you're lucky, you might hear "Great Tom," one of the heaviest bells in the world, pealing out from the bell tower. Guided tours are offered from April through September on Tuesday (10:30) and Friday (2:30), or by prior arrangement. ⊠ *Abbey Close* ☎ *01935/812452* ⊕ *www.sherborneabbey.com* ⛭ *Guided tour free Apr.–Sept., Tues. 10:30 and Fri. 2:30 (call first to check), or £3 at other times by prior arrangement* ☉ *Apr.–Sept., daily 8–6; Oct.–Mar., daily 8–4.*

Sherborne Castle, built by Sir Walter Raleigh in 1594, remained his home for 10 years before it passed to the custodianship of the Digby family. The interior has been remodeled in 19th-century Gothic style, and ceilings have splendid plaster moldings. After admiring the extensive collections of Meissen and Asian porcelain, stroll around the lake and landscaped grounds, the work of Capability Brown. The house is a half mile southeast of town. ⊠ *Off A352* ☎ *01935/813182* ⊕ *www. sherbornecastle.com* ⛭ *£9; gardens only, £4.50* ☉ *Apr.–Oct., Tues.– Thurs., Sun., and national holiday Mon. 11–5, Sat. 2–5.*

WHERE TO STAY

£   ⊡ **The Alders.** A quiet, unspoiled village 3 mi north of Sherborne contains this B&B, an old stone house with a walled garden. The lounge has an inglenook fireplace, and the bedrooms are modern and cheerfully decorated. Massage therapies are offered, and the house displays the owner's watercolors and sleek pottery, which you can view while tasting homemade jam during breakfast at the farmhouse table. Nearby pubs provide evening meals. **Pros:** peaceful setting; relaxing massages; interesting artworks. **Cons:** a bit remote; nothing to do in evening. ⊠*Sandford Orcas DT9 4SB* ☎*01963/220666* ⊕*www.thealdersbb.com* ⟳*3 rooms* ♿*In-hotel: no-smoking rooms* ⊟*No credit cards* ⦿*BP.*

STOURHEAD

15 mi northeast of Sherborne, 30 mi west of Salisbury.

ESSENTIALS

Visitor Information **Frome** (⊠*2 Bridge St.* ☎*01373/467271* ⊕*www. frometouristinfo.co.uk*).

EXPLORING

Fodor'sChoice
★

Close to the village of Stourton lies one of Wiltshire's most breathtaking sights— **Stourhead,** a country-house-and-garden combination that has few parallels for beauty anywhere in Europe. Most of Stourhead was built between 1721 and 1725 by Henry the Magnificent, the wealthy banker Henry Hoare. A fire gutted the center of the house in 1902, but it was reconstructed with only a few differences. Many rooms in the Palladian mansion contain Chinese and French porcelain, and some have furniture by Chippendale. The elegant library and floridly colored picture gallery were built for the cultural development of this exceedingly civilized family. Still, the house takes second place to the adjacent gardens designed by Hoare's son Henry Hoare II, which are the most celebrated example of the English 18th-century taste for "natural" landscaping. Temples, grottoes, and bridges have been placed among shrubs, trees, and flowers to make the grounds look like a three-dimensional oil painting. A walk around the artificial lake (1½ mi) reveals changing vistas that conjure up the 17th-century landscapes of Claude Lorrain and Nicolas Poussin; walk counterclockwise for the best views. ■TIP➔ **The best time to visit is early summer, when the massive banks of rhododendrons (introduced in Victorian times) are in full bloom, but the gardens are beautiful at any time of year.** You can get a fine view of the estate from Alfred's Tower, a 1772 folly (a structure built for picturesque effect). In summer there are occasional concerts, sometimes accompanied by fireworks and gondoliers on the lake. A restaurant and plant shop are on the grounds. From London by train, get off at Gillingham and take a five-minute cab ride to Stourton. ⊠*Off B3092, northwest of Mere, Stourton* ☎*01747/841152* ⊕*www.nationaltrust.org.uk* ⌸*£11.10; house only, £6.60; gardens only, £6.60; Alfred's Tower £2.50* ⊗*House mid-Mar.–Oct., Fri.–Tues. 11–5 or dusk; last admission 30 mins before closing; gardens daily 9–6 or dusk; Alfred's Tower mid-Mar.–Oct., daily 11–5.*

WHERE TO STAY

££ **The Spread Eagle.** You can't stay at Stourhead, but this popular hostelry, built at the beginning of the 19th century at the entrance to the landscaped park, is the next best thing (and guests are admitted free to the gardens at any time). Bedrooms are elegant and understated, with some period features. The restaurant specializes in seasonal and locally sourced fare, from mushroom-and-asparagus pie to seared duck breast. **Pros:** period character; free access to Stourhead. **Cons:** busy during the day; uneven floors an issue for those with mobility problems. ⊠ *Northwest of Mere, Stourton* ☎ *01747/840587* ⊕ *www.spreadeagleinn.com* ⇨ *5 rooms* ⚭ *In-room: no a/c, DVD, Wi-Fi. In-hotel: restaurant, bar, Wi-Fi* ⊟ *MC, V* ⊠ *BP.*

LONGLEAT HOUSE

6 mi north of Stourhead, 19 mi south of Bath, 27 mi northwest of Salisbury.

ESSENTIALS

Visitor Information Warminster (⊠ *Station Rd.* ☎ *01985/218548* ⊕ *www.visitwiltshire.co.uk*).

EXPLORING

Home of the marquess of Bath, **Longleat House** is one of southern England's most famous private estates, and possibly the most ambitiously, even eccentrically, commercialized, as evidenced by the presence of a drive-through safari park (open since 1966) with giraffes, zebras, rhinos, and lions. The blocklike Italian Renaissance building was completed in 1580 (for just more than £8,000, an astronomical sum at the time) and contains outstanding tapestries, paintings, porcelain, and furniture, as well as notable period features such as the Victorian kitchens, the Elizabethan minstrels' gallery, and the great hall with its massive wooden beams. Giant antlers of the extinct Irish elk decorate the walls, and free tours of the present Lord Bath's occasionally raunchy murals—described as "keyhole glimpses into my psyche," ranging from philosophical subjects to depictions of the Kama Sutra—can be booked separately at the front desk. Besides the safari park, Longleat has a butterfly garden, a miniature railway, an extensive (and fairly fiendish) hedge maze, and an adventure castle, all of which make it extremely popular, particularly in summer and during school vacations. ▮ TIP→ **You can easily spend a whole day here, in which case it's best to visit the house in the morning, when tours are more relaxed, and the safari park in the afternoon.** There's a safari bus service available (£5) for those arriving without their own transport. ⊠ *Off A362, Warminster* ☎ *01985/844400* ⊕ *www.longleat.co.uk* ⇨ *£23, house and grounds £12, safari park £12, gardens and grounds £4* ☉ *House Jan.–mid-Feb., weekdays guided tour at noon, weekends guided tours at 11, noon, 1, and 2; mid-Feb.–late Feb., daily 10–4:30; late Feb.–early Apr., weekdays guided tour at noon, weekends 10–4:30; early Apr.–Oct., weekdays 10–5, weekends and school vacations 10–5:30; Nov.–mid-Dec., weekdays guided tour at 1, weekends guided tours at 11, noon, 1, and 2; mid-Dec.–end Dec., daily guided tours at 11, noon, 1, and 2. Safari* *park mid-Feb.–late Feb., daily 10–3:30; late Feb.–late Mar., weekends 10–4; early Apr.–Oct., weekdays 10–5, weekends and school vacations 10–6; last entry 1 hr before closing.*

WHERE TO STAY

£££–££££ ⊞ **Bishopstrow House.** This ivy-covered Georgian house has been converted into a refreshingly relaxed hotel that combines well-chosen antiques with modern amenities such as DVD players. There's an airy conservatory and a spa where you can book pampering treatments. The lavish, classically styled guest rooms overlook either the 27-acre grounds or an interior courtyard. The Mulberry restaurant creates imaginative modern British meals with Mediterranean elements (£32 and £40 fixed-price menus). Bishopstrow House is 1½ mi east of town. **Pros:** country-house ambience; impressive suites; excellent leisure facilities. **Cons:** some rooms have poor views; less expensive rooms are small; needs general refurbishment. ⊠*Boreham Rd., Warminster* ☏*01985/212312* ⊕*www.bishopstrow.co.uk* ⇥*30 rooms, 2 suites* ⌂*In-room: no a/c, DVD, Internet, Wi-Fi (some). In-hotel: restaurant, bar, tennis courts, 2 pools, gym, spa, some pets allowed, Wi-Fi* ⊟*AE, DC, MC, V* ⦿*BP.*

EN ROUTE Four miles west of Avebury, on A4, **Cherhill Down** is a prominent hill carved with a vivid white horse and topped with a towering obelisk. It's one of a number of hillside etchings in Wiltshire, but unlike the others, this one isn't an ancient symbol—it was put there in 1780 to indicate the highest point of the downs between London and Bath. The views from the top are well worth the half-hour climb. (The best view of the horse is from A4, on the approach from Calne.)

AVEBURY

25 mi northeast of Longleat, 27 mi east of Bath, 34 mi north of Salisbury.

The village of Avebury was built much later than the stone circles that brought it fame.

GETTING HERE AND AROUND

To get here from Longleat House, drive north for about 12 mi along A36 and A350, then northeast on the A361 through Devizes to Avebury.

ESSENTIALS

Visitor Information Avebury (⊠*Avebury Chapel, Green St.* ☏*01380/734669* ⊕*www.visitwiltshire.co.uk*).

EXPLORING

★ The **Avebury Stone Circles**, which surround part of the village, are one of England's most evocative prehistoric monuments—not so famous as Stonehenge, but all the more powerful for their lack of commercial exploitation. The stones were erected around 2500 BC, some 500 years after Stonehenge was started but about 500 years before that much smaller site assumed its present form. As with Stonehenge, the purpose of this stone circle has never been ascertained, although it most likely was used for similar ritual purposes. Unlike Stonehenge, however, there are no astronomical alignments at Avebury, at least none that have survived. The main site consists of a wide, circular ditch and bank, about

1,400 feet across and more than half a mile around. Entrances break the perimeter at roughly the four points of the compass, and inside stand the remains of three stone circles. The largest one originally had 98 stones, although only 27 remain. Many stones on the site were destroyed centuries ago, especially in the 17th century when they were the target of religious fanaticism. Some were pillaged to build the thatched cottages you see flanking the fields. You can walk around the circles at

> ### WORD OF MOUTH
>
> "Having been to both Stonehenge and Avebury this past summer, I highly suggest going to Avebury in addition to passing by Stonehenge. Avebury is an excellent experience because you can actually walk around the stones (with sheep wandering the area), and it's much larger than Stonehenge."
> —padams421

any time; early morning and early evening are recommended. Be sure to visit the nearby Alexander Keiller Museum. ⊠ *1 mi north of A4* 🕾 *No phone* ⊕ *www.english-heritage.org.uk* 🎫 *Free* ⊙ *Daily.*

In the **Alexander Keiller Museum,** finds from the Avebury area, and charts, photos, models, and home movies taken by the archaeologist Keiller himself, put the Avebury Stone Circles and the site into context. Recent revelations suggest that Keiller, responsible for the excavation of Avebury in the 1930s, may have adapted the site's layout more in the interests of presentation than authenticity. The exhibits are divided between the **Stables Gallery,** showing excavated finds, and the more child-friendly, interactive **Barn Gallery.** ⊠ *1 mi north of A4* 🕾 *01672/539250* ⊕ *www.english-heritage.org.uk* 🎫 *£4.20* ⊙ *Apr.–Oct., daily 10–6; Nov.–Mar., daily 10–4.*

The Avebury monument lies at the end of **Kennett Stone Avenue,** a sort of prehistoric processional way leading to Avebury. The avenue's stones were spaced 80 feet apart, but only the half mile nearest the main monument survives intact. The lost stones are marked with concrete.

WHERE TO EAT AND STAY

£
BRITISH
✕ **Waggon and Horses.** A 16th-century thatched building created in part with stones taken from the Avebury site, this traditional inn and pub is beside the traffic circle linking A4 and A361, a two-minute drive from the prehistoric circle. Dickens mentioned the building in the *Pickwick Papers.* Excellent lunches and dinners are served beside a fire; homemade dishes include steak, kidney, and ale pie, baked Camembert, and a smoked fish platter, or you can opt for a baguette. In high season it's somewhat of a tourist hub. ⊠ *Beckhampton* 🕾 *01672/539418* ☰ *AE, MC, V* ⊙ *No dinner Sun. Oct.–May.*

££
🏠 **Manor Farm.** Views of Avebury's monoliths straggling across the field greet you from the windows of this 18th-century farmhouse right in the heart of the village. Rooms, stocked with complimentary sherry, are spacious, light, and elegantly furnished, and you have your own sitting room. The bathroom is separate, but for your exclusive use, as only one room is rented at a time (unless the same party takes both rooms). Breakfast choices include Scotch pancakes with bacon, scrambled eggs with smoked salmon, and kippers. **Pros:** ideal location; cozy and comfortable rooms; good breakfasts. **Cons:** often booked up; young children

not accepted. ✉*High St.* ☎ *01672/539294* 🛏*2 rooms without bath* 🛁*In-room: no a/c, refrigerator. In-hotel: no kids under 12, no-smoking rooms* 🚫*No credit cards* ⬤❙*BP.*

EN
ROUTE

Prehistoric relics dot the entire Avebury area; stop at the **West Kennett Long Barrow,** a chambered tomb dating from about 3250 BC, 1 mi east of Avebury on A4.

As you turn right at the traffic circle onto A4, **Silbury Hill** rises on your right. This man-made mound, 130 feet high, dates from about 2500 BC and is the largest of its kind in Europe. Excavations over 200 years have provided no clue as to its original purpose, but the generally accepted notion is that it was a massive burial chamber.

STONEHENGE

20 mi south of Avebury, 8 mi north of Salisbury.

GETTING HERE AND AROUND

Stonehenge Tour buses leave from Salisbury's train and bus stations every half hour from 9:30 from June to September and hourly from 10 from October to May. Tickets cost £11, or £17.50 with admission to Stonehenge. Other options are a taxi or an organized tour. Drivers will find the monument near the junction of A303 with A344.

EXPLORING

Fodor's Choice
★

Mysterious and ancient, **Stonehenge** has baffled archaeologists for centuries. One of England's most-visited monuments, the circle of giant stones that sits in lonely isolation on the wide sweep of Salisbury Plain still has the capacity to fascinate and move those who view it. Sadly, though, this World Heritage Site is now enclosed by barriers after incidents of vandalism, and amid fears that its popularity could threaten its existence. Visitors are kept on a path a short distance away from the stones, so that you can no longer walk among the giant stones or see up close the prehistoric carvings, some of which show axes and daggers. But if you visit in the early morning, when the crowds have not yet arrived, or in the evening, when the sky is heavy with scudding clouds, you can experience Stonehenge as it once was: a mystical, awe-inspiring place.

Stonehenge was begun about 3000 BC, enlarged between 2100 and 1900 BC, and altered yet again by 150 BC. It has been excavated and rearranged several times over the centuries. The medieval term Stonehenge means "hanging stones." Many of the huge stones that ringed the center were brought here from great distances, but it is not certain by what ancient form of transportation they were moved. The original 80 bluestones (dolerite), which made up the two internal circles, originated in the Preseli mountains, on the Atlantic coast of Wales. They may have been moved by raft over sea and river, and then dragged on rollers across country—a total journey of 130 mi as the crow flies, but closer to 240 by the practical route. Every time a reconstruction of the journey has been attempted, though, it has failed. The labor involved in quarrying, transporting, and carving these stones is astonishing, all the more so when you realize that it was accomplished about the same time that the major pyramids of Egypt were built.

Although some of the mysteries concerning the site have been solved, the reason Stonehenge was built remains unknown. It is fairly certain that it was a religious site, and that worship here involved the cycles of the sun; the alignment of the stones to point to sunrise at midsummer and sunset in midwinter makes this clear. The druids certainly had nothing to do with the construction: the monument had already been in existence for nearly 2,000 years by the time they appeared. Some historians have maintained that Stonehenge was a kind of neolithic computer, with a sophisticated astronomical purpose—an observatory of sorts—though evidence that emerged in 2007 may shed new light on the matter. Excavations at Durrington Walls, another henge a couple of miles northeast (off A345), have unearthed a substantial settlement dating from around 2500 BC, which was probably built and occupied by those who constructed Stonehenge. One other possibility is that this neolithic village was home to those who performed the religious rites at Stonehenge, where people gathered from far and wide to feast and worship. The finds show Stonehenge not to be an isolated monument, but part of a much larger complex of ceremonial structures.

A paved path for visitors at Stonehenge skirts the stones, ensuring that you don't get very close to the monoliths. Bring a pair of binoculars to help make out the details more clearly. It pays to walk all about the site, near and far, to get that magical photo and to engage your imagination. Romantics may want to view Stonehenge at dawn or dusk, or by a full moon. Your ticket entitles you to an informative audio tour, but in general, visitor amenities at Stonehenge are limited, especially for such a major tourist attraction. ■ TIP→ **English Heritage, which manages the site, can arrange entrance to the inner circle outside of regular hours on Stone Circle Access tours. These require an application and payment of £13.70 well in advance; book ahead.** ⊠ *Junction of A303 and A344/ A360, near Amesbury* ☎ *0870/333–1181, 01722/343834 for information about private access outside regular hrs* ⊕ *www.english-heritage. org.uk* ⊠ *£6.60* ⊙ *Mid-Mar.–May and Sept.–mid-Oct., daily 9:30–6; June–Aug., daily 9–7; mid-Oct.–mid-Mar., daily 9:30–4.*

NEW FOREST TO LYME REGIS

Tucked southwest of Southampton, the New Forest was once the hunting preserve of William the Conqueror and his royal descendants. Thus protected from the deforestation that has befallen most of southern England's other forests, this wild, scenic expanse offers great possibilities for walking, riding, and biking.

West of here stretches the green, hilly, and largely unspoiled county of Dorset, the setting for most of the books of Thomas Hardy, author of *Far from the Madding Crowd* and other classic Victorian-era novels. "I am convinced that it is better for a writer to know a little bit of the world remarkably well than to know a great part of the world remarkably little," he wrote as he immortalized the towns, villages, and fields of this idyllically rural area, not least the country capital, Dorchester, an ancient agricultural center. Other places of historic interest such as Maiden Castle and the chalk-cut giant of Cerne Abbas are interspersed with the bustling seaside resorts of Bournemouth and Weymouth. You may find Lyme Regis (associated with another writer, John Fowles) and the villages along the route closer to your ideal of rural England. The Jurassic Coast is the place to search for fossils.

LYNDHURST

26 mi southeast of Stonehenge, 18 mi southeast of Salisbury, 9 mi west of Southampton.

Lyndhurst is famous as the capital of the New Forest. Although some popular spots can get crowded in summer, there are ample parking lots, picnic areas, and campgrounds. Miles of walking, biking, and riding trails crisscross the region.

GETTING HERE AND AROUND

To get here from Stonehenge, head south along A360 to Salisbury, then follow A36, B3079, and continue along A337 another 4 mi or so. To explore the depths of this natural wonder, take A35 out of Lyndhurst (the road continues southwest to Bournemouth) or A337 south.

ESSENTIALS

Visitor Information Lyndhurst (✉ *Main Car Park, High St.* ☎ *023/8028–2269* ⊕ *www.thenewforest.co.uk*).

EXPLORING

The **New Forest** consists of 150 square mi of open countryside interspersed with dense woodland, a natural haven for herds of free-roaming deer, cattle, and, most famously, hardy New Forest ponies. The forest was "new" in 1079, when William the Conqueror cleared the area of farms and villages and turned it into his private hunting grounds. ⊕*www.thenewforest.co.uk*

The **New Forest Museum,** in the same building as the Visitor Information Centre, contains fascinating and informative background on the region. The exhibits focus on the area's fauna, flora, and social traditions and are linked by quizzes, and there are other interactive elements that will keep children engaged. ✉*High St.* ☎*023/8028–3444* ⊕*www. newforestmuseum.org.uk* ✎*£3* ⊗*Daily 10–4:30; last entry at 4.*

Lyndhurst's High Street is dominated by the redbrick, high Victorian church of **St. Michael and All Angels**, which holds stained glass from William Morris's studio. Fans of Lewis Carroll's *Alice in Wonderland* should note that Alice Hargreaves (*née* Liddell), the inspiration for the fictional Alice, is buried in the back of the churchyard here.

WHERE TO EAT AND STAY

££ ✕**White Buck Inn.** This traditional forest lodge makes a welcome stop
BRITISH for refreshment. The extensive menu relies on local seasonal fare, such as breast of pheasant stuffed with chestnuts, and game-and-red-wine casserole. In summer you can sit in the spacious garden, where there are regular barbecues. Live Dixieland jazz plays on Thursday evenings.

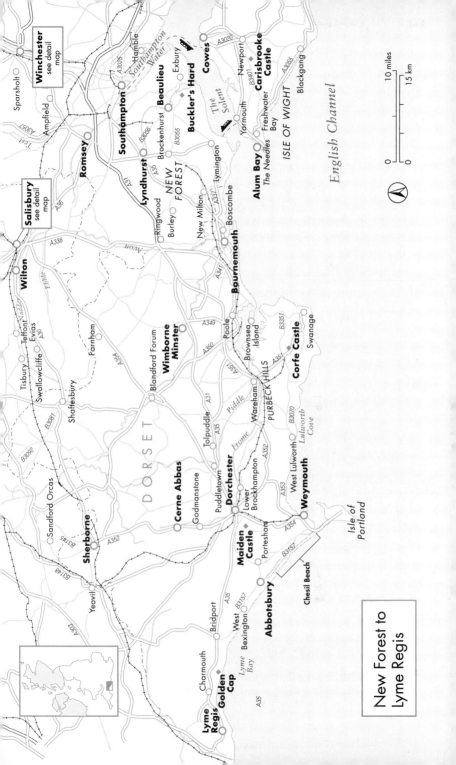

New Forest to
Lyme Regis

There are also seven guest rooms (££) ranging from functional to plush, and themed along Elizabethan or Indian lines, all with garden views. ✉*Bisterne Close, Burley, 7 mi west of Lyndhurst* ☎*01425/402264* ➡*AE, MC, V.*

££   ⛅ **The Rufus House.** If you're looking for personal service and easy access to the New Forest, book a room at this turreted Victorian house a short walk from Lyndhurst. The pastel-color rooms are bright, airy, and spotlessly clean. The two suites in the turret, both with four-poster beds, are best. As you enjoy the nourishing breakfast you can gaze out over the gardens. Self-catering cottages are also available. **Pros:** hospitable staff; delicious breakfasts; great location. **Cons:** some traffic noise in front-facing rooms; some rooms are small. ✉*Southampton Rd.* ☎*023/8028–2930* ⊕*www.rufushouse.co.uk* ➡*8 rooms, 2 suites, 2 cottages* △*In-room: no a/c, kitchen (some). In-hotel: Wi-Fi, no kids under 5, no-smoking rooms* ➡*MC, V* ◐*BP.*

SPORTS AND THE OUTDOORS

BIKING

The range of trails weaving through the New Forest make this one of Britain's best terrains for off-road biking. For £15 *per day* you can rent bikes at **Cycle Experience** (✉*2–4 Brookley Rd., Brockenhurst* ☎*01590/624204*).

HORSEBACK RIDING

The New Forest was created for riding, and there's no better way to enjoy it than on horseback. The **Burley Manor Riding Stables** (✉*Burley Manor Hotel, Ringwood Rd., Burley* ☎*01425/403489*) caters to all levels. Hour-long rides are £29. You can arrange a ride at the **Forest Park Riding Centre** (✉*Rhinefield Rd., Brockenhurst* ☎*01590/623429*). The cost is £28 per hour.

WALKING

The **New Forest** is fairly domesticated, and the walks it provides are not much more than easy strolls. For one such walk (about 4 mi), start from Lyndhurst and head directly south for Brockenhurst, a commuter village. The path goes through woods, pastureland, and heath—and you'll see plenty of New Forest ponies.

BEAULIEU

7 mi southeast of Lyndhurst.

The unspoiled village of Beaulieu (pronounced *byoo*-lee) has three major attractions in one.

EXPLORING

⟳ **Beaulieu,** with a ruined abbey, a stately home, and an automobile museum, can satisfy different interests. In 1204 King John established **Beaulieu Abbey** for the Cistercian monks, who gave their new home its name, which means "beautiful place" in French. It was badly damaged as part of the suppression of Catholicism during the reign of Henry VIII, leaving only the cloister, the doorway, the gatehouse, and two buildings. A well-planned exhibition in one building re-creates daily life in the monastery. **Palace House** incorporates the abbey's 14th-century gatehouse and has been the home of the Montagu family since they purchased it in 1538, after the dissolution of the monasteries. Inside you can see drawing rooms, dining halls, and fine family portraits. The present Lord Montagu is noted for his work in establishing the **National Motor Museum,** which traces the development of motor transport from 1895 to the present. You can see more than 250 classic cars and motorcycles. Museum attractions include a monorail, audiovisual presentations, and a trip in a 1912 London bus. ⊠ *Off B3056* ☎ *01590/612345* ⊕ *www.beaulieu.co.uk* ✆ *Abbey, Palace House, and Motor Museum £15.50–£16.75* ⏲ *Late May–Sept., daily 10–6; Oct.–late May, daily 10–5; last admission 30 mins before closing.*

Among the interesting places in the area is the museum village of **Buckler's Hard**, 2 mi south of Beaulieu. This restored 18th-century hamlet is home to a fascinating **Maritime Museum** that tells the story of Lord Nelson's favorite ship, HMS *Agamemnon*. Exhibits and model ships trace the town's shipbuilding history. Also part of the museum are four building interiors in the hamlet that re-create 18th-century village life. Easter through October, you can take a cruise on the Beaulieu River. ⊠ *Off B3056* ☎ *01590/616203* ⊕ *www.bucklershard.co.uk* ✆ *£5.90* ⏲ *Mar.–June, Sept., and Oct., daily 10–5; July and Aug., daily 10–5:30; Nov.–Feb., daily 10–4:30; last entry 30 mins before closing.*

**EN
ROUTE**

From Beaulieu, take any of the minor roads leading west through wide-open heathland to Lymington and pick up A337 for the popular seaside resort of Bournemouth, a journey of about 18 mi.

BOURNEMOUTH

26 mi southwest of Southampton, 26 mi south of Salisbury, 24 mi east of Dorchester.

The beach resort of Bournemouth was founded in 1810 by Lewis Tregonwell, an ex-army officer who had taken a liking to the area when stationed there some years before. He settled near what is now the Square and planted the first pine trees in the steep little valleys—or chines—cutting through the cliffs to the famous Bournemouth sands. The scent of fir trees was said to be healing for consumption (tuberculosis) sufferers, and the town grew steadily. Gardens laid out with trees and lawns link the Square and the beach. This is an excellent spot to relax and listen to music wafting from the Pine Walk bandstand. Regular musical programs take place at the Pavilion and at the Winter Gardens (home of the Bournemouth Symphony Orchestra) nearby.

Taking the zigzag paths through the leafy public gardens, you can descend to the seafront, where Bournemouth Pier juts into the channel from the pristine sandy beach. Bournemouth has 7 mi of beaches, and the waters are said to be some of southern England's cleanest. If you're not tempted to swim, you can stroll the promenade behind the beach. Europe's first artificial **surf reef** was being constructed here in 2009. The goal is to attract surf fans as well as create an area of calm water that's perfect for children.

GETTING HERE AND AROUND

From the New Forest, take A35 or A31/A338 southwest to Bournemouth. The center of town is best explored on foot, but to reach East Cliff or Boscombe you'll need to drive or use the frequent local buses.

ESSENTIALS

Visitor Information Bournemouth (⊠ *Westover Rd., near bandstand* ☎ *0845/051–1701* ⊕ *www.bournemouth.co.uk*).

EXPLORING

On the corner of Hinton Road stands **St. Peter's** parish church, easily recognizable by its 200-foot-high tower and spire. Lewis Tregonwell, founder and developer of Bournemouth, is buried in the churchyard. Here, too, is the elaborate tombstone of Mary Shelley, author of *Frankenstein* and wife of the great Romantic poet Percy Bysshe Shelley, whose heart is buried with her.

★ The **Russell-Cotes Art Gallery and Museum,** a late-Victorian mansion perched on East Cliff, overflows with Victorian paintings and miniatures, cases of butterflies, and treasures from Asia, including an exquisite suit of Japanese armor. Members of the Russell-Cotes family, wealthy hoteliers who traveled widely, collected the items. Fine landscaped gardens surround the house. ⊠ *East Cliff* ☎ *01202/451858* ⊕ *www.russell-cotes.bournemouth.gov.uk* ☞ *Free* ☉ *Tues.–Sun. and national holiday Mon. 10–5.*

NEED A BREAK?

For an old-fashioned tea, try the **Cumberland Hotel** (⊠ *E. Overcliffe Dr.* ☎ *01202/290722*), which serves outdoors in summer.

WHERE TO EAT AND STAY

£££
SEAFOOD
✕ **WestBeach.** Superbly positioned right on the marine promenade, close to Bournemouth Pier, this place has views over sand and sea. It also serves the best seafood in town. The menu usually lists halibut, sea bass, plaice, and shellfish (oysters, mussels, lobster). Nonfish dishes may include sirloin steak and butternut squash gnocchi. The simple wooden tables and large glass front lend a modern, minimalist feel. Live jazz bands serenade diners on the first Thursday evening of the month, and there's a narrow deck outside for eating alfresco. In summer you can pick up baguettes and other snacks from the adjacent takeout. ⊠ *Pier Approach* ☎ *01202/587785* ☐ *AE, MC, V.*

£££££
★
🛏 **Chewton Glen.** Once the home of Captain Frederick Marryat, author of *The Children of the New Forest,* this early-19th-century country house on extensive grounds is now a luxurious hotel that ranks among Britain's most acclaimed—and most expensive. All rooms are decorated in rich fabrics, with an eye to the minutest detail, and the plush spa provides the latest treatments. The restaurant, the Marryat Room (fixed-price £65), is worth a pilgrimage. It concentrates on classic meat and seafood dishes enlivened with contemporary touches, and there's a choice of more than 700 wines. Chewton Glen is 12 mi east of Bournemouth. **Pros:** classic English luxury; excellent restaurant; top-notch leisure facilities. **Cons:** astronomical prices; some updating needed. ⊠ *Christchurch Rd., New Milton* ☎ *01425/275341, 800/344–5087 in U.S.* ⊕ *www.chewtonglen.com* ⇄ *35 rooms, 21 suites* ⅋ *In-room:*

DVD, Wi-Fi. In-hotel: restaurant, golf course, tennis courts, pools, gym, spa, Internet terminal, no-smoking rooms ⊟*AE, DC, MC, V.*

££–£££ ⚇ **The Urban Beach.** Once-sedate Bournemouth has been waiting a long time for the injection of contemporary style and energy provided by this funky boutique hotel. Though located in the slightly suburban setting of Boscombe (a 10-minute drive from Bournemouth's center), and resembling a B&B from the outside, the hotel is just steps from the seafront, and boasts a tastefully minimalist interior with muted tones offset by bold splashes of color. The youthful staff are simultaneously laid-back, enthusiastic, and professional. The buzzing downstairs bistro lays out a good spread, and you have access to a health club. **Pros:** modern designer decor; friendly staff. **Cons:** not central; busy bar with occasional noise; smallish bathrooms. ⊠*23 Argyll Rd., Boscombe* ☎*01202/301509* ⊕*www.urbanbeachhotel.co.uk* ⇆*12 rooms* ⌂*In-room: no a/c, DVD, Wi-Fi. In-hotel: restaurant, bar, Wi-Fi, parking (free), no-smoking rooms* ⊟*AE, DC, MC, V* ⍾*BP.*

NIGHTLIFE AND THE ARTS

In 2010 Bournemouth celebrates its bicentenary, **Bournemouth 200** (☎*01202/451195*), with a series of cultural events taking place throughout the year.

WIMBORNE MINSTER

7 mi northwest of Bournemouth via A341.

The impressive minster of this quiet market town makes it seem like a miniature cathedral city.

GETTING HERE AND AROUND

To reach Wimborne Minster from central Bournemouth, take any main road heading west, following signs for A341 or A349, or take advantage of the regular bus service.

ESSENTIALS

Visitor Information Wimborne Minster (⊠*29 High St.* ☎*01202/886116* ⊕*www.ruraldorset.com*).

EXPLORING

The crenellated and pinnacled twin towers of **Wimborne Minster** present an attractive patchwork of gray and reddish-brown stone. The church's Norman nave has zigzag molding interspersed with carved heads, and the Gothic chancel has tall lancet windows. ■TIP→ **See the chained library (accessed via a spiral staircase), a survivor from the days when books were valuable enough to keep on chains.** Look out for the 14th-century astronomical clock on the inside wall of the west tower. ⊠*High St.* ☎*01202/884753* ⊕*www.wimborneminster.org.uk* ⍾*£2 suggested donation for church, 50p suggested donation for chained library* ⊗*Church Mar.–Dec., Mon.–Sat. 9:30–5:30, Sun. 2:30–5:30; Jan. and Feb., Mon.–Sat. 9:30–4, Sun. 2:30–4. Chained library Easter–Oct., weekdays 10:30–12:30 and 2–4, Sat. 10:30–12:30; Nov.–Easter, Sat. 10–12:30.*

The **Priest's House Museum,** on the main square in a Tudor building with a garden, includes rooms furnished in period styles and a Victorian kitchen. It also has Roman and Iron Age exhibits, including a cryptic, three-faced Celtic stone head. ✉ *23 High St.* ☎ *01202/882533* ⊕ *www. priest-house.co.uk* 🎫 *£3.50* ⊘ *Apr.–Oct., Mon.–Sat. 10–4:30; also open for 10 days after Christmas.*

Kingston Lacy, a grand 17th-century house built for the Bankes family (who had lived in Corfe Castle), was altered in the 19th century by Sir Charles Barry, co-architect of the Houses of Parliament in London. It holds a choice picture collection with works by Titian, Rubens, Van Dyck, and Velásquez, as well as the fabulous Spanish Room, lined with gilded leather and topped with an ornate Venetian ceiling. There's also a fine collection of Egyptian artifacts. Parkland with walking paths surrounds the house. ✉ *B3082, 1½ mi northwest of Wimborne Minster* ☎ *01202/883402* ⊕ *www.nationaltrust.org.uk* 🎫 *£9; park and garden only, £4.50* ⊘ *House mid-Mar.–Oct., Wed.–Sun. 11–5, last admission 4. Garden and park early Feb.–early Mar. and early Nov.–late Dec., Fri.–Sun. 10:30–4; mid-Mar.–Oct., daily 10:30–6.*

WHERE TO EAT

££
MEDITERRANEAN

✕ **Primizia.** The tangerine walls, low ceiling, and tile floor lend this popular bistro an intimate feel. The regularly changing menu, which shows French and Italian influences, may include marinated crayfish tails or saffron-and-dill risotto with king prawns and scallops. ✉ *26 West Borough* ☎ *01202/883518* ▭ *MC, V* ⊘ *Closed Sun. No dinner Mon.*

CORFE CASTLE

25 mi south of Wimborne Minster, 15 mi south of Poole, 5 mi southeast of Wareham.

ESSENTIALS

Visitor Information Wareham (✉ *Holy Trinity Church, South St.* ☎ *01929/552740* ⊕ *www.visitswanageandpurbeck.com).*

EXPLORING

★ One of the most impressive ruins in Britain, Dorset's **Corfe Castle** overlooks the appealing gray limestone village also known as Corfe Castle. The castle site guards a gap in the surrounding Purbeck Hills and has been fortified since at least 900. The present ruins are of the castle built between 1105, when the great central keep was erected, and the 1270s, when the outer walls and towers were built. It owes its ramshackle state to Cromwell's soldiers, who blew up the castle in 1646 during the Civil War, after Lady Bankes led its defense during a long siege. ✉ *A351* ☎ *01929/481294* ⊕ *www.nationaltrust.org.uk* 🎫 *£5.36* ⊘ *Mar. and Oct., daily 10–5; Apr.–Sept., daily 10–6; Nov.–Feb., daily 10–4.*

OFF THE
BEATEN
PATH

Clouds Hill. This brick-and-tile cottage served as the retreat of T. E. Lawrence (Lawrence of Arabia) before he was killed in a motorcycle accident on the road from Bovington in 1935. The house remains very much as he left it, with photos and memorabilia from the Middle East. It's particularly atmospheric on a gloomy day, as there's no electric light. ✉ *8 mi northwest of Corfe, off B3390, Wareham* ☎ *01929/405616* ⊕ *www.nationaltrust.org.uk* 🎫 *£4.50* ⊘ *Mid-Mar.–Oct., Thurs.–Sun. and national holiday Mon. noon–5 or dusk.*

WHERE TO EAT AND STAY

£ ✗**The Fox.** An age-old pub, the Fox
BRITISH has a fine view of Corfe Castle
★ from its flower garden. There's an
ancient well in the lounge bar and
more timeworn stonework in an
alcove, as well as a pre-1300 fireplace. The bar cheerfully doles out
soups and sandwiches, as well as
steaks and fish dishes. This place is
popular, and can get uncomfortably
congested in summer. ⊠ *West St., Corfe* ☎*01929/480449* ⊟*MC, V.*

WORD OF MOUTH

"The Ruins of Corfe Castle in
Dorset are also very beautiful—in
fact the whole area around Corfe
is well worth a visit: very pretty
countryside and villages—and
some excellent coastal pathways
if you like hiking." —willit

££ ♨**Castle Inn.** This thatched hotel, 10 mi west of Corfe, has a flagstone
bar and other 15th-century features. Bedrooms are individually furnished, including one with a four-poster bed. There's an extensive garden to sit in, and the sea is a 10-minute walk away. A lengthy bar
menu is available daily. **Pros:** close to Lulworth Cove; historic vibe.
Cons: needs refurbishment; cramped accommodation. ⊠ *Main Rd.,
West Lulworth* ☎*01929/400311* ⊕*www.lulworthinn.com* ⟳*10
rooms* ⟆ *In-room: no a/c, Wi-Fi. In-hotel: bar, Wi-Fi, some pets allowed*
⊟*MC, V* ⊺⊙*BP.*

DORCHESTER

*21 mi west of Corfe on A351 and A352, 30 mi west of Bournemouth,
43 mi southwest of Salisbury.*

In many ways Dorchester, the Casterbridge of Thomas Hardy's novel
The Mayor of Casterbridge, is a traditional southern country town.
The town owes much of its fame to its connection with Hardy, whose
bronze statue looks westward from a bank on Colliton Walk. Born in
a cottage in the hamlet of Higher Bockhampton, about 3 mi northeast
of Dorchester, Hardy attended school in the town and was apprenticed
to an architect here.

Dorchester has many reminders of the Roman presence in the area. The
Romans laid out the town about AD 70, and a stroll along Bowling Alley
Walk, West Walk, and Colliton Walk follows the approximate line of
the original Roman town walls. On the north side of Colliton Park lies
an excavated Roman villa with a marvelously preserved mosaic floor.

Things have changed a bit since the days when, to quote Hardy, "Bees
and butterflies in the cornfields at the top of the town, who desired
to get to the meads at the bottom, took no circuitous route, but flew
straight down High Street . . ." These days High Street is usually busy
with vehicle traffic. To appreciate the town's contemporary character,
pick up a walking itinerary from the tourist office, which will take you
past the main points of interest along quieter routes.

GETTING HERE AND AROUND

Dorchester can be reached from Corfe Castle via A351 and A352. From
Salisbury take A354. Park wherever you can (pay parking lots are scattered around the center) and explore the town on foot.

Hardy's Dorset

Among this region's proudest claims is its connection with Thomas Hardy (1840–1928), one of England's most celebrated novelists. If you read some of Hardy's novels before visiting Dorset—re-created by Hardy as his part-fact, part-fiction county of Wessex—you may well recognize some places immediately from his descriptions. The tranquil countryside surrounding Dorchester is lovingly described in *Far from the Madding Crowd*, and Casterbridge, in *The Mayor* of *Casterbridge*, stands for Dorchester itself. Any pilgrimage to Hardy's Wessex begins at the author's birthplace in Higher Bockhampton, 3 mi east of Dorchester. Salisbury makes an appearance as "Melchester" in *Jude the Obscure*. Walk in the footsteps of Jude Fawley by climbing Shaftesbury— "Shaston"—and its steeply Gold Hill, a street lined with charming cottages. Today many of these sights seem frozen in time, and Hardy's spirit is ever present.

ESSENTIALS
Visitor Information Dorchester (⊠ *11 Antelope Walk* ☎ *01305/267992* ⊕ *www.westdorset.com*).

EXPLORING
TOP ATTRACTIONS
Athelhampton House and Gardens. Fine 19th-century gardens enhance an outstanding example of 15th-century domestic architecture at Athelhampton House and Gardens, 5 mi east of Dorchester and 1 mi east of Puddletown. Thomas Hardy called this place Athelhall in some of his writings, referring to the legendary King Aethelstan, who had a palace on this site. The current house includes the Great Hall, with much of its original timber roof intact, the King's Room, and the Library, with oak paneling and more than 3,000 books. The 10 acres of landscaped gardens contain water features and the Great Court with its 12 giant yew pyramids. ⊠ *A35* ☎ *01305/848363* ⊕ *www.athelhampton.co.uk* 🎫 *£8.75, £5.75 after 2:30* ⊙ *Late Feb.–Oct., Sun.–Thurs. 11–5; Nov.– late Feb., Sun. 11–5.*

Dorset County Museum. This labyrinthine museum contains ancient Celtic remains from nearby Maiden Castle and Roman remains from town, a rural crafts gallery, and a local-history gallery. It's better known for its large collection of Hardy memorabilia, and there's a gallery focusing on the nearby Jurassic Coast. ⊠ *High West St.* ☎ *01305/262735* ⊕ *www.dorsetcountymuseum.org* 🎫 *£6.50* ⊙ *July–Sept., daily 10–5; Oct.–June, Mon.–Sat. 10–5.*

QUICK BITES Drop into **Potters Café-Bistro** (⊠ *19 Durngate St.* ☎ *01305/260312*), occupying a 17th-century cottage, for teas and delicious cakes and pastries, as well as sandwiches and lunches of fish pie or tortellini. The courtyard garden is pleasant in summer.

★ **Maiden Castle.** After Stonehenge, Maiden Castle, 2 mi southwest of Dorchester, is the most important pre-Roman archaeological site in

England. It's not an actual castle but an enormous hill fort of stone and earth with ramparts that enclose about 45 acres. England's mysterious prehistoric inhabitants built the fort, and many centuries later it was a Celtic stronghold. In AD 43 invading Romans, under the general (later emperor) Vespasian, stormed the fort. Finds from the site are on display in the Dorset County Museum in Dorchester. To experience an uncanny silence and sense of mystery, climb Maiden Castle early in the day (access to it is unrestricted). Leave your car at the lot at the end of Maiden Castle Way, a 1½-mi lane signposted off the A354. ⊠*A354.*

WORTH NOTING

Dinosaur Museum. The popular Dinosaur Museum has life-size models, interactive displays, and a hands-on Discovery Gallery. ⊠*Icen Way, off High East St.* ☎*01305/269880* ⊕*www.thedinosaurmuseum.com* ⊠*£6.95* ⊘*Apr.–Oct., daily 9:30–5:30; Nov.–Mar., daily 10–4:30.*

Hardy's Cottage. The small thatch-and-cob cottage, where the writer was born in 1840, was built by his grandfather and is little altered since that time. From here Thomas Hardy would make his daily 6-mi walk to school in Dorchester. Among other things, you can see the desk at which the author completed *Far from the Madding Crowd.* ⊠*½ mi south of Blandford Rd. (A35), Higher Bockhampton* ☎*01305/262366* ⊕*www.nationaltrust.org.uk* ⊠*£3.50* ⊘*Mid-Mar.–Oct., Sun.–Thurs. 11–5 or dusk.*

Max Gate. Thomas Hardy lived in Max Gate from 1885 until his death in 1928. An architect by profession, Hardy designed the house, in which the dining room and the light, airy drawing room are open to the public. He wrote much of his poetry here and many of his novels, including *Tess of the d'Urbervilles* and *The Mayor of Casterbridge.* ⊠*Allington Ave., 1 mi east of Dorchester on A352* ☎*01305/262538* ⊕*www.nationaltrust.org.uk* ⊠*£3* ⊘*Early Apr.–Sept., Mon., Wed., and Sun. 2–5.*

Maumbury Rings. These remains of a Roman amphitheater on the edge of town were built on a prehistoric site that later served as a place of execution. (Hardy's *Mayor of Casterbridge* contains a vivid evocation of the Rings.) As late as 1706 a girl was burned at the stake here. ⊠*Maumbury Rd.*

WHERE TO EAT AND STAY

£ ✕**Judge Jeffreys.** Relaxed and characterful, this eatery occupies the for-
ITALIAN mer residence of Judge Jeffreys, a 17th-century hanging judge. The restaurant serves a reliable menu of Italian classics. Alongside the risottos, pastas, and pizzas, you'll also find *involtini di granchio* (crab cakes) and *pollo siciliana* (char-grilled butterflied chicken breast). Both dining areas are paneled (dark at street level, lighter upstairs), with beamed ceilings, antique fireplaces, and swords on the walls. ⊠*6 High West St.* ☎*01305/259678* ☰*MC, V.*

£££££ ✕**Yalbury Cottage.** A thatch roof and inglenook fireplaces add to the
MODERN BRITISH appeal of this 300-year-old cottage, 2½ mi east of Dorchester. The restaurant's three-course fixed-price menu (£34) of superior Modern British and European fare might include seared Lyme Regis scallops, roast cannon of lamb, or glazed duck breast. There are eight functional but comfortable bedrooms (££) available in an extension overlooking

gardens or adjacent fields. Lower Bockhampton is signposted off the A35, northeast of town. ⊠ *Lower Bockhampton* ☎ *01305/262382* 🖃 *AE, MC, V* ⊗ *Closed Sun. No lunch Mon.*

££   ⌖ **The Casterbridge.** Small but full of character, this Georgian build-
★   ing (1790) reflects its age with period furniture and elegance. Guest rooms—one with its own small patio—are individually and impeccably furnished in traditional style, and the conservatory overlooks a court-yard garden. The generous breakfast includes free-range eggs and fresh fruit. **Pros:** central location; elegant period setting; congenial manage-ment. **Cons:** traffic noise in front rooms; annex rooms have less char-acter; limited parking. ⊠ *49 High East St.* ☎ *01305/264043* ⊕ *www.casterbridgehotel.co.uk* 🛏 *15 rooms* ⅏ *In-room: no a/c, Wi-Fi (some). In-hotel: bar, Wi-Fi, parking (free)* 🖃 *AE, MC, V* ⏏❙*BP.*

SHOPPING

You can find Dorset delicacies such as Blue Vinney cheese (which some connoisseurs prefer to Blue Stilton) in the **Wednesday Market** in Fairfield parking lot, off Weymouth Avenue.

THE OUTDOORS

From April through October the **Thomas Hardy Society** (◲ *Box 1438, Dorchester DT1 1YH* ☎☎ *01305/251501* ⊕ *www.hardysociety.org*) organizes walks that follow in the steps of Hardy's novels. Readings and discussions accompany the walks, which take most of a day.

OFF THE
BEATEN
PATH

Poundbury. Owned by the Duchy of Cornwall and under the aegis of the Prince of Wales, this model village a mile west of Dorchester on B3150 is a showcase of Prince Charles's vision of urban planning and community living. The emphasis is on conservation and energy effi-ciency; private houses coexist with shops, offices, small-scale factories, and leisure facilities. Central Pummery Square is dominated by the colonnaded Brownsword Hall. Here you'll find the pub and restaurant Poet Laureate (☎ *01305/251511*) and Dorchester's Farmer's Market, held the first Saturday of the month. For more information consult the Duchy of Cornwall office (⊠ *Poundbury Farmhouse, Dorchester* ☎ *01305/250533* ⊕ *www.duchyofcornwall.org*).

CERNE ABBAS

6 mi north of Dorchester.

The village of Cerne Abbas, worth a short exploration on foot, has some Tudor houses on the road beside the church. Nearby you can also see the original village stocks.

EXPLORING

Tenth-century **Cerne Abbey** is now a ruin, with little left to see except its old gateway, although the nearby Abbey House is still in use.

Cerne Abbas's main claim to fame is the colossal and unblushingly priapic **figure of a giant,** cut in chalk on a hillside overlooking the village. The 180-foot-long giant carries a huge club, and may have originated as a tribal fertility symbol long before Roman times; authorities disagree. His outlines are formed by 2-foot-wide trenches. The present giant is thought to have been carved in the chalk about AD 1200. The best place to view the figure is from the A352 itself, where you can park in any of numerous nearby turnouts.

WEYMOUTH

8 mi south of Dorchester.

Dorset's main coastal resort, Weymouth, is known for its wide, safe, sandy beaches and its royal connections. King George III took up sea bathing here for his health in 1789, setting a trend among the wealthy and fashionable people of the day. Popularity left Weymouth with many fine buildings, including the Georgian row houses lining the esplanade. Striking historical details clamor for attention: a wall on Maiden Street, for example, holds a cannonball that was embedded in it during the Civil War. Nearby, a column commemorates the launching of United States forces from Weymouth on D-Day.

ESSENTIALS

Visitor Information Weymouth (⊠ *King's Statue, The Esplanade* ☎ *01305/785747* ⊕ *www.visitweymouth.co.uk*).

EXPLORING

A 5-mi-long peninsula jutting south from Weymouth leads to the Isle of Portland, well known for its limestone. The peninsula is the eastern end of the unique geological curiosity known as **Chesil Beach**—a 200-yard-wide, 30-foot-high bank of pebbles that decrease in size from east to west. The beach extends for 18 mi. A powerful undertow makes swimming dangerous, and tombstones in local churchyards attest to the many shipwrecks the beach has caused.

WHERE TO EAT

££££ ✕**Perry's.** In a Georgian town house right by the harbor, this busy res-
SEAFOOD taurant specializes in simple dishes using the best local seafood. Try the lobster or scallops, or grilled fillet of sea bass with crab and sweet-corn polenta cake. Meat dishes, such as beef fillet and shoulder of lamb, are tasty, too. Set-price lunch menus are a good value. ⊠*The Harbourside, 4 Trinity Rd.* ☎*01305/785799* ⊟*MC, V* ⊗*Closed Mon. No lunch Sat.*

ABBOTSBURY

10 mi northwest of Weymouth.

Pretty Abbotsbury is at the western end of Chesil Beach.

EXPLORING

A lagoon outside the village serves as the **Abbotsbury Swannery,** a famous breeding place for swans. Introduced by Benedictine monks as a source of meat in winter, the swans have remained for centuries, building new nests every year in the soft, moist eelgrass. In other parts of the village, you can also visit a children's farm, housed in an impressive medieval barn, and subtropical gardens. ⊠*New Barn Rd.* ☎*01305/871858* ⊕*www.abbotsbury-tourism.co.uk* ⊠*£9* ⊗*Apr.–Sept., daily 10–6; late Mar. and Oct., daily 10–5; last admission 1 hr before closing.*

On the hills above Abbotsbury stands the **Hardy Monument**—dedicated to Sir Thomas Masterman Hardy, Lord Nelson's flag captain at Trafalgar, to whom Nelson's dying words, "Kiss me, Hardy," were addressed. The monument lacks charm, but in clear weather you can scan the whole coastline between the Isle of Wight and Start Point in Devon. ⊠ *Black Down, Portesham* 🕾 *01297/561900* ⊕ *www.nationaltrust.org.uk* 🎫 *£2* ⊗ *Apr.–Sept., weekends 11–5. May close in bad weather.*

LYME REGIS

19 mi west of Abbotsbury.

"A very strange stranger it must be, who does not see the charms of the immediate environs of Lyme, to make him wish to know it better," wrote Jane Austen in *Persuasion*. Judging from the summer crowds, most people appear to be not at all strange. The ancient, scenic town of Lyme Regis and the so-called Jurassic Coast are highlights of southwest Dorset. The crumbling seaside cliffs in this area are especially fossil rich.

GETTING HERE AND AROUND

Lyme Regis is off the A35, extending west from Bournemouth and Dorchester. First buses run here from Dorchester. Drivers should park as soon as possible—there are parking lots at the top of town, for example off Charmouth Road, on the eastern approach (A3052)—and explore the town on foot.

ESSENTIALS

Visitor Information Lyme Regis (⊠ *Guildhall Cottage, Church St.* 🕾 *01297/442138* ⊕ *www.lymeregistourism.co.uk*).

EXPLORING

Lyme Regis is famous for its curving stone breakwater, the **Cobb,** built by King Edward I in the 13th century to improve the harbor. The duke of Monmouth landed here in 1685 during his ill-fated attempt to overthrow his uncle James II. The Cobb figured prominently in the movie *The French Lieutenant's Woman,* based on John Fowles's novel set in Lyme Regis, as well as in the film version of Jane Austen's *Persuasion.* Fowles was a longtime resident of Lyme.

☉ The small but child-friendly **Marine Aquarium** offers the usual up-close look at creatures aquatic, from conger eels to spider crabs. ⊠ *End of the Cobb* 🕾 *01297/444230* 🎫 *£5* ⊗ *Mid-Mar.–Oct., daily 10–5.*

In a gabled and turreted Victorian building, the lively **Lyme Regis Museum** contains engaging items that illustrate the town's maritime and domestic history, as well as a section on local writers and a good selection of local fossils. ⊠ *Bridge St.* 🕾 *01297/443370* ⊕ *www.lymeregismuseum. co.uk* 🎫 *£3* ⊗ *Easter–Oct., Mon.–Sat. 10–5, Sun. 11–5; Nov.–Easter, Wed.–Sun. 11–4, daily during school vacations.*

☉ The **Dinosaurland Fossil Museum,** in a former church, displays an excellent collection of local fossils and gives the background on regional geology and how fossils develop. Although the museum is aimed at children, most people find it informative. Ask here about guided fossil-hunting walks. The **Lyme Regis Fossil Shop** on the ground floor sells books

CLOSE UP

Fossil Hunting on the Jurassic Coast

Fossils and fossil hunting are the lure for visitors to the coast that stretches for 95 mi between Studland Bay in the east to Exmouth (Devon) in the west. This cliff-lined coast encompasses 185 million years of the Earth's geological history, for which it has been granted World Heritage Site status. Fossils formed in the distant past are continuously being uncovered here as parts of the crumbly cliffs erode, and good examples of ammonites and dinosaur traces can be seen in museums in Dorchester and Lyme Regis. Though it is dubbed "Jurassic Coast," there are also examples of older Triassic and younger Cretaceous rocks. As a rule, the older rocks can be seen in the western parts of the coast, and younger rocks form the cliffs to the east. A good path that traces the whole coast allows you to explore the area at close quarters.

Fossil hunters are free to pick and chip away at the rocks, the best stretch being within 6 mi on either side of Lyme Regis (the beach below Stonebarrow Hill, east of Charmouth, is especially fruitful). As signs along the seafront warn, the best place to find fossils is not at the rock face but on the shore. Check weather conditions and tides—collecting on a falling tide is best, and the ideal time to do it is in winter, when heavy storms are continuously uncovering new areas.

To spot the most commonly found fossils, ammonites (chambered cephalopods from the Jurassic era, related to today's nautilus), just look down hard at the shingle (large gravel) on the beach and inspect the gaps between rocks and boulders. Ammonites are usually preserved in either calcite or iron pyrite ("fool's gold"); shinier, more fragile specimens may be found in aragonite. Visit the museums in Lyme to remind you what to look for: the lustrous spirals are similar in heft and size to a brass coin, most smaller than a 10p coin. Other fossils to be found include sea urchins, white oyster shells, and coiled worm tubes.

If you want to leave nothing to chance, hook up with a pro: information on guided walks is available from the tourist office and the Lyme Regis Museum. Publications are also available for sale in the tourist offices of Lyme Regis, Weymouth, and Dorchester; they can also tell you about coastal boat trips.

4

and fascinating fossils from around the world as well as reproductions of fossils, some fashioned into jewelry or ornaments. ⊠ *Coombe St.* ☎ *01297/443541* ⊕ *www.dinosaurland.co.uk* ⊠ *£4.50* ☉ *Mid-Feb.– mid-Oct., daily 10–5; mid-Oct.–mid-Feb., weekends 10–5, but call to check.*

WHERE TO EAT AND STAY

£ ✕ **Bell Cliff Restaurant.** This friendly little place at the bottom of Lyme's BRITISH main street makes a great spot for a light lunch or tea, although it can get noisy and cramped. Apart from teas and coffees, you can order seafood, including whitebait, plaice, and the chef's salmon cakes, or a gammon steak (a thick slice of cured ham) or leek-and-mushroom crumble. ⊠ *5–6 Broad St.* ☎ *01297/442459* ⊟ *AE, MC, V* ☉ *No dinner Oct.–May.*

£££–££££ **Alexandra.** Magnificently sited above the Cobb, the Alexandra is a rambling, old-fashioned haven with a genteel, unhurried air. Depending on the cost, some guest rooms have a restrained elegance and others are purely functional, although most have a view over the garden and sea. Bathrooms are on the small side. Informal lunches and teas are served in a conservatory that overlooks an expanse of lawn. The formal restaurant has an impressive wine list to complement the fixed-price, five-course dinners (£36.50),

> **EVEN KIDS DIG IT**
>
> In 1810 a local child named Mary Anning dug out a complete ichthyosaur near Lyme Regis (it's on display in London's Natural History Museum). Anning's obsession with Jurassic remains left her labeled locally as the "fossil woman"; throughout her life she made many valuable discoveries that were sought by museums and collectors.

featuring such entrées as grilled fillet of monkfish with citrus couscous and poached asparagus, and char-grilled fillet of beef. **Pros:** great garden; lovely views; central location. **Cons:** cheaper rooms have no sea views; restricted parking. ⊠ *Pound St.* ☎ *01297/442010* ⊕ *www. hotelalexandra.co.uk* ➳ *24 rooms* ♿ *In-room: no a/c, Wi-Fi (some). In-hotel: restaurant, bar, Internet terminal, Wi-Fi, some pets allowed, no-smoking rooms* ☰ *MC, V* ⊗ *Closed late Dec.–late Jan.* ⏉ *BP.*

£ **Coombe House.** Tucked away on one of the oldest lanes in Lyme (dating from the 16th century), this simple B&B has genial hosts and spacious, modern guest rooms in pastel shades. Breakfast, which includes homemade jams, is brought to your room. A self-catering apartment and studio are also available. **Pros:** friendly owners; pleasant rooms; central location. **Cons:** only two rooms; little parking. ⊠ *41 Coombe St.* ☎ *01297/443849* ⊕ *www.coombe-house.co.uk* ➳ *2 rooms* ♿ *In-room: no a/c, no phone, Wi-Fi. In-hotel: Wi-Fi, no-smoking rooms* ☰ *No credit cards* ⏉ *BP.*

SPORTS AND THE OUTDOORS

The 72-mi **Dorset Coast Path** (☎ *01392/383560* ⊕ *www.southwestcoast-path.com*) runs east from Lyme Regis to Poole, bypassing Weymouth and taking in the quiet bays, shingle beaches, and low chalk cliffs of the coast. Some highlights are Golden Cap, the highest point on the south coast; the Swannery at Abbotsbury; Chesil Beach; and Lulworth Cove (between Weymouth and Corfe Castle). Villages and isolated pubs dot the route, as do many rural B&Bs.

The West Country

SOMERSET, DEVON, CORNWALL

WORD OF MOUTH

"Driving from M5 to Wells is already a lovely thing—through pretty villages and countryside. Wells is a quaint little town with a pretty market, old gates, and bookshops everywhere. The cathedral is gorgeous and appears ridiculously oversized in such a small town, but this gives a proper impression how proportions were in the old times."

—traveller1959

"I'm not sure there is a central spot to really see the West Country—it sort of breaks down more into counties with North and South Cornwall being fairly large areas requiring much peninsula dipping to enjoy fully."

—opus

Updated
by Robert
Andrews

Leafy, narrow country roads all around the southwest lead through miles of buttercup meadows and cider-apple orchards to heathery heights overlooking the sea and mellow villages of stone and thatch. This can be one of England's most relaxing regions to visit. The secret of exploring it is to ignore the main highways and just follow the signposts—or, even better, to let yourself get lost, which won't be difficult. The village names alone are music to the ears: there's Tintinhull, St. Endellion, and Huish Episcopi—just to name a few hamlets that *haven't* been covered below.

Somerset, Devon, and Cornwall are the three counties that make up the long, dangling peninsula known as the West Country. Each has its own distinct flavor, and each comes with a regionalism that borders on patriotism. Somerset is noted for its subtly rolling green countryside; Devon's wild and dramatic moors—bare, boggy, upland heath dominated by heathers and gorse—contrast with the restfulness of its many sandy beaches and coves; and Cornwall has managed to retain a touch of its old insularity, despite the annual invasion of thousands of people lured by the Atlantic waves or the ripples of the English Channel.

Bristol is where you come across the first unmistakable burrs of the western brogue. Its historic port retains a strong maritime air, and Georgian architecture and a dramatic gorge create a backdrop to what has become one of Britain's most dynamic cities. You might weave south through the lovely Chew Valley on your way to the cathedral city of Wells. The county's lush countryside is best seen in a cloak of summer heat when its orchards give ample shade and its old stone houses and inns welcome you with a breath of coolness. Abutting the north coast are the Quantock and Mendip hills, and heather-covered Exmoor National Park.

Devon, farther west, is famed for its wild moorland—especially Dartmoor, where ponies roam amid an assortment of strange tors: rocky outcroppings eroded into weird shapes. Devon's large coastal towns are as interesting for their cultural and historical appeal—many were smugglers' havens—as for their scenic beauty. Some propagandists of east Devon speak of the "red cliffs" of Devon in contrast to the more famous "white cliffs of Dover." Parts of south Devon, on the other hand, resemble some balmy Mediterranean shore—hence its soubriquet, the English Riviera.

Cornwall, England's southernmost county, has always regarded itself as separate from the rest of Britain, and the Arthurian legends really took root here, not least at Tintagel Castle, the legendary birthplace of Arthur. High, jagged cliffs line Cornwall's Atlantic coast and indeed

TOP REASONS TO GO

A coastal walk: Pick almost any stretch of coast in Devon and Cornwall for a close encounter with the sea. For high, dramatic cliff scenery, choose the Exmoor coast around Lynmouth or the coast around Tintagel.

Riding or hiking on Dartmoor: Get away from it all in southern England's greatest wilderness—an empty, treeless expanse dotted with rocky outcrops called tors. Organized walks and pony-trekking operations are advertised at visitor centers.

Seafood in Padstow: Celebrity chef Rick Stein rules the roost in this small Cornish port, and any of his establishments will strongly satisfy, though the Seafood Restaurant has the wow factor. A pre- or post-dinner stroll around the harbor will allow you to soak up the spirit of this congenial town.

Tate St. Ives: There's nowhere better to absorb the local arts scene than this offshoot of London's Tate in the pretty seaside town of St. Ives. A marvelous rooftop café claims views over Porthmeor Beach.

A visit to Eden: It's worth the journey west for Cornwall's Eden Project alone: a wonderland of plant life, magnificently sited in a former clay pit. Two gigantic geodesic "biomes" are filled with flora from around the world, and the elaborate outdoor plantations are equally engaging.

Wells Cathedral: A perfect example of medieval craftsmanship, the building is a stunning spectacle. Come at the end of the day when Evensong is performed to experience its lofty interior at its most evocative.

pose a menace to passing ships. The south coast, Janus-like, is filled with sunny beaches, delightful coves, and popular resorts. England's last outposts, the flower-filled Isles of Scilly, claim the most hours of sunshine in the country.

ORIENTATION AND PLANNING

GETTING ORIENTED

Going from east to west, the counties of Somerset, Devon, and Cornwall make up the West Country. A circular tour of the West Country peninsula covers stark contrasts, from the bustling city of Bristol in the east to the remote and rocky headlands of Devon and Cornwall to the west. On the whole, the northern coast is more rugged, the cliffs dropping dramatically to tiny coves and beaches, whereas the south coast shelters many more resorts and wider expanses of sand. The crowds gravitate to the southern shore, but there are many remote inlets and estuaries, and you don't need to go far to find a degree of seclusion. The national parks of Exmoor on the northern part of the peninsula and Dartmoor, with their wilder landscapes, add even more variety.

Bristol to North Devon. Bristol is filled with remnants of its long history, but you need to explore small towns like Wells and Glastonbury to get the full flavor of the region. West of here, Exmoor has an unfettered, romantic appeal, with some entrancing coastline.

Cornwall. You're never more than 20 mi from the sea in this western outpost of Britain, and the maritime flavor imbues such port towns as Padstow and Falmouth. A string of good beaches and resort towns such as St. Ives pull in the summer crowds.

Plymouth and Dartmoor. Though modern in appearance, Plymouth has some important historical sights. To the northeast, the open heath and wild moorland of Dartmoor invites walking and horseback riding; towns such as Chagford make a good base for exploring.

Dartmouth, Torbay, and Exeter. Bustling Dartmouth and relaxed Totnes lie close to the English Riviera resorts of Torquay and Brixham (both part of the Torbay district). North of here, Exeter's sturdy cathedral dominates the historic city, from which you can make easy forays to Topsham and Honiton.

PLANNING

WHEN TO GO

In July and August, traffic chokes the roads leading into the West Country. Somehow the region squeezes in all the "grockles," or tourists, and the chances of finding a remote oasis of peace and quiet are severely curtailed. The beaches and resort towns are either bubbling with zest or unbearably tacky, depending on your point of view. In summer, your best option is to find a secluded hotel and make brief excursions from there. Avoid traveling on Saturday, when weekly rentals start and finish and the roads are jammed. Most properties that don't accept business year-round open for Easter and close in late September or October. Those that remain open have reduced hours. Winter has its own appeal: the Atlantic waves crash dramatically against the coast, and the austere Cornish cliffs are at their most spectacular.

The most notable festivals are Padstow's Obby Oss, a traditional celebration of the arrival of summer that takes place around May 1; the Cornish-themed, weeklong Golowan Festival in Penzance in late June; the Exeter Festivals in late June and November; and the St. Ives September Festival of music and art in mid-September. In addition, many West Country maritime towns host regattas over summer weekends. The best times to visit Devon are late summer and early fall, during the end-of-summer festivals, especially popular in the towns of eastern Dartmoor.

PLANNING YOUR TIME

The elongated shape of Britain's southwestern peninsula means that you may well spend more time traveling than seeing the sights. The key is to base yourself in one or two places and make day trips to the surrounding region. The cities of Bristol, Exeter, and Plymouth make handy bases from which to explore the region, but they can also swallow up a lot of time, at the expense of smaller, less demanding places. The same is true of the resorts of Torquay, Newquay, and Falmouth, which can get very busy. Choose instead towns and villages such as Wells, Lynmouth, Port Isaac, St. Mawes, and Charlestown to soak up local atmosphere. Allow

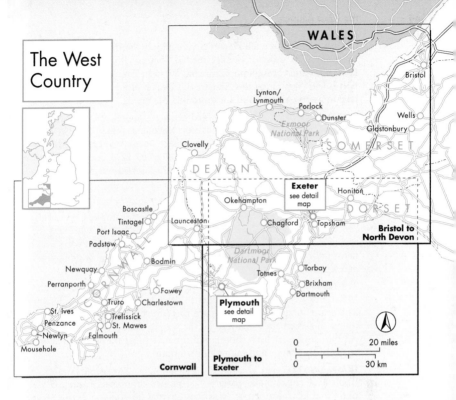

The West Country

WALES

time for aimless rambling—the best way to explore the moors and the coast—and leave enough free time for doing nothing at all.

GETTING HERE AND AROUND

AIR TRAVEL

Bristol International Airport, a few miles southwest of the city, has flights from domestic and international cities. Continental runs a direct daily service from New York. Plymouth has a small airport 4 mi north of the center. Exeter International Airport is 5 mi east of the city. Newquay Cornwall Airport, 5 mi northeast of town, has daily flights to London Stansted and London Gatwick.

Airport Information Bristol International Airport (✉ Lulsgate Bottom ☎ 0871/334–4344 ⊕ www.bristolairport.co.uk). **Exeter International Airport** ✉ Clyst Honiton (☎ 01392/367433 ⊕ www.exeter-airport.co.uk). **Plymouth City Airport** (✉ Crownhill ☎ 01752/204090 ⊕ www.plymouthairport.com). **Newquay Cornwall Airport** (✉ St. Mawgan ☎ 01637/860600 ⊕ www. newquaycornwallairport.com).

BUS TRAVEL

National Express buses leave London's Victoria Coach Station for Bristol (2½ hours), Exeter (4¼ hours), Plymouth (4¾ hours), and Penzance (about 9 hours). Megabus offers cheap service to Bristol, Exeter, Plymouth, Newquay, and Penzance. There's also a good network of regional bus services. Stagecoach Devon covers mainly South Devon. First bus company runs most of the services in Somerset, North Devon, and Plymouth, and throughout Cornwall. Western Greyhound operates in North Cornwall. First and Stagecoach Devon money-saving one- and seven-day passes are good for unlimited bus travel.

Bus Contacts First (☎ 0845/600–1420 ⊕ www.firstgroup.com). **Megabus** (☎ 0900/160–0900 ⊕ www.megabus.com). **National Express** (☎ 0871/781–8181 ⊕ www.nationalexpress.com). **Stagecoach Devon** (☎ 01392/427711 ⊕ www.stagecoachbus.com). **Traveline** (☎ 0871/200–2233 ⊕ www.traveline.org.uk). **Western Greyhound** (☎ 01637/871871 ⊕ www.westerngreyhound.com).

CAR TRAVEL

Unless you confine yourself to a few towns—for example, Exeter, Penzance, and Plymouth—you will be at a huge disadvantage without your own transportation. The region has a few main arteries, but you should take minor roads whenever possible, if only to see the real West Country at a leisurely pace.

The fastest route from London to the West Country is via the M4 and M5 motorways. Allow two hours to drive to Bristol, three to Exeter. The main roads heading west are the A30 (burrowing through the center of Devon and Cornwall all the way to the tip of Cornwall), the A39 (near the northern shore), and the A38 (near the southern shore, south of Dartmoor and taking in Plymouth).

TRAIN TRAVEL

Rail travelers can make use of a fast service connecting Exeter, Plymouth, and Penzance. First Great Western and South West Trains serve the region from London's Paddington and Waterloo stations. Average travel time to Exeter is 2½ hours, to Plymouth 3½ hours, and to Penzance about 5½ hours. Once you've arrived, however, you'll find trains to be of limited use in the West Country, as only a few branch lines leave the main line between Exeter and Penzance.

Regional Rail Rover tickets provide 8 days' unlimited travel throughout the West Country in any 15-day period, and localized Rovers cover Devon or Cornwall.

Train Contacts National Rail Enquiries (☎ 0845/748–4950 ⊕ www.nationalrail.co.uk).

RESTAURANTS

The last few years have seen a food renaissance in England's West Country. In the top restaurants, the accent is firmly on local and seasonal products. Better-known establishments are often completely booked on Friday or Saturday, so reserve well in advance.

WHAT IT COSTS IN POUNDS					
	£	££	£££	££££	£££££
Restaurants	Under £10	£10–£14	£15–£19	£20–£25	over £25
Hotels	under £70	£70–£120	£121–£160	£161–£220	over £220

Restaurant prices are for a main course at dinner. Hotel prices are for two people in a standard double room in high season, including V.A.T., with no meals or, if indicated, CP (with continental breakfast), BP (Breakfast Plan, with full breakfast), or MAP (Modified American Plan, with breakfast and dinner).

HOTELS

Availability can be limited on the coasts during August, so book well ahead. Accommodations include national hotel chains, represented in all the region's principal centers, as well as ancient inns and ubiquitous bed-and-breakfast places. Many farmhouses also rent out rooms—offering tranquility in rural surroundings—but these lodgings are often difficult to reach without a car. It's worth finding out about weekend and winter deals that many hotels offer.

VISITOR INFORMATION

Contacts Somerset Tourism (✉ *Somerset County Council, County Hall, Taunton* ☎ *01934/750833* ⊕ *www.visitsomerset.co.uk*). **South West Tourism** (☎ *0870/442–0880* ⊕ *www.visitsouthwest.co.uk*). **VisitCornwall** (✉ *Pydar House, Pydar St., Truro* ☎ *01872/322900* ⊕ *www.visitcornwall.com*). **Visit Devon** (✉ *Matford Business Centre, Waterbridge Ct., Matford Park Rd., Exeter* ☎ *01392/332828* ⊕ *www.visitdevon.co.uk*).

BRISTOL TO NORTH DEVON

On the eastern side of this region is the vibrant city of Bristol. From here, you might head south to the pretty cathedral city of Wells and continue on via Glastonbury, possibly the Avalon of Arthurian legend. Proceed west along the Somerset coast into Devon, skirting the moorlands of Exmoor and tracing the northern shore via Clovelly.

BRISTOL

120 mi west of London, 46 mi south of Birmingham, 13 mi northwest of Bath.

The West Country's biggest city, Bristol has in recent years become one of the country's most vibrant centers, with a thriving cultural scene encompassing some of the best contemporary art, theater, and music. Buzzing bars, cafés, and restaurants, and a largely youthful population make it an attractive place to spend time.

Now that the city's industries no longer rely on the docks, the historic harbor along the River Avon has been given over to recreation. Arts and entertainment complexes, museums, and galleries fill the quayside. The pubs and clubs here draw the under-25 set and make the area fairly boisterous (and best avoided) on Friday and Saturday nights.

Bristol also trails a great deal of history in its wake. It can be called the "birthplace of America" with some confidence, for John Cabot and his son Sebastian sailed from the old city docks in 1497 to touch down on the North American mainland, which he claimed for the English crown. The city had been a major center since medieval times, but in the 17th and 18th centuries it became the foremost port for trade with North America. Bristol was the home of William Penn, developer of Pennsylvania, and a haven for John Wesley, whose Methodist movement played an important role in colonial Georgia.

GETTING HERE AND AROUND

Bristol is well connected by bus and train from most cities in the country. From London, calculate about 2½ hours by bus, or 1¾ hours by train. By train, make sure you get tickets for Bristol Temple Meads station (not Bristol Parkway), which is a short bus or taxi ride (or a 20-minute walk) from the center. The bus station is more central, near the Broadmead shopping center. Most sights can be visited on foot, though a bus or a taxi is necessary to reach the Clifton neighborhood.

ESSENTIALS

Visitor Information Bristol (✉ *Explore@Bristol, Anchor Rd.* ☎ *0333/321–0101, 870/444–0654 from outside U.K.* ⊕ *www.visitbristol.co.uk*).

EXPLORING
TOP ATTRACTIONS

★ **Church of St. Mary Redcliffe.** Built by Bristol merchants who wanted a place in which to pray for the safe (and profitable) voyages of their ships, the rib-vaulted, 14th-century church was called "the fairest in England" by Queen Elizabeth I. High up on the nave wall hang the arms and armor of Sir William Penn, father of the founder of Pennsylvania. The church is a five-minute walk from Temple Meads train station toward the docks. ✉ *Redcliffe Way* ☎ *0117/929–1487* ⊕ *www. stmaryredcliffe.co.uk* ⊠ *Free* ⊙ *Mon.–Sat. 9–5 (until 4 in winter), Sun. 8–7:30.*

Clifton Suspension Bridge. In the Georgian district of Clifton—a sort of Bath in miniature—you can take in a monument to Victorian engineering, the 702-foot-long bridge that spans the Avon Gorge. Work began on Isambard Kingdom Brunel's design in 1831, but the bridge was not completed until 1864. Free hour-long guided tours take place on summer Sundays, departing from the tollbooth at the Clifton end of the bridge. At the far end of the bridge, the **Clifton Suspension Bridge Visitor Centre** (☎ *0117/974–4664* ⊕ *www.clifton-suspension-bridge.org. uk*) has a small exhibition on the bridge and its construction, including a 10-minute video. At the Bristol end of the bridge lies **Clifton Village,** which is studded with boutiques, antiques shops, and smart crafts shops in its lanes and squares. ✉ *Bridge Rd., Leigh Woods* ⊠ *Free* ⊙ *Daily 10–5. Tours Easter–mid-Sept., Sun. 3* PM.

⟳ **Explore@Bristol.** In the Harbourside area, this multimedia attraction provides a "hands-on, minds-on" exploration of science and technology. A planetarium in a gleaming stainless-steel sphere takes you on a 25-minute voyage through the galaxy. The shows are on weekdays from 11 to 2 and weekends 11 to 4. ✉ *Anchor Rd.* ☎ *0845/345–1235*

⊕*www.at-bristol.org.uk* 🎟*£10.80* 🕒*Weekdays 10–5, weekends, national holiday Mon., and school vacations 10–6; last admission 1 hr before closing.*

The excellent café-restaurant upstairs at the **Watershed Media Centre** (⊠*1 Canon's Rd.* ☎*0117/927–5100*) overlooks part of the Harborside. Sandwiches and hot snacks are served during the day, along with coffees and cakes.

★ *SS Great Britain.* On view in the harbor is the first iron ship to cross the Atlantic. Built by the great English engineer Isambard Kingdom Brunel in 1843, it remained in service until 1970, first as a transatlantic liner and ultimately as a coal storage hulk. On board, everything from the galley to the officers' quarters comes complete with sounds and smells of the time. You can descend into the ship's dry dock for a view of the hull and propeller. Moored alongside is a replica of the *Matthew,* the tiny craft that carried John Cabot to North America in 1497. Your ticket admits you to the **Dockyard Museum,** which presents the history of the *Great Britain.* ⊠*Great Western Dockyard, Gas Ferry Rd.* ☎*0117/926–0680* ⊕*www.ssgreatbritain.org* 🎟*£10.95* 🕒*Apr.–late Oct., daily 10–5:30; Feb., Mar., and late Oct., daily 10–4:30; Nov.–Jan., daily 10–4; last entry 1 hr before closing.*

WORTH NOTING

🕐 **Bristol Zoo Gardens.** Alongside the leafy expanse of Clifton Downs is one of the country's most famous zoos. More than 300 animal species live in 12 acres of gardens; the Seal and Penguin Coasts, with underwater viewing, are rival attractions for Gorilla Island, Bug World, and Twilight World. ⊠*Clifton Down* ☎*0117/974–7399* ⊕*www.bristolzoo.org.uk* 🎟*£11.86* 🕒*June–Aug., daily 9–5:30; Sept.–May, daily 9–5.*

New Room. John Wesley and Charles Wesley were among the Dissenters from the Church of England who found a home in Bristol, and in 1739 they built the New Room, a meeting place that became the first Methodist chapel. Its simplicity contrasts with the style of Anglican churches and with the modern shopping center hemming it in. Upstairs you can visit the Preachers' Rooms, now containing a small museum. ⊠*Broadmead* ☎*0117/926–4740* ⊕*www.newroombristol.org.uk* 🎟*Free* 🕒*Mon.–Sat. and national holidays 10–4.*

Tyntesfield. The National Trust is restoring this extravagant, 35-bedroom Victorian Gothic-Revival mansion. You can see the house, garden, and chapel at your own pace; entry, by timed ticket, can't be guaranteed on the busiest days. Every ornate detail of this decorative-arts showcase compels attention. Besides magnificent woodwork, stained glass, tiles, and original furniture and fabrics, the house contains the modern conveniences of the 1860s, such as a heated billiards table, and the servants' quarters are equally absorbing. Tyntesfield is 7 mi southwest of Bristol. ⊠*Wraxall* ☎*0844/800–4966* ⊕*www.nationaltrust.org.uk* 🎟*£9.45; gardens only, £4.75* 🕒*House Apr.–Oct., Sat.–Tues. 11–5; gardens Apr.–Oct., Sat.–Wed. 10:30–5:30.*

Bristol to North Devon

0 — 20 miles
0 — 30 km

WALES

Swansea
Swansea Bay

Bristol Channel

Cardiff
Newport
TO LONDON
M4
Bristol
Tyntesfield
Stanton Drew Circles
Chew Magna

Bridgwater Bay
Cheddar
Wells
Shepton Mallet
Glastonbury
Pilton
SOMERSET
A39
A37
A303

Ilfracombe
Lynton/ Lynmouth
Porlock Weir
Minehead
Dunster
Nether Stowey

Bude Bay
Combe Martin
B3358
Porlock
QUANTOCK HILLS
B3190
B3188
Taunton
A361
A303 A3088
Yeovil

Braunton Burrows Biosphere Reserve
BRENDON HILLS
Exmoor National Park
Barnstaple
A361
Dulverton
Wellington
Bradford-on-Tone
A38
A303
A30

Bideford Bay
Clovelly
A39
Bideford
Taw
Torridge
A377
Tiverton
A361
M5

Hartland Quay
DEVON
Bude
B3254
A388
A39
A30
Exe
Exeter see detail map
Gittisham
Honiton
DORSET

Okehampton
Drewsteignton
A30
A3052
Sidmouth
Lyme Regis
Bridport
Seaton
Beer

Launceston
Lewdown
A30
Lydford Gorge
Chagford
Topsham
Kenton
Budleigh Salterton
JURASSIC COAST

Bolventor

WHERE TO EAT

£££ ✕**Bell's Diner.** A local institution, this bistro occupies a former grocery
MEDITERRANEAN shop and has polished wood floors and pale gray walls lined with shelves. The inventive Mediterranean menu includes locally sourced poultry, rabbit, and seafood, as well as toothsome desserts such as crème brulée with rhubarb sorbet and shortbread. In the Montpelier area, Bell's is rather hard to find. To get there, take A38 north, then turn right on Ashley Road and immediately left at Picton Street, which will lead you to York Road. ✉*1 York Rd.* ☎*0117/924–0357* ▤*AE, MC, V* ⊘*Closed Sun. No lunch Sat. and Mon.*

£££ ✕**Bordeaux Quay.** This converted riverside warehouse is the place for
MODERN BRITISH modern, sophisticated dining in Bristol. In the more formal upstairs dining room, where a large skylight and harbor views set the scene, you can select from such dishes as rump of lamb with red pepper, eggplant, and sweet potato, and desserts such as caramelized-apple-and-raisin pudding with Calvados sauce. Sharing the space downstairs with a delicatessen and bar is a rough-and-ready brasserie where tables are allocated on a first-come, first-served basis—recommended for Sunday brunch. ✉*Canons Way* ☎*0117/943–1200* ▤*AE, MC, V* ⊘*Restaurant closed Mon. No dinner in restaurant or brasserie Sun.*

£ ✕**Boston Tea Party.** Despite the name, this laid-back and vaguely eccen-
BRITISH tric place is quintessentially English, and ideal for a relaxed lunch away

ON THE MENU

From cider to cream teas, many specialties tempt your palate in the West Country. Lamb, venison, and, in Devon and Cornwall, seafood are favored in restaurants, which have improved markedly, notably through the influence of Rick Stein's seafood-based culinary empire in Padstow, in Cornwall. In many towns the day's catch is unloaded from the harbor and transported directly to eateries. The catch varies by season, but lobster is available year-round, as is crab, stuffed into sandwiches at quayside stalls and in pubs. Seafood is celebrated at fishy frolics that include the Newlyn Fish Festival (late August) and Falmouth's Oyster Festival (early or mid–October).

Somerset is the home of Britain's most famous cheese—the ubiquitous cheddar, originally from the Mendip Hills village of the same name. Make certain that you sample a real farmhouse cheddar, made in the traditional barrel shape known as a truckle.

Devon's caloric cream teas consist of a pot of tea, homemade scones, and lots of strawberry jam and thickened clotted cream (clotted, or specially thickened cream, is a regional specialty and is sometimes called Devonshire cream).

Cornwall's specialty is the pasty, a pastry shell filled with chopped meat, onions, and potatoes. The pasty was devised as a handy way for miners to carry their dinner to work; today's versions are generally pale imitations of the original, though you can still find delicious home-cooked pasties if you're willing to search a little.

For liquid refreshment, try scrumpy, a homemade dry cider that is refreshing but carries a surprising kick. Look out, too, for perry, similar to cider but made from pears. English wine, similar to German wine, is made in all three counties (you may see it on local menus), and in Devon and Cornwall you can find a variant of age-old mead made from local honey.

from the nearby rigors of the Park Street shopping scene. Good sandwiches can be taken away or eaten in the terraced backyard or the upstairs sofa salon. Hot dishes like fish pie and generous salads are also available. ⊠*75 Park St.* ☎*0117/929–8601* ▤*MC, V* ⊗*Closes at 8* PM *daily.*

WHERE TO STAY

For a notable overture to your West Country excursion, you might book a night at Thornbury Castle, 12 mi north of Bristol in Thornbury *(⇨See Berkeley Castle in Chapter 8).*

£ ⬚**Hotel24seven.** This functional stop is Bristol's best budget option, and also offers self-catering facilities, either in the rooms or in a separate kitchen. Furnishings and decor are basic but modern and well maintained, the rooms—which come in a range of sizes—are well equipped, and there's a family apartment with its own patio. The hotel lies in the quiet Southville area of south Bristol, a 10-minute walk from the center. You must book online or by telephone before arriving. **Pros:** good value; clean rooms; self-catering. **Cons:** no reception; no breakfast. ⊠*Dean La. and*

15 Acramans Rd., Southville ☎*0844/770–9411* ⊕*www.hotel24seven. com* ⇆*30 rooms* ♿*In-room: no a/c, no phone, kitchen (some), refrigerator, DVD, Wi-Fi. In-hotel: Wi-Fi, parking (paid)* ⊟*MC, V.*

£££ 🔲 **Hotel du Vin.** This hip chain has an ambitious outlet in the Sugar House—six former sugar-refining warehouses built in 1728 when the River Frome ran outside the front door—close to the docklands and the city center. Rooms are crisply contemporary, with high-tech gadgetry, but retain many original industrial features. The restaurant specializes in modern but robust French fare. **Pros:** tastefully restored old building; great bathrooms; excellent food. **Cons:** traffic-dominated location; some noise on weekends; service can be poor. ⊠*Narrow Lewins Mead* ☎*0117/925–5577* ⊕*www.hotelduvin.com* ⇆*40 rooms* ♿*In-room: DVD, Wi-Fi. In-hotel: restaurant, bar, Wi-Fi, parking (paid)* ⊟*AE, DC, MC, V.*

££ 🔲 **Victoria Square Hotel.** In two mellow Victorian buildings overlooking one of Clifton's leafiest squares, this hotel makes an excellent base for exploring Bristol. Rooms are decorated in neutral colors and are well equipped, most with modern bathrooms; Rooms 229 and 247 open directly onto a small walled garden. Some rooms, however, are a bit cramped or are accessed via steep stairs. **Pros:** polite staff; pleasant location. **Cons:** numerous steps; needs sprucing up; occasional street noise. ⊠*Victoria Sq., Clifton* ☎*0117/973–9058* ⊕*www.vicsquare. com* ⇆*41 rooms* ♿*In-room: no a/c, Wi-Fi. In-hotel: restaurant, bar, Wi-Fi, parking (paid), no-smoking rooms* ⊟*AE, MC, V* ❘◯❘*BP.*

NIGHTLIFE AND THE ARTS

The **Arnolfini,** in a prime waterfront position, is one of the country's most prestigious contemporary-art venues, known for uncovering innovative yet accessible art. There's a cinema and a lively bar and bistro. ⊠*16 Narrow Quay* ☎*0117/917–2300* ⊕*www.arnolfini.org.uk* ⊠*Free* ⊙ *Gallery Tues.–Sun. and national holiday Mon. 10–6.*

St. George's (⊠*Great George St. off Park St.* ☎*0845/402–4001*), a church built in the 18th century, now serves as one of the country's leading acoustic venues for classical, jazz, and world music. Stop by for lunchtime concerts. The **Watershed Media Centre** (⊠*1 Canon's Rd.* ☎*0117/927–5100*) by the harbor has a movie theater that shows excellent international films.

STANTON DREW CIRCLES

6 mi south of Bristol, 10 mi west of Bath.

GETTING HERE AND AROUND

To get here from Bristol, head south on the A37 and turn right after about 5 mi onto the B3130, marked Stanton Drew. The circles are just east of the village.

EXPLORING

Three rings, two avenues of standing stones, and a burial chamber make up the **Stanton Drew Circles,** one of the grandest and most mysterious monuments in Britain, dating from 3000 to 2000 BC. It's far less well known than Stonehenge and other circles, however. The great size of the circles suggests that the site was once as important as Stonehenge for its ceremonial functions, although little of great visual impact remains. ▇TIP➡ **You have to walk through a farmyard to reach the field where the site lies, so wear sturdy shoes.** English Heritage supervises the stones, which stand on private land. Access is given at any reasonable time, and a small admission fee may be requested. ✉*B3130, Stanton Drew* ☎*0117/975–0700* ⊕*www.english-heritage.org.uk.*

WELLS

16 mi south of Stanton Drew Circles, 22 mi south of Bristol, 132 mi west of London.

England's smallest cathedral city, with a population of 10,000, lies at the foot of the Mendip Hills. Although set in what feels like a quiet country town, the great cathedral is a masterpiece of Gothic architecture—the first to be built in the Early English style. The city's name refers to the underground streams that bubble up into St. Andrew's Well within the grounds of the Bishop's Palace. Spring water has run through High Street since the 15th century. Seventeenth-century buildings surround the ancient marketplace, which hosts market days on Wednesday and Saturday.

ESSENTIALS
Visitor Information Wells (✉*Town Hall, Market Pl.* ☎*01749/672552* ⊕*www. visitsomerset.co.uk*).

EXPLORING
★ The great west towers of the medieval **Cathedral Church of St. Andrew,** the oldest surviving English Gothic church, can be seen for miles. Dating from the 12th century, the cathedral derives its beauty from the perfect harmony of all of its parts, the glowing colors of its original stained-glass windows, and its peaceful setting among stately trees and majestic lawns. To appreciate the elaborate west front facade, approach the building from the cathedral green, accessible from Market Place through a great medieval gate called "penniless porch" (named after the beggars who once waited here to collect alms from worshippers). The cathedral's west front is twice as wide as it is high, and some 300 statues of kings and saints adorn it. Inside, vast inverted arches—known as scissor arches—were added in 1338 to stop the central tower from sinking to one side. The cathedral also has a rare and beautiful medieval clock, the second-oldest working clock in the world, consisting of the seated figure of a man called Jack Blandifer, who strikes a bell on the quarter hour while mounted knights circle in a joust. Near the clock is the entrance to the Chapter House—a small wooden door opening onto a great sweep of stairs worn down on one side by the tread of pilgrims over the centuries. Free 45-minute guided tours begin at the information desk. A cloister restaurant serves tea cakes. ✉*Cathedral Green* ☎*01749/674483* ⊕*www.wellscathedral.org.uk* ✦*£5.50 suggested donation* ☯*Apr.–Sept., daily 7–7; Oct.–Mar., daily 7–6. Tours Apr.–Sept. at 10, 11, 1, 2, and 3; Oct.–Mar. at 11 and 2.*

QUICK
BITES
Goodfellows Patisserie (✉ *5 Sadler St.* ☎ *01749/673866*), a little French café near the cathedral, serves exquisite cakes and pastries, chocolate concoctions, and excellent coffee. Soups and sandwiches are also available, and there's a patio. A delicatessen and a good seafood restaurant share the premises. It's closed Sunday.

The Bishop's Eye gate leading from Market Place takes you to the magnificent, moat-ringed **Bishop's Palace,** which retains most parts of the original 12th- and 13th-century residence. You can also see the ruins of a late-13th-century great hall. The hall lost its roof in the 16th century because Edward VI needed the lead it contained. ✉ *Market Pl.* ☎ *01749/677698* ⊕ *www.bishopspalacewells.co.uk* ✇ *£5* ☉ *Apr.– Oct., Sun.–Fri., 10:30–6, Sat. 10:30–2; Nov.–late Dec., Wed.–Sun. 10:30–4:30; last admission 1 hr before closing.*

To the north of the cathedral, the cobbled **Vicar's Close,** one of Europe's oldest streets, has terraces of handsome 14th-century houses with strange, tall chimneys. A tiny medieval chapel here is still in use.

OFF THE
BEATEN ⚲
PATH
Wookey Hole Caves. Signs in Wells's town center direct you 2 mi north to limestone caves in the Mendip Hills that may have been the home of Iron Age people. Here, according to ancient legend, the Witch of Wookey turned to stone. You can tour the caves, dip your fingers in an underground river (artful lighting keeps things lively), and visit a museum, a working paper mill (that once supplied banknotes for the Confederate States of America), and a penny arcade full of Victorian amusement machines. There's plenty for kids. *Wookey Hole* ☎ *01749/672243* ⊕ *www.wookey.co.uk* ✇ *£15* ☉ *Apr.–Oct., daily 10–6; Nov.–Mar., daily 10–5; last tour 1 hr before closing.*

WHERE TO EAT AND STAY

££££   ✕ **The Old Spot.** For relaxed but top-notch dining in the heart of Wells,
MODERN BRITISH   this sociable bistro with wood paneling and creamy white walls hits all the right notes. The Modern British and Mediterranean menu (£27.50 for three courses in the evening) varies seasonally, but might include haricot bean soup with Parma ham and truffle oil for starters, and a main course of braised shoulder of lamb, goat's cheese polenta, and pepperonata. Arrive early for a table at the back, where there are views overlooking the west front of the cathedral. ✉ *12 Sadler St.* ☎ *01749/689099* ▤ *MC, V* ☉ *Closed Mon. No lunch Tues. No dinner Sun.*

££   ⚏ **Ancient Gate House.** This venerable hostelry makes a convenient base for exploring the area. The premises, dating to 1473, incorporate the Great West Gate and are full of character. There's an ancient stone staircase, and some rooms have four-posters. Rugantino's serves Italian and English dishes, made largely from local produce. Breakfast may be across the street at the White Hart. **Pros:** richly atmospheric; cathedral views. **Cons:** unsuitable for anyone with mobility problems; small rooms; not enough parking. ✉ *20 Sadler St.* ☎ *01749/672029* ⊕ *www.ancientgatehouse.co.uk* ⇘ *9 rooms* ⚬ *In-room: no a/c, Wi-Fi (some). In-hotel: restaurant, bar, Wi-Fi, some pets allowed* ▤ *AE, MC, V* ⊺◉*BP.*

££–£££   **Swan Hotel.** A former coaching inn built in the 15th century, the Swan faces the cathedral. Bedrooms, furnished with antiques, are done in subtle, restful colors; some have four-poster beds (including No. 40, which has a to-die-for view of the cathedral), and 15 are in an adjacent converted stable block, the Coach House. Check out the rooms first, as some are better than others. Costumes owned by the great Victorian actor Sir Henry Irving are displayed in the restaurant, which prepares traditional English roasts and fish dishes. **Pros:** quirky charm; friendly service; great views from some rooms. **Cons:** Coach House rooms can be cramped; some noise problems; needs refurbishing. ✉*11 Sadler St.* ☎*01749/836300* ⊕*www.swanhotelwells.co.uk* ➳*49 rooms* ⌂*In-room: no a/c, Wi-Fi. In-hotel: restaurant, bar, Wi-Fi* ☰*AE, DC, MC, V* ⊚*BP.*

> **WORD OF MOUTH**
>
> "I've never been to any place like Glastonbury. It's surreal. There's a guy playing the bagpipes with a mohawk, no shirt and a kilt over jeans. The woman who waits on me in St. Michael's Hospice, where I buy a pink fairy for my Christmas tree, wears a pentagram around her neck…There's a group of flautists, playing the most haunting music, who could have stepped off the cover of a Celtic Dreams CD, except that every conceivable body part is either tattooed or pierced. Wonderful." —rickmav

GLASTONBURY

★ *5 mi southwest of Wells, 27 mi south of Bristol, 27 mi southwest of Bath.*

A town steeped in history, myth, and legend, Glastonbury lies in the lee of Glastonbury Tor, a grassy hill rising 520 feet above the drained marshes known as the Somerset Levels. The Tor is supposedly the site of crossing ley lines (hypothetical alignments of significant places), and, in legend, Glastonbury is identified with Avalon, the paradise into which King Arthur was reborn after his death. Partly because of these associations but also because of its world-class rock-music festival, the town has acquired renown as a New Age center, mixing crystal-gazers with druids, yogis, and hippies, variously in search of Arthur, Merlin, Jesus— and even Elvis. ■TIP➔**A useful shuttle bus runs every half hour between all of Glastonbury's major sights, including the abbey, Rural Life Museum, and the base of Glastonbury Tor. Tickets (£2.50) are valid all day.**

ESSENTIALS

Visitor Information Glastonbury (✉*The Tribunal, 9 High St.* ☎*01458/832954* ⊕ *www.glastonburytic.co.uk*).

EXPLORING

At the foot of **Glastonbury Tor** is **Chalice Well,** the legendary burial place of the Grail. It's a stiff climb up the Tor, but your reward is the fabulous view across the Vale of Avalon. At the top stands a ruined tower, all that remains of **St. Michael's Church,** which collapsed after a landslide in 1271.

The ruins of the great **Glastonbury Abbey,** in the center of town, are on the site where, according to legend, Joseph of Arimathea built a church in the 1st century. A monastery had certainly been erected here by the 9th century, and the site drew many pilgrims. The ruins are those of the abbey completed in 1524 and destroyed in 1539, during Henry VIII's dissolution of the monasteries. A sign south of the Lady Chapel marks the sites where Arthur and Guinevere were supposedly buried. The visitor center has a scale model of the abbey as well as carvings and decorations salvaged from the ruins. ✉*Magdalene St.* ☎*01458/832267* ⊕*www.glastonburyabbey.com* 🎫*£5* 🕐*Feb., daily 10–5; Mar., daily 9:30–5:30; Apr., May, and Sept., daily 9:30–6; June–Aug., daily 9–6; Oct., daily 9:30–5; Nov., daily 9:30–4:30; Dec. and Jan., daily 10–4:30; last admission 30 mins before closing.*

> ### TALE OF THE GRAIL
>
> According to tradition, Glastonbury was where Joseph of Arimathea brought the Holy Grail, the chalice used by Jesus at the Last Supper. Centuries later, the Grail was said to be the objective of the quests of King Arthur and the Knights of the Round Table. When monks claimed to have found the bones of Arthur and Guinevere at Glastonbury in 1191, the popular association of the town with the mythical Avalon was sealed. Arthur and Guinevere's presumed remains were lost to history after Glastonbury Abbey was plundered for its riches in 1539.

🕐 The **Somerset Rural Life Museum** occupies a Victorian farmhouse and the large, 14th-century abbey tithe barn. More than 90 feet in length, the barn once stored the one-tenth portion of the town's produce that was owed to the church. Exhibits illustrate 19th-century farming practices, and there's a cider-apple orchard nearby. Events designed for children take place most weekends during school holidays. ■**TIP**→ **For a good walk, take the scenic footpath from the museum that leads up to the Tor, a half mile east.** ✉*Chilkwell St.* ☎*01458/831197* ⊕*www.somerset.gov.uk/museums* 🎫*Free* 🕐*Tues.–Sat. and national holiday Mon. 10–5.*

WHERE TO STAY

££ 🏨 **George and Pilgrim Hotel.** Pilgrims en route to Glastonbury Abbey stayed here in the 15th century. Today the stone-front hotel is equipped with modern comforts but retains its flagstone floors, wooden beams, and antique furniture. The rooms come in different shapes and sizes. The better ones are spacious and furnished with antiques; three rooms have four-posters. Those in the newer part of the building lack character but are cheaper. **Pros:** historic surroundings; steps from the abbey; good food. **Cons:** unreliable service; some rooms and bathrooms are small. ✉*1 High St.* ☎*01458/831146* ⊕*www.relaxinnz.co.uk* 🛏*14 rooms* ⚖*In-room: no a/c. In-hotel: restaurant, bar* ▤*AE, MC, V* ⏚*BP.*

£££ 🏨 **Number Three.** This elegant Georgian town house next to the abbey ★ has log fires in winter and a terrace and walled garden for summer relaxation. Huddled around the garden, the spacious bedrooms are individually decorated, most with traditional furniture and drapes behind the beds. Three rooms are in the separate Garden House, and the Blue Room overlooks the abbey ruins and, through the trees,

Glastonbury Tor. Breakfasts might include fresh fruit salad, ham and cheese, yogurt, and croissants. **Pros:** garden views; accommodating hosts; stylish decor. **Cons:** books up in advance. ⌂*3 Magdalene St.* ☎*01458/832129* ⊕*www.numberthree.co.uk* ⤴*5 rooms* ⌕*In-room: no a/c, Wi-Fi (some). In-hotel: Wi-Fi, parking (free), no-smoking rooms* ▭*AE, MC, V* ◑*CP.*

NIGHTLIFE AND THE ARTS

Held annually a few miles away in Pilton, the **Glastonbury Festival** (⊕*www.glastonburyfestivals.co.uk*) is England's biggest and perhaps best rock festival. For five days over the last-weekend in June, it hosts hundreds of bands—established and up-and-coming—on five stages. Tickets are steep—around £175—and sell out months in advance; they include entertainment, a camping area, and service facilities.

DUNSTER

35 mi west of Glastonbury, 43 mi north of Exeter.

Lying between the Somerset coast and the edge of Exmoor National Park, Dunster is a picture-book village with a broad main street. The eight-sided yarn-market building on High Street dates from 1589.

ESSENTIALS

Visitor Information Dunster (⌂ *Dunster Steep* ☎*01643/821835* ⊕*www. exmoor-nationalpark.gov.uk* ⊗*Mar. weekends only, closed Nov.–Feb.*) .

EXPLORING

Dunster Castle, a 13th-century fortress remodeled in 1868, dominates the village from its site on a hill. Parkland and unusual gardens with subtropical plants surround the building, which has fine plaster ceilings, stacks of family portraits (including one by Joshua Reynolds), 17th-century Dutch leather hangings, and a magnificent 17th-century oak staircase. The climb to the castle from the parking lot is steep. ⌂*Off A39* ☎*01643/823004* ⊕*www.nationaltrust.org.uk* ⤴*£7.80; gardens only, £4.30* ⊗*Castle mid-Mar.–Oct., Fri.–Wed. 11–5. Gardens mid-Mar.–Oct., daily 10–5; Nov.–mid-Mar., daily 11–4.*

EXMOOR NATIONAL PARK

20 mi northwest of Taunton.

GETTING HERE AND AROUND

A car is really necessary for getting around the inner reaches of Exmoor, though the coast is relatively well-connected by bus. The 300 bus route traces the coast between Minehead and Lynmouth. The summer-only 400 service—a vintage double-decker bus—also follows the coast between Minehead and Porlock then circles through Exmoor back to Minehead. Both services are usually open-top and are run by Quantock Motor Services.

ESSENTIALS

Bus Information Quantock Motor Services (☎*01823/251140* ⊕*www. quantockmotorservices.co.uk*)

Visitor Information Combe Martin
(⊠ *13 Cross St.* ☎ *01271/883319*
⊕ *www.visitcombemartin.co.uk*).
Dulverton (⊠ *7–9 Fore St.*
☎ *01398/323841*). **Exmoor National**
Park Authority (⊠ *Exmoor House,*
Dulverton ☎ *01398/323665* ⊕ *www.*
exmoor-nationalpark.gov.uk ✉ *Free*).
Lynmouth (⊠ *Lyndale Car Park*
☎ *01598/752509*).

EXPLORING

Less wild and forbidding than
Dartmoor to its south, 267-square-
mi **Exmoor National Park** is no less
majestic for its bare heath and
lofty views. The park extends right
up to the coast and straddles the
county border between Somerset

**SOUTH WEST
COAST PATH**

Britain's longest national trail, the
South West Coast Path, wraps
around the coast of the peninsula
for 630 mi from Minehead (near
Dunster, Somerset) to South Haven
Point, near Poole (Dorset). To complete the trail takes 50 to 60 days.

The **South West Coast Path
Association** (☎ *01752/896237*
⊕ *www.swcp.org.uk*) has information about the trail. Another Web
site, ⊕ *www.southwestcoastpath.*
com, suggests short walks.

and Devon. Some walks offer spectacular views over the Bristol Channel. Although it is interwoven with cultivated farmland and pasturage,
Exmoor can be desolate. Taking one of the more than 700 mi of paths
and bridleways through the bracken and heather (at its best in the fall),
you might glimpse the ponies and red deer for which the region is noted.
■ TIP → Be careful: the proximity of the coast means that mists and squalls
can descend with alarming suddenness.

The national park visitor centers at Combe Martin, County Gate, Dulverton, Dunster, and Lynmouth have information and maps. Guided
walks, many of which have themes (archaeology or deer, for example),
cost £3 to £5. If you're walking on your own, check the weather, take
water and a map, and tell someone where you're going. ⊠ *Exmoor*
National Park Authority, Exmoor House, Dulverton ☎ *01398/323665*
⊕ *www.exmoor-nationalpark.gov.uk* ✉ *Free*.

PORLOCK

6 mi west of Dunster, 45 mi north of Exeter.

Buried at the bottom of a valley, with the slopes of Exmoor all about,
the small, unspoiled town of Porlock lies near "Doone Country," setting for R.D. Blackmore's swashbuckling saga *Lorna Doone.* Porlock
had already achieved a place in literary history by the late 1790s, when
Samuel Taylor Coleridge declared it was a "man from Porlock" who
interrupted his opium trance while the poet was composing "Kubla
Khan."

ESSENTIALS

Visitor Information Porlock (⊠ *The Old School, High St.* ☎ *01643/863150*
⊕ *www.porlock.co.uk*).

EXPLORING

The 36-mi **Coleridge Way** (⊕*www.coleridgeway.co.uk*) trail passes through the Quantock and Brendon hills and part of Exmoor, from Nether Stowey (site of Coleridge's home) to Porlock.

The small harbor in the town of **Porlock Weir** is the starting point for an undemanding 2-mi walk along the coast through chestnut and walnut trees to **St. Culbone,** reputedly the smallest and most isolated church in England. Saxon in origin, it has a small Victorian spire and is lighted by candles. It would be hard to find a more enchanting spot.

WHERE TO EAT

£££

MODERN BRITISH

✕**Andrew's on the Weir.** Calling itself a restaurant with rooms, this waterfront Georgian hotel is pure relaxed English country house with touches of glamour. The ambitious contemporary restaurant takes advantage of local specialties like Exmoor lamb and Somerset pork. You can expect unusual desserts, such as rice pudding with rhubarb compote and cardamom syrup, and excellent local cheeses. The five guest rooms (£££) have print drapes and patchwork quilts. ⊠*Porlock Weir* ☎*01643/863300* ▤*MC, V* ⊗*Closed Mon. and Tues.*

EN
ROUTE

As you're heading west from Porlock to Lynton, the coast road A39 mounts **Porlock Hill,** an incline so steep that signs encourage drivers to "keep going." The views across Exmoor and north to the Bristol Channel and Wales are worth it. A less steep but quieter and equally scenic route up the hill on a toll road is accessed from Porlock Weir.

LYNTON AND LYNMOUTH

13 mi west of Porlock, 60 mi northwest of Exeter.

A steep hill separates this pretty pair of Devonshire villages, which are linked by a cliff railway. Lynmouth, a fishing village at the bottom of the hill, crouches below 1,000-foot-high cliffs at the mouths of the East and West Lyn rivers. Lynton is higher up. The poet Percy Bysshe Shelley visited Lynmouth in 1812, in the company of his 16-year-old bride, Harriet Westbrook. During their nine-week sojourn, the poet found time to write his polemical *Queen Mab.* The grand landscape of Exmoor lies all about, with walks to local beauty spots: Watersmeet, the Valley of the Rocks, or Hollerday Hill, where rare feral goats graze.

ESSENTIALS

Visitor Information Lynton (⊠*Lee Rd.* ☎*0845/660–3232* ⊕*www.lynton-lynmouth-tourism.co.uk).*

EXPLORING

Water and a cable system power the 862-foot **cliff railway** that connects Lynton with Lynmouth by a ride up a rocky cliff; riders get fine views over the harbor. Inaugurated in 1890, it was the gift of publisher George Newnes, who also donated Lynton's imposing Town Hall, near the top station on Lee Road. ⊠*Lee Rd., Lynton* ☎*01598/753908* ⊕*www.cliffrailwaylynton.co.uk* ▣*£2.85 round-trip* ⊗*Mid-Feb.–Mar. and early Oct.–early Nov., daily 10–5; Apr.–mid-June and mid-Sept.–early Oct., daily 10–6; mid-June–late July and early Sept., daily 10–7; late July and Aug., daily 10–9.*

Exmoor Coast Boat Cruises runs boat trips around the dramatic Devon coast from Lynmouth Harbour. A one-hour excursion goes as far as Woody Bay, allowing you to experience the clamorous birdlife on the cliffs. Other cruises include mackerel-fishing trips (£10), between May and August. ☎01598/753207 ☎£10 ⊗Apr.–Sept.

OFF THE BEATEN PATH

Braunton Burrows Biosphere Reserve. Bird-watching and miles of trails through the dunes are the draws at this sanctuary on the north side of the Taw estuary, the core of a UNESCO-designated biosphere reserve. Empty stretches of sand dunes have vistas of marram grass and the sea, and bird-watching is first-class, especially in winter. The flora is most colorful between May and August. Talks are held in the **Countryside Centre** (⊠Caen parking lot, Braunton ☎01271/817171 ⊗Apr.–Oct., Mon.–Sat. 10–4). The reserve is 18 mi southwest of Lynton. ⊠Off B3231, 2 mi west of Braunton ☎Free ⊗Daily 24 hrs.

WHERE TO EAT AND STAY

££
MODERN BRITISH

×**Rising Sun.** A 14th-century inn and a row of thatched cottages make up this restaurant and hotel with great views over the Bristol Channel. The kitchen specializes in local cuisine with Mediterranean influences such as rump of lamb with smoked-paprika-and-tomato sauce with couscous and John Dory fillet with crab-and-tomato risotto (and there's a superb game menu December through February). Corridors and creaking staircases lead to cozy guest rooms (£££) decorated in stylish print or solid fabrics. ⊠Harbourside, Lynmouth ☎01598/753223 ⊟MC, V.

££–£££
★

⊞**Shelley's Hotel.** Centrally located, this well-maintained hotel has bright and spacious rooms with generous windows and great views. Hearty breakfasts are served in the conservatory, and the service is genial and efficient. Poet Percy Bysshe Shelley is said to have stayed here during his honeymoon—and apparently left without paying the bill (he later mailed £20 of the £30 owed). **Pros:** excellent harbor views; good breakfasts; hospitable owners. **Cons:** no restaurant; Shelley link a little overplayed. ⊠8 Watermeet Rd., Lynmouth ☎01598/753219 ⊕www.shelleyshotel.co.uk ☜11 rooms ⬧In-room: no a/c, Wi-Fi (some). In-hotel: bar, Wi-Fi, no-smoking rooms ⊟AE, MC, V ⊺⊙∣BP.

CLOVELLY

Fodor'sChoice
★

40 mi southwest of Lynton, 60 mi northwest of Exeter.

Lovely Clovelly always seems to have the sun shining on its flower-lined cottages and stepped and cobbled streets. Alas, its beauty is well known, and day-trippers can overrun the village in summer. Perched precariously among cliffs, a steep, cobbled road—tumbling down at such an angle that it's closed to cars—leads to the toylike harbor with its 14th-century quay. The climb back is steep, but, happily, from Easter through October a reasonably priced shuttle service takes you to and from the parking lot at the top. Allow about two hours (more if you stop for a drink or a meal) to take in the village. A fine 10-mi walk is a cliff-top hike along the coast from Hartland Quay, near Clovelly, down to Lower Sharpnose Point, just above Bude.

EXPLORING

You pay £5.75 to park and use the **Clovelly Visitor Centre** (⊠ *Off A39* ☎ *01237/431781* ⊕ *www.clovelly. co.uk*) ; this is the only way to enter the village. The fee includes admission to a fisherman's cottage in the style of the 1930s and an exhibition about Victorian writer Charles Kingsley, who lived here as a child. All the buildings in the village are owned by the Clovelly Estate Company. ■TIP➔ **To avoid the worst crowds, visit before or after school summer vacation. If you must visit in summer, arrive early or late in the day.**

> **DONKEYS AT WORK**
>
> Donkey stables, donkey rides for kids, and abundant donkey souvenirs in Clovelly recall the days when these animals played an essential role in town life, carrying food, packages, and more up and down the village streets. Even in the 1990s, donkeys helped carry bags from the hotels. Today sledges do the work, but the animals' labor is remembered.

WHERE TO STAY

£££ 🏨 **Red Lion Hotel.** One of only two hotels in this coastal village, the 18th-century Red Lion sits right on the harbor. Guest rooms are decorated with a nautical theme; all have sea or harbor views and modern bathrooms. The climb up through Clovelly is perilously steep, but guests can bring cars via a back road to and from the hotel. The restaurant specializes in seafood dishes and homemade ice creams and sorbets. **Pros:** superb location; rooms are clean and comfortable; good service. **Cons:** gets crowded at peak times; any excursion requires steep ascent. ⊠ *The Quay* ☎ *01237/431237* ⊕ *www.clovelly.co.uk* ☞ *11 rooms* ☖ *In-room: no a/c, Wi-Fi (some). In-hotel: restaurant, bars, Wi-Fi* ▤ *AE, MC, V* ⏐◐⏐*BP*.

CORNWALL

Cornwall stretches west into the sea, with plenty of magnificent coastline to explore. One way to discover it all is to travel southwest from Boscastle and the cliff-top ruins of Tintagel Castle, the legendary birthplace of Arthur, along the north Cornish coast to Land's End. This predominantly cliff-lined coast, interspersed with broad expanses of sand, has many tempting places to stop, including Padstow (for a seafood feast), Newquay (a surfing and tourist center), or St. Ives, a delightful artists' colony.

From Land's End, the westernmost tip of Britain, known for its savage land- and seascapes and panoramic views, turn northeast, stopping in the popular seaside resort of Penzance, the harbor city of Falmouth, and a string of fishing villages, including Charlestown and Fowey. The Channel coast is less rugged than the northern coast, with more sheltered beaches. Leave time to visit the Eden Project, with its large, surrealistic-looking conservatories in an abandoned clay pit, and to explore the boggy, heath-covered expanse of Bodmin Moor.

BOSCASTLE

15 mi north of Bodmin, 30 mi south of Clovelly.

In tranquil Boscastle, some of the stone-and-slate cottages at the foot of the steep valley date from the 1300s. A good place to relax, the town is centered on a little harbor and set snug within towering cliffs. Nearby, 2 mi up the valley of the Valency, is St. Juliot's, the "Endelstow" referred to in Thomas Hardy's *A Pair of Blue Eyes*—the young author was involved with the restoration of this church while he was working as an architect.

ESSENTIALS

Visitor Information Boscastle (✉ *The Harbour* ☎ *01840/250010* ⊕ *www. visitboscastleandtintagel.com*).

WHERE TO STAY

££ **The Old Rectory.** Thomas Hardy stayed here, in what is now a delight-
Fodor'sChoice ful B&B, while restoring St. Juliot's church, and this is where he first
★ met his wife-to-be, Emma, the rector's sister-in-law. The stone house, set in 3 acres of lush grounds about 1½ mi from Boscastle, has been in the same family for five generations. The sensitive renovations are mainly in Victorian style. At the rear of the building, the Old Stable has a wood-burning stove and a separate entrance. Delicious breakfasts

usually include organic produce from the kitchen garden, and do-it-yourself barbecues can be ordered. **Pros:** secluded setting; romantic ambience; helpful hosts. **Cons:** a little hard to find; far from Boscastle. ✉ *Off B3263, St. Juliot, Boscastle* ☎ *01840/250225* ⊕ *www.stjuliot. com* 📠 *4 rooms* 🖧 *In-room: no a/c, no phone, Wi-Fi. In-hotel: Wi-Fi, some pets allowed, no kids under 12, no-smoking rooms* ☐ *MC, V* 🕑 *Closed Dec.–mid-Feb. except for 3-day packages* ⍾ *BP.*

TINTAGEL

3 mi southwest of Boscastle.

The romance of Arthurian legend thrives around Tintagel's ruined castle on the coast. Ever since the somewhat unreliable 12th-century chronicler Geoffrey of Monmouth identified Tintagel as the home of Arthur, son of Uther Pendragon and Ygrayne, devotees of the legend cycle have revered the site. In the 19th century Alfred, Lord Tennyson described Tintagel's Arthurian connection in *The Idylls of the King.* Today the village has its share of tourist junk—including Excaliburgers. Never mind: the headland around Tintagel is splendidly scenic.

ESSENTIALS

Visitor Information Tintagel (✉ *Bossiney Rd.* ☎ *01840/779084* ⊕ *www.visit-boscastleandtintagel.com*).

EXPLORING

The **Old Post Office,** a 14th-century stone manor house with yard-thick walls, smoke-blackened beams, and an undulating slate-tile roof, has been restored to its Victorian appearance, when one room served as a post office. ✉ *3–4 Tintagel Centre* ☎ *01840/770024* ⊕ *www. nationaltrust.org.uk* 💷 *£3* 🕑 *Mid-Mar.–Sept., daily 11–5:30; Oct. and late Feb., daily 11–4.*

Fodors Choice ★ Although all that remains of the ruined cliff-top **Tintagel Castle,** legendary birthplace of King Arthur, is the outline of its walls, moats, and towers, it requires only a bit of imagination to conjure up a picture of Sir Lancelot and Sir Galahad riding out in search of the Holy Grail over the narrow causeway above the seething breakers. Archaeological evidence, however, suggests that the castle dates from much later—about 1150, when it was the stronghold of the earls of Cornwall. Long before that, Romans may have occupied the site. The earliest identified remains here are of Celtic (AD 5th-century) origin, and these may have some connection with the legendary Arthur. Legends aside, nothing can detract from the castle ruins, dramatically set off by the wild, windswept Cornish coast, on an island joined to the mainland by a narrow isthmus. Paths lead down to the pebble beach and a cavern known as **Merlin's Cave.** Exploring Tintagel Castle involves some arduous climbing on steep steps, but even on a summer's day, when people swarm over the battlements and a westerly Atlantic wind sweeps through Tintagel, you can feel the proximity of the distant past. ✉ *Castle Rd., ½ mi west of village* ☎ *01840/770328* ⊕ *www.english-heritage.org.uk* 💷 *£4.90* 🕑 *Apr.–Sept., daily 10–6; Oct., daily 10–5; Nov.–Mar., daily 10–4.*

All About Arthur

Legends about King Arthur have resonated through the centuries, enthusiastically taken up by writers and poets from 7th-century Welsh and Breton troubadours to Tennyson and Mark Twain in the 19th century and T.H. White in the 20th century. The historical Arthur was probably a Christian Celtic chieftain battling against the heathen Saxons in the 6th century, although most of the tales surrounding him have a much later setting, thanks to the vivid but somewhat fanciful chronicles of his exploits by medieval scholars.

The virtuous warrior-hero of popular myth has always been treated with generous helpings of nostalgia for a golden age. For Sir Thomas Malory (circa 1408–71), author of *Le Morte d'Arthur,* the finest medieval prose collection of Arthurian romance, Arthur represented a lost era of chivalry and noble romance before the loosening of the traditional bonds of feudal society and the gradual collapse of the medieval social order.

Places associated with Arthur and his consort, Guinevere, the wizard Merlin, the knights of the Round Table, and the related legends of Tristan and Isolde (or Iseult) can be found all over Europe, but the West Country claims the closest association. Arthur was said to have had his court of Camelot at Cadbury Castle (17 mi south of Wells) and to have been buried at Glastonbury.

Cornwall holds the greatest concentration of Arthurian links, notably his supposed birthplace, Tintagel, and the site of his last battle, on Bodmin Moor. However tenuous the links—and, barring the odd, somewhat ambiguous inscription, there is nothing in the way of hard evidence of Arthur's existence—the Cornish have taken the Once and Future King to their hearts, and his spirit is said to reside in the now-rare bird, the Cornish chough.

PORT ISAAC

6 mi southwest of Tintagel.

A mixture of granite, slate, and whitewashed cottages tumbles precipitously down the cliff to the tiny harbor at Port Isaac, still dedicated to the crab and lobster trade. Low tide reveals a pebbly beach and rock pools. Relatively unscathed by tourists, it makes for a peaceful and secluded stay. For an extra slice of authentic Cornwall life, you can hear the local choir sing shanties at the harborside on Friday nights in summer.

WHERE TO STAY

££–£££ 🏨 **Slipway Hotel.** This 16th-century inn on the harborfront has low ceilings, exposed timbers, and steep staircases that lead to rooms with simple but stylish modern furnishings. Check in at the bar. The split-level restaurant, with oak beams and pillars, serves supremely fresh fish, lobster, and crab dishes. **Pros:** casual atmosphere; great location; tasty restaurant. **Cons:** few facilities; pub can get noisy; remote parking. ✉ *Harbourfront* ☎ *01208/880264* ⊕ *www.portisaachotel.com* 🛏 *8 rooms, 2 suites* ⚅ *In-room: no a/c. In-hotel: restaurant, bar, some pets allowed, no-smoking rooms* ▭ *MC, V* ⍟ *BP.*

FOUR DAYS IN CORNWALL

Here's a trip if you want to see some highlights of Cornwall. Traveling down along the North Devon coast, stop at the harbor village of **Boscastle** before steeping yourself in Arthurian legends at **Tintagel**, ideally taking a coastal walk here. Overnight in 🔲 **Padstow** and dine on excellent seafood (reserve ahead). The next day, head for **St. Ives**, popular with art lovers and beach fans, and push on to the dramatic scenery of the country's westernmost tip, **Land's End**. Stay in 🔲 **Penzance** for your second night; from here you can visit the island castle of **St. Michael's Mount**. Then either follow the coast around to tour the scenic **Lizard Peninsula**, or head straight for Pendennis Castle in **Falmouth**. Across the Carrick Roads estuary basin, explore the Roseland Peninsula, spending your third night in 🔲 **St. Mawes**, which has a fine castle. Start early the next day to visit the **Eden Project**, a must for anyone with even a passing interest in greenery, and then choose between two superb country piles: Victorian Lanhydrock, near **Bodmin**, and **Cotehele House**, a Tudor manor house.

5

PADSTOW

10 mi southwest of Port Isaac.

A small fishing port at the mouth of the Camel River, Padstow attracts attention and visitors as a center of culinary excellence, largely because of the presence here since 1975 of pioneering seafood chef Rick Stein. He has made Padstow a stop on any foodie's itinerary. Stein's empire includes two restaurants, a café, a fish-and-chips joint, a delicatessen, a patisserie, and a cooking school where classes fill up months in advance.

Even if seafood is not your favorite fare, Padstow is worth visiting. The cries of seagulls fill its lively harbor, a string of fine beaches lies within a short ride—including some choice strands highly prized by surfers—and two scenic walking routes await: the Saints Way across the peninsula to Fowey, and the Camel Trail, a footpath and cycling path that follows the river as far as Bodmin Moor. If you can avoid peak visiting times—summer weekends—so much the better.

ESSENTIALS

Visitor Information Padstow (✉ *North Quay* ☎ *01841/533449* ⊕ *www. padstowlive.com*).

WHERE TO EAT AND STAY

££££ ✕ **The Seafood Restaurant.** Rick Stein's flagship restaurant, just across
SEAFOOD from where the lobster boats and trawlers unload their catches, has
Fodor'sChoice built its reputation on the freshest fish and the highest culinary art-
★ istry. The wide-ranging menu may include ragout of turbot and scallop and Indonesian seafood curry. Don't want to move after your meal? Book one of the sunny, individually designed guest rooms (£££–££££) overlooking the harbor. ✉ *Riverside* ☎ *01841/532700* ⚔ *Reservations essential* ▤ *MC, V* ⎮◎*⎮BP*.

£££ ✕ **St. Petroc's.** Part of chef Rick Stein's empire, this bistro with contem-
FRENCH porary art adorning its walls serves French-inspired fare like rib-eye

steak with béarnaise sauce and *pommes frites (french fries)*. The food is simpler and cheaper than at his other restaurants. In fine weather you can dine in the sunny walled garden. The well-equipped bedrooms (£££–££££) are individually decorated with stylish modern pieces. ⊠*4 New St.* ☎*01841/532700* ▭*MC, V.*

££££££   ⊡ **St. Edmund's House.** The most luxurious Rick Stein venture has a sophisticated minimalist style. Excellently equipped, the bedrooms have polished oak floors, in-room DVD players, and glass doors facing the harbor and estuary. Booking here guarantees a dinner table at the Seafood Restaurant, but you should reserve as far ahead as possible. There's a two-night minimum stay on weekends. **Pros:** stylish bedrooms; select ambience. **Cons:** inflated prices; variable service. ⊠*St. Edmond's La.* ☎*01841/532700* ⊕*www.rickstein.com* ⌨*6 rooms* ⌂*In-room: refrigerator, DVD, Wi-Fi. In-hotel: Internet terminal, Wi-Fi* ▭*MC, V* ⦿*BP.*

SPORTS AND THE OUTDOORS

BIKING   Bikes of all shapes and sizes can be rented at **Trail Bike Hire** (⊠*South Quay* ☎*01841/532594* ⊕*www.trailbikehire.co.uk*), at the start of the Camel Trail.

SURFING   **Harlyn Surf School** (⊠*23 Grenville Rd.* ☎*01841/533076*) can arrange two-hour to four-day surfing courses.

WALKING   The **Saints Way,** a 30-mi inland path between Padstow and the Camel Estuary on Cornwall's north coast to Fowey on the south coast, follows a Bronze Age trading route, later used by Celtic pilgrims to cross the peninsula. Several relics of such times can be seen along the way. Contact the tourist offices in Padstow or Fowey or VisitCornwall for information.

NEWQUAY

14 mi southwest of Padstow, 30 mi southwest of Tintagel.

The biggest, most developed resort on the north Cornwall coast is a fairly large town established in 1439. It was once the center of the trade in pilchards (a small herringlike fish), and on the headland you can still see a white hut where a lookout known as a "huer" watched for pilchard schools and directed the boats to the fishing grounds. Newquay has become Britain's surfing capital, and in summer young California-dreamin' devotees can pack the wide, cliff-backed beaches.

ESSENTIALS

Visitor Information Newquay (⊠*Marcus Hill* ☎*01637/854020* ⊕*www. newquay.co.uk*).

WHERE TO EAT

££££££   ✕**Fifteen Cornwall.** One of Britain's culinary heroes, cockney chef Jamie
BRITISH   Oliver has led campaigns to encourage healthful eating in schools and to provide training in the catering arts to young people. This restaurant, part of this latter project, has won plaudits for execution, not just for its worthy intentions. To provide staff with the widest possible repertoire, the daily-changing sampling menu (£55) lists six courses that might include *taglerini* (pasta) with a sauce of local crab, parsley, and

BEACH BASICS

The beaches lining parts of the peninsula have made the West Country one of England's main family vacation destinations. Even natives have to steel themselves for the water's chilly temperature, though, and foreigners, especially those pampered by the warm waves of the Mediterranean, are understandably reluctant to brave the elements. Fortunately, wet suits are available at most resorts, making the experience more pleasurable.

At most resorts, red-and-yellow flags show the limits of safe swimming. If you see a blue flag, you can be confident that the beach and sea are unpolluted. The Blue Flag plan, which rewards cleanliness, water quality, easy access, and facilities, is run by the Foundation for Environmental Education and is used across Europe, the Caribbean, South Africa, and parts of North America. This region of England has the biggest concentration of winners—20 beaches in 2009. There can be strong undertows, and beware of fast-moving tides.

The northern coast of the peninsula has the region's best surfing beaches, and Cornwall, especially Newquay, is the center of a thriving surfing industry. Go ahead and give it a try: it's easy to rent equipment, and plenty of places offer lessons.

lemon for a starter, followed by fillet of line-caught brill with crushed Anya potatoes and purple sprouting broccoli, and pears cooked in wine with pistachio ice cream to finish. The fixed-price lunch menu costs £25.45. The dining area is modern and bright, with views over magnificent Watergate Bay—a broad beach much beloved of water-sports enthusiasts. Watergate Bay lies 3 mi east of Newquay. ⊠ *Watergate Bay* ☎ *01637/861000* ⊟ *AE, MC, V.*

ST. IVES

25 mi southwest of Newquay, 10 mi north of Penzance.

James McNeill Whistler came here to paint his landscapes, Daphne du Maurier and Virginia Woolf to write their novels. Today sand, sun, and superb art continue to attract thousands of vacationers to the fishing village of St. Ives, named after Saint Ia, a 5th-century female Irish missionary said to have arrived on a floating leaf. The town has long played host to a well-established artists' colony, and there are plenty of craftspeople, too. ■ TIP➔ **Day-trippers often crowd St. Ives, so it's best to park away from the center.**

GETTING HERE AND AROUND

St. Ives has good bus and train connections with Bristol, Exeter, and Penzance. Train journeys usually involve a change at St. Erth (the brief St. Erth–St. Ives stretch is one of the West Country's most scenic train routes). The adjacent bus and train stations are within a few minutes' walk of the center. Drivers should avoid the center—parking lots are well marked in the higher parts of town.

ESSENTIALS

Visitor Information St. Ives

(✉ *The Guildhall, Street-an-Pol* ☎ *01736/796297* ⊕ *www.visit-westcornwall.com*).

EXPLORING

The studio and garden of Dame Barbara Hepworth (1903–75), who pioneered abstract sculpture in England, are now the **Barbara Hepworth Museum and Sculpture Garden.** London's prominent Tate gallery runs the museum. The artist lived here for 26 years. ✉ *Trewyn Studio, Barnoon Hill* ☎ *01736/796226* ⊕ *www.tate.org.uk* ⊠ *£4.65, combined ticket with Tate St. Ives £8.55* ⊙ *Mar.–Oct., daily 10–5:20; Nov.–Feb., Tues.–Sun. 10–4:20.*

SURFERS WELCOME

The four-story Tate St. Ives, at the base of a cliff fronted by Porthmeor Beach, may be the only art museum with special storage space for visitors' surfboards.

★ The spectacular **Tate St. Ives** displays the work of artists who lived and worked in St. Ives, mostly from 1925 to 1975, and has selections from the rich collection of the Tate in London. It occupies a modernist building—a fantasia of seaside deco-period architecture with a panoramic view of rippling turquoise ocean. The rooftop café is excellent, for the food and views. ✉ *Porthmeor Beach* ☎ *01736/796226* ⊕ *www.tate.org.uk* ⊠ *£5.65, combined ticket with Barbara Hepworth Museum and Sculpture Garden £8.55* ⊙ *Mar.–Oct., daily 10–5:20; Nov.–Feb., Tues.–Sun. 10–4:20.*

QUICK BITES

One of Cornwall's oldest pubs (built in 1312), the harbor-front **Sloop Inn** (✉ *The Wharf* ☎ *01736/796584*) serves simple lunches as well as evening meals in wood-beam rooms that display the work of local artists. If the weather's good, you can eat at the tables outside.

At the **St. Ives Society of Artists Gallery,** local artists display selections of their current work for sale in the former Old Mariners' Church. The Mariners Gallery in the crypt is also used for private exhibitions. ✉ *Norway Sq.* ☎ *01736/795582* ⊕ *www.stisa.co.uk* ⊙ *Mar.–Easter and mid-Oct.–early Jan., Mon.–Sat. and national holidays 10:30–5:30; Easter–mid-Oct., Mon.–Sat. 10:30–5:30, Sun. 2:30–5:30.*

WHERE TO EAT AND STAY

£££   ✕**Garrack Restaurant.** This ivy-clad restaurant is known for the panoramic sea views from its hilltop location. The family-run establishment
MODERN BRITISH   offers relaxed and undemanding fine dining. The menu specializes in local fish and seafood, including rock-salt-and-coriander-crusted wild sea bass, as well as Cornish beef. Breads are made in-house, and the wine list features some Cornish vineyards. Some of the rooms (£££–££££) at the attached hotel are furnished in traditional style; others are more modern. ✉ *Burthallan La.* ☎ *01736/796199* ⊟ *AE, DC, MC, V* ⊙ *No lunch Mon.–Sat.*

£££   ✕**Porthminster Café.** Unbeatable for its location alone—on the broad,
MODERN BRITISH   golden sands of Porthminster Beach—this sleek, modern eatery prepares imaginative lunches, teas, and evening meals you can savor while you take in the marvelous vista across the bay. Typical choices are Cornish oysters, white crab risotto, and plaice fillets. The sister Porthgwidden

Beach Café, in the Downalong area of town, has a smaller and cheaper but equally varied menu. ✉ *Porthminster Beach* ☎ *01736/795352* ⚓ *Reservations essential* ☰ *MC, V* ⊘ *Closed Mon. Nov.–Easter. No dinner Sun.–Thurs. Nov.–Easter.*

££ ⚑ **Cornerways.** Everything in St. Ives seems squeezed into the tiniest of spaces, and this cottage B&B in the quiet Downalong quarter is no

exception. The light, tastefully converted rooms are pleasingly simple in design and enlivened by modern art; the more expensive have sea views. Most rooms are named after characters in Daphne du Maurier's novels (she once stayed in one of them). Fresh local fish is offered at breakfast, and guests can use complimentary tickets to visit the Tate, which is just minutes away. **Pros:** friendly owner; stylish rooms and bathrooms. **Cons:** rooms are small; narrow stairways to climb; limited parking. ✉ *1 Bethesda Pl.* ☎ *01736/796706* ⊕ *www.cornerwaysstives. com* ➥ *6 rooms* ⚒ *In-room: no a/c, no phone, Wi-Fi. In-hotel: Wi-Fi, parking (paid), no-smoking rooms* ☰ *No credit cards* �ⓞ *BP.*

£££ ⚑ **Primrose Valley Hotel.** Blending the elegance of an Edwardian villa with clean-lined modern style, this family-friendly hotel has the best of both worlds. Guest rooms are bright and contemporary, and the spacious common areas include a large lounge that opens onto the veranda. There's also an easygoing management and a great location a few steps up from Porthminster Beach. Freshly prepared "platters" of cold meats, seafood, and Cornish cheeses are available all day from the bar. There's an extra charge for sea-facing rooms with balconies, and minimums of three- or four-day stays are required in July and August, respectively. **Pros:** close to beach and train and bus stations; relaxed atmosphere; attention to detail. **Cons:** difficult to find; some rooms lack views. ✉ *Porthminster Beach* ☎ *01736/794939* ⊕ *www. primroseonline.co.uk* ➥ *9 rooms, 1 suite* ⚒ *In-room: no a/c, no phone, Wi-Fi. In-hotel: bar, Wi-Fi, parking (free), no kids under 8, no-smoking rooms* ☰ *MC, V* �ⓞ *BP.*

EN ROUTE The winding B3306 coastal road southwest from St. Ives passes through some of Cornwall's starkest yet most beautiful countryside. Barren hills crisscrossed by low stone walls drop abruptly to granite cliffs and wide bays. Evidence of the ancient tin-mining industry is everywhere. Now a fascinating mining heritage center, the early-20th-century **Geevor Tin Mine** employed 400 men, but in 1985 the collapse of the world tin market wiped Cornwall from the mining map. Wear sturdy footwear for the surface and underground tours. A museum, shop, and café are on the site. ✉ *B3306, Pendeen* ☎ *01736/788662* ⊕ *www.geevor.com* ➥ *£8.50* ⊘ *Easter–Oct., Sun.–Fri. 9–5; Nov.–Mar., Sun.–Fri. 10–4; last admission 1 hr before closing.*

LAND'S END

17 mi southwest of St. Ives, 9 mi southwest of Penzance.

The coastal road, B3306, ends at the western tip of Britain at what is, quite literally, Land's End.

EXPLORING

★ The sea crashes against the rocks at **Land's End** and lashes ships battling their way around the point. ■TIP→ **Approach from one of the coastal footpaths for the best panoramic view.** Over the years, sightseers have caused some erosion of the paths, but new ones are constantly being built, and Cornish "hedges" (granite walls covered with turf) have been planted to prevent erosion. The scenic grandeur of Land's End remains undiminished. The Land's End Hotel here is undistinguished, though the restaurant has good views.

☾ A low-key theme park, **Land's End Experience** (☎0871/720–0044 ⊕*www. landsend-landmark.co.uk*), runs a poor second to nature.

MOUSEHOLE

★ *7 mi east of Land's End, 3 mi south of Penzance.*

On B3315 between Land's End and Penzance, Mousehole (pronounced *mow*-zel, the first syllable rhyming with "cow") merits a stop—and plenty of people do stop—to see this archetypal Cornish fishing village of tiny stone cottages. It was the home of Dolly Pentreath, supposedly the last person to speak solely in Cornish, who died in 1777.

WHERE TO EAT

££–£££   ✕ **2 Fore Street.** Within view of Mousehole's tiny harbor, you can dine on
MODERN BRITISH   the freshest seafood in this popular bistro. The seasonal, Mediterranean-inspired menu takes in everything from crab Florentine and lobster to gurnard fillets with chorizo, and baked sea bream with capers and fennel. Meat eaters are also well catered to. The bright, white-walled dining room has a maritime flavor, and there are tables in the sheltered back garden. ⊠ *2 Fore St.* ☎*01736/731164* ✍*Reservations essential* ▭*AE, MC, V* ☉*Closed Jan.*

▮ EN
ROUTE   About 2 mi north of Mousehole, **Newlyn** has long been Cornwall's most important fishing port. The annual Fish Festival takes over the town for a weekend at the end of August. Newlyn became the magnet for artists at the end of the 19th century, and today has a good gallery of contemporary works, but only a few of the fishermen's cottages that first attracted artists to the area remain.

PENZANCE

1½ mi north of Newlyn, 10 mi south of St. Ives.

Superb views over Mount's Bay are one lure of this popular, unpretentious seaside resort. Even though it does get very crowded in summer, it's a good base for exploring the area. The town's isolated position has always made it vulnerable to attack from the sea. During the 16th century, Spanish raiders destroyed most of the original town, and the majority of old buildings date from as late as the 18th century. The main street is Market Jew Street, a folk mistranslation of the Cornish expression Marghas Yow, which means "Thursday Market." Where Market Jew Street meets Causeway Head is Market House, constructed in 1837, an impressive, domed granite building that now serves as a bank.

In contrast to arty St. Ives, Penzance is a no-nonsense working town. Though lacking the traffic-free lanes and quaint cottages of St. Ives, Penzance preserves pockets of handsome Georgian architecture.

GETTING HERE AND AROUND
The main train line from Plymouth terminates at Penzance, which is also served by National Express buses. Bus and train stations are next to each other at the east end of town. A car is an encumbrance here, so use one of the parking lots near the tourist office and the bus and train stations.

ESSENTIALS
Visitor Information Penzance (⊠ *Station Approach* ☎ *01736/362207* ⊕ *www. visit-westcornwall.com*).

EXPLORING
The former main street and one of the prettiest thoroughfares in Penzance, **Chapel Street** winds down from Market House to the harbor. Its predominantly Georgian and Regency houses suddenly give way to the extraordinary **Egyptian House,** whose facade recalls the Middle East. Built around 1830 as a geological museum, today it houses vacation apartments. Across Chapel Street is the 17th-century **Union Hotel,** where in 1805 the death of Lord Nelson and the victory of Trafalgar were first announced. Near the Union Hotel on Chapel Street is the **Turk's Head,** an inn said to date from the 13th century.

The small collection at the **Penlee House Gallery and Museum,** in a gracious Victorian house in a park, focuses on paintings by members of the so-called Newlyn School from about 1880 to 1930. These works evoke the life of the inhabitants of Newlyn, mostly fisherfolk. The museum also covers 5,000 years of West Cornwall history through archaeology, decorative arts, costume, and photography exhibits. ⊠ *Penlee Park* ☎ *01736/363625* ⊕ *www.penleehouse.org.uk* ⊠ *£3, Sat. free* ☉ *Easter–Sept., Mon.–Sat. 10–5; Oct.–Easter, Mon.–Sat. 10:30–4:30; last admission 30 mins before closing.*

★ Rising out of Mount's Bay just off the coast, the spectacular granite-and-slate island of **St. Michael's Mount** is one of Cornwall's greatest natural attractions. The 14th-century castle perched at the highest point—200 feet above the sea—was built on the site of a Benedictine chapel founded by Edward the Confessor. In its time, the island has served as a church (Brittany's island abbey of Mont St. Michel was an inspiration), a fortress, and a private residence. The castle rooms you can tour include the Chevy Chase Room—a name probably associated with the Cheviot Hills or the French word *chevaux* (horses), after the hunting frieze that decorates the walls of this former monks' refectory. The battlements also offer wonderful views. Around the base of the rock are buildings from medieval to Victorian, but they appear harmonious. Fascinating gardens surround the Mount, and many kinds of plants flourish in its microclimate. To get to the island, walk the cobbled causeway from the village of Marazion or, when the tide is in during the summer, take the ferry. There are pubs and restaurants in the village, but the island also has a café and restaurant. ■TIP→ **Wear stout shoes for your visit to this site, which requires a steep climb.** Visits may be canceled in severe weather. ⊠ *3 mi east of Penzance on A394, Marazion* ☎ *01736/710507* ⊕ *www.stmichaelsmount.co.uk* ⊠ *Castle £6.60, garden £3, £1.50 for ferry each way* ☉ *Castle Apr.–Oct., Sun.– Fri. 10:30–5; Nov.–Mar., tours Tues. and Fri. 11 and 2, call to check. Garden May and June, weekdays 10:30–5; July–Oct., Thurs. and Fri. 10:30–5; last admission 4:15; Nov.–Mar., phone for hrs.*

OFF THE BEATEN PATH

Isles of Scilly. Fondly regarded in folklore as the lost land of Lyonesse, this compact group of more than 100 islands 30 mi southwest of Land's End is equally famed for the warm summer climate and ferocious winter storms. In fair weather you can find peace, flowers—wild, cultivated, and subtropical—swarms of seabirds, and unspoiled beaches galore. If you have time, take the 2½-hour ferry service from Penzance; otherwise there's plane and helicopter service. These all arrive at the largest of the five inhabited islands, St. Mary's, which has the bulk of the lodgings, from palatial retreats to humble but comfortable B&Bs.

WHERE TO EAT

££
BRITISH
★

✕**Admiral Benbow.** One of the town's most famous inns, the 17th-century Admiral Benbow was once a smugglers' pub—look for the figure of a smuggler on the roof. Seafaring memorabilia, a brass cannon, model ships, and figureheads fill the place. In the restaurant area, decorated to resemble a ship's galley, you can dine on seafood or a steak-and-ale pie. ⊠ *46 Chapel St.* ☎ *01736/363448* ☰ *MC, V.*

£££
SEAFOOD

✕**Harris's.** Seafood is the main event in the two small, boldly colored rooms of this restaurant off Market Jew Street. The menu showcases whatever the boats bring: crab Florentine, grilled on a bed of spinach with a cheese sauce, is usually available. Meat dishes might include guinea fowl stuffed with Cornish Brie or Gressingham duck breast. The semiformal style is intimate, elegant, and traditional. ⊠ *46 New St.* ☎ *01736/364408* ☰ *MC, V* ☉ *Closed Sun., also Mon. Nov.–June, and 4 wks Nov.–Mar.*

WHERE TO STAY

£££–££££
★

Abbey Hotel. Owned by former 1960s model-icon Jean Shrimpton, this Wedgwood-blue-color hotel off Chapel Street is marvelously homey. Books fill the 17th-century drawing room, and antiques and chintzes decorate many of the rooms, most of which have harbor views. If you need more space, there's also a pair of comfortable apartments. **Pros:** full of character; inspiring views; solicitous staff. **Cons:** rooms slightly cramped; shabby chic style not to everyone's taste. ⊠ *Abbey St.* ☎ *01736/366906* ⊕ *www.theabbeyonline.co.uk* ➡ *6 rooms, 2 apartments* ⌂ *In-room: no a/c, Wi-Fi (some). In-hotel: restaurant, Wi-Fi, some pets allowed* ☰ *AE, MC, V* ⫶⊙⫶ *BP.*

££

Camilla House. This flower-bedecked Georgian house stands on a road parallel to the promenade, close to the harbor. Guest rooms are cheerfully decorated; those at the front have sea views. The owners are great sources of local information and offer bicycle tours around West Cornwall. Evening meals are available on request. **Pros:** friendly management; quiet location near seafront; great breakfasts. **Cons:** some rooms are small; far from bus and train stations. ⊠ *12 Regent Terr.* ☎*01736/363771* ⊕*www.camillahouse-hotel.co.uk* ⇱*8 rooms* ⬥*In-room: no a/c, no phone, DVD, Wi-Fi. In-hotel: restaurant, bar, bicycles, Internet terminal, Wi-Fi, no-smoking rooms* ⊟*AE, MC, V* ⦿*BP.*

£ ⊡**Union Hotel.** Strong on historical and nautical details, this central lodging housed the town's assembly rooms, where news of Admiral Nelson's victory at Trafalgar and of the death of Nelson himself were first announced from the minstrels' gallery in 1805. The bar, lounge, and dining rooms retain their Georgian elegance. The guest rooms, in traditional style, could use updating; some have tired-looking carpets and old-fashioned prints. A number have window seats, with views over Mount's Bay. Breakfast is served in the restored assembly rooms. **Pros:** historic character; spacious rooms; good value for the money. **Cons:** feels dowdy; weak showers. ⊠ *Chapel St.* ☎*01736/362319* ⊕*www. unionhotel.co.uk* ⇱*28 rooms* ⬥*In-room: no a/c. In-hotel: restaurant, bars, Wi-Fi, parking (free)* ⊟*AE, MC, V* ⦿*BP.*

NIGHTLIFE AND THE ARTS

★ The open-air **Minack Theatre** perches high above a beach 3 mi southeast of Land's End and about 6 mi southwest of Penzance. The slope of the cliff forms a natural amphitheater, with bench seats on the terraces and the sea as a magnificent backdrop. Different companies present plays from classic dramas to modern comedies afternoons and evenings in summer. An exhibition center tells the story of the theater's creation. ⊠ *Off B3315, Porthcurno* ☎*01736/810181* ✉*Exhibition center £3.50, performances £8.50* ⊙*Mid-Mar.–Oct., daily 9:30–5:30; Nov.–mid-Mar., daily 10–4. Exhibition center closed during matinees, currently May–Sept., Wed. and Fri. noon–4:30.*

SPORTS AND THE OUTDOORS

Many ships have foundered on Cornwall's rocky coastline, resulting in an estimated 3,600 shipwrecks. The area around Land's End has some of the best diving in Europe, in part because the convergence of the Atlantic and the Gulf Stream here results in impressive visibility and unusual subtropical marine life. **Undersea Adventures** (⊠*7 Hayle Industrial Park, Hayle* ☎*01736/751066*) offers courses and guided dives for beginners and experts.

LIZARD PENINSULA

★ *23 mi southwest of Penzance.*

The southernmost point on mainland Britain, this peninsula is a government-designated Area of Outstanding Natural Beauty, named so for the rocky, dramatic coast rather than the flat and boring interior. The huge, eerily rotating dish antennae of the Goonhilly Satellite Communications Earth Station are visible from the road as it crosses Goonhilly Downs, the backbone of the peninsula. There's no coast road, unlike Land's End, so get out and explore on foot. The beaches are good. With no large town (Helston is the biggest, and is not a tourist center), it's far less busy than the Land's End peninsula.

EXPLORING

A path close to the tip of the peninsula plunges down 200-foot cliffs to the tiny **Kynance Cove,** with its handful of pint-size islands. The sands here are reachable only during the 2½ hours before and after low tide. The peninsula's cliffs are made of greenish serpentine rock, interspersed with granite; souvenirs of the area are carved out of the stone.

FALMOUTH

8 mi northeast of Lizard Peninsula, 7 mi northeast of Gweek, 12 mi south of Truro.

The bustle of this resort town's fishing harbor, yachting center, and commercial port only adds to its charm. In the 18th century Falmouth was the main mail-boat port for North America, and in Flushing, a village across the inlet, you can see the slate-covered houses built by prosperous mail-boat captains. A ferry service now links the two towns. On Custom House Quay, off Arwenack Street, is the King's Pipe, an oven in which seized contraband was burned.

GETTING HERE AND AROUND

Falmouth can be reached from Truro on a branch rail line or on frequent buses, and it is also served by local and National Express buses from other centers. Running parallel to the seafront, the long, partly pedestrianized main drag links the town's main sights. Visitors to Pendennis Castle traveling by train should use Falmouth Docks station, from which it's a short walk. Alternatively, drive or take a local bus to the castle to save legwork.

ESSENTIALS

Visitor Information Falmouth (⊠ *11 Market Strand* ☎ *01326/312300* ⊕ *www. acornishriver.co.uk).*

EXPLORING

☺ The granite and oak-clad **National Maritime Museum Cornwall** by the harbor is an excellent place to come to grips with Cornish maritime heritage, weather lore, and navigational science. You can view the collection of 140 or so boats, examine the tools associated with Cornish boatbuilders, and study the prospect across to Flushing from the lighthouse-like Look-out, which is equipped with maps, telescopes, and binoculars. In the glass-fronted Tidal Zone below sea level, you come face-to-face with the sea itself. In summer you can reach the museum by ferry from Falmouth's Prince of Wales Pier. ⊠ *Discovery Quay* ☎ *01326/313388* ⊕ *www.nmmc.co.uk* ☜ *£8.75* ☉ *Daily 10–5.*

☺ At the end of its own peninsula stands the formidable **Pendennis Castle,** built by Henry VIII in the 1540s and improved by his daughter Elizabeth I. You can explore the defenses developed over the centuries. In the Royal Artillery Barracks, the Key to Cornwall exhibit explores the castle's history and its connection to Cornwall and England. The castle has sweeping views over the English Channel and across to St. Mawes Castle, designed as a companion fortress to guard the roads. Call about events such as concerts, plays, jousting, and shows for kids. ⊠*Pendennis Head* ☎*01326/316594* ⊕*www.english-heritage.org.uk* ☐*£5.70* ⊙*Apr.–June and Sept., Sun.–Fri. 10–5, Sat. 10–4; July and Aug., Sun.–Fri. 10–6, Sat. 10–4; Oct.–Mar., daily 10–4.*

WHERE TO EAT AND STAY

££   ×**Pandora Inn.** Four miles north of Falmouth, this thatched pub on a
SEAFOOD creek is a great retreat, with both a patio and a moored pontoon for summer dining. Maritime memorabilia and fresh flowers provide decoration, and you can eat in the bar, in the formal Upper Deck room upstairs, or outside. The menu highlight is fresh seafood—try the grilled sea bream—though there's a good selection of game in winter. ⊠*Restronguet Creek, Mylor Bridge* ☎*01326/372678* ☐*AE, MC, V.*

£££ ×**Seafood Bar.** Head down an alley off the quay to get to this restau-
SEAFOOD rant with a fish tank for a window. Beyond the door is the very best
★ local seafood, with such choices as thick crab soup, Helford River oysters, or scallops from Falmouth Bay. ⊠*Quay St.* ☎*01326/315129* ☐*MC, V* ⊙*Closed Sun. Sept.–June and Mon. Oct.–Easter. No lunch Sept.–June.*

££££ ⌂ **St. Michael's Hotel.** Colorful subtropical gardens front this seaside hotel overlooking Falmouth Bay. The public areas and spacious guest rooms are sleek and contemporary, and the young staff welcomes families. The Flying Fish restaurant is worth sampling, and the treatments in the spa's four rooms are state-of-the-art. **Pros:** great food; excellent facilities; enthusiastic and amiable staff. **Cons:** some rooms are small; poor soundproofing. ⊠*Stracey Rd.* ☎*01326/312707* ⊕*www.stmichaelshotel.co.uk* ⌂*57 rooms, 4 suites* &*In-room: Wi-Fi. In-hotel: restaurant, bar, pool, gym, spa, Internet terminal, Wi-Fi* ☐*AE, MC, V* ⊙*BP.*

TRELISSICK

6 mi northeast of Falmouth.

Trelissick has a ferry terminal as well as colorful Trelissick Garden, owned by the National Trust.

EXPLORING

The **King Harry Ferry** (☎*01872/862312* ⊕*www.kingharryscornwall. co.uk*), a chain-drawn car ferry, runs to the scenically splendid Roseland Peninsula three times hourly every day. From its decks you can see up and down the Fal, a deep, narrow river with steep, wooded banks. The river's great depth provides mooring for old ships waiting to be sold; these mammoth shapes lend a surreal touch to the riverscape.

Cornwall's mild climate has endowed it with some of the country's most spectacular gardens, among which **Trelissick Garden,** on the banks of the Fal river, is especially scenic. Famous for its camellias, azaras, and photinias, the terraced garden is set within 375 acres of wooded parkland, offering wonderful panoramic views and making this a paradise for walkers. Between May and September you can visit by river ferry from Falmouth, St. Mawes, and Truro. ⊠*Feock* ☎*01872/862090* ⊕*www.nationaltrust.org.uk* ☐*£7* ⊙*Mid-Feb.–Oct., daily 10:30–5:30 or dusk; Nov.–mid-Feb., daily 11–4 or dusk; last admission 30 mins before closing.*

ST. MAWES

16 mi east of Falmouth by road, 1½ mi east by sea, 11 mi south of Truro by ferry.

At the tip of the Roseland Peninsula is the quiet, unspoiled village of St. Mawes, where subtropical plants thrive. The peninsula itself is a lovely backwater with old churches, a lighthouse, and good coast walking. One or two sailing and boating options are available in summer, but most companies operate from Falmouth.

EXPLORING

The well-preserved Tudor-era **St. Mawes Castle,** outside the village, has a cloverleaf shape that makes it seemingly impregnable, yet during the Civil War its Royalist commander surrendered without firing a shot. (In contrast, Pendennis Castle held out at this time for 23 weeks before submitting to a siege.) ✉A3078 ☎01326/270526 ⊕www.english-heritage.org.uk ⊞£4 ⊙Apr.–June and Sept., Sun.–Fri. 10–5; July and Aug., Sun.–Fri. 10–6; Oct., daily 10–4; Nov.–Mar., Fri.–Mon. 10–4.

> **RENT A COTTAGE**
>
> There are plenty of opportunities for experiencing rural peace in a rented cottage amid the meadows and moors of England's West Country. However, the best places are often booked up from year to year in the high season (school vacation). Ask at the information centers, or try any of the following specialist companies: **Classic Cottages** (☎01326/555555 ⊕www. classic.co.uk). **Cornish Cottage Holidays** (☎01326/573808 ⊕www.cornishcottageholidays. co.uk). **Cornish Traditional Cottages** (☎01208/821666 ⊕www. corncott.com). **Helpful Holidays** (☎01647/433593 ⊕www. helpfulholidays.com).

★ North of St. Mawes on A3078 is **St. Just in Roseland,** one of the most beautiful spots in the West Country. This tiny hamlet made up of stone cottage terraces and a 13th-century church is set within a subtropical garden, often abloom with magnolias and rhododendrons on a summer's day. St. Just in Roseland is 9 mi south of Truro.

WHERE TO STAY

££££–£££££ ⬚**Lugger Hotel.** It's worth the winding drive on some of Cornwall's narrowest roads to get to this waterfront hideaway in a tiny fishing village. Several 17th-century cottages have been transformed in an eclectic modern style with bleached Portuguese wood and subdued hues in the small bedrooms. Seafood is a good choice at the excellent restaurant overlooking the diminutive harbor. There's a terrace for drinks and sunbathing, and on either side of the hotel the rugged coastline tempts you with exhilarating walks. The Lugger is 8 mi east of St. Mawes and 12 mi southeast of Truro. **Pros:** lovely location; relaxing and comfortable rooms. **Cons:** expensive for what you get; some rooms are cramped; inexperienced staff. ✉Portloe ☎01872/501322 ⊕www.luggerhotel. com ⇌21 rooms ⌂In-room: no a/c. In-hotel: restaurant, spa, Internet terminal ⊟AE, MC, V ⓘⓞⓘBP.

£££££ ⬚**Tresanton Hotel.** It's the Cornish Riviera, Italian style: this former
★ yachtsman's club, owned by Olga Polizzi, daughter of grand hotelier Charles Forte, makes for a luxuriously relaxed stay. Decorated in sunny

whites, blues, and yellows, with terra-cotta pots on the terrace, the Tresanton seems distinctly Mediterranean, and the yacht and speedboat available in summer to guests reinforce the jet-set spirit. In the fixed-price restaurant, the Italian-inspired menu includes local scallops, crab, lamb cutlets, and cannon of beef. **Pros:** efficient staff; excellent restaurant; stylishly luxurious setting. **Cons:** some steps to climb; dispersed layout inconvenient in rainy weather; distant parking lot. ⊠ *Lower Castle Rd.* ☎ *01326/270055* ⊕ *www.tresanton.com* ↩ *27 rooms, 2 suites* ⎙ *In-room: no a/c, DVD, Wi-Fi (some). In-hotel: restaurant, bar, Wi-Fi, Internet terminal* ☰ *AE, MC, V* ⎇ *BP.*

EN ROUTE

The shortest route from St. Mawes to Truro is via the King Harry Ferry. The longer way swings in a circle on A3078 for 19 mi through countryside where subtropical shrubs thrive. It takes you past Portloe and the 123-foot-tall church tower in Probus, which flaunts gargoyles and pierced stonework.

TRURO

8 mi north of Falmouth, 8 mi north of St. Mawes.

This elegant Georgian city is nestled in a crook of the River Truro. Although Bodmin is the county seat, Truro is Cornwall's only real city; it's a good option mostly for food and shopping, and for cathedral and museum buffs. For an overview of the Georgian houses, take a stroll down steep, broad Lemon Street. The 18th-century facades are of pale stone—unusual for Cornwall, where granite predominates. Like Lemon Street, Walsingham Place is a typical Georgian street, a curving, flower-lined pedestrian oasis.

GETTING HERE AND AROUND

Truro is on the main rail line between Penzance and Plymouth, and is served by local and National Express buses. The compact center can be easily walked from the bus and train stations.

ESSENTIALS

Visitor Information Truro (⊠ *City Hall, Boscawen St.* ☎ *01872/274555* ⊕ *www.acornishriver.co.uk).*

EXPLORING

The **Cathedral Church of St. Mary** dominates the city. Although built between 1880 and 1910, it evokes a medieval church, with an exterior in early-English Gothic style. The interior is filled with relics from the 16th-century parish church that stood on this site, part of which has been incorporated into a side chapel. An open, cobbled area called High Cross lies in front of the west porch, and the city's main shopping streets fan out from here. ⊠ *14 St. Mary's St.* ☎ *01872/276782* ⊕ *www. trurocathedral.org.uk* 🖾 *Free* ☉ *Mon.–Sat. 7:30–6, Sun. 9–7; tours Easter–Oct., Mon.–Thurs. and Sat. at 11, Fri. at 11:30, also weekdays at 2 during school vacations.*

The **Royal Cornwall Museum,** in a Georgian building, displays some fine examples of Cornwall-inspired art, a sampling of Cornish archaeology, an absorbing hodgepodge of local history, and an extensive collection

of minerals. There's a café and a shop. ⊠*River St.* ☎*01872/272205*
⊕*www.royalcornwallmuseum.org.uk* ☑*Free* ⊙*Mon.–Sat. 10–4:45.*

WHERE TO STAY

£££   🏠**Alverton Manor.** A bishop's house and then a convent, this atmospheric lodging still has a chapel. (These days it serves as a conference
room.) Guest rooms are large and have French cherry furniture. Quiet
elegance permeates the public areas, and in the restaurant standards
are kept high with the use of local produce in traditional and modern
English recipes. Make sure you sample the impressive selection of local
cheeses. **Pros:** old-fashioned quality; friendly and helpful staff; superb
restaurant. **Cons:** facilities need updating; slightly stuffy atmosphere.
⊠*Tregolls Rd.* ☎*01872/276633* ⊕*www.alvertonmanor.co.uk* ⇥*29
rooms, 4 suites* ⚡*In-room: no a/c, Wi-Fi (some). In-hotel: restaurant,
bar, Wi-Fi, some pets allowed* ▤*AE, MC, V* ⊙*May be closed 1 wk
over New Year's* ⦿*BP.*

CHARLESTOWN

15 mi east of Truro.

Charlestown has managed to avoid overdevelopment since its heyday
in the early 1800s. Its Georgian harbor often appears in period film and
television productions. This port was built by a local merchant in 1791
to export the huge reserves of china clay from St. Austell, 1 mi to the
north, and it became one of the ports from which 19th-century emigrants left for North America. Some spectacular gardens are nearby.

EXPLORING

★   The sprawling, popular **Lost Gardens of Heligan** have something for all
garden lovers, as well as an intriguing history. Restored in the early
1990s by former rock music producer Tim Smit (the force behind the
Eden Project garden) after decades of neglect, they were begun by the
Tremayne family in the late 18th century. In Victorian times the gardens displayed plants from around the British Empire. The Jungle zone
contains surviving plants from this era, including a lone Monterey Pine,
as well as Giant Redwood and clumps of bamboo. The Italian Garden
and walled Flower Gardens are delightful, but don't overlook the fruit
and vegetable gardens or Flora's Green, bordered by a ravine. It's easy
to spend half a day here. ■TIP→ **Travel via St. Austell to avoid confusing country lanes, then follow signs to Mevagissey.** ⊠*B3273, Pentewan*
☎*01726/845100* ⊕*www.heligan.com* ☑*£8.50* ⊙*Apr.–Sept., daily
10–6; Oct.–Mar., daily 10–5; last entry 1½ hrs before closing.*

☾   Spectacularly set in a former china-clay pit, the **Eden Project** presents the
Fodor's Choice   world's major plant systems in microcosm. The crater contains more
★   than 70,000 plants—many of them rare or endangered species—from
three climate zones. Plants from the temperate zone are outdoors, and
those from other zones are housed in hexagonally paneled geodesic
domes. In one dome, olive and citrus groves mix with cacti and other
plants indigenous to warmer climates. The tropical dome steams with
heat, resounds to the gushing of a waterfall, and blooms with exotic
flora. The emphasis is on conservation and ecology, but is free of any

editorializing. A free shuttle, the Land Train, helps the footsore, and well-informed guides provide information. An entertaining exhibition in the visitor center gives you the lowdown on the project, and the Core, an education center, provides amusement and instruction for children. Extra attractions include open-air concerts in summer and an ice-skating rink in winter. The Eden Project is 3 mi northeast of Charleston. ■ TIP→**To avoid the biggest crowds, visit on a Friday or Saturday, early in the morning, or after 2; you need at least half a day to see everything.** ⊠*Bodelva, signposted off A30, A390, and A391, St. Austell* ☏*01726/811911* ⊕*www.edenproject.com* ✍*£16, £11 if arriving by bike or on foot* ☉*Apr.–late Oct., daily 9–6; late Oct.–Mar., daily 9–4:30; last admission 1½ hrs before closing.*

FOWEY

7 mi northeast of the Eden Project, 10 mi northeast of Charlestown.

Nestled in the mouth of a wooded estuary, Fowey (pronounced Foy) is still very much a working china-clay port as well as a focal point for the sailing fraternity. Increasingly, it's also the favored home of the rich and famous. Good and varied dining and lodging options abound; these are most in demand during Regatta Week in mid-August and the annual Daphne du Maurier Festival in mid-May. The Bodinnick Ferry takes cars as well as foot passengers across the river for the coast road on to Looe.

GETTING HERE AND AROUND

Fowey is not on any train line, but the town is served by frequent buses from St. Austell. Don't attempt to drive into the steep and narrow-lane town center, which is ideal for strolling around. Parking lots are signposted on the approach roads.

ESSENTIALS

Visitor Information Fowey (⊠*5 South St.* ☏*01726/833616* ⊕*www.fowey. co.uk).*

WHERE TO EAT AND STAY

££
SEAFOOD
✕**Sam's.** Be prepared for a wait at this small and buzzing bistro with a rock-and-roll flavor. Diners squeeze onto benches and into booths to savor dishes made with local seafood, including a majestic bouillabaisse, or just a simple "Samburger." ⊠*20 Fore St.* ☏*01726/832273* ⌂*Reservations not accepted* ▭*MC, V.*

£££££
🛏**Fowey Hall.** A showy Victorian edifice, all turrets and elaborate plasterwork, this hotel with 5 acres of gardens is a great place for families. Most rooms are spacious enough for several people, and there are great

facilities for the kids. You can dine in the sumptuously oak-paneled Hansons or in the less formal Conservatory, which opens onto the terrace. **Pros:** grand manorial style; family-friendly atmosphere. **Cons:** steep climb from Fowey; some rooms are small and lack views; erratic housekeeping and service. ⊠*Hanson Dr.* ☎*01726/833866* ⊕*www. foweyhallhotel.co.uk* ⇆*25 rooms, 11 suites* ⚷*In-room: no a/c, DVD, Wi-Fi (some). In-hotel: 2 restaurants, bar, pool, laundry service, Wi-Fi, some pets allowed, no-smoking rooms* ⊟*AE, MC, V* ⥥|*BP.*

SPORTS AND THE OUTDOORS

Between May and September, **Fowey River Expeditions** (⊠*17 Passage St.* ☎*01726/833627*) runs daily canoe trips up the tranquil River Fowey, the best way to observe the abundant wildlife. Kayaks are also available to rent.

BODMIN

12 mi north of Fowey.

Bodmin, the county seat, was the only Cornish town recorded in the 11th-century Domesday Book, William the Conqueror's census. During World War I the Domesday Book and the Crown Jewels were sent to Bodmin Prison for safekeeping. From the Gilbert Memorial on Beacon Hill, you can see both of Cornwall's coasts. Lanhydrock, a stately home, is also near Bodmin.

ESSENTIALS

Visitor Information Bodmin (⊠*The Shire Hall, Mount Folly* ☎*01208/76616* ⊕*www.bodminlive.com*).

EXPLORING

Fodor'sChoice ★ One of Cornwall's greatest country piles, **Lanhydrock** gives a look into the lives of the upper classes in the 19th century. The former home of the powerful, wealthy Robartes family was originally constructed in the 17th century but was totally rebuilt after a fire in 1881. The granite exterior remains true to its original form, however, and the long picture gallery in the north wing, with its barrel-vaulted plaster ceiling depicting 24 biblical scenes, survived the devastation. A small museum in the north wing shows photographs and letters relating to the family. The house's endless pantries, sculleries, dairies, nurseries, and linen cupboards bear witness to the immense amount of work involved in maintaining this lifestyle. About 900 acres of wooded parkland border the River Fowey, and in spring the gardens present an exquisite ensemble of magnolias, azaleas, and rhododendrons. Allow two hours to see the house and more time to stroll the grounds. ⊠*3 mi southeast of Bodmin, signposted off A30, A38, and B3268* ☎*01208/265950* ⊕*www. nationaltrust.org.uk* ⛬*£9.45; grounds only, £5.30* ☉*House Mar. and Oct., Tues.–Sun. 11–5; Apr.–Sept., Tues.–Sun. and national holidays 11–5:30; garden daily 10–6; last admission 30 mins before closing.*

For a taste of Arthurian legend, follow A30 northeast out of Bodmin across the boggy, heather-clad granite plateau of Bodmin Moor. After about 10 mi, turn right at Bolventor to get to **Dozmary Pool**. A lake rather than a pool, it was here that King Arthur's legendary magic sword, Excalibur, was supposedly returned to the Lady of the Lake after Arthur's final battle.

PLYMOUTH AND DARTMOOR

Just over the border from Cornwall is Plymouth, an unprepossessing city but one with a historic old core and splendid harbor that recall a rich maritime heritage. North of Plymouth, you can explore the vast, boggy reaches of hilly Dartmoor, the setting for the Sherlock Holmes classic *The Hound of the Baskervilles*. It's a place to hike or go horseback riding away from the crowds.

PLYMOUTH

48 mi southwest of Exeter, 124 mi southwest of Bristol, 240 mi southwest of London.

Devon's largest city has long been linked with England's commercial and maritime history. The Pilgrims sailed from here to the New World in the *Mayflower* in 1620. Although much of the city center was destroyed by air raids in World War II and has been rebuilt in an uninspiring style, there are worthwhile sights. A harbor tour is also a good way to see the city.

GETTING HERE AND AROUND

Frequent trains arrive from Bodmin, Penzance, and Exeter. The train station is 1 mi north of the seafront, connected by frequent buses. Long-distance buses stop at the centrally located bus station off Royal Parade. Drivers can leave their cars in one of the numerous parking lots, including a couple right by the harbor. The seafront and central city areas are best explored on foot.

ESSENTIALS

Visitor Information Plymouth (⊠ *Plymouth Mayflower, 3–5 The Barbican* ☎ *01752/306330* ⊕ *www.plymouth.gov.uk).*

EXPLORING

TOP ATTRACTIONS

❺ **Barbican.** East of the Royal Citadel is the Barbican, the oldest surviving section of Plymouth. Here Tudor houses and warehouses rise from a maze of narrow streets leading down to the fishing docks and harbor. Many of these buildings have become antiques shops, art shops, and bookstores. It's worth a stroll.

❹ **Elizabethan House.** This former sea captain's home in the heart of the Barbican offers a fascinating insight into how well-to-do Plymothians lived during the city's golden age. The three floors of the timber-frame house are filled with 16th- and 17th-century furnishings, and there's a spiral staircase built around a ship's mast. ⊠ *32 New St.* ☎ *01752/304774* ⚓ *£2* ☾ *Apr.–Sept., Tues.–Sat. and national holidays 10–5.*

❶ **Hoe.** From the Hoe, a wide, grassy esplanade with crisscrossing walkways high above the city, you can take in a magnificent view of the inlets, bays, and harbors that make up Plymouth Sound.

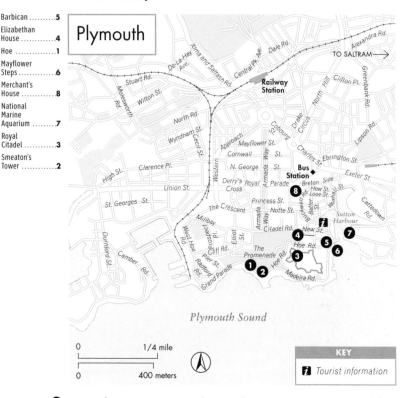

Plymouth

Plymouth Sound

0   1/4 mile

0   400 meters

KEY

i   *Tourist information*

7 **National Marine Aquarium.** This excellent aquarium, on a central harborside site, presents aqueous environments, from a freshwater stream to a seawater wave tank and a huge "shark theater." Not to be missed is the extensive collection of sea horses, part of an important breeding program, and the chance to walk under sharks in the Mediterranean tank. Explorocean highlights undersea technology with demonstrations and hands-on gizmos, and there's a 3-D cinema. ⊠ *Rope Walk, Coxside* ☎ *01752/600301* ⊕ *www.national-aquarium.co.uk* ⊠ *£11* ⊗ *Apr.–Sept., daily 10–6; Oct.–Mar., daily 10–5; last admission 1 hr before closing.*

Saltram. An exquisite 18th-century home with many of its original furnishings, Saltram was built around the remains of a late-Tudor mansion. Its jewel is one of Britain's grandest neoclassical rooms, a vast, double-cube salon designed by Robert Adam and adorned with paintings by Sir Joshua Reynolds, first president of the Royal Academy of Arts, who was born nearby in 1723. The Axminster carpet was created for the room. Fine plasterwork adorns many rooms, and three have original Chinese wallpaper. The outstanding garden includes rare trees and shrubs, and there's a restaurant and a cafeteria. Saltram is 3½ mi east of Plymouth city center. ⊠ *South of A38, Plympton* ☎ *01752/333500* ⊕ *www.nationaltrust.org.uk* ⊠ *£8.25; garden only, £4.10* ⊗ *House* *mid-Mar.–Oct., Sat.–Thurs. noon–4:30; last admission 3:45. Garden mid-Mar.–Oct., daily 11–5; Nov.–mid-Mar., Sat.–Thurs. 11–4.*

WORTH NOTING

⑥ Mayflower Steps. By the harbor you can visit the Mayflower Steps, where the Pilgrims embarked in 1620; the **Mayflower Stone** marks the exact spot. They had sailed from Southampton but had to stop in Plymouth because of damage from a storm.

⑧ Merchant's House. Near the Barbican, just off the Royal Parade, this largely 17th-century house is a museum of local history. ⊠*33 St. Andrew's St.* ☎*01752/304774* ☑*£2* ⊘*Apr.–Sept., Tues.–Sat. and national holidays 10–5.*

③ Royal Citadel. This huge citadel was built by Charles II in 1666 and still operates as a military center. ⊠*End of the Hoe* ⊕*www.english-heritage.org.uk* ☑*£4* ⊘*May–Sept., Tues. and Thurs. 1¼-hr guided tours at 2:30.*

② Smeaton's Tower. This lighthouse, transferred here at the end of the 19th century from its original site 14 mi out to sea, provides a sweeping vista over Plymouth Sound and the city as far as Dartmoor. ⊠*Hoe Rd.* ☎*01752/304774* ☑*£2* ⊘*Apr.–Sept., Tues.–Fri. 10–noon and 1–4:30, Sat. 10–noon and 1–4; Oct.–Mar., Tues.–Sat. 10–noon and 1–3.*

RIVER TOURS

Sound Cruising Ltd. This company runs harbor and river sightseeing trips all year; boats depart every 45 minutes in peak season from Phoenix Wharf (call to check November–March). ⊠*Madeira Rd., Barbican* ☎*01752/408590.*

Tamar Cruising. Harbor cruises (year-round) and longer scenic trips on the Rivers Tamar and Yealm (between Easter and October only) leave from the Mayflower Steps and Cremyll Quay. ⊠*Cremyll Quay, Cremyll, Torpoint* ☎*01752/822105.*

WHERE TO EAT

££££ ⨯**Piermasters.** Fresh seafood landed at nearby piers, notably squid, mus-
SEAFOOD sels, and oysters, appears high on the menu at this Barbican eatery. Blending modern decor in a traditional setting, the downstairs dining area has a tile floor, wooden tables, and sails on the ceiling, and upstairs is wood paneled with contemporary art on the walls. There's an excellent fixed-price menu at lunch. ⊠*33 Southside St.* ☎*01752/229345* ▭*AE, MC, V* ⊘*Closed Sun. and 10 days over Christmas.*

£££££ ⨯**Tanners.** One of the city's oldest buildings, the 15th-century Prysten
MODERN BRITISH House, is the setting for the highly regarded, inventive cuisine of brothers Chris and James Tanner. On the fixed-price menus are such lunch options as seafood; evening choices include roast beef fillet with kohlrabi gratin. One of the two lattice-windowed rooms has a well in it, and the other is hung with tapestries. The canopied courtyard is ideal for alfresco dining. The brothers also operate the Barbican Kitchen, a more relaxed, less pricey offshoot of the restaurant at the Black Friars Distillery on Southside Street. ⊠*Finewell St.* ☎*01752/252001* ⊿*Reservations essential* ▭*AE, MC, V* ⊘*Closed Sun. and Mon.*

WHERE TO STAY

£ ⊞ **Bowling Green Hotel.** Friendly and unpretentious, this Victorian house overlooks Sir Francis Drake's bowling green on Plymouth Hoe. Pine pieces and floral-print fabrics decorate the guest rooms, and there's a conservatory and garden. The house is near lots of shops. **Pros:** convenient base for sightseeing; welcoming staff. **Cons:** needs some minor maintenance; low shower pressure. ✉9–10 Osborne Pl., Lockyer St. ☎01752/ 209090 ⊕www.bowlinggreenhotel. com ⇆12 rooms ⌂In-room: no a/c, Wi-Fi. In-hotel: Wi-Fi, parking (paid), no-smoking rooms ☰MC, V ⎮◎⎮BP.

££–£££ ⊞ **Holiday Inn.** Grandly sited in a tall block overlooking Plymouth Hoe, this modern chain hotel has a businesslike tone but doesn't skimp on comforts. Rooms are contemporary and uncluttered, with a brown-and-cream color scheme. On the penthouse floor, Elliot's restaurant provides a panoramic dining area, which is also used for self-serve breakfasts. There's a good-size indoor pool. **Pros:** excellent location; fantastic views. **Cons:** impersonal feel; uninteresting food. ✉Armada Way ☎0870/225–0301 ⊕www. holidayinn.co.uk ⇆211 rooms ⌂In-room: refrigerator (some), Wi-Fi. In-hotel: restaurant, room service, bar, pool, gym, Internet terminal, Wi-Fi, parking (paid), no-smoking rooms ☰AE, DC, MC, V ⎮◎⎮BP.

> ### STAY ON A FARM
>
> Do you plan to travel by car and want to be far from resorts, traffic jams, and hubbub? One way to experience the authentic rural life in Somerset, Devon, and Cornwall is to stay on a farm. Southwest Tourism's Web site (⊕www. naturesouthwest.co.uk) gives details about working farms that supply accommodation—including bed-and-breakfasts and house rentals—throughout the region. Other reference points are Visit Devon (⊕www.visitdevon.co.uk), for farms in Devon, and Cornish Farm Holidays (⊕www.cornish-farms.co.uk), for Cornwall.

NIGHTLIFE AND THE ARTS

Plymouth's **Theatre Royal** (✉Royal Parade ☎01752/267222) presents ballet, musicals, and plays by some of Britain's best companies.

SHOPPING

At the **Black Friars Distillery,** where Plymouth's most famous export, gin, has been distilled since 1793, you can purchase bottles of sloe gin, damson liqueur, fruit cup, or the fiery "Navy Strength" gin that traditionally was issued to the Royal Navy. (✉60 Southside St., ☎01752/665292).

EN ROUTE From Plymouth you have a choice of routes northeast to Exeter. If rugged, desolate, moorland scenery appeals to you, take A386 and B3212 northeast across Dartmoor. There is plenty to stir the imagination.

DARTMOOR NATIONAL PARK

10 mi north of Plymouth, 13 mi west of Exeter.

Even on a summer's day, the brooding hills of this sprawling wilderness appear a likely haunt for such monsters as the hound of the Baskervilles,

0   20 miles

0   30 km

and it seems entirely fitting that Sir Arthur Conan Doyle set his Sherlock Holmes thriller in this landscape.

ESSENTIALS

Visitor Information **High Moorland Visitor Centre** (⊠ *High Moorland Visitor Centre, Tavistock Rd., Princetown* ☎ *01822/890414* ⊕ *www.dartmoor-npa.gov.uk*).

EXPLORING

Sometimes the wet, peaty wasteland of **Dartmoor National Park** vanishes in rain and mist, although in clear weather you can see north to Exmoor, south over the English Channel, and west far into Cornwall. Much of Dartmoor consists of open heath and moorland, unspoiled by roads—wonderful walking and horseback-riding territory but an easy place to lose your bearings. Dartmoor's earliest inhabitants left behind stone monuments and burial mounds that help you envision prehistoric man roaming these pastures. Ponies, sheep, and birds are the main animals to be seen.

Several villages scattered along the borders of this 368-square-mi reserve—one-third of which is owned by Prince Charles—make useful bases for hiking excursions. Accommodations include simple inns and some elegant havens. **Okehampton** is a main gateway, and **Chagford** is a good base for exploring North Dartmoor. Other scenic spots include **Buckland-in-the-Moor,** a hamlet with thatched-roof cottages,

Widecombe-in-the-Moor, whose church is known as the Cathedral of the Moor, and **Grimspound,** the Bronze Age site featured in Conan Doyle's most famous tale. Transmoor Link buses connect most of Dartmoor's towns and villages. Park information centers include the main **High Moorland Visitor Centre** in Princetown and centers in Newbridge, Postbridge, and Haytor. The park also works with tourist information centers in Ivybridge, Okehampton, Tavistock, and Totnes. ✉ *High Moorland Visitor Centre, Tavistock Rd., Princetown* ☎ *01822/890414* ⊕ *www.dartmoor-npa.gov.uk.*

SPORTS AND THE OUTDOORS

Tourist information centers can help you decide what to do here; another source is the **Dartmoor National Park Authority** (✉ *Parke, Haytor Rd., Bovey Tracey, Newton Abbot* ☎ *01626/832093* ⊕ *www.dartmoor-npa.gov.uk*). This is a great area for horseback riding; many towns have stables for guided rides. Hiking is popular, but longer hikes in the bleak, unpeopled region of Dartmoor—for example, the tors south of Okehampton—are appropriate only for the most experienced walkers. The areas around Widgery Cross, Becky Falls, and the Bovey Valley, and the short but dramatic walk along Lydford Gorge, have wide appeal, as do the many valleys around the southern edge of the moors. Guided hikes (£3–£8) are available through the park; reservations are not needed for most, but you can check with the High Moorland Visitor Centre in Princetown.

BUCKLAND ABBEY

8 mi north of Plymouth.

ESSENTIALS

Visitor Information Tavistock (✉ *Bedford Sq.* ☎ *01822/612938* ⊕ *www.westdevon.gov.uk).*

EXPLORING

Buckland Abbey, a 13th-century Cistercian monastery, became the home of Sir Francis Drake in 1581. Today it is filled with mementos of Drake and the Spanish Armada and has a restaurant. From Tavistock, take A386 south to Crapstone and then head west. ✉ *Yelverton* ☎ *01822/853607* ⊕ *www.nationaltrust.org.uk* 🎫 *£7.40; grounds only, £3.80 (free in winter)* ⊙ *Mid-Feb.–mid-Mar. and early Nov.– mid-Dec., Fri.–Sun. 11–4; mid-Mar.–June, Sept., and Oct., Fri.–Wed. 10:30–5:30; July and Aug., daily 10:30–5:30; last admission 45 mins before closing.*

COTEHELE HOUSE & QUAY

4 mi west of Buckland Abbey, 15 mi north of Plymouth.

ESSENTIALS

Visitor Information Tavistock (✉ *Bedford Sq.* ☎ *01822/612938* ⊕ *www.westdevon.gov.uk).*

EXPLORING

★ **Cotehele House & Quay** was formerly a busy port on the River Tamar, but it is now usually visited for the well-preserved late-medieval manor, home of the Edgcumbe family for centuries. The house has original furniture, tapestries, embroideries, and armor, and there are impressive gardens, a restored mill (in operation at 3 PM Tuesday, Thursday, and some Sundays), and a quay museum. A limited number of visitors are allowed per day, so arrive early and be prepared to wait during busy periods. Choose a bright day, because the rooms have no electric light. Shops, crafts studios, a gallery, and a restaurant provide other diversions. ■ TIP→ Take advantage of the shuttle bus that runs between the house, quay, and mill roughly every half hour. ✉ *St. Dominick, north of Saltash, signposted off A390* ☎ *01579/351346* ⊕ *www.nationaltrust.org.uk* ✉ *£8.30; gardens and mill only, £5* ⊙ *House mid-Mar.–Oct., Sat.–Thurs. 11–4:30. Mill mid-Mar.–Sept., daily 11–5; Oct., daily 11–4:30. Gardens daily 10–dusk.*

MORWELLHAM QUAY

2 mi east of Cotehele House & Quay, 5 mi southwest of Tavistock, 18 mi north of Plymouth.

ESSENTIALS

Visitor Information Tavistock (✉ *Bedford Sq.* ☎ *01822/612938* ⊕ *www.westdevon.gov.uk).*

EXPLORING

In the 19th century **Morwellham Quay** (pronounced More-*wel*-ham) was England's main copper-exporting port, and it has been carefully restored as a working museum, with quay workers and coachmen in costume, and a copper mine open to visitors. ✉ *Off A390, on minor road off B3257* ☎ *01822/832766, 01822/833808 recorded information* ⊕ *www.morwellham-quay.co.uk* ✉ *Free, attractions £8.50* ⊙ *Easter–Oct., daily 10–5:30; Nov.–Easter, daily 10–4:30.*

WHERE TO EAT

££££ ✕ **Horn of Plenty.** The restaurant within this Georgian house has mag-
MODERN BRITISH nificent views across the wooded, rhododendron-filled Tamar Valley.
★ Peter Gorton's sophisticated cooking takes its inspiration from around the world. Spiced duck breast with cherry compote and port sauce is a typical main course. There are three-course, fixed-price menus (lunch £26.50, dinner £47), but the best value is Monday evening's potluck menu (£28). A converted coach house and the main house contain eight sumptuously furnished guest rooms. ✉ *3 mi west of Tavistock on A390, Gulworthy* ☎ *01822/832528* ▭ *AE, MC, V.*

LYDFORD GORGE

12 mi north of Morwellham Quay, 7 mi north of Tavistock, 9 mi east of Launceston, 24 mi north of Plymouth.

ESSENTIALS

Visitor Information Tavistock (⊠ *Bedford Sq.* ☎ *01822/612938* ⊕ *www. westdevon.gov.uk).*

EXPLORING

★ The River Lyd has carved a spectacular 1½-mi-long chasm through the rock at **Lydford Gorge**, outside the pretty village of Lydford, midway between Okehampton and Tavistock on the edge of Dartmoor. Two paths follow the gorge past gurgling whirlpools and waterfalls with names such as the Devil's Cauldron and the White Lady. Sturdy footwear is recommended. Although the walk can be quite challenging, the paths can still get congested during busy periods. From Launceston, continue east along A30, following the signs. ⊠ *Off A386, Lydford* ☎ *01822/820320* ⊕ *www.nationaltrust.org.uk* ☎ *£5.27* ⊗ *Mid-Mar.– early Oct., daily 10–5; early Oct.–early Nov., daily 10–4; early Nov.– late Dec., weekends 11–3:30; late Dec.–mid-Feb., daily 11–3:30 (walk restricted to main waterfall and top of gorge in winter).*

WHERE TO EAT AND STAY

£££

MODERN BRITISH

✕ **Dartmoor Inn.** Locals and visitors alike make a beeline for this gastropub in a 16th-century building with a number of small dining spaces. Dishes may include rump of lamb with Indian spices, or grilled sea bass and black bream with lime-and-herb butter. There are inspired vegetarian choices as well as an "easy dining" menu in which a charcoal-grilled burger or asparagus risotto cost less than £10. The pub is at the Lydford junction. Three spacious guest rooms are furnished in a contemporary country style. ⊠ *A386, Lydford* ☎ *01822/820221* ⟐ *Reservations essential* ⊟ *MC, V* ⊗ *Closed Mon. Oct.–Mar. No dinner Sun. No lunch Mon.*

£–££

🏠 **Castle Inn.** The heart of Lydford village, this 16th-century inn is next to Lydford Castle. Rose trellises frame its rosy brick facade, and the public rooms are snug, lamp-lighted, and full of period clutter. Vivid colors are used in the guest rooms; one room has its own roof garden. A range of snacks and full bar meals is available. **Pros:** antique character; peaceful rural setting. **Cons:** shabby in places; substandard food. ⊠ *1 mi off A386, Lydford* ☎ *01822/820241* ⊕ *www.castleinnlydford. co.uk* ⟐ *8 rooms* ⟐ *In-room: no a/c, no phone, DVD, Wi-Fi. In-hotel: restaurant, bar, Wi-Fi, some pets allowed* ⊟ *MC, V* ⟐ *BP.*

SPORTS AND THE OUTDOORS

Cholwell Stables (⊠ *Mary Tavy* ☎ *01822/810526*) has one- and two-hour horseback rides through some of Dartmoor's wilder tracts. Riders of all abilities are escorted, and equipment is provided. The stables are about 6 mi south of Lydford; call for directions.

OKEHAMPTON

8 mi northeast of Lydford Gorge, 28 mi north of Plymouth, 23 mi west of Exeter.

This town at the confluence of the rivers East and West Okement is a good base for exploring North Dartmoor. It has numerous pubs and cottage tearooms (giving you a chance to have a Devon cream tea), as well as a helpful tourist office.

ESSENTIALS

Visitor Information Okehampton (⊠ *Okehampton Museum Yard, West St.* ☎ *01837/53020* ⊕ *www.okehamptondevon.co.uk).*

EXPLORING

On the riverbank a mile southwest of the town center, the jagged ruins of the Norman **Okehampton Castle** occupy a verdant site with a picnic area and woodland walks. ☎*01837/52844* ⊕*www.english-heritage. org.uk* ✆*£3.30* ⊙*Apr.–June and Sept., daily 10–5; July and Aug., daily 10–6.*

The three floors of the informative **Museum of Dartmoor Life** contain models, a working waterwheel, and photos of traditional farming methods. ⊠*3 West St.* ☎*01837/52295* ⊕*www.museumofdartmoorlife.eclipse. co.uk* ✆*£3.50* ⊙*Easter–Oct., weekdays 10:15–4:30, Sat. 10:15–3:30; Nov.–mid-Dec., Mon.–Sat. 11–3.*

WHERE TO STAY

££££–£££££ 　 🏠 **Lewtrenchard Manor.** Paneled rooms, stone fireplaces, leaded-glass windows, and handsome gardens outfit this spacious 1620 manor house on the northwestern edge of Dartmoor. Victorian hymn writer Sabine Baring Gould is responsible for the eclectic mix of architectural styles. Prints, chintzes, and upholstered furniture create comfort in the individually decorated guest rooms. The fixed-price restaurant, with its big log fire and family portraits, serves modern British fare such as roast duck breast with pickled peach. **Pros:** beautiful Jacobean setting; conscientious service; exceptional food. **Cons:** dated in parts; hushed atmosphere may feel oppressive. ⊠*Between Launceston and Okehampton, Lewdown* ☎*01566/783222* ⊕*www.lewtrenchard.co.uk* 🛏*9 rooms, 5 suites* ⚅*In-room: no a/c, DVD (some), Internet, Wi-Fi. In-hotel: restaurant, bar, Wi-Fi, some pets allowed* ⊟*AE, DC, MC, V* ⏶*BP.*

SPORTS AND THE OUTDOORS

Skaigh Stables Farm (⊠*Skaigh La., near Okehampton, Belstone* ☎*01837/ 840917* ⊕*www.skaighstables.co.uk*) arranges horseback rides by the hour, half day, and full day from Easter through September.

CHAGFORD

9 mi southeast of Okehampton, 30 mi northeast of Plymouth.

Chagford, once a tin-weighing station, was an area of fierce fighting between the Roundheads and the Cavaliers during the Civil War. Although officially a "town" since 1305, Chagford is more of a village, with old taverns grouped around a seasoned old church and a curious "pepper-pot" market house on the site of the old Stannary Court. With a handful of cafés and shops to browse around, it makes a convenient base from which to explore North Dartmoor.

EXPLORING

The intriguing **Castle Drogo,** east of Chagford across A382 above the Teign Gorge, looks like a medieval fortress, complete with battlements, but construction actually took place between 1910 and 1930. Designed by Sir Edwin Lutyens for Julius Drewe, a wealthy grocer, the castle is only half finished (funds ran out). Inside, this magisterial pile combines medieval grandeur and early-20th-century comforts like the large bathrooms. ■ TIP→ Between June and September, you can play croquet on the lawn and take in awesome views over Dartmoor. Take the A30 Exeter–Okehampton road to reach the castle, which is 4 mi northeast of Chagford and 6 mi south of A30. ⊠ *Drewsteignton* 🕾 *01647/433306* ⊕ *www.nationaltrust.org.uk* 🖼 *£7.45 or £4.77 in winter; grounds only, £4.77 or £2.19 in winter* ☉ *Castle mid-Feb.–late Feb., daily 10:30– 4:30; early Mar., early Nov.–mid-Dec., and early to late Jan., weekends 10:30–4:30; mid-Mar.–Oct., daily 10:30–5:30. Grounds early Mar., weekends 10:30–4:30; mid-Mar.–early Nov., daily 10:30–4:30; early Nov.–late Dec., Fri.–Sun. 11–4 or dusk.*

★ The **Devon Guild of Craftsmen,** the southwest's most important contemporary arts-and-crafts center, is in a converted 19th-century coach house on the edge of Dartmoor in the town of Bovey Tracey, 10 mi southeast of Chagford and 14 mi southwest of Exeter. The center has excellent exhibitions of local, national, and international crafts as well as a crafts shop and café. ⊠ *Riverside Mill, Bovey Tracey* 🕾 *01626/832223* ⊕ *www.crafts.org.uk* 🖼 *Free* ☉ *Daily 10–5:30.*

QUICK BITES   **The Old Cottage Tea Shop** (⊠ *20 Fore St., Bovey Tracey* 🕾 *01626/833430*) is the real deal, perfect for a light lunch or, even better, a cream tea served on bone china. Warm scones come in baskets, with black currant and other homemade jams and plenty of clotted cream. It's closed Wednesday afternoon and all day Sunday.

WHERE TO EAT AND STAY

££££ MODERN BRITISH ★ ✕ **Gidleigh Park.** One of England's foremost inns, lauded in poetry by Ted Hughes, occupies an enclave of landscaped gardens and streams up a lengthy, winding private drive at the edge of Dartmoor. The extremely pricey contemporary restaurant, directed by chef Michael Caines, has been showered with culinary awards. You may see why when you dig into the sea bass with shellfish mousse, roast lobster, and gazpacho sauce. The locally pumped spring water is like no other. Antiques fill the long, half-timber building, which also has luxurious guest rooms. ⊠ *Gidleigh Park* 🕾 *01647/432367* ⚓ *Reservations essential* 🖃 *AE, DC, MC, V.*

££££ ★ **Bovey Castle.** With the grandeur of a country estate and the amenities of a modern hotel, Bovey Castle, built in 1906 for Viscount Hambledon, has it all. On its vast grounds there's an outstanding golf course and 24 mi of riverbank that can be used for salmon fishing. There is a resident pianist, and children have a barn filled with activities. Enormous fireplaces and oak-panel rooms give a sense of early-20th-century pomp to the public rooms; bedrooms are luxurious, and even some of the bathrooms have great views across the valley. **Pros:** sumptuous surroundings; efficient, friendly staff; children's activities. **Cons:** some rooms are over-priced; service sometimes falters; dining occasionally disappoints. ⊠*Off B3212, North Bovey* ☎*01647/445000* ⊕*www. boveycastle.com* ⬥*63 rooms, 14 self-catering lodges* ⌂*In-room: no a/c, Wi-Fi (some). In-hotel: 3 restaurants, bar, golf course, tennis courts, pool, spa, Internet terminal, Wi-Fi, some pets allowed, no-smoking rooms* ▤*AE, MC, V* ⏁*BP.*

££ ▣ **Easton Court.** Discerning travelers such as C. P. Snow, Margaret Mead, John Steinbeck, and Evelyn Waugh—who completed *Brideshead Revisited* here—made this their Dartmoor home-away-from-home. The Tudor thatched-roof house has a 3.5-acre garden and simple but elegant cottage-style rooms in an adjoining wing; all rooms have views over the well-maintained garden. Breakfast choices include soufflé omelet. **Pros:** personal service; helpful hosts; quiet environment. **Cons:** rooms lack much character; need to drive to get anywhere. ⊠*Easton Cross* ☎*01647/433469* ⊕*www.easton.co.uk* ⬥*5 rooms* ⌂*In-room: no a/c, DVD, Wi-Fi (some). In-hotel: Wi-Fi, some pets allowed, no kids under 10, no-smoking rooms* ▤*MC, V* ⏁*BP.*

DARTMOUTH, TORBAY, AND EXETER

Sheltered by the high mass of Dartmoor to the west, the yachting center of Dartmouth and the area known as the English Riviera, Torbay, enjoy a mild, warm climate. To the north is Exeter, Devon's county seat, an ancient city that has retained some of its medieval character despite wartime bombing. From Exeter you can explore south to Exmouth.

DARTMOUTH

35 mi east of Plymouth, 35 mi south of Exeter.

An important port in the Middle Ages, Dartmouth is today a favorite haunt of yacht owners. Traces of its past include the old houses in Bayard's Cove near Lower Ferry, the 16th-century covered Butterwalk, and the two castles guarding the entrance to the River Dart. The Royal Naval College, built in 1905, dominates the town.

ESSENTIALS

Visitor Information Dartmouth (⊠*The Engine House, Mayors Ave.* ☎*01803/834224* ⊕*www.discoverdartmouth.com).*

EXPLORING

A rewarding way to experience the River Dart is to join a cruise from Dartmouth's quay to visit **Greenway,** the 16th century the riverside home of the Gilbert family (Sir Humphrey Gilbert claimed Newfoundland on behalf of Elizabeth I), more famous today for its association with the crime writer Agatha Christie. Mrs. Mallowan (Christie's married name) made it her holiday home in 1938 and the house displays collections of archaeological finds, china, and silver. The gorgeous gardens are thickly planted with magnolias, camellias, and rare shrubs, and richly endowed with panoramic views. Beware, however, that the grounds are steeply laid out, and those arriving by boat face a daunting uphill climb. **Greenway Cruises** (☎0845/489–0418 ⊕*www.greenwayferry.co.uk*) runs ferries from Dartmouth; a round-trip ticket costs £7.50. Parking spaces here are restricted and must be booked in advance. Alternatively, ask at the tourist office about walking and cycling routes to reach the house. ⊠*Galmpton* ☎*01803/842382* ⊕*www.nationaltrust.org.uk* 🎫*£7.45* ⊗*Mar.–mid-July and Sept.–late Oct., Wed.–Sun. 10:30–5; mid-July–Aug., Tues.–Sun. 10:30–5:30.*

WHERE TO EAT AND STAY

£££££
MODERN BRITISH
✕**New Angel.** John Burton Race, a celebrity chef, has a restaurant in this prime spot by the waterfront; it's yet another sign of the region's ongoing food revolution. The menu is British and European, with an emphasis on local fare such as grilled mackerel, and confit of duck leg with cherry and Banyuls (sweet fortified wine) sauce. Open in the mornings for coffee and croissants, this place is relaxed and family friendly, and guest rooms are available (££–£££). ⊠*2 S. Embankment* ☎*01803/839425* ⚓*Reservations essential* ▤*MC, V* ⊗*Closed Mon. and Jan. No dinner Sun. No lunch Tues.*

£££–££££
🏨**Royal Castle Hotel.** This hotel has truly earned the name "Royal"—several monarchs have slept here. Part of Dartmouth's historic waterfront (and consequently a hub of activity), it was built in the 17th century, reputedly of timber from wrecks of the Spanish Armada. Fireplaces and beamed ceilings are traditional features. Rooms come in different sizes and styles, but all are thoughtfully and richly furnished, with a liberal sprinkling of antiques. Number 6 has its own priest hole, a secret room used to hide Roman Catholic priests. The pricier rooms facing the river have hot tubs. **Pros:** historical resonance; superb central location. **Cons:** poor soundproofing; some facilities need modernizing. ⊠*11 The Quay* ☎*01803/833033* ⊕*www.royalcastle.co.uk* 🛏*25 rooms* ⌂*In-room: no a/c, Wi-Fi (some). In-hotel: restaurant, bars, Wi-Fi, parking (free), some pets allowed, no-smoking rooms* ▤*AE, MC, V* ⊚|*BP.*

EN ROUTE
Two ferries cross the River Dart at Dartmouth; in summer, lines can be long, and you may want to try the inland route, heading west via A3122 to Halwell and then taking A381 north to Totnes. An attractive, relaxed approach to Dartmouth is by boat down the Dart from Totnes.

TOTNES

9 mi northwest of Dartmouth, 28 mi southwest of Exeter.

This busy market town on the banks of the River Dart preserves plenty of its medieval past, and on summer Tuesdays some shopkeepers dress in Elizabethan costume. Market days proper are Friday and Saturday, when the town's status as a center of alternative medicine and culture becomes especially clear, with an abundance of crafts stalls. The historic buildings include a guildhall and St. Mary's Church.

ESSENTIALS

Visitor Information Totnes (⊠*The Town Mill, Coronation Rd.* ☎*01803/ 863168* ⊕*www.totnesinformation.co.uk*).

EXPLORING

You can climb up the hill in town to the ruins of **Totnes Castle**—a fine Norman motte and bailey design—for a wonderful view of Totnes and the River Dart. *TQ9 5NU* ☎*01803/864406* ⊕*www.english-heritage. org.uk* ⊠*£3* ⊙*Apr.–June and Sept., daily 10–5; July and Aug., daily 10–6; Oct., daily 10–4.*

⟳ Steam trains of the **South Devon Railway** run through 7 mi of the wooded Dart Valley between Totnes and Buckfastleigh, on the edge of Dartmoor. There are often special trips around Christmas. ⊠*Near Totnes, Little-hempston* ☎*0845/345–1466* ⊕*www.southdevonrailway.org* ⊠*£9.90 round-trip* ⊙*Late Mar.–Oct., daily; call for winter operation.*

WHERE TO STAY

££ 🏨 **Royal Seven Stars Hotel.** Conveniently located at the bottom of the main street, this centuries-old coaching inn has counted Daniel Defoe and Edward VII among its former guests. A modern makeover has transformed the interior without sacrificing its period features. The well-equipped bedrooms are clean and elegant, and some have spa baths. You can order hot and cold snacks in the traditional Saloon Bar or the contemporary Bar 7, whereas the stylish TQ9 restaurant has more substantial fare. **Pros:** central location; friendly staff. **Cons:** some traffic noise; bar food sometimes disappoints. ⊠*The Plains* ☎*01803/862125* ⊕*www.royalsevenstars.co.uk* ⇆*16 rooms* ♿*In-room: no a/c, Wi-Fi. In-hotel: restaurant, bars, Wi-Fi, parking (free), some pets allowed* ⊟*AE, MC, V* ⦿*BP*

NIGHTLIFE AND THE ARTS

★ One of the foremost arts centers of the West Country, **Dartington Hall** (⊠*Dartington* ☎*01803/847070* ⊕*www.dartington.org/arts*) lies 2 mi northwest of Totnes. The medieval estate was an experimental school before it evolved into an arts and education center. There are concerts, a respected summer school of classical music with master classes and performances, film screenings, and exhibitions, usually with a contemporary slant. The gardens, free year-round, are the setting for outdoor performances of Shakespeare in summer. There's a café, and you can stay overnight in some rooms in the hall.

SHOPPING

Near Dartington Hall, 15 stores and two restaurants in and around an old cider press make up the **Dartington Cider Press Centre** (⊠*Shinners Bridge, Dartington* ☎*01803/847500* ⊕*www.dartington.org/cider-press-centre*), open daily, which markets handmade Dartington crystal glassware, kitchenware, high-quality crafts, books, and toys from Devon and elsewhere. The farm shop sells fudge, ice cream, and cider, and Cranks is an excellent vegetarian restaurant.

BRIXHAM

10 mi southeast of Totnes by A385 and A3022.

Brixham, at the southern point of Tor Bay, has kept much of its original charm, partly because it is still an active fishing village. Much of the catch goes straight to restaurants as far away as London. Sample fish-and-chips on the quayside, where there is a (surprisingly petite) full-scale reproduction of the vessel on which Sir Francis Drake circumnavigated the world.

ESSENTIALS

Visitor Information Brixham (✉ *The Old Market House, The Quay* ☎ *01803/211211* ⊕ *www.englishriviera.co.uk).*

TORQUAY

5 mi north of Brixham via A3022, 23 mi south of Exeter.

The most important resort area in South Devon, Torquay envisions itself as the center of the "English Riviera." Since 1968 the towns of Paignton and Torquay (pronounced tor-*kee*) have been amalgamated under the common moniker of Torbay. Torquay is the supposed site of the hotel in the popular British television comedy *Fawlty Towers* and was the home of mystery writer Agatha Christie. Fans should check out the exhibit devoted to Christie at the town museum. Torre Abbey Mansion holds one of Devon's best collections of 19th-century art.

The town has shed some of its old-fashioned image in recent years, with modern hotels, luxury villas, and apartments that climb the hillsides above the harbor. Still, Torquay is more like Brighton's maiden aunt in terms of energy and fizz, though a pubs-and-clubs culture makes an appearance on Friday and Saturday nights. Palm trees and other semitropical plants (a benefit of being near the warming Gulf Stream) flourish in the seafront gardens; the sea is a clear and intense blue.

GETTING HERE AND AROUND

Buses arrive near Torquay's harbor and the tourist office. The train station is close to Torre Abbey Mansion, but other points in town are best reached on local buses or by taxi. Drivers should take A385 from Totnes or A38 and A380 from Exeter.

ESSENTIALS

Visitor Information Torquay (✉ *Vaughan Parade* ☎ *01803/211211* ⊕ *www. englishriviera.co.uk).*

EXPLORING

Torbay's **beaches**, a mixture of sand and shingle (coarse gravel), have won awards for their water quality and facilities, and can get very crowded in summer. Apart from the central Torre Abbey Sands, they are scattered around town, often separated by the crumbly red cliffs characteristic of the area. To sun and swim, head for Anstey's Cove, a favorite spot for scuba divers, with more beaches farther along at neighboring Babbacombe.

★ For lovers of fine things, Torquay's chief attraction is the **Torre Abbey Mansion,** surrounded by parkland but close to the seafront. It was built on the site of the abbey razed in 1539, and you can still see traces of the old construction. The artistic riches lie within the main building: marine paintings, Victorian sculptures, Pre-Raphaelite window designs, and drawings by William Blake. ✉ *King's Dr.* ☎ *01803/293593* ⊕ *www. torre-abbey.org.uk* 🎟 *£5.75* ⊙ *Mar.–Oct., daily 10–6; Nov., Dec., and*

Feb., daily 10–5; last admission 1 hr before closing.

Just outside Torbay lies a chocolate-box Devon village, **Cockington**, which has thatched cottages, a 14th-century forge, and the square-tower Church of St. George and St. Mary. Repair to the Old Mill for a café lunch or head to the Drum Inn, designed by Sir Edwin Lutyens to be an archetypal pub. On the village outskirts lies Cockington Court—a grand estate with crafts studios, shops, and an eatery. Cockington has, however, more than a touch of the faux: cottages that don't sell anything put up signs to this effect.

5

WHERE TO EAT AND STAY

££ ✕ **Elephant.** Set back from Torquay's harbor, this elegant eatery offers
MODERN BRITISH sophisticated but relaxed dining, either in the dining room upstairs
★ with views over Tor Bay or in the less formal street-level brasserie. In the latter, you can tuck into such dishes as steamed Brixham mussels, Dover sole, and fillet steaks. Upstairs, with its high-back chairs, antique lighting fixtures, and polished floorboards, has more innovative concoctions, available on fixed-price tasting menus, which may include risotto of squid and cauliflower as a starter, fillet of halibut with parsnip puree for the main course, and black currant mousse with licorice and crème fraiche for dessert. ⊠ *3–4 Beacon Terr.* ☎ *01803/200044* ▤ *MC, V* ⊘ *Closed Mon. and 2 wks early Jan. No dinner Sun.*

£££ ✕ **Number 7 Fish Bistro.** Seafood fans can indulge their passion at this
SEAFOOD unpretentious, convivial spot near the harbor. Fresh, locally caught fish are brought to your table for inspection before being simply but imaginatively prepared. The extensive menu offers dishes ranging from humble—but abundant and beautifully cooked—fish-and-chips to curried prawns, and lobster and crab grilled with garlic and brandy. ⊠ *7 Beacon Terr.* ☎ *01803/295055* ⚓ *Reservations essential* ▤ *AE, MC, V* ⊘ *Closed Sun. Oct.–June, Mon. Nov.–May. No lunch Sun.–Tues.*

£££–££££ 🏨 **The Imperial.** This enormous pile perched above the sea, overlooking Torbay, exudes slightly faded Victorian splendor. Magnificent gardens surround the property, and the interior of the 1866 hotel is, well, imperial, with chandeliers, marble floors, and the general air of a bygone world. Most of the traditionally furnished bedrooms are large and comfortable—it's worth paying a bit extra for front-facing ones that have balconies and entrancing views across the bay. **Pros:** stunning location; great views; spacious rooms. **Cons:** steep climb from town; inland-facing rooms overlook parking lot. ⊠ *Park Hill Rd.* ☎ *01803/294301* ⊕ *www.barcelo-hotels.co.uk* 🛏 *140 rooms, 13 suites* ⚑ *In-room: no a/c, refrigerator, Internet, Wi-Fi (some). In-hotel: 2 restaurants, bar, tennis court, pools, gym, spa, parking (paid), some pets allowed* ▤ *AE, DC, MC, V* ⏹ *BP.*

££   🖼️**Lanscombe House.** Located in the postcard-pretty village of Cockington, a rural hideaway within Torquay, this family-run Victorian guesthouse offers spacious bedrooms with Laura Ashley wallpaper and period furnishings, and a walled garden where you can try your hand at croquet. Though Cockington gets quite busy at peak periods, the place preserves a blissfully peaceful ambience in the morning and late afternoon, and the Country Park is just steps away. **Pros:** quiet, traditional setting; pleasant garden. **Cons:** touristy environment; car necessary for local sights. ⊠*Cockington* ☎*01803/606938* ⊕*www.lanscombehouse. co.uk* ⇄*8 rooms* ♿*In-room: no a/c, no phone. In-hotel: bar, parking (free)* ▭*MC, V* ⊗*Closed Nov.–Easter* ⦿*BP*

EXETER

23 mi north of Torbay, 48 mi northeast of Plymouth, 85 mi southwest of Bristol, 205 mi southwest of London.

Devon's county seat, Exeter, has been the capital of the region since the Romans established a fortress here 2,000 years ago. Evidence of the Roman occupation remains in the city walls. Although it was heavily bombed in 1942, Exeter retains much of its medieval character, as well as examples of the gracious architecture of the 18th and 19th centuries.

GETTING HERE AND AROUND

Exeter is a major transportation hub for Devon. Trains from Bristol, Salisbury, and Plymouth stop at Exeter St David's, and connect to the center by frequent buses. Some trains also stop at the more useful Exeter Central. The bus station is off Paris Street near the tourist office. Cars are unnecessary in town, so park yours as soon as possible—all the sights are within an easy walk.

TOURS   Free 90-minute walking tours of Exeter by Red Coat guides take place daily all year, focusing on different aspects of the city. See ⊕*www. exeter.gov.uk/guidedtours* for details, or contact the tourist office. You can also pick up a leaflet on self-guided walks from here.

ESSENTIALS

Visitor Information Exeter (⊠*Dix's Field, Paris St.* ☎*01392/665700* ⊕*www. exeterandessentialdevon.com*).

EXPLORING
TOP ATTRACTIONS

❶ **Cathedral of St. Peter.** At the heart of Exeter, the great Gothic cathedral ★ was begun in 1275 and completed almost a century later. Its twin towers are even older survivors of an earlier Norman cathedral. Rising from a forest of ribbed columns, the nave's 300-foot stretch of unbroken Gothic vaulting is the longest in the world. Myriad statues, tombs, and memorial plaques adorn the interior. In the minstrels' gallery, high up on the left of the nave, stands a group of carved figures singing and playing musical instruments, including bagpipes. The **Close,** a pleasant green space for relaxing, surrounds the cathedral. Don't miss the 400-year-old door to No. 10, the bishop of Crediton's house, ornately carved with angels' and lions' heads. ⊠*Cathedral Close* ☎*01392/285983*

⊕*www.exeter-cathedral.org.uk* 🎫*£5* ⊙*Mon.–Sat. 9:30–5, Sun. open for services only. Guided tours Mar.–June and Oct., weekdays at 11 and 2:30, Sat. at 11; July–Sept., weekdays at 11, 12:30, and 2:30, Sat. at 11 and 12:30.*

OFF THE BEATEN PATH

Powderham Castle. Seat of the earls of Devon, this notable stately home 8 mi south of Exeter is famed for its staircase hall, a soaring fantasia of white stuccowork on a turquoise background, constructed in 1739–69. Other sumptuous rooms, adorned with family portraits by Sir Godfrey Kneller and Sir Joshua Reynolds, were used in the Merchant Ivory film *Remains of the Day.* A tower built in 1400 by Sir Philip Courtenay, ancestor of the current owners, stands in the deer park. The restaurant serves traditional English fare, and there's a farm shop and plant center. ⊠*A379, Kenton* 🕾*01626/890243* ⊕*www.powderham.co.uk* 🎫*£8.95* ⊙*Apr.–mid-July, Sept., and Oct., Sun.–Fri. 11–4:30; mid-July–Aug., Sun.–Fri. 11–5:30.*

❺ Royal Albert Memorial Museum. This museum houses natural-history displays, superb Exeter silverware, and the work of some West Country artists. There is also an excellent international gallery and a fine archaeological section. The property is undergoing a major refurbishment project and will be closed until early 2011. ⊠*Queen St.* 🕾*01392/665858* ⊕*www.exeter.gov.uk* 🎫*Free* ⊙*Mon.–Sat. 10–5.*

WORTH NOTING

❽ Custom House. Exeter's historic waterfront on the River Exe was the center of the city's medieval wool industry, and the Custom House, built in 1682 on the quay, attests to the city's prosperity. Victorian warehouses flank the city's earliest surviving brick building.

❸ Guildhall. Just behind the Close, this is said to be the oldest municipal building in the country still in use. The current hall, with its Renaissance portico, dates from 1330, although a guildhall has occupied this site since at least 1160. Its timber-braced roof, one of the earliest in England, dates from about 1460. The building may be closed during civic functions—call to check. ⊠*High St.* 🕾*01392/265500* 🎫*Free* ⊙*Weekdays 11–1 and 2–4, Sat. 10:30–12:30 (alternate Sat. only in winter).*

❷ Mol's Coffee House. With its half-timber facade bearing the coat of arms of Elizabeth I, this building (now a shoe shop), on the corner of Cathedral Close, is redolent of bygone times. It is said that Sir Francis Drake met his admirals here to plan strategy against the Spanish Armada in 1588.

❼ Quay House. This late-17th-century stone warehouse houses the Heritage Centre, with documents on the city's maritime history and an audiovisual display. ⊠*The Quay* 🕾*01392/271611* 🎫*Free* ⊙*Apr.–Oct., daily 10–5; Nov.–Mar., weekends 11–4.*

NEED A BREAK?

At the **Prospect Inn** (⊠*The Quay* 🕾*01392/273152*) you can contemplate the quayside comings and goings over a pint of real ale and a hot or cold meal. The nautical theme comes through in pictures and the ship's wheel hanging from the ceiling.

Railway Station

TO BARNSTAPLE

Northernhay Gardens

New North Rd.

Sidwell St.

Bampflyde St.

Bus Station

Queen St.

Gandy St.

Paris St.

Princesshay Shopping Centre

Northernhay St.

Iron Bridge

Paul St.

Bedford St.

Westernway

North St.

High St.

Cathedral Close

Princesshay

West

East

Southernhay

Southernhay

Mary Arches St.

South St.

City Wall

Fore St.

Market St.

Magdalen St.

Bartholomew St.

Bridge St.

Preston St.

Bull Meadow

New

Western Way

Quay Hill

Holloway St.

Commercial Rd.

TO TOPSHAM

0   200 yards
0   200 meters

Exe

KEY

i *Tourist information*

Exeter

④ Rougemont Gardens. These gardens behind the Royal Albert Memorial Museum were laid out at the end of the 18th century. The land was once part of the defensive ditch of Rougemont Castle, built in 1068 by decree of William the Conqueror. The gardens contain the original Norman gatehouse and the remains of the Roman city wall, the latter forming part of the ancient castle's outer wall; nothing else remains of the castle. ⊠*Off Queen St.*

⑥ Underground Passages. Exeter's Underground Passages, which once served as conduits for fresh water, are the only medieval vaulted passages open to the public in Britain. They date to the mid-14th century, although some were enlarged by the Victorians. An exhibition and video precede the 40-minute guided tour. Many of the passages are narrow and low: be prepared to stoop. Children under five are not permitted. ⊠*2 Paris St.* ☎*01392/665887* ⊕*www.exeter.gov.uk* ⊡*£4.90* ⊗*June–Sept. and school vacations, Mon.–Sat. 10–5, Sun. 10:30–3; Oct.–May, Tues.–Fri. noon–4:30, Sat. 10–5, Sun. 10:30–3; last tours 1 hr before closing.*

WHERE TO EAT

£

ITALIAN

✕**Ask.** This outpost of an Italian chain has secured an enviable site in a part-medieval, part-Georgian building opposite the cathedral. There are three dining areas. The large-windowed rooms offer superb views across the Close, the back room is older and has more atmosphere, and the courtyard is perfect for warm days. The food is unadventurous, with a generous choice of pizzas and pastas, but everything is prepared to high standards, including good antipasti and salads. ✉ *5 Cathedral Close* ☎ *01392/427127* ⊟ *AE, DC, MC, V.*

£ ✕ **Herbie's.** A mellow stop, this friendly vegetarian bistro is ideal for
VEGETARIAN unwinding over leisurely conversation. You can snack on pita bread
★ with hummus, or tackle the butternut squash and cashew nut loaf or spinach-and-mushroom lasagna. All the wines and the superb ice cream are organic. ✉ *15 North St.* ☎ *01392/258473* ⊟ *MC, V* ⊘ *Closed Sun. No dinner Mon.*

££££ ✕ **Michael Caines Restaurant.** Perfectly located within the Cathedral Close,
FRENCH this ultrachic restaurant is in the centuries-old building that is now the
★ Abode Exeter. Run by master chef Michael Caines (of Gidleigh Park fame), the kitchen serves French-accented contemporary fare such as beef sirloin with roasted shallots or fillet of sea bass with stir-fried mange-tout (snow peas), shiitake mushrooms, and lemongrass foam. Fixed-price early-evening menus offer a good value. Alternatively, a more relaxed (and more affordable) café-bar next door serves meals all day, including good fixed-price lunches; there's live jazz on alternate Friday evenings. The hotel's beautifully designed bedrooms have the same clean-line style. ✉ *Cathedral Yard* ☎ *01392/223638* ⊟ *AE, DC, MC, V* ⊘ *Restaurant closed Sun.*

£ ✕ **Ship Inn.** Here you can lift a tankard of stout in the very rooms where
BRITISH Sir Francis Drake and Sir Walter Raleigh enjoyed their ale. Drake, in fact, once wrote, "Next to mine own shippe, I do most love that old 'Shippe' in Exon." The pub dishes out casual bar fare, from curries to sausage and mash, either in the bar or the more secluded upstairs restaurant (lunchtime only). ✉ *St. Martin's La.* ☎ *01392/272040* ⊟ *MC, V.*

WHERE TO STAY

£–££ ⊡ **Georgian Lodge.** There's nothing fancy in this quiet hotel close by Exeter Central train station—just clean, modern, and functional rooms, small but more than adequate for a night or two. The main benefit is the location in a calm Georgian square, just a stroll away from all the sights. **Pros:** good value; central location; clean and tidy. **Cons:** small rooms; no parking. ✉ *5 Bystock Terr.* ☎ *01392/213079* ⊕ *www. georgianlodge.com* ⇆ *11 rooms* ⌂ *In-room: no a/c, Wi-Fi. In-hotel: Wi-Fi, no-smoking rooms,* ⊟ *MC, V* ⊘ *Closed 3 wks at Christmas* ⍟ *BP.*

££ ⊡ **St. Olaves Court Hotel.** In a hushed enclave in an unattractive part of Exeter's center, this hotel occupies a Georgian house with a walled garden. A privileged but unfussy air prevails, with an old-fashioned elegance in the spacious, pastel-color bedrooms. The first-rate Treasury Restaurant provides a sedate setting for fine dining. The bar menu is a cheaper lunchtime option. The shops nearby are lackluster, but the cathedral is only a few minutes away. **Pros:** intimate and refined atmosphere; secluded location in city center. **Cons:** some facilities rather dated; inadequate soundproofing. ✉ *Mary Arches St.* ☎ *01392/217736* ⊕ *www.olaves.co.uk* ⇆ *12 rooms, 2 suites* ⌂ *In-room: no a/c, Wi-Fi (some). In-hotel: restaurant, bar, Wi-Fi* ⊟ *MC, V.*

5

£ ⚄**White Hart.** Guests have been welcomed to this inn since the 15th century, and it is said that Oliver Cromwell stabled his horses here. Beyond the lovely cobbled entrance, the main building retains all the trappings of a period inn—beams, stone walls, courtyard—but there are more modern bedrooms in a separate wing. The hotel has a casual bar-restaurant where you can order such dishes as slow-cooked gammon, curries, and char-grills. **Pros:** plenty of atmosphere; friendly service. **Cons:** worn-down in places; modern wing lacks charm. ✉*66 South St.* ☎*01392/279897* ⊕*www.marstonsinnsandtaverns.co.uk* ↩*55 rooms* ⚘*In-room: Wi-Fi, no a/c. In-hotel: restaurant, bar, Wi-Fi, parking (free)* ▭*AE, MC, V* ⦿*BP.*

NIGHTLIFE AND THE ARTS

Among the best known of the West Country's festivals, the **Exeter Festival** (☎*01392/265200* ⊕*www.exeter.gov.uk/festival*) mixes musical and theater events over two weeks in June. The **Exeter Festival of South West Food and Drink** (⊕*www.exeterfoodanddrinkfestival.co.uk*) showcases local producers, chefs, and their gastronomic specialties, taking place in Rougemont Gardens and Northernhay Gardens in mid-April. Live music is staged in the evenings.Some of London's best companies often stage plays at the **Northcott Theatre** (✉*Stocker Rd.* ☎*01392/493493* ⊕*www.exeternorthcott.co.uk*).

SHOPPING

Many of Exeter's most interesting shops are along Gandy Street, off the main High Street drag, with several good food and clothes outlets. Exeter was the silver-assay office for the West Country, and the earliest example of Exeter silver (now a museum piece) dates from 1218; Victorian pieces are still sold. The Exeter assay mark is three castles. **Bruford's of Exeter** (✉*17 The Guildhall Centre, Queen St.* ☎*01392/254901*) stocks antique jewelry and silver.

SPORTS AND THE OUTDOORS

Saddles and Paddles (✉*4 Kings Wharf, the Quay* ☎*01392/424241*) rents bikes, kayaks, and canoes and is handily placed for a 7-mi route along the scenic Exeter Canal Trail, which follows the River Exe and the Exeter Ship Canal.

TOPSHAM

4 mi southeast of Exeter on B3182.

This town full of narrow streets and hidden courtyards was once a bustling port, and it remains rich in 18th-century houses and inns.

EXPLORING

Occupying a 17th-century Dutch-style merchant's house beside the river, the **Topsham Museum** has period-furnished rooms and displays on local and maritime history. One room has memorabilia belonging to the late actress Vivien Leigh. ✉*25 The Strand* ☎*01392/873244* ▭*Free* ☾*Apr.–Oct., Mon., Wed., and weekends 2–5.*

★ The 16-sided, nearly circular **A la Ronde,** surely one of the most unusual houses in England, was built in 1798 by two cousins inspired by the Church of San Vitale in Ravenna, Italy. Among the 18th- and

19th-century curiosities here is an elaborate display of feathers and shells. The house is 5 mi south of Topsham. ⊠*Summer La., on A376 near Exmouth* ☎*01395/265514* ⊕*www.nationaltrust.org.uk* ⊠*£6.40* ⊗*Mid-Mar.–Oct., Sat.–Wed. 11–5; last admission at 4:30.*

EN ROUTE

The **Jurassic Coast** (⊕*www.jurassiccoast.com*), from Exmouth to Studland Bay in Dorset, 95 mi to the east, has been designated a World Heritage Site because of the rich geological record of ancient rocks and fossils exposed here. The reddish, grass-topped cliffs of the region are punctuated by quiet seaside resorts such as Budleigh Salterton, Sidmouth, and Seaton. *For more information about the Jurassic Coast, see Lyme Regis in Chapter 4.*

HONITON

20 mi east of Topsham, 20 mi east of Exeter.

Handsome Georgian houses line Honiton's long High Street. Modern storefronts have intruded, but the original facades remain at second-floor level. For 300 years the town was known for lace making, and the industry was revived when Queen Victoria selected the fabric for her wedding veil in 1840. Lace has not been made here commercially since the early 20th century, but individuals keep up the craft.

ESSENTIALS
Visitor Information Honiton (⊠*Lace Walk Car Park, Dowell St.* ☎*01404/ 43716* ⊕*www.honiton.com*).

EXPLORING
After viewing the glorious collection of lace at **Allhallows Museum**—in what is claimed to be the town's oldest building—it's worth delving into the antiques shops where prized early examples are sold. ⊠*High St.* ☎*01404/44966* ⊕*www.honitonmuseum.co.uk* ⊠*£2* ⊗*Easter–Sept., weekdays 9:30–4:30, Sat. 9:30–1; Oct., weekdays 9:30–3:30, Sat. 9:30–12:30.*

WHERE TO EAT AND STAY

££ MODERN BRITISH

✕**The Holt.** For a satisfying lunch or dinner, try this pub and restaurant at the bottom of High Street. Downstairs is a vibrant, chattery pub with soft orange walls and fine Otter real ales; the buzz wafts upstairs, where you can dine on such dishes as smoked haddock and spiced risotto with tiger prawns, peas, and poached egg, and grilled sausage with chive mash. ⊠*178 High St.* ☎*01404/47707* ▤*MC, V* ⊗*Closed Sun. and Mon.*

££££ ★

▦**Combe House.** Rolling parkland surrounds this luxurious Elizabethan manor house. From the imposing Great Hall, with its huge, open fireplace, to the spacious, individually decorated bedrooms, the emphasis is on country-house style that unites antiques and modern comfort. The fixed-price restaurant prepares such sophisticated creations as quail ballotine with morels, and roast chicken breast with Jerusalem artichoke puree. You can fish on a 1½-mi stretch of the River Otter and explore Gittisham, just west of Honiton, once described as "the ideal English village" by Prince Charles. There's a two-night minimum stay on weekends. **Pros:** beautiful rural surroundings; romantic ambience;

attentive staff. **Cons:** a bit unkempt in places; rather remote. ⊠ *Gittisham* ☎*01404/540400* ⊕*www.thishotel.com* ⬚*13 rooms, 2 suites, 1 cottage* ⬚*In-room: no a/c, Internet, Wi-Fi (some). In-hotel: restaurant, Wi-Fi, some pets allowed* ⊟*MC, V* ⦶*BP.*

SHOPPING

Honiton has several dozen fine antiques stores. The **Grove Antiques Centre** (⊠ *55 High St.* ☎ *01404/43377*) is a good stop for antiques of all kinds, including art, furniture, and jewelry.

The Thames Valley

WINDSOR, HENLEY-ON-THAMES,
OXFORD, BLENHEIM PALACE

WORD OF MOUTH

"At Windsor Castle, the free audioguide is very good; they also offer tours (free). If you arrive after opening time, expect a line. I spent the first hour around the grounds, plus seeing St George's Chapel. I watched the Changing of the Guard (40 minutes) and got in line for the Doll's House and State Apartments. So, allot 3 to 4 hours"

—yk

"Christ Church Chapel is excellent and the dining hall is worth a look. Pleasant main quad. Magdalen College is definitely the best of Oxford's many colleges to visit. Has a very nice chapel, several striking towers, and an extensive park and grounds to walk in."

—bachslunch

Updated by
Kate Hughes

Once an aquatic highway connecting London to the rest of England and the world, the River Thames was critical to the power of the city when the sun never set on the British Empire. Easy proximity to the capital made the Thames Valley enormously popular with the rich and powerful throughout the country's history. They built the lavish country estates and castles, including Windsor, that form the area's most popular tourist attractions today. Some of these, as well as Oxford with its university, are easy day trips from London.

By the 18th century the Thames was one of the world's busiest water systems, declining in commercial importance only when the 20th century brought other means of transportation to the forefront. Along its 215-mi course the river runs from the Cotswolds through London and on to where it pours into the sea in Essex. Traditionally, the area west of London is known as the Thames Valley, and the area to the east is called the Thames Gateway.

Anyone who wants to understand the mystique of the British monarchy should visit Windsor, home to the medieval and massive Windsor Castle. Farther upstream, the green quadrangles and graceful spires of Oxford are the hallmarks of one of the world's most famous universities. Within 10 mi of Oxford the storybook village of Woodstock and gracious Blenheim Palace, one of the grandest houses in England, are both well worth your time.

The railroads and motorways carrying traffic to and from London have turned much of this area into commuter territory, but you can still find timeless villages and miles of relaxing countryside. The stretches of the Thames near Marlow, Henley, and Sonning-on-Thames are lovely, with rowing clubs, piers, and sturdy waterside cottages and villas. It all conspires to make the Thames Valley a wonderful find, even for experienced travelers.

ORIENTATION AND PLANNING

GETTING ORIENTED

An ideal place to begin any exploration of the Thames Valley is the town of Windsor, a journey of 1½ hours by car from central London. From there you can follow the river to Marlow and to Henley-on-Thames, site of the famous regatta, and then make a counterclockwise sweep west to the area around Sonning-on-Thames, the countryside immortalized by Kenneth Grahame's *The Wind in the Willows*. To the north is Oxford, with its pubs, colleges, and museums; it can make a good base

TOP REASONS TO GO

Windsor Castle: The mystique of eight successive royal houses of the British monarchy permeates Windsor and its famous castle, where a fraction of the current Queen's vast wealth is displayed in heraldic splendor.

Mapledurham House: While at this house that inspired Toad Hall from *The Wind in the Willows*, you can picnic on the grounds and drink in the views of the sleepy countryside.

Oxford: While scholars' noses are buried in their books, you get to sightsee among Oxford University's ancient stone buildings (look out for gargoyles around New College) and memorable museums. Try your luck at punting, too. You'll either proudly exhibit your balance and strength, or take a humiliating plunge into a slow-moving river.

Blenheim Palace: The only British historic home to be named a World Heritage Site has magnificent baroque architecture, stunning gardens and parkland, and remembrances of Winston Churchill. For a special treat, attend an outdoor summer concert.

for exploring some of the area's charming towns and notable stately homes. If you're extending your itinerary, west of the region but nearby are both the Cotswolds and Stratford-upon-Avon.

Windsor, Marlow, and Environs. Gorgeous Windsor has its fairy-tale palace, stone cottages, and tea shops, and nearby Eton is also charming. The meadows and villages around Marlow and Henley are lovely in summer when the flowers are in bloom. Mapledurham House near Sonning-on-Thames is an idyllic stop; you can take a boat here.

Oxford. Wonderfully walkable, this university town has one golden-stone building after another to explore. Take a punt on the local waterways for a break. Oxford's good bars, pubs, and restaurants keep you going late at night as well.

Blenheim Palace to Althorp. So many grand manor houses, so little time: around the Thames Valley are many intriguing stops. Blenheim is a vast, ornate, extraordinary place that takes the better part of a day to see. Althorp, home of the late Princess Diana, seems almost small by comparison, although it's actually enormous.

THAMES VALLEY PLANNER

WHEN TO GO

High summer is lovely, but droves of visitors have the same effect on some travelers as bad weather. Consider visiting in late spring or early fall, when the weather is not too bad and the crowds have headed home for the school year. Book tickets and accommodations well in advance for Henley's Royal Regatta at the cusp of June and July or Ascot's Royal Meeting in mid-June. Visiting at Eton and the Oxford colleges is much more restricted during term time (generally September to late March and late April to mid-July). Most stately homes are open March through September or October only—call in advance if you're planning an itinerary. Avoid any driving in the London area during afternoon and morning rush hours.

PLANNING YOUR TIME

The major towns of the Thames Valley are easy to visit on a day trip from London. A train to Windsor, for example, takes about an hour, and you can fully explore Windsor and its environs in a day. Base yourself in Oxford for a couple of days, though, if you want to make a thorough exploration of the town and the surrounding countryside. To visit the great houses and the rural castles you'll need to either rent a car or join an organized tour.

GETTING HERE AND AROUND

BUS TRAVEL

The area's main towns and also Oxford are convenient by bus from London, as is Windsor (although trains are faster), but St. Albans is best reached by train.

You can travel between the major towns by local bus, but it's complicated and can require changing more than once. For information, contact Traveline. If you want to see more than one town in this area in a day, it would be best to rent a car or join a tour.

Contacts Arriva (☎0871/200–2233 ⊕ www.arriva.co.uk.). **First** (☎01344/782200 ⊕ www.firstgroup.com). **Megabus** (⊕ www.megabus.co.uk). **Oxford Bus Company** (☎01865/785400 ⊕ www.oxfordbus.co.uk). **Reading Buses** (☎0118/959–4000 ⊕ www.reading-buses.co.uk). **Stagecoach Oxford Tube** (☎01865/772250 ⊕ www.oxfordtube.com) . **Traveline** (☎0871/200–2233 ⊕ www.traveline.org.uk).

CAR TRAVEL

Most towns in this area are within a one- or two-hour drive of central London—except during rush hour, of course. Although the roads are good, this wealthy section of the commuter belt has heavy traffic, even on the smaller roads. Parking in towns can be a problem, so expect to park in public parking lots near the outskirts of town centers.

TRAIN TRAVEL

Trains to Oxford (one hour) and the region depart from London's Paddington Station. Trains bound for Ascot (50 minutes) leave Waterloo on the half hour. Trains to St. Albans (30 minutes) leave from St. Pancras Station. A number of lines, including Chiltern and First Great Western, serve the area; National Rail Enquiries has information.

Contacts National Rail Enquiries (☎0845/748–4950 ⊕ www.nationalrail.co.uk).

RESTAURANTS

Londoners weekend here, and where they go, stellar restaurants follow. Windsor, Henley, and Great Milton (near Oxford) claim some excellent tables. Simple pub food, as well as classic French cuisine, can be enjoyed in waterside settings at many restaurants beside the Thames. Even in towns away from the river, well-heeled commuters and Oxford professors support top-flight establishments. Reservations are strongly recommended, especially on weekends.

HOTELS

From converted country houses to refurbished Elizabethan inns, the region's accommodations are rich in history and distinctive in appeal. Many hotels cultivate traditional gardens and retain a sense of the past with impressive collections of antiques. Book ahead, particularly in summer; you're competing for rooms with many Londoners in search of a getaway.

	£	££	£££	££££	£££££
WHAT IT COSTS IN POUNDS					
Restaurants	Under £10	£10–£14	£15–£19	£20–£25	over £25
Hotels	Under £70	£70–£120	£121–£160	£161–£220	over £220

Restaurant prices are for a main course at dinner. Hotel prices are for two people in a standard double room in high season, including V.A.T., with no meals or, if indicated, CP (with continental breakfast), BP (Breakfast Plan, with full breakfast), or MAP (Modified American Plan, with breakfast and dinner).

VISITOR INFORMATION

Contacts Southern and Southeast England Tourist Board (☎ *0238/062–5400* ⊕ *www.visitsoutheastengland.com*). **River Thames Alliance** (⊕ *www. visitthames.co.uk*).

WINDSOR, MARLOW, AND ENVIRONS

Windsor Castle is one of the jewels of the area known as Royal Windsor, but a journey around this section of the Thames has other classic pleasures. The town of Eton holds the eponymous public school, Ascot has its famous racecourse, and Cliveden is a stately home turned into a grand hotel.

The stretch of the Thames Valley from Marlow to Sonning-on-Thames is enchanting. Walking through its fields and along its waterways, it's easy to see how it inspired Kenneth Grahame's classic 1908 children's book *The Wind in the Willows*. Whether by boat or on foot, you can discover some of the region's most delightful scenery here. On each bank are fine wooded hills, with spacious homes, greenhouses, flower beds, and neat lawns that stretch to the water's edge. Grahame wrote his book in Pangbourne, and his illustrator, E.H. Shepard, used the great house at Mapledurham as the model for Toad Hall. It all still has the power to inspire.

WINDSOR

21 mi west of London.

Only a small part of old Windsor—the settlement that grew up around the town's famous castle in the Middle Ages—has survived. The town isn't what it was in the time of Sir John Falstaff and the *Merry Wives of Windsor,* when it was famous for its convivial inns—in 1650, it had about 70 of them. Only a handful remain, with the others replaced, it seems, by endless tea shops. Windsor can feel overrun by tourists in summer, but even so, romantics will appreciate cobbled Church Lane and noble Queen Charlotte Street, opposite the castle entrance.

GETTING HERE AND AROUND

Fast Green Line buses leave from the Colonnades opposite London's Victoria Coach Station every half hour for the 70-minute trip to Windsor. National Express has frequent service from Heathrow Airport's Terminal 5; the journey takes less than an hour. First Group offers regional bus services to small towns and villages near Windsor.

South West Trains travel from London Waterloo every 30 minutes, or you can catch a more frequent train from Paddington and change at Slough. The trip takes 50 minutes from Waterloo and 30 minutes from Paddington. If you're driving, take the M4 from London; journey time is about 1½ hours. Park in one of the public lots near the edge of the town center.

TOURS   Orchard Poyle Carriage Rides offers 30-minute (£20) and one-hour (£40) horse-drawn carriage rides around the historic district. Tours leave from the Harte & Garter Hotel in central Windsor and tour the town and Windsor Great Park. City Sightseeing has hop-on, hop-off tours of Windsor and Eton, though it's easy to explore compact Windsor on foot; the price is £8.

Windsor, Marlow, and Environs

TIMING

Windsor is at its best in the winter and fall when it's not as crowded with tour groups. In the summer it can be uncomfortably packed. Queen Elizabeth is in residence when her banner flies above the palace—everybody perks up a bit when that happens.

ESSENTIALS

Bus Contacts First (☎ 0175/352–4144 ⊕ www.firstgroup.com). **Green Line** (☎ 0870/608–7261 ⊕ www.greenline.co.uk). **National Express** (☎ 0871/781–8181 ⊕ www.nationalexpress.com).

Tour Information City Sightseeing (☎ 01789/299123 ⊕ www.city-sightseeing. com). **Orchard Poyle Carriage Rides** (☎ 01784/435983 ⊕ www.orchardpoyle. co.uk).

Visitor Information Windsor (✉ Old Booking Hall, Windsor Royal Station, Thames St. ☎ 01753/743900, 01753/743907 for accommodation ⊕ www. windsor.gov.uk).

EXPLORING

★ From William the Conqueror to Queen Victoria, the kings and queens of England added towers and wings to brooding, imposing **Windsor Castle,** visible for miles and now the largest inhabited castle in the world. Despite the multiplicity of hands involved in its design, the palace manages to have a unity of style and character. The most impressive view of Windsor Castle is from the A332 road, coming into town from the south. Admission includes an audio guide and, if you wish, a guided tour of the castle precincts. Entrance lines can be long in season, so come early.

William the Conqueror began work on the castle in the 11th century, and Edward III modified and extended it in the mid-1300s. One of Edward's largest contributions was the enormous and distinctive **Round Tower.** Finally, between 1824 and 1837, George IV transformed the still essentially medieval castle into the fortified royal palace you see today. Most of England's kings and queens have demonstrated their undying attachment to the castle, the only royal residence in continuous use by the Royal Family since the Middle Ages.

As you enter the castle, **Henry VIII's gateway** leads uphill into the wide castle precincts, where you are free to wander. Across from the entrance is the exquisite **St. George's Chapel** (closed Sunday). Here lie 10 of the kings of England, including Henry VI, Charles I, and Henry VIII (Jane Seymour is the only one of his six wives buried here). One of the noblest buildings in England, the chapel was built in the Perpendicular style popular in the 15th and 16th centuries, with elegant stained-glass windows, a high, vaulted ceiling, and intricately carved choir stalls. The colorful heraldic banners of the Knights of the Garter—the oldest British Order of Chivalry, founded by Edward III in 1348—hang in the choir. The ceremony in which the knights are installed as members of the order has been held here with much pageantry for more than five centuries.

The **North Terrace** provides especially good views across the Thames to Eton College, perhaps the most famous of Britain's exclusive "public" boys' schools. From the terrace, you enter the **State Apartments,** which are open to the public when the Queen is not in residence (call in advance to see if they're open). Queen Elizabeth uses the castle far more than any of her predecessors did, as a sort of country weekend home.

▬ TIP→ **To see the castle come magnificently alive, check out the Changing of the Guard, which takes place at 11** AM **Monday to Saturday from April through July and on alternate weekdays and Saturday from August through March.** Because the dates are changeable, confirm the exact schedule before traveling to Windsor. When the Queen is in town, the guard and a regimental band parade through town to the castle gate; when she is away, a drum-and-fife band takes over.

Although a fire in 1992 gutted some of the State Apartments, hardly any works of art were lost. Phenomenal repair work restored the **Grand Reception Room,** the **Green and Crimson Drawing Rooms,** and the **State and Octagonal Dining Rooms.** A green oak hammer-beam (a short horizontal roof beam that projects from the tops of walls for support) roof looms magnificently over the 600-year-old **St. George's Hall,** where the Queen gives state banquets. The State Apartments contain priceless furniture, including a magnificent Louis XVI bed and Gobelin tapestries; and paintings by Canaletto, Rubens, Van Dyck, Holbein, Dürer, and del Sarto. The tour's high points are the **Throne Room** and the **Waterloo Chamber,** where Sir Thomas Lawrence's portraits of Napoléon's victorious foes line the walls. You can also see arms and armor and an exhibition on the restoration of Windsor Castle.

🕙 **Queen Mary's Doll's House,** on display to the left of the entrance to the State Apartments, is a perfect miniature Georgian palace-within-a-palace, created in 1923. Electric lights glow, the doors all have tiny little keys, and water pours from the small faucets. A miniature library holds Lilliputian-size books especially written for the young Queen by famous authors of the 1920s. ⊠ *Castle Hill* ☎ *020/7766–7304 tickets, 01753/831118 recorded information* ⊕ *www.royalcollection. org.uk* 🖃 *£15.50 for Precincts, State Apartments, Gallery, St. George's Chapel, Albert Memorial Chapel, and Doll's House; £7.50 when State Apartments are closed* ☉ *Mar.–Oct., daily 9:45–5:15, last admission at 4; Nov.–Feb., daily 9:45–4:15, last admission at 3.*

> ### TIME FOR A CUPPA
>
> This is a tea-and-scones town, so having some in one of Windsor's many charming tearooms simply feels right. After taking in the castle and wandering the town's winding medieval lanes, a nice "cuppa," as the locals call it, is just perfect. **Crooked House of Windsor** (⊠ *51 High St.* ☎ *01753/857534*), with two tiny rooms in a 300-year-old house, is a traditional favorite for tea and plates of cakes and scones for £4–£7. It's open daily.

Just outside the castle, on St. Albans Street, the royal horses are kept in the **Royal Mews,** along with coaches and splendid crimson-and-gold harnesses. You can see the carriages and sometimes the horses.

The **Jubilee Garden,** created in 2002, has a stone bandstand used for concerts on summer Sunday afternoons. The garden begins at the main gates and extends to St. George's Gate on Castle Hill.

Windsor Great Park (☎ *01753/860222* ⊕ *www.theroyallandscape.co.uk*), the remains of an ancient royal hunting forest, stretches for some 5,000 acres south of Windsor Castle. Much of it is open to the public and can be seen by car (parking charges apply) or on foot, including its geographical focal points, the romantic 3-mi **Long Walk,** designed by Charles II to join castle and park, and **Virginia Water,** a 2-mi-long lake. A spectacular visitor center offers a good introduction to the surrounding landscape. The park contains one of Queen Victoria's most treasured residences, **Frogmore House** (☎ *020/7766–7305* ⊕ *www.royalcollection.org* 🖃 *House, gardens, and mausoleum £9.50 in May, £7 in Aug.* ☉ *May and Aug., selected days 10–5:30*). The sprawling white mansion is still a retreat for the Royal Family. The main horticultural delight of Windsor Great Park, the exquisite **Savill Garden** (⊠ *Wick La., Englefield Green, Egham* ☎ *01753/847518* ⊕ *www.theroyallandscape.co.uk* 🖃 *£7.50, £5.75 in winter* ☉ *Mar.–Oct., daily 10–6; Nov.–Feb., daily 10–4:30*), contains a tremendous diversity of trees and shrubs. You need a car to get to Savill Garden; it's 4 mi from Windsor castle.

WHERE TO EAT

Bray, a tiny village 6 mi outside Windsor, is known for its restaurants more than anything else.

££££££ ✕**Fat Duck.** One of the top restaurants in the country, and ranked by
MODERN BRITISH some reviewers among the best in the world, this extraordinary, discreet
Fodor'sChoice (there's no sign; look for the duck-inspired implements hanging outside)
★ Bray establishment packs in fans of hyper-creative, hyper-expensive cuisine. Reserve a table two months in advance. Innovative chef Heston
Blumenthal is famed for bizarre taste combinations—scrambled-egg-and-
bacon ice cream, for example—and the laboratory-like kitchen in which
this advocate of molecular gastronomy creates his dishes. The chef's
taster menu (£130) features the most adventuresome items, including
such dishes as snail porridge. The à la carte menu (£98 for three courses)
offers more approachable fare—sole Véronique with champagne gel, for
instance. Like the food, the interior blends traditional and contemporary
elements—modern art, exposed brick walls, and ancient wooden beams.
⊠*High St., Bray-on-Thames* ☎*01628/580333* ♨*Reservations essential* ▤*AE, DC, MC, V* ⊗*Closed Mon. No dinner Sun.*

£££ ✕**Hinds Head.** The Fat Duck's esteemed chef Heston Blumenthal also
BRITISH owns this traditional pub across the road, where he sells less extreme
dishes at more reasonable prices. The atmosphere and dress code are
relaxed, and the look of the place is historic, with low beams, polished
wood-panel walls, and brick fireplaces. A brilliant modern take on
traditional English cuisine, the food includes oxtail-and-kidney pudding, and rump steak with bone-marrow sauce and triple-cooked fries.
Bar snacks and sandwiches are available for weekday lunches as well.
⊠*High St., Bray-on-Thames* ☎*01628/626151* ▤*AE, MC, V* ⊗*No
dinner Sun.*

££££ ✕**Strok's Restaurant.** In Sir Christopher Wren's House Hotel—a man-
MODERN BRITISH sion built in 1676 by the architect who designed St. Paul's Cathedral—
Strok's offers an ever-changing modern British menu and a Thames-side
wooden terrace that swells with crowds in summer. Dishes may include
oak-smoked salmon with Avruga (herring) caviar followed by rump of
lamb with ratatouille and potato cake. ⊠*Thames St. at Eton Bridge*
☎*01753/861354* ▤*AE, DC, MC, V.*

££ ✕**Two Brewers.** Locals congregate in the two small, low-ceiling rooms
BRITISH of this 17th-century pub, right by the gates of Windsor Great Park.
Children are not welcome, but adults will find a suitable collection of
wine, espresso, and local beer, plus an excellent little menu with dishes
from salmon and lamb cutlets to salads. Reservations are essential on
Sunday, when the pub serves a traditional lunchtime roast. Fridays and
Saturdays are tapas nights. ⊠*34 Park St.* ☎*01753/855426* ▤*AE, MC,
V* ⊗*No dinner Sun.*

WHERE TO STAY

££ ▥**Alma Lodge.** This friendly little bed-and-breakfast in an early-
Victorian town house is just one of many that can be booked through
the Windsor tourist office. Ornate ceilings and ornamental fireplaces are
some of the house's original features, and each well-maintained room
is decorated in an uncluttered Victorian style. **Pros:** very welcoming;
beautiful fireplaces; good location. **Cons:** few frills; can be too quiet for
some. ⊠*58 Alma Rd.* ⊕*www.almalodge.co.uk* ➶*4 rooms* ♨*In-room:
no a/c, no phone, Wi-Fi. In-hotel: parking (free), some pets allowed,
no-smoking rooms* ▤*MC, V* ⦶*BP.*

££ ⊞**Langton House.** A former residence for Queen Victoria's local gov-
✄ ernment officials, this big Victorian mansion on a quiet, leafy road
is a 10-minute walk from Windsor Castle. Rooms are spacious and
unfussy, and the owner is eco-conscious. Guests have access to a small
kitchen with refrigerator, toaster, microwave, and kettle. This place
is very child-friendly, with supplies for babies. **Pros:** soothing decor;
family-friendly environment. **Cons:** not for those who prefer their privacy; a little out of town. ⊠*46 Alma Rd.* ☏*01753/858299* ⊕*www.
langtonhouse.co.uk* ✄*4 rooms* ⚡*In-room: Wi-Fi. In-hotel: Internet
terminal, parking (free), no-smoking rooms* ▭*MC, V* ⦶*BP.*

£££–££££ ⊞**Mercure Castle Hotel.** You get an exceptional view of the Changing
of the Guard from this Georgian hotel, parts of which date back much
further to its start in the 16th century as a coaching inn. In the older
section guest rooms have gently tilting floors, whereas elsewhere it's
smooth elegance, with tasteful fabrics in neutral tones juxtaposed
against original architectural detail. The cozy lounges are perfect for
afternoon tea. **Pros:** excellent location; wonderful afternoon tea. **Cons:**
older rooms are small; you can get a good bump on the head from the
low beams. ⊠*High St.* ☏*01753/851577* ⊕*www.mercure.com* ✄*108
rooms, 4 suites* ⚡*In-room: Internet. In-hotel: restaurant, room service,
bar, laundry service, parking (paid), no-smoking rooms* ⦶*BP* ▭*AE,
DC, MC, V.*

£££–££££ ⊞**Oakley Court.** A romantic getaway with plenty of pampering amenities, this Victorian-era Gothic mansion stands on landscaped grounds
beside the Thames, 3 mi west of Windsor. Its bristling towers and
spires have been used in several films, including *The Rocky Horror
Picture Show* and *Dracula*; note, however, that half the rooms are in
a modern annex. Guest rooms have an old-fashioned charm, though
the color schemes of the traditional stripes and prints may seem to
clash. The Dining Room restaurant (££££) serves continental cuisine
in plush surroundings. **Pros:** stunning mansion; tranquil riverside setting. **Cons:** many rooms in modern wing; snacks and drink can be
expensive. ⊠*Windsor Rd., Water Oakley* ☏*01753/609988* ⊕*www.
oakleycourt.co.uk* ✄*106 rooms, 12 suites* ⚡*In-room: safe, Wi-Fi. In-
hotel: restaurant, room service, bar, golf course, tennis courts, pool,
gym, spa, laundry service, parking (free), no-smoking rooms* ▭*AE,
DC, MC, V.*

NIGHTLIFE AND THE ARTS

Windsor's **Theatre Royal** (⊠*Thames St.* ☏*01753/853888*), where productions have been staged since 1910, is one of Britain's leading provincial theaters. It puts on plays and musicals year-round, including a
pantomime for the six weeks after Christmas.

Concerts, poetry readings, and children's events highlight the two-week
Windsor Festival (☏*01753/714364* ⊕*www.windsorfestival.com*), usually held in early September or October, with events occasionally taking
place in the castle.

6

SPORTS AND THE OUTDOORS

From Easter to September, **John Logie Motorboats** (✉ *Barry Ave.* 📧 *07774/ 983809*) rents motorboats and rowboats by the half hour and hour.

SHOPPING

Most Windsor stores are open Sunday as well as the rest of the week, particularly the antiques stores along Peascod Street, High Street, and King Edward Court. **Windsor Royal Station** (✉ *5 Goswell Hill* 📧 *01753/797070*), a collection of stores in a Victorian train station, includes Jaeger, Ghost, and arts-and-crafts stores.

ETON

23 mi west of London, linked by a footbridge across the Thames to Windsor.

Some observers may find it symbolic that almost opposite Windsor Castle—which embodies the continuity of the royal tradition—stands Eton, a school that for centuries has educated many future leaders of the country. With High Street, its single main street, leading from the river to the famous school, the old-fashioned town of Eton is much quieter than Windsor.

EXPLORING

★ The splendid redbrick Tudor-style buildings of **Eton College,** founded in 1440 by King Henry VI, border the north end of High Street; signs warn drivers of BOYS CROSSING. During the college semesters, the schoolboys dress in their distinctive pinstripe trousers, swallow-tail coats, and stiff collars (top hats have not been worn by the boys since the 1940s) to walk to class, and it's all terrifically photogenic. The Gothic **Chapel** rivals St. George's at Windsor in size and magnificence, and is both impressively austere and intimate. Beyond the cloisters are the school's playing fields where, according to the duke of Wellington, the Battle of Waterloo was really won, since so many of his officers had learned discipline and strategy during their school days there. The **Museum of Eton Life** has displays on the school's history. ✉ *Main entrance Brewhouse Yard* 📧 *01753/671177* 🌐 *www.etoncollege.com* 🎟 *£5* 🕐 *Guided tours at 2 and 3:15: mid-Mar.–mid-Apr. and July–early Sept., daily; mid-Apr.–June and mid-Sept.–early Oct., Wed. and Fri.–Sun.; early Oct.–Nov., Wed. and Fri.*

WHERE TO EAT AND STAY

£££   ✕ **Gilbey's Bar & Restaurant.** Just over the bridge from Windsor, this res-
BRITISH   taurant at the center of Eton's Antiques Row serves a fine, changing menu of imaginative fare, from goat cheese on thyme-and-honey French toast to pigeon and quail with a pistachio-and-herb risotto. There's a fixed-price lunch and early dinner menu for £14.50. Well-priced French wines are a specialty. The conservatory, with its colorful scattering of cushions, is a particularly pleasant place to sit in fine weather. ✉ *82–83 High St.* 📧 *01753/854921* 🚪 *AE, DC, MC, V.*

£££–££££   🏨 **Christopher Hotel.** Sister to Sir Christopher Wren's Hotel in Windsor, this former coaching inn on the main shopping street has spacious rooms in the main building as well as in the courtyard mews. Rooms have been renovated in a sleek, modern style; those in the courtyard have more privacy and space. Christopher's Bar and Grill serves classic English and American dishes, including hamburgers, rib-eye steaks, and braised lamb shank with mashed sweet potatoes. **Pros:** a nice mix of modern and historic; good restaurant. **Cons:** steep stairs and no elevator; restaurant can get booked up early. ⊠*110 High St.* ☎*01753/852359* ⊕*www.thechristopher.co.uk* *33 rooms* In-room: Internet In-hotel: restaurant, room service, bar, Wi-Fi, parking (free), some pets allowed, no-smoking rooms ⊟*AE, MC, V.*

ASCOT

8 mi southwest of Windsor, 28 mi southwest from London.

The town of Ascot (pronounced *as*-cut) has for centuries been famous for horse racing and for style. Queen Anne chose to have a racecourse here, and the first race meeting took place in 1711. The impressive show of millinery for which the Royal Meeting, or Royal Ascot, is also known was immortalized in *My Fair Lady,* in which osprey feathers and black-and-white silk roses transformed Eliza Doolittle into a grand lady. Betting on the races is as important as dressing up; it's all part of the fun.

EXPLORING

Ascot Racecourse (⊠*A329* ☎*0870/727–1234* ⊕*www.ascot.co.uk*) continues to look gloriously upper class. The races run regularly throughout the year, and Royal Ascot takes place annually in June. ■**TIP→Purchase tickets well in advance. Tickets for Royal Ascot generally go on sale in January.** Prices range from £16 for standing room on the heath to £60 for seats in the stands.

WHERE TO STAY

£££　**MacDonald Berystede Hotel & Spa.** With its turrets and half-timbering, this Victorian-era hotel is a magnificent neo-Gothic fantasy on 9 acres of countryside. The overall feeling is traditional, thanks to the patterned curtains and busy carpets. Most rooms have been renovated with a modern style, and dark brown and toffee shades predominate. Notable amenities are the luxurious spa, indoor pool, and high-tech gym. The Hyperion restaurant serves modern British cuisine. **Pros:** lovely historic building; relaxing spa; all the modern conveniences. **Cons:** restaurant is a bit old-fashioned; pool tends to be crowded. ⊠*Bagshot Rd.* ☎*0844/879–9104* ⊕*www.macdonaldhotels.co.uk/berystede* *119 rooms, 10 suites* In-room: safe, Internet. In-hotel: restaurant, room service, bar, pool, gym, spa, laundry service, some pets allowed, no-smoking rooms ⊟*AE, DC, MC, V* *BP.*

CLIVEDEN

8 mi northwest of Windsor, 16 mi north of Ascot, 26 mi west of London.

EXPLORING

Described by Queen Victoria as a "bijou of taste," **Cliveden** is a magnificent country mansion that has for more than 300 years lived up to its Georgian heritage as a bastion of aesthetic delights. The house, set in 376 acres of gardens and parkland above the River Thames, was rebuilt for the duke of Sutherland by Sir Charles Barry in 1861; the Astors, who purchased it in 1893, made it famous. In the 1920s and '30s the Cliveden Set met here at the strongly conservative (not to say fascist) salon presided over by Nancy Astor, who—though she was an American—was the first woman to sit in Parliament, in 1919. Cliveden now belongs to the National Trust, which leases it as a *very* exclusive hotel. The public can visit the spectacular grounds that run down to bluffs overlooking the Thames and, by timed ticket (£1) on a limited basis, three rooms in the house. ⊠ *Off A404, Taplow* ⊕ *Near Maidenhead* ☎ *01628/605069, 01494/755562 recorded information* ⊕ *www.nationaltrust.org.uk* ✉ *Grounds £8, woodlands £3, house £1.* ⊙ *Grounds Mar.–Oct., daily 11–6; Nov. and Dec., daily 11–4. House Apr.–Oct., Thurs. and Sun. 3–5:30.*

WHERE TO STAY

££££ ⓣ**Cliveden.** If you've ever wondered what it would feel like to be an
Fodor's Choice Edwardian grandee, splurge for a stay at this stately home, one of
★ Britain's grandest hotels. Cliveden's opulent interior includes art such as John Singer Sargent's portrait of Nancy Astor (in the Great Hall), suits of armor, and a paneled staircase. The plush traditional bedrooms each bear the name of someone famous who has stayed here. Waldo's, one of three restaurants, serves excellent contemporary British and French cuisine. If your pocket doesn't rise to a night here, you can drop in for a luxurious afternoon tea (£25). **Pros:** like stepping back in time; outstanding sense of luxury. **Cons:** can be rather stuffy; you might feel underdressed if you don't have designer duds. ⊠ *Off A404 near Maidenhead, Taplow* ☎ *01628/668561* ⊕ *www.clivedenhouse. co.uk* ↙ *38 rooms, 1 cottage* ⅂ *In-room: no a/c (some), safe, Wi-Fi. In-hotel: 3 restaurants, room service, bar, tennis courts, pool, gym, spa, laundry service, no-smoking rooms, some pets allowed* ⊟ *AE, DC, MC, V* ⦿ *BP.*

OUTDOORS

Cliveden Boathouse (⊠ *Off A404 near Maidenhead, Taplow* ☎ *01628/ 668561*) at Cliveden hotel has two vintage boats and a vintage electric canoe that ply the Thames. The champagne sunset cruise (most days April through September at 5 and 6:15) is the most affordable at £45 per person; you can rent the boats, too.

MARLOW

7 mi west of Cliveden, 15 mi northwest of Windsor.

Just inside the Buckinghamshire border, Marlow and the surrounding area overflow with Thames-side prettiness. The unusual suspension bridge was built in the 1830s by William Tierney Clark, architect of the bridge linking Buda and Pest. Marlow has a number of striking old buildings, particularly the privately owned Georgian houses along Peter and West streets. In 1817 the Romantic poet Percy Bysshe Shelley stayed with friends at 67 West Street and then bought **Albion House** on the same street. His second wife, Mary, completed her Gothic novel *Frankenstein* here. **Marlow Place**, on Station Road, dates from 1721 and has been home to several princes.

Marlow hosts its own one-day regatta in mid-June. The town is a good base from which to join the **Thames Path** to Henley-on-Thames. On summer weekends, tourism can often overwhelm the town.

ESSENTIALS

Visitor Information Marlow (⊠ *31 High St.* ☎ *01628/483597*).

EXPLORING

Swan-Upping (☎ *01628/523030*), a traditional event that dates back 800 years, takes places in Marlow during the third week of July. By bizarre ancient laws, the Queen owns the country's swans, so each year swan-markers in skiffs start from Sunbury-on-Thames, catching the new cygnets and marking their beaks to establish ownership. The Queen's swan keeper, dressed in scarlet livery, presides over this colorful ceremony.

WHERE TO EAT AND STAY

££££ ✕**Vanilla Pod.** Discreet and intimate, this restaurant is a showcase for
FRENCH French-inspired cuisine by chef Michael Macdonald. Some of the best choices on the fixed-price menu are the pork with maple syrup carrot risotto, and the poached sea bass with fennel and pollen cream. For dessert, indulge in hazelnut mille-feuille and bitter-chocolate ice cream. The £19.50 fixed-price lunch menu offers a fantastic bargain, and the seven-course *menu gourmand* for £50 is a tour de force. ⊠ *31 West St.* ☎ *01628/898101* ⚑ *Reservations essential* ⊟ *AE, MC, V* ⊘ *Closed Sun. and Mon.*

£££–££££ ⊞**Macdonald Compleat Angler.** Although fishing aficionados consider this luxurious 17th-century Thames-side inn the ideal place to stay, the place is stylish enough to attract those with no interest in casting a line. The name comes from Isaak Walton's 1653 masterpiece of angling advice and philosophy, which he wrote in this area. Rooms are subtly decorated in earth tones and cozy fabrics, and many have views over the Thames. The hotel's two restaurants offer outstanding modern British cooking with waterside views. A sunny conservatory serves afternoon tea. **Pros:** gorgeous rooms; great views of the Thames. **Cons:** nonanglers might find dinner conversation dull; need a car to get around; breakfast not included in rate. ⊠ *Marlow Bridge, Bisham Rd.* ☎ *0844/879–9128* ⊕ *www.macdonaldhotels.co.uk/compleatangler* ⇌ *61 rooms, 3 suites* ⚏ *In-room: no a/c, safe, refrigerator, Internet,*

BOATING ALONG THE THAMES

One ideal way to see the Thames region is from the water. Water-based tours can range from 30 minutes to all day. Hobbs and Sons covers the Henley Reach and also rents boats if you want to take the active approach. Salter's Steamers runs daily steamer cruises, mid-May to mid-September from Windsor, Oxford, Abingdon, Henley, Marlow, and Reading. Thames River Cruises conducts outings from Caversham Bridge in Reading, Easter through September. French Brothers operates river trips from the Promenade in Windsor, and from Runnymede going as far as Hampton Court.

The Environment Agency's Visit Thames Web site and telephone hotline provide information about boating, fishing, and walking the Thames.

CONTACTS AND RESOURCES
Environment Agency Visit Thames (☎ *0845/601–5336* ⊕ *www. visitthames.com*). **French Brothers** (✉ *The Promenade, Windsor* ☎ *01753/851900* ⊕ *www. boat-trips.co.uk*). **Hobbs and Sons** (✉ *Station Rd., Henley-on-Thames* ☎ *01491/572035* ⊕ *www. hobbs-of-henley.com*). **Salter's Steamers** (✉ *Folly Bridge, Oxford* ☎ *01865/243421* ⊕ *www. salterssteamers.co.uk*). **Thames River Cruises** (✉ *Caversham Bridge, Reading* ☎ *0118/948–1088* ⊕ *www.thamesrivercruise.co.uk*).

Wi-Fi. In-hotel: 2 restaurants, room service, bars, some pets allowed, no-smoking rooms ▭ *AE, DC, MC, V.*

HENLEY-ON-THAMES

7 mi southwest of Marlow, 8 mi north of Reading, 36 mi west of central London.

Henley's fame is based on one thing: rowing. The Henley Royal Regatta, held at the cusp of June and July on a long, straight stretch of the River Thames, has made the little riverside town famous throughout the world. Townspeople launched the Henley Regatta in 1839, initiating the Grand Challenge Cup, the most famous of its many trophies. The best amateur oarsmen from around the globe compete in crews of eight, four, or two, or as single scullers. For many spectators, however, the event is on par with Royal Ascot and Wimbledon.

The town is set in a broad valley between gentle hillsides. Henley's historic buildings, including half-timber Georgian cottages and inns (as well as one of Britain's oldest theaters, the Kenton), are all within a few minutes' walk. The river near Henley is alive with boats of every shape and size, from luxury cabin cruisers to tiny rowboats.

GETTING HERE AND AROUND

There are frequent First Great Western trains to Henley from London Paddington; journey time is around an hour. If you're driving from London or from the west, leave M4 at Junction 8/9; follow A404(M) and then A4130 to Henley Bridge. From Marlow, Henley is a 7-mi drive southwest on A4155.

ESSENTIALS

Visitor Information Henley-on-Thames (✉ *King's Arms Barn, Kings Rd.* ☎ *01491/578034* ⊕ *www.henley-on-thames.org*).

EXPLORING

The 16th-century "checkerboard" tower of **St. Mary's Church** overlooks Henley's bridge on Hart Street. If the church's rector is about, ask permission to climb to the top to take in the superb views up and down the river. The adjacent, yellow-washed **Chantry House,** built in 1420, is one of England's few remaining merchant houses from the period. It is an unspoiled example of the rare timber-frame design, with upper floors jutting out. ✉ *Hart St.* ☎ *01491/577062* ☞ *Free* ☉ *By appointment.*

☾ The handsome **River & Rowing Museum** focuses not just on the history and sport of rowing but on the Thames and the town itself. One gallery interprets the Thames and its surroundings as the river flows from its source to the ocean; another explores Henley's history and the regatta. Galleries devoted to rowing display models and actual boats, from Greek triremes to lifeboats to sleek modern rowing boats. A *Wind in the Willows* exhibit evokes the settings of the famous children's book. ✉ *Mill Meadows* ☎ *01491/415600* ⊕ *www.rrm.co.uk* ☞ *£7* ☉ *May–Aug., daily 10–5:30; Sept.–Apr., daily 10–5.*

This section of the Thames inspired Kenneth Grahame's 1908 *The Wind in the Willows,* which began as a bedtime story for Grahame's son Alastair while the family lived at Pangbourne. Some of E. F. Shepard's illustrations are of specific sites along the river—none more fabled than ★ **Mapledurham House,** a redbrick Elizabethan mansion, bristling with tall chimneys, mullioned windows, and battlements. It became the inspiration for Shepard's vision of Toad Hall. The Eyston family, descendants of longtime owners of the estate, still lives at Mapledurham, and the house seems warm and friendly even with all the family portraits, magnificent oak staircases, and Tudor plasterwork ceilings. There's also a 15th-century working grain mill on the river. The house is 5 mi west of Sonning-on-Thames and 10 mi southwest of Henley-on-Thames. On summer weekends you can reach the house by a **Thames River Cruises** (☎ *0118/948–1088*) boat from Caversham Promenade in Reading. Departures are at 2 PM, and travel time is 45 minutes. You can linger at one of the seven rental cottages around the estate (from £335 a week). ✉ *Off A074, Mapledurham* ⊹ *Near Reading* ☎ *0118/972–3350* ⊕ *www.mapledurham.co.uk* ☞ *House and mill £6.75; house only, £4.25; grounds and mill £3.25* ☉ *Easter–Sept., weekends and national holiday Mon. 2–5:30.*

WHERE TO EAT AND STAY

£££ ✕**Crooked Billet.** The notice on the door of this cozy 17th-century coun-
BRITISH try pub, offering an exchange of local, homegrown produce for lunch, tells you what you might expect inside. Local rabbit and free-range chicken may be served with wild garlic, field mushrooms, or braised barley; partridge with sloe gin; and British cheeses with homemade oatcakes. There's a garden for alfresco dining and regular music evenings. Foodies come from far and wide, so book ahead. Fixed-price lunches are another option. ✉ *Newlands La., Stoke Row* ⊹ *6 mi west*

6

of Henley-on-Thames, off B481
☎*01491/681048* ☰*MC, V.*

££   🖼️ **Falaise House.** The rooms in this Georgian town house in the center of Henley are furnished in a sympathetic contemporary style, with a mixture of antique and modern décor that is soft and warm. There are luxurious Egyptian cotton sheets on the beds and crisp white linens on the breakfast tables, where the long menu lists choices from scrambled eggs with smoked salmon to eggs with ham and mushrooms. **Pros:** family-run; great breakfasts. **Cons:** some rooms face the main road. ⊠*37 Market Pl. RG9 2AA* ☎*01491/573388* ⊕*www.falaisehouse.com* ⇆*6 rooms* ♿*In-room: no a/c, no phone, Internet, Wi-Fi. In hotel: no kids under 8* ☰*MC, V* ⦿|*BP.*

WALK THE CHILTERNS

Part of the Chiltern Hills is an Area of Outstanding Beauty (⊕*www.chilternsaonb.org*), a nature reserve that stretches over 320 square mi, taking in chalk hills, valleys, forests, lakes, and pretty towns. Its springtime bluebell woods are famed, and its autumn colors are glorious. The distinctive chestnut-color birds soaring above you will be red kites. You'll likely drive in and out of the Chilterns as you explore, or you could walk part of the circular 124-mi Chiltern Way. A 13-mi section starts in Henley, runs north through the Hambleden Valley, and returns to Henley via the Assendons.

£££–££££   🖼️ **Hotel du Vin.** A sprawling brick brewery near the river has been transformed into a distinctively modern architectural showplace. Bedrooms have beige carpeting and whitewashed walls—everything else is black. The original brewery windows appear in strange places, and staircases are contorted to fit the space. Still, the minimalist ethic makes this hotel a pleasure. Wine gets special attention in the bar and bistro. **Pros:** astonishing decor; lovely river views from upper floors; good for oenophiles. **Cons:** won't thrill traditionalists; not everyone will like the stark black-and-white decor; there's a charge for parking. ⊠*New St.* ☎*01491/848400* ⊕*www.hotelduvin.com* ⇆*43 rooms* ♿*In-room: DVD, refrigerator, Internet, Wi-Fi. In-hotel: restaurant, room service, bar, no-smoking rooms* ☰*AE, MC, V.*

NIGHTLIFE AND THE ARTS

A floating stage and spectacular musical events from classical to folk, as well as some art activities, draw a dress-code-abiding crowd to the upscale **Henley Festival** (☎*01491/843404* ⊕*www.henley-festival.co.uk*) during the week after the regatta in July. Book tickets ahead.

ROWING

Henley Royal Regatta (☎*01491/572153* ⊕*www.hrr.co.uk*), a series of rowing competitions that draw participants from many countries, takes place in late June and early July each year. Large tents are erected along both sides of the unique straight stretch of river here known as Henley Reach, and every surrounding field becomes a parking lot. There is plenty of space on the public towpath from which to watch the early stages of the races. ■**TIP→** **If you want to attend, book a room months in advance.** After all, 500,000 people, including members of the Royal Family, attend the event.

OXFORD

With arguably the most famous university in the world, Oxford has been a center of learning since 1167, with only the Sorbonne preceding it. It doesn't take more than a day or two to explore its winding medieval streets, snap some photographs of its ivy-covered stone buildings and ancient churches and libraries, and even take a punt down one of its placid, picturesque waterways. The town center is compact and walkable, and at its heart is Oxford University. Alumni of this prestigious institution include 47 Nobel Prize winners, 25 British prime ministers (including former Prime Minister Tony Blair), and 28 foreign presidents (including former U.S. President Bill Clinton), along with poets, authors, and artists such as Percy Bysshe Shelley, Oscar Wilde, and W.H. Auden. Except for its modern storefronts, the city looks much as it has for hundreds of years, in part because Adolf Hitler had vague plans to make it his European capital and so spared it from bombings. Victorian writer Matthew Arnold described Oxford's "dreaming spires," a phrase that has become famous. Students rush past you on the sidewalks on the way to their exams, clad with marvelous antiquarian style in their requisite mortar caps, flowing dark gowns, stiff collars, and crisp white bow ties. ■ TIP→ **Tip: In term time the city is awash with bikes. Watch your back when crossing roads; cycles are silent.**

Oxford is 55 mi northwest of London, at the junction of the Thames and Cherwell rivers. The city is more interesting and more cosmopolitan than Cambridge, and although it's also bigger, its suburbs are not remotely interesting to visitors. The interest is all at the center, where the old town curls around the grand stone buildings, good restaurants, and historic pubs.

GETTING HERE AND AROUND

Megabus, Oxford Bus Company, and Oxford Tube all have buses traveling from London 24 hours a day; the trip takes about one hour and 40 or 50 minutes. In London, Megabus departs from Victoria Coach Station, and Oxford Bus Company and Oxford Tube have pickup points near Victoria Train Station and Baker Street and Marble Arch Underground stations. Oxford Bus Company also offers round-trip shuttle service from Gatwick (£30) every hour and Heathrow (£22) every half hour. Most of the companies have multiple stops in Oxford, with the final stop being the most convenient for most travelers. You can easily traverse the town center on foot, but the Oxford Bus Company offers a one-day ticket (£6) and seven-day (£19) passes for unlimited travel within Oxford.

Trains to Oxford depart from London's Paddington station for the one-hour trip. Oxford Station is just at the edge of the historic town center on Botley Road.

By car, the M40 heads northwest from London. It's an hour's drive, except during rush hour, when it can take twice as long. In-town parking is notoriously difficult, so use one of the five park-and-ride lots (free) and pay for the bus to the city. The Thornhill Park and Ride and the St. Clement's parking lot before the roundabout that leads to Magdalen Bridge are convenient for the M40.

Oxford

TO SUMMERTOWN

TO WALTON STREET AND JERICHO

University Parks

Science Area

0   220 yards
0   200 meters

Little Clarendon St.

Woodstock Rd.

Banbury Rd.

Keble Rd.

Keble College

Museum Rd.

11   **10**

South Parks Rd.

St. Cross Rd.

Mansfield College

Mansfield Rd.

Pusey St.

St. Giles

8

Trinity College

Parks Rd.

Wadham College

Savile Rd.

Jowett Walk

St. Cross Rd.

Magdalen Grove

Deer Park

St. John St.

Pusey La.

9

Magdalen St.

Beaumont St.

Holywell St.

Gloucester Green

Broad St.

Bodleian Library

6   **5**

Catte St.

New College La.

7

Queen's La.

Bus Station

George St.

TO TRAIN STATION

St. Michael's St.

Ship St.

Turl St.

4

3

Queen's College

Longwall St.

TO ADDISON'S WALK

Magdalen Grove

New Inn Hall St.

Cornmarket

Clarendon Shopping Centre

Market St.

Covered Market

High St.

(The High)

Oriel College

Bear Lane

Magpie La.

All Souls College

High St.

Rose La.

1

New Rd.

Castle St.

St. Ebb's St.

Queen St.

Shoe La.

12

St. Aldate's

Blue Boar St.

Main Post Office

Pembroke St.

Oriel St.

14

13

Merton St.

Merton College

Dead Man's Walk

2

TO A40 AND M40

TO MAGDALEN BRIDGE

Norfolk St.

Westgate Shopping Center

Brewer St.

Rose Pl.

Corpus Cristi College

Merton Field

Clarks Row

Speedwell St.

Thames St.

Broad Walk

New Walk

Christ Church Meadow

Cherwell

Thames

Folly Bridge

Abingdon Rd.

Isis

KEY

𝑖   Tourist information

TOURS The Oxford Tourist Information Centre has information on the many guided walking tours of the city. The best way of gaining access to the collegiate buildings is to take the university and city tour, which leaves the Tourist Information Centre daily at 11 and 2. City Sightseeing offers hop-on, hop-off bus tours (£11.50) with 20 stops around Oxford; your ticket, purchased from the driver, is good for 24 hours.

TIMING

You can explore major sights in town in a day or so, but you'll need more than a day to spend an hour in all of the key museums and absorb the scene at the colleges. Some colleges are open only in the afternoons during university terms. When the undergraduates are in residence, access is often restricted to the chapels, dining rooms, and libraries, too, and you are requested to refrain from picnicking in the quadrangles. All are closed certain days during exams, usually from mid-April to late June.

ESSENTIALS

Bus Contacts Oxford Bus Company (☎ *01865/785400* ⊕ *www.oxfordbus. co.uk*). **Stagecoach Oxford Tube** (☎ *01865/772250* ⊕ *www.oxfordtube.com*).

Visitor and Tour Information City Sightseeing (☎ *01865/790522* ⊕ *www. citysightseeingoxford.com*). **Oxford Tourist Information Centre** (✉ *15/16 Broad St.* ☎ *01865/252200* ⊕ *www.visitoxford.org*).

EXPLORING OXFORD

Oxford University is not one easily identifiable campus, but a sprawling mixture of 38 colleges scattered around the city center, each with its own distinctive identity and focus. Oxford students live and study at their own college, and also use the centralized resources of the overarching university. The individual colleges are deeply competitive. Most of the grounds and magnificent dining halls and chapels are open to visitors, though the opening times (displayed at the entrance gates) vary greatly.

The city center of Oxford is bordered by High Street, St. Giles, and Longwall Street. Most of Oxford University's most famous buildings are within this area. Jericho, the neighborhood where many students live, is west of St. Giles, just outside the city center. Its narrow streets are lined with lovely cottages. The area north of the center around Banbury and Marston Ferry roads is called Summertown, and the area east of the center, along St. Clement's Street, is known as St. Clement's.

TOP ATTRACTIONS

❾ **Ashmolean Museum.** Britain's oldest public museum, due to reopen in ★ late 2009, displays its rich and varied collections over five floors. Innovative galleries on the theme of "Crossing Cultures, Crossing Time" explore connections between the priceless Egyptian, Greek, Roman, and Indian artifacts, and also display more recent art. Among the highlights are drawings by Raphael, the mantle of Powhatan (father of Pocahontas), and the Alfred Jewel. This ancient piece features a large semiprecious stone set in gold carved with the words AELFRED MEC HEHT GEWYRCAN, which translates from old English as "Alfred ordered me to be made." The piece dates from the reign of King Alfred the Great (ruled 871–899). ✉ *Beaumont St.* ☎ *01865/278000* ⊕ *www. ashmolean.org* ☞ *Free* ☉ *Tues.–Sat. 10–5, Sun. noon–5.*

⓭ **Christ Church.** Built in 1546, the college of Christ Church is referred to by its members as "The House." This is the site of Oxford's largest quadrangle, Tom Quad, named after the huge bell (6¼ tons) that hangs in the Christopher Wren–designed gate tower and rings 101 times at five past nine every evening in honor of the original number of Christ Church scholars. The vaulted, 800-year-old chapel in one corner has been Oxford's cathedral since the time of Henry VIII. The college's medieval dining hall contains portraits of many famous alumni, including John Wesley, William Penn, and 13 of Britain's prime ministers. A reproduction of this room appears in the banquet scenes at Hogwarts School in the *Harry Potter* films. Lewis Carroll, author of *Alice in Wonderland,* was a teacher of mathematics here for many years; a shop opposite the meadows on St. Aldate's sells Alice paraphernalia. ✉ *St. Aldate's* ☎ *01865/276492* ⊕ *www.chch. ox.ac.uk* ☞ *£6* ☉ *Mon.–Sat. 9–5, Sun. 2–5.*

⓮ **Christ Church Picture Gallery.** This connoisseur's delight in Canterbury Quadrangle exhibits works by the Italian masters as well as Hals, Rubens, and Van Dyck. Drawings in the 2,000-strong collection are shown on a changing basis. ✉ *Oriel Sq.* ☎ *01865/276172* ⊕ *www. chch.ox.ac.uk* ☞ *£3* ☉ *May–Sept., Mon.–Sat. 10:30–5, Sun. 2–5; Oct.–Apr., Mon.–Sat. 10:30–1 and 2–4:30, Sun. 2–4:30.*

❶ **Magdalen College.** Founded in 1458, with a handsome main quadrangle ★ and a supremely monastic air, Magdalen (pronounced *maud*-lin) is one of the most impressive of Oxford's colleges and attracts its most artistic students. Alumni include such diverse people as Cardinal Wolsey, P.G. Wodehouse, Edward Gibbon, Oscar Wilde, Dudley Moore, and U.S. Supreme Court Justice David Souter. The school's large, square tower is a famous local landmark. ■TIP→ **A stroll around the Deer Park and along Addison's Walk is a good way to appreciate the place.** ✉ *High St.* ☎ *01865/276000* ⊕ *www.magd.ox.ac.uk* ☞ *£4* ☉ *July–Sept., daily noon–6; Oct.–June, daily 1–6.*

⓫ **Oxford University Museum of Natural History.** This highly decorative Victorian Gothic creation of cast iron and glass, more a cathedral than a museum, is worth a visit for its architecture alone. Among the eclectic collections of entomology, geology, mineralogy, and zoology are the towering skeleton of a Tyrannosaurus rex and casts of a dodo's foot and head. There's plenty for children to explore and touch. The museum is adjacent to the Pitt Rivers Museum. ✉ *Parks Rd.* ☎ *01865/272950* ⊕ *www.oum.ox.ac.uk* ☞ *Free* ☉ *Daily 10–5.*

⑩ **Pitt Rivers Museum.** More than half a
☾ million archaeological and anthro-
Fodor'sChoice pological items from around the
★ globe, based on the collection
bequeathed by Lieutenant-General
Augustus Henry Lane Fox Pitt
Rivers in 1884, are crammed into
glass cases and drawers. Items are
organized thematically rather than
geographically, which may seem
eccentric but is actually thought-
provoking. Labels are handwritten,
and children are given flashlights to

> **LIBRARIES OF OLD**
>
> Disappointed that you can't get
> inside Radcliffe Camera? Those
> eager to see the inside of another
> scholarly library, this one medi-
> eval in vintage, can check out
> the library at Merton College, on
> Merton Street. There are daily
> tours in the afternoon from July to
> September.

explore the farthest corners and spot the world's smallest dolly. Give
yourself plenty of time to wander through the displays of shrunken
heads, Hawaiian feather cloaks, masks, jewelry, amulets, canoes;
the list is endless. Children will have a field day. ⊠ *S. Parks Rd.*
☏ *01865/270927* ⊕ *www.prm.ox.ac.uk* ▤ *Free* ⊙ *Mon. noon–4:30,*
Tues.–Sun. 10–4:30.

④ **Radcliffe Camera and Bodleian Library.** A vast library, the round, domed
★ Radcliffe Camera is Oxford's most spectacular building, built in 1737–
49 by James Gibbs in Italian baroque style. It's usually surrounded by
tourists with cameras trained at its golden-stone walls. The Camera
(closed to the public) contains part of the Bodleian Library's enormous
collection, which was begun in 1602 and has grown to more than 8
million volumes. Much like the Library of Congress in the United States,
the Bodleian contains a copy of every book printed in Great Britain.
You can tour parts of the library, which is made up of multiple buildings
connected by tunnels; the old buildings are magnificent and hold lovely
art and ancient tomes. Most of the library's books are in underground
spaces beneath the square in which the Camera sits. Another part of
the Bodleian, the Divinity School, a superbly vaulted room dating to
1462, is also worth visiting. Along with other parts of the Bodleian, it
was used for Hogwarts School in the Harry Potter films. ⊠ *Broad St.*
☏ *01865/277224 for information on tour* ⊕ *www.shop.bodley.ox.ac.*
uk ▤ *Free; audio tour £2.50; guided tour £6, extended tour (Sat. only)*
£12 ⊙ *Bodleian weekdays 9–4:15, Sat. 9–3:30. Divinity School week-*
days 9–4:45, Sat. 9–4:30.

⑧ **St. John's College.** One of Oxford's most attractive campuses, St. John's
has seven quiet quadrangles surrounded by elaborately carved, clois-
terlike buildings. You enter the first through a low wooden door. This
college dates to 1555, when Sir Thomas White, a merchant, founded
it. His heart is buried in the chapel (by tradition, students curse as
they walk over it). The Canterbury Quad represented the first example of Italian Renaissance architecture in Oxford, and the Front Quad
includes the buildings of the old St. Bernard's Monastery. St. John's is
Oxford's wealthiest college, with an estimated endowment of half a billion dollars. ⊠ *St. Giles* ☏ *01865/277300* ⊕ *www.sjc.ox.ac.uk* ▤ *Free*
⊙ *Daily 1–dusk.*

6

The **Eagle and Child pub** (⊠ *49 St. Giles* ☎ *01865/302925*) is a favorite not only for its good ales (try the local Old Hooky) and sense of history, but also for its literary associations. From the 1930s to the 1960s this was the meeting place of C. S. Lewis, J. R. R. Tolkien, and their circle of literary friends who called themselves the "Inklings." The pub is so close to St. John's College, and such a favorite of its students, that the college purchased it, although it remains open to the public.

❺ **Sheldonian Theatre.** This fabulously ornate theater is where Oxford's impressive graduation ceremonies are held, conducted almost entirely in Latin. Dating to 1663, it was the first building designed by Sir Christopher Wren when he served as professor of astronomy. The D-shape theater has pillars, balconies, and an elaborately painted ceiling. The stone pillars outside are topped by 18 massive stone heads, sculpted in the 1970s to replace originals destroyed by air pollution. ⊠ *Broad St.* ☎ *01865/277299* ⊕ *www.sheldon.ox.ac.uk* ✆ *£2* ⊙ *Mon.–Sat. 10–12:30 and 2–4:30; Nov.–Mar., closes at 3:30. Closed for 10 days at Christmas and Easter and for degree ceremonies and events.*

WORTH NOTING

⓬ **Carfax Tower.** Passing through Carfax, the center of Oxford and where four roads meet, you can spot this tower. It's all that remains of **St. Martin's Church,** where Shakespeare stood as godfather for William Davenant, who himself became a playwright. Every 15 minutes, little mechanical "quarter boys" mark the passage of time on the tower front. ■TIP➔ **You can climb up the dark stairwell for a good view of the town center.** ⊠ *Corner of Queen St. and Cornmarket* ☎ *01865/792653* ✆ *£2.10* ⊙ *Apr.–Sept., daily 10–5:30; Oct.–Mar., daily 10–dusk.*

❻ **Museum of the History of Science.** The Ashmolean, the world's oldest public museum, was originally housed in this 1638 building, which now holds scientific and mathematical instruments, from astrolabes to quadrants to medical equipment. The restored 18th-century chemical laboratory in the basement has the chalkboard Einstein used in a lecture on the theory of relativity. ⊠ *Broad St.* ☎ *01865/277280* ⊕ *www.mhs.ox.ac. uk* ✆ *Free* ⊙ *Tues.–Fri. noon–5, Sat. 10–5, Sun. 2–5.*

❼ **New College.** One of the university's best-known and oldest colleges (dating to 1379), New College stands alongside New College Lane, known for its Italianate Bridge of Sighs. Its grounds are big and enticing, with acres of soft green grass and pristinely maintained gardens. The college buildings, in ivory stone, are partly enclosed by the medieval city wall, and feature one of the city's best displays of Gothic gargoyles. Famous alumni include the actors Hugh Grant and Kate Beckinsale. ⊠ *Holywell St.* ☎ *01865/279555* ⊕ *www.new.ox.ac.uk* ✆ *Easter–Sept. £2, Oct.– Easter free* ⊙ *Easter–Sept., daily 11–5; Oct.–Easter, daily 2–4.*

❸ **University Church of St. Mary the Virgin.** Seven hundred years' worth of funeral monuments crowd this church, including the tombstone of Amy Robsart, the wife of Robert Dudley, Elizabeth I's favorite. One pillar marks the site of Thomas Cranmer's trial under Queen Mary for his marital machinations on behalf of Henry VIII. ■TIP➔ **From the top of the church's 14th-century tower, you get a panoramic view of the city's** skyline. **It's worth the 127 steps.** The Vaults Café and Garden, a part of the church accessible from Radcliffe Square, serves generous portions of warm food—cafeteria style—under the room in which the charity Oxfam was founded. ⊠*High St.* ☎*01865/279111* ⊕*www.university-church.ox.ac.uk* ⊠*Church free, tower £3* ⊙*Sept.–June, Mon.–Sat. 9–5, Sun. noon–5; July and Aug., Mon.–Sat. 9–6, Sun. noon–6; last admission to tower 30 mins before closing.*

❷ University of Oxford Botanic Garden. Founded in 1621 as a physic (healing) garden, this is the oldest of its kind in the British Isles. The compact but diverse garden displays 7,000 species from lilies to palms in greenhouses, a small walled garden, and special gardens (such as rock and bog gardens) outside the walled area. ⊠*Rose La.* ☎*01865/286690* ⊕*www.botanic-garden.ox.ac.uk* ⊠*£3* ⊙*Mar., Apr., Sept., and Oct., daily 9–5; May–Aug., daily 9–6; Nov.–Feb., daily 9–4:30.*

WHERE TO EAT

The city's pubs offer more options for a quick bite.

£ ✕**Big Bang.** Sausage and mash (mashed potatoes) is the theme of this
BRITISH friendly and buzzy little restaurant in the Jericho district, where the meat is ethically sourced from the local area. You're encouraged to mix and match, and could choose a carrot-and-swede (rutabaga) or a green onion mash for the traditional Oxford sausages, or a rose-hue mash (beets give the color) to accompany the wild-mushroom-and-garlic sausages. ⊠ *124 Walton St.* ☎*01865/511441* ▭*MC, V.*

£££ ✕**Brasserie Blanc.** Raymond Blanc's sophisticated brasserie in the Jer-
FRENCH icho neighborhood, a hipper cousin of Le Manoir aux Quat' Saisons in
★ Great Milton, is one of the best places to eat in Oxford. The changing menu always lists innovative, visually stunning adaptations of bourgeois French fare, sometimes with Mediterranean or Asian influences. Try the steamed Loch Fyne mussels in a white-wine-and-cream sauce. The fixed-price menus (which start at £11.35 for lunch) are a good value. ⊠*71–72 Walton St.* ☎*01865/510999* ▭*AE, MC, V.*

££ ✕**Fishers.** Everything is remarkably fresh at what is widely viewed as
SEAFOOD the city's best seafood restaurant. Seafood is prepared with a European touch and frequently comes with butter, cream, and other sauces: baked bream with olive-and-chive butter, for instance. Hot and cold shellfish platters are popular, as are the oysters, served either on ice or in a tempura batter. The interior has a casual nautical theme with wooden floors and tables, porthole windows, and red sails overhead. Bustling but relaxed, this place is often fully booked. Lunches are a very good value. ⊠*36–37 St. Clement's St.* ☎*01865/243003* ⚞*Reservations essential* ▭*MC, V* ⊙*No lunch Mon.*

£££ ✕**Gee's.** With its glass-and-steel framework, this former florist's shop just
BRITISH north of the town center makes a charming conservatory dining room. The constantly changing menu features locally raised meats and vegetables in modern versions of traditional English dishes, such as a rabbit cottage pie with spring greens. ⊠*61 Banbury Rd.* ☎*01865/553540* ▭*AE, MC, V.*

£   ✗**Grand Café.** Golden-hue tiles, towering columns, and antique marble
CAFÉ   tables make this café both architecturally impressive and an excellent
spot for a light meal (sandwiches, salads, and some hot fare) or leisurely
drink. It's touristy and service can be slow, but this is still a pretty spot
for afternoon tea. At night it transforms into a popular cocktail bar.
⊠ *84 High St.* ☎*01865/204463* ▤*AE, MC, V.*

£££££   ✗**Le Manoir aux Quat' Saisons.** Standards are high at this 15th-century
FRENCH   stone manor house, a hotel with one of the country's finest kitchens;
Fodor'sChoice   there's also a cooking school. Chef Raymond Blanc's epicurean touch
★   shows at every turn. Decide from among the innovative French creations (about £40 for a main course), such as braised brill and scallops
with wild asparagus, cucumber, and wasabi, or try one of the fixed-
price menus from £95 to £116; a fixed-price lunch can be a good deal
at £50. A stroll through the hotel's herb and Japanese gardens is de
rigueur; you may want to linger for a night in one of the 32 luxurious
rooms. The pretty town of Great Milton is 7 mi southeast of Oxford.
⊠ *Church Rd., Great Milton* ☎*01844/278881* ⚏*Reservations essential* ▤*AE, DC, MC, V.*

££   ✗**Trout Inn.** More than a century ago, Lewis Carroll took three children
BRITISH   on a Thames picnic. "We rowed up to Godstow, and had tea beside
a haystack," he told a friend at Christ Church; "I told them the fairy
tale of Alice's adventures in Wonderland." The haystacks are gone,
but you can stop at the creeper-covered Thames-side pub 2 mi north
of the city center for steaks, roasted chicken, and burgers as well as
pastas and pizzas. There's a corner devoted to Carroll, and a "Morse
Bar" with ample Inspector Morse memorabilia, as the fictional inspector often drank here. This place is at the heart of the tourist trail and
can get crowded; service may falter. ⊠*195 Godstow Rd., Wolvercote*
☎*01865/510930* ▤*AE, MC, V.*

WHERE TO STAY

Oxford is pricey; for the cheapest lodging, contact the tourist information office for bed-and-breakfasts in locals' homes.

£   ⊞**Brown's Guest House.** At the edge of central Oxford, this redbrick Victorian house is a good bet in a town that has precious few affordable guesthouses. Rooms are spacious and simply decorated in fresh colors; most
rooms have two beds and lots of light. The breakfast room is big and
homey, and the food is good and hearty. One downside is the 15-minute
walk or a bus ride into the center. **Pros:** comfortable rooms; friendly owners. **Cons:** a long walk to the center; some rooms without private bathroom. ⊠*281 Iffley Rd.* ☎*01865/246822* ⊕*www.brownsguesthouse.
co.uk* ⇦*11 rooms, 6 with bath* ⚘*In room: no a/c, no phone, Wi-Fi. In
hotel: parking (free), no-smoking rooms* ▤*MC, V* ⎥◎⎥*BP.*

££   ⊞**Burlington House.** This Victorian guesthouse in Summertown, on the
outskirts of Oxford, shows flair in its decoration, breakfasts, and attentive, helpful service. Guest rooms are beautifully furnished in contemporary style in muted, neutral colors, and have flat-screen TVs with Internet
access. Homemade bread, preserves, yogurt, and Gruyère omelets make
breakfasts luxurious. **Pros:** friendly; superior breakfasts; double-glazed

windows throughout. **Cons:** 10-minute bus ride to the center; main road location. ⊠*374 Banbury Rd.* ☎*01865/513513* ⊕*www.burlingtonhouse.co.uk* ⊋*12 rooms* ⚊*In-room: DVD, Internet, Wi-Fi. In-hotel: parking (free), no kids under 12* ⊟*MC, V* ⊚*BP.*

£££££ 🖼 **Macdonald Randolph.** A 19th-century neo-Gothic landmark, the hotel faces both the Ashmolean and the Martyrs' Memorial. If their parents are feeling generous, undergraduates are treated to tea in the Morse Bar or dinner in the hotel restaurant. Rooms are large and elegantly designed in tones of coffee and cream; some have antique desks, and many have views of Oxford's spires. A tiled, vaulted spa with four treatment rooms is the latest pampering amenity. **Pros:** handy location; grand building. **Cons:** on a busy street; rooms can be a bit noisy. ⊠*Beaumont St.* ☎*0844/879–9132* ⊕*www.macdonaldhotels.co.uk/ randolph* ⊋*151 rooms* ⚊*In-room: no a/c, Wi-Fi. In-hotel: restaurant, room service, bar, spa, laundry service, Internet terminal, parking (fee), some pets allowed, no-smoking rooms* ⊟*AE, DC, MC, V.*

£££££ 🖼 **Malmaison Oxford Castle.** Inside a 19th-century prison, this high-concept boutique hotel was designed to remain sympathetic to the building's history. Guest rooms, modern in style and with pampering bathrooms, are divided into the old prison wings: A-Wing rooms are comfortably sized, C-Wing rooms include two semicircular suites. With its metal doors, exposed brick walls, and clever embrace of its incarcerating past, this hotel is not for all. You half expect guests to come out and bang their spoons on the white metal railing if breakfast isn't served on time. But then, breakfast is always served on time. **Pros:** modern luxury; historic building; great bar and restaurant. **Cons:** prison life isn't for everyone; expensive parking. ⊠*3 Oxford Castle* ☎*01865/248432* ⊕*www.malmaison.com* ⊋*86 rooms, 8 suites* ⚊*In-room: DVD, Internet, Wi-Fi. In-hotel: restaurant, room service, bar, laundry service, parking (paid), no-smoking rooms* ⊟*AE, MC, V* ⊚*BP.*

££–£££ 🖼 **Newton House.** A handsome Victorian mansion just a five-minute walk from all of Oxford's action, the Newton is a sprawling, friendly place on three floors. Decent-size rooms are brightly decorated in rich reds and autumn golds; some have original Victorian features. The breakfast is varied, with yogurt and croissants along with the usual eggs and bacon. This is one of the best deals in the city center, so book early. **Pros:** great breakfasts; parking lot. **Cons:** on a main road; no elevator. ⊠*82 Abingdon Rd.* ☎*01865/240561* ✉*newton.house@btinternet. com* ⊋*11 rooms* ⚊*In-room: no a/c, Wi-Fi. In-hotel: parking (free)* ⊟*AE, MC, V* ⊚*BP.*

££££–£££££ 🖼 **Old Bank Hotel.** From its sleek lobby to the 20th-century British paintings on display and the modern furnishings in the guest rooms, this stately converted bank offers contemporary style in a city that favors the traditional. Oxford's most centrally located hotel also holds the contemporary Quod Bar and Grill, serving creative pastas and dishes such as duck confit. **Pros:** excellent location; great city views. **Cons:** standard rooms can be small; extra charge for breakfast. ⊠*92–94 High St.* ☎*01865/799599* ⊕*www.oldbank-hotel.co.uk* ⊋*42 rooms* ⚊*In-room: safe, DVD, Internet, Wi-Fi. In-hotel: restaurant, room service, bar, laundry service, parking (free), no-smoking rooms* ⊟*AE, MC, V.*

6

££££ · ⌂ **Old Parsonage.** A 17th-century gabled stone house in a small garden
★ next to St. Giles Church, this hotel provides a dignified escape from
the surrounding city center. Dark red walls, eclectic art, and a crackling
wood fire make the lobby a distinguished retreat. The fresh guest rooms
are done in crisp white shades with bright splashes of color; bathrooms
are marble. Memorable meals by the fire (or in the walled garden terrace
in summer) keep people coming back. Afternoon teas with scones and
clotted cream are excellent. **Pros:** interesting building; complimentary
walking tours; great afternoon tea. **Cons:** pricey given what's on offer;
bathrooms are small. ⌂*1 Banbury Rd.* ☎*01865/310210* ⊕*www.
oldparsonage-hotel.co.uk* ⇆*26 rooms, 4 suites* ⌂*In-room: no a/c,
safe, Internet, Wi-Fi. In-hotel: restaurant, room service, bar, laundry
service, parking (free), no-smoking rooms* ⊟*AE, MC, V.*

£££ · ⌂ **Royal Oxford Hotel.** This hotel, a few steps from the train station, has
simply furnished but bright, light, and modern rooms with contemporary furniture. Bathrooms are well equipped. Tea- and coffeemakers, and hospitality trays of chocolates, fruit, and cookies are welcome
touches. **Pros:** comfortable rooms; good for train travelers. **Cons:** rooms
are plain; not many amenities. ⌂*17 Park End St.* ☎*01865/248432*
⊕*www.royaloxfordhotel.co.uk* ⇆*26 rooms* ⌂*In-room: Wi-Fi. In-
hotel: restaurant, room service, laundry service, Wi-Fi, no-smoking
rooms* ⊟*AE, MC, V* ⍥*BP.*

NIGHTLIFE AND THE ARTS

NIGHTLIFE AND PUBS

Nightlife in Oxford centers around student life, which in turn focuses
on the local pubs, though you may find a few surprises, too. The popular Jericho area, around Walton Street north of the old city walls and
within walking distance of the center of town, has good restaurants
and pubs. **Frevd** (⌂*119 Walton St.* ☎*01865/311171*), in a renovated
neoclassical church, serves light meals and cocktails and offers nightly
live jazz or funk. The **Kings Arms** (⌂*40 Holywell St.* ☎*01865/242369*),
popular with students and fairly quiet during the day, carries excellent
local brews as well as inexpensive pub grub.

Raoul's (⌂*32 Walton St.* ☎*01865/553732*) is a trendy cocktail bar in
the equally trendy Jericho neighborhood. The **Turf Tavern** (⌂*Bath Pl.*
☎*01865/243235*), off Holywell Street, includes a higgledy-piggledy
collection of little rooms and outdoor space good for a quiet drink and
inexpensive pub food.

THE ARTS

FESTIVALS **Choral music** at the city's churches is a calming way to spend the early
AND evening. Drop by weekdays during term time at 6 PM at Magdalen
CONCERTS (except Tuesday), New College (except Wednesday), or Christ Church
(except Monday) to hear evensong.

The **Jacqueline Du Pre Music Building** (⌂*St. Hilda's College, Cowley Pl.*
☎*01865/276821*), endowed with the city's best acoustics, showcases
rising talent at recitals. **Music at Oxford** (☎*01865/242865*), an acclaimed
series of weekend classical concerts, takes place mid-September
through June in such surroundings as Christ Church Cathedral and

Sir Christopher Wren's Sheldonian Theatre. At the **Oxford Coffee Concerts** (⊠*Holywell Music Room, Holywell Rd.*), a program of Sunday morning chamber concerts, string quartets, piano trios, and soloists presents baroque and classical pieces in a 1748 hall. Reasonably priced tickets are available from the **Oxford Playhouse** (⊠*Beaumont St.* ☎*01865/305305*).

Blenheim Palace (☎*01993/811091* ⊕*www.blenheimpalace.com*) in nearby Woodstock puts on marvelous classical and pop concerts in summer, sometimes combined with fireworks displays. ■**TIP➡Pack a picnic of Champagne, Kent strawberries, and fresh Henley cream, and head out for a true, elegant English summertime experience.**

OPERA The **Garsington Opera** (⊠*Garsington* ☎*01865/361636*), a well-regarded event staged in a covered outdoor auditorium, uses Garsington Manor's magical gardens as a backdrop for classic and little-known operas each June and July. The manor is 5 mi southeast of Oxford; you can dine in the Great Barn. Book well ahead.

THEATERS During term time, undergraduate productions are often given in the colleges or local halls. In summer, outdoor performances may take place in quadrangles or college gardens. Look for announcement posters and take a chance.

New Theatre (⊠*George St.* ☎*0870/606–3500*), Oxford's main theater, stages plays, opera, ballet, pantomime, and concerts. It's the second home of the Welsh National Opera and the Glyndebourne Touring Opera. **OFS Studio Theatre** (⊠*40 George St.* ☎*01865/297170*), an alternative theater, showcases student productions, small-scale opera, and new musicals. The **Oxford Playhouse** (⊠*Beaumont St.* ☎*01865/305305*) is a serious theater presenting classic and modern dramas as well as dance and music performances.

SPORTS AND THE OUTDOORS

BIKING

Bikes can be rented at **Summertown Cycles** (⊠*200–202 Banbury Rd,* ☎*01865/316885*), north of the city center in Summertown.

PUNTING

Fodor'sChoice
★

You may choose, like many an Oxford student, to spend a summer afternoon **punting,** while dangling your champagne bottle in the water to keep it cool. Punts—shallow-bottom boats that are poled slowly up the river—can be rented in several places, including at the foot of the Magdalen Bridge.

From mid-March through mid-October, **Cherwell Boathouse** (⊠*Bardwell Rd.* ☎*01865/515978*), a punt station and restaurant a mile north of the heart of Oxford, will rent you a boat and, if you wish, someone (usually an Oxford student) to punt it. Rentals are £12–£14 per hour; £60–£70 per day. At the St. Aldates Road end of Folly Bridge, **Salter's Steamers** (☎*01865/243421*) rents out punts and skiffs (rowboats) for £20 per hour, £60 per half day, and £100 per day. Their chauffeured punts are £60 per hour, booked in advance.

At the end of May, during **Oxford's Eights Week,** men and women rowers from the university's colleges compete to be "Head of the River." Because the river is too narrow for teams of eight to race side by side, the boats set off, 13 at a time, one behind another. Each boat tries to catch and bump the one in front.

Oxford University Cricket Club competes against leading county teams in late spring and summer and also, each summer, the major foreign teams visiting Britain. In the middle of the sprawling University Parks—itself worthy of a walk—the club's playing field is truly lovely.

SHOPPING

Small shops line High Street, Cornmarket, and Queen Street, and the Clarendon and Westgate shopping centers, which lead off them, have branches of several nationally known stores. **Alice's Shop** (✉ 83 St. Aldate's ☎ 01865/723793) sells all manner of *Alice in Wonder-* ★ *land* paraphernalia. **Blackwell's** (✉ 48–51 Broad St. ☎ 01865/792792), family-owned and family-run since 1879, stocks an excellent selection of books. The **Covered Market** (✉ Off High St.), which has good food as well as clothes and more in its stalls, is a fine place for a cheap sandwich and a leisurely browse; the smell of pastries and coffee follows you from cobbler to jeweler to cheesemonger. **Shepherd & Woodward** (✉ 109–113 High St. ☎ 01865/249491), a traditional tailor, specializes in university gowns, ties, and scarves. The **University of Oxford Shop** (✉ 106 High St. ☎ 01865/247414), run by the university, sells authorized clothing, ceramics, and tea towels, all emblazoned with university crests.

BLENHEIM PALACE TO ALTHORP

The River Thames takes on a new graciousness as it flows along the borders of Oxfordshire for 71 mi; each league it increases in size and importance. Three tributaries swell the river as it passes through the landscape: the Windrush, the Evenlode, and the Cherwell. Tucked among the hills and dales are one of England's impressive stately homes, an Edenic village, and a former Rothschild estate. Closer to London in Hertfordshire is St. Albans, with its cathedral and Roman remains.

WOODSTOCK AND BLENHEIM PALACE

★ *8 mi northwest of Oxford on A44.*

Handsome 17th- and 18th-century houses line the trim streets of Woodstock, at the eastern edge of the Cotswolds. It's best known for nearby Blenheim Palace, and in the summer, tour buses clog the village's ancient streets. On a quiet fall or spring afternoon, however, Woodstock is a sublime experience: a mellowed 18th-century church and town hall mark the central square, and along its backstreets you can find flower-bedecked houses and quiet lanes right out of a 19th-century etching.

GETTING HERE AND AROUND

The public bus service S3 runs (usually every half hour) between Oxford to Woodstock and costs £3 one-way.

ESSENTIALS

Visitor Information Woodstock (⊠ *Oxfordshire Museum, Park St.* ☎ *01993/813276*).

EXPLORING

Fodor'sChoice ★

So grandiose is **Blenheim Palace** and so breathtaking are its articulations of splendor that it was named a World Heritage Site, the only historic house in Britain to receive the honor. Built by Sir John Vanbrugh in the early 1700s, Blenheim was given by Queen Anne and the nation to General John Churchill, first duke of Marlborough, in gratitude for his military victories against the French in 1704. The exterior is mind-boggling, with its huge columns, enormous pediments, and obelisks, all exemplars of English baroque. Inside, lavishness continues in monumental extremes. In most of the opulent rooms great family portraits look down at sumptuous furniture, elaborate carpets, and immense pieces of silver. Exquisite tapestries in the three state rooms illustrate the first duke's victories. For some visitors, however, the most memorable room is the small, low-ceiling chamber where Winston Churchill (his father was the younger brother of the then-duke) was born in 1874; he is buried in nearby Bladon.

Sir Winston wrote that the unique beauty of Blenheim lay in its perfect adaptation of English parkland to an Italian palace. Indeed the 2,000 acres of grounds, the work of Capability Brown, 18th-century England's most gifted landscape gardener, are arguably the best example of the "cunningly natural" park in the country. It's well worth a stroll. Tucked away here is the Temple of Diana, where Winston Churchill proposed to his future wife, Clementine. Blenheim's formal gardens include notable water terraces and an Italian garden with a mermaid fountain, all built in the 1920s.

The Pleasure Gardens, reached by a train that stops outside the main entrance to the palace, contain some child-pleasers: a butterfly house, notable 1-acre hedge maze, playground, and giant chess set. The herb-and-lavender garden is also delightful. In summer a miniature train runs every 30 minutes from 11 until 5, connecting the palace with the pleasure gardens. It's easy to spend half a day here. ⊠ *Off A4095, Woodstock* ☎ *0870/060–2080* ⊕ *www.blenheimpalace.com* ⊠ *Palace, park, and gardens: mid-Feb. and Apr.–Oct. £17.50; late Feb., Mar., and Nov.–mid-Dec. £14.50. Park and gardens only: mid-Feb. and Apr.–Oct. £10; late Feb., Mar., and Nov.–mid-Dec. £7.70* ⊙ *Palace mid-Feb.– Oct., daily 10:30–4:45; Nov.–mid-Dec., Wed.–Sun. 10:30–4:45; park daily 9–4:45.*

WHERE TO EAT AND STAY

££
BRITISH
Fodor'sChoice
★

✕ **Falkland Arms.** It's worth detouring a bit for this supremely appealing pub on the village green at Great Tew, about 8 mi northwest of Woodstock. The bar has impressive malt whiskies, and mugs and jugs hang from the beams. The small restaurant chalks up a traditional but creative menu, which includes such items as spinach-and-mushroom risotto

6

Blenheim Palace to Althorp

10 miles

15 km

St. Albans

Watford
Rickmansworth

Woburn Abbey
Leighton Buzzard
Dunstable

Amersham

High Wycombe
Beaconsfield

Cliveden
Stoke Poges
Cookham

Marlow

BUCKINGHAMSHIRE

Castle Ashby

Milton Keynes

A509

A428

A5

Northampton

M1

A413

Buckingham

Althorp

Great Brington
Harlestone

Stowe Landscape Gardens

Waddesdon Manor

Aylesbury

Stonor

Great Milton

A40

M40

CHILTERN HILLS

Ewelme

Nuffield

A421

Bicester

OXFORDSHIRE

A43

A41

Garsington

Dorchester-on-Thames

Abingdon

Weston-on-the-Green

Oxford
see detail
map

Thames

Cumnor

Wolvercote

Bladon

Banbury

Lower Tysoe
Middle Tysoe
Upper Tysoe

Chipping Norton

Woodstock

Blenheim Palace

Witney

Thames

VALE OF THE WHITE HORSE

Wantage

Uffington

Faringdon

Warwick

Stratford-upon-Avon

Bourton-on-the-Water

Burford

and slow-cooked lamb shank. A spiral stone staircase leads to five guest rooms (££), which have brass bedsteads or four-posters. Reservations are essential for both staying and eating here. ⊠ *Great Tew OX7 4DB* ☎ *01608/683653* ⌂ *Reservations essential* ⊟ *AE, MC, V* ⊗ *No dinner Sun.*

£ 🏠 **Blenheim Guest House & Tea Rooms.** Small and unassuming, this three-story guesthouse stands in the quiet village cul-de-sac that leads to the back gates of Blenheim Palace. You can still just make out the Victorian-era banner that says VIEWS AND POSTCARDS OF BLENHEIM. The guest rooms have modest period furnishings, with pretty sheer curtains, but the Marlborough room is unique—its bathroom offers a view of Blenheim. **Pros:** handy tearoom downstairs; bathroom views of Blenheim Palace. **Cons:** plain decor; floors are a bit creaky. ⊠ *17 Park St.* ☎ *01993/813814* ⊕ *www.theblenheim.com* ⇆ *6 rooms* ⌂ *In-room: no a/c. In-hotel: Wi-Fi, no-smoking rooms* ⊟ *MC, V* ⊚ *BP.*

££££ 🏠 **The Feathers.** Antiques-bedecked guest rooms with floral prints and ★ striped fabrics fill this stylish hotel in the heart of town. The inn was cobbled together from five 17th-century houses, and its elegant courtyard is favored for a summertime meal. In winter, log fires make the public rooms cozy. The seasonal menu and upscale dining room are worth the restaurant's hefty prices, though the bistro is a cheaper option. You might opt for Cornish lobster with pineapple and fennel, followed by chilled strawberry soup and ice cream. **Pros:** cozy lounges with fireplaces; great food. **Cons:** prices are high given what's on offer; minimum two-night stay on weekends. ⊠ *Market St.* ☎ *01993/812291* ⊕ *www.feathers.co.uk* ⇆ *16 rooms, 4 suites* ⌂ *In-room: no a/c, Wi-Fi. In-hotel: 2 restaurants, room service, bar, laundry service* ⊟ *AE, DC, MC, V* ⊚ *BP.*

£££–££££ 🏠 **Macdonald Bear.** Tudoresque wood paneling, beamed ceilings, wattle-and-daub walls, and blazing fireplaces in winter help define this as an archetypal English coaching inn. The guest rooms, overlooking either a quiet churchyard or the town square, have plenty of carved oak; the duplex suites would make a king feel at home, thanks to their timbered loft-balconies and gargantuan four-posters. Legend has it that the Bear is where Richard Burton finally popped the question to Elizabeth Taylor. **Pros:** true luxury; historic house. **Cons:** creaky floors; you can knock yourself silly on those old beams. ⊠ *Park St.* ☎ *0844/879–9143* ⊕ *www.macdonaldhotels.co.uk/bear* ⇆ *46 rooms, 8 suites* ⌂ *In-room: no a/c (some), Wi-Fi. In-hotel: restaurant, room service, bar, laundry service, no-smoking rooms* ⊟ *AE, MC, V* ⊚ *BP.*

EN ROUTE

After taking in Blenheim Palace, stop by **Bladon,** 2 mi southeast of Woodstock on A4095 and 6 mi northwest of Oxford, to see the small, tree-lined churchyard that is the burial place of Sir Winston Churchill. His grave is all the more impressive for its simplicity.

DORCHESTER-ON-THAMES

16 mi southeast of Woodstock, 15 mi east of Uffington, 9 mi southeast of Oxford.

An important center in Saxon times, when it was the seat of a bishopric, Dorchester merits a visit chiefly because of its ancient abbey, but also because it's a charming little town. The main street, once a leg of the Roman road to Silchester, has timber houses, thatched cottages, and ancient inns. Crossing the Thames at Day's Lock and turning left at Little Wittenham takes you on a bucolic and historic walk past the remains of the village's Iron Age settlements. Pricey and alluring antiques shops line the High Street.

GETTING HERE AND AROUND

Thames Travel runs a regular hourly bus service from Oxford (40 minutes). Drivers from Oxford should take A4074, which also connects with A4130 and Junction 8/9 of M4 for London.

ESSENTIALS

Bus Contacts Thames Travel (☎ *0871/200–2233* ⊕ *www.thames-travel.co.uk*).

EXPLORING

In addition to secluded cloisters and gardens, **Dorchester Abbey** has a spacious church (1170) with traceried medieval windows and a lead baptismal font. The great tower was rebuilt in 1602, but incorporated the old 14th-century spiral staircase. ■ TIP→ **Climb the tower for sweeping views of verdant pastures, graceful willows, and water meadows.** ⊠ *Off A4074* ☏ *01865/340007* ⊕ *www.dorchester-abbey.org.uk* ✉ *Free* ☽ *May–Sept., daily 8:30–7; Oct.–Apr., daily 8:30–dusk, except during services.*

OFF THE BEATEN PATH

Vale of the White Horse. Stretching up into the foothills of the Berkshire Downs between Swindon and Oxford is a wide fertile plain known as the Vale of the White Horse. Here, off B4507, cut into the turf of the hillside to expose the underlying chalk, is the 374-foot-long, 110-foot-high **figure of a white horse,** an important prehistoric site. Some historians believed that the figure might have been carved to commemorate King Alfred's victory over the Danes in 871, whereas others dated it to the Iron Age, around 750 BC. More current research suggests that it is at least 1,000 years older, created at the beginning of the second millennium BC. **Uffington Castle,** above the horse, is a prehistoric fort. English Heritage maintains these sites. To reach the Vale of the White Horse from Oxford (about 20 mi), follow A420, then B4508 to the village of Uffington.

AYLESBURY

22 mi east of Oxford, 46 mi northwest of London.

Aylesbury makes a good base for exploring the surrounding countryside, including stately homes and gardens. It's a pretty, historic town with a 13th-century church surrounded by small Tudor lanes and cottages. From the 18th century this market town has been associated

HIKING AND BIKING ALONG THE THAMES

The Thames Valley is a great area to explore by foot or bike. It's not too hilly, and pubs and easily accessible lodgings dot the riverside and small towns. The Thames is almost completely free of car traffic along the Thames Path, a 180-mi national trail that traces the river from the London flood barrier to the river's source near Kemble, in the Cotswolds. The path follows towpaths from the outskirts of London, through Windsor, to Oxford and Lechlade. Good public transportation in the region makes it possible to start and stop easily anywhere along this route. In summer the walking is fine and no special gear is necessary, but in winter the path often floods—check before you head out.

The Countryside Agency has been charting and preserving Thames paths for years, and through its Natural England branch it offers publications and information about them. For maps and advice, contact the National Trails Office or the Ramblers' Association. The Chiltern Conservation Board promotes walking in the Chilterns peaks.

Biking is perhaps the best way to see the Chilterns. Routes include the 99-mi Thames Valley Cycle Route from London to Oxford, the 200-mi Oxfordshire Cycleway around the county's countryside, and the 87-mi Ridgeway Path from Uffington that follows the Chilterns; the National Trails Office has information. The Thames Path also has plenty of biking opportunities.

CONTACTS AND RESOURCES

Chiltern Conservation Board (☎01844/355500 ⊕www.chilternsaonb.org). **Chiltern Way** (☎01494/771250 ⊕www.chilternsociety.org.uk). **National Trails Office** (☎01865/810224 ⊕www.nationaltrail.co.uk). **Natural England** (☎0845/600–3078 ⊕www.naturalengland.org.uk). **Ramblers' Association** (☎020/7339-8500 ⊕www.ramblers.org.uk). **Sustrans (Thames Valley Cycle Route)** (☎0845/113–0065 ⊕www.sustrans.org.uk).

with the Aylesbury duck. Flocks would have been walked the 40 mi to the London markets.

GETTING HERE AND AROUND

From London, Chiltern Railways runs frequent trains from Marylebone station (1 hour). The town is easily accessible from Oxford by Arriva Bus 280, which runs every 30 minutes; travel time is 80 minutes. If you're driving from Oxford, take A40 and A418. From London, follow M1 and A41 and allow 90 minutes.

ESSENTIALS

Visitor Information Aylesbury (⊠ King's Head Passage, off Market Sq. ☎01296/330559).

EXPLORING

Many of the regal residences created by the Rothschild family throughout Europe are gone now, but **Waddesdon Manor** remains, a vision of the 19th century at its most sumptuous. G.H. Destailleur built the house in the 1880s for Baron Ferdinand de Rothschild in the style of a French chateau, with perfectly balanced turrets and towers and

Fodor'sChoice
★

walls of creamy stone. Although intended only for summer weekend house parties, it was lovingly furnished over the course of 35 years with Savonnerie carpets, Sèvres porcelain, furniture made by Riesener for Marie Antoinette, and paintings by Guardi, Dutch and Flemish masters, Gainsborough, and Reynolds. An exquisite 21st-century broken porcelain chandelier by Ingo Maurer in the Blue Dining Room brings the collection up to date. The gardens are equally extraordinary, with an aviary, colorful plantings, and winding trails that provide panoramic views. In the restaurant you can dine on English or French fare and order excellent Rothschild wines if your pocketbook can take the hit. Admission prices are a bit higher on weekends. ■TIP→ **Admission is by timed ticket; arrive early or book in advance.** ⊠ *Waddesdon* ✛ *On A41 west of Aylesbury* ☎ *01296/653226* ⊕ *www.waddesdon.org.uk* ⊠ *House and grounds £13.20–£15; grounds only, £5.50–£7* ⊙ *House Apr.–Oct., Wed.–Fri. and national holiday Mon. noon–4, weekends 11–4; gardens Jan.–Mar., weekends 10–5; Apr.–Oct., Wed.–Sun. and national holiday Mon. 10–5.*

★ A superb example of a Georgian garden, **Stowe Landscape Gardens** was created for the Temple family by the most famous gardeners of the 18th century. Capability Brown, Charles Bridgeman, and William Kent all worked on the land to create 980 acres of pleasing greenery in the valleys and meadows. More than 40 striking monuments, follies, and temples dot the landscape of lakes, rivers, and pleasant vistas. Allow at least half a day if you want to explore the extensive grounds. Stowe House, at its center, is now a fancy school with some magnificently restored rooms; it's closed to the public, apart from irregular tours throughout the year (call for dates and times). The gardens are about 3 mi northwest of Buckingham, which is 14 mi northwest of Aylesbury. ⊠ *Stowe Ave., off 422 Buckingham–Banbury Rd., Buckingham* ☎ *01280/822850, 01494/755568 information line, 01280/818166 house tours* ⊕ *www.nationaltrust.org.uk* ⊠ *Gardens only, £6.50; house and gardens £10.20; house £4.20* ⊙ *Mar.–Oct., Wed.–Sun. and national holiday Mon. 10:30–5:30; Nov.–Feb., weekends 10:30–4; last admission 90 mins before closing.*

WHERE TO STAY

££ ▦ **Five Arrows.** Fancifully patterned brick chimneys and purple gables decorate this baroque building next to the main entrance of Waddesdon Manor. Constructed to house the manor's workers, it now holds a hotel with traditional-style bedrooms. The delightful suites in the Courtyard Stables are big enough for families, or for couples who just want to stretch out a little. A fine restaurant and pub serves inspired modern fare with a Mediterranean twist; the wine list is excellent. The in-house "wine pub" is a regular award winner. **Pros:** charming historic building; lovely grounds. **Cons:** some rooms are small; on a busy main road. ⊠ *High St., Waddesdon* ☎ *01296/651727* ⊕ *www.waddesdon.org.uk/ five_arrows* ⇆ *9 rooms, 2 suites* ⌂ *In-room: no a/c, Wi-Fi. In-hotel: restaurant, bar, no-smoking rooms* ▭ *MC, V* ⧉ *BP.*

£££££ ▦ **Hartwell House.** Part Jacobean, part Georgian, this magnificent stately home, now owned by the National Trust, offers formal luxury in an opulent countryside setting. The building is decorated with a masterful touch—crystal chandeliers, original oil paintings, and carved ceilings adorn the ornate public areas, and bedrooms with well-chosen antiques and comfortable beds are suitably grand. There are also guest rooms in the nearby Old Rectory. Some rooms have direct access to the gardens, which sprawl over 90 acres of landscaped parkland, perfect for strolls. This is the kind of place where you must dress to impress for dinner. **Pros:** truly elegant; soothing views of the gardens. **Cons:** atmosphere feels too formal; spa is open to the public; breakfast not included. ⊠ *Oxford Rd. (A418)* ☎ *01296/747444* ⊕ *www.hartwell-house.com* ↪ *33 rooms, 13 suites* ⊛ *In-room: no a/c (some), Internet, Wi-Fi. In-hotel: restaurant, room service, bar, tennis courts, pool, gym, spa, laundry service, some pets allowed, no kids under 8, no-smoking rooms* ☐ *AE, MC, V* ⦿ *CP*

ST. ALBANS

25 mi east of Aylesbury, 20 mi northwest of London.

A lively town on the outskirts of London, St. Albans is known for its historic cathedral, and it also holds reminders of its long history. From AD 50 to 440, the town then known as Verulamium was one of the largest communities in Roman Britain. You can explore this past in the Verulamium Museum and splendid Roman sites around the area. For activities more focused on the present, every Wednesday and Saturday the Market Place on St. Peter's Street bustles with traders from all over England, selling everything from fish and farm produce to clothing and CDs.

GETTING HERE AND AROUND

About 20 mi northwest of London, St. Albans is off the M1 and M25 highways, about an hour's drive from the center of the capital. First Capital Connect trains leave every half hour from London's St. Pancras Station, arriving in St. Albans in 30 minutes. The main train station is on Victoria Street, in the town center. A second station on the south side of town, St. Albans Abbey Station, serves smaller towns in the surrounding area. Bus service is not direct; take the train. Central St. Albans is small and walkable. There's a local bus service, but you're unlikely to need it. Taxis usually line up outside the train stations.

ESSENTIALS

Train Contacts First Capital Connect (☎ *0845/026–4700* ⊕ *www. firstcapitalconnect.co.uk).*

Visitor Information St. Albans (⊠ *Town Hall, Market Pl.* ☎ *01727/864511* ⊕ *www.stalbans.gov.uk).*

EXPLORING

Medieval pilgrims came from far and wide to hilltop **St. Albans Cathedral** to honor its patron saint, a Roman soldier turned Christian martyr. Construction of the impressive, mainly Norman cathedral began in the early 11th century, but the nearly 300-foot-long nave dates from 1235. The tower is even more historic, and contains bricks from ancient Roman buildings. ⊠ *Holywell Hill at High St.* ☎ *01727/860780* ⊕ *www. stalbanscathedral.org.uk* ⊡ *£3 suggested donation* ⊘ *Daily 8–5:45; guided tours weekdays 11:30 and 2:30, Sat. 11:30 and 2, Sun. 2:30.*

With exhibits on everything from Roman food to burial practices, the ☉ **Verulamium Museum,** on the site of the ancient Roman city, explores life 2,000 years ago. The re-created Roman rooms contain colorful mosaics that are some of the finest in Britain. Every second weekend of the month, "Roman soldiers" invade the museum and demonstrate the skills of the Imperial Army. ⊠ *St. Michael's St.* ☎ *01727/751810* ⊕ *www.stalbansmuseums.org.uk* 🎟 *£3.50* ☉ *Mon.–Sat. 10–5:30, Sun. 2–5:30.*

☉ **Verulamium Park,** adjacent to the Verulamium Museum, contains the usual—playground, wading pool, lake—and the unusual—**Roman ruins** that include part of the Roman town hall and a hypocaust, a central-heating system. The hypocaust dates to AD 200 and included one of the first heated floors in Britain. Brick columns supported the floor, and hot air from a nearby fire was drawn underneath the floor to keep bathers warm. ⊠ *St. Michael's St.* ☎ *01727/751810* ⊕ *www.stalbansmuseums. org.uk* 🎟 *Free* ☉ *Hypocaust Mon.–Sat. 10–5:30, Sun. 2–5:30.*

Imagination can take you back to AD 130 and to a Roman stage drama as you walk around the ruins of the **Roman Theater,** one of the few in this country. Next to the theater are the ruins of a Roman town house, shops, and a shrine. ⊠ *Bluehouse Hill* ☎ *01727/835035* ⊕ *www. romantheatre.co.uk* 🎟 *£2.50* ☉ *Easter–Nov., daily 10–5; Dec.–Easter, daily 10–4.*

Six miles east of St. Albans, **Hatfield House,** an outstanding brick mansion surrounded by lovely formal gardens, stands as a testament to the magnificence of Jacobean architecture. Robert Cecil, earl of Salisbury, built Hatfield in 1611, and his descendants still live here. The interior, with its dark-wood paneling, lush tapestries, and Tudor and Jacobean portraits, reveals much about the era. Perhaps the finest feature is the ornate Grand Staircase, with carved wooden figures on the banisters. Thursday is the only day on which the East Garden, with topiaries, parterres, and rare plants, is open. The **Elizabethan Banquet** (☎ *01707/262055* ⊕ *www.hatfield-house.co.uk* 🎟 *£45* ☉ *Tues., Fri., and Sat. 7:30 PM–11 PM*) is a hearty five-course dinner accompanied by kitschy entertainment from King Henry VIII, Queen Elizabeth I, minstrels, and jokers. ⊠ *Off A1 Hatfield* ☎ *01707/287010* ⊕ *www.hatfield-house.co.uk* 🎟 *House, gardens, and park £10.50 (£14 on Thurs., if you wish to see East Garden), gardens £6, park £3* ☉ *Easter–Sept., mansion Wed.–Sun. and national holiday Mon. noon–4, west gardens Wed.–Sun. and national holiday Mon. 11–5, east gardens Thurs. 11–5; guided tours weekdays only (not in Aug.).*

From 1906 to his death in 1950, the famed Irish playwright George Bernard Shaw lived in the small village of Ayot St. Lawrence, 9 mi northeast of St. Albans. Today his small Edwardian home, **Shaw's Corner,** remains much as he left it. The most delightful curiosity is his little writing hut in the garden, which can be turned to face the sun. Take care when driving here; the access roads are very narrow. ⊠ *Off Hill Farm La., Ayot St. Lawrence* ☎ *01438/820307* ⊕ *www.nationaltrust. org.uk* 🎟 *£5.20* ☉ *House mid-Mar.–Oct., Wed.–Sun. 1–5; gardens mid-Mar.–Oct., Wed.–Sun. noon–5:30.*

WHERE TO EAT AND STAY

£

BELGIAN

✕**Waffle House.** Indoors or outside, you can have a great budget meal at the 16th-century Kingsbury Watermill, near the Verulamium Museum. The organic flour for the high-quality, sweet and savory Belgian waffles comes from Redbournbury Watermill just north of the city; daily specials add variety. In the main dining room you can see the wheel churn the water of the River Ver. Waffle House is open 10 to 5 in winter, to 6 in summer. ✉*Kingsbury Watermill, St. Michael's St.* ☎*01727/853502* ⊟*MC, V* ☉*No dinner.*

£

BRITISH

✕**Ye Olde Fighting Cocks.** Some claim this is England's oldest pub, although that's a contentious category. Still, this octagonal building certainly looks suitably aged. The building was moved to this location in the 16th century, but the foundations date back to the 8th century. The small rooms with low ceilings make a cozy stop for a pint and simple pub grub. Be prepared for crowds. ✉*16 Abbey Mill La.* ☎*01727/869152* ⊟*MC, V.*

£££–££££

⌂**St. Michael's Manor.** The Newling Ward family has owned this luxurious 16th-century manor house close to the center of St. Albans for three generations. The 5 acres of grounds, complete with a lake, add a sense of seclusion, and plush furniture helps make the antiques- and paintings-filled public areas inviting. The contemporary-style bedrooms are equipped with thoughtful extras like complimentary bottled water, fruit, and cookies. The conservatory restaurant (£££) serves modern British cuisine, including such dishes as tea-smoked fillet of beef with forest mushrooms and Guinness sauce. Champagne afternoon tea is a treat. **Pros:** spacious rooms; excellent food; beautiful grounds. **Cons:** a little too grand for some. ✉*Fishpool St.* ☎*01727/864444* ⊕*www. stmichaelsmanor.com* ⇔*30 rooms* ♿*In-room: no a/c, DVD, Internet, Wi-Fi (some). In-hotel: restaurant, room service, bar, laundry service, no-smoking rooms* ⊟*AE, DC, MC, V* ⏹*BP.*

WOBURN ABBEY

30 mi west of St. Albans, 10 mi northeast of Aylesbury.

EXPLORING

✪ **Woburn Abbey** is the stately home as big business. Still the ancestral residence of the duke of Bedford, it houses countless Grand Tour treasures and old master paintings, including 20 stunning Canalettos that practically wallpaper the crimson dining salon, and excellent works by Gainsborough and Reynolds. The Palladian mansion contains a number of etchings by Queen Victoria, who left them behind after she stayed here. Outside, 10 species of deer roam grounds that include an antiques center and small restaurant. The adjacent **Woburn Safari Park** is a popular drive-through wildlife experience, home to big game from around the world. Jeep tours, walks with elephants, and other special packages are available. There are plenty of play areas, a boating lake with swan boats, and walkabouts with small animals such as wallabies. ▪TIP➔ **Allow at least half a day for the safari park. If you buy a joint ticket with the house, you can use it on another day.** ✉*A4012, off A5 Woburn* ☎*01525/290333* ⊕*www.woburnabbey.co.uk* ✉*House and deer park*

£13, safari £18 in summer, £17 off-season; deer park only, £2.50; joint ticket for house and safari £22.50 ⊗ House Apr.–Sept., daily 11–4. Safari Park Mar.–Oct., daily 10–5; Nov. and Feb., weekends 10–5. Deer park daily 10–4.30.

WHERE TO STAY

£££ ⊡ **The Inn at Woburn.** In the center of Woburn village, a small Georgian town, this modern hotel has uncluttered and comfortable bedrooms. Some rooms have beamed ceilings and skylights, and others have two levels. Olivier's serves contemporary British cuisine with an Italian accent, and the pub is a snug place for a pint. ■ TIP → **Ask about packages that include entrance to Woburn Abbey and Safari Park.** Pros: close to Woburn Abbey; light-filled spaces. Cons: decor lacks character; small bathrooms. ⊠ George St., Woburn 🕾 01525/290441 ⊕ www. theinnatwoburn.com 🛏 50 rooms, 7 suites △ In-room: no a/c, safe (some). In-hotel: restaurant, room service, bar, laundry service, Wi-Fi, some pets allowed, no-smoking rooms ⊟ AE, DC, MC, V.

ALTHORP

5 mi west of Northampton, 27 mi northwest of Woburn Abbey.

EXPLORING

Deep in the heart of Northamptonshire sits **Althorp,** the ancestral home of the Spencers, the family of Diana, Princess of Wales. Here, on a tiny island within the estate park, is Diana's final resting place. Diana and her siblings found the house too melancholy, calling it "Deadlock Hall." What the house does have are rooms filled with Van Dycks, Reynoldses, and Rubenses—all portraits of the Spencers going back 500 years—and an entry hall that architectural historian Nikolaus Pevsner called "the noblest Georgian room in the country." To these attractions, Diana's brother, Earl Spencer, has added a visitor center devoted to her, which includes her wedding dress, childhood memorabilia, and an exhibition on her charitable work. A percentage of ticket income is donated to the Diana Princess of Wales Memorial Fund. On the west side of the estate park is Great Brington, the neighboring village where the church of **St. Mary the Virgin** (⊗ Daily noon–5) holds the Spencer family crypt; it's best reached by the designated path from Althorp. ⊠ Rugby Rd., off A428 🕾 01604/770107 ⊕ www.althorp.com 🖭 £12.50 (£14, including 2nd floor of house) ⊗ July and Aug., daily 11–5.

Shakespeare Country

STRATFORD-UPON-AVON AND ENVIRONS

WORD OF MOUTH

"Stratford's waterfront area is entertaining in summer, and while I wouldn't push too many of the Shakespeare sights in town, your kids would enjoy Mary Arden's House in the country. Warwick Castle is superb, and you could also visit Kenilworth in the same day. Kenilworth has a beautiful castle in semi-ruins—very evocative."

—palatino82

"If you are doing the Shakespeare properties and Warwick Castle and some similar sites, then by all means investigate the Great British Heritage Pass as it could save you big bucks—it's sold only to foreign tourists."

—PalenQ

Updated
by Christi
Daugherty

You get new insight into William Shakespeare when you visit the stretch of country where he was born and raised. The hills of sculpted farmland may look nothing like the forested countryside of the 16th century, but some sturdy Tudor houses that Shakespeare knew survive to this day. You can walk down streets he might have traveled up and cross streams where, as a child, he might have dangled his feet in the cool water. There's beauty in this—and also the possibility of tourist overkill.

Stratford-upon-Avon, with its carefully preserved Shakespeare sites and the theaters of the famed Royal Shakespeare Company, veers toward becoming "Shakespeare World." Still, it's a fascinating place, and there's much more to see—castles, churches, and countryside—in this famously lovely part of Britain.

Driving down Warwickshire's country lanes is one of the best ways to explore this area. Stop in at Charlecote, a grand Elizabethan manor house, and Baddesley Clinton, a superb example of late-medieval domestic architecture. Other treasure houses are Ragley Hall and Coughton Court, brimming with art and antiques; Compton Verney is a stately home that has been converted to an art gallery. Warwick Castle, a huge fortress, provides a glimpse into the country's turbulent history.

The price you pay for visiting Stratford is being caught among vast crowds of people, especially in peak season when the volume of visitors and the commercialization can be too much. If the hurly-burly bothers you, take a hint from the young Shakespeare. He often followed the Avon through quiet meadows and peaceful villages. You, too, can wander though a tranquil landscape and spend an afternoon picnicking in peace by a quiet river.

ORIENTATION AND PLANNING

GETTING ORIENTED

Stratford-upon-Avon, the heart of this small region, is surrounded by tiny villages, some with Shakespearean connections. The countryside around these hamlets is littered with stately "piles," as the British call the sprawling mansions built over the centuries. Many are open to the public, and each requires a few hours to explore. To the north lie two magnificent castles, Warwick and Kenilworth. The town of Warwick has much to offer besides its castle, and it's worth a visit.

Stratford-upon-Avon. The birthplace of Shakespeare, this bustling historic town is liberally dotted with 16th-century buildings the playwright

TOP REASONS TO GO

Shakespeare in Stratford: To see a play by Shakespeare in the town where he was born—and perhaps after you've visited his birthplace or other sites—is a magical experience. The Royal Shakespeare Company's productions are often outstanding.

A stroll to Anne Hathaway's Cottage: Taking the mile or so walk here from Stratford is as memorable as seeing the home of Shakespeare's wife. In spring and summer, flowers and soft green grass surround the path. The thatched cottage itself has rare period furniture and lush gardens.

Warwick Castle: Taking in the history—and some modern kitsch—at this sprawling medieval castle is a fun day out and great for the whole family. The castle is more than just the armory, great hall, and Tussauds waxworks. Expect year-round activities and events from jousting tournaments to demonstrations of falconry.

Kenilworth Castle: Exploring the sprawling, red-stone ruins of Kenilworth helps you appreciate the great amount of history that took place here. Check out the castle's massive Norman keep as well as buildings constructed for a visit from Elizabeth I. Cromwell may have ravaged this fortress, but it still commands the tranquil countryside. This is a great place to picnic.

would recognize. Turn down the quieter old lanes for a more peaceful experience.

Around Shakespeare Country. Warwickshire—the county of which Stratford is the southern nexus—is a land of sleepy villages, thatch-roof cottages, and solitary farmhouses. Explore these as well as stately homes and sprawling Warwick Castle.

PLANNING

WHEN TO GO

The Shakespeare sights get very crowded on weekends and school vacations; Warwick Castle usually brims with visitors, so arrive early in the day to beat the rush. Some country properties fill up quickly on weekends, and most close in winter. Some stately homes have limited hours even in summer, and many close in winter.

PLANNING YOUR TIME

Stratford-upon-Avon is ideal for day visits from London or as a convenient base; depending on the depth of your love of Shakespeare, you probably won't need more than a day or two here. Warwick is small and can be explored in an hour or two. Castle lovers could spend half a day in the many lines at popular Warwick Castle. A drive through the villages along the area's country lanes is a pleasant way to spend a day; a stop at any of the stately homes (check hours, which can be limited) will take a couple of hours. You're also near the northern Cotswolds if you want to explore further.

BUS TRAVEL

The cheapest way to travel is by bus, and National Express serves the region from London's Victoria Coach Station; there's ample service to Stratford. Buses run from London's Heathrow and Gatwick airports to Coventry (change there for Warwick), and Stagecoach serves local routes throughout the Stratford, Birmingham, and Coventry areas. Megabus, a budget service booked online, runs double-decker buses from Victoria station in London as well. They can take you to the same destinations as National Express.

Contacts Megabus (⊕ www.megabus.co.uk). **National Express** (☎0871/781–8181 ⊕ www.nationalexpress.com). **Stagecoach** (☎01788/535555 or 0845/600–1314 ⊕ www.stagecoachbus.com).

CAR TRAVEL

Main roads provide easy access between towns, but one pleasure of this rural area is exploring the smaller "B" roads, which lead deep into the countryside, by car. Local public bus service is not sufficient for most sightseeing journeys, as buses are infrequent and unpredictable. Renting a car or taking a tour bus are the two best options, although trains go to all the major towns.

TRAIN TRAVEL

Stratford has good train service and can be seen as a day trip from London if your time is limited. First Great Western Link and Virgin Trains serve the area. A seven-day Heart of England Rover ticket (£63) is valid for unlimited rail travel over any three days within a seven-day period in the region; contact National Rail Enquiries for purchasing information. Visit First Great Western's Web site, or phone the company, before your trip, as there are frequently Stratford-related packages and deals.

Contacts National Rail Enquiries (☎0845/748–4950 ⊕ www.nationalrail. co.uk). **First Great Western Link** (☎01789/293127 ⊕ www.firstgreatwestern. co.uk). **Virgin Trains** (☎0845/722–2333 ⊕ www.virgin.co.uk/trains).

RESTAURANTS

Stratford has many reasonably priced bistros and unpretentious eateries offering a broad choice of international fare. Warwick and Kenilworth both have good restaurant options.

HOTELS

Stratford and Warwick hold the highest concentration of lodgings in the area, from bed-and-breakfasts to hotels. Here you can find accommodations to fit every wallet. Because Stratford is *so* popular with theatergoers, book well ahead whenever possible. Most hotels offer discounted two- and three-day packages. Outside the towns, a number of top-notch country hotels guarantee discreet but attentive service—at fancy prices. At the other end of the scale, almost every village has an old inn with rooms at reasonable rates. If you're stuck, you can book a B&B through the local Tourist Information Centre.

WHAT IT COSTS IN POUNDS					
	£	££	£££	££££	£££££
Restaurants	Under £10	£10–£14	£15–£19	£20–£25	over £25
Hotels	Under £70	£70–£120	£121–£160	£161–£220	over £220

Restaurant prices are for a main course at dinner. Hotel prices are for two people in a standard double room in high season, including V.A.T., with no meals or, if indicated, CP (with continental breakfast), BP (Breakfast Plan, with full breakfast), or MAP (Modified American Plan, with breakfast and dinner).

VISITOR INFORMATION

Contacts Heart of England Tourist Board (☎ 01905/761100 ⊕ www.visittheheart.co.uk). **Shakespeare Country** (☎ 0870/160–7930 ⊕ www.shakespeare-country.co.uk).

STRATFORD-UPON-AVON

Even under the weight of busloads of visitors, Stratford, on the banks of the slow-flowing River Avon, has somehow hung on to much of its ancient character and can, on a good day, still feel like an English market town. It doesn't take long to figure out who's the center of attention here. Born in a half-timber, early-16th-century building in the center of Stratford on April 23, 1564, Shakespeare died on April 23, 1616, his 52nd birthday, in a more imposing house at New Place. Although he spent much of his life in London, the world still associates him with "Shakespeare's Avon." Here, in the years between his birth and 1587, he played as a young lad, attended grammar school, and married Anne Hathaway; and here he returned, as a prosperous man. You can see Shakespeare's whole life here: his birthplace on Henley Street; his burial place in Holy Trinity Church; Anne Hathaway's Cottage; his mother's home at Wilmcote; New Place; and the neighboring Nash's House, home of Shakespeare's granddaughter.

Take Antonio's advice (*Twelfth Night*, act 3, scene 3) and "beguile the time, and feed your knowledge with viewing the town." By the 16th century Stratford was a prosperous market town with thriving guilds and industries. Half-timber houses from this era have been preserved, and they are set off by later architecture, such as the elegant Georgian storefronts on Bridge Street, with their 18th-century porticoes and arched doorways.

GETTING HERE AND AROUND

Stratford lies about 100 mi northwest of London; take M40 to Junction 15. The town is 37 mi southeast of Birmingham by A435 and A46 or by M40 to Junction 15.

First Great Western Link and Virgin Trains serve the area. Four direct trains (two in the morning and two in the afternoon) from London's Paddington Station take two hours to reach Stratford; other trains require you to change, usually at Leamington Spa. Stratford's train station is at the edge of the town center on Alcester Road. Taxis are usually available to pick up arriving passengers. If you have a map, you can walk into town.

Stratford's center is small and easily walkable—it's unlikely you'd need to use the local bus service. City Sightseeing runs guided tours of Stratford (£11). The bus tours are rather run-of-the-mill and don't include admission to the Stratford sights (most of which are within walking distance in town). Shakespeare Town Walk offers a number of walks and cruises, including a ghost-theme walk. For information about the Shakespeare's Life in Stratford walk, led by actors, ask at the tourism office.

TIMING

If you have only a day here, arrive early and confine your visit to two or three Shakespeare Birthplace Trust properties, a few other town sights, a pub lunch, and a walk along the river, capped off by a stroll to the cottage of Anne Hathaway.

If you don't like crowds, avoid visiting on weekends and school vacations, and take in the main Shakespeare shrines in the early morning to see them at their least frenetic. One high point of Stratford's calendar is the Shakespeare Birthday Celebrations, usually on the weekend nearest to April 23.

ESSENTIALS

Tour Information **City Sightseeing** (☎ *01789/294466* ⊕ *www.city-sightseeing. com)*. **Shakespeare Town Walk** (☎ *01789/292478* ⊕ *www.stratfordtownwalk. co.uk)*.

Visitor Information **Stratford-upon-Avon** (⊠ *Bridgefoot* ☎ *0870/160–7930* ⊕ *www.stratford-upon-avon.co.uk)*.

EXPLORING

Most sights cluster around Henley Street (off the roundabout as you come in on the A3400 Birmingham road), High Street, and Waterside, which skirts the public gardens through which the River Avon flows. Bridge Street and Sheep Street (parallel to Bridge) are Stratford's main thoroughfares and the site of most banks, shops, and eating places. The town's tourist office lies at Bridgefoot, between the canal and the river, next to Clopton Bridge—"a sumptuous new bridge and large of stone"— built in the 15th century by Sir Hugh Clopton, once lord mayor of London and one of Stratford's richest and most philanthropic residents.

The **Shakespeare Birthplace Trust** runs the main places of Shakespearean interest: Anne Hathaway's Cottage, Hall's Croft, Mary Arden's House, Nash's House and New Place, and Shakespeare's Birthplace. They have similar opening times. ■ TIP→ **You can buy a money-saving combination ticket to all five properties, or pay separate entry fees if you're visiting only one or two. Family tickets are an option, too.** At the time of this writing, tickets for Hall's Croft and Nash's House and New Place were available only as a rather pricey (£10) joint ticket that includes the birthplace: unfortunate if you're interested in only one of them. You can check out special events at the properties, from talks about Tudor life to performances of Shakespeare's plays. ☎ *01789/204016* ⊕ *www.shakespeare. org.uk* ✉ *Joint ticket to 5 properties £16; joint ticket to Shakespeare's Birthplace, Hall's Croft, and Nash's House–New Place £10.*

TOP ATTRACTIONS

8 **★** **Anne Hathaway's Cottage.** The most picturesque of the Shakespeare Trust properties, on the western outskirts of Stratford, was the family home of the woman Shakespeare married in 1582. The "cottage," actually a substantial Tudor farmhouse, has latticed windows and a grand thatch roof. Inside is period furniture, including a rare carved Elizabethan bed; outside is a garden planted in lush Victorian style with herbs and flowers. In a nearby field the **Shakespeare Tree Garden** has 40 trees mentioned in the playwright's works, a yew maze, and sculptures with Shakespearean themes. ■ TIP→ **The best way to get here is to walk, especially in late spring when the apple trees are in blossom.** There are two main footpaths, one via Greenhill Street by the railroad bridge, the other leaving from Holy Trinity Church up Old Town and Chestnut Walk. ⊠ *Cottage La., Shottery* ☎ *01789/204016* ⊕ *www.shakespeare. org.uk* ✉ *£6.50, Shakespeare Trust 5-property ticket £16* ☉ *Apr., May, Sept., and Oct., Mon.–Sat. 9:30–5, Sun. 10–5; June–Aug., Mon.–Sat. 9–5, Sun. 9:30–5; Nov.–Mar., Mon.–Sat. 10–4, Sun. 10:30–4; last entry 30 mins before closing.*

Stratford-upon-Avon

TO
A3400 AND MARY
ARDEN'S HOUSE

← TO TRAIN
STATION

Birmingham Rd.

Shakespeare St.

Mulberry St.

Gt. William St.

Stratford-upon-Avon Canal

St. Gregory Rd.

Welcombe Rd.

Warwick Rd.

Maidenhead Rd.

Lock Cl.

Tyler St.

Payton St.

John St.

Arden St.

Windsor St.

Henley St.

Mansell St.

Union St.

Guild St.

Bus Station

Bridgeway

Meer St.

Greenhill St.

Wood St.

Bridge St.

Bridgefoot

Clopton Bridge

High St.

Rother Rd.

Grove Rd.

Ely St.

Sheep St.

Bancroft Gardens

Waterside

Tramway Bridge

Chapel St.

Scholars La.

Chapel La.

Swan Theatre

Church St.

Chestnut Walk

Courtyard Theatre

Southern La.

Broad St.

Old Town

Avon

West St.

Bull St.

Broad Walk

Narrow La.

New Broad St.

Sanctus St.

College St.

College La.

Hollom St.

New St.

Trinity St.

Mill La.

❶ ❷ ❸ ❹ ❺ ❻ ❼ ❽ ❾ ❿ ⓫ ⓬

0   200 yds

0   200 m

KEY
🛈 *Tourist information*

❾ Holy Trinity Church. The burial place of William Shakespeare, this 13th-century church sits on the banks of the Avon, with a graceful avenue of lime trees framing its entrance. Shakespeare's final resting place is in the chancel, rebuilt in 1465–91 in the late Perpendicular style. He was buried here not because he was a famed poet but because he was a lay rector of Stratford, owning a portion of the township tithes. On the north wall of the sanctuary, over the altar steps, is the famous marble bust created by Gerard Jansen in 1623, and thought to be a true likeness of Shakespeare. The bust offers a more human, even humorous, per-spective when viewed from the side. Also in the chancel are the graves of Shakespeare's wife, Anne; his daughter Susanna; his son-in-law John Hall; and his granddaughter's husband, Thomas Nash. Nearby, the Par-ish Register is displayed, containing both Shakespeare's baptismal entry (1564) and his burial notice (1616). The church is trying to raise more than £2 million for restoration work. Its vicar warns that, without that work, all or part of the building will have to close within five years. ⊠ *Trinity St.* ⊕ *www.stratford-upon-avon.org* ✉ *£1.50 for chancel* ⊙ *Mar., Mon.–Sat. 9–5, Sun. 12:30–5; Apr.–Oct., Mon.–Sat. 8:30–6, Sun. 12:30–5; Nov.–Feb., Mon.–Sat. 9–4, Sun. 12:30–5; last admission 20 mins before closing.*

⓬ Mary Arden's House. A working farm, where food is grown using meth-ods common in the 16th century, is the main attraction at Mary Arden's House (the childhood home of Shakespeare's mother) and Palmer's Farm. This bucolic stop is great for kids, who can see the lambs, listen as the farmers explain their work in the fields, and watch the cooks pre-pare food in the Tudor farmhouse kitchen. It all brings the past to life. There are crafts exhibits, a café, and a garden. The site is 3 mi north-west of Stratford; you need to walk or drive here, or else go with a tour. ⊠ *Off A3400, Wilmcote* ☎ *01789/204016, 01789/293455 information on special events* ⊕ *www.shakespeare.org.uk* ✉ *£8, Shakespeare Trust 5-property ticket £16* ⊙ *Nov.–Mar., daily 10–4; Sept., Oct., Apr., and May, daily 10–5; June–Aug., daily 9:30–5; last entry 30 mins before closing.*

❿ Royal Shakespeare Theatre. The Stratford home of the Royal Shakespeare Company (RSC), amid lovely gardens along the River Avon, has been closed for a massive renovation since 2007 but is scheduled to be com-plete in 2010. The new theater will have better sightlines, better seating, and better acoustics than the old 1932 building ever had. The company, which presents some of the finest productions of Shakespeare's plays in the world, has existed since 1879. Shows are also staged in its other the-aters, including the adjacent **Swan**, a Victorian theater that follows the lines of Shakespeare's original Globe and is considered to be one of the most exciting performing spaces in Britain. There's also the Courtyard Theatre just up the street from the Royal Shakespeare Theatre. Between the two there's an art gallery with theater-related exhibitions, portraits, and depictions of scenes from the plays. ⊠ *Waterside* ☎ *0844/800–1114 ticket hotline, 01789/296655 information* 🖷 *01789/403444 box office* ⊕ *www.rsc.org.uk.*

❶ Shakespeare's Birthplace. A half-timber house typical of its time, the playwright's birthplace is a much-visited shrine that has been altered and restored since he lived here. You enter through the somewhat over-the-top **Shakespeare Centre,** where the exhibits consist mostly of poster-size Shakespeare quotations, with written information about the age in which he lived. It's mainly geared to the groups of schoolchildren who often fill the place, so don't feel bad about hustling on to the house itself, which is across the garden from the large, modern center. The few furnishings in the actual house reflect comfortable, middle-class Elizabethan domestic life. Shakespeare's father, John, a glove maker and wool dealer, purchased the house; a reconstructed workshop shows the tools of the glover's trade. An auction notice describes the property as it was when it was offered for sale in 1847. You can also see the signatures of earlier pilgrims, including Mark Twain and Charles Dickens, who according to the Shakespeare Trust, scratched with their diamond rings into Shakespeare's windowpanes. ⊠ *Henley St.* ☎ *01789/204016* ⊕ *www. shakespeare.org.uk* ✉ *£10, includes entry to Hall's Croft and Nash's House, 5-property ticket £16* ⊙ *Nov.–Mar., Mon.–Sat. 10–4, Sun. 10:30–4; Apr. and May, Mon.–Sat. 10–5, Sun. 10:30–5; June–Aug., Mon.–Sat. 9–5, Sun. 9:30–5; Sept. and Oct., Mon.–Sat. 10–5, Sun. 10:30–5; last entry 30 mins before closing.*

> **WILL FOR SALE**
>
> In 1847 two widowed ladies were maintaining Shakespeare's birthplace in a somewhat ramshackle state. With the approach of the tercentennial of the playwright's birth, and in response to a rumor that the building was to be purchased by P. T. Barnum and shipped across the Atlantic, the city shelled out £3,000 for the relic. It was tidied up and opened to a growing throng of Shakespeare devotees.

WORTH SEEING

⓫ **Butterfly Farm.** Europe's largest display of butterflies, a mock rain forest, and spiders, caterpillars, and insects from all over the world are a two-minute walk past the Bridgefoot footbridge. ⊠ *Swan's Nest La.* ☎ *01789/299288* ⊕ *www.butterflyfarm.co.uk* ✉ *£6* ⊙ *June–Aug., daily 10–6; Sept.–May, daily 10–dusk.*

❺ **Guild Chapel.** This chapel is the noble centerpiece of Stratford's Guild buildings, including the Guildhall, the Grammar School, and the almshouses—all structures well known to Shakespeare. The ancient structure was rebuilt in the late Perpendicular style in the first half of the 15th century, thanks to the largesse of Stratford resident Hugh Clopton. The otherwise plain interior includes fragments of a remarkable medieval fresco of the Last Judgment uncovered in a 20th-century reconstruction. The painting had been painted over in the 16th century and forgotten. The bell, also given by Sir Hugh, still rings as it did to tell Shakespeare the time of day. ⊠ *Chapel La. at Church St.* ☎ *01789/293351* ✉ *Free, donations welcome* ⊙ *Daily 9–5.*

❻ **Guildhall.** Dating to 1416–18, the Guildhall is occupied by **King Edward's Grammar School,** which Shakespeare probably attended as a boy; it's still used as a school. On the first floor is the Guildhall proper, where traveling acting companies performed. Many historians believe that it was after seeing the troupe known as the Earl of Leicester's Men in 1587 that Shakespeare got the acting bug and set off for London. Upstairs is the classroom in which he is reputed to have learned "little Latin and less Greek." Students use the classroom today, so visits may be made by prior arrangement only, during after-school hours or vacation time; contact the tourist information office. Immediately beyond the Guildhall on Church Street is a row of timber-and-daub almshouses, built for the poor by the Guild of the Holy Cross in the early 15th century and still serving as housing for pensioners. ⊠ *Church St.*

⑦ Hall's Croft. One of the finest surviving Jacobean (early-17th-century) town houses, this impressive residence has a delightful walled garden. Tradition has it that Hall's Croft was the home of Shakespeare's elder daughter, Susanna, and her husband, Dr. John Hall, whose medical dispensary is on view along with the other rooms, all containing Jacobean furniture of heavy oak and some 17th-century portraits ⊠ *Old Town* ☎ *01789/204016* ⊕ *www.shakespeare.org.uk* ✉ *£10, includes admission to Shakespeare's Birthplace and New Place, 5-property ticket £16* ☉ *Nov.–Mar., daily 11–4; Apr., May, Sept., and Oct., daily 11–5; June–Aug., Mon.–Sat. 9:30–5, Sun. 10–5; last entry 30 mins before closing.*

② Harvard House. This is the grand, half-timber, 16th-century home of Katherine Rogers, mother of the John Harvard who founded Harvard University in 1636. The twin-gabled facade, dating from about 1600, is one of Stratford's glories. Note the exterior beams carved with fleurs-de-lis in relief, the sculpted human faces on the corbels, and the bear and staff (symbols of the Warwick earls) on the bracket heads. Inside, the **Museum of British Pewter** displays pewter toys, tankards, and teapots, dating from Roman times to the present. ⊠ *High St.* ☎ *01789/204507* ⊕ *www.shakespeare.org.uk* ✉ *£3.50, free if you have a 5-property ticket* ☉ *May, June, and Sept.–Nov., Fri.–Sun. 11:30–4:30; July and Aug., Thurs.–Sun. 11:30–4:30.*

QUICK BITES

Duck into the quaint **Hathaway Tea Rooms** (⊠ **19 High St.** ☎ **01789/ 292404**), above the shops on the busy High Street in a 17th-century building, for wonderful tea and scones. It can be packed in summer.

④ Nash's House and New Place. This is the home of Thomas Nash, who married Shakespeare's last direct descendant, his granddaughter Elizabeth Hall. The heavily restored house has been furnished in 17th-century style, and it also contains a local museum. In the gardens (note the intricately laid-out Elizabethan knot garden) are the foundations of **New Place**, the house in which Shakespeare died in 1616. Built in 1483 "of brike and tymber" for a lord mayor of London, New Place was Stratford's grandest piece of real estate when Shakespeare bought it in 1597 for £60; tragically, it was torn down in 1759 by the Reverend Francis Gastrell, who was angry at the hordes of Shakespeare-related sightseers. The **Great Garden** of New Place, beyond the knot garden, has a sculpture trail with bronze works inspired by Shakespeare's plays. ⊠ *Chapel St.* ☎ *01789/204016* ⊕ *www.shakespeare.org.uk* ✉ *£10, includes admission to Shakespeare's Birthplace and Hall's Croft, 5-property ticket £16* ☉ *Nov.–Mar., daily 11–4; Apr., May, Sept., and Oct., daily 11–5; June–Aug., Mon.–Sat. 9:30–5, Sun. 10–5; last entry 30 mins before closing.*

③ **Tudor World at the Falstaff Experience.** Designed like a traditional Victorian museum, this place is G-rated but for the claim that the building is haunted—which is most of the draw. Tudor World examines the 16th century with displays of historic detritus and memorabilia that explore the plague years, early medicine, and alleged ghosts. At night, adult-only "ghost tours" (£7.50; on the hour nightly from 6 to 9) and "vigils" explore the house's paranormal history in spooky detail. ⊠ *The Shrieves House Barn, 40 Sheep St.* ☎ *0870/350–2770* ⊕ *www.falstaffexperience.co.uk* ✉ *£4.955; kids ages 5–12 admitted free if accompanied by an adult* ⊙ *Daily 10:30–5:30.*

WHERE TO EAT

£ ✗ **Black Swan.** Known locally as the Dirty Duck, one of Stratford's
BRITISH   most celebrated pubs has attracted actors since Garrick's days. Its little
★   veranda overlooks the theaters and the river. You can sample English grill specialties as well as bar meals such as mussels and fries. Few people come here for the food, which is mediocre: the real attraction is the ambience and the other customers. ⊠ *Southern La.* ☎ *01789/297312* ▤ *AE, MC, V* ⊙ *No dinner Sun.*

££ ✗ **Georgetown Restaurant.** Small and somewhat eccentric, this restau-
MALAYSIAN rant serves exotic Malaysian cuisine from a menu divided to represent the country's diverse population. You can choose Malaysian Malay dishes, Malaysian Indian, or Malaysian Chinese, and mix and mingle the options—perhaps starting with the Malay fried fish *ikan goring,* and moving on to the *rending daging* dish of beef and coconut milk. The food is excellent, but portions are tiny. Palm trees, gilded mirrors, and teak strike a Colonial note. ⊠ *23 Sheep St.* ☎ *01789/204445* ▤ *AE, MC, V.*

£££ ✗ **Lambs of Sheep Street.** Sit downstairs to appreciate the hardwood floors
BRITISH   and oak beams of this local epicurean favorite; upstairs, the look is a bit more contemporary. The updates of tried-and-true dishes include salmon cakes with wilted spinach, and char-grilled sausages with leek mash. Desserts are fantastic here, and daily specials keep the menu seasonal. The two- and three-course fixed-price menus (£10 and £15) for lunch or pretheater dining on weekdays are good deals. ⊠ *12 Sheep St.* ☎ *01789/292554* ⌂ *Reservations essential* ▤ *AE, MC, V.*

£££ ✗ **Malbec.** Blending French and British styles seamlessly, this laid-back,
FRENCH   sophisticated little restaurant has been stacking up kudos for French-influenced dishes such as roast lamb with mint hollandaise and Cornish bream (a freshwater fish) with braised cabbage, mussels, and tarragon. You can dine in the main-floor space or in the cellar, with its flagstone floors and light oak tables. The constantly changing wine list is very well chosen. The fixed-price lunch (two courses for £9) is a great deal. ⊠ *6 Union St.* ☎ *01789/269106* ▤ *AE, MC, V.*

££ ✗ **Oppo.** Hearty, warming meals are offered at this informal, family-
BRITISH   style restaurant in a 16th-century building on the main dining street near the theaters. The English and European dishes on the menu win praise from the locals, or you could try the sausages and mash, roasted chicken, and toasted sandwiches. Make reservations a month ahead in summer. ⊠ *13 Sheep St.* ☎ *01789/269980* ▤ *MC, V.*

££ ✕ **Russons.** Popular with theatergoers, this restaurant occupies a16th-
BRITISH century building furnished with prints of the area. The fare, though
reasonably priced, doesn't skimp on quality. On the daily-changing
menu, chalked on a blackboard, are English specialties such as roast
lamb and guinea fowl, along with seafood choices from shrimp to sole.
⊠ *8 Church St.* ☎ *01789/268822* ⌖ *Reservations essential* ▤ *AE, MC,
V* ⊘ *Closed Mon.*

££ ✕ **Sorrento.** Somewhat formal, this family-run Italian restaurant takes
ITALIAN a respectable, old-fashioned approach to service. Upon arrival, guests
have an aperitif in the lounge before they're escorted to their tables for
a silver-service, white-tablecloth meal. The menu of traditional favorites
is cooked from family recipes, and includes salmon and lemon sole with
capers, steak flambéed in brandy, and a pasta of the day. Pretheater dinners are a good value. ⊠ *8 Ely St.* ☎ *01789/297999* ▤ *AE, MC, V.*

££ ✕ **Thespian's Indian Restaurant.** A buzzing crowd of regulars frequents this
INDIAN casual Indian restaurant, drawn by its extensive menu of spicy dishes
from the subcontinent and its friendly atmosphere. Dishes like lamb
rogan josh (a curry) or the sweet chicken korma are professionally
turned out, and served on heated trays by the able staff. It's an excellent option when you're bored with meat and potatoes. ⊠ *26 Sheep St.*
☎ *01789/267187* ▤ *AE, MC, V.*

££ ✕ **The Vintner.** The imaginative, bistro-inspired menu varies each day at
BISTRO this café and wine bar. Shoulder of lamb is a popular main course, as
is the steak; a children's menu is available. To dine before curtain time,
arrive early or make a reservation. The building, largely unaltered since
the late 1400s, has lovely flagstone floors and oak beams. ⊠ *5 Sheep
St.* ☎ *01789/297259* ▤ *AE, MC, V.*

WHERE TO STAY

The Ettington Park Hotel and the Fox & Goose, both near Alderminster, are excellent rural hotels a few miles from Stratford.

£ ⊞ **Heron Lodge.** Just a mile outside of Stratford town center, this B&B
combines budget accommodation in a family home with high-quality
service. Rooms are individually decorated, and the casual conservatory
is perfect for an afternoon cup of tea. Owners David and Sarah Rus-
son are serious about breakfast, serving pancakes, omelets, and more;
locally sourced ingredients—from tea to jam and sausages—appear on
the menu. You can also get a top-quality English breakfast. There's a bus
stop near the house. **Pros:** unusual and relaxing place; excellent service.
Cons: outside of town. ⊠ *260 Alcester Rd.* ☎ *01789/299169* ⊕ *www.*
heronlodge.com ⇘ *5 rooms* ⌖ *In-room: no a/c. In-hotel: bar, parking*
(free), no kids under 5, no-smoking rooms ▤ *AE, MC, V* ⦿ *BP.*

££–£££ ⊞ **Holiday Inn Stratford-upon-Avon.** This good-value, modern chain hotel's
♺ best selling points are its excellent location in the center of the historic
district, on the banks of the Avon, and its views across the river and
town center. It also has plenty of modern amenities. Rooms are large
and full of light, but bathrooms are a bit of a squeeze. Children are welcomed enthusiastically (if you don't appreciate kids, you might find this
place annoying). Ask for rooms away from the elevators, as those can be

a bit noisy. Package-tour groups spilling out of their buses add a steady background roar. **Pros:** good location; handy for families. **Cons:** modern and featureless; big and impersonal. ⊠*Bridgefoot* ☎*01789/279988* ⊕*www.holidayinn.com* ⌨*251 rooms, 2 suites* ⚓*In-room: Wi-Fi. In-hotel: restaurant, room service, bar, pool, gym, parking (paid), no-smoking rooms* ☰*AE, MC, V* ⫶⊙⫶*BP.*

£££–££££ 🏠**Legacy Falcon Hotel.** Licensed as an alehouse since 1640, this black-and-white timber-frame hotel in the center of town has an excellent location, and a 2008 renovation has brought a bright new look inside. The heavily beamed rooms in the older part are small and a bit more interesting, but the creaky, uneven antique floors might bother some. The ordinary rooms in the modern extension have more space. All guest rooms have neutral modern decor in shades of chocolate and cream, along with new, comfortable beds. Downstairs, the Oak Bar and Will's Restaurant have been sympathetically upgraded to keep their lovely, antique look. **Pros:** great location; old portion of the building is charming. **Cons:** modern rooms are uninspiring; so-so restaurant. ⊠*Chapel St.* ☎*01789/279953 or 0845/602–6787* ⊕*www.legacy-hotels.co.uk* ⌨*84 rooms* ⚓*In-room: no a/c, Wi-Fi. In-hotel: restaurant, room service, bars, laundry service, parking (free)* ☰*AE, DC, MC, V* ⫶⊙⫶*BP.*

£££ 🏠**Macdonald Alveston Manor.** This redbrick Elizabethan manor house across the River Avon from central Stratford has plenty of historic details, as well as a modern spa. Rooms are comfortably sized, with faux antiques—a few Tudor-style rooms in the main building have four-poster beds. Although much of the building is modern, one section dates back to the 18th century, and original fireplaces and paneling have been preserved in the comfortable lounges, where you can sip a cup of tea by a roaring fire. Legend says the grounds were the setting for the first production of *A Midsummer Night's Dream.* **Pros:** nice mix of historic and modern; good spa facilities; you can warm yourself by a fire in winter. **Cons:** modern rooms are less interesting; there's no elevator and lots of stairs. ⊠*Clopton Bridge* ☎*08704/008181* ⊕*www. macdonald-hotels.co.uk* ⌨*110 rooms, 4 suites* ⚓*In-room: refrigerator, Internet. In-hotel: restaurant, room service, bar, pool, spa, laundry service, parking (free), some pets allowed (fee), no-smoking rooms* ☰*AE, DC, MC, V* ⫶⊙⫶*BP.*

££££–£££££ 🏠**Menzies Welcombe Hotel Spa & Golf Club.** With its mullioned bay windows, gables, and tall chimneys, this hotel in an 1886 neo-Jacobean-style building evokes the luxury of bygone days. You can relax in the clubby bar or on the Italianate terrace. Public rooms such as the Great Hall, with wood paneling, chandeliers, and marble fireplace, complement the main-house guest rooms, which have faux-antique furnishings and beds that are not particularly comfortable. The fancy Trevelyan Restaurant (jacket and tie required) relies on a French foundation to present English cuisine, and although the setting is not as formal as you might expect, the atmosphere certainly is. The hotel is about a 10-minute drive from Stratford. **Pros:** great for golfers; good spa facilities; indoor pool. **Cons:** formal dining; atmosphere a bit stuffy. ⊠*Warwick Rd.* ☎*01789/295252* ⊕*www.menzies-hotels.co.uk* ⌨*64 rooms* ⚓*In-room: no a/c, Internet. In-hotel: 2 restaurants, room service, bar,* *golf course, tennis court, pool, gym, spa, laundry service, parking (free), no-smoking rooms* ▤*AE, D, MC, V* ⏀*BP.*

£–££ 🏠 **Penryn House.** Traditional English prints and furnishings as well as some simple modern pieces fill the small but cheerful rooms here. The helpful proprietors, Robert and Anne Dawkes, take pride in the hearty breakfast, and they always have options for vegetarians. The B&B is an easy walk from the city center, Anne Hathaway's Cottage, and the rail station. **Pros:** charming little place; great breakfasts. **Cons:** rooms are quite tiny; too floral for some. ✉*126 Alcester Rd.* ☎*01789/293718* ⊕*www.penrynguesthouse.co.uk* ⇆*7 rooms, 6 with bath* ⏁*In-room: no a/c. In-hotel: Wi-Fi, laundry service, parking (free), no-smoking rooms* ▤*MC, V* ⏀*BP.*

£££–££££ 🏠 **Shakespeare Hotel.** Built in the 1400s, this Elizabethan town house ★ in the heart of town is a vision right out of *The Merry Wives of Windsor,* with its five gables and long, stunning, black-and-white half-timber facade. Its restaurant, bar, and lounge have blackened beams and a pleasantly aged look. The intelligently modernized interiors have a touch of luxury; Shakespeareana and old playbills decorate the public areas. Upstairs, rooms are named after Shakespeare's characters and the actors who have portrayed them. Hewn timbers carved with rose-and-thistle patterns decorate some rooms; all have new beds and a clean, neutral decor. There are good deals on room rates in the off-season. **Pros:** historic building; great lounge to relax in. **Cons:** prices are quite high for what's on offer; some very small bedrooms. ✉*Chapel St.* ☎*0870/400–8182* ⊕*www.mercure.com* ⇆*64 rooms, 6 suites* ⏁*In-room: no a/c, Internet. In-hotel: restaurant, room service, bar, laundry service, parking (paid), some pets allowed (fee), no-smoking rooms* ▤*AE, DC, MC, V.*

£££–££££ 🏠 **The Stratford.** Although this modern hotel may lack the period charm of older hotels, its up-to-date facilities, spacious rooms, and ample grounds make it a good option for those for whom Tudor beamed ceilings are nothing more than something to bump your head into. Rooms, all in polished oak wood with burgundy-and-green color schemes, come in several shapes: some have four-poster beds, others are geared to the business traveler. You can use the leisure facilities, including an indoor pool, at a sister hotel, the Stratford Manor, 3 mi away. **Pros:** handy location; lots of modern conveniences. **Cons:** service a bit impersonal; rooms lack personality. ✉*Arden St.* ☎*01789/271000* ⊕*www.qhotels. co.uk* ⇆*102 rooms* ⏁*In-room: no a/c, Internet. In-hotel: restaurant, room service, bar, gym, laundry service, parking (free), no-smoking rooms* ▤*AE, DC, MC, V* ⏀*BP.*

£ 🏠 **Victoria Spa Lodge.** This good-value B&B lies 1½ mi outside town, within view of the Stratford Canal. The grand, clematis-draped building dates from 1837; you can see Queen Victoria's coat of arms in two of its gables. Dark wood and floral fabrics decorating the lounge–breakfast room and spacious guest rooms are a bit dated, but the bathrooms are modern and the price is attractive. **Pros:** beautiful buildings; spacious guest rooms. **Cons:** decor is old-fashioned; could use refurbishment. ✉*Bishopton La., Bishopton* ☎*01789/267985* ⊕*www.victoriaspa. co.uk* ⇆*7 rooms* ⏁*In-room: no a/c, no phone, Wi-Fi. In-hotel: parking (free), no-smoking rooms* ▤*MC, V* ⏀*BP.*

££ ⚞⚟**White Swan.** Exposed beams,
★ low ceilings, and winding corridors
make this cozy hotel a delight for
those who like a little authenticity.
It claims to be the oldest building
in Stratford, and the look of the
exterior (circa 1450) reinforces
that boast. Each room is individually decorated, and although fabrics
are not luxurious, admirable effort
has been made to avoid traditional
chintz. Heavy antiques mix with
reproductions; some rooms have
fireplaces, and some have four-

> **THE PUB'S THE THING**
>
> Take a break from Shakespeare.
> Having a pint of ale at the **White
> Swan**, on a cool night when the
> fires are lighted and the mood is
> jovial, is a true English experience.
> You never know which direction
> the conversation will turn. Or stop
> by another of Stratford's pubs,
> such as the **Black Swan** (also
> known as the Dirty Duck).

poster beds. Bathrooms are tucked into what little space is available.
■TIP➡**The popular pub, a traditional English boozer with ancient beams,
attracts visitors and locals. Pros:** great for those who like ancient buildings; unique decor. **Cons:** some rooms are small; most bathrooms are
even tinier. ⊠*Rother St.* ☎*01789/297022* ⊕*www.pebblehotels.com*
⤴*41 rooms* ⚑*In-room: no a/c (some), Internet (some). In-hotel: restaurant, room service, parking (no fee)* ⊟*MC, V* ⦿*BP.*

NIGHTLIFE AND THE ARTS

FESTIVALS

The **Shakespeare Birthday Celebrations** (☎*01789/415536* ⊕*www.
shakespeare.org.uk*) take place on and around the weekend closest to
April 23 (unless Easter occurs during that time). The events, spread over
four or five days, include a formal reception, lectures, free concerts,
processions, and a special performance of a play.

THEATER

Fodor's Choice The **Royal Shakespeare Company** (⊠ *Waterside* ☎*0844/800–1114 ticket
★ hotline, 01789/296655 general information* ⊕*www.rsc.org.uk*) performs Shakespeare plays year-round in Stratford, as well as in other
venues around Britain. Stratford's Royal Shakespeare Theatre is the
home of the RSC, one of the finest repertory troupes in the world and
long the backbone of the country's theatrical life. The company's new
theater is scheduled to open in 2010 on the site of the old, and performances also take place at other theaters throughout town, including the
1,000-seat Courtyard Theatre on Southern Lane. The Swan Theatre,
behind the Royal Shakespeare Theatre, stages plays by Shakespeare
and contemporaries such as Christopher Marlowe and Ben Jonson.
Prices usually are £7 to £45. ■TIP➡**Book ahead through the RSC, as
seats go fast, but day-of-performance (two per person to personal callers
only) and returned tickets are often available.** You can book tickets from
London with **Ticketmaster** (☎*0870/534–4444* ⊕*www.ticketmaster.
co.uk*), operating 24 hours a day. You can book tickets in the United
States (a 20% surcharge applies) with **Keith Prowse** (☎*212/398–1430
or 800/669–8687* ⊕*www.keithprowse.com*).

SPORTS AND THE OUTDOORS

Avon Cruises ($\boxtimes$ *The Boatyard, Swan's Nest La.* ☎☎01789/267073) rents boats and punts, and provides half-hour river excursions for a welcome escape from the crowds; the company can arrange longer trips from Easter to October. **Bancroft Cruises** ($\boxtimes$ *Moathouse, Bridgefoot* ☎01789/269669) runs half-hourly excursions on the river. Hour-long trips farther afield can also be scheduled.

SHOPPING

Chain stores and shops sell tourist junk, but this is also a good place to shop for high-quality (and high-price) silver, jewelry, and china. There's an open **market** (great for bargains) every Friday in the Market Place at Greenhill and Meer streets. **Antique Arms & Armour** ($\boxtimes$ *Poet's Arbour, Sheep St.* ☎01789/293453) sells antique swords, sabers, and armor. The **Antique Market** ($\boxtimes$ *Ely St.*) contains 50 stalls of jewelry, silver, linens, porcelain, and memorabilia. **B&W Thornton** ($\boxtimes$ *23 Henley St.* ☎01789/269405), above Shakespeare's Birthplace, stocks Moorcroft pottery and glass. **Chaucer Head Bookshop** ($\boxtimes$ *21 Chapel St.* ☎01789/415691) is the best of Stratford's many secondhand bookshops. The **Shakespeare Bookshop** ($\boxtimes$ *39 Henley St.* ☎01789/201820), run by the Shakespeare Birthplace, carries Elizabethan plays, Tudor history books, children's books, and general paraphernalia.

7

AROUND SHAKESPEARE COUNTRY

This section of Warwickshire is marked by gentle hills, green fields, slow-moving rivers, quiet villages, and time-burnished halls, castles (Warwick and Kenilworth are the best examples, and well worth visiting), and churches. Historic houses such as Baddesley Clinton and Charlecote Court are another reason to explore. All the sights are close enough to Stratford-upon-Avon that you can easily use the town as a base if you wish.

HENLEY-IN-ARDEN

8 mi northwest of Stratford.

A brief drive out of Stratford will take you under the Stratford-upon-Avon Canal aqueduct to pretty Henley-in-Arden, whose wide main street is an architectural pageant of many periods. This area was once the Forest of Arden, where Shakespeare set one of his greatest comedies, *As You Like It.* Among the buildings to look for are the former Guildhall, dating from the 15th century, and the White Swan pub, built in the early 1600s. Near Henley-in Arden are two stately homes worth a stop, Packwood House and Baddesley Clinton.

GETTING HERE AND AROUND

The town is on the A3400. London Midland trains for Henley-in-Arden depart every half hour from Stratford; the journey takes about 15 minutes. Train service from Birmingham takes about 30 minutes, and trains leave every half hour. The town heritage center is not an official Tourist

Information Centre but does have brochures; it's open Easter through October but is closed on Monday.

ESSENTIALS

Visitor Information Henley-in-Arden Heritage and Visitors Center (✉ *Joseph Hardy House, 150 High St.* ☎ *01564/795919* ⊕ *www. heritagehenley.org.uk*).

EXPLORING

Packwood House draws garden enthusiasts to its re-created 17th-century gardens, highlighted by an ambitious topiary Tudor garden in which yew trees depict Jesus' Sermon on the Mount. The house combines redbrick and half-timbering, and its tall chimneys are also typical of the period. Exquisite collections of 16th-century furniture and textiles in the interior's 20th-century version of Tudor architecture make this one of the area's finest historic houses open to the public. It's 5 mi north of Henley-in-Arden and 12 mi north of Stratford-upon-Avon. ✉ *Off B4439, 2 mi east of Hockley Heath* ☎ *01564/783294* ⊕ *www.nationaltrust.org.uk* ✉ *£7, garden only £4.40, combined ticket with Baddesley Clinton £12.70* ⊙ *House Feb.–Oct., Wed.–Sun. noon–4:30. Garden Mar., Apr., and Oct., Wed.–Sun. 11–4:30; May–Sept., Wed.–Sun. 11–5:30.*

★ **Baddesley Clinton** struck the eminent architectural historian Sir Nikolaus Pevsner as "the perfect late medieval manor house. The entrance side of grey stone, the small, creeper-clad Queen Anne brick bridge across the moat, the gateway with a porch higher than the roof and embattled—it could not be better." Set off a winding back road, this grand manor dating from the 15th century retains its great fireplaces, 17th-century paneling, and three priest holes (secret chambers for Roman Catholic priests, who were hidden by sympathizers when Catholicism was banned in the 16th and 17th centuries). The café is an idyllic spot. Admission to the house is by timed ticket; Baddesley Clinton is 2 mi east of Packwood House and 15 mi north of Stratford-upon-Avon. ✉ *Rising La., off A4141 near Chadwick End* ☎ *01564/783294* ⊕ *www.nationaltrust.org.uk* ✉ *£8.80, garden only £4.40, combined ticket with Packwood House £12.70* ⊙ *House Feb.–Oct., Wed.–Sun. 11–5. Garden Feb.–Oct., Wed.–Sun. 11–5; Nov. and Dec., Wed.–Sun. 11–4.*

COUNTRY WALKS

The gentle countryside rewards exploration on foot. Ambitious walkers can try the 26-mi Arden Way loop (⊕ *www.ardenway.org*) that takes in Henley-in-Arden and the Forest of Arden. On the 3-mi walk from Stratford to Wilmcote and Mary Arden's House, you can see beautiful scenery. Parkland with trails surrounds stately homes such as Charlecote Park, Coughton Court, and Ragley Hall. Even Stratford can be the base for easy walks along the River Avon or on the path bordering the Stratford-upon-Avon Canal. Stratford's Tourist Information Centre has pamphlets with walks.

WARWICK

7½ mi southeast of Baddesley Clinton, 4 mi south of Kenilworth, 9 mi northeast of Stratford-upon-Avon.

Most famous for Warwick Castle—that vision out of the feudal ages—the town of Warwick (pronounced *war*-ick) is an interesting architectural mix of Georgian redbrick and Elizabethan half-timbering.

GETTING HERE AND AROUND

Trains from London to Warwick run every hour or so from London's Marylebone Station. The journey takes about 90 minutes. National Express coaches make the same journey in about three hours several times a day from Victoria Coach Station.

To travel between Stratford-upon-Avon and Warwick, catch a National Express bus from Stratford-upon-Avon's riverside bus station to Warwick's Castle Hill. These buses run every 90 minutes, and the journey takes about 20 minutes. Trains also make the 20-minute journey between Stratford and Warwick every half hour during the day.

ESSENTIALS

Visitor Information Warwick (⊠ *Court House, Jury St.* ☎ *01926/492212* ⊕ *www.warwick-uk.co.uk).*

EXPLORING

Unattractive postwar development has spoiled much of the town center, but look for the 15th-century half-timber **Lord Leycester Hospital,** a home for old soldiers since the earl of Leicester dedicated it to that purpose in 1571. Within the complex are a chapel and a fine courtyard, complete with a wattle-and-daub balcony and 500-year-old gardens. Try a cream tea in the Brethren's Kitchen. ⊠ *High St.* ☎ *01926/491422* ⊕ *www.lordleycester.com* 🎫 *£4.90* ☉ *Apr.–Sept., Tues.–Sun. 10–5; Oct.–Mar., Tues.–Sun. 10–4.*

Crowded with gilded, carved, and painted tombs, the **Beauchamp Chapel** of the **Collegiate Church of St. Mary** is the essence of late-medieval and Tudor chivalry—although it was built (1443–64) to honor the somewhat-less-than-chivalrous Richard Beauchamp, who consigned Joan of Arc to the flames. Colored bosses (projecting blocks), fan tracery, and flying ribs distinguish the chapel, which holds monuments to the Beauchamps (several of whom became earl of Warwick), including Richard Beauchamp's impressive effigy in bronze and the alabaster table tomb of Thomas Beauchamp and his wife. Robert Dudley, earl of Leicester, adviser and favorite of Elizabeth I, is buried here. There's a brass-rubbing center, and you can climb the tower in summer. It's a five-minute walk from Warwick Castle. ⊠ *Church St., Old Sq.* ☎ *01926/403940* ⊕ *www.saintmaryschurch.co.uk* 🎫 *£2 donation requested* ☉ *Apr.–Oct., daily 10–6; Nov.–Mar., daily 10–4:30.*

Kids as well as adults appreciate **St. John's House,** a Jacobean building near the castle; beautiful gardens surround it. Inside are period costumes and scenes of domestic life, as well as a Victorian schoolroom. ⊠ *Smith St.* ☎ *01926/412132* 🎫 *Free* ☉ *Tues.–Sat. 10–5, Sun. 2:30–5.*

★ ☺ The vast bulk of medieval **Warwick Castle** rests on a cliff overlooking the Avon—"the fairest monument of ancient and chivalrous splendor which yet remains uninjured by time," to use the words of Sir Walter Scott. Today the castle is owned by the people who run the Madame Tussauds wax museums, and the exhibits and diversions can occupy a full day; it's a great castle experience for kids, though it's pricey (there are family prices). Warwick's two soaring towers can be seen for miles: the 147-foot-high Caesar's Tower, built in 1356, and the 128-foot-high Guy's Tower, built in 1380. The towers bristle with battlements, and their irregular forms allowed defenders to shoot from numerous points. The castle's most powerful commander was Richard Neville, earl of Warwick, known during the 15th-century Wars of the Roses as the Kingmaker. Warwick Castle's monumental walls enclose an impressive armory of medieval weapons, as well as state rooms with historic furnishings and paintings by Peter Paul Rubens, Anthony Van Dyck, and other old masters. Twelve rooms are devoted to an imaginative wax exhibition, "A Royal Weekend Party—1898." Another exhibit displays the sights and sounds of a great medieval household as it prepares for an important battle. At the Mill and Engine House, you can see the turning water mill and the engines used to generate electricity early in the 20th century. In the spooky dungeon exhibit, you (or perhaps any teenagers you know) can wander by wax re-creations of decaying bodies, chanting monks, executions, and "the labyrinth of lost souls"—a modern mirror maze. Below the castle, along the Avon, strutting peacocks patrol 60 acres of grounds elegantly landscaped by Capability Brown in the 18th century. ■ TIP➔**The castle is popular; arrive early to beat the crowds. If you book online, you can save on ticket prices.** Lavish medieval banquets (extra charge) and special events, including festivals, jousting tournaments, and a Christmas market, take place throughout the year, and plenty of food stalls serve lunches. ⊠ *Castle La. off Mill St., Warwick* ☎ *01926/495421, 08704/422000 24-hr information line* ⊕ *www.warwick-castle.co.uk* ✉ *£16.95 without dungeon, £19.95 with dungeon* ☉ *Nov.–Jan. and Apr.–Sept., daily 10–6; Oct.–Dec. and Jan.–Mar., daily 10–5.*

> ### WORD OF MOUTH
>
> "Warwick is the epitome of a medieval castle but has been 'Disneyfied.' The grand hall and the building are interesting, and if you are able to ignore somewhat of the carnival and circus atmosphere, you might enjoy the day."
> —traveller1959
>
> "It is not 'Disneyfied.' If anything, I like it more now. But yes, there are some exhibits I'd skip. They are easy to spot. The castle state rooms, inner ward, grounds/gardens, and the family quarters are worth a visit, for sure." —JanisJ

QUICK BITES

After a vigorous walk around the ramparts at Warwick Castle, you can drop by the cream-, crimson-, and gold-vaulted, 14th-century **Undercroft** (☎ *01926/495421*) for a refreshing spot of tea or a hot meal from the cafeteria.

WHERE TO EAT AND STAY

£££
ECLECTIC
✕**Findon's.** The imaginative menu at this posh Georgian town house restaurant takes its inspiration from Asia and Europe as well as England. Among the delicious choices are Gressingham duck with blackberry and green peppercorn sauce, and scallops with apple couscous, creamed sweet potatoes, and lime broth. The terrace is a lovely spot to dine in summer. For the best deal, try the fixed-price menus. ✉ *7 Old Sq.* ☎ *01926/411755* ▭ *MC, V* ☺ *Closed Sun.*

£££
BRITISH
✕ **Rose & Crown.** Stripped pine floorboards, red walls, big wooden tables, and solidly good food and drink set the tone at this contemporary gastro-pub with rooms on the town's main square; it's very popular with locals. The owners take pride in offering seasonal food that mixes British and international influences. The deli board lists marinated anchovies and crayfish tails; other options are coq au vin with sweet potato and ginger puree, and Aberdeen rump steak and chips. Five moderately priced bedrooms are simple but clean and modern. ✉ *30 Market Pl.* ☎ *01926/411117* ▭ *MC, V.*

££
🏨 **Lord Leycester Hotel.** Built in 1726, this house with an appealing central location became a hotel in 1925, and signs of age and history abound. The small, plainly furnished rooms and even smaller bathrooms look and feel cheap. Still, they're pleasant enough, and clean and quiet. **Pros:** good price; great location. **Cons:** nothing fancy here; everything could use a refurbishment. ✉ *17 Jury St.* ☎ *01926/491481* ⊕ *www.hobyhotels.com* 🛏 *49 rooms* ⌁ *In-room: no a/c, Internet. In-hotel: 2 restaurants, room service, bar, laundry service, parking (free), some pets allowed, no-smoking rooms* ▭ *AE, DC, MC, V* ❢ *BP.*

££££–£££££
🏨 **Mallory Court Hotel.** Just outside of Warwick, this elegant country-house hotel makes a quiet, luxurious getaway. It has 30 rooms but still manages to feel as if you're just visiting wealthy friends. The style in the comfortably designed bedrooms is country chic, with clever touches of chintz and plaid. One of the biggest attractions is the hotel restaurant (£££££), acclaimed for its exquisite French cuisine; the more casual brasserie is also good. You can use a nearby health club and also book spa treatments in your room. **Pros:** good for pampering; excellent restaurant. **Cons:** outside of town; chintz decor will not appeal to all. ✉ *Harbury La., Bishops Tachbrook* ☎ *01926/330214* ⊕ *www.mallory.co.uk* 🛏 *30 rooms* ⌁ *In-room: no a/c, refrigerator, Internet. In-hotel: 2 restaurants, room service, no-smoking rooms* ▭ *MC, V* ❢ *BP.*

KENILWORTH CASTLE

5 mi north of Warwick.

GETTING HERE AND AROUND

The local Stagecoach bus company offers services between Stratford and Kenilworth on the X16 and X17 buses. Catch the buses at Stratford's Riverside bus terminal near Bridgeway Road. The castle is a mile and a half from the town center.

ESSENTIALS

Visitor Information Kenilworth (✉ *Kenilworth Library, 11 Smalley Pl.* ☎ *01926/852595* ⊕ *www.kenilworthweb.co.uk*).

EXPLORING

★ The sprawling, graceful red ruins of **Kenilworth Castle** loom over the green fields of Warwickshire, surrounded by the low grassy impression of what was once a lake that surrounded it completely. The top of the keep (central tower) has commanding views of the countryside, one good indication of why this was such a formidable fortress from 1120 until it was dismantled by Oliver Cromwell after the Civil War in the mid-17th century. Still intact are its keep, with 20-foot-thick walls; its great hall built by John of Gaunt in the 14th century; and its curtain walls, the low outer walls forming the castle's first line of defense. Even more than Warwick Castle, these ruins reflect English history. In 1326 King Edward II was imprisoned here and forced to renounce the throne, before he was transferred to Berkeley Castle and allegedly murdered with a red-hot poker. Here the ambitious Robert Dudley, earl of Leicester, one of Elizabeth I's favorites, entertained her four times, most notably in 1575 with 19 days of revelry. An exhibition in the restored gatehouse discusses the relationship between Leicester and Elizabeth, and a re-created Elizabethan garden with arbors and a fountain provides further interest for a visit for an hour or two. Sir Walter Scott's novel *Kenilworth* (1821) presented tales about the earl and Elizabeth, adding to a national fascination with the castle. This is a good place for a picnic and contemplation of the passage of time. The fine gift shop sells excellent replicas of tapestries and swords. ⊠*Off A452, Kenilworth* ☎*01926/852078* ⊕*www.english-heritage.org.uk* ⊠*£7* ☉*Apr.–Sept., daily 10–6; Oct., daily 10–5; Nov.–Mar., daily 10–4.*

WHERE TO EAT

£ ✕**Clarendon Arms.** A location close to Kenilworth Castle helps make this
BRITISH   pub a good spot for lunch. You can order fine home-cooked food at the small bar downstairs. A larger, slightly pricier restaurant upstairs serves complete meals, from English roasts to more international fare. ⊠*44 Castle Hill, Kenilworth* ☎*01926/852017* ▤*AE, DC, MC, V.*

££ ✕**Petit Gourmand.** New owners have renamed the former Simply Simp-
FRENCH   sons but kept it as a relaxed, elegant restaurant with the look of an upscale modern French brasserie. The menu is still a creative mixture of classic English dishes done with French flair. Seasonal and local produce and meats are well represented in dishes such as warm Severn & Wye smoked salmon, Scotch beef bourguignon with mashed potatoes, and the duck-leg confit cassoulet with Toulouse sausage. ⊠*101 Warwick Rd., Kenilworth* ☎*01926/864567* ▤*AE, MC, V* ☉*Closed Sun. and Mon.*

COVENTRY

7 mi northeast of Warwick, 16 mi northeast of Stratford-upon-Avon.

Coventry, which thrived in medieval times as a center for the cloth and dyeing industries, is where, according to lore, a naked Lady Godiva allegedly rode through the streets in the 11th century to protest high taxes. In the 19th century the city became an industrial powerhouse, and the first British automobiles were manufactured here (the Coventry Transport Museum heralds the now largely lost British auto industry).

In World Wars I and II, Coventry was a center for weapons manufacturing, a fact that made it a favorite German target. On November 14, 1940, it suffered one of the worst air raids of the war: hundreds died, and the historic St. Michael's Cathedral was destroyed. Rapid postwar rebuilding was done in the cold architectural style of the 1950s and '60s, and Coventry is not a pretty town today, but it attracts history buffs and those who honor its past.

GETTING HERE AND AROUND

Virgin trains leave for Coventry every 20 minutes from London Euston station; it's a one-hour journey. Bus service from National Express and Megabus takes just over two hours from Victoria Coach station.

If you're driving into town, use the city's hop on, hop off Park and Ride services. Park at the War Memorial Park off Kenilworth Road on the south side of town, or on the north side on Austin Drive, Courthouse Green. Park and Ride operates Monday to Saturday with frequent buses.

ESSENTIALS

Visitor Information Coventry (⊠ Bayley La. ☎ 024/7622–7264 ⊕ www. visitcoventry.org).

EXPLORING

Before World War II, Coventry, like York and Canterbury, was virtually defined by its cathedral. After the war, to raise national morale, Sir Basil Spence was given the task of building a new cathedral. Wisely, he made no attempt to re-create the building that had been lost to German bombs. The striking, modern **Coventry Cathedral**, completed in 1962, stands beside the ruins of the blitzed St. Michael's, a powerful symbol of rebirth and reconciliation. Outside the sandstone building is Sir Jacob Epstein's *St. Michael Defeating the Devil*; the modern artworks inside include Graham Sutherland's stunning 70-foot-high tapestry *Christ in Glory* and unusual abstract stained glass. The visitor center in the undercroft shows a film about the cathedral; there's also a charred cross wired together from timbers from the bombed building. ⊠ *Priory Row* ☎ *024/7622–1200* ⊕ *www.coventrycathedral.org. uk* ✉ *Suggested cathedral donation £3.50, visitor center £2* ⊗ *Daily 9–5, services permitting.*

CHARLECOTE PARK

13 mi south of Coventry, 6 mi northeast of Stratford.

EXPLORING

A celebrated house in the village of Hampton Lucy, **Charlecote Park** was built in 1572 by Sir Thomas Lucy to entertain Queen Elizabeth I (in her honor, the house is shaped like the letter "E"). Shakespeare knew the house and may even have poached deer here. Standing at the edge of a glassy lake, the redbrick manor is striking and sprawling. It was renovated in neo-Elizabethan style by the Lucy family during the mid-19th century; a carved ebony bed is one of many spectacular pieces of furniture. The Tudor gatehouse is unchanged since Shakespeare's day, and a collection of carriages, a Victorian kitchen, and a small brewery occupy the outbuildings. Indulge in a game of croquet near the quirky, Victorian-era summer hut, or explore the deer park landscaped by Capability Brown. There are interesting themed tours and walks throughout the summer—call in advance to find out what's on offer. ⊠ *B4086, off A429, Hampton Lucy* ☎ *01789/470277* ⊕ *www.nationaltrust.org.uk* 🎟 *£7.80, grounds only £4.40* ⊙ *House Mar.–Oct., Fri.–Tues. noon–5; Dec., weekends noon–4. Gardens Mar.–Oct., Fri.–Tues. 10:30–6; Feb. and Oct., Fri.–Tues. 10:30–4.*

> ### BARD'S REVENGE?
>
> According to tradition, Shakespeare was caught poaching deer at Charlecote Park soon after his marriage and fled to London. Years later he supposedly retaliated by portraying Sir Thomas Lucy in *Henry IV Part 2* and the *Merry Wives of Windsor* as the foolish Justice Shallow. Some historians doubt the reference, but Shakespeare does mention the "dozen white luces"—which figure in the Lucy coat of arms—and Shallow does tax Falstaff with killing his deer.

COMPTON VERNEY

6 mi southeast of Charlecote Park.

EXPLORING

A neoclassical country mansion remodeled in the 1760s by Robert Adam, **Compton Verney** has been repurposed by the Peter Moores Foundation as an art museum with more than 800 works. The house, set in 120 acres of parkland landscaped by Capability Brown, was decaying before the museum opened in 2004. The works of art are intriguingly varied and beautifully displayed in restored rooms: British folk art and portraits, textiles, Chinese pottery and bronzes, southern Italian art from 1600 to 1800, and German art from 1450 to 1600 are the main focus. Special exhibitions round out the program. ⊠ *Off B4086, near Kineton* ☎ *01926/645500* ⊕ *www.comptonverney.org.uk* 🎟 *£8; grounds free* ⊙ *Mid-Mar.–mid-Dec., Tues.–Sun. 10–5.*

ALDERMINSTER

5 mi south of Stratford-upon-Avon.

Alderminster is one of the most interesting of the so-called "Stour villages"—those places so characteristic of Shakespeare Country, strung along the winding route of the River Stour south of Stratford. The main street holds an unusual row of old stone cottages, and the church has a Norman nave and a tower dating from the 13th century. Although the interior of the church has been much restored, it's worth a peek for the carved faces between the arches and the old altar stone.

Other Stour villages include Honington, Shipston-on-Stour, and Tredington. A village green anchors Honington, where a lovely five-arched bridge crosses the river. Shipston, the largest of the group, is an old sheep-market town, its handsome batch of Georgian houses formerly owned by wealthy wool merchants. Tredington, an exquisite nutshell of a village, has an old stone church.

GETTING HERE AND AROUND

Alderminster, on A3400, is very small. Stagecoach bus services from Stratford-upon-Avon and Warwick stop there throughout the day.

WHERE TO STAY

£££–££££ ⬆ **Ettington Park Hotel.** Victorian Gothic in style and with a modern wing, ★ this mansion built on land owned by the Shirley family since the 12th century is a soothing retreat for theatergoers who don't want to cope with Stratford's crowds. Some of the individually decorated rooms have four-poster beds; rooms are grandly traditional in decor, and the fancier doubles are larger and cost more. The oak-paneled restaurant (fixed-price menu; £££££) offers extremely good modern British cuisine. For a break, take tea or a whisky in antiques-filled public rooms or stroll on the 40-acre grounds, which contain the ruins of a 12th-century church. **Pros:** gorgeous building; spacious rooms; relaxing lounge. **Cons:** a bit too formal for some; well out of Stratford. ✉ *Off A3400, Alderminster* ☎*0845/072–7454* 🖷*01789/450472* ⬆*www.handpicked.co.uk/ ettingtonpark* ⬟*37 rooms, 11 suites* ⬧*In-room: safe, DVD, Wi-Fi. In-hotel: restaurant, room service, bar, tennis courts, pool, gym, bicycles, laundry service, Wi-Fi* ▭*AE, DC, MC, V* ⬤*BP.*

£–££ ⬆ **Fox & Goose.** A quirky style and fabulous fresh food make this place ★ in the wee, unspoiled village of Armscote, 8 mi south of Stratford, more than just a pub with rooms. Everything is in place for relaxation: Victorian claw-foot tubs with candles, a CD player, and a satisfying English breakfast served until noon. Rooms are themed around Clue (Cluedo in England) characters: Colonel Mustard's room is yellow, and Miss Scarlet's Boudoir is red and dimly lighted. The gastro-pub downstairs (££) serves a fusion menu and local ales. **Pros:** relaxing rooms; great restaurant. **Cons:** restaurant gets booked up; room decor can be bright and a bit quirky. ✉*Middle St., Armscote* ☎*01608/682293* ⬆*www. foxandgoosearmscote.co.uk* ⬟*4 rooms* ⬧*In-room: no a/c, no phone. In-hotel: restaurant, bar* ▭*MC, V* ⬤*BP.*

ALCESTER

8 mi west of Stratford-upon-Avon.

The small market town of Alcester (pronounced *al*-ster) holds ancient buildings and Tudor houses. Search out the narrow **Butter Street,** off High Street, site of the 17th-century Churchill House, and on Malt Mill Lane (off Church Street) the **Old Malt House,** dating from 1500.

Two stately homes, Ragley Hall and Coughton Court, are a few miles from Alcester.

GETTING HERE AND AROUND

A car is needed to get here unless you find an organized tour that includes the stately homes.

EXPLORING

James Wyatt and other outstanding architects worked on **Ragley Hall,** a Palladian-style mansion with more than 100 rooms. Inside are architectural and decorative treasures as well as magnificent views of the parkland laid out by Capability Brown in the 1750s. The Great Hall has fine baroque plasterwork by James Gibb, and there are portraits by Joshua Reynolds and Dutch masters, among others, as well as some striking 20th-century murals by Graham Rust. This is the ancestral home of the marquesses of Hertford, the third of whom figured in Thackeray's *Vanity Fair* and the fourth of whom collected many of the treasures in London's Wallace Collection. Between the large house and vast grounds, you can spend about three hours here. ■TIP➡ **Let the kids blow off energy in the adventure playground and picnic area.** The house is 2 mi southwest of Alcester. ✉ *Off A435 and A46* ☎*01789/762090* ⊕*www.ragleyhall.com* ☜*£8.50* ◷*House mid-Mar.–mid-July, Sept., and Oct., Sun. noon–4; mid-July–Aug., Sun.–Fri. noon–4. Park mid-Mar.–mid-July, Sept., and Oct., weekends 10–6; mid-July–Aug., daily 10–6. Call to confirm, as schedule may vary on particular wks.*

A grand Elizabethan manor house, **Coughton Court** is the home of the Catholic Throckmorton family, as it has been since 1409. The impressive gatehouse, the centerpiece of a half-timber courtyard, contains a fine fan-vaulted ceiling and memorabilia, including the dress worn by Mary, Queen of Scots at her execution. There are children's clothes and a Gunpowder Plot exhibition, and you can wander in the excellent formal gardens (the roses are notable) and along a river and lake; allot an hour or so for a visit. The house is 2 mi north of Alcester and 8 mi northwest of Stratford. ✉*A435* ☎*01789/400777* ⊕*www.nationaltrust.org.uk* ☜*£9.50, gardens only £5.80, parking £1* ◷*Mid-Mar.–June and Sept., Wed.–Sun. 11–5:30; July and Aug., Tues.–Sun. 11–5:30; Oct., Thurs.–Sun. 11–5.*

WHERE TO STAY

££££ ▥**Barceló Billesley Manor.** Cozy public rooms with fireplaces and antiques and 11 acres of grounds with a topiary garden enhance this 16th-century manor house, now a luxurious country retreat with the requisite spa. Guest rooms retain period features and are richly decorated in modern or traditional country style; a few have four-poster beds. Some are in the main house, others in converted barns. The excellent wine list complements the wood-paneled restaurant's sophisticated dishes. **Pros:** online deals if you book in advance; large garden. **Cons:** a bit too formal; some double rooms are quite small. ✉*Off A46, Billesley* ✛*Near Alcester* ☎*01789/279955* 🖷*01789/764145* ⊕*www.barcelo-hotels.co.uk* ⇱*69 rooms, 2 suites* ♿*In-room: no a/c, Internet. In-hotel: restaurant, room service, tennis court, pool, gym, spa, laundry service, no-smoking rooms* ▤*AE, D, MC, V* ¶○|*BP.*

Bath and the Cotswolds

WORD OF MOUTH

"If you enjoy walking, then you can explore this delightful landscape by following some of the Cotswold Way, a public footpath that allows you to take in the breathtaking scenery of the Cotswolds. Village after village has its own individual feel, but each and every one is well worth a visit."

—lynbes 1

"One of my fondest memories of visiting Bath was an afternoon I spent at Prior Park, a National Trust site. It is a beautiful house and garden, perched on a hill with a gorgeous view of Bath and the countryside. A city bus goes to the entrance."

—tekwriter

Updated
by Robert
Andrews

The rolling uplands of the Cotswold Hills represent the quintessence of rural England, as immortalized in countless books, paintings, and films. Here you can taste the glories of the old English village—its stone slate roofs, low-ceiling rooms, and gardens; the atmosphere is as thick as honey, and equally as sweet. On the edge of the Cotswolds is Bath, among the most alluring small cities in Europe.

The blissfully unspoiled Cotswolds, deservedly popular with visitors and convenient to London, occupies much of the county of Gloucestershire, in west-central England. It also takes in slices of neighboring Oxfordshire, Worcestershire, and Somerset. Together these make up a sweep of land stretching from Shakespeare Country in the north almost as far as the Bristol Channel in the south. On the edge of the area, three historic towns have absorbed, rather than compromised, the flavor of the Cotswolds: Bath, offering up "18th-century England in all its urban glory," to use a phrase by writer Nigel Nicolson; Regency-era Cheltenham, like Bath, a spa town with elegant architecture; and Gloucester, which holds an outstanding medieval cathedral and gives access to the ancient Forest of Dean, on the western edge of the area.

Bath rightly boasts of being the best-planned town in England. Although the Romans founded the city when they discovered here the only true hot springs in England, its popularity during the 17th and 18th centuries ensured its aesthetic immortality. Bath's fashionable period luckily coincided with one of Britain's most creative architectural eras, producing virtually an entire town of stylish buildings. Today people come to walk in the footsteps of Jane Austen, visit Bath Abbey and the excavated Roman baths, shop in an elegant setting, or have a modern spa experience at the stunning Thermae spa.

North of Bath are the Cotswolds—a region that more than one writer has called the very soul of England. Is it the pretty-as-a-picture villages with the perfectly clipped hedges? The mellow, centuries-old stone cottages festooned with honeysuckle? Whatever the reason, this idyllic region, which from medieval times grew prosperous on the wool trade, remains a vision of rural England. Here are time-defying churches, sleepy hamlets, and ancient farmsteads so sequestered that they seem to offer everyone the thrill of personal discovery. Hidden in sheltered valleys are fabled abodes—Sudeley Castle, Stanway House, and Snowshill Manor among them. The Cotswolds can hardly claim to be undiscovered, but, happily, the area's poetic appeal has survived the tour buses, crowds, and antiques shops.

TOP REASONS TO GO

Cotswold pubs: The classic pubs here press all the right buttons—low wooden beams, horse brasses, and inglenook fireplaces. Many pubs date back 300 years or more, but some have added smart dining areas. Most now offer tea and coffee, and also welcome children.

Perfect villages: With their stone cottages, Cotswold villages tend to be improbably picturesque; the hamlets of Upper and Lower Slaughter are among the most seductive. Part of the fun is to take almost any scenic lane or head for any evocatively named spot on the map.

Gloucester Cathedral: The Great East Window, Whispering Gallery, and cloisters are especially noteworthy in this ancient monument, one of the country's finest cathedrals. Look

out, too, for the settings of scenes in the Harry Potter movies.

Hidcote Manor Gardens: In a region rich with imaginative garden displays, Hidcote lays good claim to eminence. Exotic shrubs from around the world and the famous "garden rooms" are the highlights of this Arts and Crafts masterpiece.

Roman Baths, Bath: Take a break from the town's Georgian elegance and return to its Roman days on a tour around this beautifully preserved bath complex, built around the country's only hot springs.

Shops in Cheltenham: The grand Regency terraces of Cheltenham make a wonderful setting for "country chic" boutiques, antiques shops, and gift stores that attract people from the entire region.

ORIENTATION AND PLANNING

8

GETTING ORIENTED

The region's major points of interest—Bath, the Cotswold Hills, and the Gloucester–Cheltenham axis—are one way to organize your explorations. Bath, in the southwestern corner of this area, is a good place to start; it can also be visited on a day out from London. The Cotswold Hills, about two hours west of London by car, cover some of southern England's most beautiful terrain. The area's small roads make for wonderful exploring, but public transportation is limited. To the west of the Cotswolds lie the cities of Gloucester and Cheltenham, a former spa town; beyond them, between the River Severn and the border of Wales, is the Forest of Dean. The road from Gloucester to Bath takes you by the castle at Berkeley.

Bath and Environs. With the Roman Baths—renovated and embellished in the 18th century—and the late-medieval Bath Abbey at its heart, Bath is one of the country's comeliest towns. You can also soak up its thriving cultural scene.

The Cotswolds. With a scattering of picture-postcard towns and villages separated by rolling dales and woods, the Cotswold Hills are rural England at its best. Nearby Cheltenham, with busy cafés and shops, provides a lively counterpoint.

Gloucester to the Forest of Dean. Sturdy Norman cathedrals dominate the towns of Gloucester and Tewkesbury. South of Gloucester, Berkeley Castle offers more medieval grandeur, and the Forest of Dean, to the west, offers a chance to stretch your legs.

PLANNING

WHEN TO GO

This area contains some of England's most popular destinations, and you would do well to avoid weekends in the busier areas of the Cotswolds. During the week, even in summer, you may hardly see a soul in the more remote spots. Bath is particularly congested in summer, when students flock to its language schools. On the other hand, Gloucester and Cheltenham are workaday places that can absorb many tour buses comfortably.

Book your room well ahead if you visit during the two weeks in May and June when the Bath International Music Festival hits town, or if you visit Cheltenham during the National Hunt Festival in mid-March. Note that the private properties of Hidcote Manor, Snowshill Manor, and Sudeley Castle close in winter. Hidcote Manor Garden is at its best in spring and fall, Bowood Gardens in May.

PLANNING YOUR TIME

Bath and Cheltenham are the most compelling towns in the region, and the obvious centers for an exploration of the Cotswolds Hills. Cheltenham is closer to the heart of the Cotswolds and is far less touristy, but has less immediate appeal. Bath is 29 mi from Cirencester in the southern Cotswolds, and 45 mi from Stow-in the-Wold in the north.

It's also worth finding accommodation in the smaller Cotswold settlements, though overnight stops in this well-heeled area can be costly. Good choices include Cirencester, Stow-on-the-Wold, and Broadway. Gloucester is not such an attractive place for a stay, though it would make a feasible base for Tewkesbury to the north and Slimbridge and Berkeley Castle to the south. If you have more time, consider a foray to the Forest of Dean, west of Gloucester.

You can get a taste of Bath and the Cotswolds in three hurried days; a weeklong visit gives you plenty of time for the slow wandering this small region deserves. Near Bath, it's an easy drive to Lacock and Castle Combe, two stately villages on the southern edge of the Cotswolds, and Winchcombe makes a good entry into the area from Cheltenham. At the heart of the Cotswolds, Stow-on-the-Wold and Broadway should on no account be missed. Within a short distance of these, Chipping Campden and Moreton-in-Marsh are less showy, with a more relaxed feel. Bourton-on-the-Water and Northleach are fairly low-key but still picturesque examples of the Cotswold hamlet, and Bibury, Owlpen, and Upper and Lower Slaughter are tiny settlements that can easily be appreciated on a brief passage. On the southern fringes of the area, Burford, Tetbury, and Cirencester have antiques and tea shops stores galore while avoiding the worst of the crowds.

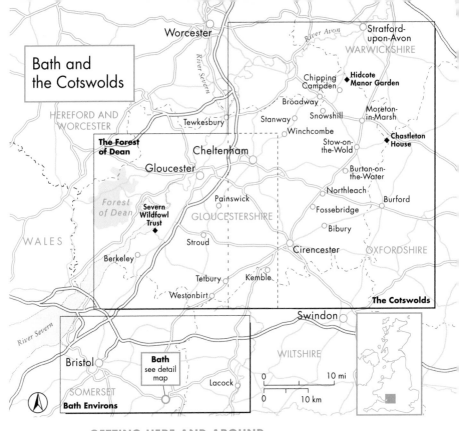

Bath and
the Cotswolds

GETTING HERE AND AROUND

AIR TRAVEL

This area is about two hours from London; Bristol and Birmingham
have the closest regional airports. Bristol's airport is 8 mi south of the
city; it also has limited service from New York.

BUS TRAVEL

National Express buses head to the region from London's Victoria
Coach Station. Megabus, a budget bus company, serves Cheltenham
and Gloucester. It can take about three hours to get to Cheltenham,
three to four hours to get to Bath. Bus service between some towns can
be extremely limited. The First company covers the area around Bath.
Stagecoach, Castleways, Johnson's Coaches, Swanbrook, and Pulhams
operate in the Gloucestershire and Cotswolds region. Traveline has
information about public transportation.

Contacts Castleways (☎01242/602949 ⊕www.castleways.co.uk) .
First (☎0845/606–4446 ⊕www.firstgroup.com). **Johnson's Coaches**
(☎01564/797070 ⊕www. johnsoncoaches.co.uk). **Megabus** (☎0900/160–
0900 premium-rate number ⊕www.megabus.com). **National Express**
(☎0871/781–8181 ⊕www.nationalexpress.com). **Pulhams** (☎01451/820369
⊕www.pulhamscoaches.com). **Stagecoach** (⊕www.stagecoachbus.

com). **Swanbrook** (☎ 01452/712386 ⊕ www.swanbrook.co.uk). **Traveline**
(☎ 0871/200–2233 ⊕ www.traveline.org.uk).

CAR TRAVEL

A car is the best way to make a thorough tour of the area, given the
limitations of public transportation. M4 is the main route west from
London to Bath and southern Gloucestershire; expect about a two-hour
drive. From Exit 18, take A46 south to Bath. From Exit 20, take M5
north to Gloucester (25 mi), Cheltenham, and Tewkesbury; from Exit
15, take A419 to A429 north to the Cotswolds. From London you can
also take M40 and A40 to the Cotswolds, where a network of minor
roads link the villages.

TRAIN TRAVEL

First Great Western trains serve the region from London's Paddington
Station; First Great Western and CrossCountry trains connect Gloucester, Cheltenham, and Birmingham. Travel time from Paddington to Bath
is about 90 minutes. Most trains to Cheltenham (2 hours) and Gloucester (1¾ hours) involve a change at Swindon. Train service within the
Cotswold area is extremely limited, with Kemble (near Cirencester)
and Moreton-in-Marsh being the most useful stops, both serviced by
daily trains from London Paddington. A three-day or seven-day Heart
of England Rover train ticket is valid for unlimited travel within the
region.

Contacts National Rail Enquiries (☎ 0845/748–4950 ⊕ www.nationalrail.
co.uk).

RESTAURANTS

Good restaurants dot the region, thanks to a steady flow of fine chefs
seeking to cater to wealthy locals and waves of demanding visitors. The
country's food revolution is in full evidence here. Restaurants have never
had a problem with a fresh food supply: excellent regional produce,
salmon from the Rivers Severn and Wye, local lamb and pork, venison
from the Forest of Dean, and pheasant, partridge, quail, and grouse in
season. Also look for Gloucestershire Old Spot pork, bacon (try a delicious Old Spot bacon sandwich), and sausage on area menus.

HOTELS

The hotels of this region are among Britain's most highly rated—from
bed-and-breakfasts in village homes and farmhouses to luxurious
country-house hotels. Many hotels present themselves as deeply traditional rural retreats, but some have opted for a sleeker, fresher style,
with boldly contemporary or minimalist furnishings. Spas are becoming increasingly popular at these hotels, too. Book ahead whenever
possible and brace yourself for some high prices. B&Bs are a cheaper
alternative to the fancier hotels, and most hotels offer two- and three-
day packages. Note that most lodgings in Bath require a two-night minimum stay on weekends and national holidays; rates are often higher on
weekends. Hotels can front on heavily trafficked roads; ask for quiet
rooms in the back.

WHAT IT COSTS IN POUNDS					
	£	££	£££	££££	£££££
Restaurants	Under £10	£10–£14	£15–£19	£20–£25	over £25
Hotels	Under £70	£70–£120	£121–£160	£161–£220	over £220

Restaurant prices are for a main course at dinner. Hotel prices are for two people in a standard double room in high season, including V.A.T., with no meals or, if indicated, CP (with continental breakfast), BP (Breakfast Plan, with full breakfast), or MAP (Modified American Plan, with breakfast and dinner).

VISITOR INFORMATION

The South West Tourism Web site has information about the entire region; the Cotswold site is a government one that has a useful section on tourism. The major towns have Tourist Information Centres that provide advice and help with accommodations.

Contacts Cotswolds (⊕ www.cotswold.gov.uk). **Forest of Dean** (☎ 01594/812388 ⊕ www.visitforestofdean.co.uk). **South West Tourism** (☎ 0870/442–0880 ⊕ www.visitsouthwest.co.uk).

BATH AND ENVIRONS

Anyone who listens to the local speech of Bath will note the inflections that herald the closeness of England's West Country. The city, however, has strong links with the Cotswold Hills stretching north, and the Georgian architecture and mellow stone that are such features of Bath recall the stone mansions and cottages of that region. The hinterland of the county of Somerset has plenty of gentle, green countryside.

BATH

★ *13 mi southeast of Bristol, 115 mi west of London.*

"I really believe I shall always be talking of Bath . . . Oh! who can ever be tired of Bath," enthuses Catherine Morland in Jane Austen's *Northanger Abbey,* and today plenty of people agree with these sentiments. In Bath, a UNESCO World Heritage Site, you are surrounded by magnificent 18th-century architecture, a lasting reminder of the vanished world described by Austen. In the 19th century the city lost its fashionable luster and slid into a refined gentility that is still palpable. Although the 20th century saw some slight harm from World War II bombing and slightly more from urban renewal, the damage was halted before it could ruin the city's Georgian elegance.

Bath is no museum, though: it's lively, with good dining and shopping, excellent art galleries and museums, the remarkable excavated Roman baths, and theater, music, and other performances all year. The Thermae Bath Spa allows you to take advantage of the hot springs that gave the city its fame. Many people rush through Bath in a day, but there's enough to do to merit an overnight stay—or more. In summer, the sheer volume of sightseers may hamper your progress on a stroll.

The Romans put Bath on the map in the 1st century, when they built a temple here, in honor of the goddess Minerva, and a sophisticated network of baths to make full use of the mineral springs that gush from the earth at a constant temperature of 116°F (46.5°C). ■TIP→ **Don't miss the remains of these baths, one of the city's glories.** Visits by Queen Anne in 1702 and 1703 brought attention to the town, and soon 18th-century "people of quality" took it to heart. Bath became the most fashionable spa in Britain. Assembly rooms, theaters, and pleasure gardens were built to entertain the rich and titled when they weren't busy attending the parties of Beau Nash (the city's master of ceremonies and chief social organizer, who helped increase Bath's popularity) and having their portraits painted by Gainsborough.

GETTING HERE AND AROUND

Frequent trains from Paddington and National Express buses from Victoria connect Bath with London. The bus and train stations are close to each other south of the center. By car from London, take M4 to Exit 18, from which A46 leads 10 mi south to Bath.

Drivers should note that parking is extremely limited within the city, and any car illegally parked is likely to be ticketed. Fees for towed cars can be hundreds of pounds. Public parking lots in the historic area fill up early, but the Park and Ride lots on the outskirts provide inexpensive shuttle service into the center, which is pleasant to stroll around.

TOURS   Free, two-hour walking tours of Bath are offered year-round by the Mayor of Bath's Honorary Guides. Individuals can just show up outside the main entrance to the Pump Room. Tours are Sunday through Friday at 10:30 and 2, Saturday at 10:30. There's also a tour at 7 PM Tuesday and Friday from May to September. The Jane Austen Centre arranges Jane-themed walking tours on weekends. City Sightseeing runs 50-minute guided tours of Bath on open-top buses year-round, leaving two–four times an hour from High Street, near the abbey. Tickets, valid for 24 hours, give a 10% reduction on entry to some of Bath's top attractions.

Mad Max Tours runs full-day tours from Bath through the Cotswolds, stopping at Tetbury, Upper Slaughter and Lower Slaughter, and either Bourton-on-the-Water or Stow-on-the-Wold. The departure point is the Glass House Shop on Orange Grove, near Bath Abbey, at 8:45. The company also has tours to Castle Combe, Lacock, Avebury, and Stonehenge.

TIMING

Schedule a visit to Bath during the week, as weekends see an influx of visitors. The city gets similarly crowded during its various festivals, though the added conviviality and cultural activity during these events are big draws in themselves.

ESSENTIALS

Visitor and Tour Information Bath (⊠ *Abbey Chambers, Abbey Churchyard* ☎ *0906/711–2000 [calls cost 50p per minute], +44 844/847–5257 [from abroad], or 0844/847–5256 [booking accommodation service]* ⊕ *www.visitbath. co.uk).* **City Sightseeing** (☎ *01225/330444 in Bath* ⊕ *www.city-sightseeing.*

com). **Mad Max Tours** (☎ *0799/050–5970* ⊕ *www.madmax.abel.co.uk*). **Mayor of Bath's Honorary Guides** (☎ 01225/477411).

EXPLORING
TOP ATTRACTIONS

❷ **Bath Abbey.** Dominating Bath's center, this 15th-century edifice of golden, glowing stone has a splendid west front, with carved figures of angels ascending ladders on either side. Notice, too, the miter, olive tree, and crown motif, a play on the name of the current building's founder, Bishop Oliver King. More than 50 stained-glass windows fill about 80% of the building's wall space, giving the interior an impression of lightness. The abbey was built in the Perpendicular (English late-Gothic) style on the site of a Saxon abbey, and the nave and side aisles contain superb fan-vaulted ceilings. There are six services on Sunday, including Choral Evensong at 3:30. Forty-five-minute **tower tours,** allowing close-up views of the massive bells and panoramic cityscapes from the roof, take place most days; the 212 dizzying steps demand a level of fitness. The small, low-key **Heritage Vaults,** accessible from the abbey's south wall (the right-hand aisle), has an informative audiovisual presentation of the abbey's history, along with a reconstruction of the Norman cathedral that preceded it, some statuary, and a petition from 4th-century Bath that includes what is thought to be the first mention of the word Christian in Britain. ⊠ *Abbey Churchyard* ☎ 01225/422462 ⊕ *www. bathabbey.org* ⌕ *Abbey £2.50 donation suggested, tower tours £5, Heritage Vaults free* ☉ *Abbey Apr.–Oct., Mon.–Sat. 9–6, Sun. 1–2:30 and 4:30–5:30; Nov.–Mar., Mon.–Sat. 9–4:30, Sun. 1–2:30 and 4:30–5:30. Tower tours Mon.–Sat. 11, noon, and 2 (but check); Heritage Vaults Mon.–Sat. 10–3:30.*

❾ **Circus.** John Wood designed the masterful Circus, a circle of curving,
★ perfectly proportioned Georgian houses interrupted just three times for intersecting streets. Wood died shortly after work on the Circus began; his son, the younger John Wood, completed the project. Notice the carved acorns atop the houses: Wood nurtured the myth that Prince Bladud founded Bath, ostensibly with the help of an errant pig rooting for acorns (this is one of a number of variations of Bladud's story), and the architect adopted the acorn motif in a number of places. A garden fills the center of the Circus. The painter Thomas Gainsborough (1727–88) lived at No. 17 from 1760 to 1774.

❼ **Fashion Museum and Assembly Rooms.** In its role as the **Assembly Rooms,**
★ this neoclassical building was the leading center for social life in 18th-century Bath, with a schedule of dress balls, concerts, and choral nights. Jane Austen came here often, and it is here, in the Ballroom, that Catherine Morland has her first, disappointing encounter with Bath's beau monde in *Northanger Abbey;* the Octagon Room is the setting for an important encounter between Anne Elliot and Captain Wentworth in *Persuasion.* Built by John Wood the Younger in 1771, the building was badly damaged by wartime bombing in 1942 but was faithfully restored. Its stunning chandeliers are the 18th-century originals. Today the Assembly Rooms are well known for the entertaining **Fashion Museum,** displaying apparel from Jacobean times up to the

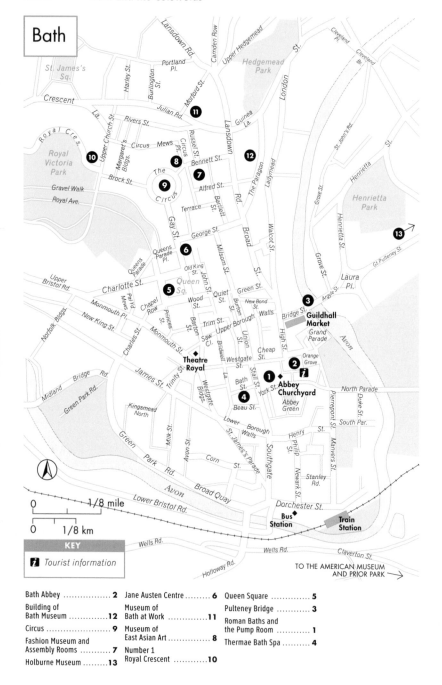

Bath

KEY

🔢 *Tourist information*

present (audio guide included). You might see displays of pockets or punk fashions in changing exhibits. Throughout the year, classical concerts are given here, just as they were in bygone days. ⊠ *Bennett St.* ☎ *01225/477173* ⊕ *www.museumofcostume.co.uk* 🖃 *£7; combined ticket with Roman Baths, valid 7 days, £14.50* ⊙ *Mar.–Oct., daily 10:30–6; Nov.–Feb., daily 10:30–5; last admission 1 hr before closing.*

⓭ **Holburne Museum.** One of Bath's
★ gems, this elegant 18th-century building houses a small but superb collection of 17th- and 18th-century decorative arts, ceramics, and silverware. Highlights include paintings by Gainsborough (*The Byam Family,* on indefinite loan) and George Stubbs (*Reverend Carter Thelwall and Family*), and Rachmaninoff's

Steinway piano. In its original incarnation as the Sydney Hotel, the house was one of the pivots of Bath's high society, which came to perambulate in the pleasure gardens (Sydney Gardens) that still lie behind it. One visitor was Jane Austen, whose main Bath residence was No. 4 Sydney Place, a brief stroll across the road from the museum. At the time of this writing, the interior of the museum was closed for a major renovation scheduled to be finished in late 2010. ⊠ *Great Pulteney St.* ☎ *01225/466669* ⊕ *www.bath.ac.uk/holburne* 🖃 *£5.50* ⊙ *Mid-Jan.–mid-Dec., Tues.–Sat. 10–5, Sun. and national holidays 11–5.*

❻ **Jane Austen Centre.** The one place in Bath that gives Austen any space provides a briefly diverting exhibition about the influence of Bath on her writings; *Northanger Abbey* and *Persuasion* are both set primarily in the city. There's a 15-minute introductory talk, and displays give a pictorial overview of life in Bath around 1800, putting Austen's world in context. The cozy Georgian house, a few doors up from where the writer lived in 1805 (one of several addresses she had in Bath at different times), also includes the Austen-theme Regency Tea Rooms, open to the public. ■TIP➔ **You can buy tickets here for Jane Austen walking tours, which leave from the Abbey Churchyard at 11 on weekends and national holidays (also at 4 on Friday and Saturday in July and August).** A tour ticket entitles you to a 20% reduction for entry to the exhibition. ⊠ *40 Gay St.* ☎ *01225/443000* ⊕ *www.janeausten.co.uk* 🖃 *£6.95, tours £6* ⊙ *Mid-Mar.–early Nov., daily 9:45–5:30, until 7 Thurs.–Sat. in July and Aug.; early Nov.–mid-Mar., Sun.–Fri. 11–4:30, Sat. 9:45–5:30.*

❿ **Number 1 Royal Crescent.** The majestic arc of the Royal Crescent, much
Fodor's Choice used as a film location, is the crowning glory of Palladian architecture
★ in Bath; Number 1 offers you a glimpse inside this splendor. The work of John Wood the Younger, the 30 houses fronted by 114 columns

were laid out between 1767 and 1774. A house in the center is now the Royal Crescent Hotel. On the corner of Brock Street and the Royal Crescent, Number 1 Royal Crescent has been turned into a museum and furnished as it might have been in the 18th century. The museum crystallizes a view of the English class system—upstairs all is elegance, and downstairs is a kitchen display. ⊠ *Royal Crescent* ☎*01225/428126* ⊕*www.bath-preservation-trust.org.uk* ⊠*£5* ⊗*Mid-Feb.–late Oct., Tues.–Sun. and national holidays 10:30–5; late Oct.–early Dec., Tues.–Sun. 10:30–4; last admission 30 mins before closing.*

❸ **Pulteney Bridge.** Florence's Ponte Vecchio inspired this 18th-century span, one of the most famous landmarks in the city and the only work of Robert Adam in Bath. It's unique in Great Britain because shops line both sides of the bridge.

❺ **Queen Square.** Houses and the Francis Hotel surround the garden in the center of this small, peaceful square. An obelisk designed by the older John Wood and financed by Beau Nash celebrates the 1738 visit of Frederick, prince of Wales.

❶ **Roman Baths and the Pump Room.** The hot springs have drawn people here since prehistoric times, so it's quite appropriate to begin an exploration of Bath at this excellent museum on the site of the ancient city's temple complex and primary "watering hole." Here Roman patricians would gather to immerse themselves, drink the mineral waters, and socialize. With the departure of the Romans, the baths fell into disuse and were partially covered. When bathing again became fashionable, the site was reopened; the magnificent Georgian building now standing was erected at the end of the 18th century. During the 19th century almost the entire Roman bath complex was rediscovered and excavated, and the museum displays relics of the temple once dedicated to Sulis Minerva. Exhibits include a memorable mustachioed, Celtic-influenced Gorgon's head, fragments of colorful curses invoked by the Romans against some of their neighbors, and information about Roman bathing practices. The **Great Bath** is now roofless, and the statuary and pillars belong to the 19th century, but much remains from the original complex, and the steaming, somewhat murky waters are undeniably evocative. ■TIP➔ There are free hourly tours of the baths, and in August you can take torch-lighted tours at night.

Adjacent to the Roman bath complex is the famed **Pump Room,** built in 1792–96, a rendezvous for members of 18th-century and 19th-century Bath society, who liked to check on the new arrivals to the city. Here Catherine Morland and Mrs. Allen "paraded up and down for an hour, looking at everybody and speaking to no one," to quote from Jane Austen's *Northanger Abbey.* Today you can take in the elegant space—or you can simply, for a small fee, taste the fairly vile mineral water. Charles Dickens described it as tasting like warm flatirons. ⊠*Abbey Churchyard* ☎*01225/477785* ⊕*www.romanbaths.co.uk* ⊠*Pump Room free, Roman Baths £11, £11.50 in July and Aug. with audio guide; combined ticket with Fashion Museum and Assembly Rooms (valid 7 days) £14.50* ⊗*Mar.–June, Sept., and Oct., daily 9–6; July and Aug., daily 9 AM–10 PM; Nov.–Feb., daily 9:30–5:30; last admission 1 hr before closing.*

Fodor'sChoice
★

The quiet courtyard of two adjacent cafés, the **Café René and Café Parisien** (⊠ *2 Shires Yard, off Broad St.* ☎ *01225/447147*), is handy for coffee or a lunchtime baguette. This is a prime spot for watching the locals go about their daily lives. You can linger in the **Pump Room** (⊠ *Abbey Churchyard* ☎ *01225/444477*) for morning coffee or afternoon tea after seeing the Roman Baths.

4 Thermae Bath Spa. The only place in Britain where you can bathe in natural hot-spring water, and in an open-air rooftop location as well, this striking complex designed by Nicholas Grimshaw consists of a Bath-stone building surrounded by a glass curtain wall. The only difficulty is in deciding where to spend more time—in the sleekly luxurious, light-filled Minerva Bath, with its curves and gentle currents; in the smaller, open-air rooftop pool for the unique sensation of bathing with views of Bath's operatic skyline (don't miss this); in the aromatic steam rooms; or in the treatment rooms. Two 18th-century thermal baths, the Cross Bath and the Hot Bath, are back in use, too. End your session in the crisp third-floor café and restaurant. ■ TIP→ **It's recommended that you book spa treatments ahead.** Towels, robes, and slippers are available for rent. Weekdays are the quietest time to visit. A separate, free **Visitor Centre** (Monday–Saturday 10–5, Sunday 10–4) opposite the entrance gives an overview of the project and provides audio guides (£2) for a brief tour of the outside of the complex. ⊠ *Hot Bath St.* ☎ *0844/888–0844* ⊕ *www.thermaebathspa.com* 🎟 *£22 for 2 hrs, £32 for 4 hrs, £52 all day; extra charges for treatments* 🕙 *Daily 9* AM*–10* PM*; last entry at 7:30* PM.

WORTH NOTING

American Museum in Britain. A Greek-Revival (19th-century) mansion in a majestic setting on a hill southeast of the city holds the only museum of American decorative arts outside the United States. In the vaulted basement, the American Heritage Exhibition focuses on such aspects of U.S. history as the War of Independence, the settlement of the West, Native Americans, slavery, and the Civil War. Rooms are furnished in historical styles, such as a 17th-century keeping room from Massachusetts and a richly red New Orleans bedroom from the 1860s. Other galleries contain rugs and quilts, porcelain, and Shaker objects, and a separate building is devoted to folk art. The parkland includes a reproduction of George Washington's garden at Mount Vernon. You can take a bus headed for the University of Bath and get off at the Avenue, where signs point to the museum, half a mile away. ⊠ *Claverton Manor, off A36, 2½ mi southeast of Bath* ☎ *01225/460503* ⊕ *www.americanmuseum. org* 🎟 *Museum, special exhibitions, and grounds £8; special exhibitions and grounds £5.50* 🕙 *Mid-Mar.–July, Sept., and Oct., Tues.–Sun. and national holidays noon–5; Aug., daily noon–5; late Nov.–mid-Dec., Tues.–Sun. and national holidays noon–4:30.*

12 Building of Bath Museum. This absorbing museum in the Georgian Gothic–style Countess of Huntingdon's Chapel is an essential stop on any exploration of Bath, particularly for fans of Georgian architecture. It explains and illustrates the evolution of the city, with examples of everything from window design and wrought-iron railings to marquetry

8

A GOOD WALK IN BATH

For an hour-long stroll that takes in Bath's architectural showpieces, start in the traffic-free Abbey Churchyard, a lively piazza (often filled with musicians and street artists) dominated by Bath Abbey and the Roman Baths complex. Work your way east to Grand Parade and look out over flower-filled gardens and the River Avon, crossed by the graceful, Italianate Pulteney Bridge.

Stroll over the shop-lined bridge to gaze up the broad thoroughfare of Great Pulteney Street; then cross back over the bridge and head east up Bridge Street, turning right at High Street to follow up Broad Street and its northern extension, Lansdown Road. Turn left onto Bennett Street, passing the 18th-century

Assembly Rooms and the Fashion Museum. Bennett Street ends at the Circus, an architectural tour de force compared by some to an inverted Colosseum.

The graceful arc of Bath's most dazzling terrace, the Royal Crescent, embraces a swath of green lawns at one end of Brock Street. Return to the Circus and walk south down Gay Street, which brings you past dignified Queen Square, with its obelisk, to the Theatre Royal. Wander east from here along tiny alleys packed with stores, galleries, and eating places, back to your starting point at Abbey Churchyard, where you could have a well-earned sit-down and tea at the Pump Room, or perhaps a soak in a pool at Thermae Bath Spa.

and other interior ornamentation. ⊠*The Paragon* ☎*01225/333895* ⊕*www.bath-preservation-trust.org.uk* 🖭*£4* ☉*Mid-Apr.–Oct., Sat.– Mon. 10:30–5; last admission at 4:30.*

⑪ Museum of Bath at Work. The core of this industrial-history collection, which gives a novel perspective on the city, is a complete engineering works and fizzy drinks factory, relocated to this building. It once belonged to Bath entrepreneur Jonathan Bowler, who started his many businesses in 1872. The tour includes the original clanking machinery and offers glimpses into Bath's stone industry and cabinetmaking. ⊠*Julian Rd.* ☎*01225/318348* ⊕*www.bath-at-work.org.uk* 🖭*£4.50* ☉*Apr.–Oct., daily 10:30–5; Nov.–Mar., weekends 10:30–5; last admission at 4:30.*

❽ Museum of East Asian Art. Intimate galleries on three floors finely display ancient and modern pieces, mostly from China but with other exhibits from Japan, Korea, and Southeast Asia. Highlights are a graphic 19th-century watercolor depicting the Chinese idea of hell, Chinese ivory figures, Buddhist objects, and Japanese lacquerware and prints. ⊠*12 Bennett St.* ☎*01225/464640* ⊕*www.meaa.org.uk* 🖭*£5* ☉*Tues.–Sat. 10–5, Sun. noon–5; last admission at 4:30.*

Prior Park. A vision to warm Jane Austen's heart, Bath's grandest house lies a mile or so southeast of the center, with splendid views over the Georgian townscape. Built around 1738 by John Wood the Elder of honey-color limestone, the Palladian mansion was the home of quarry owner and philanthropist Ralph Allen (1693–1764), whose guests included such luminaries as poet Alexander Pope and novelists Henry

Bath's Georgian Architecture

Bath wouldn't be Bath without its distinctive 18th-century Georgian architecture, much of which was conceived by John Wood the Elder (1704–54), an antiquarian and architect. Wood saw Bath as a city destined for almost mythic greatness along the lines of Winchester and Glastonbury. Arriving in Bath in 1727, he sought an architectural style that would do justice to his concept, and found it in the Palladian style, made popular in Britain by Inigo Jones.

Wood created a harmonious city, building graceful terraces (row houses), crescents (curving rows of houses), and villas of the same golden local limestone used by the Romans. Influenced by nearby ancient stone circles as well as round Roman temples, Wood broke from convention in his design for Bath's Circus, a circle of houses broken only three times for intersecting streets.

After the death of Wood the Elder, John Wood the Younger (1728–82) carried out his father's plans for the Royal Crescent, an obtuse crescent of 30 interconnected houses. Today you can stop in at No. 1 Royal Crescent for a look at one of these homes—it's like eavesdropping on the 18th century. He also built the Assembly Rooms, now open to the public.

Fielding and Samuel Richardson. Today it is a Roman Catholic school and the interior is not open to the public, but you may wander through the beautiful grounds, designed by Capability Brown and embellished with a Palladian bridge and lake. A leisurely circuit of the park should take around an hour. ■TIP➡ **The parking here is only for people with disabilities: unless you relish the uphill trudge, take a taxi or Bus 2 from the center.** ⊠ *Ralph Allen Dr.* 🕾 *01225/833422* ⊕ *www.nationaltrust. org.uk* 🖼 *£4.75* ⊘ *Mid-Feb.–Oct., Wed.–Mon. 11–5:30 or dusk; Nov.– mid-Feb., weekends 11–dusk; last admission 1 hr before closing.*

8

⟲ **Royal Victoria Park.** Originally designed as an arboretum, this tidy expanse of lawns and shady walks just west of the Royal Crescent provides the perfect setting for pleasant strolls and leisurely picnics. It's a different way to enjoy Bath other than its museums and sights. The park has a pond, an aviary, a **Botanic Garden,** and an adventure playground with plenty for kids. Hot-air balloon launches and open-air shows at festival time enliven the atmosphere. ⊠ *Upper Bristol Rd.* 🖼 *Free* ⊘ *Daily 24 hrs.*

WHERE TO EAT

Among hotel restaurants, the Dower House in the Royal Crescent Hotel is outstanding; the Cavendish in Dukes Hotel and the Olive Tree in the Queensberry Hotel are noteworthy.

££ ✕**Firehouse Rotisserie.** California comes to Bath. Tex-Mex, Pacific Rim, AMERICAN and creole influences are also evident on a menu that showcases dishes from the rotisserie and grill, such as spice-rubbed chicken with barbecue sauce, and rib eye of Angus steak with fiery steak sauce. Brick-fired pizzas entice with creative toppings; try goat cheese, pesto, and artichokes. Rustic decor, wooden floors and tables, and an easy, sociable vibe set the scene. ⊠ *2 John St.* ☎ *01225/482070* ⊟ *AE, DC, MC, V* ⊘ *Closed Sun.*

£££   ✕ **Hole in the Wall.** Escape from Bath's busyness at this relaxed eatery
MODERN BRITISH   serving sophisticated modern English fare in an 18th-century town house. At the bottom of a flight of stairs, the unfussy, stone-tile dining area—warmed by a generous open fire in winter—exudes calm and poise. (The piped-in music can be intrusive, however.) It's a great environment to indulge in such dishes as baked cod steak, panfried pork fillet, and Cheddar cheese and chive polenta. While you wait for your order, nibble on the complimentary freshly baked bread. Lunches and pretheater meals are a good value. ⊠ *16 George St.* ☎ *01225/425242* ⊟ *AE, MC, V* ⊘ *No lunch Sun.*

££   ✕ **Jamie's Italian.** Recently opened by celebrity chef Jamie Oliver, this
ITALIAN   buzzing brasserie is a cheerful counterpoint to Bath's predominantly sedate tone. The dining areas, spread over two floors and including a rooftop terrace, have a contemporary, slightly industrial feel. Expect dishes typical of Oliver's straightforward Italian rustic style, such as bruschetta, lavish antipasti, rich and meaty lasagna, and beef carpaccio and rocket (arugula) salad. Desserts include *affogato* (vanilla ice cream with espresso) and Amalfi orange tart. There's always a line outside at busy times, but you can take advantage of the all-day service by coming at off-peak hours. ⊠ *10 Milsom Pl.* ☎ *01225/510051* ⟵ *Reservations not accepted* ⊟ *MC, V.*

£   ✕ **Jazz Café.** Snack to a background of jazz classics in this cramped but
BRITISH   cozy café. Famous for its all-day breakfasts, the café is also a good spot for a quick lunch, with soups, salads, sandwiches, and fine vegetarian choices. Daily specials might include Cuban pork stew, cassoulet, or grilled salmon skewers. Last orders are taken at 9 PM. ⊠ *Kingsmead Sq.* ☎ *01225/329002* ⊟ *MC, V* ⊘ *No dinner Sun.–Thurs.*

£££   ✕ **No. 5 Restaurant.** An ideal spot for a light lunch, this airy bistro deco-
FRENCH   rated with pretty plants and framed posters is just over Pulteney Bridge from the center of town. The menu changes daily but lists soups and such dishes as crostini (toasted bread) of goat cheese with cherry tomatoes, and grilled rib of beef with red wine and shallots. There's a good-value early-evening menu on weekdays. You can bring your own wine on Monday and Tuesday evenings. ⊠ *5 Argyle St.* ☎ *01225/444499* ⊟ *AE, MC, V.*

££££   ✕ **Olive Tree.** A sleek space in the basement of the Queensberry Hotel
★   makes a calm, contemporary setting for top-notch English and Medi-
MODERN BRITISH   terranean dishes. The range of seductive, sophisticated choices includes confit salmon and potato terrine for starters and such main courses as loin of venison with poached blackberries and spinach. Some dessert picks are quince-and-pear trifle and chocolate délice, a mousselike pudding with caramel sauce. Fixed-price menus are available at lunchtime. ⊠ *Russel St.* ☎ *01225/447928* ⊟ *AE, MC, V* ⊘ *No lunch Mon.*

££   ✕ **Pump Room.** The 18th-century Pump Room, next to the Roman Baths,
BRITISH   serves morning coffee, lunches of chicken, beef, and lamb dishes, and afternoon tea, often to music by a pianist or string trio. Its stately setting is the selling point rather than the food, but do sample the English cheese board and homemade Bath biscuits. The Terrace Restaurant has

views over the Baths and is also open occasionally for fixed-price dinners (reservations are essential). Be prepared to wait in line for a table during the day. ⊠ *Abbey Churchyard* ☎ *01225/444477* ▤ *AE, MC, V* ⊘ *No dinner except during July, Aug., Dec., and festivals.*

££
BRITISH
✕ **Sally Lunn's.** Small and slightly twee, this tourist magnet near Bath Abbey occupies the oldest house in Bath, dating to 1482. It's famous for the Sally Lunn bun, actually a semisweet bread served here since 1680. You can choose from more than 40 sweet and savory toppings to accompany your bun, or turn it into a meal with such dishes as trencher pork with sherry-and-tarragon sauce. There's also an economical early-bird two-course evening menu. Daytime diners can view the small kitchen museum in the cellar (30p for nondining visitors). ⊠ *4 N. Parade Passage* ☎ *01225/461634* ▤ *MC, V.*

££
ITALIAN
✕ **Strada.** The former home of Richard "Beau" Nash—the dictator of fashion for mid-18th-century society in Bath—and his mistress Juliana Popjoy provides an elegant setting for this outpost of a reliable chain of Italian eateries. Modern wooden furnishings blend smoothly with the Georgian tone of the dining areas on two levels. Pizzas and pasta appear on the menu with dishes based on classics, including *saltimbocca di maiale* (fillet of pork in a sage-and-butter sauce). ⊠ *Beau Nash House, Saw Close* ☎ *01225/337753* ▤ *AE, MC, V.*

££
FRENCH
✕ **Tilleys Bistro.** This intimate, bow-windowed French eatery presents alluring meat and vegetarian dishes offered in small, medium, and large portions. Choices include *escargots à la bourguignonne* (snails baked in a garlic-and-butter sauce), ratatouille niçoise (vegetables cooked in a flavorsome tomato sauce), and roasted magret duck breast. Pretheater meals are available on weekdays between 6 and 7 PM. ⊠ *3 North Parade Passage* ☎ *01225/484200* ▤ *MC, V* ⊘ *Closed Sun.*

WHERE TO STAY

££
▦ **Albany Guest House.** Homey and friendly, this Edwardian house close to the Royal Crescent has contemporary, simply furnished rooms. Most are decorated with neutral, beige, and cream colors. The attic room is the largest and best. Vegetarian and other dietary preferences are accommodated at breakfast, which may include tasty homemade vegetarian sausages. **Pros:** spotless rooms; close to sights; excellent breakfasts. **Cons:** some rooms are very small; limited parking. ⊠ *24 Crescent Gardens* ☎ *01225/313339* ⊕ *www.albanybath.co.uk* ⌫ *5 rooms* ⌂ *In-room: no a/c, no phone, Wi-Fi. In-hotel: Wi-Fi, parking (free), no-smoking rooms* ▤ *AE, MC, V* ⎮⎮ *BP.*

£££–££££
▦ **Bath Paradise House.** Don't be put off by the 10-minute uphill walk from the center of Bath—you'll be rewarded by a wonderful prospect of the city from the garden and upper stories of this Georgian guesthouse. Cool pastels and traditional furnishings decorate the rooms attractively, and there are open fires in winter and a lush garden for spring and summer. Rooms 3, 4, and 5 have the best views; Nos. 9, 10, 11, and 12 open straight onto the garden. If the full English breakfast is too daunting, indulge in coffee and croissants in bed. **Pros:** great attention to detail; spectacular views from some rooms; high-quality toiletries. **Cons:** uphill walk; books up far in advance. ⊠ *88 Holloway* ☎ *01225/317723* ⊕ *www.paradise-house.co.uk* ⌫ *11 rooms* ⌂ *In-room: no a/c, DVD,*

Wi-Fi (some). In-hotel: bar, Internet terminal, Wi-Fi, parking (free), no-smoking rooms ☐AE, MC, V ⊚BP.

££ ⌂**Cranleigh.** In a quiet location on the hill above the city center, this Victorian guesthouse has wonderful views of the Avon Valley. Rooms are richly decorated. Large breakfasts—pancakes with maple syrup, kippers, scrambled eggs with smoked salmon, and vegetarian options—are served in the dining room, which overlooks the garden. There's a hot tub, but it costs £20 for two hours. The Cranleigh is a 15-minute walk from the city center, or you can take one of three buses that stop nearby. **Pros:** quiet rooms; period furnishings; many choices at breakfast. **Cons:** far from center; along a busy road; steps to climb. ⊠*159 Newbridge Hill* ☎*01225/310197* ⊕*www.cranleighguesthouse.com* ➥*9 rooms* ⌂*In-room: no a/c, Wi-Fi. In-hotel: Internet terminal, parking (free), no kids under 5, no-smoking rooms* ☐MC, V ⊚BP.

£££–££££ ⌂**Dukes Hotel.** True Georgian grandeur is evident in the refurbished rooms of this Palladian-style mansion turned elegant small hotel. Guest rooms are individually decorated in English-, French-, or Italian-inspired style, and some have elaborate plasterwork and large windows facing the street. The airy Cavendish Restaurant relies on locally sourced and organic ingredients, and light lunches are served in the bar. **Pros:** excellent central location; graceful surroundings; friendly and helpful service. **Cons:** some rooms are small; steps to climb; parking (with permit) can be tricky to find. ⊠*Great Pulteney St. (entrance on Edward St.)* ☎*01225/787960* ⊕*www.dukesbath.co.uk* ➥*11 rooms, 6 suites* ⌂*In-room: no a/c, Wi-Fi. In-hotel: restaurant, bar, Internet terminal, Wi-Fi, some pets allowed* ☐AE, MC, V ⊚BP.

££–£££ ⌂**Harington's Hotel.** It's rare to find a compact hotel in the cobblestone heart of Bath, and this informal three-story lodging converted from a group of Georgian town houses fits the bill nicely. Bedrooms aren't spacious, there are no views from the windows, and the parking facilities can be tricky to find; however, the polite but friendly service and the central location outweigh these minuses. The bar serves snacks all day. **Pros:** bright rooms; helpful staff. **Cons:** tricky to locate; some street noise from revelers; steps to climb. ⊠*Queen St.* ☎*01225/461728* ⊕*www. haringtons.co.uk* ➥*13 rooms* ⌂*In-room: no a/c, Wi-Fi (some). In-hotel: bar, parking (paid), no-smoking rooms* ☐AE, MC, V ⊚BP.

££–£££ ⌂**Marlborough House.** A warm, informal welcome greets all who stay at this Victorian establishment close to the Royal Crescent. Each room charms with period furniture, fresh flowers, and antique beds, and there's complimentary sherry for evening relaxation. Leisurely breakfasts are encouraged; choose from scones, yogurts, and savory omelets. All the food is organic and vegetarian, and vegans and those with special diets will find their needs amply supplied. **Pros:** obliging and helpful hosts; great breakfasts. **Cons:** some traffic noise; the walk to the center is along a noisy road. ⊠*1 Marlborough La.* ☎*01225/318175* ⊕*www. marlborough-house.net* ➥*6 rooms* ⌂*In-room: no a/c, Wi-Fi. In-hotel: Wi-Fi, some pets allowed, no-smoking rooms* ☐MC, V ⊚BP.

£££–££££ ⌂**Queensberry Hotel.** Intimate and elegant, this boutique hotel in a resi-
FodorsChoice   dential street near the Circus occupies three 1772 town houses built by
★   John Wood the Younger for the marquis of Queensberry. It's a perfect

marriage of chic sophistication, homey comforts, and attentive service. Renovations have preserved the Regency stucco ceilings and cornices and marble tile on the fireplaces, and each room is individually decorated in contemporary style. Four secluded, terraced gardens invite a summer aperitif, and downstairs is the excellent semiformal, understated Olive Tree restaurant. **Pros:** efficient service; good location; comfortable accommodations. **Cons:** some street noise; no tea/coffee-making facilities in rooms. ⊠*Russel St.* ☎*01225/447928* ⊕*www.thequeensberry.co.uk* ↻*26 rooms, 3 suites* ⌂*In-room: no a/c, Wi-Fi (some). In-hotel: restaurant, bar, Internet terminal, Wi-Fi, parking (free)* ▭*AE, MC, V.*

£££-£££   🏠 **Three Abbey Green.** Just steps away from Bath Abbey, a majestic plane tree dominates the gorgeous square that is home to this welcoming B&B. Parts of the building date from 1689, but contemporary design lightens the spacious, pastel-hue rooms. The Lord Nelson room is extra big, with a four-poster, separate sitting area, and handsome fireplace; there are also family rooms. The only downsides are Bath's perennial shortage of parking space—though parking lots are nearby—and the occasional noise at night. The hosts are ready with tips for visiting the city and beyond. Four apartments with kitchens are also available. **Pros:** superb location; airy rooms. **Cons:** some noise from pub goers; only one suite has a bathtub; no parking. ⊠*3 Abbey Green* ☎*01225/428558* ⊕*www.threeabbeygreen.com* ↻*7 rooms* ⌂*In-room: no a/c, Wi-Fi. In-hotel: Internet terminal, no-smoking rooms* ▭*MC, V* ❘⊚❘*BP.*

NIGHTLIFE AND THE ARTS

BARS AND PUBS

The **Porter** (⊠*2 Miles's Buildings, George St.* ☎*01225/424104*), the city's only vegetarian pub, features nightly music and comedy performances in its grungy cellar bar.Pub aficionados will relish the friendly, unspoiled ambience of the **Raven** (⊠*Queen St.* ☎*01225/425045*), a great spot for a pint, with regular poetry readings, storytelling nights, and live music upstairs.

FESTIVALS
★

Bath Comedy Festival (⊠*Bath Festivals Box Office, 2 Church St., Abbey Green* ☎*01225/463362* ⊕*www.bathcomedyfestival.co.uk*) kicks off on April Fool's Day (April 1) for 12 days of comedy events at venues throughout the city.

The **Bath International Music Festival** (⊠*Bath Festivals Box Office, 2 Church St., Abbey Green* ☎*01225/463362* ⊕*www.bathmusicfest.org. uk*), held for two weeks in May and June, presents concerts (classical, jazz, and world music), dance performances, and exhibitions in and around Bath, many in the Assembly Rooms and Bath Abbey.

The weeklong **Bath Literature Festival** (⊠*Bath Festivals Box Office, 2 Church St., Abbey Green* ☎*01225/463362* ⊕*www.bathlitfest.org.uk*) in early March features readings and talks by writers, mostly in the 18th-century Guildhall on High Street.

The **Jane Austen Festival** (☎*01225/443000* ⊕*www.janeausten.co.uk/ festival*) celebrates the great writer with films, plays, walks, and talks over 10 days in late September. It's a feast for Janeites.

THEATER

The **Theatre Royal** (⊠*Box Office, Saw Close* ☎*01225/448844*), a gemlike Regency playhouse from 1805, has a year-round program that often includes pre- or post-London tours. You must reserve the best

8

seats well in advance, but you can line up for same-day standby seats or standing room. Tours usually take place on the first Wednesday and the following Saturday of the month. ■ TIP→ **Take care with your seat location—sight lines can be poor.**

SPORTS AND THE OUTDOORS

To explore the River Avon by rented punt or canoe, head for the **Bath Boating Station** (⊠ *Forester Rd.* ☎ *01225/312900*), behind the Holburne Museum. It's open Easter to October.

SHOPPING

Bath has excellent small, family-run, and specialty shops; many close on Sunday. The shopping district centers on Stall and Union streets (modern stores), Milsom Street (traditional stores), and Walcot Street (arts and crafts). Leading off these main streets are alleyways and passages lined with galleries and antiques shops.

For 10 days in late November and early December, the outdoor **Bath Christmas Market** (⊠ *Abbey Green, Abbey Gate St., and Kingston Parade* ☎ *01225/396417*) sells gift items—from handcrafted toys to candles, cards, and edible delights—in stalls around the abbey and Roman Baths.

★ **Bartlett Street Antiques Centre** (⊠ *Bartlett St.* ☎ *No phone*) has more than 50 showcases and stands selling every kind of antique imaginable, including silver, porcelain, and jewelry. **Bath Sweet Shop** (⊠ *8 North Parade Passage* ☎ *01225/428040*), the city's oldest candy store, boasts of stocking some 350 different sweets, including traditional licorice torpedoes, pear drops, and aniseed balls. Sugar-free varieties are available. **Beaux Arts Ceramics** (⊠ *12–13 York St.* ☎ *01225/464850*) carries the work of prominent potters. The covered **Guildhall Market** (⊠ *Entrances on High St. and Grand Parade*), open Monday through Saturday 9 to 5, is the place for everything from jewelry and gifts to delicatessen food, secondhand books, bags, and batteries; there's a café, too. **Margaret's Buildings** (⊠ *Halfway between the Circus and Royal Crescent*) is a lane with gift shops and several stores selling secondhand and antiquarian books.

CASTLE COMBE

Fodor's Choice   *12 mi northeast of Bath, 5 mi northwest of Chippenham.*

★ This Wiltshire village lived a sleepy existence until 1962, when it was voted the "prettiest village" in England—without any of its inhabitants knowing that it had even been a contender. The village's magic is that it's so toylike, so delightfully all-of-a-piece: you can see almost the whole town at one glance from any one position. Castle Combe consists of little more than a brook, a pack bridge, a street (which is called the Street) of simple stone cottages, a market cross from the 13th century, and the Perpendicular-style church of St. Andrew. The grandest house in the village (on its outskirts) is the Upper Manor House, built in the 15th century by Sir John Fastolf and now the Manor House Hotel.

GETTING HERE AND AROUND

All buses from Bath to Lacock involve a change and take 60 to 110 minutes, so it's best to drive or join a tour.

Bath
see detail
map

WHERE TO STAY

££££–£££££ [image] **Manor House Hotel.** This partly 14th-century manor house, outside
★ the village in a 23-acre park, is a baronial swirl of solid chimney stacks,
carvings, and columns. Inside, a stone frieze depicts characters from
Shakespeare's Falstaff plays, to commemorate the fact that Sir John
Fastolf, thought to be the model for the character, was lord of this
manor. Guest rooms—some in mews cottages—brim with antique
character, and the secluded, landscaped setting is soothing, with green
vistas on every side, though the village is only a few steps away. The
golf course is excellent. The well-regarded Bybrook restaurant serves
imaginative fixed-price meals. **Pros:** romantic getaway; rich historical
setting; good golf course. **Cons:** cottage rooms lack ambience; expensive restaurant. ⊠ *Castle Combe SN14 7HR* ☎ *01249/782206* ⊕ *www.
manorhouse.co.uk* ⇴ *48 rooms* ⏚ *In-room: no a/c, Internet. In-hotel:
restaurant, bar, golf course, tennis court, Internet terminal, Wi-Fi, some
pets allowed* ⊟ *AE, MC, V.*

LACOCK

Fodor's Choice 8 mi southeast of Castle Combe, 12 mi east of Bath.
★
Owned by the National Trust, this lovely Wiltshire village is the victim
of its own charm, its unspoiled gabled and stone-tile cottages drawing tour buses aplenty. Off-season, however, Lacock slips back into its
profound slumber, the mellow stone and brick buildings little changed
in 500 years and well worth a wander. Besides Lacock Abbey, there are
a few antiques shops, the handsome church of St. Cyriac (built with
money earned in the wool trade), a 14th-century tithe barn, and a scattering of pubs that serve bar meals in atmospheric surroundings.

GETTING HERE AND AROUND

All buses from Bath to Castle Combe involve one or two changes and
take 70 to 100 minutes, so it's best to drive or join a tour.

EXPLORING

Well-preserved **Lacock Abbey** reflects the fate of many religious establishments in England—a spiritual center became a home. The abbey, at the town's center, was founded in the 13th century and closed down during the dissolution of the monasteries in 1539, when its new owner, Sir William Sharington, demolished the church and converted the clois-

ters, sacristy, chapter house, and monastic quarters into a private dwelling. His last descendant, Mathilda Talbot, donated the property as well as Lacock itself to the National Trust in the 1940s. The abbey's grounds are also worth a wander, with a Victorian woodland garden and an 18th-century summerhouse. Harry Potter fans, take note: Lacock Abbey was used for some scenes at Hogwarts School in the film *Harry Potter and the Sorcerer's Stone.*

The **Fox Talbot Museum,** in a 16th-century barn at the gates of Lacock Abbey, illustrates the early history of photography with works by pioneers in the field and also exhibits contemporary artists. The museum commemorates the work of William Henry Fox Talbot (1800–77), who developed the first photographic negative at Lacock Abbey, showing an oriel window in his family home. Look for a copy of this and other results of Fox Talbot's experiments in the 1830s. ✉ *Just east of A350* ☎ *01249/730459* ⊕ *www.nationaltrust.org.uk* ✉ *Abbey, museum, gardens, and cloisters £9.50; abbey, garden, and cloisters £7.60; museum, gardens, and cloisters £5.70* ⊙ *Abbey mid-Mar.–Oct., Thurs.–Mon. 11–5. Museum, gardens, and cloisters late Feb.–Oct., daily 11–5:30; early Nov.–late Dec. and Jan.–late Feb., weekends 11–4; last admission 30 mins before closing.*

WHERE TO EAT

£££   ✕**Sign of the Angel.** An inn since the 15th century, this atmospheric res-
BRITISH   taurant is known for its roasts, casseroles, and specialties like Stilton and walnut pâté. Don't pass up such desserts as meringues with clotted cream. There are also somewhat cramped accommodations (£££)—some rooms are in comfortable older buildings, others are in a newer annex. ✉ *6 Church St.* ☎ *01249/730230* ▭ *AE, DC, MC, V* ⊙ *Closed Mon. lunch and last wk of Dec.*

THE COTSWOLDS

The Thames rises among the limestone Cotswold Hills, a delightful cradle for that historic river. The Cotswolds are among England's best-preserved rural districts, and the quiet but lovely grays and ambers of the stone buildings here are truly unsurpassed. Much has been written about the area's age-mellowed towns, but the architecture of the villages actually differs little from that of villages elsewhere in England. Their distinction lies in their surroundings: the valleys are deep and rolling, and cozy hamlets appear to drip in foliage from church tower to garden gate. Beyond the town limits, you can explore, on foot or by car, the "high wild hills and rough uneven ways" that Shakespeare wrote about.

Over the centuries, quarries of honey-color stone have yielded building blocks for many Cotswold houses and churches and have transformed little towns into realms of gold. Nowhere else in Britain does that superb combination of church tower and gabled manor house shine so brightly. There's an elusive spirit about the Cotswolds, so make Chipping Campden, Moreton-in-Marsh, or Stow-on-the-Wold your headquarters and wander for a few days. Then ask yourself what the area is all about. Its secret seems shared by two things—sheep and stone. The combination isn't as strange as it may sound. These were once the great sheep-rearing areas of England, and during the peak of prosperity in the Middle Ages, Cotswold wool was in demand the world over. This made the local merchants rich, but many gave back to the Cotswolds by restoring old churches (the famous "wool churches" of the region) or building rows of almshouses, of limestone now seasoned to a glorious golden-gray.

Begin with Cheltenham—the largest town in the area and a gateway to the Cotswolds, but slightly outside the boundaries—then move on to the beauty spots in and around Winchcombe. Next are Sudeley Castle, Stanway House, and Snowshill Manor, among the most impressive houses of the region; the oversold village of Broadway; Chipping Campden—the Cotswold cognoscenti's favorite; and Hidcote Manor, one of the most spectacular gardens in England. Then circle back south, down through Moreton-in-Marsh, Stow-on-the-Wold, Upper Slaughter, Lower Slaughter, and Bourton-on-the-Water, and end with Bibury, Tetbury, and Owlpen. This is definitely a region where it pays to go off the beaten track to take a look at that village among the trees.

CHELTENHAM

50 mi north of Bath, 13 mi east of Gloucester, 99 mi west of London.

Although Cheltenham has acquired a reputation as snooty—the population (around 110,000) is generally well heeled and conservative—it's also cosmopolitan. The town has excellent restaurants and bars, fashionable stores, and a thriving cultural life. Its primary claim to renown, however, is its architecture, rivaling Bath's in its Georgian elegance, with wide, tree-lined streets, crescents, and terraces with row houses, balconies, and iron railings.

Like Bath, Cheltenham owes part of its fame to mineral springs. By 1740 the first spa was built, and after a visit from George III and Queen Charlotte in 1788, the town dedicated itself to idleness and enjoyment. "A polka, parson-worshipping place"—in the words of resident Lord Tennyson—Cheltenham gained its reputation for snobbishness when stiff-collared Raj majordomos returned from India to find that the springs—the only purely natural alkaline waters in England—were the most effective cure for their "tropical ailments."

Great Regency architectural set pieces—Lansdown Crescent, Pittville Spa, and the Lower Assembly Rooms, among them—were built solely

The Cotswolds

to adorn the town. The Rotunda building (1826) at the top of Montpellier Walk—now a bank—contains the spa's original "pump room," in which the mineral waters were on tap. More than 30 statues adorn the storefronts of Montpellier Walk. Wander past Imperial Square, with its ironwork balconies, past the ornate Neptune's Fountain, and along the Promenade. In spring and summer lush flower gardens enhance the town's buildings, attracting many visitors.

GETTING HERE AND AROUND

Trains from London Paddington and buses from London Victoria head to Cheltenham. The train station is west of the center, and the bus station is centrally located off Royal Well Road. Drivers should leave their vehicles in one of the numerous parking lots. The town center is easily negotiable on foot. Cheltenham's tourist office arranges walking tours (£4) of the town late June through mid-September.

ESSENTIALS

Visitor Information Cheltenham (✉ 77 Promenade ☎ 01242/522878 ⊕ www.visitcheltenham.info).

EXPLORING

From the 1880s onward, Cheltenham was at the forefront of the Arts and Crafts movement, and the **Cheltenham Art Gallery and Museum** contains fine displays of William Morris textiles, furniture by Charles Voysey, and wood and metal pieces by Ernest Gimson. Decorative arts, such as Chinese ceramics, are represented, and British artists, including Stanley Spencer and Vanessa Bell, make their mark in the art gallery. Other exhibits focus on local archaeology and history; one is devoted to Edward Wilson, who traveled with Robert Scott to the Antarctic on Scott's ill-fated 1912 expedition. ✉ *Clarence St.* ☎ *01242/237431* ⊕ *www.cheltenhammuseum.org.uk* ✉ *Free* ☉ *Apr.–Oct., daily 10–5 (11–5 1st Thurs. of month, 10–8 3rd Thurs. of month); Nov.–Mar., daily 10–4 (11–4 1st Thurs. of month, 10–8 3rd Thurs. of month).*

The grandest of the remaining spa buildings, the **Pittville Pump Room** is set amid parkland, a 20-minute walk from the town center. The classic Regency structure, built in the late 1820s, now serves mainly as a concert hall and a theatrical venue but still offers its musty mineral waters to the strong of stomach. The Pump Room may not be accessible during functions, so call ahead. ✉ *E. Approach Dr., Pittville* ☎ *01242/523852* ⊕ *www.pittvillepumproom.org.uk* ✉ *Free* ☉ *Wed.–Mon. 10–4.*

WHERE TO EAT

£££ ✕ **Brasserie Blanc.** Housed in the former ballroom of Queen's Hotel,
FRENCH this offshoot of renowned chef Raymond Blanc's Manoir aux Quat' Saisons in Great Milton offers French provincial cooking in contemporary surroundings that harmonize well with the expansive Regency windows. The impressive menu takes in everything from Burgundian snails in garlic to seared sea bream fillet in a bouillabaisse sauce. Among the lip-smacking desserts is flaming baked Alaska. ✉ *The Promenade* ☎ *01242/266800* ⊟ *AE, MC, V.*

£££ ✕ **Hotel du Vin.** Town movers and shakers have made the restaurant in
MODERN FRENCH the trendy Hotel du Vin a favorite dining spot. Casual but sophisticated, the basement-level bistro lies at the bottom of a grand staircase

beneath an artful chandelier made of wine glasses. The numerous bottles incorporated into the decor are a subtle boast about the formidable wine list. Don't be distracted from the French menu, which includes char-grilled rib-eye steak and butternut squash risotto. For dessert, dip into the lavender panna cotta with roast figs or lemon meringue pie. In fine weather, you can enjoy your lunch alfresco. ⊠ *Parabola Rd., Montpellier* ☎*01242/588450* ♥*AE, MC, V.*

> ### FLOWERS AND FESTIVALS
>
> Parts of the town may look like something out of a Gilbert and Sullivan stage set, but Cheltenham is the site of two of England's most progressive arts festivals— the Cheltenham Festival of Literature and the town's music festival—as well as a jazz fest.

£££££ ✕**Le Champignon Sauvage.** The relatively short, perfectly balanced menu
FRENCH at this well-established restaurant showcases the contemporary French
★ cooking of David Everitt-Matthias. Relax in a room with cream walls and modern art as you indulge in dishes such as pressed terrine of young goat followed by Cinderford lamb. Desserts, including warm prune cake, are worth the calories; you can choose among many cheeses as well. Fixed-price menus at lunch (£25–£30) and dinner (£25–£58) help keep the cost down. ⊠*24 Suffolk Rd.* ☎*01242/573449* ▱*AE, DC, MC, V* ♥*Closed Sun., Mon., 3 wks in June, and 10 days in Dec. and Jan.*

££ ✕**Montpellier Wine Bar.** An ideal place for a light afternoon snack or a full
BRITISH evening meal, this busy, informal wine bar is on two floors—upstairs is more casual and downstairs is more formal. In Cheltenham's fashionable Montpellier shopping district, it serves tapas, pastas, salads, and dishes such as Hereford beef fillet. Get in early for fast service. ⊠*Bayshill Lodge, Montpellier St.* ☎*01242/527774* ▱*AE, DC, MC, V.*

WHERE TO STAY

££ ▢**Abbey Hotel.** Relaxed and family-run, this hotel in a quiet terrace near the center of town offers great value. Bedrooms are simple but pleasant, decorated in subtle tones, and the breakfast area overlooks the well-stocked garden. There's an honesty bar for guests. **Pros:** easygoing atmosphere; good breakfasts; discounts for longer stays. **Cons:** limited parking; some bathrooms are small. ⊠*14–16 Bath Parade* ☎*01242/516053* ⊕*www.abbeyhotel-cheltenham.com* ◿*13 rooms* ♤*In-room: no a/c, Wi-Fi. In-hotel: Wi-Fi, no-smoking rooms* ▱*MC, V* ▯◉▯*BP.*

£££££ ▢**Cowley Manor.** Good-bye, floral prints: this Georgian mansion on 55 acres brings country-house style into the 21st century with a mellow atmosphere and modern fabrics and furniture. The comfort level is high enough to soothe a chic clientele. Witty sculptures and lighting complement the public rooms, beds are huge and comfortable, and bathrooms are trendy, with glass walls and expansive showers. Half the rooms are in the house; the rest fill a transformed stable. There's a two-night minimum stay on weekends. The spa, set into the ground, looks like a work of art. Cowley Manor is 5 mi south of Cheltenham. **Pros:** beautiful grounds; family-friendly atmosphere, superb pools. **Cons:** food can be patchy; occasionally slack service for the steep prices. ✉*Off A435, Cowley* 🕿*01242/870900* ⊕*www.cowleymanor.com* 🛏*30 rooms* ♨*In-room: DVD, Internet, Wi-Fi (some). In-hotel: restaurant, pools, gym, spa, Internet terminal, Wi-Fi* ▭*AE, DC, MC, V* ⫶❙*BP.*

££ 🔲 **Lypiatt House Hotel.** A short walk from central Cheltenham in the chic Montpellier area, this splendid Victorian villa offers attentive service in elegant surroundings. Guest rooms are mostly spacious and have chic bathrooms. The restful drawing room is done in deep pink, and the conservatory makes a good place for a drink. **Pros:** clean and elegant; capacious parking; discounts for longer stays. **Cons:** stiff atmosphere. ✉*Lypiatt Rd.* 🕿*01242/224994* ⊕*www.lypiatt.co.uk* 🛏*10 rooms* ♨*In-room: no a/c, Wi-Fi. In-hotel: bar, laundry service, Wi-Fi, parking (free), no kids under 12, no-smoking rooms* ▭*AE, MC, V* ⫶❙*BP.*

£££–££££ 🔲 **Mercure Queen's Hotel.** Grandly dominating Imperial Gardens, this hotel in a classic Regency mansion has welcomed visitors to Cheltenham since 1838. Public areas and rooms leading off the stunning inner stairway are traditionally British (and rather old-fashioned) in style, and every bedroom is individually decorated. Top-floor rooms afford the best views. **Pros:** central location; grand style. **Cons:** front-facing rooms can be noisy; charges for all the extras. ✉*The Promenade* 🕿*01242/514754* ⊕*www.mercure.com* 🛏*79 rooms* ♨*In-room: Internet, Wi-Fi. In-hotel: restaurant, bar, Internet terminal, Wi-Fi, parking (paid), some pets allowed* ▭*AE, DC, MC, V.*

NIGHTLIFE AND THE ARTS

The late-Victorian **Everyman Theatre** (✉*Regent St.* 🕿*01242/572573*) is an intimate venue for opera, dance, concerts, and plays. ■**TIP→ You can often catch pre– or post–West End productions here, at a fraction of big city prices.**

For information on the town's ambitious lineup of festivals, contact the **Festival Office** (✉*109 Bath Rd., Cheltenham* 🕿*0844/576–8970* ⊕*www.cheltenhamfestivals.co.uk*). The **Cheltenham Jazz Festival,** held over a week in late April/early May, presents noted musicians. The

★ 10-day **Literature Festival** in October brings together world-renowned authors, actors, and critics for hundreds of readings and events. Cheltenham's famous **Music Festival,** in early to mid-July, highlights new compositions, often conducted by the composers, and classical pieces. The **Science Festival,** which takes place over five days in early June, attracts leading scientists and writers.

SPORTS

Important steeplechase races take place at **Cheltenham Racecourse** (✉*Prestbury Park* 🕿*0844/579–3003*), north of the town center. The Gold Cup awards crown the last day of the National Hunt Festival in mid-March.

SHOPPING

This is serious shopping territory. A stroll along Montpellier Walk and then along the flower-bedecked Promenade brings you to high-quality specialty stores and boutiques. A bubble-blowing Wishing Fish Clock, designed by Kit Williams, dominates the Regent Arcade, a modern

8

shopping area behind the Promenade. General markets are held every Sunday at the Cheltenham Racecourse and every Thursday morning off Lower High Street. An indoor antiques market is open Monday through Saturday at 54 Suffolk Road; there are other antiques shops in the Suffolk Road area. A farmers' market takes place on the Promenade on the second and fourth Friday of the month.

Cavendish House (✉ *32–48 The Promenade* ☎*01242/521300*) is a high-quality department store with designer fashions. **Feva** (✉*20 Regent St.* ☎*01242/222998*) sells eye-catching lines of clothes for women in bright, splashy colors, as well as shoes, belts, and handbags. More-formal wear is sold on the upper floor. **Martin** (✉*19 The Promenade* ☎*01242/522821*) carries a good stock of modern jewelry. **Q and C Militaria** (✉*22 Suffolk Rd.* ☎*01242/519815*) a treasure trove for military buffs, offers badges and medals, breastplates, helmets, coats of arms, and books.

WINCHCOMBE

7 mi northeast of Cheltenham.

The sleepy, unspoiled village of Winchcombe (population 4,500), once the capital of the Anglo-Saxon kingdom of Mercia, has some attractive half-timber and stone houses, as well as a clutch of appealing old inns serving food. A good place to escape the crowds, it's near Sudeley Castle and is also the start of both the Warden's Way and Windrush Way walking trails.

ESSENTIALS

Visitor Information Winchcombe (✉ *Town Hall, High St.* ☎*01242/602925* ⊕*www.visitcotswoldsandsevernvale.gov.uk*).

EXPLORING

Almost 40 outlandish gargoyles adorn the mid-15th-century Perpendicular-style **St. Peter's Church** (✉*Gloucester St.*), a typical Cotswold wool church.

One of the grand showpieces of the Cotswolds, **Sudeley Castle** was the home and burial place of Catherine Parr (1512–48), Henry VIII's sixth and last wife, who outlived him by one year. Here Catherine undertook, in her later years, the education of the ill-fated Lady Jane Grey and the future queen, Princess Elizabeth. Sudeley, for good reason, has been called a woman's castle. The term castle is misleading, though, for it looks more like a Tudor-era palace, with a peaceful air that belies its turbulent history. In the 17th century Charles I took refuge here, causing Oliver Cromwell's army to besiege the castle, leaving it in ruins until the Dent-Brocklehurst family stepped in with a 19th-century renovation.

The 14 acres of gardens, which include the spectacular roses of the Queen's Garden and a Tudor knot garden, are the setting for Shakespeare performances, concerts, and other events in summer. Inside the castle, however, visitors see only the West Wing, with the Long Room and temporary exhibitions that focus on such subjects as the Tudors, the Civil War, and the Victorians. The private apartments of Lord and Lady Ashcombe, where you can see paintings by Van Dyck, Rubens,

Turner, and Reynolds, are viewable only on Connoisseur Tours on Tuesday, Wednesday, and Thursday (£15, including entry to the public rooms and a guidebook). Garden tours are available Monday and Friday (£11). The 11 cottages on the grounds are booked for a minimum of three-night stays. The castle is a mile southeast of Winchcombe. ⊠ *Off B4632* ☎ *01242/602308* ⊕ *www.sudeleycastle.co.uk* ⊠ *£7.20* ⊗ *Apr.–Oct., daily 10:30–5.*

A bracing 2-mi walk south of Winchcombe on the **Cotswold Way,** one of Britain's national walking trails, leads to the hilltop site of **Belas Knap,** a neolithic long barrow, or submerged burial chamber, above

★ **Humblebee Wood.** ■TIP➔ **The site isn't much to see, but you hike next to and through one of the most enchanting natural domains in England, with views stretching over to Sudeley Castle.** If you have a car, take the scenic Humblebee Wood road down to the villages of Sevenhampton and Brockhampton.

A mile east of Winchcombe, at Greet, you can board a steam-hauled ⌚ train of the **Gloucestershire and Warwickshire Railway,** which chugs its way along a 13-mi stretch at the foot of the Cotswolds between Toddington Station and Cheltenham Racecourse. The round-trip journey takes around 90 minutes. ⊠ *Station Rd., Greet* ☎ *01242/621405* ⊕ *www. gwsr.com* ⊠ *£10 round-trip* ⊗ *Mar.–Dec., weekends 10:30–5; call for other days of operation.*

WHERE TO EAT

£££££ ✕ **Wesley House.** Wooden beams and stone walls distinguish this 15th-
MEDITERRANEAN century half-timber building, where the red-carpeted dining room makes a fine backdrop for superior Mediterranean-style food. The fixed-price menus (£32.50–£38) include halibut with Jerusalem artichoke and brown shrimps, and caramelized duck breast with parsnip purée, gratin potatoes, and Madeira sauce. You can eat and drink less formally in the adjoining wine bar and grill, with a choice of pastas, risottos, steaks, and seafood. Upstairs, five small guest rooms have twisted beams and sloping ceilings, including the Preacher's Room, where John Wesley used to stay. ⊠ *High St.* ☎ *01242/602366* ⊟ *AE, MC, V* ⊗ *No dinner Sun.*

BROADWAY

8 mi north of Winchcombe, 17 mi northeast of Cheltenham.

The Cotswold town to end all Cotswold towns, Broadway has become a favorite of day-trippers. William Morris first discovered the delights of this village, and J. M. Barrie, Vaughan Williams, and Edward Elgar soon followed. Today you may want to avoid Broadway in summer, when it's clogged with cars and buses. Named for its handsome, wide main street (well worth a stroll), the village includes the renowned Lygon Arms hotel and numerous antiques shops, tea parlors, and boutiques. Step off onto Broadway's back roads and alleys and you can discover any number of honey-color houses and colorful gardens.

GETTING HERE AND AROUND

Broadway can be reached by car via A44; drivers should park in one of the car parks signposted from the main street. Johnson's Coaches connect the town with Stratford-upon-Avon, Chipping Campden, and Moreton-in-Marsh; Castleways connect Broadway with Winchcombe and Cheltenham. No services run on Sundays. You'll need a car to reach Broadway Tower, Stanway House, and Snowshill Manor.

ESSENTIALS

Visitor Information Broadway (⊠ *Russell Sq.* ☎ *01386/852937* ⊕ *www. beautifulbroadway.com*).

EXPLORING

Among the attractions of **Broadway Tower Country Park,** on the outskirts of town, is its **tower,** an 18th-century "folly" built by the sixth earl of Coventry and later used by William Morris as a retreat. Exhibits describe the tower's past and the local Arts and Crafts movement, and the view from the top takes in three counties. (The tower normally stays open longer than the advertised times in fine weather.) Peaceful countryside surrounds you on the nature trails and picnic grounds. ⊠ *Off A44* ☎ *01386/852390* ⊠ *Park free, tower £4* ⊙ *Tower Apr.–Oct., daily 10:30–5; Nov.–Mar., weekends 10:30–3.*

★
⊙
Snowshill, 3 mi south of Broadway and 13 mi northeast of Cheltenham, is one of the most unspoiled of all Cotswold villages. Snuggled beneath Oat Hill, with little room for expansion, the hamlet is centered around an old burial ground, the 19th-century St. Barnabas Church, and **Snowshill Manor,** a splendid 17th-century house that brims with the collections of Charles Paget Wade, gathered between 1919 and 1956. Over the door of the house is Wade's family motto, *Nequid pereat* ("Let nothing perish"). The rooms are bursting with Tibetan scrolls, spinners' tools, ship models, Persian lamps, and bric-a-brac. The Green Room displays 26 suits of Japanese samurai armor. Children love the place. Outside, an imaginative terraced garden provides an exquisite frame for the house. ■ TIP→ **Admission is by timed tickets issued on a first-come, first-served basis, so arrive early in peak season.** ⊠ *Off A44, Snowshill* ☎ *01386/852410* ⊕ *www.nationaltrust.org.uk* ⊠ *£7.70; garden only, £4.10* ⊙ *House: mid-Mar.–Oct., Wed.–Sun. noon–5. Garden: mid-Mar.–Oct., Wed.–Sun. 11–5:30.*

★
Stanway House, a perfect Cotswold manor of glowing limestone in the small village of Stanway, dates from the Jacobean era. Its triple-gabled gatehouse is a Cotswold landmark, and towering windows dominate the house's Great Hall. They illuminate a 22-foot-long shuffleboard table from 1620 and an 18th-century bouncing exercise machine. The other well-worn rooms are adorned with family portraits, tattered tapestries, vintage armchairs, and, at times, Lord or Lady Neidpath themselves, the current owners. The partly restored baroque water garden has a fountain, built in 2004, that shoots up 300 feet. The tallest in Britain, it shoots at 2:45 and 4. To get to Stanway, about 5 mi south of Broadway, take B4632 south from town, turning left at B4077. ⊠ *Off B4077, Stanway* ☎ *01386/584469* ⊕ *www.stanwayfountain.co.uk* ⊠ *House*

and fountain £6; fountain only, £4
⊙House and fountain: June–Aug.,
Tues. and Thurs. 2–5.

WHERE TO EAT

£££ ✕ **Russell's.** With a courtyard at the
MODERN BRITISH back and a patio at the front, this chic "restaurant with rooms" is perfect for a light lunch at midday or a full meal in the evening. The restaurant, in a furniture factory once belonging to local designer George Russell, is modern and plush. A la carte and fixed-price menus concentrate on modern British dishes, with such temptations as baked goat cheese in filo pastry, roast pheasant with braised red cabbage, and grilled plaice (a fish). The seven boutique-style rooms upstairs (£££) are very sleek. ⊠20 High St. ☎01386/853555 ⊟AE, MC, V ⊙No dinner Sun.

WHERE TO STAY

£££–££££ ⊞ **Barceló Lygon Arms.** Modern luxury, epitomized in the luxurious spa and health club, exists in perfect symbiosis with old-fashioned charm right in the heart of Broadway. In business since 1532, the inn (pronounced Liggon) has a gabled roof and mullioned windows dating to 1620. Inside, look for antiques-bedecked parlors, baronial fireplaces, rich paneling, and rooms that once sheltered Charles I and Oliver Cromwell. Behind the house are more modern (and less expensive) bedrooms and 3 acres of formal gardens. One restaurant, the Great Hall (££££–£££££), complete with a minstrels' gallery, focuses on creative adaptations of traditional dishes. A good and cheaper option is Goblets Bistro. **Pros:** historic main building; great spa facilities; indoor pool. **Cons:** annex lacks character; disappointing breakfast, service sometimes sloppy. ⊠High St. ☎01386/852255 ⊕www.barcelo-hotels.co.uk ⇆71 rooms, 7 suites ⌂In-room: no a/c (some), Internet. In-hotel: 2 restaurants, bar, tennis court, pool, spa, Wi-Fi, some pets allowed ⊟AE, MC, V ⓄBP.

£££££ ⊞ **Buckland Manor.** As an alternative to the hustle and bustle of Broad-
★ way, you can splurge at this exceptional traditional country-house hotel 2 mi away in the idyllic hamlet of Buckland. The land was valued at £9 in the 11th-century Domesday Book, and the sprawling stone building dates back to Jacobean times. Public areas and guest rooms are plushly comfortable, with old paintings, fine rugs, and antiques everywhere. The gardens are well groomed and tranquil. The baronial restaurant (£££££, jacket and tie required) features largely traditional fare enhanced with modern trimmings. **Pros:** beautiful setting; cozy public rooms; large bathrooms with high-quality toiletries. **Cons:** service can be spotty; not a place for families with small children. ⊠Off B4632, Buckland ☎01386/852626 ⊕www.bucklandmanor.co.uk ⇆13 rooms ⌂In-room: no a/c, Internet. In-hotel: restaurant, bar, tennis courts, no kids under 10 ⊟AE, MC, V ⓄBP.

££££ ⊞ **Dormy House Hotel.** Guest rooms in this converted 17th-century
★ farmhouse overlook the Vale of Evesham from high on the Cotswolds

8

ridge—one of the region's most celebrated vistas. Luxury rules at this establishment, where you can relax by a fireplace or play a game of croquet on the lawn. Modern furnishings blend comfortably with traditional pieces in the beamed bedrooms. Noted in the region, the restaurant (£37 fixed-price menu) has a superlative wine list and specializes in English. A more economical option is the beamed Barn Owl bar and brasserie. The hotel is 2 mi north of Broadway. **Pros:** professional staff; well-equipped rooms; great location; discount at nearby golf course. **Cons:** hard to find; standard rooms may be rather small and dark. ⊠ *Willersey Hill* ☎ *01386/852711* ⊕ *www.dormyhouse.co.uk* ⬅ *45 rooms* ♿ *In-room: no a/c, Internet (some), Wi-Fi (some). In-hotel: restaurant, bars, gym, Wi-Fi* ⊟ *AE, DC, MC, V* ⦿ *BP.*

£££   ⛅ **Mill Hay House.** If the rose garden, trout-filled pond, and pet sheep at this 18th-century Queen Anne house aren't appealing enough, then the stone-flagged floors, leather sofas, and grandfather clocks should satisfy. Booking ahead is essential to secure one of the three beautiful, traditional-style pastel bedrooms at this B&B. Ask about discounted midweek and weekend packages. It's 1 mi from Broadway on Snowshill Road. **Pros:** stunning views; beautifully landscaped gardens; gourmet breakfasts. **Cons:** books up quickly; no young children admitted. ⊠ *Snowshill Rd.* ☎ *01386/852498* ⊕ *www.millhay.co.uk* ⬅ *2 rooms, 1 suite* ♿ *In-room: no a/c, safe, kitchen, Wi-Fi. In-hotel: Wi-Fi, no kids under 12, no-smoking rooms* ⊟ *MC, V* ⦿ *BP.*

CHIPPING CAMPDEN

4 mi east of Broadway, 18 mi northeast of Cheltenham.

Undoubtedly one of the most beautiful towns in the area, Chipping Campden, with its population of about 2,500, is the Cotswolds in a microcosm. It has St. James, the region's most impressive church; frozen-in-time streets; a silk mill that was once the center of the Guild of Handicrafts; and pleasant, un-touristy shops. One of the area's most seductive settings unfolds before you as you travel on B4081 through sublime English countryside and happen upon the town, tucked in a slight valley. North of town is lovely Hidcote Manor Gardens. ■ TIP➜ **Chipping Campden can easily be reached on foot along a level section of the Cotswold Way from Broadway Tower; the walk takes about 75 minutes.**

GETTING HERE AND AROUND

By car, Chipping Campden can be reached on minor roads from A44 or A429. There's a small car park in the center and spaces on the outskirts of the village. By bus, take Johnson's Coaches from Stratford-upon-Avon, Broadway, and Moreton-in-Marsh, or Pulhams Coaches from Bourton-on-the-Water and Cheltenham (both services do not run on Sunday). Hidcote Manor Garden is accessible only by car.

ESSENTIALS

Visitor Information Chipping Campden (⊠ *The Old Police Station, High St.* ☎ *01386/841206* ⊕ *www.chippingcampdenonline.org*).

EXPLORING

The soaring pinnacled tower of **St. James,** a prime example of a Cotswold wool church (it was rebuilt in the 15th century with money from wool merchants), announces the town from a distance; it's worth stepping inside to see the lofty nave. The church recalls the old saying, which became popular because of the vast numbers of houses of worship in the Cotswolds, "As sure as God's in Gloucestershire." ⊠*Church St.* ☎*01386/841927* ⊕*www.stjameschurchcampden.co.uk* ☜*£1 donation suggested* ☾*Mar.–Oct., Mon.–Sat. 10–5, Sun. 2–6; Nov and Feb., Mon.–Sat. 11–4, Sun. 2–4; Dec. and Jan., Mon.–Sat. 11–3, Sun. 2–3.*

Near the church of St. James, the **Court Barn Museum** occupies an old agricultural building that has been smartly renovated to showcase the area's prominence in the fields of craft and design. You can admire examples of silverware, bookbinding, printing, furniture, and jewelry. Opposite the barn is an important row of almshouses dating from the reign of King James I. ⊠*Church St.* ☎*01386/841951* ⊕*www.courtbarn.org.uk* ☜*£3.75* ☾*Apr.–Sept., Tues.–Sat. 10:30–5:30, Sun. 11:30–5:30; Oct.–Mar., Tues.–Sat. 11–4, Sun. 11:30–4.*

The broad High Street, lined with stone houses and shops, follows a captivating curve; in the center, on Market Street, is the **Market Hall,** a gabled Jacobean structure built by Sir Baptiste Hycks in 1627 "for the sale of local produce."

In 1902 the Guild of Handicrafts took over the **Silk Mill,** and Arts and Crafts evangelist Charles Robert Ashbee (1863–1942) brought 150 acolytes here from London, including 50 guildsmen, to revive and practice such skills as cabinetmaking and bookbinding. The operation folded in 1920, but the refurbished building houses an exhibition and workshops, including those of a silversmith, jeweler, and stone carver. ⊠*Sheep St.* ☎ *No phone* ☜*Free* ☾*Weekdays 9–5, Sat. 9–1.*

Fodor'sChoice ★ Laid out around a Cotswold manor house, **Hidcote Manor Garden** is arguably the most interesting and attractive large garden in Britain. Crowds are large at the height of the season, but it's worthwhile anytime. A horticulturist from the United States, Major Lawrence Johnstone, created the garden in 1907 in the Arts and Crafts style. Johnstone was an imaginative gardener and widely traveled plantsman who brought back specimens from all over the world. The formal part of the garden is arranged in "rooms" separated by hedges and often with fine topiary work and walls. Besides the variety of plants, what's impressive are the different effects created, from calm open spaces to areas packed with flowers. ■TIP➔ **Look out for one of Johnson's earliest schemes, the red borders of dahlias, poppies, fuchsias, lobelias, and roses; the tall hornbeam hedges; and the Bathing Pool garden, where the pool is so wide there's scarcely space to walk.** The White Garden was probably the forerunner of the popular white gardens at Sissinghurst and Glyndebourne. If you have time, explore tiny Hidcote Bartrim with its thatched stone houses; it borders the garden and fills a storybook dell. A five-minute stroll from Hidcote Manor is Kiftsgate Court Gardens, smaller but captivating. ⊠*Off B4081, Hidcote Bartrim, 4 mi northeast of Chipping Campden* ☎*01386/438333* ⊕*www.nationaltrust.org.uk* ☜*£8.10*

8

CLOSE UP

Arts and Crafts in the Cotswolds

The Arts and Crafts movement flourished throughout Britain in the late 19th and early 20th centuries, but the Cotswolds are most closely associated with it. The godfather of the movement was designer William Morris (1834–96), whose home for the last 25 years of his life, Kelmscott Manor in Gloucestershire, became the headquarters of the school. A lecture by Morris, "The Beauty of Life," delivered in Birmingham in 1880, included the injunction that became the guiding principle of the movement: "Have nothing in your houses which you do not know to be useful or believe to be beautiful."

Driven by the belief that the spirit of medieval arts and crafts was being degraded and destroyed by the mass production and aggressive capitalism of the Victorian era, and aided by a dedicated core of artisans, Morris revolutionized the art of house design and decoration. His work with textiles was particularly influential.

Many of Morris's followers were influenced by the Cotswold countryside, such as the designer and architect Charles Robert Ashbee, who transferred his Guild of Handicrafts from London to Chipping Campden in 1902. The village holds a small museum dedicated to local craftwork, including a permanent exhibition of pieces by the original group and those who followed in their wake. Their work can also be seen at Cheltenham's Art Gallery and Museum, and, in its original context, at Rodmarton Manor outside Tetbury—which Ashbee declared the finest application of the movement's ideals—and at Owlpen Manor. (Farther afield, Blackwell in the Lake District is a notable Arts and Crafts house.) To see the Arts and Crafts ethic applied to horticulture, visit Hidcote Manor Garden, near Chipping Campden.

⊙ *Mid-Mar.–June and Sept., Mon.–Wed. and weekends 10–6 ; July and Aug., daily 10–6; Oct., Mon.–Wed. and weekends 10–5; early Nov.–late Dec., weekends noon–4; last admission 1 hr before closing.*

WHERE TO EAT

££ ✕**Churchill Arms.** In this small country pub just outside Chipping Camp-
BRITISH den, plain wooden tables and benches, a flagstone floor, and a roaring fire provide the backdrop for excellent food. Daily specials—grilled sea bass on a bed of spinach, and roasted partridge with cognac-and-grape jus—appear on the blackboard. If you feel like staying overnight, upstairs are four traditionally furnished bedrooms (££). ⊠ *Off B4035, Paxford* ☎*01386/594000* ▤*MC, V.*

WHERE TO STAY

££ �456**Badgers Hall.** Expect a friendly welcome at this antique B&B above a tearoom just across from the Market Hall. The spacious, spotless rooms have low, beamed ceilings and exposed stonework. Guests are greeted with a cream tea on arrival, and the excellent breakfast will set you up for the day. Two nights is the minimum stay. **Pros:** atmospheric building; central location; spacious rooms. **Cons:** low ceilings; entrance is through tea shop. ⊠ *High St.* ☎*01386/840839* ⊕*www.badgershall.com* ⤴*3*

rooms ⟨In-hotel: Wi-Fi, no kids under 10, no-smoking rooms ☰MC,
V ⦙⊙⦙BP.

£££–££££ ⊞**Charingworth Manor.** Views of the countryside are limitless from this
14th-century manor house hotel a short distance outside town. Mullioned windows and oak beams enhance the sofa-filled sitting room, and
bedrooms have antique furniture. T. S. Eliot, a guest in the 1930s, used
to enjoy walking the 50 acres of grounds. The restaurant (£££), with
its low-beam ceilings, is attractive and serves both traditional English
and Mediterranean-inspired dishes such as local rack of lamb. The hotel
is 3 mi east of Chipping Campden. **Pros:** great views; peaceful setting;
lots of amenities. **Cons:** slightly dated feel; some rooms are near a road.
⊠*Charingworth* ☎*01386/593555* ⊕*www.classiclodges.co.uk* ⇱*23
rooms, 3 suites* ⟨*In-room: no a/c, safe. In-hotel: restaurant, tennis
court, pool, gym* ☰*AE, MC, V* ⦙⊙⦙*BP.*

£££–££££ ⊞**Cotswold House.** This luxury hotel in the center of Chipping Campden
injects contemporary design into a stately 18th-century manor house.
From the swirling staircase in the entrance to the guest rooms studded
with contemporary art and high-tech gadgetry, it's a winning formula.
The lounges invite lingering, and the patio and spacious garden offer
seclusion. The formal Juliana's Restaurant (£££££) and the livelier and
cheaper Hicks' Brasserie (££) both offer creative takes on English and
Mediterranean dishes. Hicks' is open all day and is worth a stop even
if you aren't staying here. **Pros:** huge beds; plenty of pampering; lovely
garden. **Cons:** piped-in music in public rooms, rooms can be overheated; staff sometimes aloof. ⊠*The Square* ☎*01386/840330* ⊕*www.
cotswoldhouse.com* ⇱*26 rooms, 4 suites* ⟨*In-room: no a/c (some),
refrigerator, DVD, Internet, Wi-Fi (some). In-hotel: 2 restaurants, bars,
Wi-Fi, parking (free), no-smoking rooms* ☰*AE, MC, V* ⦙⊙⦙*BP.*

£££–£££££ ⊞**Noel Arms Hotel.** Dating to the 14th century, Chipping Campden's
oldest inn was built to accommodate foreign wool traders. Even though
it has been enlarged, the building retains its exposed beams and stonework. Guest rooms—some in the 14th-century portion—are full of
warm colors and dark oak furniture, and fully equipped with modern
amenities. Breakfast can be taken in the flagstone conservatory. The
same owners run the nearby Cotswold House, and guests have access
to its facilities. **Pros:** historic charm; friendly staff. **Cons:** some facilities are dated; some rooms creaky and noisy; room rates rather steep.
⊠*High St.* ☎*01386/840317* ⊕*www.noelarmshotel.com* ⇱*26 rooms*
⟨*In-room: no a/c. In-hotel: restaurant, bar, parking (free), some pets
allowed, no-smoking rooms* ☰*AE, MC, V* ⦙⊙⦙*BP.*

SHOPPING

At **Hart** (⊠*The Silk Mill, Sheep St.* ☎*01386/841100*), descendants of an
original member of the Guild of Handicrafts specialize in making silver
items. **Martin Gotrel** (⊠*Camperdene House, High St.* ☎*01386/841360*)
crafts fine traditional and contemporary jewelry.

8

MORETON-IN-MARSH

5 mi south of Chipping Campden, 18 mi northeast of Cheltenham, 5 mi north of Stow-on-the-Wold.

In Moreton-in-Marsh, the houses have been built not around a central square but along a street wide enough to accommodate a market. The village has fine views across the hills. One local landmark, St. David's Church, has a tower of honey-gold ashlar. This town of about 3,500 also possesses one of the last remaining curfew towers, dated 1633; curfew dates to the time of the Norman Conquest, when a bell was rung to "cover-fire" for the night against any invaders.

GETTING HERE AND AROUND

Moreton-in-Marsh is on the A429 north of Cirencester. Park along the main street or in the lot on Station Road. The town has a train station with daily connections to London Paddington. Pulhams buses arrive here from Cirencester (not Sunday) or Cheltenham (not Sunday in winter). There's also service to and from Stratford-upon-Avon, Stow-on-the-Wold, and Bourton-on-the-Water. For Sezincote, a car is necessary.

ESSENTIALS

Visitor Information Moreton-in-Marsh (⊠ *High St.* ☎ *01608/650881* ⊕ *www. cotswolds.gov.uk).*

EXPLORING

Supposed to be the largest street market in the Cotswolds, the **Tuesday Market** takes over the center of the main street between 8 and 2:30, with a mix of household goods, fruits and vegetables, and some arts-and-crafts and jewelry stalls. Check out this market, which is no newcomer: it was chartered in 1227.

It comes as somewhat of an architectural surprise to see the blue onion domes and miniature minarets of **Sezincote,** a mellow stone house and garden tucked into a valley near Moreton-in-Marsh. Created in the early 19th century, the house and estate were the vision of Sir Charles Cockerell, who made a fortune in the East India Company. He employed his architect brother, Samuel Pepys Cockerell, to "Indianize" the residence with Hindu and Muslim motifs. Note the peacock-tail arches surrounding the windows of the first floor. The exotic garden, Hindu temple folly, and Indian-style bridge have appealed to visitors ever since the future George IV came to the estate in 1807 (and was inspired to create that Xanadu of Brighton, the Royal Pavilion). If you come in spring, glorious aconites and snowdrops greet you. Note that children are allowed indoors only at the owners' discretion. ⊠ *Off A44* ☎ *01386/700444* ⊕ *www.sezincote.co.uk* ⊡ *House and grounds £8, grounds £5* ⊙ *House May–Sept., Thurs. and Fri. 2:30–5:30; grounds Jan.–Nov., Thurs. and Fri. and national holidays 2–6 or dusk.*

WHERE TO EAT AND STAY

£   ✕**Ask.** Two stone Cotswold cottages have been tastefully converted to
ITALIAN   form this warm, relaxed eating space in the center of Moreton. Part of a chain specializing in Italian standards, the restaurant has flagstone floors, modern art on the walls, and a menu that ranges from stone-baked pizzas to *polpette al forno* (meatballs). Antipasti, salads,

CLOSE UP

Visiting Cotswold Gardens

Perhaps it's the sheer beauty of this area that has inspired the creation of so many superb gardens. Gardening is an English passion, and even nongardeners may be tempted by the choices large and small. The Arts and Crafts movement in Britain transformed not only interior design but also the world of gardening; at Hidcote Manor Garden, an influential, much-visited masterpiece of the style, hedges and walls set off vistas and surround distinct themed garden rooms. Rodmarton Manor also has a garden in this style.

In the Cotswolds, as elsewhere in England, gardens often complement a stately home and deserve as close a look as the house. At Sudeley Castle, the home of Catherine Parr (Henry VIII's last wife), for example, explore the 19th-century Queen's Garden, beloved for its roses. Also large in scale but entirely different is Westonbirt National Arboreturm,

near Tetbury, with its magnificent collection of trees. In contrast, the 18th-century Painswick Rococo Garden, with its Gothic screen and other intriguing structures, has a pleasant intimacy. Britain wouldn't be Britain without a touch of eccentricity, and in the Cotswolds the garden at the Indian-style manor of Sezincote, with its temple to a Hindu god, supplies a satisfying blend of the stately and the exotic.

Eager to see more? The National Garden Scheme (⊕ www.ngs.org.uk) publishes annual "yellow books" that list all gardens open throughout the country (£8.99). Bookstores sell these, too. Depending on your itinerary, buying a Great British Heritage Pass or joining the National Trust (⊕ www. nationaltrust.org.uk) may save you money on garden admissions. You can also contact Cheltenham's tourist office for information on garden tours in the Cotswolds.

and espresso coffee complete the meal. ⊠ *High St.* ☏*01608/651119* ⊕*www.askcentral.co.uk* ▤*AE, MC, V.*

££££–£££££ 🖼 **Manor House Hotel.** Secret passageways and a priest's hole testify to the age of this 16th-century building, set back from the main thoroughfare. Wing chairs and chintz-covered sofas and drapes adorn the public rooms, setting a traditional note. Bedrooms, revealing original stonework, mix stylish modern furnishings and fabrics with antiques. The Mulberry restaurant serves an adventurous English menu. **Pros:** accommodating staff; historical ambience; top-notch toiletries. **Cons:** some traffic noise in front rooms; occasionally malfunctioning plumbing and heating. ⊠*High St.* ☏*01608/650501* ⊕*www.cotswold-inns-hotels. co.uk* 🛏*35 rooms* ♿*In-room: no a/c, Wi-Fi. In-hotel: restaurant, bar, Wi-Fi, no-smoking rooms* ▤*AE, DC, MC, V* ⦿*BP.*

STOW-ON-THE-WOLD

5 mi south of Moreton-in-Marsh, 15 mi east of Cheltenham.

At an elevation of 800 feet, Stow is the highest town in the Cotswolds— "Stow-on-the-Wold, where the wind blows cold" is the age-old saying. Built around a wide square, Stow's imposing golden stone houses have been discreetly converted into many high-quality antiques stores. The Square, as it is known, has a fascinating history. In the 18th century Daniel Defoe wrote that more than 20,000 sheep could be sold here on a busy day; such was the press of livestock that sheep runs, known as "tures," were used to control the sheep, and these narrow streets still run off the main square. Today pubs and cafés fill the area.

Also here are St. Edward's Church and the Kings Arms Old Posting House, its wide entrance still seeming to wait for the stagecoaches that used to stop here on their way to Cheltenham. As well as being a lure for the antiques hunter, Stow is a convenient base: eight main Cotswolds roads intersect here, but all—happily—bypass the town center. The town's current population is about 2,800.

GETTING HERE AND AROUND
Stow-on-the-Wold is well connected by road (A429, A424, and A436) and bus (from Moreton-in-Marsh, Bourton-on-the-Water, Northleach, Cirencester, and Cheltenham). Parking is usually easy to find near the center. Chastleton House is only reachable by car.

ESSENTIALS
Visitor Information Stow-on-the-Wold (⊠ *Hollis House, The Square* ☎ *01451/831082* ⊕ *www.cotswold.gov.uk).*

EXPLORING
★ **Chastleton House,** one of the most complete Jacobean properties in Britain, opts for a beguilingly lived-in appearance, taking advantage of almost 400 years' worth of furniture and trappings accumulated by many generations of the single family that owned it until 1991. The house was built between 1605 and 1612 for William Jones, a wealthy wool merchant, and has an appealing authenticity: cobwebs and bric-a-brac are strewn around, wood and pewter are unpolished, upholstery is uncleaned. The top floor is a glorious, barrel-vaulted long gallery, and throughout the house you can see exquisite plasterwork, paneling, and tapestries. The gardens include England's first croquet lawn (the rules of croquet were codified here in 1865) and rotund topiaries. ■ TIP➔ **Admission is by timed ticket, so it's a good idea to call ahead to reserve.** Chastleton is 6 mi northeast of Stow, signposted off A436 between Stow and A44. ⊠ *Off A436, Moreton-in-Marsh* ☎ *01608/674981, 01494/755560 for recorded information* ⊕ *www.nationaltrust.org.uk* ⊠ *£7.50* ☉ *Apr.– Sept., Wed.–Sat. 1–5; Oct., Wed.–Sat. 1–4.*

WHERE TO EAT AND STAY
£ × **Queen's Head.** An excellent stopping-off spot for lunch or dinner,
BRITISH this pub has a courtyard out back that's a quiet retreat on a summer day. The bench in front, under a climbing rose, makes a relaxing spot for imbibing outdoor refreshment. Besides standard pub grub, including ploughman's lunches, sandwiches, sausage and mash, and chicken pie, there are daily specials such as lamb chops. ⊠ *The Square* ☎ *01451/830563* ⊟ *MC, V.*

£–££ 🏠 **Number Nine.** Beyond the traditional stone-and-creeper exterior of this former coaching inn—now a bed-and-breakfast—are unfussy, spacious bedrooms done in soothing white and pale colors. The inglenook fireplace is a draw in winter, and wholesome breakfasts include poached fruits and specialty breads. **Pros:** helpful and welcoming hosts; excellent breakfasts; attention to detail. **Cons:** not all bathrooms have showers; many steps to climb. ✉9 *Park St.* ☎*01451/870333* ⊕*www.number-nine.info* ⇆*3 rooms* ♿*In-room: no a/c, no phone, Wi-Fi. In-hotel: Internet terminal, no-smoking rooms* ⊟*MC, V* ⦿*BP.*

£££ 🏠**Royalist Hotel.** Dating from the 10th century, this hostelry is jammed with interesting features, including witches' marks on the beams, and a tunnel to the church across the road. The owners have stylishly integrated designer bedrooms and the sleek 947AD restaurant (££££). If the elegant modern English dishes here don't appeal, the adjacent Eagle and Child (££) offers a hearty brasserie-style menu from the same kitchen. **Pros:** lots of character; comfortable beds; great breakfasts. **Cons:** two-night minimum stay on weekends; some rooms are noisy. ✉*Digbeth St.* ☎*01451/830670* ⊕*www.theroyalisthotel.com* ⇆*12 rooms, 2 suites* ♿*In-room: no a/c, Wi-Fi. In-hotel: restaurant, bars, Wi-Fi, no-smoking rooms* ⊟*AE, DC, MC, V* ⦿*BP.*

> ## COTSWOLD WALKS
>
> Short walks thread the gentle countryside and are a great way to appreciate the Cotswolds, an **Area of Outstanding National Beauty** (⊕ *www.cotswoldsaonb.org.uk*). Tourist information centers carry walking maps and have information about longer trails. You can also track the rivers on which many towns are built, following the **towpaths** that run near the water. The **Cotswold Way** (⊕ *www.nationaltrail.co.uk*), a 100-mi national trail between Bath and Chipping Campden, traces the ridge marking the edge of the Cotswolds and the Severn Valley and has incomparable views. You can walk just part of it.

SHOPPING

Stow-on-the-Wold is the leading center for antiques stores in the Cotswolds, with more than 40 dealers centered on the Square, Sheep Street, and Church Street.

Duncan Baggott Antiques (✉*Woolcomber House, Sheep St.* ☎*01451/830662*) displays fine old English furniture, portraits and landscape paintings, and garden statuary and ornaments. **Roger Lamb Antiques** (✉*The Square* ☎*01451/831371*) specializes in objets d'art and small pieces of furniture from the Georgian and Regency periods, with Regency "faux bamboo," tea caddies, and antique needlework the particular fortes. Head for **Talbot Galleries** (✉*7 Talbot Ct.* ☎*01451/832169*) if you're interested in antique maps and prints.

BOURTON-ON-THE-WATER

4 mi southwest of Stow-on-the-Wold, 12 mi northeast of Cheltenham.

Bourton-on-the-Water, off A429 on the eastern edge of the Cotswold Hills, is deservedly famous as a classic Cotswold village. Like many others, it became wealthy in the Middle Ages because of wool. The little River Windrush runs through Bourton, crossed by low stone bridges; it's as pretty as it sounds. This village makes a good touring base and has a collection of quirky small museums, but in summer it can be

CLOSE UP

Antiques and Markets in the Cotswolds

The Cotswolds contain one of the largest concentrations of art and antiques dealers outside London. The famous antiques shops here are, it is sometimes whispered, "temporary" storerooms for the great families of the region, filled with tole-ware, treen, faience firedogs, toby jugs, and silhouettes, plus country furniture, Edwardiana, and ravishing 17th- to 19th-century furniture. The center of antiquing is Stow-on-the-Wold, in terms of volume of dealers. Other towns that have a number of antiques shops are Burford, Cirencester, Tetbury, and Moreton-in-Marsh. The Cotswolds have few of those "anything in this tray for £10" shops, however. For information about dealers and special events, contact the **Cotswold Antique Dealers' Association**

(CADA ⌧ Broadwell House, Sheep St., Stow-on-the-Wold ☏ 07789/968319 ⊕ www.cotswolds-antiques-art.com), which represents more than 40 dealers in the area.

As across England, many towns in the region have market days, when you can purchase local produce (including special treats ranging from Cotswold cheeses to fruit juices), crafts, and items such as clothes, books, and toys. Attending a farmers' market or a general market is a great way to mingle with the locals and perhaps find a special treasure or a tasty treat. Head for Moreton-in-Marsh on Tuesday and Cirencester on Friday and some Saturdays; tourist information offices have information on market days, or check out **Country Markets** (⊕ www. country-markets.co.uk).

overcrowded. A stroll through Bourton takes you past stone cottages, many converted to small stores and coffee shops.

ESSSENTIALS

Visitor Information Bourton-on-the-Water (⌧ Victoria St. ☏ 01451/820211 ⊕ www.bourtoninfo.com).

EXPLORING

↻ An old mill, now the **Cotswold Motoring Museum and Toy Collection,** contains more than 30 vintage motor vehicles and a collection of old advertising signs (supposedly the largest in Europe), as well as two caravans (trailers) from the 1920s, ancient bicycles, and children's toys. ⌧ Sherborne St. ☏ 01451/821255 ⊕ www.cotswold-motor-museum.co.uk ☐ £3.80 ⊙ Mid-Feb.–early Dec., daily 10–6.

↻ The **Model Railway Exhibition** displays more than 40 British and continental trains running on 500 square feet of scenic layout. There are plenty of trains and toys to buy in the shop. ⌧ Box Bush, High St. ☏ 01451/820686 ⊕ www.bourtonmodelrailway.co.uk ☐ £2.50 ⊙ June–Aug., daily 11–5; Sept.–May, weekends 11–5 (call ahead in Jan.).

An outdoor reproduction of Bourton, the **Model Village** was built in 1937 to a scale of one-ninth; you can walk through it. ⌧ Old New Inn ☏ 01451/820467 ☐ £3.25 ⊙ Late Mar.–Oct., daily 10–5:45; Nov.–late Mar., daily 10–3:45 ⊕ www.theoldnewinn.co.uk.

WHERE TO STAY

££ ▣ **The Old Manse.** Built in 1748 for the local Baptist pastor, this stone house is only steps away from the River Windrush. The smallish bedrooms are decorated in cream and maroon hues; one has a four-poster, another a canopied French half-sleigh bed. Some rooms can be noisy—avoid those facing Sherborne Street if you can. Traditional English fare with a contemporary touch is served in the restaurant. There's a patio at the rear, and one at the front looking onto the river. **Pros:** central location; helpful staff. **Cons:** restricted parking; some rooms are noisy; tired-looking in places. ✉ *Victoria St.* ☎ *01451/820082* ⊕ *www. oldmansehotel.com* 🛏 *15 rooms* ♿ *In-room: no a/c. In-hotel: restaurant, bar, no-smoking rooms* ▭ *AE, MC, V* ◎*BP.*

SHOPPING

The **Cotswold Perfumery** carries many perfumes that are manufactured here, and also stocks perfume bottles and jewelry. You can exercise your olfactory skills in the Perfumed Garden, part of a prebooked factory tour that takes in the laboratory, compounding room, and bottling process. ✉ *Victoria St.* ☎ *01451/820698* ▤ *Factory tour £5* ⊙ *Mon.–Sat. 9:30–5:30, Sun. 10:30–5:30 (closes at 5 in winter).*

LOWER SLAUGHTER AND UPPER SLAUGHTER

Fodor's Choice ★ *2 mi north of Bourton-on-the-Water, 15 mi east of Cheltenham.*

To see the quieter, more typical Cotswold villages, seek out the evocatively named Lower Slaughter and Upper Slaughter (the names have nothing to do with mass murder, but come from the Saxon word *sloh*, which means "a marshy place"). Lower Slaughter is one of the "water villages," with Slaughter Brook running down the center road of the town. Little stone footbridges cross the brook, and the town's resident gaggle of geese can often be seen paddling through the sparkling water. Lower and Upper Swell are two other quiet towns to explore.

EXPLORING

Connecting the two Slaughters is **Warden's Way** (⊕ *www.cotswoldsaonb. org.uk*), a mile-long pathway that begins in Upper Slaughter at the town-center parking lot and passes stone houses, green meadows, ancient trees, and a 19th-century corn mill with a waterwheel and brick chimney. Warden's Way continues south to Bourton-on-the-Water; the full walk from Winchcombe to Bourton is 14 mi. You can pick up an itinerary from Winchcombe's tourist office.

WHERE TO STAY

££££ ▣ **Lords of the Manor Hotel.** A fishing stream winds through the rolling fields that surround this rambling 17th-century manor house with Victorian additions. It offers comfort and a warm welcome in a quintessential Cotswold village, with a choice of traditional bedrooms in the main house or more modern ones in the converted granary and barn. Country-house chintzes and antiques set the style in the bedrooms and in the acclaimed restaurant, which has creative British-French fixed-price menus (££££). Ask about midweek rates that include dinner. **Pros:** heavenly setting; outstanding food. **Cons:** little to do within walking distance; some rooms lack charm; two-night minimum stay on week-ends. ⊠*Upper Slaughter* ☎*01451/820243* ⊕*www.lordsofthemanor. com* ⌁*26 rooms* ⌂*In-room: no a/c, DVD. In-hotel: restaurant, bar, Wi-Fi* ⊟*AE, DC, MC, V* ⦿*BP.*

NORTHLEACH

7 mi southwest of Lower and Upper Slaughter, 14 mi southeast of Cheltenham.

Just off the Fosse Way (and bypassed by the busy A40), little North-leach—population around 2,000—has remained one of the least spoiled of Cotswold towns. Trim cottages, many with traditional stone-tile roofs, line the streets that converge on the spacious central square. By the 13th century Northleach had acquired substantial wealth thanks to the wool trade. The wool of the local Cotswold Lion sheep (so-called because of their thick, manelike fleeces) was praised above all other by weavers in Flanders, to whom it was exported.

EXPLORING

The 15th-century church of **St. Peter and St. Paul,** with its soaring pillars and clerestory windows, contains notable memorial brasses, monuments to the merchants who endowed the church; each merchant has a wool sack and sheep at his feet. ⊠*Mill End* ☎*01451/860314* ▨*Free* ⊙*Apr.–Oct., daily 8–6; Nov.–Mar., daily 8–dusk.*

At **Keith Harding's World of Mechanical Music,** the diverting tour explores pianolas, music boxes, and other mechanical instruments from times past, which you can hear played. You can even listen to the maestros Grieg, Paderewski, Rachmaninov, and Gershwin on piano rolls. The shop stocks antique and modern music boxes and more. ⊠*The Oak House, High St.* ☎*01451/860181* ⊕*www.mechanicalmusic.co.uk* ▨*£8* ⊙*Daily 10–6; last tour at 5.*

WHERE TO EAT AND STAY

££ ✕**Wheatsheaf Inn.** This traditional pub has a cool, modern coffee lounge
MODERN BRITISH and adjoining restaurant specializing in modern British fare. On the menu you might find prawns, oysters, and butternut-squash-and-coriander soup, and more substantial dishes include roast partridge with Toulouse sausage-and-lentil cassoulet. The inn also offers nine stylish, uncluttered bedrooms (££). ⊠*West End* ☎*01451/860244* ⊟*AE, MC, V.*

£–££ ▥**Blanche House.** A traditional Cotswold building, imaginatively con-verted and run as an upmarket B&B by a young interior designer and a chef and furniture maker, adds up to a winning formula. Located in the hamlet of Turkdean, a couple of miles northwest of Northleach, the house was originally four separate cottages, and has a bright, spacious feel. Rooms share baths, but you can pay extra to make a bathroom private. Organic breakfasts can be taken in the modern conservatory, or "glass barn," overlooking the garden. The surrounding Leygore Estate offers opportunities for longer walks. **Pros:** rural peace; stylish mix of traditional and contemporary. **Cons:** no private bathrooms; hard to find. ⊠*Turkdean* ☎*01451/861176* ⊕*www.blanchehousebandb.*

co.uk 🛏4 *rooms without bath* ⚿*In-room: no a/c, no phone, no TV, Wi-Fi. In-hotel: Wi-Fi, some pets allowed, no kids under 3* ☰*No credit cards* ⊺⃝⃒*BP.*

BURFORD

9 mi east of Northleach, 18 mi north of Swindon, 18 mi west of Oxford.

Burford's broad main street leads steeply down to a narrow bridge across the River Windrush. The village served as a stagecoach stop for centuries and has many historic inns; it's now a popular stop for tour buses and seekers of antiques.

ESSENTIALS

Visitor Information Burford (✉ *The Brewery, Sheep St.* ☎*01993/823558* ⊕ *www.oxfordshirecotswolds.org*).

EXPLORING

Hidden away at the end of a lane at the bottom of High Street is the splendid parish church of **St. John,** its interior a warren of arches, chapels, and shrines. The church was remodeled in the 15th century from Norman beginnings. Among the monuments is one dedicated to Henry VIII's barber, Edmund Harman, that depicts four Amazonian Indians; it's said to be the first depiction of native people from the Americas in Britain. Look also for the elaborate Tanfield monument and its poignant widow's epitaph. ✉*Church Green* ☎*01993/822275* ✉*Free* ⊙*Apr.– Oct., daily 9–5; Nov.–Mar., daily 9–4.*

WHERE TO EAT AND STAY

£££ ✕**The Angel at Burford.** Contemporary dishes you might see at the
BRITISH farmhouse-style tables of this informal brasserie in a 16th-century former coaching inn (now a restaurant with rooms) include salmon fillet with dill-and-chive gnocchi and roast breast of pheasant. Upstairs, the three delightful guest rooms (££) are furnished in different styles: Indian in rich reds, French with wooden sleigh bed, or cool-blue contemporary Italian. ✉*14 Witney St.,* ☎*01993/822714* ☰*MC, V.*

£££ ⌗**Burford House.** Family photographs, books, and toys scattered throughout this 17th-century building make it feel more like home than a hotel. The richly decorated bedrooms, filled with antiques, come with freestanding baths and power showers. Intimate sitting rooms and a courtyard garden add to the charm. Lunch and afternoon tea are offered, and you can arrange evening meals on Thursday, Friday, and Saturday. **Pros:** family-friendly establishment; warm ambience; lots of character. **Cons:** sometimes overheated; traffic noise in front rooms; no parking. ✉*99 High St.* ☎*01993/823151* ⊕*www.burford-house. co.uk* 🛏*8 rooms* ⚿*In-room: no a/c, DVD, Internet, Wi-Fi. In-hotel: restaurant, bar, Wi-Fi* ☰*AE, MC, V* ⊺⃝⃒*BP.*

8

BIBURY

10 mi southwest of Burford, 6 mi northeast of Cirencester, 15 mi north of Swindon.

The tiny town of Bibury, with a population of less than 1,000, sits idyllically beside the little River Coln on B4425; it was famed Arts and Crafts designer William Morris's choice for Britain's most beautiful village. Fine old cottages, a river meadow, and the church of St. Mary's are some of the delights here.

EXPLORING

Arlington Row is a famously pretty and much-photographed group of 17th-century weavers' cottages made of stone.

☾ The remains of a mile of walls are what's left of **Chedworth Roman Villa,** one of the largest Roman villas in England, beautifully set in a wooded valley on the eastern fringe of the Cotswolds. Thirty-two rooms, including two complete bath suites, have been identified, and the colorful mosaics are some of the most complete in England. Audio guides are available, and the visitor center and museum give a detailed picture of Roman life in Britain. ■TIP➔ **Look carefully for the signs for the villa: from Bibury, go across A429 to Yanworth and Chedworth. The villa is also signposted from A40.** The site is 6 mi northwest of Bibury and 10 mi southeast of Cheltenham. ⊠*Yanworth* ☎*01242/890256* ⊕*www. nationaltrust.org.uk* ⊠*£6* ☉*Mar. and late Oct.–mid-Nov., Tues.–Sun. 10–4; Apr.–late Oct., Tues.–Sun. 10–5.*

QUICK BITES
For a fireside pint, a hearty meal, or just a sandwich, the **Seven Tuns** (⊠*Queen St., Chedworth* ☎*01285/720242*) fits the bill—a traditional pub with a strong menu and outdoor seating. It lies just a few minutes from the Roman villa, by a splashing stream and a handsome Perpendicular church.

WHERE TO STAY

£££–££££ ⊡ **Swan Hotel.** Crystal chandeliers and displays of plates and glassware adorn this mid-17th-century coaching inn on the banks of the River Coln. Guest rooms, all different though most are traditional in style, come with splendid modern bathrooms—Room 3 is dramatically tiled in black and white. The formal Gallery restaurant has fixed-price dinners, and there are also meals at the cheerful, cheaper Café Swan. **Pros:** idyllic spot; discounts on packages. **Cons:** busy with day-trippers on weekends; restaurant can be disappointing. ⊠*Off B4425* ☎*01285/740695* ⊕*www.cotswold-inns-hotels.co.uk* ⇋*18 rooms, 3 suites* ⌂*In-room: no a/c, Wi-Fi. In-hotel: 2 restaurants, bar, Wi-Fi, some pets allowed, no-smoking rooms* ▤*AE, DC, MC, V* ¶◎*BP.*

CIRENCESTER

9 mi south of Chedworth, 14 mi southeast of Cheltenham.

Cirencester (pronounced sirensester) has been a hub of the Cotswolds since Roman times, when it was called Corinium; the town was second only to Londinium (London) in importance. It lay at the intersection of two major Roman roads, the Fosse Way and Ermin Street (today A429 and A417). In the Middle Ages Cirencester grew rich on wool, which funded its 15th-century parish church. Today this old market town is the area's largest, with a population of 19,000. It preserves many mellow stone buildings dating mainly from the 17th and 18th centuries, and bow-fronted shops that still have one foot in the past.

ESSENTIALS

Visitor Information Cirencester (⊠ *Corinium Museum, Park St.* ☎ *01285/654180* ⊕ *www.cotswolds. com*).

> ## WORD OF MOUTH
>
> "There is much more to the Cotswolds than just the northeast part. Farther south the hills get steeper, the valleys deeper and narrower, the stone grayer. But it is still incredibly lovely. And there are relatively few visitors, except on weekends when our fellow Englishmen come to see this glorious part of England." —julia_t

EXPLORING

At the top of Market Place is the magnificent Gothic parish church of **St. John the Baptist,** known as the cathedral of the "woolgothic" style. Its elaborate, three-tier, three-bay south porch, the largest in England, once served as the town hall. The chantry chapels and many coats of arms bear witness to the importance of the wool merchants as benefactors of the church. A rare example of a 15th-century wineglass pulpit sits in the nave. ⊠ *Market Pl.* ☎ *01285/659317* ☒ *Free, £2 donation suggested* ☉ *Mon.–Sat. 10–5 (10:30–4 in winter), Sun. 2:15–5.*

★ Not much of the Roman town remains visible, but the **Corinium Museum** displays an outstanding collection of Roman artifacts, including jewelry and coins, as well as mosaic pavements and full-scale reconstructions of local Roman interiors. Spacious galleries explore the town's history in Roman and Anglo-Saxon times and in the 18th century; they include plenty of hands-on exhibits. ⊠ *Park St.* ☎ *01285/655611* ⊕ *www. cotswold.gov.uk* ☒ *£4.25* ☉ *Mon.–Sat. 10–5, Sun. 2–5.*

WHERE TO EAT AND STAY

£££££   ╳ **Barnsley House.** Fine dining in the Cotswolds doesn't get much better
ITALIAN   than at this honey-and-cream Georgian mansion, the former home of garden designer Rosemary Verey. Discreetly modernized, the building has jettisoned none of its charm. The well-tended gardens, overlooked by the dining room, continue to be an attraction. The fixed-price meals (£19.50–£21.50 for a two-course lunch, and £42.50 for a three-course dinner) reveal a strong Italian and Mediterranean influence in dishes like the classic *vincisgrassi* (baked pasta with Parma ham, porcini mushrooms, and truffles). The desserts include such extravagances as praline-and-amaretti parfait with fruit salad and lemon yogurt sorbet. Chic, pricey rooms (£££££) are also available. ⊠ *B4425, 4 mi northeast of Cirencester, Barnsley* ☎ *01285/740000* ⊕ *www.barnsleyhouse.com* ⌕ *Reservations essential* ▭ *AE, MC, V.*

££   ╳ **Wild Duck Inn.** The deep-red dining room of this Elizabethan inn 3 mi
BRITISH   southwest of Cirencester has an abundance of wood beams and oil portraits. Fresh fish is a strong suit here—try it in a beer batter—or sample such meat dishes as grilled Aberdeen Angus steaks. There's a

That Special Cotswold Stone

If there's one feature of the Cotswold landscape that sums up its special flavor, it's the oolitic limestone that is the area's primary building material. This stone can be seen in everything from drystone walls (whose total length in the region is said to equal or exceed that of the Great Wall of China) to snug cottages and manor houses. Even roof tiles are fashioned from the stone, contributing to a harmonious ensemble despite the different ages of the buildings.

Malleable when first quarried, and gradually hardening with age, the stone lends itself to every use. During the late-medieval heyday of the great churches funded by wool merchants, it was used to brilliant effect in the mullions, gargoyles, and other intricate decorations on ecclesiastical buildings. Some quarries are still active, producing stone that is used mainly for restoration and repair purposes. The varying colors of the stone are caused by impurities in the rock. They include the honey hues of the northern reaches of the Cotswolds, and modulate to a more golden tone in the central area, with a paler hue in and around Bath.

Writer and commentator J. B. Priestley, however, wrote of Cotswold stone that "the truth is that it has no color that can be described. Even when the sun is obscured and the light is cold, these walls are still faintly warm and luminous, as if they knew the trick of keeping the lost sunlight of centuries glimmering about them." Walk or drive around Cotswold villages and towns for even a day, and you will know what he meant.

garden for alfresco dining. Upstairs are 12 small but comfortable guest rooms (££–£££), mostly modern in style and with dark-wood furniture; reservations should be made well in advance. ⊠ *Off A429, Ewen* ☎ *01285/770310* ▤ *AE, MC, V.*

£ 📷 **Ivy House.** Personal touches such as chocolates and bottled water in the rooms enhance a stay at this stone Victorian house, close to the center of town. The B&B's simple bedrooms, done up in pastels, are an excellent value, with double-glazed windows to block out traffic noise. The owners are friendly, and cyclists and walkers are welcomed. **Pros:** central location; good common areas. **Cons:** books up far in advance; two-night minimum stay on weekends. ⊠ *2 Victoria Rd.* ☎ *01285/656626* ⊕ *www.ivyhousecotswolds.com* ➾ *4 rooms* ⌂ *In-room: no a/c, no phone, Wi-Fi. In-hotel: parking (free), no-smoking rooms* ▤ *AE, MC, V* ⊗|*BP.*

NIGHTLIFE AND THE ARTS

New Brewery Arts (⊠ *Brewery Ct.* ☎ *01285/657181*) includes a theater, exhibition space, and a café.

SPORTS AND THE OUTDOORS

Ⓢ You can indulge in water sports such as waterskiing and windsurfing at the **Cotswold Water Park,** 3 mi south of Cirencester. This group of 130 lakes covers 40 square mi and has multiple entrances. There's swimming June through September; the park also draws wildlife enthusiasts, walkers, cyclists, and horseback riders. You pay individual charges for the activities April through October, and you can rent equipment on-site. ⊠*Keynes Country Park, off B4696, Shorncote* ☎*01285/868096* ⊕*www. waterpark.org* ✉*£1–£4, depending on when you visit* ☼*Apr. and Sept., daily 9–7; May, daily 9–8; June–Aug., daily 9–9; Oct.–Mar., daily 9–5.*

SHOPPING

The **Corn Hall** (⊠*Market Pl.*) is the venue for an antiques market on Friday and a crafts market on Saturday. Every Monday and Friday, Cirencester's central **Market Place** is packed with stalls selling a motley assortment of goods, mainly household items but some local produce and crafts, too. A farmers' market takes place here every second and fourth Saturday of the month. **William H. Stokes** (⊠*6–8 Dollar St.* ☎*01285/653907*) specializes in oak furniture from the 16th and 17th centuries.

SPECIAL DAYS

Painswick's annual Clypping Ceremony, on the first Sunday after September 19, has nothing to do with topiaries—the name derives from the Anglo-Saxon word clyppan, meaning "encircle." Children with garlands make a ring around the parish church as traditional hymns are sung; the idea is to affirm the church and the faith it stands for. Another good time to visit is the town's Victorian Market Day in early July.

PAINSWICK

16 mi northwest of Cirencester, 8 mi southwest of Cheltenham, 5 mi south of Gloucester.

An old Cotswold wool town of around 2,000 inhabitants, Painswick has become a chocolate-box picture of quaintness, attracting day-trippers and tour buses. But come during the week and you can discover the place in relative tranquillity. The huddled gray stone houses and inns date from as early as the 14th century and include a notable group from the Georgian era. The churchyard of St. Mary's is renowned for its table tombs and monuments and its yew trees (100 of them now) planted in 1792.

ESSENTIALS
Visitor Information Painswick (⊠*The Library, Stroud Rd.* ☎*01452/813552*).

EXPLORING

The **Painswick Rococo Garden,** ½ mi north of town, is a delightful survivor from the exuberant rococo period of English garden design (1720–60). After 50 years in its original form, the 6-acre garden became overgrown with woodland. Beginning in 1984, after the rediscovery of a 1748 painting of the garden by Thomas Robins, the garden was restored. Now you can view the original architectural structures—such as the vaguely Gothic Eagle House and Exedra—and asymmetrical vistas. There's also a restaurant and a shop. ⊠*B4073* ☎*01452/813204* ⊕*www.rococogarden.org.uk* ✉*£5.50* ☼*Mid-Jan.–Oct., daily 11–6; last admission at 5.*

WHERE TO STAY

££ **Cardynham House.** In the heart of the village, this 15th- to 16th-
★ century former wool merchant's house, which retains its beamed ceilings, Jacobean staircase, and Elizabethan fireplace, has four-poster beds
in almost all its rooms. The rooms have creative themes such as the
Medieval Garden, Dovecote, and Arabian Nights; one pricier option
has a private pool. The adjoining restaurant serves simple English and
European dishes. **Pros:** friendly welcome; romantic ambience; good-
size rooms. **Cons:** slightly worn around the edges; staff sometimes
hard to find; pool could be cleaner. ⊠ *The Cross* ☎ *01452/814006,
01452/810030 restaurant* ⊕ *www.cardynham.co.uk* 🛏 *9 rooms* ⚷ *In-
room: no a/c, dial-up. In-hotel: restaurant, no-smoking rooms* ⊟ *AE,
MC, V* ⊙ *BP.*

OWLPEN

★ *10 mi southwest of Painswick.*

Prince Charles described the beauty spot of Owlpen, an off-the-beaten-
path hamlet, as "the epitome of the English village." First settled in
Saxon days as Olla's Pen (meaning "valley"), the village centers on a
church, a Tudor manor house, and pearl-gray stone cottages, all set
against a hillside. A graceful grouping of tithe barns, garden buildings,
and a gristmill softens the seignorial bearing of the manor house.

EXPLORING

The triple-gabled stone **Owlpen Manor** was built between 1450 and 1616,
but was restored in the 1920s by local Arts and Crafts artisans, who also
created some of the furnishings. Today Nicholas and Karin Mander live
here with their family. Inside are oak chests fashioned by William Morris, family portraits, painted cloths from the Tudor and Stuart eras, and
Queen Margaret's Room, said to be haunted by the spirit of Margaret
of Anjou, wife of Henry VI, who visited here during the Wars of the
Roses. You can also explore the terraced garden with its yew topiary,
the envy of gardening masters such as Gertrude Jekyll. A restaurant is
on the premises, and there are some cottages for rent. ⊠ *Off B4066,
near Uley* ☎ *01453/860261* ⊕ *www.owlpen.com* 🎟 *£5.75; gardens
only, £3.75* ⊙ *May–Sept., Tues., Thurs., and Sun. 2–5.*

TETBURY

*6 mi southeast of Owlpen, 8 mi southwest of Cirencester, 12 mi south
of Painswick.*

Tetbury, with about 5,300 inhabitants, claims right royal connections.
Indeed, the soaring spire of the church that presides over this Elizabethan market town is within sight of Highgrove House, the Prince of
Wales's abode (not open to the public). The town is known as one of
the area's antiques centers.

ESSENTIALS

Visitor Information Tetbury (⊠ *33 Church St.* ☎ *01666/503552* ⊕ *www.
visittetbury.co.uk*).

EXPLORING

In the center of the village, look for the eye-catching, white-painted stone **Market House** on Market Square, dating from 1655 and built up on rows of Tuscan pillars. Various markets are held here during the week.

The church of **St. Mary the Virgin** (⊠*Church St.* ☎*01666/502333*), in 18th-century neo-Gothic style, has a galleried interior with pews.

QUICK BITES Just steps from Market House, **Blue Zucchini** (⊠ *7–9 Church St.* ☎*01666/ 505852*) is a brasserie that also makes a relaxed spot for coffee, light lunches, and afternoon tea. The interior has wooden floorboards and sofas, and you can dine alfresco at tables in the front and in the patio garden.

★ The 600-acre **Westonbirt National Arboretum**, 3 mi southwest of Tetbury (and about 10 mi north of Bath), contains one of the most extensive collections of trees and shrubs in Europe; it's a lovely place to spend an hour or two. The best times to come for color are in late spring, when the rhododendrons, azaleas, and magnolias are blooming, and in fall, when the maples come into their own. A gift shop, café, and restaurant are on the grounds. Open-air concerts take place in summer, and there are exhibitions throughout the year. ⊠*Off A433, near Tetbury* ☎*01666/880220* ⊕*www.forestry.gov.uk/westonbirt* ☜*£5 Jan. and Feb.; £7 Mar.–Sept.; £8 Oct. and Nov.; Dec., free.* ☉*Apr.–Nov., weekdays 9–8 or dusk, weekends 8–8 or dusk; Dec.–Mar., 9–5 or dusk, weekends 8–5 or dusk.*

One of the last English country houses constructed using traditional methods and materials, **Rodmarton Manor** (built 1909–29) is furnished with specially commissioned pieces in the Arts and Crafts style. Ernest Barnsley, a follower of William Morris, worked on the house and gardens. The notable gardens—wild, winter, sunken, and white—are divided into "rooms" bounded by hedges of holly, beech, and yew. The manor is 5 mi northeast of Tetbury. ⊠*Off A433, Rodmarton* ☎*01285/841253* ⊕*www.rodmarton-manor.co.uk* ☜*£7; garden only, £4* ☉*May–Sept., Wed., Sat., and national holidays 2–5.*

WHERE TO EAT AND STAY

££

MODERN BRITISH

×**The Chef's Table.** On Tetbury's Antiques Alley, this trendy eatery is a blend of farmhouse kitchen and designer chic, with a few tables and chairs next to an open kitchen. You can come for breakfast, snack lunches, or more substantial fare such as wild mushroom risotto or pheasant sausages. Reserve ahead because of the limited dining space. If you can't get a seat, however, do not despair—the downstairs delicatessen supplies a lip-smacking range of cheeses, hams, and homemade organic breads for a takeout lunch. ⊠ *49 Long St.* ☎*01666/504466* ☰*MC, V* ☉*Closed Sun. No dinner Mon. and Tues.*

£££££

Calcot Manor. Comfortable country-house furnishings in pale-hued rooms characterize this former farmhouse and the surrounding converted barns and stables. This is a family-friendly establishment with a high-tech children's play area as well as the usual luxurious spa. Guest rooms are airy and spacious; family suites have bunk beds in a separate room and refrigerators. Dishes at the elegant Conservatory restaurant

(£££) are a blend of traditional and modern elements, whereas the Gumstool Inn provides more farmhouse-style fare; dinner is included in the price on weekends and during the peak summer period. The hotel is 3 mi west of town. **Pros:** pleasant rural setting; informal ambience; child-friendly. **Cons:** patchy service in restaurants; leisure facilities can get busy. ⊠*A4135* ☎*01666/890391* ⊕*www.calcotmanor.co.uk* ☏*26 rooms, 9 suites* ⊘*In-room: no a/c, Wi-Fi. In-hotel: 2 restaurants, bars, tennis courts, pool, gym, spa, Wi-Fi* ⊟*AE, DC, MC, V* ⦿*BP.*

SHOPPING

Tetbury is home to more than 30 antiques shops, some of which are incorporated into small malls. **Day Antiques** (⊠*5 New Church St.* ☎*01666/502413*) specializes in oak furniture.

Highgrove Shop (⊠*10 Long St.* ☎*0166/505666*) sells organic products and gifts inspired by Prince Charles's interests. **House of Cheese** (⊠*13 Church St.* ☎*01666/502865*) retails fine, farm-produced cheeses, all wonderfully fresh and flavorsome. Pâtés, preserves, and chocolates are other goodies at this tiny shop.

GLOUCESTER TO THE FOREST OF DEAN

West of the Cotswolds a rather urbanized axis connects Gloucester with Cheltenham. Despite their proximity on either side of the M5 motorway, the towns are very different; the down-to-earth Gloucester, built around docks connected to the River Severn, contrasts with the gentrified spa town of Cheltenham. North of Gloucester lies the riverside town of Tewkesbury with its imposing abbey; to the south, easily accessible from M5, stands battlemented Berkeley Castle. Southwest of Gloucester, the low-lying Forest of Dean (officially the Royal Forest of Dean), once a private hunting ground of kings, is now a recreation area for the public, with some of the country's most beautiful woodlands.

GLOUCESTER

13 mi southwest of Cheltenham, 56 mi south of Birmingham, 105 mi west of London.

Although much of the ancient heritage of this county seat has been lost to nondescript modern stores and offices, Gloucester (population about 111,000) has a number of worthwhile sights, most notably its cathedral.

GETTING HERE AND AROUND

Gloucester can be reached on trains from London Paddington, Bristol, Cheltenham, and Birmingham, and by bus on National Express and Megabus from London Victoria. The train and bus stations are close to each other near the center. The city is easily reached by road from the M5 motorway. Walking is the best way to tour the central sights—the dock area is 10 minutes southwest of the cathedral.

Between mid-June and mid-September, Gloucester Civic Trust organizes walking tours of the city (£2.50) that begin at 2 from the tourist office

(Monday to Saturday) and from the Mariners' Chapel in the center of the historic docks (weekends).

ESSENTIALS

Visitor and Tour Information Gloucester (✉ *28 Southgate St.* ☎ *01452/ 396572* ⊕ *www.visitgloucester.info*). **Gloucester Civic Trust** (☎ *01452/396572*).

EXPLORING

★ Magnificent **Gloucester Cathedral**, with its soaring, elegant exterior, was originally a Norman abbey church, consecrated in 1100. Reflecting different periods, the cathedral mirrors perfectly the slow growth of ecclesiastical taste and the development of the Perpendicular style. The interior has largely been spared the sterilizing attentions of modern architects and is almost completely Norman, with the massive pillars of the nave left untouched since their completion. The fan-vaulted roof of the 14th-century cloisters is the finest in Europe, and the cloisters enclose a peaceful garden (used in the filming of *Harry Potter and the Sorcerer's Stone* for some Hogwarts School scenes). ■ TIP→ **Don't miss the Whispering Gallery, which has a permanent exhibition devoted to the splendid, 14th-century stained glass of the Great East Window.** Tours of the tower (269 steps up) are also available. ✉ *Westgate St.* ☎ *01452/528095* ⊕ *www.gloucestercathedral.org.uk* ✉ *£3 donation* *requested, photography permit £3. Tower tours £3, exhibition £2 ☉ Daily 7:30–6, except during services and special events. Tower tours Apr.–Oct., Wed.–Fri. 2:30, Sat. and national holidays 1:30 and 2:30; also Mon. and Tues. at 2:30 during school vacations. Whispering Gallery Apr.–Oct., weekdays 10:30–4, Sat. 10:30–3:30.*

QUICK
BITES

After a visit to the cathedral, drop in at **Lily's Restaurant** (⊠ *5A College Ct.* ☏ *01452/307060*) for a relaxed morning coffee, afternoon cream tea, or lunch of quiche or shepherd's pie. The tearoom and restaurant is in a narrow alley just steps from the cathedral, opposite the Beatrix Potter shop and museum.

The **Gloucester Folk Museum,** close to the cathedral, fills a row of fine Tudor and Jacobean half-timber houses. Exhibits on the Civil War, crafts, and domestic life illustrate the history of Gloucester and the surrounding areas, and one room has a Toys and Childhood gallery. ⊠ *99–103 Westgate St.* ☏ *01452/396868* ⊕ *www.gloucester.gov.uk* ▣ *Free* ☉ *Tues.–Sat. 10–5.*

The historic **Gloucester Docks,** a short walk from the cathedral along the canal, still function but now cater mainly to pleasure craft. The vast Victorian warehouses have been restored, and shops and cafés added, reviving the area. One warehouse is now the Antiques Centre, and others hold good museums.

☉
Fodor'sChoice
★

The **National Waterways Museum,** in a converted Victorian warehouse, contains examples of canal houseboats, including gaily painted "canal ware"—ornaments and utensils found on barges. The three stories are full of the sounds and smells of the docks and canals around Gloucester, enhanced by interactive gizmos. From dredger buckets to full-size vessels moored at the two quaysides, the imaginatively presented exhibits explain the role of canals in the 18th and 19th centuries. You can try your foot at "walking the wall," the boatmen's way of propelling barges through tunnels with their feet. From the **pier** outside the National Waterways Museum, boats leave for a 45-minute tour of the Gloucester Docks or all-day cruises that head as far north as Tewkesbury or south to the Severn Estuary at Sharpness. ⊠ *Llanthony Warehouse, Llanthony Rd., Gloucester Docks* ☏ *01452/318200* ⊕ *www.nwm.org.uk* ▣ *£3.95* ☉ *Sept.–June., Wed.–Sun. 11–4; July, Aug., and school vacations daily 11–4; last admission 1 hr before closing.*

WHERE TO EAT

££
BRITISH

✕ **The New Inn.** This rambling coaching inn is a few steps down from the Cross—the historic heart of the old city where Northgate, Westgate, Southgate, and Eastgate streets meet. The galleried courtyard, overgrown with creepers, adds to the impression of age. There are plenty of seafood choices, and an extensive carvery menu with plenty of roasted meats is added on Sunday. ⊠ *16 Northgate St.* ☏ *01452/522177* ▤ *MC, V*

SHOPPING

The locals say it's best to look in Cheltenham and buy in Gloucester, where prices are lower. The more than 140 dealers in the **Antiques Centre** (⊠*1 Severn Rd.* ☎*01452/529716*) offer some good buys on items—clocks, silver, china, military collectibles, and more—in a five-floor Victorian warehouse by the Gloucester Docks.

The **Beatrix Potter Shop and Museum** (⊠*9 College Ct.* ☎*01452/422856*), next to the Cathedral Gate, is in the house that served as a model for the tailor's house in Potter's illustrated children's story *The Tailor of Gloucester*. The shop sells Potter-related items, and the small museum upstairs is dedicated to the author and her works.

TEWKESBURY

12 mi northeast of Gloucester.

Tewkesbury is an ancient town of black-and-white half-timber buildings, as well as some fine Georgian ones, on the River Avon. Its abbey is worth a look, too.

ESSENTIALS

Visitor Information Tewkesbury (⊠*100 Church St.* ☎*01684/855040* ⊕*www.visitcotswoldsandsevernvale.gov.uk*).

EXPLORING

The stonework in the Norman **Tewkesbury Abbey** has much in common with that of Gloucester Cathedral, but this church was built in the Romanesque (12th-century) and Decorated Gothic (14th-century) styles. Its exterior makes an impressive sight, with the largest Norman tower in the world—148 feet high and 46 feet square—and the 65-foot-high arch of the west front. Fourteen stout Norman pillars and myriad gilded bosses on the roof of the nave and choir (best viewed through a mirror on wheels) grace the beautifully kept interior. Book tours in advance. ⊠*Church St.* ☎*01684/850959* ⊕*www.tewkesburyabbey.org.uk* ⊡*£5 donation requested, tours £4, tower tours £3* ☉*Easter–Oct., daily 7:30–6:30; Nov.–Easter, daily 7:30–6.*

WHERE TO EAT AND STAY

££ ✕**Aubergine.** A few steps from the abbey, this traditional, family-run
BRITISH restaurant has a relaxed, intimate atmosphere. Pies, casseroles, and steaks are regular items on the menu, and there's a full English Sunday lunch. Leave room for such time-honored desserts as fruit crumble and treacle tart. Special diets are well catered for. ⊠*73 Church St.* ☎*01684/292703* ▤*MC, V* ☉*Closed Mon and Tues. No dinner Wed. and Sun.*

££ ▥**Jessop Townhouse.** Restrained elegance and friendly management are hallmarks of this three-story Georgian B&B just across from the abbey. The spacious rooms are a tasteful blend of traditional and modern (some have couches and extra-wide beds), though those at the front may suffer from traffic noise. Breakfast options include kippers, smoked salmon and scrambled eggs, and pancakes with maple syrup. **Pros:** relaxed atmosphere; comfortable beds; family-friendly. **Cons:** some traffic and church bell noise; limited parking. ⊠*65 Church St.* ☎*01684/292017*

8

⊕*www.jessophousehotel.com* ◆8 *rooms* ⌂ *In-room: no a/c, Internet, Wi-Fi. In-hotel: bar, Wi-Fi, parking (free)* ▤*AE, MC, V* ◎*BP.*

SOUDLEY

27 mi southwest of Tewkesbury, 15 mi west of Gloucester.

Soudley has a museum that provides a useful introduction to the surrounding forest.

EXPLORING

★ The ancient **Forest of Dean** (⊕*www.visitforestofdean.co.uk*) covers much of the valley between the Rivers Severn and Wye. Although the primordial forest has long since been cut down and replanted, the landscape here remains one of strange beauty, hiding in its folds and under its hills deposits of iron, silver, and coal that have been mined for thousands of years. Of the original forest established in 1016 by King Canute, 27,000 acres are preserved by the Forestry Commission. It's still a source of timber, but parking lots and picnic grounds have been created and eight nature trails marked. ■TIP→ **For a driving tour of the forest, head to Littledean, where signs direct you through the best of the forest.** To get to Littledean from Soudley, backtrack north on B4227, and turn east on A4151.

★ The **Dean Heritage Centre,** in a restored mill building in a wooded valley
۞ on the forest's eastern edge, tells the history of the forest, with reconstructions of a forester's cottage, a waterwheel, and a "beam engine" (a primitive steam engine used to pump water from flooded coal mines). Other galleries show art with local themes as well as furniture, ornaments, and the like made from local oak. Also within the grounds is a smallholding (a small farm), with a couple of resident pigs, and a charcoal burner's hut. Craftspeople work in the outbuildings. ⊠*B4227, near Cinderford* ☎*01594/822170* ⊕*www.deanheritagemuseum.com* ☞*£4.90* ۞*Apr.–Oct., daily 10–5; Nov.–Mar., daily 10–4.*

COLEFORD

5 mi west of Soudley, 10 mi south of Ross-on-Wye.

The area around Coleford, a large village of more than 8,000 people, is a maze of moss-covered rocks, huge ferns, and ancient yew trees—a shady haven on a summer's day. The tourist information center has details of picnic grounds, nature and sculpture trails, and tours of the forest.

ESSENTIALS

Visitor Information Coleford Tourist Information Center (⊠*High St.* ☎*01594/812388* ⊕*www.visitforestofdean.co.uk*).

EXPLORING

۞ A visit to the workings in the spectacular **Clearwell Caves,** 1½ mi south of Coleford, provides insight into the region's mining for iron and coal, which went on continuously from Roman times to 1945. Ocher (for paint pigments and cosmetics) is still mined here. ⊠*Off B4228* ☎*01594/832535* ⊕*www.clearwellcaves.co.uk* ☞*£5.80, £7.50*

Christmas Fantasy displays ⊙ *Mid-Feb.–Oct. and late Nov.–late Dec., daily 10–5 (closes at 8 on Thurs. late Nov.–late Dec.).*

WHERE TO STAY

££ ⊞ **Tudor Farmhouse.** Despite its name, this former farmhouse has some sections dating to the 13th century. Polished oak staircases, mullioned windows, and a huge stone fireplace in the sitting room imbue the place with plenty of charm. Most of the traditionally styled bedrooms are in a converted barn, and two have four-poster beds. The restaurant (£££) serves good-quality fare using seasonal ingredients. **Pros:** lovely setting; pleasant staff; good food. **Cons:** often booked with wedding parties; limited cell phone reception. ⊠*High St., near Coleford, Clearwell* ☎*01594/833046* ⊕*www.tudorfarmhousehotel.co.uk* ⇨*18 rooms, 2 suites* ⚐*In-room: no a/c, Wi-Fi. In-hotel: restaurant, some pets allowed, no-smoking rooms* ⊟*AE, MC, V* ⦿*BP.*

SPORTS AND THE OUTDOORS

The densely wooded Forest of Dean is quite special for walking, with interesting villages and monastic ruins. There are easy walks out of Newland, around New Fancy (great view) and Mallards Pike Lake, and there's a slightly longer one (three hours) that takes in Wench Ford, Danby Lodge, and Blackpool Bridge. The area has picnic grounds, car parking, and, hidden away, old pubs where you can wet your whistle. For information on hiking in the Forest of Dean, contact the **Forestry Commission** (⊠*Bank House, Bank St., Coleford* ☎*01594/833057* ⊕*www.forestry.gov.uk*).

SLIMBRIDGE WILDFOWL AND WETLANDS TRUST

38 mi east of Coleford (via Severn Bridge to the south), 12 mi south of Gloucester, 20 mi northeast of Bristol.

GETTING HERE AND AROUND

To drive here from the Forest of Dean, you can take the Severn Bridge to the south of the area and then take A38 or M5 north.

EXPLORING

↻ On the banks of the River Severn, the 73-acre **Slimbridge Wildfowl and Wetlands Trust** encompasses rich marshland that harbors Britain's largest collection of wildfowl. Thousands of swans, ducks, and geese come to winter here; spring and early summer are the times to see cygnets, ducklings, and goslings. Trails with blinds (called "hides" in Britain) thread the preserve. The visitor center has an observation tower, cinema, gift shop, and restaurant; a gallery of wildlife art presents changing exhibitions. The preserve is outside the village of Slimbridge (head west and across the Sharpness Canal). ⊠*Off A38, or off Exit 13 or 14 of M5* ☎*01453/891900* ⊕*www.wwt.org.uk* ⊡*£7.95* ⊙*Apr.–Oct., daily 9:30–5:30; Nov.–Mar., daily 9:30–5.*

BERKELEY CASTLE

4 mi southwest of Slimbridge, 17 mi southwest of Gloucester, 21 mi north of Bristol.

EXPLORING

★ **Berkeley Castle,** in the sleepy village of Berkeley (pronounced *bark*-ley), is perfectly preserved, down to its medieval turrets, and full of family treasures. It witnessed the murder of King Edward II in 1327—the cell in which it occurred can still be seen. Edward was deposed by his French consort, Queen Isabella, and her paramour, the earl of Mortimer. They then connived at his imprisonment and subsequent death. Roger De Berkeley, a Norman knight, began work on the castle in 1153, and it has remained in the family ever since. Magnificent furniture, tapestries, and pictures fill the state apartments, but even the ancient buttery and kitchen are interesting. The surrounding meadows, now the setting for pleasant Elizabethan gardens that include a tropical Butterfly House, were once flooded to make a formidable moat. Special events take place year-round. ⊠ *Off A38, Berkeley* ☎ *01453/810332* ⊕ *www. berkeley-castle.com* ⊠ *£7.50; gardens only, £4; Butterfly House only, £2* ⊘ *House and gardens: late Apr., May, Sept., and Oct., Sun. and national holidays 11–5:30; June–Aug., Sun.–Thurs. and national holidays 11–5:30.*

WHERE TO STAY

££ **Drakestone House.** Lovely and reasonably priced, this Cotswold Arts
★ and Crafts house 3 mi east of Berkeley has wooden floors and beamed and plasterwork ceilings. Fine antiques and period furniture complement the architecture, and in the impressive garden clipped yew hedges surround an immaculate lawn and sunken pond. If you have a car, it's a good place to get away from it all. **Pros:** beautiful furnishings; secluded setting. **Cons:** no evening diversions nearby; hard to find. ⊠ *Off B4060, Stinchcombe, Dursley* ☎ *01453/542140* ⊕ *www.wolseylodges.com* ⊠ *3 rooms* ⌂ *In-room: no a/c, no phone, no TV, Wi-Fi. In-hotel: Wi-Fi, some pets allowed, no-smoking rooms* ⊟ *No credit cards* ⊺ *BP.*

££££–££££ **Thornbury Castle.** An impressive lodging, Thornbury has everything
★ a genuine 16th-century Tudor castle needs: huge fireplaces, moody paintings, and mullioned windows, along with a large garden. There's also plenty of history: Henry VIII, Anne Boleyn, and Mary Tudor all spent time here. The standards of comfort are famous, and the pampering touches in the "bedchambers" include well-appointed bathrooms. People come from all over to dine in the restaurant, where you'll find sophisticated fare such as loin of venison, poached brill, quail, and duck. The hotel is 12 mi north of Bristol. **Pros:** grand medieval surroundings; romantic ambience; professional staff. **Cons:** many steps to climb; rooms overheated; village of Thornbury is dull. ⊠ *Castle St., off A38, Thornbury* ☎ *01454/281182* ⊕ *www.thornburycastle.co.uk* ⊠ *21 rooms, 4 suites* ⌂ *In-room: no a/c, Internet. In-hotel: restaurant, bar, some pets allowed* ⊟ *AE, DC, MC, V* ⊺ *BP.*

The Welsh Borders

WORD OF MOUTH

"I lived in Brindleyplace in Birmingham. This is a great area with loads of restaurants and is effectively canal central (narrowboat tours of the canal system are always available) for the country. Also worth a visit is the Ikon art gallery. For great cheap Indian food, check out the Balti Triangle."

—crellston

"Shropshire is very near Birmingham and has plenty of stuff kids would be interested in. Ironbridge is literally packed with museums and other things, including one museum especially for kids and teens, Enginuity. Blists Hill Victorian Town in Ironbridge had a lot of kids when we were there. Shrewsbury is a great medieval town, too."

—semiramis

9

Updated by
Kate Hughes

Some of England's prettiest countryside lies along the 108-mi border with Wales, which stretches from the town of Chepstow on the Severn estuary in the south to the appealing walled city of Chester in the north. Much of the land along this border, in the counties of Herefordshire, Shropshire, and southern Cheshire, is remote and tranquil, and, except for a few highlights, attracts fewer travelers than more well-known areas of England. The large, culturally rich city of Birmingham can be a gateway to exploring the Welsh Borders.

Herefordshire, in the south, is a county of rich, rolling countryside and river valleys, gradually opening out in the high hills and plateaus of Shropshire. North of the Shropshire hills, the gentler Cheshire plain stretches toward Liverpool and Manchester. This is dairy country, dotted with small villages and market towns that have many of the 13th- and 14th-century black-and-white, half-timber buildings typical of northwestern England. These are the legacy of a forested countryside. (The Victorians, however, are responsible for the more recent fashion of painting these structures black and white.) In the market towns of Chester and Shrewsbury, the more elaborately decorated half-timber buildings are monuments to wealth, dating mostly from the early 17th century. More half-timbered structures are found in Ludlow, now a culinary center nestled in the lee of its majestic ruined castle.

Today's rural peace belies a turbulent past, when relations between the English and the Welsh were difficult. The 177-mi Offa's Dyke Path, a National Trail that runs near the border (two-thirds is in Wales), follows part of the 8th-century earthen wall built by King Offa as protection against Welsh raiders. A string of medieval castles also bears witness to this history.

In the 18th century, one small corner of Shropshire heralded the tumultuous birth of the Industrial Revolution. Here, in a wooded stretch of the Severn Gorge, the coke blast furnace was invented and the first iron bridge was erected (1779). You can get a sense of this history at the museums at Ironbridge Gorge.

The ramifications of that technological leap led to the growth of Britain's second-largest city, Birmingham, the capital of the Midlands. Birmingham has transcended its reputation as one of the country's least attractive cities; its imaginative makeover and active, varied cultural life, together with its historic architecture, are draws for anyone interested in modern urban Britain.

TOP REASONS TO GO

The city of Birmingham: The revamped city center shows off its superb art collections and cultural facilities, international cuisine, and renowned Jewellery Quarter amid full-bodied redbrick architecture, a link to Birmingham's industrial heritage.

Taste of the East: Spice up your life and make the most of the swath of Indian restaurants in and around Birmingham. After all, a curry is now regarded as a traditional English dish.

Half-timber architecture: Black-and-white half-timber houses are a mark of pride throughout the region;

there are notable concentrations of buildings from medieval times to the Jacobean era in Chester, Shrewsbury, and Ludlow.

Walks on the Malverns: Take inspiration as composer Elgar did, as you stride across these hills and look across the fields and orchards to the Cotswolds in the east and misty Welsh mountains to the west.

Ironbridge Gorge: Recall the burgeoning of England's Industrial Revolution at the complex of museums within the shadow of this graceful bridge, the first of its kind in the world.

ORIENTATION AND PLANNING

ORIENTATION

The main eastern gateway to the region is bustling Birmingham, one of the best places in England for the performing arts, but many people visiting the region are seeking rural peace rather than urban action. The city of Worcester, to the south, is renowned for its proud cathedral and fine bone china. Farther south and west, along the lovely Malvern Hills, lie the peaceful spa town of Great Malvern and the prosperous agricultural city of Hereford. West of Birmingham is Bewdley, a terminus of the Severn Valley Railway, and beyond, the West Midlands—birthplace of modern British industry. In the western part of the region, hugged by the River Severn, the small city of Shrewsbury is near a cluster of excellent Ironbridge museums interpreting the region's industrial heritage. To its south lies Ludlow, an architectural and culinary hot spot; at the northwestern edge of the region is the ancient city of Chester, popular with visitors.

Birmingham. On the eastern edge of the region, Britain's second-largest city, once known as "the city of 1,001 trades," now recalls its past through excellent museums and a network of canals. Business sets the pace here, but so do an adventurous arts program, buzzing nightlife, and an excellent restaurant scene.

Worcester, Hereford and Environs. A couple of cathedral towns—Worcester and Hereford—and genteel Malvern contrast with Dudley, where the Black Country Living Museum preserves reminders of the grim conditions of an industrial past.

9

Shrewsbury to Chester. The northern, most varied part of the region, studded with its characteristic half-timber buildings, embraces the World Heritage Site of Ironbridge Gorge, the Shropshire hills, and ancient Shrewsbury and Chester, as well as Ludlow with its gastronomic delights.

PLANNING

WHEN TO GO

Most attractions are open and the countryside is most appealing in the warmer weather between April and September. The open-air performances at Ludlow Castle take place at the end of June; the Three Choirs Festival, rotating from year to year among Gloucester (2010), Hereford, and Worcester, is held in mid-August, and the Autumn in Malvern Festival happens on weekends in October. Most rural sights have limited opening hours in winter. Even in the towns and cities, the majority of attractions close at 5.

PLANNING YOUR TIME

Birmingham makes a logical base if you're looking for cosmopolitan city life. The museums and sights will take you a full day to explore, and from here Worcester and Avoncroft to the south, as well as Dudley and Lichfield to the north, are feasible day trips.

It's easy to reach the countryside from the smaller cities of Hereford, Worcester, and Chester, but if you want to walk the hills, Ludlow is a good gateway for Wenlock Edge, as is Great Malvern or Ledbury for the Malvern Hills.

To the north of the region, Ironbridge Gorge and Chester demand a full day each. Ludlow and Shrewsbury take less time, though it would be a shame to leave Ludlow without sampling its fine food and dining. Shrewsbury makes a good central base, from which Chester and the north are easily reached. Once you've gone as far north as this, you might consider going on to Liverpool, if the Beatles and maritime history have any appeal, or to north Wales.

GETTING HERE AND AROUND

AIR TRAVEL

The region is served by Birmingham International Airport, 6 mi east of the city center, and the country's second-busiest airport. It has connections to all of Britain's major cities, and limited service to the United States.

Contacts Birmingham International Airport (✉ *A45, off Junction 6 of M42* ☎ *0870/733–5511* ⊕ *www.bhx.co.uk).*

BUS TRAVEL

National Express runs buses from London's Victoria Coach Station. You can reach Birmingham in less than three hours; Hereford, Shrewsbury, and Worcester take between four and five hours. It also operates services from London's Heathrow (2¾ hours) and Gatwick (4 hours) airports to Birmingham.

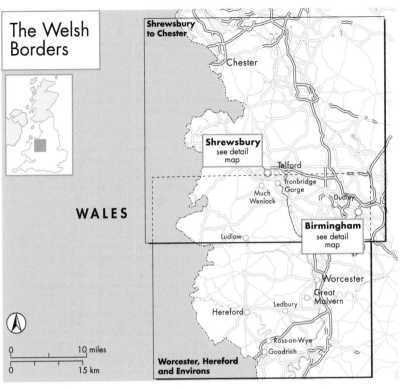

The Welsh Borders

Shrewsbury to Chester

Chester

Shrewsbury
see detail map

Telford

Ironbridge Gorge

Much Wenlock

Dudley

WALES

Birmingham
see detail map

Ludlow

Worcester

Great Malvern

Ledbury

Hereford

Ross-on-Wye

Goodrich

Worcester, Hereford and Environs

0 — 10 miles
0 — 15 km

The First bus company has service between Birmingham, Worcester, Hereford, Kidderminster, and Ludlow.

Contacts First (☎ *0871/200–2233* ⊕ *www.firstgroup.com*). **National Express** (☎ *0871/781–8181* ⊕ *www.nationalexpress.com*).

CAR TRAVEL

Although all major towns are served by public transport, a car allows greater flexibility and the ability to get off the beaten track. To reach Birmingham (120 mi), Shrewsbury (150 mi), Ludlow (140 mi), and Chester (180 mi) from London, take M40 and keep on it until it becomes M42, or take M1/M6. M4 and then M5 from London take you to Worcester and Hereford in just under three hours. Driving can be difficult in the region's western reaches—especially in the hills and valleys west of Hereford, where steep, twisting roads often narrow down into mere trackways.

TRAIN TRAVEL

For travel to and between the main towns and cities, trains are more frequent and much quicker than the buses, though more expensive. From London, First Great Western and Arriva trains serve the region from Paddington Station, and Virgin, Central, and Silverlink trains leave from Euston (call National Rail Enquiries for all schedules and information). Travel times are Paddington to Hereford, 3 hours, and

Ludlow, 3¼ hours (both changing at Newport); to Worcester, 2¼ hours; Euston to Birmingham, 1½ hours; Euston to Shrewsbury, with a change at Crewe or Birmingham, 2¾ hours; or to Chester, with a change at Crewe, 2¾ hours. West Midlands Day Ranger tickets (£16.20) and three- and seven-day Heart of England Rover tickets (£63 and £82.40) allow unlimited travel on trains throughout the region.

Contacts National Rail Enquiries (☎0845/748–4950 ⊕ www.nationalrail.co.uk).

RESTAURANTS

Birmingham has splendid international restaurants but is probably most famous for its Indian and Pakistani eateries; you'll find good choices both in the city center and out of town. The city has more Michelin-starred restaurants than any other British city outside of London and hosts the annual Taste of Birmingham Festival in July. In the rest of the area, casual spots dominate, though Ludlow is a culinary center.

HOTELS

The Welsh Borders are full of ancient inns and venerable Regency-style houses converted into hotels. Although some places are pricey, bargains can be found; Internet deals are always worth searching out. Birmingham's hotels, geared to the convention crowd and often booked up well in advance, are mostly bland and impersonal, but sophisticated; weekend rates may be heavily discounted.

WHAT IT COSTS IN POUNDS					
	£	££	£££	££££	£££££
Restaurants	Under £10	£10–£14	£15–£19	£20–£25	over £25
Hotels	Under £70	£70–£120	£121–£160	£161–£220	over £220

Restaurant prices are for a main course at dinner. Hotel prices are for two people in a standard double room in high season, including V.A.T., with no meals or, if indicated, CP (with continental breakfast), BP (Breakfast Plan, with full breakfast), or MAP (Modified American Plan, with breakfast and dinner).

VISITOR INFORMATION

Traveline can field all general transportation inquiries. Local tourist offices can recommend day or half-day tours of the region and will have the names of registered Blue Badge guides. The Heart of England tourist board Web site covers Birmingham, the Black Country, Herefordshire, Ironbridge, and Worcestershire.

Contacts Heart of England Tourist Board (⊕ www.visittheheart.co.uk).**Traveline** (☎0871/200–2233 ⊕ www.traveline.org.uk).

BIRMINGHAM

The dynamic cultural life of Birmingham—the result of the museums, art galleries, theater, ballet, and symphony that thrive here—comes as a refreshing surprise. The city's visual appeal, thanks to heavy industry, German bombing during World War II, and some unfortunate late-20th-century civic architecture, may be less than instantly evident, but treasures and historic civic architecture remain. Creative redevelopment and public art are increasingly making areas more attractive, too. The redeveloped Bullring shopping center, part of which has a striking, curving facade of 15,000 aluminum disks, is one creation that has won praise.

Birmingham, with a metropolitan area population of 2.6 million, lies 25 mi north of Stratford and 120 mi northwest of London. "Brum," as it's known, is one of the country's most ethnically diverse urban areas, with nearly a third of its residents from minority groups. The city first flourished in the boom years of the 19th-century's Industrial Revolution. Its inventive citizens accumulated enormous wealth, and at one time the city had some of the finest Victorian buildings in the country. It still has some of the most ravishingly beautiful Pre-Raphaelite paintings, on view in the Birmingham Museum and Art Gallery.

GETTING HERE AND AROUND

Bus 900 runs from the airport to the city center every 20 minutes; a taxi will cost you around £20. It's advisable to avoid negotiating the city's convoluted road network. Drivers are often surprised that Birmingham's inner ring road twists right through the city center. Parking in the center is free between 6 PM to 8 SM.

New Street train station is right in the center of the city, close to the Bullring. The bus station is at Oxford Street, a few minutes' walk from the Bullring shopping center. The easiest way to get around the city is by foot, though you'll need a bus for the Barber Institute and Cadbury World, and a short metro (tram) trip for the Jewellery Quarter. A Daytripper ticket covering bus, train, and metro travel costs £5.20.

ESSENTIALS

Transportation Contacts Traveline (☎ *0870/200–2233* ⊕ *www.traveline.org. uk*).

Visitor Information Birmingham (⊠ *The Rotunda, 150 New St.* ☎ *0844/888– 3883* ⊕ *www.visitbirmingham.com*).

EXPLORING

A full day gives you time to linger in the Jewellery Quarter and browse the art museums. Much of Birmingham is now pedestrian-friendly, the downtown shopping area transformed into arcades and buses-only streets. You can also explore restored canals and canal towpaths. Most of the central sights, which are well signposted, form a tight-knit group. The tourist information center, the best place to pick up a map, is close to public bus and rail stations. It has details of heritage walks.

TOP ATTRACTIONS

Avoncroft Museum of Historic Buildings. You can see the architecture typical of the Midlands in microcosm at this 15-acre open-air museum, which has rescued more than 25 structures from destruction. Alongside the half-timber buildings are Victorian chimneys, a collection of phone booths, a three-seater earth closet (lavatory), a 1946 prefabricated house, and a working windmill. Avoncroft is 17 mi southwest of Birmingham. ■TIP→ School groups usually arrive at the museum in

OFF THE BEATEN PATH

9

Birmingham

Jewellery Quarter

St. George's St.

Buckingham St.

Mott St.

St. George's St.

Summer Lane (B4498)

New Town Row

Kenyon St.

Constitution Hill

Henrietta St.

Lower Loveday St.

Northwood St.

Caroline St.

Cox St.

Livery St.

Water St.

Shadwell St.

Birmingham & Fazeley Canal

St. Chads Queensway

James St.

St. Paul's Square

Frederick St.

Vittoria St.

Graham St.

St. Chad's Circus

Draw St.

General Hospital

George St.

Newhall Hill

King Edward Rd.

Charlotte St.

Lionel St.

Newhall St.

Ludgate Hill

Gt. Charles St. Queensway

Cornwall St.

Edmund St.

Church St.

Colmore Row

Snow Hill Station

Livery St.

Steelhouse Lane

Colmore Circus

Priory

Summer Row

Paradise Circus

Queensway

Waterloo St.

Temple Row

Bull St.

Corporation St.

Queensway

Dale End

Albert St.

Cambridge St.

Alfred's Pl.

Cannon St.

Carr's Ln.

High St.

Moor St. Queensway

Symphony Hall and International Convention Centre

BRINDLEYPLACE

Centenary Way

Town Hall ◆

Victoria Sq.

New Street

Centenary Sq.

Paradise St.

Pinfold St.

Moor Street Station

Broad St.

Bridge St.

Gas Street Basin

Holliday St.

Gas St.

Suffolk St. Queensway

Navigation St.

New Street Station

The Bullring

TO OXFORD ST. AND BUS STATION

The Mailbox

Severn St.

John Bright St.

Hill St.

Station St.

Worcester & Birmingham Canal

Commercial St.

Smallbrook Queensway

Hurst St.

9 10

0 ———— 1/8 mile

0 ———— 200 meters

the morning, making afternoons a less crowded time to visit. Wear sensible shoes. ⊠*Stokeheath, Bromsgrove* ☎*01527/831363* ⊕*www.avoncroft.org.uk* 🖃*£6.60* ⊗*Mar., Nov., and Dec., Fri.–Sun. 10:30–4; Apr.–June, Tues.–Sun. 10:30–5; July and Aug., daily 10:30–5; Sept. and Oct., Tues.–Sun. 10:30–5.*

❾ ★ Barber Institute of Fine Art. Part of the University of Birmingham, the museum has a small but astounding collection of European paintings, prints, drawings, and sculpture, including works by Bellini, Holbein, Poussin, Turner, Whistler, Degas, Monet, and van Gogh. There are also changing exhibitions. The museum is 3 mi from the city center; to get here, take a train from New Street Station south to University Station, or Bus 61, 62, or 63 from the city center. ⊠*Off Edgbaston Park Rd. near East Gate, Edgbaston* ☎*0121/414–7333* ⊕*www.barber.org.uk* 🖃*Free* ⊗*Mon.–Sat. 10–5, Sun. noon–5.*

❽ Birmingham Back to Backs. Of the 20,000 courts of back-to-back houses (constructed around a courtyard and thus backing onto each other) built in the 19th century for the city's expanding working-class population, this is the only survivor. Three houses tell the stories of families, headed by a watchmaker, a locksmith, and a glassworker, who lived here between the 1840s and the 1930s. A few houses are available for overnight stays. Admission is by timed ticket, booked in advance; allow one hour for the tour and be prepared for steep stairs. The houses are closed the Tuesday after a national holiday. ⊠*Hurst St., City Centre* ☎*0121/666–7671* ⊕*www.nationaltrust.co.uk* 🖃*£5.15* ⊗*Feb.–Dec., Tues.–Sun. and national holidays 10–5.*

❺ Birmingham Museum and Art Gallery. Vast and impressive, this museum Fodor'sChoice holds a magnificent collection of Victorian art and is known interna- ★ tionally for its works by the Pre-Raphaelites. All the big names are here, including William Holman Hunt, John Everett Millais, and Dante Gabriel Rossetti—reflecting the enormous wealth of 19th-century Birmingham and the aesthetic taste of its industrialists. Galleries of metalwork, silver, and ceramics reveal some of the city's history, and works from the Renaissance, the Arts and Crafts movement, and the present day are also well represented. Allow at least a couple of hours for your visit, and you might want to stop off in the impressive Edwardian Tea Room along the way. ⊠*Chamberlain Sq., City Centre* ☎*0121/303–2834* ⊕*www.bmag.org.uk* 🖃*Free* ⊗*Mon.–Thurs. and Sat. 10–5, Fri. 10:30–5, Sun. 12:30–5.*

❹ Jewellery Quarter. For more than two centuries, jewelers have worked in the district of Hockley, northwest of the city center; today around 200 manufacturing jewelers continue the tradition, producing more than a third of the jewelry made in Britain. ◼TIP➔ **The Jewellery Quarter is a great place to shop for jewelry. The free** *Jewellery Quarter* **booklet from the tourist office or library will give you the lowdown on all the history and the shops.** The city's Assay Office hallmarks 12 million items each year with

9

the anchor symbol denoting Birmingham origin. The ornate green and gilded Chamberlain Clock, at the intersection of Vyse Street, Warstone Lane, and Frederick Street, marks the center of the district. Note that shops are closed on Sunday. The quarter is two stops along Metro Line 1 from Snow Hill station. ⊠ *Hockley* ⊕ *www.the-quarter.com.*

OFF THE BEATEN PATH

Lichfield Cathedral. It's worth a detour (14 mi northeast of Birmingham on A38) to explore the only English cathedral with three spires. The sandstone building, beautifully sited by a tree-fringed pool, dates mainly from the 12th and 13th centuries, and the Lady Chapel glows with some fine 16th-century stained glass from the Cistercian abbey of Herkenrode, near Liège, in Belgium. Half-timber houses surround the peaceful grounds, and the town itself has attractive Georgian buildings as well as the birthplace (now a museum) of lexicographer Dr. Samuel Johnson. Frequent trains from Birmingham New Street station take 35 minutes. ⊠ *19A The Close, Lichfield* ☎ *01543/306100* ⊕ *www. lichfield-cathedral.org* ⊠ *Suggested donation £4* ⊙ *Daily 7:30–6:15; closes Sun. at 5 in winter.*

❸ Museum of the Jewellery Quarter. The museum is built around the workshops of Smith & Pepper, a firm that operated here for more than 80 years until 1981; little has changed since the early 1900s. A factory tour (about an hour) and exhibits explain the history of the neighborhood and the jeweler's craft, and you can watch demonstrations of jewelry being made in the traditional way. ⊠ *75–79 Vyse St., Jewellery Quarter* ☎ *0121/554–3598* ⊕ *www.bmag.org.uk* ⊠ *Free* ⊙ *Tues.–Sat. and national holidays 11:30–4; last admission 1 hr before closing.*

❼ Thinktank. This interactive museum in the state-of-the-art Millennium Point center allows you to explore science and the history of Birmingham over four floors of galleries. You can watch giant steam engines at work, explore deep space, program a robot to play the drums, and help perform a hip operation. The IMAX cinema and planetarium put on shows throughout the day. The museum is a 10-minute walk from Moor Street railway station. ⊠ *Curzon St., Digbeth* ☎ *0121/202–2222* ⊕ *www.thinktank.ac* ⊠ *£9; IMAX cinema £8, planetarium £2.45* ⊙ *Daily 10–5; last admission at 4.*

WORTH NOTING

❻ Birmingham Cathedral. The early-18th-century Cathedral of St. Philip, a few blocks from Victoria Square, contains some lovely plasterwork in its elegant, gilded Georgian interior. The stunning stained-glass windows behind the altar, designed by the Pre-Raphaelite Edward Burne-Jones (1833–98) and executed by William Morris (1834–96), glow with sensuous hues. ⊠ *Colmore Row, City Centre* ☎ *0121/262–1840* ⊕ *www.birminghamcathedral.com* ⊠ *Suggested donation £2* ⊙ *Daily 8:30–5.*

❿ Cadbury World. The village of Bournville (4 mi south of the city center) contains this museum devoted to—what else?—chocolate. In 1879 the Quaker Cadbury brothers moved the family business to this "factory in a garden" from the city; they also constructed a model village for workers. The museum traces the history of the cocoa bean and the Cadbury dynasty. The rain-forest walk, Cadabra ride, and exhibits

Cruising Birmingham's Canals

With eight canals and 34 mi of waterways, Birmingham has more canals in its center than Venice. The city is at the heart of a system of waterways built during the Industrial Revolution to connect inland factories to rivers and seaports—by 1840 the canals extended more than 4,000 mi throughout the British Isles. These canals, which carried 9 million tons of cargo a year in the late 19th century and helped make the city an industrial powerhouse, have undergone extensive cleanup and renovation, and are now a tourist attraction.

A walk along the Birmingham Canal Main Line near the Gas Street Basin will bring you to modern shops, restaurants, and more developments such as Brindleyplace in one direction and the Mailbox in the other, and you can see the city from an attractive new perspective. Contact the city tourist offices for maps of pleasant walks along the towpaths and for details about canal cruises on colorfully painted barges.

You can take an hour ride on a canal barge from **Sherborne Wharf** (✉ *Sherborne St., City Centre* ☎ *0121/455–6163* ⊕ *www. sherbornewharf.co.uk*). Trips leave daily April through October at 11:30, 1, 2:30, and 4, and on weekends the rest of the year, departing from the International Convention Centre Quayside.

---

may seem kitschy, and some are perhaps tired, but Cadbury World is extremely popular. You can watch (and smell) chocolates being made by hand, enjoy free samples, and then stock up from the cut-price shop. The restaurant has specialty chocolate cakes as well as lunches. ✉ *Off A38 (take train from New St. to Bournville Train Station), Bournville* ☎ *0845/450–3599* ⊕ *www.cadburyworld.co.uk* 💷 *£13.45* ⏱ *Feb.– Oct., daily; late Jan., Nov. and Dec., Tues.–Thurs. and weekends; times vary; reservations strongly advised, and essential at busy times.*

❶ **Ikon Gallery.** Converted from a Victorian Gothic–style school, this gallery serves as the city's main venue for exhibitions of contemporary art from Britain and abroad. The bright, white interior is divided into comparatively small display areas, making the shows easily digestible. If you need fortifying, however, try the attached tapas bar. ✉ *1 Oozells Sq., Brindleyplace, City Centre* ☎ *0121/248–0708* ⊕ *www.ikon-gallery. co.uk* 💷 *Free* ⏱ *Tues.–Sun. and national holiday Mon. 11–6.*

QUICK BITES The balcony of the redbrick **Malt House** (✉ *75 King Edward's Rd.* ☎ *0121/633–4171*) is just the place to linger over a drink as you watch canal life go by.

❷ **Pen Room.** During the 19th century Birmingham was the hub of the world pen trade. This compact museum in a former pen factory illustrates that heyday through an overwhelming and decorative array of nibs, quills, fountain pens, inks, and all the paraphernalia of the preballpoint era. You can try your hand at calligraphy and make your own nib. ✉ *60 Frederick St., Jewellery Quarter* ☎ *0121/236–9834* ⊕ *www. penroom.co.uk* 💷 *Free* ⏱ *Mon.–Sat. 11–4, Sun. 1–4.*

9

WHERE TO EAT

£   ✕**Canalside Café.** This snug old lockkeeper's cottage on the canal favors
BRITISH   homemade organic meat and vegetarian food. Your preferred option
might be beef or vegetable chili topped with Parmesan cheese, then
apple pie and custard. Snacks are available all day, and the Cornish clotted cream tea is well priced. ⊠*35 Worcester Bar, Gas St., City Centre*
☎ *0785/441–9862* ⊟*No credit cards.*

£   ✕**Henry's.** A popular spot, this traditional Cantonese restaurant on the
CHINESE   edge of the Jewellery Quarter is a haven for lunch during a shopping
spree. The menu lists more than 170 items and also includes a good-
value fixed-price menu and a Sunday buffet. The sizzling dishes, which
arrive at your table on a metal plate, are a good choice. ⊠*27 St. Paul's
Sq., City Centre* ☎*0121/200–1136* ⊟*AE, MC, V.*

££   ✕**Itihaas.** Birmingham has some of Britain's finest Indian restaurants,
INDIAN   and this is one upbeat choice. The style is traditional and colonial; pot-
★   ted palms and pictures rub shoulders with antiques. Cooking concentrates on North Indian dishes, and some good choices are *koila murgh,*
chicken marinated in yogurt, with herb paste, seared over charcoal,
or *hara bara gosth,* a casserole of lamb cooked with garlic, chili, and
spinach. The weekday lunchtime tapas menu is a deal at £8.95. ⊠*18
Fleet St., City Centre* ☎*0121/212–3383* ⊟*AE, MC, V* ⊘*No lunch
weekends.*

£££   ✕**Opus.** The best seasonal and market choices are freshly prepared for
MODERN BRITISH   discerning diners—anyone from ladies out on the town to intimate
couples—enjoying this modern, light space. The accent is on local and
British, so expect quince, pumpkins, air-dried Cumbrian ham, wild
mushrooms, and British cheeses on the menu. Meat is free range and fish
is wild caught; the three-course fixed-price menu weekdays offers excellent value at £18.50. Service is unobtrusive and unstuffy. ⊠ *54 Cornwall
St., City Centre* ☎*0121/200–2323* ⊟*AE, MC, V* ⊘*Closed Sun.*

££   ✕**The Oriental.** Exoticism is the keyword for this Asian restaurant.
ECLECTIC   Silver-gray crushed velvet lines the walls, red flowers paper the ceiling, and, uniquely, the chairs are upholstered with photographic portraits. The food doesn't disappoint, and dishes such as *rendang* chicken
(slow-cooked in spicy coconut sauce) and *sambal* lamb cooked in a dry
sauce (lemongrass, chili, and shrimp paste) reflect the Malaysian focus,
though Thai and Chinese dishes are also on the menu. Lunch and bar
menus are good value. ⊠*128–130 Wharfside St., The Mailbox, City
Centre* ☎*0121/633–9988* ⊟*AE, MC, V.*

£££££   ✕**Purnell's.** Business moguls along with sophisticated foodies can be
MODERN BRITISH   found sampling an aperitif in a comfy armchair before moving on to
superb modern British fare in the sleek, slate-floor dining room. This
high spot in the business district, in a Victorian terra-cotta and redbrick building, is where chef Glyn Purnell creates his individual culinary
stamp. Cornish lamb comes with toffee-and-cumin carrots and Indian
lentils, and marjoram custard enhances slow-cooked banana. Set-price
dinners (two courses for £34, three courses for £40) are complemented
by a tasting menu (£65). Lunches (£17 for two courses) are a good
value. ⊠*55 Cornwall St., City Centre* ☎*0121/212–9799* ⊟*AE, MC,
V* ⊘*Closed Sun. and Mon. No lunch Sat.*

££££ ✗**Simpsons.** Choose between the
FRENCH conservatory with garden views or
Fodor'sChoice the inner dining space of this ele-
★ gant and gleaming Georgian villa
known for fine French-influenced
modern cuisine. Either way, the
light and immaculate surroundings,
and assured and welcoming service
make it easy to savor specialties
such as pavé of Aberdeenshire beef
with slow-cooked ox cheek, and
pear tarte tatin with Roquefort
ice cream. There are four luxurious theme guest rooms for those
who wish to stray no farther, and
a cooking school. It's a mile south
of the city center. ⊠*20 Highfield
Rd., Edgbaston* ☎*0121/454–3434*
⊟*AE, MC, V* ☻*No dinner Sun.*

££ ✗**Thai Edge.** The elegant, contem-
THAI porary Asian design is a welcoming
draw at this well-regarded restaurant. Dishes such as *gaeng keow waan*
(green curry cooked in coconut milk with eggplant, lime leaves, and
basil) are excellent. Lunches are a good value. ⊠*7 Oozells Sq., City
Centre* ☎*0121/643–3993* ⊟*AE, MC, V.*

> ### EAT BALTI IN BRUM
>
> Birmingham is home to the Balti,
> a popular cuisine invented in the
> mid-1970s by the Pakistani com-
> munity. The food is cooked and
> brought to the table in a woklike
> dish and eaten with naan bread,
> not rice. Curry and other spices
> season the meat and vegetables.
> The more than 30 restaurants in
> the "Balti Triangle" of the Moseley
> and Sparkbrook districts include
> **Punjab Paradise** (⊠*377 Lady-
> pool Rd.* ☎*0121/499–4110*) and
> **Al Frash** (⊠*186 Ladypool Rd.*
> ☎*0121/753–3120*). Buses 6, 12,
> 13, and 37 go to this area a few
> miles south of the center.

WHERE TO STAY

££–£££ ⊞**City Inn.** This bustling hotel has an excellent central location near the
waterside nightlife scene. The crisp, modern bedrooms and bathrooms,
though on the small side, are beautifully equipped and furnished in
calm, neutral tones; all guest rooms come with iMacs. Floors 6 and 7
have the best views. Breakfast is included in the good weekend deals.
Pros: fine restaurant; free Wi-Fi and Skype; windows can be opened.
Cons: oriented to business sector. ⊠*1 Brunswick Sq., Brindleyplace,
City Centre* ☎*0121/643–1003* ⊕*www.cityinn.com* ⇗*238 rooms*
⚘*In-room: DVD, Internet, Wi-Fi. In-hotel: restaurant, room service,
gym, laundry service, parking (paid), no-smoking rooms* ⊟*AE, DC,
MC, V.*

£ ⊞**Fountain Court.** A five-minute drive from the city center, this cheerful,
family-run small hotel is in a leafy, well-heeled neighborhood. Bedrooms are modern and bright, and the more traditional public rooms
have dark-wood furniture. You can arrange dinner here if you wish.
Pros: free Wi-Fi; family rooms available. **Cons:** on busy main road; a
couple of miles out of city center. ⊠*339–343 Hagley Rd., Edgbaston*
☎*0121/429–1754* ⊕*www.fountain-court.co.uk* ⇗*22 rooms* ⚘*In-
room: no a/c. In-hotel: bar, Wi-Fi, parking (free), no-smoking rooms*
⊟*MC, V* ℞*BP.*

££££ ⊞**Hotel du Vin & Bistro.** A Victorian eye hospital in the city center received
a makeover from this *très* hip mini-chain but retains details such as the
ironwork double stairway and marble columns. Beyond the imposing

redbrick exterior is an inner courtyard with a fountain and garden. Bedrooms are sleek and contemporary, with huge, fluffy towels and white linens. The bistro is redolent of fin-de-siècle Paris, and in the Bubble Lounge you can drown in more than 50 varieties of champagne. **Pros:** good for celebrity spotting; central location. **Cons:** no private parking lot; breakfast costs extra. ⊠ *25 Church St., City Centre* ☎ *0121/200– 0600* ⊕ *www.hotelduvin.com* ⌨ *56 rooms, 10 suites* ⌂ *In-room: no a/c, Wi-Fi. In-hotel: restaurant, room service, bars, gym, spa, laundry service, parking (paid), no-smoking rooms* ▭ *AE, MC, V.*

££££–££££ **Macdonald Burlington Hotel.** Wood paneling and marble abound at this traditional hotel in one of the city's grand Victorian buildings. Guest rooms are decorated either with conservative dark woods and print fabrics or, for a slightly higher rate, in a modern, minimalist style using warm muted colors. At the sumptuous Berlioz restaurant, the menu is organically sourced and features Scottish steaks, oysters, and salmon. **Pros:** close to New Street station and shops; very good weekend rates. **Cons:** attracts a mainly business clientele. ⊠ *Burlington Arcade, 126 New St., City Centre* ☎ *0844/879–9019* ⊕ *www.burlingtonhotel. com* ⌨ *112 rooms* ⌂ *In-room: Wi-Fi. In-hotel: restaurant, room service, bar, gym, laundry service, parking (paid), some pets allowed, no-smoking rooms* ▭ *AE, DC, MC, V* ⏐○⏐*BP.*

££££ **Malmaison.** Retail therapy is on your doorstep at this chic, up-to-the-minute hotel in the Mailbox shopping center. Large windows make the guest rooms light and airy by day, and there's subtle lighting by night. Furnishings are smoothly modern, in chocolate and cream colors; bathrooms indulge you with tailor-made toiletries and soothing showers. A plush red carpet winds upstairs to the upbeat Brasserie, which concentrates on French cuisine. **Pros:** handy for Mailbox shopping and restaurants; within easy reach of canal-side attractions; good Internet rates. **Cons:** expensive parking (cheaper alternatives are close by); over-the-top marketing may be annoying; breakfast not included. ⊠ *1 Wharfside St., City Centre* ☎ *0121/246–5000* ⊕ *www.malmaison. com* ⌨ *189 rooms, 10 suites* ⌂ *In-room: Internet. In-hotel: restaurant, room service, bar, gym, spa, laundry service, Wi-Fi, parking (paid), no-smoking rooms* ▭ *AE, DC, MC, V.*

££–£££ **New Hall Hotel & Spa.** A tree-lined drive leads through 26 acres of
★ gardens and open land to this moated, 12th-century manor-house-turned-country-hotel. Public rooms reflect the house's long history with touches such as the 16th-century oak paneling and Flemish glass, 18th-century chandeliers, and a stone fireplace from the 17th century. Guest rooms, most in a more modern section, are done in contemporary English country style with plain and print fabrics and marble-tile baths. Both the formal Bridge restaurant and the more relaxed Terrace Brasserie serve sophisticated English and French cuisine. The hotel is 7 mi northeast of the city center. **Pros:** historic building; beautiful grounds; plenty of sports facilities. **Cons:** a little difficult to locate; away from city center. ⊠ *Walmley Rd., Sutton Coldfield* ☎ *0121/378–2442* ⊕ *www.handpickedhotels.co.uk* ⌨ *49 rooms, 10 suites* ⌂ *In-room: no a/c (some), Wi-Fi. In-hotel: restaurant, room service, bar, golf course, tennis court, pool, gym, spa, laundry service, parking (free), no-smoking rooms* ▭ *AE, MC, V* ⏐○⏐*BP.*

££££–£££ ▫️**Staying Cool.** The 19th and 20th floors of the Rotunda, an iconic office building erected in the 1960s, now contain spacious, wedge-shape serviced apartments, designed to the hilt in sleek '60s style. Good for those who like their surroundings light and white—floor-to-ceiling windows, white decor punctuated by colorful, specially commissioned furniture—each apartment comes with an Apple Mac and all the latest technology. One- and two-bed apartments are available, with one apartment on the second floor. Organic breakfasts can be delivered. **Pros:** beautifully fitted and well-stocked kitchens; memory-foam beds, free Wi-Fi. **Cons:** not for those with fear of heights; no designated parking. ✉️*150 New St., City Centre* ☎️*0121/643–0815* ⊕*www.stayingcool. com* ⇆*15 apartments* ♿*In-room: no a/c, no phone, kitchen, refrigerator, Internet, Wi-Fi. In-hotel: no-smoking rooms* ▤*AE, MC, V.*

££ ▫️**Totel.** These serviced apartments, 1½ mi from Birmingham's center and off the main A456, make for a secluded and peaceful retreat. The large redbrick house, once a 19th-century private residence, now consists of one- and two-bedroom suites that are spacious and furnished in crisp, contemporary style. **Pros:** plenty of room; undisturbed by service staff; frequent buses to center. **Cons:** not in city center; no shops or restaurants in immediate vicinity. ✉️*Asquith House, 19 Portland Rd., Edgbaston* ☎️*0121/454–5282* ⊕*www.toteluk.com* ⇆*10 apartments* ♿*In-room: no a/c, kitchen, DVD, Wi-Fi. In-hotel: parking (free), no-smoking rooms* ▤*AE, MC, V* ⏧*BP.*

NIGHTLIFE AND THE ARTS

NIGHTLIFE

The city's thriving nightlife scene is concentrated around Broad Street and Hurst Street, as well as the Brindleyplace and Mailbox areas.

Colorful **Asha's** (✉️*12–22 Newhall St., City Centre* ☎️*0121/200–2767*), a bar and restaurant, has superb fresh fruit cocktails, with Asian cuisine available. **Bar Epernay** (✉️*171 Wharfside St., City Centre* ☎️*0121/632–1430*), a champagne bar and brasserie in the Mailbox, has a revolving piano and central, warming brazier, making it perfect for relaxing after a day's sightseeing. The **Jam House** (✉️*3–5 St. Paul's Sq., Jewellery Quarter* ☎️*0121/200–3030*), an excellent drinking, dining, and dancing venue, benefits from nightly live entertainment—jazz, soul, or funk. It's directed by musician Jools Holland.

The spacious and high-domed **Old Joint Stock** (✉️*4 Temple Row West, off Colmore Row, City Centre* ☎️*0121/200–1892*) serves good ales and pies, and there's a theater attached. The bar at the **Vaults** (✉️*Newhall Pl., Newhall Hill, Jewellery Quarter* ☎️*0121/212–9837*) is perfect for an intimate drink. Another option is to reserve your own private, brick-vaulted booth, draw the curtain, adjust the music, and settle down.

THE ARTS

Birmingham's performing arts companies are well regarded throughout the country. Catch a performance if you can.

BALLET The **Birmingham Royal Ballet** (✉️*Hurst St., City Centre* ☎️*0870/730–1234*), the second company of the Royal Ballet, is based at the

Hippodrome Theatre, which also plays host to visiting companies such as the Welsh National Opera.

CONCERTS
★   **Symphony Hall** (⊠*International Convention Centre, Broad St., City Centre* ☎*0121/780–3333*) is the home of the distinguished City of Birmingham Symphony Orchestra and a venue for jazz, pop, and world as well as classical concerts. The **National Exhibition Centre** (⊠*M42, Junction 6, close to airport* ☎*0844/338–8000*) promotes top names in rock and pop.

The splendidly refurbished neoclassical **Town Hall Birmingham** (⊠*Paradise St.* ☎*0121/780–3333*) holds a wide range of events, including organ recitals, opera, and folk concerts.

THEATER   The **Alexandra Theatre** (⊠*Station St., City Centre* ☎*0870/607–7533*) welcomes touring companies on their way to or from London's West End. The **Birmingham Repertory Theatre** (⊠*Centenary Sq., Broad St., City Centre* ☎*0121/236–4455*), founded in 1913, is equally at home with modern or classical work as one of England's oldest and most esteemed theater companies.

FILM   The **Electric Cinema** (⊠*47–49 Station St., City Centre* ☎*0121/643–7879*), the country's oldest working cinema if not the smartest, has sofas and waiter service to enhance the viewing experience at this individualistic art deco survivor.

SHOPPING

★   The glass-roof **Bullring** (⊠*Between New St. and High St., City Centre* ☎*0121/632–1500*) has three floors of retail enticement, including two department stores, Debenhams and the stunningly curved Selfridges, covered with aluminum disks. Don't miss Selfridges's awesome Food Hall.

The **Mailbox** (⊠*150 Wharfside St., City Centre* ☎*0121/632–1000*), once a Royal Mail sorting office, entices with trendy shops and designer outlets such as Harvey Nichols and Armani, restaurants, and hotels.

JEWELLERY
QUARTER   The **Jewellery Quarter** (⊠*Hockley* ☎*0121/604–7700*) has more than 100 shops that sell and repair gold and silver handcrafted jewelry, clocks, and watches. The Information Centre at 120 Vyse Street provides information on artisans and retail outlets.

Crescent Silver (⊠*83–85 Spencer St., Jewellery Quarter* ☎*0121/236–9006*) sells an interesting range of silver jewelry and gifts.

St. Paul's Gallery (⊠*94–108 Norwood St., Jewellery Quarter* ☎*0121/236–5800*), an entertaining treasure trove, specializes in hand-signed fine-art prints of album covers, past and present.

WORCESTER, HEREFORD, AND ENVIRONS

In the arc of towns to the west of Birmingham and the cluster of places around the banks of the River Wye to the south, history and tradition rub up against deepest rural England. The cathedral towns of Worcester and Hereford make great bases from which to soak up the bucolic flavor of the Malvern Hills and Elgar country, or to view the spectacular swing of the Wye at Symond's Yat. En route, there's a taste of Georgian architecture at Bewdley, and reminders of the old industrial Midlands at Dudley.

WORCESTER

27 mi southwest of Birmingham, 118 mi northwest of London.

Worcester (pronounced *wuss*-ter), on the River Severn in the center of Worcestershire, is an ancient cathedral city proud of its history and in particular of its nickname, "the Faithful City," bestowed on the town for steadfast allegiance to the crown during the English Civil War. In that conflict between king and Parliament, two major battles were waged here. The second one, the decisive Battle of Worcester of 1651, resulted in the exile of the future Charles II.

Since the mid-18th century the town's name has become synonymous with fine bone china it once produced; Royal Worcester was purchased by Portmeirion Potteries in 2009. Despite unfortunate modernization in the 1960s, some of medieval Worcester remains. This ancient section forms a convenient and pleasant walking route around the great cathedral.

Southwest of Worcester lie the Malvern Hills, their long, low, purple profiles rising from the surrounding plain. These hills, great for walking, inspired much of the music of Sir Edward Elgar (1857–1934), who composed "Pomp and Circumstance." They also inspired his remark that "there is music in the air, music all around us."

GETTING HERE AND AROUND

Trains from London Paddington (2¼ hours) and Birmingham (1 hour) arrive at the Foregate Street station, half a mile north of the city center. The bus station is close by on the Butts. First buses serve the local area. Worcester is just under three hours by car from London on M4 and then M5; a prettier but slower route is M40 to Oxford and then A44, which skirts the Cotswolds. Take care if you're driving on A44 west of Worcester, as there are frequent, sudden bends in the road.

Worcester itself is easily covered on foot; the city's mainly pedestrianized High Street runs through the center of town, from the cathedral to Foregate Street station.

ESSENTIALS

Bus Contact First (☎ *0871/200–2233* ⊕ *www.firstgroup.com*).

Visitor information Worcester (✉ *The Guildhall, High St.* ☎ *01905/726311* ⊕ *www.visitworcester.com*).

EXPLORING

TOP ATTRACTIONS

Commandery. Occupying a cluster of 15th-century half-timber buildings that later became the headquarters of the Royalist troops during the Battle of Worcester, the Commandery has a large exhibit about the English Civil War. A state-of-the-art audio guide tells the story of the building, and the magnificent, oak-beam Great Hall alone is worth a visit. The building is across the road from Worcester Porcelain Museum,

9

minutes from the cathedral. ⊠*Sidbury* ☎*01905/361821* ⊕*www. worcestercitymuseums.org.uk* ⊠*£5.40* ⊙*Easter–Oct., Mon.–Sat. 10–5, Sun. 1:30–5; Nov.–Easter, Mon.–Thurs. and Sat. 10–5, Sun. 1:30–5.*

★ **Worcester Cathedral.** There are few more quintessentially English sights than that of Worcester Cathedral, its towers overlooking the green expanse of the county cricket ground, and its majestic image reflected in the swift-flowing—and frequently flooding—waters of the River Severn. A cathedral has stood on this site since 680, and much of what remains dates from the 13th and 14th centuries. Notable exceptions are the Norman crypt (built in the 1080s), the largest in England, and the ambulatory, a cloister built around the east end. The most important tomb in the cathedral is that of King John (1167–1216), one of the country's least-admired monarchs, who alienated his barons and subjects through bad administration and heavy taxation and in 1215 was forced to sign the Magna Carta, the great charter of liberty. ■TIP→**Don't miss the beautiful decoration in the vaulted chantry chapel of Prince Arthur, Henry VII's elder son, whose body was brought to Worcester after his death at Ludlow in 1502.** The wealthy endowed chantry chapels to enable priests to celebrate Masses there for the souls of the deceased. ⊠*College Yard at High St.* ☎*01905/732900* ⊕*www.worcestercathedral.co.uk* ⊠*Donations welcome, tours £3* ⊙*Daily 7:30–6, tours Apr.–Oct., Mon.–Sat. 11 and 2:30.*

Worcester Porcelain Museum. The world's largest collection of Worcester porcelain, bone china, and earthenware is displayed here, representing work from the start of manufacturing in 1751 to the present. Tableware, doll-house miniatures, and ornamental birds and animals are characteristically ornate, and the Victorian gallery presents pieces made on the Worcester site. The museum lies south of Worcester Cathedral (follow Severn Street). ⊠*Severn St.* ☎*01905/21247* ⊕*www. worcesterporcelainmuseum.org* ⊠ *£5* ⊙*Easter–Oct., Mon.–Sat. 10–5; Nov.–Easter, Tues.–Sat. 10:30–4.*

WORTH NOTING

Elgar Birthplace Museum. The composer Sir Edward Elgar was born in the village of Lower Broadheath—on B4204, 2 mi west of Worcester—in this tiny brick cottage, now a museum. Set in a peaceful little garden, the house contains personal memorabilia, and the Elgar Centre exhibits photographs, musical scores, and letters. ⊠*Crown East La., Lower Broadheath* ☎*01905/333224* ⊕*www.elgar.org* ⊠*£6* ⊙*Feb.–Dec., daily 11–5; last admission 45 mins before closing.*

Greyfriars. The wood-panel rooms in the black-and-white Greyfriars building, a merchant's house that dates to the 15th century, contain fine period textiles and furniture. The parlor has some rare Georgian hunting wallpaper. ⊠*Friar St.* ☎*01905/23571* ⊕*www.nationaltrust. org.uk* ⊠*£4* ⊙*Mar.–June and Sept.–mid-Dec., Wed.–Sat. 1–5; July and Aug., Wed.–Sun. 1–5.*

Guildhall. Also the location of the tourist information office, the Guildhall, set back behind ornate iron railings, has an 18th-century facade with gilded statues of Queen Anne, Charles I, and Charles II. Note the carving of Cromwell's head pinned up by the ears. In the Assembly

Worcester,
Hereford
and Environs

Room on the second floor, impressive patrician portraits hang under a painted ceiling; you can admire them while having a good-value lunch or tea and buns. ⊠*High St.* ☎*01905/723471* ▣*Free* ☉*Weekdays 8:30–4:30, Sat. 8:30–4.*

Worcester River Cruises. In summer, this company offers 45-minute river cruises daily on a 1926 launch, departing from South Quay. ⊠*22 Britannia Rd.* ☎*01905/611060.*

WHERE TO EAT

£££
MODERN BRITISH
★

✕**Brown's.** A former grain mill is home to this light, airy riverside restaurant serving daily specialties that revolve around varied, well-prepared modern English dishes. You might start with Wye Valley smoked salmon with hot goat cheese, continue with Herefordshire beef fillet, and finish with apple tart, prunes, and Armagnac. Two-course lunches are a good deal. ⊠*Old Cornmill, South Quay* ☎*01905/26263* ▤*AE, MC, V* ☉*No dinner Sun.*

£££
BRASSERIE

✕**Glasshouse Brasserie.** You can watch city life go by through all the glass—that is, if you can divert yourself from the excellent offerings on your plate at this very contemporary and sleek brasserie. Striped blue-and-black banquettes complement the soft gray upholstered chairs and wood floor. Steak tartare, slow-roast pork belly with Worcester apples, and strawberry-and-jam sponge with custard are all winners.

The restaurant is at the southern end of City Walls Road. ⊠*Danesbury House, Sidbury* ☎*01905/611120* ⊟*AE, MC, V* ⊗*Closed Sun.*

££   ✕**King Charles II Restaurant.** A half-timber house in which Charles II hid
CONTINENTAL   after the Battle of Worcester is now a discreet, oak-paneled restaurant
that likes its lace tablecloths and curtains. The cuisine is mainly French
and Italian, but traditional English selections such as beef Wellington,
and fish dishes including Dover sole also appear on the menu. ⊠*29 New St.* ☎*01905/22449* ⊟*AE, MC, V* ⊗*Closed Sun.*

WHERE TO STAY

£   ⬚**Burgage House.** You couldn't stay closer to the cathedral than this
tall, red-brick terraced Georgian house, facing onto a quiet, cobbled
street. An impressive stone staircase winds up to the traditionally furnished, spacious bedrooms, which are kept impeccably fresh and neat.
The cathedral chimes are silenced at night. **Pros:** close to cathedral;
good breakfasts; ground-floor room available **Cons:** no credit cards;
too quiet for some. ⊠*4 College Precincts* ☎*01905/25396* ⊕*www.
burgagehouse.co.uk* ◔*4 rooms* ⬚*In-room: no a/c, no phone. In-hotel:
parking (free)* ⊟*No credit cards* ⦿*BP.*

££   ⬚**Ye Olde Talbot Hotel.** The Olde Talbot was originally a courtroom
belonging to the cathedral, which stands close by. Modern extensions
supplement the 16th-century core of the building. The spacious bedrooms have double-glazed windows and are done in green, blue, and
burgundy tones with patterned fabrics. Be sure to try a cask ale in
the Victorian bar. **Pros:** very central; all-morning breakfasts; power
showers. **Cons:** no private parking; location on main road. ⊠*Friar St.*
☎*01905/235730* ⊕*www.yeoldetalbot.com* ◔*29 rooms* ⬚*In-room:
no a/c, DVD, Wi-Fi. In-hotel: restaurant, room service, bar, laundry
service, parking (paid), no-smoking rooms* ⊟*AE, MC, V* ⦿*BP.*

NIGHTLIFE AND THE ARTS

Huntingdon Hall (⊠*Crowngate* ☎*01905/611427*), a refurbished Methodist chapel founded in 1773, puts on a varied program of music,
interspersed with some theater and dance. The original pews are—
thankfully—provided with cushions.

SHOPPING

★   **Bygones** (⊠*3 College Precincts* ☎*01905/23132*) sells antiques, finely
crafted items, and small gifts in silver, glass, and porcelain. **G. R. Pratley**
(⊠*The Shambles* ☎*01905/22678*) has tables piled high with glassware
and fine china; it's closed Thursday afternoon.

GREAT MALVERN

7 mi south of Worcester.

Great Malvern, off the A449, is a Victorian spa town whose architecture has changed little since the mid-1800s. Great Malvern is known
both as an educational center and as a place for retirement homes. The
town also has a Winter Gardens complex with a theater, cinema, and
gardens. This is a good base for walks in the Malvern Hills.

GETTING HERE AND AROUND

To get here from Worcester will take 20 minutes or so by car. There are also frequent trains and buses run by First (15 minutes by train, 1 hour by bus). On weekends and national holidays from April through August, the Hills Hopper bus gives access to the Malvern Hills.

ESSENTIALS

Bus Contact Malvern Hills Hopper (☎ *01905/765765*).

Visitor Information Great Malvern (✉ *21 Church St.* ☎ *01684/892289* ⊕ *www.malvernhills.gov.uk*).

EXPLORING

The **Priory**, a solidly built early-Norman Benedictine abbey with later Perpendicular elements, dominates the steep streets downtown. The fine glass spans from the 15th century—including a magnificent east window and the vibrantly blue Magnificat window in the north transept—to the evocative Millennium Windows. There's a splendid set of misericords (the elaborately carved undersides of choir seats). ✉ *Church St.* ☎ *01684/561020* ⊕ *www.greatmalvernpriory.org.uk* 🎟 *Free; donations welcome* ⏰ *Daily 9–5.*

During three days in mid-June, the agricultural **Three Counties Show** (☎ *01684/584900* ⊕ *www.threecounties.co.uk*) showcases rare animal breeds, equestrian events, competitions for the best cows, pigs, and sheep, and plenty of food.

WHERE TO STAY

£££–££££ 🏨**Cottage in the Wood.** On shady grounds, this family-run hotel sits high up the side of the Malvern Hills, with splendid views of the countryside. Country-house touches in the three buildings include floral prints and white bedspreads; rooms with a view are equipped with binoculars. The mirrored restaurant, which has the best panorama, serves modern English fare and offers more than 600 wines, among them many local vintages. **Pros:** family run; tremendous views; good food. **Cons:** three separate buildings (umbrellas provided if necessary); steep and narrow approach. ✉ *Holywell Rd.* ☎ *01684/588860* ⊕ *www.cottageinthewood.co.uk* 🛏 *30 rooms* ♿ *In-room: no a/c, Wi-Fi (some). In-hotel: restaurant, bar, some pets allowed, no-smoking rooms* 🍴 *AE, MC, V* ⊙*BP.*

£–££ 🏨**Sidney House.** In addition to having stunning views, this dignified early-19th-century bed-and-breakfast, run by a friendly husband-and-wife team, is near the town center. Rooms, done in pastel hues, are furnished with stripped pine and period pieces. On a clear afternoon you can sit on the terrace and gaze out over the Vale of Evesham to the Cotswolds. **Pros:** great views; easy access to Malvern Hills. **Cons:** main road location, though rooms at rear are quiet. ✉ *40 Worcester Rd.* ☎ *01684/574994* ⊕ *www.sidneyhouse.co.uk* 🛏 *8 rooms* ♿ *In-room: no a/c, no phone. In-hotel: parking (free), some pets allowed, no-smoking rooms* 🍴 *MC, V* ⊙*BP.*

9

ON THE MENU

Outside Birmingham, this area is all rich farming country where, for centuries, the orchards have produced succulent fruit, especially apples and plums. Hereford cider, for example, is popular because it tastes much sweeter than the cider brewed farther south in Devon.

The meat and milk products, which come from the local red-and-white Hereford breed of cattle, are second to none. Cheshire cheese, one of the country's oldest cheeses, is noted for its rich, crumbly texture; blue-veined Shropshire cheese is more unusual and worth trying. In May the sheltered Vale of Evesham is the center for the asparagus crop. Ludlow produces a formidable assortment of local meat products and is noted for its sausages.

Something else to try is Malvern spring water. "The Malvern water," said Dr. John Wall in 1756, "is famous for containing nothing at all." The famously pure water is still bottled in the town and exported worldwide; it is said that the Queen never travels without it.

NIGHTLIFE AND THE ARTS

Malvern has links with Sir Edward Elgar as well as with George Bernard Shaw, who premiered many of his plays here. The **Autumn in Malvern Festival** (☎01684/892277 or 01684/892289 ⊕*www.malvernfestival. co.uk*) takes place on weekends throughout October and concentrates on classical music, including Elgar, as well as literary events.

LEDBURY

10 mi southwest of Great Malvern on A449.

Among the black-and-white half-timber buildings that make up the market town of Ledbury, take special note of two late-16th-century ones: the Feathers Hotel and the Talbot Inn. The cobbled Church Lane, almost hidden behind the 17th-century market house, is crowded with medieval half-timber buildings and leads to St. Michael's Church.

ESSENTIALS

Visitor Information Ledbury (✉ *The Master's House, St. Katherine's* ☎ *01531/636147* ⊕ *www.visitherefordshire.co.uk*).

EXPLORING

Ledbury Heritage Centre, in the old grammar school, traces the history of the building, town, railroad, and canal, mostly through local photographic postcards. It also has displays on two literary celebrities linked to the area, John Masefield and Elizabeth Barrett Browning. ✉*Church La.* ☎*01531/636147* 🎫*Free* ☉*Easter–Oct., daily 10–4.*

★ Completed in 1820, **Eastnor Castle,** a turreted, stone, Norman Revival extravaganza on the eastern outskirts of Ledbury, includes some magnificent, ornate, neo-Gothic salons designed by 19th-century architect Augustus Pugin. The Hervey-Bathurst family has restored other grand rooms, full of tapestries, gilt-framed paintings, Regency chandeliers, and Auntie's old armchairs and enormous sofas, making Eastnor a must-see for lovers of English interior decoration. In the Little Library, look out for the rare game of Life Pool, originally played on the billiards table. Eastnor hosts the innovative Big Chill arts festival each August. ⊠*A438* ☎*01531/633160* ⊕*www.eastnorcastle.com* ✉*House and grounds £8.50; grounds only, £5.50* ☉*Mid-July and Aug., Sun.–Thurs. 11–4:30; June and Sept., Sun. and national holiday Mon. 11–4:30; last admission 30 mins before closing.*

Just outside the village of Much Marcle, 4 mi southwest of Ledbury, lies the beautiful 17th-century manor of **Hellens,** still in authentic condition. Part of the house dates from the 13th century and contains fine old-master paintings. The gloom and dust are part of the experience of visiting; candles illuminate the house, and central heating has been scorned. Take a walk in the gardens and, if you have time, also check out the 13th-century village church. ⊠*½ mi east of A449, off B4024 and Monks Walk, Much Marcle* ☎*01531/660504* ⊕*www.hellensmanor.com* ✉*£5* ☉*Apr.–Sept., Wed., Thurs., Sun., and national holiday Mon. 2–5; tours at 2, 3, and 4.*

> ## WALKS AND DRIVES IN THE MALVERNS
>
> The Malvern Hills have climbs and walks of varying length and difficulty; the seasonal Malvern Hills Hopper bus gives useful access on weekends April through August. The best places to start are Great Malvern and Ledbury. The Elgar Route, a drive, extends for 45 mi and touches on Malvern and Worcester as it threads through the Malverns. The hilltop vistas across the countryside are spectacular—isolated hills rise up from the fairly flat plain. The area around Ross-on-Wye has ideal walks with scenic river views. For information on hiking the Malverns, contact the Malvern or Ross-on-Wye tourist office.

WHERE TO STAY

££££–££££ 🏨 **Feathers Hotel.** You can't miss the striking black-and-white facade of this central hostelry, which dates from the 16th century. Its interior has a satisfyingly antique flavor, with creaking staircases and ancient floorboards, and some rooms have four-posters. The hop-bedecked Fuggles Brasserie (named after a variety of hop) and the more formal Quills restaurant serve plenty of fresh fish, as well as lighter meals. **Pros:** guest rooms retain wooden beams and period feel; indoor heated pool. **Cons:** some guest rooms on the small side; can be creaky; no elevator. ⊠*High St.* ☎*01531/635266* ⊕*www.feathers-ledbury.co.uk* ➫*19 rooms* ⚒*In-room: no a/c, Wi-Fi. In-hotel: 2 restaurants, bar, pool, gym, some pets allowed, no-smoking rooms* ⊟*AE, MC, V* ⛙*BP.*

ROSS-ON-WYE

10 mi southwest of Ledbury.

Perched high above the River Wye in the Malvern Hills, Ross-on-Wye seems oblivious to modern-day intrusions and remains at heart a small market town. Its steep streets come alive on Thursday and Saturday—market days—but they're always a happy hunting ground for antiques. Nearby towns have sights from a castle to a scenic overlook on the river.

GETTING HERE AND AROUND

A449 connects Ross-on-Wye with Great Malvern and Ledbury, and M50 leads directly to Ross from Junction 8 of M5. Stagecoach buses run from Ledbury (30 minutes) and have frequent connections with Hereford (50 minutes) and Gloucester (45 minutes).

ESSENTIALS

Bus Contact Stagecoach (☎0871/200–2233 ⊕ www.stagecoachbus.com).

Visitor Information Ross-on-Wye (✉ Swan House, Edde Cross St. ☎01989/562768 ⊕ www.visitherefordshire.co.uk).

EXPLORING

Looming dramatically over the River Wye at Kerne Bridge, **Goodrich Castle** from the south looks like a fortress from the Rhineland amid the green fields; you quickly see its grimmer face from the battlements on its north side. Dating from the late 12th century, the red sandstone castle is surrounded by a deep moat carved out of solid rock, from which its walls appear to soar upward. Built to repel Welsh raiders, it was destroyed in the 17th century during the Civil War. The town of Goodrich is 3 mi south of Ross-on-Wye on B4234. ✉ Off A40, Goodrich ☎01600/890538 ⊕ www.english-heritage.org.uk ✍£5.20, parking charge ☉ Mar., daily 10–5; Apr.–June, daily 10–5; July and Aug., daily 10–6; Sept. and Oct., daily 10–5; Nov.–Feb., Wed.–Sun. 10–4.

Six miles south of Ross-on-Wye, outside the village of **Symond's Yat** ("gate"), the 473-foot-high Yat Rock commands superb views of the River Wye as it winds through a narrow gorge and swings around in a great 5-mi loop. It's best approached from the south on B4432, from which it's a short walk. A small ferry takes passengers across the river (80p).

SPORTS AND THE OUTDOORS

Symond's Yat Canoe Hire hires out canoes and kayaks by the hour or for full days or more; it's a popular way to experience the River Wye. ✉ The Leisure Park, Symonds Yat West, ☎01600/891069 ⊕ www. canoehire.com.

WHERE TO STAY

££–£££   ⌸ **Chase Hotel.** The public areas in this well-renovated Georgian-style country-house hotel on 11 acres of grounds retain some original elements. Bedrooms in the main house are simply and comfortably furnished in pastels and print fabrics, and those in the newer wing are more modern. **Pros:** peaceful grounds; country-house appeal. **Cons:** guest rooms furnished in traditional, conventional style. ✉ Gloucester Rd. ☎01989/763161 ⊕ www.chasehotel.co.uk ↩36 rooms ♿ In-room: no a/c, Wi-Fi. In-hotel: restaurant, room service, bar, gym, no-smoking rooms ☰ AE, DC, MC, V ⏁◖BP.

HEREFORD

23 mi southwest of Worcester, 56 mi southwest of Birmingham, 54 mi northeast of Cardiff.

A busy country town, Hereford is the center of a wealthy agricultural area known for its cider, fruit, and cattle—the white-faced Hereford breed has spread across the world. It's also an important cathedral city, and the massive Norman building towers proudly over the River Wye. Before 1066 Hereford was the capital of the Anglo-Saxon kingdom of Mercia and, earlier still, the site of Roman, Celtic, and Iron Age settlements. Today people come primarily to see the cathedral but quickly discover the charms of a town that has changed slowly but unobtrusively with the passing centuries.

GETTING HERE AND AROUND

The bus and train stations are about half a mile northeast of the center. A train from Birmingham will take around 1¾ hours. Traveling by car, take M50 at junction 8 of M5, then A417 and A438 to Hereford. First buses cover the local area, and the city is compact enough to cover on foot.

ESSENTIALS

Visitor Information Hereford (⊠ *1 King St.* ☏ *01432/268430* ⊕ *www. visitherefordshire.co.uk*).

EXPLORING

Built of local red sandstone with a large central tower, **Hereford Cathedral** retains some fine 11th-century Norman carvings but suffered considerable "restoration" in the 19th century. Inside, its greatest glories include a 12th-century chair, to the left of the high altar, one of the earliest pieces of furniture in the country and reputedly used by King Stephen, and some fine misericords. ⊠ *Cathedral Close* ☏ *01432/374200* ⊕ *www. herefordcathedral.org* ✉ *Suggested donation £5, cathedral tours free, garden tours £5* ⊙ *Mon.–Sat. 9:15–5:30, Sun. 8–3:30; cathedral tours Apr.–Oct., Mon.–Sat. 11 and 2, garden tours Apr.–Oct., Wed. and Sat. at 3.*

★ The **Mappa Mundi and Chained Library Exhibition**, an extraordinary double attraction, includes the more than 20-square-foot parchment Mappa Mundi. Hereford's own picture of the medieval world shows the Earth as flat, with Jerusalem at its center. It's thought that the map was originally the central section of an altarpiece dating from 1290. The chained library contains some 1,500 books, among them an 8th-century copy of the Four Gospels. Chained libraries, in which books were attached to cupboards to discourage theft, are extremely rare: they date from medieval times, when books were as precious as gold. ⊠ *Cathedral Close* ☏ *01432/374219* ⊕ *www.herefordcathedral.org* ✉ *£4.50* ⊙ *Apr.–late May, Sept., and Oct., Mon.–Sat. 10–5; late May–Aug., Mon.–Sat. 10–5, Sun. 11–4; Nov., Dec., Feb., and Mar., Mon.–Sat. 10–4; last admission 30 mins before closing.*

The half-timber **Old House** is a fine example of domestic Jacobean architecture, furnished in 17th-century style on three floors. You can see a kitchen, dining hall, parlor, and bedrooms. Look for the dog's door between the nursery and master bedroom. ⊠*High Town* ☎*01432/260694* ☒*Free* ⊘*Apr.–Sept., Tues.–Sat. 10–5, Sun. and national holidays Mon. 10–4; Oct.–Mar., Tues.–Sat. 10–5.*

The 13th-century **All Saints Church**, on the west side of High Town, contains superb canopied choir stalls and misericords, as well as an unusual Queen Anne reredos in the south chapel. It also has an excellent coffee bar and restaurant. ⊠*High St.* ☎*01432/370414.*

A farm cider house and a cooper's workshop have been re-created at the **Cider Museum,** where you can tour ancient cider cellars with huge oak vats. Cider brandy (applejack) is made here, and the museum sells its own brand, along with other cider items. ⊠*Pomona Pl. at Whitecross Rd.* ☎*01432/354207* ⊕*www.cidermuseum.co.uk* ☒*£3.50* ⊘*Apr.–Oct., Tues.–Sat. and national holidays Mon. 10–5; Nov.–Mar., Tues.–Sat. 11–3; last admission 1 hr before closing.*

OFF THE BEATEN PATH

Kilpeck church. One of Britain's best-preserved Norman churches, built of red sandstone in the mid-12th century, is lavishly decorated inside and out with sculpture exceptional for a country church. The carvings depict all manner of subjects, including animals. Much of the tiny hamlet is protected as a Scheduled Ancient Monument. ⊠*Off A465, 7 mi southwest of Hereford, Kilpeck* ☎*01981/570315* ☒*Donations accepted* ⊘*Daily 9–dusk.*

WHERE TO EAT AND STAY

£
VEGETARIAN
★

✕**Café @ All Saints.** Open 8 to 5 and a good spot for lunch, the west end and gallery of this community-minded church are given over to a coffee bar and restaurant, granting a rare opportunity to indulge body and spirit at one sitting. The imaginative vegetarian menu is worth every penny, but for something lighter, try the tasty sandwiches (roast mushroom and tofu, for example), salads, cakes, and local ice creams. Or come for breakfast or coffee—scrambled eggs and smoked salmon is one option. ⊠*High St.* ☎*01432/370415* ☰*MC, V* ⊘*Closed Sun. No dinner.*

££££

▦**Castle House.** These conjoined Georgian villas next to the moat (all that remains of Hereford Castle) offer luxury, a warm welcome, and good food. Delicate plasterwork graces the public areas. Spacious guest rooms vary in style, with yellow, cream, and red the preferred colors; each bedroom contains a decanter of cider brandy. The excellent restaurant relies on locally sourced and regional fare, such as Hereford beef and Gloucester Old Spot pork; the bistro, with terrace, is open all day for light refreshment. **Pros:** close to cathedral; quiet; lovely garden. **Cons:** not cheap; some report slow service. ⊠*Castle St.* ☎*01432/356321* ⊕*www.castlehse.co.uk* ⇱*10 suites, 5 rooms* ♿*In-room: no a/c, safe, refrigerator, Internet. In-hotel: restaurant, room service, bar, Wi-Fi, parking (free), some pets allowed, no-smoking rooms* ☰*AE, MC, V* ⏐◎⏐*BP.*

£ ⊞ **Sink Green Farm.** Benefits of staying on this informal working farm, which dates back to the 16th century, include views of the Wye Valley and use of the barbecue and outdoor hot tub in a summerhouse. Guest rooms in the stone farmhouse are prettily furnished with period pieces, and breakfasts, including local bacon and eggs, are taken at the communal dining table. The location is 3 mi southeast of the city. **Pros:** friendly and casual; garden, river walks. **Cons:** car needed; not in town. ⊠*B4399, Rotherwas* ☎*01432/870223* ⊕*www.sinkgreenfarm.co.uk* ☞*4 rooms* ⌂*In-room: no a/c, no phone, Wi-Fi. In-hotel: parking (free), some pets allowed, no-smoking rooms* ⊟*No credit cards* ♦⦶*BP.*

SHOPPING

Hereford has a market for livestock on Wednesday and for general retail on Saturday. The stores in **Capuchin Yard** (⊠*Off 29 Church St.*) display crafts, including handmade shoes and knitwear; other outlets sell haberdashery and ceramics.

BEWDLEY

14 mi north of Worcester, 3 mi west of Kidderminster.

In Bewdley, an exceptionally attractive Severn Valley town, tall, narrow-front Georgian buildings cluster around the river bridge. You can take a scenic train or boat ride from here to appreciate the rural landscape.

ESSENTIALS

Visitor Information Bewdley (⊠*Load St.* ☎*01299/404740* ⊕*www.visit-worcestershire.org).*

EXPLORING

The 18th-century butchers' market, the Shambles, now holds **Bewdley Museum,** which documents local history, trades, and crafts with exhibits and demonstrations of rope making and clay-pipe making. Craftspeople working in wood, ceramics, stained glass, and textiles occupy the nearby workshops. ⊠*Load St.* ☎*01299/403573* ☒*Free* ⊗*Easter–Sept., daily 10–4:30; Oct., daily 11–4.*

⟳ Bewdley is the southern terminus of the **Severn Valley Railway,** a steam railroad running 16 mi north along the river to Bridgnorth, a lovely market town on a ridge above the Severn. The train stops at a handful of sleepy stations where time has apparently stood still since the age of steam. You can get off at any of these stations, picnic by the river, and walk to the next station to get a train back. Perching on a high sandstone ridge on the banks of the Severn, Bridgnorth has two distinct parts, High Town and Low Town, connected by a winding road, flights of steep steps, and—best of all—a cliff railroad. Even the tower of the Norman castle seems to suffer from vertigo, having a 17-degree list. ⊠*Railway Station* ☎*01299/403816* ⊕*www.svr.co.uk* ☒*£14 round-trip* ⊗*Apr.–Sept., trains run daily; Oct.–Mar., weekends only.*

The **Stourport Steamer Co.** has short river trips, or you can take longer journeys as far as Worcester on Wednesday from the last week in July through August. Stourport is a few miles south of Bewdley. ⊠*Riverside Walk, Stourport* ☎*01299/871177 or 0786/046-8792* ⊕*www.*

9

riverboathire.co.uk ☎£4–£12 ⊘ *Mar.–mid-July and Sept., Sun.; mid-July–Aug., daily.*

DUDLEY

14 mi northeast of Bewdley, 8 mi west of central Birmingham.

It was in Dudley, in the 17th century, that coal was first used for smelting iron. The town subsequently became known as the capital of the Black Country, a term that arose from the air pollution caused by ironworks foundries and coal mining.

ESSENTIALS

Visitor Information Black Country Tourism (☎08458/151516 ⊕*www.blackcountrytourism.co.uk).*

EXPLORING

☼ The **Black Country Living Museum,** established to interpret the area's indus-
★ trial heritage, consists of an entire village made up of disused buildings from around the region. Among the exhibits on 26 acres are a chain maker's house and workshop that demonstrates the craft; a trap-works that made animal traps; his-and-hers hardware stores; a druggist and general store, where costumed women describe life in a poor industrial community in the 19th century; a Methodist chapel; and a coal mine and wharf. The brick-and-terra-cotta Rolfe Street Baths building, brought here from Smethwick, gives an overview of the Black Country. You can also sit on a hard bench and watch Charlie Chaplin in the 1920s cinema, or ride on a barge (extra charge) through a tunnel to experience the canal travel of yesteryear. For sustenance the 1930s-era Fried Fish Shop serves fish-and-chips cooked in beef drippings, and there are two cafés and the Bottle & Glass pub for ales and drinks. ◼TIP→ **To avoid the numerous school parties, visit on the weekend or during school vacations.** The museum, 3 mi from the M5, is best reached by car. Leave M5 at Junction 2 by A4123, and then take A4037 at Tipton. Trains from Birmingham stop at Tipton; the museum is a mile away by bus. ✉ *Tipton Rd.* ☎*0121/557–9643* ⊕*www.bclm.co.uk* ☎*£12.95, barge trip £4.95, parking £1* ⊘ *Mar.–Oct., daily 10–5; Nov.–Feb., Wed.–Sun. 10–4.*

SHREWSBURY TO CHESTER

Rural Shropshire, one of the least populated English counties, is far removed from most people's preconceptions of the industrial Midlands. Within its spread are towns long famed for their beauty, such as Bridgnorth and Ludlow. Two important cities of the Welsh Border region, Shrewsbury and Chester, are both renowned for their medieval heritage and their wealth of half-timber buildings. The 6-mi stretch of the Ironbridge Gorge, however, gives you the chance to experience the cradle of the Industrial Revolution with none of the reeking smoke that gave this region west of Birmingham its name—the Black Country—during the mid-19th century. Now taken over by the Ironbridge Gorge Museum Trust, the bridge, the first in the world to be built of iron and opened in 1781, is the centerpiece of this vast museum complex.

SHREWSBURY

47 mi northwest of Dudley, 55 mi north of Hereford, 46 mi south of Chester, 48 mi northwest of Birmingham.

One of England's most important medieval towns, Shrewsbury (usually pronounced *shrose*-bury), the county seat of Shropshire, lies within a great horseshoe loop of the Severn. It has numerous 16th-century half-timber buildings—many built by well-to-do wool merchants—plus elegant ones from later periods. Today the town retains a romantic air (indeed, there are many bridal shops, along with churches), and it can be a lovely experience to stroll the Shrewsbury "shuts." These narrow alleys overhung with timbered gables lead off the central market square, which was designed to be closed off at night to protect local residents. You can also relax in Quarry Park on the river.

A good starting point for exploring the city is the small square between Fish Street and Butcher Row. These streets are little changed since medieval times, when some of them took their names from the principal trades carried on there, but Peacock Alley, Gullet Passage, and Grope Lane clearly got their names from somewhere else.

GETTING HERE AND AROUND

The train station is at the neck of the river that loops the center, a little farther out than the bus station on Raven Meadows. A direct train service runs here from Hereford (50 minutes) and Birmingham (1 hour). If you're coming from London by car, take M40 and M42 north, then M6 and M54, which becomes A5 to Shrewsbury; it's 150 mi. The streets are full of twists, but it's small enough not to get lost. Walking tours of Shrewsbury depart daily from the tourist office at 2:30 from May through September and on Saturday the rest of the year (£3.50).

ESSENTIALS

Visitor Information Shrewsbury (⊠ *Rowley's House, Barker St.* ☎ *01743/ 281200* ⊕ *www.visitshrewsbury.com*).

EXPLORING

TOP ATTRACTIONS

Attingham Park. Built in 1785 by George Steuart (architect of the church of St. Chad in Shrewsbury) for the first Lord Berwick, this elegant stone mansion has a three-story portico, with a pediment carried on four tall columns. The building overlooks a sweep of parkland, including a deer park landscaped by Humphrey Repton (1752–1818), and there are walks by the river and in the deer park. Inside the house are painted ceilings and delicate plasterwork, a fine picture gallery designed by John Nash (1752–1835), and 19th-century Neapolitan furniture. Attingham Park is 4 mi southeast of Shrewsbury. ⊠ *B4380, off A5, Atcham* ☎ *01743/708162* ⊕ *www.nationaltrust.org.uk* ☎ *£7.63, park and grounds only, £3.80* ☉ *House early Mar., weekends 1–4; mid-Mar.– Oct., Thurs.–Tues. 1–5:30, national holiday Mon. 11–5:30; last admission 1 hr before closing. Park and grounds mid-Feb.–Oct., daily 9–6; Nov.–mid-Feb., daily 9–5.*

❷ St. Chad. On a hilltop west of the town center, this church designed by George Steuart, the architect of Attingham Park, is one of England's

Shrewsbury

| 0 | 440 yards |
| 0 | 400 meters |

KEY

🛈 *Tourist information*

most original ecclesiastical buildings. Completed in 1792, the round Georgian church is surmounted by a tower that is in turn square, octagonal, and circular—and finally topped by a dome. When being built, it provoked riots among townsfolk averse to its radical style. The interior has a fine Venetian east window and a brass Arts and Crafts pulpit. ✉ *St. Chad's Terr.* ☎ *01743/365478* 🎫 *Free* 🕐 *Apr.–Oct., daily 8–5; Nov.–Mar., daily 8–1.*

❺ **Shrewsbury Abbey.** Now unbecomingly surrounded by busy roads, the abbey was founded in 1083 and later became a powerful Benedictine monastery. The abbey church has survived many vicissitudes and retains a 14th-century west window above a Norman doorway. The abbey figures in the Brother Cadfael whodunits by Ellis Peters; the novels provide an excellent idea of local life in the Middle Ages. To reach the abbey from the center, cross the river by the English Bridge. ✉ *Abbey Church, Abbey Foregate* ☎ *01743/232723* 🌐 *www.shrewsburyabbey. com* 🎫 *Donations welcome* 🕐 *Mon.–Sat. 10:30–3, Sun. 9:30–2:30.*

❹ **Shrewsbury Castle.** Guarding the northern approaches to the town, the castle rises over the River Severn at the bottom of Pride Hill. Originally Norman, it was dismantled during the Civil War and later rebuilt by Thomas Telford, the Scottish engineer who designed many notable buildings and bridges in the early 19th century. The castle holds the

Shropshire Regimental Museum, containing enough social history to engage the non–military buff. ■TIP→ The numerous benches in the gardens are good for a quiet sit-down. ✉ *Shrewsbury Castle, Castle Gates* ☎ *01743/358516* ⊕ *www. shrewsburymuseums.com* 🖾 *£2.50* ⊙ *Mid-Feb.–May and mid-Sept.– Dec., Tues.–Sat. and national holi-day Mon. 10:30–4; June–mid-Sept., Tues.–Sun. and bank holiday Mon. 10:30–5. Castle grounds Mon.–Sat. 9–5, Sun. 10:30–5.*

WORTH NOTING

❶ Ireland's Mansion. The cluster of restored half-timber buildings that link Fish Street with Market Square is known as Bear Steps; this mansion, built in 1575 with elaborate Jacobean timbering and richly decorated with quatrefoils, is the most notable. It's not open to the public.

❸ Shrewsbury Museum and Art Gallery. The museum holds Shropshire pottery and ceramics, as well as items of local history and Roman finds such as a unique silver mirror from nearby Wroxeter. A reconstructed 17th-century paneled bedroom showcases an elaborate four-poster bed (1593), enlivened with richly embroidered silk and velvet hangings. The Darwin Exhibition explores the life of Shrewsbury's famous son, Charles Darwin. ✉ *Barker St.* ☎ *01743/361196 or 01743/281205* ⊕ *www.shrewsburymuseums.com* 🖾 *Free* ⊙ *May–Sept., Mon.–Sat. 10–5, Sun. 10–4; Oct.–Apr., Mon.–Sat. 10–4.*

WHERE TO EAT

££
BRITISH
✕ **The Armoury.** This smartly converted warehouse, whose arched windows overlook the river, is well stocked with books, prints, and curiosities, as well as good food, wines, and real ales. Among the appetizers are leek-and-Stilton quiche. Braised lamb shoulder is a popular main course, and you can try bread-and-butter pudding with apricot sauce for dessert. Appetizing sandwiches—a lamb-and-yogurt tortilla, for example—are an alternative at lunchtime. ✉ *Victoria Quay* ☎ *01743/340525* ▱ *AE, MC, V.*

£££
BRITISH
✕ **Draper's Hall.** The dark-wood paneling, antique furniture, and warm, intimate lighting of this 16th-century hall make it a distinctive dining spot for up-to-date English cuisine. You might try the crispy-roasted duck with juniper-scented jus; leave room for desserts such as chocolate fondant with homemade mint ice cream. There are plenty of cheeses and salads, as well as good fish and vegetarian choices; special diets are accommodated. Another option is the lighter brasserie menu. ✉ *10 St. Mary's Pl.* ☎ *01743/344679* ▱ *AE, MC, V* ⊙ *No dinner Sun.*

££
MODERN BRITISH
✕ **Mad Jack's.** Whether you eat in the sleek, dark-wood restaurant or the elegant foliage-filled courtyard, you'll be tucking into good local and seasonal produce. Look out for the rare-breed Shropshire steak and, in winter, local venison with Shropshire blue cheese. It's a good spot for plump sandwiches at lunchtime, or afternoon tea or cocktails

9

later in the day. Four contemporary rooms are available should you wish to linger longer. ⊠ *15 St. Mary's St.* ☏*01743/358870* ▭*MC, V* ☾*No dinner Sun.*

WHERE TO STAY

££–£££ ⛨**Albright Hussey Hotel.** Lovely gardens surround this Tudor manor house, originally the home of the Hussey family, which dates back to 1524 and combines black-and-white half-timbering with a later (1560) redbrick-and-stone extension. Beams, oak paneling, four-poster beds, and antiques enhance rooms in the original building, for which you should book well ahead; those in the extension are plainer. The hotel is 2½ mi north of Shrewsbury on A5228. **Pros:** friendly service; beautiful grounds. **Cons:** popular venue for weddings; books up for weekends; rooms in extension less attractive. ⊠*Ellesmere Rd.* ☏*01939/290571* ⊕*www.albrighthussey.co.uk* ⇆*22 rooms, 4 suites* ⌂*In-room: no a/c, Wi-Fi. In-hotel: restaurant, room service, bar, laundry service, parking (free), some pets allowed, no-smoking rooms* ▭*AE, DC, MC, V* ☉❘*BP.*

££ ⛨**The Lion Hotel.** Parts of this once-renowned coaching inn in the heart of town date to the 14th century; today the hotel envelops you in the 17th-century-style luxury for which it became famous. Rooms are small and traditionally furnished, but the glorious lounge, with its high ceiling, oil paintings, and carved-stone fireplace, sets the Lion apart. Add to this the magnificent Adam Ballroom, and you can see the appeal for former guests such as Charles Dickens, Benjamin Disraeli, and Paganini. **Pros:** historic appeal; good breakfasts. **Cons:** prone to wedding parties on weekends; smallish rooms. ⊠*Wyle Cop* ☏*01743/353107* ⊕*www.thelionhotelshrewsbury.co.uk* ⇆*59 rooms* ⌂*In-room: no a/c. In-hotel: restaurant, room service, bar, laundry service, Wi-Fi, no-smoking rooms* ▭*AE, MC, V* ☉❘*BP.*

£ ⛨**Sandford House Hotel.** The Richards family runs this small Georgian hotel close to the river and the town center. Beautiful original decorative plasterwork is still in evidence; modern pine furnishes the bedrooms. Room 5 is seven-sided, with a beautiful molded ceiling, and there are eight modern rooms in the garden lodge. **Pros:** central location; some rooms for people with disabilities; nice garden. **Cons:** some bedrooms face busy road; no parking. ⊠*St. Julian Friars* ☏*01743/343829* ⊕*www.sandfordhouse.co.uk* ⇆*20 rooms* ⌂*In-room: no a/c, no phone, Wi-Fi. In-hotel: Wi-Fi, some pets allowed, no-smoking rooms* ▭*AE, MC, V* ☉❘*BP.*

NIGHTLIFE AND THE ARTS

The brand-new **Theatre Severn** (⊠*Frankwell Quay* ☏*01743/281281*) covers all the performance arts: music, both classical and popular; dance; and drama.

SHOPPING

The **Parade** (⊠*St. Mary's Pl.* ☏*01743/343178*), just behind St. Mary's church, is a shopping center created from the neoclassical former Royal Infirmary, built in 1830. One of the most appealing malls in England, it has 25 attractive boutiques, a coffee shop, and a river terrace.

EN
ROUTE

If you head south of Shrewsbury on B4380 for around 5 mi, you can see, rising on the left, the **Wrekin,** a strange, wooded, conical, extinct volcano that is 1,335 feet high. The walk to the summit, which has panoramic views, is about 5 mi. A few miles farther on, you enter the wooded gorge of the River Severn.

MUCH WENLOCK

12 mi southeast of Shrewsbury.

Much Wenlock, a town on A458, is full of half-timber buildings, including a 16th-century guildhall. Nearby are popular places to walk; you can ask the tourist office for information.

GETTING HERE AND AROUND
The town is a half hour by car from Shrewsbury on A458, or you can take the Arriva bus service that runs hourly (35 minutes).

ESSENTIALS
Bus Contact Arriva (☎ *0871/200–2233* ⊕ *www.arrivabusbus.co.uk*).

Visitor Information Much Wenlock (⊠ *The Museum, High St.* ☎ *01952/ 727679* ⊕ *www.muchwenlockguide.info*).

EXPLORING
The romantic ruins of Norman **Wenlock Priory,** with their elaborate decoration, are in a topiary garden. It's an appealing combination. ⊠ *High St.* ☎ *01952/727466* ⊕ *www.english-heritage.org.uk* 🎫 *£3.50* ⊙ *Late Mar.–Apr., Sept., and Oct., Wed.–Sun. and national holiday Mon. 10–5; May–Aug., daily 10–5; Nov.–Feb., Thurs.–Sun. 10–4.*

SPORTS AND THE OUTDOORS
The high escarpment of **Wenlock Edge** runs southwest from Much Wenlock and provides a splendid view. This is hiking country, and if a healthful walk sounds inviting, turn off B4371 through Church Stretton into Cardingmill Valley, or to the wide heather uplands on top of Long Mynd. You can park and set off on foot.

9

IRONBRIDGE GORGE

15 mi east of Shrewsbury, 28 mi northwest of Birmingham.

Ironbridge Gorge is the name given to a group of villages south of Telford that were crucial in ushering in the Industrial Revolution. The Shropshire coalfields were of enormous importance to the development of the coke-smelting process, which helped make producing anything in iron much easier.

ESSENTIALS
Visitor Information Ironbridge Visitor Information (⊠ *The Toll House* ☎ *01952/884391* ⊕ *www.ironbridge.org.uk*).

EXPLORING
The 10 component sections of the **Ironbridge Gorge Museum,** spread over 6 square mi, preserve and interpret the area's fascinating industrial history. ■ TIP➜ Allow at least a full day to appreciate all the major sights, and perhaps to take a stroll around the famous iron bridge or hunt for Coalport

Shrewsbury to Chester

0 _____ 10 miles

0 _____ 15 km

china in the stores clustered near it. If you're without a vehicle, visit on a weekend or national holiday (April through October), when a shuttle bus takes you between sites. The best starting point is the **Museum of the Gorge,** which has a good selection of literature and an audiovisual show on the gorge's history. In nearby Coalbrookdale, the **Museum of Iron** explains the production of iron and steel. You can see the blast furnace built by Abraham Darby, who developed the original coke process in 1709. Adjacent to this, the **Enginuity** exhibition is a hands-on, feet-on, interactive exploration of engineering; it's good for kids. From here, drive the few miles along the river until the arches of the **Iron Bridge** come into view. Designed by T. F. Pritchard, smelted by Darby, and erected between 1777 and 1779, this graceful arch spanning the River Severn can best be seen—and photographed or painted—from the towpath, a riverside walk edged with wildflowers and shrubs. The tollhouse on the far side houses an exhibition on the bridge's history and restoration.

A mile farther along the river is the **Jackfield Tile Museum,** a repository of decorative tiles from the 19th and 20th centuries. Another half mile brings you to the **Coalport China Museum.** Exhibits show some of the factory's most beautiful wares, and craftspeople give demonstrations; visit the restrooms for the unique communal washbasins.

Above Coalport is **Blists Hill Victorian Town,** where you can see old mines, furnaces, and a wrought-iron works. But the main draw is the re-creation of the "town" itself, with its doctor's office, bakery, grocer's, candle maker's, sawmill, printing shop, and candy store. At the entrance you can change some money for specially minted pennies and make purchases from the shops. Shopkeepers, the bank manager, and the doctor's wife are on hand to give you advice. Craft demonstrations are scheduled in summer. If you don't fancy the refreshments at the Fried Fish shop, drop into the **New Inn** pub (in Blists Hill) for a traditional ale or ginger beer, and join in the sing-along around the piano at 1 and 3:30 (3 in winter), or tuck into a steak-and-kidney pudding from the butcher's next door. ⊠ *B4380, Ironbridge, Telford* ☎ *01952/884391* ⊕ *www.ironbridge.org.uk* ⊠ *Ticket to all sights £19.95; parking £1* ⊙ *Daily 10–5; Blists Hill Apr.–Oct., daily 10–5; Nov.–Mar., daily 10–4.*

WHERE TO EAT AND STAY

££££
MODERN BRITISH
✗ **Restaurant Severn.** This discreet restaurant, set back from the main road in the center of Ironbridge, delivers fine quality with care and attention. Fixed-price menus (around £25 for dinner) of up-to-date English fare might feature wild mushroom soufflé with Madeira sauce and crispy leeks, or duckling with orange sauce and caramelized apricots; pear-and-almond tart rounds off the meal well. The warm yellow walls cast a glow on elegant surroundings. ⊠ *33 High St., Ironbridge* ☎ *01952/432233* ⊟ *AE, MC, V* ⊙ *Closed Mon. and Tues. No dinner Sun.; no lunch Wed.–Sat.*

££
🏨 **Hundred House Hotel.** The low beams, stained glass, wood paneling, flowers and herbs, and patchwork cushions that greet you as you enter this Georgian inn set the tone for the whimsical guest rooms. Feel thoroughly cocooned by the antique beds, floral quilts, and lavender-scented sheets, and take a lulling sway on a velvet swing (many rooms have one). The excellent restaurant uses herbs and vegetables from the well-tended gardens. It's 3 mi from both Ironbridge and Bridgnorth. **Pros:** cozy and full of nooks and corners; good food. **Cons:** not for those who favor the plain and simple. ⊠ *A442, Norton* ☎ *01952/730353* ⊕ *www.hundredhouse.co.uk* 🛏 *10 rooms* ⊘ *In-room: no a/c, Wi-Fi. In-hotel: restaurant, bar, some pets allowed* ⊟ *MC, V* ⊙ *BP.*

££
★
🏨 **Library House.** At one point the village's library, this small guesthouse on the hillside near the Ironbridge museums (and only a few steps from the bridge itself) has kept its attractive Victorian style while allowing for modern-day luxuries—a DVD library, for instance. Rooms are furnished with elegance, and service is warm without being obtrusive. **Pros:** welcoming hosts; close to Iron Bridge; free parking-lot passes for the town. **Cons:** not for families with young children. ⊠ *11 Severn Bank, Telford* ☎ *01952/432299* ⊕ *www.libraryhouse.com* 🛏 *3 rooms* ⊘ *In-room: no a/c, no phone, DVD, Wi-Fi. In-hotel: bar, no kids under 12, no-smoking rooms* ⊟ *MC, V* ⊙ *BP.*

£
🏨 **Severn Trow.** This whitewashed 17th-century house, formerly known as the Boatman's Brothel (a trow is a type of boat), is bang on the river, and a step away from the Jackfield Tile Museum. Low-beamed rooms showcase Jackfield tiles and are stuffed with antique furniture and pictures. **Pros:** peaceful; intimate; delicious breakfasts. **Cons:** no

9

family rooms; difficult to reach without a car. ✉ *Church Rd., Jackfield* ☎ *01952/883551* ⊕ *www.severntrow.co.uk* 🛏 *3 rooms* 🔑 *In-room: no a/c, no phone, safe. In-hotel: Wi-Fi* ⊟ *MC, V* ⏹ *BP.*

LUDLOW

29 mi south of Shrewsbury, 24 mi north of Hereford.

Pretty Ludlow has medieval, Georgian, and Victorian buildings and a finer display of black-and-white half-timber buildings than even Shrewsbury. The Church of St. Lawrence on College Street dominates the center, its extravagant size a testimony to the town's prosperous wool trade. Cross the River Teme and climb Whitcliff for a spectacular view. Several outstanding restaurants have given the town of 10,000 a reputation as a culinary hot spot. Ludlow is now the national headquarters of the Slow Food movement, which focuses on food traditions and responsible production.

GETTING HERE AND AROUND
Ludlow has good train connections. From London Paddington, the journey time is 3¼ hours (changing at Newport), from Birmingham 1¾ hours, and from Shrewsbury 30 minutes. The train station is a 15-minute walk southwest to the center. Driving from London, take M40, M42, and then A448 to Kidderminster, A456, and A4117 to Ludlow. The town has good parking and is easily walkable.

ESSENTIALS
Visitor Information Ludlow (✉ *Castle St.* ☎ *01584/875053* ⊕ *www.ludlow. org.uk, www.visitsouthshropshire.co.uk*).

EXPLORING
The **Ludlow and the Marches Food Festival** (☎ *01584/873957* ⊕ *www. foodfestival.co.uk*) takes place over a weekend in mid-September and has demonstrations and tastings of local sausages, ale, and cider.

Dating from 1085, the massive, ruined, red sandstone **Ludlow Castle** dwarfs the town; it served as a vital stronghold for centuries and was the seat of the Marcher Lords who ruled "the Marches," the local name for the border region. The two sons of Edward IV—the little princes of the Tower of London—spent time here before being dispatched to London and their death in 1483. The earl of Powys owns the castle. Follow the terraced walk around the castle for a lovely view of the countryside. ✉ *Castle Sq.* ☎ *01584/873355* ⊕ *www.ludlowcastle.com* 💷 *£4.50* 🕙 *Jan. and Dec., weekends 10–4; Feb., Mar., Oct., and Nov., daily 10–4; Apr.–July and Sept., daily 10–5; Aug., daily 10–7; last admission 30 mins before closing.*

OFF THE BEATEN PATH

Stokesay Castle. This 13th-century fortified manor house built by a wealthy merchant is arguably the finest of its kind in England. Inside the main hall, the wooden cruck roof and timber staircase (a rare survival) demonstrate state-of-the-art building methods of the day. Outside, the cottage-style garden creates a bewitching backdrop for the magnificent Jacobean timber-frame gatehouse. ✉ *Craven Arms* ✛ *Off A49 Shrewsbury road, 7 mi northwest of Ludlow* ☎ *01588/672544* ⊕ *www.english-heritage.org.uk* 💷 *£5.20* 🕙 *Mar. and Oct., Wed.–Sun.*

and national holidays 10–5; Apr.–Sept., daily 10–5; Nov.–Feb., Thurs.–
Sun. 10–4.

WHERE TO EAT

Ludlow is known for some pricier fine-dining establishments, but options from excellent tea rooms to pubs and ethnic restaurants are also available.

££££ ✕**La Bécasse.** Dip into the past—the intimate building dates to 1349, the
FRENCH warm oak paneling merely to the 17th century—as you savor a fixed-price menu (around £50) of French food that's bang up to the minute. Rose-color glass chargers on crisp white table linen signal the artistry with which dishes such as salad of duck with bay leaf jelly, and plaice (an ocean fish) with sage potatoes, smoked bacon, and hazelnut butter are presented. Vegetarians are well served with a separate menu. Reservations are essential on weekends. ⊠ *17 Corve St.* ☎*01584/872325* ▤*MC, V* ⊘*Closed Mon. No dinner Sun. No lunch Tues.*

££££ ✕ **Mr. Underhill's.** Occupying a converted mill building beneath the castle,
MODERN BRITISH this secluded establishment looks onto the wooded River Teme. The
★ restaurant is light and informal, but stylish and warm at the same time. The superb modern-British, fixed-price menu (£45–£55), customized when you book, uses only fresh seasonal ingredients. A main dish could be local venison with red wine, elderberry, and thyme, and a dessert, plum sponge with star anise ice cream. Book well ahead, especially on weekends; there are rooms and suites available should you want to make a night of it. ⊠*Dinham Weir* ☎*01584/874431* ▤*MC, V* ⊘*Closed Mon. and Tues. No lunch.*

WHERE TO STAY

£££–££££ 🏨 **Dinham Hall.** A converted merchant's town house dating from 1792,
this hotel near Ludlow Castle formerly served as a boys' dormitory for the local grammar school. The owners have successfully integrated modern amenities—including comfortable furniture and print fabrics—with historic elements. The elegant dining room serves creative fixed-price meals. **Pros:** light and intimate; great views over walled garden; good restaurant. **Cons:** no Internet access. ⊠*Off Market Sq.* ☎*01584/876464* ⊕*www.dinhamhall.co.uk* 🛏*10 rooms, 3 suites* ♿*In-room: no a/c. In-hotel: restaurant, room service, bar, laundry service, some pets allowed, no-smoking rooms* ▤*MC, V* ⦿*BP.*

£££–££££ 🏨 **The Feathers.** Even if you're not staying here, take time to admire the
extravagant half-timber facade of this building, described by the architectural historian Nicholas Pevsner as "that prodigy of timber-framed houses." The interior is equally impressive—dripping with ornate plaster ceilings, carved oak, paneling, beams, and creaking floors. Some guest rooms are done in modern style, but others preserve the antique look. **Pros:** ornate plasterwork a must-see; unpretentious. **Cons:** most guest rooms are in newer part of the hotel and lack antique look. ⊠*The Bull Ring* ☎*01584/875261* ⊕*www.feathersatludlow.co.uk* 🛏*40 rooms* ♿*In-room: no a/c. In-hotel: restaurant, room service, bar, laundry service, Wi-Fi, some pets allowed, no-smoking rooms* ▤*AE, MC, V* ⦿*BP.*

9

££ 🔲**Timberstone.** The welcoming Read family has made a go-slow B&B
☾ haven out of its rambling stone cottage, run on ecological principles, in
the Clee Hills. Rooms are furnished in neutral tones in a soothing, contemporary style; the Clay Room has its own veranda, and in summer the
Garden Studio (no television) makes the perfect peaceful retreat. Books
and games abound, and reflexology treatment, a sauna, and evening
meals (by request) are options if you wish to stay put. The owners have
young children and are used to them. There's shuttle service to and from
Ludlow, which is 5 mi away. **Pros:** relaxing and hospitable; geared to
families; great food. **Cons:** out of center of Ludlow; twisty lanes to follow.
✉*B4363, Clee Stanton* ☎*01584/823519* ⊕*www.timberstoneludlow.*
co.uk ⤶*4 rooms* ⚷*In-room: no a/c, no phone, Wi-Fi. In-hotel: some*
pets allowed, no-smoking rooms ▭*MC, V* ⏀*BP.*

NIGHTLIFE AND THE ARTS

The two-week **Ludlow Festival** (☎*01584/872150* ⊕*www.ludlowfestival.*
co.uk), starting in late June, includes Shakespeare performed near the
ruined castle, and opera, dance, and concerts around town.

CHESTER

75 mi north of Ludlow, 46 mi north of Shrewsbury.

Cheshire is mainly a land of well-kept farms, supporting their herds of
cattle, but numerous places here are steeped in history. Villages contain
many fine examples of the black-and-white timber-frame architecture
more often associated with areas to the east. The region's thriving center is Chester, a city similar in some ways to Shrewsbury, though it has
many more black-and-white half-timber buildings (some built in Georgian and Victorian times), and its medieval walls still stand.

Chester has been a prominent city since the late 1st century, when the
Roman Empire expanded north to the banks of the River Dee. The
original Roman town plan is still evident: the principal streets, Eastgate,
Northgate, Watergate, and Bridge Street, lead out from the Cross—the
site of the central area of the Roman fortress—to the four city gates, and
the partly excavated remains of what is thought to have been the country's largest Roman amphitheater lie to the south of Chester's medieval
castle. Since Roman times ships have sailed up the estuary of the Dee
and anchored under the city walls. The port enjoyed its most prosperous period during the 12th and 13th centuries.

History seems more tangible in Chester than in many other ancient cities. Much medieval architecture remains in the compact town center,
and modern buildings have not been allowed to intrude. A negative
result of this perfection is that Chester has become a favorite bus-tour
destination, with gift shops, noise, and crowds.

GETTING HERE AND AROUND

There's a free shuttle bus to the center if you arrive by train, and buses
pull up at Vicar's Lane in the center. Chester is 180 mi from London,
and about 2¾ hours by train (change at Crewe). If you're driving and
here for a day only, use the city's Park and Ride lots, as central parking
lots fill quickly, especially in summer.

Guided walks leave the town hall daily at 10:30, and City Sightseeing operates daily tours of Chester in open-top buses from May to September.

ESSENTIALS

Visitor and Tour Information Chester (⊠ *Town Hall, Northgate St.* ⊠ *Vicar's La.* ☎ *01244/402111* ⊕ *www.chestertourism.com*). **City Sightseeing** (⊠ *Chester* ☎ *01244/381461* ⊕ *www.city-sightseeing.com*).

EXPLORING

TOP ATTRACTIONS

Chester Cathedral. Tradition has it that a church of some sort stood on the site of what is now Chester Cathedral in Roman times, but records indicate construction around AD 900. The earliest work traceable today, mainly in the north transept, is that of the 11th-century Benedictine abbey. After Henry VIII dissolved the monasteries in the 16th century, the abbey church became the cathedral church of the new diocese of Chester. The misericords in the choir stalls reveal intricately carved figures of people and animals, both real and mythical, and above is a gilded and colorful vaulted ceiling. In the small inner garden, a striking modern bronze statue depicts the woman of Samaria offering water to Jesus. ⊠ *St. Werburgh St., off Market Sq.* ☎ *01244/324756* ⊕ *www. chestercathedral.com* ⊠ *£4, includes audio guide* ⊗ *Mon.–Sat. 9–5, Sun. 12:30–4.*

City walls. The city walls, accessible from several points, provide splendid views of the city and its surroundings. The whole circuit is 2 mi, but if your time is short, climb the steps at Newgate and walk along toward Eastgate to see the great ornamental **Eastgate Clock,** erected to commemorate Queen Victoria's Diamond Jubilee in 1897. Lots of small shops near this part of the walls sell old books, old postcards, antiques, and jewelry. Where the **Bridge of Sighs** (named after the enclosed bridge in Venice that it closely resembles) crosses the canal, descend to street level and walk up Northgate Street into Market Square.

★ **Rows.** Chester's unique Rows, which originated in the 12th and 13th centuries, are essentially double rows of stores, one at street level and the other on the second floor with galleries overlooking the street. The Rows line the junction of the four streets in the old town. They have medieval crypts below them, and some reveal Roman foundations.

WORTH NOTING

ChesterBoat. This company runs excursions on the River Dee every 30 minutes daily (April through October) and hourly on weekends (November through March). Saturday evening cruises in summer feature discos. ⊠ *Boating Station, Souters La., The Groves* ☎ *01244/325394* ⊕ *www. chesterboat.co.uk.*

Chester Zoo. Well-landscaped grounds and natural enclosures make the 80-acre zoo one of Britain's most popular, as well as the largest. Highlights include Chimpanzee Island, the jaguar enclosure, and the Islands in Danger tropical habitat. Baby animals are often on display. Eleven miles of paths wend through the zoo, and you can use the waterbus boats or the overhead train to tour the grounds. ⊠ *A41, 2 mi north of*

9

Chester ☎ *01244/380280* ⊕ *www.chesterzoo.org* ☞ *Apr.–Oct. £14.95; Nov.–Mar. £11.75, bus £2, train £2* ⊙ *Daily 10–dusk.*

Grosvenor Museum. Start a visit with a look at Roman Chester, particularly in the Roman Stones Gallery, which houses tombstones previously used to repair the walls; look out for the wounded barbarian. Then skip a few centuries to explore the period house for a tour from 1680 to the 1920s. ⊠ *27 Grosvenor St.* ☎ *01244/402008* ☞ *Free* ⊕ *www. grosvenormuseum.co.uk* ⊙ *Mon.–Sat. 10:30–5, Sun. 1–4.*

WHERE TO EAT

£ ✕**Albion.** Traditional is the name of this Victorian pub; the posters,
BRITISH advertisements, flags, and curios tell you the idiosyncratic landlord keeps it as it would have been during World War I. The candlelit restaurant forms one of the three snug rooms and, unsurprisingly, serves up ultratraditional fare such as corned beef hash, Staffordshire oatcakes, and gammon (thick-sliced ham) with pease pudding. You can stay overnight here as well. ⊠ *Park St.* ☎ *01244/340345* ▤ *No credit cards* ⊙ *No dinner Sun.*

££ ✕**Chez Jules.** Once a fire station, this bustling bistro is now unasham-
BISTRO edly French and rustic, with red-and-white-check tablecloths and a menu chalked up on the blackboard. Start perhaps with a tomato tarte tatin, and then follow with pork fillet with caramelized pear and a Calvados-and-white-wine sauce, or lemon sole filled with salmon-and-prawn mousse. ⊠ *71 Northgate St.* ☎ *01244/400014* ▤ *MC, V.*

£££££ ✕**Simon Radley at the Chester Grosvenor.** Named for its noted chef, this
FRENCH restaurant is elegant in the extreme, the dishes cheekily titled; all comes with a sophisticated panache. Expect the seasonal but not the usual: Oysters and Pearls is scallop-and-fennel panna cotta with poached oysters and caviar, and the dessert Coffee is a chocolate cup with iced latte, espresso jelly, and coffee-bean brittle. There's a fixed-price dinner (£59) as well as a daily gastronomic menu (£70). The wine cellar has more than 1,000 bins. Reservations are essential on weekends, and children must be at least 12. ⊠ *Chester Grosvenor Hotel, Eastgate St.* ☎ *01244/895618* ▤ *AE, DC, MC, V* ⊙ *No dinner Mon. and Sun. Closed 1st 3 wks in Jan.*

WHERE TO STAY

£££££ ▥**Chester Grosvenor Hotel.** Handmade Italian furniture and French silk
★ furnishings fill this deluxe hotel in a Tudor-style building downtown. Molton Brown toiletries, CD and DVD players, and a luxury spa are among the pampering amenities. There are two restaurants, including the well-regarded Simon Radley at the Chester Grosvenor, and the intimate library is a perfect spot for afternoon tea. Breakfast is included in the weekend rates. **Pros:** pampering luxury; superb food; excellent service and facilities. **Cons:** breakfast included only with special rates; spa entails extra cost; no private parking lot. ⊠ *Eastgate St.* ☎ *01244/324024* ⊕ *www.chestergrosvenor.com* ⇱ *66 rooms, 14 suites* ♿ *In-room: safe, Internet. In-hotel: 2 restaurants, room service, bar, gym, spa, laundry service, Wi-Fi, no-smoking rooms* ▤ *AE, DC, MC, V.*

££–£££
★

Frogg Manor. Leave the modern world behind, dance foxtrots after dinner in the party room, and sleep in sumptuous tranquility. Lavishly furnished with antiques, drapes, and ornaments (frogs in particular), this hotel makes its individualist statement and never fails its faithful devotees. Lady Guinevere is the only tree-house suite in the country, and the conservatory restaurant has a gourmet (£42) and set-price menu (£37). The hotel is 15 minutes' drive south of Chester. **Pros:** English eccentricity at its best; plenty of frills and furbelows in the individually furnished rooms; sense of fun. **Cons:** not for minimalists; outside town. ⊠*A534, Nantwich Rd., Broxton* ☎*01829/782629* ⊕*www.froggmanorhotel. co.uk* ⬮*8 rooms* ☐*In-room: no a/c, Wi-Fi. In-hotel: restaurant, bar, parking (free), no-smoking rooms* ☐*AE, MC, V* ❘○❘*CP.*

££££

Green Bough Hotel. Chester's leafy outskirts are the setting for this memorable small hotel a mile from the town center. Furnished with antiques, including cast-iron and carved wooden beds, and decorated with Italian fabrics and wall coverings, the individually designed guest rooms make luxurious and soothing retreats. The Olive Tree restaurant provides top-notch contemporary British fare in intimate surroundings. Head to the rooftop garden for a relaxing drink in summer. **Pros:** warm, attentive service; individual and well-designed rooms. **Cons:** no young children allowed; ducks and teddy bears for adults. ⊠*60 Hoole Rd.* ☎*01244/326241* ⊕*www.greenbough.co.uk* ⬮*6 rooms, 7 suites* ☐*In-room: no a/c, DVD, Wi-Fi. In-hotel: restaurant, room service, bar, bicycles, laundry service, parking (free), no kids under 13, no-smoking rooms* ☐*AE, DC, MC, V* ❘○❘*BP.*

£
★

Grove Villa. The location of this family-run B&B, an early-19th-century house on the banks of the River Dee, enhances its appeal. Add antique furniture and a sense of calm, and you are guaranteed a soothing stay. **Pros:** beautiful river location; family-run; breakfast around a communal table. **Cons:** cash or checks only; no Internet facilities. ⊠*18 The Groves* ☎*01244/349713* ⊕*www.grovevillachester.com* ⬮*3 rooms* ☐*In-room: no a/c, no phone. In-hotel: parking (free), no-smoking rooms* ☐*No credit cards* ❘○❘*BP.*

££

Recorder House. This Georgian redbrick house has the perfect location right on the city wall and overlooking the River Dee. Meander through the picture-filled passages to find your rooms, the best of which have a four-poster bed and a view. Rooms are named after astrological signs, but the furnishings are straightforwardly traditional. The amiable hosts don't stint on breakfast choices: Parma ham and fresh pineapple, bacon and mushroom sandwich are but two of them. **Pros:** within easy reach of the center; parking; excellent breakfasts. **Cons:** no elevator. ⊠*19 City Walls* ☎*01244/326580* ⊕*www.recorderhotel.co.uk* ⬮*11 rooms* ☐*In-room: no a/c, Wi-Fi. In-hotel: parking (free), no-smoking rooms* ☐*AE, MC, V* ❘○❘ *BP.*

NIGHTLIFE AND THE ARTS

Oddfellows (⊠*20 Lower Bridge St.* ☎*01244/40000)* is the swankiest bar in town. Sip champagne cocktails or afternoon tea and admire the big wallpaper and big candelabra. You can dine here, too.

9

SHOPPING

Chester has an **indoor market** in the Forum, near the Town Hall, every day except Sunday. Watergate Street hosts antiques shops with anything from ceramics to furniture. **Bluecoat Books** (✉*1 City Walls* ☎*01244/318752*) specializes in travel, art, architecture, and history.

Lancashire and the Peaks

MANCHESTER, LIVERPOOL, AND THE PEAK DISTRICT

WORD OF MOUTH

"Next it was back to Liverpool's Mathew Street, touristy shops, and the Cavern Club. Even though it's not the original, it's a fantastic, atmospheric bar. It was about 9:30 and the place was hopping with tourists, young people, and locals. The band played early Beatles songs. Everyone was singing along; everything about it was perfect."

—saysull55

"I was very impressed with the Peak District. We spent a day in Buxton, which is a charming spa town. Our kids enjoyed Poole's cavern there. (Derbyshire is known for its show caverns, and there are quite a few others to visit)."

—Vttraveler

Updated by
Kate Hughes

For those looking for the postcard England of little villages and churches, the northwest region of England might not appear at the top of a sightseeing list. Manchester, Britain's third-largest city, today bustles with redevelopment and the energy of youth culture, and Liverpool's stint as the European Union's Capital of Culture in 2008 has brought exciting changes. However, the 200 years of smokestack industry that abated only in the 1980s have taken a toll on the east Lancashire landscape.

The region does have some lovely scenery inland, in Derbyshire (pronounced Darbyshire)—notably the spectacular Peak District, a huge national park at the southern end of the Pennines range. In and around this area are Victorian-era spas such as Buxton, pretty towns such as Bakewell, and magnificent stately houses such as Chatsworth, Hardwick Hall, and Haddon Hall. Manchester and Liverpool, the economic engines that propelled Britain in the 18th and 19th centuries, are sloughing off their mid-20th-century decline and celebrating their rich industrial and maritime heritage in their excellent museums—in imposing Victorian edifices, or, in Manchester's case, in strikingly modern buildings. The cities, each with a population of about 450,000, have reestablished themselves as centers of sporting and musical excellence, and as nightlife hot spots. Since 1962 the Manchester United, Everton, and Liverpool football (soccer in the United States) clubs have won everything worth winning in Britain and Europe. The Beatles launched the Mersey sound of the '60s; contemporary Manchester groups ride both British and U.S. airwaves. On the classical side of music, Manchester is also the home of Britain's oldest leading orchestra, the Hallé (founded in 1857)—just one legacy of 19th-century industrialists' investments in culture.

The Peak District is a wilder part of England, a region of crags that rear violently out of the plain. The Pennines, a line of hills that begins in the Peak District and runs as far north as Scotland, are sometimes called the "backbone of England." In this landscape of rocky outcrops and vaulting meadowland, you'll see nothing for miles but sheep, drystone (without mortar) walls, and farms, interrupted—spectacularly—by 19th-century villages and treasure houses. The delight of the Peak District is being able to ramble for days in rugged countryside but still enjoy the pleasures of civilization.

TOP REASONS TO GO

The Beatles: Whether you want to relive the Fab Four's moments of glory, visit their haunts, see their childhood homes, or just buy a Beatle pencil sharpener, a magical mystery tour in Liverpool will provide it all.

Museums in Manchester and Liverpool: You don't need the excuse of rain to learn about these cities' industrial and maritime pasts; visit even on a sunny day. Take history lessons at the Museum of Science and Industry and the Imperial War Museum North in Manchester, and the Merseyside Maritime Museum in Liverpool. Then opt for art appreciation in the cities' galleries.

Manchester nightspots: Catch the city at night in any of its humming café-bars and pubs; strut your stuff, soak up the latest sounds, or just enjoy a good beer in a gloriously ornate Victorian-era pub.

Chatsworth House and Haddon Hall: Engage the past and imagine yourself as a country landowner roaming the great pile that is Chatsworth, or as a Tudor noble exercising in the intricate long gallery of the quintessentially English Haddon Hall. Haddon can take you a half day—Chatsworth a full day—to explore.

Walking in the Peak District: Even a short walk in Edale or High Peak reveals the rocky yet intimate scenery that is unique to the area—dales rubbing shoulders with moors, and drystone walls patterning the fields. Civilization, in the form of welcoming pubs and peaceful towns, is always close at hand; that's part of the pleasure.

ORIENTATION AND PLANNING

GETTING ORIENTED

Manchester lies at the heart of a tangle of motorways in the northwest of England, about a half hour across the Pennines from Yorkshire. It's 70 mi from the southern edge of the Lake District. The city spreads west toward the coast and the mouth of the River Mersey, where Liverpool is still centered on its port. For the Northwest's most dramatic scenery—indeed, its only real geological feature of interest—you must travel to the Peak District, a national park less than an hour's drive southeast of Manchester. England at its grandest and most ducal can be seen in the great houses of Derbyshire's Wye valley.

Manchester. The skies may be gray, but the vibrant city of Manchester is known for its modern urban design and its thriving music and club scenes. Great museums justify its status as the leading city of the Northwest.

Liverpool. Now in the midst of a postindustrial rebirth, this city is more than the Beatles. The imposing waterfront, the pair of cathedrals, and the grand architecture make this clear. But the museums don't forget to mention the city's place in rock-and-roll history.

10

The Peak District. Britain's first national park, the Peak District is studded with an array of stately homes, the most impressive being Chatsworth House. Dramatic moors, intimate dales, and limestone caverns invite exploration.

PLANNING

WHEN TO GO

Manchester has a reputation as one of the wettest cities in Britain, and visiting in summer won't guarantee fine weather. Nevertheless, wet or cold weather shouldn't spoil a visit because of the many indoor sights and cultural activities here and in Liverpool. Summer is the optimum time to see the Peak District, especially because traditional festivities take place in many villages at its start. The *only* time to see the great houses of Derbyshire's Wye valley is from spring through fall.

PLANNING YOUR TIME

It's possible to see the main sights of Manchester or Liverpool in a day, but you'd have to take the museums at a gallop. In Manchester, the Museum of Science and Industry and the Imperial War Museum could easily absorb a day, as could the Waterfront area of Liverpool, where the Beatles Story, Tate Liverpool, Merseyside Maritime, and International Slavery museums all vie for your attention. In Liverpool, you'd need an additional half day to see the homes of John Lennon and Paul McCartney. The buzzing nightlife of each city demands at least an overnight stay. You can explore the Peak District on a day trip from Manchester in a pinch, but allow longer to visit the stately homes or to hike.

GETTING HERE AND AROUND

AIR TRAVEL

Both Manchester and Liverpool are well served by their international airports. Manchester, the third largest airport in the country, has the greater number of flights, including some from the United States.

Airports Manchester Airport (☎ 0871/271-0711 ⊕ www.manchesterairport. co.uk). **Liverpool John Lennon Airport** (☎ 0871/521-8484 ⊕ www. liverpoolairport.com).

BUS TRAVEL

National Express buses serve the region from London's Victoria Coach Station. Average travel time to Manchester or Liverpool is five hours. To reach Matlock, Bakewell, and Buxton you can take a bus from London to Derby and change to the TransPeak bus service, though you might find it more convenient to travel first to Manchester.

Bus Contacts National Express (☎ 0871/781-8181 ⊕ www.nationalexpress. com). **TransPeak** (☎ 01733/712265 ⊕ www.transpeak.co.uk). **Traveline** (☎ 0871/200-2233 ⊕ www.traveline.org.uk).

CAR TRAVEL

If you're traveling by road, expect heavy traffic out of London on weekends. Travel time to Manchester or Liverpool from London via the M6 is 3 to 3½ hours. Although a car may not be an asset in touring the centers of Manchester and Liverpool, it is helpful in getting around

Lancashire and the Peaks

TO THE LAKE DISTRICT

Preston
Lytham St. Anne's
A584
Burnley
Blackburn
Bradford
M65

LANCASHIRE

Southport
Irish Sea
Formby
Bolton
Manchester see detail map
Huddersfield
M62
A62
Holmfirth
Woodhead
Oldham

TO DOUGLAS, ISLE OF MAN
Kirkby
Wigan
Liverpool see detail map
Glossop
A617 and M

Birkenhead
Warrington
Stockport
Hayfield
Edale
Castleton
Eyam
Baslow

Flint
Widnes
Speke
River Mersey
Wilmslow
Macclesfield
Buxton
Chatsworth House
Haddon Hall

CHESHIRE
Little Moreton Hall
Bakewell
Hardwick Hall
Winster
Matlock
Matlock Bath

WALES
Chester
Crewe
Kidsgrove
Leek
Ashbourne

Wrexham
Nantwich
Stoke-on-Trent

Whitchurch
Newcastle-under-Lyme
Uttoxeter

0   10 miles
0   10 kilometers

the Peak District. Bus service there is quite good, but a car allows the most flexibility.

Roads within the region are generally very good. In Manchester and Liverpool, try to sightsee on foot to avoid parking problems. In the Peak District, park in signposted parking lots whenever possible. In summer, Peak District traffic is very heavy; watch out for speeding motorbikes, especially on the A6. In winter, know the weather forecast, as moorland roads can quickly become impassable.

TRAIN TRAVEL

Virgin Trains serves the region from London's Euston Station. Direct service to Manchester and Liverpool takes 2½ hours. There are trains between Manchester's Piccadilly Station and Liverpool's Lime Street every half hour during the day; the trip takes 50 minutes.

To reach Buxton, in the Peak District, from London, take the Manchester train; switch at Stockport. Local service—one train an hour—from Manchester to Buxton takes one hour. Call National Rail Enquiries for timetable information.

Train Contacts **National Rail Enquiries** (☎ 0845/748–4950 ⊕ www.nationalrail.co.uk).

10

DISCOUNTS AND DEALS

A Wayfarer ticket (£9.20), which covers a day's travel on all forms of transport in Manchester and the Peak District, is a good deal. Contact National Rail Enquiries for information.

RESTAURANTS

Dining options in Manchester and Liverpool vary from smart cafés offering modern British and continental fare to excellent ethnic restaurants. Manchester has one of Britain's biggest Chinatowns, and locals also favor the 40-odd Bangladeshi, Pakistani, and Indian restaurants along Wilmslow Road in Rusholme, a mile south of the city center, known as Curry Mile (check out ⊕*www.rusholmecurry.co.uk*).

One local dish that has survived is Bakewell pudding (*never* called "tart" in these areas, as its imitations are elsewhere in England). Served with custard or cream, the pudding—a pastry covered with jam and a thin layer of almond-flavor filling—is the joy of Bakewell. Another regional creation is Lancashire hot pot, a hearty meat stew.

HOTELS

Because the larger city-center hotels in Manchester and Liverpool rely on business travelers during the week, they often markedly reduce their rates on weekends. Smaller hotels and guesthouses abound in nearby suburbs, many just a short bus ride from downtown. The Manchester and Liverpool visitor centers operate room-booking services. Also worth investigating are serviced apartments, which are becoming more popular in the cities. The Peak District has inns, bed-and-breakfasts, and hotels, as well as a network of youth hostels. Local tourist offices have details; reserve well in advance for Easter and summer.

WHAT IT COSTS IN POUNDS					
	£	££	£££	££££	£££££
Restaurants	Under £10	£10–£14	£15–£19	£20–£25	over £25
Hotels	Under £70	£70–£120	£121–£160	£161–£220	over £220

Restaurant prices are for a main course at dinner. Hotel prices are for two people in a standard double room in high season, including V.A.T., with no meals or, if indicated, CP (with continental breakfast), BP (Breakfast Plan, with full breakfast), or MAP (Modified American Plan, with breakfast and dinner).

VISITOR INFORMATION

England's Northwest (⊕ *www.visitenglandsnorthwest.com*).

MANCHESTER

Manchester's center hums with the vibe of cutting-edge popular music and a swank café culture. The city's once-grim industrial landscape, redeveloped since the late 1980s, includes tidied-up canals, cotton mills transformed into loft apartments, and stylish contemporary architecture that has pushed the skyline ever higher. Beetham Tower, the second-tallest building in Britain after London's Canary Wharf, can't be overlooked. Bridgewater Hall and the Lowry, as well as the Imperial War

Museum North, are outstanding cultural facilities. Sure, it still rains here, but the rain-soaked streets are part of the city's charm, in a bleak, northern kind of way.

For most of its existence Manchester, Britain's third-largest city, has been a thriving and prosperous place. The Romans built a fort here in AD 79 and named it Mamucium, but the city that stands today—with the imposing Town Hall, Royal Exchange, Midland Hotel, the waterways, and railway—is a product of the Industrial Revolution and the wealth it created.

It's impossible to talk about 20th-century Manchester without mentioning music and football. Out of poverty and unemployment came the brash sounds of punk and the indie record labels, and a thriving club scene. In the 1980s the band New Order produced a unique Mancunian sound that mixed live instruments with digital sound. The now-defunct Haçienda Club marketed New Order to the world, and Manchester became the clubbing capital of England. Joy Division, Morrissey, Stone Roses, Happy Mondays, and Oasis rose to the top of the charts. The triumphant reign of the Manchester United football club, which now faces challenges from Liverpool and southern rivals Arsenal, Aston Villa, and Chelsea, has kept many eyes on Manchester.

GETTING HERE AND AROUND

Manchester Airport has many international flights, so you might not even have to travel through London. There are frequent trains from the airport to Piccadilly Railway Station (15–20 minutes) and buses to Piccadilly Gardens Bus Station (1 hour). A taxi from the airport to Manchester city center costs between £18 and £20. For details about public transportation in Manchester, call the Greater Manchester Passenger Transport Executive (GMPTE) information line.

Driving to Manchester from London (3 to 3½ hours), take M1 north to M6, then the M62 east, which becomes M602 as it enters Greater Manchester. Trains from London's Euston Station drop passengers at the centrally located Piccadilly Railway Station. The journey takes 2½ hours. Chorlton Street Coach Station, a few hundred yards west of Piccadilly Railway Station, is the main bus station for regional and long-distance buses.

You can cover the center-city sights easily enough on foot, except for the Whitworth Art Gallery, which requires taking a bus or a taxi. Most local buses leave from Piccadilly Gardens Bus Station, the hub of the urban bus network. Metroshuttle operates three free circular routes around the city center; service runs every 5 to 10 minutes Monday to Saturday 7 to 7 and Sunday 10 to 6. Metrolink electric tram service runs through the city center and out to the suburbs. The Eccles extension has stops for the Lowry (Harbour City) and for the Manchester United Stadium (Old Trafford). Buy a ticket from the platform machine before you board. A £5.80 one-day tram and bus ticket is a good value.

Blue Badge Guides can arrange dozens of different tours of the city, and City Centre Cruises offers a three-hour Sunday lunch round-trip on a barge to the Manchester Ship Canal.

ESSENTIALS
Transportation Contacts **Greater Manchester Passenger Transport Executive** (☎ *0161/228–7811 or 0871/200–2233* ⊕ *www.gmpte.com*). **Metrolink**
(☎ *0161/205–2000* ⊕ *www.metrolink.co.uk*).

Visitor and Tour Information **Blue Badge Guides** (☎ *0161/440–0277*).
City Centre Cruises (☎ *0161/902–0222* ⊕ *www.citycentrecruises.co.uk*).
Manchester Visitor Centre (✉ *Town Hall Extension, Lloyd St., City Centre*
☎ *0871/222–8223* ⊕ *www.visitmanchester.com*).

EXPLORING

Manchester is compact enough that you can easily walk across the
city center in 40 minutes, but buses and Metrolink trams make it easy
to navigate. Deansgate and Princess Street, the main thoroughfares,
run roughly north–south and west–east; the lofty terra-cotta Victorian
Town Hall sits in the middle, close to the visitor center and the fine
Manchester Art Gallery. Dominating the skyline at the southern end of
Deansgate is Manchester's newest and highest building, Beetham Tower,
which houses a Hilton Hotel and marks the beginning of the **Castlefield Urban Heritage Park,** with the Museum of Science and Industry
and the canal system. The **Whitworth Art Gallery** is a bus ride from
downtown; otherwise, all other central sights are within easy walking
distance of the Town Hall. Take a Metrolink tram 2 mi south for the
Salford Quays dockland area, with the **Lowry** and the **Imperial War
Museum;** you can spend half a day or more in this area. ■TIP→ **Keep
in mind that the museums are both excellent and free.**

TOP ATTRACTIONS

❹ **Castlefield Urban Heritage Park.** Site of an early Roman fort, the district
of Castlefield was later the center of the city's industrial boom, which
resulted in the building of Britain's first modern canal in 1764 and the
world's first railway station in 1830. What had become an urban wasteland has been beautifully restored into an urban park with canal-side
walks, landscaped open spaces, and refurbished warehouses. The 7-acre
site contains the reconstructed gate to the Roman fort of Mamucium,
the buildings of the **Museum of Science and Industry,** and several of
the city's hippest bars and restaurants. You can spend half a day here,
including the museum. ✉ *Off Liverpool Rd., Castlefield.*

★ **Imperial War Museum North.** The thought-provoking exhibits in this
striking, aluminum-clad building, which architect Daniel Libeskind
described as representing three shards of an exploded globe, present
the reasons for war and show its effects on society. Three Big Picture
audiovisual shows envelop you in the sights and sounds of conflicts
from 1914 to the present, and a storage system allows you to select
trays of objects to examine, including artifacts from the 2003 war in
Iraq. A 100-foot viewing platform gives a bird's-eye view of the city.
The museum is on the banks of the Manchester Ship Canal in Salford Quays, across the footbridge from the Lowry. It's a 10-minute
(often breezy) walk from the Harbour City stop of the Metrolink tram.
✉ *Trafford Wharf Rd., Salford Quays* ☎ *0161/836–4000* ⊕ *www.iwm.*

Manchester

org.uk ✉*Free* ⊙*Mar.–Oct., daily 10–6; Nov.–Feb., daily 10–5; last admission 30 mins before closing.*

The Lowry. This impressive arts center in Manchester's Salford Quays waterways occupies a dramatic modern building with a steel-gray metallic and glass exterior that reflects the light. L. S. Lowry (1887–1976) was a local artist, and one of the few who painted the industrial landscape. Galleries showcase Lowry's and other contemporary artists' work. The theater, Britain's largest outside London, presents an impressive lineup of touring companies. The nearest Metrolink tram stop is Harbour City, a 10-minute walk from the Lowry. ✉*Pier 8, Salford Quays* ☎*0870/111–2020* ⊕*www.thelowry.com* ✉*Free; prices vary for theater tickets and exhibitions; tours £3* ⊙*Building Sun. and Mon. 10–6, Tues.–Sat. 10–8, or last performance; galleries Sun.–Fri. 11–5, Sat. 10–5.*

➋ ★ **Manchester Art Gallery.** Behind its impressive classical portico, this splendid museum presents its collections in both a Victorian and contemporary setting. Don't miss the outstanding examples of the vibrant paintings of the Pre-Raphaelites and their circle, notably Ford Madox Brown's masterpiece *Work* and Holman Hunt's *The Hireling Shepherd*. British works from the 18th century—*Cheetah and Stag with Two Indians* by George Stubbs, for instance—and the 20th century are also well represented. The Manchester Gallery illustrates the city's contribution to art, and the second-floor Craft and Design Gallery shows off the best of the decorative arts in ceramics and glass, metalwork, and furniture. ✉*Mosely St., City Centre* ☎*0161/235–8888* ⊕*www.manchestergalleries.org.uk* ✉*Free* ⊙*Tues.–Sun. and national holidays 10–5.*

➎ **Fodor'sChoice** ★ **Museum of Science and Industry.** The museum's five buildings, one of which is the world's oldest passenger rail station (1830), hold marvelous collections relating to the city's industrial past and present. You can walk through a reconstructed Victorian sewer, be blasted by the heat and noise of working steam engines, and see cotton looms whirring in action. The Air and Space Gallery fills a graceful cast-iron-and-glass building, constructed as a market hall in 1877. ■**TIP→ Allow at least half a day to get the most out of all the sites, which are in the Castlefield Urban Heritage Park.** ✉*Liverpool Rd., main entrance on Lower Byrom St., Castlefield* ☎*0161/832–2244* ⊕*www.msim.org.uk* ✉*Free, charges vary for special exhibitions; parking £3–£7, depending on time of day* ⊙*Daily 10–5.*

➐ ☼ **People's History Museum.** Not everyone in 19th-century Manchester owned a cotton mill or made a fortune on the trading floor. This newly refurbished and extended museum recounts powerfully the struggles of working people in the city since the Industrial Revolution. It tells the story of the 1819 Peterloo Massacre and has an unrivaled collection of trade-union banners, tools, toys, utensils, and photographs, all illustrating the working lives and pastimes of the city's people. At this writing, the museum was due to reopen in late 2009. ✉*Left Bank, City Centre* ⊕*www.phm.org.uk* ✉*Free* ⊙*Daily 10–5.*

■ **NEED A BREAK?**
The brick-vaulted, waterside **Mark Addy pub** (✉*Stanley St. off Bridge St., City Centre* ☎*0161/832–4080*) is a good spot to have a relaxing drink and sample an excellent spread of pâtés and cheeses. The pub is named for the

Manchester: Cottonopolis

Manchester's spectacular rise from a small town to the world's cotton capital—with the nickname Cottonopolis—in only 100 years began with the first steam-powered cotton mill, built in 1783. Dredging made the rivers Irwell and Mersey navigable to ship coal to the factories. The world's first passenger railway opened in 1830, and construction of the Manchester Ship Canal in 1894 provided the infrastructure for Manchester to dominate the industrial world. Check out ⊕ *www.industrialpowerhouse.co.uk* for information about seeing more of this industrial heritage.

A few people acquired great wealth, but factory hands worked under appalling conditions. Working-class discontent came to a head in 1819 in the Peterloo Massacre, when soldiers killed 11 workers at a protest meeting. The conditions under which factory hands worked were later recorded by Friedrich Engels (co-author with Karl Marx of the *Communist Manifesto*), who managed a cotton mill in the city. More formal political opposition to the government emerged in the shape of the Chartist movement (which campaigned for universal suffrage) and the Anti–Corn Law League (which opposed trade tariffs), forerunners of the British trade unions. From Victorian times until the 1960s, daily life for the average Mancunian was so oppressive that it bred the desire to escape, although most stayed put and endured the harsh conditions.

19th-century boatman who rescued more than 50 people from the River Irwell.

❾ **Royal Exchange.** Throughout its commercial heyday, this was the city's most important building—the cotton market. Built with Victorian exuberance in 1874, the existing structure accommodated 7,000 traders. The building was refurbished and the giant glass-dome roof restored after damage by the 1996 IRA bombing. Visit to see the lunar module–inspired Royal Exchange Theatre, have a drink in the café, and browse the crafts shop or the clothes outlets in the arcade. ✉*St. Ann's Sq., City Centre* ☎*0161/834–3731* ⊕*www.royalexchange.co.uk.*

10

❶ **Town Hall.** Manchester's imposing Town Hall, with its 280-foot-tall clock tower, speaks volumes about the city's 19th-century sense of self-importance. Alfred Waterhouse designed the Victorian Gothic building (1867–76); extensions were added just before World War II. Over the main entrance is a statue of Roman general Agricola, who founded Mamucium in AD 79. Above him are Henry III, Elizabeth I, and St. George, the patron saint of England. Murals of the city's history, painted between 1852 and 1865 by the Pre-Raphaelite Ford Madox Brown, decorate the Great Hall, with its emblazoned hammer-beam roof. Guided tours (twice a month) include the murals, but ask at the front desk: if the rooms aren't being used, you may be allowed to wander in. ✉*Albert Sq., public entrance on Lloyd St., City Centre* ☎*0161/234–5000* 🎟*Free; guided tours £6* ☉*Mon.–Sat. 8:45–5; ask at tourist office about tour information.*

⑫ **Whitworth Art Gallery.** This University of Manchester–run art museum has strong collections of British watercolors, old-master drawings, and post-impressionist works, as well as wallpapers. The excellent textile gallery—befitting a city built on textile manufacture—demonstrates the meaning and power of clothing in such items as a 16th-century Spanish funeral cope, 18th-century babies' vests, and a modern-day Turkish circumcision suit. A good bistro and a gift shop are also here. To get here, catch any southbound bus with a number in the 40s (except 47) on Oxford Road, or from St. Peter's Square or Piccadilly Gardens. ⌧ *Oxford Rd., University Quarter* ☎ *0161/275–7450* ⊕ *www.whitworth.manchester. ac.uk* ⌨ *Free* ⊘ *Mon.–Sat. 10–5, Sun. noon–4.*

WORTH NOTING

❸ **Central Library.** The circular exterior of the city's main library, topped by a line of Doric columns and a massive Corinthian portico facing St. Peter's Square, is a major focus for Manchester's most prestigious civic quarter. Erected in 1930, it was at one time the biggest municipal library in the world. The glass-top reading room, inspired by the Pantheon, is worth seeing. The **Library Theatre** is part of the complex. ⌧ *St. Peter's Sq., City Centre* ☎ *0161/234–1900* ⊘ *Mon.–Thurs. 9–8, Fri. and Sat. 9–5.*

❻ **John Rylands Library.** Owned by the University of Manchester, this Gothic Revival masterpiece designed by Alfred Waterhouse was built by Enriqueta Augustina Rylands as a memorial to her husband, a cotton magnate. Constructed of red sandstone in the 1890s, the library resembles a cathedral and contains outstanding collections of illuminated manuscripts and personal papers of famous writers. Excellent exhibitions tell the story of the library. ⌧ *150 Deansgate, City Centre* ☎ *0161/306–0555* ⊕ *www.library.manchester.ac.uk* ⊘ *Tues.–Sat. 10–5, Sun. and Mon. noon–5.*

❿ **Manchester Cathedral.** The city's sandstone cathedral, set beside the River Irwell and originally a medieval parish church dating in part from the 15th century, is unusually broad for its length and has the widest medieval nave in Britain. Inside, angels with gilded instruments look down from the roof of the nave, and misericords (the undersides of choristers' seats) in the early-16th-century choir stalls reveal intriguing carvings. The octagonal chapter house dates from 1485. ⌧ *Victoria St., Millennium Quarter* ☎ *0161/833–2220* ⌨ *Free, donations welcome* ⊕ *www.manchestercathedral.org* ⊘ *Weekdays 8:30–7, Sat. 8:30–5, Sun. 8:30–7:30.*

❽ **St. Ann's Church.** Built in 1712 and sometimes wrongly attributed to Christopher Wren, St. Ann's is Manchester's oldest surviving classical building. The plain, elegant interior has a gallery supported by Tuscan columns, and light from the clear windows enhances the dark-wood pews and chancel. ⌧ *St. Ann's Sq., City Centre* ☎ *0161/834–0239* ⌨ *Free, donations welcome* ⊕ *www.stannsmanchester.com* ⊘ *Mon.–Sat. 9:45–4:45, Sun. 8:45–4:45 and 6–7:30.*

Urbis. A high-tech museum in this striking, glass-skinned triangle of a building dissects the modern urban condition through a program of changing exhibitions on such themes as the Black Panther movement and video games, as well as Manchester itself. There is a good variety of tours in and around the building; an introductory tour begins daily at 1. ⊠ *Cathedral Gardens, Millennium Quarter* ☎*0161/605–8200* ⊕*www.urbis.org.uk* ✉*Free* ☉*Daily 10–6.*

WHERE TO EAT

The city's dining scene, with everything from Indian (go to Rusholme) to modern British fare, is lively. The Manchester Food & Drink Festival, held the first two weeks of October, showcases the city's chefs and regional products with special events. The city's pubs are also good for lunch or dinner.

£ INDIAN ✕ **Akbar's.** Locals line up for this big, bright, and buzzing contemporary restaurant just opposite the Museum of Science and Industry. If they're not tucking into sizzling Balti dishes, they might be enjoying a mild and creamy korma, rogan josh (with tomatoes and coriander) or a sweet-and-sour dhansak dish (with pineapple and lentils)—all popular staples. Vegetarians have plenty of choices, too. The restaurant doesn't take reservations, so be prepared to wait at busy times. ⊠ *73–83 Liverpool Rd., Castlefield* ☎*0161/834–8444* ☐*MC, V.*

££ ECLECTIC ✕ **Albert's Shed.** From the outside it's a plate-glass oblong box, but inside, this restaurant is warm, relaxed, and welcoming. The menu has an Italian slant with plenty of pizzas, pastas, and risottos on offer, but you might prefer to choose from the good selection of steaks. Take note: the specialty sundae—strawberry, chocolate, and vanilla ice cream with berries, brandy-soaked panettone, and whipped cream—might defeat you. In summer you can dine *alfresco* by the canal. ⊠ *20 Castle St., Deansgate* ☎*0161/839–9818* ☐*MC, V.*

£ INDIAN ✕ **Lal Haweli.** One of Rusholme's string of Indian restaurants, this bright and spacious establishment specializes in tandoori chicken and other Indian staples. What sets it apart are Nepalese offerings such as chicken sultani (with orange, pineapple, and chilies) and stir-fried Balti dishes from northern Pakistan. This mostly Asian (mainly Pakistani) area is full of bright neon signs and waiters trying to lure you into their restaurants. A mile south of the city center, it's easily accessible by Buses 41, 42, 43, 44, and 45, or a short taxi ride. ⊠*68–72 Wilmslow Rd., Rusholme* ☎*0161/248–9700* ☐*AE, MC, V.*

£££ SEAFOOD ✕ **Livebait.** An offshoot of the London-based restaurant serves fresh fish from around the world in an old building across from Albert Square. Tall windows, cool cream-and-green decor, and dark-wood furniture add fresh style. Among the many good choices are Cornish sardines, Thai fish curry, or traditional cockles and mussels. Dine early for the fixed-price pretheater menu or try the excellent-value lunches. ⊠*22 Lloyd St., City Centre* ☎*0161/817–4110* ☐*AE, DC, MC, V.*

££ BRITISH ✕ **Mr. Thomas's Chophouse.** The city's oldest restaurant (1872) dishes out good old British favorites such as brown onion soup, steak-and-kidney

10

pudding, Lancashire hot pot, and corned-beef hash to crowds of city types and shoppers. This hearty food is served in a Victorian-style room with a black-and-white-checked floor and dark green tiling. The wine list is exceptional. Mr. Sam's Chophouse in Chapel Walks is just as busy and serves similar fare. ⊠ *52 Cross St., City Centre* ☎ *0161/832–2245* ⊟ *AE, MC, V.*

£££   ✕ **Stock.** The Edwardian building
ITALIAN   that houses this buzzing Italian restaurant was once the city's stock exchange—hence its name and grand domed setting. Chef Enzo Mauro emphasizes the flavors of southern Italy on a menu that might include fish and shellfish broth on a garlicky bruschetta or rump of lamb marinated in mint and chili. You can accompany this with a fine-quality wine. Bonuses are a good-value lunch deal, jazz on Friday, and occasional opera nights. ⊠ *4 Norfolk St., City Centre* ☎ *0161/839–6644* ⊟ *AE, MC, V* ⊗ *Closed Sun.*

££   ✕ **Yang Sing.** One of Manchester's best Chinese restaurants, this elegant
CHINESE   place is filled with Chinese families gathered around the huge round
★   tables, which is always a good sign. The menu of Cantonese dishes is endless, the dim sum are legendary, and there's plenty for the adventurous—ox tripe with pickled vegetables or shark's fin soup, for example. Vegetarians won't be disappointed, either. ⊠ *34 Princess St., City Centre* ☎ *0161/236–2200* ⊟ *AE, MC, V.*

CHINATOWN

The large red-and-gold Imperial Chinese Arch, erected in 1987, marks Manchester's Chinatown, one of the largest Chinese communities outside London. Bordered by Portland Street, Mosley Street, Princess Street, and Charlotte Street, the area buzzes on Sunday, when traders from all over the country stock up from the supermarkets, food stalls, herbalists, and gift shops. The restaurants offer excellent choices of authentic Cantonese cooking, so consider a stop here when your shopping energies run low.

WHERE TO STAY

£££–££££   🏠 **Arora International.** The centrally located Arora International, opposite the Manchester Art Gallery, occupies one of the city's grand Victorian buildings. Its interior design, however, is minimalist modern. Chunky contemporary upholstered furnishings fill the public areas and guest rooms, where favored colors are beiges and muted reds and purples. Five rooms inspired by Cliff Richard songs contain artwork and memorabilia from the singer's own collection. The luxurious bathrooms have music speakers so you can listen to his tunes (or anyone else's, for that matter). Each floor has its own cooking facilities. **Pros:** fun theme rooms; historic building; good deals on weekends. **Cons:** no parking; smallish rooms. ⊠ *18–24 Princess St., City Centre* ☎ *0161/236–8999* ⊕ *www.arorainternational.com* ⇆ *141 rooms* ♿ *In-room: safe, refrigerator, Internet. In-hotel: restaurant, room service, bar, gym, laundry service, Wi-Fi, no-smoking rooms* ⊟ *AE, DC, MC, V* ⦿ *BP, EP.*

£–££   🏠 **Castlefield Hotel.** This popular modern hotel sits near the water's edge in the Castlefield Basin. Public rooms are cheery and traditional; subdued tones help make the bedrooms restful. The amenities are plentiful for a hotel in this price range. There's a gym with a range of exercise classes, an indoor running track, and a dance studio. **Pros:** excellent leisure facilities; reasonable rates. **Cons:** rooms can feel stuffy; a bit far from downtown. ⊠*Liverpool Rd., Castlefield* ☎*0161/832–7073* ⊕*www.castlefield-hotel.co.uk* ⬦*48 rooms* ⬦*In-room: no a/c, Wi-Fi. In-hotel: restaurant, room service, bar, pool, gym, laundry service, parking (paid)* ⊟*AE, MC, V* ❙⊚❙*BP.*

£££££   🏨 **Great John Street.** Once a Victorian schoolhouse, this plush boutique hotel next to the Granada TV studios now attracts well-heeled business executives, television stars, and anyone seeking something truly special. Duplex rooms have huge windows. Baroque furnishings, rich fabrics, and deep colors create a chic contrast with the original wooden flooring and exposed brick walls. Bathrooms, on a separate level, are equally spacious and luxurious. Unwind in the cozy Oyster Bar or head up to the rooftop garden with its outdoor hot tub. **Pros:** luxurious rooms; unique design; good online deals. **Cons:** valet parking is expensive; breakfast is extra. ⊠*Great John St., City Centre* ☎*0161/831–3211* ⊕*www.greatjohnstreet.co.uk* ⬦*14 rooms, 16 suites* ⬦*In-room: DVD, Internet, Wi-Fi. In-hotel: room service, bar, gym, parking (paid), no-smoking rooms* ⊟*AE, MC, V.*

££–£££   🏨 **Jurys Inn.** A good value, this link in the Irish-based chain has a sleek wooden lobby and attractive contemporary design. Guest rooms are spacious and comfortable. The location is excellent—next to Bridgewater Hall and close to shopping on King Street and the café-bar scenes on Whitworth Street and in Castlefield. A Metrolink tram stop is nearby. **Pros:** family-friendly rooms; affordable rates. **Cons:** impersonal feel; bland decor. ⊠*56 Great Bridgewater St., Peter's Fields* ☎*0161/953–8888* ⊕*www.jurysinns.com* ⬦*265 rooms* ⬦*In-room: Internet. In-hotel: restaurant, room service, bar, laundry service, Wi-Fi, parking (paid), no-smoking rooms* ⊟*AE, DC, MC, V* ❙⊚❙*BP.*

££££–£££££   🏨 **The Lowry Hotel.** The strikingly modern design of this glass edifice exudes luxury and spaciousness. The clean-lined public areas and guest rooms are washed in soothing neutral tones, enlivened by brilliant splashes of color. Marble bathrooms and walk-in closets are nice touches. Classic British dishes are served in the elegant River Room restaurant. The hotel is next to the River Irwell across from the landmark Trinity Bridge designed by Santiago Calatrava. **Pros:** luxury at every turn; spacious rooms; good deals online. **Cons:** you feel swallowed up in the vast lobby; view of office blocks is less than inspiring. ⊠*50 Dearman's Pl., Chapel Wharf, City Centre* ☎*0161/827–4000* ⊕*www.thelowryhotel.com* ⬦*157 rooms, 7 suites* ⬦*In-room: safe, DVD, Internet, Wi-Fi. In-hotel: restaurant, room service, bar, pool, gym, spa, laundry service, parking (paid), no-smoking rooms* ⊟*AE, DC, MC, V* ❙⊚❙*BP.*

£££   🏨 **The Midland Hotel.** The Edwardian splendor of the hotel's public rooms manages to shine through a contemporary makeover, evoking the days when this was the city's railroad station hotel. To get in the spirit, enjoy high tea in the grand lobby. Guest rooms, with huge photos of Manchester as headboards, are pleasant and light, with contemporary walnut furniture and dark-purple-and-cream furnishings. You're

10

in the heart of the city, close to Town Hall and a Metrolink stop. **Pros:** central location; historic building; good for business travelers. **Cons:** impersonal feel; rooms facing road can be noisy. ⊠*Peter St., City Centre* ☎*0161/236–3333* ⊕*www.qhotels.co.uk* ⥏*298 rooms, 14 suites* ⚷*In-room: safe, Internet, Wi-Fi. In-hotel: 2 restaurants, room service, bars, pool, gym, laundry service, parking (paid), some pets allowed, no-smoking rooms* ▤*AE, DC, MC, V* ⍐*BP.*

£ 🏠 **The Ox.** Friendly and relaxed, this gastro-pub with rooms is a real find for those who just want the basics. Guest rooms are simple, creamy cool and modern in style. The buzz-filled restaurant, decorated with local artwork, serves modern British cuisine. Guest ales are on tap, complemented by a good selection of wines. The Ox is close to the Museum of Science and Industry, at the southern end of the city center. **Pros:** friendly staff; bargain prices. **Cons:** breakfast not included; no-frills decor. ⊠*71 Liverpool Rd., Castlefield* ☎*0161/839–7740* ⊕*www. theox.co.uk* ⥏*9 rooms* ⚷*In-room: no a/c. In-hotel: restaurant, bar, no-smoking rooms* ▤*MC, V.*

££££ 🏠 **The Place Apartment Hotel.** Cast-iron columns rise side by side with palm trees in an elegantly converted former cotton warehouse with modern, loft-style apartments. It's a good alternative for people who want the convenience of a kitchen or a second bedroom. The spacious rooms, centered on an airy atrium, still retain the original redbrick work but are fitted out in cool tones and pale-wood furniture. One- and two-bedroom apartments are available. **Pros:** restaurant open for breakfast and dinner; plenty of space. **Cons:** central atrium makes sound reverberate; floors a little worn. ⊠*Ducie St., Piccadilly, City Centre* ☎*0161/778–7500* ⊕*www.theplacehotel.com* ⥏*100 apartments, 8 penthouses* ⚷*In-room: no a/c, kitchen, DVD, Internet, Wi-Fi. In-hotel: restaurant, parking (paid), no-smoking rooms* ▤*AE, MC, V.*

NIGHTLIFE AND THE ARTS

Manchester vies with London as Britain's capital of youth culture, but has vibrant nightlife and entertainment options for all ages. Spending time at a bar, pub, or club is definitely an essential part of any trip. For event listings, check out the free *Manchester Evening News* or *Manchester Metro News*, both widely available.

NIGHTLIFE

The action after dark centers on the Deansgate, Northern Quarter, and Gay Village areas.

CAFÉ-BARS AND PUBS

Barça (⊠*8–9 Catalan Sq., Castlefield* ☎*0161/839–7099*) is a hip canal-side bar-restaurant that has won awards for its interesting architecture. **Cloud 23** (⊠*Beetham Tower, 303 Deansgate, City Centre* ☎*0161/870–1688*) in the Hilton has a stunning 360-degree view of the city that you'll pay for; but at 23 floors up, this swanky bar is not for the vertiginous. Book well ahead.

Dry Bar (⊠*28–30 Oldham St., Northern Quarter* ☎*0161/236–9840*), the original café-bar in town, is still full of young people drinking and dancing. Whether you come to see or be seen, the **Living Room**

(⊠*80 Deansgate, City Centre* ☎*0161/832–0083*) is the city's top spot; a pianist plays in the early evening. **Obsidian** (⊠*18–24 Princess St., City Centre* ☎*0161/238–4348*) has a huge frosted-glass bar and great cocktails. **Revolution** (⊠*Arch 7, Whitworth St. W, Peter's Fields* ☎*0161/839–7558*), one of the trendy bars converted from a railway arch in Deansgate Locks, is a vodka bar. **Tiger Tiger** (⊠*5–6 The Printworks, City Centre* ☎*0161/385–8080*) is the place to go for a relaxed meal and to drink or dance.

★ The **Gay Village,** which came to television in the British series *Queer as Folk,* has stylish bars and cafés along the Rochdale Canal; Canal Street is its heart. The area is not only the center of Manchester's good-size gay scene but also the nightlife center for the young and trendy. The chic **Manto** (⊠*46 Canal St., Gay Village* ☎*0161/236–2667*) draws a mostly gay crowd to its split-level, postindustrial interior.

Fodor'sChoice The **Britons Protection** (⊠*50 Great Bridgewater St., Peter's Fields*
★ ☎*0161/236–5895*) is a relaxed pub with stained-glass windows, cozy back rooms, and a mural of the Peterloo Massacre. You can sample more than 230 whiskies and bourbons. **Dukes 92** (⊠*18 Castle St., Castlefield* ☎*0161/839–3522*) has a perfect canal-side setting for a summer pub lunch or drink. **Peveril of the Peak** (⊠*127 Great Bridgewater St., Peter's Fields* ☎*0161/236–6364*), a nifty Victorian pub with a green-tile exterior, draws a crush of locals to its tiny rooms. **Sinclair's Oyster Bar** (⊠*2 Cathedral Gates, Millennium Quarter* ☎*0161/834–0430*), a half-timber pub built in the 17th century, specializes in fresh oyster dishes.

DANCE CLUBS
42nd Street (⊠*2 Bootle St., off Deansgate, City Centre* ☎*0161/831–7108*) plays retro, indie, sing-along anthems, and classic rock. **Sankey's** (⊠*Beehive Mill, Jersey St., Ancoats* ☎*0161/236–5444*) covers electro, techno, and hard-core music.

LIVE MUSIC
The recently revamped **Band on the Wall** (⊠*25 Swan St., Northern Quarter* ☎*0161/834–1786*) has a reputation for both established and pioneering music. Past performers include Joy Division, Simply Red, and Bjork. **Manchester Apollo** (⊠*Stockport Rd., Ardwick Green* ☎*0870/401–8000*) showcases live performances for all musical tastes. Major rock and pop stars appear at the **Manchester Evening News Arena** (⊠*21 Hunt's Bank, Hunt's Bank* ☎*0844/847–8000*). The **Roadhouse** (⊠*8 Newton St., City Centre* ☎*0161/228–1789*), an intimate band venue, also hosts funk and indie nights.

THE ARTS
PERFORMING ARTS VENUES
★ Dramatically modern **Bridgewater Hall** (⊠*Lower Mosley St., Peter's Fields* ☎*0161/907–9000*) has concerts by Manchester's renowned Hallé Orchestra and hosts both classical music and a varied light-entertainment program. The **Lowry** (⊠*Pier 8, Salford Quays* ☎*0870/787–5780*) contains two theaters and presents everything from musicals to dance and performance poetry. The **Opera House** (⊠*Quay St., City Centre* ☎*0844/847–2295*) is a venue for West End musicals, opera,

10

and classical ballet. The **Palace Theatre** (⊠ *Oxford St., City Centre* ☎ *0844/847–2275*) presents large touring shows—major plays, ballet, and opera. **Royal Northern College of Music** (⊠ *124 Oxford Rd., University Quarter* ☎ *0161/907–5555*) hosts classical and contemporary music concerts, jazz, and opera.

THEATER

Green Room (⊠ *54–56 Whitworth St. W, City Centre* ☎ *0161/615–0500*) is an alternative space for theater, poetry, dance, and performance art. **Library Theatre** (⊠ *St. Peter's Sq., City Centre* ☎ *0161/236–7110*) in the Central Library stages classical drama, Shakespeare, chamber musicals, and new work from local playwrights. **Royal Exchange Theatre** (⊠ *St. Ann's Sq., City Centre* ☎ *0161/833–9833*) serves as the city's main venue for innovative contemporary theater.

FOOTBALL

Football (soccer in the United States) is *the* reigning passion in Manchester. Locals support the local club, Manchester City, and glory seekers come from afar to root for Manchester United, based in neighboring Trafford. Matches for both clubs are usually sold out months in advance, though you have more of a chance with Manchester City. **Manchester City** (⊠ *Rowsley St., SportCity* ☎ *0870/062–1894*) plays at the City of Manchester Stadium. At the **Manchester City Museum and Stadium Tours** (⊠ *Rowsley St., SportCity* ☎ *0870/062–1894*) you can see club memorabilia, visit the players' changing rooms, and go down the tunnel to pitch side. Excluding match days, there are three tours daily Monday through Saturday, two on Sunday; admission is £9.50.

★ **Manchester United** (⊠ *Sir Matt Busby Way, Trafford Wharf* ☎ *0161/868–8000*) has home matches at Old Trafford. You can take a trip to the Theatre of Dreams at the **Manchester United Museum and Tour** (⊠ *Sir Matt Busby Way, Trafford Wharf* ☎ *0161/868–8000*), which tells the history of the football club. It's best to prebook the tour (not available on match days), which takes you behind the scenes, into the changing rooms and players' lounge, and down the tunnel. The museum is open daily 9:30 to 5; admission for the museum and tour is £11.74; for the museum only, £8.32. Take the tram to the Old Trafford stop and walk five minutes.

SHOPPING

The city is nothing if not fashion conscious; take your pick from glitzy department stores, huge retail outlets, designer shops, and idiosyncratic boutiques. Famous names are centered on Exchange Square, Deansgate, and King Street; the Northern Quarter provides style for younger trendsetters.

Afflecks Palace (⊠ *52 Church St., Northern Quarter* ☎ *0161/839–0718*) attracts young Mancunians with four floors of bohemian glam, ethnic crafts and jewelry, and innovative gift ideas. **Barton Arcade** (⊠ *51–63 Deansgate, City Centre* ☎ *No phone*) has specialty shopping inside a lovely Victorian arcade.

★ **Harvey Nichols** (⊠*21 New Cathedral St., City Centre* ☎*0161/828–8888*), an outpost of London's chic luxury department store, is packed with designer goods and has an excellent second-floor restaurant and brasserie. The **Lowry Designer Outlet** (⊠*Salford Quays* ☎*0161/848–1850*), with 80 stores, has good discounts on top brands at stores such as Nike and Karen Millen. The **Manchester Craft and Design Centre** (⊠*17 Oak St., Northern Quarter* ☎*0161/832–4274*) houses 18 workshop-cum-retail outlets. The world's largest **Marks & Spencer** (⊠*7 Market St., City Centre* ☎*0161/831–7341*) department store offers its own brand of fashion and has an excellent food department. The **Triangle** (⊠*Millennium Quarter* ☎*0161/834–8961*), a stylish mall in the Victorian Corn Exchange, has more than 30 stores, including independent designer shops.

Oldham Street, in the Northern Quarter, is littered with urban hip-hop boutiques and music shops.

LIVERPOOL

A city lined with one of the most famous waterfronts in England, celebrated around the world as the birthplace of the Beatles, and still the place to catch that "Ferry 'Cross the Mersey," Liverpool reversed a downturn in its fortunes with developments in the late 1980s, such as the impressively refurbished Albert Dock area and Tate Liverpool. Its stint as the European Union's Capital of Culture in 2008, when three billion pounds was invested in the city, acted as a catalyst for further regeneration. UNESCO named six historic areas in the city center a World Heritage Site, in recognition of its maritime and mercantile achievements. This heritage, together with the renowned attractions and a legacy of cultural vibrancy now draw in an ever increasing number of visitors.

Liverpool, on the east bank of the Mersey River estuary, at the point where it merges with the Irish Sea, developed from the 17th century through the slave trade. It became Britain's leading port for ferrying Africans to North America and for handling sugar, tobacco, rum, and cotton, which began to dominate the local economy after the abolition of the slave trade in 1807. Because of its proximity to Ireland, the city was also the first port of call for those fleeing famine, poverty, and persecution in that country. Liverpool was often the last British port of call for thousands of mostly Jewish refugees fleeing Eastern Europe.

Many of the best-known liner companies were based in Liverpool, including Cunard and White Star, whose best-known vessel, the *Titanic,* was registered in Liverpool. The city was dealt an economic blow in 1894 with the opening of the Manchester Ship Canal, which allowed traders to bypass Liverpool and head to Manchester, 35 mi east. Britain's entry into the European Common Market saw more trade move from the west coast to the east, and the postwar growth of air travel diverted passengers from the sea. Ocean–going liners however returned to the city in 2008 after the building of a new cruise liner terminal at the Pier Head.

10

The 1960s produced Liverpool's most famous export—the Beatles. The group was one of hundreds that copied the rock and roll they heard from visiting American GIs and merchant seamen in the late 1950s, and one of many that played local venues such as the Cavern (demolished but rebuilt nearby). All four Beatles were born in Liverpool, but the group's success dates from the time they left for London. Nevertheless, the city has milked the group's Liverpool connections for all they are worth, with a multitude of local attractions such as Paul McCartney's and John Lennon's childhood homes.

GETTING HERE AND AROUND

Liverpool John Lennon Airport, about 8 mi southeast of the city, receives mostly domestic and European flights. The Airlink 500 bus service runs to the city center every 30 minutes, and a taxi to the center of Liverpool costs around £15.

Long-distance National Express coaches, including service from London, use the Norton Street Coach Station, and local buses depart from Sir Thomas Street, Queen Square, and the Paradise Street Interchange. Traveline has information on long-distance and local routes. Train service on Virgin Trains from London's Euston Station takes 2½ hours.

If you're walking (which is easier than driving), you'll find the downtown sights well signposted. Take care when crossing the busy inner ring road separating the Albert Dock from the rest of the city. The circular C4 bus links Queen Square bus station with the Albert Dock (Gower Street stop).

TOURS   Blue Badge Guides can arrange dozens of different tours, which can be booked through the tourist office. Cavern City Tours offers a Beatles Magical Mystery Tour of Liverpool, departing from the Albert Dock Visitor Centre. The two-hour bus tour, which costs £13.95, runs past Penny Lane, Strawberry Field, and other mop-top landmarks. Liverpool Beatles Tours has personalized tours of Beatles sites. The oddly named Yellow Duckmarines runs daily tours on amphibious vehicles from World War II. The trips, which cost between £9.95 and £11.95, leave from the Gower Street bus stop in Albert Dock.

DISCOUNTS AND DEALS

If you're staying in Liverpool, you could make use of Your Ticket for Liverpool, a visitor card that gives free admission to selected sights, free bus travel in the city, and restaurant discounts over three consecutive days. It costs £24.99 and is available from tourist offices and online at ⊕ *www.yourticketforliverpool.com.*

ESSENTIALS

Bus Contacts Airlink 500 (☎ *0871/200–2233* ⊕ *www.arrivabus.co.uk*). **Traveline** (☎ *0871/200–2233* ⊕ *www.traveline.org.uk*).

Tour Contacts Blue Badge Guides (☎ *0796/451–5681 or 0791/865–5113*). **Cavern City Tours** (✉ *Mathew St., City Centre, Liverpool* ☎ *0151/236–9091* ⊕ *www.cavernclub.org*). **Liverpool Beatles Tours** (✉ *25 Victoria St., City Centre, Liverpool* ☎ *0151/281–7738* ⊕ *www.beatlestours.co.uk*). **YellowDuckmarines** (☎ *0151/708–7799* ⊕ *www.theyellowduckmarine.co.uk*).

Visitor Information Liverpool (✉ 36–38 Whitechapel, City Centre ☎0151/ 233-2008 or 0151/233-2459, 0844/870-0123 for accommodations ✉Anchor Courtyard, Albert Dock ☎0151/707-0729 ✉Arrival Hall, South Terminal, John Lennon Airport ☎0151/907-1057 ⊕ www.visitliverpool.com).

EXPLORING LIVERPOOL

Liverpool has a fairly compact center, and you can see most of the city highlights on foot. The skyline helps with orientation: the Radio City tower on **Queen Square** marks the center of the city and is a stone's throw away from the '08 Place, which gives tourist information. The Liver Birds, on top of the **Royal Liver Building**, signal the waterfront and River Mersey. North of the Radio City tower lie Lime Street station and William Brown Street, a showcase boulevard of municipal buildings, including the outstanding **Walker Art Gallery and Liverpool World Museum.** The city's other museums and the **Beatles Story** are concentrated westward on the waterfront in the **Albert Dock** area, a 20-minute walk or 5-minute bus ride away. The Museum of Liverpool is undergoing construction on nearby Mann Island, and is due to open in late 2010. **Hope Street**, to the east of the center, connects the city's two cathedrals, both easily recognizable on the skyline. On nearby Berry Street the red, green, and gold **Chinese Arch,** the largest outside China, marks the small Chinatown area. ■ TIP→ **Allow extra time to visit the childhood homes of Paul McCartney and John Lennon, as they lie outside the city center.**

ON THE TRAIL OF THE BEATLES

⑫ ★ **Beatles Story.** You can follow in the footsteps of the Fab Four at one of the more popular attractions in the Albert Dock complex. Entertaining scenes re-create stages in their career, from the enthusiastic early days in Germany and the Cavern Club to the White Room, where "Imagine" seems to emanate from softly billowing curtains. Artifacts included are the glasses John Lennon wore when he composed "Imagine" and the blue felt bedspread used in the famous "Bed-in" in 1969. The "Going Solo" section follows the members' separate careers. ■ TIP→ **Avoid the crowds of July and August by visiting in the late afternoon.** You can purchase tickets online in advance. A shop sells everything from wallets to alarm clocks emblazoned with the Beatles logo. ✉*Britannia Vaults, Albert Dock, Waterfront* ☎*0151/709-1963* ⊕*www.beatlesstory.com* ✉*£12.50* ⊙*Daily 9–7; last admission 2 hrs before closing.*

❺ **Mathew Street.** At the Cavern on this street Brian Epstein, who became the Beatles' manager, first heard the group in 1961. The Cavern had opened at No. 10 as a jazz venue in 1957, but beat groups, of whom the Beatles were clearly the most talented, had taken it over. Epstein became their manager a few months after first visiting the club, and within two years the group was the most talked-about phenomenon in music. The club was demolished in 1973; it was rebuilt a few yards from the original site. At No. 5 is the Cavern Pub, opened in 1994, with Beatles memorabilia and plenty of nostalgia. ■ TIP→ **At No. 31, check out the well-stocked Beatles Shop.**

10

Liverpool

KEY

🛈 *Tourist information*

0 _____ 1/4 mile

0 _____ 400 meters

QUICK BITES

Not far from Mathew Street, **Delifonseca** (✉ *12 Stanley St., City Centre* ☎ *0151/255–0808*) offers reviving coffee and cake, as well as excellent sandwiches and salads. You could also stock up on munchies from the capacious downstairs deli.

Mendips. The National Trust (overseers of such landmarks as Blenheim Palace) maintains the 1930s middle-class, semidetached house that was the home of John Lennon from 1946 to 1963 and is a must-see for Beatles pilgrims. After his parents separated, John joined his aunt Mimi here; she gave him his first guitar but banished him to the porch, saying, "The guitar's all very well, John, but you'll never make a living out of it." The house can be seen only on a tour, for which you must book a seat on the minibus that connects the site with the Jurys Inn next to Albert Dock (mornings) or Speke Hall (afternoons). You can book online. ✉ *251 Menlove Ave., Woolton* ☎ *0844/800–4791 or 0151/427–7231* ⊕ *www.nationaltrust.org.uk* ✉ *£16, includes 20 Forthlin Road and Speke Hall gardens* ⊙ *Mid-Mar.–Oct., Wed.–Sun. and national holidays, 4 departures a day; early Mar. and Nov., Wed.– Sun., 3 departures a day. Call for times.*

20 Forthlin Road. From 1955 to 1964, Paul McCartney lived with his family in this modest 1950s council house (a building rented from the

Beatles Discovered ... and Rediscovered

Brian Epstein was led to the Beatles in 1961 by a teenager who came into his record shop, NEMS (North End Music Stores) at 12–14 Whitechapel, and asked for a record by Tony Sheridan and the Beat Brothers. He couldn't find it in his catalog, but discovered that the backing band was the Beatles, a local group, playing at the nearby Cavern Club. Epstein heard the group, and the rest is history.

History lives on, though. If the Beatles Story, Mathew Street, Mendips, and 20 Forthlin Road can't sate your Beatlemania in Liverpool, consider adding a guided tour of the essential and more off-the-beaten-path landmarks.

The faithful celebrate the Beatles' enduring appeal at the annual **International Beatle Week** (⊕ www. cavernclub.org), usually held the last week in August when what seems to be the entire city takes time out to dance, attend John and Yoko fancy-dress parties, and listen to Beatle bands from around the world. The event includes concerts, a convention, flea markets, and more. If you have the money to spend, stay at—or at least visit the bar of—the Beatle-themed **Hard Day's Night Hotel** on Mathew Street. Yeah, yeah, yeah!

local government). A number of the Beatles' songs, including "Love Me Do" and "When I'm Sixty-Four," were written here. Inside is an exhibit of photographs of Paul taken by his brother, Mike. The house is viewable only on a tour, for which you must prebook a seat on the minibus that connects the site with the Jurys Inn next to Albert Dock (mornings) or Speke Hall (afternoons). You can book online. ⊠ *20 Forthlin Rd., Allerton* ☎ *0844/800–4791 or 0151/427–7231* ⊕ *www.nationaltrust. org.uk* ⊠ *£16, includes Mendips and Speke Hall gardens* ☽ *Mid-Mar.– Oct., Wed.–Sun. and national holidays, 4 departures a day; early Mar. and Nov., 3 departures a day. Call for times.*

TOP ATTRACTIONS

⓭ **Albert Dock.** To understand the city's prosperous maritime past, head for
★ waterfront Albert Dock, 7 acres of restored warehouses built in 1846. Named after Queen Victoria's consort, Prince Albert, the dock provided storage for silk, tea, and tobacco from the Far East until it was closed in 1972. Rescued by the Merseyside Development Corporation, the fine colonnaded brick warehouse buildings are England's largest heritage attraction, containing the **Merseyside Maritime Museum**, the **International Slavery Museum**, **Tate Liverpool**, and the **Beatles Story.** When weather allows, sit at an outdoor café overlooking the dock or take a boat trip through the docks and onto the river. Albert Dock is part of the area known as **Liverpool's Historic Waterfront.** ■ TIP→ **Much of the pedestrian area of the Albert Dock and Waterfront area is made of cobbled stone, so be sure to wear comfortable shoes.** ⊕ *www.albertdock.com.*

⓽ **International Slavery Museum.** On the third floor of the Maritime Museum, this museum's three dynamic galleries recount the history of transatlantic slavery and trace its significance in contemporary society. "Life in

10

West Africa" reproduces a Nigerian Igbo compound, all the shackles of slavery are shown in the "Enslavement" section, and many stories, some never heard before, are told in "Legacies of Slavery." ⊠*Albert Dock Waterfront* ☎*0151/478–4499* ⊕*www.liverpoolmuseums.org. uk* ⊠*Free* ☉*Daily 10–5.*

⑩ Merseyside Maritime Museum. Part of the Albert Dock complex, this is a wonderful place to explore the role of the sea in the life of the city. The museum captures the triumphs and tragedies of Liverpool's seafaring history over five floors. As well as maritime paintings, models, ceramics, and ships in bottles, the main museum brings to life the ill-fated stories of the *Titanic* and *Lusitania*, the Battle of the Atlantic, and the city's role during World War II. The basement is home to Seized, the Customs and Excise National Museum, which explores the heroes and villains of the world of smuggling, together with the story of mass emigration from the port in the 19th century. In summer full-size vessels are on display. ⊠*Albert Dock, Waterfront* ☎*0151/478–4499* ⊕*www. liverpoolmuseums.org.uk* ⊠*Free* ☉*Daily 10–5.*

Fodor'sChoice ★

⑦ Pier Head. Here you can take a ferry across the River Mersey from Pierhead to Birkenhead and Seacombe and back. Boats leave regularly and offer fine views of the city—a journey celebrated in "Ferry 'Cross the Mersey," Gerry and the Pacemakers' 1964 hit song. It was from Pier Head that 9 million British, Irish, and other European emigrants set sail between 1830 and 1930 for new lives in the United States, Canada, Australia, and Africa. ■TIP→ Take a short ferry ride or the longer cruise with commentary ("Scousers," as locals are known, are famous for their patter); the city views are worth the time and money. ⊠*Pier Head Ferry Terminal, Mersey Ferries, Waterfront* ☎*0151/330–1444* ⊕*www. merseyferries.co.uk* ⊠*£2.30 round-trip, cruises £5.30* ☉*Ferries every 30 mins weekdays 7:30–9:30 AM (Seacombe only) and 4:15–6:45 PM; cruises hourly weekdays 10–3, weekends 10–6.*

⑥ Royal Liver Building. Best seen from the ferry, the 322-foot-tall Royal Liver (pronounced lie-ver) Building with its twin towers is topped by two 18-foot-high copper birds. They represent the mythical Liver Birds, the town symbol; local legend has it that if they fly away, Liverpool will cease to exist. For decades Liverpudlians looked to the Royal Liver Society for assistance—it was originally a burial club to which families paid contributions to ensure a decent send-off. ⊠*Water St., Waterfront.*

⑪ Tate Liverpool. An offshoot of the London-based art galleries of the same name, the Liverpool museum, a handsome conversion of existing Albert Dock warehouses, was designed in the 1990s by the late James Stirling, one of Britain's leading 20th-century architects. Galleries display changing exhibits of challenging modern art. A free introductory tour begins daily at 12:30. The excellent shop sells art books, prints, and posters, and there's a children's art-play area and a dockside café-restaurant. ⊠*The Colonnades, Albert Dock, Waterfront* ☎*0151/702–7400* ⊕*www.tate.org.uk* ⊠*Free, charge for special exhibitions* ☉*Apr.–Sept., daily 10–5:50; Oct.–Mar., Tues.–Sun. and national holidays 10–5:50.*

❸ **Walker Art Gallery.** With a superb
Fodor's Choice display of British art and some out-
★ standing Italian and Flemish works,
the Walker maintains its position as
one of the best British art collections outside London. Don't miss
the unrivaled collection of paintings by 18th-century Liverpudlian
equestrian artist George Stubbs,
and works by J. M. W. Turner, John
Constable, Sir Edwin Henry Landseer, and the Pre-Raphaelites. Mod-

ern artists are included, too—on display is one of David Hockney's
typically Californian pool scenes. Other excellent exhibits showcase
china, silver, and furniture that once adorned the mansions of Liverpool's industrial barons. The Tea Room holds center stage in the airy
museum lobby. ✉ *William Brown St., City Centre* ☎ *0151/478–4199*
⊕ *www.liverpoolmuseums.org.uk* ✉ *Free* ⊙ *Daily 10–5.*

❶ **World Museum Liverpool.** You can travel from the prehistoric to the space
⊙ age through stunning displays in these state-of-the-art galleries. Ethnol-
ogy, the natural and physical sciences, and archaeology all get their due
on five floors. The World Cultures gallery colorfully illustrates the cosmopolitan history of the city. If the kids aren't grabbed by the monster
bugs in the Bug House or afternoon shows in the Treasure House Theatre and Planetarium, they'll find plenty to do in the hands-on centers.
✉ *William Brown St.* ☎ *0151/478–4393* ⊕ *www.liverpoolmuseums.
org.uk* ✉ *Free* ⊙ *Daily 10–5.*

WORTH NOTING

⓮ **Anglican Cathedral.** The largest church in northern Britain overlooks the
city and the River Mersey. Built of local sandstone, the Gothic-style
cathedral was begun in 1903 by architect Giles Gilbert Scott; it was
finally finished in 1978. Take a look at the grand interior on your own
or experience the Great Space film and audio tour to help you appreciate the building. The 331-foot-tall tower is a popular climb; two
elevators and 108 steps take you to breathtaking views. Take in the
Embroidery Gallery on your way up. A refectory serves light meals and
coffee. ✉ *St. James's Mount, City Centre* ☎ *0151/709–6271* ⊕ *www.
liverpoolcathedral.org.uk* ✉ *£3 suggested donation, tower and embroidery exhibition £4.25, film and audio tour £4.25, combined ticket £6.75*
⊙ *Daily 8–6. Tower Mar.–Sept., Mon.–Sat. 10–4:30; Oct.–Feb., Mon.–
Sat. 10–3:30. Film and audio tour Mon.–Sat. 9–4, Sun. noon–2.30.*

Another Place. A hundred naked, life-size, cast iron figures by sculptor
Antony Gormley stand proudly on the 2 mi of foreshore at Crosby
Beach, weathered by sand and sea. Unlike most other statues, you are
permitted to interact with these and even clothe them as you wish.
Check tide times before you go and be aware that it's not safe to
walk out to the farthest figures. The site is 6 mi north of Liverpool
center; to get here take the Merseyrail train to Waterloo from Moor-
fields station. A taxi will cost around £15. ✉ *Mariners Rd., Crosby*

10

Beach ☎*0151/237–3945, 0151/934–2967 for tide times* ⊕*www. visitsouthport.com* ✉*Free.*

❹ **Metropolitan Cathedral of Christ the King.** This Roman Catholic cathedral consecrated in 1967 is a modernistic, funnel-like structure of concrete, stone, and mosaic, topped with a glass lantern. Long, narrow, blue-glass windows separate chapels, each with modern works of art. An earlier design by classically inspired architect Edwin Lutyens was abandoned when World War II began (the current design is by Frederick Gibberd), but you can still take a look at Lutyen's vast brick-and-granite crypt and barrel-vaulted ceilings. ⊠*Mount Pleasant, City Centre* ☎*0151/709–9222* ⊕*www.liverpoolmetrocathedral.org.uk* ✉*£3 suggested donation* ⊙*Mon.–Sat. 8–6, Sun. 8–5.*

❷ **St. George's Hall.** Built between 1839 and 1847, St. George's Hall is among the world's best Greek Revival buildings. When Queen Victoria visited Liverpool in 1851, she declared it "worthy of ancient Athens." Today the hall serves as a home for music festivals, concerts, and fairs. Self-guided tours tell the story of the building as a Crown court and cultural venue. ⊠*Lime St., City Centre* ☎*0151/225–6909* ⊙*Daily10–5.*

Speke Hall and Gardens. This black-and-white mansion only 6 mi from downtown Liverpool is one of the best examples of half-timbering in Britain. Built around a cobbled courtyard, the great hall dates to 1490; an elaborate western bay with a vast chimneypiece was added in 1560. The house, owned by the National Trust, was heavily restored in the 19th century, though a Tudor priest hole and Jacobean plasterwork remain intact. Speke Hall is on the east side of the airport; the Airportxpress 500 bus drops you a pleasant 10-minute walk away. ⊠*The Walk, Speke* ☎*0151/427–7231* ⊕*www.nationaltrust.org.uk* ✉*£7.27; gardens only, £4.31* ⊙*House mid-Mar.–Oct., Wed.–Sun. and national holidays 11–5; Nov.–early Dec., weekends 11–4:30. Gardens daily 11–5:30 or dusk. Last admission 30 mins before closing.*

❽ **Western Approaches Museum.** Be taken right back to the 1940s when you explore the warren of rooms under the city streets, once the top-secret headquarters for the Battle of the Atlantic during World War II. The lofty Operations Room, full of the state-of-the-art technology of the time, is especially evocative. ⊠*1–3 Rumford St., off Chapel St., City Centre* ☎*0151/227–2008* ⊕*www.liverpoolwarmuseum.co.uk* ✉*£4.75* ⊙*Mar.–Oct., Mon.–Thurs. and Sat. 10:30–4:30*

WHERE TO EAT

£££ ✕**60 Hope Street.** The combination of a ground-floor restaurant and a
MODERN BRITISH more informal basement bistro make this a popular choice. A light, polished wood floor and blue-and-cream walls help create an uncluttered backdrop for dishes that reflect a Mediterranean clime, but found only on British shores are fish in beer batter and the deep-fried jam sandwich with condensed-milk ice cream. ⊠*60 Hope St., City Centre* ☎*0151/707–6060* ▤*AE, MC, V* ⊙*Closed Sun. No lunch Sat. in restaurant.*

£££ ✕**Blue Bar and Grill.** Expect to rub shoulders with local celebrities in
BRITISH this sophisticated modern restaurant and bar on the waterfront. The
focal point is the beautiful Venetian crystal chandelier, a counterpoint
to the original open brickwork, chunky furnishings, and plasma video
monitors. Downstairs (less expensive) you can sample tapas, dim sum,
and bruschetta; the fare in the upstairs gallery includes pork with pea
purée and black pudding mash, and a large selection of meat and fish
steaks, accompanied by different sauces. ⊠*Edward Pavilion, Albert
Dock, Waterfront* ☎*0151/709–7097* ⊟*AE, MC, V.*

£ ✕**Everyman Bistro.** A cosmopolitan crowd can always be found at the
BRITISH simple wooden tables in the crypt of the Everyman Theatre. The hearty,
★ varied menu changes twice daily and might include lamb scouse (stew)
with beetroot and red cabbage or smoked haddock with horseradish and
pea-fish cakes, with apple-and-almond pudding for a notable dessert.
Vegetarians have plenty of choices, and there are good soups, cheeses,
and salads for lunch. ⊠*5–9 Hope St., City Centre* ☎*0151/708–9545*
⊟*AE, MC, V* ☙*Closed Sun.*

££ ✕**Side Door.** You'll often find couples enjoying a meal before a play or
BRITISH concert at this intimate and unpretentious bistro. The menu changes
every week, but there is always plenty of fish, such as hake with rosemary potatoes, and the sticky toffee pudding is legendary. Pretheater
fixed-price meals are good value. ⊠*29a Hope St.,* ☎*0151/707–
7888* ⊟*MC, V* ☙*Closed Sun.*

£££ ✕**Simply Heathcote's.** This chic contemporary restaurant, an outpost of
BRITISH chef Paul Heathcote's empire, has a curved glass front, cherry furnishings, and a granite floor. The menu has a local accent—fried black
pudding with rhubarb chutney, duck with potato dumplings, and bread-
and-butter pudding—along with dishes from warmer climes. Vegetarians are well served, too. The restaurant is opposite the Royal Liver
and Cunard buildings. ⊠*25 The Strand, Waterfront* ☎*0151/236–3536*
⊟*AE, MC, V.*

£ ✕**Tate Café.** The Tate Liverpool's café-bar is a winner for daytime sus-
BRITISH tenance whether or not you're visiting the museum. Dockside seats
are great on warm summer days, and you can choose from among the
salads and open sandwiches, including steak with Wirral watercress as
well as main dishes such as chicken breast with Savoy cabbage. Fruit
scones with jam and cream also make an appearance. ⊠*The Colonnades, Albert Dock, Waterfront* ☎*0151/702–7581* ⊟*MC, V* ☙*Closed
Mon in winter. No dinner.*

£ ✕**Yuet Ben.** The name means "Welcome, Honored Guest," and this
CHINESE warm greeting stays with you throughout your visit to this longtime
institution. Tantalizingly aromatic dishes such as crispy duck and sweet-
and-sour cherry chicken are presented with a smile. There's always a
good vegetarian choice. The restaurant is just opposite the Chinese
Arch. ⊠*1 Upper Duke St., City Centre* ☎*0151/709–5772* ⊟*AE, MC,
V* ☙*Closed Mon.*

10

WHERE TO STAY

££–£££ [] **Crowne Plaza Liverpool.** Many of the city's main sights are at the doorstep of this modern hotel on the waterfront next to the Royal Liver Building. A bright, bustling atrium leads to well-equipped and spacious bedrooms, done in soothing colors. Family rooms have two double beds; children under 12 stay free and even get free meals in the Plaza Brasserie. **Pros:** on waterfront; friendly staff; plenty of activities. **Cons:** chain-hotel furnishings; guest room windows cannot be opened. ⊠ *St. Nicholas Pl., Waterfront* ☎ *0151/243–8000* ⊕ *www.cpliverpool.com* ⇨ *159 rooms* ⅓ *In-room: Internet. In-hotel: 2 restaurants, room service, bar, pool, gym, laundry service, Wi-Fi, parking (paid), no-smoking rooms* ⊟ *AE, DC, MC, V.*

££££ [] **Hard Day's Night Hotel.** "Everything seems to be right" since the
Fodor's Choice marble-columned office block on the corner of Mathew Street was
★ transformed into a hotel in homage to the Beatles. Their music is played in the public rooms and their photos (many original) loom large on the walls, but it's all done with finesse. A wide staircase spirals up from the humming brasserie and bar, the hub of the hotel, to sleek and luxurious guest rooms hung with original paintings. The unashamedly modern ambience, emboldened with bright orange, blue, and green fabrics, includes electronic gadgets that control everything. The moody red-and-black Hari's Bar is the place to see and be seen; Blakes restaurant provides the nourishment you need for your tour of Beatles sites. **Pros:** welcoming staff; sophisticated rooms; close to Beatles attractions. **Cons:** rumbling trains and street noise heard in some rooms; breakfast costs extra; no parking. ⊠ *Central Bldgs., N. John St., City Centre* ☎ *0151/236–1964* ⊕ *www.harddaysnighthotel.com* ⇨ *108 rooms, 2 suites* ⅓ *In-room: safe, Wi-Fi. In-hotel: restaurant, room service, bars, laundry service, no-smoking rooms* ⊟ *AE, DC, MC, V.*

£££ [] **Hope Street Hotel.** Liverpool's first boutique hotel is in a converted
★ carriage warehouse built in the style of a Venetian palazzo. Hope Street Hotel puts the emphasis on traditional, natural materials and retains the exposed brickwork and cast-iron columns from the 1860s. A stunning oak staircase runs the height of the building. Light, elegant bedrooms are minimalist in style, with crisp white bed linens and custom-made walnut and cherry pieces; the rooms benefit from underfloor heating. The London Carriage Works concentrates on local and seasonal produce. **Pros:** beautiful design; plenty of space. **Cons:** service can be inconsistent; parking difficult to find; rooms face a busy street. ⊠ *40 Hope St., City Centre* ☎ *0151/709–3000* ⊕ *www.hopestreethotel.co.uk* ⇨ *41 rooms, 7 suites* ⅓ *In-room: no a/c, DVD, Internet. In-hotel: restaurant, room service, bars, laundry service, Wi-Fi, parking (paid), no-smoking rooms* ⊟ *AE, MC, V.*

£ [] **Liverpool Youth Hostel.** This hostel a few minutes' walk from Albert Dock really should change its name, because it offers modest hotel standards for bargain prices. The smart rooms (for two, three, four, or six people) are fully carpeted, with private bathrooms and heated towel rails. **Pros:** breakfast included; plenty of parking. **Cons:** far from the center; limited number of double rooms. ⊠ *25 Tabley St., off Wapping Waterfront* ☎ *0870/770–5924* ⊕ *www.yha.org.uk* ⇨ *100 beds*

✪ *In-room: no a/c, no TV. In-hotel: restaurant, laundry facilities, Internet terminal, Wi-Fi* ▤ *MC, V* ⦿*BP.*

££££ ▦ **Malmaison.** The only purpose-built hotel in this chic chain combines extreme glamour with sleek industrial modernity and a great sense of space. It's a five-minute walk north of the Liver Building. It's right on the waterfront, so request a riverside room with a view. Guest rooms, though not large, favor plum and orange and rich textures; walk-in "wet rooms" have a shower and a tub. Public areas are transformed in the evening when chairs change their livery and candlelight abounds, and a cocktail in the Plum Bar is an almost theatrical experience. **Pros:** buzzy atmosphere; rich decor. **Cons:** dim lighting in guest rooms; no parking; views to the back are disappointing. ⊠*Princes Dock* ☎*0151/229–5000* ⊕*www.malmaison.com* ⇆*128 rooms, 2 suites* ✪*In-room: safe, refrigerator, DVD, Internet, Wi-Fi. In-hotel: restaurant, room service, bar, gym, laundry service, no-smoking rooms* ▤ *AE, MC, V.*

££–£££ ▦ **Premier Apartments.** These apartments have everything you need for an independent stay—including groceries, which can be delivered to your door. Spacious and airy apartments have either one or two bedrooms and are furnished in cheerful contemporary style. Lime Street station is a five-minute walk away. **Pros:** great for travelers who don't need hotel services; plenty of room; breakfast delivered every morning. **Cons:** more expensive on weekends; limited parking. ⊠*11 Hatton Gardens, City Centre* ☎*0151/227–9467 or 0845/070–0907* ⊕*www. premierapartments.com* ⇆*62 apartments* ✪*In-room: no a/c, Internet, Wi-Fi. In-hotel: laundry facilities, laundry service, parking (paid), no-smoking rooms* ▤ *AE, MC, V.*

££–£££ ▦ **Staybridge Apartments.** These up-to-the-minute and well-fitted
★ apartments close to the Liverpool Arena make for a great stay on the waterfront. Rooms are filled with light and contain compact kitchens, modern-style furnishings, and spare sofa beds. You can have breakfast (included in the price) with other guests, or stock up on food from the on-site shop. Reception, available 24 hours, is friendly and helpful. **Pros:** upbeat atmosphere; complimentary receptions on weekday evenings; public spaces for socializing. **Cons:** limited parking; no nice views. ⊠*21 Keel Wharf, Waterfront* ☎*0151/703–9700* ⊕*www.staybridge.co.uk* ⇆*132 apartments* ✪*In-room: kitchen, refrigerator, Internet, Wi-Fi. In-hotel: gym, laundry facilities, laundry service, parking (paid)* ▤ *AE, MC, V* ⦿*BP.*

NIGHTLIFE AND THE ARTS

NIGHTLIFE

The many bars, clubs, and pubs of Liverpool are an experience in themselves, from the trendy to the traditional. **Alma de Cuba** (⊠*Seel St.,*
Fodor's Choice *City Centre* ☎*0151/702–7394*), a church transformed into a luxuri-
★ ous bar, uses a huge mirrored altar and hundreds of dripping candles to great effect. **Baby Cream** (⊠*Atlantic Pavilion, Albert Dock, Waterfront* ☎*0151/709–7097*) is known for its weekend DJs. The ladies can pamper themselves in the glitzy black powder room. The **Cavern Club** (⊠*8–10 Mathew St., City Centre* ☎*0151/236–1965*) draws many on the Beatles trail, some of whom don't realize it's not the original

10

spot—that was demolished years ago. The **Cavern Pub** (⌧5 Mathew St., City Centre ☎0151/236–4041) merits a stop for nostalgia's sake; here are recorded the names of the groups and artists who played in the Cavern Club between 1957 and 1973. Opposite Philharmonic Hall, the **Philharmonic** (⌧36 Hope St., City Centre ☎0151/707–2837) is a Victorian-era extravaganza decorated in colorful marble. Make sure to check out the ornate loos. **Ye Cracke** (⌧13 Rice St., off Hope St., City Centre ☎0151/709–4171), one of the city's oldest pubs, was much visited by John Lennon in the 1960s.

THE ARTS

FILM

The **FACT Centre** (⌧88 Wood St., City Centre ☎0151/707–4450) (Foundation for Art and Creative Technology) shows art-house and independent films on three screens; galleries display experimental film, video, and new media.

PERFORMING ARTS VENUES

The well-regarded Royal Liverpool Philharmonic Orchestra plays its
★ concert season at **Philharmonic Hall** (⌧Hope St., City Centre ☎0151/709–3789). The venue also hosts contemporary music, jazz, and world concerts, and shows classic films.

Bluecoat (⌧School La., City Centre ☎0151/702–5324) features contemporary visual and performing arts. The **Liverpool Arena and Convention Centre** (⌧Monarch's Quay, Waterfront ☎0844/8000–400) hosts large-scale concerts and exhibitions. The **Liverpool Empire** (⌧Lime St., City Centre ☎0844/847–2525) presents major ballet, opera, drama, and musical performances.

THEATER

Everyman Theatre (⌧5–9 Hope St., City Centre ☎0151/709–4776) focuses on works by British playwrights as well as experimental productions from around the world. **Royal Court Theatre** (⌧1 Roe St., City Centre ☎0870/787–1866), an art deco building, is one of the city's most appealing sites for stand-up comedy and theater.

SPORTS AND THE OUTDOORS

FOOTBALL

Football (soccer) matches are played on weekends and, increasingly, weekdays. Tickets for Liverpool are sold out months in advance, but you should have more luck with Everton.

Liverpool (☎0844/844–0844), one of England's top clubs, plays at Anfield, 2 mi north of the city center. The **Liverpool Museum and Stadium Tour** (⌧Anfield Rd., Anfield ☎0151/260–6677 ⌧£5 ☉Daily 10–3) takes you into the dressing rooms and down the tunnel, and gives you a sense of match day. There are no tours on match days. **Everton** (☎0870/442–1878), now reestablishing its historic competitiveness, plays at Goodison Park, about ½ mi north of Anfield.

HORSE RACING

★ Britain's most famous horse race, the Grand National steeplechase, has been run at Liverpool's **Aintree Racecourse** (⊠*Ormskirk Rd., Aintree* ☎*0844/579–3001*) almost every year since 1839. The race is held in March or April; book well ahead. Admission on most race days is £18.

SHOPPING

Circa 1900 (⊠*11–13 Holts Arcade, India Buildings, Water St., City Centre* ☎*0151/236–1282*) specializes in authentic art nouveau and art deco pieces, from ceramics and glass to furniture. **From Me to You** (⊠*Cavern Walks, Mathew St., City Centre* ☎*0151/227–1963*) may stock the mop-top knickknack of your dreams. **Liverpool One** (⊠*Off Paradise St.City Centre* ☎*No phone*), the city's latest and largest shopping complex, has more than 160 stores, including John Lewis. **Metquarter** (⊠*35 Whitechapel, City Centre* ☎*0151/224–2390*), with more than 40 stores, is the place for designer names and the latest fashions. The **Stanley Dock Sunday Market** (⊠*Great Howard St. and Regent Rd., City Centre*) operates each Sunday, selling bric-a-brac, clothes, and toys. The **Walker Art Gallery** (⊠*William Brown St., City Centre* ☎*0151/478–4199*) has a small lobby shop with high-quality glassware, ceramics, and jewelry by local designers.

THE PEAK DISTRICT

Heading southeast, away from the urban congestion of Manchester and Liverpool, it's not far to the southernmost contortions of the Pennine Hills. Here, about an hour from Manchester, sheltered in a great natural bowl, is the spa town of Buxton: at an elevation of more than 1,000 feet, it's the second-highest town in England. Buxton makes a convenient base for exploring the 540 square mi of the Peak District, Britain's oldest—and, some say, most beautiful—national park. About 38,000 people live in the towns throughout the park. "Peak" is perhaps misleading; despite being a hilly area, it contains only gentle rises that don't reach much higher than 2,000 feet. Yet a trip around destinations such as Bakewell, Matlock, Castleton, and Edale, and the grand estates of Chatsworth House, Haddon Hall, and Hardwick Hall involves negotiating fairly perilous country roads, each of which repays the effort with enchanting views. Outdoor activities are popular in the Peaks, particularly caving (or "potholing"), walking, and hiking. Bring all-weather clothing and waterproof shoes.

10

BUXTON

25 mi southeast of Manchester.

Buxton's spa days left a notable legacy of 18th- and 19th-century buildings, parks, and open spaces that give the town an air of faded grandeur. The Romans arrived in AD 79 and named Buxton Aquae Arnemetiae, loosely translated as "Waters of the Goddess of the Grove," suggesting they considered this area in the Derbyshire hills special. The mineral springs, which emerge from 3,500 to 5,000 feet below ground at a constant 82°F, were believed to cure assorted ailments; in the 18th century the town became established as a popular spa, a minor rival to Bath. You can still drink water from the ancient St. Anne's Well, and it's also bottled and sold throughout Britain.

GETTING HERE AND AROUND

Both the National Express and TransPeak bus services from Manchester stop at Buxton. There are departures every two to three hours from Manchester's Chorlton Street Bus Station. If you're driving from Manchester, take A6 southeast to Buxton. The journey takes one hour. The hourly train from Manchester to Buxton takes an hour.

ESSENTIALS

Bus Contacts GMPTE information line (☎ *0161/228–7811* or *0871/200– 2233* ⊕ *www.gmpte.com*). **National Express** (☎ *0871/781–8181* ⊕ *www. nationalexpress.com*). **TransPeak** (☎ *01733/712265* ⊕ *www.transpeak.co.uk*).

Visitor Information Buxton (✉ *The Crescent* ☎ *01298/25106* ⊕ *www. visitpeakdistrict.com*).

EXPLORING

A good place to start exploring is the **Crescent** on the northwest side of the Slopes park (the town hall is on the opposite side); almost all out-of-town roads lead toward this central green. The three former hotels that make up the Georgian-era Crescent, with its arches, Doric colonnades, and 378 windows, were built in 1780 by fashionable architect John Carr for the fifth duke of Devonshire (of nearby Chatsworth House). The thermal baths at the end of the Crescent now house a shopping center.

The **Devonshire Royal Hospital,** behind the Crescent, also by John Carr, was originally a stable with room for 110 horses. In 1859 the circular area for exercising horses was covered with a massive 156-foot-wide slate-color dome and incorporated into the hospital. The University of Derby has taken over the building and, when school is in session, runs an informal bistro open during the day and a restaurant serving excellent lunches (weekdays) and dinners (Thursday).

The **Buxton Museum** contains a collection of Blue John stone, a semi-precious mineral found only in the Peak District. It also displays local archaeological finds and pieces made from Derbyshire black marble, and there's a small art gallery. The museum is on the eastern side of the Slopes. ✉ *Terrace Rd.* ☎ *01298/24658* ✉ *Free* ☉ *Tues.–Fri. 9:30–5:30, Sat. 9:30–5, Sun. and national holidays (Apr.–Sept. only) 10:30–5.*

The **Pavilion** (✉ *Pavilion Gardens* ☎ *01298/23114*), with its ornate iron-and-glass roof, was a concert hall and ballroom. Erected in the 1870s, it remains a lively place, with a plant-filled conservatory, several bars, a cafeteria, and a restaurant, surrounded by 25 acres of gardens. The Pavilion is adjacent to the Crescent and the Slopes on the west.

The Peak District's extraordinary geology is revealed close to Buxton at **Poole's Cavern,** a large limestone cave far beneath the 100 wooded acres of Buxton Country Park. The cave was inhabited in prehistoric times and contains, in addition to the standard stalactites and stalagmites, the source of the River Wye, which flows through Buxton. ✉*Green La.* ☏*01298/26978* ⊕*www.poolescavern.co.uk* 🎫*£7.50, including 50-min guided tour. Park and visitor center free* ⊙*Dec.–mid-Feb., weekends 10–4; mid-Feb.–Oct., daily 9:30–5; Nov., daily 10–4. Tours every 20 mins.*

★

The epitome of "magpie" black-and-white half-timber buildings, **Little Moreton Hall**, in the words of Olive Cook's *The English Country House*, "exaggerates and exalts the typical and humble medieval timber-framed dwelling, making of it a bizarre, unforgettable phenomenon." Covered with zigzags, crosses, and lozenge shapes crafted of timber and daub, the house was built by the Moreton family between 1450 and 1580. The long gallery and colorful Tudor-era wall paintings are spectacular, and the staggered lavatories are intriguing. Little Moreton Hall lies to the west of the Peak District; to get here from Liverpool, take the M6 to the A534 east to Congleton. The house is 20 mi southwest of Buxton. ✉*A34, Congleton* ☏*01260/272018* ⊕*www.nationaltrust.org.uk* 🎫*£6.10 Mar.–Nov., £3.30 Dec.* ⊙*Early–mid-Mar., weekends 11–4; late Mar.–early Nov., Wed.–Sun. and national holidays 11–5; mid-Nov.–late Nov., weekends 11–4; early to mid-Dec., ground fl. only, weekends 11–4.*

WHERE TO EAT AND STAY

££
BRITISH

✕**Columbine.** The husband-and-wife team behind Columbine always go for local flavor, no matter if the dishes are traditional, such as High Peak lamb's liver with black pudding and smoked bacon, or more retro, like duckling with oranges and Grand Marnier. The cozy venue, with upstairs and downstairs seating, is a good spot for pre- and post-theater meals. ✉*7 Hall Bank* ☏*01298/78752* ▭*MC, V* ⊙*Closed Sun. May–Oct. and Sun. and Tues. Nov.–Apr. No lunch Aug.–June.*

££
★

🏠**Buxton's Victorian Guesthouse.** One of a terrace (a group of row houses) built by the duke of Devonshire in 1860, this beautifully decorated house stands a stone's throw away from the Opera House. Victorian and Edwardian antiques and prints furnish the individually decorated rooms. Imaginative breakfasts are taken in the beautifully decorated dining room. **Pros:** peaceful location on Pavilion Gardens; family suite available. **Cons:** many stairs to climb; surcharge for credit cards. ✉*3A Broad Walk* ☏*01298/78759* ⊕*www.buxtonvictorian.co.uk* 🛏*7 rooms, 1 suite* ♿*In-room: no a/c, no phone. In-hotel: parking (free), no kids under 4, no-smoking rooms* ▭*AE, MC, V* ⊙*BP.*

££–£££

🏠**Old Hall.** In a refurbished 16th-century building, this hotel overlooks the Opera House. The individually decorated rooms are furnished in a mixture of period and modern styles. One room in the oldest section, Mary's Bower, retains its original ceiling moldings. The Cockerel Bar is popular with theatergoers, who stoke up on its hearty dishes; there's a more formal restaurant as well. **Pros:** unpretentious atmosphere; good dining choices. **Cons:** conventional furnishings; no private parking. ✉*The Square* ☏*01298/22841* ⊕*www.oldhallhotelbuxton.co.uk* 🛏*38 rooms* ♿*In-room: no a/c. In-hotel: restaurant, room service, bar, Wi-Fi, some pets allowed* ▭*AE, MC, V* ⊙*BP.*

£

🏠**Stoneridge.** Built of stone, this Edwardian B&B close to the Opera House has been richly restored. Bedrooms are done out in brown and

10

cream and furnished with modern pieces. Hearty breakfasts include fresh fruit, omelets, and potato scones; packed lunches, afternoon teas, and three-course evening meals can be provided on request. **Pros:** excellent food choices; secluded and tranquil garden. **Cons:** no tubs in bathrooms; credit cards not accepted. ⊠*9 Park Rd.* ☎*01298/26120* ⊕*www.stoneridge.co.uk* ⇆*4 rooms* ⌂*In-room: no a/c, no phone, Wi-Fi. In-hotel: parking (free), some pets allowed, no kids under 5, no-smoking rooms* ⊟*No credit cards* ⦿*BP.*

NIGHTLIFE AND THE ARTS

★ **Buxton Opera House** (⊠*Water St.* ☎*0845/127–2190*), bedecked with carved cupids, presents excellent theater, ballet, and jazz performances year-round; in late February it also hosts the annual Four-Four Time festival of world, jazz, blues, and folk music.

The renowned **Buxton Festival** (⊠*Festival Office, The Square* ☎*01298/ 70395* ⊕*www.buxtonfestival.co.uk*), held for two weeks during mid-July each year, includes opera, drama, and concerts.

SHOPPING

Buxton has many kinds of stores, especially around Spring Gardens, the main shopping street. Stores in the beautifully tiled **Cavendish Arcade** (⊠*The Crescent*), on the site of the old thermal baths, sell antiques, jewelry, fashions, and leather goods in stylish surroundings. A **market,** selling mainly food and clothes, is held in Buxton every Tuesday and Saturday.

EN ROUTE   As you head southeast from Buxton on the A6, you pass through the spectacular valleys of Ashwood Dale, Wyedale, and Monsal Dale before reaching Bakewell.

BAKEWELL

12 mi southeast of Buxton, 32 mi northeast of Little Moreton Hall.

In Bakewell, a medieval bridge crosses the winding River Wye in five graceful arches, and the 9th-century Saxon cross that stands outside the parish church reveals the town's great age. Narrow streets and houses built out of the local gray-brown stone also make the town extremely appealing. Ceaseless traffic through the streets can take the shine off—though there's respite down on the quiet riverside paths.

This market town is the commercial hub of the Peak District, for locals and visitors. The crowds are really substantial on market day (Monday), attended by area farmers; a similarly popular traditional agricultural show takes place the first week of August. For a self-guided hour-long stroll, pick up a map at the tourist office, where the town trail begins. A small exhibition upstairs explains the landscape of the Peak District. Worth exploring nearby are two distinguished houses: Haddon Hall and Chatsworth.

GETTING HERE AND AROUND

National Express and TransPeak offer bus services from Manchester's Chorlton Street Bus Station to Bakewell. By car, Bakewell is a one-hour, 30-minute drive southeast on the A6 from Manchester.

Stoke-on-Trent: The Potteries

The area known as the Potteries, about 55 mi southeast of Liverpool, is still the center of Britain's ceramics industry, though production is increasingly being transferred overseas. The novels of Arnold Bennett (1867–1931), including *Anna of the Five Towns,* realistically describe life in the area as an "architecture of ovens and chimneys" with an atmosphere "as black as mud." There are, in fact, six towns, now administered as "the city of Stoke-on-Trent." Famous names such as Wedgwood, Royal Doulton, Spode, and Coalport carry on, though they were taken over by other companies in 2009.

The most famous manufacturer, Josiah Wedgwood, established his pottery works at Etruria, near Burslem, in 1759, and created the cream-color ware (creamware), which so pleased Queen Charlotte that in 1762 she appointed him royal supplier of dinnerware. Perhaps Wedgwood's best-known innovation was his blue jasperware, decorated with white cameo figures by the British artist John Flaxman. More recent innovators include the very collectible Clarice Cliff, who strove to brighten plain whiteware in the 1920s with her colorful geometric and floral designs, notably the bold crocus pattern. Also bold and colorful were the classic art deco pieces of Susie Cooper. Four museums evocatively portray the history of this area.

Ceramica occupies an ornate former town hall and uses displays, videos, and interactive technology to explore the area's history, the process of creating china, and some noted companies. In Bizarreland (the name comes from Clarice Cliff's art deco designs), kids can dig for relics from the past and take a virtual ride over the Potteries. A shop sells local wares. ⊠ *Market Pl., Burslem* ☎ *01782/832001* ⊕ *www.ceramicauk.com* 🎫 *£4.10* ⊗ *Tues.–Sat. 10:30–4:30.*

The **Gladstone Pottery Museum,** the city's only remaining Victorian pottery factory, contains examples of the old bottle kilns, surrounded by original workshops where you can watch the traditional skills of throwing, casting, and decorating. The Flushed with Pride galleries tell the story of the toilet from the 1840s onward. ⊠ *Uttoxeter Rd., Longton* ☎ *01782/237777* ⊕ *www.stokemuseums.org.uk* 🎫 *£5.95* ⊗ *Daily 10–5; last admission at 4.*

The modern **Potteries Museum and Art Gallery** displays a 5,000-piece ceramic collection of international repute, and is recognized worldwide for its unique Staffordshire pottery. ⊠ *Bethesda St., Hanley* ☎ *01782/232323* ⊕ *www.stoke.gov. uk* 🎫 *Free* ⊗ *Mar.–Oct., Mon.–Sat. 10–5, Sun. 2–5; Nov.–Feb., Mon.–Sat. 10–4, Sun. 1–4.*

At the **Wedgwood Museum and Visitor Centre** you can learn about the history of Wedgwood, and see samples of its ware. Look out for portrait medallions, cauliflower ware and the innovative black basalt—the hedgehog bulb pot is a charming example. The visitor center has craft demonstrations and also displays Doulton and Minton ware. Both the museum and visitor center have shops where you can buy "firsts" and "seconds." ⊠ *Off A5035, Barlaston* ☎ *01782/371911* ⊕ *www. wedgwoodmuseum.org.uk* 🎫 *£9.25 joint ticket, £6 museum only* ⊗ *Weekdays 9–5, weekends 10–5.*

10

ESSENTIALS

Visitor Information Bakewell
(✉ *Old Market Hall, Bridge St.* ☎ *01629/813227* ⊕ *www. visitpeakdistrict.com*).

EXPLORING

Fodor'sChoice
★

Stately house scholar Hugo Montgomery-Massingberd has called **Haddon Hall**, a romantic, storybook medieval manor set along the River Wye 2 mi southeast of Bakewell, "the *beau idéal* of the English country house." Unlike other trophy homes that are marble Palladian monuments to a European grand tour, Haddon Hall remains quintessentially English in appearance, bristling with crenellations and stepped roofs and landscaped with rose gardens.

> ### PRIDE AND CHATSWORTH
>
> You may recognize the exterior and parkland of Chatsworth as Pemberley, home of Mr. Darcy, in the 2005 film version of *Pride and Prejudice*. It was Hollywood exaggeration to give him one of England's grandest country mansions, but no matter. The film also has some enticing views of the Peak District. The interior of the house is revealed in the 2008 film *The Duchess* with Keira Knightley.

The house, built between 1180 and 1565, passed into the ownership of the dukes of Rutland and remained largely unaltered until the early 20th century, when the ninth duke undertook a superlative restoration. This revealed a series of early decorative 15th-century frescoes in the chapel. The finest of the intricate plasterwork and wooden paneling is best seen in the superb Long Gallery on the first floor. Baking is still done in the bread ovens in the well-preserved Tudor kitchen. Here, too, is the unique collection of Gothic dole cupboards, some original to the house, which would have been filled with food and placed outside for those in need. The wider world saw the hall in *Jane Eyre* (both Franco Zeffirelli's 1996 version and the BBC's 2006 version), *Pride and Prejudice* with Keira Knightley (2005), and *The Other Boleyn Girl* (2008). ✉*A6* ☎*01629/812855* ⊕*www.haddonhall.co.uk* ☑*£8.75, parking £1* ☉*May–Sept., daily noon–5; Apr. and Oct., Sat.–Mon. noon–5; last admission 1 hr before closing.*

☺
★

Glorious parkland leads to **Chatsworth House,** ancestral home of the dukes of Devonshire and one of England's greatest country houses. The vast expanse of greenery, grazed by deer and sheep, sets off the Palladian-style elegance of "the Palace of the Peak." Originally an Elizabethan house, Chatsworth was conceived on a monumental scale. It was altered over several generations starting in 1686, and the architecture now has a hodgepodge look, though the Palladian facade remains splendid. The house is surrounded by woods, elaborate gardens, greenhouses, rock gardens, and the most famous water cascade in the kingdom—all designed by two great landscape artists, Capability Brown and, in the 19th century, Joseph Paxton, an engineer as well as a brilliant gardener. The gravity-fed Emperor Fountain can shoot as high as 300 feet. Perennially popular with children, the farmyard area has milking demonstrations at 3 and an adventure playground. ■TIP➜ **Plan on at least a half day to explore the grounds; avoid Sunday if you prefer not to be with the heaviest** crowds. Although death duties have taken a toll on the interior grandeur, as duke after duke has been forced to sell off treasures to keep the place going, there is more than enough to look at. Inside are intricate carvings, Van Dyck portraits, superb furniture, and a few fabulous rooms, including the Sculpture Gallery, the library, and the Blue Drawing Room, where you can see two of the most famous portraits in Britain, Sir Joshua Reynolds's *Georgiana, Duchess of Devonshire, and Her Baby*, and John Singer Sargent's enormous *Acheson Sisters.* Chatsworth is 4 mi northeast of Bakewell. ⊠ *Off B6012* ☎ *01246/582204* ⊕ *www.chatsworth.org* ✉ *House, gardens, and farmyard £16; house and gardens £11.50; gardens only, £7.50; farmyard and adventure playground £5; parking £2* ☉ *Mid-Mar.–late Dec., house daily 11–5:30, gardens daily 11–6, farmyard and adventure playground daily 10:30–5:30; last admission 1 hr before closing.*

WHERE TO EAT

££
BRITISH

✕ **The Albert.** Contemporary blends with traditional in this centrally located restaurant. Massive plate glass windows and discreet lighting show off the old wooden paneling and stone walls. The attentive service enhances the comfort factor. If you're in the mood for tradition, opt for the grilled Derbyshire beef or lamb with horseradish or Stilton cream sauce. If you feel adventurous, try the sea bass with a tapenade crust, or maybe a James Bond cocktail from the bar menu. Weekday fixed-price menus are a good value. ⊠ *Unit 6, Theme Court, Bridge St.* ☎ *01629/810077* ▤ *MC, V* ☉ *Closed Mon. No dinner Sun.*

££
BRITISH

✕ **Devonshire Arms.** This stone 18th-century coaching inn, which counts Charles Dickens as one of its many famous visitors, is divided into a cozy bar area and a modern brasserie, both serving great homemade fare. Typical dishes include Chatsworth shoulder of lamb with potato curry, and rice pudding with raisins and orange marmalade. There's an excellent snack menu, too. The inn is 2 mi south of Chatsworth and also has eight bedrooms. ⊠ *B6012, Beeley* ☎ *01629/733259* ▤ *AE, MC, V.*

££££
BRITISH
★

✕ **Fischer's.** The Fischer family bought this stately Edwardian manor on the edge of the Chatsworth estate to house their restaurant. Intimate and formal, the restaurant takes pride in using high-quality local products; on the menu you'll find wild venison, Derbyshire pork and lamb, and Yorkshire rhubarb, all presented with care and aplomb. If you can't decide, there's an eight-course tasting menu of specialty dishes (£63). With 11 elegant bedrooms here as well, you might consider staying the night. Sunday dinner is for overnight guests only. ⊠ *Baslow Hall, Calver Rd., Baslow* ☎ *01246/583259* ▤ *AE, MC, V.*

£
MODERN BRITISH

✕ **The Old Original Bakewell Pudding Shop.** Given the plethora of local rivals, it takes a bold establishment to claim its Bakewell puddings as

10

"original," but there's certainly nothing wrong with those served here, eaten hot with custard or cream. The oak-beam dining room also turns out commendable main courses of Yorkshireman (batter pudding with meat and vegetables) and steak-and-ale pie. ⊠ *The Square* ☎ *01629/812193* ⊟ *MC, V.*

WHERE TO STAY

££ ★ 🏠 **Haddon House Farm.** This may be a working farm, but there's nothing workaday about the fresh and imaginatively designed rooms (with themes such as Monet and Shakespeare) that the Nicholls husband-and-wife team created. The peaceful valley location, lovely antiques, and bouquets of flowers all contribute to a relaxing stay. Bathrooms have tiles hand-painted with insects and bamboo. Breakfasts are taken casually around the kitchen table. The location on the A6 lies between Haddon Hall and Bakewell. **Pros:** charming and obliging hosts; outdoor hot tub (extra fee); easily accessible by bus. **Cons:** no credit cards; no single rooms. ⊠ *Haddon Rd.* ☎ *01629/814024* ⊕ *www.great-place. co.uk* 🛏 *4 rooms* ⚒ *In-room: no a/c, no phone, Wi-Fi. In-hotel: parking (free), no kids under 5, no-smoking rooms* ⊟ *No credit cards* ⏹ *BP.*

SPORTS AND THE OUTDOORS

Dragon Balloons (⊠ *Mam House Farm, Hope Valley, Castleton* ☎ *01433/ 623007* ⊕ *www.dragonballoon.co.uk*) fly over Chatsworth House and Haddon Hall and surroundings in a hot-air balloon from the Bakewell Showground. The hour-long morning or evening flights cost from £135.

> ### BAKEWELL PUDDING
>
> Bakewell is the source of Bakewell pudding, said to have been created inadvertently when, sometime in the 19th century, a cook at the town's Rutland Arms Hotel (which is still in business) dropped some rich cake mixture over jam tarts and baked it. Every local bakery and tearoom claims an original recipe, so it's easy to spend a gustatory afternoon tasting rival puddings.

MATLOCK

5 mi south of Haddon Hall, 8 mi southeast of Bakewell.

In the heart of the Derbyshire Dales, Matlock and its near neighbor Matlock Bath are former spa towns compressed into a narrow gorge on the River Derwent. Some surviving Regency buildings in Matlock testify to its former importance, although it's less impressive an ensemble than that presented by Buxton. The surroundings, however, are particularly beautiful.

GETTING HERE AND AROUND

Matlock is served by National Express and TransPeak buses from Manchester's Chorlton Street Bus Station. The town is about a one-hour, 40-minute drive southeast on the A6 from Manchester.

ESSENTIALS

Visitor Information Matlock (⊠ *Crown Sq.* ☎ *01629/583388* ⊕ *www. visitpeakdistrict.com*).

EXPLORING

The **Matlock River Illuminations,** a flotilla of lighted boats shimmering after dark along the still waters of the river, takes place on weekends September through late October.

At Matlock Bath, 2 mi south of Matlock, river and valley views unfold from the curving line of buildings that makes up the village. Aside from riverside strolls, the major attraction is the cable-car ride across the River Derwent that takes you to the **Heights of Abraham Country Park and Caverns** on the crags above, with a visitor center and café. The all-inclusive ticket allows access to the woodland walks and nature trails of the 60-acre park, as well as entry to a cavern and a guided descent into an old lead mine, where workers toiled by candlelight. ⊠*A6, Matlock Bath* ☎*01629/582365* ⊕*www.heightsofabraham.com* ☎*£10.80* ⊙*Cable car and visitor center mid-Feb.–late Feb., daily 10–4:30; early to mid-Mar., weekends 10–4:30; late Mar.–Sept., daily 10–5 (and later in summer); Oct., daily 10–4:30.*

OFF THE BEATEN PATH

★ Few houses in England evoke the late Elizabethan era as vividly as **Hardwick Hall,** a beautiful stone mansion and all its treasures. The facade glitters with myriad windows, making it easy to see why the house came to be known as "Hardwick Hall, more glass than wall." ■TIP➔ Choose a sunny day to see the rooms and their treasures at their best. The vast state apartments well befit their original chatelaine, Bess of Hardwick. By marrying a succession of four rich husbands, she had become second only to Elizabeth in her wealth when work on this house began. She took possession in 1597, and four years later made an inventory of the important rooms and their contents—furniture, tapestries, and embroideries. The wonder is that these items still remain here. Unique patchwork hangings, probably made from clerical copes and altar frontals taken from monasteries and abbeys, grace the entrance hall, and superb 16th- and 17th-century tapestries cover the walls of the main staircase and first-floor High Great Chamber. The collection of Elizabethan embroideries—table carpets, cushions, bed hangings, and pillowcases—is second to none. There are also fine examples of plasterwork, painted friezes, and ornamental chimneypieces. Outside, you can visit the walled gardens. Hardwick Hall is 10 mi east of Matlock. Access is signposted from Junction 29 of the M1 motorway. ⊠*Doe Lea, Chesterfield* ☎*01246/850430* ⊕*www.nationaltrust.org.uk* ☎*£9.09; gardens only, £5.54; parking £2* ⊙*House mid-Mar.–Oct., Wed.–Sun. and national holidays, noon–4:30; Dec., weekends noon–3. Gardens mid-Mar.–Oct., Wed.–Sun. and national holidays noon–4:30; Dec. weekends 11–3; last admission 30 mins before closing. Grounds daily 8–dusk.*

WHERE TO STAY

££ **Dower House.** This charming 16th-century stone house sitting at the head of the pretty village of Winster, about 6 mi west of Matlock, has all you expect from a small country-house stay. Mullioned windows throw plenty of light into warmly furnished and spacious rooms, and the beamed dining room focuses on a wood fire. Courteous hosts prepare scrumptious breakfasts and, should you want, packed lunches, and the lovely walled garden is a perfect spot for relaxation. **Pros:**

10

Well Dressing

Unique to the Peak District is the custom of well dressing, when certain wells or springs are decorated with elaborate pictures made of flowers. Frames up to 4 feet wide and 6 feet high, covered with a base of clay, are filled with a colorful mosaic of seeds, grasses, berries, and moss as well as flowers and flower petals, a process that involves a team of workers and takes about a week to complete. Although the designs usually incorporate religious themes such as biblical stories, they are a Christian veneer over an ancient pagan celebration of the water's life-giving powers. The well dressing and blessing ceremony, usually accompanied by a brass band, heralds the start of several days of festivities. Of the 70 or so towns and villages that continue this summertime tradition, Tissington (May), south of Matlock; Bakewell (early July); and, near Chatsworth, Eyam (late August) are among the most popular. Check with local tourist offices for information.

country house character; very peaceful; beautifully furnished. **Cons:** no credit cards; minimum two-night stay on weekends; not easily accessible without a car. ⊠ *Main St., Winster* ☎ *01629/650–931* ⊕ *www. thedowerhousewinster.com* ⇔ *4 rooms* ⌂ *In-room: no a/c. In-hotel: no kids under 12* ▭ *No credit cards* ⍾*BP.*

SPORTS AND THE OUTDOORS

One of the major trails in the Peak District, **High Peak Trail** runs for 17 mi from Cromford (south of Matlock Bath) to Dowlow, following the route of an old railroad. For information, guidebooks, guide services, and maps, contact any Peak District National Park Office.

Red House Stables (⊠ *Old Rd., Darley Dale, Matlock* ☎ *01629/733–583* ⊕ *www.workingcarriages.com*) arranges carriage trips through the local countryside. An hour-long ride costs £30.

CASTLETON

10 mi northwest of Chatsworth, 9 mi northeast of Buxton.

The area around Castleton, in Hope Valley, contains the most famous manifestations of the geology of the Peak District. A number of caves and mines are open to the public, including some former lead mines and Blue John mines (amethystine spar; the unusual name is a corruption of the French *bleu-jaune* (meaning "blue yellow"). The limestone caverns attract many people, which means that pretty Castleton shows a certain commercialization. Summer brings the crowds, many of whom poke around in the numerous shops displaying Blue John jewelry and wares.

EXPLORING

In 1176 Henry II added the square tower to the Norman **Peveril Castle,** whose ruins occupy a dramatic crag above the town. The castle has superb views—from here you can clearly see a curving section of the medieval defensive earthworks still visible in the town center below.

Peveril Castle is protected on its west side by a 230-foot-deep gorge formed by a collapsed cave. Park in the town center, from which it's a steep climb up. ⊠*Market Pl., A1687* ☎*01433/620613* ⊕*www. english-heritage.org.uk* ☜*£3.70* ☉*Apr.–June, Sept., and Oct., daily 10–5; July and Aug., daily 10–6; Nov.–Mar., Thurs.–Mon. 10–4.*

Caves riddle the entire town and the surrounding area, and in the massive **Peak Cavern**—reputedly Derbyshire's largest natural cave—rope making has been done on a great ropewalk for more than 400 years. You can still see the remains of the 17th-century rope makers' village. ⊠*Hope Valley* ☎*01433/620285* ⊕*www.devilsarse.com* ☜*£7.25; £12 joint ticket with Speedwell Cavern* ☉*Apr.–Oct., daily 10–5; Nov.–Mar., weekends 10–5, call ahead for weekday hrs.*

The area's most exciting cavern by far is **Speedwell Cavern,** where 105 slippery steps lead down to old lead-mine tunnels, blasted out by 19th-century miners. Here you transfer to a small boat for the claustrophobic ¼-mi chug through an illuminated access tunnel to the cavern itself. At this point you're 600 feet underground, in the deepest public-access cave in Britain, with views farther down to the so-called Bottomless Pit, a water-filled cavern. A shop on-site sells items made of the Blue John mineral. Speedwell Cavern is at the bottom of Winnats Pass, 1 mi west of Castleton. ⊠*Winnats Pass* ☎*01433/620512* ⊕*www. speedwellcavern.co.uk* ☜*£7.75; £12 joint ticket with Peak Cavern; parking £2* ☉*Daily 10–5; last tour 1 hr before closing.*

WHERE TO STAY

£ 🖼**Bargate Cottage.** This cottage dating to 1650, at the top of Market Place below the castle, is one of Castleton's B&B treasures. The kindly owners scatter teddy bears with abandon, and the cutesy oak-beam rooms incorporate the necessary facilities. Breakfast is served at one table, with plenty of bonhomie and hiking advice on tap. **Pros:** peaceful location; great Derbyshire breakfasts. **Cons:** small rooms; no credit cards. ⊠*Market Pl.* ☎*01433/620201* ⊕*www.bargatecottage.co.uk* ➬*3 rooms* ⚙*In-room: no a/c. In-hotel: no kids under 12, no-smoking rooms* ⊟*No credit cards* ⍥*BP.*

££ 🖼**Underleigh House.** Peaceful is the word for the location of this creeper-clad cottage and barn at the end of a lane in lovely walking country. The big lounge has a fireplace, and the flagstone entrance hall has one big table for breakfasts (expect local specialties such as fruit compotes, oatcakes, and black pudding). There are games for rainy days, and books, sweets, and flowers in the tidy modern bedrooms. Hope is 1 mi east of Castleton on A617. **Pros:** superb views; ample breakfasts. **Cons:** minimum stays on weekends; surcharge for credit cards. ⊠*Off Edale Rd., Hope* ☎*01433/621372* ⊕*www.underleighhouse.co.uk* ➬*3 rooms, 2 suites* ⚙*In-room: no a/c, DVD. In-hotel: parking (free), some pets allowed, no kids under 12, no-smoking rooms* ⊟*MC, V* ⍥*BP.*

EN ROUTE Heading northwest to Edale, the most spectacular driving route is over **Winnats Pass,** through a narrow, boulder-strewn valley. Beyond are the tops of Mam Tor (where there's a lookout point) and the hamlet of Barber Booth, after which you run into Edale.

10

EDALE

5 mi northwest of Castleton.

At Edale you're truly in the Peak District wilds. This sleepy, straggling village, in the shadow of Mam Tor and Lose Hill and the moorlands of the high plateau known as Kinder Scout (2,088 feet), lies among some of the most breathtaking scenery in Derbyshire. England can show little wilder scenery than Kinder Scout, with its ragged edges of grit stone and its interminable leagues of heather and peat. Late summer brings a covering of reddish purple as the heather flowers, but the time to really appreciate the somber beauties of Kinder and its neighbors is in late fall or early winter, when the moors seem to brood under low clouds.

EXPLORING

The **Old Nag's Head** (☎*01433/670291*), a pub at the top of the village, has marked the official start of the Pennine Way since 1965. Call in at the Hiker's Bar, sit by the fire, and tuck into hearty bar meals and hot toddies. On Monday and Tuesday in winter, when this pub is closed, the Ramblers' Inn, at the other end of the village, is open.

In the village, the Edale **National Park Information Centre** has maps, guides, and information on all the walks in the area. There's limited accommodation in the village (all B&B-style), but the information center can provide a list or point you toward the local youth hostel. ⊠*Fieldhead, Edale Village* ☎*01433/670207* ⊕*www.peakdistrict.org* ☉*Apr.–Oct., daily 9:30–5; Nov.–Mar., weekdays 10–3:30, weekends 9:30–4:30.*

SPORTS AND THE OUTDOORS

An extremely popular walking center, Edale is the starting point of the 250-mi-long **Pennine Way** (⊕*www.nationaltrail.co.uk*), which crosses Kinder Scout. If you plan to attempt this, seek local advice first, because bad weather can make the walk treacherous. However, several much shorter routes into the Edale Valley, like the 8-mi route west to Hayfield, give you a taste of dramatic scenery.

The Lake District

WINDERMERE, GRASMERE, KENDAL, KESWICK

WORD OF MOUTH

"I loved Beatrix Potter's Hill Top farm and the solicitor's offices in town (Hawkshead) that were her husband's firm's; they are now a gallery of rotating illustrations from the books. We also thought Wordsworth's Dove Cottage in Grasmere was interesting, primarily for an excellent commentary."

—Cathinjoetown

"It's not a hike, but you will love the walk around Derwentwater. My favorite in England. No hills but stunning views of the hills and plenty of good hotels and pubs for lunch. You can also cheat by taking the old wooden launch that runs on the lake and stops at various points."

—markrosy

www.fodors.com/community

Updated by
Julius Honnor

"Let nature be your teacher . . ." Wordsworth's ideal comes true in this popular region of jagged mountains, waterfalls, wooded valleys, and stone-built villages. No mountains in Britain give a greater impression of majesty; deeper and bluer lakes can be found, but none that fit so readily into the surrounding scene.

The poets Wordsworth and Coleridge, and other English writers, found the Lake District an inspiring setting for their work, and outdoor enthusiasts have followed ever since, to walk, go boating, or just relax and take in the views. Other literary figures who made their homes in the Lake District include Thomas De Quincey, John Ruskin, and later, the children's writer Beatrix Potter.

In 1951 the Lake District National Park was created here from parts of the counties of Cumberland, Westmorland, and Lancashire. The Lake District is a contour map come to life, covering an area of approximately 885 square mi and holding 16 major lakes and countless smaller stretches of water. You can cross it by car in about an hour, though that would be a shame: this is an area meant to be walked. The mountains are not high by international standards—Scafell Pike, England's highest peak, is only 3,210 feet above sea level—but they can be tricky to climb. In spring, many of the higher summits remain snowcapped long after the weather below has turned mild.

This area can be one of Britain's most appealing reservoirs of calm, but not in summer. A lakeside town, however appealing, loses its charm when cars and tour buses clog its narrow streets. Similarly, the walks and hiking trails that crisscross the region seem less inviting when you share them with a crowd. Despite the challenges of popularity, the Lake District has managed tourism and the landscape in a manner that retains the character of the villages and the natural environment. Today, too, a new generation of hotel and restaurant owners is making more creative use of the edible and other assets of the Lakeland fells, and chic modern establishments are springing up next to traditional tea rooms and chintz-filled inns.

Off-season visits can be a real treat. All those inns and bed-and-breakfasts that turn away crowds in summer are eager for business the rest of the year (and their rates drop accordingly). It's not an easy task to find a succession of sunny days in the Lake District—some malicious statisticians allot to it about 250 rainy days a year—but when the sun breaks through and brightens the surfaces of the lakes, it is an away-from-it-all place to remember.

TOP REASONS TO GO

Hiking the trails: Whether it's a demanding trek up England's highest mountain, or a gentle wander around a tarn (a small mountain lake), walking is the number-one pleasure and the way to see the Lake District at its rugged and spectacular best. Even in summer, there are fantastic opportunities to escape the crowds.

Mucking around in boats: There's nowhere better for renting a small boat or taking a cruise on a vintage boat and discovering the pleasures of bobbing around on the water. You'll get a different perspective on the mountains, too. The Coniston Boating Centre and Derwentwater Marina near Keswick are possible places to start.

Wordsworth's daffodils and literary landscapes: The Lake District has a rich literary history, in the children's books of Beatrix Potter such as *The Tale of Peter Rabbit*, in the writings of John Ruskin, and in the poems of Wordsworth, which resonate more deeply after you've seen his flowers dancing in the breeze. A stop at any of the writers' homes will enrich the experience.

Pints and pubs: Cumbria has some great microbreweries, and a pint of real ale in one of the region's atmospheric rural inns may never taste as good as after a long hard day up a mountain.

Sunrise at Castlerigg: The stone circle at Castlerigg, in a natural hollow ringed by peaks, is a reminder of the region's ancient history. Blencathra and other mountains provide an awesome backdrop for the 38 stones. Sunrise is magical.

ORIENTATION AND PLANNING

GETTING ORIENTED

The Lake District is in northwest England, some 70 mi north of the industrial belt along the River Mersey that stretches from Liverpool to Manchester, and south of Scotland. The major gateway from the south is Kendal, and from the north, Penrith. Both are on the M6 motorway. Main-line trains stop at Oxenholme, near Kendal, with a branch linking Oxenholme to Kendal and Windermere. Windermere, in the south, is the most obvious starting point and has plenty of man-made attractions—museums, cafés, and gift shops. But the farther (and higher) you can get from the southern towns, the more you'll appreciate the area's spectacular landscapes. The Lake District National Park breaks into two reasonably distinct sections: the gentler, rolling south and the craggier, wilder north.

The Southern Lakes. The southern lakes and valleys contain the park's most popular, and thus most overcrowded in summer, destinations, incorporating the largest body of water, Windermere, as well as most of the quintessential Lakeland towns and villages: Kendal, Bowness, Ambleside, Grasmere, Elterwater, Coniston, and Hawkshead.

Penrith and the Northern Lakes. In the north, the landscape opens out across the bleaker fells to reveal challenging, spectacular walking

country. Here, in the northern lakes, south of Keswick and Cockermouth, you have the best chance to get away from the crowds.

LAKE DISTRICT PLANNER

WHEN TO GO

The Lake District is one of the rainiest areas in Britain, but June, July,
and August hold the best hope of fine weather and are the time for all
the major festivals. You will, however, be sharing the lakes with thousands of other people. If you must travel at this time, turn up early at
popular museums and attractions, and expect to work to find parking.
April and May, as well as September and October, are alternatives.
Later and earlier in the year there will be even more space and freedom, but many attractions close, and from December to March, snow
on high ground may preclude serious hill-walking without heavy-duty
equipment.

PLANNING YOUR TIME

You could spend months tramping the hills, valleys, and fells of the Lake
District, or, in three days, you could drive through the major towns and
villages. The key is not to do too much in too short a time. If you are
traveling by public transportation, many places will be off-limits. As a
base, Windermere has the best transport links, but it can be crowded
and it has less character than some of the smaller towns. Ambleside
and Keswick also have plenty of sleeping and eating options; for real
village life, try Coniston, Hawkshead, or Grasmere. Keep in mind that
the northern lakes have the most dramatic scenery and offer the opportunity to escape the summertime hordes.

The Lake District is compact but is not a place to hurry. Allow plenty of
time for walking: paths can be steep and rocky, and in any case you'll
want to stop frequently to look at the great views. A good day's walking
with a picnic can be done from nearly anywhere. Driving brings its own
speed inhibitors, from sheep on the roads to slow tractors.

You're likely to be based down at lake level, but try to experience the
hills, too. If you're short of time, a drive over one of the high passes
such as Hardknott, Honister, or Kirkstone will give you a glimpse of
the enormity of the landscape.

GETTING HERE AND AROUND

AIR TRAVEL

Manchester Airport has its own rail station with direct service to Carlisle, Windermere, and Barrow-in-Furness. Manchester is 70 mi from
the southern part of the Lake District.

Contact Manchester Airport (⊠ *Near Junctions 5 and 6 of M56* ☎ *0161/489–
3000* ⊕ *www.manchesterairport.co.uk*).

BOAT TRAVEL

Whether you rent a boat or take a ride on a modern launch or vintage
vessels, getting out on the water is a fun (and often useful) way to see
the Lake District. Windermere, Coniston Water, and Derwentwater all
have boat rental facilities.

The Lake District

BUS TRAVEL

National Express serves the region from London's Victoria Coach Station and from Manchester's Chorlton Street Station. Average travel time to Kendal is just over 7 hours from London; to Windermere, 7½ hours; and to Keswick, 8¼ hours. From Manchester there's one bus a day to Windermere via Ambleside, Grasmere, and Keswick. There's direct bus service to the Lake District from Carlisle, Lancaster, and York. Traveline handles public transportation inquiries.

Stagecoach in Cumbria provides local service between Lakeland towns and through the valleys and high passes. Contact Traveline for an up-to-date timetable. Bus service between main tourist centers is fairly frequent on weekdays, but much reduced on weekends and bank holidays. Don't count on reaching the more remote parts of the area by bus. Off-the-beaten-track touring requires a car or strong legs. A one-week Cumbria Goldrider ticket (£23), available on the bus, is valid on all routes. Explorer tickets (£9) are valid for a day on all routes.

Contacts National Express (☎ 0870/580–8080 ⊕ www.nationalexpress.com). **Traveline** (☎ 0870/608–2608 ⊕ www.traveline.org.uk).

CAR TRAVEL

A car is almost essential in the Lake District; bus service is limited and trains can get you to the edge of the national park but no farther. You can rent cars in Penrith and Kendal. Roads within the region are generally good, although minor routes and mountain passes can be steep and narrow. Warning signs are often posted if snow or ice has made a road impassable; listen to local weather forecasts in winter before heading out. In July and August and during the long public holiday weekends, expect heavy traffic. The Lake District has plenty of parking lots; use them to avoid blocking narrow lanes.

To reach the Lake District by car from London, take M1 north to M6, getting off either at Junction 36 and joining A590/A591 west (around the Kendal bypass to Windermere) or at Junction 40, joining A66 direct to Keswick and the northern lakes region. Travel time to Kendal is about four hours, to Keswick five to six hours. Expect heavy traffic out of London on weekends.

TRAIN TRAVEL

There are direct trains from Manchester and Manchester airport to Windermere. From London you'll need to change at Oxenholme for the branch line service to Kendal and Windermere. For schedule information, call National Rail Enquiries. Two train companies serve the region from London's Euston Station: take a Virgin or Northern Rail train bound for Carlisle, Edinburgh, or Glasgow and change at Oxenholme for the branch line service to Kendal and Windermere. Average travel time to Windermere (including the change) is 4½ hours. If you're heading for Keswick, you can either take the train to Windermere and continue from there by Stagecoach bus (Bus 554/555/556; 70 minutes), or stay on the main London–Carlisle train to Penrith Station (four hours), from which Stagecoach buses (Bus X5) also run to Keswick (45 minutes). Direct trains from Manchester depart for Windermere five times daily (travel time two hours). First North Western runs a local service from Windermere and Barrow-in-Furness to Manchester Airport. National Rail can handle all questions about trains.

Train connections are good around the edges of the Lake District, but these services aren't useful for getting around the central Lakeland region (you must take the bus or drive), and they are reduced, or non-existent, on Sunday.

Contacts National Rail Enquiries (☎0845/748–4950 ⊕www.nationalrail. co.uk). **Northern Rail** (☎0845/600–1159 ⊕www.northernrail.org). **Virgin Trains** (☎0845/722–2333 ⊕www.virgintrains.co.uk).

NATIONAL PARK

The Lake District National Park head office (and main visitor center) is at Brockhole, north of Windermere. It's closed November through mid-February. Helpful regional national-park information centers sell books and maps, book accommodations, and provide walking advice.

Contacts Lake District National Park (✉Brockhole, A591, Ambleside Rd., Windermere ☎015394/46601 ⊕www.lake-district.gov.uk). **Bowness Bay** (✉Glebe Rd., Bowness-on-Windermere ☎015394/42895). **Keswick** (✉Moot Hall, Main St. ☎017687/72645). **Ullswater** (✉Beckside Car Park, Glenridding ☎017684/82414).

TOURS

Mountain Goat and Lakes Supertours provide minibus sightseeing tours with skilled local guides. Half- and full-day tours, some of which really get off the beaten track, depart from Bowness, Windermere, Ambleside, and Grasmere.

Walks range from gentle, literary-oriented strolls to challenging ridge hikes. The Lake District National Park or tourist information centers can put you in touch with qualified guides. Blue Badge Guides can provide experts on the area. English Lakeland Ramblers organizes single-base and inn-to-inn guided tours of the Lake District. Lake District Walker offers guide day hikes for different abilities. Go Higher will take you on challenging routes and provides technical gear and courses on mountaineering skills.

Contacts Blue Badge Guides (☎020/7403–1115 ⊕www.blue-badge.org. uk). **English Lakeland Ramblers** (✉18 Stuyvesant Oval, #1A, New York, NY ☎01229/587382 or 212/505–1020, 800/724–8801 in U.S. ⊕www.ramblers. com). **Go Higher** (✉High Dyon Side, Distington ☎01946/830476 ⊕www. gohigher.co.uk). **Lake District Walker** (☎01900/822448 ⊕www.lakedistrict walker.co.uk). **Lakes Supertours** (✉1 High St., Windermere ☎015394/42751 ⊕www.lakes-supertours.co.uk). **Mountain Goat** (✉Victoria St., Windermere ☎015394/45161 ⊕www.mountain-goat.com).

RESTAURANTS

Lakeland restaurants increasingly reflect a growing British awareness of good food. Local sourcing and international influences are common, and even old Cumberland favourites are being creatively reinvented. Some of the area's better restaurants are at hotels. If you aren't a guest but want to dine at the hotel, though, make reservations in advance. Pub dining in the Lake District can be excellent—the hearty fare often makes use of local ingredients such as Herdwick lamb. If you're going walking, ask your hotel or B&B about making you a packed lunch. Some local delicatessens also offer this service.

HOTELS

Your choices include everything from small country inns to grand lakeside hotels; many hotels offer the option of paying a higher price that includes dinner as well as breakfast. The regional mainstay is the bed-and-breakfast, from the house on Main Street to isolated farmhouses. Most country hotels and B&Bs gladly cater to hikers and can provide on-the-spot information.

Wherever you stay, book well in advance for summer visits, especially those in late July and August. In winter many accommodations close for a month or two. On weekends and in summer it may be hard to find places willing to take bookings for a single night. Internet access in the Lakes is improving, and an increasing number of hotels and cafés offer Wi-Fi access.

WHAT IT COSTS IN POUNDS					
	£	££	£££	££££	£££££
Restaurants	under £10	£10–£14	£15–£19	£20–£25	over £25
Hotels	under £70	£70–£120	£121–£160	£161–£220	over £220

Restaurant prices are for a main course at dinner. Hotel prices are for two people in a standard double room in high season, including V.A.T., with no meals or, if indicated, CP (with continental breakfast), BP (Breakfast Plan, with full breakfast), or MAP (Modified American Plan, with breakfast and dinner).

VISITOR INFORMATION

Contacts Cumbria Tourism (✉ *Windermere Rd, Staverley, Kendal* ☎ *015398/22222* ⊕ *www.golakes.co.uk*).

THE SOUTHERN LAKES

Among the many attractions here are the small resort towns clustered around Windermere, England's largest lake, and the area's hideaway valleys, rugged walking centers, and monuments rich in literary associations. This is the easiest part of the Lake District to reach, with Kendal, the largest town, just a short distance from the M6 motorway. An obvious route from Kendal takes in Windermere, the area's natural touring center, before moving north through Ambleside and Rydal Water to Grasmere. Some of the loveliest Lakeland scenery is to be found by then turning south, through Elterwater, Hawkshead, and Coniston.

KENDAL

70 mi north of Manchester.

The southern gateway to the Lake District is the "Auld Gray Town" of Kendal, outside the national park and less touristy than the towns to the north. You may want to stay closer to the action, but the town has some worthwhile sights. Nearby hills frame Kendal's gray stone houses and provide some delightful walks; you can also explore the ruins of Kendal Castle. ■ TIP➔ Pack a slab of Kendal mint cake, the local peppermint candy that all British walkers and climbers swear by to provide them with energy. It's on sale in town gift shops and around the region.

The town's motto, "Wool Is My Bread," refers to its importance as a textile center in northern England before the Industrial Revolution. It was known for manufacturing woolen cloth, especially Kendal Green, which archers favored. Away from the main road are quiet courtyards and winding medieval streets known as "ginnels." Wool merchants used these for easy access to the River Kent.

GETTING HERE AND AROUND
Kendal is just off the M6, about 70 mi north of Manchester. It's the largest town in the area but is still plenty small enough to walk around.

ESSENTIALS
Visitor Information Kendal (⊠ *Town Hall, Highgate* ☎ *01539/725758*).

EXPLORING
One of the region's finest art galleries, **Abbot Hall**, occupies a Palladian-style Georgian mansion built in 1759. The permanent collection includes works by Victorian artist and critic John Ruskin, who lived near Coniston, and by 18th-century portrait painter George Romney, who worked (and died) in Kendal. The gallery also has a changing calendar of high-profile, often fascinating exhibitions of 20th- and 21st-century art. There's an excellent café. Abbot Hall is on the River Kent, next to the parish church; the Museum of Lakeland Life, with exhibits on blacksmithing and wheelwrighting and some great old black-and-white photos, is in the former stable block of the hall, on the same site. ⊠ *Off Highgate* ☎ *01539/722464* ⊕ *www.abbothall. org.uk* ⊠ *£5.75, £7.50 combined ticket with Museum of Lakeland Life* ⊗ *Apr.–Oct., Mon.–Sat. 10:30–5; Nov., Dec., and mid-Jan.–Mar., Mon.–Sat. 10:30–4.*

★ **Levens Hall**, a handsome Elizabethan house and the home of the Bagot family, is famous for its topiary garden, probably the most distinctive in the world. Laid out in 1694, the garden retains its original design, and the yew and beech hedges, cut into complex shapes that resemble enormous chess pieces, rise among a profusion of flowers. The house contains a stunning medieval hall with oak paneling, ornate plasterwork, Jacobean furniture, and Cordova goat-leather wallpaper. You can spend a couple of hours here. Levens Hall is 4 mi south of Kendal. ⊠ *Off A590, Levens* ☎ *015395/60321* ⊕ *www.levenshall.co.uk* ⊠ *£10.50; gardens only, £7.50* ⊗ *Apr.–mid-Oct., Sun.–Thurs.; house noon–4:30, last admission at 4, gardens 10–5.*

Sizergh Castle, one of the Lake District's finest fortified houses, has a 58-foot-tall defensive peel tower that dates from 1340, when Scottish raids were feared. It has been the home of the Strickland family for more than 760 years. Expanded in Elizabethan times, the castle includes outstanding oak-paneled interiors with intricately carved chimneypieces and oak furniture. The estate has a rock garden with a large collection of ferns, two lakes, and an ancient woodland; there are good walks here, too. Sizergh is 3½ mi south of Kendal. ✉*Off A591, Sizergh* ☎*015395/60070* ⊕*www.nationaltrust.org.uk* ✍*£6.80; gardens only, £4.90* ⊙*Castle mid-Mar.–Oct., Sun.–Thurs. 1–5 (also noon–1 by guided tour); gardens mid-Mar.–Oct., Sun.–Thurs. 11–5.*

WHERE TO EAT AND STAY

The Brewery Arts Centre is another good dining option in Kendal, as is the café at Abbot Hall.

££

MODERN BRITISH

✗**The New Moon.** This small but sleek restaurant, decorated in tones of warm off-white and pale, earthy brown, has won a good local reputation for high-quality dishes. The vegetarian selections are always worthwhile, and the sometimes adventurous modern English cooking shows Mediterranean flourishes. Duck breast is served on sweet-potato puree with caramelized orange sauce. Lunch and the fixed-price early dinner (5:30–7 weekdays) are especially good values. ✉*129 Highgate* ☎*01539/729254* ▤*MC, V* ⊙*Closed Sun. and Mon.*

£

VEGETARIAN

✗**Waterside Wholefoods Café.** In summer, grab one of the outdoor picnic tables overlooking the River Kent and order from the delicious, filling vegetarian menu of soups, quiches, cottage pies, salads, and cakes and scones. For the full Lakeland experience, stay at Lakeland Natural, the café's inexpensive guesthouse. ✉*2 Kent View, Waterside* ☎*01539/729743* ▤*MC, V* ⊙*Closed Sun. No dinner.*

££

★

🏠**Beech House.** Old-fashioned qualities combine with modern luxuries such as heated bathroom floors in this comfortable, ivy-clad town house a five-minute walk up the hill from the center of town in a conservation area. Rooms are individually designed but share a contemporary feel. There's a well-stocked shared refrigerator. A full English breakfast includes local bacon, honey-glazed sausages, and pancakes. **Pros:** stylish, homey rooms; heated bathroom floors, private parking. **Cons:** steep walk up the hill to get here; Kendal is outside the national park. ✉*40 Greenside* ☎*01539/720385* 🖶*01539/724082* ⊕*www.beechhouse-kendal.co.uk* ⇆*6 rooms* ⌂*In-room: no a/c, DVD, Wi-Fi. In-hotel: Wi-Fi* ▤*MC, V* ⎮⊙⎮*BP.*

NIGHTLIFE AND THE ARTS

★ The **Brewery Arts Centre,** a contemporary complex in a converted brewery, includes an art gallery, theater, cinemas, and workshop spaces. It gives Kendal a good, artsy vibe. The Grain Store, overlooking lovely gardens, serves lunch and dinner, and Vats Bar offers pizza and ales, lagers, and wines. In November the Mountain Film Festival presents productions aimed at climbers and walkers. ✉*Highgate* ☎*01539/725133* ✍*Free, except for special exhibitions* ⊙*Mon.–Sat. 9* AM–11 PM.

SHOPPING

Kendal has a pleasant mix of chain names, factory outlet stores, specialty shops, and traditional markets. The most interesting stores are tucked away in the quiet lanes and courtyards around Market Place, Finkle Street, and Stramongate. There's been a **market** in Kendal since 1189, and outdoor market stalls still line the center of town along Stramongate and Market Place every Wednesday and Saturday.

Henry Roberts Bookshop (✉*7 Stramongate* ☎*01539/720425*), in Kendal's oldest house (a 16th-century cottage), stocks a superb selection of regional books. **K Village Outlet Centre** (⊠ *20 Stricklandgate* ☎ *01539/732363*) sells some brand names at a discount: the wares include clothing, shoes, and china. The **Kentdale Rambler** (⊠ *34 Market Pl.* ☎ *01539/729188*) is the best local store for walking boots and equipment, maps, and guides, including Wainwright's Lakeland guides. **Peter Hall & Son** (⊠ *Danes Rd., Staveley* ☎ *01539/821633*), a woodcraft workshop 5 mi north of Kendal along A591, sells ornamental bowls and gifts.

WINDERMERE AND BOWNESS-ON-WINDERMERE

10 mi northwest of Kendal.

For a natural touring base for the southern half of the Lake District, you don't need to look much farther than Windermere, though it does get crowded in summer. The resort became popular in the Victorian era when the arrival of the railway made the remote and rugged area accessible. Wordsworth and Ruskin opposed the railway, fearing an influx of tourists would ruin the tranquil place. Sure enough, the railway terminus in 1847 brought with it Victorian day-trippers, and the original hamlet of Birthwaite was subsumed by the new town of Windermere, named after the lake.

The town has continued to flourish, despite being a mile or so from the water; the development now spreads to envelop the slate-gray lakeside village of Bowness-on-Windermere. Bowness is the more attractive, but they are so close it doesn't matter where you stay.

GETTING HERE AND AROUND

Windermere is easily reached by car, less than a half hour off the M6. There's also a train station at the eastern edge of town; change at Oxenholme for the branch line to Kendal and Windermere.

Bus 599, leaving every 20 minutes in summer (hourly the rest of the year) from outside Windermere train station, links the town with Bowness.

ESSENTIALS

Visitor Information Windermere (⊠ *Victoria St.* ☎ *015394/46499* ⊕ *www.southlakeland.gov.uk*).

EXPLORING

TOP ATTRACTIONS

Fodor's Choice ★

Blackwell. From 1898 to 1900, architect Mackay Hugh Baillie Scott (1865–1945) designed Blackwell, a quintessential Arts and Crafts house with carved paneling, delicate plasterwork, and a startling sense of light and space. Originally a retreat for a Manchester brewery owner, the house is a refined mix of modern style and the local vernacular.

Whitewashed walls and sloping slate roofs make it fit elegantly into the landscape above Windermere, and the artful integration of decorative features into stained glass, stonework, friezes, and wrought iron gives the house a sleekly contemporary feel. Rooms showcase works from different periods that embody Arts and Crafts ideals. Peruse the shop, try homemade soup in the tearoom, or take in one of the occasional classical concerts. ⊠*B5360, Windermere* ☎*015394/46139* ⊕*www. blackwell.org.uk* ☜*£6.30* ⊗*Apr.–Oct., daily 10:30–5; Nov., Dec., and mid-Jan.–Mar., daily 10:30–4.*

☾ ★ **Lakes Aquarium.** On the quayside at the southern end of Windermere, this excellent aquarium has wildlife and waterside exhibits that focus mostly on the region. The highlight is an underwater tunnel walk along a re-created lake bed, complete with diving ducks, though the piranhas and the bumblebee poison arrow frogs also have their fans. Friendly staff are eager to talk about the exhibits. You can take a boat to Lakeside from the town of Windermere or drive here. ⊠*C5062, Lakeside* ☎*015394/30153* ⊕*www.lakesaquarium.co.uk* ☜*£8.75* ⊗*Apr.–Oct., daily 9–6; Nov.–Mar., daily 9–5.*

OFF THE BEATEN PATH

Orrest Head. To escape the traffic and have a view of Windermere, set out on foot and follow the signs to the left of the Windermere Hotel (across from the train station) to Orrest Head. The shady, uphill path winds through Elleray Wood, and after a 20-minute hike you arrive at a rocky little summit (784 feet) with a panoramic view that encompasses the Yorkshire fells, Morecambe Bay, and Troutbeck Valley.

★ **Windermere.** No sights in Windermere or Bowness compete with that of Windermere itself. At 11 mi long, 1½ mi wide, and 200 feet deep, the lake is England's largest and stretches from Newby Bridge almost to Ambleside, filling a rocky gorge between steep, thickly wooded hills. The cold waters are superb for fishing, especially for Windermere char, a rare lake trout. In summer, steamers and pleasure craft travel the lake, and a trip across the island-studded waters, particularly the round-trip from Bowness to Ambleside or down to Lakeside, is wonderful. Although the lake's marinas and piers have some charm, you can bypass the busier stretches of shoreline (in summer they can be packed solid) by walking beyond the boathouses. Here, from among the pine trees, are fine views across the lake. The **car ferry**, which also carries pedestrians, crosses from Ferry Nab on the Bowness side of the lake to reach Far Sawrey and the road to Hawkshead. A ferry has been running this route since the 15th century. ☎*07860/813427* ☜*Car ferry £3.50 cars, 50p foot passengers* ⊗*Ferries every 20 mins Mon.–Sat. 6:50 AM–9:50 PM, Sun. 9:10 AM–9:50 PM; Nov.–Mar. until 8:50 PM.*

WORTH NOTING

☾ **Lakeside & Haverthwaite Railway Company.** Vintage steam trains run on the 4-mi branch line between Lakeside and Haverthwaite along the lake's southern tip; you can add on a lake cruise. Departures coincide with ferry arrivals from Windermere. ☎*015395/31594* ⊕*www. lakesiderailway.co.uk* ☜*£5.70* ⊗*Apr.–Oct., daily 10:30–6.*

☾ **Lake District National Park Visitor Centre at Brockhole.** Brockhole, a lakeside 19th-century mansion with 30 acres of terraced gardens sloping down to the water, serves as the park's official visitor center and has exhibits about the local ecology, flora, and fauna. It's a good stop at the start of your visit. The gardens are at their best in spring, when daffodils cover the lawns and azaleas burst into bloom. Among the park activities are lectures, guided walks, and demonstrations of traditional crafts such as drystone wall building. Some programs are geared to children, who appreciate the adventure playground here. You can also try the croquet lawn. The bookstore carries hiking guides and maps, and you can picnic here or eat at the café-restaurant. Bus 555/556 goes to the visitor center from the Windermere train station; the center is 3 mi north of Windermere. **Windermere Lake Cruises** (☎015394/43360 ⊕*www.windermere-lakecruises.co.uk*) runs a ferry service to the center from Ambleside. ✉*A591, Ambleside Rd., Windermere* ☎*015394/46601* ⊕*www.lake-district.gov.uk* ✉*Free; parking £2.20 for 2 hrs, £4 for 4 hrs, £6 full day, £2 out of season* ⊙ *Mid-Feb.–Oct., daily 10–5.*

> ### ARTS AND CRAFTS TRAIL
>
> The Arts and Crafts movement of the late 19th century flourished in the Lake District, inspired by the landscape as well as the writings of John Ruskin, who lived here. The search for meaningful style produced many artistic gems in the area's houses, churches, and hotels. At Blackwell you can purchase an Arts and Crafts Trail map and explore the best of them. Blackwell's Web site, ⊕ *www.blackwell.org.uk,* has extensive information about sites on the trail.

Windermere Lake Cruises. This company employs modern launches and vintage cruisers year-round between Ambleside, Bowness, Brockhole, and Lakeside. Ticket prices vary; a Freedom of the Lake ticket (£16) gives unlimited travel on any of the ferries for 24 hours. ☎*015394/73360* ⊕*www.windermere-lakecruises.co.uk.*

☺ **The World of Beatrix Potter.** A touristy attraction aimed at kids interprets the author's 23 tales with three-dimensional scenes of Peter Rabbit and more. Skip it if you can and visit Potter's former home at Hill Top and the Beatrix Potter Gallery in Hawkshead. ✉*The Old Laundry, Crag Brow, Bowness-on-Windermere* ☎*015394/88444* ⊕*www.hopskip-jump.com* ✉*£6.75* ⊙*Easter–Sept., daily 10–5:30; Oct.–Easter, daily 10–4:30.*

WHERE TO EAT

£££ ✗ **Jerichos at the Waverley.** The town's most stylish restaurant has recently
MODERN BRITISH relocated to this 1870 Victorian building near the center of town and gained 10 smart bedrooms upstairs. An open kitchen, bare wood, stone, and candles give the place a contemporary look and make for a sophisticated evening out. Choices from the brief, frequently changing modern British menu might include pigeon on grilled black pudding, halibut on mushroom-and-truffle risotto, and roast pork on mashed colcannon. ✉*College Rd., Windermere* ☎*015394/42522* ▭*MC, V* ⊙*No lunch. Closed Thurs., last 2 wks of Nov., and 1st wk of Dec.*

£   ✕**Lucy4 at the Porthole.** Tapas with a Lakeland twist are the specialty
MEDITERRANEAN   at this cheerful bistro and wine bar: Latin tunes and friendly service
★   make it a laid-back place to spend an evening. You can have fun combining dishes from the complex menu. The wine list is extensive, and
you should leave room for desserts. The patio is ideal for alfresco dining. ⊠*3 Ash St., Bowness-on-Windermere* ☎*015394/42793* ▭*MC,
V* ☺*No lunch weekdays.*

££   ✕**The Queen's Head Hotel.** A high-quality pub but one with few pre-
BRITISH   tensions, this 17th-century inn north of Windermere is renowned for
★   innovative pub food such as bobotie, a curried South African dish with
minced lamb, almonds and apricots. It's also noted for real ales served
from what was once an Elizabethan four-poster bed. The intimate dining rooms have oak beams, flagged floors, and log fires. Lunches can
be less hearty than the excellent evening meals. If you want to stay
overnight, 7 of the 15 guest rooms have four-posters, and all offer colorful fabrics and splendid views. ⊠*A592, Troutbeck* ☎*015394/32174*
▭*MC, V.*

££   ✕**Wicked Windermere.** The tasty modern adaptations of Lakeland favor-
BRITISH   ites work better than the name in this sleek little restaurant. White
walls and dark tablecloths set off dishes such as Cumbrian lamb with
Cabernet sauce or panfried duck breast with a port-and-apricot sauce.
Don't pass up the sticky toffee pudding. ⊠*4 High St., Windermere*
☎*015394/44954* ▭*MC, V.*

WHERE TO STAY

££   ▦**1 Park Road.** On a quiet street, this fine example of a new breed of
upmarket boutique B&Bs has spacious guest rooms with carefully chosen fabrics and contemporary touches such as iPod docking stations.
Stained glass, books, and a piano help give the place a cultured air.
Breakfast options include local sausages, fresh fruit and kedgeree; dinner
is also available on Friday and Saturday. **Pros:** welcoming and stylish;
good-size family room; good food, wine, and beer. **Cons:** a 15-minute
walk to the lake. ⊠*1 Park Rd., Windermere* ☎*015394/42107*
⊕*www.1parkroad.com* ⇦*6 rooms* ⌂*In-room: no a/c, no phone,
Wi-Fi, DVD. In-hotel: Wi-Fi, restaurant* ▭*MC, V* ⦿*BP.*

£££££   ▦**Gilpin Lodge.** Hidden in 22 acres of grounds with meandering paths
★   and six resident llamas, this family-run, rambling country-house hotel
2 mi east of Windermere pampers its guests in a low-key way. The hotel,
in a converted 1901 house with two modern wings, has plush but understated public rooms furnished with comfy sofas and rugs and warmed
by log fires. Bedrooms embody contemporary rustic chic, and most have
sitting areas; six contemporary garden suites have outdoor hot tubs.
Therapists provide spa treatments in your room. The superb restaurant
(reservations essential; fixed-price menu £52) serves imaginative modern dishes using local products such as venison wrapped in pancetta or
monkfish with cèpe mushrooms. You can use a well-equipped nearby
health club, and the hotel helps arrange outdoor activities. **Pros:** high-
class but laid-back pampering with a smile; notable food; a policy of no
weddings or conferences. **Cons:** location is beautiful, but it's a little out
of the way if you want to eat out; expensive. ⊠*Crook Rd., off B5284,
Bowness-on-Windermere* ☎*015394/88818* ⊕*www.gilpinlodge.co.uk*

↩14 rooms, 6 suites ⏾In-room: no a/c, safe. In-hotel: restaurant, room service, bars, Internet terminal, no kids under 7, no-smoking rooms ⊟AE, DC, MC, V ⍟BP.

££ ⊞ **Ivy Bank.** One of Windermere's smarter bed-and-breakfasts, Ivy Bank is in a quiet, leafy part of town. The guest rooms have handsome wooden furniture and views over the rooftops. The owner is a qualified masseuse and aromatherapist and offers treatments to guests. You can use the local health club for free. **Pros:** bike storage; near good walks. **Cons:** no bathtub in most rooms (shower only). ⊠Holly Rd., Windermere ☎015394/42601 ⊕www.ivy-bank.co.uk ↩5 rooms ⏾In-room: no a/c, no phone, DVD (some), Wi-Fi. In-hotel: Wi-Fi, no-smoking rooms ⊟MC, V ⍟BP.

> **STAY ON A FARM**
>
> The Cumbrian Web site ⊕www.luxuryinafarm.co.uk is a good place to start checking out farm stays, whether B&B-style or self-catering (with kitchen); ⊕www.golakes.co.uk has a wider selection of less luxurious options. Prices can be reasonable, but you'll need a car for most.

£££££ ⊞ **Miller Howe.** Location, lake views, and superb service help set this
Fodor's Choice luxurious Edwardian country-house hotel apart. The sumptuous guest
★ rooms have been given an Arts and Crafts makeover, with William Morris wallpaper, fresh flowers, and contemporary art brightening the individually decorated rooms. Some have lake views, so ask; or you can relax in the conservatory and look at Windermere. The modern British restaurant (££££) serves sophisticated fare, and the hotel arranges activities from archery to pony trekking. **Pros:** more than 5 acres of grounds; great lake views; staff that take care of the little extras. **Cons:** sometimes closes for a couple of weeks in winter. ⊠Rayrigg Rd., Bowness-on-Windermere ☎015394/42536 ⌨015394/45664 ⊕www.millerhowe.com ↩15 rooms ⏾In-room: no a/c. In-hotel: restaurant, some pets allowed, no kids under 8 ⊟AE, MC, V ⍟MAP.

££££ ⊞ **The Punch Bowl.** Under the same management as the celebrated
★ Drunken Duck Inn near Hawkshead, this outstanding inn and restaurant is a pleasantly modern retreat in the peaceful Lyth Valley, between Windermere and Kendal. The bright, airy bedrooms have high oak-beam ceilings and chic fabric designs and big baths. Health and beauty treatments are available if you book in advance. Sleek and slate-floored, the bar serves fine real ales, and you can sample good locally sourced dishes in the bright, contemporary restaurant. The pub has taken over duties from the local post office, so you can even post a letter here. **Pros:** contemporary-yet-relaxed design will make you look at beer and Lakeland lodgings in a new light; excellent food. **Cons:** a little way from the area's main sights. ⊠Off A5074, Crosthwaite, Lyth Valley ☎015395/68237 ⊕www.the-punchbowl.co.uk ↩9 rooms ⏾In-room: Wi-Fi (some), no a/c. In-hotel: restaurant, Wi-Fi, no-smoking rooms ⊟AE, MC, V ⍟BP.

£££££ ⊞ **The Samling.** On its own sculpture-dotted 67 acres above Wind-
★ ermere, this place oozes exclusivity from every carefully fashioned corner. Wordsworth used to come here to pay his rent. Today the hotel is favored by the rich and famous, but it avoids the snobbishness

sometimes found in such establishments. Rooms are elegantly traditional but not fussy—all come with roll-top baths and some have fireplaces. Service is a good mix of professional and friendly, and the lake views are fantastic. The restaurant (£55 fixed-price dinner menu) specializes in creative local fare; it's open to nonguests for dinner, afternoon tea, and Sunday lunch. **Pros:** you'll feel like a star, and may sit next to one at breakfast, too. **Cons:** you'll likely miss the steep turn off the road the first time you arrive; the exclusivity doesn't come cheap. ⊠ *Ambleside Rd., Windermere* ☎ *015394/31922* ⊕ *www.thesamling.com* ⤙ *11 suites* ⟳ *In-room: no a/c, DVD, Internet. In-hotel: restaurant, Wi-Fi* ⊟ *AE, D, MC, V* ⦿ *BP.*

SPORTS AND THE OUTDOORS

Windermere Cycle Hire (⊠ *Railway Station, Windermere* ☎ *015394/44544*) rents bikes for £5 per hour or £15 per day, and is right next to the train station.

Windermere Lake Holidays Afloat (⊠ *Mereside, Ferry Nab, Bowness-on-Windermere* ☎ *015394/43415*) rents boats, from small sailboats to houseboats.

SHOPPING

The best selection of shops is at the Bowness end of Windermere, on Lake Road and around Queen's Square: clothing stores, crafts shops, and souvenir stores of all kinds. At **Lakeland Jewellers** (⊠ *Crag Brow, Bowness-on-Windermere* ☎ *015394/42992*) the local experts set semiprecious stones in necklaces and brooches. **Lakeland Leather** (⊠ *Lake Rd., Bowness-on-Windermere* ☎ *015394/44466*), which also has branches in Ambleside and Keswick, stocks moderately priced leather and sheepskin goods.

AMBLESIDE

7 mi northwest of Windermere.

Unlike Kendal and Windermere, Ambleside seems almost part of the hills and fells. Its buildings, mainly of local stone and many built in the traditional style that forgoes the use of mortar in the outer walls, blend perfectly into their setting. The small town sits at the northern end of Windermere along A591, making it a popular center for Lake District excursions. It has a better choice of restaurants than Windermere or Bowness, and the numerous outdoor shops are handy for fell walkers. The town does, however, suffer from overcrowding in high season. Wednesday, when the local market takes place, is particularly busy.

ESSENTIALS

Visitor Information Ambleside (⊠ *Central Bldgs., Market Cross, Rydal Rd.* ☎ *015394/32582*).

EXPLORING

Bridge House, a tiny 17th-century stone former apple store, perches on an arched stone bridge that spans Stone Beck. It may have been built here to avoid land tax. This much-photographed building holds a National Trust shop and information center. ⊠ *Rydal Rd.* ☎ *015394/35599* ⊡ *Free* ⊙ *Easter–Oct., daily 10–5.*

QUICK BITES

Cozy Sheila's Cottage (⊠ *The Slack* ☎ *015394/33079*), serving great homemade cakes and desserts, is a good place to gather the strength for a walk or to relax after one. Try a good-value afternoon tea with tea bread or, for the full calorie replenishment, go for a hot chocolate loaded with cream.

The **Armitt Museum,** a fine local-history gallery and library, explores Ambleside's past and its surroundings through the eyes of local people such as William Wordsworth, Thomas De Quincey, Robert Southey, John Ruskin, and Beatrix Potter. You can study Beatrix Potter's natural-history watercolors or watch a Victorian lantern slide show. ⊠ *Rydal Rd.* ☎ *015394/31212* ⊕ *www.armitt.com* ☎ *£2.50* ⏰ *Daily 10–5; last admission at 4:30.*

Windermere Lake Cruises (☎ *015394/43360* ⊕ *www.windermere-lakecruises.co.uk*) has year-round service between Ambleside, Bowness, Brockhole, and Lakeside. It's a pleasant way to experience the lake.

WHERE TO EAT

££
MODERN BRITISH
★

✕ **Glass House.** A converted medieval mill with a working waterwheel is an atmospheric setting for this restaurant serving modern British cuisine. Look for an international twist in dishes such as grilled snapper with warm fennel salad or rib-eye steak with mushroom noodles. You can have an elegant dinner or just sip a cappuccino in the courtyard. There's a well-priced early-evening menu (two courses £15) weekdays from 6:30 to 7:30. ⊠ *Rydal Rd.* ☎ *015394/32137* ⌔ *Reservations essential* ⊟ *MC, V.*

£££
BRITISH
★

✕ **Lucy's on a Plate.** This informal café by day, restaurant by night is the perfect spot to relax, whether with mushroom stroganoff for lunch, a chocolate almond torte for afternoon tea, or grilled char for dinner by candlelight. One room has scrubbed pine tables; a conservatory provides additional seating. Lucy's is famous for its puddings (desserts), and on the first Wednesday of every month the "up the duff" pudding night includes a menu with at least 30 choices. A nearby delicatessen sells high-class Cumbrian foods: sticky toffee pudding, farm cheeses, Cumberland sausage, jams, chutneys, and biscuits. Lucy's growing empire now includes cooking courses as well as a wine bar on nearby St. Mary's Lane: Lucy4. ⊠ *Church St.* ☎ *015394/31191* ⊟ *MC, V.*

£
BRITISH

✕ **Matthew's Bistro.** Food photos decorate the otherwise plain white walls in this straightforward but high-quality little eatery, where the hearty food, perfect after a day of walking, is English rather than French. The char-grilled chicken is free range and the fish pie is a favorite; the game pie is also recommended. Prices are especially good value if you get your order in by 7 PM: three courses for £15 or two for £13. ✉ *Compston Rd., Ambleside* ☎*015394/31234* 🖃*MC, V* ⊘*Closed Sun. No lunch.*

WHERE TO STAY

£   🏠 **3 Cambridge Villas.** Ambleside has a lot of inexpensive B&Bs, many clumped along the western end of the town, but it's hard to find a more welcoming spot than this lofty Victorian house right in the center, with hosts who know a thing or two about local walks. They'll also supply a packed lunch if you plan to be out exploring all day. Although space is at a premium, the rooms are pleasantly decorated with prints and wood furniture. **Pros:** especially good value for single travelers; warm family welcome; central. **Cons:** some rooms are a little cramped; can occasionally be noisy. ✉*3 Church St.* ☎*015394/32307* ⊕*www.3cambridgevillas.co.uk* 🛏*7 rooms, 5 with bath* ⌂*In-room: no a/c, no phone, Wi-Fi. In-hotel: Wi-Fi, no-smoking rooms* 🖃*MC, V* ⦿*BP.*

££   🏠 **The Old Vicarage.** A quiet edge of Ambleside's old center is the peace-
★   ful setting for this excellent-value B&B in a large Victorian former vicar-age. Rooms are furnished in traditional English country style, with floral and print fabrics and dark-wood furniture; some are well equipped for families; those in the new wing are more modern. A log fire and great breakfasts help make this a good deal even without the swimming pool. **Pros:** friendly welcome; indoor heated pool. **Cons:** some rooms are on the plain side of stylish; cuddly owls won't be to everybody's taste. ✉*Vicarage Rd.* ☎*015394/33364* ⊕*www.oldvicarageambleside.co.uk* 🛏*15 rooms* ⌂*In-room: no a/c, DVD, Wi-Fi. In-hotel: pool* 🖃*MC, V* ⦿*BP.*

SPORTS AND THE OUTDOORS

The fine walks in the vicinity include routes north to Rydal Mount or southeast over Wansfell to Troutbeck. Each walk will take up to a half day, there and back. Ferries from Bowness-on-Windermere dock at Ambleside's harbor, called Waterhead. ■**TIP→** You can rent rowboats at the harbor for an hour or two to escape the crowds and get a different view of the area.

Biketreks (✉*Rydal Rd.* ☎*015394/31245*) is a good source for bike rentals.

RYDAL

1 mi northwest of Ambleside.

The village of Rydal, on the small glacial lake called Rydal Water, is rich with Wordsworthian associations.

EXPLORING

One famous beauty spot linked with Wordsworth is **Dora's Field,** below Rydal Mount next to the church of **St. Mary's** (where you can still see the poet's pew). In spring the field is awash in yellow daffodils, planted by William Wordsworth and his wife in memory of their beloved daugh-ter Dora, who died in 1847.

If there's one poet associated with the Lake District, it is Words-worth, who made his home at **Rydal Mount** from 1813 until his death.

Wordsworth and his family moved to these grand surroundings when he was nearing the height of his career, and his descendants still live here, surrounded by his furniture, books, and portraits. You can see the study in which he worked, the family dining room, and the 4½-acre garden, laid out by the poet himself, that gave him so much pleasure. ■ TIP➡ Surrounding Rydal Mount and the areas around Dove Cottage and Grasmere are many footpaths where Wordsworth wandered. His favorite can be found on the hill past White Moss Common and the River Rothay. Spend an hour or two walking them and you may understand why the great poet composed most of his verse in the open air. ✉A591 ☎015394/33002 ⊕www.rydalmount.co.uk ✉£6; garden only, £4 ⊙Mar.–Oct., daily 9:30–5; Nov., Dec., and Feb., Wed.–Sun. 11–4.

WHERE TO STAY

£££ ☆ **Cote How Organic Guest House.** Elegant, peaceful, and with a focus on organic and sustainable fare, Cote How is a cut above most of the B&Bs in the Lakes. Woodrow Wilson had his portrait painted here, and the sophistication of the house's former existences as the home of painter Frederick Yates lives on its subtle decoration. Big bathrooms have views over the 11 acres of gardens, beds are king size, and Herdwick carpets (made from the wool of local sheep) and homemade candles add to the homey, welcoming feel. Vegetarians are well catered for at breakfast, but there is organic, locally sourced meat on the menu. A tearoom is open to all on summer weekends. **Pros:** beautiful gardens; great food; spacious rooms. **Cons:** location is great for walks, less so if you want other amenities. ✉Rydal ☎015394/32765 ⊕www.cotehow.co.uk ➥3 rooms ♨In-room: no a/c, no phone, no TV, Wi-Fi. In-hotel: no-smoking rooms ☰MC, V ⊙|BP.

GRASMERE

3 mi north of Rydal, 4 mi northwest of Ambleside.

Lovely Grasmere, on a tiny, wood-fringed lake, is made up of crooked lanes in which Westmorland slate–built cottages hold shops and galleries. The village is a focal point for literary and landscape associations because this area was the adopted heartland of the Romantic poets, notably Wordsworth and Coleridge. The Vale of Grasmere has changed over the years, but many features Wordsworth wrote about are still visible. Wordsworth lived on the town's outskirts for almost 50 years and described the area as "the loveliest spot that man hath ever known."

EXPLORING

Wordsworth, his wife, Mary, his sister, Dorothy, and four of his children are buried in the churchyard of **St. Oswald's,** which is on the River Rothay. The poet planted eight of the yew trees here. As you leave the churchyard, stop at the Gingerbread Shop, in a tiny cottage, for a special local treat.

★ William Wordsworth lived in **Dove Cottage** from 1799 to 1808, a prolific and happy time for the poet. During this time he wrote some of his most famous works, including "Ode: Intimations of Immortality" and *The Prelude;* Wordsworth was also married here. Built in the early

ON THE MENU

In Cumbria, which encompasses the Lake District, food is more than fuel for hiking. The area has earned a reputation for good country food using Herdwick lamb, beef, and game, as well as fish from the freshwater streams and lakes, such as salmon, Windermere char, and Borrowdale and Ullswater trout. Sold in one long strip, the thick pork-and-herb Cumberland sausage is another specialty.

Local breads, cakes, pastries, and scones are scrumptious, as is the ubiquitous sticky toffee pudding. Brown sugar, molasses, nutmeg, cinnamon, ginger, and rum—favorite ingredients in traditional cakes—were imported from the West Indies in exchange for wool and are integral to the cakes' and puddings' flavor. Lyth Valley damsons (a kind of plum) have a nutty taste used in everything from beverages and desserts to cheese. Grasmere gingerbread is baked from a secret recipe, and Kendal mint cake (a candy marketed as survival food) has a home in many hikers' backpacks.

17th century as an inn, this tiny, dim, and, in some places, dank, house is beautifully preserved, with an oak-paneled hall and floors of Westmorland slate. It first opened to the public in 1891 and remains as it was when Wordsworth lived here with his sister, Dorothy, and wife, Mary. Bedrooms and living areas contain much of Wordsworth's furniture and many personal belongings. Coleridge was a frequent visitor, as was Thomas De Quincey, best known for his 1822 autobiographical masterpiece *Confessions of an English Opium-Eater*. De Quincey moved in after the Wordsworths left. You visit the house on a timed guided tour, and the ticket includes admission to the spacious, modern **Wordsworth Museum and Art Gallery,** which documents the poet's life and the literary contributions of Wordsworth and the Lake Poets. Besides seeing the poet's original manuscripts, you can hear his poems read aloud on headphones. Books, manuscripts, and artwork capture the spirit of the Romantic movement. The museum includes space for major art exhibitions. The **Jerwood Centre,** open to researchers by appointment, houses 50,000 letters, first editions, and manuscripts. Afternoon tea is served at **Villa Colombina.** Opposite the restaurant, the **3°W Gallery,** another Wordsworth Trust property (free; ring the bell for entry), has innovative contemporary art exhibitions. ✉*A591, 1 mi south of Grasmere* ☎*015394/35544* ⊕*www.wordsworth.org.uk* ✉*£7.50* ⊙*Daily 9:30–5:30.*

QUICK BITES

Heidi's ✉*Red Lion Sq.* ☎*015394/35248*) is a buzzing, cozy little café and deli lined with jars of locally made jams and chutneys. Bang in the center of Grasmere, it's great for coffee and a delicious homemade pastry or flapjack (bars made with syrup, butter, and oats).

WHERE TO EAT

££   ✕**The Jumble Room.** This small, stone-built restaurant, dating to the
BRITISH   18th century, was Grasmere's first shop and is a friendly, fashionable, and colorful place, with children's books, bold animal paintings, fans,

and hanging lamps. The food is an eclectic mix of international and traditional English: excellent fish-and-chips and beefsteak appear on the menu with crab crostini and polenta with Parmesan and roasted pumpkin. Lunches are lighter and cheaper, with good soups and homemade puddings. ⊠ *Langdale Rd.* ☎ *015394/35188* ▤ *MC, V* ⊘ *Closed Mon. and Tues. Easter–Nov.; Sun. evening and Mon.–Wed. Dec.–Easter.*

£££ ✕ **Tweedies Bar.** Attached to the Dale Lodge Hotel, Tweedies is one of
BRITISH the region's best gastro-pubs and attracts many locals as well as visi-
★ tors. Delicious contemporary British food such as smoked pork loin and sweet chili king prawn skewers is served in a smart, cozy, contemporary pub with laid-back music and a wood-burning fire. Several of Cumbria's best beers are on tap alongside a good selection of world beers; you can also try a number of real ales. Freshly made pizzas are another good option. ⊠ *Langdale Rd.* ☎ *15394/35300* ▤ *MC, V.*

WHERE TO STAY

£ 🛏 **Banerigg House.** You don't have to spend a fortune to find appealing
★ lakeside lodgings in Grasmere. This cozy, early-20th-century house, ¾ mi south of the village on A591, has unfussy, well-appointed rooms, most with lake views. Games and books fill the guest lounge. The B&B is walker-friendly, which means you get hiking advice from the owners, drying facilities, and a roaring fire when needed. **Pros:** very welcoming hosts; good value for single rooms; canoes available. **Cons:** a little out of town; the house has an awkward, and potentially dangerous, turn onto the road. ⊠ *Lake Rd.* ☎ *015394/35204* ⊕ *www.baneriggguesthouse. co.uk* 🛏 *6 rooms, 5 with bath* ♿ *In-room: no a/c, no phone, no TV, Wi-Fi. In-hotel: no-smoking rooms* ▤ *No credit cards* ⏸ *BP.*

£££ 🛏 **Harwood Hotel.** A romantically decorated hotel, the small but sumptuous Harwood has a distinctly feminine feel, with floral wallpaper, curly steel lamps, and painted woodwork. State-of-the-art contemporary touches such as TVs in the bathrooms and under-floor heating add extra luxury. Two rooms have private terraces. Dig into a generous and tasty breakfast downstairs in Heidi's Café. **Pros:** colorful, fantastic bathrooms with whirlpool tubs; warm welcome. **Cons:** not good for families; so pristine you may worry about your muddy boots; fee to use Internet. ⊠ *Red Lion Sq.* ☎ *015394/35248* ⊕ *www.harwoodhotel. co.uk* 🛏 *6 rooms* ♿ *In-room: no a/c, no phone, Internet. In-hotel: restaurant, no kids under 18* ▤ *MC, V* ⏸ *BP.*

£££££ 🛏 **Moss Grove.** A Victorian building in the heart of Grasmere, Moss Grove has been refurbished to the highest quality, with an emphasis on its environmental credentials. Private hot tubs, balconies, luxurious duck-down duvets, and flat-screen TVs appear along with reclaimed stained glass, old timbers, and organic clay paints. Spacious and luxurious yet chicly informal and a long way from quaint, this hotel adds a newly hip angle to posh Lake District accommodation. For a special treat, request the champagne truffles on arrival. **Pros:** plenty of room; huge chunky furniture; modern design with a conscience. **Cons:** tight parking; not the place for a big fry-up breakfast. ⊠ *Red Lion Square* ☎ *015394 35251* ⊕ *www.mossgrove.com* 🛏 *11 rooms* ♿ *In-room: no a/c, DVD, Internet (some). In-hotel: some pets allowed* ▤ *AE, D, DC, MC, V* ⏸ *BP.*

SPORTS AND THE OUTDOORS

The most panoramic views of lake and village are from the south of Grasmere, from the bare slopes of **Loughrigg Terrace,** reached along a signposted track on the western side of the lake. It's less than an hour's walk, though your stroll can be extended by continuing around Rydal Water, passing Rydal Mount and Dove Cottage before returning to Grasmere, a 4-mi (three-hour) walk in total.

SHOPPING

Elkhome (⊠ *College St.* ☎ *01539/435154*), an elegant small palace of modern design and homewares, is an unexpected find in Grasmere. Traditional Lakeland crafts are nowhere to be seen, but it's a great place to find a gift.

★ The smells wafting across the churchyard draw many people to the **Grasmere Gingerbread Shop** (⊠ *Church Cottage* ☎ *015394/35428*). Since 1854 Sarah Nelson's gingerbread has been sold from this cramped 17th-century cottage, which was once the village school. The delicious treats, still made from a secret recipe, are available in attractive tins for the journey home or to eat right away.

ELTERWATER

2½ mi south of Grasmere, 4 mi west of Ambleside.

The delightful village of Elterwater, at the eastern end of the Great Langdale Valley on B5343, is a good stop for hikers. It's barely more than a cluster of houses around a village green, but from here you can choose from a selection of excellent circular walks.

WHERE TO EAT AND STAY

££ ✕ **Britannia Inn.** At this family-owned, 500-year-old pub, restaurant, and
BRITISH inn in the heart of superb walking country, antiques, comfortable chairs, and prints and oil paintings furnish the cozy, beamed public rooms. You can relax with a bar meal and Cumbrian ale on the terrace while taking in the village green and the rolling scenery beyond. The hearty traditional English food—from grilled Hawkshead trout to chicken, ham, and leek pie—is popular with locals, as are the many ales and whiskies. Things can get hectic in the evening; the restaurant is in the center of town. The nine smallish guest rooms are more modern in style; ask about discounts for midweek stays. ⊠ *B5343* ☎ *015394/37210* ▭ *MC, V.*

££ ⬚ **Old Dungeon Ghyll Hotel.** There's no more comforting stop after a
★ day outdoors than the Hiker's Bar of this 300-year-old hotel at the head of the Great Langdale Valley. The stone floor and wooden beams echo to the clatter of hikers' boots, and the roaring stove rapidly dries out wet walking gear. Thick slabs of flapjack (dense bar cookies) from behind the bar will get you up the surrounding Langdale Pikes. Guest rooms are decorated with traditional patterned carpets and flowered bed linens, though the hotel exudes a rougher version of Lakeland life far away from Beatrix Potter quaintness. You can include dinner in the rate. **Pros:** ideally situated for walking; spectacular views all around. **Cons:** no-nonsense approach leaves little room for frippery and won't

be to everyone's taste. ✉ *Off B5343, Great Langdale* ☎ *015394/37272* ⊕ *www.odg.co.uk* ⇄ *13 rooms, 8 with bath* ⚒ *In-room: no a/c, no phone, no TV. In-hotel: restaurant, bars, Wi-Fi* ▤ *AE, MC, V* �ΙΟΙ *BP.*

SPORTS AND THE OUTDOORS

There are access points to Langdale Fell from several spots along B5343, the main road; look for information boards at local parking places. You can also stroll up the river valley or embark on more energetic hikes to Stickle Tarn or to one of the summits of the Langdale Pikes.

CONISTON

5 mi south of Elterwater.

This small lake resort and boating center attracts climbers to the steep peak known as the **Old Man of Coniston** (2,635 feet), which towers above the slate-roof houses. It also has sites related to John Ruskin. Quieter than Windermere, Coniston is a good introduction to the pastoral and watery charms of the area, though the small town itself can get crowded in summer.

ESSENTIALS

Visitor Information Coniston (✉ *Ruskin Ave.* ☎ *015394/41533* ⊕ *www. conistontic.org*).

EXPLORING

Coniston Water, the lake on which Coniston stands, came to prominence in the 1930s when Arthur Ransome made it the setting for *Swallows and Amazons,* one of a series of novels about a group of children and their adventures. The lake is about 5 mi long, a tempting stretch that drew boat and car racer Donald Campbell here in 1959 to set a water-speed record of 260 mph. He was killed when trying to beat it in 1967. His body and the wreckage of *Bluebird K7* were retrieved from the lake in 2001. Campbell is buried in St. Andrew's church in Coniston, and a stone memorial on the village green commemorates him.

The **Ruskin Museum** holds fascinating and thought-provoking manuscripts, personal items, and watercolors by John Ruskin that illuminate his thinking and influence. There is also a focus on Donald Campbell; the tailfin of his *Bluebird K7,* dragged up from Coniston Water, is here, and a reconstruction project is under way. (A new Bluebird wing will open in 2010 or 2011.) Good local-interest exhibits include copper mining, geology, lace, and more. ✉ *Yewdale Rd.* ☎ *015394/41164* ⊕ *www. ruskinmuseum.com* ⊡ *£4.50* ⊙ *Mid-Mar.–mid-Nov., daily 10–5:30; mid-Nov.–mid-Mar., Wed.–Sun. 10:30–3:30.*

★ **Brantwood,** on the eastern shore of Coniston Water, was the cherished home of John Ruskin (1819–1900), the noted Victorian artist, writer, critic, and social reformer, after 1872. The rambling, white, 18th-century house (with Victorian alterations) is on a 250-acre estate that stretches high above the lake. Here, alongside mementos such as his mahogany desk, are Ruskin's own paintings, drawings, and books. There is art that this great connoisseur collected, and there are cerebral corners such as the Ideas Room, where visitors are encouraged to think about meaning and change. A video on Ruskin's life shows the lasting influence of his thoughts, and the **Severn Studio** has rotating art exhibitions. Ruskin himself laid out the extensive grounds; take time to explore the gardens and woodland walks. ■TIP→ **It's an easy drive to Brantwood from Coniston, but it's pleasant to travel here by ferry across the lake, via either the Coniston Launch or the *Gondola*, a 19th-century steam yacht. Both depart from Coniston Pier through the summer.** ⊠ *Off B5285* ☎ *015394/41396* ⊕ *www.brantwood.org.uk* ☜ *£5.95; gardens only, £4* ☉ *Mid-Mar.–mid-Nov., daily 11–5:30; mid-Nov.–mid-Mar., Wed.–Sun. 11–4:30.*

Coniston Launch (☎ *017687/75753* ⊕ *www.conistonlaunch.co.uk*) connects Coniston Pier with Ruskin's home at Brantwood, offering hourly service (£7.40 round-trip, with more extensive routes mid-March through November) on its wooden *Ruskin* and *Ransome* launches, which run on a solar–electric power system. Thematic sightseeing tours are also available.

Steam Yacht *Gondola* (☎ *015394/41288* ⊕ *www.nationaltrust.org.uk*) runs the National Trust's luxurious Victorian steam yacht between Coniston Pier, Brantwood, and Park-a-Moor at the south end of Coniston Water, daily from April through October (£7 round-trip). A stop at Monk Coniston jetty connects to the footpaths through the Monk Coniston Estate, linking Coniston Water to the beauty spot of Tarn Hows.

WHERE TO EAT AND STAY

£   ╳**Jumping Jenny's.** Named after Ruskin's beloved boat, the wood-
BRITISH   beamed tearoom at Brantwood occupies the converted coach house. It has an open log fire and mountain views, and serves morning coffee, lunch (sophisticated soups, pastas, sandwiches, and salads), and afternoon tea with tasty homemade cakes. You can sit on the terrace in warmer weather. ⊠ *Off B5285* ☎ *015394/41715* ▭ *MC, V* ☉ *Closed Mon. and Tues. mid-Nov.–mid-Mar. No dinner.*

£   ▥**Beech Tree Guest House.** This Victorian stone house with friendly own-
★   ers and a garden is within walking distance of the town center. The individually furnished rooms, some of which look out over an ancient beech tree, are done in a country theme, and breakfast is hearty and vegetarian. There's a TV in the sitting room. **Pros:** cozy, family atmosphere; excellent breakfast. **Cons:** not for those wanting all the mod cons; no meat with breakfast. ⊠ *Yewdale Rd.* ☎ *015394/413717* ↩*8 rooms, 4 with bath* ☖ *In-room: no a/c, no TV. In-hotel: some pets allowed, no-smoking rooms* ▭ *No credit cards* ⑩*BP.*

££   ▥**Yew Tree Farm.** Homemade cakes on arrival set the scene for this friendly, working farm bed-and-breakfast 5 mi north of Coniston toward Skelwith Bridge. Once owned by Beatrix Potter, and later used in filming the story of her life, Yew Tree Farm is nestled in some especially attractive hills, and its tearoom retains Potter's original furnishings. Guests have free access to a local health club. All this means that it's very popular, and you'll need to book in advance. **Pros:** pretty location; bacon from the farm for breakfast; two rooms have four-poster beds. **Cons:** often booked up far in advance. ⊠ *A593* ☎ *015394/41433* ⊕ *www.yewtree-farm.com* ↩*3 rooms* ☖ *In-room: no a/c, no phone, no TV, Wi-Fi. In-hotel: no-smoking rooms* ▭ *MC, V* ⑩*BP.*

WALKING IN THE LAKE DISTRICT

You can choose gentle rambles near the most popular towns and villages or challenging hikes and climbs up some of England's most impressive peaks. Information boards at parking lots throughout the region point out the possibilities.

British mountaineering began in the Lake District, with its notable hikes: the famous Old Man of Coniston, the Langdale Pikes, Scafell Pike, Skiddaw, and Helvellyn are all popular, though these require experience, energy, and proper hiking boots and clothing. The Cumbria Way (70 mi) crosses the Lake District, starting at the market town of Ulverston and finishing at Carlisle. The Coast-to-Coast Walk (190 mi) runs from St. Bees on the Irish Sea through the Lake District and across the Yorkshire Dales and the North York Moors; it ends at Robin Hood's Bay at the edge of the North Sea in Yorkshire. Guidebooks to these and other Lakeland walks are available in local bookstores—check out Alfred Wainwright's classic guides.

For short walks, consult the tourist information centers: those at Ambleside, Cockermouth, Grasmere, Kendal, Keswick, and Windermere provide maps and advice. The other main sources of information are the Lake District National Park information centers. Cumbria Tourism's general Web site, www.golakes.co.uk, and its outdoor site, www.lakedistrictoutdoors.co.uk, are helpful for planning. Several climbing organizations offer guided hikes as well as technical rock climbing.

SPORTS AND THE OUTDOORS

Steep tracks lead up from the village to the **Old Man of Coniston.** The trail starts near the Sun Hotel on Brow Hill and goes past an old copper mine to the peak, which you can reach in about two hours. It's one of the Lake District's most satisfying—not too arduous but high enough to feel a real sense of accomplishment and get some fantastic views (west to the sea, south to Morecambe Bay, and east to Windermere). Experienced hikers include the peak in a seven-hour circular walk from the village, also taking in the dramatic heights and ridges of Swirl How and Wetherlam.

★ **Coniston Boating Centre** (⊠ *Lake Rd.* ☎ *015394/41366* ⊕ *www.lake-district.gov.uk*) is a good place to help you enjoy the water. You can rent launches, canoes, kayaks, and wooden rowboats, or even take a sailing lesson. A picnic area and café are near the center, too.

HAWKSHEAD

3 mi east of Coniston.

In the Vale of Esthwaite, this small market town, with a pleasing hodge-podge of tiny squares, cobbled lanes, and whitewashed houses, is perhaps the Lake District's most picturesque village. There's a good deal more history here than in most local villages, however. The Hawkshead Courthouse, just outside town, was built by the monks of Furness Abbey in the 15th century. Hawkshead later derived much wealth from the wool trade, which flourished here in the 17th and 18th centuries.

As a thriving market center, it could afford to maintain the **Hawkshead Grammar School**, at which William Wordsworth was a pupil from 1779 to 1787; he carved his name on a desk inside, now on display. In the village, Ann Tyson's House claims the honor of having provided the young William with lodgings. The twin draws of Wordsworth and Beatrix Potter—apart from her home, Hill Top, there's a Potter gallery—conspire to make Hawkshead crowded year-round.

ESSENTIALS

Visitor Information Hawkshead (⊠ *Main St.* ☎ *015394/36946* ⊕ *www. hawksheadtouristinfo.org.uk*).

BIKING THE LAKE DISTRICT

Cycling along the numerous bicycle paths and quiet forest roads in Cumbria is pleasurable and safe. Some flat paths are beside the lakes, but the best routes involve plenty of ups and downs. The Cumbria Cycle Way circles the county, and for local excursions guided bike tours are often available, starting at about £25 per day. Contact local tourist offices or bike-rental places for details on cycle routes.

EXPLORING

The **Beatrix Potter Gallery,** in the solicitor's offices formerly used by Potter's husband, displays an annually changing selection of the artist-writer's original watercolors and drawings, as well as information on her interests as a naturalist. Potter was a conservationist and an early supporter of the National Trust. The house looks almost as it would have in her day. Admission is by timed ticket. ⊠ *Main St.* ☎ *015394/36355* ⊕ *www.nationaltrust.org.uk* ☜ *£4.20* ⊘ *Mid-Feb.–mid-Mar., Sat.– Thurs. 11–3:30; mid-Mar.–Oct., Sat.–Thurs. 10–4:30.*

Hill Top was the home of children's author and illustrator Beatrix Potter (1866–1943), most famous for her *Peter Rabbit* stories. The house looks much the same as when Potter bequeathed it to the National Trust, and fans will recognize details such as the porch and garden gate, old kitchen range, Victorian dollhouse, and four-poster bed, which were depicted in the book illustrations. ■ TIP➡ **Admission to this often-crowded spot is by timed ticket; you can book in advance. Try to avoid visiting on summer weekends and during school vacations.** Hill Top lies 2 mi south of Hawkshead by car or foot, though you can also approach via the car ferry from Bowness-on-Windermere. ⊠ *Off B5285, Near Sawrey* ☎ *015394/36269* ⊕ *www.nationaltrust.org.uk* ☜ *£6.20, gardens free when house closed* ⊘ *House mid-Feb.–mid-Mar., Sat.–Thurs. 11–3:30; mid-Mar.–Oct., Sat.–Thurs. 10–4:30. Gardens and shop mid-Mar.–Oct., daily 10:30–5; Nov., Dec., and Feb., daily 10–4.*

Two miles northwest of the village (follow signs on B5285) is one of the Lake District's most celebrated beauty spots, **Tarn Hows,** a tree-lined lake. Scenic overlooks let you drink it all in, or you can take an hour to putter along the paths. A free National Trust bus runs here from Hawkshead and Coniston (Easter–October, Sunday only).

WHERE TO EAT AND STAY

££££ ✕**L'Enclume.** Cartmel, one of the most attractive southern Lakeland vil-
MODERN BRITISH lages, has earned a place on England's culinary map with this ambitious
restaurant with rooms that has converted a forge into a bright, contemporary, and airy space. Chef Simon Rogan's innovative food incorporate
long-forgotten herbs; choose from menu 1 (£55) or the more extensive
menu 2 (£75) or 3 (£95). Your choices might include carrots in honey
wine and ham fat, mallow soup with iced ginger and shrimp, and bay
crab with kohlrabi and yellow clover. Some dishes work better than
others at this outpost of molecular gastronomy, but boredom is never
a risk. You can stay the night in one of the nine unfussy but luxurious
bedrooms, too. Cartmel is 17 mi south of Hawkshead and 12 mi south
of Kendal. ⊠*Cavendish St., Cartmel* ☎*015395/36362* ☰*AE, MC, V*
⊗*No dinner Mon.; no lunch Mon.–Wed.*

£££–££££ ⌂**Drunken Duck Inn.** After four centuries, this friendly old coaching inn
Fodor's Choice remains an outstanding place for both food and lodging. Bedrooms,
★ bright, contemporary, and exceptionally comfortable, make good use
of natural materials and have wonderful views of the Langdale Pikes.
The price includes afternoon tea and breakfast. Nestle into the cozy bar
with oak settles and order a tasty real ale from the Duck's Barnsgate
Brewery. There's an open fire, and hops hang over the bar. The two dining spaces have dark-wood furniture and hunting prints; breast of duck
with salsify and mashed potatoes with star anise jus is typical of the
modern British fare. The inn is 2½ mi from both Ambleside and Hawkshead. **Pros:** super-chic rural style; excellent dining and drinking. **Cons:**
hunting paraphernalia may put you off your beer; not in heart of town.
⊠*Off B5286, Barngates* ☎*015394/36347* ⊕*www.drunkenduckinn.
co.uk* ⋈*16 rooms* ⌂*In-room: no a/c, Wi-Fi. In-hotel: restaurant, bar,
no-smoking rooms* ☰*AE, MC, V* ⍉*BP* ⟨*Reservations essential.*

££££ ⌂**Randy Pike.** The owners of the successful Jumble Room restaurant
in Grasmere have found the perfect spot for this chic new B&B, a
labor of love. Built in the 19th century as the shooting lodge for Wray
Castle, Randy Pike is filled with stylish, imaginative, and personal
touches. Playful design influences range from Gothic to Rococo. The
large guest rooms use slate and reclaimed timber, bathrooms are huge,
and instead of a minibar there's a "boudoir larder" with local beers
and cheeses. A three-course breakfast is delivered to your room. **Pros:**
space, style, and good food; big garden. **Cons:** a little out of the way.
⊠*Off B5286 between Outgate and Clappersgate* ☎*015394/36088*
⊕*www.randypike.co.uk* ⋈*2 rooms* ⌂*In-room: no a/c, refrigerator*
☰*MC, V* ⍉*BP.*

££ ⌂**Yewfield.** With the laid-back friendliness of a B&B but with most
of the style of a fancier country-house hotel, this is a very good value
for the money—especially if you can get one of the rooms with a great
view across the valley from the front of the house. The 19th-century
Gothic house, between Hawkshead and Tarn Hows, has a large lounge
and sits on 30 acres of land. Breakfast is wholesome and vegetarian.
Pros: a great out-of-the-way location; garden; apartments a convenient
option for weeklong stays. **Cons:** laid-back service can occasionally
be too relaxed; not good for families with young kids. ⊠*Hawkshead*

CLOSE UP

What's Real About Real Ale?

The English can be passionate about their drink, as the growing interest in real ale shows. It differs from other ales by the use of natural ingredients and the fact that it is matured by fermentation in the barrel from which the ale is served. The process doesn't use carbon dioxide, so pure taste wins out over fizz.

The Directory of U.K. Real Ale Breweries (⊕ www.quaffale.org.uk) lists 26 operating real-ale breweries in Cumbria, of which the Coniston Brewing Company, Barngates Brewery (at the Drunken Duck Inn), and Jennings (in Cockermouth) are three of the best. Most real ales are caramel in color and hoppy, malty, and slightly bitter to taste. A pint of ale is the usual quantity to be consumed, though a half is acceptable; you can also find it in bottles.

Most pubs in the Lake District offer some sort of local brew—the better ones take enormous pride in their careful tending of the beer, from barrel to glass. Interested in the subject, or just in the taste? Check out the Web site of the Campaign for Real Ale (⊕ www.camra.org.uk).

Hill ☎ *015394/36765* 🖷 *015394/36096* ⊕ *www.yewfield.co.uk* 🛏 *6 rooms, 2 apartments* & *In-room: no a/c, DVD, Wi-Fi (some). In-hotel: bar, Wi-Fi, no kids under 9* ═ *MC, V* ☉ *Closed Dec. and Jan.* ⍑ *BP.*

PENRITH AND THE NORTHERN LAKES

The scenery of the northern lakes is considerably more dramatic—some would say bleaker—than much of the landscape to the south, a change that becomes apparent on your way north from Kendal to Penrith. Your easiest approach is a 30-mi drive on the A6 that takes you through the wild and desolate Shap Fells, which rise to a height of 1,304 feet. This is one of the most notorious moorland crossings in the country: even in summer it's a lonely place to be, and in winter snow on the road can be dangerous. From Penrith the road leads to Ullswater, possibly the grandest of all the lakes; then there's a winding route west past Keswick, south through the marvelous Borrowdale Valley, and on to Bassenthwaite and Cockermouth.

PENRITH

30 mi north of Kendal.

The red-sandstone town of Penrith was the capital of Cumbria, part of the Scottish kingdom of Strathclyde in the 9th and 10th centuries. It was rather neglected after the Normans arrived, and the Scots sacked it on several occasions. Penrith has been a thriving market town for centuries; the market still takes place on Tuesday, and it continues to be known for good shopping.

The tourist information center, in the Penrith Museum, has information about the historic town trail, which takes you through narrow byways to the plague stone on King Street, where food was left for the stricken, to St. Andrew's churchyard and its 1,000-year-old "hog back" tombstones (stones carved as stylized "houses of the dead"), and finally to the ruins of Penrith Castle.

GETTING HERE AND AROUND
Penrith is just off the M6, 30 mi north of Kendal and 100 mi north of Manchester. Both the M6 and the alternative A6 cross the Pennines spectacularly at Shap Fells. From Windermere, you can reach Penrith by going over the Kirkstone Pass to Ullswater. There are some direct trains from Euston Station in London to Penrith; sometimes it's necessary to change.

ESSENTIALS
Visitor Information Penrith (✉ *Penrith Museum, Middlegate* ☎ *01768/867466* ⊕ *www.visiteden.co.uk*).

EXPLORING
The evocative remains of the 15th-century redbrick **Penrith Castle** stand high above a steep, now-dry moat. Home of the maligned Richard, duke of Gloucester (later Richard III), who was responsible for keeping peace along the border, it was one of England's first lines of defense against the Scots. By the Civil War the castle was in ruins, and the townsfolk used some of the fallen stones to build their houses. The ruins stand across from the town's train station. ✉ *Off Castlegate* ☎ *No phone* ⊕ *www.english-heritage.org.uk* ✉ *Free* ◷ *June–Sept., daily 7:30 AM– 9 PM; Oct.–May, daily 7:30–4:30.*

The **Penrith Museum**, in a 16th-century building that served as a school from 1670 to the 1970s, contains displays on the history of the Eden Valley, including Roman pottery and a medieval cauldron. The Penrith Tourist Information Centre is here. ✉ *Robinson's School, Middlegate* ☎ *01768/212228* ⊕ *www.eden.gov.uk* ✉ *Free* ◷ *Apr.–Oct., Mon.–Sat. 10–5, Sun. 1–4:45; Nov.–Mar., Mon.–Sat. 10–5.*

🔄 **Rheged,** the name of the Celtic kingdom of Cumbria, is the theme of this grass-covered visitor center with activities for kids and some interesting free exhibits about the history, culture, and other aspects of the Lake District. Its centerpiece, a large-format cinema (fee), shows *Rheged—The Movie,* a mix of history and fantasy introducing Celtic warriors and more. Shops showcase Cumbrian produce and crafts, and the Rheged Café and Bluebird bar offer drinks and light meals. Rheged is 2 mi southwest of Penrith and 1 mi west of Junction 40 on the M6. ✉ *A66* ☎ *01768/868000* ⊕ *www.rheged.com* ✉ *Free, movie £4.95* ◷ *Daily 10–5:30.*

Home of the Hasell family since 1679, **Dalemain,** 3 mi southwest of Penrith, began with a 12th-century peel tower built to protect the occupants from raiding Scots, and is now a delightful hodgepodge of architectural styles. An imposing Georgian facade of local pink sandstone encompasses a medieval hall and extensions from the 16th through the 18th century. Inside are a magnificent oak staircase, furniture dating from the mid-17th century, a Chinese drawing room, a 16th-century room with intricate plasterwork, and many fine paintings, including masterpieces by Van Dyck. The gardens are worth a look. ✉ *A592*

☎01768/486450 ⊕*www.dalemain.com* 🎫*£8.50; gardens only, £6* ⊙*House Apr.–Sept., Sun.–Thurs. 11:15–4; Oct., Sun.–Thurs. 11:15–3. Gardens Apr.–Oct., Sun.–Thurs. 10:30–5; Nov.–mid-Dec., Feb., and Mar., Sun.–Thurs. 11–4.*

WHERE TO EAT AND STAY

£ ✕**No. 15.** A laid-back, spacious contemporary gallery and café with a
CAFÉ large range of teas and coffees also serves light meals such as homemade soups and quiches and great cakes and desserts. Wi-Fi can be used for 30 minutes for £2. ✉*15 Victoria Rd.* ☎*01768/867453* ▭*MC, V.*

££ ✕**George and Dragon.** Just south of Penrith, this freshly updated pub
BRITISH owned by the nearby Lowther estate makes good use of the estate's resources for its traditional organic dishes, such as shorthorn beef burger and chips, and lamb-shank-and-parsley pie. It's also a well-tended spot to pop in for a pint of local beer, with handsome slate floors and hanging hops. Bonnie Prince Charlie was once involved in a battle here, and the remains of 12 Scottish rebels were discovered in the pub's back garden. Ten individually designed guest rooms with some furnishings from the Lowther family's collection are available for overnight stays. ✉*A6, Clifton* ☎*01768/865381* ⊕*www.georgeanddragonclifton. co.uk* ▭*MC, V* ⊙*No lunch Mon.*

£–££ 🏠**Brooklands.** Pristinely refurbished in soothing, mostly neutral tones, Brooklands is one of a cluster of B&Bs on Portland Place, a short walk north of Penrith's center. The welcome is friendly, the breakfast is hearty (salmon fishcakes and omelets are among the options), and rooms are bright and simple. **Pros:** well-looked-after B&B; bathrobes in room; fancy toiletries. **Cons:** Penrith is outside the national park and a drive from the spectacular Lakeland scenery. ✉*2 Portland Pl.* ☎*01768/863395* ⊕*www.brooklandsguesthouse.com* 🛏*8 rooms* ⅼ*In-room: no a/c, Wi-Fi. In-hotel: Wi-Fi, no-smoking rooms* ▭*MC, V* ⓧⓘ*BP.*

SHOPPING

Penrith is a diverting place to shop, with its narrow streets and arcades chockablock with family-run specialty shops. Major shopping areas include Devonshire Arcade, with its brand-name stores; the pedestrian-only Angel Lane and Little Dockray; and Angel Square. The stalls of the outdoor **market** line Dockray, Corn Market, and Market Square every Tuesday and sell fine local produce and original crafts.

The excellent **Bluebell Bookshop** (✉*8 Angel La.* ☎*01768/866660*) sometimes hosts special events and readings. **James & John Graham of Penrith Ltd.** (✉*Market Sq.* ☎*01768/862281*) has a great bakery and a well-stocked delicatessen that specializes in cheese and local products. The **Toffee Shop** (✉*7 Brunswick Rd.* ☎*01768/862008*), where the Queen buys her toffee, may also have England's best fudge.

ULLSWATER

3 mi southwest of Dalemain, 6 mi southwest of Penrith.

Hemmed in by towering hills, Ullswater, the region's second-largest lake, draws outdoorsy types. Some superb views are from the A592 as it sticks to the lake's western shore, through the adjacent hamlets of

Glenridding and Patterdale at the southern end. Lakeside strolls, tea shops, and rowboat rentals provide the usual Lakeland experience.

ESSENTIALS

Visitor Information Ullswater (⊠ *Main Car Park, Glenridding* ☎ *017684/ 82414*).

EXPLORING

Ullswater Steamers (☎ *017684/82229* ⊕ *www.ullswater-steamers.co.uk*) sends its antique vessels, including an oil-burning, 19th-century steamer, the length of Ullswater between Glenridding and Pooley Bridge; it's a pleasant tour and combines well with a lakeside walk. The service operates 363 days a year from the pier at Glenridding. A one-way trip the full length of the lake is £7.50, or you can do any three stages for £10.50.

At **Aira Force** (⊠ *Off A592, 5 mi north of Patterdale*) a spectacular waterfall pounds under a stone bridge and through a wooded ravine to feed into Ullswater. From the parking lot (£3.50–£5.50 fee, depending on how long you stay), it's a 10-minute walk to the falls, with more serious walks on Gowbarrow Fell and to the village of Dockray beyond. Bring sturdy shoes in wet weather. Just above Aira Force in the woods of Gowbarrow Park is the spot where, in 1802, William Wordsworth's sister, Dorothy, observed daffodils that, as she wrote, ". . . tossed and reeled and danced and seemed as if they verily laughed with the wind that blew upon them." Two years later Wordsworth transformed his sister's words into the famous poem "I Wandered Lonely as a Cloud." And two centuries later, national park wardens patrol Gowbarrow Park in season to prevent tourists from picking the few remaining daffodils.

★ West of Ullswater's southern end, the brooding presence of **Helvellyn** (3,118 feet), one of the Lake District's most formidable mountains, recalls the region's fundamental character. It's an arduous climb to the top, especially via the challenging ridge known as Striding Edge, and the ascent shouldn't be attempted in poor weather or by inexperienced hikers. Signposted paths to the peak run from the road between Glenridding and Patterdale and pass by **Red Tarn**, at 2,356 feet the highest small mountain lake in the region.

WHERE TO STAY

£££ 🏨 **Howtown Hotel.** Near the end of the road down the isolated eastern side of Ullswater, this gloriously quiet, welcoming, family-run hotel is low-key and low-tech, though the Ullswater Steamer connects it to the outside world. Cut flowers, antiques, and stuffed deer heads decorate the steadfastly old-fashioned interior, and there are fireplaces and views over the lake from some rooms. The restaurant, open to nonguests, serves hearty Lakeland fare, and good take-out lunches are available. Howtown is popular, so book ahead. **Pros:** exceptionally quiet; spectacular location; dinner included in price. **Cons:** not for those who must be plugged in; a bit remote. ⊠ *4 mi south of Pooley Bridge* ☎ *017684/86514* ⊕ *www. howtown-hotel.com* 🛏 *12 rooms* ⚬ *In-room: no a/c, no phone, no TV. In-hotel: restaurant, 2 bars, some pets allowed, no kids under 7* ☰ *No credit cards* ⊗ *Closed Nov.–Mar.* ⏐⊙⏐*MAP*.

CLOSE UP

Poetry, Prose, and the Lakes

The Lake District's beauty has whetted the creativity of many a famous poet and artist over the centuries. Here's a quick rundown of some of the writers inspired by the area's vistas.

William Wordsworth (1770–1850), one of the first English Romantics, redefined poetry by replacing the mannered style of his predecessors with a more conversational style. Many of his greatest works, such as *The Prelude*, draw directly from his experiences in the Lake District, where he spent the first 20 and last 50 years of his life. Wordsworth and his work had an enormous effect on Coleridge, Keats, Shelley, Byron, and countless other writers.

John Ruskin (1819–1900), writer, art critic, and early conservationist, was an impassioned champion of new ways of seeing. He defended contemporary artists such as William Turner and the Pre-Raphaelites. His five-volume masterwork, *Modern Painters*, changed the role of the art critic from that of approver or naysayer to that of interpreter.

Thomas De Quincey (1785–1859) wrote essays whose impressionistic style influenced many 19th-century writers, including Poe and Baudelaire. His most famous work, *Confessions of an English Opium-Eater* (1822), is an imaginative memoir of his young life, which indeed included opium addiction. He settled in Grasmere in 1809.

Beatrix Potter (1866–1943) never had a formal education; instead, she spent her childhood studying nature. Her love of the outdoors, and Lakeland scenery in particular, influenced her delightfully illustrated children's books, including *The Tale of Peter Rabbit* and *The Tale of Jemima Puddle-Duck*. Potter also became a noted conservationist who donated land to the National Trust. The story of her life was made into the 2006 film *Miss Potter,* starring Renée Zellweger and Ewan McGregor.

£££££–£££££
★
Sharrow Bay. Sublime views and exceptional service and cuisine add distinction to this country-house hotel on the shores of Ullswater. Salons with oil paintings and fringed lamp shades represent classic Lakeland style. The traditional bedrooms are plushly opulent, although those in the Edwardian Gatehouse and in the Bank House, an Elizabethan farmhouse about 1½ mi away, are somewhat simpler. Your sophisticated dinner (reservations essential, £70 fixed-price menu) might include roast salmon on scallop risotto or venison with sweet-potato confit; choose a wine from the excellent list. Be sure to request the lake-view dining room. Afternoon tea is another option (£19). **Pros:** elegant in the extreme; great views across Ullswater; pretty garden. **Cons:** not for the faint of wallet; some distance from other facilities. ⊠ *Howtown Rd., Pooley Bridge* ☎ *017684/86301* ⊕ *www.sharrowbay.co.uk* � *16 rooms, 8 suites* ⚙ *In-room: no a/c (some). In-hotel: 2 restaurants, bars, Wi-Fi, no kids under 13* ⊟ *AE, MC, V* ⚲ *MAP.*

KESWICK

14 mi west of Ullswater.

The great mountains of Skiddaw and Blencathra brood over the gray slate houses of Keswick (pronounced *kezz*-ick), on the scenic shores of Derwentwater. The town is a natural base for exploring the rounded, heather-clad Skiddaw range to the north, and the hidden valleys of Borrowdale and Buttermere (the latter reached by stunning Honister Pass) take you into the rugged heart of the Lake District. Nearby, five beautiful lakes are set among the three highest mountain ranges in England. The tourist information center here has regional information and is the place to get fishing permits for Derwentwater and Bassenthwaite.

Although tourists pack its cobbled, narrow streets, Keswick doesn't have quite the Victorian charm of Grasmere or Ambleside, or the specialty shops of Penrith. However, it is the best spot in the Lake District to purchase mountaineering gear and outdoor clothing. There are also many hotels, guesthouses, restaurants, and pubs, making it a good base.

GETTING HERE AND AROUND

It's easily reached along A66 from Penrith, though you can get to Keswick more scenically via Grasmere in the south. Buses run from the train station in Penrith to Keswick. The town center is pedestrianized.

■ TIP→ Because traffic congestion can be horrendous in summer, and parking is difficult in the higher valleys, consider leaving your car in Keswick. The open-top Borrowdale bus service between Keswick and Seatoller runs frequently, and the Honister Rambler minibus is perfect for walkers aiming for the high fells of the central lakes; it makes many stops from Keswick to Buttermere. The Keswick Launch service on Derwentwater links to many walks as well as the Borrowdale bus service.

ESSENTIALS

Visitor Information Keswick (⊠ *Moot Hall, Market Sq.* ☎ *017687/72645* ⊕ *www.keswick.org*).

EXPLORING

★ To understand why **Derwentwater** is considered one of England's finest lakes, take a short walk from Keswick's town center to the lakeshore and past the jetty, and follow the **Friar's Crag** path, about a 15-minute level walk from the center. This pine-tree-fringed peninsula is a favorite vantage point, with its view of the lake, the ring of mountains, and many tiny islands. Ahead, crags line the **Jaws of Borrowdale** and overhang a mountain ravine—a scene that looks as if it emerged from a Romantic painting.

For the best lake views, take a wooden-launch cruise with **Keswick-on-Derwentwater Launch Co.** (☎ *017687/72263* ⊕ *www.keswick-launch. co.uk*) around Derwentwater. Between late March and November, cruises set off every hour in each direction from a dock at the shore; there is also a limited winter timetable. You can also rent a rowboat here. Buy a hop-on, hop-off Around the Lake ticket (£8.50) and take advantage of the seven landing stages around the lake that provide access to hiking trails, such as the two-hour climb up and down Cat Bells, a celebrated lookout point on the western shore of Derwentwater.

Borrowdale's long connection with graphite is celebrated at the entertaining **Cumberland Pencil Museum.** Legend has it that shepherds found graphite on Seathwaite Fell after a storm uprooted trees in the 16th century. The Derwent company still makes pencils here, and the museum contains the world's longest pencil, a pencil produced for World War II spies that contains a rolled-up map, and displays about graphite mining and pencil making. There's a café and quizzes for kids. ⊠*Southey Works* ☎*017687/73626* ⊕*www.pencilmuseum.co.uk* ⊡*£3.25* ⊗*Daily 9:30–5; last admission at 4.*

★ A Neolithic monument about 100 feet in diameter, the **Castlerigg Stone Circle** (⊠*Off A66, 4 mi east of Keswick*) lies in a brooding natural hollow called St. John's Vale, ringed by magnificent peaks and ranged by sheep. The 38 stones aren't large, but the site makes them particularly impressive. Wordsworth described them as "a dismal cirque of Druid stones upon a forlorn moor." A marked route leads to a 200-foot-long path through a pasture. You can visit at any time, no charge.

WHERE TO EAT

£   ✕ **Café Bar 26.** A metropolitan bar in the rural Lake District, where cozy
BRITISH   tearooms are more the norm, Café Bar 26 has wooden beams, mellow brick-color walls, candlelight, and live music every Saturday. The wine list is on the short side, but there are good nibbles at night, though no dinner. During the day light lunches are served, including tuna on roasted vegetables, linguine with sun-dried tomatoes, and Caesar salad. The three bedrooms upstairs are an excellent value for an overnight. ⊠*26 Lake Rd.* ☎*017687/80863* ⊟*MC, V* ⊗*No dinner.*

£   ✕ **Lakeland Pedlar.** Colorful and cheerful, this café and bike shop serves
VEGETARIAN   inspired vegetarian and vegan cuisine: hearty breakfast burritos, Tex-Mex and Mediterranean food, and a homemade, fresh-daily "monster main course soup." You can also check out the fresh juices, espresso, and homemade cakes. Admire the fells (or the parking lot) from the outdoor tables, or take food with you for the trail. ⊠*Henderson's Yard, Bell Close* ☎*017687/74492* ⊟*MC, V* ⊗*Closed Wed. No dinner Sept.–June.*

££   ✕ **Morrel's.** One of the town's better eating places has cinematically
BRITISH   themed art, and wooden floors that give a contemporary edge to the bar and dining area. Updated British fare is the specialty at this mellow restaurant: the pork fillet is stuffed with prunes and Calvados, and the duck breast comes with puy lentils and black cherries. A couple of equally stylish apartments upstairs are available for short-term rentals. ⊠*34 Lake Rd.* ☎*017687/72666* ⊕*www.morrels.co.uk* ⊟*MC, V* ⊗*Closed Mon.*

£   ✕ **Square Orange Café.** Young locals and windblown walkers gather here
CAFÉ   for excellent coffee, tea, cordials, and some serious hot chocolate; cakes,
★   paninis, and tapas are served as well. Music is laid-back, the walls have paintings and photos, and there are games, pizza (some days and nights) and snacks, and pints of local beer for long rainy days or cold winter nights. ⊠*20 St. John's St.* ☎*017687/73888* ⊟*MC, V.*

£   ✕ **Star of Siam.** Good value and charmingly welcoming, this elegant
THAI   restaurant has an eclectic mix of decoration, including old clock faces and Asian masks and mirrors. The food on the long menu is authentic

Thai, with a rich mix of lime, lemongrass, coconut, and chili flavors. Green and red curries, stir-fries, and noodle dishes are among the options. It's all a nice change from the usual Lakeland fare. ⊠ *89 Main St.* ☎*017687/71444* ⊕*www. starofsiam.co.uk* ⊟*MC, V.*

WHERE TO STAY

£ 🏠 **Ferndene.** Exceptionally friendly, this spotless B&B has a warm, family atmosphere and is carefully cared for by its kind owners. Comfortable rooms are decorated in neutral tones, breakfast is hearty, and there's always plenty of local advice on walking and local sights when you want it. Good-size family rooms have views over the mountains of Blencathra and Skiddaw. **Pros:** family-focused; good value; bicycle storage. **Cons:** can't compete with stylishness of more expensive lodgings. ⊠*6 St. John's Terr.* ☎*017687/74612* ⊕*www.ferndene-keswick.co.uk* ☞*7 rooms* ♿*In-room: Wi-Fi. In-hotel: no-smoking rooms* ⊟*MC, V* ⦿*BP.*

£££–££££ 🏠 **Highfield Hotel.** Slightly austere-looking on the outside but excep-
★ tionally friendly within, this family-run Victorian hotel overlooks the lawns of Hope Park and has lodging with great character, including turret rooms and a former chapel that holds a four-poster. Smaller rooms downstairs are simpler and less impressive. The balconies of the common areas have superb valley views, and some rooms look out to Derwentwater or Skiddaw. The well-regarded restaurant's daily-changing fixed-price menu (£29.50 or £42.50) uses local ingredients. A four-course dinner is included in the room rate, adding value. Check out the fine wine list and 25 whiskies in the bar. **Pros:** good service and food; great views. **Cons:** some small downstairs bedrooms; meal plan may not appeal to those who want to dine around. ⊠*The Heads* ☎*017687/72508* ⊕*www.highfieldkeswick.co.uk* ☞*18 rooms* ♿*In-room: DVD, no a/c. In-hotel: restaurant, bar, Internet terminal, no-smoking rooms* ⊟*AE, MC, V* ⊘*Closed Jan.–mid-Feb.* ⦿*MAP.*

££ 🏠 **Howe Keld.** In a town that overflows with B&Bs, this comfortable town house–hotel combines local touches with contemporary flair and pampering touches. Some rooms have wood floors, and many have wooden furniture by local craftsman Danny Frost; the style is streamlined and neutral. Howe Keld also stands out because of its high-quality breakfasts that can include home-baked bread and pancakes as well as meaty Cumbrian fry-ups. **Pros:** freshly renovated; famously good breakfasts; one room is accessible for people with disabilities. **Cons:** a short distance from the heart of town; can get a little crowded. ⊠*5–7 The Heads* ☎*017687/72417* ⊕*www.howekeld.co.uk* ☞*15 rooms* ♿*In-room: no a/c, no phone. In-hotel: restaurant, bar, Wi-Fi, some pets allowed, no-smoking rooms* ⊟*MC, V* ⊘*Closed Jan.* ⦿*BP.*

NIGHTLIFE AND THE ARTS

The **Keswick Film Club** (☎*017687/72398*) has an excellent festival in February and a program of international and classic films, screened at the old redbrick Alhambra Cinema on St. John's Street and at the Theatre by the Lake. The popular **Keswick Jazz Festival** (☎*017687/74411*), held each May, consists of four days of music. Reservations are taken as early as before Christmas.

The company at the **Theatre by the Lake** (✉*Lake Rd.* ☎*017687/74411*) presents classic and contemporary productions year-round. Touring music and dance companies also perform. The Keswick Music Society season runs from September through January, and the Words on the Water literary festival takes place in February and March.

SPORTS AND THE OUTDOORS

BIKING **Keswick Mountain Bike Centre** (✉*Southey Hill* ☎*017687/75202*) rents bikes and provides information on trails; it also stocks accessories and clothing. Guided tours can be arranged with advance notice.

WATER SPORTS **Derwentwater Marina** (✉*Portinscale* ☎*017687/72912*) offers boat rentals in all shapes and sizes, and instruction in canoeing, sailing, windsurfing, and rowing as well as in other water-related activities such as ghyll scrambling—the fine art of walking up a steep Lakeland stream. A two-day sailing or windsurfing course costs £175. The marina is open year-round but has shorter hours November through February.

SHOPPING

Keswick has a good choice of bookstores, crafts shops, and wool-clothing stores tucked away in its cobbled streets, as well as excellent outdoor shops. Keswick's **market** is held Saturday.

George Fisher (✉*2 Borrowdale Rd.* ☎*017687/72178*), the area's largest and best outdoor equipment store, sells sportswear, travel books, and maps. Daily weather information is posted in the window. **Needle Sports** (✉*56 Main St.* ☎*017687/72227*) supplies equipment for mountaineering and for rock and ice climbing. The **Northern Lights Gallery** (✉*22 St. John's St.* ☎*01768/775402*) carries a good selection of contemporary paintings, photography, sculpture, jewelry, and ceramics by around 80 local artists. **Thomasons** (✉*8–10 Station St.* ☎*017687/80169*), a butcher and delicatessen, sells some very good meat pies—just the thing for putting in your pocket before you climb a Lakeland fell.

EN ROUTE
The most scenic route from Keswick, B5289 south, runs along the eastern edge of Derwentwater, past turnoffs to natural attractions such as Ashness Bridge, the idyllic tarn of Watendlath, the Lodore Falls (best in wet weather), and the precariously balanced Bowder Stone. Farther south is the tiny village of **Grange,** a walking center at the head of Borrowdale, where there's a riverside café.

BORROWDALE

FodorsChoice
★
7 mi south of Keswick.

South of Keswick and its lake lies the valley of Borrowdale, whose varied landscape of green valley floor and surrounding crags has long been considered one of the region's most magnificent treasures. **Rosthwaite,** a tranquil farming village, and **Seatoller,** the southernmost settlement, are the two main centers (both are accessible by bus from Keswick), though they are little more than clusters of aged buildings surrounded by glorious countryside.

CLOSE UP

Festivals and Folk Sports

11

With everything from rushbearing to Westmorland wrestling to traditional music, the Lake District hosts some of Britain's most unusual country festivals as well as some excellent but more typical ones. Major festivals include the Keswick Film Festival (February), Words by the Water (a literary festival in Keswick, February–March), Keswick Jazz Festival (May), Cockermouth and Keswick carnivals (June), Ambleside rushbearing (August) and sports (July), Grasmere rushbearing (August) and sports (August), and Lake District Summer Music (regionwide, in August), but some sort of event or festival happens somewhere during most weeks throughout the year.

Rushbearing dates back to medieval times, when rushes covered church floors; today processions of flower-bedecked children and adults bring rushes to churches in a number of villages. Folk sports, often the highlights at local festivals, include Cumberland and Westmorland wrestling, in which the opponents must maintain a grip around each other's body. Fell running, a sort of cross-country run where the route goes roughly straight up and down a mountain, is also popular.

A calendar of events is available at tourist information centers or on the Cumbria Tourism Web site, ⊕ *www.golakes.co.uk.*

EXPLORING

The steep **Borrowdale Fells** rise up dramatically behind Seatoller. Get out and walk whenever inspiration strikes. Trails are well signposted, or you can pick up maps and any gear in Keswick.

England's highest mountain, the 3,210-foot **Scafell Pike** (pronounced *scar*-fell) is visible from Seatoller. One route up the mountain, for experienced walkers, is from the hamlet of Seathwaite, a mile south of Seatoller.

WHERE TO EAT AND STAY

£ ✕ **Yew Tree Restaurant.** Two 17th-century miners' cottages make up this BRITISH intimate restaurant at the foot of Honister Pass. A low-beam ceiling, open fireplace, and excellent bar serving local Hesket Newmarket Brewery beers add appeal. The menu focuses on regional ingredients: Ullswater trout, Derwentwater pike, Herdwick lamb burgers ("herdy burgers"), and wonderful Cumbrian cheeses and sausages. ⊠ *B5289, Seatoller* ☎ *017687/77634* ⊟ *D, MC, V* ⊗ *Closed Mon. and 3 wks in Jan.*

££ ☷ **Hazel Bank Country House.** Hikers and others of a less energetic bent appreciate the comforts of this stately, carefully restored Victorian home, which retains original elements such as the stained-glass windows. Immaculate, spacious bedrooms are done in a faux-Victorian theme, and some have four-posters and window seats. All rooms, including the sitting area, have splendid views across the carpetlike lawns to the Borrowdale Valley and the central Lakeland peaks. Four-course dinners in the restaurant focus on local ingredients prepared with modern British flair. The owners claim that 85% of visitors return. **Pros:** serene location; immaculate gardens; packed lunches made on request.

Cons: some distance from a lake; not for families with younger children. ✉*Off B5289, Rosthwaite* ☎*017687/77248* 📠*017687/77373* 🌐*www.hazelbankhotel.co.uk* 📞*8 rooms, 1 cottage* 🏠*In-room: no a/c. In-hotel: restaurant, bar, Internet terminal, no kids under 12, no-smoking rooms* ▤*MC, V* 🍽*BP.*

EN ROUTE

Beyond Seatoller, B5289 turns westward through **Honister Pass** (1,176 feet) and Buttermere Fell. Boulders line the road, which is one of the most dramatic in the region; at times it channels through soaring rock canyons. The road sweeps down from the pass to the village of Buttermere, sandwiched between Buttermere (the lake) and Crummock Water at the foot of high, craggy fells. Just beyond the pass toward Buttermere, Syke House Farm sells fantastic ice cream made from the milk of their Ayrshire herd.

COCKERMOUTH

14 mi northwest of Seatoller.

This small but bustling town, at the confluence of the rivers Derwent and Cocker, has a maze of narrow streets that are a delight to wander. It's a bit off the usual tourist path, and a bit bohemian. The ruined 13th-century castle is open only on special occasions.

ESSENTIALS

Visitor Information Cockermouth (✉*The Town Hall, Market St.* ☎*01900/ 822634*).

EXPLORING

You can tour **Jennings Brewery** and learn how real ales are made. The tour includes the history of the company and allows you to see inside the huge fermentation casks, which hold up to 150 barrels of beer. It finishes up in the bar for some tastes of the finished product. There are one or two tours a day (more in summer), but no Sunday tours November through February. ✉*Castle Brewery* ☎*0845/129–7190* 🌐*www. jenningsbrewery.co.uk* 💷*£5.50 tour* ⏰*Shop Sept.–June, weekdays 9–5, Sat. 10–4; July and Aug., weekdays 9–5, weekends 10–4.*

From late June through July, the **Cockermouth Summer Festival** (🌐*www. cockermouth.org.uk*) presents art, music, and theater in town.

Cockermouth was the birthplace of William Wordsworth (and his sister, Dorothy), whose childhood home, **Wordsworth House,** is an 18th-century town house. The restored house looks somewhat close to what the poet would have known. You see it complete with clutter, costumed interpreters, and period cooking in the kitchen. Live harpsichord recitals take place regularly. Wordsworth's father is buried in the All Saints' churchyard, and the church has a stained-glass window in memory of the poet. ✉*Main St.* ☎*01900/824805* 🌐*www.nationaltrust.org. uk* 💷*£5.90* ⏰*Mar., weekends 11–5; Apr.–Oct., Mon.–Sat. 11–5; last admission at 4.*

★ **Castlegate House Gallery,** one of the region's best galleries, displays and sells an outstanding collection of works, many by Cumbrian artists. Eight exhibitions a year focus on paintings, sculpture, glass, ceramics, and jewelry. ⊠*Castlegate* ☎*01900/822149* ⊕*www.castlegatehouse. co.uk* ☽*Mar.–Dec., Mon.–Wed., Fri., and Sat. 10:30–5, Sun. 2–5.*

WHERE TO EAT AND STAY

£

BRITISH

✕**Bitter End.** Flocked floral wallpaper, old lamps, an open fire, and a handsome wooden floor set the tone at this appealing pub attached to Cumbria's smallest brewery, whose beers it sells. In contrast to big brother Jennings nearby, this outfit is homey and intimate, serving big, tasty portions of traditional English food such as lamb cobbler and fish-and-chips. ⊠*15 Kirkgate* ☎*01900/828993* ⊟*MC, V.*

£££

VEGETARIAN

★

✕**Quince & Medlar.** Sophisticated and imaginative vegetarian cuisine, served by candlelight, is the specialty at this refined, wood-paneled Georgian town house. Diners are offered a drink in the sitting room before being called to their table and can choose from at least six main courses, such as pecan-and-celeriac gateau with blue cheese and cran-berries; all come with seasonal vegetables. Desserts are delicious, espe-cially the lemon-and-almond sponge. ⊠*13 Castlegate* ☎*01900/823579* ⊟*MC, V* ☽*Closed Sun. and Mon. No lunch.*

£

🖭**Six Castlegate.** After a day of exploring, relax in stylish accommoda-tion in an elegant B&B in a Grade 2–listed (considered to be of special architectural or historic interest) Georgian town house. The spacious rooms, named after local mountains, are decorated in pale, natural tones and have good views, generous showers, and big, comfortable beds. Breakfasts entice with local ingredients. You can use the pool and parking lot at the nearby leisure center. **Pros:** modern facilities and antique style blend nicely; near galleries and attractions. **Cons:** some road noise in some rooms. ⊠*6 Castlegate* ☎*01900/826786* ⊕*www. sixcastlegate.co.uk* 🛏*6 rooms* ⚘*In-room: no a/c, DVD (some), Wi-Fi. In-hotel: no-smoking rooms* ⊟*MC, V* ⦿*BP.*

BASSENTHWAITE LAKE

5 mi east of Cockermouth, 3 mi north of Keswick.

Bassenthwaite is the only body of water officially called a lake in the Lake District; the others are known as "meres" or "waters." Bird-watchers know this less-frequented lake well because of the many spe-cies of migratory birds found here, including ospreys (check out www. ospreywatch.co.uk). The shoreline habitat is the best-preserved in the national park—in part because most of it is privately owned, and also because motorboats are not allowed.

Posh accommodations and good restaurants dot the area, and popular walks include the climb up Skiddaw (3,054 feet), which, on a clear day, has panoramic views of the Lake District, the Pennines, Scotland, and the Isle of Man from its summit.

WHERE TO STAY

£££–££££

★

🖭**The Pheasant.** Halfway between Cockermouth and Keswick at the northern end of Bassenthwaite Lake, this traditional 17th-century coaching inn exudes English coziness without the usual Lakeland fussi-ness. Tasteful, modern bedrooms have soft but comfortable beds and tiled bathrooms with large tubs, and they overlook a garden and 60 acres of forest. You can request a TV; superior rooms come with iPod docks. A wood-beamed restaurant (£33 and £37 for fixed-price menus) serves superb English fare as well as afternoon tea; lighter lunches are an option in the lounges. Varnished walls, oak settles, and a smattering of locals set the mood in the popular bar. **Pros:** upmarket option with the atmosphere of a well-loved local inn; nice bar. **Cons:** a little out of the way for the Lakes' sights. ✉ *Off A66, Bassenthwaite Lake* ☎ *017687/76234* ⊕ *www.the-pheasant.co.uk* ⟳ *15 rooms, 3 suites* ♿ *In-room: no a/c. In-hotel: restaurant, bar, Wi-Fi, some pets allowed* ▭ *MC, V* ⏀ *BP.*

East Anglia

CAMBRIDGE, BURY ST. EDMUNDS,
NORWICH, LINCOLN

WORD OF MOUTH

"Try and visit King's College Chapel; it's only open at certain times but free to enter. We were there on a Sunday morning and heard the choir singing. The sun shining through the stained glass and the whole atmosphere of the massive church was amazing."

—KayF

"Suffolk and Norfolk have some delightful small towns and villages, many with big churches built with money from the wool trade. It's not far from London but seems off the main tourist track. Lavenham is charming. The houses were made from unseasoned oak, so they are crooked."

—MissPrism

Updated by
Jack Jewers

One of those beautiful English inconsistencies, East Anglia has no spectacular mountains or rivers to disturb the storied, quiet land, full of quiet rural delights. Occupying an area of southeastern England that bulges out into the North Sea, its counties of Essex, Norfolk, Suffolk, Lincolnshire, and Cambridgeshire feel cut off from the central routes and pulse of the country.

In times past, East Anglia was one of the most important centers of power in Northern Europe. The towns of Colchester and Lincoln were major Roman settlements, and the medieval wool trade brought huge prosperity to the higgledy-piggledy streets of tiny Lavenham. Thanks to its relative lack of thoroughfares and canals, however, East Anglia was mercifully untouched by the Industrial Revolution. The area is rich in idyllic, quintessentially English villages: sleepy, sylvan settlements in the midst of otherwise deserted lowlands. Even the towns feel small and manageable; the biggest city, Norwich, has a population of just 125,000.

East Anglia also boasts four of the country's greatest stately homes: Holkham Hall, Blickling Hall, Houghton Hall, and Sandringham—where the Queen spends the summer. There are incomparable cathedrals, at Ely and Lincoln particularly, and one of the finest Gothic buildings in Europe, King's College Chapel in Cambridge.

And yet, despite all of these treasures, the real joy of exploring East Anglia is making your own discoveries. Spend a couple of days exploring the hidden byways of the Fens, or just taking in the subtle beauties of the many England-like-it-looks-in-the-movies villages. If you find yourself driving down a small country lane and an old church or mysterious, ivy-covered ruin peeks out from behind the trees, give in to your curiosity and look inside. Such hidden places are East Anglia's best-kept secret, and there are real gems to be found.

ORIENTATION AND PLANNING

GETTING ORIENTED

For purposes of sightseeing, East Anglia can be divided into distinct areas: the central area surrounding the ancient university city of Cambridge and including Ely, with its magnificent cathedral rising out of the flatlands, and the towns of inland Suffolk; the southeast, taking in the ancient Roman town of Colchester and sweeping upward along the Suffolk Heritage Coast; and the northeast, with the region's capital, Norwich, the waterways of the Broads, and the beaches and salt marshes of the North Norfolk coast. Farther north, in Lincolnshire, are

12

TOP REASONS TO GO

Cambridge: A walk though the colleges is grand, but the best views of the university's colleges and immaculate lawns (and some famous bridges) are from a punt on the river. Try not to let your pole get stuck in the mud.

Constable country: In the area where Constable grew up, you can walk or row downstream from the pastel-shaded village of Dedham straight into the setting of one of the English landscape painter's masterpieces at Flatford Mill.

Grand houses: When the Queen's not in residence, you can visit the Royal Family's holiday home of Sandringham. If that's out of bounds, other options, including Holkham Hall and Burghley House, are just as spectacular.

Lincoln's old center: The ancient center of the city has a vast, soaring cathedral, a proper rampart-ringed castle, and winding medieval streets lined with small shops, restaurants, and cafés.

Wild North Sea coast: North Norfolk has enormous sandy beaches (great for walking) and opportunities to see seals and birdlife, especially on the salt marshes around Blakeney.

Lavenham: This medieval town is the most comely of the tight-knit cluster of places that did well from the wool trade: nearby are Sudbury and Long Melford. All have perhaps the region's most memorable architecture, including timber-frame houses gnarled into crookedness by age.

the city of Lincoln, landmarked by its tall, fluted cathedral towers, and the historic town of Stamford.

Cambridge. The home of the famous university may be East Anglia's liveliest town, but it's also refreshingly free of noise and traffic. The city center is perfect for ambling around the ancient colleges, museums, and King's College Chapel, one of England's greatest monuments.

Ely to Bury St. Edmunds. The villages within a short drive of Cambridge remain largely unspoiled. Ely's lofty cathedral dominates the surrounding flatlands, and Sudbury, Long Melford, Lavenham, and Bury St. Edmunds preserve their rich historical flavor.

Colchester and the Suffolk Coast. North of Colchester, with its Roman and Norman remains, and Dedham, the center of Constable Country, the Suffolk Coast includes such atmospheric seaside towns as Woodbridge and Aldeburgh.

Norwich to North Norfolk. Sights in Norwich include its soaring cathedral and sturdy castle. To the north and west you'll find the stately homes of Blickling Hall, Houghton Hall, and Sandringham and a string of quiet coastal resorts such as Blakeney and Wells-next-the-Sea.

Stamford and Lincoln. On the western fringes of East Anglia, Lincoln is worth visiting for its Norman cathedral, whereas Stamford is best known for Burghley House, an impressive Elizabethan mansion.

PLANNING

WHEN TO GO

Summer and late spring are the best times to visit East Anglia. Late fall and winter can be cold, windy, and rainy, though this is England's driest region and crisp, frosty days here are beautiful. To escape crowds, avoid the popular Norfolk Broads in late July and August. The Aldeburgh Festival of Music and the Arts, one of the biggest events on the British classical music calendar, takes place in June.

PLANNING YOUR TIME

Cambridge is the region's most interesting city, and you should allow two or three days to absorb its various sights. You could easily use the city as a base for exploring Ely, Bury St. Edmunds, Lavenham, Long Melford, and Sudbury, although you will also find accommodations in these towns. The Suffolk Coast offers enticing overnight stops in such small towns as Dedham and Aldeburgh. In the northern part of the region, Norwich makes a good place to stop for the night, and has enough sights to keep you interested for a day. If you're here to see the coast, you'd do better staying in villages such as Blakeney or Wells. Allow a full day for seeing large houses such as Blickling Hall, near Norwich, and Burghley House, outside Stamford. Lincoln, notable for its cathedral, and Stamford are west and north of Norfolk if you want to work them into an itinerary.

GETTING HERE AND AROUND

AIR TRAVEL

Norwich International Airport serves a limited number of domestic and international destinations, though not the United States. The vast majority of travelers to the region, however, arrive by train, car, or bus.

Airport Norwich International Airport (✉ *Amsterdam Way, A140, Norwich* ☎ *0844/748–0112* ⊕ *www.norwichinternational.com*).

BUS TRAVEL

National Express buses serve the region from London's Victoria Coach Station. Average travel times are 3 hours to Cambridge, 2 hours (with one transfer) to Colchester, 2½ hours to Bury St. Edmunds, 5 hours (with one transfer) to Norwich, and 4 hours to Lincoln.

Trains and long-distance buses are useful for reaching the region and traveling between its major centers, but for smaller hops, local buses are best. Local First and Stagecoach buses cover the Cambridge, Lincolnshire, and Norwich areas. Information about local Norfolk service and county service is available from the Norfolk Bus Information Centre. Traveline can answer public transportation questions.

A FirstDay ticket from First gives a day's unlimited bus travel around Norwich and the Norfolk coast for £10. A family pass for two adults and two children costs £20.

Bus Contacts First (☎ *0845/601–8020* ⊕ *www.firstgroup.com*). **National Express** (☎ *0845/600–7245* ⊕ *www.nationalexpress.com*). **Norfolk Bus Information Centre** (☎ *0845/300–6116*). **Stagecoach** (☎ *01223/423578* ⊕ *www.stagecoachbus.com/cambridge*). **Traveline** (☎ *0871/200–2233* ⊕ *www. traveline.org.uk*).

Norwich,
North Norfolk,
and Lincoln

East Anglia

Wells-next-
the-Sea   Blakeney

TO LINCOLN

Norwich
see detail
map

N O R F O L K

Stamford

Ely

C A M B R I D G E S H I R E

Cambridge
see detail
map

Bury St.
Edmunds

S U F F O L K   Aldeburgh

Lavenham   Woodbridge

Orford

Long Melford
Sudbury

Dedham

E S S E X

Colchester

0   20 miles

0   30 km

**Ely to the
Suffolk Coast**

CAR TRAVEL

If you're driving from London, Cambridge (54 mi) is off M11. At Exit
9, M11 connects with A11 to Norwich (114 mi); A14 off A11 goes to
Bury St. Edmunds. A12 from London goes through east Suffolk via
Colchester and Ipswich. For Lincoln (131 mi), take A1 via Huntingdon,
Peterborough, and Grantham to A46 at Newark-on-Trent. A more sce-
nic alternative is to leave A1 at Grantham and take A607 to Lincoln.

East Anglia has few fast main roads. The principal routes are those mentioned above. Once off the A roads, traveling within the region often
means taking country lanes that have many twists and turns.

TRAIN TRAVEL

The entire region is well served by trains from London's Liverpool
Street, King's Cross, and St. Pancras stations. The quality and convenience of these services varies enormously, however. Cambridge trains
leave from King's Cross and Liverpool Street, take around one hour,
and cost just under £20. On the other hand, getting to Lincoln from
St. Pancras entails at least two transfers, takes two to three hours, and
costs £60 to £100. (A much-hyped new direct service, which started in
2008, leaves only once a day—in the evening.)

A good way to save money on local trains in East Anglia is to buy an
Anglia Plus Ranger Pass. It costs £13.50 for one day or £27 for three

days, and allows unlimited rail travel in Norfolk, Suffolk, and part of Cambridgeshire.

Train Contacts National Rail Enquiries (☎ *0845/748–4950* ⊕ *www. nationalrail.co.uk*).

RESTAURANTS

In summer the coast gets so packed with people that reservations are essential at restaurants. Getting something to eat at other than regular mealtime hours is not always possible in small towns; look for cafés if you want a mid-morning or after-lunch snack.

HOTELS

The region is full of centuries-old, half-timber inns with rooms full of roaring fires and cozy bars. Bed-and-breakfasts are a good option in pricey Cambridge. It's always busy in Cambridge and along the coast in summer, so reserve well in advance.

WHAT IT COSTS IN POUNDS					
	£	££	£££	££££	£££££
Restaurants	Under £10	£10–£14	£15–£19	£20–£25	over £25
Hotels	Under £70	£70–£120	£121–£160	£161–£220	over £220

Restaurant prices are for a main course at dinner. Hotel prices are for two people in a standard double room in high season, including V.A.T., with no meals or, if indicated, CP (with continental breakfast), BP (Breakfast Plan, with full breakfast), or MAP (Modified American Plan, with breakfast and dinner).

Visitor Information East of England Tourism (✉ *Dettingen House, Dettingen Way, Bury St. Edmunds* ☎ *01284/727470* ⊕ *www.visiteastofengland.com*). **Broads Authority** (✉ *Dragonfly House, 2 Gilders Way, Norwich* ☎ *01603/ 610734* ⊕ *www.broads-authority.gov.uk*).

CAMBRIDGE

With the spires of its university buildings framed by towering trees and expansive meadows, its medieval streets and passages enhanced by gardens and riverbanks, the city of Cambridge is among the loveliest in England. The city predates the Roman occupation of Britain, but there's confusion over exactly how the university was founded. The most widely accepted story is that it was established in 1209 by a pair of scholars from Oxford, who left their university in protest over the wrongful execution of a colleague for murder.

Today Cambridge embodies a certain genteel, intellectual, and sometimes anachronistically idealized image of Englishness. Think Rupert Brooke, the short-lived World War I–era poet ("There is some corner of a foreign field/That is forever England"), a Cambridgeshire lad who called his county "The shire for Men who Understand," as well as William Wordsworth, Thackeray, Byron, Tennyson, E. M. Forster, and C.S. Lewis. The exquisite King's College choir defines the traditional English Christmas, when the *Festival of Nine Lessons and Carols* is broadcast live on Christmas Eve. On top of all this tradition and history,

Cambridge remains a lively city and an extraordinary center of learning and research where innovation and discovery still happen behind its ancient walls.

Keep in mind there is no recognizable campus: the scattered colleges *are* the university. The town reveals itself only slowly, filled with tiny gardens, ancient courtyards, imposing classic buildings, alleyways that lead past medieval churches, and wisteria-hung facades. Perhaps the best views are from the Backs, the green parkland that extends along the River Cam behind several colleges. This broad, sweeping openness, a result of the larger size of the colleges and from the lack of industrialization in the city center, is just what distinguishes Cambridge from Oxford.

GETTING HERE AND AROUND

Good bus (three hours) and train (one hour) services connect London and Cambridge. The train station is a mile or so southeast of the center and is connected by the frequent Citi 3 bus service, run by Stagecoach, to Emmanuel Street, which is just around the corner from the long-distance bus terminus on Drummer Street. If you're driving, don't attempt to venture very far into the center—parking is scarce and pricey. The center is amenable to explorations on foot, or you could join the throng by renting a bicycle.

Stagecoach sells Dayrider (£3) tickets for all-day bus travel within Cambridge, and Megarider tickets (£11) for seven days of travel within the city. You can extend these to cover the whole county for a few extra pounds.

City Sightseeing operates open-top bus tours of Cambridge—the Backs, the colleges, the Imperial War Museum in Duxford, and the Grafton shopping center. Tours can be joined at marked bus stops in the city. Tickets are £10. Also ask the tourist office about tours.

TIMING

During the summer and over the Easter and Christmas holidays, Cambridge is devoid of students, its heart and soul. To see the city in full swing, visit from October through June. In summer there are festivals, notably the Strawberry Fair (June) and the Folk Festival and Arts Festival (both July). The May Bumps, intercollegiate boat races, are, confusingly, held the first week of June. This is also the month when students celebrate the end of exam season, so expect to encounter some boisterous nightlife.

ESSENTIALS

Bus Contacts First (☎ 0845/601–8020 ⊕ www.firstgroup.com). **Stagecoach** (☎ 01223/423578 ⊕ www.stagecoachbus.com/cambridge).

Visitor and Tour Information Cambridge (✉ Wheeler St. ☎ 0871/226–8006, 44/1223/464732 from abroad ⊕ www.visitcambridge.org). **Cambridge University** (☎ 01223/337733 ⊕ www.cam.ac.uk). **City Sightseeing** (✉ Cambridge train station, Station Road ☎ 01223/423578 ⊕ www.city-sightseeing.com).

EXPLORING CAMBRIDGE

Exploring the city means, in large part, exploring the university. Each of the 25 oldest colleges is built around a series of courts, or quadrangles, framing manicured, velvety lawns. Because students and fellows (faculty) live and work in these courts, access is sometimes restricted, and at *all* times you are asked not to picnic in the quadrangles.

Visitors are not normally allowed into college buildings other than chapels, dining halls, and some libraries; some colleges charge admission for certain buildings. The university's Web site, ⊕*www.cam.ac.uk*, has information about the colleges and other institutions associated with it. Public visiting hours vary from college to college, depending on the time of year, and it's best to call or to check with the city tourist office. Colleges close to visitors during the main exam time, late May to mid-June. Term time (when classes are in session) means roughly October to December, January to March, and April to June; summer term, or vacation, runs from July to September.

■ TIP ➜ When the colleges are open, the best way to gain access is to join a walking tour led by an official Blue Badge guide—many areas are off-limits unless you do. The two-hour tours (£8.50–£10) leave up to four times daily from the city tourist office. The other traditional view of the colleges is gained from a punt—the boats propelled by pole on the River Cam.

TOP ATTRACTIONS

⓭ Christ's College. To see the way a college has grown over the centuries you could not do better than visit here. The main gateway bears the enormous coat of arms of its patroness, Lady Margaret Beaufort, mother of Henry VII, who established the institution in 1505. It leads into a fine courtyard, with the chapel framed by an ancient magnolia. In the dining hall hang portraits of John Milton and Charles Darwin, two of the college's more famous students. You next walk past a fellows' building credited to Inigo Jones, to the spacious garden (once the haunt of Milton), and finally to a modern ziggurat-like confection. ⊠*St. Andrew's St.* ☎*01223/334900* ⊕*www.christs.cam.ac.uk* ⊗*Term time, except exam period, daily 9:30–dusk; out of term, daily 9:30–noon. Fellows' Garden: term time, except exam period, daily 9:30–noon, 2–4; out of term, weekdays 9:30–noon.*

⓫ Corpus Christi College. If you visit only one quadrangle, make it the beautiful, serene, 14th-century Old Court here. Founded in 1352, it's the longest continuously inhabited college quadrangle in Cambridge. ⊠*King's Parade* ☎*01223/338000* ⊕*www.corpus.cam.ac.uk* ▣*Free* ⊗*Daily dawn–dusk.*

⓮ Emmanuel College. The master hand of architect Christopher Wren (1632–1723) is evident throughout much of Cambridge, particularly at Emmanuel, built on the site of a Dominican friary, where he designed the chapel and colonnade. A stained-glass window in the chapel has a likeness of John Harvard, founder of Harvard University, who studied here. The college, founded in 1584, was an early center of Puritan learning; a number of the Pilgrims were Emmanuel alumni, and they

Cambridge

KEY

i *Tourist information*

12

remembered their alma mater in naming Cambridge, Massachusetts. ✉ *St. Andrew's St.* ☎ *01223/334200* ⊕ *www.emma.cam.ac.uk* ☉ *Daily 9–6, except exam period.*

⑱ Fitzwilliam Museum. In a Classical Revival building renowned for its grand Corinthian portico, the Fitzwilliam, founded by the seventh viscount Fitzwilliam of Merrion in 1816, has one of Britain's most outstanding collections of art and antiquities. Highlights include two large Titians, an extensive collection of French Impressionist painting, and many paintings by Matisse and Picasso. The opulent interior displays its treasures to marvelous effect, from Egyptian pieces such as inch-high figurines and painted coffins to sculptures from the Chinese Han dynasty of the 3rd century BC. Besides its archaeological collections, the Fitzwilliam contains English Staffordshire and other pottery, as well as a fascinating room of armor and muskets. The gallery holds occasional free classical music concerts. Guided tours beginning at 2:30 PM on Saturday cost £3.50; you can buy tickets that day or in advance from the Tourism Office. ✉ *Trumpington St.* ☎ *01223/332900* ⊕ *www. fitzmuseum.cam.ac.uk* ⛁ *Free* ☉ *Tues.–Sat. 10–5, Sun. noon–5.*

Fodor'sChoice
★

❻ Great St. Mary's. Known as the "university church," Great St. Mary's has its origins in the 11th century, although the current building dates from 1478. The main reason to visit is to climb the 113-foot tower, which has a superb view over the colleges and marketplace. Also here is the **Michaelhouse Centre,** a small café, gallery, and performing arts venue, where free lunchtime concerts are occasionally held. ✉ *Market Hill, King's Parade* ☎ *01223/741716* ⊕ *www.gsm.cam.ac.uk* ⛁ *Free, tower £2.50* ☉ *Mon.–Sat. 9:30–5, Sun. 12:30–5; Sept.–Apr. closes at 4.*

OFF THE
BEATEN
PATH

Imperial War Museum Duxford. The buildings and grounds of this former airfield, now Europe's leading aviation museum, house a remarkable collection of 180 aircraft from Europe and the United States. It's effectively a complex of several museums under one banner, and the ticket price covers admission to everything, save for occasional special events. The **Land Warfare Hall** features tanks and other military vehicles. The **American Air Museum,** housed in a striking Norman Foster–designed building, honors the 30,000 Americans who were killed in action flying from Britain during World War II. It contains the largest display of American fighter planes outside the United States. (Duxford itself was the headquarters of the American 78th Fighter Group.) **AirSpace** contains a vast array of military and civil aircraft in a 3-acre hangar, including Concorde. Directly underneath is the new **Airborne Assault Museum,** which chronicles the history of airborne forces, such as the British Parachute Regiment, which played a pivotal role in the Normandy Landings. On a handful of dates every summer and fall, the Imperial War Museum holds very popular air shows at Duxford, some featuring historic warplanes. Check in advance for dates and ticket prices. ✉ *A505, Duxford* ☎ *01223/835000* ⊕ *duxford.iwm.org.uk* ⛁ *£16* ☉ *Mid-Mar.–Oct., daily 10–6; late Oct.–mid-Mar., daily 10–4. Last admission 1 hr before closing.*

❹ Jesus College. Unique in Cambridge, the spacious grounds of Jesus College incorporate cloisters, a remnant of the nunnery of St. Radegund,

12

which existed on the site before the college was founded in 1496. Cloister Court exudes a quiet medieval charm, an attribute evident in the adjacent chapel, another part of the nunnery. Victorian restoration of the building includes some Pre-Raphaelite stained-glass windows and ceiling designs by William Morris. ⊠*Jesus La.* 🕾*01223/339339* ⊕*www.jesus.cam.ac.uk* ⏾*Daily 8–7, except exam period.*

9 **King's College.** Founded in 1441 by Henry VI, King's College's most famous landmark is its late-15th-century chapel. Other architecture of note is the neo-Gothic Porters' Lodge, facing King's Parade, which was a relatively recent addition in the 1830s, and the classical Gibbs building. ▇TIP➔ **Follow the college's Back Lawn down to the river, from where the panorama of college and chapel is one of the university's most photographed views.** Past students of King's College include the novelist E. M. Forster, the economist John Maynard Keynes, and the World War I poet Rupert Brooke. ⊠*King's Parade* 🕾*01223/331100* ⊕*www.kings.cam.ac.uk* 🎫*£5, includes chapel* ⏾*Term time, weekdays 9:30–3:30, Sat. 9:30–3:15, Sun. 1:15–2:15; out of term, Mon.–Sat. 9:30–4:30, Sun. 10–5.*

8 **King's College Chapel.** Based on Sainte Chapelle, the 13th-century royal chapel in Paris, this house of worship is the final, perhaps most glorious flowering of Perpendicular Gothic in Britain. Henry VI, the king after whom the college is named, oversaw the work. This was the last period before the classical architecture of the ancient Greeks and Romans, then being rediscovered by the Italians, began to make its influence felt in Northern Europe. From the outside, the most prominent features are the expanses of glass, the massive flying buttresses, and the fingerlike spires that line the length of the building. Inside, the most obvious impression is of great space—the chapel has been described as "the noblest barn in Europe"—and of light flooding in from its huge windows. The brilliantly colored bosses (carved panels at the intersections of the roof ribs) are particularly intense, although hard to see without binoculars. An exhibition in the chantries, or side chapels, explains more about the chapel's construction. Behind the altar is *The Adoration of the Magi,* an enormous painting by Peter Paul Rubens. Every Christmas Eve a festival of carols sung by the chapel's famous choir is broadcast worldwide from here. A small number of tickets to this service are available for the general public, but competition is fierce. To try your luck, join the line at the college's main front entrance early—doors open at 7AM. ⊠*King's Parade* 🕾*01223/331155* ⊕*www.kings.cam.ac.uk* 🎫*£5, includes college and grounds* ⏾*Term time, weekdays 9:30–3:30, Sat. 9:30–3:15, Sun. 1:15–2:30; out of term, Mon.–Sat. 9:30–4:30, Sun. 10–5; hrs vary, so call ahead.*

Fodor'sChoice ★

QUICK BITES

The 600-year-old **Pickerel Inn** (⊠ *30 Magdalene St.* 🕾*01223/355068*), one of the city's oldest pubs, makes for a good stop for a soothing afternoon pint of real ale or lager and a bowl of potato wedges. Watch for the low beams.

10 **Queens' College.** One of the most eye-catching colleges is Queens', named after Margaret, queen of Henry VI, and Elizabeth, queen of Edward IV. Founded in 1448, the college is tucked away on Queens' Lane, next to the wide lawns that lead down from King's College to the Backs. The secluded "cloister court" looks untouched since its completion in the 1540s. Queens' masterpiece is the **Mathematical Bridge,** the original version of which is said to have been built without any fastenings. The current bridge (1902) is securely bolted. ⊠ *Queens' La.* ☎ *01223/335511* ⊕ *www.quns.cam.ac.uk* 🖃 *£2, free Nov.–mid-Mar. and weekdays in Oct.* ⊙ *Mid-Mar.–mid-May, weekdays 11–3, weekends 10–4:30; late June–late Sept., daily 10–4:30; late Sept.–late Oct., weekdays 1:45–4:30, weekends 10–4:30; late Oct.–mid Mar., daily 1:45–4:30* ⊙ *Closed mid-May–mid-June for examinations; call for special closures.*

❸ St. John's College. Two mythical beasts called "yales," with the bodies of antelopes and heads of goats, hold up the coat of arms and guard the gateway of Cambridge's second-largest college. St. John's was founded in 1511 by Henry VII's mother, Lady Margaret Beaufort. Its structures lie on two sites: from the main entrance, walk to the left through the courts to the 1831 **"Bridge of Sighs,"** whose only resemblance to its Venetian counterpart is its covering. The windowed, covered stone bridge reaches across the Cam to the mock-Gothic New Court (1825), nicknamed "the wedding cake." If you walk through to the riverbank, you can stroll along the Backs and photograph the elegant bridge. ⊠ *St. John's St.* ☎ *01223/338600* ⊕ *www.joh.cam.ac.uk* 🖃 *£2.80* ⊙ *Mar.–Oct., daily 10–5:30; Nov.–Feb., weekends only, hrs vary.*

❺ Trinity College. Founded in 1546 by Henry VIII, Trinity replaced a 14th-century educational foundation and is the largest college in either Cambridge or Oxford, with nearly 700 undergraduates. Many of the buildings match its size, not least its 17th-century "great court." Here the massive gatehouse holds "Great Tom," a giant clock that strikes each hour with high and low notes. The college's greatest masterpiece is Christopher Wren's **library,** colonnaded and seemingly constructed with as much light as stone. Alongside the books, you can also see A. A. Milne's handwritten manuscript of *The House at Pooh Corner.* Alumni include Sir Isaac Newton, William Thackeray, Lords George Byron, Alfred Tennyson, and Thomas Macaulay, and 31 Nobel Prize winners. Prince Charles was an undergraduate here in the late 1960s. ⊠ *St. John's St.* ☎ *01223/338400* ⊕ *www.trin.cam.ac.uk* 🖃 *£2.50, free late Oct.–mid-Mar.* ⊙ *College and chapel daily 10–5, except exam period and occasional event days; library weekdays noon–2, Sat. in term time 10:30–12:30; hall weekdays 3–5, except during services and rehearsals.*

WORTH NOTING

❶ Kettle's Yard. Originally a private house owned by a former curator of London's Tate galleries, Kettle's Yard contains a fine collection of 20th-century art, sculpture, furniture, and decorative arts, including works by Henry Moore, Barbara Hepworth, and Henri Gaudier-Brzeska. One gallery shows changing exhibitions of modern art and crafts, and weekly concerts (term time only) and lectures attract an eclectic mix of enthusiasts. Ring the bell for admission. ⊠ *Castle St.* ☎ *01223/748100* ⊕ *www.kettlesyard.co.uk* 🖃 *Free* ⊙ *House early Apr.–Sept., Tues.–Sun. 1:30–4:30; Oct.–early Apr., Tues.–Sun. 2–4. Gallery Tues.–Sun. 11:30–5.*

12

② **Magdalene College.** Across Magdalene (pronounced *maud*-lin) Bridge, a cast-iron 1820 structure, lies the only one of the older colleges to be sited across the river. Magdalene Street itself is traffic-heavy, but there's relative calm inside the red-brick courts. It was a hostel for Benedictine monks for more than 100 years before the college was founded in 1542. In the second court, the college's **Pepys Library** (☎01223/332187 ⊘ *Mid-Apr.–Aug., Mon.–Sat. 11:30–12:30 and 2:30–3:30; Oct.–early Dec. and mid-Jan.–mid-Mar., Mon.–Sat. 2:30–3:30*) —labeled *Bibliotecha Pepysiana*—contains the books and desk of the famed 17th-century diarist Samuel Pepys. Beyond, quiet gardens overlook the river. ✉ *Magdalene St.* ☎*01223/332100* ⊕*www.magd.cam.ac.uk* ✉*Free* ⊘ *Daily 9–6, except exam period.*

A GIFT FOR SCIENCE
For centuries the University of Cambridge has been among the greatest universities, rivaled in Britain only by Oxford. Since the time of its most famous scientific alumnus, Sir Isaac Newton, it has outshone Oxford in the natural sciences. The university has taken advantage of its scientific prestige, pooling its research facilities with high-tech industries. As a result, Cambridge is surrounded by IT companies and has been dubbed "Silicon Fen" in comparison to California's Silicon Valley. The prosperity brought by these businesses is evident around the city.

⑮ **Museum of Archaeology and Anthropology.** The university maintains some fine museums in its research halls on Downing Street—the wonder is that they are not better known to visitors. Geological collections at the Sedgwick Museum and the exhibits at the Zoological Museum are extensive, but be sure to see the Museum of Archaeology and Anthropology, which houses a superb collection of ethnographic objects brought back by early explorers, including members of Captain Cook's pioneering voyages to the Pacific. ✉ *Downing St.* ☎*01223/333516* ⊕*maa.cam.ac.uk* ✉*Free* ⊘ *Tues.–Sat. 10:30–4:30.*

⑯ **Pembroke College.** Established in 1347, Pembroke has some buildings dating from the 14th century in its first court. On the south side, Christopher Wren's chapel—his first major commission, completed in 1665—looks like a distinctly modern intrusion. You can walk through the college, around a delightful garden, and past the fellows' bowling green. Outside the library you can't miss the resplendent, toga-clad statue of the precocious William Pitt the Younger; he came up to Pembroke at age 15 and was appointed prime minister of Great Britain in 1783, when he was just 24. ✉ *Trumpington St.* ☎*01223/338100* ⊕*www.pem.cam.ac.uk* ⊘ *Daily 9–5, except exam period.*

⑫ **Peterhouse College.** The bishop of Ely founded Cambridge's oldest college in 1281. Parts of the dining hall date from 1290, although the hall is most notable for powerful, 19th-century stained glass by William Morris and his contemporaries. The adjacent church of Little St. Mary's served as the college chapel until 1632, when the current late-Gothic chapel was built. ✉ *Trumpington St.* ☎*01223/338200* ⊕*www.pet.cam.ac.uk* ⊘ *Daily 9–5, except exam period.*

⑦ Trinity Hall. The green parkland of the Backs is best appreciated from Trinity's 14th-century neighboring college, Trinity Hall, where you can sit on a wall by the river and watch students in punts maneuver under the ancient ornamental bridges of Clare and King's. Access to the river is down Trinity Lane, off Trinity Street. The **Senate House** (⊠*King's Parade*), which stands between Clare College and Trinity Hall, is not part of a particular college. A classical building of the 1720s, it's used for graduation ceremonies and other events. There is no official public access, but if the gate is open, you can wander into the court. ⊠*Trinity La.* ☎*01223/332500* ⊕*www.trinhall.cam.ac.uk* ⊙*Daily 9:15–noon and 2–5:30, except exam period and summer term.*

⑰ University Botanic Gardens. Laid out in 1846, these gardens contain rare specimens, conservatories, and a rock garden. They are a five-minute walk from the Fitzwilliam Museum. ⊠*Cory Lodge, Bateman St.* ☎*01223/336265* ⊕*www.botanic.cam.ac.uk* ⊡*£4* ⊙*Feb., Mar., and Oct., daily 10–5; Apr.–Sept., daily 10–6; Nov.–Jan., daily 10–4. Conservatories close ½ hr before gardens.*

WHERE TO EAT

££
CAFÉ
⊠**Fitzbillies.** Usually filled with students' parents who are visiting in town, Fitzbillies is rightly famous for its exceptionally sticky Chelsea buns (a sweet bun flavored with currants, lemon peel, and spices). If you don't want to sit down, the bakery next door has the same range of pastries to take away. It also serves filling and tasty lunches, and more formal evening meals, with dishes such as lamb *noisettes,* small, round boneless cuts, and sirloin steak. ⊠*52 Trumpington St.* ☎*01223/352500* ⊟*AE, MC, V* ⊙*No dinner Sun.*

££
SEAFOOD
⊠**Loch Fyne.** Part of a midsize Scottish chain that harvests oysters and runs seafood restaurants, this airy, casual place across the street from the Fitzwilliam Museum is open for breakfast, lunch, and dinner. The oysters and other seafood are deservedly popular—mussels and salmon are fresh and well prepared, and line-caught tuna is served with a mint-and-caper salsa. ⊠*37 Trumpington St.* ☎*01223/362433* ⊟*AE, MC, V.*

£££££
FRENCH
★
⊠**Midsummer House.** An elegant restaurant beside the River Cam on the edge of Midsummer Common, the gray-brick Midsummer House has a comfortable conservatory and a handful of tables in a lush secluded garden under fruit trees. Fixed-price menus for lunch and dinner offer innovative French and Mediterranean dishes. Choices might include braised turbot, smoked eel salad, or grilled pigeon. ⊠*Midsummer Common* ☎*01223/369299* ⚖*Reservations essential* ⊟*AE, MC, V* ⊙*Closed Sun. and Mon. No lunch Tues.*

£££££
BRITISH
⊠**Restaurant 22.** Pretty stained-glass windows separate this sophisticated little restaurant from the busy Chesterton Road. The setting, in a terrace of houses, is low-key, but the food is creative and eye-catching. The fixed-price menu changes monthly and features dishes such as roast breast of guinea fowl with root vegetables and crab apple jelly. ⊠*22 Chesterton Rd.* ☎*01223/351880* ⊟*AE, MC, V* ⊙*Closed Sun. and Mon. No lunch.*

ON THE MENU

Farmland and the rivers and sea provide ample bounty for the table in East Anglia. Look for area specialties, such as duckling, Norfolk black turkey, hare, and partridge, on menus around the region. In Norwich, there's no escaping the hot, bright yellow Colman's mustard, which is perfect smeared gingerly on some sausage and mash.

Among the culinary treats from the sea is samphire, a delicious plant that grows in the salt marshes along the North Norfolk and Suffolk coasts. The long coastline also provides tasty Cromer crabs and Yarmouth bloaters (a kind of smoked herring), whereas the Essex coast near Colchester has been producing oysters since Roman times. Brancaster and Stiffkey mussels, Sheringham lobster, and Thornham oysters are all seafood highlights worth indulging in while visiting North Norfolk. Eel, a delicacy in the Fens, is served smoked or jellied. Maldon sea salt is another famous, high-quality local product. When you're traveling the coast, sample fresh fish-and-chips on the Suffolk coast, especially in Aldeburgh, where local creations have gained national recognition.

For liquid refreshment, Adnams, Greene King, and Tolly Cobbold are major ale producers, and a pint of Suffolk cider is usually a good accompaniment to the local food. There's an equally venerable tradition in wine making in the region. The Romans first introduced vines to Britain and they took especially well here. Today East Anglia has more than 40 vineyards; check wine lists in local restaurants.

££ ✕**River Bar & Kitchen.** Fashionable and stylish, this waterfront eatery
MODERN BRITISH designed by Terence Conran focuses on contemporary food with the occasional Eastern influence, such as spicy lamb samosas with mint-and-cucumber dip and Moroccan tagine. Light lunches are served between noon and 3, and cocktails are what most people come in for in the evening. Dinner service begins at 6:30. ✉*Quayside, off Bridge St.* ☎*01223/307030* ✍*Reservations essential* ▤*AE, MC, V* ⊘*Closed Mon. (except bank holidays). No dinner Sun.*

£££ ✕**Three Horseshoes.** This early-19th-century pub-restaurant in a thatched
ITALIAN cottage has an elegant dining space in the conservatory, and more infor-
★ mal tables in the airy bar area. The tempting, beautifully presented, and carefully sourced dishes are modern Italian with a British slant. Appetizers include risotto with slow-cooked beef shin, and among the main courses is grilled scallops and monkfish. The bar menu of two- and three-course meals (£12 to £17) is especially good value. It's 5 mi west of Cambridge, about a 10-minute taxi ride. ✉*High St., Madingley* ☎*01954/210221* ▤*MC, V.*

£ ✕**The Vaults.** Ochre and deep red walls and metal chairs on slate floors
ECLECTIC bring a sleek, contemporary edge to this popular basement restaurant. The menu is an eclectic mix of "fusion tapas"—you order lots of small portions from an imaginative, if ethnically confused, selection of dishes. Lunchtime menus are more traditional. The zinc-top bar with black sofas is the perfect place for lounging with a cocktail, and there is live

music two nights a week. Reservations are a good idea, especially on weekends. ⊠*14A Trinity St.* ☎*01223/506090* 🖃*AE, MC, V.*

WHERE TO STAY

There aren't many hotels downtown. For more (and cheaper) options, consider one of the numerous guesthouses on the arterial roads and in the suburbs. These start at £25 per person per night and can be booked through the tourist information center.

££–£££ 🖭**Arundel House Hotel.** Elegantly proportioned, this Victorian hotel made up of connected town houses has a fine location overlooking the River Cam, with Jesus Green in the background. The comfortable bedrooms, modern in style, have locally made mahogany furniture. Rattan chairs, trailing plants, and a patio garden add a certain cachet to meals and afternoon teas in the Victorian-style conservatory. The weekend rates are an excellent value. **Pros:** short walk to town center; comfortable rooms; free parking. **Cons:** unhelpful staff; old-fashioned furnishings; no elevator; few choices at breakfast. ⊠*53 Chesterton Rd.* ☎*01223/367701* ⊕*www.arundelhousehotels.co.uk* 🖅*103 rooms* △*In-room: no a/c, safe. In-hotel: 2 restaurants, bar, Wi-Fi, parking (free), no-smoking rooms* 🖃*AE, DC, MC, V* ⦿*CP.*

££–£££ 🖭**Ashley Hotel.** Sister to the Arundel House Hotel, this plainer and smaller establishment near the center of Cambridge was converted from two Victorian houses. The bedrooms won't win any interior design prizes, but they are a good value. You can take advantage of the facilities of nearby Arundel House, where you go to check in. **Pros:** cheerful staff; free parking. **Cons:** tiny bathrooms; plain rooms; off-site check-in. ⊠*74 Chesterton Rd.* ☎*01223/350059* ⊕*www.arundelhousehotels.co.uk/ashleyhotel.html* 🖅*16 rooms* △*In-room: no a/c. In-hotel: parking (free), no-smoking rooms* 🖃*AE, DC, MC, V* ⦿*BP.*

£ 🖭**Cityroomz.** A good budget option, this low-key hostelry outside the train station has small bedrooms with wood floors, white walls, and futon beds. Most double rooms have bunk beds. The sparsely furnished spaces are for those who want a cheap, clean place to sleep. **Pros:** tidy and clean; handy for train station. **Cons:** minuscule rooms; can be noisy; reserved parking very limited. ⊠*Station Rd.* ☎*01223/304050* ⊕*www.cityroomz.com* 🖅*25 rooms* △*In-room: no a/c, no phone. In-hotel: parking (free), no-smoking rooms* 🖃*MC, V* ⦿*CP.*

££–£££ 🖭**De Vere University Arms Hotel.** The 19th-century De Vere is well placed in the city center, with comfortable, traditionally furnished guest rooms. Many rooms have views of Parker's Piece, the green backing the hotel, although you pay slightly more for these; Parker's Bar also overlooks the green. The lounge serves afternoon tea by the fireplace. You can use a nearby swimming pool and a health club 2 mi away. **Pros:** good location; tasty food; some rooms have Playstations. **Cons:** small rooms; faded décor; unhelpful service. ⊠*Regent St.* ☎*01223/351241* ⊕*www.devere-hotels.com* 🖅*117 rooms, 2 suites* △*In-room: safe, Internet. In-hotel: restaurant, room service, bars, Wi-Fi, parking (paid), some pets allowed* 🖃*AE, DC, MC, V.*

12

££££   🏨 **Doubletree by Hilton.** Many of the rooms have views of the water at this modern establishment that makes the most of its peaceful riverside location. The gardens, conservatories, and bar also overlook the Cam. The hotel is set among the colleges on 3 acres of private grounds. Although the architecture exhibits a brutal use of concrete, the rooms are more stylish. Ask about lower-price packages that include breakfast. **Pros:** very central position; good facilities; spacious rooms. **Cons:** poor service; disappointing breakfasts. ⊠ *Granta Pl. and Mill La.* ☎ *01223/259988* ⊕ *www.doubletreebyhilton.co.uk* 🛏 *118 rooms, 4 suites* ⚫ *In-room: no a/c (some), refrigerator, Wi-Fi. In-hotel: restaurant, room service, bar, pool, gym, parking (paid), no-smoking rooms* 🖃 *AE, DC, MC, V.*

££££   🏨 **Hotel Felix.** This contemporary hotel has spacious bedrooms with clean-lined, stylish modern furnishings in neutral colors. The main part of the building is a converted Victorian mansion; today it contains some bedrooms as well as the sophisticated Graffiti restaurant and bar, serving Mediterranean food. You can use a health club and spa in the center of the city. **Pros:** up-to-the-minute furnishings; quiet location; easy to reach from motorway. **Cons:** impersonal feel; spotty service; can be noisy; 3 mi walk from center. ⊠ *Whitehouse La., off Huntingdon Rd.* ☎ *01223/277977* ⊕ *www.hotelfelix.co.uk* 🛏 *52 rooms* ⚫ *In-room: safe, refrigerator, Wi-Fi. In-hotel: restaurant, room service, bar, laundry service, parking (free), some pets allowed, no-smoking rooms* 🖃 *AE, DC, MC, V* 🍴 *CP.*

££–£££   🏨 **Regent Hotel.** A rare smaller hotel in Cambridge's city center, this handsome smaller Georgian town house looks across Parker's Piece, a tree-lined park, through wooden sash windows. The cozy licensed bar has an open fire; bedrooms are a little more anonymous but are decorated in pale modern tones, and all have bathtubs. **Pros:** good view from top rooms; close to bars and restaurants. **Cons:** no parking; a tad scruffy; disappointing breakfasts. ⊠ *41 Regent St.* ☎ *01223/351470* ⊕ *www. regenthotel.co.uk* 🛏 *22 rooms* ⚫ *In-room: Wi-Fi. In-hotel: bar, no-smoking rooms* 🖃 *AE, DC, MC, V.*

NIGHTLIFE AND THE ARTS

NIGHTLIFE

The city's pubs provide the mainstay of Cambridge's nightlife and shouldn't be missed. The **Eagle** (⊠ *8 Benet St.* ☎ *01223/505020*), first among equals, is a 16th-century coaching inn with several bars and a cobbled courtyard that's lost none of its old-time character. It's extremely busy on weekends. **Fort St. George** (⊠ *Midsummer Common* ☎ *01223/354327*), which overlooks the university boathouses, gets the honors for riverside views. The **Free Press** (⊠ *Prospect Row* ☎ *01223/368337*) is a small, mobile phone–free pub, attracting a student rowing clientele.

THE ARTS

CONCERTS   Cambridge supports its own symphony orchestra, and regular musical events are held in many colleges, especially those with large chapels. During regular terms, **King's College Chapel** (☎ *01223/331155*) has evensong services Monday through Saturday at 5:30, Sunday at 3:30. The **Corn Exchange** (✉ *Wheeler St.* ☎ *01223/357851*), beautifully restored, presents concerts (classical and rock), stand-up comedy, musicals, opera, and ballet.

The **Cambridge Folk Festival** (☎ *01223/357851* ⊕ *www.cambridgefolk festival.co.uk*), spread over a weekend in late July or early August at Cherry Hinton Hall, attracts major international folk singers and groups. Camping is available on the park grounds—reservations are essential.

THEATER The **ADC Theatre** (✉ *Park St.* ☎ *01223/300085* ⊕ *www.adctheatre. com*) hosts mainly student and fringe theater productions, including the famous Cambridge Footlights revue, training ground for much comic talent since the 1970s. The **Arts Theatre** (✉ *6 St. Edward's Passage* ☎ *01223/503333* ⊕ *www.cambridgeartstheatre.com*), the city's main repertory theater, was built by economist John Maynard Keynes in 1936 and supports a full program of theater, concerts, and events. It also has a good ground-floor bar and two restaurants.

SPORTS AND THE OUTDOORS

BIKING

It's fun to explore by bike. **City Cycle Hire** (✉ *61 Newnham Rd.* ☎ *01223/ 365629*) charges from £5 for a half day, £8 per day, and £15 for a week. Advance reservations are essential in July and August.

PUNTING

You can rent punts at several places, notably at Silver Street Bridge–Mill Lane, at Magdalene Bridge, and from outside the Rat and Parrot pub on Thompson's Lane on Jesus Green. Hourly rental costs £16 to £18. Chauffeured punting on the River Cam is also possible at most rental places. Around £12 per head is the usual rate, and your chauffeur will likely be a Cambridge student. **Scudamore's Punting Co.** (✉ *Mill La. and Quayside* ☎ *01223/359750* ⊕ *www.scudamores.com*) rents chauffeured and self-drive punts. They also offer various tour packages, ranging from a punt-and-walk **Ghost Tour** for £16 to a more extravagant **Evening Champagne Punt Tour** for £200.

SHOPPING

Cambridge is a main shopping area for a wide region, and it has all the usual chain stores, many in the Grafton Centre and Lion's Yard shopping precincts. More interesting are the specialty shops found among the colleges in the center of Cambridge, especially in and around Rose Crescent and King's Parade. Bookshops, including antiquarian stores, are Cambridge's pride and joy.

All Saints Garden Art & Craft Market (✉ *Trinity St.* ⊕ *www.cambridge-art-craft.co.uk*) displays the wares of local artists outdoors on Saturday. It's also open Friday from June to August and Wednesday to Friday in December. **Ryder & Amies** (✉ *22 King's Parade* ☎ *01223/350371* ⊕ *www.ryderamies.co.uk*) carries official university wear and even straw boaters.

CLOSE UP

Punting on the Cam

To punt is to maneuver a flat-bottom, wooden, gondolalike boat—in this case, through the shallow River Cam along the verdant Backs behind the colleges of the University of Cambridge. One benefit of this popular activity is that you get a better view of the ivy-covered walls from the water than from the front. Mastery of the sport lies in your ability to control a 15-foot pole, used to propel the punt. Collect a bottle of wine, some food, and a few friends, and you may find yourself saying things such as, "It doesn't get any better than this." One piece of advice: if your pole gets stuck, let go. You can use the smaller paddle to go back and retrieve it.

The lazier-at-heart may prefer chauffeured punting, with food supplied. Students from Cambridge may do the work, and you get a fairly informative spiel on the colleges. For a romantic evening trip, there are illuminated punts.

One university punting society has recently placed a helpful "Bluffers Guide to Punting" on its Web site, featuring detailed instructions and tips on how to master the art. Go to ⊕ *www.joh.cam.ac.uk/college_life/ student_life/societies/punt* and click on "How to Punt."

BOOKS **Cambridge University Press bookshop** (✉ *1 Trinity St.* ☎ *01223/333333* ⊕ *www.cambridge.org/uk/bookshop*) stands on one of the oldest bookstore sites in Britain; books have been sold here since at least 1581. Three-story **Galloway & Porter** (✉ *30 Sidney St.* ☎ *01223/367876* ⊕ *www.gallowayandporter.co.uk*) has an extensive collection of new and secondhand books. **G. David** (✉ *16 St. Edward's Passage* ☎ *01223/ 354619*), near the Arts Theatre, sells antiquarian books. The **Haunted Bookshop** (✉ *9 St. Edward's Passage* ☎ *01223/312913* ⊕ *www.sarah-keybooks.co.uk*) carries a great selection of old, illustrated books and British classics. **Heffer's** (✉ *20 Trinity St.* ☎ *01223/568568*) stocks many rare and imported books.

ELY TO BURY ST. EDMUNDS

This central area of towns and villages within easy reach of Cambridge is testament to the amazing changeability of the English landscape. The town of Ely is set in an eerie, flat, and apparently endless fenland, or marsh. Only a few miles south and east into Suffolk, however, all this changes to pastoral landscapes of gently undulating hills, and clusters of villages including pretty Sudbury and Lavenham.

ELY

16 mi north of Cambridge.

Known for its magnificent cathedral, Ely is the "capital" of the fens, the center of what used to be a separate county called the Isle of Ely (literally "island of eels"). Until the land was drained in the 17th century,

Ely was surrounded by treacherous marshland, which inhabitants crossed wearing stilts. Today Wicken Fen, a nature reserve 9 mi southeast of town (off A1123), preserves the sole remaining example of fenland in an undrained state.

Enveloped by fields of wheat, sugar beets, and carrots, Ely is a small, dense town that fails to live up to the high expectations created by its big attraction, its cathedral. The shopping area and market square lie to the north and lead down to the riverside, and the medieval buildings of the cathedral grounds and the King's School (which trains cathedral choristers) spread out to the south and west. Ely's most famous resident was Oliver Cromwell, whose house is now a museum.

GETTING HERE AND AROUND
The 9 and X9 buses leave from the Drummer Street bus station in Cambridge, twice an hour. The journey to Ely takes about 45 minutes. Ely is quite small, so if you're driving it's best to find somewhere to park and walk to the center. To get there from Cambridge, simply take the A10 road going north out of the city. Trains from Cambridge to Ely leave three times an hour and take 15 minutes.

ESSENTIALS
Visitor Information Ely (✉ *Oliver Cromwell's House, 29 St. Mary's St.* ☎ *01353/662062* ⊕ *visitely.eastcambs.gov.uk*).

EXPLORING
★ Known affectionately as the Ship of the Fens, **Ely Cathedral** can be seen for miles, towering above the flat landscape on one of the few ridges in the fens. In 1083 the Normans began work on the cathedral, which stands on the site of a Benedictine monastery founded by the Anglo-Saxon princess Etheldreda in 673. In the center of the cathedral you see a marvel of medieval construction—the unique octagonal **Lantern Tower,** a sort of stained-glass skylight of colossal proportions, built to replace the central tower after it collapsed in 1322. Tours of the tower are daily between April and October and on weekends between November and March. The cathedral is also notable for its 248-foot-long **nave,** with its simple Norman arches and Victorian painted ceiling. Much of the decorative carving of the 14th-century **Lady Chapel** was defaced during the Reformation (mostly by knocking off the heads of the statuary), but enough traces remain to show its original beauty. The fan-vaulted, carved ceiling remains intact, as it was too high for the iconoclasts to reach. Guided tours begin daily at 10:45, 1, and 2, with an additional tour at 3 between April and October. The cathedral houses a superior **Stained Glass Museum** (☎ *01353/660347* ⊕ *www.stainedglassmuseum. com* 🔳 *£3.50* 🕙 *Easter–Oct., weekdays 10:30–5, Sat. 10:30–5:30, Sun. noon–6; Nov.–Easter, weekdays and Sat. 10:30–5, Sun. noon–4:30*), up a flight of 42 steps. Exhibits trace the history of stained glass from medieval to modern times. ✉ *The Gallery* ☎ *01353/667735* ⊕ *www.*

cathedral.ely.anglican.org ⊠*£5.50, free on Sun. Tower tours £3.50, £5 on Sun.* ⊙*May–Oct., daily 7–7; Nov.–Apr., Mon.–Sat. 7:30–6, Sun. 7:30–5.*

Oliver Cromwell's House, the half-timber medieval building that was the home of Cromwell and his family, stands in the shadows of Ely Cathedral. During the 10 years he lived here, from 1636, Cromwell was leading the rebellious Roundheads in their eventually victorious struggle against King Charles I in the English Civil War. The house contains an exhibit about its former occupant. It's also the site of Ely's tourist information center. ⊠*29 St. Mary's St.* ☎*01353/662062* ⊠*£4.30* ⊙*Apr.–Oct., daily 10–5; Nov.–Mar., weekdays 11–4, Sat. 10–5, Sun. 11–4.*

> **DRAINING EAST ANGLIA**
>
> Large areas of East Anglia were originally barely inhabited, swampy marshes. Drainage of the wetlands by the creation of waterways was carried out most energetically in the 17th and 18th centuries. The process was far from smooth. Locals, whose fishing rights were threatened, sometimes destroyed the work. Also, as the marshland dried out, it shrank and sank, requiring pumps to stop renewed flooding. Hundreds of windmills were used to pump water away; some of them can still be seen today.

12

WHERE TO EAT AND STAY

£££
BRITISH
★

✕**Old Fire Engine House.** Scrubbed pine tables fill the main dining room of this restaurant in a converted fire station near the cathedral. Another room, used only for overflow, has an open fireplace and a polished wood floor, and also serves as an art gallery. Among the English dishes are traditional fenland recipes such as pike baked in white wine, as well as eel pie and game in season. ⊠*25 St. Mary's St.* ☎*01353/662582* ▭*MC, V* ⊙*Closed 2 wks at Christmas. No dinner Sun.*

££

Cathedral House. Run by Jenny and Robin Farndale, this Georgian house makes a pleasant overnight stop in Ely. The cozy bedrooms have antique furniture and coffeemakers, and an oriel window and handsome staircase are original features. In the back is a walled garden filled with flowers. **Pros:** heaps of character; steps from the cathedral; free parking. **Cons:** small bathrooms; on a busy road. ⊠*17 St. Mary's St.* ☎*01353/662124* ⊕*www.cathedralhouse.co.uk* ⊷*3 rooms, 1 cottage* &*In-room: no a/c. In-hotel: no-smoking rooms* ▭*No credit cards* ⏏*BP.*

SUDBURY

32 mi southeast of Ely, 16 mi south of Bury St. Edmunds, 14 mi northwest of Colchester.

An early silk-weaving industry (still in existence, on a smaller scale) as well as the wool trade brought prosperity to Sudbury, which has three fine Perpendicular Gothic churches and some half-timber houses. Today this town of 20,000 is the largest in this part of the Stour Valley. The Stour River was once navigable to the sea, and quays filled the town. In Charles Dickens's first novel, *The Pickwick Papers,* Sudbury

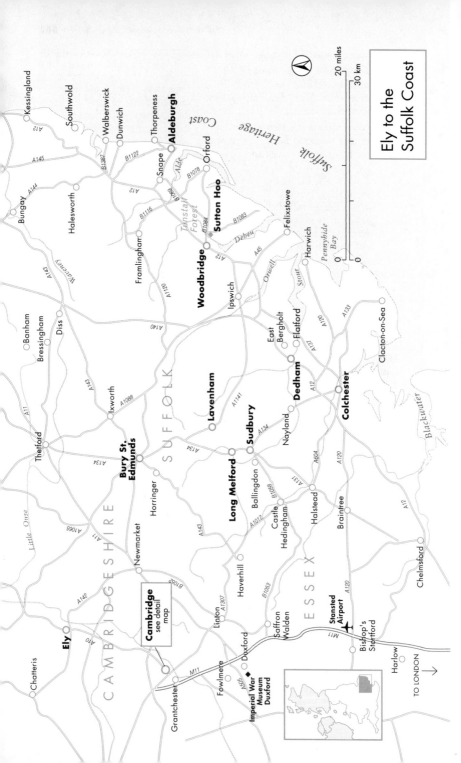

Ely to the
Suffolk Coast

20 miles
30 km

was the model for the fictional Eatanswill, where Mr. Pickwick stands for Parliament.

ESSENTIALS

Visitor Information Sudbury (⊠ *Town Hall, Market Hill* ☎ *01787/881320* ⊕ *www.babergh-south-suffolk.gov.uk*).

EXPLORING

Thomas Gainsborough, one of the greatest English portrait and landscape painters, was born here in 1727; a **statue of Gainsborough** holding his palette stands on Market Hill.

The birthplace and family home of Thomas Gainsborough (1727–88), **Gainsborough's House,** contains many paintings and drawings by the artist and his contemporaries. Although it presents a Georgian facade, with touches of the 18th-century neo-Gothic style, the building is essentially Tudor. The walled garden has a mulberry tree planted in 1620 and a printmaking workshop. The entrance is through the café and shop on Weavers Lane. ⊠ *46 Gainsborough St.* ☎ *01787/372958* ⊕ *www.gainsborough.org* 🎫 *£4.50, free Tues. 1–5* ⊙ *Mon.–Sat. 10–5.*

LONG MELFORD

2 mi north of Sudbury, 14 mi south of Bury St. Edmunds.

It's easy to see how this village got its name, especially if you walk the full length of its 2-mi-long main street, which gradually broadens to include green squares and trees and finally opens into the large triangular green on the hill. Long Melford grew rich on its wool trade in the 15th century, and the town's buildings are an appealing mix, mostly Tudor half-timber or Georgian. Many house antiques shops. Away from the main road, Long Melford returns to its resolutely latemedieval roots.

EXPLORING

The largely 15th-century **Holy Trinity Church,** founded by the rich clothiers of Long Melford, stands on a hill at the north end of the village. Close up, the delicate flint flush-work (shaped flints set into a pattern) and huge Perpendicular Gothic windows that take up most of the church's walls have great impact, especially because the nave is 150 feet long. The Clopton Chapel, with an ornate ceiling, predates the rest of the church by 150 years. The beautiful Lady Chapel has an unusual cloister; the stone on the wall in the corner is an ancient multiplication table, used when the chapel served as a school in the 17th and 18th centuries. ⊠ *Main St.* ☎ *01787/310845* ⊕ *www.stedmundsbury.anglican.org/longmelford* ⊙ *Mar.–Oct., daily 10–4; Nov.–Feb., daily 10–3.*

Melford Hall, distinguished from the outside by its turrets and topiaries, is an Elizabethan house with its original banqueting hall, a fair number of 18th-century additions, and pleasant gardens. Much of the porcelain and other fine pieces here come from the *Santissima Trinidad,* a ship loaded with gifts from the emperor of China and bound for Spain that was captured by one of the house's owners in the 18th century. Children's writer Beatrix Potter, who was related to the owners, visited the house often; there's a small collection of Potter memorabilia. ⊠ *Off*

A134 ☎*01787/376395* ⊕*www.nationaltrust.co.uk* 🎫*£6* ⊗*Apr. and Oct., weekends 1:30–5; May–Sept., Wed.–Sun. 1:30–5.*

↻   A wide moat surrounds **Kentwell Hall**, a redbrick Tudor manor house with tall chimneys and domed turrets. Built between 1520 and 1550, it was heavily restored inside after a fire in the early 19th century. On some weekends from mid-April through September, costumed "servants" and "farmworkers" perform reenactments of Tudor life or life during World War II. There's also an organic farm with rare-breed farm animals. The house is a half mile north of Long Melford Green. Call ahead, as hours sometimes vary—charming though it is, this place has a frustrating habit of not sticking to its advertised opening times. ⊠*Off A134* ☎*01787/310207* ⊕*www.kentwell.co.uk* 🎫*£9.15, £6.40 farm and garden only* ⊗*Late Mar.–mid-Apr., daily 11–5; late Apr.–mid-May, Sun.–Wed. 11–5; early June, Mon.–Wed. 11–5; mid-July–early Sept., daily 11–5; early Sept.–late Sept., Sun.–Wed. 11–5; various dates in Oct. 11–5.*

WHERE TO STAY

£££   🏠**The Bull.** This half-timber Elizabethan building reveals its long history with stone-flagged floors, bowed and twisted oak beams, and heavy antique furniture. Creature comforts offset the smallish size of the bedrooms here, which retain their original character—some are crooked, with sloping floors. The food is very good here too. **Pros:** historic atmosphere; comfortable bedrooms; friendly staff; good restaurant. **Cons:** very popular wedding venue in summer. ⊠*Hall St.* ☎*01787/378494* ⊕*www.thebull-hotel.com* ⤶*25 rooms* ⟁*In-room: DVD. In-hotel: Restaurant, bar* ☰*AE, DC, MC, V* ⎁*MAP.*

LAVENHAM

Fodor'sChoice   *4 mi northeast of Long Melford, 10 mi southeast of Bury St.*
★   *Edmunds.*

Virtually unchanged since the height of its wealth in the 15th and 16th centuries, Lavenham is one of the most perfectly preserved examples of a Tudor village in England. The weavers' and wool merchants' houses occupy not just one show street but most of the town. The houses are timber-frame in black oak, the main posts looking as if they could last another 400 years, though their walls are often no longer entirely perpendicular to the ground. The town has many examples of Suffolk pink buildings, in hues from pale pink to apricot, and many of these house small galleries selling paintings and crafts.

ESSENTIALS

Visitor Information Lavenham (⊠*Lady St.* ☎*01787/248207* ⊕*www. babergh-south-suffolk.gov.uk*).

EXPLORING

The timber-frame **Guildhall of Corpus Christi** (1529) dominates Market Place, a square with barely a foot in the present. Upstairs is a rather dull exhibition on the Wool Trade, although looking around the building itself is worth the admission charge. ⊠*Market Pl.* ☎*01787/ 247646* ⊕*www.nationaltrust.org.uk* 🎫*£4.20* ⊗*Early Mar.–late Mar.,*

Wed.–Sun. 11–4; Apr.–early Nov., daily 11–5; early Nov.–late Nov., weekends 11–4.

Little Hall, a timber-frame former wool merchant's house, shows the building's progress from its creation in the 14th century to its subsequent "modernization" through the 17th century and has a beautiful garden. ⊠*Market Pl.* ☎*01787/247019* ⊕*www.littlehall.org.uk* ⊡*£2.50* ◷*Easter–Oct., Wed., Thurs., and weekends 2–5:30.*

12

QUICK
BITES
In a haphazardly leaning old house, the **Tickled Pink Tea Room** (⊠17 High St. ☎01787/248438) has fresh cakes and coffee as well as soup and sandwiches.

The grand 15th-century Perpendicular **Church of St. Peter and St. Paul** (⊠*Church St.* ☎*01787/247244*), set apart from the village on a hill, was built with wool money by cloth merchant Thomas Spring between 1480 and 1520. The height of its tower (141 feet) was meant to surpass those of the neighboring churches—and perhaps to impress rival towns. The rest of the church is perfectly proportioned, with intricate wood carving.

WHERE TO EAT

££££
CONTINENTAL
★

✕**Great House.** The town's finest "restaurant with rooms" occupies a 15th-century building on the medieval market square. Run by Régis and Martine Crépy, the dining room serves European fare with a French touch. The five spacious bedrooms have sloping floors, beamed ceilings, well-appointed bathrooms, and antique furnishings. ⊠*Market Pl.* ☎*01787/247431* ▭*MC, V* ◷*Closed Mon. and Jan. No dinner Sun. No lunch Tues.*

£££
INDIAN
Fodor'sChoice
★

✕**Memsaab.** In a town ready to burst with cream teas and fussy hotel food, it comes as something of a surprise to find an Indian restaurant at all here, let alone such an exceptional one as Memsaab. Among the classics one would expect from a British curry house—from mild kormas to spicy madrases and jalfrezies (traditional curries made with chili and tomato)—are some finely executed specialties, including Nizami chicken, a fiery dish prepared with yogurt and fresh ginger, and duck bhujon, a fusion dish made with orange and Madeira sauce. The menu also contains regional specialties from Goa and Hyderabad. ⊠*2 Church St.* ☎*01787/249431* ▭*MC, V.*

WHERE TO STAY

£

Guinea House. Still a private home 600 years after it was built, Guinea House is a good budget option for travelers seeking something a little more authentic than your average B&B. This certainly isn't a hotel, but rooms have exceptionally comfortable beds and modern bathrooms. Bill and Gillian Delucy are warm hosts with an encyclopedic knowledge of the area, and are happy to help with planning day trips and booking restaurants for evening meals. Gillian's breakfasts are hearty and filling, although you have to be precise about when you want them. **Pros:** quiet central location; intimate feel. **Cons:** guests are confined to bedrooms; some doorways are extremely small. ⊠*16 Bolton St.* ☎*01787/249046* ⊕*www.guineahouse.co.uk* ⇥*2 rooms* ⌂*In-room: no a/c, no phone* ▭*Credit cards accepted only if arranged in advance* ◷*BP.*

£££   ⊡ **Lavenham Priory.** You can immerse yourself in Lavenham's Tudor his-
★   tory at this luxurious B&B in a sprawling house that dates in part to
the 13th century. The great hall, sitting room, and 3 acres of gardens
are great places to relax, and a walled herb garden is the scene for
evening drinks in warm weather. Prints and wood furnishings fill the
bedrooms; each has oak floors and timber ceilings, and some have four-
posters. **Pros:** historic ambience; charming rooms; lovely garden. **Cons:**
sloping floors are difficult for those with mobility problems; no locks
on room doors; service can be surly. ⊠ *Water St.* ☎*01787/247404*
⊕*www.lavenhampriory.co.uk* ⟿*5 rooms, 1 suite* &*In-room: no a/c,
no phone, Wi-Fi (some). In-hotel: bar, Wi-Fi, no kids under 10, no-
smoking rooms* ⊟*MC, V* ❏|*BP.*

££££–£££££   ⊡ **Swan Hotel.** This half-timber 14th-century lodging has aging beams,
rambling public rooms, and roaring fireplaces. Along corridors so low
that cushions are strategically placed on beams, most of the individually styled bedrooms have rich oak cabinets and original wood paneling. Bathrooms have been fashioned around ancient timbers and
hidden rooms. The bar, which is a popular local meeting place, is full
of memorabilia from the days when this was the favorite pub among
the American airmen who were stationed in Lavenham during World
War II. One wall is entirely covered with autographs and messages
from the vets who loved this place. **Pros:** lovely building; atmospheric
rooms. **Cons:** indifferent service; creaky floors; steps to climb. ⊠*High
St.* ☎*01787/247477* ⊕*www.theswanatlavenham.co.uk* ⟿*47 rooms,
2 suites* &*In-room: no a/c, refrigerator, DVD, Internet. In-hotel: restaurant, bar, Wi-Fi, some pets allowed* ⊟*AE, MC, V.*

BURY ST. EDMUNDS

★   *10 mi north of Lavenham, 28 mi east of Cambridge.*

Bury St. Edmunds owes its name, and indeed its existence, to Edmund,
the last king of East Anglia and medieval patron saint of England, who
was hacked to death by marauding Danes in 869. He was subsequently
canonized, and his shrine attracted pilgrims, settlement, and commerce.
In the 11th century the erection of a great Norman abbey (now only
ruins) confirmed the town's importance as a religious center. The tourist
office has a leaflet about the ruins and can arrange a guided tour. Robert
Adam designed the town hall in 1774. The Georgian streetscape helps
make the town one of the area's prettiest, and the nearby Greene King
Westgate Brewery adds the smell of sweet hops to the air.

GETTING HERE AND AROUND

The 11 bus leaves from Cambridge's Drummer Street bus station, and
takes about an hour to reach Bury St. Edmunds. By car, the town is a
short drive from either Lavenham or Cambridge. Trains from Cambridge
to Bury St. Edmunds leave once or twice an hour and take 40 minutes.

ESSENTIALS

Visitor Information Bury St. Edmunds (⊠*6 Angel Hill* ☎*01284/764667*
⊕ *www.stedmundsbury.gov.uk*).

EXPLORING

A walk along **Angel Hill** is a journey through the history of Bury St. Edmunds. Along one side, the Abbey Gate, cathedral, Norman Gate Tower, and St. Mary's church make up a continuous display of medieval architecture.

Elegant Georgian houses line Angel Hill on the side opposite St. Mary's Church; these include the **Athenaeum**, an 18th-century social and cultural meeting place, which has a fine Adam-style ballroom.

Originally three churches stood within the walls of the Abbey of St. Edmunds, but only two have survived, including **St. Mary's,** built in the 15th century. It has a blue-and-gold embossed "wagon" (barrel-shape) roof over the choir. Mary Tudor, Henry VIII's sister and queen of France, is buried here. ⊠ *Angel Hill at Honey Hill* ☎ *01284/706668* ⊕ *www.stmarystpeter.net* ☉ *Daily 10–4; call to confirm.*

St. Edmundsbury Cathedral dates from the 15th century, but the brilliant paint on its ceiling and the gleaming stained-glass windows are the result of 19th-century restoration by the architect Sir Gilbert Scott. Don't miss the memorial (near the altar) to an event in 1214, when the barons of England took an oath here to force King John to grant the Magna Carta. The cathedral's original Abbey Gate was destroyed in a riot, and it was rebuilt in the 14th century with defense in mind—you can see the arrow slits. Guided tours are available every day except Sunday during the summer months. There's no need to prebook. ■ TIP→ **After your visit, stop by the modest café filled with locals.** ⊠ *Angel Hill* ☎ *01284/754933* ⊕ *www. stedscathedral.co.uk* ✉ *Free, suggested donation £3* ☉ *Daily 8:30–6.*

The **Abbey Ruins and Botanical Gardens** are all that remain of the Abbey of Bury St. Edmunds, which fell during Henry VIII's dissolution of the monasteries. The Benedictine abbey's enormous scale is evident in the surviving Norman Gate Tower on Angel Hill; besides this, only the fortified Abbot's Bridge over the River Lark and a few ruins remain. There are explanatory plaques amid the ruins, which are now the site of the Abbey Botanical Gardens, with roses, elegant hedges, and rare trees, including a Chinese tree of heaven planted in the 1830s. There's also an aviary, a putting green, and a children's play area on-site. ⊠ *Angel Hill* ✉ *Free* ☉ *Mon.–Sat. 7:30 AM–dusk, Sun. 9 AM–dusk.*

The 12th-century **Moyse's Hall,** probably the oldest building in East Anglia, is a rare surviving example of a Norman house. The rooms hold local history and archaeological collections. One macabre display relates to the Red Barn murder, a local case that gained notoriety in a 19th-century play. ⊠ *Cornhill* ☎ *01284/706183* ⊕ *www.stedmundsbury.gov. uk* ✉ *£3* ☉ *Daily 10–5; last entry 4.*

WHERE TO EAT

£ ✕ **Harriet's Café Tearooms.** In an elegant dining room, Harriet's brings
CAFÉ back the tearooms of yesteryear. Munch on a savory sandwich or have a full cream tea while listening to hits from the 1940s. ⊠ *57 Cornhill* ☎ *01284/756256* ▤ *MC, V* ☉ *No dinner.*

£££ ✕ **Maison Bleue.** This stylish French restaurant, with the same owners
FRENCH as the Great House in nearby Lavenham, specializes in locally caught seafood and serves some tasty meat dishes, too. The seafood depends on

the day's catch, but grilled sole and roast cod are always available, as are cheeses imported from Paris. ⊠*31 Churchgate St.* ☎*01284/760623* ⊕*www.maisonbleue.co.uk* ⚓*Reservations essential* ⊟*AE, MC, V* ⊘*Closed Sun., Mon., Jan., and 2 wks in summer.*

WHERE TO STAY

££££–£££££ ★ ♻ **Ickworth Hotel.** You can live like nobility in the east wing of the Italianate Ickworth House, a National Trust property with 1,800 acres of grounds just outside Horringer, 5 mi southwest of Bury St. Edmunds. (If it's too pricey, you can just visit the grounds and see the fine art in the west wing for £7.90.) The splendid public rooms have stylish 1950s and '60s furniture and striking modern art. This look extends to most bedrooms, though some still have luxe period furnishings. The rows of tiny wellies in the porch attest to the hotel's emphasis on being family-friendly. Children are catered to with a free day-care room (for kids under 6) and a game center. Adults can dine in the more formal Frederick's restaurant and the casual Conservatory Restaurant. **Pros:** gorgeous grounds; relaxed atmosphere; family-friendly vibe. **Cons:** inconsistent service; some rooms are small; family-friendly vibe gets tiresome if you don't like kids. ⊠*Off A143, Horringer* ☎*01284/735350* ⊕*www.ickworthhotel.co.uk* ⊨*24 rooms, 11 apartments* ⚹*In-room: no a/c, kitchen (some), DVD, Wi-Fi. In-hotel: 2 restaurants, room service, bar, tennis court, pool, spa, bicycles, laundry service, some pets allowed, no-smoking rooms* ⊟*AE, DC, MC, V* ⦿*BP.*

£££ ★ **Ounce House.** Small and friendly, this Victorian B&B has a great deal of charm. Print fabrics and wooden furniture adorn the generous and stylish guest rooms. You can unwind in the antiques-filled drawing room and library, and have a drink from the honor bar. The house is a three-minute walk from the abbey ruins. **Pros:** spotlessly clean; spacious and comfortable rooms; generous breakfasts. **Cons:** fussy decor; often booked up far in advance. ⊠*Northgate St.* ☎*01284/761779* ⊕*www.ouncehouse.co.uk* ⊨*4 rooms* ⚹*In-room: no a/c, Internet. In-hotel: bar, no-smoking rooms* ⊟*AE, MC, V* ⦿*BP.*

NIGHTLIFE AND THE ARTS

The **Theatre Royal,** which presents touring shows, was built in 1819 and is a perfect example of Regency theater design. Guided tours (spring and summer only) can be booked at the box office. ⊠*Westgate St.* ☎*01284/769505.* ⊕*www.theatreroyal.org.*

COLCHESTER AND THE SUFFOLK COAST

Colchester is the oldest town on record in England, dating back to the Iron Age, and the reminders of its long history are well worth visiting. The town also serves as a traditional base for exploring Constable Country, that quintessentially English rural landscape on the borders of Suffolk and Essex made famous by the early-19th-century painter John Constable. This area runs north and west of Colchester along the valley of the River Stour. The 40-mi Suffolk Heritage Coast, which wanders northward from Felixstowe up to Kessingland, is one of the most unspoiled shorelines in the country. The lower part of the coast is the most impressive; try to avoid the area between Lowestoft and Great Yarmouth, a region of run-down beach resorts.

12

COLCHESTER

59 mi northeast of London, 47 mi southeast of Cambridge, 68 mi south of Norwich.

Evidence of Colchester's four centuries of Roman history is visible everywhere in this ancient town. The Roman walls still stand, together with a Norman castle, a Victorian town hall, and Dutch-style houses built by refugee weavers from the Low Countries in the late 16th century. Archaeological research indicates a settlement at the head of the Colne estuary at least as early as 1100 BC. Two thousand years ago it was the domain of Cunobelin (Shakespeare's Cymbeline), who was king of the Catuvellauni. On Cunobelin's death, the Romans invaded in AD 43. The emperor Claudius made it the first Roman colony in Britain, renaming the town *Colonia Victricensis,* the Colony of Victory. The settlement was burned during the failed revolt in AD 60 by Boudicca, queen of the Iceni. The English Civil War saw further conflict in Colchester, as the city endured a three-month siege in 1648 before the Royalist forces surrendered. Colchester has always had a strategic importance and still has a military base; a tattoo (military spectacle) is held in even-numbered years.

GETTING HERE AND AROUND

Drivers should take the A12 from London or the A134 from Bury St. Edmunds. Of Colchester's two train stations, Colchester North, half a mile north of the center, is for trains from London. The bus station is more central. Most of the sights can be visited on foot.

The tourism office offers walking tours around Colchester; tickets are £3. From April through September, City Sightseeing operates hour-long hop-on, hop-off bus tours of the town for £7.50. They depart from the castle.

ESSENTIALS

Visitor and Tour Information City Sightseeing (☎01206/252472 ⊕www. city-sightseeing.com).**Colchester** (✉1 Queen St. ☎01206/282920 ⊕www. visitcolchester.com).

EXPLORING

Colchester was important enough for the Romans to build massive fortifications around it, and the **Roman Walls,** dating largely from the reign of Emperor Vespasian (AD 69–79), can still be seen, especially along Balkerne Hill (to the west of the town center), with its splendid Balkerne Gate.

Near the castle, the remains of a 3,000-seat **Roman amphitheater** (✉*Maidenburgh St.*) are visible. The curve of the foundations is outlined in the paving stones of the roadway, and parts of the walls and floor have been preserved in a building, where they can be viewed alongside an image of how the amphitheater would have looked.

The castle built by William the Conqueror between 1076 and 1125, reusing brick and tiles from the ruins of the Roman town, is today the superb **Colchester Castle Museum.** All that remains is the keep, the largest the Normans built. The castle was constructed over the foundations of the huge Roman Temple of Claudius, and in the vaults you can descend through 1,000 years of history. Among the items on show in the museum are the beautifully carved tombstones of Facilis and Longinus, two Roman soldiers. ⊠*Castle Park* ☎*01206/282939* ⊕*www.colchestermuseums.org.uk* ⊠*£5.50, guided tours £2* ⊗*Mon.–Sat. 10–5, Sun. 11–5.*

> ### QUEEN OF THE ICENI
>
> After King Prasutagus died around AD 60, his wife, Boudicca, became queen of the Iceni kingdom, which covered roughly the same area as modern-day Norfolk. Alas, the occupying Romans annexed Iceni. They flogged Boudicca and raped her daughters; in revenge the queen led an uprising, destroying first Roman Colchester, then London and St. Albans. By the time Boudicca met with the army of the Roman governor, Suetonius, her army outnumbered the occupiers. The queen, however, was defeated. With her flowing red hair and her chariot, the warrior queen has become something of a national symbol of Britain.

The excellent interactive **Hollytrees Museum,** in a Georgian mansion near the castle, tells the story of the daily lives of local people through objects. There are chances to create a silhouette portrait or play with Victorian toys, and there are occasional children's events, such as puppet making. ⊠*Castle Park, High St.* ☎*01206/282940* ⊕*www.colchestermuseums. org.uk* ⊠*Free* ⊗*Mon.–Sat. 10–5, Sun. 11–5.*

The narrow medieval streets behind the Town Hall, off High Street, are called the **Dutch Quarter,** because refugee weavers from the Low Countries settled here in the 16th century, when Colchester was the center of a thriving cloth trade.

WHERE TO EAT

££
BRITISH ✕ **The Lemon Tree.** Jazz evenings in the cellar enhance the atmosphere at this popular restaurant. Well-presented dishes such as seared king scallops or rack of lamb with a garlic-and-herb crust are served in a building that incorporates part of the original Roman city wall. Set-price lunches and dinners are good value. ⊠*48 St. Johns St.* ☎*01206/767337* ▤*AE, MC, V* ⊗*Closed Sun.*

DEDHAM

Fodor'sChoice
★ *8 mi northeast of Colchester, off A12 on B1029.*

Dedham is the heart of Constable Country. Here gentle hills and the cornfields of Dedham Vale, set under the district's delicate, pale skies, inspired John Constable (1776–1837) to paint some of his most celebrated canvases. He went to school in Dedham, a picture-book village that did well from the wool trade in the 15th and 16th centuries and has retained a well-off air ever since. The 15th-century church looms large over handsomely sturdy, pastel-color houses.

EXPLORING

Two miles northeast of Dedham, off A12, the Constable trail continues in **East Bergholt**, where Constable was born in 1776. Most of the village is modern and rather unattractive, but if you arrive from Flatford Mill, you'll see the older part—including **St. Mary-the-Virgin** (⊠ *Flatford Rd.* ☉ *Daily; hrs vary but usually 10–5, except during services* ☎ *Free*), one of the most remarkable churches in the region. It was painted by Constable, but that's least among the reasons that make it worth a visit. The church was started just before the Reformation; the doors underneath the ruined archways outside (remnants of a much older church) contain a coded message left by Catholic sympathizers of the time. The striking interior is full of little treasures, including an ancient wall painting of the Virgin Mary in one of the rear chapels, a 14th-century chest, and an extraordinary series of florid memorial stones on the nave wall opposite the main entrance.

From Dedham, on the banks of the River Stour, you can rent a rowboat from the **Boathouse Restaurant** (⊠ *Mill La.* ☉ *Easter–Sept., daily 10–5, weather permitting* ☎ *£12 per hr* ☎ *01206/323153* ⊕ *www.dedhamboathouse.com/*). It's an idyllic way to travel the 2 mi downriver to **Flatford**, where you can see Flatford Mill, one of the two water mills owned by Constable's father, and the subject of his most famous painting, *The Hay Wain* (1821).

Near Flatford Mill is the 16th-century **Willy Lott's House**, which is instantly recognizable from Constable's painting *The Hay Wain*. Although the house itself is not open to the public, the road is a public thoroughfare, so you don't have to buy a ticket to see the famous—and completely unchanged—view for yourself. Just stand across from the two trees on the far bank, with the mill on your right, and look upstream. ▪**TIP→** **The display board on the outside wall of the mill contains a handy reproduction of** *The Hay Wain* **to help you compose your own photo.**

The National Trust owns Flatford Mill and the houses around it, including the thatched 16th-century **Bridge Cottage**, on the north bank of the Stour, which has a shop and an exhibition about Constable's life. You can also rent rowboats from here. ⊠ *Off B1070, East Bergholt* ☎ *01206/298260* ⊕ *www.nationaltrust.org.uk* ☎ *Free, guided tours £2.50* ☉ *Jan. and Feb., weekends 11–3:30; Mar. and Apr., Wed.–Sun. 11–5; May–Sept., daily 10:30–5:30; Oct., daily 11–4; Nov. and Dec., Wed.–Sun. 11–3:30. Guided tours Apr.–Oct. on most days, at 11:30, 1:30, and 3.*

WHERE TO EAT

££££
BRITISH
★

✕ **Le Talbooth.** A longtime favorite, this sophisticated restaurant in a Tudor house is idyllically set beside the River Stour. There are floodlighted terraces where food and drinks are served in summer and where jazz and steel bands play on summer Sunday nights. Inside, original beams, leaded-glass windows, and a brick fireplace add to the sense of age. The superb English fare at lunch and dinner may include loin of venison, local sea bass, or duck breast. ⊠*Gun Hill* ☎*01206/323150* ⌂*Reservations essential* ☐*AE, DC, MC, V* ⊘*No dinner Sun. Nov.–May.*

£ ✕**Marlborough Head.** This friendly, BIRITSH 300-year-old pub across from Constable's school in Dedham serves traditional bar food with a flourish. Dishes such as salmon in champagne share the menu with fish-and-chips and burgers. There are also rooms available (one with a four-poster bed) for £52–£100 per night, depending on the season. ⊠*Mill La.* ☎*01206/323250* ☐*MC, V.*

> ### CHANGING TASTES
>
> Constable's landscape paintings may be popular today, but *The Hay Wain*, now in London's National Gallery, did not sell after the Royal Academy displayed it. The artist sold only 20 paintings in England during his lifetime. He was elected to the Royal Academy with a majority of one vote at age 52.

WOODBRIDGE

18 mi northeast of Dedham.

One of the first good ports of call on the Suffolk Heritage Coast, Woodbridge, off A12, is a town whose upper reaches center on a fine old market square, site of the 16th-century Shire Hall. Woodbridge is at its best around its old quayside, where boatbuilding has been carried out since the 16th century. The most prominent building is a white-clapboard mill, which dates from the 18th century and is powered by the tides.

ESSENTIALS

Visitor Information Woodbridge (⊠ *The Station* ☎ *01394/382240* ⊕ *www. suffolkcoastal.gov.uk).*

EXPLORING

The visitor center at **Sutton Hoo** helps interpret one of Britain's most significant Anglo-Saxon archaeological sites. In 1938 a local archaeologist excavated a series of earth mounds and discovered a 7th-century burial ship, probably that of King Raedwald of East Anglia. Many artifacts uncovered are now in the British Museum in London. A replica of the 40-oar, 90-foot-long ship stands in the visitor center, which has artifacts and displays about Anglo-Saxon society. Trails around the 245-acre site explore the area along the River Deben. ⊠*Signposted on the B1083, 2 mi east of Woodbridge* ☎*01394/389700* ⊕*www.nationaltrust.org. uk* ⤳*£5.90* ⊘*Mid-Mar.–late Oct., Wed.–Sun. (some wks also Mon. and Tues.) 10:30–5; early Nov.–early Mar. weekends (some wks also weekdays) 11–4.*

WHERE TO STAY

£££–££££ ▦**Seckford Hall.** The sense of history at this delightfully old-school hotel FodorsChoice comes from more than just the magnificent Tudor architecture. Several
★ pieces of furniture are castoffs from Buckingham Palace (King Edward VII died on one of the chairs in the drawing room) and one of the beds was supposedly slept in by Elizabeth I. Bedrooms are large and comfortable, with recently renovated bathrooms (some have whirlpool baths). The landscaped grounds are perfect for a stroll to admire the roses or

the duck-filled lake. The main restaurant specializes in local lobster; for cheaper meals, grab a table in the Club House. Staff are happy to share some of the Hall's taller tales if asked (including its secret passage and fabulously Bacchanalian ghost). **Pros:** antique charm; lovely setting; great atmosphere. **Cons:** no elevator; creaky old beds; fussy service in restaurant. ⊠*Off the A12 outside Woodbridge* ☎*01394/385678* ⊕*www.seckford.co.uk* ⇖*32 rooms* ⌂*In-room: no a/c, Internet. In-hotel: 2 restaurants, room service, bar, pool, gym, spa, laundry service, some pets allowed* ⊟*AE, DC, MC, V* ⦾*BP.*

ALDEBURGH

15 mi northeast of Woodbridge, 41 mi northeast of Colchester.

Aldeburgh (pronounced orl-bruh) is a quiet seaside resort, except in June, when the town fills up with people attending the noted Aldeburgh Festival. Its beach is backed by a promenade lined with candy-color dwellings. Twentieth-century composer Benjamin Britten lived here for some time—he was born in the busy port of Lowestoft, 30 mi to the north. Britten grew interested in the story of Aldeburgh's native son, the poet George Crabbe (1754–1832), and turned his life story into the celebrated modern opera *Peter Grimes,* a piece that perfectly captures the atmosphere of the Suffolk coast.

ESSENTIALS

Visitor Information Aldeburgh (⊠ *High St.* ☎ *01728/453637* ⊕ *www. suffolkcoastal.gov.uk*).

EXPLORING

The Elizabethan **Moot Hall**, built of flint and timber, stood in the center of a thriving 16th-century town when first erected. Now it's just a few steps from the beach, a mute witness to the erosive powers of the North Sea. It's the home of the Aldeburgh Museum, a low-key collection that includes finds from an Anglo-Saxon ship burial. ⊠*Market Cross Pl., Sea Front* ☎*01728/454666* ⊕*www.aldeburghmuseum.org.uk* ✉*£1* ☉*Easter–Apr., weekends 2:30–5; May, Sept., and Oct., daily 2:30–5; June–Aug., daily noon–5.*

WHERE TO EAT AND STAY

£   ✕**The Fish and Chip Shop.** When frying time approaches, Aldeburgh's
BRITISH   most celebrated fish-and-chip shop always has a long line of eager customers, especially in summer. Popularity ensures a high turnover, so you know the fish is always freshly cooked. The batter melts in your mouth, and the chips are satisfyingly chunky. Upstairs you can bring your own wine or beer and sit at tables. But for the full experience, join a line for the paper-wrapped version. The deep-fried delicacies are equally good at the **Golden Galleon**, just along the road and run by the same team. ⊠*226 High St.* ☎*01728/452250* ⊟*No credit cards.*

££   ✕**The Lighthouse.** An excellent value, this low-key brasserie with tightly
MODERN BRITISH   packed wooden tables relies exclusively on local products. The menu
Fodor'sChoice   focuses on seafood, including oysters and Cromer crabs. All the con-
★   temporary British dishes are imaginatively prepared. Desserts, such as

the chocolate-and–Grand Marnier fudge cake, are particularly good. ⊠*77 High St.* ☎*01728/453377* ⊟*MC, V.*

£££–££££ 🏨 **Brudenell.** The best rooms at this bright, stylish, contemporary seaside hotel face the water. Its restaurant serves fresh, uncomplicated seafood dishes. The accommodating staff here make it easy for guests to relax. The White Lion hotel, dating to 1563, is the Brudenell's historic sister property. **Pros:** great setting; pleasant staff; spacious rooms. **Cons:** some beds are small; limited parking. ⊠*The Parade* ☎*01728/452071* ⊕*www.brudenellhotel.co.uk* ⟿*42 rooms* ♿*In-room: no a/c, Wi-Fi. In-hotel: restaurant, room service, bar, Wi-Fi, some pets allowed, no-smoking rooms* ⊟*AE, MC, V* ⟦◯⟧*BP.*

NIGHTLIFE AND THE ARTS

★ East Anglia's most important arts festival, and one of the best known in Great Britain, is the **Aldeburgh Festival** (☎*01728/687110* ⊕*www. aldeburgh.co.uk*). It's held for two weeks in June in the small village of Snape, 5 mi west of Aldeburgh. Founded by Benjamin Britten, the festival concentrates on music but includes related exhibitions, poetry readings, and even walks. A less hectic calendar of events continues through the year.

It's well worth a stop to take in the peaceful River Alde location of the **Snape Maltings** cultural center. It includes art galleries and crafts shops in distinctive large brick buildings once used to malt barley. You can pause at the tea shop or the Plough & Sail pub. Snape Maltings has special events year-round, such as the Britten Festival in October. Leisurely river cruises (£6) leave from the Quayside during high tide. ⊠*Snape* ✛*Near Saxmundham* ☎*01728/688303* ⊕*www.snapemaltings.co.uk* ☯*Daily 10–5.*

NORWICH TO NORTH NORFOLK

Norwich, unofficial capital of East Anglia, is dominated by the 15th-century spire of its impressive cathedral. Norfolk's continuing isolation from the rest of the country, and its unspoiled landscape and architecture—largely bypassed by the Industrial Revolution—have proved to be a draw. Many of the flint-knapped (decorated with broken flint) houses in North Norfolk's newly trendy villages are now weekend or holiday homes. Windmills, churches, and waterways are the area's chief defining characteristics. A few miles inland from the Norfolk coast, the Broads begin, a national park made up of a network of shallow, reed-bordered lakes, many linked by wide rivers. Boating and fishing are great lures; rent a boat for a day or a week and the waterside pubs, churches, villages, and nature reserves are all within easy reach.

NORWICH

63 mi northeast of Cambridge.

It used to be said that Norwich had a pub for each day of the year and a church in which to repent for every Sunday of the year. Although this is no longer true, real ales and steeples are still much in evidence in this pleasant city of about 130,000. Established by the Saxons because of its prime trading position on the rivers Yare and Wensum, the town has its heart in the triangle between the two waterways. The inner beltway follows the line of the old city wall, much of which is still visible. It's worth walking or driving around after dark to see the floodlit older buildings. By the time of the Norman Conquest, Norwich was one of the largest towns in England, although much was destroyed by the Normans to create a new town.

You can see the old flint buildings as you walk down the medieval streets and alleyways. Despite some industrial sites and many shopping centers, the town remains historic and engaging. The University of East Anglia brings a cosmopolitan touch, including a lively arts scene, to an otherwise remote urban area. It's a good base from which to explore the Norfolk Broads and the coast.

GETTING HERE AND AROUND

There are regular bus and train connections from London; the trip takes about three hours. The bus and train stations are a 10-minute walk from the center. If you're driving, leave your car in any of the numerous parking lots scattered around the center.

City Sightseeing operates 45-minute open-top bus tours of Norwich, leaving hourly from Theatre Street. Tours cost £8.

ESSENTIALS

Visitor and Tour Information City Sightseeing (⊠ *Theatre St., across from Theatre Royal* ☎ *01263/587005* ⊕ *www.city-sightseeing.com*). **Norwich** (⊠ *The Forum, Millennium Plain* ☎ *01603/213999* ⊕ *www.visitnorwich.co.uk*).

EXPLORING

TOP ATTRACTIONS

★ **Blickling Hall.** Behind the wrought-iron entrance gate to Blickling Hall, two mighty yew hedges form an imposing allée, creating a magnificent frame for this perfectly symmetrical Jacobean masterpiece. The redbrick mansion, 15 mi north of Norwich, has towers and chimneys, baroque Dutch gables, and, in the center, a three-story timber clock tower. The grounds include a formal flower garden and parkland with woods that conceal a temple, an orangery, and a pyramid. Blickling belonged to a succession of historic figures, including Sir John Fastolf, the model for Shakespeare's Falstaff; Anne Boleyn's family; and finally, Lord Lothian, ambassador to the United States at the outbreak of the Second World War, who left Blickling Hall to the people of Britain when he died. The Long Gallery (127 feet) has an intricate plasterwork ceiling with Jacobean emblems. Most of the interior is handsome but somewhat austere, although a sumptuous tapestry of Peter the Great at the Battle of Poltawa hangs in its own room. ⊠ *B1354, Blickling* ☎ *01263/738030* ⊕ *www. nationaltrust.org.uk* ✉ *£8.85; gardens only, £5.90* ⊙ *House late Feb.– mid-July, early Sept., and Oct., Wed.–Sun. 11–5; mid-July–early Sept., Wed.–Mon. 11–5. Gardens early–late Feb. 11–4; late Feb.–mid-July and early Sept.–late Oct., Wed.–Sun. 10:15–5:15; mid-July–early Sept., Wed.–Mon. 10:15–5:15; Nov.–Jan., Thurs.–Sun. 11–4.*

❺ Norwich Castle. The decorated stone facing of this castle, now a museum on the hill in the center of the city, makes it look like a children's-book illustration. The castle is Norman (1130), but a stone keep replaced the original wooden bailey (wall). The thick walls and other defenses attest to its military function. Interactive displays explore topics from ancient Egypt to life in Norman times. You can even try out a copy of Queen Boudicca's chariot to relive her attack on Roman Colchester. The art section includes a gallery devoted to the Norwich School of painters who, like John Constable, focused on the everyday landscape and seascape. Daily tours explore the castle's battlements or dungeons. ⊠ *Castle Meadow* ☎ *01603/495897* ⊕ *www.museums. norfolk.gov.uk* ✉ *Gallery, museum, and castle £5.70 (£1 last hr before closing); special exhibitions £2.90; tours of battlements or dungeons £2* ☉ *Weekdays 10–4:30, Sat. 10–5, Sun. 1–5. Closes 5:30 Mon.–Sat. when schools not in session.*

❸ ★ **Norwich Cathedral.** The grandest example of Norman architecture in Norwich has the second-largest monastic cloisters in Britain (only Salisbury's are bigger). Although its spire, at 315 feet tall (also second only to Salisbury's), is visible from everywhere in the city, you cannot see the building itself until you pass through St. Ethelbert's Gate. The cathedral was begun in 1096 by Herbert de Losinga, who had come from Normandy in 1091 to be its first bishop; his splendid tomb is by the high altar. Distinctly Norman elements are the plain west front and dramatic crossing tower, with its austere, geometrical decoration. The remarkable length of the nave is immediately impressive; the similarly striking height of the vaulted ceiling makes it a strain to study the delightful colored bosses, which illustrate Bible stories with great vigor and detail. (Binoculars are handy.) The grave of Norfolk-born nurse Edith Cavell, the British World War I heroine shot by the Germans in 1915, is at the east end of the cathedral. There's also a small medieval-style herb garden, plus a restaurant and coffee shop. ⊠ *62 The Close* ☎ *01603/218300* ⊕ *www.cathedral.org.uk* ✉ *Free* ☉ *Daily 7:30–6; call ahead to check, as times can vary. Herb garden Tues.–Thurs. 9:30–4:30.*

❻ **Sainsbury Centre for the Visual Arts.** A modern, hangarlike building designed by Norman Foster on the University of East Anglia campus holds the important private art collection of the Sainsbury family, owners of a supermarket chain. It includes a remarkable quantity of tribal art and 20th-century works, especially art nouveau, and has pieces by Pablo Picasso and Alberto Giacometti. Rotating exhibitions include big-name photography and art shows. Buses 22, 25, 26, and 27 run from downtown Norwich to the university. ⊠ *Earlham Rd.* ☎ *01603/593199* ⊕ *www.scva.org.uk* ✉ *Free; special exhibits vary* ☉ *Tues. and Thurs.– Sun. 10–5, Wed. 10–8.*

WORTH NOTING

❶ Elm Hill. Off Tombland, this neighborhood is a cobbled and pleasing mixture of Tudor and Georgian houses that hold gift shops and tearooms.

❹ Pulls Ferry. The Cathedral **Close** (grounds) is one of the most idyllic places in Norwich; past the mixture of medieval and Georgian houses, a path leads down to the ancient water gate, Pulls Ferry.

❷ Tombland. Narrow lanes and alleys that used to be the main streets of medieval Norwich lead away from the market and end at Tombland by the cathedral. Neither a graveyard nor a plague pit, Tombland was the site of the Anglo-Saxon trading place, now a busy thoroughfare.

WHERE TO EAT AND STAY

£ ✕ **Adam and Eve.** Said to be Norwich's oldest pub, this place dates back
BRITISH   to 1249. From noon until 7, the kitchen serves such hearty pub staples as beef-and-mushroom pie or cheese-and-ale soup from the short but solid bar menu. Theakston's and Adnams beer are available on tap, as is Aspall's cider. ✉*Bishopsgate* ☎*01603/667423* ▭*MC, V.*

£££ ✕ **Adlard's Restaurant.** This restaurant with pine floors and white walls
FRENCH   couldn't feel more relaxed. The kitchen serves beautifully presented dishes such as roasted salmon fillet with purple sprouting broccoli. Desserts such as lemon tart with mango sorbet compete against excellent

local cheeses. There's a small à la carte menu as well as a set-price meal for lunch. ⊠*79 Upper St. Giles St.* ☎*01603/633522* ▤*AE, DC, MC, V* ⊘*No dinner Sun. No lunch Mon.*

£   ✕**Britons Arms.** A converted pub, this cozy, thatched café and eatery
BRITISH   has famously good homemade cakes as well as some pies and tarts.
★   The 15th-century building has low ceilings, a garden in summer, and an open fire in winter. ⊠*9 Elm Hill* ☎*01603/623367* ▤*No credit cards* ⊘*Closed Sun.*

£££–££££   🏨**Dunston Hall Hotel & Country Club.** Gables and tall chimneys give this redbrick mansion built in 1859 an Elizabethan look, and extensive modern additions have transformed a country house into a luxurious retreat. The peaceful landscaped gardens and woodland are ideal for relaxing after a day's sightseeing. If you seek a sense of the past, ask for a four-poster bedroom or one of the small attic bedrooms with original low-beamed ceilings. The hotel is 4 mi south of the city center, on the A140. **Pros:** beautiful setting; friendly and efficient service; good for golfers. **Cons:** rooms can be noisy; food is mediocre and pricey. ⊠*Ipswich Rd.* ☎*01508/470444* ⊕*www.devere-hotels.com* ↪*157 rooms, 12 suites, 1 penthouse* ♿*In-room: no a/c (some), Internet. In-hotel: 2 restaurants, bars, room service, golf course, tennis courts, pool, gym, spa, laundry service, no-smoking rooms* ▤*AE, DC, MC, V* ⑩*BP.*

NIGHTLIFE AND THE ARTS

The **King of Hearts** (⊠*7–15 Fye Bridge St.* ☎*01603/766129* ⊕*www. kingofhearts.org.uk*), a restored 15th-century merchant's house, serves as a small arts center that presents chamber concerts, recitals, and poetry readings. It also has a good café. The **Maddermarket Theatre** (⊠*St. John's Alley* ☎*01603/620917* ⊕*www.maddermarket.co.uk*), patterned after Elizabethan theaters, has been the base of amateur and community theater in Norwich since 1911. **Norwich Arts Centre** (⊠*St. Benedict's St.* ☎*01603/660352* ⊕*www.norwichartscentre.co.uk*) puts on an eclectic program of live music, dance, and stand-up comedy. It too has a good café, with free Internet access.

Norwich Playhouse (⊠*Gun Wharf, St. George's St.* ☎*01603/598598* ⊕*www.norwichplayhouse.org.uk*), a professional repertory group, performs everything from Shakespeare to world premieres of new plays; it also runs a bookshop. Norwich's biggest and best-known theater, the **Theatre Royal** (⊠*Theatre St.* ☎*01603/630000* ⊕*www. theatreroyalnorwich.co.uk*) hosts touring companies staging musicals, ballet, opera, and plays.

SPORTS AND THE OUTDOORS

Traffic on the River Yare is now mostly for pleasure rather than commerce, and a summer trip with **City Boats** (⊠*Elm Hill, Pulls Ferry, Station, Whitlingham Park, and Griffin Lane quays; head office Highcraft Marina, Griffin Lane* ☎*01603/701701*) gives a fresh perspective on Norwich. Longer trips are available down the Rivers Wensum and Yare to the nearer Broads.

Introducing Fens and Broads

For many people, the joy of East Anglia is its separateness, its desolate landscapes and isolated beaches. Of these, the Broads (expanded rivers) of Norfolk are the most dramatic. The water in the marshes and dikes reflects the arching sky, whose cloudscapes are ever-changing, stretching toward seemingly infinite horizons. The sunsets are to be treasured.

The reed-bordered **Norfolk Broads** (⊕ *www.broads-authority.gov.uk*) make a gentle landscape of canals and lakes that are ideal for boating and are alive with birds and animals. Touring by car isn't really an option if you want to see something of the Broads, because much of this area of shallow lakes linked by wide rivers is inaccessible by road. However, there are boat tours through the 150 mi of waterways. There's also an extensive network of bicycle paths.

Explore the Broads by bicycle with **Broadland Cycle Hire** (⊠ *The Rhond, Hoverton* ☎ *07887/480331* ⊕ *www. norfolkbroadscycling.co.uk*), 8 mi northeast of Norwich. Rentals (£14 per day) are available from Easter through October and during school vacations. The company can recommend routes 7 to 20 mi from their base.

Broads Tours (☎ *01603/782207 Wroxham, 01692/670711 Potter Heigham* ⊕ *www.broads.co.uk*), based at the quaysides in Wroxham, 7 mi northeast of Norwich, and Potter Heigham, 15 mi northeast of Norwich, offers day cruises in the Broads as well as half-day and full-day launch rental (lessons included).

SHOPPING

The medieval lanes of Norwich, around Elm Hill and Tombland, contain the best antiques, book, and crafts stores. The **Mustard Shop** (⊠ *15 Royal Arcade* ☎ *01603/627889*) pays homage to Colman's Mustard, a company founded in Norwich in the early 19th century; it sells collectibles and more than 15 varieties of mustard. The **Tombland Antiques Centre** (⊠ *14 Tombland* ☎ *01603/619129*), opposite the cathedral, is an old house crammed full of shops. **Norwich Market** (⊠ *Market Pl., Gentleman's Walk* ☎ *01603/212414* ⊕ *www.norwich-market.co.uk*), the city's main outdoor market, is open daily; it sells everything from jewelry to clothes and food and has been the heart of the city for 900 years.

BLAKENEY

28 mi northwest of Norwich.

The Norfolk coast begins to feel wild and remote near Blakeney, 14 mi west of Cromer. Driving the coast road from Cromer, you pass marshes, sandbanks, and coves, as well as villages. Blakeney is one of the most appealing, with harbors for small fishing boats and yachts. Once a bustling port town exporting corn and salt, it enjoys a quiet existence today, and a reputation for wildlife viewing at Blakeney Point.

EXPLORING

Blakeney Point, 1,000 acres of grassy dunes, is home to nesting terns and about 500 common and gray seals. You can walk 3½ mi from Cley Beach to get here, but a boat trip from Blakeney or Morston Quay is fun and educational. An information center and a tearoom at Morston Quay open according to tides and weather. **Bishop's Boats** (⊠*Ticket Office Blakeney Quay, opposite junction with High St.* ☎*01263/740753* ⊕*www.norfolksealtrips.co.uk*) runs one- or two-hour trips daily between February and October from Morston Quay and Blakeney harbor for £8 per person. ⊠*A149* ☎*01263/740241* ⊕*www.nationaltrust.org.uk* ☞*Free.*

WHERE TO EAT AND STAY

£   ✕ **Anchor Inn.** This delightful little gastro-pub in Morston, a mile and a
SEAFOOD   half west of Blakeney, has a cozy, pelagic atmosphere. The menu doesn't just consist of seafood, but why would you order anything else when the fresh, locally sourced catch is this good? Platters of mussels and oysters are popular, and prawns are served the way purists like them—in a pint glass, shells on, with a twist of lemon and a pot of homemade mayo. The fish-and-chips here are outstanding. ⊠*22 The Street, Morston* ☎*01263/741392* ▤*MC, V.*

£££   ✕ **White Horse at Blakeney.** Fine food is the draw at this former coach-
MODERN BRITISH   ing inn. Goat's-cheese parcels, smoked eel, and roast pork tenderloin appear on the menu, along with pub classics such as ploughman's lunch and cod-and-chips. You can dine in the bar, an airy conservatory, or the more intimate Long Room. A few of the pleasant, simply furnished guest rooms have sea views that are worth the extra pence. ⊠*4 High St.* ☎*01263/740574* ▤*MC, V.*

£££–££££   ☷ **Byfords.** In a market town 5 mi southeast of Blakeney, Byfords epito-
★   mizes the increasing trendiness of North Norfolk. The self-styled "Posh B&B" rooms are stylish and comfortable, with Egyptian cotton linens, elegantly modern hi-fi sound systems, and fresh flowers. Seven rooms are in an annex, and the rest are in the main building. The busy café by day turns into a restaurant offering Mediterranean and English fare in the evening. There's also a superb delicatessen—excellent for preparing a picnic. **Pros:** plush rooms; amiable staff; relaxed atmosphere. **Cons:** gets busy on weekends; service occasionally slow. ⊠*1–3 Shirehall Plain, Holt* ☎*01263/711400* ⊕*www.byfords.org.uk* ⬗*16 rooms* ☖*In-room: no a/c, DVD. In-hotel: restaurant* ▤*MC, V* ☷*BP.*

SPORTS AND THE OUTDOORS

Temples Seal Watching Trips (☎*01263/740791* ⊕*www.sealtrips.co.uk*) organizes two-hour boat trips out to Blakeney Point, where you can watch seals in their natural environment. Tours cost £8 for adults, and £4 for children; call ahead for sailing times. The ticket office is located in the Anchor Inn in Morston, a mile and a half west of Blakeney.

WELLS-NEXT-THE-SEA

10 mi west of Blakeney, 34 mi northwest of Norwich.

A quiet base from which to explore other nearby towns, the harbor town of Wells-next-the-Sea and the nearby coastline remain untouched,

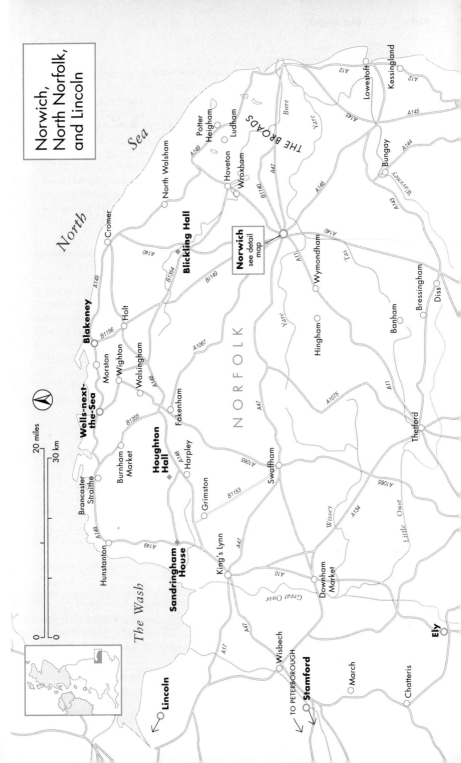

Norwich,
North Norfolk,
and Lincoln

North Sea

The Wash

NORFOLK

THE BROADS

20 miles
30 km

Lincoln

Ely

Stamford

TO PETERBOROUGH

March

Chatteris

Wisbech

King's Lynn

Downham
Market

**Sandringham
House**

Hunstanton

Brancaster
Staithe

Burnham
Market

**Wells-next-
the-Sea**

Blakeney

Morston

Wighton

Walsingham

Fakenham

**Houghton
Hall**

Harpley

Grimston

Swaffham

Thetford

Holt

Cromer

North Walsham

Blickling Hall

Hingham

Wymondham

Banham

Bressingham

Diss

Norwich
see detail
map

Hoveton
Wroxham

Ludham

Potter
Heigham

Lowestoft

Kessingland

Bungay

Great Ouse

Little Ouse

Wissey

Yare

Tas

Bure

Yare

Waveney

A17

A47

A10

A47

A149

A148

B1355

A148

A1067

B1149

B1354

A140

A149

B1156

A148

A1065

B1153

A134

A1075

A1065

A11

A47

A140

A11

A146

A47

B1140

A149

A144

A143

A145

A12

A12

A143

Popular Paths

East Anglia is a walker's dream, especially if a relatively flat trail appeals to you. The long-distance footpath known as the Peddars Way follows the line of a pre-Roman road, running from near Thetford through heathland, pine forests, and arable fields, and on through rolling chalk lands to the Norfolk coast near Hunstanton. The Norfolk Coastal Path then continues eastward along the coast, joining at Cromer with the delightfully varied

Weaver's Way, which passes through medieval weaving villages and deeply rural parts of the Norfolk Broads on its 56-mi route from Cromer to Great Yarmouth. Birders or anyone interested in birds should carry binoculars and a bird identification book, as both of these routes have abundant avian life—both local and migratory. Tourist information centers and the regional Web site ⊕ *www.visiteastofengland. com* have further details.

with many excellent places for bird-watching and walking on the sandy beaches of Holkham Bay, near Holkham Hall. Today the town is a mile from the sea, but in Tudor times, when it was closer to the ocean, it served as one of the main ports of East Anglia. The remains of a medieval priory and two holy wells point to the town's past as a major pilgrimage destination in the Middle Ages. Along the nearby beach a narrow-gauge steam train makes the short journey to Walsingham between Easter and October.

ESSENTIALS
Visitor Information Wells-next-the-Sea (✉ *Staithe St.* ☎ *01328/711022*).

EXPLORING
Fodor'sChoice ★ The Palladian **Holkham Hall,** one of the most splendid mansions in Britain, is the seat of the Coke family, the earls of Leicester. In the late 18th century, Thomas Coke went on the fashionable grand tour of the Continent, returning with art treasures and determined to build a house according to the new Italian ideas. Centered by a grand staircase and modeled after the Baths of Diocletian, the entryway, the 60-foot-tall Marble Hall (mostly alabaster, in fact), may be the most spectacular room in Britain. Beyond this hall lie salons brilliant with gold and alabaster, each filled with works from Coke's collection of masterpieces, including paintings by Gainsborough, Sir Anthony Van Dyck, Peter Paul Rubens, and Raphael. Surrounding this transplant from neoclassical Italy is parkland landscaped by Capability Brown in 1762. The **Bygones Museum,** in the stable block, has more than 5,000 items, from gramophones to fire engines. ✉ *Off A149* ☎ *01328/710227* ⊕ *www. holkham.co.uk* ✉ *Hall £8, museum £5, combined ticket £10; lake cruise £3; deer park and grounds free* ☉ *June–Sept., Sun.–Tues. and Thurs. noon–4; May and Oct., Sun., Mon., and Thurs. noon–4.*

WHERE TO STAY
££££ ☺ Fodor'sChoice ★ 🏨**Victoria at Holkham.** A colorful, whimsical hideaway, this hotel on the Holkham Hall estate is managed by the earl of Leicester's family. The atmosphere is more laid-back and family-friendly than the austere

exterior may suggest. Inside, subtle lighting and artsy, shabby-chic
decor contrasts with a young and
rather sophisticated vibe. Bedrooms
are on the small side, but comfortable, with elegant, handmade furniture and modern bathrooms. Most
romantic is the Raj Room, with
its claw-foot tub and ornate, precipitously tall (if somewhat creaky)
bed. The hotel restaurant is one of
the finest in the region, with an
emphasis on modern European
cuisine, expertly prepared using

local produce. In the summer months, the Victoria also holds a highly
popular nightly alfresco barbecue. The dune-backed Holkham Beach
(where the final scene of *Shakespeare in Love* was filmed) is a just a
few minutes down the dirt road opposite the hotel; show your room
key to avoid paying the toll if you're driving. **Pros:** original character;
excellent location; outstanding food. **Cons:** gets extremely busy in summer; no elevator. ⊠ *A149* ☎ *01328/711008* ⊕ *www.holkham.co.uk/
victoria* 🛏 *9 rooms, 1 suite, 4 lodges (self-contained accommodations)
on grounds* ⚙ *In-room: no a/c (some), DVD. In-hotel: restaurant, room
service, bar* ⊟ *MC, V* ❍ *CP.*

SPORTS AND THE OUTDOORS

On Yer Bike Cycle Hire (⊠ *The Laurels, Nutwood Farm, Wighton*
☎ *01328/820719* ⊕ *www.norfolkcyclehire.co.uk*) will deliver and collect bikes; rentals are £13 per day, and reservations are required.

HOUGHTON HALL

14 mi southwest of Wells-next-the-Sea, 35 mi northwest of Norwich.

GETTING HERE AND AROUND

Houghton Hall is in the tiny hamlet of Houghton, which is just outside
Harpley, on the A148 between King's Lynn and Fakenham.

EXPLORING

Houghton Hall, a grand Palladian pile built by the first British prime minister, Sir Robert Walpole, in the 1720s, has been carefully restored by
its current owner, the seventh marquess of Cholmondeley. The double-
height Stone Hall and the sumptuous rooms, perfect for gatherings of
the powerful, reveal designer William Kent's preference for gilt, plush
fabrics, stucco, and elaborate carvings. The Common Parlour, one of
the original family rooms, is elegant but far simpler. New landscaping,
including a 5-acre walled garden, is also part of the picture. ⊠ *Off
A148, near Harpley* ☎ *01485/528569* ⊕ *www.houghtonhall.com*
🎫 *£8.80; park and grounds only, £6* ❍ *Late Mar.–late Sept., Wed.,
Thurs., Sun., and bank holiday Mon. 1:30–5; grounds 11–5:30; last
admission 4:30.*

SANDRINGHAM HOUSE

8 mi west of Houghton Hall, 20 mi southwest of Wells-next-the-Sea, 43 mi northwest of Norwich.

GETTING HERE AND AROUND

Sandringham is just off the B1440, between Dersingham and Hillington.

EXPLORING

Not far from the old-fashioned but still popular seaside resort of Hunstanton, **Sandringham House** is where the Royal Family traditionally spends Christmas. The redbrick Victorian mansion was clearly designed for enormous country-house parties, with a ballroom, billiard room, and bowling alley, as well as a shooting lodge on the grounds. The house and gardens close when the Queen is in residence, but the woodlands, nature walks, and museum of royal memorabilia (in the old stables) remain open, as does the church, medieval but in heavy Victorian disguise. Tours have access to most rooms but steer clear of personal effects of current royals. ✉*Sandringham* ☎*01553/772675* ⊕*www.sandringhamestate.co.uk* 🖼*House, gardens, and museum £10, gardens and museum £8.50* ⊙*Mid-Apr.–late July and early Aug.–early Nov., daily 11–5. Gardens open ½ hr early.*

STAMFORD AND LINCOLN

The fens of northern Cambridgeshire pass imperceptibly into the three divisions of Lincolnshire: Holland, Kesteven, and Lindsey are parts of the county, divided administratively. Holland borders the Isle of Ely and the Soke of Peterborough. This marshland spreads far and wide south of the Wash. The chief attractions are two towns: Stamford, to the southwest, and Lincoln, with its magnificent cathedral.

STAMFORD

48 mi northwest of Cambridge.

Serene, honey-hued Stamford, on a hillside overlooking the River Welland, has a well-preserved center, in part because in 1967 it was designated England's first conservation area. This unspoiled town, which grew rich in the medieval wool and cloth trades, is a delightful place to study the harmonious mixture of Georgian and medieval architecture.

ESSENTIALS

Visitor Information Stamford (✉ *Stamford Arts Centre, St. Mary's St.* ☎*01780/755611* ⊕ *www.stamfordartscentre.com*).

EXPLORING

★ **Burghley House,** an architectural masterpiece that many consider the grandest house of the first Elizabethan age, is celebrated for its roofscape bristling with pepper-pot chimneys and slate-roof towers. It was built between 1565 and 1587 to the design of William Cecil, first Baron Burghley, when he was Elizabeth I's high treasurer; his descendants still occupy the house. The interior was remodeled in the late 17th century with treasures from Europe. The house contains 18 sumptuous rooms, with carvings by Grinling Gibbons and ceiling paintings by Antonio Verrio (including the dramatic Heaven Room and the Hell Staircase), as well as innumerable paintings and priceless porcelain. You can tour on your own or join a free 80-minute guided tour beginning daily at 3:30. In the 18th century Capability Brown landscaped the grounds (where deer now roam and open-air concerts are staged in summer), dug the lake, and added the Gothic Revival orangery, where today you can have tea or lunch. In early September Burghley is host to the international Burghley Horse Trials. The house is a mile southeast of Stamford. ⊠ *Off A1* ☎ *01780/752451* ⊕ *www.burghley.co.uk* 🏠 *House and gardens £11.30; gardens only, £6.50* ◷ *Easter–late Oct., Sat.–Thurs. 11–5.*

LINCOLN

★ *53 mi north of Stamford, 93 mi northwest of Cambridge, 97 mi northwest of Norwich.*

Celts, Romans, and Danes all had important settlements here, but it was the Normans who gave Lincoln its medieval stature after William the Conqueror founded Lincoln Castle as a stronghold in 1068. Four years later William appointed Bishop Remigius to run the huge diocese stretching from the Humber to the Thames, resulting in the construction of Lincoln Cathedral, the third largest in England after York Minster and St. Paul's. Since medieval times Lincoln's status has declined. However, its somewhat remote location (there are no major motorways or railways nearby) has helped preserve its traditional character.

The cathedral is on the aptly named Steep Hill; to its south, narrow medieval streets cling to the hillside. Jew's House, on the Strait, dating from the early 12th century, is one of several well-preserved domestic buildings in this area. The rather prosaic name is almost as old as the house itself—it refers to a former resident, Belaset of Wallingford, a Jewish woman who was murdered by a mob in 1290, the same year the Jews were expelled from England. The River Witham flows unobtrusively under the incongruously named High Bridge, a low, vaulted Norman bridge topped by timber-frame houses from the 16th century. West from here you can rent boats, or, in summer, go on a river cruise.

GETTING HERE AND AROUND

There are direct buses (four hours) from London, but most rail journeys (two–four hours) involve changing trains. The bus and train stations are south of the center, and it's a steep walk uphill to the cathedral and castle. You can avoid the climb by taking the Walk & Ride electric bus service from the stop on St. Mary's Street. You can purchase tickets on board. Drivers will find parking lots around the bus and train stations and in the center at The Lawn and Westgate.

ESSENTIALS

Visitor Information Lincoln (⊠ *9 Castle Hill* ☎ *01522/873800* ⊕ *www.lincoln. gov.uk*).

EXPLORING

★ Lincoln's crowning glory, the great **Cathedral of St. Mary,** was for hundreds of years the tallest building in Europe, but this magnificent medieval building is now among the least known of European cathedrals. The Norman bishop Remigius began work in 1072. The Romanesque church he built was irremediably damaged, first by fire, then by earthquake (in 1185), but you can still see parts of the ancient structure at the west front. The next great phase of building, initiated by Bishop Hugh of Avalon, is mainly 13th century in character. The west front, topped by two strikingly tall towers, gives tremendous breadth to the entrance. It is best seen from the 14th-century Exchequer Gate arch in front of the cathedral, or from the castle battlements beyond.

Inside, a breathtaking impression of space and unity belies the many centuries of building and rebuilding. The stained-glass window at the north end of the transept, known as the Dean's Eye, is one of the earliest (13th-century) traceried windows, whereas its opposite number at the south end shows a 14th-century sophistication in its interlaced designs. ■**TIP→ Look for the Lincoln Imp upon the pillar nearest St. Hugh's shrine; an angel turned this creature to stone, according to legend.** Through a door on the north side is the chapter house, a 10-sided building that sometimes housed the medieval Parliament of England during the reigns of Edward I and Edward II. The chapter house is connected to the 13th-century cloister, notable for its amusing ceiling bosses. The cathedral library, a restrained building by Christopher Wren, was built onto the north side of the cloisters after the original library collapsed. Tours of the cathedral roof and tower are fascinating. (No children under 14 are allowed.) ⊠*Minster Yard* ☎*01522/561600* ⊕*www.lincolncathedral. com* ☎*£4* ⊗*June–Aug., weekdays 7:15 AM–8 PM, weekends 7:15 AM– 6 PM; Sept.–May, Mon.–Sat. 7:15 AM–6 PM, Sun. 7:15 AM–5 PM. Guided tours 11 and at least one other time (varies according to season—call ahead); roof tours weekdays 1:30, Sat. 11 and 2; tower tours Apr. and Oct., Sat. 1:30 and 3, May–Sept., Sat. 12:15, 1:30, and 3. All tour times can vary, so check beforehand.*

QUICK BITES

After climbing Steep Hill, you'll need at least one of the 23 different teas or 15 coffees available at **Pimento** (⊠*27 Steep Hill* ☎*01522/544880*). Choose a cake or snack to go along with your pick-me-up.

The **Minster Yard,** which surrounds the cathedral on three sides, contains buildings of different periods, including graceful Georgian architecture. A statue of Alfred, Lord Tennyson, who was born in Lincolnshire, stands on the green near the chapter house.

The **Medieval Bishop's Palace,** on the south side of Minster Yard, has exhibits about the former administrative center of the diocese, plus a garden and working vineyard. ⊠*Minster Yard* ☎*01522/527468* ⊕*www.english-heritage.org.uk* ☎*£4* ⊗*July and Aug., daily 10–6; late Mar.–June, Sept., and Oct., daily 10–5; Nov.–Mar., Thurs.–Mon. 10–4.*

Ⅽ **Lincoln Castle,** facing the cathedral across Exchequer Gate, was built on two great mounds by William the Conqueror in 1068, incorporating part of the remains of Roman garrison walls. The castle was a military base until the 17th century, after which it operated as a prison. In the extraordinary prison chapel you can see the cagelike stalls in which Victorian convicts listened to sermons. ■TIP→ One of the four surviving copies of the Magna Carta, signed by King John at Runnymede in 1215, is on display in the same building. ⊠*Castle Hill* ☎*01522/511068* ⊕*www.lincolnshire.gov.uk/lincolncastle* ⊠*£4* ⊙*Apr. and Sept., daily 10–5; May–Aug., daily 10–6; Oct.–Mar., daily 10–4; last entry 1 hr before closing.*

⟲ The **Collection** is made up of the **Usher Gallery,** an art gallery with paintings by Turner, Lowry, and Hitchens as well as some more contemporary works, and the modern **Archaeology Collection** next door, an interactive museum with a sound installation, games to play, and local artifacts spanning 3,000 years of history. Look out for good temporary exhibitions at the Usher Gallery. ⊠*Danes Terrace* ☎*01522/550990* ⊕*www.thecollection.lincoln.museum* ⊠*Free* ⊙*Daily 10–4.*

WHERE TO EAT AND STAY

££   ✕**Brown's Pie Shop.** More than you might imagine from the modest
BRITISH   name, Brown's Pie Shop serves the best of traditional English cuisine: succulent beef, great puddings, and, of course, some very good, freshly made savory pies. This restaurant, close to the cathedral, serves an economical early-evening menu. ⊠*33 Steep Hill* ☎*01522/527330* ▭*MC, V.*

£££   ✕**Jew's House.** This intimate restaurant, with restrained tones and open
MODERN BRITISH   stonework, is in one of Lincoln's oldest buildings, a rare survivor of
★   12th-century Norman domestic architecture. The cosmopolitan fixed-price menu of continental specialties changes daily, and the restaurant is renowned for its fresh fish and rich desserts, all homemade. ⊠*15 The Strait* ☎*01522/524851* ▭*MC, V* ⊙*Closed Sun. and Mon.*

££–£££   ▦**Bailhouse & Mews.** In a 14th-century baronial hall near the cathedral, the welcoming Bailhouse & Mews offers good-value accommodation, with four-poster beds in some rooms and plenty of antique features, such as flagstones and wooden beams. The gardens have a swimming pool and a stone chapel, and you can help yourself to tea or coffee at any time from the kitchen. The hotel also has three self-catering cottages and one house available. **Pros:** historic building; views of cathedral and castle; convenient parking. **Cons:** some street noise; feels understaffed. ⊠*34 Bailgate* ☎*01522/541000* ⊕*www.bailhouse.co.uk* ⇆*10 rooms, 3 cottages, 1 house* ⌂*In-room: no a/c, DVD (some), Wi-Fi. In-hotel: bar, pool, no-smoking rooms* ▭*AE, MC, V* ⋔*BP.*

£££   ▦**White Hart.** Luxuriously furnished with a wealth of antiques, among
★   them some fine clocks and china, the establishment has been a hotel for 600 years. Bedrooms are individually decorated in traditional style; many are outfitted with antiques, and hardwoods such as walnut and mahogany abound. **Pros:** excellent location; blend of period and modern furnishings. **Cons:** slow service; overpriced food. ⊠*Bailgate* ☎*01522/563293* ⊕*www.whitehart-lincoln.co.uk* ⇆*39 rooms, 11 suites* ⌂*In-room: no a/c, Internet. In-hotel: restaurant, room service, bar, laundry service, Wi-Fi, some pets allowed, no-smoking rooms* ▭*AE, MC, V* ⋔*BP.*

NIGHTLIFE AND THE ARTS

The **Theatre Royal** (⊠ *Clasketgate* ☎ *01522/525555* ⊕ *www.theatre-royallincoln.com*), a fine Victorian theater, previews plays and musicals before their London runs and also hosts touring productions and comedy.

SHOPPING

Chain stores fill the Bailgate Mall and High Street. The best stores, however, are on Bailgate, Steep Hill, and the medieval streets leading directly down from the cathedral and castle. Just off Steep Hill, the **Cheese Society** (⊠ *1 St. Martin's La.* ☎ *01522/511003* ⊕ *www.thecheesesociety.co.uk*) has a great selection of English and French cheeses and an attached café. **Cobb Hall Craft Centre** (⊠ *St. Paul's La. off Bailgate*), a small mall of crafts shops and workshops, sells clocks, candles, and ornaments. Steep Hill has good bookstores, antiques shops, and crafts and art galleries, including **Harding House Galleries** (⊠ *Steep Hill* ☎ *01522/523537*).

Yorkshire

LEEDS, HAWORTH, YORK,
WHITBY, CASTLE HOWARD

WORD OF MOUTH

"The first thing we chose to do was visit the [York] Minster. Like the Duomo in Florence, it looms over the entire town and is truly beautiful and impressive . . . The main part of the cathedral is breathtaking and nearly defies description. If you do only one thing in the town, this is what I would choose."

—penel523

"From Castle Howard, head north and explore the North Yorkshire Moors, as you won't need a full day at CH. The drive from Pickering over the moors to Whitby is spectacular, or you can take the steam railway which more or less follows the same route, Pickering to Whitby."

—Cathinjoetown

Updated
by Christi
Daugherty

A hauntingly beautiful region, Yorkshire is known for its wide-open spaces and dramatic landscapes. The hills of the moors and dales glow pink with heather in summer, and turn black with it in winter. Hearty fishing villages and ruined monasteries cling to the edges of cliffs in one of England's last remaining wildernesses.

Some of the region's biggest attractions are the result of human endeavor: the towering cathedral in medieval York; Castle Howard, a baroque masterpiece near York; and the old haunts of the Brontë sisters in the hillside town of Haworth.

The most rugged land is the North York Moors, a vast, lonely area free of fences, and dotted with fluffy sheep that wander at will in summer. (It is said that if the grazing sheep ever disappeared, the ancient forests would return.) Between the bleak moors and the rocky Pennine hills lie lush, green valleys known as the Yorkshire Dales, where the high rainfall produces luxuriant vegetation, swift rivers, sparkling streams, and waterfalls. The villages here, immortalized in the books of the Brontës and the late veterinarian Alf Wight (1916–95)—who wrote under the name James Herriot—are wonderfully peaceful, bursting into life only in summer as hundreds of hikers (or "ramblers" as they're known in England) appear over the hills.

The area is not all green fields and perfect villages—there's also a gritty, urban aspect to Yorkshire, whose manufacturing towns changed the course of British history. In West Yorkshire, once down-at-the-heels Leeds has remade itself with trendy restaurants and cafés, and its buzzing music industry and nightlife scene.

ORIENTATION AND PLANNING

GETTING ORIENTED

Yorkshire is the largest English region to explore (its fiercely proud inhabitants would say it's the only English region *worth* exploring). The industrial heartland is West Yorkshire, with the cities of Leeds and Bradford. What the tourist office likes to call Brontë Country—basically Haworth, home of the Brontë family—is just to the northwest, and northward spread the hills, valleys, and villages of the Yorkshire Dales. To the east is the ancient city of York, with its famous cathedral.

Along the coast, Yorkshire reveals itself as a seaside vacation destination, although never one that will win prizes for summerlike weather. But fine beaches and a fascinating history await you in the resort of Scarborough, the former whaling port of Whitby, and Robin Hood's Bay—a cliff-top, onetime smuggler's haunt. Finally, you can strike

TOP REASONS TO GO

York Minster: The largest Gothic cathedral in England helps make York one of the country's most-visited towns. The building's history is told in its crypt, brilliantly converted into a museum.

North York Moors: There's enough space for walkers to experience isolation amid the heather-covered hills that glow crimson and purple in late summer and early fall. Make way for the passing sheep.

Rievaulx Abbey: Heading down the tiny lane that leads to the ruins of one of the great Cistercian abbeys only serves to make it all the more dramatic when its soaring arches appear out of the trees.

Whitby: This bustling coastal town inspired Bram Stoker to write *Dracula*. At night, its gloomy cliff-top church and skeletal abbey ruins loom over Whitby dramatically.

Robin Hood's Bay: Test your balance on the steep roads of this seaside village set in a ravine, and then breathe easy on the miles of outstanding beach.

13

inland to the North York Moors National Park. Isolated stone villages, moorland walks, and Rievaulx Abbey are within easy reach.

West Yorkshire and Brontë Country. Rocky and bleak, this windswept stretch of country makes sense of all those tragedies penned by the Brontë sisters in prettily gloomy Haworth. Leeds is a reviving former industrial center worth a stop.

The Yorkshire Dales. This mountainous region, a bit off the beaten track, has windswept moors and valleys that offer extraordinary views. Gorgeous villages like Bolton Abbey and Grassington are well worth exploring.

York. Still wrapped up in its medieval city walls, this beautifully preserved city makes the perfect introduction to Yorkshire. Its towering Minster and crooked little streets entrance history buffs.

York Environs. This rural region holds the exquisite Victorian spa town, Harrogate, as well as charming villages like Knaresborough, tucked away in a steep valley. Baroque Castle Howard is also near York.

The North Yorkshire Coast. Along this part of the coast, tiny fishing villages cling to the cliffs where the earth rushes down to meet the cold sea. Scarborough and adorable Robin Hood's Bay make ideal getaways.

The North Yorkshire Moors. A short drive north from York, these heather-covered hills are a perfect place to wander. Hutton-le-Hole and Helmsley are pleasant towns, and the ruins of Rievaulx Abbey are nearby.

PLANNING

WHEN TO GO

To see the heather at its lushest, visit in summer (but despite the season, be prepared for some chilly days). It's also the best time for the coast, when colorful regattas and arts festivals are under way. York Minster makes a splendid focal point for the prestigious York Early

Music Festival in early July. Spring and fall bring their own rewards: far fewer crowds and crisp, clear days, although there's an increased risk of rain and fog. The harsh winter is hard to call: with glistening snow and bright days, the coast, moors, and dales are beautiful, but storms and blizzards set in quickly. The moorland roads become impassable, and villages can be cut off entirely. In winter, stick to York and the main towns.

PLANNING YOUR TIME

Yorkshire is a vast region, which makes it difficult to explore in a short amount of time. If you're in a hurry, you could visit York or Leeds as a day trip from London; the fastest trains take just two hours. But proper exploration of the region—especially of the countryside—requires time and effort. In a few days you could explore York and some nearby highlights such as Castle Howard and Studley Royal. You'd need the better part of a week to take in the small towns, abandoned abbeys, and inspiring moors and coast. But it's well worth it. This is the path less traveled.

GETTING HERE AND AROUND

AIR TRAVEL

Leeds Bradford Airport, 8 mi northwest of Leeds, has frequent flights from other cities in England and Europe. Look for cheap fares from London on BMI Baby, Easyjet, or British Airways. Another good choice for this region is Manchester Airport, about 40 mi southwest of Leeds. This larger airport is well served by domestic and international carriers.

Airports Leeds Bradford International Airport (⊠ *A658, Yeadon* ☎ *0113/ 250–9696* ⊕ *www.lbia.co.uk*). **Manchester Airport** (⊠ *Near Junctions 5 and 6 of M56* ☎ *0161/489–3000* ⊕ *www.manairport.co.uk*).

BUS TRAVEL

National Express and Megabus both have numerous buses a day from London's Victoria Coach Station to major cities in Yorkshire. Average travel times are 4¼ hours to Leeds, 6 hours to York, and 8 hours to Scarborough. Once you're in the region, local bus companies take over the routes. There are Metro buses from Leeds and Bradford into the more remote parts of the Yorkshire Dales. Other companies are Harrogate & District for services to Ripon, Harrogate, and Leeds; Yorkshire Coastliner for Castle Howard, Scarborough, Whitby, Malton, and Leeds; and Arriva for Whitby, Scarborough, and Middlesbrough. In York the main local bus operator is First. Traveline has route information.

Bus Contacts Arriva (☎ *0870/120–1088* ⊕ *www.arriva.co.uk*). **First** (☎ *01904/ 883000* ⊕ *www.firstgroup.com*). **Harrogate & District** (☎ *01423/566061*). **Megabus** (☎ *0900/160–0900* ⊕ *www.megabus.co.uk*). **Metroline** (☎ *0113/ 245–7676* ⊕ *www.wymetro.com*). **National Express** (☎ *0871/781–8181* ⊕ *www.nationalexpress.com*). **Traveline** (☎ *0870/608–2608* ⊕ *www.traveline. org.uk*). **Yorkshire Coastliner** (☎ *01653/692556* ⊕ *www.yorkshirecoastliner. co.uk*).

CAR TRAVEL

If you're driving, the M1 is the principal route north from London. This major thoroughfare gets you to Leeds in about two hours. For York (193 mi) and the Scarborough areas, stay on M1 to Leeds (189 mi), and then take A64. For the Yorkshire Dales, take M1 to Leeds, then A660 to A65 north and west to Skipton. For the North York Moors, take either B1363 north from York to Helmsley, or the A64 through Malton to Whitby. The trans-Pennine motorway, the M62, between Liverpool and Hull, crosses the bottom of this region. North of Leeds, A1 is the major north–south road, although narrow stretches, roadwork, and heavy traffic make this route slow going at times.

Some of the steep, narrow roads in the countryside off the main routes are difficult drives and can be perilous (or closed altogether) in winter. Main roads often closed by snowdrifts are the moorland A169 and the coast-and-moor A171. If you plan to drive in the dales or moors in winter, check the weather forecast in advance.

TRAIN TRAVEL

National Express trains travel to Leeds and York from London's King's Cross station. Average travel times from King's Cross are 2½ hours to Leeds and 2 hours to York. At this writing, the National Express transportation system was undergoing changes, so call ahead to confirm schedules. Two Regional Rover tickets for seven days of unlimited travel are available: North East (£75) and Coast and Peaks (£55). For the East Yorkshire area, which includes Scarborough and York, an unlimited travel pass valid for four days (within an eight-day period) costs £32.50. Contact National Rail for information.

Train Contacts National Express (☎0870/522-5125 ⊕ www.nationalexpress. com). **National Rail Enquiries** (☎0845/748-4950 ⊕ www.nationalrail.co.uk).

RESTAURANTS

Generally speaking, Yorkshire is not known for its cuisine, and bacon-based breakfasts and pork pies do tend to pale fairly quickly. Luckily, in the larger towns and cities, particularly in Leeds, a foodie culture has developed. Indian restaurants (called "curry restaurants") are very good in the north. Out in the countryside, pubs are your best bet for dining. Many offer excellent home-cooked food and locally produced meat (especially lamb) and vegetables. Roast beef dinners generally come with Yorkshire pudding, the tasty, light bread that is called a popover in the United States and Canada. It's generally served with lots of gravy. Be sure to sample local cheeses, especially Wensleydale, which has a delicate flavor and honeyed aftertaste.

HOTELS

Traditional hotels are limited primarily to major towns and cities; those in the country tend to be guesthouses. Many of the better guesthouses are at the edge of town, but some proprietors will pick you up at the main station if you're relying on public transportation—verify before booking. Rooms fill quickly at seaside resorts in July and August, and some places in the moors and dales close in winter. Always call ahead to make sure a hotel is open and has space available.

WHAT IT COSTS IN POUNDS					
	£	££	£££	££££	£££££
Restaurants	Under £10	£10–£14	£15–£19	£20–£25	over £25
Hotels	Under £70	£70–£120	£121–£160	£161–£220	over £220

Restaurant prices are for a main course at dinner. Hotel prices are for two people in a standard double room in high season, including V.A.T., with no meals or, if indicated, CP (with continental breakfast), BP (Breakfast Plan, with full breakfast), or MAP (Modified American Plan, with breakfast and dinner).

VISITOR INFORMATION

Contact Yorkshire Tourist Board (✉312 Tadcaster Rd., York ☎01904/707961 ⊕ www.yorkshire.com).

WEST YORKSHIRE AND BRONTË COUNTRY

The busy city of Leeds provides an obvious starting point for a tour of West Yorkshire. From there you can strike out for the traditional wool towns, such as Saltaire, a UNESCO-protected gem, and the Magna museum at Rotherham, which draws long lines for its surprisingly interesting exploration of steel. But the main thrust of many visits to West

Yorkshire is to the west of Leeds, where the gaunt hills north of the Calder Valley and south of the River Aire form the district immortalized by the mournful writings of the Brontë sisters. Haworth, an otherwise gray village, might have faded into obscurity were it not for the magnetism of the literary sisters. Every summer, thousands toil up the steep main street to visit their hometown, but to truly understand their writing you need to go farther afield to the ruined farm of Top Withins, which is by legend, if not fact, Wuthering Heights.

LEEDS

43 mi northeast of Manchester, 25 mi southwest of York.

It may be one of the cultural centers of the north, but Leeds is still living down a reputation as a grim, northern industrial town. However, since 1990, the city has successfully transformed itself. Its Victorian buildings have been polished and restored, its old factories and warehouses converted into pricey loft housing and modern offices. Everywhere are cafés with outdoor tables defying the northern weather, sleek bars, modern hotels, and upscale restaurants. Leeds University keeps the town young and hip, supporting the city's good music shops and funky clothing and jewelry boutiques.

GETTING HERE AND AROUND

Leeds Bradford Airport, 8 mi northwest of the city, is the main gateway to this part of the country. National Express and Megabus have frequent buses here from London's Victoria Coach Station. The journey takes about four hours. National Express trains depart from London's King's Cross Station to Leeds Station about every 30 minutes during the week. The trip takes about 2½ hours. Leeds Station is in the middle of central Leeds and usually has a line of taxis waiting out front.

A city of nearly half a million people, Leeds has an efficient local bus service. Most visitors will never use it, as most sights are in the easily walkable downtown.

ESSENTIALS

Visitor Information Leeds (✉ *Leeds City Station* ☎ *0113/242–5242* ⊕ *www. visitleeds.co.uk*).

EXPLORING

TOP ATTRACTIONS

The Calls. The Calls, east of Granary Wharf by the river, has converted redbrick warehouses with more snazzy bars and restaurants that enliven the cobbled streets and quayside. This is definitely the area to wander at lunchtime and when you're craving an afternoon coffee.

City Square. One of the city's best examples of Victorian architecture is City Square, right in front of the train station. Busy streets surround the traffic-free oasis where benches make a good place to get your bearings as you take in the 19th-century statues. On the east side is the 18th-century Mill Hill Chapel.

★ **Harewood House.** The home of the earl of Harewood, a cousin of the Queen, Harewood House (pronounced *har*-wood) is a spectacular neoclassical mansion, built in 1759 by John Carr of York. Highlights include Robert Adam interiors, important paintings and ceramics, and a large, ravishingly beautiful collection of Chippendale furniture (Chippendale was born in nearby Otley), notably the magnificent State Bed. The Old Kitchen and Below Stairs exhibition illustrates life from the servants' point of view. Capability Brown designed the handsome grounds, and Charles Barry created a notable Italian garden with fountains in the 1840s. Also here are a bird garden with 120 rare and endangered species, an adventure playground, and a butterfly house. The house is 7 mi north of Leeds; you can take Harrogate & District Bus 36. ⊠ *Junction of A61 and A659, Harewood* ☎ *0113/218–1010* ⊕ *www.harewood. org* ⊠ *£14.50* ⊘ *House Apr.–Oct., daily noon–4.*

★ **Leeds Art Gallery.** Next door to the Victorian Town Hall, the recently renovated Leeds Art Gallery is Yorkshire's most impressive art museum, with a strong core collection of works by Courbet, Sisley, Constable, Crome, and the internationally acclaimed Yorkshire sculptor Henry Moore, who studied at the Leeds School of Art. The graceful statue on the steps outside the gallery is Moore's *Reclining Woman.* More works by Moore are at the adjacent **Henry Moore Institute,** which also has regular exhibitions of modern sculpture. The **Craft Centre and Design Gallery,** also in the museum, exhibits and sells fine contemporary crafts. ⊠ *The Headrow* ☎ *0113/247–8248* ⊕ *www.leeds.gov.uk/artgallery* ⊠ *Free* ⊘ *Mon., Tues., and Thurs.–Sat. 10–5, Wed. 10–8, Sun. 1–5.*

QUICK BITES | Step down to the cozy, book-lined **New Conservatory** (⊠ *The Albions, Albion Pl., off Briggate* ☎ *0113/246–1853*) for fresh sandwiches, wraps, and cakes. You can also sit and relax with a cup of tea or coffee.

WORTH NOTING

Granary Wharf. Once the center of Leeds' decayed industrial area, two adjacent neighborhoods along the River Aire have been revitalized into a trendy area of pricey loft apartments, chic bars, and pleasant cafés. Granary Wharf, in the Canal Basin, reached via the Dark Arches where the River Aire flows under City Station, is a good place to go exploring design and crafts shops, music shops, and a regular festival market.

☾ **Royal Armouries.** Much of the legendary arms and armor originally collected in the Tower of London fills the Royal Armouries, which occupies a redeveloped 13-acre dockland site, a 15-minute walk from the city center. Five theme galleries—War, Tournament, Self-Defense, Hunting, and Arms and Armor of the Orient—trace the history of weaponry. The state-of-the-art building is stunningly designed: expect a full-size elephant in armor, warriors on horseback, and floor-to-ceiling tents, as well as spirited interactive displays and live demonstrations. Shoot a crossbow, direct operations on a battlefield, experience a Wild West gunfight or an Elizabethan joust: it's your choice. ⊠ *Armouries Dr., off M1 or M621* ☎ *0113/220–1916* ⊕ *www.armouries.org.uk* ⊠ *Free* ⊘ *Daily 10–5.*

Temple Newsam. The Leeds City Council uses Temple Newsam, a huge Elizabethan and Jacobean building, to display its impressive collections of furniture, paintings, and ceramics. The house was the birthplace in 1545 of Lord Darnley, the doomed husband of Mary, Queen of Scots.

West Yorkshire and the Dales

Richmond
Catterick
Northallerton
A167
A1
A684
Leeming
Bedale
Hawes
A684
Aysgarth
Ure
Swale
A167
A168
B6160
A6108
Thirsk
A61
TO YORK
YORKSHIRE
DALES
NATIONAL
PARK
Masham
Grewelthorpe
North Stainley
A6108
Ripon
B6265
Newby Hall
Kettlewell
Gouthwaite
Res.
Studley Royal &
Fountains Abbey
A61
WHARFEDALE
Pateley
Bridge
B6165
A1(M)
Grassington
B6265
TO MALHAM
Cracoe
Nidd
B6165
B6055
TO YORK
Hetton
Bolton Priory
Blubberhouses
A59
Knaresborough
B6265
Bolton Abbey
Harrogate
A661
Wharfe
Skipton
A65
Ilkley
Askwith
B1224
AIREDALE
Pool
A658
A61
Wetherby
A629(T)
A660
A659
Keighley
A650
Aire
Harewood
House
A61
A64
Haworth
A629
B6144
Saltaire
A63
Oxenhope
Bradford
Leeds
Temple
Newsam
M1
TO MANCHESTER
M62
TO SHEFFIELD
AND MAGNA
Aire

Surrounding the house is a public park with rose gardens, greenhouses, and miles of woodland walks, all laid out by Capability Brown in 1762. Temple Newsam is 4 mi east of Leeds on A63; Buses 18, 40, 88, and 163–165 leave from Leeds Central Bus Station every 30 minutes and stop at the Irwin Arms, a 10-minute walk from the site. ⊠ *Off Selby Rd.* ☎ *0113/264–7321* ⊕ *www.leeds.gov.uk/templenewsam* ☒ *House £3.50, farm £3, joint ticket £5.60; parking £3.60* ⊙ *Apr.–Oct., Tues.–Sun. and national holiday Mon. 10:30–5; Nov.–Mar., Tues.–Sun. and national holiday Mon. 10:30–4. Last admission 45 mins before closing.*

OFF THE BEATEN PATH

Magna. A 45-minute drive south from Leeds to Rotherham brings you squarely in view of Yorkshire's industrial past. The sheer scale of the former steelworks that houses Magna, a widely respected science museum, is impressive, but the power of the Big Melt show really hits the spot. Smoke, flames, and sparking electricity bring one of the original six arc furnaces roaring to life in a sound-and-light show. Steel workers lost their jobs in the 1970s and '80s when the British coal and steel industries collapsed, and a permanent exhibit explores what happened to those workers afterward. In summer, former steel workers give tours here. Four pavilions engagingly illustrate the elements of fire, earth, air, and water used in the production of steel. ⊠ *Junction 33 or 34 off M1, Sheffield Rd., Rotherham* ☎ *01709/720002* ⊕ *www.visitmagna.co.uk* ☒ *£8.60* ⊙ *Daily 10–5.*

WHERE TO EAT

£££
MODERN BRITISH
✕ **Anthony's.** A well-regarded outpost of innovative cuisine influenced by molecular gastronomy, this intimate basement restaurant takes a lot of chances and is hugely rewarding to lovers of daring food. Main courses change daily but can include risotto with white onion, espresso, and Parmesan, or roasted duck with chocolate truffles. These unusual combinations work well in the formal, fine-dining setting. Other Anthony's outposts are a lunch spot at Flannels (a store) on Vicar Lane and a patisserie in the Victoria Quarter shopping arcade on Briggate. ⊠ *19 Boar La.* ☎ *0113/245–5922* ☒ *AE, DC, MC, V* ⊙ *Closed Sun. and Mon.*

£££
MODERN BRITISH
✕ **Brasserie Forty 4.** Within the elegant 44 The Calls Hotel, the Brasserie is one of the city's best restaurants. The atmosphere, like the menu, is modern and upscale, but not snobby. Starters include chicken-liver parfait, and Parma ham with Gorgonzola and hazelnuts, and main courses might be confit of duck with poached figs or herb-crusted salmon with black fettuccine. Book in advance. ⊠ *42–44 The Calls* ☎ *0113/234–3232* ☒ *AE, DC, MC, V.*

££
MODERN BRITISH
✕ **Fourth Floor Restaurant.** If the Harvey Nichols department store has been a roaring success, it's partly because of the lure of its swank Fourth Floor eatery, a standout for both food and dramatic, high-tech design. The well-crafted modern British menu changes several times a week, but is sure to have stylish takes on dishes such as saffron risotto with spiced eggplant, char-grilled rib-eye steak, and the freshest lemon sole. ⊠ *Harvey Nichols, 107–111 Briggate* ☎ *0113/204–8000* ☒ *AE, DC, MC, V* ⊙ *No dinner Sun.–Wed.*

£
BRITISH
✕ **Whitelocks.** The city's oldest pub, dating from 1715, is tucked away in an alley in the city center. It's been known for years for traditional

Yorkshire pudding and gravy, homemade pies, and real ale. The long, narrow bar has all the trappings of the Victorian era—stained glass, etched mirrors, copper-top tables, and red-plush banquettes. Service is brisk and friendly, and during the day the emphasis is more on food than drink. ⊠*Turks Head Yard, off Briggate* ☎*0113/245–3950* ⊟*AE, MC, V.*

WHERE TO STAY

£££–£££££   ⌧ **42 The Calls.** This high-tech, high-concept hotel in the trendy waterfront area was once a grain mill. Each room shows creative flair but retains such original elements as exposed beams and atmospheric brickwork. The amenities are up-to-the-minute, including in-room CD players: some rooms even come with fishing rods (bring your own bait). **Pros:** laid-back vibe; luxurious rooms; clever use of space. **Cons:** some find it too trendy; rather pricey. ⊠*42 The Calls* ☎*0113/244–0099* ⊕*www.42thecalls.co.uk* ⟿*41 rooms* ♿*In-room: no a/c, refrigerator, Internet. In-hotel: restaurant, room service, bar, some pets allowed, no-smoking rooms* ⊟*AE, DC, MC, V.*

£££   ⌧ **Malmaison.** Passengers who used this building as a tram and bus ter-
★ minal could hardly have envisioned its rebirth as a chic hotel exuding contemporary class and comfort. Guest rooms have color themes of subtle tones—plum, charcoal, and ocher—and are beautifully outfitted with velvet pillows and floor-to-ceiling windows. The dark-panel brasserie concentrates on French food with a Mediterranean twist. **Pros:** beautiful design; spacious rooms; comfortable beds. **Cons:** restaurant is often booked up; overly trendy. ⊠*1 Swinegate* ☎*0113/398–1000* ⊕*www.malmaison.com* ⟿*100 rooms* ♿*In-room: Internet. In-hotel: restaurant, bar, gym, spa, laundry service* ⊟*AE, DC, MC, V.*

£££   ⌧ **Quebecs.** The grand Leeds and County Liberal Club may have changed its identity when it became a boutique hotel, but the building has lost none of its Victorian verve. The sweeping oak staircase, lighted by tall stained-glass windows, leads up to classy bedrooms of different shapes and sizes, all sympathetically decorated in muted colors. The paneled Oak Room, an unusual circular design, is a must for a drink. Lower weekend rates include breakfast. **Pros:** gorgeous building; spacious rooms; great bar. **Cons:** a bit too formal; some rooms are better than others. ⊠*9 Quebec St.* ☎*0113/244–8989* ⊕*www.theetoncollection.com* ⟿*45 rooms, 6 suites* ♿*In-room: safe, refrigerator, Internet. In-hotel: restaurant, room service, bar* ⊟*AE, DC, MC, V.*

NIGHTLIFE AND THE ARTS

NIGHTLIFE

At fashionable café-bars all over Leeds, you can grab a bite or sip cappuccino or designer beer until late into the night. There's no shortage of clubs, either; Leeds has one of the best party scenes outside London. The **Atrium** (⊠*6–9 The Grand Arcade* ☎*0113/242–6116*) is the place for deep soul and funk. **Bar Norman** (⊠*36 Call La.* ☎*0113/234–3988*) has won the local in-crowd with its weird and wonderful design, including curved walls. Japanese food and music are other draws. **Cuban Heels** (⊠*The Arches, 28–30 Assembly St.* ☎*0113/234–6115*) kicks out salsa sounds most nights. **Mojo** (⊠*18 Merrion St.* ☎*0113/244–6387*) is a real rock-and-roll bar, with the music and the look to match.

THE ARTS

Opera North, a leading provincial opera company, has its home in Leeds at the **Grand Theatre** (✉ *46 New Briggate* ☎ *0113/222–6222*); the opulent auditorium is modeled on that of La Scala. Opera North also plays for free each summer at Temple Newsam.

The Victorian **Town Hall** (✉ *The Headrow* ☎ *0113/224–3801*) hosts an international concert season (October through May) that attracts top performers and conductors. In September it is the site of the fourth and final stage of the prestigious Leeds International Piano Competition.

The ultramodern **West Yorkshire Playhouse** (✉ *Playhouse Sq., Quarry Hill* ☎ *0113/213–7700*) was built on the slope of an old quarry. Its adaptable staging makes it eminently suitable for new and classic productions.

SHOPPING

★ For funky and cheap ethnic clothes, handmade gifts, artisan jewelry, and accessories, visit the shops inside the old, circular **Corn Exchange** (✉ *Call La.* ☎ *0113/234–0363*). The city has some excellent markets, notably **Kirkgate Market** (✉ *34 George St.* ☎ *0113/214–5162* ⊗ *Closed Wed. morning and Sun.*), an Edwardian beauty that's the largest in the north of England. Specialty stores and designer boutiques fill the Victorian shopping arcades; the glistening **Victoria Quarter** (✉ *Briggate* ☎ *0113/245–5333*), with its 70 stores, epitomizes fin-de-siècle style and 21st-century chic.

SALTAIRE

12 mi east of Leeds, 8 mi east of Haworth.

GETTING HERE AND AROUND

Saltaire is 4 mi north of Bradford, an old wool-market town. There are regular bus and train services to Saltaire from Bradford. Drivers should take A650 to Shipley and follow the signs.

ESSENTIALS

Visitor Information **Saltaire Tourist Information Center** (✉ *2 Victoria Rd., Saltaire* ☎ *01274/774993* ⊕ *www.saltaire-village.co.uk*).

EXPLORING

★ A UNESCO World Heritage Site, the former model town of **Saltaire** was built in the mid-19th century by textile magnate Sir Titus Salt, who was trying to create the ideal industrial world. When he decided to relocate his factories from the dark mills of Bradford to the countryside, he hoped to create a beautiful environment in which his workers would be happy. Fashioned in Italianate style, the town is remarkably well preserved, its former mills and houses now turned into shops, restaurants, and galleries. Salt's Mill, built in 1853, resembles a palazzo and was the largest factory in the world when it was built. Today it holds an art gallery and crafts and furniture shops. One-hour guided tours (£3) depart every Saturday at 2 PM and Sunday at 11 AM and 2 PM from the **tourist information center** (✉ *2 Victoria Rd., Saltaire* ☎ *01274/774993* ⊕ *www.saltaire-village.co.uk*). The **1853 Gallery** (✉ *Salt's Mill, Victoria Rd.* ☎ *01274/531163* ⊠ *Free* ⊗ *Daily 10–6*) holds a remarkable exhibition of 400 works by Bradford-born artist David Hockney. There are two restaurants on-site.

OFF THE BEATEN PATH

Most people come to Bradford, 10 mi west of Leeds, for the museums, particularly the renowned **National Media Museum,** which traces the history of photographic media. It's a huge and hugely entertaining place, with interactive models, machines, and related ephemera spread out over five galleries, encompassing the world's first negative, up-to-the-minute digital imaging, and all stages between. ■ TIP➔ The museum's popularity with children means you should come early or late in the day if you want to see the displays in peace. ⊠ *Pictureville, Prince's Way* ☎ *01274/202030 or 0870/701-0200* ⊕ *www.nationalmediamuseum. org.uk* ⊠ *Free* ⊗ *Tues.–Sun. and bank holidays 10–6.*

13

HAWORTH: HEART OF BRONTË COUNTRY

★ *8 mi west of Saltaire, 10 mi northwest of Bradford, 4 mi southwest of Keighley.*

Whatever Haworth might have been in the past, today it is Brontë country. This old stone-built village on the edge of the Yorkshire Moors long ago gave up its own personality and allowed itself to be taken over by the doomed sisters, their mournful books, and their millions of fans. In 1820, when Anne, Emily, and Charlotte were very young, their father moved them and their other three siblings away from their old home in Bradford to Haworth. The sisters—Emily (author of *Wuthering Heights,* 1847), Charlotte (*Jane Eyre,* 1847), and Anne (*The Tenant of Wildfell Hall,* 1848) were all affected by the stark, dramatic countryside. These days it seems that every building they ever glanced at has been turned into a memorial, shop, or museum.

GETTING HERE AND AROUND

To reach Haworth by bus or train, buy a Metro Day Rover for bus and rail and take the Metro train from Leeds train station to Keighley. There are about three hourly. From Keighley, take the Keighley & Worth Valley Railway for the trip to Haworth (weekends only; £7 round-trip), or Keighley and District Bus 663, 664, or 665 (Monday–Saturday, every 20 minutes; Sunday, every half hour). From Bradford station, Interchange buses run every half hour to Keighley.

The Haworth Visitor Center has information about accommodations, maps, books on the Brontës, and inexpensive leaflets to help you find your way to such outlying *Wuthering Heights* sites as Ponden Hall (Thrushcross Grange) and Ponden Kirk (Penistone Crag).

ESSENTIALS

Visitor Information Haworth Visitor Center (⊠ *2–4 West La.* ☎ *01535/ 642329*).

EXPLORING

Haworth's steep, cobbled **Main Street** has changed little in outward appearance since the early 19th century, but today acts as a funnel for the people who crowd into the points of interest: the **Black Bull** pub, where the reprobate Branwell, the Brontës' only brother, drank himself into an early grave; the **post office** from which Charlotte, Emily, and Anne sent their manuscripts to their London publishers; and the **church,** with its gloomy graveyard (Charlotte and Emily are buried inside the church; Anne is buried in Scarborough).

The best of the Brontë sights in Haworth is the **Brontë Parsonage Museum.** In the somber Georgian house in which the sisters grew up, it displays original furniture (some bought by Charlotte after the success of *Jane Eyre*), portraits, and books. The Brontës moved to this simple house when the Reverend Patrick Brontë was appointed to the local church, but tragedy soon struck—his wife, Maria, and their two eldest children died within five years. They

were done in, along with hundreds of others, by water wells tainted by seepage from the neighboring graveyard. The museum explains the family's tragic life story and makes it real with a strong collection of enchanting mementos of the four children, including tiny books they made when they were still very young, Charlotte's wedding bonnet and the sisters' spidery, youthful graffiti on the nursery wall. Branwell painted several of the portraits on display. ⊠*Church St.* ☎*01535/642323* ⊕*www. bronte.info* ⊠*£6* ☉*Apr.–Sept., daily 10–5:30; Oct.–Mar., daily 11–5; last admission 30 mins before closing.*

If you have the time, you can pack a lunch and walk an hour or so along a field path, a lane, and a moorland track to the lovely, isolated waterfall that has, inevitably, been renamed the **Brontë Waterfall.** It was a favorite of the sisters, who wrote about it in poems and letters.

Top Withins, a ruined, gloomy house on a bleak hilltop farm 3 mi from Haworth, is often taken to be the inspiration for Heathcliff's gloomy mansion, Wuthering Heights. Brontë scholars say it probably isn't; the ruins never looked the way the book describes them. Still, it's an inspirational walk across the moors. There and back from Haworth is a two-hour walk. ∎TIP➔ If you've read *Wuthering Heights*, you don't need to be reminded to wear sturdy shoes and protective clothing.

☺ Haworth is on the **Keighley & Worth Valley Railway,** a gorgeous 5-mi-long branch line along which steam engines run between Keighley (4 mi northeast of Haworth) and Oxenhope. On special days, family fairs en route add to the fun. The **Museum of Rail Travel** (⊠*£2* ☉*Daily 11–4*), at Ingrow along the line, exhibits vintage train cars. ⊠*Railway Station, Keighley* ☎*01535/645214, 01535/647777 for 24-hr information* ⊕*www.kwvr.co.uk* ⊠*£9 round-trip, £12 Day Rover ticket* ☉*Sept.– June, weekends; July and Aug., daily; call for schedules.*

WHERE TO EAT AND STAY

£££ ✕**Weavers.** Although Weavers is known primarily as a restaurant,
BRITISH upstairs there are a few chintz-filled rooms with antique French beds. The restaurant serves traditional, organic Yorkshire fare like smoked haddock soup and duck in brandy sauce, served with home-baked bread. ⊠*15 West La.* ☎*01535/643822* ▭*AE, DC, MC, V* ⊗*Closed Mon. No dinner Sun.*

£ 🏠**Aitches.** This intimate 19th-century stone house is close to the Brontë Parsonage. The guest rooms are modern, with pine pieces and colorful quilts and drapes. A fixed-price meal in the elegant small restaurant, open to nonguests on weekends only, might include pork cutlet with Stilton crumble followed by a bread-and-butter pudding. **Pros:** intimate building; friendly staff; great restaurant. **Cons:** the rustic decor won't appeal to everyone. ⊠*11 West La.* ☎*01535/642501* ⊕*www.aitches. co.uk* ⌖*5 rooms* ⌂*In-room: no a/c, no phone. In-hotel: restaurant, no-smoking rooms* ▭*MC, V* ⊙*BP.*

££–£££ 🏠**Ashmount Country House.** This charming stone building at the top of the hill was once home to the Brontë sisters' physician, Dr. Amos Ingham. Today it's a peaceful hideaway a short walk from the Parsonage and surrounded by gardens with sweeping views over the valley. Spacious and sunny rooms are cheerfully decorated with fluffy floral comforters. Some have four-posters, others have whirlpool tubs. The owners are friendly and helpful, the atmosphere is relaxed, and breakfasts are delicious. **Pros:** lovely old building; ideal location; great views. **Cons:** books up in advance; it's one of the priciest places in town. ⊠*Mytholmes La.* ☎*01535/646726* ⊕*www.ashmounthaworth.co.uk* ⌖*8 rooms* ⌂*In-room: no a/c, no phone, Wi-Fi. In-hotel: no-smoking rooms* ▭*MC, V* ⊙*BP.*

THE YORKSHIRE DALES

The western equivalent of the North York Moors, the Yorkshire Dales are just as beautiful and nearly as wild. The word dale comes from the Viking word for valley, which gives you an indication that, although the moors have steep hills, the dales are more rugged, with sharper, higher hills culminating in the mountains Pen-y-ghent, Ingleborough, and Whernside. These river valleys fall south and east from the Pennines, and beyond Skipton they present an almost wholly rural aspect. Ruined priories, narrow roads, drystone walls made without mortar, and babbling rivers make for a quintessentially English landscape, full of paths and trails to explore.

BOLTON ABBEY

12 mi north of Haworth, 24 mi northwest of Leeds.

A leafy, picturesque village amid the rolling hills of the Yorkshire Dales, Bolton Abbey is a famously attractive town with a stone church and evocative priory ruins. Much of the area is still technically owned by the duke of Devonshire, who has a huge estate nearby—a lingering remnant of the country's feudal past.

EXPLORING

★ Some of the loveliest Wharfedale scenery comes into view around **Bolton Priory,** the ruins of an Augustinian priory, which sits on a grassy embankment inside a great curve of the River Wharfe. The priory is just a short walk or drive from the village of Bolton Abbey. You can wander through the 13th-century ruins or visit the priory church, which is still the local parish church. The duke of Devonshire owns the Bolton Abbey estate, including the ruins. John Ruskin, the Victorian art critic, rated it the most beautiful of all English ruins.Close to Bolton Priory, surrounded by romantic woodland scenery, the River Wharfe plunges between a narrow chasm in the rocks (called the Strid) before reaching **Barden Tower,** a medieval hunting lodge. This lodge is now a ruin and can be visited just as easily as Bolton Priory, in whose grounds it stands. ⊠*B6160, off A59* ☎*01756/718009* ⊕*www.boltonabbey.com* ✉*Free, parking £6* ☉*Daily 9–dusk.*

You can ride the scenic 4-mi **Embsay & Bolton Abbey Steam Railway** (☎*01756/710614, 01756/795189 recorded timetable*), which has a station in Bolton Abbey.

WHERE TO STAY

££££   ⓘ **Devonshire Arms.** Originally an 18th-century coaching inn, and still belonging to the dukes of Devonshire, this luxurious country-house hotel is near the River Wharfe, an easy walk from Bolton Abbey. The bedrooms are tastefully decorated with antiques and family memorabilia from the family home, Chatsworth House in Derbyshire. The Burlington restaurant has a fixed-price menu (£55) of superb traditional fare that uses game and fish from the estate. The brasserie serves modestly priced fare. **Pros:** one of the region's best hotels; real manor-house style. **Cons:** you pay for all that charm. ⊠*Bolton Abbey, Skipton* ☎*01756/710441, 01756/718111 reservation line* ⊕*www. thedevonshirearms.co.uk* ⬐*37 rooms, 3 suites* ⬧*In-room: no a/c, Internet. In-hotel: 2 restaurants, bars, tennis court, pool, gym, some pets allowed* ▤*AE, DC, MC, V* ⦿*BP.*

SKIPTON

6 mi west of Bolton Abbey, 12 mi north of Haworth, 22 mi west of Harrogate.

Skipton in Airedale, capital of the limestone district of Craven, is a typical Dales market town with as many farmers as visitors milling in the streets. There are markets Monday, Wednesday, Friday, and Saturday, and shops selling local produce predominate.

ESSENTIALS

Visitor Information Skipton (⊠*35 Coach St.* ☎*01756/792809* ⊕*www. skiptononline.co.uk*).

EXPLORING

★ **Skipton Castle,** built by the Normans in 1090 and unaltered since the 17th century, is one of the best-preserved of English medieval castles. After the Battle of Marston Moor during the Civil War, it remained the only Royalist stronghold in the north of England. So sturdy was the squat little fortification with its rounded battlements (in places the walls are 12 feet thick) that Oliver Cromwell ordered that the roof be removed, as it had survived one bombardment after another during a three-year siege. When the castle's owner, Lady Anne Clifford, later asked if she could replace the roof, he allowed her do so, as long as it was not strong enough to withstand cannon fire. Today the buildings are marvelously complete, and in the central courtyard a yew tree, planted more than 300 years ago by Lady Anne herself, flourishes. ⊠*High St.* ☎*01756/792442* ⊕*www.skiptoncastle.co.uk* ▨*£6* ☻*Mar.–Sept., Mon.–Sat. 10–6, Sun. noon–6; Oct.–Feb., Mon.–Sat. 10–4, Sun. noon–4.*

WHERE TO EAT

£££ ✕**Angel Inn.** Diners at the Angel clog the hidden-away hamlet of Hetton
BRITISH with their vehicles, such is the attraction of this place with its casual brasserie and more formal restaurant. Roasted lamb and duck are specialties in the restaurant. The ancient stone barn across the road has well-equipped guest rooms in unfussy country styles, from rustic to French, as do a scattering of adorable cottages. The inn is 5 mi north of Skipton. ⊠*Off B6265, Hetton* ☎*01756/730263* ▭*AE, DC, MC, V.*

GRASSINGTON

10 mi north of Skipton, 14 mi northwest of Ilkley, 25 mi west of Ripon.

A small, stone village built around an ancient cobbled marketplace, Grassington makes a good base for exploring Upper Wharfedale. The Dales Way footpath passes through the village, and there's a mix of guesthouses, stores, pubs, and cafés. In summer it becomes overwhelmed by day-trippers and walkers. There are plenty of local walks, however, and if you're prepared to make a day of it, you can soon leave the crowds behind.

EXPLORING

The **National Park Centre** has guidebooks, maps, and bus schedules to help you enjoy a day in the Yorkshire Dales National Park. ⊠*Colvend, Hebdon Rd.* ☎*01756/752774* ⊕*www.yorkshiredales.org.uk* ☻*Apr.– Oct., daily 10–5; Nov.–Mar., Wed. and Fri.–Sun. 10–4.*

WHERE TO EAT AND STAY

££ ✕**Devonshire Hotel.** This traditional inn makes a comfortable rural dining
BRITISH spot, with its oak-paneled dining room aglow with flickering candles. Local lamb, beef, and dishes such as fish hot pot (stew with vegetables) and gammon (cured ham) steak appear on the menu alongside stir-fries and curries. ⊠*Main St.* ☎*01756/752525* ▭*MC, V.*

££ 🏠**Grassington Lodge.** Light and airy, this Victorian house has made the most of its original features with tasteful and uncluttered decoration. Bedrooms have been refurbished, with a modern touch. A roaring log fire in the sitting room takes the edge off cold days. **Pros:** lovely building; spacious rooms. **Cons:** can feel a bit crowded; not a lot of amenities. ⊠*8 Wood La.* ☎*01756/752518* ⊕*www.grassingtonlodge.co.uk* ☞*9 rooms* ⚭*In-room: no a/c, no phone, refrigerator, Wi-Fi. In-hotel:*

13

HIKING IN MALHAM

Avid summer hikers descend in droves on Malham to tour the remarkable limestone formations Malham Cove and Gordale Scar, and Malham Tarn. The three sites are on a circular walk of 8 mi that takes most people four to five hours. Those with less time should cut out the tarn (a small lake): a circular walk from the village to the limestone formations Malham Cove and Gordale Scar can be completed in just over two hours.

Malham's **National Park Centre** (☎01729/830363 ⊕www.yorkshiredales.org.uk ⊙Apr.–Oct., daily 10–5; Nov.–Mar., Fri.–Sun. 10–4) has displays and will give you ideas of what to do locally and in Yorkshire Dales National Park. You can get a list of bed-and-breakfast and pub accommodations, too.

Malham Cove, a huge, 300-foot-high natural rock amphitheater, is a mile north of the village and provides the easiest local walk. Following the path *up* to the top is a brutal climb, though rewarded by magnificent views.

At **Gordale Scar,** a deep natural chasm between overhanging limestone cliffs, the white waters of a moorland stream plunge 300 feet. It's a mile northeast of Malham by a lovely riverside path.

A walk of more than 3 mi leads north from Malham to **Malham Tarn,** an attractive lake in windswept isolation. There's a nature reserve on the west bank and an easy-to-follow trail on the east bank. Malham is 10 mi west of Grassington: take B6265 south 2 mi through Cracoe, then branch west onto the minor road past Hetton and Calton. Malham is also 12 mi northwest of Skipton, off A65.

no kids under 12, no-smoking rooms ▤*No credit cards* ⊙*Call ahead in winter* ⎪◎⎪*BP.*

HAWES

28 mi north of Grassington.

The best time to visit the so-called cheesiest town in Yorkshire is on Tuesday, when farmers crowd into town for the weekly market. Hawes is the business center for Wensleydale's traditional cheese making. Crumbly, white Wensleydale cheese has been made in the valley for centuries, and it is sold in local stores and at the market. Allow yourself time to wander the cobbled side streets, some of which are filled with antiques shops and tearooms.

EXPLORING

The **Wensleydale Creamery Visitor Centre,** in a working dairy farm, includes a museum that tells the story of the famed local cheese so beloved by the cartoon characters Wallace and Gromit. You can watch production (best seen between 10 and 2) from the viewing gallery, and then taste the output in the shop. A restaurant on-site has plenty of cheese samples as well, such as smoked, with ginger, or with apple pie. ✉*Gayle La.* ☎*01969/667664* ⊕*www.wensleydale.co.uk* ▱*Museum*

£2.50 ⊙ *Apr.–Oct., daily 9–5:30; Nov.–Mar., daily 9:30–4:30.*

The Yorkshire Dales National Park Information Centre in the old train station contains the **Dales Country-side Museum,** which gives a picture of Dales life in past centuries. A traditional rope-making shop here also welcomes visitors. ⊠*Station Yard* 🕾*01969/667450* ⊕*www. yorkshiredales.org.uk* ⊠*Museum £3* ⊙*Daily 10–5.*

13

RICHMOND

22 mi northeast of Hawes, 25 mi northwest of Ripon.

Richmond tucks itself into a curve above the foaming River Swale, with a network of narrow Georgian streets and terraces opening onto a large cobbled marketplace. Despite appearances, it would be a mistake to date the town to the 18th century. The Normans swept in during the late 11th century, determined to subdue the local population and establish their rule in the north. This they did by building a mighty castle, around which the town grew, and throughout the Middle Ages Richmond was effectively a garrison town.

GETTING HERE AND AROUND

Trains run to Richmond from Darlington every 30 minutes or so; the journey takes half an hour. There is no direct train service to Richmond from London. By car, Richmond is on the rural B6274—follow signs off A1.

ESSENTIALS

Visitor Information Richmond (⊠*Friary Gardens, Victoria Rd.* 🕾*01748/ 850252* ⊕*www.yorkshiredales.org*).

EXPLORING

The immense keep of Norman **Richmond Castle** towers above the river, providing excellent views of the countryside. Built around 1071 by Alan Rufus, first earl of Richmond, it was used as a prison for William "the Lion" of Scotland 100 years later. The castle is a well-preserved monument of this era, retaining its thick curtain wall and chapel, and a great hall that has been restored to its medieval splendor; even the 14th-century graffiti remains. There's a heritage garden, and a path along the river leads to the ruins of golden-stone Easby Abbey. One historical note: when Henry Tudor (son of Edmund Tudor, earl of Richmond) became Henry VII in 1485, he began calling his palace in southwest London by the name Richmond after his family seat in Richmond. The name gradually came to be used to describe that area of London. 🕾*01748/822493* ⊕*www.english-heritage.org.uk* ⊠*£3.90* ⊙*Apr.– Sept., daily 10–6; Oct.–Mar., Thurs.–Mon. 10–4.*

The tiny Georgian **Theatre Royal,** a jewel box built in 1788, retains original features such as the wooden seating from the days of the

18th-century Shakespearean actor David Garrick. The museum holds scenery dating from 1836. There are tours of the theater every weekday between 10 and 4. ⊠ *Victoria Rd.* ☎ *01748/823710, 01748/825252 box office* ⊕ *www.georgiantheatreroyal.co.uk* 🖼 *Museum £2.50 suggested donation* ☉ *Museum mid-Feb.–Dec., Mon.–Sat. 10–4:30.*

WHERE TO EAT AND STAY

££

MEDITERRANEAN

✕**Frenchgate Café.** Blue wicker chairs and yellow walls capture a bit of the bright Mediterranean at this little bistro just below the main cobbled square. Try one of the pastas, such as penne with smoked salmon and prawns. Cappuccino, scones, and sandwiches are available. ⊠ *29 Frenchgate* ☎ *01748/824949* ⊟ *AE, MC, V* ☉ *Closed Mon.*

££

🏨 **Frenchgate Hotel.** This three-story Georgian town house on a quiet cobbled street has a secluded walled garden for summer days. The bright and welcoming interior is furnished with some flair. Public rooms hark back to the 17th century, but the decorative mice (symbol of local craftsman Mousey Thompson) hidden in the woodwork are more recent. Works by area artists fill the hotel, and the spacious bedrooms are subtly decorated in soothing cream and taupe. Some bathrooms have deep, roll-top baths. The in-house restaurant creates tasty French fare. **Pros:** lovely gardens; quiet neighborhood. **Cons:** restaurant can be a bit noisy; not a lot of amenities. ⊠ *59–61 Frenchgate* ☎ *01748/822087* ⊕ *www.thefrenchgate.co.uk* 🛏 *11 rooms* ⚿ *In-room: no a/c. In-hotel: restaurant, bar* ⊟ *MC, V* ⦿ *BP.*

££–£££

🏨 **Millgate House.** This 18th-century house in the center of Richmond has been beautifully restored, as you'll note from the elegant dining room and lounge. The bedrooms are spacious havens in creams and whites. All have views of the town or the extraordinary gardens, which have won Royal Horticultural Society awards. Big claw-foot tubs lure you into the bathrooms—some of which have their own fireplaces. Breakfasts here win raves for their variety and freshness. In addition to the five rooms, there are two self-catering apartments. **Pros:** fantastic location in the middle of town; grand historic house. **Cons:** rooms can be a bit chilly. ⊠ *Millgate* ☎ *01748/823571* ⊕ *www.millgatehouse. com* 🛏 *5 rooms* ⚿ *In-room: no a/c, no phone, kitchen (some)* ⊟ *MC, V* ⦿ *BP.*

YORK

48 mi southeast of Richmond, 25 mi northeast of Leeds, 82 mi south of Newcastle.

It would be unthinkable to visit North Yorkshire without first visiting the historic cathedral city of York, and not just because of its central location. Much of the city's medieval and 18th-century architecture has survived, making this city a delight to explore. ■ **TIP**➡ **The city is one of the most popular short-stay destinations in Britain, and only two hours by train from London's King's Cross Station.**

Named "Eboracum" by the Romans, York was the military capital of Roman Britain, and traces of garrison buildings survive throughout the city. After the Roman Empire collapsed in the 5th century, the Saxons built "Eoforwic" upon the ruins of a fort, but were soon defeated by Vikings who called the town Jorvik and used it as a base from which to subjugate the countryside. The Normans came in the 11th century and emulated the Vikings by using the town as a military base. It was during Norman times that the foundations of York Minster, the largest medieval cathedral in England, were laid. The only changes the 19th century brought were large houses, built mostly on the outskirts of the city center.

GETTING HERE AND AROUND

If you're driving, take the M1 north from London. Stay on it to Leeds, and then take the A64 to York. The journey should take around three hours. National Express and Megabus have motor coaches traveling from London's Victoria Coach Station every hour. The journey takes 4½ hours. National Express trains run from London's King's Cross Station about every 30 minutes during the week. The trip takes about two hours. York Station, just outside the city walls, has a line of taxis out front to take you to your hotel. If you don't have bags, the walk to town takes eight minutes.

York's city center is mostly closed to traffic and is very walkable. The old center is a compact, dense web of narrow streets and tiny medieval alleys called "snickleways." These provide shortcuts across the city center, but they're not on maps, so you never quite know where you'll end up, which in York is more often a pleasant surprise.

TOURS City Sightseeing runs frequent bus tours of York that stop at the Castle Museum, the Shambles, and Jorvik. You can get on and off as often as you please. York Association of Voluntary Guides arranges short walking tours around the city, which depart daily at 10:15. There are additional tours at 2:15 April through October and at 6:45 July and August. The tours are free, but tips are appreciated. Yorktour can arrange city tours.

TIMING

In July and August tourists choke the narrow streets and form long lines at the Minster. April, May, June, and September are less crowded, but the weather can be unpredictable. April is also the time to see the embankments beneath the city walls filled with the pale gold ripple of daffodils.

ESSENTIALS

Tour Information City Sightseeing (☎ 01904/655585 ⊕ www.citysightseeing. co.uk). **York Association of Voluntary Guides** (✉ De Grey Rooms, Exhibition Sq. ☎ 01904/640780). **Yorktour** (☎ 01423/321240 ⊕ www.eddiebrowntours.com).

SAVING MONEY IN YORK

The **York Pass** (☎ 0870/242–9988 or 01904/621756 ⊕ www.yorkpass.com) offers unlimited free admission to more than 30 attractions in or near the city, including Castle Howard. You also get free transportation on City Sightseeing buses and discounts at restaurants and theaters. Adult passes cost £28 (one day), £36 (two days), and £42 (three days), and can be purchased online, by phone, or at the York Tourist Information Centre.

13

Visitor Information York (⊠ *De Grey Rooms, Exhibition Sq.* ☎ *01904/550099* ⊕ *www.visityork.org* ⊠ *York Train Station* ☎ *01904/621756)*

EXPLORING

TOP ATTRACTIONS

❶ City walls. York's almost 3 mi of ancient stone walls are among the best-preserved in England. A walk on the narrow paved path along the top leads you through 1,900 years of history, from the time the earthen ramparts were raised by the Romans and York's Viking kings to repel raiders, to their fortification by the Normans, to their current colorful landscaping by the city council. The walls are crossed periodically by York's distinctive fortified gates or "bars": the portcullis on Monk's Bar on Goodramgate is still in working order, and Walmgate Bar in the east is the only gate in England with an intact barbican. It also has scars from the cannon balls hurled at it during the Civil War. Bootham Bar in Exhibition Square was the defensive bastion for the north road, and Micklegate Bar, in the city's southwest corner, was traditionally the monarch's entrance. For a small fee you can explore all of these gates. To access the path and the lookout towers, find a staircase at one of the many breaks in the walls. *Free* ☉ *Daily 8* AM–*dusk.*

❾ Dig. This venture from the people behind the Jorvik Viking Centre is a great way to get young people inspired about history and archaeology. It's an ongoing archaeological dig in and beneath an old church; kids, supervised by knowledgeable experts, help with the work. After your dig, record your findings and head to the lab to learn what archaeological finds discovered on the site reveal about how people lived in the past. It's an educational, fun, fascinating way to spend a couple of hours. ⊠ *St. Saviour's Church, St. Saviourgate* ☎ *01904/543403* ⊕ *www.vikingjorvik.com* *£5.50; joint admission to Jorvik Viking Centre £11* ☉ *Apr.–Oct., daily 10–5; Nov.–Mar., daily 10–4.*

❻ Guildhall. The mid-15th-century guildhall, by the River Ouse, was a meeting place for the city's powerful guilds. It was also used for mystery plays (medieval dramas based on biblical stories and the lives of saints). Restoration after World War II bombing damage has given it something of its erstwhile glory. The guildhall is behind the 18th-century Mansion House; you can visit it when no function is in progress. ⊠ *St. Helen's Sq.* ☎ *01904/613161* *Free* ☉ *May–Oct., weekdays 9–5, Sat. 10–5, Sun. 2–5; Nov.–Apr., weekdays 9–5.*

❿ Jorvik Viking Centre. This exhibition re-creates a 10th-century Viking village. A mixture of museum and carnival ride, it requires you to "travel through time." You climb into a Disney-esque machine that propels you above straw huts and mannequins in Viking garb. Commentary is provided in 10 languages (click on the British flag to hear it in English). Kids will get a lot out of it, but adults are unlikely to learn anything new. A small collection of Viking-era artifacts is on display at the end of the ride. ⊠ *Coppergate* ☎ *01904/643211, 01904/543403 advance booking* ⊕ *www.vikingjorvik.com* *£8.50; joint admission to Dig £11* ☉ *Apr.–Oct., daily 10–5; Nov.–Mar., daily 10–4.*

13

York

200 yards
200 meters

Train Station

Bus Station

KEY

🛈 *Tourist information*

7 **National Railway Museum.** For train-lovers one and all: here Britain's national collection of locomotives forms part of a massive train museum. Among the exhibits are gleaming giants of the steam era, including the *Mallard,* holder of the world speed record for a steam engine (126 mph). Passenger cars used by Queen Victoria are on display, as well as the only Japanese bullet train to be seen outside Japan. You can clamber aboard the trains, some of which are started up regularly to keep the engines working. ✉*Leeman Rd.* ☎*01904/621261, 01904/686286 information line* ⊕*www.nrm.org.uk* 🎫*Museum free* ☉*Daily 10–6.*

> ### WHERE ARE THE GATES?
>
> The Viking conquerors of northern England held the region for more than a century and made York their capital. Gate was the Viking word for "street," hence the street names such as Goodramgate and Micklegate. Adding to the confusion, the city's entrances, or gates, are called "bars," from an Old English term. As local tour guides like to say, "In York, our streets are called gates, our gates are called bars, and our bars are called pubs."

8 **The Shambles.** York's best-preserved medieval street has half-timber stores and houses with overhangs so massive you could almost reach across the street from one second-floor window to another. Once the city's street of butchers (meat hooks are still fastened outside some of the doors), today it's filled with touristy shops of scant interest to most visitors. Still, it's beautiful to walk down for the atmosphere.

5 **Stonegate.** This narrow, pedestrian-only street of Tudor and 18th-century storefronts and courtyards retains considerable charm. It has been in daily use for almost 2,000 years, since first being paved in Roman times. Today it's lined with jewelry stores, knickknack shops, tea shops, and ancient pubs. A passage just off Stonegate, at 52A, leads to the remnants of a 12th-century Norman stone house attached to a more recent structure. You can see the old Norman wall and window. Look out for the little red devil high up on a doorpost. ■ TIP→ **Keep an eye out throughout the area for similar tiny statues that once acted as signs for businesses.** The devil announced a printer's shop. There's another statue at the intersection of Stonegate and High Petergate, where Minerva lounges on a stack of books. She once advertised a bookseller.

NEED A BREAK?   At the opposite end of Stonegate from the Minster, Betty's (✉*6–8 Helen's Sq., off Stonegate* ☎*01904/659142*) has been a York institution since 1912. This tea-and-cakes salon in an attractive art nouveau building is more beloved for its history and ambience than for its so-so food. Still, it's a piece of history, and a good place to take a rest. There's always a line out front, so expect a short wait for a table.

2 **York Minster.** Focal point of the city, this vast cathedral is the largest Gothic church in England and attracts almost as many visitors as London's Westminster Abbey. Inside, the effect created by its soaring pillars and lofty vaulted ceilings is almost overpowering. Come with binoculars if you wish to study the dazzling 128 stained-glass windows. Glowing

Fodor's Choice ★

with deep wine reds and cobalt blues, they are bested only by those in Chartres Cathedral in France. Mere statistics cannot convey the scale of the building; however, the central towers are 184 feet high, and the church is 534 feet long, 249 feet across its transepts, and 90 feet from floor to roof. Contributing to the cold, crushing splendor are the ornamentation of the 14th-century nave; the east window, one of the greatest pieces of medieval glazing in the world; the north transept's **Five Sisters** windows, five tall lancets of frosted 13th-century glass; the enormous choir screen portraying somewhat whimsical images of every king of England from William the Conqueror to Henry VI; and the imposing tracery of the **Rose Window,** commemorating the marriage of Henry VII and Elizabeth of York in 1486 (the event that ended the Wars of the Roses and began the Tudor dynasty). Don't miss the exquisite 13th-century **Chapter House** and the **Undercroft, Treasury, and Crypt.** Finds during the latest renovation date back to Roman times, and include a Saxon child's coffin. After exploring the interior, you might take the 275 winding steps to the roof of the great **Central Tower** (strictly for those with a head for heights), not only for the close-up view of the cathedral's detailed carving but for a panorama of York and the surrounding moors. ■ TIP→ Attending Evensong here is a memorable experience. ⊠*Duncombe Pl.* ☎*01904/557216* ⊕*www. yorkminster.org* ⊠*Minster £6; Undercroft, Treasury, and Crypt £4; Minster, Undercroft, Treasury, and Crypt ticket £9.50; Central Tower £4* ⊘*Apr.–Oct., Mon.–Sat. 9–5, Sun. noon–3:45; Nov.–Mar., Mon.– Sat. 9:30–4:45, Sun. noon–3:45.*

WORTH NOTING

⑭ **Castle Museum.** A former 18th-century debtors' prison, this quirky museum of everyday items presents detailed exhibitions and re-creations, including a Victorian street complete with crafts shops and a working water mill, as well as notable domestic, costume, and arms and armor displays. One treasure is the Coppergate Helmet, a 1,200-year-old Anglo-Saxon helmet discovered during excavations of the city; it's one of only three such objects found. You can also visit the cell where Dick Turpin, the 18th-century highwayman and folk hero, spent the night before his execution. ⊠*Clifford St.* ☎*01904/687687* ⊕*www. yorkcastlemuseum.org.uk* ⊠*£7.50* ⊘*Daily 9:30–5.*

⑬ **Clifford's Tower.** Apart from the city walls, this rather battered-looking keep is all that remains of the old York castle. The stone tower, which sits on a grassy mound surrounded by a parking lot, dates from the mid-12th century. The Norman version that preceded it was infamously destroyed in 1190, when more than 150 Jews locked themselves inside with no food or water to protect themselves from a violent mob. In the end, they committed mass suicide by setting their own prison aflame. These days the tower's future is threatened, as the city is planning to approve the construction of a shopping center around it. ⊠*Tower St.* ☎*01904/646940* ⊕*www.cliffordstower.com* ⊠*£3* ⊘*Apr.–June and Sept., daily 10–6; July and Aug., daily 9:30–7; Oct.–Mar., daily 10–4.*

⑫ **Fairfax House.** This 1762 Georgian town house is a museum of decorative arts. The house is beautifully decorated with period furniture, crystal chandeliers, and silk wallpaper. ⊠*Castlegate* ☎*01904/655543*

⊕www.fairfaxhouse.co.uk 🎫*£6*
🕐*Mon.–Thurs. and Sat. 11–5,*
Sun. 1:30–5; last admission 4:30;
Fri., guided tours 11 and 2.

⑪ **Merchant Adventurers' Hall.** Built
between 1357 and 1368 by a
wealthy medieval guild, this is the
largest half-timber hall in York. Portraits, silver, and furniture are on display, and the house itself is much of
the attraction. A riverfront garden
lies behind the hall. On most Saturdays antiques fairs are held inside
the building. ⊠*Fossgate* 🕿*01904/*
654818 *⊕www.theyorkcompany.*
co.uk 🎫*£3* 🕐*Apr.–Sept., Mon.–*
Thurs. 9–5, Fri. and Sat. 9–3:30,
Sun. noon–4; Oct.–Mar., Mon.–Sat.
9–3:30; closed 1st wk in Dec.

❸ **Treasurer's House.** Surprises await
inside this large 17th-century house,
the home from 1897 to 1930 of
industrialist Frank Green. With a fine eye for texture, decoration, and
pattern, Green created period rooms—including a medieval great hall—
as a showcase for his collection of antique furniture. Delft tiles decorate
the kitchen, copies of medieval stenciling cover the vibrant Red Room,
and 17th-century stump work adorns the Tapestry Room. ⊠*Minster
Yard* 🕿*01904/624247* *⊕www.nationaltrust.org.uk* 🎫*House and
garden £5.35; £7 with cellar tour* 🕐*Apr.–Oct., Sat.–Thurs. 11–5; last
admission 30 mins before closing.*

❹ **Yorkshire Museum.** The natural and archaeological history of the county,
including material on the Roman, Anglo-Saxon, and Viking aspects of
York, is the focus of this museum. Also on display in the solid, Doric-
style building is the 15th-century Middleham Jewel, a pendant gleaming with a large sapphire. The museum lies just outside the walled city,
through Bootham Bar, one of York's old gates on the site of the medieval
St. Mary's Abbey. The museum is undergoing renovation, and will be
closed from the end of November 2009 until August 2010. ⊠*Museum
Gardens, Museum St.* 🕿*01904/551805* *⊕www.yorkshiremuseum.org.
uk* 🎫*£5* 🕐*Daily 10–5.*

> **A WALK IN YORK**
>
> York is a fine city for walk-
> ing, especially along the walls
> embracing the old center. Start at
> the Minster and head down the
> medieval lane, Stonegate, which
> is lined with shops and leads
> directly to Betty's tea shop. From
> there you can swing right to find
> antiques shops, or left for more
> modern shops, and eventually
> the shopping area known as the
> Shambles, and the remains of the
> old castle. At any point, climb the
> steps to the top of the city walls
> for perspective on where you are
> in town. The Ouse River, by the
> way, is more like an undeveloped
> canal, hidden away by buildings.

WHERE TO EAT

£££   ✕**Blue Bicycle.** One of York's best restaurants is in a building that once
BRITISH   served as a brothel. Downstairs are intimate walled booths, and at
★   street level is a lively room lighted with candles. The menu concentrates on local beef and seafood. You might start with crab cannelloni
on spinach salad, and move on to seared salmon or the fillet of Yorkshire beef on smoked-bacon mashed potatoes. The wine list is good,
and the service couldn't be friendlier. The restaurant has launched a

small guesthouse—a handful of luxury rooms in a mews nearby, called Blue Rooms. ✉*34 Fossgate* ☎*01904/673990* ⌕*Reservations essential* ☰*MC, V.*

££ ✕**Café Concerto.** Music is the theme at this relaxed, intimate bistro in
MODERN BRITISH sight of York Minster. The kitchen serves updated versions of British classics. You could have pork stuffed with carmelized onion, bacon, and rosemary in a brandy cream sauce, or chicken breast marinated in lemon, mint, and chili. ✉*21 High Petergate* ☎*01904/610478* ☰*No credit cards.*

£££ ✕**Melton's.** Once a private house, this unpretentious restaurant has
MODERN BRITISH local art on the walls, but you'll more likely be watching the open kitchen. The excellent seasonal menus are highly imaginative with modern English and European fare, such as venison with red wine and mulled pears, and roast partridge with mascarpone and grilled polenta. Melton's is a 10-minute walk from York Minster. ✉*7 Scarcroft Rd.* ☎*01904/634341* ⌕*Reservations essential* ☰*MC, V* ⊘*Closed 3 wks at Christmas, and 1 wk in Aug. No lunch Mon.; no dinner Sun.*

£ ✕**Spurriergate Centre.** Churches are not just for services, as this decon-
BRITISH secrated 15th-century house of worship proves. Resurrected as a cafeteria by a community organization, St. Michael's is a favorite spot for travelers and mothers with strollers to refuel spiritually as well as gastronomically. You may end up eating bean-and-cabbage hot pot on the spot where John Wesley prayed in 1768. Don't pass up the cream scones. ✉*Spurriergate* ☎*01904/629393* ⊘*Closed Sun. No dinner.*

WHERE TO STAY

£–££ ▦**Dairy Guest House.** Victorian stained glass, pine woodwork, and intricate plaster cornices are original features of this former dairy near the city walls. Bedrooms, done in pleasant pastels, come with books and games, and the imaginative breakfasts can accommodate vegetarians and vegans. The flower-filled internal courtyard is lovely. **Pros:** great breakfast; interesting building. **Cons:** a bit of a walk to the center; few amenities. ✉*3 Scarcroft Rd.* ☎*01904/639367* ⊕*www. dairyguesthouse.co.uk* ⏎*5 rooms* ⌂*In-room: no a/c, no phone. In-hotel: some pets allowed, no-smoking rooms* ☰*MC, V* ⟊*BP.*

£££–££££ ▦**Grange Hotel.** Built in the early 19th century as a home for high-
★ ranking clergy from York Minster, the Grange is now a luxury boutique hotel. The decor in the public rooms is reminiscent of a grand country home, and bedrooms are all open and airy. Look for lovely period details like fireplaces. **Pros:** spacious rooms; lovely decor. **Cons:** can feel a bit fussy. ✉*1 Clifton* ☎*01904/644744* ⊕*www.grangehotel.co.uk* ⏎*30 rooms* ⌂*In-room: no a/c, refrigerator, Wi-Fi. In-hotel: restaurant, bar, gym, parking (free), no-smoking rooms* ☰*AE, MC, V* ⟊*BP.*

££ ▦**The Hazelwood.** Close to York Minster, this tall Victorian town house stands in a peaceful cul-de-sac, away from the hustle and bustle. Reds and golds dominate bedrooms furnished with rich fabrics and handsome traditional wood pieces. The memorable breakfasts include black pudding, Danish pastries, and vegetarian sausages. **Pros:** quiet neighborhood; lovely building. **Cons:** not much privacy; few amenities. ✉*24–25 Portland St.* ☎*01904/626548* ⊕*www.thehazelwoodyork.com* ⏎*14*

13

rooms 🚫 In-room: no a/c, no phone. In-hotel: parking (free), no kids under 8, no-smoking rooms ⊟MC, V ⓄBP.

££££–£££££   🏠**Hotel Du Vin.** Oliver Twist would have been pleasantly surprised by what's become of this 19th-century orphanage. Converted into a swanky hotel, it still has the original brick walls and arched doorways, but now filling the rooms are leather furnishings, impressive pieces of art, and lots of flickering candles. Rooms are spacious and very quiet; some are on two levels, with the bathrooms upstairs. Most have claw-foot tubs and showers big enough for two. The in-house restaurant specializes in buttery French cuisine. Workers are helpful and jovial. There's a two-night minimum stay on weekends. **Pros:** makes great use of the space; jovial staff; comfortable beds. **Cons:** minimum stay on weekends. ⊠89 The Mount ☎01904/557350 ⊕www.hotelduvin.com ⟳44 rooms 🚫 In-room: safe, refrigerator, Internet. In-hotel: restaurant, room service, bar, parking (free) ⊟AE, DC, MC, V ⓄBP.

££££–£££££   🏠**Middlethorpe Hall & Spa.** This splendidly restored 18th-century man-
★   sion, about 1½ mi from the city center, was the sometime home of the traveler and diarist Lady Mary Wortley Montagu (1689–1762), and is now a part of the National Trust. Antiques, paintings, and fresh flow-ers fill the traditionally decorated rooms, some in cottage-style accom-modations around an 18th-century courtyard. The extensive grounds include a lake and a 17th-century dovecote. The British menu of the wood-paneled restaurant changes seasonally, but always has more than a hint of luxury—like the hotel itself. **Pros:** traditional splendor; gor-geous grounds. **Cons:** some rooms are getting a bit worn; has an old-fashioned approach. ⊠Bishopthorpe Rd. ☎01904/641241 ⊕www.middlethorpe.com ⟳23 rooms, 8 suites 🚫 In-room: no a/c, Internet. In-hotel: restaurant, bar, pool, gym, spa, laundry service, parking (free), no kids under 8, no-smoking rooms ⊟AE, MC, V ⓄCP.

££–£££   🏠**Mount Royale Hotel.** In a quiet country house in the upscale residential part of west York, this hotel offers excellent service that is both profes-sional and friendly. Outside near the pool, discover orange, lemon, and fig trees mingling with the sprays of flowers in the pristine English gar-den. Rooms are spacious and decorated simply with subtle colors; four have walk-in closets and verandas that lead to the garden. ■TIP➔**The Mediterranean restaurant, One19 The Mount, is one of York's most popular; if you drive, expect to fight for parking.** **Pros:** country-club feel; lovely pool and garden. **Cons:** well outside the town center. ⊠117–119 The Mount ☎01904/628856 ⊕www.mountroyale.co.uk ⟳23 rooms 🚫 In-room: no a/c. In-hotel: restaurant, room service, bar, pool, laundry service ⊟AE, DC, MC, V ⓄBP.

NIGHTLIFE AND THE ARTS

NIGHTLIFE

York is full of historic pubs where you can while away an hour over a pint. The **Black Swan** (⊠Peasholme Green ☎01904/686911) is the city's oldest pub, in a 16th-century Tudor building. It's said to be haunted by a young girl that sits by the fireplace. The **Old White Swan** (⊠Goodram-gate ☎01904/540911) is vast, spreading across five medieval, half-timbered buildings on busy Goodramgate. It's known for good pub lunches and its ghosts—it claims to have more than the Black Swan. The **Snickleway Inn** (⊠ *Goodramgate* ☎ *01904/656138*) is in a 15th-century building with open fireplaces and a real sense of history.

THE ARTS

The **Early Music Festival** (☎ *01904/658338 festival office, 01904/621756 Tourist Information Centre* ⊕ *www.ncem.co.uk*), featuring pre-18th-century music, is held each July. The **Viking Festival** (⊠ *Jorvik, Coppergate* ☎ *01904/543402* ⊕ *www.vikingjorvik.com*) takes place each February. The celebrations, including a parade and long-ship regatta, end with the Jorvik Viking combat reenactment, when Norsemen confront their Anglo-Saxon enemies.

In a lovely 18th-century building, the **York Theatre Royal** (⊠ *St. Leonard's Pl.* ☎ *01904/623568*) presents plays, music, poetry readings, and art exhibitions.

SHOPPING

The new and secondhand bookstores around Petergate, Stonegate, and the Shambles are excellent. The **Minster Gate Bookshop** (⊠ *8 Minster Gate* ☎ *01904/621812*) sells secondhand books, old maps, and prints. **Mulberry Hall** (⊠ *Stonegate* ☎ *01904/620736*) is a sales center for all the famous names in fine bone china and crystal. It also has a neat café. The **York Antiques Centre** (⊠ *2 Lendal* ☎ *01904/641445*) has 25 shops selling antiques, bric-a-brac, books, and jewelry.

YORK ENVIRONS

West and north of York a number of sights make easy, appealing day trips from the city: the spa town of Harrogate, atmospheric Knaresborough, the ruins of Fountain Abbey, the market town of Ripon and nearby Newby Hall, and Thirsk, with its James Herriot connection. If you're heading northwest from York to Harrogate, you might take the less direct B1224 across Marston Moor, where, in 1644, Oliver Cromwell won a decisive victory over the Royalists during the Civil War. A few miles beyond, at Wetherby, you can cut northwest along the A661 to Harrogate. Also nearby, northeast of York, is Castle Howard, a magnificent stately home.

HARROGATE

★ *21 mi west of York, 11 mi south of Ripon, 16 mi north of Leeds.*

During the Regency and early-Victorian periods, it became fashionable for the noble and wealthy to retire to a spa to "take the waters" for relaxation. In Yorkshire the trend reached its grandest heights in Harrogate, an elegant town that flourished during the 19th century. Today the Regency buildings, parks, and spas built during that time make Harrogate an absorbing getaway.

York Environs

0 — 6 miles
0 — 6 kilometers

GETTING HERE AND AROUND

Northern Rail trains to Harrogate leave from York every hour or so, and the journey takes about 30 minutes. There are no direct trains from London to Harrogate. By car, Harrogate is off A59, and is well marked. It's a walkable town, so you can park in one of its central parking lots, or at your hotel, and explore on foot. National Express buses run to Harrogate from York every hour most days; the journey takes about 40 minutes.

Within and around Harrogate, the Transdev bus company provides area services, but the town itself is easily walkable and taxis are plentiful.

ESSENTIALS

Visitor Information Harrogate (⊠ *Royal Baths, Crescent Rd.* ☎ *01423/537300* ⊕ *www.harrogate.gov.uk*).

EXPLORING

The **Royal Pump Room Museum** is in the octagonal structure built in 1842 over the original sulfur well that brought great prosperity to the town. You can still drink the evil-smelling (and nasty-tasting) spa waters here. The museum displays some equipment of spa days gone by, alongside a rather eccentric collection of fine 19th-century china, clothes, and bicycles. ⊠ *Crown Pl.* ☎ *01423/556188* ⊕ *www.harrogate.gov.uk*

✉£3 ⊙ *Apr.–Oct., Mon.–Sat. 10–5, Sun. 2–5; Nov.–Mar., Mon.–Sat. 10–4, Sun. 2–4.*

★ The exotic and fully restored **Turkish Baths** (1897) allow you to experience what brought so many Victorians to Harrogate. After changing into your bathing suit, you can relax on luxurious lounge chairs in the mosaic-tile warming room. Move on to increasingly hot sauna rooms, and then soak up eucalyptus mist in the steam room before braving the icy plunge pool. You can also book a massage or facial. Open hours are divided into women-only, men-only, and couples-only nights, so book in advance. ✉ *Parliament St.* ☎ *01423/556746* ⊕ *www.harrogate.gov.uk/ turkishbaths* ✉ *£11.50–£17.20 per bath and sauna session, massages and treatments additional* ⊙ *Daily; call for schedules.*

At the edge of the town center, the 200-acre grassy parkland known as the **Stray** is a riot of color in spring.

The **Valley Gardens,** southwest of the town center, include a boating lake, tennis courts, and a little café.

WHERE TO EAT AND STAY

£ ✕**Betty's.** The celebrated Yorkshire tearoom began life in Harrogate
CAFÉ in the 1920s, when Swiss restaurateur Frederic Belmont brought his Alpine specialties to England. The elegant surroundings have changed little since then, the cakes, pastries, and teas not at all. A pianist plays nightly. ✉ *1 Parliament St.* ☎ *01423/502746* ▭ *MC, V.*

££ ⊟**Balmoral Hotel.** Luxurious contemporary furnishings and antique pieces, patterned wallpapers, and colorful ornaments fill this mock-Tudor edifice. Ten pastel-hue bedrooms have mahogany, walnut, or oak four-poster beds, all frilled and draped. The Harrogate Grille restaurant looks like a gentlemen's club, with leather seats, and has a high-quality contemporary British menu. Guests have access to a nearby health club. **Pros:** spacious rooms; attractive restaurant. **Cons:** a bit too old-fashioned; very formal atmosphere. ✉ *Franklin Mt.* ☎ *01423/508208* ⊕ *www.balmoralhotel.co.uk* ⇋ *20 rooms, 1 suite* ⌂ *In-room: no a/c. In-hotel: restaurant, bar, some pets allowed* ▭ *AE, MC, V* ❘❍❘ *BP.*

£££ ⊟**Hotel du Vin.** Tired of chintz? This hip hotel chain has taken over eight Georgian houses, using stripped wood floors, clubby leather armchairs, and a purple billiard table to set the tone. Bedrooms, clean-lined and modern, are done in beige and cream tones. The pampering bathrooms are a nice touch, with deep tubs and spacious showers. The bar is a serious place to drink, and the popular bistro offers classics like roasted lamb, smoked salmon, and vegetarian linguine. **Pros:** relaxed lounge; wonderful wine list; modern vibe. **Cons:** looks a bit battered around the edges; the bar can take over the lounge. ✉ *Prospect Pl.* ☎ *01423/856800* ⊕ *www.hotelduvin.com* ⇋ *35 rooms, 8 suites* ⌂ *In-room: no a/c, safe, Internet. In-hotel: restaurant, bar, gym, no-smoking rooms* ▭ *AE, MC, V.*

NIGHTLIFE AND THE ARTS

★ Harrogate's annual **International Festival** (☎ *01423/562303* ⊕ *www. harrogate-festival.org.uk*) of ballet, music, contemporary dance, film, comedy, street theater, and more takes place during two weeks at the end of July and beginning of August.

13

KNARESBOROUGH

3 mi northeast of Harrogate, 17 mi west of York.

At the bottom of a precipitously deep rocky gorge along the River Nidd, the little town of Knaresborough couldn't be more photogenic. It's best seen from a train, crossing the high viaduct above. Once you leave the train, there's a steep descent down a rocky footpath to the riverside. In summer you can rent a boat and paddle down the slow-moving river and wander the town's little marketplace, and year-round you can climb to the hilltop ruins of the castle where Richard II was imprisoned in 1399.

EXPLORING

The touristy **Mother Shipton's Cave,** across the river from the main riverside attractions, is tucked in a pleasant park. The cave is, according to local lore, the birthplace of the titular 16th-century prophetess. Events supposedly foretold by her include the defeat of the Spanish Armada. The mineral-rich well beside her cave is famed for its ability to turn any object to stone in just a few hours. It's all good fun. ✉ *Prophesy House, High Bridge* ☎ *01423/864600* ⊕ *www.mothershipton.co.uk* 🎫 *£6* ⊘ *Mar.–Oct., daily 10–5:45, last admission 5; Nov. and Feb.– Mar., weekends only 10–4:30.*

RIPON

11 mi north of Harrogate, 24 mi northwest of York.

Ripon was thriving as early as the 9th century as an important market center. A relatively small church has been designated a cathedral since the mid-19th century, which makes Ripon, with only about 15,000 inhabitants, technically a city. Market day, Thursday, is probably the best day to stop by.

EXPLORING

★ **Studley Royal Water Garden & Fountains Abbey.** You can easily spend a day at this World Heritage Site, an 822-acre complex made up of an 18th-century water garden and deer park and the majestic ruins of medieval Fountains Abbey. Here a neoclassical vision of an ordered universe— with spectacular terraces, classical temples, and a grotto—blends with the glories of English Gothic architecture. The abbey, on the banks of the River Skell, was founded in 1132 and completed in the early 1500s. The Cistercian monks here, called "White Monks" for the color of their robes, devoted their lives to silence, prayer, and work. Of the surviving buildings, the lay brothers' echoing refectory and dormitory impresses most; the Gothic tower was a 16th-century addition. Fountains Mill, with sections dating back to 1140, displays reconstructed mill machinery (wool was the monks' large and profitable business). The 17th-century Fountains Hall, partially built with stones taken from the abbey, has an exhibition and video display. The water garden and Fountains Abbey is 9 mi northwest of Knaresborough, 4 mi southwest of Ripon. ✉ *Off B6265* ☎ *01765/608888* ⊕ *www.fountainsabbey.org.uk* 🎫 *£8* ⊘ *Mar.–Oct., daily 10–6; Feb. and Nov., daily 10–4. Free guided tours*

CLOSE UP

The Monastic Past

The sheer number of once richly decorated monastic buildings here is a testament to the power of the Catholic monks of medieval Yorkshire. They became some of the richest in Europe by virtue of the international wool trade that they conducted, with the help of lay workers, from their vast religious estates. The buildings lie mostly in romantic ruins, a result of the dissolution of the monasteries during the 16th century, part of Henry VIII's struggle with the Catholic church over finances and his divorce request (the rejection of which he perceived as a calculated way to deny him a male heir). Henry's break with

Rome was made official in 1534 with the Act of Supremacy, which made him head of the Church of England. By 1540 no monasteries or abbeys remained; the king confiscated all their property, distributed the lands, and destroyed or gave away many buildings. Today the ruined abbeys at Fountains, Rievaulx, and Whitby are top attractions where you can learn about the religious and business worlds of the great monasteries, and the political machinations that destroyed them. They serve as vivid reminders of what life was like in the Middle Ages.

of abbey and gardens Apr.–Oct., daily at 11, 1:30, and 2:30 (June–Aug. extra tour at 3:30); water garden tour Apr.–Oct., daily at 2.

Successive churches here were destroyed by the Vikings and the Normans, and the current **Ripon Cathedral,** dating from the 12th and 13th centuries, is notable for its finely carved choir stalls. The Saxon crypt (AD 672), now an empty series of chambers, housed sacred relics. ⊠ *Minster Rd.* ☎ *01765/602072* ⊕ *www.riponcathedral.org.uk* ✉ *£3 donation requested* ⊘ *Daily 8–5.*

☪ An early-18th-century house redecorated later in the same century by Robert Adam for his patron William Weddell, **Newby Hall** contains fine decorative art of its period, particularly ornamental plasterwork and Chippendale furniture. The domed Sculpture Hall with Roman works, and the Tapestry Hall, with its priceless Gobelin tapestries, are gorgeous; both are Adams designs. The 25 acres of gardens are justifiably famous; a double herbaceous border, which runs down to the river, separates garden "rooms," each flowering during a different season. A miniature railroad, playground, and pedal boats amuse kids. The house is 5 mi southeast of Ripon. ⊠ *Skelton-on-Ure* ☎ *01423/322583* ⊕ *www.newbyhall.co.uk* ✉ *£11; gardens only, £8* ⊘ *Apr.–Sept., Tues.– Sun. and national holiday Mon., house noon–5, grounds 11–5:30; last admission 30 mins before closing.*

WHERE TO STAY

££££–£££££ ⊞ **Swinton Park.** The Cunliffe-Lister family operates part of its ancestral castle—a stately pile rebuilt in the 18th and 19th centuries with battlements and a turret —as a hotel. The plush public rooms give you space to relax, and the traditionally decorated bedrooms are named and themed after towns in Yorkshire. About 200 acres of parkland near Yorkshire Dales National Park guarantee seclusion and abundant outdoor pursuits. Chef-author Rosemary Shrager has a cooking school on the grounds. Masham is 8 mi north of Ripon and 35 mi north of Leeds and York. **Pros:** eye-popping castle; gorgeous rooms. **Cons:** some rooms have better views than others. ⊠*Off A1, Swinton Park, Masham* ☎*01765/680900* ⊕*www.swintonpark.com* ⌂*26 rooms, 4 suites* ⚹*In-room: no a/c, Internet. In-hotel: restaurant, gym, bicycles, some pets allowed* ☰*AE, DC, MC, V* ⦿*BP.*

THIRSK

13 mi north of Newby Hall, 23 mi north of York.

This busy market town on the western edge of the moors was once a thriving stopover on the main east–west route from the dales to the coast. Today it's a busy, affluent farm town. Lovely Georgian houses abound, and the cobbled medieval Market Place is handsome; Saturday and Monday are market days. Thirsk is best known as the place where veterinarian Alf Wight (who wrote about his experiences under the name James Herriot) had his practice.

EXPLORING

The popular **World of James Herriot,** in the author's actual office, recreates the operating room and the living spaces of the 1940s and '50s; it also displays veterinary artifacts. The interactive displays upstairs appeal to kids and adults alike. ⊠*23 Kirkgate* ☎*01845/524234* ⊕*www.worldofjamesherriot.org* ⛁*£5.50* ⊙*Apr.–Oct., daily 10–6; Nov.–Mar., daily 11–4; last admission 1 hr before closing.*

CASTLE HOWARD

15 mi northeast of York, 14 mi southeast of Rievaulx Abbey, 12 mi southeast of Helmsley.

GETTING HERE AND AROUND

There is no public transportation to Castle Howard, which is well outside any town and several miles off any public road. To get there by car, follow signs off A64.

EXPLORING

Standing serene among the Howardian Hills to the west of Malton, **Castle Howard** is an opulent, stately home whose magnificent profile is punctuated by stone chimneys and a graceful central dome. Many people know it best as Brideshead, the home of the Flyte family in Evelyn Waugh's tale of aristocratic woe, *Brideshead Revisited,* because much of the 1981 TV series was filmed here. The house was designed by Sir John Vanbrugh (1664–1726) for the Howard family. Considering its many theatrical, even flamboyant features, it seems fitting that Vanbrugh was praised more as a playwright than an architect (he also had careers as a soldier and adventurer). In 18th-century London his plays were second in popularity only to Congreve's. This was Vanbrugh's first building design; his self-assurance knowing no bounds, he went on to create Blenheim Palace, the Versailles of England. For Castle Howard, Vanbrugh sought assistance, and turned to the brilliant Nicholas Hawksmoor (1661–1736), who at 18 had been under the tutelage of

Fodor'sChoice ★

Christopher Wren. Hawksmoor encouraged adding bodies of water to the landscape, and he designed the imposing Mausoleum; many consider it a masterpiece equal to his churches in London.

The audacity of the great baroque house is startling, proclaiming the wealth and importance of the Howards. This was the first private residence in Britain built with a stone dome. A magnificent central hallway spanned by a hand-painted (in the 20th century) ceiling dwarfs all visitors, and there is no shortage of grandeur: vast family portraits, delicate marble fireplaces, immense and fading tapestries, huge pieces of Victorian silver on polished tables, and a great many marble busts. Outside, the stunning neoclassical landscape of carefully arranged woods, lakes, bridges, and obelisks led Horace Walpole, the 18th-century connoisseur, to comment that a pheasant at Castle Howard lives better than most dukes elsewhere. The grounds sprawl for miles, and hidden away among the hills and lakes (there's even a fanciful playground for children) are the Temple of the Four Winds and the Mausoleum, whose magnificence caused Walpole to quip that all who view it would wish to be buried alive. Hourly tours, included in the admission price, fill you in on more background and history. ⊠ *Off A64 and B1257, Coneysthorpe* ☎ *01653/648333* ⊕ *www.castlehoward.co.uk* ✉ *£11; gardens only, £8.50* ⊙ *House Mar.–Oct., daily 11–6; last admission 4. Grounds daily 10–6:30 or dusk; last admission 4:30.*

THE NORTH YORKSHIRE COAST

The North York Moors plummet down to the sea in spectacular cliffs that stretch down the coastline, creating a dramatic view of pink heather and white cliffs hundreds of feet above the dark sea. The red roofs of Robin Hood's Bay, the sharply curved bay at Whitby, and the gold-and-white buildings of Scarborough capture the imagination at first sight. Most coastal towns still support an active fishing industry, and every harbor offers fishing and leisure trips throughout summer. Beaches at Scarborough, Whitby, and Filey have patrolled areas: swim (in cold water) between the red-and-yellow flags, and don't swim when a red flag is flying. All the North Sea beaches are ideal for fossil hunting and seashell collecting.

From Scarborough, you can take the main road (A171) north to Robin Hood's Bay and Whitby. Otherwise, you can head directly across the moors to Whitby, which makes for a wilder and more beautiful journey not to be taken lightly in winter.

SCARBOROUGH

34 mi northeast of York.

There is no Scarborough Fair, and historians are divided on whether there ever was one, but don't let that stop you from heading to this classic English seaside resort, where lemon-hued Victorian houses top cliffs overlooking the dark blue sea. The older, more genteel side of Scarborough is in the southern half of town, with carefully laid-out crescents and squares, the ruins of its castle, and views across Cayton Bay. The northern side is a riot of tacky seaside arcades, ice-cream stands, bingo halls, and stores selling "rock" (luridly colored hard candy). The huddle of streets, alleyways, and red-roof cottages around the harbor gives an idea of what the town was like before the resort days.

GETTING HERE AND AROUND

Scarborough is rather difficult to get to by public transportation. Transpennine Express trains to Scarborough leave from York every hour or so; the journey takes just under an hour. There are no direct trains from London to Scarborough. By bus, a trip from London takes all day, and involves changing buses in Leeds. The journey from Leeds to Scarborough by National Express bus takes about four hours. By car, Scarborough is on the coastal A165 road.

ESSENTIALS

Train Information Transpennine Express (☎ 0845/600–1671 ⊕ www. tpexpress.co.uk).

Visitor Information Scarborough (✉ Unit 3, Pavilion House, Valley Bridge Rd. ☎ 01723/383636 ⊕ www.discoveryorkshirecoast.com).

13

EXPLORING

For nearly 900 years the rambling ruins of **Scarborough Castle** have dominated the northern headland. The Romans used the site as a signaling station in the 4th century, and archaeological digs have uncovered evidence that people lived here in the Bronze age. The current structure dates to 1136, when it was built by William de Gros to replace a wooden fort. Henry II later took the castle for himself because he believed it was impossible to invade. He was right: although the castle was repeatedly besieged, it was never taken by force. ■TIP➔**The castle has spectacular views across the North Bay and the shore gardens.** ⊠*Castle Rd.* ☎*01723/372451* ⊕*www.english-heritage.org.uk* 🎫*£4* ☉*Apr.–Sept., daily 10–6; Oct.–Mar., Thurs.–Mon. 10–4.*

> ### A SPA IS BORN
>
> In 1626 Elizabeth Farrow came upon a stream of acidic water running from a cliff south of Scarborough. This led to the town's establishment as a hugely popular spa on a par with Harrogate. By the 18th century, when icy sea bathing came into vogue, no beaches were busier than Scarborough's. Donkeys and horses drew wheeled cabins called bathing machines into the surf and anchored there. The city's prosperity manifested itself in the handsome Regency and early-Victorian residences and hotels you see today.

Most visitors to the little medieval church of **St. Mary** (⊠*Castle Rd.* ☎*01723/500541*) are attracted by the churchyard's most famous occupant: Anne, the youngest Brontë sister. She was taken to Scarborough from Haworth when suffering from tuberculosis in a futile effort to save her life by exposing her to the sea air. She died in 1849. The church is near the castle on the way into town.

The extraordinary circular building that holds the **Rotunda Museum** was constructed in 1829 for William Smith of the Scarborough Philosophical Society to display his geological collection. It now contains important archaeological and local history collections, and changing temporary exhibits. It's largely geared toward children (it's free for everyone under 18 years old), but its archaeological finds can be interesting for adults, too. ⊠*Vernon Rd.* ☎*01723/353665* 🎫*£4.50* ☉*Tues.–Sun. 10–5.*

Recognizable by its white pyramids, **Scarborough Sea Life Centre** is a great—if expensive—way to entertain the kids for an afternoon. Fish, crabs, and stingrays are presented in an engaging way, with all the marine habitats native to Great Britain. ⊠*Scalby Mills, North Bay* ☎*01723/373414* ⊕*www.sealifeeurope.com* 🎫*£13* ☉*Mar.–Oct., daily 10–6; Nov.–Feb., daily 10–4; last admission 1 hr before closing.*

WHERE TO EAT AND STAY

£
SEAFOOD
✕**The Golden Grid.** Everyone has to have fish-and-chips at least once in Scarborough, and this harbor-front spot is a classic of its kind. Choose an upstairs window table and tuck into freshly fried cod or haddock. ⊠*4 Sandside* ☎*01723/360922* ▤*MC, V* ☉*No dinner Sun.–Thurs. Sept.–Mar.*

£££ ✕ **Lanterna Ristorante.** This unpretentious restaurant prides itself on *not*
ITALIAN being modern. Instead it offers classic Italian dishes, including tender
steak cooked with ham and cheese, and seafood chosen fresh off the boats
in the harbor. Opt for seasonal specials using fresh vegetables, fish, and
white truffles (October to January). ⊠*33 Queen St.* ☎*01723/363616*
▤*MC, V* ⊘*No lunch. Closed Sun. and 2 wks late Oct.*

££–£££ 🛏 **The Crown Spa.** The centerpiece of the Regency Esplanade, this 19th-
century hotel overlooks South Bay and the castle headland. Built to
accommodate fashionable visitors to Scarborough Spa, it has been considerably refurbished; rooms are modern and done in muted colors.
Rates drop for some two-night stays. **Pros:** pure Victorian style; rooms
have modern amenities. **Cons:** bathrooms can be quite small. ⊠*The
Esplanade* ☎*01723/357426* ⊕*www.crownspahotel.com* ⇗*87 rooms*
♿*In-room: no a/c. In-hotel: 2 restaurants, bars, pool, spa, gym, some
pets allowed* ▤*AE, MC, V* �PO|*BP.*

NIGHTLIFE AND THE ARTS

Scarborough is one of England's busy theater towns, especially for summer repertory, with most of the activity buzzing around the **Stephen
Joseph Theatre** (⊠ *Westborough* ☎*01723/370541*). It presents productions on two stages and also has a cinema, a restaurant, and a bar. The
tourist office also has box-office details.

ROBIN HOOD'S BAY

★ *15 mi northwest of Scarborough.*

This tiny fishing village squeezed into a steep narrow ravine is absolutely
adorable, from its name right down to its little red-roof cottages and
cobbled roads. The village has no connection to the famous medieval
outlaw, though. It was once a smuggling center that passed contraband
up the streambed beneath the cottages, linked to one another by secret
passages. The attraction here is the town itself, with its winding stone
staircases that eventually wander off across the headland. ▀ TIP→ **Park
in the pay lots at the top of the hill. Do not attempt to drive down the hill.**

EXPLORING

The **beach** is lovely, but mercurial—the tide rushes in quickly, so take
care not to get cut off. Provided the tide is out, you can stroll for a
couple of hours south from the town, along a rough stone shore full of
rock pools, inlets, and sandy strands. A few stretches of sand are suitable for sunbathers. To the south, at the curiously named **Boggle Hole,**
a ravine nestles an old water mill, now an atmospheric youth hostel
(signs mark the way on the cliff-top path). Farther south is **Ravenscar,**
a Victorian village that now consists of little more than a hotel, which
can be reached by a hazardous but exhilarating path up the cliff. The
walk back, along the cliff, is less tricky but no less energetic.

WHERE TO EAT AND STAY

£ ✕ **Bay Hotel.** The village's most favored pub is this friendly Victorian
SEAFOOD retreat, perfectly positioned at the bottom of the village. It sits on a
rocky outcrop lapped by the sea, so there are nice views. The bar is
festooned with oak and brass; in winter, a roaring fire warms all comers.

Whitby scampi and chestnut-and-butter-bean casserole are often on the menu. ✉ *The Dock* ☎ *01947/880278* ▭ *MC, V.*

££££–£££££ 🏨 **Raven Hall Hotel.** This superb Georgian hotel with landscaped grounds offers unrivaled coastal views from the headland of Ravenscar, 3 mi southeast of Robin Hood's Bay. All rooms have lovely views, but the best ones look out over the bay. The hotel is known for its good sports facilities; the bar marks the traditional end of the punishing, long-distance Lyke-Wake Walk, so on occasion you may share the lounge with exhausted walkers. There are also skeet shooting and themed murder-mystery dinners and wine tastings. It's worth checking for dinner and B&B deals year-round. **Pros:** breathtaking coastal views; great for sports fanatics. **Cons:** a bit off the beaten track; need a car to get around. ✉ *Ravenscar YO13 0ET* ☎ *01723/870353* ⊕ *www.ravenhall. co.uk* ⇦ *53 rooms* ⚙ *In-room: no a/c, Internet. In-hotel: restaurant, bar, golf course, tennis courts, pool, gym* ▭ *AE, MC, V* �‖ *BP.*

SPORTS AND THE OUTDOORS

Several superb long-distance walks start at, finish in, or run through Robin Hood's Bay. The coastal part of **Cleveland Way** (⊕ *www. nationaltrail.co.uk*) runs north to Whitby and south to Scarborough. The village marks one end of the 190-mi **Coast-to-Coast Walk**; the other is at St. Bees Head on the Irish Sea. Walkers finish at the Bay Hotel, above the harbor. The trans-moor **Lyke-Wake Walk** (⊕ *www.lykewakewalk. co.uk*) finishes 3 mi away at Ravenscar. **Wellington Lodge** (✉ *Staintondale* ☎ *01723/871234* ⊕ *www.llamatreks.co.uk*), 3 mi south of Ravenscar, schedules llama treks along the moors or the coast; you walk, and the llamas carry your lunch.

WHITBY

Fodor's Choice
★ *7 mi northwest of Robin Hood's Bay, 20 mi northeast of Pickering.*

A scenic seaside town with a Gothic edge, Whitby is a busy tourist hub, but it handles that fact so well you might not notice (except at dinnertime, when it's hard to get a seat in a restaurant). Whitby curves around its symmetrical harbor and winds its way up the cliffs. The glassy waters of the slow-moving River Esk cut through the town. Fine Georgian houses dominate the west side of the river (known as West Cliff), and across the swing bridge smaller 17th-century buildings mark the old town (known as East Cliff). Here cobbled Church Street is packed in summer with people exploring the shop-lined alleyways.

Whitby came to prominence as a whaling port. The first ships sailed from here to Greenland in the mid-18th century, captained by local men such as William Scoresby. Herman Melville paid tribute to this inventor of the crow's nest in *Moby Dick*. Whaling brought Whitby wealth, and shipbuilding made it famous: Captain James Cook (1728–79), explorer and navigator, sailed on his first ship from Whitby in 1747, and all four of his subsequent discovery vessels were built in the town.

GETTING HERE AND AROUND

A car is a must, as there are no direct buses or trains from London. National Express and Megabus have buses to the region, but you must change at least once, and the journey can take up to 10 hours. National

Express trains from London's King's Cross Station go to Leeds, where you can change to a local train. The entire journey can take six hours.

Whitby has a very small town center, and it's easily walkable. The train station is in the town center, between its two cliffs. If you're looking for a taxi, they tend to line up outside the station.

ESSENTIALS

Visitor Information Whitby (✉ *Langbourne Rd.* ☎ *01947/602674*).

EXPLORING

On top of the East Cliff—reached by climbing 199 stone steps—the Gothic church of **St. Mary** overlooks the town, while it in turn is watched over by the gaunt ruins of Whitby Abbey. Bram Stoker lived in Whitby briefly and later said his stay inspired him to write *Dracula*. He was particularly struck by the image of pallbearers carrying coffins up the long stone staircase to St. Mary's spooky churchyard. The unusual-looking church with its ship's-deck roof, triple-decker pulpit, and enclosed box pews dates from the 12th century, although almost everything you see today is the result of 19th- and 20th-century renovations. The weather-beaten churchyard is filled with the crooked old gravestones of ancient mariners. ■TIP➔ **Rather than walking the 199 steps, you can drive to the hilltop and park in the abbey's large parking lot for a small fee.** ✉ *Church La., East Cliff* ☎ *01947/603421* ✉ *Free, donation suggested* ⏱ *Apr., daily 10–4; May–Aug., daily 10–5; Sept. and Oct., daily 10–3; Nov.–Mar., daily 10–2.*

★ The glorious ruins of **Whitby Abbey,** high on the East Cliff, dominate the area. The skeletal remains of the once grand church can even be seen from the hills of the moors miles away. The cutting-edge abbess St. Hilda founded the abbey in AD 657. It was one of very few founded by a woman, and operated with a mixed population of monks and nuns. Caedmon (died circa 670), the first identifiable poet of the English language, was a monk here. Sacked by the Vikings in the 9th century, the monastery was refounded in the 11th century and enlarged in the 13th century, from which point these ruins date. It flourished until Henry VIII destroyed it. The visitor center is excellent, with exhibits on Hilda and Bram Stoker, artifacts from the site, interactive displays on the medieval abbey, and a tea shop. ✉ *Abbey La., East Cliff* ☎ *01947/603568* ⊕ *www.english-heritage.org.uk* ✉ *£5.25* ⏱ *Apr.–Sept., daily 10–6; Oct., daily 10–5; Nov.–Mar., Thurs.–Mon. 10–4.*

Filled with exhibits relating to the man and explorer, the **Captain Cook Memorial Museum** is in the 18th-century house belonging to ship owner John Walker. Cook lived here as an apprentice from 1746 to 1749. On display are mementos of his epic expeditions, including maps, diaries, and

CLOSE UP

Whitby Jet

In the 19th century Whitby became famous around the western world for jet, a very hard, black form of natural carbon, found in thin seams along the coast here and worked into jewelry and ornaments. Known since prehistoric times and sometimes used to ward off the evil eye, it reached the peak of its popularity in the 1850s when 1,400 men and boys, supplied by 200 miners, made a good living in jewelry workshops all over the town. The queen of Bavaria was impressed enough to order a chain more than 4 feet long. On the death of her husband, Albert, in 1861, Queen Victoria introduced jet into court circles and set the fashion for mourning memorabilia.

You can see fine examples in the Whitby Museum on St. Hilda's Terrace and in the shop displays in the old town along Church Street and parallel to Sandgate. If you buy a piece, keep it shiny with baby oil.

drawings. ✉ *Grape La.* ☎ *01947/601900* ⊕ *www.cookmuseumwhitby. co.uk* 🖻 *£4* ⊙ *Apr.–Oct., daily 9:45–5; Mar., daily 11–3.*

Exhibits in the quirky **Whitby Museum** wander from local geology and natural history to archaeology, whaling, and trade routes in Asia. It's interesting for its old-fashioned approach—displays have handwritten cards. ✉ *St. Hilda's La., Pannett Park* ☎ *01947/602908* ⊕ *www. whitbymuseum.org.uk* 🖻 *£3* ⊙ *May–Sept., Mon.–Sat. 9:30–5:30, Sun. 2–5; Oct.–Apr., Tues. 10–1, Wed.–Sat. 10–4, Sun. 2–4.*

OFF THE BEATEN PATH

Goathland. This moorland village, 8 mi southwest of Whitby, attracts walkers and people who want to see the fictional Aidensfield of the British TV series *Heartbeat.* Its cute 1865 train station served as Hogsmeade Station for students arriving at the school of wizardry in the film *Harry Potter and the Sorcerer's Stone.* The 18-mi **North Yorkshire Moors Railway** (✉ *Pickering Station, Park St., Pickering* ☎ *01751/472508, 01751/473535 recorded information* ⊕ *www.nymr.co.uk* 🖻 *£14.50 round-trip* ⊙ *Late Mar.–early Nov., daily; early Nov.–Feb., some weekends and holiday periods*), between Grosmont and Pickering, passes through neat towns and moorland. Steam-powered trains provide a great outing.

WHERE TO EAT

£ **SEAFOOD** ✕ **Magpie Café.** Whitby is full of fish-and-chip places, but this is the one that draws the biggest crowd with a well-stocked menu that includes plaice, cod, and haddock along with grilled fish and meat platters. The food is good and fans say it's worth the wait, which can stretch to an hour on busy nights. ✉ *14 Pier Rd.* ☎ *01947/602058* ⚓ *Reservations not accepted* ▤ *MC, V* ⊙ *Closed Jan.*

WHERE TO STAY

£ 🛏 **Broom House.** Tucked away in the tiny village of Egton Bridge, about 5 mi outside of Whitby, this two-story stone house sits beside a babbling brook at the base of forested hills. The rooms are decorated with impeccable taste, and all have plenty of space and peaceful views. Breakfasts are fresh and tasty. During the day you can wander through the orchard, and in the evening sit by the crackling fire. At the time of this writing, the owners were developing a new bistro and adding additional guest rooms, which were expected to be available in 2010. **Pros:** gorgeous setting; beautifully decorated rooms. **Cons:** far from Whitby; need a car to get around. ⊠*Broom House La., Egton Bridge* ☎*01947/895279* ⊕*www.egton-bridge.co.uk* ⇄*6 rooms* ☂*In-room: no a/c, no phone* ⊟*MC, V* ⏐◎⏐*BP.*

£££–££££   ⌧ **Dunsley Hall Hotel.** Built as the home of a shipping magnate, this family-run Victorian country-house hotel has 4 acres of gardens and grounds. Stained- and leaded-glass windows and plenty of wood paneling complement rich carpets, rocking chairs, and leather armchairs. Bedrooms are spacious, and the only intrusion is the occasional screech of a peacock. A new wing opened in 2007 added eight modern guest rooms. The hotel is 4 mi west of Whitby. **Pros:** acres and acres of gardens; spacious bedrooms. **Cons:** peacocks might wake you up early; modern rooms not as charming. ⊠*Dunsley* ☎*01947/893437* ⊕*www.dunsleyhall.com* ⇄*26 rooms* ☂*In-room: no a/c. In-hotel: restaurant, bar, tennis court, pool, gym* ⊟*AE, MC, V* ⏐◎⏐*BP.*

£   ⌧ **Shepherd's Purse.** This splendid little complex in the cobbled old town consists of boutique-style guest rooms, an organic café, and a health-food store. There are two less-expensive bedrooms above the stores and others in the galleried courtyard at the back. Although small, many rooms have four-poster or brass bedsteads; floors are wooden, the furniture is country style, and two rooms have balconies. **Pros:** quirky style; comfortable rooms. **Cons:** health-conscious focus not for everyone; some rooms are quite small; no elevator. ⊠*95 Church St.* ☎*01947/820228* ⇄*9 rooms, 5 with bath* ☂*In-room: no a/c, no phone. In-hotel: restaurant, some pets allowed* ⊟*MC, V* ⏐◎⏐*BP.*

££   ⌧ **White Horse and Griffin.** When looking for the perfect inn, you want an old building with character, a roaring fire, and food to thrill. This 18th-century establishment, in which Charles Dickens once slept and railway pioneer George Stephenson lectured, fills the bill. The tidy rooms, done in an uncluttered traditional style, are warmly decorated in muted colors, and downstairs the cozy bistro serves a fine, changing menu with locally caught fish and game in season. **Pros:** Charles Dickens slept here; lots of character; tasty food. **Cons:** old-fashioned style; few amenities; no elevator. ⊠*Church St.* ☎*01947/604857* ⊕*www.whitehorseandgriffin.co.uk* ⇄*10 rooms* ☂*In-room: no a/c, no phone. In-hotel: restaurant, bar, no-smoking rooms, some pets allowed* ⊟*MC, V* ⏐◎⏐*BP.*

NIGHTLIFE AND THE ARTS

★   The **Whitby Regatta** (⊕*www.whitbyregatta.co.uk*), held at the beginning of August, is a three-day jamboree of boat races, fair rides, lifeboat rescue displays, fireworks, and music. Music (but also traditional dance and storytelling) predominates during **Whitby Folk Week** (⊕*www.whitbyfolk.co.uk*), usually held the week before the late-August bank holiday, when pubs, sidewalks, and halls become venues for more than 600 traditional folk events by British performers.

THE NORTH YORK MOORS

The North York Moors are a dramatic swath of high moorland starting 25 mi north of the city of York and stretching east to the coast and west to the Cleveland Hills. Once covered in forest, of which a few pockets survive, the landscape changed when the monks at Rievaulx and Whitby abbeys began raising huge flocks of sheep in medieval times. Over the course of centuries, the sheep have kept the moors deforested, and still ensure that the pink heather on which they feed spreads lushly across the hills. A series of isolated, medieval "standing stones" that once acted as signposts on the paths between the abbeys are now handy for hikers.

13

For more than four decades the area has been a national park, ensuring the protection of the bleak moors and grassy valleys that shelter brown-stone villages and hamlets. Minor roads and tracks crisscross the hills, and there's no single, obvious route through the region. Perhaps the most rewarding approach is west from the coast at Whitby, along the Esk Valley to Danby, which is also accessible on the Esk Valley branch train line between Middlesbrough and Whitby. From Danby, minor roads run south over the high moors reaching Hutton-le-Hole, beyond which main roads lead to interesting towns on the moors' edge, such as Helmsley. Completing the route in this direction leaves you with an easy side trip to Castle Howard before returning to nearby York.

DANBY

15 mi west of Whitby.

The old stone village of Danby nestles in a green valley, just a short walk from the tops of the moors. It's been settled since Viking times—Danby means "village where the Danes lived"—and these days it bumbles along in a semitourised way. There's a pub, and a cozy bakery with a tearoom, and if you bring hiking boots, within 10 minutes you can be above the village looking down, surrounded by moorland. To get here from Whitby, take A171 west and turn north for Danby after 12 mi, after which it's a 3-mi drive over Danby Low Moor to the village.

EXPLORING

In a house on the eastern outskirts of Danby, the North York Moors National Park's **Moors Centre** underwent a full renovation in 2007, and now features displays on the flora and fauna of the moors. Local arts and crafts, a tearoom, and a picnic area are also here. The summer Moorsbus operates from the center for the 30-minute journey south to Hutton-le-Hole. ⊠*Danby Lodge* ☎*01439/772737* ⊕*www.visitnorthyorkshiremoors.co.uk* ✆*Free; parking £2* ⊙*Jan. and Feb., weekends 11–4; Mar., Nov., and Dec., daily 11–4; Apr.–Oct., daily 10–5.*

EN ROUTE From Danby take the road due west for 2 mi to Castleton, and then turn south over the top of the moors toward Hutton-le-Hole. The narrow road offers magnificent views over North York Moors National Park, especially at the old stone **Ralph Cross** (5 mi), which marks the park's highest point. Drive carefully: sheep-dodging is a necessary art.

HUTTON-LE-HOLE

13 mi south of Danby.

Similar to many other area villages, sleepy Hutton-le-Hole is a charming little place based around a wide village green, with fluffy sheep snoozing in the shade of stone cottages. Unfortunately, because of its frequent selection by guidebooks as *the* village to see in the area, it can be unbearably crowded in summer. You can always keep driving to either the charming nearby burg of Thorton-le-Dale or to the medieval market towns of Helmsley or Pickering.

EXPLORING

The excellent open-air **Ryedale Folk Museum** interprets life in the Dales from prehistory onward through craft demonstrations and 13 historic buildings, including a medieval kiln, 16th-century cottages, and a 19th-century blacksmith's shop. ☎01751/417367 ⊕*www.ryedalefolkmuseum.co.uk* £5.25 ☉*Early Mar.–Oct., daily 10–5:30; Nov.–Feb., daily 10–dusk; last admission 4:30.*

HELMSLEY

8 mi southwest of Hutton-le-Hole, 27 mi north of York.

The market town of Helmsley, with its flowering window boxes, stone cottages, arched bridges across streams, and churchyard, is the perfect place to spend a relaxing afternoon. You can while away a few hours lingering in its tea shops and tiny boutiques, and exploring the craggy ruins of its Norman castle (destroyed during the Civil War). Market day is Friday. Nearby are the impressive ruins of Rievaulx Abbey.

GETTING HERE AND AROUND

There is no train station in Helmsley, and it has no major bus service. The Moorsbus stops in Helmsley once a day during the summer. By car, Helmsley is on A170.

ESSENTIALS

Bus Information Moorsbus (☎01845/597000) .

Visitor Information Helmsley (✉*Town Hall, Market Pl.* ☎01439/770173 ⊕*www.ryedale.gov.uk*).

EXPLORING

Fodor'sChoice ★ The perfect marriage of architecture and countryside, **Rievaulx** (pronounced ree-*voh*) Abbey has a dramatic setting 2 mi northwest of Helmsley; its sweeping arches soar at the precise point where a forested hillside rushes down to the River Rye. A French Cistercian sect founded this abbey in 1132, and though its monks led a life of isolation and silence, they were active in the wool business. By the end of the 13th century the abbey was massively wealthy, with hundreds of lay workers and farmland filling the valley. The evocative ruins give a good indication of how vast the abbey once was. Tiny plaques indicate where the dormitories, kitchen, chapter house, and nave once stood. Medieval mosaic tiling can still be seen here and there, and part of the symmetrical cloisters remains. The Chapter House retains the original shrine of the first abbot, William, by the entrance. By the time of Henry VIII the abbey had shrunk dramatically; only 20 or so monks lived here when the king's soldiers arrived to destroy the building in 1538. After that, the earl of Rutland owned Rievaulx, and he demolished what was left to the best of his ability. The abbey is a 1½-hour walk northwest from Helmsley by signposted footpath, or 2 mi by vehicle. ⊠*Off B1257* ☎*01439/798228* ⊕*www.english-heritage.org.uk* 🎫£5 ⊙*Apr.–Sept., daily 10–6; Oct., daily 10–5; Nov.–Mar., Thurs.–Mon. 10–4.*

**OFF THE
BEATEN
PATH**

Rievaulx Terrace and Temples. From Rievaulx Abbey it's a short walk or drive up to the hill where Rievaulx Terraces have a magnificent view of the abbey. The long, grassy walkway on the hillside ends at the remains of several Tuscan- and Ionic-style classical temples, once maintained by the earl of Rutland. Unfortunately, the terrace and the abbey are overseen by different organizations, so there's no joint admission. If you must choose between the two, visit the abbey. ⊠*Off B1257* ☎*01439/798340* ⊕*www.nationaltrust.org.uk* 🎫£4.40 ⊙*Late Mar.– Sept., daily 10:30–6; Oct., daily 10:30–5; last admission 1 hr before closing.*

13

WHERE TO STAY

£££–££££ 🍽 **Black Swan.** A splendid base for exploring the area, this ivy-covered property sits on the edge of the market square. The building is a hybrid—part 16th-century coaching inn, part Georgian house. Cozy rooms overlook either the square or the fine walled garden at the back. The restaurant serves traditional British and local dishes. **Pros:** ivy-covered charm; great location in the center of town. **Cons:** decor is a bit old-fashioned; bathrooms need updating. ⊠*Market Pl.* ☎*01439/770466, 0870/400–8112 for reservations* ⊕*www.blackswan-helmsley.co.uk* 📠*45 rooms* ♿*In-room: no a/c. In-hotel: restaurant, bar, some pets allowed* ⊟*AE, DC, MC, V* ⏝⏝*BP.*

££ 🍽 **No. 54.** Tea and cakes provide a tasty welcome in this stone cottage just off market square. The light-filled rooms are decorated in creamy hues. Owner Lizzie Would knows everything about the area and is happy to help. She'll cook you a fine dinner for £22 if you book in advance. **Pros:** tea and cakes for everyone; comfy beds. **Cons:** small rooms; not much privacy. ⊠*Bondgate* ☎*01439/771533* ⊕*www.no54.co.uk* 📠*3 rooms* ♿*In-room: no a/c, no phone* ⊟*No credit cards* ⏝⏝*BP.*

SPORTS AND THE OUTDOORS

Helmsley, on the southern edge of the moors, is the starting point of the **Cleveland Way** (⊕*www.nationaltrail.co.uk*), the long-distance moor-and-coastal footpath. Boots are donned at the old cross in the market square; it's 50 mi or so across the moors to the coast and then a similar distance south to Filey along the cliff tops. The footpath is 110 mi long and takes around nine days start to finish. The trail passes close to Rievaulx Abbey, a few miles outside town, and walking to Rievaulx is a good way to sample the trail. Maps are available at the tourist center in town, but the Rievaulx section is well signposted.

The Northeast

WORD OF MOUTH

"My husband is from Newcastle and there are loads of picturesque castles to visit on the coast and around the Northeast. It is also easy to get to the Lake District from there (about 3 hours) . . . This is prime farming territory—I'm sure you would love it and it is off the beaten path for many Americans."

—palatino82

"Hadrian's Wall, Housesteads, and Vindolanda were favorites. . . . The museum at Vindolanda has incredible artifacts from the Roman garrison's garbage dump. The countryside is amazing—you can imagine that the Romans stationed there thought they were at the end of the earth!"

—Marsha

Updated
by Christi
Daugherty

For many Britons the words the Northeast provoke a vision of near-Siberian isolation. The truth is a revelation. For although there are wind-hammered, wide-open spaces and empty roads threading the wild high moorland, the Northeast also has simple fishing towns, small villages of remarkable charm, and historic abbeys and castles that are all the more romantic for their often ruinous state.

Even the remoteness can be relative. Suddenly, around the next bend of a country road, you may come across an imposing church, a tall monastery, or a gorgeous country house built by a Victorian-era millionaire. The value found in the shops and accommodations, the uncrowded beaches ideal for walking, and the friendliness of the people also add to the region's appeal. Still, outside of a few key sights, the Northeast is off the well-trodden tourist path.

Mainly composed of the two large counties of Durham and Northumberland, the Northeast includes English villages adjacent to the Scottish border area, renowned in ballads and romantic literature for feuds, raids, and battles. Fittingly, Durham Cathedral, the seat of bishops for nearly 800 years, has been described as "half church of God, half castle 'gainst the Scot." Hadrian's Wall, which marked the northern limit of the Roman Empire, stretches across prehistoric remains and moorland in this region. Not far north of Hadrian's Wall are some of the most interesting parts of Northumberland National Park. Steel, coal, railroads, and shipbuilding made prosperous towns such as Newcastle upon Tyne (now re-creating itself as a cultural center) and Darlington.

The region's 100 mi of largely undeveloped coast is one of the least-visited and most dramatic in all Europe. Several outstanding castles perch on headlands and promontories along here, including Bamburgh, which according to legend was the site of Joyous Garde, the castle of Sir Lancelot du Lac.

ORIENTATION AND PLANNING

GETTING ORIENTED

The historic cathedral city of Durham, one of the region's top attractions, sits to the east of the wooded foothills of the Pennines mountain range. Farther north, busy Newcastle straddles the region's main river, the muddy Tyne. West of Newcastle, the remains of Hadrian's Wall snake through rugged scenery. Head northwest for the wilderness of Northumberland National Park. Along the far northeastern coast, towering castles and misty islands punctuate the stunning, final miles of England's eastern shoreline.

TOP REASONS TO GO

Castles, castles, castles: Fought over for centuries by the Scots and the English, and prey to Viking raiders, the Northeast was one of the most heavily fortified regions in England.

Medieval Durham: A splendid Norman cathedral that dates back to the 11th century is just one of the city's charms. Take a stroll on its ancient winding streets or along the River Wear; this is a fairy-tale town hewn from stone.

Hadrian's Wall: The ancient Roman wall is a wonder for the wild countryside around it and the resiliency of its stones. For an awe-inspiring sense of history, nothing beats a hike along part of the Hadrian's Wall Path national trail or a ride on Hadrian's Cycleway.

Lindisfarne (Holy Island): Just getting to this historic island is an unusual experience; you drive across a causeway that floods at high tide. This remote spot includes the ruins of Lindisfarne Priory.

Alnwick Castle and Gardens: The inland seat of the dukes of Northumberland is fascinating with its formidable walls, luxurious interiors, and multimillion-dollar gardens.

14

Durham, Newcastle, and Environs. The historic city of Durham, set on a rocky spur, has a stunning castle and cathedral. South and west are scenic towns with castles and industrial heritage sites. Newcastle, to the north, is a sprawling metropolis with a lively regional arts scene.

Hadrian's Wall Country. England's wildest countryside is traversed by the remains of the wall that marked the northern border of the Roman Empire. Hexham is a useful base, and Housesteads Roman Fort is a key site. It's stunning country for walking or biking.

The Far Northeast Coast. In this dramatic landscape, rocky hillsides plunge into the sea. The ruins of castle towers such as Dunstanburgh and Bamburgh stand guard over windswept beaches, and Lindisfarne has a long religious history. Alnwick, inland, has spectacular gardens.

PLANNING

WHEN TO GO

The best time to see the Northeast is in summer. This ensures that the museums—and the roads—will be open, and you can take advantage of the countryside walks that are one of the region's greatest pleasures. Rough seas and inclement weather make it dangerous to swim at any of the beaches except in July and August. At the end of June, Alnwick hosts its annual fair, with a medieval market, art shows, and concerts. The Durham Regatta also takes place in June. The Northumberland Traditional Music Festival runs over two weeks in October.

PLANNING YOUR TIME

If you're interested in exploring Hadrian's Wall and the Roman ruins, you will probably want to base yourself at a guesthouse in or around Hexham. From there you can easily take in Housesteads and the other local landmarks. It's worth taking a day trip to Durham to see its lovely ancient buildings, and Newcastle's museums are a favorite destination of art lovers. Make Newcastle a day trip, as the city's tourist offerings are limited. Romantics will want to spend a day or two driving up the coast to take in the incredible castle views.

GETTING HERE AND AROUND

AIR TRAVEL

Newcastle has an airport (a 15-minute drive from the city center), which has flights from British and European cities.

Contact **Newcastle Airport** (⊠ *Off A696* ☎ *0870/122–1488* ⊕ *www. newcastleairport.com*).

BUS TRAVEL

National Express and Megabus (book online to avoid phone charges) travel to Durham and Newcastle and leave from London's Victoria Coach Station, but the journey isn't quick. Expect it to take between six and eight hours. Connecting services to other parts of the region leave from those cities. Traveline has information.

The North East Explorer Pass (£8, one day) allows unlimited travel on most local bus and Metro train services in the region and is available from the bus driver or local bus or Metro stations.

Contacts **Megabus** (☎ *0900/160–0900* ⊕ *www.megabus.co.uk*). **National Express** (☎ *0871/781–8181* ⊕ *www.nationalexpress.com*). **North East Explorer Pass** ⊕ *www.explorernortheast.co.uk/*). **Traveline** (☎ *0870/608–2608* ⊕ *www.traveline.org.uk*).

CAR TRAVEL

If you're headed to small villages, remote castles, or Hadrian's Wall, traveling by car is the best alternative. The A1 highway links London and Newcastle (five to six hours). The scenic route is the A697, which branches west off A1 north of Morpeth. For the coast, leave the A1 at Alnwick and follow the minor B1340 and B1339 for Craster, Seahouses, and Bamburgh. Holy Island is reached from the A1.

TRAIN TRAVEL

Within England, the train is still the best way to reach this region. National Express runs the train service from London to the Northeast. The average travel times from London are 2½ hours to Darlington, and 3 hours to Durham and Newcastle. At this writing, the National Express transportation system was undergoing changes, so call ahead to confirm schedules. From Newcastle, you can catch local trains to Alnwick, Corbridge, Hexham, and Carlisle; these journeys take about a half hour. National Rail Enquiries has information.

Contacts **National Express** (☎ *0870/522–5125* ⊕ *www.nationalexpress.com*). **National Rail Enquiries** (☎ *0845/748–4950* ⊕ *www.nationalrail.co.uk*).

RESTAURANTS

Make sure to sample fine local meats and produce. Look for restaurants that serve game from the Kielder Forest, local lamb from the hillsides, salmon and trout from the rivers, and shellfish, crab, and oysters from the coast. Don't wait until 9 PM to have dinner or you may have a hard time finding a place that is still serving.

HOTELS

The large hotel chains don't have much of a presence in the Northeast, outside the few cities. Instead, you can expect to find country houses converted into welcoming hotels, old coaching inns that still greet guests after 300 years, and cozy bed-and-breakfasts convenient to hiking trails. Many budget accommodations close in winter.

WHAT IT COSTS IN POUNDS				
£	££	£££	££££	£££££
Restaurants	Under £10	£10–£14	£15–£19	£20–£25	over £25
Hotels	Under £70	£70–£120	£121–£160	£161–£220	over £220

Restaurant prices are for a main course at dinner. Hotel prices are for two people in a standard double room in high season, including V.A.T., with no meals or, if indicated, CP (with continental breakfast), BP (Breakfast Plan, with full breakfast), or MAP (Modified American Plan, with breakfast and dinner).

VISITOR INFORMATION

Contacts Hadrian's Wall Country (⊕ *www.hadrians-wall.org*). **Northumbria Regional Tourist Board** (⊠ *Stella House, Goldcrest Way, Newburn Riverside, Newcastle-upon-Tyne* ☎ *01271/336182* ⊕ *www.visitnorthumbria.com*).

DURHAM, NEWCASTLE, AND ENVIRONS

Durham—the first major northeastern town on the main road up from London—is by far the region's most interesting historic city. Its cobblestone streets and towering cathedral make it a charming place to visit. The city is surrounded on all sides by scenic countryside, ruined castles, and isolated villages. Newcastle, though, is the region's biggest, liveliest, and most cosmopolitan city. Most other towns in the area made their fortunes during the Industrial Revolution and have since subsided into slow decline. Several, such as bustling Darlington, birthplace of the modern railroad, hold interesting relics of their 19th-century heyday.

DURHAM

250 mi north of London, 15 mi south of Newcastle.

The great medieval city of Durham, seat of County Durham, stands dramatically on a rocky spur, overlooking the countryside. Its cathedral and castle, a World Heritage Site, rise together on a wooded peninsula almost entirely encircled by the River Wear (rhymes with "beer"). For centuries these two ancient structures have dominated Durham—now a thriving university town, the Northeast's equivalent of Oxford or Cambridge. Steep, narrow streets overlooked by perilously angled medieval houses and 18th-century town houses make for fun exploring. In the most attractive part of the city, near the Palace Green and along the river, people go boating, anglers cast their lines, and strollers walk along the shaded paths.

Despite the military advantages of its location, Durham was founded surprisingly late, probably in about the year 1000, growing up around a small Saxon church erected to house the remains of St. Cuthbert. It was the Normans, under William the Conqueror, who put Durham on the map, building the first defensive castle and beginning work on the cathedral. From here, Durham's prince-bishops, granted almost dictatorial local powers by William in 1072, kept a tight rein on the county, coining their own money and maintaining their own laws and courts; not until 1836 were these rights finally restored to the English Crown.

GETTING HERE AND AROUND

National Express trains from London's King's Cross Station arrive at the centrally located Durham Station once an hour during the day. The journey takes about three hours. Trains from York arrive about every 15 minutes; that journey takes an hour. A handful of National Express and Megabus buses from London arrive daily. The trip takes about seven hours.

Between 10 and 4 on Monday through Saturday, cars are charged £2 (on top of parking charges) to enter the Palace Green area. Bus 40 links parking lots and the train and bus stations with the cathedral.

ESSENTIALS

Visitor Information Durham (✉ *Millennium Pl.* ☎ *0191/384-3720* ⊕ *www.durhamtourism.co.uk*).

14

EXPLORING

❷ Durham Castle. For almost 800 years the castle was the home of successive prince-bishops; from here they ruled large tracts of northern England and kept the Scots at bay. Facing the cathedral across Palace Green, the castle commands a strategic position above the River Wear. It has required many renovations and repairs through the ages because of less-than-stable foundations, but it remains an impressive pile. Henry VIII first curtailed the bishops' independence, although it wasn't until the 19th century that the prince-bishops finally had their powers annulled. They abandoned the castle, turning it over to University College, one of several colleges of the University of Durham (founded 1832), the oldest in England after Oxford and Cambridge. You can visit the castle only on a 45-minute guided tour. ✉*Palace Green* ☎*0191/334–4106* ⊕*www.durhamcastle.com* 💷*£5* ◷*Call for guided tour hrs.*

QUICK BITES

Drop into the **Almshouse Café** (✉*Palace Green* ☎*0191/386–1054*), in an ancient almshouse between the cathedral and castle, for fat brownies or tasty cheesecake. These sweet treats are perfect with your tea.

❶ Durham Cathedral. A Norman masterpiece in the heart of the city, the cathedral is an amazing vision of solidity and strength, a far cry from the airy lightness of later, Gothic cathedrals. Construction began in about

Fodor'sChoice
★

1090, and the main body was finished in about 1150. The round arches of the nave and the deep zigzag patterns carved into them typify the heavy, gaunt style of Norman, or Romanesque, building. The technology of Durham, however, was revolutionary. This was the first European cathedral to be given a stone, rather than a wooden, roof. When you consider the means of construction available to its builders—the stones that form the ribs of the roof had to be hoisted by hand and set on a wooden structure, which was then knocked away—the achievement seems staggering.

The origins of the cathedral go back to the 10th century. In 995 monks brought to this site the remains of St. Cuthbert, which had been removed from the monastery at Lindisfarne after a Viking raid in 875. Soon the wealth attracted by Cuthbert's shrine paid for the construction of a cathedral. The bishop's throne here was claimed to be the loftiest in medieval Christendom; the miter of the bishop is the only one to be encircled by a coronet, and his coat of arms is the only one to be crossed with a sword as well as a crosier. **Cuthbert's shrine** lies surrounded by columns of local marble, with the saint's remains buried below a simple slab. An unobtrusive tomb at the west end of the cathedral, in the handsome, Moorish-influenced **Galilee Chapel,** is the final resting place of the **Venerable Bede,** an 8th-century Northumbrian monk whose contemporary account of the English people made him the country's first reliable historian. He died in Jarrow in 735, and his remains were placed here in 1020.

Upon entering the cathedral, note the 12th-century bronze **Sanctuary Knocker,** shaped like the head of a ferocious mythological beast, mounted on the massive northwestern door. By grasping the ring clenched in the animal's mouth, medieval felons could claim sanctuary; cathedral records show that 331 criminals sought this protection between 1464 and 1524. The current knocker is, in fact, a reproduction. The original is kept in the cathedral **Treasury,** along with ancient illuminated manuscripts, fragments of St. Cuthbert's oak coffin, and more church treasures well worth a look. You can view a film and an exhibit about building the cathedral, and in good weather you can climb the **tower.** There's also a restaurant in the atmospheric undercroft, and a lovely shop. ⊠ *Palace Green* ☎ *0191/386–4266* ⊕ *www. durhamcathedral.co.uk* 🖃 *£4 donation requested; Treasury £2.50, tower £3, guided tours £4* ⊗ *Cathedral mid-June–early Sept., daily 7:30 AM–8 PM; early Sept.–mid-June, Mon.–Sat. 7:30–6, Sun. 7:45–5. Treasury and tower Mon.–Sat. 10–4:30, Sun. 2–4:30. Choral evensong service Tues.–Sat. 5:15, Sun. 3:30. Guided tours mid-Apr.–Sept., Mon.– Sat. 11 and 2:30.*

❹ Framwellgate Bridge. If you follow the far side of the Wear north from Prebends Footbridge, you can recross the river at this 12th-century bridge. Many of the elegant town houses that line the narrow lanes back up to the cathedral now house departments of the University of Durham.

❸ Prebends Footbridge. Delightful views are the reward of a short stroll along the River Wear's leafy banks, especially as you cross this footbridge, reached from the southern end of Palace Green. J. M. W. Turner reveled in the view from here and painted a celebrated scene of Durham from the bridge.

❺ University of Durham Oriental Museum. The museum displays fine art and craft work from all parts of Asia. The collection of Chinese ceramics is notable, and don't miss the nearby 18-acre Botanic Gardens. ⊠*Elvet Hill, off South Rd. (A1050)* ☎*0191/334–5694* ⊕*www.dur.ac.uk/oriental.museum* 🎫*£1.50* ☉*Weekdays 10–5, weekends noon–5.*

> ### ROW THEIR BOATS
>
> The pretty River Wear winds through Durham, curving beneath the cathedral and castle. In mid-June each year the city hosts the prestigious Durham Regatta, Britain's oldest rowing event. Three hundred racing crews compete in events, including races for single sculls and teams of eight.

WHERE TO EAT

££ **FRENCH** ✕**Bistro 21.** A few miles northwest of the center, Durham's most fashionable restaurant is in a superbly restored farmhouse. The eclectic, seasonal menu has a pronounced French accent. Look for such dishes as poached salmon and lamb with lemon polenta, as well as rich desserts. ⊠*Aykley Heads* ☎*0191/384–4354* ▤*AE, DC, MC, V* ☉*Closed Sun.*

££ **THAI** ✕**Numjai.** This Thai restaurant provides variety to the north's meat-and-vegetables diet. To top it all off, it has a lovely setting in the Milburngate shopping center. Its wraparound windows let you gaze out over your coconut green curry at the cathedral. ⊠*19 Milburngate* ☎*0191/386–2020* ▤*MC, V.*

££ **BRITISH** ✕**Oldfields Restaurant.** This excellent eatery specializes in organic vegetables and free-range meat, and most comes from the surrounding region. The seasonal menu of steaks, panfried pheasant, and braised mutton tends to be served with hearty root vegetables in the winter, and greens and beans in the summer. ⊠*18 Clay Path* ☎*0191/370–9595* ▤*MC, V.*

WHERE TO STAY

During college vacations (late March through April, July through September, and December), reasonably priced accommodations are available at the **University of Durham** (☎*0191/334–2886* ⊕*www.dur.ac.uk/conferences*), in Durham Castle and in buildings throughout the city.

££ 🏠**Georgian Town House.** At the top of a cobbled street overlooking the cathedral and castle, this family-run guesthouse has a location almost good enough to make you overlook the sometimes startling decor (such as burgundy curtains with lime green accents). Rooms are small and snug and have pleasant city views. Every bit of space is crowded with knickknacks, but the place is friendly and the breakfasts are big. **Pros:** great location; jovial owners; laid-back atmosphere. **Cons:** small rooms; odd design choices. ⊠*10 Crossgate* ☎*0191/386–8070* ⊕*www.thegeorgiantownhouse.co.uk* 🛏*8 rooms* ⚘*In-room: no a/c. In-hotel: no-smoking rooms* ▤*No credit cards* ☉*Closed last wk of Dec.* ⦿*BP.*

££ 🏠**Seven Stars Inn.** Warm oranges and tartans in the public areas enhance the coziness of this good-value early-18th-century coaching inn. The simple bedrooms are done in creamy yellows and reds and have modern pine furniture. At the restaurant, tuck into such dishes as rib-eye steak with black pudding and bacon. The inn is 2 mi south of the city. **Pros:** cozy lounge; reasonable rates. **Cons:** far from the center; on a main road; it's nothing fancy. ⊠*High St. N, Shincliffe Village* ☎*0191/384–8454* ⊕ *www.sevenstarsinn.co.uk* ⇥*8 rooms* ⧖*In-room: no a/c. In-hotel: restaurant, some pets allowed* ▤*MC, V* ⊺⏘*BP.*

££–£££   ⧉**Three Tuns Hotel.** This 16th-century inn has echoes of its solid country past. Some sections retain the old oak beams and fireplaces. The bedrooms are more contemporary, although antiques keep the historic feel going. Guests can use the indoor pool and health club at the nearby Swallow Royal County Hotel. Browns restaurant serves staples such as veal, steak, and salmon. **Pros:** nice mix of the old and the new; lots of atmosphere. **Cons:** it's a bit of a walk to use the pool and health club. ⊠*New Elvet* ☎*0191/386–4326* ⊕*www.swallowhotels.com* ⇥*50 rooms* ⧖*In-room: no a/c. In-hotel: restaurant, bar, parking (free), some pets allowed* ▤*AE, DC, MC, V* ⊺⏘*BP.*

NIGHTLIFE AND THE ARTS

Durham's nightlife is geared to university students. The **Coach-and-Eight** (⊠*Bridge House, Framwellgate Bridge* ☎*0191/386–3284*) can get noisy, but outdoor seating makes it appealing. The **Hogshead** (⊠*58 Saddler St.* ☎*0191/386–9550*) pub is a true student haunt.

SHOPPING

Bramwells Jewellers (⊠*24 Elvet Bridge* ☎*0191/386–8006*) has its own store specialty, a pendant copy of the gold-and-silver cross of St. Cuthbert. The food and bric-a-brac stalls in **Durham Indoor Market** (⊠*Market Pl.* ☎*0191/384–6153*), a Victorian arcade, are open Monday through Saturday 9 to 5.

SPORTS AND THE OUTDOORS

Brown's Boat House (⊠*Elvet Bridge* ☎*0191/386–3779*) rents rowboats April through early November and offers short cruises all year.

BISHOP AUCKLAND

10 mi southwest of Durham.

For 700 years, between the 12th and 19th century, the powerful prince-bishops of Durham had their country residence in Auckland Castle, in the town of Bishop Auckland. When finally deprived of their powers in 1836, the bishops left Durham and made Bishop Auckland their official home.

GETTING HERE AND AROUND

Bishop Auckland is just off the A1 motorway from London (260 mi) or Durham (13 mi). There's no direct train service here from London or Durham. However, you can take a train from either city to Darlington and change. The journey takes about three hours from London and one hour from Durham. National Express offers a regional bus service between Bishop Auckland and Durham. This trip takes about 30 minutes.

ESSENTIALS

Visitor Information Bishop Auckland (⊠ *Town Hall, Market Pl.* ☎ *01388/ 604922* ⊕ *www.durham.gov.uk*).

EXPLORING

Arguably the greatest of the prince-bishops of Durham's properties is the episcopal palace of **Auckland Castle,** which you enter through an elaborate stone arch. Much of what you see today dates from the 16th century, although the limestone-and-marble chapel, with its dazzling stained-glass windows, was built in 1665 from the ruins of a 12th-century hall. ■TIP→ Don't miss some of the palace's greatest treasures: paintings by the 17th-century Spanish artist Zurbarán of Jacob and his 12 sons. ⊠ *Off Market Pl.* ☎ *01388/601627* ⊕ *www.auckland-castle. co.uk* 🎫 *£4* ⊗ *Apr.–June and Sept., Mon. and Sun. 2–5; July and Aug., Mon. and Wed. 11–5, Sun. 2–5; park daily 7 AM–sunset.*

★ The stone battlements and turrets of moated **Raby Castle,** once the seat of the powerful Nevills and currently the home of the 11th baron Barnard, stand amid a 200-acre deer park and ornamental gardens. Charles Nevill supported Mary, Queen of Scots in the 1569 uprising against Elizabeth I; when the Rising of the North failed, the estate was confiscated. Dating mostly from the 14th century (using stone plundered from

Barnard Castle) and renovated in the 18th and 19th centuries, the luxuriously furnished castle has displays of art and other treasures, including an important Meissen collection. Rooms in wonderfully elaborate Gothic Revival, Regency, and Victorian styles are open for viewing. Raby Castle is 7 mi southwest of Bishop Auckland, 19 mi southwest of Durham. ⊠*A688, 1 mi north of Staindrop* ☎*01833/660202* ⊕*www.rabycastle.com* ☜*Castle, park, and gardens £9.75, park and gardens £5* ⊘*Castle: May, June, and Sept., Sun.–Wed. 12:30–5; July and Aug., Sun.–Fri. 12:30–5.*

UPSTAIRS, DOWNSTAIRS

Gorgeous Raby Castle acts as a living museum for castle life through the centuries. It's especially good at juxtaposing life as a servant with life as a lord. In the lord's dining room, rich red carpets and patterned silk wallpaper glow under a soaring, intricately carved ceiling. Downstairs, the servants had their meals in the bare, low-ceilinged medieval servants' hall, sitting at a rough pine table on hard wooden benches. Ouch!

BARNARD CASTLE

14 mi south of Bishop Auckland, 25 mi southwest of Durham.

The handsome market town of Barnard Castle has sights of its own and can also serve as a base for venturing into the Teesdale Valley to the northwest. Its unusual butter-market hall (known locally as Market Cross), surmounted by an old fire-alarm bell, marks the junction of the streets Thorngate, Newgate, and Market Place. Stores, pubs, and cafés line these thoroughfares. In 1838 Charles Dickens stayed at the **King's Head Inn** here while doing research for his novel *Nicholas Nickleby*. The local tourist office has a free *In the Footsteps of Charles Dickens* leaflet.

GETTING HERE AND AROUND

Barnard Castle is about a 20-minute drive from Bishop Auckland on A688. It's small, and walking is an easy way to explore the town.

ESSENTIALS

Visitor Information Barnard Castle (⊠*Woodleigh, Flatts Rd.* ☎*01833/ 690909* ⊕*www.teesdalediscovery.com*).

EXPLORING

The substantial ruins of **Barnard Castle,** which gave its name to the town, cling to an aerie overlooking the River Tees. Inside you can see parts of the 14th-century Great Hall and the cylindrical, 13th-century tower, built by the castle's original owners, the Anglo-Scottish Balliol family. ⊠*Off Galgate* ☎*01833/638212* ⊕*www.english-heritage.org. uk* ☜*£4.20* ⊘*Apr.–Sept., daily 10–6; Oct., daily 10–4; Nov.–Mar., Thurs.–Mon. 10–4; call ahead in winter.*

★ The **Bowes Museum,** a vast French-inspired château a mile west of the town center, was built between 1862 and 1875 to house the art and artifacts accumulated by philanthropists John and Josephine Bowes. Highlights include paintings by Canaletto, El Greco, Francisco Goya, and François Boucher, and 18th-century French furniture. ■TIP➔ **Time** your visit so you can see the extraordinary 18th-century life-size, mechanical silver swan in action. It sits on a stream of twisted glass and catches and swallows a silver fish every day at 2. ⊠ *Up Newgate, follow signs from town center* ☎ *01833/690606* ⊕ *www.thebowesmuseum.org.uk* ⊠ *£6* ⊗ *Mar.–Oct., daily 10–5; Nov.–Feb., daily 11–5.*

The Upper Teesdale Valley's elemental nature shows its most volatile aspect in the sprays of England's highest waterfall, the 72-foot **High Force**. From the roadside parking lot it's a 10-minute walk through woodland to the massive rocks over which the water tumbles. A precarious viewpoint puts you right above the falls, at their best in springtime after a rain. The waterfall is 15 mi northwest of Barnard Castle. ⊠ *Off B6277* ☎ *01833/640209* ⊠ *£1; parking £1.50* ⊗ *Mid-Apr.–Oct., daily 9:30–5; Nov.–mid-Apr., open but unattended.*

14

WHERE TO EAT

£

BRITISH

✕ **Market Place Teashop.** A nicely old-fashioned air pervades this 17th-century building on the main square. Waitresses clad in striped uniforms serve such dishes as parsnip and bacon with Mornay sauce, as well as many vegetarian options. Afternoon tea comes in silver teapots. ⊠ *29 Market Pl.* ☎ *01833/690110* ▭ *MC, V* ⊗ *Closed Sun. except afternoons Apr.–Oct. No dinner.*

DARLINGTON

15 mi east of Barnard Castle, 21 mi south of Durham.

Still rooted in its 19th-century industrial past, the town of Darlington gained fame in 1825, when George Stephenson piloted his steam-powered *Locomotion* along newly laid tracks the few miles to nearby Stockton, thus kick-starting the railway age.

ESSENTIALS

Visitor Information Darlington (⊠ *13 Horsemarket* ☎ *01325/388666* ⊕ *www.visitdarlington.net).*

EXPLORING

⟳
★
Head of Steam: The Darlington Railway Centre and Museum tells the story of the early days of rail travel. It occupies the town's 1842 train station, a 20-minute walk from the town center. Its interactive exhibits and big steam trains are great for kids. Antique engines and scale models help bring history to life. ⊠ *North Rd. Station, Station Rd.* ☎ *01325/460532* ⊕ *www.drcm.org.uk* ⊠ *£5* ⊗ *Tues–Sun. 10–5.*

WHERE TO STAY

££–£££

BRITISH

⌂ **Hall Garth Hotel, Golf & Country Club.** In a lovely early-19th-century building, this hotel is surrounded by 67 acres of parkland, complete with lakes and woodlands, as well as a 9-hole golf course. At the edge of Darlington, it's a pleasant option even for nongolfers, with an indoor swimming pool and sauna, bucolic views, and lots of peaceful grounds to wander. The recently renovated rooms have a modern, tasteful decor. The hotel restaurant serves traditional British cuisine. **Pros:** gorgeous pastoral setting; relaxing rooms; good golfing. **Cons:** rooms aren't as charming as the common areas. ⊠ *Coatham Mundeville, Darlington* ☎ *0870/609–6131* ⊕ *www.foliohotels.com/hallgarth* ⇢ *51 rooms*

&In-room: no a/c. In-hotel: restaurant, bar, golf course, pool, no-smoking rooms ☐AE, MC, V ♥⃝BP.

WASHINGTON

12 mi north of Durham.

The little town of Washington has a direct link to the history of the United States.

EXPLORING

Washington Old Hall is the ancestral home of the first U.S. president. George Washington's direct forebears, the de Wessyngtons, lived here between 1183 and 1288. Other family members resided in the house until 1613, when the property was rebuilt in its current form, using parts of the medieval manor. The stone house retains a Jacobean (17th-century) appearance, particularly in the fine wood paneling and the heavy furniture. ✉ *From A1(M), 5 mi west of Sunderland, follow signs to Washington New Town, District 4, and on to Washington Village* ☎ *0191/416–6879* ⊕ *www.nationaltrust.org.uk* ⧖ *£4.40* ♥⃝ *Apr.–Oct., Sun.–Wed. 11–5; last admission 4:30.*

BEAMISH OPEN-AIR MUSEUM

8 mi west of Washington, 8 mi south of Durham

EXPLORING

★ The sprawling **Beamish Open-Air Museum** village, with buildings moved here from throughout the region, explores the way people in the Northeast lived and worked from the early 1800s to the early 1900s. A streetcar takes you around the site and to a reconstructed 1920s shopping street with a dentist's office, pub, and grocery store. Other attractions include a small manor house, a railroad station, and a coal mine. In summer, a steam train makes a short run. ■TIP➔ **Allow at least a half day if you come in summer.** ✉ *Off A693, between Chester-le-Street and Stanley* ☎ *0191/370–4000* ⊕ *www.beamish.org.uk* ⧖ *£16 Apr.–Oct., £6 Nov.–Mar.* ♥⃝ *Apr.–Oct., daily 10–5; Nov.–mid-Dec. and Jan.–Mar., Tues.–Thurs. and weekends 10–4; last admission 3.*

WHERE TO STAY

££££–£££££ ⊡**Lumley Castle Hotel.** This is a real Norman castle, right down to the
Fodor'sChoice dungeons and maze of dark flagstone corridors. Antiques, silks, and
★ deep, rich fabrics furnish all the sumptuous rooms, which are designed with clever touches such as a bathroom hidden behind a bookcase. The rooms in the courtyard annex are less expensive. You can join in the merriment of the Friday and Saturday night Elizabethan banquets or dine in the Black Knight restaurant. The hotel is just east of town via the B1284. **Pros:** great for antiques lovers; delightful hidden rooms. **Cons:** it's easy to get lost down the winding corridors. ✉ *Chester-le-Street* ☎ *0191/389–1111* ⊕ *www.lumleycastle.com* ⮑ *59 rooms* & *In-room: no a/c, Internet. In-hotel: restaurant, bar* ☐ *AE, DC, MC, V.*

NEWCASTLE UPON TYNE

8 mi north of Beamish Open-Air Museum, 16 mi north of Durham.

Durham may have the glories of its castle, cathedral, and university, but the liveliest city of the Northeast is Newcastle. It is reinventing itself as a regional center for culture and modern architecture after years of decline. Settled since Roman times on the Tyne River, the city made its fortune twice—first by exporting coal and later by shipbuilding. As a 19th-century industrial center, Newcastle had few equals in Britain, showing off its wealth in grand Victorian buildings lining the broad streets. Some of these remain, particularly on Grey Street.

Much of the regeneration since the early 1990s has been based around the Gateshead Quays. Here the Baltic Centre for Contemporary Art and the pedestrian-only Millennium Bridge—the world's first tilting bridge, which opens and shuts like an eyelid—have risen from wasteland.

14

GETTING HERE AND AROUND

Newcastle Airport, a 15-minute drive from the city center, has flights from British and European cities. Metro trains connect to the center. The A1 highway links London and Newcastle (five to six hours).

National Express trains from London's King Cross take about three hours. National Express and Megabus have buses departing from London's Victoria Coach Station several times a day for the six- to eight-hour trip.

Newcastle has a good public transportation system. Its Metro light rail network is easy to use, well signposted, and has stops near most sights. Buses go all the places Metro doesn't reach.

ESSENTIALS

Visitor Information Newcastle upon Tyne (✉ *Central Arcade, 132 Grainger St.* ☎ *0191/277–8000* ✉ *Main Concourse, Central Station* ☎ *0191/277–8000* ⊕ *www.visitnewcastlegateshead.com*).

EXPLORING

TOP ATTRACTIONS

★ ***Angel of the North.*** If you're approaching Newcastle from the south, 8 mi from the city center, at the junction of A1(M) and A1 at Gateshead, stands England's largest—and one of its most popular—sculptures, the powerful *Angel of the North*. Created by Antony Gormley in 1998, the rust-color steel sculpture is a sturdy, abstract human figure with airplane-like wings rather than arms. It stands 65 feet tall and has a horizontal wingspan of 175 feet. There's parking nearby, signposted on A167.

Baltic Centre for Contemporary Art. Formerly a grain warehouse and now the country's largest national gallery for contemporary art outside London, Baltic has changing exhibitions. ✉ *Gateshead Quays* ☎ *0191/478–1810* ⊕ *www.balticmill.com* 🎟 *Free* 🕐 *Daily 10–6.*

☺ **Great North Museum.** This museum opened in 2009, combining the collections of the erstwhile University of Newcastle upon Tyne's Museum of Antiquities and the Shefton Museum of Greek Art and Archaeology. The modern, £26 million facility contains an impressive collection of ancient archaeological finds, including remnants left behind by the Roman builders of Hadrian's Wall. It also holds a superb array of ancient Greek artifacts, as well as a reconstruction of the 1st-century Temple of Mithras at Carrawburgh. It's a very kid-friendly museum, with a planetarium and an exhibit of live animals alongside dusty Victorian stuffed specimens. ⊠ *Barras Bridge* ☎ *0191/222–6765* ⊕ *www. greatnorthmuseum.org* ▣ *Free* ⊙ *Mon.–Sat. 10–5; Sun. 2–5.*

NEED A BREAK? The popular art deco **Tyneside Coffee Rooms** (⊠ *10 Pilgrim St.* ☎ *0191/ 261–9291*), on the second floor above the Tyneside Cinema, make an intriguing place to stop for teas, coffee, and a snack. It's open daily.

★ **Laing Art Gallery.** The Northeast's finest art museum merits at least an hour's visit for its selection of British art. Some of the most extraordinary paintings are those by 19th-century local artist John Martin, who produced dramatic biblical landscapes. The Pre-Raphaelites are on show, too, and the Art on Tyneside exhibition traces 400 years of local arts, highlighting glassware, pottery, and engraving. ⊠ *Higham Pl. near John Dobson St.* ☎ *0191/232–7734* ⊕ *www.twmuseums.org. uk* ▣ *Free* ⊙ *Mon.–Sat. 10–5, Sun. 2–5.*

WORTH NOTING

☼ **Discovery Museum.** Kids and history buffs will get the most out of the
★ Discovery Museum, which tells Newcastle's story. Reconstructed streets and homes lead you from Roman times to the present day, and the Tyne galleries show off maritime and industrial achievements. *Turbinia* is a model of the 1897 ship that was the world's first to be powered by steam turbines. ⊠ *Blandford Sq.* ☎ *0191/232–6789* ⊕ *www.twmuseums.org. uk/discovery* ▣ *Free* ⊙ *Mon.–Sat. 10–5, Sun. 2–5.*

Norman castle. Overlooking the Tyne River, the remains of the Norman castle recall the city's earlier status as a defensive stronghold. This was the "new castle," built in 1080, that gave the city its name. ⊠ *St. Nicholas St.* ☎ *0191/232–7938* ⊕ *museums.ncl.ac.uk/keep* ▣ *£2.50* ⊙ *Apr.–Sept., daily 9:30–5:30; Oct.–Mar., daily 9:30–4:30; last admission 30 mins before closing.*

Segedunum Roman Fort, Baths and Museum. For a good introduction to Britain's Roman history, dip into this museum. It includes the remains of the substantial Roman fort of Segedunum, built around AD 125 as an eastern extension to Hadrian's Wall, and part of the original wall as well as a reproduction section. There's also a reconstructed Roman bath complex and an observation tower. ⊠ *Buddle St., Wallsend* ☎ *0191/ 236–9347* ⊕ *www.twmuseums.org.uk/segedunum* ▣ *£4* ⊙ *Apr.–Oct., daily 10–5; Nov.–Mar., daily 10–3:30.*

Tyne Bridge. By the old quayside, this bridge (built in 1929) is the symbol of Newcastle, and is one of seven bridges spanning the river in the city.

WHERE TO EAT AND STAY

£££ ✕ **Café 21.** A Newcastle classic, this sleek brasserie has been a favor-
MODERN BRITISH ite for business lunches and romantic dinners for years. Warm wood,
★ leather banquettes, and crisp white table linens lend a polished look. The menu focuses on modern versions of classic British cuisine. Try the

Northumbrian venison with poached apples and wild mushrooms, or the grilled rib-eye steak with roasted bone marrow. Desserts such as custard tart with nutmeg ice cream are excellent. The three-course dinner special (£18) is a good way to try it all. ⊠*Trinity Gardens, Quayside* ☎*0191/222–0755* ☰*AE, MC, V* ☽*No dinner Sun.*

££££–£££££ ⊡**Jesmond Dene House.** In a sprawling 19th-century mansion, this hotel
★ has been racking up accolades since it opened in 2007. It's surrounded by lush gardens and filled with polished oak floors, huge windows, and wandering staircases. You can read the papers by the inglenook fireplace in the lounge or curl up on a firm bed in one of the spacious, modern guest rooms. The elegant restaurant has become a local favorite for its use of regional meat and produce. **Pros:** beautiful light-filled rooms; lovely gardens. **Cons:** the restaurant is popular, so you need to book in advance. ⊠*Jesmend Dene Rd.* ☎*0191/212–3000* ⊕*www.jesmonddenehouse.co.uk* ➽*40 rooms* ⌂*In-room: dial-up. In-hotel: restaurant, bar, pool, gym, spa* ☰*AE, DC, MC, V* ⊺⊙*BP.*

£££ ⊡**Malmaison.** Converted from an old riverside warehouse, this member of a glamorous, design-conscious chain sits right beside the pedestrian Millennium Bridge. Guest rooms, done in a modern style with clever rococo-esque touches of gilt and velvet, are spacious, and the huge beds are piled high with pillows. The discreet Mal restaurant presents modern French fare in a room overlooking the Tyne. **Pros:** interesting building; gorgeous restaurant; irresistible claw-foot tubs. **Cons:** bar and restaurant get very crowded. ⊠*Quayside* ☎*0191/245–5000* ⊕*www.malmaison.com* ➽*116 rooms* ⌂*In-room: Internet. In-hotel: restaurant, room service, bar, gym, spa, laundry service, some pets allowed* ☰*AE, DC, MC, V.*

£££££ ⊡**Seaham Hall.** Byron married Annabella Milbanke in this foursquare
★ mansion in 1815; today the sumptuous contemporary interior filled with warm natural hues is a haven of luxury. Elegant bedrooms have their own fireplaces, original artwork, two-person baths, and exotic flowers. At the equally elegant restaurant (£££££), indulge in dishes such as loin of venison and root vegetables flavored with chocolate. Make some time for the spa inspired by feng shui principles. Seaham is 15 mi south of the center of Newcastle, off A19. **Pros:** luxurious rooms; full of atmosphere. **Cons:** far outside town; you'll have to dress up for dinner. ⊠*Lord Byron's Walk, Seaham* ☎*0191/516–1400* ⊕*www.seaham-hall.com* ➽*19 suites* ⌂*In-room: Internet. In-hotel: restaurant, bar, pool, gym, spa* ☰*AE, DC, MC, V* ⊺⊙*BP.*

NIGHTLIFE AND THE ARTS

★ **Offshore 44** (⊠*40–44 Sandhill* ☎*0191/261–0921*) is an old pub with a nautical theme. The upstairs terrace of the **Pitcher and Piano** (⊠*108 Quayside* ☎*0191/232–4110*), a popular pub with floor-to-ceiling windows, is the perfect viewing point for the Millennium Bridge.

★ The **Sage Gateshead** (⊠*West St., Gateshead Quays* ☎*0870/703–4555*) hosts concerts—jazz, world, pop, classical, folk, and rock—in a curving, modern building designed by Sir Norman Foster.

Theatre Royal (⊠*Grey St.* ☎*0870/905–5060*), the region's most established theater, has high-quality productions and is also a venue for opera and dance.

JARROW

4 mi east of Newcastle.

Jarrow had a noted shipyard until 1036, but the town's much more ancient history is what attracts visitors today.

EXPLORING

Bede's World holds substantial monastic ruins, a visitor center–museum, and the church of St. Paul, all reflecting the long tradition of religion and learning that began here in AD 681, when the first Saxon church was established on the site. The Venerable Bede, deemed to be England's earliest historian, moved into the monastery when he was seven and remained until his death in AD 735. You can gain a sense of medieval life from the reconstructed farm buildings and the rare breeds of pigs and cattle on the 11-acre Anglo-Saxon farm. From the southern exit traffic circle at South Tyne tunnel, take A185 to South Shields and follow signs to St. Paul's Church and Jarrow Hall. ⊠ *Church Bank* ☎ *0191/489–2106* ⊕ *www.bedesworld.co.uk* ☎ *£5.50* ⊗ *Apr.–Oct., Mon.–Sat. 10–5:30, Sun. noon–5:30; Nov.–Mar., Mon.–Sat. 10–4:30, Sun. noon–4:30; last admission 1 hr before closing.*

HADRIAN'S WALL COUNTRY

A formidable line of Roman fortifications, Hadrian's Wall was the Romans' most ambitious construction in Britain. The land through which the old wall wanders is wild and inhospitable in places, but that seems only to add to the powerful sense of history it evokes. Museums and information centers along the wall make it possible to learn as much as you want about the Roman era.

HADRIAN'S WALL

73 mi from Wallsend, north of Newcastle, to Bowness-on-Solway, beyond Carlisle.

ESSENTIALS

Visitor Information Hexham Tourism Information Centre (⊠ *Wentworth Car Park* ☎ *01434/652220* ⊕ *www.hadrianswallcountry.org*). **Once Brewed National Park Visitor Centre**. (⊠ *In Northumberland National Park, B6318 Once Brewed* ☎ *01434/344396* ⊕ *www.northumberland-national-park.org.uk* ⊗ *Mid-Mar.–Nov., daily 9:30–5.*)

EXPLORING

Fodor's Choice ★ Dedicated to the Roman god Terminus, the massive span of **Hadrian's Wall** once marked the northern frontier of the Roman Empire. Today remnants of the wall wander across pastures and hills, stretching 73 mi from Wallsend ("Wall's End," north of Newcastle) in the east, to Bowness-on-Solway in the west.

Today, the wall is a World Heritage Site, and excavating, interpreting, repairing, and generally managing the Roman remains is a Northumbrian growth industry. ■ TIP→ **At Chesters, Housesteads (the best-preserved fort), and Vindolanda, and at the Roman Army Museum near**

Greenhead, you get a good introduction to the life led by Roman soldiers on the frontier. In summer most sites sponsor talks, Roman drama, and festivals; local tourist offices and the sites have details.

At Emperor Hadrian's command, three legions of soldiers began building the wall in AD 122, and finished it in four years. It was constructed after repeated invasions from troublesome Pictish tribes in Scotland. During the Roman era it was the most heavily fortified wall in the world, with walls 15 feet high and 9 feet thick; behind it lay the vallum, a ditch about 20 feet wide and 10 feet deep. Spaced at 5-mi intervals along the wall were massive forts (such as those at Housesteads and Chesters), which could house up to 1,000 soldiers. Every mile was marked by a thick-walled milecastle (a fort that housed about 30 soldiers), and between each milecastle were two turrets, each lodging four men who kept watch. For more than 250 years the Roman army used the wall to control travel and trade and to fortify Roman Britain against the barbarians to the north.

> **FAST WALL FACTS**
>
> ■ No slaves were used to build the wall; it was built by skilled Roman masons with the labor of thousands of soldiers.
>
> ■ The wall was a multicultural military zone, with soldiers (and their families) coming from places such as Germany, Spain, and North Africa. Lively wall communities were made up of people with different languages and customs.
>
> ■ Only 5% of the Roman remains in the region around the wall have been excavated.

During the Jacobite Rebellion of 1745, the English dismantled much of the Roman wall and used the stones to pave what is now the B6318 highway. The most substantial stretches of the remaining wall are between Housesteads and Birdoswald (west of Greenhead). Running through the southern edge of Northumberland National Park and along the sheer escarpment of Whin Sill, this section is also an area of dramatic natural beauty. The ancient ruins, rugged cliffs, dramatic vistas, and spreading pastures make it a good area for hiking. For information about the wall, check out ⊕*www.hadrians-wall.org.*

A special **Hadrian's Wall Bus** (☎*01434/322002* ⊕*www.hadrians-wall. org*) offers day passes (£7.50) for service between Wallsend and Carlisle, stopping at Newcastle, Hexham, and the major Roman forts. The service runs daily from late May to mid-September and on Sunday throughout the year. Another bus runs daily from Wallsend to Bowness, and another from Hexham to Vindolanda (£2.55).

SPORTS AND THE OUTDOORS

BIKING

Hadrian's Cycleway (⊕*www.cycle-routes.org/hadrianscycleway*), between Tynemouth and Whitehaven, follows the river Tyne from the east coast until Newcastle, before chasing the entire length of Hadrian's Wall. It then continues west to the Irish Sea. Maps and guides are available at the Tourist Information Centre in Newcastle or online. **Eden's Lawn Cycle Hire** (✉*Eden's Lawn Garage, Haltwhistle* ☎*01434/320443*) rents mountain bikes for £12 per day. Bikes in the **Bike Shop** (✉ *16–17 St. Mary's, Hexham* ☎ *01434/601032*) cost £15 per day.

HIKING

Hadrian's Wall Path (☎ *01434/322022* ⊕ *www.nationaltrail.co.uk/ hadrianswall*) runs the entire 73-mi length of the wall. If you don't have time for it all, take one of the less challenging circular routes. One of the most scenic but also most rugged sections is the 12-mi western stretch between Sewingshields and Greenhead.

HEXHAM

22 mi west of Newcastle, 31 mi northwest of Durham.

The area around the busy market town of Hexham is a popular base for visiting Hadrian's Wall. Just a few miles from the most significant remains, it's a bustling working town, but it has enough historic buildings and winding medieval streets to warrant a stop in its own right. First settled in the 7th century, around a Benedictine monastery, Hexham later became a byword for monastic learning, famous for its book painting, sculpture, and singing.

GETTING HERE AND AROUND

No major bus companies travel to this region. National Express trains take about three hours to travel from London's King Cross to Newcastle. From there, catch a local train. The A1 highway links London and the region (five to six hours).

Hexham is a small, walkable town. It has infrequent local bus service, but you're unlikely to need it. If you're driving, park in the lot by the tourism office and walk into town. The tourism office has free maps and will point you in the right direction.

ESSENTIALS

Visitor Information Hexham Tourism Information Centre (✉ *Wentworth Car Park* ☎ *01434/652220* ⊕ *www.hadrianswallcountry.org*).

EXPLORING

★ Ancient **Hexham Abbey,** a site of Christian worship for more than 1,300 years, forms one side of the town's main square. Inside, you can climb the 35 worn stone "night stairs," which once led from the main part of the abbey to the canon's dormitory, to overlook the whole ensemble. Most of the current building dates from the 12th and 13th centuries, and much of the stone, including that of the Anglo-Saxon crypt, was taken from the Roman fort at Corbridge. Note the portraits on the 16th-century wooden rood screen and the four panels from a 15th-century Dance of Death in the sanctuary. ✉ *Beaumont St.* ☎ *01434/602031* ⊕ *www.hexhamabbey.org.uk* ✉ *Requested donation £2* ⊗ *May–Sept., daily 9:30–7; Oct.–Apr., daily 9:30–5. Crypt daily at 11:30 and 3.*

Since 1239, Hexham's central **Market Place** has been the site of a weekly market, now held each Tuesday. Crowded stalls are set out under the long slate roof of the Shambles; other stalls, protected only by bright awnings, take their chances with the weather.

Dating from 1330, Hexham's **Old Gaol,** across Market Place from the abbey, houses fascinating exhibits about Border history. Photographs, models, a house interior, and weapons tell the story of the "Middle March," the medieval administrative area governed by a warden and centered on Hexham. A glass elevator takes you to four floors, including the dungeon. ⊠ *Hallgate* 🕾 *01434/652351* 🖭 *£3* 🕙 *Apr.–Oct., daily 10–4:30; Nov., Feb., and Mar., Mon., Tues., and Sat. 10–4:30.*

Chesters Roman Fort, a cavalry fort in a wooded valley on the banks of the North Tyne River, was known as Cilurnum in Roman times, when it protected the point where Hadrian's Wall crossed the river. You approach the fort directly from the parking lot, and, although the site cannot compete with Housesteads in setting, the recently renovated museum here holds a fascinating collection of Roman artifacts, including statues of river and water gods, altars, milestones, iron tools, weapons, and jewelry. The military bathhouse by the river is well preserved. The fort is 4 mi north of Hexham ⊠ *B6318, ½ mi southwest of Chollerford* 🕾 *01434/681379* ⊕ *www.english-heritage.org.uk* 🖭 *£4.10* 🕙 *Apr.–Sept., daily 9:30–5; Oct.–Mar., daily 10–4.*

WHERE TO EAT AND STAY

££££ ✕ **Langley Castle.** Rescued from decline by a professor from the United
BRITISH States in the mid-1980s, this 14th-century castle with turrets and battlements is thoroughly lavish. The baronial dining room is romantic, with little candlelit alcoves draped in rich fabric. It serves an excellent menu of traditional English dishes and game—try the saddle of rabbit with wild mushrooms and chestnuts, or the fillet of beef with twice-cooked oxtail. It is 6 mi west of Hexham. ⊠ *Langley-on-Tyne* 🕾 *01434/688888* 🖃 *AE, DC, MC, V.*

£ 🏠 **Dene House.** Peaceful and stone-built, this former farmhouse on 9 acres of lovely countryside has beamed ceilings and homey rooms with pine pieces and colorful quilts. Breakfasts, taken in the cozy kitchen, include homemade bread and preserves. The house is 4 mi south of Hexham; follow signs for Dye House. **Pros:** tasty breakfasts; warm atmosphere. **Cons:** not a lot of privacy. ⊠ *B6303, Juniper, Hexham* 🕾 *01434/673413* ⊕ *www.denehouse-hexham.co.uk* 🛏 *3 rooms, 1 with private bath* 🚫 *In-room: no a/c, no phone, no TV. In-hotel: bar, no-smoking rooms* 🖃 *AE, MC, V* ⊠ *BP.*

£ 🏠 **Montcoffer.** This charming guesthouse sits in cozy, whitewashed stables that were converted in 1999. Its three guest rooms are spacious, with pine floors warmed with soft rugs, and comfortable beds covered in thick white comforters and blankets. The knowledgeable owners can suggest sights off the beaten track. Breakfasts, served in the attractive, beamed dining room, are hearty, and vegetarians are well cared for. All rooms are on the ground floor and accessible to those with mobility problems. **Pros:** big rooms; helpful owners. **Cons:** it gets booked up early. ⊠ *Bardon Mill, Hexham* 🕾 *01434/344138* ⊕ *www.montcoffer. co.uk* 🛏 *3 rooms* 🚫 *In-room: no a/c, refrigerator. In-hotel: no-smoking rooms* 🖃 *No credit cards* ⊠ *BP.*

££ 🏠 **Shieldhall Guesthouse.** A lovely 19th-century farmhouse and its origi-
★ nal outbuildings have been converted into this charming guesthouse about 15 mi into the countryside outside Hexham. Surrounded by miles

of rolling farmland, it's an ideal place to base yourself if you are in search of remote stretches of Hadrian's Wall. Rooms are small but beautifully decorated, with lots of draped fabric; bathrooms are big and modern. The friendly owners have a woodworking shop nearby where they make all the furniture in the house Elegant dinners are served at the main house's large dining table with advance notice. **Pros:** lots of peace and quiet; dinners are exceptional. **Cons:** well outside town; need a car to get around. ⊠ *Off B6342, about 15 mi east of Hexham, Belsay* ☎*01830/540387* ⊕*www.shieldhallguesthouse.co.uk* ⇋*3 rooms* ⬦*In-room: no a/c. In-hotel: restaurant* ☰*MC, V* ❙⦾❙*BP.*

NIGHTLIFE AND THE ARTS

The **Queen's Hall Arts Centre** (⊠*Beaumont St.* ☎*01434/652477*) presents theater, dance, and art exhibitions. It also sponsors events such as June's jazz festival.

GREENHEAD

18 mi west of Hexham, 49 mi northwest of Durham.

Tiny Greenhead has the Roman Army Museum, an informative Hadrian's Wall site. Other important sites are nearby, too.

EXPLORING

The **Roman Army Museum**, at the garrison fort of Carvoran, near the village, makes an excellent introduction to Hadrian's Wall. Full-size models and excavations bring this remote outpost of the empire to life; authentic Roman graffiti adorn the walls of an excavated barracks. Opposite the museum, at Walltown Crags on the Pennine Way (a long-distance hiking route), are 400 yards of the best-preserved section of the wall. ⊠*Off B6318, 1 mi northeast of Greenhead* ☎*016977/47485* ⊕*www.vindolanda.com* ▭*£4.40, joint ticket with Vindolanda £8* ☉*Mid-Feb.–Mar., Oct., and Nov., daily 10–5; Dec. and Jan., daily 10–4; Apr.–Sept., daily 10–6.*

★ If you have time to visit only one Hadrian's Wall site, **Housesteads Roman Fort**, Britain's most complete example of a Roman fort, is your best bet. It includes an interpretive center, views of long sections of the wall, the excavated 5-acre fort itself, and a small but interesting museum containing statues and other items uncovered at the fort. The steep, 10-minute walk up from the parking lot by B6318 to the site rewards the effort, especially for the sight of the wall disappearing over hills and crags into the distance. Excavations have revealed remains of granaries, gateways, barracks, a hospital, and the commandant's house. The fort is 11 mi east of Greenhead, and about 35 mi from Durham. ⊠*B6318* ☎*01434/344363* ⊕*www.english-heritage.org.uk* ▭*£4.40* ☉*Apr.–Sept., daily 10–6; Oct.–Mar., daily 10–4.*

The great garrison fort of **Vindolanda**, 8 mi east of Greenhead, holds the remains of eight successive Roman forts and civilian settlements, which have provided intriguing information about daily life in a military compound. Most of the visible remains date from the 2nd and 3rd centuries, and excavations are always under way. There are a reconstructed Roman temple, house, and shop to explore, and the museum displays rare artifacts such as writing tablets. A full-size reproduction of a section of the wall gives a sense of its massiveness. ✉*Near Bardon Mill* ☎*01434/344277* ⊕*www.vindolanda.com* 🖻*£5.20, joint ticket with Roman Army Museum £8* ⊙*Mid-Nov.–mid-Jan., Wed.–Sun. 10–4; mid-Feb.–Mar., Oct., and Nov., daily 10–5; Apr.–Sept., daily 10–6; call to confirm times in winter.*

In Northumberland National Park, **Once Brewed National Park Visitor Centre,** ½ mi north of Vindolanda, has informative displays about Hadrian's Wall and can advise about local walks. ✉*B6318 Once Brewed* ☎*01434/344396* ⊕*www.northumberland-national-park.org.uk* 🖻*Free* ⊙*Mid-Mar.–Nov., daily 9:30–5.*

WHERE TO EAT AND STAY

££
BRITISH
★

✕**Milecastle Inn.** The snug traditional bar and restaurant of this remote, peaceful 17th-century pub make an excellent place to dine. Fine local meat goes into its famous pies; take your pick from rabbit, venison, and duckling. The inn is on the north side of Haltwhistle on B6318. ✉*Military Rd., Haltwhistle* ☎*01434/321372* ⊟*AE, MC, V.*

££
🛏**Holmhead Guest House.** This former farmhouse in open countryside is not only built *on* Hadrian's Wall but also *of* it. Stone arches and exposed beams add to the feeling of history. Rooms are small but comfortable, the beds covered with soft, white eiderdown. You can book a fixed-priced dinner that may include organic vegetables. There's also an apartment in a cottage (prices start at £265 per week) and eight hostel-style beds in a barn. **Pros:** perfect for history buffs; close to Hadrian's Wall. **Cons:** rooms are a bit of a squeeze; you need a car out here. ✉*Off A69* ☎*016977/47402* ⊕*www.bandbhadrianswall.com* 🛏*4 rooms, 8 beds, 1 apartment* ♿*In-room: no a/c, no TV. In-hotel: restaurant, no-smoking rooms* ⊟*MC, V* ⊙*BP.*

THE FAR NORTHEAST COAST

Extraordinary medieval fortresses and monasteries line the final 40 mi of the Northeast coast before England gives way to Scotland. Northumbria was an enclave where the flame of learning was kept alive during Europe's Dark Ages, most notably at Lindisfarne, home of saints and scholars. Castles abound, including the spectacularly sited Bamburgh and the desolate Dunstanburgh. The region also has some magnificent beaches, which, because of the cold water and rough seas, are far better for walking than swimming. The 3-mi walk from Seahouses to Bamburgh gives splendid views of the Farne Islands, and the 2-mi hike from Craster to Dunstanburgh Castle is unforgettable. A bit inland are a few other pretty towns and other castles. This area was badly flooded in 2008, and towns like Morpeth found themselves virtually submerged for several days. You may still see signs of flood damage when you travel, although it was all being cleaned up and rebuilt as the time of this writing.

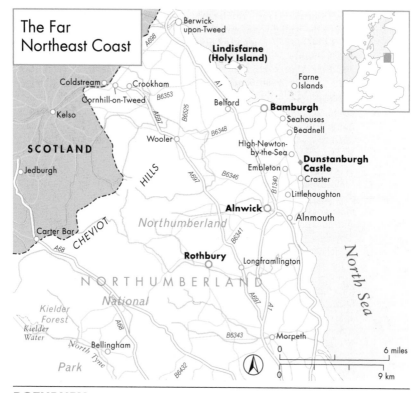

The Far
Northeast Coast

Berwick-
upon-Tweed

**Lindisfarne
(Holy Island)**

Farne
Islands

Coldstream Crookham
Cornhill-on-Tweed   B6353

Belford   **Bamburgh**

Seahouses
Beadnell

Kelso

B6348

Wooler

High-Newton-
by-the-Sea

**Dunstanburgh
Castle**

SCOTLAND

Embleton   Craster

Jedburgh

B6346

Littlehoughton

Alnwick   Alnmouth

Carter Bar

Northumberland

Rothbury   Longframlington

CHEVIOT   *HILLS*

A68

NORTHUMBERLAND

North Sea

*Kielder
Forest*
*Kielder
Water*

National

B6343   Morpeth

Bellingham   0   6 miles

North Tyne

Park   0   9 km

ROTHBURY

39 mi north of Greenhead, 9 mi southwest of Alnwick.

The small market town of Rothbury, surrounded by stunning countryside, originally developed as a Victorian resort, attracting the gentry
who roamed its hills and glades. Buildings from the era survive in the
handsome center, although, as with many such towns, the sheer weight
of modern traffic has blunted its appeal.

EXPLORING

The helpful staff at the **Northumberland National Park Visitor Centre** can
discuss walking routes through the Simonside Hills. It's also a national
tourist information center. ⊠*4 Bridge St.* ☎*01669/620887* ⊕*www.
northumberland-national-park.org.uk* ⊗*Apr.–Oct., daily 10–5.*

★   The turrets and towers of Tudor-style **Cragside** look out over the edge
of a forested hillside. This Victorian country house was built between
1864 and 1895 by Lord Armstrong, an early electrical engineer and
inventor, and designed by Richard Norman Shaw, a well-regarded
architect. Among Armstrong's contemporaries it was called "the
palace of a modern magician" because it contained so many of his
inventions. This was the first house to be lighted by hydroelectricity;
the grounds also hold an energy center with restored mid-Victorian

machinery. There are Pre-Raphaelite paintings and an elaborate mock-Renaissance marble chimneypiece. The gardens, including a rock garden and a sculpture trail, are as impressive as the house; in June rhododendrons bloom in the 660-acre park surrounding the mansion. In 2009, the old iron bridge was restored and opened after being closed for 30 years. ■ TIP➔ **Paths around the grounds are steep and distances can be long; wear comfortable shoes.** ✉ *Off A697 and B6341, 1 mi north of Rothbury* ☎*01669/620333* ⊕*www.nationaltrust.org.uk* ◈*Grounds £8.50; grounds and house £12* ⊙*House mid-Mar.–early Oct., Tues.–Sun. 1–5:30; early Oct.–Nov., Tues.–Sun. 1–4:30. Grounds mid-Mar.–Dec., Tues.–Sun. 11–5:30.*

WHERE TO STAY

££   ▧**Embleton Hall.** The 5 acres of beautiful grounds are reason enough to stay in this stone country mansion, parts of which date to 1730. Some lovely antiques and paintings decorate the individually furnished guest rooms. The chintz draperies and cut-glass chandeliers in the restaurant make perfect accompaniments to English dishes such as noisettes of lamb with mint-and-rosemary sauce. Bar options are cheaper. **Pros:** sprawling grounds; elegant restaurant. **Cons:** well outside town; few amenities. ✉*A697, 5 mi east of Rothbury, Longframlington* ☎*01665/570249* ⊕*www.embletonhallmorpeth.co.uk* ⇆*14 rooms* ⌂*In-room: no a/c. In-hotel: restaurant, bar, some pets allowed* ▤*AE, DC, MC, V* ⦿|*BP.*

14

ALNWICK

30 mi north of Newcastle, 46 mi north of Durham.

Dominated by a grand castle, the little market town of Alnwick (pronounced *ahn*-ick) is the best base from which to explore the dramatic coast and countryside of northern Northumberland.

ESSENTIALS

Visitor Information Alnwick (✉*2 the Shambles* ☎*01665/510665* ⊕*www.visitalnwick.org.uk*).

EXPLORING

A weekly open-air market (every Saturday) has been held in Alnwick's cobbled **Market Place** for more than 800 years. Note the market cross, built on the base of an older cross; the town crier once made his proclamations from here. In the last week of June, this site is host to the **Alnwick Fair,** a festival noteworthy for the enthusiastic participation of locals in medieval costume.

★   The grandly scaled **Alnwick Castle,** on the edge of the town center, is known for its gardens as well as the castle itself. This is still the home of the dukes of Northumberland, whose family, the regal Percys, dominated the Northeast for centuries. Known as "the Windsor of the North," it has been remodeled several times since Henry de Percy adapted the original Norman keep. Nowadays Alnwick is in favor as a set for films such as *Robin Hood: Prince of Thieves, Elizabeth,* and the first two Harry Potter movies (in the first, the castle grounds appear as the exterior of Hogwarts School in scenes such as the Quidditch match). In contrast with the cold, formidable exterior, the interior has all the opulence of the palatial home it still is. You see only 6 of the more than 150 rooms, but among the treasures on show are a galleried library, niches with larger-than-life-size marble statues, and Venetian-mosaic floors. The castle's extensive gardens, developed since 2000, are the big news: they include a modern, 260-foot-long stepped water cascade as well as rose and ornamental gardens and a large tree house. ⊠ *Above junction of Narrowgate and Bailiffgate* ☎ *01665/510777* ⊕ *www.alnwickcastle.com* ✉ *£12* ☯ *Castle late Mar.–late Oct., daily 11–5; last admission 4:15. Garden daily 10–dusk; last admission 45 mins before closing.*

> **GARDEN VISION**
>
> A marvelous flight of fancy, the Alnwick Gardens represent the vision of the duchess of Northumberland. Centering on modern terraced fountains by Belgian designers Jacques and Peter Wirtz, the gardens include traditional features (shaded woodland walks) and funkier elements such as a Poison Garden and a labyrinth of towering bamboo.

WHERE TO STAY

££ 🏨**White Swan Hotel.** The surprise feature of this 18th-century coaching inn near the town square is that one lounge, the Olympic Suite, has been reconstructed with the paneling, stained glass, and mirrors of the *Olympic,* sister ship of the ill-fated *Titanic.* It's used as a function room, but guests can take a look. The whole property underwent a refurbishment in 2007, and the once old-fashioned rooms now have a sleeker look. A bistro offers French-influenced British cooking. **Pros:** modern and comfortable rooms; relaxed restaurant. **Cons:** lost some of its charm. ⊠ *Bondgate Within* ☎ *01665/602109* ⊕ *www.classiclodges. co.uk* ⇘ *57 rooms* ♿ *In-room: no a/c. In-hotel: restaurant, bar, some pets allowed* ⊟ *AE, MC, V* ⫟ *BP.*

SHOPPING

The **House of Hardy** (☎ *01665/602771*), just outside Alnwick (from downtown, take A1 south to just beyond the traffic circle on the left, clearly marked), is one of Britain's finest stores for country sports. It has a worldwide reputation for handcrafted fishing tackle.

DUNSTANBURGH CASTLE

8 mi northeast of Alnwick.

GETTING HERE AND AROUND

The castle is 8 mi northeast of Alnwick, and is accessible only by footpaths from the villages of Craster or Embleton off the B1339 rural road. Follow the signs to the castle. To get here you'll need a car—there is no public transportation to or near the site.

EXPLORING

Perched romantically on a cliff 100 feet above the shore, the **Dunstanburgh Castle** ruins can be reached along a windy, mile-long coastal footpath that heads north from the tiny fishing village of Craster. Built in 1316 by the earl of Lancaster as a defense against the Scots (or perhaps as a symbol of Lancaster's deteriorating relationship with King Edward II), and later enlarged by John of Gaunt (the powerful duke of Lancaster who virtually ruled England in the late 14th century), the castle is known to many from the popular paintings by 19th-century artist J. M. W. Turner. Several handsome sandy bays indent the coastline immediately to the north. ■TIP→If you're making the hike from Craster, take time to sample the great kippers—salted and smoked herring—produced in smokehouses here and served in local pubs there. ☎01665/576231 ⊕*www.english-heritage.org.uk* ☜*£3.50* ☼*Apr.– Sept., daily 10–5; Oct., daily 10–4; Nov.–Mar., Thurs.–Mon. 10–4.*

> ### WALK AND BIKE
>
> Wide vistas, quiet roads, and fresh air make hikes and bike rides appealing in the Northeast. Long-distance footpaths include the 90-mi Teesdale Way, which follows the River Tees through Barnard Castle and Middleton-in-Teesdale. Otherwise, the russet hills and dales of Northumberland National Park will please any serious walker. Bike routes to explore—in whole or in part—are the 220-mi Northumbria's Cycling Kingdom loop and the 81-mi Coast and Castles cycle route, which takes in Dunstanburgh and Bamburgh castles.

14

BAMBURGH

14 mi north of Alnwick.

Tiny Bamburgh has a splendid castle, and several beaches are a few minutes' walk away.

EXPLORING

Especially stunning when floodlighted at night, **Bamburgh Castle** dominates the coastal view for miles, set atop a great crag to the north of Seahouses and overlooking a magnificent sweep of sand and sea backed by high dunes. It was once believed to be the legendary Joyous Garde of Sir Lancelot du Lac, one of King Arthur's fabled knights. A fortification of some kind has stood here since the 6th century, but the Norman castle was damaged during the 15th century. Much of the castle—the home of the Armstrong family since 1894—was restored during the 18th and 19th centuries, including the Victorian Great Hall, although the great Norman keep (central tower) remains intact. Exhibits include armor, porcelain, jade, furniture, and paintings. Parts of the castle are now rented as apartments. ⊠ *3 mi north of Seahouses, Bamburgh* ☎01668/214515 ⊕*www.bamburghcastle.com* ☜*£7.50; parking £1* ☼*Mid-Mar.–Oct., daily 10–5; last admission 4* PM.

WHERE TO EAT AND STAY

££££ ✕**Waren House.** Six acres of woodland surround this Georgian house
BRITISH on a quiet bay between Bamburgh and Holy Island. The crisply elegant restaurant has romantic views of Holy Island when the trees are bare; two- to four-course fixed-price dinners might include zucchini-and-apple soup, local game or trout, and ginger cheesecake. Public areas are furnished comfortably in period style, and there are a few guest rooms (£180–£240) done up in country-house style. ⊠ *Waren Mill,*

Belford ☎*01668/214581* ⊕*www.warenhousehotel.co.uk* ▭*AE, DC, MC, V.*

££–£££   ⌂**Lord Crewe Arms.** This cozy, stone-walled inn with oak beams is in the heart of the village, close to Bamburgh Castle. It's an ideal spot for lunch while you're touring the area. Pine furnishings decorate the simple guest rooms, and the food, especially seafood dishes, is excellent. **Pros:** in the center of the village; good restaurant. **Cons:** pub can get quite crowded. ⊠*Front St.* ☎*01668/214243* ⊕*www.lordcrewe.co.uk* ⟻*18 rooms* ⌂*In-room: no a/c. In-hotel: restaurant, bar, no kids under 5, some pets allowed* ▭*MC, V* ⊘*Closed Dec. and Jan.* ⟟◎⟞*BP.*

LINDISFARNE (HOLY ISLAND)

★ *6 mi east of A1, north of Bamburgh, 22 mi north of Alnwick.*

Cradle of northern England's Christianity and home of St. Cuthbert, Lindisfarne (or Holy Island) has a religious history that dates from AD 635, when St. Aidan established a monastery here. Under its greatest abbot, the sainted Cuthbert, Lindisfarne became one of the foremost centers of learning in Christendom. ■TIP➡ **The island is reached from the mainland by a long drive along a causeway that floods at high tide, so check when crossing is safe.** The times, which change daily, are displayed at the causeway and printed in local newspapers. Traffic can be heavy; allow at least a half hour for your return trip.

EXPLORING

In the year 875, Vikings destroyed the Lindisfarne community; only a few monks managed to escape, carrying with them Cuthbert's bones, which they reburied in Durham. The sandstone Norman ruins of **Lindisfarne Priory**, reestablished in the 11th century by monks from Durham, remain both impressive and beautiful. A museum here displays Anglo-Saxon carvings. ⊠*Lindisfarne* ☎*01289/389200* ⊕*www.english-heritage.org.uk* ⌂*£3.90* ⊘*Feb. and Mar., daily 10–4; Apr.–Sept., daily 9:30–5; Oct., daily 9:30–4; Nov.–Jan., Mon. and weekends 10–2.*

Reached during low tide via a causeway from the mainland, **Lindisfarne Castle** appears to grow out of the rocky pinnacle on which it was built 400 years ago, looking for all the world like a fairy-tale illustration. In 1903 architect Sir Edwin Lutyens converted the former Tudor fort into a private home that retains the original's ancient features. Across several fields from the castle is a walled garden designed by Gertrude Jekyll. Call ahead for times, as these change with the tides. ⊠*Lindisfarne* ☎*01289/389244* ⊕*www.nationaltrust.org.uk* ⌂*£5.70; garden only, £1* ⊘*Castle late Mar.–Oct., Tues.–Sun. call for hrs; garden daily 10–dusk.*

Wales

WORD OF MOUTH

"Okay, I'm biased seeing as I live there, but South Wales is so beautiful in the summer! . . . I'm from Swansea and we have the Gower coast . . . miles and miles of stunning coastline and beaches. . . . Cardiff is near, of course, and so is Pembroke. Tenby is a great little town, too."

—Lea_Lea

"I vote for Conwy so you can walk the town walls in the evening after a day of exploring. Lots of choices for eats in Conwy. I spent a week there and found it very centrally located for exploring."

—irishface

Updated by
Roger Thomas

Known as the Land of the Song, Wales is also a land of mountain and flood, where wild peaks challenge the sky and waterfalls thunder down steep, rocky chasms. It is a land of gray-stone castles, ruined abbeys, male-voice choirs, and a handful of cities. Pockets of the southeast and northeast were heavily industrialized in the 19th century, largely with mining and steelmaking, but long stretches of the coast and the mountainous interior remain areas of unmarred beauty.

Small, self-contained Wales has three national parks (Snowdonia, including Snowdon, highest mountain in England and Wales; the Brecon Beacons; and the Pembrokeshire Coast) and five official Areas of Outstanding Natural Beauty (the Wye Valley, Gower Peninsula, Llŷn Peninsula, Isle of Anglesey, and Clwydian Range), as well as large tracts of unspoiled moor and mountain in Mid Wales, the least traveled part of the country. Riches of other sorts fill the country: medieval castles, seaside resorts, traditional market towns, the glorious Bodnant Garden and the National Botanic Garden, the stately houses of Powis and Plas Newydd, steam-powered trains running through Snowdonia and central Wales, and the cosmopolitan capital of Cardiff.

The 1941 film *How Green Was My Valley* depicted Wales as an industrial cauldron filled with coal mines. Although mining did take place in Wales, the picture was not accurate then and is certainly not accurate now. One of the glories of visiting Wales is the drive through beautiful countryside from south to north without passing through any large towns. On such a drive, it's easy to believe that Wales has a population of about 2.9 million but is home to 5.5 million sheep. The country's 750 mi of coast consists mainly of sandy beaches, grassy headlands, cliffs, and estuaries.

The Welsh are a Celtic race. When the Anglo-Saxons spread through Britain beginning around AD 500, they pushed the indigenous Celts farther back into their Welsh mountain strongholds. In fact, "Wales" comes from the Saxon word *Weallas,* which means "strangers," the name impertinently given by the new arrivals to the natives. The Welsh, however, have always called themselves Y *Cymry,* the companions. Not until the English king Edward I (1272–1307) waged a brutal campaign to conquer Wales was English supremacy established. Welsh hopes were finally crushed with the death in battle of Llywelyn ap Gruffudd, last native prince of Wales, in 1282.

Today Wales has achieved a measure of independence from its English neighbor. In a 1999 referendum, a narrow majority of the Welsh people voted for partial devolution for the country. Elections were held and the Welsh Assembly was born. Unlike the Scottish Parliament, the Welsh Assembly has no lawmaking powers, but it does have significant administrative responsibilities and considerable control over Welsh affairs.

TOP REASONS TO GO

Castle country: Wales is the "Land of Castles." With more than 400 historic sites, it has one of the highest concentrations of castles in Europe. They range from evocative ruins of the native Welsh princes, such as Criccieth Castle, and the fairy-tale Victorian extravaganza of Castell Coch to the huge, mighty fortresses of Caernarfon and Harlech.

Cardiff old and new: The capital of Wales is young and vibrant. Compare the stately architecture of Cardiff's neoclassical Civic Centre with the futuristic form of Wales Millennium Centre, the new arts complex on lively Cardiff Bay.

Coast and mountain walks: Hike along the coast at St. David's, one of the most magical sections of the long-distance Pembrokeshire Coast Path. Or take a hike to the top of Pen y Fan, the highest peak in the grassy Brecon Beacons National Park.

A ride on the rails: Wales has 13 mostly narrow-gauge railways that transport you at the more leisurely pace of a bygone era along scenic routes throughout the country. The rack-and-pinion Snowdon Mountain Railway takes you to the summit of the highest mountain in England and Wales.

Pump the pedals: Brecon is great for biking. From this attractive town country roads lead into the national park; mountain bikers can climb grassy trails and tracks up into the hills.

The Welsh Assembly is housed in a building on Cardiff Bay designed by the world-famous British architect Sir Richard Rogers.

The Welsh language continues to flourish. Although spoken by only a fifth of the population, it has a high profile within the country. Welsh-language schools are popular, there is a Welsh TV channel, and road signs are bilingual. Ironically, although in the 15th and 16th centuries the Tudor kings Henry VII and Henry VIII continued England's domination of the Welsh, principally by attempting to abolish the language, another Tudor monarch, Elizabeth I, ensured its survival by authorizing a Welsh translation of the Bible in 1588. Many older people say they owe their knowledge of Welsh to the Bible. You may see (and hear) Welsh throughout your travels, but everyone in Wales speaks English, too.

ORIENTATION AND PLANNING

GETTING ORIENTED

Wales has three main regions: North, Mid, and South. North Wales is a mixture of mountains, popular sandy beaches, and coastal hideaways. Although dominated by the rocky Snowdonia National Park, the north has a gentler, greener side along the border with England. Mid Wales is pure countryside, fringed on its western shores by the arc of Cardigan Bay. Here you'll find Wales's rural heartland, with mountain lakes, quiet roads, hill sheep farms, and traditional market towns. The south is the most varied, for its boundaries include everything from Wales's capital city, Cardiff, to unspoiled coastline, grassy mountains, and wooded valleys. It's a landscape of dramatic, sudden contrasts—within minutes of urban areas you can be among national parklands, moors, and mountains.

North Wales. Wales's most famous castles are found in its northern region. The cream of the crop is Caernarfon, a medieval palace dominating the waterfront on the Menai Strait. Conwy (castle and town) is popular, too. Snowdonia's mountains are a major draw, as is quirky Portmeirion, a faux-Italian village.

Mid Wales. The quietest part of Wales is home to scenic countryside, from rolling hills to more rugged mountains. Dolgellau is in the mountainous southern part of Snowdonia National Park. Hay-on-Wye is famous for its secondhand and antiquarian bookstores.

South Wales. Cardiff, the lively young capital city, is here, as are two very different national parks: the green, swooping hills of the Brecon Beacons and, in the far west, the sea cliffs, beaches, and estuaries of the Pembrokeshire Coast. Both are excellent for outdoor activities such as sailing, walking, and mountain biking,

PLANNING

WHEN TO GO

The weather in Wales, as in the rest of Britain, is a lottery. It can be warm in spring and cool in summer; come prepared for rain or shine. Generally speaking, southwest Wales enjoys a milder climate than elsewhere in Britain, thanks to the moderating effects of the sea. Spring and autumn can be surprisingly dry and sunny. Spring may arrive very early in Pembrokeshire, in the southwest. In contrast, mountainous areas like Snowdonia and the Brecon Beacons can be chilly at any time of the year. Book ahead for major festivals such as the literary Hay Festival, Brecon Jazz, Abergavenny Food Festival, and Llangollen's International Musical Eisteddfod.

PLANNING YOUR TIME

First-time visitors often try to cover too much ground in too little time. Wales is often perceived as a destination to be covered in just a few days. If you have limited time, base yourself in one region—North or South Wales, for example—and see the surrounding sights. From Cardiff, it's easy to visit the Wye Valley, Brecon Beacons, and the Gower Peninsula. Along the North Wales coast, Llandudno is a good base for Snowdonia and a sandy seashore. But many people return for a longer visit and get to know the country, its history, culture, and off-the-beaten-track locations.

The location of Wales lends itself to a border-hopping trip. Well-known locations like Bath (near South Wales) and Chester (near North Wales) are no more than an hour from the Welsh border, so it is easy to create an itinerary that combines both Wales and England.

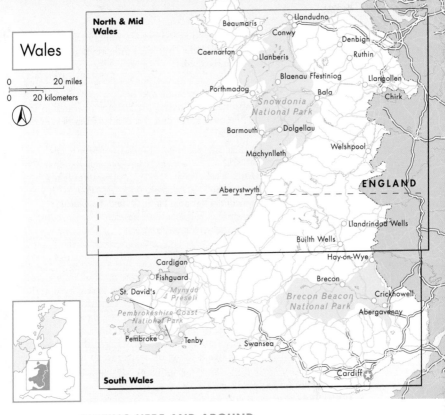

North & Mid Wales

Wales

0   20 miles
0   20 kilometers

Beaumaris
Llandudno
Conwy
Denbigh
Caernarfon
Llanberis
Ruthin
Blaenau Ffestiniog
Llangollen
Porthmadog
Bala
Chirk
Snowdonia National Park
Barmouth
Dolgellau
Machynlleth
Welshpool
Aberystwyth
ENGLAND
Llandrindod Wells
Builth Wells
Hay-on-Wye
Cardigan
Fishguard
Brecon
St. David's
Mynydd Preseli
Crickhowell
Pembrokeshire Coast National Park
Brecon Beacon National Park
Abergavenny
Pembroke
Tenby
Swansea
Cardiff
South Wales

GETTING HERE AND AROUND

AIR TRAVEL

If you're arriving from the United States, London's Heathrow and Gatwick airports are usually your best options because of their large number of international flights. Heathrow (2 hours) is slightly closer than Gatwick (2½ hours), but both have excellent motorway links with South Wales. For North Wales, the quickest access is via Manchester Airport, with a travel time of less than an hour to the Welsh border.

Cardiff International Airport, 19 mi from downtown Cardiff, is the only airport in Wales with international flights. These are mostly from Europe and Canada, however. A bus service runs from the airport to Cardiff's central train and bus stations.

Airports Cardiff International Airport (⊠ A4226, Rhoose ☎ 01446/711111 ⊕ www.cwlfly.com). **Manchester Airport** (⊠ Near Junctions 5 and 6 of M56 ☎ 08712/710711, 0161/489–3000 ⊕ www.manchesterairport.co.uk).

BUS TRAVEL

Most parts of Wales are accessible by bus. National Express serves Wales from London's Victoria Coach Station and also direct from London's Heathrow and Gatwick airports. It also has routes into Wales from many major towns and cities in England and Scotland. Average travel times from London to Wales are 3½ hours to Cardiff, 4 hours to Swansea, 5½ hours to Aberystwyth, and 4½ hours to Llandudno. Regional buses fan out across Wales, but local timetables and connections can be somewhat complicated.

Wales's three national parks run summer bus services. The Snowdon Sherpa runs into and around Snowdonia and links with main rail and bus services. The Pembrokeshire Coastal Bus Service operates in the Pembrokeshire Coast National Park, and the Beacons Bus serves the Brecon Beacons National Park.

Bus Contacts Brecon Beacons National Park (✉ *Plas-y-Ffynnon, Cambrian Way, Brecon* ☏ *01874/624437* ⊕ *www.breconbeacons.org*). **National Express** (☏ *0871/781–8181* ⊕ *www.nationalexpress.com*).**Pembrokeshire Coast National Park** (✉ *Llannion Park, Pembroke Dock* ☏ *0845/345–7275* ⊕ *www.pcnpa.org.uk*). **Snowdonia National Park** (✉ *Penrhyndeudraeth* ☏ *01766/770274* ⊕ *www.eryri-npa.gov.uk or www.snowdoniagreenkey.co.uk*). **Traveline** (☏ *0871/200–2233* ⊕ *www.traveline.org.uk*).

CAR TRAVEL

The easiest way to get around Wales is by car. Bus and train service is available, but in the rural areas—which constitute most of Wales—you will find that progress can be slow. If you don't want to rent a car at the airport, you can do so at major destinations like Cardiff or Swansea. Distances in miles may not be great in Wales, but getting around takes time because there are few major highways. There is no single fast route from north to south (the mountains have discouraged that); A470 is good and scenic, and A487 runs along or near most of the coastline. Many smaller mountain roads are winding and difficult to maneuver, but they have magnificent views.

TRAIN TRAVEL

Travel time on the fast InterCity rail service from London's Paddington Station is about two hours to Cardiff and three hours to Swansea. InterCity trains also run between London's Euston Station and North Wales. Average travel times from Euston are 3¾ hours and 5 hours to Aberystwyth. Regional train service covers much of Wales. There are many scenic routes, such as the Cambrian Coast Railway, running 70 mi between Aberystwyth and Pwllheli, and the Heart of Wales line, linking Swansea and Craven Arms, near Shrewsbury.

Train Contacts Flexi Pass information (☏ *0845/606–1660* ⊕ *www. walesflexipass.co.uk*). **Great Little Trains of Wales** (✉ *Wharf Station, Tywyn* ☏ *01654/710472* ⊕ *www.greatlittletrainsofwales.co.uk*). **National Rail Enquiries** (☏ *0845/748–4950* ⊕ *www.nationalrail.co.uk*). **Regional & Intercity Railways** (☏ *0845/748–4950* ⊕ *www.thetrainline.com*). **Snowdon Mountain Railway** (✉ *Llanberis, Caernarfon* ☏ *0871/720–0033* ⊕ *www.snowdonrailway. co.uk*).

DISCOUNTS AND DEALS

For travel within Wales, ask about money-saving unlimited-travel tickets (such as Freedom of Wales Flexi Pass, North and Mid Wales Rover, and the South Wales Flexi Rover), which include the use of bus services. A discount card offering a 20% reduction on each of the narrow-gauge

Great Little Trains of Wales is also available. It costs £10 and is valid for 12 months.

The Cadw/Welsh Historic Monuments Explorer Pass is good for unlimited admission to most of Wales's historic sites. The seven-day pass costs £17.50 (single adult), £29 (two adults), or £36 (family ticket); the three-day pass costs £11, £18, and £26, respectively. Passes are available at any site covered by the Cadw program. All national museums and galleries in Wales are free.

Discount Information Cadw/Welsh Historic Monuments (✉ *Plas Carew, Unit 5–7, Cefn Coed, Parc Nantgarw, Treforest* ☎ *01443/336000* ⊕ *www. cadw.wales.gov.uk*). **National Museums and Galleries of Wales** (⊕ *www. museumwales.ac.uk*).

TOURS

A good way to see Wales is by local tour bus; in summer there are day and half-day excursions to most parts of the country. In major resorts and cities, ask for details at a tourist information center or bus station.

The Wales Official Tourist Guide Association (WOTGA) uses only guides recognized by VisitWales and will create tailor-made tours. You can book a driver-guide or someone to accompany you as you drive.

Tour Information Wales Official Tourist Guide Association (☎ *01633/ 774796* ⊕ *www.walestourguides.com*).

RESTAURANTS

Today even many rural pubs are more interested in offering meals than serving pints of beer, so do consider them as a dining option. Don't overlook hotel restaurants in Wales; many, particularly those in country inns or hotels, are excellent. More and more restaurants are creating dishes using local produce—Welsh lamb, Welsh Black beef, Welsh cheeses, and seafood from the Welsh coast—that show off the best of the region's cuisine.

HOTELS

A 19th-century dictum, "I sleeps where I dines," still holds true in Wales, where good hotels and good restaurants often go together. Castles, country mansions, and even small railway stations are being transformed into interesting hotels and restaurants. Traditional inns with low, beamed ceilings, wood paneling, and fireplaces remain Wales's pride, but they, as well as farmhouse accommodations, tend to be off the beaten track. Cardiff and Swansea have some large chain hotels, and, for luxury, Wales has good country-house hotels. An added attraction is that prices are generally lower than they are for equivalent properties in the Cotswolds, Scotland, or southeast England. A service charge may be added to the room cost; ask if it's included.

WHAT IT COSTS IN POUNDS				
£	££	£££	££££	£££££
Restaurants	Under £10	£10–£14	£15–£19	£20–£25	over £25
Hotels	Under £70	£70–£120	£121–£160	£161–£220	over £220

Restaurant prices are for a main course at dinner. Hotel prices are for two people in a standard double room in high season, including V.A.T., with no meals or, if indicated, CP (with continental breakfast), BP (Breakfast Plan, with full breakfast), or MAP (Modified American Plan, with breakfast and dinner).

VISITOR INFORMATION

VisitWales Centre (☎ 08708/300306 ⊕ www.visitwales.com). **Wales in Style** (⊕ www.walesinstyle.com).

NORTH WALES

Wales masses all its savage splendor and fierce beauty in the north. Dominating the area is Snowdon, at 3,560 feet, the highest peak in England and Wales. It is impossible to describe the magnificence of the view from the mountain on a clear day: to the northwest the Menai Strait, Anglesey, and beyond to the Irish Sea; to the south the mountains of Merionethshire, Harlech Castle, and the Cadair Idris mountain range; and all around towering masses of wild and barren rock. ■ TIP→ If you ascend the peak by the Snowdon Mountain Railway from Llanberis, telephone from the terminus to check if Snowdon is free from mist. You lose much when clouds encircle the monster's brow, as often happens.

The peak gives its name to **Snowdonia National Park,** which extends southward all the way to Machynlleth in Mid Wales. The park consists of 840 square mi of rocky mountains, valleys clothed in oak woods, moorlands, lakes, and rivers, all guaranteeing natural beauty and, to a lesser extent, solitude. As in other British national parks, much of the land is privately owned, so inside the park are towns, villages, and farms. The park has become a popular climbing center, and some fear that Snowdon itself is becoming worn away by the boots of walkers.

Along the sandy, north-facing coast, seaside resorts have attracted people for well over a century. Llandudno, the dignified "Queen of the North Wales coast," was built in Victorian times as a seaside watering hole. Nearby Conwy, with its medieval castle and town walls, deserves a look, as do other great North Wales castles such as Harlech and Caernarfon. There are two official Areas of Outstanding Beauty: the Isle of Anglesey (connected by bridge to the mainland), and the Llŷn Peninsula, dotted with quieter small resorts and villages. Portmeirion, a mock-Italianate village, is a different kind of escape.

CHIRK AND THE CEIRIOG VALLEY

22 mi southwest of Chester, 60 mi southwest of Manchester.

Chirk, poised on the border between England and Wales, is a handy gateway to the Ceiriog Valley, a narrowing vale that penetrates the silent, green foothills of the lofty Berwyn Mountains.

EXPLORING

The impressive medieval fortress of **Chirk Castle,** finished in its original form in 1310, has evolved into a grand home (albeit one with a medieval dungeon), complete with an 18th-century servants hall and interiors furnished in 16th- to 19th-century styles. Surrounding the castle are beautiful formal gardens and parkland. ☒ *Off B4500* ☎ *01691/777701* ⊕ *www.nationaltrust.org.uk* ☒ *£9.20; garden only, £6.50* ☉ *Castle mid-Mar.–June, Wed.–Sun. 11–5; July and Aug., Tues.–Sun. 11–5; Sept., Wed.–Sun. 11–5; Oct., Wed.–Sun. 11–4. Garden mid-Mar.–June, Wed.– Sun. 10–6; July and Aug., Tues.–Sun. 10–6; Sept., Wed.–Sun. 10–6; Oct., Wed.–Sun. 10–5.*

West of Chirk is the **Vale of Ceiriog,** nicknamed Little Switzerland. Take B4500 west 6 mi through the lovely valley to the village of Glyn Ceiriog, at the foothills of the remote Berwyn Mountains. The area attracts pony trekkers, walkers, and anglers.

WHERE TO STAY

£ 🏠 **Bron Heulog.** Carefully restored in period style as a guesthouse, this former home of a Victorian, liberal politician was built in 1861 and stands in 2 acres of gardens. Fireplaces, high ceilings, and an oak staircase are original elements of the large stone house. Rooms have showers only—no bathtubs. **Pros:** all rooms have good views; self-catering option; peaceful location in Berwyn Mountains. **Cons:** no evening meal; need a car to get around. ☒ *Waterfall Rd., off B4396, Llanrhaeadr ym Mochnant* ☎ *01691/780521* ⊕ *www.bronheulog.co.uk* ☒ *3 rooms* ☒ *In-room: no a/c, no phone. In-hotel: laundry service* ☒ *MC, V* ☒ *BP.*

EN ROUTE The peat-brown water of **Pistyll Rhaeadr,** the highest waterfall in Wales, thunders down a 290-foot double cascade. To get here, take B4500 southwest from Glyn Ceiriog, and then its unnumbered continuation, to reach Llanrhaeadr ym Mochnant, in the peaceful Tanat Valley. Here, in 1588, the Bible was translated into Welsh, thus ensuring the survival of the language. Turn northwest and go 4 mi up the road to the waterfall.

LLANGOLLEN

5 mi northwest of Chirk, 23 mi southwest of Chester.

Llangollen's setting in a deep valley carved by the River Dee gives it a typically Welsh appearance. The bridge over the Dee, a 14th-century stone structure, is named in a traditional Welsh folk song as one of the "Seven Wonders of Wales." In July the very popular International Musical Eisteddfod brings crowds to town. For a particularly scenic drive in this area, head for the Horseshoe Pass.

ESSENTIALS

Visitor Information Llangollen (✉ *Y Chapel, Castle St.* ☎ *01978/860828*).

EXPLORING

Plas Newydd (not to be confused with the estate on the Isle of Anglesey with the same name) was the home from 1778 to 1828 of Lady Eleanor Butler and Sarah Ponsonby, the eccentric Ladies of Llangollen, who set up a then-scandalous single-sex household, collected curios and magnificent wood carvings, and made it into a tourist attraction even during their lifetimes. The terraced gardens have original features such as a font from an abbey. ✉ *Hill St.* ☎ *01824/708274* ⊕ *www.denbighshire. gov.uk* 💷 *£3.50* ⏱ *Easter–Oct., daily 10–5.*

From the **canal wharf** (☎ *01978/860702*) you can take a horse-drawn boat or a narrow boat (a slender barge) along the Llangollen Canal to the largest navigable aqueduct in the world at Pontcysyllte.

Ⓒ The **Llangollen Railway,** a restored standard-gauge steam line, runs for a few miles along the scenic Dee Valley. The terminus is near the town's bridge. ☎ *01978/860979* ⊕ *www.llangollen-railway.co.uk* 💷 *£10 round-trip* ⏱ *May–Sept., daily 10:30-5; Oct.–Apr., weekends, limited service.*

WHERE TO STAY

££ ⬚**Oakmere.** This sandstone Victorian residence with landscaped grounds succeeds in preserving its period flavor. Special features include tile or polished pine floors, 19th-century furniture in walnut and mahogany, a conservatory, and spacious, high-ceiling bedrooms. There are excellent views of the valley and mountains. **Pros:** spacious bedrooms; walking distance to town center; ample off-road parking. **Cons:** upper floors accessed by stairs; small TVs. ✉ *Regent St.* ☎ *01978/861126* ⊕ *www. oakmere.llangollen.co.uk* 🛏 *6 rooms* ⏏ *In-room: no a/c, no phone, Wi-Fi* ⊟ *No credit cards* ⏹ *BP.*

NIGHTLIFE AND THE ARTS

★ The six-day **International Musical Eisteddfod** (☎ *01978/862001* ⊕ *www. international-eisteddfod.co.uk*), held in early July, brings together amateur choirs and dancers—more than 12,000 participants in all—from all corners of the globe for a large, colorful folk-arts festival. The tradition of the *eisteddfod,* held throughout Wales, goes back to the 12th century. Originally gatherings of bards, the *eisteddfodau* of today are more like competitions or festivals.

SPORTS AND THE OUTDOORS

There are easy walks along the banks of the River Dee or along part of the **Offa's Dyke Path** (⊕ *www.offasdyke.demon.co.uk*), which passes through hills, river valleys, and lowlands. This 177-mi-long National Trail follows the line of an ancient earthen wall, still surviving in parts, which was built along the border with England in the 8th century by King Offa of Mercia to keep out Welsh raiders.

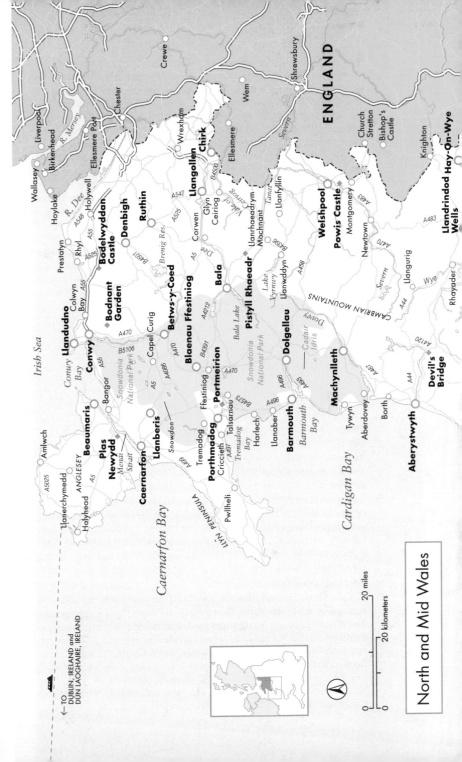

North and Mid Wales

All Aboard: Steam Railways

Wales is the best place in Britain for narrow-gauge steam railways, many of which wind through extraordinary landscapes. The Great Little Trains of Wales (⊕ *www.greatlittletrainsofwales. co.uk*) operate in spring, summer, and fall through the mountains of Snowdonia and central Wales (there are also a few lines in South Wales). The ride is just part of the fun; a good deal of history is associated with the old trains and train stations, some of which served industry before they became attractions for visitors. The Ffestiniog Railway, which links two British Rail lines at the old slate town of Blaenau Ffestiniog and Porth-madog, climbs the mountainside in Snowdonia National Park around an ascending loop. Snowdonia also has Britain's only alpine-style steam-rack railway, the Snowdon Mountain Railway, where little sloping boiler engines on a rack-and-pinion track push their trains 3,000 feet up from Llanberis to the summit of Snowdon.

BALA

18 mi southwest of Llangollen.

The staunchly Welsh town of Bala makes a good base for exploring the eastern and southern sections of Snowdonia National Park as well as the gentler landscapes of borderland Wales. It stands at the head of Llŷn Tegid (Bala Lake), at 4 mi long the largest natural lake in Wales. This is a fine place for kayaking and windsurfing.

ESSENTIALS

Visitor Information Bala (⊠ *Pensarn Rd.* ☎ *01678/521021).*

EXPLORING

♺ The scenic, narrow-gauge **Bala Lake Railway** (☎ *01678/540666* ⊕ *www. bala-lake-railway.co.uk*), one of the Great Little Trains of Wales, runs along the lake's southern shore. The station in Llanuwchllyn has parking.

★ To experience Wales at its wildest, you can drive over **Bwlch y Groes** *(Pass of the Cross)*, the highest road in Wales, whose sweeping panoramas are breathtaking. To get here, take the narrow road south from Bala through Cwm Hirnant and over the mountain to Lake Vyrnwy. Turn right at the lake and drive for a mile on B4393 before heading west on the mountain road.

WHERE TO STAY

££ 🏠 **Cyfie Farm.** This refurbished, ivy-clad 17th-century farmhouse in a tranquil area close to Lake Vyrnwy has oak beams and log fireplaces. The luxurious suites, in converted barns and stables, offer all the sophis-tication of those in a top hotel. **Pros:** in-room log fireplaces; outdoor hot tub with valley views; hosts are trained chefs. **Cons:** remote location; need a car to get around. ⊠ *Off B4393, near Llanfyllin, Llanfihangel-yng-Ngwynfa* ☎ *01691/648451* ⊕ *www.cyfiefarm.co.uk* ⌖ *4 suites* ⚐ *In-room: no a/c, no phone, DVD. In-hotel: Internet terminal, no kids under 10* ⊟ *AE, MC, V* ⓧ *BP.*

££££–££££
★

🏠 **Lake Vyrnwy Hotel.** Awesome views of mountain-ringed Lake Vyrnwy are just one asset of this country mansion within a 24,000-acre estate. For the ultimate sporting vacation you can fish, bird-watch, play tennis, or take long hikes. Sailboats are also available. The less energetic can linger in the superb spa. Leather chairs, log fires, and antiques add luxury, and the bedrooms are full of pampering touches. The sophisticated contemporary cuisine (£40 fixed-price menu only) includes lamb from their very own flock and seasonal game from the estate. **Pros:** perfect for outdoor pursuits; dramatic lakeside location; luxurious spa. **Cons:** too remote for some; no nearby sights. ⊠ *Off B4393, Llanwddyn* ☎ *01691/870692* ⊕ *www.lakevyrnwy.com* ⊋ *52 rooms* 🛏 *In-room: no a/c. In-hotel: restaurant, room service, bars, tennis court, gym, spa, water sports, bicycles, laundry service, Wi-Fi, some pets allowed* ⊟ *AE, DC, MC, V* ⏺|*BP.*

BLAENAU FFESTINIOG

22 mi northwest of Bala, 10 mi southwest of Betws-y-Coed.

Most of the world's roofing tiles used to come from this former "slate capital of North Wales," and commercial quarrying continues here. On the hillsides around the town is the evidence of decades of mining. The enterprises that attract attention nowadays, however, remain the old slate mines, which opened to the public in the 1970s. The narrow-gauge Ffestiniog Railway, which begins in Porthmadog, ends in the town, near the caverns.

ESSENTIALS
Visitor Information Blaenau Ffestiniog (⊠ *High St.* ☎ *01766/830360).*

EXPLORING
At the **Llechwedd Slate Caverns,** you can take two trips: a tram ride through floodlighted tunnels where Victorian working conditions have been re-created, and a ride on Britain's deepest underground railway to a mine where you can walk by an eerie underground lake. Either tour gives a good idea of the difficult working conditions the miners endured. On the surface of this popular site are a re-created Victorian village and slate-splitting demonstrations. ⊠ *Off A470* ☎ *01766/830306* ⊕ *www. llechwedd-slate-caverns.co.uk* 🎟 *Tour £9.45, grounds free* ⊗ *Apr.– Sept., daily 10–5:15; Oct.–Mar., daily 10–4:15.*

PORTHMADOG

12 mi southwest of Blaenau Ffestiniog, 16 mi southeast of Caernarfon.

The little seaside town of Porthmadog, built as a harbor to export slate from Blaenau Ffestiniog, stands at the gateway to Llŷn, an unspoiled peninsula of beaches, wildflowers, and country lanes. It's also near Harlech Castle. The location between Snowdonia and Llŷn, as well as the good beaches nearby and the many attractions around town, makes the town a lively place in summer. A mile-long embankment known as the Cob serves as the eastern approach to Porthmadog.

ESSENTIALS
Visitor Information Porthmadog (⊠ *High St.* ☎ *01766/512981).*

EXPLORING

The oldest Welsh narrow-gauge line (founded in the early 19th century to carry slate), the **Ffestiniog Railway,** runs from a quayside terminus along the Cob and continues through a wooded vale into the mountains. Its northern terminus is Blaenau Ffestiniog, where you can visit the slate caverns. ☎01766/516000 ⊕*www.festrail.co.uk* ✆*£17.95 round-trip* ⊙*Apr.–Oct., daily, plus limited winter service; call for exact times.*

Fodor'sChoice   One not-to-be-missed site in North Wales is **Portmeirion,** a tiny fantasy-
★   Italianate village on a private peninsula surrounded by hills, which is said to be loosely modeled after Portofino. Begun in 1926 by architect Clough Williams-Ellis (1883–1978), the village has a hotel, restaurant, town hall, shops (selling books, gifts, and Portmeirion pottery), rental cottages, and woodland walks; beaches are nearby. Williams-Ellis called it his "light-opera approach to architecture," and the result is magical, though distinctly un-Welsh. Royalty, political figures, artists, and other celebrities have stayed here, and the cult 1967 TV series *The Prisoner* was filmed here. Portmeirion is a short trip east of Porthmadog over the Cob. ⊠*A487* ☎*01766/770000* ⊕*www.portmeirion-village.com* ✆*£7* ⊙*Daily 9:30–5:30.*

North of Porthmadog is **Tremadog,** a handsome village that was the birthplace of T. E. Lawrence (1888–1935), better known as Lawrence of Arabia.

In the Victorian seaside resort of **Criccieth,** a few miles west of Porth-madog on A497, a medieval castle with sweeping views crowns the headland. David Lloyd George, the prime minister of Britain from 1916 to 1922, grew up in Wales and lived here; a small museum in his child-hood home honors him.

A wealth of legend, poetry, and song is conjured up by the 13th-century
★   **Harlech Castle,** built by Edward I to help subdue the Welsh; it's now a UNESCO World Heritage Site. The castle, on a promontory, domi-nates the little coastal town of Harlech, 12 mi south of Porthmadog. Its mighty ruins, visible for miles and commanding wide views, are as dramatic as its history (though you have to imagine the sea, which has since receded, edging the castle site). Harlech was occupied by Owain Glyndŵr from 1404 to 1408 during his revolt against the English. The music of Ceiriog's song *Men of Harlech* reflects the heroic defense of this castle in 1468 by Dafydd ap Eynion, who, summoned to surrender, replied: "I held a castle in France until every old woman in Wales heard of it, and I will hold a castle in Wales until every old woman in France hears of it!" Later in the 15th century the Lancastrians survived an eight-year siege during the Wars of the Roses here, and it was the last Welsh stronghold to fall in the 17th-century Civil War. ⊠*Off B4573* ☎*01766/780552* ⊕*www.cadw.wales.gov.uk* ✆*£3.60* ⊙*Apr.–Oct., daily 9–5; Nov.–Mar., Mon.–Sat. 9:30–4, Sun. 11–4.*

OFF THE BEATEN PATH   **Nant Gwrtheyrn.** This is a worthwhile stop—for awesome views of Caer-narfon Bay as well as cultural information—if you're exploring the Llŷn Peninsula. A former village for granite-quarry workers serves as the Welsh Language and Heritage Centre, offering Welsh-language classes and cultural courses (in Welsh). The chapel is a tourist information

ON THE MENU

Talented chefs making use of the country's bountiful resources have put Wales firmly on the culinary map. Welsh Black beef and succulent Welsh lamb are world renowned, and the supply of fish and seafood (including mussels and oysters) from coasts and rivers is excellent. Organic products are available to restaurants and the public from specialty companies, farm shops, and farmers' markets.

Tŷ Nant Welsh spring water graces restaurant tables worldwide, and wines, such as Cariad, have won medals at French wine festivals; there's even a Welsh whisky.

Cheese making has undergone a remarkable revival. You can try traditionally named cheeses such as Llanboidy and Caws Cenarth or an extra-mature cheddar called Black Bomber.

Contemporary cuisine has the buzz, but traditional dishes are worth seeking out. Cawl, for example, is a nourishing broth of lamb and vegetables, and laverbread is a distinctive-tasting pureed seaweed that's usually fried with eggs and bacon.

For information on high-quality Welsh food, check out the Web site Wales—the True Taste (⊕ www. walesthetruetaste.com).

15

center and has modest historical exhibits, and a café serves good sandwiches and snacks. ⊠ *Off B4417, Llithfaen* ☎ *01758/750334* ⊕ *www. nantgwrtheyrn.org* ⊠ *Free* ⊙ *Apr.–Sept., daily 11–3.*

WHERE TO EAT AND STAY

££££ ✕ **Castle Cottage.** Close to Harlech's mighty castle, this friendly "restau-
BRITISH rant with rooms" is a wonderful find. The emphasis is on the excep-
★ tional cuisine of chef-proprietor Glyn Roberts, who uses ingredients from lobster to Welsh lamb to create imaginative, beautifully presented contemporary dishes. There's a fixed-price dinner menu (£34), but no lunch. The hotel has three spacious modern rooms with four more in the annex, a former 16th-century pub. ⊠ *Near B4573, Harlech* ☎ *01766/780479* ⊟ *MC, V.*

£££–££££ ⊞ **Hotel Maes-y-Neuadd.** Eight acres of gardens and parkland create a
★ glorious setting for this luxurious country hotel in a manor house dating from the 14th century. Walls of local granite, oak-beam ceilings, and an inglenook fireplace add character; the updated bedrooms have different shapes and details but use prints and pastel fabrics. The restaurant's three-course, fixed-price (£35) menu of Welsh, English, and French specialties uses herbs and vegetables grown in the hotel's own prolific walled garden to complement local meat, fish, and cheeses. The hotel is 3½ mi northeast of Harlech. **Pros:** magnificent location above Tremadog Bay; close to many attractions. **Cons:** on a narrow road; need a car to get around. ⊠ *Off B4573, Talsarnau* ☎ *01766/780200 or 800/635–3602* ⊕ *www.neuadd.com* ⊲ *15 rooms* ⊘ *In-room: no a/c, Wi-Fi. In-hotel: restaurant, room service, bar, laundry service, Wi-Fi, some pets allowed* ⊟ *MC, V* ⊚ *BP.*

££££–£££££ ⊞ **Hotel Portmeirion.** One of the most elegant and unusual places to stay
★ in Wales is also supremely relaxing. Clough Williams-Ellis built his

Italianate fantasy village around this waterside Victorian mansion with a library and curved, colonnaded dining room. The hotel bedrooms are comfortable and richly decorated. Accommodation is also available in cottage suites around the village and in chic, minimalistic suites in Castell Deudraeth, a castellated 19th-century house. The restaurant, which serves breakfast and has a fixed-price dinner menu (£37.50), highlights local foods with a sophisticated contemporary style. **Pros:** unique architecture; beautiful woodland walks; far-reaching estuary views. **Cons:** long walk from some rooms to the dining room; grounds can be crowded with day-trippers; some rooms are a bit shabby. ⊠*A487, Portmeirion* ☎*01766/770000* ⊕*www.portmeirion-village.com* ⮐*14 rooms in main hotel, 28 rooms in cottages, 11 suites in Castell Deudraeth* ⌂*In-room: no a/c, Internet (some). In-hotel: restaurant, room service, bar, tennis court, pool, laundry service, Wi-Fi* ▤*AE, MC, V* ﹖❙*BP.*

BETWS-Y-COED

25 mi northeast of Porthmadog, 19 mi south of Llandudno.

The rivers Llugwy and Conwy meet at Betws-y-Coed, a popular resort village set among wooded hills with excellent views of Snowdonia. Busy in summer, the village has a good selection of hotels and crafts shops. The chief landmark here is the ornate iron Waterloo Bridge (1815) over the Conwy, designed by Thomas Telford (1757–1834), and the magnificent Bodnant Garden south of the town of Conwy makes a delightful excursion.

ESSENTIALS
Visitor Information Betws-y-Coed (⊠*Royal Oak Stables* ☎*01690/710426).*

EXPLORING
On the western (A5) approach to Betws-y-Coed are the **Swallow Falls** (£1 admission charge), a famous North Wales beauty spot where the River Llugwy tumbles down through a wooded chasm.

WHERE TO EAT AND STAY

££

MODERN BRITISH

✕**Ty Gwyn.** The restaurant in this 17th-century coaching inn overlooking Waterloo Bridge on the outskirts of Betws-y-Coed is a delight for lovers of antiques, old beams, and rustic, uneven floors. Fresh local produce is used in the good-value bar meals and full à la carte menu. Chicken liver, port, whisky, and walnut terrine, and baked Welsh lamb fillet with a roast-onion-and-peppercorn marmalade are good choices on the contemporary menu. ⊠*A5* ☎*01690/710383* ▤*MC, V.*

£–££

🏠**Aberconwy House.** This luxurious Victorian house has panoramic views over Betws-y-Coed and Snowdonia. Built in the 1870s, the bed-and-breakfast successfully combines period features and contemporary style. The bedrooms are well equipped and the owners are extremely hospitable. The village is only a 10-minute walk away. **Pros:** reasonable rates; great breakfasts. **Cons:** no bar; stairs to climb. ⊠*Turn onto Lôn Muriau off A470, then Llanrwst, Betws-y-Coed* ☎*01690/710202* ⊕*www.aberconwy-house.co.uk* ⮐*8 rooms* ⌂*In-room: no a/c, Wi-Fi* ▤*MC, V* ﹖❙*BP.*

£–££ Pengwern Country House. In Victorian times this stone-and-slate country house on 2 acres of woodland was an artists' colony. Today the polished slate floors, beamed bedrooms, and traditional furnishings reflect the house's original charm. The house is about a mile south of Betws-y-Coed. **Pros:** scenic woodland location; wealth of Victorian features. **Cons:** close to main road; car essential to reach town. ✉ A5, Allt Dinas ☎ 01690/710480 ⊕ www.snowdoniaaccommodation.co.uk ⇆ 3 rooms ⚬ In-room: no a/c, no phone, no TV, Wi-Fi. In-hotel: Internet terminal, no kids under 13 ⊟ MC, V ⦿ BP.

£££–££££ Tan-y-Foel Country House. Hidden away on a wooded hillside outside Betws-y-Coed, this quiet, contemporary hideaway has views over the Conwy Valley and Snowdonia mountain range. The vibrant hues of the stylish interior contrast with the dark stone exterior, and some bedrooms have four-posters. Chef-owner Janet Pitman, a Master Chef of Great Britain, prepares exquisite food with French and Asian influences. **Pros:** strikingly contemporary decor; inventive cuisine; views over Conwy Valley to Snowdon. **Cons:** meals by arrangement only; too far to walk into town. ✉ Off A5, Capel Garmon ☎ 01690/710507 ⊕ www.tyfhotel.co.uk ⇆ 6 rooms ⚬ In-room: no a/c, DVD. In-hotel: restaurant, bar, no kids under 12 ⊟ MC, V ⦿ BP.

TRAINING FOR EVEREST

Lord Hunt, Sir Edmund Hillary, and their team used the rock-strewn slopes of Snowdonia to train for the first successful ascent of Mount Everest in 1953. The Pen-y-Gwryd Hotel, a famous climbing inn just beyond the summit of Llanberis Pass, has memorabilia from those times.

15

LLANBERIS

17 mi west of Betws-y-Coed, 7 mi southeast of Caernarfon.

Llanberis, like Betws-y-Coed, is a focal point for people visiting Snowdonia National Park.

ESSENTIALS

Visitor Information Llanberis (✉ 41b High St. ☎ 01286/870765).

EXPLORING

The town stands beside twin lakes at the foot of the rocky **Llanberis Pass,** which cuts through the highest mountains in the park and is lined with slabs popular with rock climbers. There are hiking trails from the top of the pass, but the going can be rough for the inexperienced. Ask for local advice before starting any ramble.

Llanberis's most famous attraction is the rack-and-pinion **Snowdon Mountain Railway,** with some of its track at a gradient of 1 in 5; the train terminates within 70 feet of the 3,560-foot-high summit. Snowdon, Yr Wyddfa in Welsh, is the highest peak south of Scotland and lies within the 840-square-mi national park. From May through September, weather permitting, trains go all the way to the summit; on a clear day you can see as far as the Wicklow Mountains in Ireland, about 90 mi away. In 1998 the National Trust bought the mountain, ensuring its long-term protection. ☎*0870/458–0033* ⊕*www.snowdonrailway. co.uk* ⊠*£23 round-trip* ⊙*Mar.–Oct., daily; schedule depends on customer demand.*

Perched at the top of Snowdon is **Hafod Eryri,** the eco-friendly replacement for the previous visitor center (once described by Prince Charles as "the highest slum in Wales"). The new building has a curved granite roof and huge panoramic windows, and it blends beautifully into the rocky landscape. Inside there's a café and exhibitions about the mountain, its ecology, and its history.

On Lake Padarn in the Padarn Country Park, the old Dinorwig slate quarry serves as the **National Slate Museum,** dedicated to what was an important industry here: Welsh slate roofed many a building. The museum has quarry workshops and slate-splitting demonstrations, as well as restored worker housing, all of which convey the development of the industry and the challenges faced by those who worked in it. The narrow-gauge Llanberis Lake Railway runs from here. ⊠*A4086* ☎*01286/870630* ⊕*www.museumwales.ac.uk* ⊠*Free* ⊙*Easter–Oct., daily 10–5; Nov.–Easter, Sun.–Fri. 10–4.*

CAERNARFON

7 mi northwest of Llanberis, 26 mi southwest of Llandudno.

The town of Caernarfon, which has a historic pedigree as a walled medieval settlement, has nothing to rival the considerable splendor of its castle and is now overrun with tourist buses. Still, don't miss the garrison church of St. Mary, built into the city walls.

ESSENTIALS

Visitor Information Caernarfon (⊠ *Oriel Pendeitsh, opposite castle entrance* ☎ *01286/672232).*

EXPLORING

★ Standing like a warning finger, the grim, majestic mass of **Caernarfon Castle,** "that most magnificent badge of our subjection," wrote Thomas Pennant (1726–98), looms over the waters of the River Seiont. It's a UNESCO World Heritage Site. Numerous bloody encounters were witnessed by these sullen walls, erected by Edward I in 1283 as a symbol of his determination to subdue the Welsh. The castle's towers, unlike those of Edward I's other castles, are polygonal and patterned with bands of different-color stone. In 1284 the monarch thought of a scheme to steal the Welsh throne. Knowing that the Welsh chieftains would accept no foreign prince, Edward promised to designate a ruler who could speak no word of English. His long-suffering queen, Eleanor of Castile, was dispatched to this cold stone fortress, where she gave birth to a son. Edward presented the infant to the assembled chieftains as their prince "who spoke no English, had been born on Welsh soil, and whose first words would be spoken in Welsh." The ruse worked, and on that day was created the first prince of Wales of English lineage. This tradition still holds: in July 1969, Elizabeth II presented Prince Charles to the people of Wales as their prince from this castle. In the Queen's Tower, a museum charts the history of the local regiment, the Royal

Welsh Fusiliers. ⊠*Castle Hill* ☎*01286/677617* ⊕*www.caernarfon. com* ◎*£5.10* ⊙*Apr.–Oct., daily 9–5; Nov.–Mar., Mon.–Sat. 9:30–4, Sun. 11–4.*

Outside Caernarfon, the **Segontium Roman Museum** tells the story of the Roman presence in Wales; it includes material from one of Britain's most famous Roman forts. The extensive excavation site of the fort is here, too. ⊠*Beddgelert Rd. (A4085)* ☎*01286/675625* ⊕*www.segontium. org.uk/* ◎*Free* ⊙*Excavation site Tues.–Sun. 10–4:30. Museum Tues.– Sun. 12:30–4:30. Also open national holiday Mon. 12:30–4:30.*

You can take a workshop tour and short trip on a coal-fired steam loco-
ᗑ motive at the **Welsh Highland Railway–Rheilffordd Eryri,** a narrow-gauge line that operates on the route of an abandoned railway. The terminus is on the quay near Caernarfon Castle. ⊠*St. Helens Rd.* ☎*01766/516000* ⊕*www.welshhighlandrailway.net* ◎*£17.50 round-trip* ⊙*Apr.–Oct., daily 10–4; Nov.–Mar., limited weekend service.*

WHERE TO STAY

£££–£££ 🏠**Meifod Country House.** Former home of the high sheriff of Caernarfon, this opulent Victorian house has polished tile floors, wood-burning fire-places, and bedrooms with features such as Victorian claw-foot baths and chandeliers. The atmosphere is luxurious but unpretentious. The house stands on lush grounds less than 2 mi south of Caernarfon, making it a convenient base for exploring Snowdonia. **Pros:** authentic atmosphere; good food. **Cons:** gets booked up with wedding parties; not walking distance to town. ⊠*Off A487, Bontnewydd* ☎*01286/673351* ⊕*www.meifodcountryhouse.co.uk* ⌂*5 rooms* ⌂*In-room: no a/c. In-hotel: restaurant, room service, bars, tennis court, laundry service* ▭*MC, V* ⌂◎*BP.*

BEAUMARIS

13 mi northeast of Caernarfon.

Elegant Beaumaris is on the Isle of Anglesey, the largest island directly off the shore of Wales and England. It's linked to the mainland by the Britannia road and rail bridge and by Thomas Telford's remarkable chain suspension bridge, built in 1826 over the Menai Strait. Though its name means "beautiful marsh," Beaumaris has become a town of pretty cottages, Georgian houses, and bright shops. The nearest main-line train station is in Bangor, 6 mi away on the mainland; bus service operates between the station and Beaumaris. Ferries and catamarans to Ireland leave from Holyhead, on the island's western side.

EXPLORING

The town dates from 1295, when Edward I commenced work on impressive **Beaumaris Castle,** the last and largest link in an "iron ring" of fortifications around North Wales built to contain the Welsh. Guard-ing the western approach to the Menai Strait, the unfinished castle (a World Heritage Site) is solid and symmetrical, with concentric lines of fortification, arrow slits, and a moat: a superb example of medi-eval defensive planning. ⊠*Castle St.* ☎*01248/810361* ⊕*www.cadw.*

wales.gov.uk ⚏£3.70 ⊗*Apr.–Oct., daily 9–5; Nov.–Mar., Mon.–Sat. 9:30–4, Sun. 11–4.*

On Castle Street the **Tudor Rose,** a house dating from 1400, is an excellent example of Tudor timberwork.

To learn about the grim life of a Victorian prisoner, head to the old **gaol,** built in 1829 by Joseph Hansom (1803–82), who was also the designer of the Hansom cab. ⊠*Steeple La.* ☎*01248/810921* ⚏£3.50 ⊗*Easter–Sept., daily 10:30–5.*

The 14th-century **Church of St. Mary and St. Nicholas,** opposite the gaol in Steeple Lane, houses the stone coffin of Princess Joan, daughter of King John (1167–1216) and wife of Welsh leader Llewelyn the Great.

OFF THE BEATEN PATH

Plas Newydd. Some historians rate this mansion on the Isle of Anglesey the finest house in Wales. Remodeled in the 18th century by James Wyatt (1747–1813) for the marquesses of Anglesey (who still live here), it stands on the Menai Strait about 7 mi southwest of Beaumaris (don't confuse it with the Plas Newydd at Llangollen). The interior has some fine 18th-century Gothic Revival decorations. In 1936–40 the society artist Rex Whistler (1905–44) painted the mural in the dining room. A museum commemorates the Battle of Waterloo, where the first marquess, Wellington's cavalry commander, lost his leg. The woodland walk and garden are worth exploring, and you can ask about boat trips on the strait. The views of Snowdonia are magnificent. ⊠*Off A4080, southwest of Britannia Bridge, Llanfairpwll* ☎*01248/714795* ⊕*www. nationaltrust.org.uk* ⚏*House £7.50; garden only, £5.50* ⊗*House mid-Mar.–early Nov., Sat.–Wed. noon–5; last admission ½ hr before closing. Garden mid-Mar.–early Nov., Sat.–Wed. 11–5:30.*

WHERE TO EAT AND STAY

£££££
BRITISH
✗**Ye Olde Bull's Head.** Originally a coaching inn built in 1472, this small place is filled with history. Samuel Johnson and Charles Dickens were both guests here. Eat in the stylish brasserie with its slate floors and oak tables or the excellent oak-beam dining room dating from 1617. Contemporary dinner specialties (£38.50 fixed-price menu) include truffled goat cheese mousse and saddle of wild venison; seafood dishes win praise, too. ⊠*Castle St.* ☎*01248/810329* ▭*AE, MC, V.*

££
★
Ⓣ**Cleifiog.** This cozy gem of a Georgian house overlooks the Menai Strait just a short stroll from Beaumaris Castle. Its charms include contemporary comforts, wood-panel walls, limestone floors, and a magnificent staircase dating from 1680. **Pros:** seafront location; close to town; house with interesting history. **Cons:** minimum stay on weekends; a little claustrophobic for some. ⊠*Townsend, Beaumaris* ☎*01248/811507* ⊕*www.cleifiogbandb.co.uk* ☞*3 rooms* ⚙*In-room: no a/c, no phone, DVD. In-hotel: Internet terminal, no kids under 3* ▭*MC, V* Ⓘ*BP.*

NIGHTLIFE AND THE ARTS

The **Beaumaris Festival** (☎*01248/810218* ⊕*www.beaumarisfestival. com*) takes place annually in late May. The whole town is used as a site for special concerts, dance performances, and plays.

CONWY

★ *23 mi east of Beaumaris, 48 mi northwest of Chester.*

The still-authentic medieval town of Conwy grew up around its castle on the west bank of the River Conwy. A ring of ancient but well-preserved walls, built in the 13th century to protect the English merchants who lived here, enclose the old town and add to the strong sense of history. It's well worth strolling the streets and walking on top of sections of the wall, which has 21 towers. A walk on the walls rewards with impressive views across huddled rooftops to the castle on the estuary, with mountains in the distance.

GETTING HERE AND AROUND

The A55 expressway links Conwy into the central U.K. motorway system via the M56. The town is also on the North Wales coast rail route, which ends at Holyhead on Anglesey. The town itself—surrounded by its wonderfully preserved walls—is perfect for pedestrians.

ESSENTIALS

Visitor Information Conwy (⊠ *Castle Bldg.* ☎ *01492/592248*).

EXPLORING

Fodor'sChoice Of all Edward I's fortresses, **Conwy Castle,** a mighty, many-turreted
★ stronghold built between 1283 and 1287, preserves most convincingly the spirit of medieval times. Along with Conwy's town walls, the castle is a UNESCO World Heritage Site. The eight large round towers and tall curtain wall, set on a rocky promontory, provide sweeping views of the area and the town walls. Although the castle is roofless (and floorless in places), you can read the signs, take a tour, or buy a guidebook to help you visualize the Great Hall and other chambers. Narrow stairs lead into towers such as the Chapel Tower. Conwy Castle can be approached on foot by a dramatic suspension bridge completed in 1825; engineer Thomas Telford designed the bridge with turrets to blend in with the fortress's presence. ⊠ *Rose Hill St.* ☎ *01492/592358* ⊕ *www.cadw. wales.gov.uk* ⊠ *£4.60; £6.85 joint ticket with Plas Mawr* ⊗ *Apr.–Oct., daily 9–5; Nov.–Mar., Mon.–Sat. 9:30–4, Sun. 11–4.*

What is said to be the **smallest house in Britain** (⊠ *Lower Gate St.* ☎ *01492/593484* ⊠ *£0.75* ⊗ *Apr.–Oct., daily 10–4:30*) is furnished in mid-Victorian Welsh style. The house, which is 6 feet wide and 10 feet high, was reputedly last occupied in 1900 by a fisherman who was more than 6 feet tall.

Plas Mawr, a jewel in the heart of Conwy, is the best-preserved Elizabethan town house in Britain. Built in 1576 by Robert Wynn (who later became both a member of Parliament and sheriff of Caernarfonshire), this richly decorated house with its ornamental plasterwork gives a unique insight into the lives of the Tudor gentry and their servants. ⊠ *High St.* ☎ *01492/580167* ⊕ *www.cadw.wales.gov.uk* ⊠ *£4.95; £6.85 joint ticket with Conwy Castle* ⊗ *Apr.–Sept., Tues.–Sun. 9–5; Oct., Tues.–Sun. 9:30–4.*

Built in the 14th century, **Aberconwy House** is the only surviving medieval merchant's house in Conwy. Each room in the restored building reflects different eras of its long history. ⊠ *Castle St.* ☎ *01492/592246* ⊕ *www.*

15

nationaltrust.org.uk ✉£3 ⊙ *Mar.–Nov., Wed.–Mon. 11–5.*

Fodor's Choice
★

With a reputation as the finest garden in Wales, **Bodnant Garden** remains a pilgrimage spot for horticulturists from around the world. Laid out in 1875, the 87 acres are particularly famed for rhododendrons, camellias, and magnolias. ■ TIP→ **Visit in May to see the laburnum arch that forms a huge tunnel of golden blooms.** The mountains of Snowdonia form a magnificent backdrop to the Italianate terraces, rock and rose gardens, and pinetum. The gardens are about 5 mi south of Conwy. ✉ *Off A470, Tal-y-Cafn* ☎*01492/650460* ⊕*www.nationaltrust.org.uk* ✉£7.50 ⊙*Mar.–Nov., daily 10–5.*

WHERE TO EAT AND STAY

£££
MODERN BRITISH

✕**Le Gallois.** Just off the coast road 4 mi west of Conwy, this small and unpretentious restaurant is a culinary oasis. The chef-proprietor offers a changing chalkboard menu using the best local produce. Dishes like juicy scallops with a beurre blanc, Conwy crab au gratin, and local lamb cooked pink with a mint-and-Madeira sauce are typical daily fare. ✉*Pant yr Afon, Penmaenmawr* ☎*01492/623820* ▭*MC, V* ⊙*Closed Mon.–Wed. No lunch.*

£££
Castle Hotel. Sitting snugly within Conwy's medieval walls, this former coaching inn has wooden beams, old fireplaces, and plenty of antiques. Illustrious former guests include William Wordsworth, Samuel Johnson, and Charlotte Brontë. The bedrooms are smallish but plushly luxurious, with elaborate modern bathrooms. Dawson's Cuisine and Bar is decorated with paintings of scenes from Shakespeare's plays, traded by distinguished Victorian artist John Dawson-Watson in return for lodgings. Here you can enjoy excellent modern British cuisine, such as salmon on a creamy Conwy crab risotto. **Pros:** oozes history; in the heart of medieval Conwy; good food. **Cons:** small rooms; noisy seagulls; narrow town center streets. ✉*High St.* ☎*01492/582800* ⊕*www.castlewales.co.uk* ⇆*28 rooms* ⚐*In-room: no a/c, Wi-Fi. In-hotel: restaurant, bar, some pets allowed* ▭*AE, MC, V* ❢❶*BP.*

££
Sychnant Pass House. On a peaceful wooded hillside above Conwy, this hotel has all the qualities of a country-house hotel but without any unnecessary formality. The enthusiastic owners, Bre and Graham Carrington-Sykes, provide a genuine welcome and good food with a set-price dinner menu (£30). There are spacious sitting rooms with big comfortable sofas and nicely furnished bedrooms, some with French windows opening out onto an attractive decked terrace. The leisure facilities are excellent. **Pros:** great indoor pool and hot tub; beautiful grounds; unforced hospitality.

CASTLE COUNTRY

More than 400 fortresses in Wales provide an inexhaustible supply of inspiration for any lover of history. These ancient strongholds, some of which were built by Edward I in the 13th century during his struggles with the rebellious Welsh, punctuate the landscape from south (Caerphilly) to north (Harlech, Beaumaris, Conwy), and include romantic ruins and well-preserved fortresses. To make the most of a visit, buy a guidebook or take a tour of a site so that you can best appreciate the remains of a distant era. The great North Wales castles, such as Caernarfon, are particularly famous; four are World Heritage Sites.

Cons: pets allowed in rooms; far outside Conwy. ⊠*Sychnant Pass Rd.* ☎*01492/596868* ⊕*www.sychnant-pass-house.co.uk* ☞*12 rooms* ⚲*In-room: no a/c, no phone, safe, DVD. In-hotel: restaurant, pool, gym, Wi-Fi, some pets allowed* ⊟*MC, V* ⏀*BP.*

LLANDUDNO

3 mi north of Conwy, 50 mi northwest of Chester.

This appealingly old-fashioned North Wales seaside resort has a wealth of well-preserved Victorian architecture and an ornate amusement pier with entertainments, shops, and places to eat. Attractively painted hotels line the wide promenade, and the shopping streets behind also look the part, thanks to their original canopied walkways. Llandudno has the largest choice of lodging of any resort in Wales.

GETTING HERE AND AROUND

Llandudno is on the North Wales railway line, with fast access from London and other major cities. By road, it is connected to the motorway system via the A55 expressway. It is a good gateway for travel to the nearby mountains of Snowdonia. The scenic Conwy Valley rail line runs via the popular mountain resort of Betws-y-Coed to Blaenau Ffestiniog. It is also on the network covered by the convenient "hop-on, hop-off" Snowdon Sherpa bus service.

ESSENTIALS

Visitor Information Llandudno (⊠*Mostyn St.* ☎*01492/876413*).

EXPLORING

Llandudno has little in the way of garish arcades, preferring to stick to the faithful **Great Orme Tramway** (☎*01492/879306* ⊕*www.greatorme-tramway.co.uk* ☞*£5.40 round-trip* ⏀*Mar.–Oct., daily 10–6*) that climbs to the summit of the Great Orme headland above the resort.

Besides a tram, the town has an **aerial cable car** (☎*01492/879306* ⊕*www.llandudnoskislope.co.uk* ☞*£6.50 round-trip* ⏀*Easter–Sept., daily 10–5*) to the top of the Great Orme. There's also a large, dry ski slope (with an artificial surface you can ski on year-round) and year-round toboggan run (£4.50).

The prehistoric **Great Orme Mines** are at the summit of the Great Orme (*orme*, a Norse word meaning "sea monster"), with its views of the coast and mountains of Snowdonia. Copper was first mined here in the Bronze Age, and you can tour the ancient underground workings. ⊠*Great Orme* ☎*01492/870447* ⊕*www.greatormemines.info* ☞*£6* ⏀*Mar.–Nov., daily 10–5*.

WHERE TO STAY

££££–£££££

★ 🏨**Bodysgallen Hall.** Antiques, comfortable chairs by cheery fires, pictures, and polished wood distinguish one of Wales's most luxurious country-house hotels. The part 17th-, part 18th-century building is set in walled gardens 2 mi out of town. Bedrooms in the house combine elegance and practicality; seekers of privacy may prefer the cottage suites scattered around the estate and parkland. The outstanding restaurant uses local ingredients in creative ways, such as roe deer with choucroute, truffled gnocchi and cauliflower, or pavé of turbot with mustard-glazed ham knuckle. **Pros:** superb spa and swimming pool; rare 17th-century knot garden; elegant dining. **Cons:** too formal for some; very expensive. ⊠ *Off A470* ☎*01492/584466* ⊕ *www.bodysgallen.com* ⇨*15 rooms, 16 cottage suites* ⌂*In-room: no a/c (some), DVD, Wi-Fi. In-hotel:restaurant, room service, bar, pool, gym, spa, laundry service, Internet terminal, Wi-Fi, some pets allowed, no kids under 6* ⊟*AE, MC, V* ⊺⊙*BP.*

££ ⊞**Bryn Derwen Hotel.** Many hoteliers at British seaside resorts have not upgraded their accommodations and food, but this immaculate Victorian hotel exemplifies how it should be done. Fresh flowers, plush period furnishings in the public areas, and soothing, warm-hued bedrooms show the owners' attention to detail. Bryn Derwen offers truly excellent value for the price. **Pros:** on-site beauty salon; plenty of parking; close to the beach. **Cons:** no sea views; not child friendly. ⊠*34 Abbey Rd.* ⊕*www.bryn-derwen.co.uk* ☎*01492/876804* ⇨*9 rooms* ⌂*In-room: no a/c, no phone, DVD, Wi-Fi. In-hotel: restaurant, bar, no kids under 12* ⊟*MC, V* ⊺⊙*BP.*

£££–££££ ⊞**St. Tudno Hotel.** From the outside, one of Britain's best small seaside hotels blends unobtrusively with its neighbors. But the interior contains opulently furnished guest rooms and public areas with plenty of print fabrics and chintz. It's perfectly situated on the seafront promenade overlooking the beach and the pier. The fine contemporary cuisine includes dishes such as poached halibut steak with salsify, local mussel-and-orange hollandaise, and a medley of game with honey, blackberry, and truffle dressing. **Pros:** ocean views; friendly well-trained staff; good food. **Cons:** some rooms are snug; overly fussy decor; small pool. ⊠*Promenade* ☎*01492/874411* ⊕*www.st-tudno.co.uk* ⇨*18 rooms* ⌂*In-room: no a/c (some). In-hotel: restaurant, room service, bar, pool, laundry service, some pets allowed* ⊟*AE, DC, MC, V* ⊺⊙*BP.*

EN ROUTE Inland from Rhyl, **Bodelwyddan Castle**, between Abergele and St. Asaph, is the Welsh home of London's National Portrait Gallery. Gardens, including a maze, aviary, and woodland walks, surround the Victorian castle. Galleries display Regency and Victorian portraits by artists such as John Singer Sargent, Thomas Lawrence, Dante Gabriel Rossetti, and Edwin Landseer. There are also hands-on galleries of Victorian amusements and inventions. ⊠*Off A55, Bodelwyddan* ☎*01745/584060* ⊕*www.bodelwyddan-castle.co.uk* ⊠*£6* ⊙*Mar.–July, Sept., and Oct., Sat.–Thurs. 10:30–5; Aug., daily 10:30–5; Nov. and Dec., Thurs. and weekends 10:30–4; Jan. and Feb., weekends 10:30–4.*

ADVENTURES IN WONDERLAND

Llandudno was the summer home of the family of Dr. Liddell, the Oxford don and father of the immortal Alice, inspiration for Lewis Carroll's *Alice's Adventures in Wonderland.* The book's Walrus and the Carpenter may be based on two rocks on Llandudno's West Shore close to the now demolished Liddell home. A statue of the White Rabbit stands on the West Shore.

DENBIGH

25 mi southeast of Llandudno.

This market town (market day is Wednesday) was much admired by the great English literary figure and lexicographer Dr. Samuel Johnson (1709–84). A walk along the riverbank at Lawnt (a village just south of Denbigh), which he loved, brings you to a monumental urn placed in his honor. Not that it pleased him: "It looks like an intention to bury me alive," he thundered.

EXPLORING

Denbigh Castle, begun in 1282 as one of Edward I's ring of castles built to control the Welsh, is known as "the hollow crown" because it is not much more than a shell—though an impressive one—set on high ground, dominating the town. H. M. Stanley (1841–1904), the intrepid 19th-century journalist and explorer who found Dr. Livingstone in Africa, was born in a cottage below the castle. ☎*01745/813385* ⊕*www.cadw.wales.gov.uk* ✉*£3* ⊙*Apr.–Sept., daily 10–5.*

15

RUTHIN

8 mi southeast of Denbigh, 23 mi southwest of Chester.

Once a stronghold of Welsh hero Owain Glyndŵr (circa 1354–1416), Ruthin is a delightful market town with elegant shops, good inns, and a fascinating architectural mix of medieval, Tudor, and Georgian buildings. The town also hosts medieval-style banquets and has a crafts complex with displays of the artisans' creations.

EXPLORING

The 17th-century **Myddleton Arms** in the town square has seven Dutch-style dormer windows, known as the "eyes of Ruthin," set into its red-tile roof.

You can tour **Ruthin Gaol,** where from 1654 to 1916 thousands of prisoners were incarcerated, and learn about prison conditions over the centuries. ✉*Clwyd St.* ☎*01824/708281* ⊕*www.ruthingaol.co.uk* ✉*£3.50* ⊙*Apr.–Oct., daily 10–5; Nov.–Mar., weekends 10–5.*

WHERE TO STAY

££ ▦**Eyarth Old Railway Station.** This Victorian railway station 2 mi south of Ruthin has been converted into an outstanding B&B. The modern bedrooms are spacious, with large windows looking out over the Vale of Clwyd. **Pros:** good base for exploring the area; secluded garden; extensive views. **Cons:** a little dated; basic accommodations. ✉*Off A525, Llanfair Dyffryn Clwyd* ☎*01824/703643* ⊕*www.eyarthstation.com* ⌨*6 rooms* ⌂*In-room: no a/c, no phone, no TV, Wi-Fi. In-hotel: bar, pool, Internet terminal, Wi-Fi, some pets allowed* ▤*MC, V* ⦿*BP.*

£££ ▦**manorhaus.** A Georgian town house in the heart of Ruthin has been converted into a simply stunning boutique hotel. Each entirely original room is a mini–art gallery, designed and decorated in collaboration with the artist whose work hangs on the walls. There's also a library, gallery, sauna, steam room, private cinema, and restaurant serving fresh, locally sourced food. **Pros:** cutting-edge design; art lover's paradise; trendy bistro. **Cons:** small rooms; limited parking. ✉ *Well St.* ☎*01824/704830* ⊕*www.manorhaus.com* ⇔*8 rooms* ♿*In-room: DVD, Wi-Fi. In-hotel: restaurant, bar, gym, spa* ➠ *AE, MC, V* ⦿*BP.*

MID WALES

Traditional market towns and country villages, small seaside resorts, quiet roads, and rolling landscapes filled with sheep farms, forests, and lakes make up Mid Wales, the country's green and rural heart. Because this is Wales's quietest vacation region, lodgings are scattered thinly. Outside of one or two large centers, Aberystwyth and Llandrindod Wells, accommodations are mainly country inns, small hotels, and farmhouses. This area also has some splendid country-house hotels.

Although green is the predominant color here, the landscape differs around the region. The borderlands with England are gentle and undulating, rising to the west into high, wild mountains. Farther north, around Dolgellau, mountainous scenery becomes even more pronounced in the southern section of the Snowdonia National Park. Mountains meet the sea along Cardigan Bay, a long coastline of headlands, peaceful sandy beaches, and beautiful estuaries that has long been a refuge from the crowd. In the 19th century Tennyson, Darwin, Shelley, and Ruskin came to this area to work and relax; today thousands more come to delight in the numerous antiquarian bookstores of Hay-on-Wye.

HAY-ON-WYE

★ *57 mi north of Cardiff, 25 mi north of Abergavenny.*

Bookshops and a mostly ruined castle dominate this town on the border of Wales and England. Hay is a lively place, especially on Sunday, when the rest of central Wales seems to be closed down. In 1961 Richard Booth established a small secondhand and antiquarian bookshop here. Other booksellers soon got in on the act, and bookshops now fill several houses, a movie theater, shops, and a pub. At last count there were about 40 bookstores, all in a town of only 1,300 inhabitants. It's now the largest secondhand bookselling center in the world, and priceless 14th-century manuscripts rub spines with "job lots" selling for a few pounds. Hay also has antiques and crafts centers.

GETTING HERE AND AROUND

You'll need a car to get to Hay. Once you're there, parking is plentiful and everything is accessible by foot.

ESSENTIALS

Visitor Information Hay-on-Wye (✉*Craft Centre* ☎*01497/820144).*

EXPLORING

★ Things buzz in early summer during the 10-day **Hay Festival** (☎*0870/990–1299* ⊕*www.hayfestival.com*), a celebration of literature that attracts famous writers from all over the world.

QUICK BITES

After some hard browsing, stop off at the Granary (✉*Broad St.* ☎*01497/ 820790), a wood-beamed former grain store by the clock tower. The**

chalkboard menu lists soups, lamb-and-spinach curry, and cheese-and-garlic toasties (open, toasted sandwiches).

WHERE TO EAT AND STAY

£££
BRITISH

✕ **Old Black Lion.** A 17th-century coaching inn close to Hay's center is ideal for a lunch break while you're ransacking the bookshops. The oak-beamed bar serves food, and the breakfasts are especially good. The restaurant's sophisticated cooking has an international flavor and emphasizes local meats and produce. You can even opt for an overnight stay in one of the country-style rooms. ⊠*Lion St.* ☎*01497/820841* ▤*AE, MC, V.*

££££–£££££

⊡ **Llangoed Hall.** This magnificent Jacobean mansion on the banks of the River Wye close to Hay was renovated by Sir Bernard Ashley, the recently deceased husband of the late Welsh fabric designer Laura Ashley. There are antiques everywhere, beautiful fabrics and furnishings, open fireplaces, a sweeping carved staircase, and a paneled library dating back to 1632. Bernard Ashley's personal collection of paintings adorns the walls. Savor main courses like grilled salmon fillet with saffron crushed potatoes and crayfish sauce on the fixed-price (£45 for four courses) menu. **Pros:** exclusive fabric shop; private fishing on River Wye; wonderful art collection. **Cons:** very expensive; often filled with wedding parties; no attractions within walking distance. ⊠*Llyswen* ☎*01874/754525* ⊕*www.llangoedhall.com* ⇖*23 rooms* ⌂*In-room: no a/c, DVD (some), Wi-Fi. In-hotel: restaurant, no kids under 8* ▤*AE, MC, V* ⑩*BP.*

15

SHOPPING

Boz Books (⊠*13A Castle St.* ☎*01497/821277*) specializes in 19th-century novels, including first editions of Dickens. A former movie theater houses the town's largest book outpost, the **Hay Cinema Bookshop** (⊠*Castle St.* ☎*01497/820071* ⊕*www.haycinemabookshop.co.uk*), which stocks 200,000 volumes on subjects from art to zoology at prices from 50p to £5,000.

LLANDRINDOD WELLS

27 mi north of Hay-on-Wye, 67 mi north of Cardiff.

Also known as Llandod, the old spa town of Llandrindod Wells preserves its Victorian layout and look, with turrets, cupolas, loggias, and balustrades, and greenery everywhere. On a branch-line rail route and with good bus service, Llandrindod makes a useful base for exploring the region, and the town itself is easily explored on foot. Cross over to South Crescent, passing the Glen Usk Hotel with its wrought-iron balustrade and the Victorian bandstand in the gardens opposite, and you reach Middleton Street, another Victorian thoroughfare. From there, head to Rock Park and the path that leads to the Pump Room. This historic building is now an alternative health center, but visitors can freely "take the waters" that the Victorians found so beneficial. On the other side of town, the lake, with its boathouse, café, and gift shop, has wooded hills on one side and a broad common on the other.

ESSENTIALS

Visitor Information Llandrindod
Wells (⊠ *The Groe Car Park* ☎ *01982/
553307*).

EXPLORING

The **Radnorshire Museum,** in Memorial Gardens, presents the spa's development from Roman times and explains some Victorian "cures" in gruesome detail. ☎ *01597/824513* ⊡ *£1* ⊘ *Apr.–Sept., Tues.–Fri. 10–4, Sun. 1–5; Oct.–Mar., Tues.– Fri. 10–4, Sat. 10–1.*

WHERE TO STAY

£ 🏠 **Brynhir Farm.** You get a warm welcome at this immaculate, creamwashed farmhouse tucked into the hills on a 200-acre sheep-and-cattle farm. Country-style furnishings enhance the rooms. The farm is 2 mi from Llandrindod. **Pros:** bird-watcher's delight; serves homegrown Welsh lamb; extensive views. **Cons:** too rural for some; not walking distance to town. ⊠ *Chapel Rd., Howey* ☎ *01597/822425* ⊕ *www. brynhir.farm.btinternet.co.uk* ⇆ *3 rooms* ⚙ *In-room: no a/c, no phone. In-hotel: restaurant, Internet terminal, Wi-Fi, no kids under 6* ⊟ *MC, V* ⏏ *BP.*

££ 🏠 **Guidfa House.** Friendly hosts Tony and Anne Millan run this stylish Georgian guesthouse with a welcoming log fire and bright, individually furnished bedrooms. Cordon Bleu–trained Anne prepares dinners (for guests only) from fresh local produce; the guinea fowl with apple brandy and mushroom sauce is delicious. **Pros:** good base for exploring the countryside; great wine list; romantic coach house suite. **Cons:** overlooks a road junction; far from Llandod. ⊠ *Crossgates, near Llandrindod Wells* ☎ *01597/851241* ⊕ *www.guidfa-house.co.uk* ⇆ *6 rooms* ⚙ *In-room: no a/c, no phone, DVD. In-hotel: restaurant, Wi-Fi, no kids under 10* ⊟ *MC, V* ⏏ *BP.*

EN ROUTE
From Llandrindod, take A4081/A470 to Rhayader, a good ponytrekking center and gateway town for the **Elan Valley,** Wales's Lake District. This 7-mi chain of lakes, winding between gray-green hills, was created in the 1890s by a system of dams designed to supply water to Birmingham, 73 mi to the east.

From the Elan Valley you can follow the narrow Cwmystwyth mountain road west to **Devil's Bridge,** a famous (and popular) beauty spot where three bridges set one on top of the other span a chasm over the raging River Mynach, before continuing on to Aberystwyth. You can also take the Vale of Rheidol Railway to this site from Aberystwyth.

ABERYSTWYTH

41 mi northwest of Llandrindod Wells via A44, 118 mi northwest of Cardiff.

Aberystwyth makes the best of several worlds as a seaside resort (complete with promenade and amusement pier) and a long-established university town that is home to the impressive National Library of Wales. It also has a small harbor and is a major shopping center for Mid Wales. More than 5,000 students expand the full-time population of 12,000. The town, midway along Cardigan Bay, came to prominence as a Victorian watering hole thanks to a curving beach set beneath a prominent headland. Aberystwyth is a good gateway for exploring Mid Wales: few towns in Wales present such varied scenery within their immediate neighborhood, from the Devil's Bridge to the green Rheidol Valley.

GETTING HERE AND AROUND

A resort that was born with the coming of the railways, Aberystwyth is easily reached by train. A cross-country line still runs from the main hub of Shrewsbury just across the border of England. Of interest to visitors is the Cambrian Coast line, which runs along the northern arc of Cardigan Bay from Aberystwyth to Pwllheli on the Llyn Peninsula. This is one of Britain's great scenic rail routes, with views of coast and mountains. Another must is a trip on the narrow-gauge Vale of Rheidol Railway that runs into the mountains from Aberystwyth. If you're arriving by car, the scenic A470 connects to the A44. You won't need a car to get around town, as all the attractions are within easy walking distance.

TIMING

Aberystwyth is a busy resort and university town, so if you have specific accommodation in mind, it is advisable to book ahead.

ESSENTIALS

Visitor Information Aberystwyth (✉ *Terrace Rd.* ☎ *01970/612125*).

EXPLORING

The massive, neoclassical **National Library of Wales**, on a hill amid the buildings of the modern University of Wales–Aberystwyth houses notable Welsh and other Celtic literary works among its more than 4.5 million printed volumes. This self-described national treasure house also has enormous archives of maps, photographs, films, and sound recordings. ■TIP➔ **Material doesn't circulate, but the public can do research; many people pursue genealogical history here (there's a family history center).** The gallery has art shows (works may be for sale, too), and exhibitions highlight Welsh and other subjects. Films and concerts are presented in the auditorium. ✉ *Off Penglais Rd.* ☎ *01970/632800* ⊕ *www.llgc.org.uk* ⊠ *Free* ⊙ *Weekdays 9:30–6, Sat. 9:30–5*.

Housed in a flamboyant 1905 Edwardian theater, the **Ceredigion Museum** has fine collections related to folk history. Highlights include a reconstructed mud-walled cottage from 1850, exhibits from the building's music-hall past, and items illustrating the region's seafaring, lead-mining, and farming history. ✉ *Terrace Rd.* ☎ *01970/633088* ⊕ *museum.ceredigion.gov.uk* ⊠ *Free* ⊙ *Mon.–Sat. 10–5*.

15

The Language of Cymru

Welsh, the native language of Wales (Cymru, in Welsh), is revered in the country, but it was not legally recognized in Britain until the 1960s. Today Welsh schoolchildren under 14 are required to take classes to learn the language, and Welsh is surviving more successfully than its Celtic cousin, Breton, which is spoken in northwestern France. Welsh may look daunting to pronounce, but it is a phonetic language; pronunciation is fairly easy once the alphabet is learned. Remember that "dd" is sounded like "th" in they, "f" sounds like "v" in save, and "ff" is the equivalent of the English "f" in forest. The "ll" sound has no English equivalent; the closest match is the "cl" sound in "close."

Terms that crop up frequently in Welsh are *bach* or *fach* (small), *craig* or *graig* (rock), *cwm* (valley; pronounced cum), *dyffryn* (valley), *eglwys* (church), *glyn* (glen), *llyn* (lake), *mawr* or *fawr* (great, big), *mynydd* or *fynydd* (mountain, moorland), *pentre* (village, homestead), *plas* (hall, mansion), and *pont* or *bont* (bridge).

At the southern end of the bay near the New Promenade, **the castle.** was built in 1277 and rebuilt in 1282 by Edward I. It was one of several strongholds to fall, in 1404, to the Welsh leader Owain Glyndŵr. Today it is a romantic ruin on a headland.

At the northern end of the beach promenade a zigzag cliff path–nature trail at **Constitution Hill** leads to a view from the hilltop.An enjoyable way to reach the summit of Constitution Hill is by the **Aberystwyth Cliff Railway** (☎01970/617642 ⊕*www.aberystwythcliffrailway.co.uk* ≦*£3.20 round-trip* ☉*Nov.–Feb., Wed.–Sun. 10–4; Mar.–Oct., daily 10–5*), the longest electric cliff railway in Britain. Opened in 1896, it retains its Victorian look. At the 430-foot summit of Constitution Hill is the **Great Aberystwyth Camera Obscura** (☎*01970/617642*), a free modern version of a Victorian amusement: a massive 14-inch lens gives a bird's-eye view of the whole of Cardigan Bay and 26 Welsh mountain peaks. It has the same hours as the railway.

At Aberystwyth Station you can hop on the narrow-gauge, steam-operated **Vale of Rheidol Railway** for an hour ride to the **Devil's Bridge,** where the rivers Rheidol and Mynach meet in a series of spectacular falls. Clamped between two rocky cliffs where a torrent of water pours unceasingly, this bridge well deserves its name—Pont y Gwr Drwg, or Bridge of the Evil One. There are actually three bridges (the oldest is 800 years old), and the walk down to the lowest bridge, "the devil's," is magnificent but strictly for the sure-footed. ⊠*Park Ave.* ☎*01970/625819* ⊕*www.rheidolrailway.co.uk* ≦*£13.50 round-trip* ☉*Easter–Oct.; call for schedule.*

OFF THE BEATEN PATH

Llanerchaeron. This late-18th-century Welsh gentry estate in the Aeron Valley, 17 mi south of Aberystwyth, near Aberaeron, is a superb example of the early work of John Nash (1752–1835). Nash was the leading architect of the Regency and the designer of Brighton's Royal Pavilion. The estate survived with few changes until the present; it is a self-contained world with stables, barns, dairy, and brewery. The walled gardens are spectacular. ✉ *Off A482, Ciliau Aeron* ☎*01545/570200* ⊕*www.nationaltrust.org.uk* ✐*£6.90; farm and garden only, £5.90* ⊙*House Mar.–July, Wed.–Sun. 11:30–4; Aug., daily 11:30–4; Sept. and Oct., Wed.–Sun. 11:30–4:30. Farm and garden Mar.–July, Wed.–Sun. 11–5; Aug., daily 11–5; Sept. and Oct., Wed.–Sun. 11–5.*

WHERE TO EAT AND STAY

££
BISTRO
✕**Gannets.** A simple, good-value bistro, Gannets specializes in hearty roasts and pies produced from locally supplied meat, fish, and game. Organically grown vegetables and a good French house wine are further draws for a university crowd. ✉*7 St. James's Sq.* ☎*01970/617164* ▤*MC, V* ⊙*Closed Sun.–Tues.*

££ 🛏**Gwesty Cymru.** This seafront Edwardian home makes the perfect guesthouse for the 21st century. The hotel makes abundant and stylish use of the natural materials of Wales, so there's plenty of slate and oak. There are also spectacular sea views, designer bathrooms, original paintings, and illuminated Welsh poetry. **Pros:** Welsh atmosphere; sea views. **Cons:** no guest lounge; tiny entrance hall; small restaurant. ✉*19 Marine Terr.* ☎*01970/612252* ⊕*www.gwestycymru.com* 🛏*8 rooms* ♿*In-room: no a/c, DVD, Wi-Fi. In-hotel: restaurant, bar* ▤*MC, V* ⦿*BP.*

£££–££££ 🛏**Harbourmaster Hotel.** A drive south on the coast road from Aberystwyth brings you to Aberaeron and the delights of this early-19th-century Georgian-style building, right on the harbor among colorfully painted structures. Modern design and strong colors dominate the public areas and bedrooms, which have wonderful harbor views. The brasserie produces sophisticated fare such as deviled lamb kidneys and whole baked sea bream with fennel-and-olive gratin. **Pros:** huge zinc-top bar; stunning harbor location; friendly hosts. **Cons:** difficult parking; often booked up; minimum stay on weekends. ✉*Pen Cei, 15 mi south of Aberystwyth, Aberaeron* ☎*01545/570755* ⊕*www.harbour-master. com* 🛏*13 rooms* ♿*In-room: no a/c, DVD, Wi-Fi. In-hotel: restaurant, bar, Wi-Fi, no kids under 5* ▤*MC, V* ⦿*BP.*

15

MACHYNLLETH

18 mi northeast of Aberystwyth.

Machynlleth, at the head of the beautiful Dovey Estuary, does not look like a typical Welsh country town. Its long and wide main street (Heol Maengwyn), lined with a mixed style of buildings from sober gray stone to well-proportioned Georgian, creates an atypical sense of openness and space. Machynlleth's busiest day is Wednesday, when the stalls of market traders fill the main street.

ESSENTIALS

Visitor Information Aberdyfi (✉ *The Wharf Gardens* ☎*01654/767321* ⊙*Easter–Oct., daily 9:30–5:30*).

EXPLORING

At the **Owain Glyndŵr Centre,** a small exhibition celebrates Wales's last native leader, who established a Welsh parliament at Machynlleth in the early 15th century. ✉*End of Heol Maengwyn* ☎*01654/702827*

⊕*www.canolfanowainglyndwrcentre.org.uk* ✉*£1.50* ⊙*Easter–Sept.,*
Mon.–Sat. and Sun. in summer 10–4.

In a former chapel that's now a cultural and performing-arts center
is **Y Tabernacl Museum of Modern Art,** a superb gallery with permanent
displays, including works by the recently deceased Welsh artist Kyffin
Williams. ⊠*Heol Penrallt* ☎*01654/703355* ⊕*www.momawales.org.*
uk ✉*Free* ⊙*Mon.–Sat. 10–4.*

Ⓒ At the unique **Centre for Alternative Technology,** in an abandoned slate
quarry in the forested hills just north of Machynlleth, a water-balanced
cliff railway transports you to a futuristic, educational village equipped
with all things green: alternative energy sources (solar roofs, wood-
chip boilers), organic gardens, and a vegetarian café. Interactive displays present practical ideas about renewable resources, and the store
is full of inspirational books and eco-friendly products. ⊠*Off A487*
☎*01654/705950* ⊕*www.cat.org.uk* ✉*£8.40; lower prices in off-sea-*
son ⊙*Easter–June, daily 10–5:30; July and Aug., daily 10–6; Nov.–*
Easter, daily 10–dusk.

WHERE TO STAY

£££ 🛏 **Llety Bodfor.** The delightful little sailing center of Aberdovey is perched
at the mouth of the Dovey Estuary, west of Machynlleth. This contemporary Victorian town house has bright bedrooms that look out over
Cardigan Bay. All were decorated by owner and interior designer Ann
Hughes. The open-plan guest lounge/dining room has capacious leather
sofas, a small bar, and a piano. You can even buy items of hotel decor
that take your fancy at Seld Interiors, the on-site shop. **Pros:** stylish
decor; sea views; great shopping. **Cons:** no evening meals; no parking.
⊠*Bodfor Terrace, Aberdovey* ☎*01654/767475* ⊕*www.lletybodfor.*
co.uk ➘*8 rooms* △*In-room: no a/c, DVD. In-hotel: bar* ☰*MC, V*
†Ⓞ|*BP.*

£££££ 🛏 **Ynyshir Hall.** Idyllic gardens and grounds surround this supremely
★ luxurious Georgian mansion once owned by Queen Victoria. Inside,
the place glows with jewel-like tones and vibrant paintings by the former owner, artist Rob Reen. Antiques and Welsh pottery fill the public
areas; the pampering guest rooms, named after artists (Hogarth, Matisse, Goya), have antique beds. The outstanding contemporary cuisine
in the candlelit restaurant uses local favorites, from wild salmon and
venison to farmhouse cheeses. **Pros:** arty ambience; unabashed luxury;
great food. **Cons:** very expensive; isolated location. ⊠*Off A487, south-*
west of Machynlleth, Eglwysfach ☎*01654/781209 or 800/777–6536*
⊕*www.ynyshir-hall.co.uk* ➘*9 rooms* △*In-room: no a/c. In-hotel: res-*
taurant, room service, bar, laundry service, Internet terminal, no kids
under 9 ☰*AE, DC, MC, V* †Ⓞ|*BP.*

OUTDOORS

The 128-mi **Glyndŵr's Way** (⊕*www.glyndwrsway.org.uk*) walking route
passes through Machynlleth before it turns east to climb above the
Dovey with wonderful views north to Cadair Idris.

DOLGELLAU

16 mi north of Machynlleth, 34 mi northeast of Aberystwyth.

A solidly Welsh town with dark stone buildings and old coaching inns made of the local gray dolerite and slate, Dolgellau (pronounced dol-*geth*-lee) thrived with the wool trade until the mid-19th century. Sheep are still auctioned here, but now they're valued for meat rather than wool. Prosperity left striking architecture, with buildings of different eras side by side on crooked streets that are a pre-Norman legacy. The town trail booklet, sold in the tourist office on Eldon Square, tells the story. Dolgellau, in a valley, has long been a popular base for people eager to walk the surrounding countryside. Look down the streets or above the buildings, and you'll see mountains rising up in the distance.

The town became the center of the Welsh gold trade in the 19th century, when high-quality gold was discovered locally. A nugget of Dolgellau gold is used to make royal wedding rings. You can still try your luck and pan for gold in the Mawddach.

15

ESSENTIALS

Visitor Information Dolgellau (⊠ *Ty Meirion, Eldon Sq.* ☎ *01341/422888*).

EXPLORING

The **Museum of the Quakers,** in the town square, commemorates the area's strong links with the Quaker movement and the Quakers' emigration to the American colonies. ⊠ *Eldon Sq.* ☎ *01341/422888* ☑ *Free* ☉ *Easter–Oct., daily 9:30–5:30; Nov.–Easter, Thurs.–Mon. 9:30–4:30.*

℃ The National Centre for Welsh Folk Music, **Ty Siamas,** in the converted Victorian Market Hall and Assembly Rooms, has a fascinating interactive folk music exhibition, performance auditorium, and café and bar. ⊠ *Neuadd Idris, Eldon Sq.* ☎ *01341/421800* ⊕ *www.tysiamas.com* ☑ *£3.90 (exhibition)* ☉ *Easter–Sept., Wed.–Fri. 10–4, Sat. 10–1. Call for off-season times.*

To the south of Dolgellau rises the menacing bulk of **Cadair Idris** (2,927 feet); the name means "the Chair of Idris," though no one is completely sure who Idris was—probably a warrior bard. It is said that anyone sleeping for a night on a certain part of the mountain will awaken either a poet or a madman, or not at all.

BARMOUTH

10 mi west of Dolgellau.

Barmouth, on the northern mouth of the Mawddach Estuary, is one of the few places along the Welsh coast that can be described as a full-fledged seaside resort, although it's now a bit tired. It has a 2-mi-long promenade, wide expanses of golden beach, and facilities for sea, river, and mountain-lake fishing. To appreciate the splendid location, walk along the footpath beside the railway bridge that crosses the mouth of the estuary: the bay stretches out on one side, and on the other are rugged, looming mountains and the river.

The arrival of the railroad in the 19th century made Barmouth a popular vacation spot. Alfred, Lord Tennyson was inspired to write *Crossing the Bar* by the spectacle of the Mawddach rushing to meet the sea. Charles Darwin worked on *The Origin of Species* and *The Descent of Man* in a house by the shore. Essayist and art critic John Ruskin was a frequent visitor and was trustee of the St. George's cottages built in 1871 by the Guild of St. George (Ruskin's organization, dedicated to founding agrarian communities) in 1871. Ruskin loved the walk from Barmouth up the river to Dolgellau.

ESSENTIALS

Visitor Information Barmouth (⊠ *The Station* ☎ *01341/280787*).

WHERE TO STAY

£££ 🏠 **Bae Abermaw.** Perched high above the sea with panoramic views across the bay, this traditional Victorian stone house encloses a surprisingly contemporary, minimalist interior. Clean lines and pale natural tones make for a relaxed atmosphere. The excellent restaurant serves sophisticated local fare. **Pros:** bay views; successful blend of old and new. **Cons:** on a narrow road; steep driveway. ⊠*Panorama Rd.* ☎*01341/280550* ⊕*www.baeabermaw.com* ⇆*14 rooms* ⌂*In-room: no a/c, Wi-Fi. In-hotel: restaurant, bars, Wi-Fi* ▤*MC, V* ⏁*BP.*

WELSHPOOL

48 mi east of Barmouth, 19 mi southwest of Shrewsbury.

The border town of Welshpool, "Trallwng" in Welsh, is famous as the home of Powis Castle, one of Mid Wales's greatest treasures, but it also has an appealing town center.

ESSENTIALS

Visitor Information Welshpool (⊠ *Vicarage Gardens Car Park, Church St.* ☎*01938/552043*).

EXPLORING

★ Continuously occupied since the 13th century, **Powis Castle** is one of the most opulent residential castles in Britain, with gardens that are equally renowned. Its battlements rear high on a hilltop, and Italian- and French-influenced terraced gardens surround the castle. Below gigantic yew hedges, the grounds fall steeply down to wide lawns and neat Elizabethan gardens. The interior contains many treasures: Greek vases; paintings by Thomas Gainsborough, Joshua Reynolds, and George Romney, among others; superb furniture; and the **Clive of India Museum,** with a good collection of Indian art. The tearoom is excellent. A timed-ticket system may be in effect on busy days. ⊠*Off A483* ☎*01938/551944* ⊕*www.nationaltrust.org.uk* 🎫*£11; gardens only, £7.50* ⊗*Castle and museum Apr.–June and Sept., Thurs.–Mon. 1–5; July and Aug., Wed.–Mon. 1–5; Oct., Thurs.–Mon. 1–4. Gardens Thurs.–Mon. 11–5:30; July and Aug., Wed.–Mon. 11–5:30; Oct., Thurs.–Mon. 11–5.*

The excellent **Powysland Museum,** in a converted warehouse on the banks of the Montgomery Canal, focuses on local history from the Stone

Age to Victorian times. ✉ *Canal Wharf* ☎ *01938/554656* ✍ *£1* ⊗ *May–Sept., Mon., Tues., Thurs., and Fri. 11–1 and 2–5, weekends 10–1 and 2–5; Oct.–Apr., Mon., Tues., Thurs., and Fri. 11–1 and 2–5, Sat. 11–2.*

SOUTH WALES

The most diverse of Wales's three regions, the south covers not only the immediate region around Cardiff and the border of Wales and England, but also the southwest as far as the rugged coastline of Pembrokeshire. The very different natures of its two national parks reveal South Wales's scenic variety. The Brecon Beacons park, a short drive north of Cardiff, is an area of high, grassy mountains, lakes, and craggy limestone gorges. In contrast, the Pembrokeshire Coast National Park holds one of Europe's finest stretches of coastal natural beauty, with mile after mile of spectacular sea cliffs, beaches, headlands, and coves. Other pieces of the complicated South Wales jigsaw include traditional farmlands, cosmopolitan urban areas, rolling border country, wooded vales, and the former industrial valleys where coal was mined in huge quantities during the 19th and early 20th centuries.

15

CARDIFF

20 mi southwest of the Second Severn Bridge, which carries the M4 motorway across the Severn Estuary into Wales.

Home to the Welsh Assembly and with a population of 306,000, Cardiff is financially, industrially, and commercially the most important city in Wales. It's also one of Europe's youngest and most vibrant capital cities, with an appealing blend of old and brand-new. Attracting increasing numbers of tourists are its handsome Civic Centre, magnificent parklands, canopied shopping arcades, and a castle with abundant Victorian verve. These traditional sights stand alongside new landmarks like the Millennium Stadium and Cardiff Bay, a onetime coal-exporting hub that has undergone a dazzling waterfront regeneration. Here a dam across the Taff and Ely rivers has created a freshwater lake edged by 8 mi of prime waterfront, an area of promenades, shops, restaurants, attractions, and exciting modern buildings like the Wales Millennium Centre.

True to the Welsh tradition of vocal excellence, Cardiff is home base for Britain's adventurous and acclaimed Welsh National Opera. Cardiff is also the sporting center of Wales and the Welsh capital of rugby football. To hear crowds singing their support for the Welsh team is a stirring experience.

GETTING HERE AND AROUND

The capital is a major transportation hub with good connections to other parts of Wales and with England. A local rail network runs north into the South Wales valleys, and there are fast mainline rail and bus services to Swansea and southwest Wales. Cardiff is easily accessible by road, with the M4 motorway running to its doorstep. For walkers there are two Cardiffs: the established city center and the waterfront a mile or so to the south. Bus and rail links connect the two.

SeeWales offers day trips from Cardiff to destinations including Brecon Beacons National Park and the Gower Peninsula.

TIMING

If you don't like crowds, avoid Cardiff during international rugby tournaments or other major sporting events.

ESSENTIALS

Visitor and Tour Information Cardiff (✉ *The Old Library, The Hayes* ☎ *08701/211258* ⊕ *www.visitcardiff.com*). SeeWales (☎ *029/20–227227* ⊕ *www.seewales.com*).

EXPLORING

TOP ATTRACTIONS

Cardiff Bay. Panoramic bay views, promenades, shops, restaurants, museums, and prestigious buildings make Cardiff Bay well worth a visit. The revitalized dockland, 1 mi south of the city center, can be reached by bus, train, or taxi. The **Cardiff Bay Visitor Centre,** a futuristic building known locally as "the Tube" (because of its shape), tells the story of the transformation of the bay area. Next door and overlooking the bay is the timber Norwegian seamen's church where Roald Dahl (noted author whose children's books include *James and the Giant Peach* and *Charlie and the Chocolate Factory*) was baptized. It's now known as the **Norwegian Church Arts Centre** and houses a performance space, a gallery, and a café. North of the visitor center is the **National Assembly Debating Chamber,** a canopied glass structure designed by Richard Rogers that complements the neighboring modern buildings. The lively exhibition about the workings of the National Assembly, however, is across the street in the imposing Victorian building, the **Pierhead.**

❶ ★ Cardiff Castle. In Bute Park, one section of the city's hundreds of acres of parkland, is an unusual historic site, with Roman, Norman, and Victorian associations. Parts of the walls are Roman, the solid keep is Norman, and the whole complex was restored and transformed into a Victorian ego flight by the third marquess of Bute. He employed William Burges (1827–81), an architect obsessed by the Gothic period, and Burges transformed the castle into an extravaganza of medieval color and careful craftsmanship. It is the perfect expression of the anything-goes Victorian spirit, and a reflection of the fortune made by the marquess in Cardiff's booming docklands. ✉ *Bute Park* ☎ *029/2087–8100* ⊕ *www.cardiffcastle.com* ✆ *Grounds and guided tour of castle £8.95; grounds only, £3.75* ☉ *Mar.–Oct., daily 9:30–6; Nov.–Feb., daily 9:30–5; call for tour times.*

QUICK BITES

Café Minuet (✉ *42 Castle Arcade* ☎ *029/2034-1794* ☉ *Mon.-Sat. 11-5*), in the Victorian shopping arcade opposite Cardiff Castle, has pale wood floors and checked tablecloths and serves tasty rustic Italian food like homemade soups, pasta, and pizzas. Service is prompt and friendly.

❺ ★ Castell Coch. Perched on a hillside is the Red Castle, a turreted Victorian vision. It was built (on the site of a medieval stronghold) in the 1870s, about the time that Ludwig II of Bavaria was creating his fairy-tale castles, and it could almost be one of them. The castle was another collaboration of the third marquess of Bute and William Burges, builders

Cardiff

KEY

i Tourist information

Corbett Rd.

Central Station i

Museum Ave.

King Edward VII. Ave.

College Rd.

Cathays Park

North Road

City Hall Rd.

Gorsedd Gardens Rd.

St. Andrews Pl.

Senghennydd Rd.

Park Place

Park Grove

Blvd. de Nantes

Greyfriars Rd.

Stuttgarter Strasse

Dumfries Pl.

Windsor Pl.

Talbot St.

Cathedral Rd.

Sophia Grdns.

Cooper's Field

Bute Park

Cowbridge Road East

Lower Cathedral Rd.

Green St.

Brook St.

Despenser St.

Despenser Pl.

Clare St.

Taff

Fitzhamon Embankment

Castle Street

Westgate St.

Duke St.

Kings Way

High St.

St. John St.

Trinity St.

Queen St.

The Friary

Park Place

Charles St.

Churchill Way

Guildford St.

Cardiff Bay Visitor Centre i

Hill St.

Cardiff International Arena & World Trade Center

Mary Ann St.

Bridge St.

Tudor St.

Wood St.

Bus Station

St. Mary St.

Mill La.

Customhouse St.

Bute Terrace

Bute St.

↓ TO CARDIFF BAY,
↓ 1 mile south of city center

0 · · · 1/8 mile

0 · · · 1/8 kilometer

Cardiff Bay Area

Mount Stuart Sq.

West Bute St.

Bute St.

James St.

Adelaide St.

Lloyd George Av.

New George St.

Bute Place

Pierhead St.

A4232

A4232

Stuart St.

Oval Basin

Pierhead Building

National Assembly Debating Chamber

Britannia Quay

Harbour Dr.

Lightship 2000

Cardiff Bay Visitor Centre i

Mermaid Quay

Cardiff Bay

Wetlands Nature Reserve

0 · · · 1/8 mile

0 · · · 1/8 kilometer

of Cardiff Castle. Burges created everything—architecture, furnishings, murals—in a remarkable exercise in Victorian-Gothic whimsy. ⊠*A470, 4 mi north of Cardiff, Tongwynlais* ☎*029/2081–0101* ⊕*www.cadw. wales.gov.uk* ⊠*£3.60* ⊙*Apr.–Oct., daily 9–5; Nov.–Mar., Mon.–Sat. 9:30–4, Sun. 11–4.*

Civic Centre. Two blocks north and east of Cardiff Castle is a well-designed complex of tree-lined avenues and Edwardian civic buildings with white Portland stone facades; Cathays Park is in the center. A Welsh dragon sits atop the domed City Hall, and inside the Marble Hall contains statues of Welsh heroes, including St. David, Henry Tudor, and Owain Glyndŵr (although he razed Cardiff in 1404). Neoclassical law courts and university campus buildings are also here. ⊠*Bordered by North Rd. on the west and Park Pl. on the east.*

❹ **National Museum Cardiff.** This splendid museum, next to City Hall in the Civic Centre, tells the story of Wales through its plants, rocks, archaeology, zoology, art, and industry. The Evolution of Wales gallery gives a dazzling run through Wales's past using robotics and audiovisual effects. There's a fine collection of modern European art, including the largest collection of French impressionist and postimpressionist works in the country. Allow at least half a day at the museum, and don't miss *La Parisienne,* by Renoir. ⊠*Cathays Park* ☎*029/2039–7951* ⊕*www. museumwales.ac.uk* ⊠*Free* ⊙*Tues.–Sun. 10–5.*

Fodor'sChoice

★

❸ **St. David's Centre.** South of the Civic Centre are the shopping and business areas of Cardiff. A large, modern shopping mall holds **St. David's Hall,** one of Europe's best concert halls, with outstanding acoustics. People come here for classical music, jazz, rock, ballet, and even snooker championships. At the time of this writing, St. David's 2, a large mall with stores, cafés, public areas, and a library, was scheduled to be completed in late 2009. Nearby is the **Cardiff International Arena,** a multipurpose center for exhibitions, concerts, and conferences. ⊠*Queen St. and St. John St.*

OFF THE BEATEN PATH

Tintern Abbey. When Wordsworth penned "Lines Written a Few Miles Above Tintern Abbey," he had no idea of all the people who would flock to Tintern to gaze at the abbey's substantial ruins. Remote and hauntingly beautiful as the site is, its appeal is diminished in summer because of crowds, so visit early or late in the day to best appreciate the complex stonework and tracery of the Gothic church. The abbey, 5 mi north of Chepstow and 30 mi northeast of Cardiff, is on the banks of the River Wye. ⊠*A466, Tintern* ☎*01291/689251* ⊕*www.cadw. wales.gov.uk* ⊠*£3.60* ⊙*Apr.–Oct., daily 9–5; Nov.–Mar., Mon.–Sat. 9:30–4, Sun. 11–4.*

WORTH NOTING

Caerphilly Castle. The largest and one of the most impressive fortresses in Wales was remarkable at the time of its construction in the 13th century. Built by an Anglo-Norman lord, the concentric fortification contained inner and outer defenses. More than 30 acres of grounds and a moat surround the castle, but Caerphilly is no longer on guard; some walls have toppled and others lean haphazardly. Exhibits in the gatehouse trace its turbulent history. The castle is 7 mi north of Cardiff. ⊠*Access* *off A470–A468, Caerphilly* ☎*029/ 2088–3143* ⊕*www.cadw.wales. gov.uk* ☑*£3.60* ⊘*Apr.–Oct., daily 9:30–5; Nov.–Mar., Mon.–Sat. 9:30–4, Sun. 11–4.*

6 **Llandaff.** In a suburb that retains its village feeling, you can visit **Llandaff Cathedral,** which was repaired after serious bomb damage in World War II. The cathedral includes the work of a number of Pre-Raphaelites as well as *Christ in Majesty,* a 15-foot-tall aluminum figure by sculptor Jacob Epstein (1880–1959). To get here from Cardiff, cross the River Taff and follow Cathedral Road for about 2 mi. Guided tours are available by arrangement. *CF5 2LA* ☎*029/2056– 4554* ⊕*www.llandaffcathedral.org.uk.*

15

2 **Millennium Stadium.** The modern, 72,000-seat stadium stands beside the River Taff on the site of the famous Cardiff Arms Park, the spiritual home of Welsh rugby. The stadium's retractable roof enables it to be used for concerts and special events throughout the year, as well as for rugby. On a one-hour tour you can walk the players' tunnel and see the Royal Box, dressing rooms, pitch, and broadcasting suite. ✉*Entrance Gate 3, Westgate St.* ☎*029/2082–2228* ⊕*www.millenniumstadium. com* ☑*Tours £6.50* ⊘*Call for tour times.*

7 **St. Fagans National History Museum.** On 100 acres of parkland and gardens, this excellent open-air museum has farmhouses, cottages, shops, a school, chapels, St. Fagans castle (a 16th-century manor house), and terraced houses that celebrate Wales's rich rural culture and show the evolution of building styles. All but two of the structures were brought here from places around Wales. Galleries display clothing and articles from daily life. There are farming demonstrations and special events that highlight ancient rural festivals. The museum is accessible from Junction 33 on the M4. ✉*St. Fagans* ☎*029/2057–3500* ⊕*www. museumwales.ac.uk* ☑*Free* ⊘*Daily 10–5.*

9 **Techniquest.** A large science-discovery center on the waterfront, Techniquest has 160 interactive exhibits, a planetarium, and a science theater. ✉*Stuart St., Cardiff Bay* ☎*029/2047–5475* ⊕*www.techniquest.org* ☑*£6.90* ⊘*Weekdays 9:30–4:30, weekends 10:30–5.*

8 **Wales Millennium Centre.** This huge arts complex with a curving golden steel roof and purple slate walls is a world-class stage for full-scale ballet, opera, and musical performances. The center contains dance and recording studios, an orchestra hall, and a 1,900-seat auditorium. Seven leading Welsh cultural organizations make this their home base, including the Welsh National Opera Company and the Dance Company of Wales. There are shops, bars, and restaurants; one-hour tours are available from WMC's guides. ✉*Cardiff Bay* ☎*08700/402000* ⊕*www. wmc.org.uk* ✍*Free. Tours £5.50* ⊘*Call to arrange tour.*

WHERE TO EAT

£££
MODERN BRITISH
✗**Armless Dragon.** It's worth the five-minute drive from the city center to eat at this comfortable restaurant with a contemporary menu that changes daily. Dishes such as Monmouthshire woodland pork with smoked bacon and creamed leeks are created from seasonal, local ingredients. There are always excellent vegetarian options, too. ✉*97 Wyverne Rd.* ☎*029/2038–2357* ⊟*AE, MC, V* ⊘*Closed Sun. and Mon.*

£££
BRITISH
✗**Harry Ramsden's.** You can dine on the (reputedly) world's most famous fish-and-chips in a chandeliered, 200-seat dining room with wonderful views across Cardiff Bay. If you like live music with your meal, call to ask for dates of gala nights and sing-along evenings. ✉*Landsea House, Stuart St.* ☎*029/2046–3334* ⊟*MC, V.*

£££
MODERN BRITISH
★
✗**Le Gallois.** Its minimalist furnishings and varied menu help make this sophisticated restaurant, close to Sophia Gardens, one of the city's most popular. The cooking is European in style and takes advantage of local ingredients. Try the haunch of venison steak with mushroom duxelle and suet pastry pudding. A good-value fixed-price menu (£18.95 for three courses) is available at lunch. ✉*8 Romilly Crescent* ☎*029/2034–1264* ⊟*MC, V* ⊘*Closed Mon.*

££
ITALIAN
✗**Valentino's.** With its cozily rustic decor and friendly Italian staff, this little restaurant simply drips with authenticity. In addition to the usual pizzas and pastas, there is an ever-changing selection of fresh, locally sourced meat and fish dishes. ✉*5 Windsor Pl.* ☎*029/2022–9697* ⊟*AE, DC, MC, V* ⊘*Closed Sun.*

WHERE TO STAY

££–£££
▦ **Jolyons Hotel.** Every room has different antiques, design, and fabrics at this sumptuous little boutique hotel close to the Millennium Centre. All the beds are king-size, so you can spread out with the morning paper. The lively Bar Cwtch (which means "cuddle" or "cubbyhole" in Welsh) has a wood-burning stove (order a pizza and watch it cook in the log fire). It's a great location from which to explore all the attractions of Cardiff Bay. **Pros:** bursting with character; comfortable bar; in the heart of Cardiff Bay. **Cons:** not near the city center; Cardiff Bay area can lack atmosphere in off-peak times. ✉*Bute Cres., Cardiff Bay* ☎*029/2048–8775* ⊕*www.jolyons.co.uk* ⇆*6 rooms* ⌂*In-room: no a/c, DVD, Wi-Fi. In-hotel: room service, bar, laundry service, Wi-Fi, no kids under 13* ⊟*AE, DC, MC, V* ⦿*BP.*

££
▦ **Llanerch Vineyard.** The pine-furnished, country-style rooms in the farmhouse and spacious converted outbuildings of this Vale of Glamorgan vineyard are only 15 minutes from Cardiff center, but you are deep in the green countryside here. You can walk in the surrounding vineyard and woodlands and arrange your own personal Welsh wine tasting. Take Junction 34 off M4 and follow the brown signs. **Pros:** wine lover's delight; cooking school on-site; excellent restaurant. **Cons:** not that close to Cardiff; rooms vary greatly in size. ✉*Hensol, Pendoylan* ☎*01443/225877* ⊕*www.llanerch-vineyard.co.uk* ⇆*11 rooms* ⌂*In-room: no a/c, DVD, Wi-Fi. In-hotel: restaurant* ⊟*MC, V* ⦿*BP.*

££££–£££££   **Park Plaza.** At this award-winning hotel just off Cardiff's main pedestrianized shopping street, spacious rooms are individually designed in a clean-lined, uncluttered style with sumptuous fabrics. After a hard day's retail therapy unwind in the luxury health club and enjoy the simple, locally sourced food served in the restaurant. **Pros:** central location; excellent fitness center; stainless-steel pool. **Cons:** a bit corporate; no Welsh atmosphere. ⊠ *Greyfriars Rd.* ☎ *029/2011–1111* ⊕ *www.parkplaza.com* ⇄ *129 rooms* & *In-room: safe, Wi-Fi. In-hotel: restaurant, room service, bar, pool, gym, spa, laundry service, Wi-Fi* ⊟ *AE, MC, V* ⊚ *BP.*

£££–£££££   **St. David's Hotel and Spa.** Natural light from a glass atrium floods ★ this stylish, up-to-the-minute luxury hotel along the waterfront. Every room, done in soothing neutral tones with sleek modern furniture, has a private balcony and views over Cardiff Bay. You can indulge in a relaxing hydrotherapy spa treatment or feast at the Tides restaurant, which specializes in modern French fare. Special promotional deals are often available. **Pros:** a bit like staying on a cruise ship; relaxing spa; close to Cardiff Bay amenities. **Cons:** entrance rather stark; not convenient to downtown. ⊠ *Havannah St.* ☎ *029/2045–4045* ⊕ *stdavidshotelcardiff.co.uk* ⇄ *132 rooms* & *In-room: safe, DVD, Internet. In-hotel: restaurant, room service, pool, gym, spa, laundry service, Internet terminal, Wi-Fi, no-smoking rooms* ⊟ *AE, DC, MC, V.*

££   **Town House.** Cosmopolitan in style, this immaculate guesthouse near the city center (the castle is a short walk away) is considered Cardiff's best B&B. The elegant Victorian building retains many original features and has neat, well-equipped bedrooms. You can have traditional British or American breakfasts in the formal dining room. **Pros:** close to Cardiff Castle; near shops. **Cons:** rooms quite small; guests share a table at breakfast. ⊠ *70 Cathedral Rd.* ☎ *029/2023–9399* ⊕ *www.thetownhousecardiff.co.uk* ⇄ *8 rooms* & *In-room: no a/c, Wi-Fi. In-hotel: bar, Wi-Fi, some pets allowed* ⊟ *AE, MC, V* ⊚ *BP.*

NIGHTLIFE AND THE ARTS

NIGHTLIFE   Cardiff's clubs and pubs make up a lively nighttime scene. **Café Jazz** (⊠ *21 St. Mary St.* ☎ *029/2038–7026*) presents live jazz five nights a week and has TV screens in the bar and restaurant so you can view the on-stage action. **Clwb Ifor Bach** (⊠ *Womanby St.* ☎ *029/2023–2199* ⊕ *www.clwb. net*), a distinctively Welsh club (its name means "Little Ivor's Club"), has three floors of eclectic music, from funk to folk to rock.

THE ARTS   The big theaters present a full program of entertainment: drama and comedy, pop and the classics. The huge **Cardiff International Arena** (⊠ *Mary Ann St.* ☎ *029/2022–4488*) showcases artists who can draw huge crowds, from Tom Jones to Bob Dylan. **St. David's Hall** (⊠ *The Hayes* ☎ *029/2087–8444* ⊕ *www.stdavidshallcardiff.co.uk*), a popular venue, presents the Welsh Proms in July, attracting major international orchestras and soloists, and every two years hosts the prestigious Cardiff Singer of the World competition. It also stages rock, pop, jazz, and folk events.

New Theatre (⊠ *Park Pl.* ☎ *029/2087–8889* ⊕ *www.newtheatrecardiff. co.uk*), a refurbished Edwardian playhouse, presents big names, including the Royal Shakespeare Company, the National Theatre, and the Northern Ballet.

Wales has one of Britain's four major opera companies, the outstanding **Welsh National Opera** (✉ *Wales Millennium Centre, Cardiff Bay* ☎*029/2063–5000 for info, 08700/402000 for tickets* ⊕*www.wno. org.uk*). The company spends most of its time touring Wales and England.

SHOPPING

Canopied Victorian and Edwardian shopping arcades lined with specialty stores weave in and out of the city's modern shopping complexes. The **Cardiff Antiques Centre** (✉*Royal Arcade* ☎*029/2039–8891*), in an 1856 arcade, is a good place to buy antique jewelry. Cardiff's traditional **covered market** (✉*The Hayes* ☎*029/2087–1214* ⊕*www.cardiff-market. co.uk*) sells tempting fresh foods beneath its Victorian glass canopy. **Melin Tregwynt** (✉*26 Royal Arcade* ☎*08700/424562 or 029/20224997* ⊕*www.melintregwynt.co.uk*) is an elegant shop selling woolen clothing, bags, and cushions woven in an old Pembrokeshire mill. The result is a wonderfully textured blend of traditional and contemporary.

ABERGAVENNY

28 mi north of Cardiff.

The market town of Abergavenny, near Brecon Beacons National Park, is a popular base for walkers and hikers.

ESSENTIALS

Visitor Information Abergavenny (✉*Swan Meadow, Monmouth Rd.* ☎*01873/853254*).

EXPLORING

The popular **Abergavenny Food Festival** (☎*01873/851643 general information, 01873/850805 tickets* ⊕*www.abergavennyfoodfestival.com*), held over a weekend in September, has lectures, discussions, demonstrations, and a food market. It's another sign of the growing interest in regional Welsh food.

Ruined **Abergavenny Castle,** built early in the 11th century, has a good local museum. The castle witnessed a tragic event on Christmas in 1176: the Norman knight William de Braose invited the neighboring Welsh chieftains to a feast and, in a crude attempt to gain control of the area, had them all slaughtered as they sat at dinner. Afterward, the Welsh attacked and virtually demolished the castle. Most of what now remains dates from the 13th and 14th centuries. The castle's 19th-century hunting lodge houses the museum, with exhibits about area history from the Iron Age to the present. The re-creation of a Victorian Welsh farmhouse kitchen includes old utensils and butter molds. ✉*Castle Museum, Castle St.* ☎*01873/854282* ⊡*Free* ⊘*Mar.–Oct., Mon.–Sat. 11–1 and 2–5, Sun. 2–5; Nov.–Feb., Mon.–Sat. 11–1 and 2–4.*

West of Abergavenny lie the valleys—the Rhondda is the most famous—so well described by Richard Llewellyn in his 1939 novel *How Green Was My Valley* (the basis for the 1941 film). The slag heaps of the coal mines are green now, thanks to land reclamation plans. The area south-west of Abergavenny, around the former iron- and coal-mining town of Blaenavon, has been named a World Heritage Site by UNESCO; it provides a fascinating glimpse into Wales's industrial past. At the **Big Pit: National Coal Museum,** ex-miners take you underground on a tour of an authentic coal mine for a look at the hard life of the South Wales miner. You can also see the pithead baths and workshops. ⊠ *Off A4043, Blaenavon* ☎ *01495/790311* ⊕ *www.museumwales.ac.uk* ▣ *Free* ⊙ *Feb.–Nov., daily 9:30–5; underground tours 10–3:30.*

Fodor's Choice
★

The **Blaenavon Ironworks,** dating from 1789, trace the entire process of iron production in that era. Well-preserved blast furnaces, a water-balance lift used to transport materials to higher ground, and a terraced row of workers' cottages show how the business operated. ⊠ *A4043, Blaenavon* ☎ *01495/792615* ⊕ *www.cadw.wales.gov.uk* ▣ *Free* ⊙ *Apr.–Oct., daily 10–5; Nov.–Mar., Fri. and Sat. 9:30–4, Sun. 11–4.*

WHERE TO EAT AND STAY

££
MODERN BRITISH

✕ **Clytha Arms.** A converted house on the banks of the River Usk near Abergavenny serves imaginative modern food in a relaxed setting. Try the wild sea bass with crab-and-laver sauce. You can eat very cheaply in the bar (try the real ales) or pay a little more in the restaurant. ⊠ *Off B4598, Clytha* ☎ *01873/840206* ▤ *AE, MC, V* ⊙ *Closed Mon.*

£££–££££

🏠 **Llansantffraed Court Hotel.** This grand country house dating from 1400 is set on 20 acres of well-tended grounds with a trout lake and views of the Brecon Beacons. The rooms are large and have four-poster beds. There's a log fire in the lounge, and the terrace is perfect for afternoon tea. The acclaimed restaurant is known for using organic meats. **Pros:** excellent foodie reputation; peaceful setting; great for anglers. **Cons:** unexciting decor; out-of-the-way location between Abergavenny and Raglan. ⊠ *Old Raglan Rd., Clytha* ☎ *01873/840678* ⊕ *www.llch. co.uk* ⮑ *21 rooms* ⚭ *In-room: no a/c, Wi-Fi. In-hotel: restaurant, room service, bar, laundry service, Internet terminal, Wi-Fi, some pets allowed* ▤ *AE, MC, V* ⦿|*BP.*

15

CRICKHOWELL

5 mi northwest of Abergavenny.

If you take A40 northwest out of Abergavenny, you pass Sugar Loaf mountain and come to Crickhowell, a charming town on the banks of the River Usk with little shops, an ancient bridge, and a ruined castle.

ESSENTIALS

Visitor Information Crickhowell (⊠ *Beaufort St.* ☎ *01873/811970*).

EXPLORING

Tretower Court, 3 mi northwest of Crickhowell, is a splendid example of a fortified medieval manor house. Nearby, and part of the site, are the ruins of a Norman castle. ⊠ *A479* ☎ *01874/730279* ⊕ *www.cadw. wales.gov.uk* ▣ *£2.90* ⊙ *Apr.–Sept., Tues.–Sun. 10–5; Oct., Tues.–Sun. 9–4.*

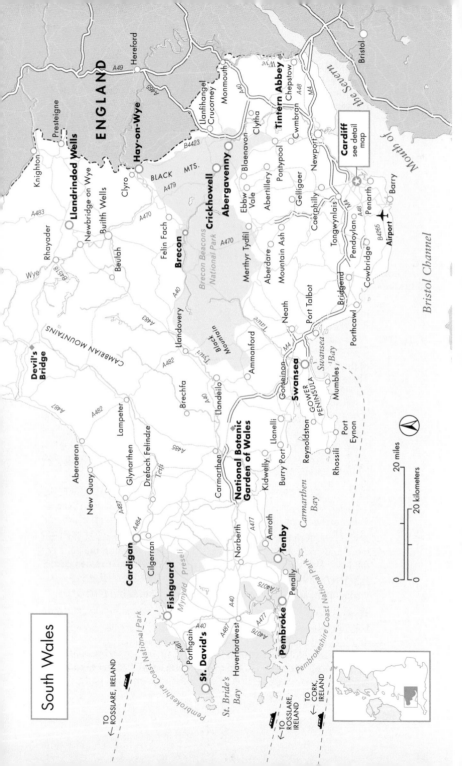

WHERE TO STAY

££–£££   🛏 **Bear Hotel.** In the middle of town, this coaching inn is full of character. The low-beamed bar, decorated with memorabilia from the days when stagecoaches stopped here, has a log fire in winter. Rooms in the hotel or in a modern addition in the former stable yard vary widely (some are fairly small); the most luxurious have four-poster beds and antiques. The Bear serves creative contemporary cuisine, including excellent-value bar food. **Pros:** friendly bar; in the heart of Crickhowell; good food. **Cons:** some rooms overlook the road; rooms vary in quality; can get busy on weekends. ⊠*A40* ☎*01873/810408* ⊕*www.bearhotel.co.uk* 🛏*35 rooms* &*In-room: no a/c, DVD, Wi-Fi. In-hotel: restaurant, room service, bar, laundry service, Wi-Fi, some pets allowed* ⊟*AE, MC, V* 🍽*BP.*

> **WORD OF MOUTH**

> "Our base was Crickhowell, a very pretty small village on the eastern edge of the Brecon Beacons. From there you can easily reach several important castles. There is a somewhat larger town, Abergavenny, even closer. I'd think either would make a good base."
> —Fra_Diavolo

££   🛏 **Ty Croeso Hotel.** A hillside location with views over the Usk Valley adds to the appeal of this hotel (its name means "House of Welcome"). The early-19th-century gray-stone building has comfortable rooms with print fabrics, a lounge with a log fire, and imaginative food with a Welsh emphasis. **Pros:** borders a lovely canal; good walking in the area; mountain views. **Cons:** on a narrow lane; very steep walk from Crickhowell. ⊠*The Dardy, off B4558* ☎*01873/810573* ⊕*www.ty-croeso. co.uk* 🛏*8 rooms* &*In-room: no a/c, Wi-Fi. In-hotel: restaurant, room service, bar, laundry service, Wi-Fi* ⊟*AE, MC, V* 🍽*BP.*

BRECON

14 mi northwest of Crickhowell, 19 mi northwest of Abergavenny, 41 mi north of Cardiff.

Brecon, a historic market town of narrow passageways, Georgian buildings, and pleasant riverside walks, is also the gateway to Brecon Beacons National Park. It's particularly appealing on market days (Tuesday and Friday). You may want to purchase a hand-carved wooden love spoon similar to those on display in the Brecknock Museum.

ESSENTIALS

Visitor Information Brecon (⊠*Market Car Park* ☎*01874/622485*).

EXPLORING

Cavernous **Brecon Cathedral** (☎*01874/623344* ⊕*www.breconcathedral. org.uk*), with a heritage center that traces its history, stands on the hill above the middle of town.

In the colonnaded Shire Hall built in 1842 is the **Brecknock Museum** (⊠*Captain's Walk* ☎*01874/624121*), with its artifacts from rural life, art exhibits, superb collection of carved love spoons, and perfectly preserved 19th-century assize court.

15

The military exhibits in the **South Wales Borderers' Museum** span centuries of conflict; some relate to battles in which this regiment participated. The Zulu Room recalls the Borderers' defense of Rorke's Drift in the Anglo-Zulu war of 1879, an action dramatized in the 1964 film *Zulu*, starring Michael Caine. ⊠ *The Barracks* ☏ *01874/613310* ⊕ *www. rrw.org.uk* 🎟️ *£3* 🕑 *Oct.–Mar., weekdays 10–5; Apr.–Sept., weekdays 10–5, weekends 10–4.*

> **LOVE SPOONS**
>
> The rural Welsh custom of giving one's beloved a wooden spoon intricately hand carved with symbols of love dates from the mid-17th century. Motifs include hearts, flowers, doves, intertwined vines, and chain links. These days you don't have to make the effort yourself, because shops all over Wales sell the spoons as souvenirs.

South of Brecon the skyline fills with mountains, and wild, windswept uplands stretch to the horizon in Brecon Beacons National Park. The **Brecon Beacons National Park Visitor Centre** on Mynydd Illtyd, a high, grassy stretch of upland west of A470, is an excellent source of information for attractions and activities within this 519-square-mi park of hills and open moorlands. It also gives wonderful panoramic views across to Pen-y-fan, at 2,907 feet the highest peak in South Wales. If you plan to explore Wales's high country on foot, come well equipped. Mist and rain can quickly descend, and the Beacons' summits are exposed to high winds. ⊠ *Off A470, Libanus, Brecon* ✛ *5½ mi southwest of Brecon* ☏ *01874/623366* ⊕ *www.breconbeacons.org* 🎟️ *Free; fee for parking* 🕑 *Daily 9:30–5; until 4:30 Nov.–Feb.*

WHERE TO EAT AND STAY

£   ✕ **Brecon Beacons National Park Visitor Centre Tearoom and Restaurant.** The
BISTRO spectacular view across the Beacons and homemade dishes make this a very popular spot. The parsnip-and-apple soup and the Welsh Black beef pie are among the good choices. You can indulge in a cream tea or fresh-baked cake, or just have coffee and enjoy the view. ⊠ *Off A470, Libanus, Brecon* ☏ *01874/624979* ▭ *MC, V* 🕑 *No dinner.*

£££   ✕ **Felin Fach Griffin.** Old and new blend perfectly in this modern country-
BRITISH style inn with old wood floors, comfy leather sofas, and terra-cotta–color stone walls hung with bright prints. The excellent menu makes use of fresh local produce, much of it coming from the Griffin's own organic garden. Try the Welsh venison, with autumn fruits and squash mashed potatoes with thyme jus. ⊠ *A470, east of Brecon, Felin Fach* ☏ *01874/620111* ▭ *MC, V.*

££   🏠 **The Coach House.** This former coach house provides contemporary town-house accommodation. The friendly Welsh-speaking owners are fonts of local information on where to go and what to do in the Brecon Beacons, and at the end of a hectic day's activities offer relaxing holistic massages. Inventive Welsh breakfasts and evening meals are served in the small stylish restaurant. **Pros:** friendly hosts; great massages; central location. **Cons:** on a main road; garden is small. ⊠ *Orchard St.* ☏ *01874/620043* ⊕ *www.coachhousebrecon.co.uk* 🛏️ *7 rooms* ⚘ *In-room: no a/c, DVD, Wi-Fi. In-hotel: restaurant, room service, bar, Wi-Fi, no kids under 16* ▭ *MC, V* 🍴 *BP.*

HIKING AND BIKING IN WALES

Hiking and walking are the most popular outdoor activities in Wales, and a great way to see the country. Long-distance paths include the Pembrokeshire Coast Path (which runs all along the spectacular shores of southwest Wales), the south–north Offa's Dyke Path, based on the border between England and Wales established by King Offa in the 8th century, and the Glyndŵr Way, a 128-mi-long highland route that traverses Mid Wales from the border town of Knighton via Machynlleth to Welshpool. Signposted footpaths in Wales's forested areas are short and easy to follow. Dedicated enthusiasts might prefer the wide-open spaces of Brecon Beacons National Park or the mountains of Snowdonia.

Wales's reputation as both an on-road and off-road cycling mecca is well established. There's an amazing choice of scenic routes and terrain from challenging off-road tracks (⊕ www.mtbwales.com is for the serious cyclist) to long-distance road rides and gentle family trails; VisitWales has information to get you started.

CONTACTS AND RESOURCES
Cycling Wales (⊕ www.cycling.visitwales.com). **Offa's Dyke Centre** (☎ 01547/528753 ⊕ www.offasdyke.demon.co.uk). **Pembrokeshire Coast Path** (⊕ www.nationaltrail.co.uk). **Ramblers' Association in Wales** (☎ 029/2064-4308 ⊕ www.ramblers.org.uk/wales).

15

£–££ 📺 **Felin Glais.** In the 17th century Felin Glais was a barn; now, renovated and extended but without losing its ancient character, it provides spacious and comfortable accommodation. The owners are extremely sociable, and many of their customers become friends. They are also enthusiastic about food (available for guests only) and make good use of locally sourced produce. **Pros:** beautiful building; spacious rooms; good food. **Cons:** dogs allowed in rooms; communal dining table. ✉ *Abersycir, near Brecon* ☎ *01874/623107* ⊕ *www.felinglais.co.uk* 📞 *4 rooms* ☐ *In-room: no a/c, no phone, refrigerator, DVD, Wi-Fi. In-hotel: restaurant, laundry service, Wi-Fi, some pets allowed* ☐ *No credit cards* ⦿ *BP.*

NIGHTLIFE AND THE ARTS
Each summer the town hosts **Brecon Jazz** (☎ 01874/625875 ⊕ *www.breconjazz.co.uk*), an international jazz festival that attracts top performers.

Theatr Brycheiniog (✉ *Canal Wharf* ☎ *01874/611622* ⊕ *www.theatrbrycheiniog.co.uk*), on the canal, is the town's impressive venue for the arts. It also has a gallery and waterfront bistro.

SPORTS AND THE OUTDOORS
Crickhowell Adventure Gear (✉ *Ship St.* ☎ *01874/611586*), which also has a smaller shop in Crickhowell, sells outdoor gear such as clothes and climbing equipment.

Brecon is an ideal center for on- and off-road cycling. **Biped Cycles** (✉ *10 Ship St.* ☎ *01874/622296* ⊕ *www.bipedcycles.co.uk*) will rent you the right bike and equipment to take to the hills.

SWANSEA

36 mi southwest of Brecon, 40 mi west of Cardiff.

Swansea, the birthplace of poet Dylan Thomas (1914–53), marks the end of the industrial region of South Wales. Despite some undistinguished postwar architecture, Wales's second-largest city (population 224,000) has a number of appealing sights, including the waterfront pedestrian Sail Bridge, which has a 300-foot-high mast.

GETTING HERE AND AROUND

There's an hourly rail service between Swansea and London's Paddington Station, and regular rail services from Swansea to the Midlands and north of England. The city has direct National Express coach services to the rest of Wales, London, and other U.K. cities. The city is best explored on foot; it takes only 10 minutes to walk from the shopping center to the beach.

ESSENTIALS

Visitor Information Swansea (⊠ *Plymouth St.* ☎ *01792/468321* ⊕ *www.visitswanseabay.com*).

EXPLORING

TOP ATTRACTIONS

Dylan Thomas Centre. Situated on the banks of the Tawe close to the Maritime Quarter, the Dylan Thomas Centre is the National Literature Centre for Wales. The center houses a permanent Dylan Thomas exhibition, art gallery, restaurant, and café-bookshop, and hosts literary events such as the annual Dylan Thomas Festival. ■ TIP→ **Those interested in following in the poet's footsteps can pick up a leaflet that outlines the Dylan Thomas Trail around South Wales.** ⊠ *Somerset Pl.* ☎ *01792/463980* ⊕ *www.dylanthomas.com* ⊠ *Free* ⊙ *Daily 10–4:30.*

Maritime Quarter. Swansea was extensively bombed during World War II, and its old dockland has reemerged as the splendid Maritime Quarter, a modern marina with attractive housing and shops and a seafront that commands views across the sweep of Swansea Bay.

National Waterfront Museum. Housed in a construction of steel, slate, and glass grafted onto a historic redbrick building, the National Waterfront Museum's galleries have 15 theme areas. State-of-the-art interactive technology and artifacts bring Welsh industrial and maritime history to a 21st-century audience. ⊠ *Oystermouth Rd., Maritime Quarter* ☎ *01792/638950* ⊕ *www.museumwales.ac.uk* ⊠ *Free* ⊙ *Daily 10–5.*

WORTH NOTING

Covered market. Swansea's modern shopping center is nothing special, but the covered market, part of Quadrant Shopping Centre, is the best fresh-foods market in Wales. You can buy cockles from the Penclawdd beds on the nearby Gower Peninsula, and laverbread, that unique Welsh delicacy made from seaweed, which is usually served with bacon and eggs.

Egypt Centre. A substantial collection of ancient Egyptian artifacts is on display here, including bead necklaces from the time of Tutankhamen and the beautiful painted coffin of a Theban musician. ⊠ *University* *of Wales–Swansea, Singleton Park* ☎*01792/295960* ⊕*www.swansea. ac.uk/egypt* 🎟*Free* ⊘*Tues.–Sat. 10–4.*

★ **Gower Peninsula.** The 14-mi-long Gower Peninsula, only minutes away from Swansea's center, was the first part of Britain to be declared an area of Outstanding Natural Beauty. Its shores are a succession of sheltered sandy bays and awesome headlands. Actress Catherine Zeta-Jones was born here, in the Victorian seaside resort of Mumbles. ∎**TIP**➔ **For the area's most breathtaking views, head to Rhossili on its western tip.**

Swansea Museum. Founded in 1841, this museum contains a quirky and eclectic collection that includes an Egyptian mummy, china, local archaeological exhibits, and the intriguing Cabinet of Curiosity, which holds artifacts from Swansea's past. The museum is close to the Maritime Quarter. ✉*Victoria Rd.* ☎*01792/653763* ⊕*www.swanseaheritage.net* 🎟*Free* ⊘*Tues.–Sun. 10–5.*

WHERE TO EAT AND STAY

£££
SPANISH
✕**La Braseria.** This lively, welcoming spot resembles a Spanish restaurant, with its flamenco music, oak barrels, and whitewashed walls. Among the house specialties are sea bass in rock salt, roast suckling pig, and pheasant (in season, of course). There's a good choice of 140 Spanish and French wines. ✉*28 Wind St.* ☎*01792/469683* ⊟*AE, MC, V* ⊘*Closed Sun.*

£££–££££
★
🏨**Fairyhill.** Luxuriously furnished public rooms, spacious bedrooms, and 24 acres of wooded grounds make this 18th-century country house in the western part of the scenic Gower Peninsula a restful retreat. The hotel is renowned for sophisticated cuisine and a well-chosen wine list. There's a fixed-price dinner menu (£35 for two courses, £45 for three). **Pros:** peaceful surroundings; local seafood a specialty. **Cons:** difficult to find; restaurant always busy. ✉*Off B4295, 11 mi southwest of Swansea, Reynoldston* ☎*01792/390139* ⊕*www.fairyhill.net* 🛏*8 rooms* ⚒*In-room: no a/c, DVD, Wi-Fi. In-hotel: restaurant, bar, laundry service, Internet terminal, Wi-Fi, no kids under 8* ⊟*AE, MC, V* ⊚|*BP.*

£££–££££
🏨**Morgans.** This old Victorian Port Authority building in the Maritime Quarter has been transformed into a strikingly modern hotel without losing any of its period features: moldings, pillars, stained glass, and wood floors. The rooms, in both the main building and in the Town House across the road, are immaculate with crisp cotton sheets and drapes of satin, silk, and suede. The stylish restaurant serves dishes like panfried fillet of local sea bass with crushed-pea-and-potato cake and watercress sauce, and lighter treats at the café-bar. **Pros:** near the marina; short walk to shops; building reflects city's maritime heritage. **Cons:** no outdoor space; busy bars; popular with wedding parties. ✉*Somerset Pl.* ☎*01792/484848* ⊕*www.morganshotel.co.uk* 🛏*41 rooms* ⚒*In-room: no a/c (some), DVD, Internet (some), Wi-Fi (some). In-hotel: restaurant, room service, bars, gym, laundry service, Internet terminal, Wi-Fi* ⊟*AE, MC, V.*

15

NATIONAL BOTANIC GARDEN OF WALES

20 mi northwest of Swansea, 60 mi northwest of Cardiff.

EXPLORING

The first modern botanic garden in Britain, opened in 2000, the **National Botanic Garden of Wales** celebrates conservation and education. It's based at Middleton Park, a 568-acre, 18th-century estate with seven lakes, cascades, fountains, and a Japanese garden. The garden's centerpiece is the Norman Foster–designed Great Glass House, the largest single-span greenhouse in the world, which blends into the curving landforms of the Tywi Valley. The interior landscape includes a 40-foot-deep ravine and thousands of plants from all the Mediterranean climates of the world. The garden is signposted off the main road between Swansea and Carmarthen. *⊠ Off A48 or B4310, Llanarthne ☎ 01558/6687688 ⊕ www.gardenofwales.org.uk ⊠ £8 ⊙ Apr.–Oct., daily 10–6; Nov.–Mar., daily 10–4:30.*

TENBY

53 mi west of Swansea.

Pastel-color Georgian houses cluster around a harbor in this seaside resort, where two golden sandy beaches stretch below the hotel-lined cliff top. Medieval Tenby's ancient town walls still stand, enclosing narrow streets and passageways full of shops, inns, and places to eat. From the harbor you can take a short boat trip to beautiful Caldey Island and visit the monastery, where monks make a famous perfume from the local plants.

GETTING HERE AND AROUND

Tenby is on the southwest Wales rail route from London's Paddington Station. You have to change trains at Swansea. The center of Tenby, a maze of narrow medieval streets, has parking restrictions. During the summer the downtown area is closed to traffic, so you'll have to park in more remote lots and take the park-and-ride shuttle buses.

TIMING

Tenby, Pembrokeshire's most popular seaside resort, is very busy in summer and on holiday weekends. During these times booking ahead is essential.

ESSENTIALS

Visitor Information Tenby (*⊠ Unit 2, The Gateway Complex ☎ 01834/842402).*

EXPLORING

The ruins of a castle stand on a headland overlooking the sea, close to the informative **Tenby Museum and Art Gallery** (*⊠ Castle Hill ☎ 01834/842809 ⊕ www.tenbymuseum.org.uk*), which recalls the town's maritime history and its growth as a fashionable resort.

The late-15th-century **Tudor Merchant's House,** in town, shows how a prosperous trader would have lived in the Tenby of old. *⊠ Quay Hill ☎ 01834/842279 ⊕ www.nationaltrust.org.uk ⊠ £2.70 ⊙ Apr.–early Nov., Sun.–Fri. 11–5.*

WHERE TO EAT AND STAY

£££ ✕ **Plantagenet House.** Candlelit dining, open fires, exposed stone walls,
BRITISH and top-notch locally sourced food are hallmarks of this popular restaurant and bar in a beautiful 15th-century Merchant's House in the heart of Tenby. ⊠ *Quay Hill* ☎ *01834/842350* ☰ *MC, V* ⊗ *Easter–Oct., daily noon–2:30, 6–late; off-season, weekends only. Closed Jan.–mid-Feb.*

£ 🏠 **Ivy Bank Guest House.** This comfortable and immaculate Victorian house is just a five-minute stroll from the sea. The breakfast menu is extensive and the rooms are furnished with light flowery fabrics. **Pros:** reasonable rates; walled garden; close to sea. **Cons:** no designated parking lot; no sea views; a little dated. ⊠ *Harding St., Tenby* ☎ *01834/842311* ⊕ *www.ivybanktenby.co.uk* ⇋ *5 rooms* ♿ *In-room: no a/c, no phone. In-hotel: bar* ☰ *AE, MC, V* ⍾ *BP.*

£££–££££ 🏠 **Penally Abbey.** Built on the site of a 6th-century abbey on 5 acres of lush forest overlooking Camarthen Bay, this dignified 18th-century house is awash with period details. Bedrooms in the house are furnished with antiques and four-poster beds, whereas those in the light and airy lodges have a touch of urban chic. The hotel is relaxed rather than stuffy, but service is first-class. **Pros:** informal luxury; great views; friendly hosts. **Cons:** small pool; 2 mi from Tenby. ⊠ *Off A4139, 2 mi west of Tenby, Penally* ☎ *01834/843033* ⊕ *www.penally-abbey.com* ⇋ *17 rooms* ♿ *In-room: no a/c, Wi-Fi. In-hotel: restaurant, bar, pool, Wi-Fi* ☰ *AE, MC, V* ⍾ *BP.*

££££–£££££ 🏠 **St. Brides Spa Hotel.** This luxury hotel perches in a breathtaking location above Carmarthen Bay between Amroth and Tenby. Most of the superbly appointed rooms have stunning sea views, and there's a state-of-the-art spa with infinity pool, steam room, sauna, salt infusion room, and ice fountain. The restaurant specializes in locally sourced produce, seafood being a particular highlight. **Pros:** amazing view; wonderful marine spa; displays of contemporary Welsh art. **Cons:** steep walk up from beach; area lacks charm. ⊠ *Saundersfoot* ☎ *01834/812304* ⊕ *www.stbridesspahotel.com* ⇋ *35 rooms* ♿ *In-room: no a/c, DVD, Wi-Fi (some), Internet (some). In-hotel: restaurant, room service, bar, pool, spa, laundry service, Wi-Fi* ☰ *AE, DC, MC, V* ⍾ *BP.*

15

PEMBROKE

13 mi west of Tenby, 13 mi south of Haverfordwest.

In Pembroke you are entering the heart of Pembrokeshire, one of the most curious regions of Wales. All around are English names such as Deeplake, New Hedges, and Rudbaxton. Locals more often than not don't understand Welsh, and South Pembrokeshire is known as "Little England beyond Wales." History is responsible: in the 11th century the English conquered this region with the aid of the Normans, and the English and Normans intermarried and set about building castles.

ESSENTIALS

Visitor Information Pembroke (⊠ *Commons Rd.* ☎ *01646/622388).*

EXPLORING

One of the most magnificent Norman fortresses is massive **Pembroke Castle,** dating from 1190. Its walls remain stout, its gatehouse mighty, and the enormous cylindrical keep proved so impregnable to cannon fire in the Civil War that Cromwell's men had to starve out its Royalist defenders. You can climb the towers and walk the walls for fine views. This was the birthplace, in 1457, of Henry Tudor, who seized the throne of England as Henry VII in 1485, and whose son Henry VIII united Wales and England in 1536. ☎ *01646/684585* ⊕ *www.pembroke-castle.co.uk* ✉ *£3.50* ♥ *Apr.–Sept., daily 9:30–6; Oct. and Mar., daily 10–5; Nov.–Feb., daily 10–4.*

> **FISH WEEK**
>
> Pembrokeshire Fish Week takes place in late June and early July, celebrating all things fishy. Events include gourmet seafood evenings, mackerel barbecues, sea fishing, and kayak trips. For dates and locations, visit ⊕ *www.pembrokeshirefishweek.co.uk.*

ST. DAVID'S

25 mi northwest of Pembroke, 16 mi southwest of Fishguard.

This tiny village holds what has been described as the holiest ground in Great Britain, the Cathedral of St. David and the shrine of the patron saint of Wales, who founded a monastic community here in the 6th century. The entire area around St. David's, steeped in sanctity and history, was a place of pilgrimage for many centuries, two journeys to St. David's equaling, in spiritual value, one to Rome. Here, on the savagely beautiful coastline, edged by the Pembrokeshire Coast Path, Pembrokeshire is at its unspoiled best. You can almost recapture the feeling of those days nearly 1,500 years ago, when this shrine was very nearly the sole outpost of Christianity in the British Isles. If you have a day to spare, the 6.5-mi walk along the coastal path around the St. David's headland from St. Justinian to Caerfai Bay is magnificent. ■ **TIP →** Come in May and June to see the hedgerows and coastal path full of wildflowers.

ESSENTIALS

Visitor Information St. David's Oriel y Parc (✉ *1 High St.* ☎ *01437/720392* ⊕ *www.orielyparc.co.uk*).

EXPLORING

Unlike any other cathedral, the venerable 12th-century **St. David's Cathedral** (⊕ *www.stdavidscathedral.org.uk*) does not seek to dominate the surrounding countryside with its enormous mass; it is in a vast hollow. You must climb down 39 steps (called locally the Thirty-Nine Articles) to enter the cathedral. Its location helped protect the church from Viking raiders by hiding it from the view of invaders who came by sea. From the outside, purple-stone St. David's has a simple austerity that harmonizes with the beautiful windswept countryside, but the interior is more intricate. Treasures include the fan vaulting in Bishop Vaughan's Chapel, the delicate carving on the choir stalls, and the oaken roof over the nave. Across the brook are the ruins of the medieval **Bishop's Palace.**

☎️*01437/720517* ⊕*www.cadw.wales.gov.uk* 💷*£3* 🕙*Apr.–Oct., daily 9–5; Nov.–Mar., Mon.–Sat. 9:30–4, Sun. 11–4.*

St. David's Oriel y Parc was built entirely using green technology. The 180-degree monopitch roof is aligned with the path of the sun and supported by conical pillars, and the building houses a visitor information center and gallery dedicated to the interpretation of landscape. The exhibits are drawn from the huge collection of art and artifacts at the National Museum Wales. ✉️*1 High St.* ☎️*01437/720392* ⊕*www.orielyparc.co.uk* 🕙*Easter–Oct., daily 9:30–5:30; Nov.–Easter, daily 10–4:30.*

WHERE TO EAT AND STAY

£££   ✕**Morgan's Brasserie.** One choice sounds more delicious than the next
BISTRO   at this classic bistro in the heart of town, which has an inventive menu based on local and organic ingredients. A blackboard lists daily specials, including local fish. Try the trio of Pembrokeshire lamb or sea bass with leek foam, Solva lobster sauce, and truffle oil. ✉️*20 Nun St.* ☎️*01437/720508* ▭*MC, V* 🕙*Closed Tues.*

££££–£££££   🏨**Warpool Court Hotel.** Overlooking a stunning stretch of coastline, this hotel sits on a bluff above St. Non's Bay. Many rooms have sea views; decorative tiles adorn public areas and some bedrooms. The building dates from the 1860s, when it housed St. David's Cathedral Choir School. The well-equipped hotel offers contemporary cuisine, with fish, including roast halibut and wild bass fillets, as a specialty; the dining room overlooks the water. **Pros:** on the coastal path; peaceful gardens; good food. **Cons:** unattractive entrance; not a beautiful building; expensive rates. ✉️*Off Goat St.* ☎️*01437/720300* ⊕*www.warpoolcourthotel. com* ⏏*25 rooms* ♿*In-room: no a/c, Wi-Fi. In-hotel: restaurant, room service, bar, tennis court, pool, gym, laundry service, Internet terminal, Wi-Fi, some pets allowed* ▭*AE, MC, V* ⭘|*BP.*

FISHGUARD

16 mi northeast of St. David's, 26 mi north of Pembroke.

Fishguard is a town of three parts. The ferry terminal at Goodwick across the waters of Fishguard Bay sees activity year-round as boats sail to Rosslare, Ireland, across the Irish Sea. Fishguard's main town stands on high ground just south of Goodwick, separating the modern port from its old harbor in the Lower Town, where gabled cottages are grouped around the quayside. The Lower Town was the setting for the 1973 film of Dylan Thomas's play *Under Milkwood*, which starred Elizabeth Taylor and Welsh actor Richard Burton.

ESSENTIALS

Visitor Information Fishguard (✉️*Town Hall, Market Sq.* ☎️*01437/776636*).

EXPLORING

The 100-foot-long **Last Invasion Tapestry,** on display in a gallery in the Town Hall, is modeled on the famous Bayeux Tapestry that celebrates the Norman invasion of 1066, but this work commemorates a far less successful assault. In 1797 a small French force, commanded by a U.S. citizen, landed near Fishguard. After some skirmishing the group was allegedly forced to surrender by local women. In 1997, 70 Fishguard women spent 40,000 hours stitching this impressive tapestry. ⊠ *Town Hall, Market Sq.* ☏ *01437/776639* ✉ *Free* ⊘ *Apr.–Sept., Mon.–Wed., Fri., and Sat. 9:30–5, Thurs. 9:30–6:30; Oct.–Mar., Mon.–Wed. and Fri. 9:30–5, Thurs. 9:30–6:30, Sat. 9:30–1.*

CARDIGAN AND THE TEIFI VALLEY

18 mi northeast of Fishguard.

The little market town of Cardigan, with its ancient bridge, was the scene of a never-to-be-forgotten victory by the Welsh over the Norman army in 1136. The town is near the mouth of the Teifi, a river that runs through a wooded valley with traditional market towns and villages. The valley also contains reminders of the area's once-flourishing woolen industry. Wales's first eisteddfod, or folk festival, took place in Cardigan Castle in 1176. The eisteddfod tradition, based on the Welsh language and arts—a sort of Welsh cultural Olympics—remains strong in Wales, and events large and small are held here (mainly in summer months).

ESSENTIALS

Visitor Information Cardigan (⊠ *Theatr Mwldan, Bath House Rd.* ☏ *01239/613230*).

EXPLORING

Cilgerran, a village a few miles south of Cardigan, has the dramatic ruins of 13th-century **Cilgerran Castle,** which stands above a deep, wooded gorge where the River Teifi flows. ⊠ *Off A478* ☏ *01239/615136 or 01443/336104* ⊕ *www.cadw.wales.gov.uk* ✉ *£3* ⊘ *Apr.–Oct., daily 10–5; Nov.–Mar., daily 10–4.*

> **OFF THE BEATEN PATH**
>
> **National Wool Museum.** Working exhibits and displays at this museum in what was once Wales's most important wool-producing area trace the evolution of the industry. The National Textile Collection is showcased. There are also crafts workshops, and a woolen mill produces reproduction fabrics. A shop sells the best of Welsh textiles. The museum is east of Cenarth, a few miles past Newcastle Emlyn. ⊠ *Off A484, Drefach Felindre* ☏ *01559/370929* ⊕ *www.museumwales.ac.uk* ✉ *Free* ⊘ *Apr.–Sept., daily 10–5; Oct.–Mar., Tues.–Sat. 10–5.*

WHERE TO STAY

£ 🏠 **Wervil Grange Farm.** Here you can experience high-quality accommodation at an immaculate Georgian farmhouse on a traditional working farm rearing sheep and Welsh Black cattle. The rooms are beautifully furnished with antiques and fine fabrics patterned in flowers and stripes. There's free fishing on the farm and easy access to the beach. **Pros:** real working farm; great for anglers; dolphin spotting on the coast. **Cons:** no sea views. ⊠ *Off A487, 8 mi northeast of Cardigan, Pentregat* ☏ *01239/654252* ⊕ *www.tiscover.co.uk/wervil-grange* 🛏 *4 rooms* ⌕ *In-room: no a/c, no phone. In-hotel: some pets allowed* 🚫 *No credit cards* ❘◯❘ *BP.*

UNDERSTANDING ENGLAND

ENGLISH ARCHITECTURAL STYLES

In England you can see structures that go back to the dawn of history, such as the hauntingly mysterious circles of monoliths at Stonehenge or Avebury, or view the resurrected remains of Roman empire builders preserved in Bath, Cirencester, and other towns. On the other hand, you can startle your eyes with the very current designs of contemporary architects in areas such as London's Docklands or the City. Knowing a few hallmarks of particular styles can enhance your enjoyment. Here, then, is a primer of a millennium of architectural styles.

Norman

Duke William of Normandy brought the solid Norman style to Britain when he invaded and conquered England in 1066, although William's predecessor, King Edward (the Confessor) used the style in the building of Westminster Abbey a little earlier, in 1042. Until around 1200 it was favored for buildings of any importance, and William's castles and churches soon dominated the countryside.

Norman towers tended to be hefty and square, arches were always round-top, and the vaulting was barrel shaped. Decoration was mostly geometrical, but within those limits, ornate. Norman motte-and-bailey castles had two connecting stockaded mounds, with the keep on the higher mound, and other buildings on the lower mound. *Best seen in the Tower of London and in the cathedrals of St. Albans, Ely, Gloucester, Durham, and Norwich, and at Tewkesbury Abbey.*

Gothic Early English

From 1130 to 1300, pointed arches began to supplant rounded ones, buttresses became heavier than the Norman variety, and windows lost their rounded tops to become more pointed and lancet shaped. Buildings climbed skyward and were less squat and heavy, with the soaring effect accentuated by steep roofs and spires. *Best seen in the cathedrals of York, Salisbury, Ely, Worcester, Wells (interior), and*

Canterbury (east end), and Westminster Abbey's Chapter House.

Decorated. From the late 1100s until around 1400, elegance and ornament became fully integrated into architectural design, rather than applied to the surface of a solid, basic form. Windows filled more of the walls and were divided into sections by carved mullions. Vaulting grew increasingly complex, with ribs and ornamental bosses proliferating; spires became even more pointed; arches took on the ogee shape, with its unique double curve. This style was one of England's greatest gifts to world architecture. *Best seen at the cathedrals of Wells, Lincoln, Exeter, Durham (east transept), and Ely (Lady Chapel and Octagon).*

Perpendicular. In later Gothic architecture, the emphasis on the vertical grew more pronounced, as shown in features such as slender pillars, huge expanses of glass, and superb fan vaulting resembling the formalized branches of frozen trees. Walls were divided by panels. One of the chief areas in which to see Perpendicular architecture is East Anglia, where towns that grew rich from the wool trade built magnificent churches in the style. Houses, too, began to reflect the prevailing taste. Perpendicular Gothic lasted for well over two centuries from its advent around 1330. *Best seen at St. George's Chapel in Windsor, Gloucester Cathedral (cloister), Henry VII's Chapel in Westminster Abbey, Bath Abbey, and King's College Chapel in Cambridge.*

Tudor

With the great period of cathedral building over, from 1500 to 1560 the nation's attention turned to the construction of spacious homes characterized by this latest fashionable architectural style. The rapidly expanding, newly rich middle class, created by the two Tudor Henrys (VII and VIII) to challenge the power of the aristocracy, built spacious manor houses, often on the foundations of pillaged monasteries. Thus began the era of the great stately homes. Brick replaced stone as the most popular medium, and plasterwork and carved wood displayed the elaborate motifs of the age.

Timber-frame and plaster buildings were also popular in this period for domestic and commercial use. Many "black-and-white" structures, as they are called, are copies made in later eras, but notable originals survive. (The Victorians are responsible for the fashion of painting half-timber buildings, of whatever era, black and white.) Wealthier individuals could afford to have the exposed wood beams carved or shaped; Little Moreton Hall, in Congleton near the Peak District, has wonderfully intricate patterns. Speke Hall in Liverpool and Harvard House in Stratford-upon-Avon are other notable examples of the style.

Another way the social climbers could make their mark, and ensure their place in the next world, was by building churches. Money earned in the wool trade continued to fund splendid parish churches. Some of the most magnificent are in Suffolk, Norfolk, and the Cotswolds. *Domestic architecture is best seen at Hampton Court and St. James's Palace, London; for wool churches, Lavenham and Long Melford (though its tower is much later) in Suffolk, and Cirencester, Chipping Campden, Northleach, and Winchcombe in the Cotswolds.*

Renaissance Elizabethan

For a short period under Elizabeth I, 1560–1600, this development of Tudor style flourished as Italian influences began to seep into England, seen especially in symmetrical facades. The most notable example was Hardwick Hall in Derbyshire, built in the 1590s by Bess of Hardwick; the jingle that describes it goes "Hardwick Hall, more glass than wall." However grand the houses were, they were still on a human scale, warm and livable, built of a mellow amalgam of brick and stone. *Other great Elizabe-than houses are Longleat in Wiltshire and Burghley House in Cambridgeshire.*

Jacobean

At the beginning of the 17th century, for the first 15 years of the reign of James I (the name Jacobean is taken from the Latin word for James, Jacobus), architecture did not change noticeably. Windows were still large in proportion to the wall surfaces. Gables, in the style of the Netherlands, were popular. Carved decoration in wood and plaster (especially the geometrical patterning called "strapwork," another element of Dutch origin, which resembled intertwined leather belts) remained exuberant, now even more so.

A change was on the way, though. Inigo Jones (1573–1652), the first great modern British architect, attempted to synthesize the architectural heritage of England with current Italian theories. Two of his finest remaining buildings—the Banqueting House in London and the Queen's House at Greenwich—epitomize his genius, which was to introduce to England the Italian-created Palladian style that would dominate England's architecture for centuries. It uses the classical Greek orders: Doric, Ionic, and Corinthian. The grand classical style that proved so monumentally effective under a hot Mediterranean sun was transformed in England, domesticated and tamed. Columns and pediments decorated the facades, and huge frescoes provided acres of color to interior walls and ceilings, all in the Italian manner.

There were in fact two quite distinct styles running concurrently: the comfortably domestic and the purer classical in public buildings. They were finally fused by the talent of Christopher Wren. *Jacobean is best seen at the Bodleian Library, Oxford; Chastleton House, near Stow-on-the Wold; Hatfield House, near St. Albans; and Emmanuel College, Cambridge.*

Wren and the English Baroque

The work of Sir Christopher Wren (1632–1723) constituted an architectural era all by itself. Not only was he one of the world's greatest architects, but he was also given an unparalleled opportunity in 1666 when the disastrous Great Fire of London wiped out the center of the capital, destroying no fewer than 89 churches and 13,200 houses. Although Wren's great scheme for a modern city center was rejected, he did build 52 churches in London, the greatest of which was St. Paul's, completed in just 35 years. The range of Wren's designs is extremely wide, from simple classical shapes to the extravagantly dramatic baroque. He was also at home with domestic architecture, where his combinations of brick and stone produced a warm, homey effect.

The influence of the Italian baroque can be seen in Sir John Vanbrugh's Blenheim Palace, where the facade echoes the piazza of St. Peter's in Rome, and at Vanbrugh's exuberant Castle Howard in Yorkshire.

Nicholas Hawksmoor, Wren's pupil, designed some notable London churches and also the baroque Mausoleum at Castle Howard. The baroque had only a brief heyday in England; by 1725 the Palladian style was firmly in favor and the vast pile of Blenheim was being mocked by trendsetters. *Wren's ecclesiastical architecture is best seen at St. Paul's Cathedral (baroque with classical touches) and his other remaining London churches, his domestic style at Hampton Court Palace, Kensington Palace, the Royal Hospital in Chelsea, and the Old Royal Naval College in Greenwich. English baroque is best seen at Blenheim Palace (Oxfordshire) and Castle Howard (Yorkshire).*

Palladian

In Britain this style is often referred to as Georgian, so-called from the Hanoverian kings George I through IV, although it was introduced as early as Inigo Jones's time. During the 18th century, classical inspiration was thoroughly acclimatized.

Though they looked completely at home among the hills, lakes, and trees of the English countryside, Palladian buildings were derived from the Roman-inspired designs of the Italian architectural theorist Andrea Palladio (1508–80), with pillared porticoes, triangular pediments, and strictly balanced windows. In domestic architecture, this large-scale classicism was usually modified to quiet simplicity, preserving mathematical proportions of windows, doors, and the exactly calculated volume of room space, to create a feeling of balance and harmony.

The occasional departures from the classical manner at this time included the over-the-top Indian-style Royal Pavilion in Brighton, built for the prince regent (later George IV) by John Nash. The Regency style comes under the Palladian heading, though strictly speaking it lasted only for the few years of the actual Regency (1811–20).

Architects such as the brilliant Robert Adam, who was born in Scotland but also worked in England, handled the Palladian style with more freedom than their counterparts elsewhere in Europe, and the United States took its cue from the British. *Among the best Palladian examples are Regent's Park Terraces (London), the library at Kenwood (London), the Royal Crescent and other streets in Bath, Stourhead (Wiltshire), and Holkham Hall (Norfolk).*

Victorian

Elements of imaginative fantasy, already seen in the Palladian era, came to the fore during the long reign of Victoria (1837–1901). The country's vast profits made from the Industrial Revolution were spent lavishly. Civic building accelerated in all the major cities, with town halls modeled after medieval castles or French châteaux.

The Victorians plundered the past for styles, with Gothic, about which the scholarly Victorians were very knowledgeable, leading the field. The supreme examples here are the Houses of Parliament by Charles Barry and Augustus Pugin, and the Albert Memorial by George Gilbert Scott, both in London. (To distinguish between the Victorian variety and a version of the style that flourished in the late 1700s, the earlier one is commonly spelled "Gothick.") Among the other styles in the running was the attractively named, and self-explanatory, "Wrenaissance." *Other striking examples of Victorian architecture are Truro Cathedral, Manchester Town Hall, Ironbridge, and Cragside (Northumberland).*

Edwardian

Toward the end of the Victorian era, in the late 1800s, architecture calmed down considerably, with a return to a solid sort of classicism, and even to a muted baroque. The Arts and Crafts movement, especially the work of William Morris (1834–96) and work inspired by Morris, produced simpler designs, sometimes returning to medieval models. In an age of increasing mechanization, craftsmanship was emphasized. Architectural elements incorporated stylized natural motifs. *Best seen in Buckingham Palace and the Admiralty Arch in London. Rodmarton Manor near Tetbury (the Cotswolds), and Blackwell in Windermere (Cumbria) are notable Arts and Crafts houses.*

Modern

A furious public debate has raged here for years between traditionalists and the adherents of modernistic architecture. Britons tend to be strongly conservative when it comes to their environment. These arguments have been highlighted by the intervention of such notable figures as Prince Charles, who derides excessive modernism and who said, for instance, that the design for the Sainsbury Wing of the National Gallery in London's Trafalgar Square would be like "a monstrous carbuncle on the face of a much-loved and elegant friend."

One reason for the strength of this attitude is that the country suffered from much ill-conceived development after World War II, when large areas of city centers had to be rebuilt after the devastation caused by German bombs. Town planners and architects created badly built and worse-designed towers and shopping areas. Today, however, there appears to be an increased readiness to embrace the new, as designers draw people into user-friendly, lighthearted buildings such as City Hall in London and the Sage Gateshead in Newcastle. The situation created in the '50s and '60s is slowly being reversed. High-rise apartment blocks are being taken down and replaced by more humanly scaled housing. Commercial areas in a number of cities are slowly being rebuilt. The emphasis has gradually moved to planning, design, and construction that pays more attention to the needs of inhabitants. A healthier attitude also exists toward the conservation of old buildings. Happily, many that survived the wreckers' ball are being restored and put back to use.

Nowadays, a number of architectural styles prevail. A predominant one draws largely on the past, with nostalgic echoes of the country cottage, and leans heavily on variegated brickwork and close attention to decorative detail. Urban centers have buildings in the most innovative styles, which are exciting and ecologically sensitive, too, using light to more thoughtful effect. These new designs have turned many fatigued or declining areas, from Newcastle to Manchester, into destinations to see and be seen in.

In London, the Lloyd's of London tower in the City, by Sir Richard Rogers, designer of the Pompidou Center in Paris, began the trend toward modernism in the 1980s. The Millennium Dome, Rogers's tour de force, transformed the industrial blot of Greenwich peninsula; it closed but reopened in 2007 as O2, a performance venue. Sir Norman Foster's graceful Millennium Bridge became a landmark almost as soon as it opened.

Foster's glassy masterpiece, City Hall, near Tower Bridge, has been knocked as a "glass testicle," but it is one of the boldest designs in London.

Skyscrapers in the City of London are the exception rather than the rule, although the regenerated space of the old Docklands has allowed more room for imagination, as at Canary Wharf. Other buildings, such as Barclays Bank with its jukebox dome, and Swiss Re's "Gherkin" at 30 St. Mary Axe, the latter by Foster and looking akin to a glittering carousel pole, have begun to push height limitations established because of the proximity of historic buildings.

Other centers of modern architectural excellence include Manchester, with the Imperial War Museum North by Daniel Libeskind. After the city center was bombed by the Irish Republican Army in 1996, Manchester received an impressive face-lift. Also in the north, Gateshead Quays is the spectacularly renovated industrial area around the River Tyne and Newcastle. The tilting Millennium Bridge in Newcastle is as dramatic as London's, and the city has opened the largest arts space in Europe, the Baltic Centre for Contemporary Art, as well as the Sage, a curvaceous steel-and-glass music venue; both have a vista that could rival Sydney Harbor's. Birmingham has the Selfridges department store, with its coat of shimmering disks, and Cornwall the Eden Project, the world's largest conservatories, which are set in a former china-clay pit and massed to make a giant glass crater.

Numerous cultural institutions, particularly in London, have undergone innovative renovations, in part to add visitor-friendly, interactive technology. The Royal Opera House, Tate Modern and Tate Britain, the Great Court at the British Museum, the Queen's Gallery, St. Pancras Station, and the Wellcome Wing at the Science Museum are among the noteworthy projects that have embraced the new, with a subtle emphasis on complementing the old. Anyone with an interest in architecture should visit the headquarters of the Royal Institute of British Architects (RIBA) in Portland Place, London, for exhibits on buildings great and small, new and old.

What's next? The approach of the 2012 Summer Olympics in London has prompted some ambitious building plans. Everyone's waiting for a swimming pool by world-renowned architect Zaha Hadid and the 1,016-foot "Shard" designed by Italian Renzo Piano—it will be the tallest building in London by 2012. *Among other buildings to see are Richmond House and the Clore Building at Tate Britain (in London), the campus of Sussex University (outside Brighton), the Royal Regatta Building (Henley), the Sainsbury Centre for the Visual Arts (Norwich), and the Lowry Centre (Manchester).*

BOOKS AND MOVIES

Fiction and Poetry

Many writers' names have become inextricably linked with the regions in which they set their books or plays. Hardy's Wessex, Daphne Du Maurier's Cornwall, Wordsworth's Lake District, Shakespeare's Arden, and Brontë Country in Yorkshire are now evocative catchphrases, treasured by local tourist boards. However hackneyed the tags may be, you *can* still get a heightened insight into an area through the eyes of authors of genius, even though they may have written a century or more ago. Here are a few works that may provide you with an understanding of their authors' loved territory.

Thomas Hardy's novels *The Mayor of Casterbridge, Tess of the d'Urbervilles,* and *Far from the Madding Crowd* (and indeed almost everything he wrote) are solidly based on his Wessex (Dorset) homeland. Daphne Du Maurier had a deep love of Cornwall from her childhood; *Frenchman's Creek, Jamaica Inn,* and *The King's General* all capture the county's Celtic mood. The wildness of Exmoor in Devon is captured in the historical novel *Lorna Doone* by R.D. Blackmore. The Brontë sisters' *Wuthering Heights, The Tenant of Wildfell Hall,* and *Jane Eyre* breathe the sharp air of the moors around the writers' Haworth home. William Wordsworth, who was born at Cockermouth in the Lake District, depicts the area's rugged beauty in many of his poems, especially the *Lyrical Ballads.*

Virginia Woolf's visits to Vita Sackville-West at her ancestral home of Knole, in Sevenoaks, inspired the novel *Orlando.* The stately home is now a National Trust property. American writer Henry James lived at Lamb House in Rye, also in East Sussex, as did E.F. Benson, whose delicious Lucia novels take place in a thinly disguised version of the town. Lamb House is a National Trust building.

A highly irreverent and very funny version of academic life, *Porterhouse Blue,* by Tom Sharpe, will guarantee that you look at Oxford and Cambridge with a totally different eye. Also irreverent is *England, England* by Julian Barnes, in which an entrepreneur takes over the Isle of Wight and establishes a theme park based on national cliches. John Fowles's *The French Lieutenant's Woman,* largely set in Lyme Regis, is full of local color about Dorset, and Laurie Lee's *Cider with Rosie* is a poignant reminiscence about Cotswold village life in the 1920s.

Mysteries are almost a way of life, partly because many of the best English mystery writers set their plots in their home territories. Modern whodunits by P.D. James and Ruth Rendell convey a fine sense of place, and Ellis Peters's Brother Cadfael stories re-create life in medieval Shrewsbury with a wealth of telling detail. Colin Dexter's Inspector Morse mysteries capture the flavor of Oxford's town and gown. There are also always the villages, vicarages, and scandals of Agatha Christie's "Miss Marple" books.

The fans of Arthurian legends can turn to some excellent, imaginative novels that not only tell the stories but also give fine descriptions of the countryside. Among them are *Sword at Sunset,* by Rosemary Sutcliffe, *The Once and Future King,* by T.H. White, and the four Merlin novels by Mary Stewart: *The Crystal Cave, The Hollow Hills, The Last Enchantment,* and *The Wicked Day.* Edward Rutherfurd's historical novels *Sarum, London,* and *The Forest* deal with British history with a grand sweep from the prehistoric past to the present.

The late James Herriot's veterinary surgeon books, among them *All Creatures Great and Small,* give evocative accounts of life in the Yorkshire Dales during much of the 20th century; the books were made into popular television shows.

An animal's close-to-the-earth viewpoint can reveal all kinds of countryside insights. *Watership Down,* a runaway best seller about rabbits, was written by Richard Adam in the early '70s. *The Wind in the Willows,* by Kenneth Grahame, gives a vivid impression of the Thames Valley almost 100 years ago that still holds largely true today. Devon, the northern part in particular, is the setting of Henry Williamson's *Tarka the Otter,* a beloved nature story published in the 1920s; many paths in the region are signposted as part of the Tarka Trail.

Nonfiction

Those interested in writers and the surroundings that influenced their works should look at *Bloom's Literary Guide to London,* by Donna Dailey, and *The Oxford Literary Guide to the British Isles,* edited by Dorothy Eagle and Hilary Carnell (now out of print). One author currently in vogue is Jane Austen: Janeites will want to read Maggie Lane's *Jane Austen's World* and Nigel Nicolson's wonderful *World of Jane Austen (now out of print).*

Good background books on English history are *The Oxford Illustrated History of Britain,* edited by Kenneth O. Morgan, and *The Story of England,* by Christopher Hibbert. *The Isles,* a long history by Norman Davies, challenges conventional Anglocentric assumptions. *The English: A Portrait of a People,* by Jeremy Paxman, examines the concept of Englishness in a changing world. Simon Schama's three-volume *History of Britain,* with handsome color illustrations, was written to accompany the BBC–History Channel television series. Peter Ackroyd's illustrated *London: A Biography* captures the city's energy and its quirks from prehistory to the present. Ronald Blythe's well-regarded *Akenfield: Portrait of an English Village,* written in the 1960s, gives a perceptive account of life in the English countryside.

The finest book on the country's stately homes is Nigel Nicolson's *Great Houses of Britain,* written for the National Trust (now out of print). Also spectacular is the picture book *Great Houses of Britain and Wales,* by Hugh Montgomery-Massingberd. *The Buildings of England,* written by Nikolaus Pevsner but much updated since his death, is part of a multivolume series, organized by county. Pevsner's *Best Buildings of Britain* is a grand anthology with lush photographs. New Pevsner Architectural Guides continue to be published. For the golden era of Georgian architecture, check out John Summerson's definitive *Architecture in Britain 1530–1830.*

Simon Jenkins's *England's Thousand Best Churches,* with photographs, describes parish churches (not cathedrals) large and small. The same author's delightful *England's Thousand Best Houses* has pithy descriptions (and star ratings) of small and large houses open to the public. Mark Girouard's *Life in the English Country House* focuses on houses over the centuries, and *The Victorian Country House* (out of print) addresses the lifestyles of the rich and famous of the 19th century. For a scenic look at English villages, see *The Most Beautiful Villages of England,* by James Bentley, with ravishing photographs by Hugh Palmer.

There are many delightful travel books about Britain. Bill Bryson's *Notes from a Small Island* is perennially popular, though it is becoming a bit dated. Few of today's authors have managed to top the wit and perception of Henry James's magisterial *English Hours.*

Movies

From *Wuthering Heights* to *Jane Eyre,* great classics of literature have been rendered into great classics of film. It's surprising to learn, however, how many of them were creations of Hollywood and not the British film industry (which had its heyday from the 1940s to the 1960s). From Laurence Olivier to Kenneth Branagh, noted director-actors have cross-pollinated the cinema in Britain and the United States.

Films can motivate travelers to visit specific locations and sights in a favorite film. VisitBritain (⊕*www.visitbritain.com*) has recognized this by including a movies section on its Web site. It has even produced "movie maps" with the locations for certain films such as the Harry Potter series.

A survey can begin with the dramas of Shakespeare: Olivier gave the world a memorable *Othello* and *Hamlet,* Orson Welles a moody *Macbeth,* and Branagh gave up mod versions of *Hamlet* and *Much Ado About Nothing.* Leonardo DiCaprio graced Australian Baz Luhrmann's contemporary version of *Romeo and Juliet.* Going behind the scenes, so to speak, Tom Stoppard created the Oscar winner *Shakespeare in Love.* Charles Dickens has also provided the foundation for film favorites: David Lean's immortal *Great Expectations,* George Cukor's *David Copperfield,* and *A Christmas Carol,* with Alastair Sim as Scrooge, top this list, which continues to grow with additions such as Douglas McGrath's *Nicholas Nickleby.*

McGrath's *Emma,* starring Gwyneth Paltrow, and Ang Lee's *Sense and Sensibility,* starring Emma Thompson and Kate Winslet, are just two of the recent film versions of Jane Austen's works. Keira Knightley had the role of Elizabeth Bennet in the latest *Pride and Prejudice* (2005). Anne Hathaway played Jane Austen herself in *Becoming Jane,* which imagines an early love affair for the novelist.

Harry Potter and the Sorcerer's Stone (in Britain, *Harry Potter and the Philosopher's Stone*), based on the wildly popular children's books by J.K. Rowling, was filmed in many British locations, including London, Gloucester, the Cotswolds, Northumbria, Yorkshire, and Scotland. The second movie, *Harry Potter and the Chamber of Secrets,* used some of the same settings as the first. *Harry Potter and the Prisoner of Azkaban, Harry Potter and the Goblet of Fire, Harry Potter and the Order of the Phoenix,* and *Harry Potter and the Half-Blood Prince* are additional installments; *Harry Potter and the Deathly Hallows* will appear in late 2010.

Of the film versions of Agatha Christie's books, one is especially treasured: *Murder, She Said,* which starred the inimitable Margaret Rutherford. With its quiet English village setting, harpsichord score, and the dotty Miss Marple as portrayed by Rutherford, this must be the most English of all Christie films.

Lovers of opulence, spectacle, and history (or just juicy costume dramas) have choices that grow each year—including Robert Bolt's classic version of Sir Thomas More's life and death, *A Man for All Seasons.* His *Lady Caroline Lamb* is surely the most beautiful historical film ever made. Richard Harris made a stirring Lord Protector in *Cromwell,* and the miniseries on Queen Elizabeth I, starring Glenda Jackson, is a great BBC addition to a DVD library. Elizabeth's adversary came to breathless life in Vanessa Redgrave's rendition of *Mary, Queen of Scots,* certainly one of her finest performances. More recent and a chilling performance of tortuous times is Cate Blanchett as *Elizabeth*; 2007 saw the release of *The Golden Age,* a sequel. Helen Mirren played a dignified Elizabeth II as she faces the dilemmas caused by the death of Princess Diana in the excellent *The Queen. Miss Potter,* with Renée Zellweger, explored the life of the beloved children's book writer and illustrator Beatrix Potter, who had a home in the Lake District. Keira Knightley starred in *The Duchess,* the story of Georgiana, duchess of Devonshire, a flamboyant 18th-century aristocrat. Emily Blunt plays the young Queen Victoria in *The Young Victoria* (2009). The television series *The Tudors* has won fans on both sides of the Atlantic.

Musicals? Near the top of anyone's list are four films set in England—three of them in Hollywood's England—that rank among the greatest musicals of all time: Walt Disney's *Mary Poppins,* George Cukor's *My Fair Lady,* Carol Reed's Oscar-winner *Oliver!,* and—yeah, yeah, yeah!—the Beatles' *A Hard Day's Night,* a British production.

If you're seeking a look at contemporary England, you might view *My Beautiful Laundrette,* about Asians in London, or *Secrets and Lies,* about a dysfunctional London family. Manchester's rocking music scene from the 1970s to early 1990s is the subject of the well-named *24 Hour Party People.* Mods, New Romantics, and Skinheads feature in *This Is England,* a sensitive tale of working-class life in the Midlands in the early 1980s.

Closer, adapted from Patrick Marber's play, takes a dark look at love in modern London. Woody Allen set his movies *Match Point* and *Scoop* in London; there are gorgeous shots of historic and modern locations in both.

You might lighten up with *The Full Monty,* about six former steelworkers in Sheffield who become strippers, or one of numerous romantic comedies: *Notting Hill,* with Julia Roberts and Hugh Grant; Hugh Grant again in *Four Weddings and a Funeral*; Gwyneth Paltrow in *Sliding Doors*; and Renée Zellweger (and Hugh Grant, again) in *Bridget Jones's Diary* and *Bridget Jones: The Edge of Reason.* *Calendar Girls,* filmed in rural Yorkshire, follows the true story of middle-aged women who raise money for charity with an (almost) bare-all calendar.

Quintessentially British are some comedies of the 1950s and '60s: Alec Guinness's *Kind Hearts and Coronets,* Peter Sellers's *The Mouse That Roared,* and Tony Richardson's Oscar winner and cinematic style setter, *Tom Jones,* starring Albert Finney, are best bets.

In 2001 American director Robert Altman took a biting look at the country's class system in *Gosford Park,* a country-house murder mystery set in the 1930s that stars mostly British actors, including Jeremy Northam and Maggie Smith. *Atonement* (2007), based on Ian McEwan's novel and starring Keira Knightley, also explores class tensions and depicts a small country estate between the world wars. A more staid, upstairs-downstairs look at the class system is the film of Kazuo Ishiguro's novel *The Remains of the Day,* featuring Anthony Hopkins as the stalwart butler, with Emma Thompson. Today some people's visions of turn-of-the-20th-century England have been captured by the Merchant and Ivory films, notably their *Howard's End,* which won many awards.

CHRONOLOGY

3000 BC   First building of Stonehenge (later building 2100–1900 BC)

54 BC–AD 43   Julius Caesar's exploratory invasion of England. Romans conquer England, led by Emperor Claudius

60   Boudicca, a native British queen, razes the first Roman London (Londinium)

122–27   Emperor Hadrian completes the Roman conquest and builds a wall across the north to keep back the Scottish Picts

300–50   Height of Roman colonization, administered from such towns as Verulamium (St. Albans), Colchester, Lincoln, and York

410   Roman rule of Britain ends, after waves of invasion by Jutes, Angles, and Saxons

ca. 490   Possible period for the legendary King Arthur, who may have led resistance to Anglo-Saxon invaders

550–700   Seven Anglo-Saxon kingdoms emerge—Essex, Wessex, Sussex, Kent, Anglia, Mercia, and Northumbria—to become the core of English social and political organization for centuries

597   St. Augustine arrives in Canterbury to Christianize Britain

871–99   Alfred the Great, king of Wessex, unifies the English against Viking invaders, who are then confined to the Northeast

1040   Edward the Confessor moves his court to Westminster and founds Westminster Abbey

1066   William, duke of Normandy, invades, defeats King Harold at the Battle of Hastings, and is crowned William I at Westminster in December

1086   Domesday Book completed, a survey of all taxpayers in England, drawn up to assist administration of the realm

1167   Oxford University founded

1170   Thomas à Becket murdered in Canterbury; his shrine becomes center for international pilgrimage

1209   Cambridge University founded

1215   King John forced to sign Magna Carta at Runnymede. It promulgates basic principles of English law: no taxation except through Parliament, trial by jury, and property guarantees

1272–1307   Reign of Edward I, a great legislator; in 1282–83 he conquers Wales and reinforces his rule with a chain of massive castles

1337–1453   Edward III claims the French throne, starting the Hundred Years War. In spite of dramatic English victories—1346 at Crécy, 1356 at Poitiers, 1415 at Agincourt—the long war of attrition ends with the French driving the English out from everywhere but Calais, which finally falls in 1558

1348–49 The Black Death (bubonic plague) reduces the population of Britain from around 4¼ million to around 2½ million; decades of social unrest follow

1399 Henry Bolingbroke (Henry IV) deposes and murders his cousin Richard II; beginning of the rivalry between houses of York and Lancaster

1402–10 The Welsh, led by Owain Glendŵr, rebel against English rule

1455–85 The Wars of the Roses; the York–Lancaster struggle erupts into civil war

1477 William Caxton prints first book in England

1485 Henry Tudor (Henry VII) defeats Richard III at the Battle of Bosworth and founds the Tudor dynasty; he suppresses private armies, develops administrative efficiency and royal absolutism

1530s Under Henry VIII the Reformation takes hold; he dissolves the monasteries and finally demolishes medieval England. The land goes to wealthy merchant families, creating new gentry

1555 During the reign of papal supporter Mary I (reigned 1553–58), Protestant bishops Ridley and Latimer are burned in Oxford; in 1556 Archbishop Cranmer is burned

1558–1603 Reign of Elizabeth I: Protestantism reestablished; Drake, Raleigh, and other freebooters establish English claims in the West Indies and North America

1568 Mary, Queen of Scots, flees to England; in 1587 she is executed

1588 Spanish Armada fails to invade England

1603 James VI of Scotland, son of Mary, Queen of Scots and Lord Darnley, becomes James I of England

1605 Guy Fawkes and friends plot to blow up Parliament

1611 King James Authorized Version of the Bible published

1620 Pilgrims sail from Plymouth on the *Mayflower* and settle in what becomes New England

1629 Charles I dissolves Parliament, decides to rule alone

1642–49 Civil War between the Royalists and Parliamentarians (Cavaliers and Roundheads); the Parliamentarians win

1649 Charles I executed; England is a republic

1653 Oliver Cromwell becomes Lord Protector, establishing England's only dictatorship

1660 The Restoration: Charles II restored to the throne; accepts limits to royal power

1666 The Great Fire: London burns for three days; its medieval center is destroyed

1689 Accession of William III (of Orange) and his wife, Mary II, as joint monarchs; royal power further limited

1700s Under the first four Georges, the Industrial Revolution develops and with it Britain's domination of world trade

1707 Union of English and Scots parliaments under Queen Anne

1714 The German Hanoverians succeed to the throne; George I's deficiency in English leads to the establishment of a council of ministers, the beginning of the cabinet system of government

1715, 1745–46 Two Jacobite rebellions fail to restore the House of Stuart to the throne; in 1746 Charles Edward Stuart (Bonnie Prince Charlie) is decisively defeated at Culloden Moor in Scotland

1775–83 Britain loses the American colonies that become the United States

1795–1815 Britain and its allies defeat France in the Napoleonic Wars; in 1805, Admiral Lord Nelson is killed at Trafalgar; in 1815, Battle of Waterloo is fought

1801 Union with Ireland

1811–20 Prince Regent rules during his father's (George III) madness, the Regency period

1825 The Stockton to Darlington railway, the world's first passenger line with regular service, is established

1832 The Reform Bill extends the franchise, limiting the power of the great landowners

1837–1901 During the long reign of Victoria, Britain becomes the world's richest country, and the British Empire reaches its height

1887 Victoria celebrates her Golden Jubilee; in 1901 she dies, marking the end of an era

1914–18 World War I: fighting against Germany, Britain loses a whole generation, with 750,000 men killed in trench warfare alone; enormous debts and inept diplomacy in the postwar years undermine Britain's position as a world power

1919 Ireland declares independence from England; bloody Black-and-Tan struggle is one result

1936 Edward VIII abdicates to marry American divorcée Wallis Simpson

1939–45 World War II: Britain declares war on Germany when Germany invades Poland in September 1939. London badly damaged during the Blitz, September 1940–May 1941; Britain's economy shattered

1945 Labour wins a landslide victory; stays in power for six years, transforming Britain into a welfare state

1952 Queen Elizabeth II accedes to the throne

1973 Britain joins the European Economic Community after referendum

1975 Britain begins to pump North Sea oil

1981 Marriage of Prince Charles and Lady Diana Spencer

1982 Falklands regained in war with Argentina

1987 Conservatives under Margaret Thatcher win a third term in office

1992 Great Britain and European countries join to form one European Community (EC), whose name changed to European Union in 1993

1994 The Channel Tunnel opens a direct rail link between Britain and Europe

1996 The Prince and Princess of Wales receive a divorce

1997 "New Labour" comes to power, with Tony Blair as prime minister. Diana, Princess of Wales, dies at 36 in a car crash in Paris. She is buried at Althorp in Northamptonshire

2002 Queen Elizabeth celebrates her Golden Jubilee. Queen Elizabeth (the Queen Mother) and Princess Margaret die. Euro coins and notes enter circulation; Britain continues to ponder adopting the euro

2003 Britain joins U.S. and coalition forces in invading Iraq

2005 Prince Charles and Camilla Parker Bowles wed in a civil ceremony. The ban on the traditional sport of fox hunting with hounds is put into effect. Tony Blair is elected to a historic third term as prime minister. London wins the bid for the 2012 Olympics in July

2007 Gordon Brown becomes prime minister

2009 British economy suffers as part of the global recession; Brown and the Labour Party lose some popularity

Travel Smart England

GETTING HERE AND AROUND

▌ AIR TRAVEL

The least expensive airfares to England are often priced for round-trip travel and must usually be purchased in advance. Airlines generally allow you to change your return date for a fee; most low-fare tickets, however, are nonrefundable.

Flying time to London is about 6½ hours from New York, 7½ hours from Chicago, 9½ hours from Dallas, 10 hours from Los Angeles, and 21½ hours from Sydney. From London, flights take an hour to Paris or Amsterdam, 1½ hours to cities in Switzerland or Luxembourg, and 2 hours to Rome.

If you're flying to Europe from England, plan to arrive at the airport two hours in advance. Security at Gatwick and Heathrow airports is always fairly intense. Most people can expect to be frisked after they pass through metal detectors. Travelers are randomly searched again at the gate before transatlantic flights.

Airline Security Issues Transportation Security Administration (⊕ www.tsa.gov).

AIRPORTS

Most international flights to London arrive at either Heathrow Airport (LHR), 15 mi west of London, or at Gatwick Airport (LGW), 27 mi south of the capital. Most flights from the United States go to Heathrow, with Terminals 4 and 5 handling transatlantic flights (British Airways uses Terminal 5). Gatwick is London's second gateway, serving many U.S. destinations. A third, much smaller airport, Stansted (STN), is 35 mi northeast of the city. It handles mainly European and domestic traffic. Luton Airport (LLA), 30 mi north of the city, is also quite small, and serves British and European destinations. Luton is the hub for the low-cost easyJet airline. Manchester (MAN) in northwest England handles some bmi/British Midland flights from the United States. Birmingham (BHX), in the Midlands, handles mainly

European and British flights as well as flights from Chicago, Philadelphia, Newark, New York, and Orlando. Bristol (BRS) has limited service from New York.

Heathrow and Gatwick are enormous and can seem like shopping malls where planes just happen to land. Both airports have bars and pubs, and dining options. There are several hotels connected to each airport, and both Gatwick and Heathrow are near dozens of hotels that run free shuttles to the airports. Heathrow has a Hotel Hoppa service that runs shuttles between the airport and nearby major hotels for £3 each way. You can find out more at the bus center in Arrivals at Terminal 4. Yotel has budget pod hotels in both Heathrow and Gatwick with cabin-size rooms to be booked in advance in four-hour blocks (£25) or overnight (£56).

In comparison, other airports, including Manchester, Birmingham, and London's Luton and Stansted, have much more limited shopping, hotel, and dining options; a delay of a few hours can seem like years.

Airport Information Birmingham Airport (☎ 0870/733–5511 ⊕ www.bhx.com). **Gatwick Airport** (☎ 0870/000–2468 ⊕ www. gatwickairport.com). **Heathrow Airport** (☎ 0870/000–0123 ⊕ www.heathrowairport. com). **Luton Airport** (☎ 01582/405100 ⊕ www.london-luton.co.uk). **Manchester Airport** (☎ 0161/489–3000 ⊕ www. manchesterairport.co.uk). **Stansted Airport** (☎ 0870/850–2825 ⊕ www.stanstedairport. com).

GROUND TRANSPORTATION

London has excellent bus and train connections between its airports and downtown. The Transport for London Web site has helpful information, and airport Web sites have links to transportation services. You can get discounts on many tickets if you book on the Internet.

Train service can be quick, but the downside (for trains from all airports) is that you must get yourself and your luggage to the train via a series of escalators and connecting trams. Airport link buses (generally National Express Airport buses) may ease the luggage factor and drop you closer to central hotels, but they're subject to London traffic, which can be horrendous. Taxis can be more convenient than buses, but prices can go through the roof. Airport Travel Line has additional transfer information and takes advance booking for transfers between airports and into London.

Heathrow: From Heathrow, the cheapest route into London is via the Piccadilly line of the Underground. Trains on the Tube run every four to eight minutes from all five terminals; the 50-minute trip costs around £6 one-way and connects with London's Tube system. The first train departs around 5:13 AM (5:57 AM Sunday); the last train departs from the airport at 11:49 PM (11:30 PM Sunday). The quickest way into London is the Heathrow Express train, which takes 15 minutes to and from Paddington Station in the city center. It's considered "the most expensive train journey in Europe," however, as one-way tickets cost £16.50 for standard class (£32 round-trip). Daily service departs every 15 minutes from 5:15 AM to around 11:30 PM.

Bus service to London is available from the Heathrow Central Bus Station. National Express A2 service costs £7 one-way, £14 round-trip; travel time is about one hour and 40 minutes. Buses leave for Victoria Station and St. Pancras station, with stops at Marble Arch and Russell Square, every 30 minutes 5:30 AM to 9:45 PM, but are tedious because there are more than a dozen stops en route. Faster National Express buses leave every 30 minutes 5:40 AM to 9:35 PM to Victoria Coach Station from Heathrow Central Bus Station—connected to arrival terminals by a pedestrian underpass, and next to Heathrow Underground Station for Terminals 1–3: the cost is cheaper if you book in advance, but averages around £8 one-way.

Gatwick: To get to Gatwick, you can take a commuter train to either London Bridge or Victoria stations (approximately £11 one-way), or in the opposite direction to Brighton, but these trains can be crowded with little room for baggage. During rush hour harried commuters can be impatient with weary air travelers, and you can find yourself standing up all the way. The better option is the fast, nonstop Gatwick Express train that leaves the airport approximately every 15 minutes from 4:35 AM to 1:35 AM. The 30-minute trip costs £17 one-way standard, £30 round-trip.

Hourly bus service runs from Gatwick's south terminal to Victoria Station in the city center, with stops along the way at Hooley, Coulsdon, Mitcham, Streatham, Stockwell, and Pimlico. The journey takes 90 minutes and costs £11 one-way. Make sure you get on a direct bus not requiring a change—otherwise the journey could take hours.

Stansted: Stansted, 35 mi northeast of London, serves mainly European destinations but also receives some transatlantic flights. The 45-minute journey on Stansted Express to Liverpool Street Station runs every 15 minutes 8 AM to 5 PM weekdays, and every 30 minutes 5 PM to midnight and 6 AM to 8 AM weekdays, and all day on weekends. The trip costs £16 one-way, £28 round-trip. By bus, there's hourly service on National Express Airport Bus A6 (24 hours a day) to Victoria Coach Station. The journey costs £11 one-way, £16 round-trip, and takes about 1 hour and 40 minutes. Stops include Golders Green, Finchley Road, St. John's Wood, Baker Street, Marble Arch, and Hyde Park Corner.

Luton: From Luton (30 mi north of London), which, like Stansted, serves mainly British and European airlines, you can take a free shuttle to the nearby Luton Airport Parkway Station, from which you can take a train or bus into London. The Thameslink train service runs to several London stations, terminating at St.

Pancras Station, adjacent to King's Cross station, which takes about 35 minutes. Trains leave every 15 minutes or so 24 hours a day and cost approximately £10 one-way, £19 round-trip. For a cheaper journey, take the Green Line 757 bus service from Luton to Victoria Station. It runs three times an hour, takes about 90 minutes, and costs around £8.

Heathrow, Gatwick, Stansted, and Luton by Taxi: If you are thinking of taking a taxi from Heathrow and Gatwick into the city center, remember that they can get caught in traffic; the trip from Heathrow, for example, can take more than an hour and costs from £35 to more than £50. From Gatwick, the taxi fare is about £75; the ride takes about an hour and 20 minutes. From Stansted, the £75 journey takes a little over an hour. From Luton, the approximately one-hour journey should cost around £65. Your hotel may be able to recommend a car service for airport transfers; charges are usually about £35 to any of the airports.

TRANSFERS BETWEEN AIRPORTS

For transfers between airports, allow at least two to three hours. The cheapest option is public transportation: from Gatwick to Stansted, for instance, you can catch the nonexpress commuter train from Gatwick to Victoria Station in London, take the Tube to Liverpool Street Station, then catch the train to Stansted from there. To get from Heathrow to Gatwick by public transport, take the Tube to King's Cross, then change to the Victoria Line, get to Victoria Station, and take the commuter train to Gatwick. Both of these trips would take about two hours.

The National Express Airport bus is the most direct option between Gatwick and Heathrow. Buses pick up passengers every 15 minutes from 5 AM to 10 PM from both airports. The trip takes 1½ to 2 hours, and the fare is around £20 one-way, £39 round-trip. It's advisable to book tickets in advance via National Express, especially during peak travel seasons, but you can buy also tickets in the terminals. National

Express also runs shuttles between all the other airports, except between Luton and Stansted. Finally, some airlines may offer shuttle services as well—check with your travel agent in advance of your journey.

Contacts Airport Travel Line (☎ 0870/574–7777). **Gatwick Express** (☎ 0845/850–1530 ⊕ www.gatwickexpress.com). **Heathrow Express** (☎ 0845/600–1515 ⊕ www. heathrowexpress.com). **National Express** (☎ 0870/580–8080 ⊕ www.nationalexpress. com). **Stansted Express** (☎ 0845/850–0150 ⊕ www.stanstedexpress.co.uk). **Transport for London** (☎ 020/7222–1234 ⊕ www.tfl.gov.uk).

FLIGHTS

British Airways offers mostly nonstop flights from 18 U.S. cities to Heathrow, along with flights to Manchester and Birmingham. It offers myriad add-on options that help bring down ticket costs. In addition, it has a vast program of discount airfare-hotel packages. Britain-based Virgin Atlantic is a strong competitor in terms of packages. London is a very popular destination, so many U.S. carriers have flights and packages there, too.

Because England is such a small country, internal air travel is much less important than it is in the United States. For trips of less than 200 mi, the train is often quicker, with rail stations more centrally located. Flying tends to cost more, but for longer trips air travel has a considerable time advantage (you need to factor in time to get to and from the airport, though).

British Airways operates shuttle services between Heathrow or Gatwick and Manchester. bmi/British Midland operates from Heathrow to Leeds and Manchester, as well as to Washington, D.C., Chicago, Las Vegas, and major cities in eastern Canada.

Low-cost airlines such as easyJet, bmi baby, and Ryanair offer flights within the United Kingdom as well as to cities in Ireland and continental Europe. Prices are low, but these airlines usually use satellite cities and fly out of smaller British airports such as Stansted and Luton (both near London). Check ⊕*www.cheapflights. com* for price comparisons.

Major Airline Contacts American Airlines (☎ *800/433-7300, 020/7365-0777 in London* ⊕ *www.aa.com*) to Heathrow, Gatwick, Manchester, Newcastle. **British Airways** (☎ *800/247-9297, 0844/493-0787 in London* ⊕ *www.britishairways.com*) to Heathrow. **Continental Airlines** (☎ *800/231-0856 for international reservations, 0845/607-6760 in London* ⊕ *www.continental.com*) to Heathrow, Bristol, Gatwick. **Delta Airlines** (☎ *800/221-1212 for U.S. reservations, 800/241-4141 for international reservations, 0845/600-0950 in London* ⊕ *www.delta.com*) to Gatwick. **Virgin Atlantic** (☎ *800/862-8621, 08705/747-747 in London* ⊕ *www.virgin-atlantic.com*) to Heathrow, Gatwick.

Within England and to Europe bmi baby (☎ *0870/607-0555 in London* ⊕ *www. bmibaby.com*). **easyJet** (☎ *0870/600-0000 in London* ⊕ *www.easyjet.com*). **Ryanair** (☎ *0871/246-0000 in London* ⊕ *www.ryanair. com*).

PASSES

The Discover Europe Airpass from bmi is available on the airline's British and European flights. The pass is valid for up to 90 days and allows passengers to travel to a combination of European cities for reduced fares. The Visit Europe Pass from British Airways offers travelers a way to choose from the airline's and its partners' networks.

Air Pass Info bmi (☎ *800/788-0555, 020/8745-7321 in U.K.* ⊕ *www.flybmi. com*). **British Airways** (☎ *800/247-9297, 0870/850-9850 in U.K* ⊕ *www.britishairways. com*). **DER Travel Services** (☎ *800/782-2424* ⊕ *www.der.com*). **FlightPass** (*EuropebyAir* ☎ *888/387-2479* ⊕ *www.europebyair.com*).

∎ BOAT TRAVEL

Ferries, hovercraft, and Seacats (a kind of ferry) travel regular routes to France, Spain, Ireland, and Scandinavia. Hoverspeed provides fast travel to France and Belgium. P&O runs ferries between Belgium, Great Britain, Ireland, France, the Netherlands, and Spain. DFDS Seaways covers Denmark, Holland, Germany, Norway, Poland, and Sweden. Stena Line serves Ireland and the Netherlands.

Low-cost airlines and Eurostar (which lets you take a car to France on the train) have cut into ferry travel, but companies have responded by cutting fares and upgrading equipment.

For fares and schedules, contact companies directly. Traveler's checks (in pounds), cash, and major credit cards are accepted for payments. Prices vary; booking early ensures cheaper fares, but also ask about special deals. Seaview is a comprehensive online ferry- and cruise-booking portal for Great Britain and continental Europe. Ferry Cheap is a discount Web site.

Information DFDS Seaways (☎ *01255/ 240240 or 0870/533-3000* ⊕ *www. dfdsseaways.co.uk*). **Ferry Cheap** (⊕ *www. ferrycheap.com*). **Hoverspeed** (☎ *0870/240-8070* ⊕ *www.hoverspeed.com*). **P&O Irish Sea** (☎ *0870/242-4777* ⊕ *www.poirishsea.com*). **P&O North Sea** (☎ *0870/129-6002* ⊕ *www. ponsf.com*). **Seaview** (⊕ *www.seaview.co.uk*). **Stena Line** (☎ *0870/570-7070* ⊕ *www. stenaline.co.uk*).

CRUISES

Most cruise ships leave from southern England—particularly Southampton and Portsmouth. Some ships leave from Liverpool and Dover as well, or from Harwich, near London. Each cruise company has its own journeys and policies, so check their Web sites or contact a travel agent if you're interested in more information about cruising from England to Europe. *For information about cruising England's rivers, lakes, and canals, see Sports and the Outdoors in Essentials, below.*

Cruise Lines Cunard Line (☎ *661/753-1000 or 800/728-6273* ⊕ *www.cunard.com*). **Holland America Line** (☎ *206/281-3535 or 877/932-4259* ⊕ *www.hollandamerica.com*). **Norwegian Cruise Line** (☎ *305/436-4000 or 800/327-7030* ⊕ *www.ncl.com*). **Princess Cruises** (☎ *661/753-0000 or 800/774-6237*

⊕www.princess.com). **Royal Caribbean International** (☎305/539–6000 or 800/327–6700 ⊕www.royalcaribbean.com).

▌BUS TRAVEL

Britain has a comprehensive bus (short-haul) and coach (the British term for long-distance buses) network that offers an inexpensive way of seeing England and Wales. National Express is the major coach operator, and Victoria Coach Station, near Victoria Station in central London, is the hub of the National Express network, serving around 1,200 destinations within Great Britain and, via Eurolines, continental Europe. Tickets and information are available from any of the company's 2,500 agents nationwide, including offices at London's Heathrow and Gatwick airport coach stations.

Green Line is the next-largest national service, serving airports and major tourist towns.

A well-priced budget option on the long-distance bus travel scene, Megabus has double-decker buses that serve cities across Britain. (Note: Megabus does not accommodate wheelchairs, and the company strictly limits luggage to one checked piece per person and one piece of hand luggage.) In London the company's buses depart from the Green Line bus stand at Victoria Station. At this writing, Greyhound was planning to launch low-cost, long-distance bus service in the U.K. as well.

Coach tickets can be as low as half the price of a train ticket (even lower if you take advantage of special deals), and buses are just as comfortable as trains. For example, an Oxford Tube bus ticket from London to Oxford is £8, whereas a train ticket is £25. However, most bus services take twice as long as trains. All bus services forbid smoking, and National Express has onboard refreshments and toilets. There is only one class of service.

Double-decker buses make up many of the extensive networks of local bus services, run by private companies. Check with the local bus station or tourist information center for bus schedules. Most companies offer day or week Explorer or Rover unlimited-travel tickets, and those in popular tourist areas operate special scenic tours in summer. The top deck of a double-decker bus is a great place from which to view the countryside.

DISCOUNTS AND DEALS

A Discount Coach Card for students, 16–26, and over-50, which costs £10 and is good for one year, qualifies you for 20% to 30% discounts off many fares. At the time of this writing, National Express was reviewing its service. Check the Web site for information on this and other discounts.

Apex tickets (cheap advance-purchase tickets) save money on standard fares, and traveling midweek is cheaper than over weekends and at holiday periods. Most companies offer a discount for children under 15.

FARES AND SCHEDULES

You can find schedules online, pick them up from tourist information offices, or get them by phone from the bus companies. Fares vary based on how close to the time of travel you book—Megabus tickets, for example, are cheaper if ordered in advance online.

PAYING

Tickets for National Express can be bought from the Victoria, Heathrow, or Gatwick coach stations, or by phone with a credit card, or via the National Express Web site, or from most British travel agencies. Reservations are advised. Tickets for Megabus must be purchased online in advance, or by phone (avoid this, as the surcharge is at least 60p per minute). Surcharges for tickets bought online in advance rarely rise above £5.

Most companies will accept MasterCard and Visa for advance purchases, but it's cash-only if you're purchasing your tickets on the bus on the day of travel.

RESERVATIONS

There are no surcharges for booking in advance; in fact, it's a much better idea, as busy routes and times can book up quickly. With most bus companies (National Express, Megabus, Green Line), if you pay in advance your receipt can be e-mailed to you, and your name is placed on a list given to the bus driver.

Bus Contacts Greyhound (⊕ www. greyhounduk.com). **Green Line** (☎ 0870/608–7261 ⊕ www.greenline.co.uk). **Megabus** (☎ 0900/160–0900 ⊕ www.megabus.com), 60p per minute for calls from landlines in U.K. **National Express** (☎ 0870/580–8080 ⊕ www. nationalexpress.com). **Victoria Coach Station** (✉ 164 Buckingham Palace Rd., London SW1 ☎ 020/7730–3466 for station, 020/7730–3499 for booking ⊕ www.tfl.gov.uk/vcs).

▌ CAR TRAVEL

With more than 50 million inhabitants in England and Wales, and a road system designed in part for horse-drawn carriages, Britain can be a challenging place in which to drive. That's even without considering that people drive on the left side of the road, most rental cars have standard transmissions, and the gearshift is on the wrong side entirely.

There's no reason to rent a car for a stay in London, since the city and its suburbs are well served by public transportation, and traffic is desperately congested. Here and in other major cities it's best to rely on the comprehensive public transportation network.

Outside the cities, a car can be very handy. Many sights are not easily reached without one—castles, for example, are rarely connected to any public transportation system. Small villages might have only one or two buses a day pass through them. Driving between the tall hedgerows or on country roads is a truly English experi-

ence. Buy good maps either at home or in England.

In England and Wales your own driver's license is acceptable. However, you may choose to get an International Driving Permit (IDP), which can be used only in conjunction with a valid driver's license and which translates your license into 10 languages. Check the AAA Web site for more info as well as for IDPs ($10) themselves. These permits are universally recognized, and having one in your wallet may save you a problem with the local authorities.

GASOLINE

Gasoline is called petrol in England and is sold by the liter. The price you see posted at a petrol station is the price of a liter, and there are about four liters in a U.S. gallon. Petrol is expensive; it was around 90 pence per liter at this writing. Supermarket pumps just outside city centers frequently offer the best prices. Unleaded petrol is predominant, denoted by green stickers on fuel pumps and pump lines. Premium and super premium are the two varieties, and most cars run on regular premium. Diesel is prevalent; be sure not to use it by mistake. Along busy motorways, most large stations are open 24 hours a day, seven days a week. In rural areas, hours can vary. Most service stations accept major credit cards, and most are self-service.

PARKING

Parking regulations are strictly enforced everywhere, so look out for signs that display the rules where you're thinking of parking. If there are no signs on a street, it's free to park there. However, many streets have centralized "pay and display" machines, in which you deposit the required money and get a ticket allowing you to park for a set period of time. You display that ticket in your windshield. In town centers your best bet is usually to park in a public car lot. Square blue street signs with a white P in the center direct you to the nearest lot.

If you park on the street, follow these basic rules: Do not park within 15 yards of an intersection. Do not park on double yellow lines or in bus lanes. Park as close to the curb as possible. On "Red Routes"—busy roads with red lines painted on the street—you cannot park or stop to let a passenger out of the car.

RENTALS

Rental rates are generally reasonable, and insurance costs are lower than in most U.S. cities. If you want the car only for country trips, consider renting your car in a medium-size town in the area where you'll be traveling, and journeying there by train and picking up the car once you arrive. Rental rates are slightly cheaper out in the country, and you can avoid traversing London's notoriously complex road system.

Rental rates vary widely, beginning at £25 a day and £160 a week for a midsize car, usually with manual transmission. Air-conditioning and unlimited mileage generally come with larger automatic transmission cars. As in the United States, prices are higher at times of heaviest use—summer and holidays. Car seats for children usually cost about £20 extra. Adding one extra driver is usually included in the original rental price. Major car rental agencies are much the same in Britain as in the United States: Alamo, Avis, Budget, Enterprise, Hertz, and National all have offices in Britain, and you can reserve a car in advance on their Web sites. Europcar is another large company.

Companies may not rent cars to people who are under 23 or over 75.

ROAD CONDITIONS

There's a very good network of highways (motorways) and divided highways (dual carriageways) throughout most of England and Wales, although in remote areas (including parts of Wales), where unclassified roads join villages and are little more than glorified one-lane paths, travel is slower. Motorways (with the prefix M), shown in blue on most maps and road signs, are mainly two or three lanes in each direction. Other major roads (with the prefix A) are shown on maps in green and red. Sections of fast dual carriageways (with black-edged, thick outlines on maps) have both traffic lights and traffic circles; right turns are sometimes permitted. Turnoffs are often marked by highway numbers, rather than place names. An exit is called a junction in Britain.

The vast network of lesser roads, for the most part old coach and turnpike roads, might make your trip take twice the time but show you twice as much. Minor roads drawn in yellow or white, the former prefixed by B, the latter unlettered and unnumbered, are the ancient lanes and byways, a way of discovering the real England. Some of these (the white roads, in the main) are pothole-filled switchbacks. Should you take one of these, be prepared to back up into a passing place if you meet an oncoming car.

ROADSIDE EMERGENCIES

On major highways emergency roadside telephone booths are positioned within walking-distance intervals. Contact your car-rental company (there should be an emergency assistance phone number on the car's paperwork), or call the police. You can also call the British Automobile Association toll-free. You can join and receive assistance from the AA on the spot, but the charge (around £75) is higher than a simple membership fee. If you are a member of AAA (the American Automobile Association), check before you travel; reciprocal agreements may give you free roadside aid.

Emergency Services Ambulance, fire, police (☎ *999*). **Automobile Association** (☎ *0800/085–2721* ⊕ *www.theaa.co.uk*).

RULES OF THE ROAD

You must drive on the left side of the road. You may find it's easier than you expected, as the steering and mirrors on British cars are designed for driving on the left. You use the side mirrors much more this way. If you have a standard transmission car, you have to shift gears with your left hand. Study your map before leaving the rental-car lot, and give yourself time to adjust. Seat belts are obligatory in the front and back seats. It is illegal to talk on a hand-held cell phone while driving.

Pick up a copy of the official Highway Code (£4.50) at a service station, news-stand, or bookstore, or check it out online by going to ⊕*www.direct.gov.uk* and putting 'Highway Code' in the search bar. Besides driving rules and illustrations of signs and road markings, this booklet contains information for motorcyclists, cyclists, and pedestrians.

Speed limits are complicated, and there are speed cameras everywhere. The speed limit (shown on circular red signs) is generally 30 mph in towns, 60 mph on two-lane highways, and 70 mph on motorways. At traffic circles (called roundabouts), you turn clockwise; you will see signs before the roundabout that indicate where each exiting road is headed. As cars enter the circle, they must yield to those already in the circle. If you're taking an exit all the way around the circle, stay to the center until just before your own exit.

Pedestrians have the right-of-way on "zebra" crossings (black-and-white-stripe crosswalks between two orange-flashing globe lights). If there's a person waiting to cross the street, treat the crossing like a stop sign. The curb on each side of the zebra crossing has zigzag markings. It is illegal to park within zigzag areas or to pass a vehicle at a zebra crossing. At other crossings, pedestrians must yield to traffic, but they do have the right-of-way over traffic turning left.

Drunk-driving laws are strictly enforced. The legal limit is 80 milligrams of alcohol, which means two units of alcohol—two glasses of wine, one pint of beer, or one glass of whisky—but these amounts vary, depending on your body weight or the amount you have eaten that day.

■ TRAIN TRAVEL

Operated by private companies, the train system in Britain is extensive and useful, though less than perfect. Some regional trains are old, and virtually all lines suffer from occasional delays, schedule changes, and periodic crippling strikes. Worst of all, you will pay quite a lot for all of that. Work is under way to improve the situation, and at this writing, changes on some lines seem likely. All major cities and many small towns are served by trains, and despite the difficulties, rail travel is the most pleasant way to cover long distances.

On long-distance runs some rail lines have buffet cars; on others you can purchase snacks from a mobile snack cart. Most train companies now have "quiet cars" on trains, where mobile-phone use is forbidden and conversation is meant to be kept at a low volume.

CLASSES

Most rail lines have first-class and second-class cars. In virtually all cases, second class is perfectly comfortable. First class generally has superior seating and tables, and seats are marginally larger. First class usually costs two to three times the price of second class, though, so it's not always worth the cost. However, first class is also usually quieter and less crowded.

FARES AND SCHEDULES

The best way to find out which train to take, which station to catch the train, and what times trains travel to your destination is to call National Rail Enquiries. It's a helpful, comprehensive, free service that covers all the country's rail lines. National Rail will help you choose the best train to take, and then connect you with the ticket office for that train company.

The monthly *OAG Rail Guide* (about £7 and available from WH Smith branches at most larger main-line rail stations) covers all national rail services and Eurostar, as well as buses, ferries, and rail-based tourist facilities, but it's dizzyingly comprehensive. You can find timetables of rail services in Britain and some ferry services in the *Thomas Cook European Timetable,* issued monthly and available at travel agents and some bookstores in the United States.

Ticket prices are set on a sliding scale, and they cost more the closer you get to the day of travel. Book several weeks in advance and tickets can be half or one-third of what you might pay if you bought the ticket the same day you traveled. A journey from London to Cardiff will cost around £38 if purchased more than two weeks in advance, but if purchased on the day you travel, the ticket can cost more than £150. However, this is the case only for long-distance travel—journeys within commuting distance of city centers are sold at set prices, and those can be purchased on the day you expect to make your journey.

In all cases ticket prices are more expensive during rush hour, so, whether your journey will be short or long, plan to travel after 9:30 AM, and before 4:30 PM or after 6:30 PM if you want the best prices.

National Rail Enquiries has information about rail passes such as Rovers, which save you money on individual railroads. Purchasing a BritRail Pass before you leave home may save money.

■ TIP→ **Ask the local tourist board about hotel and local transportation packages that include tickets to major events.**

Information National Rail Enquiries (☎ *0845/748–4950, 020/7278–5240 outside Britain* ⊕ *www.nationalrail.co.uk).*

PASSES

If you plan to travel a lot by train in England and Wales, consider purchasing a BritRail Pass, which gives unlimited travel over the entire British rail network and can save you money. If you don't plan to cover many miles, you may come out ahead by buying individual tickets. You must buy your BritRail Pass before you leave home. They are available from most travel agents or from ACP Rail

International, BritRail, Flight Centre, or Rail Europe. Note that Eurail Passes are not honored in Britain and that the rates listed here are subject to change.

BritRail passes come in two basic varieties. The Classic pass allows travel on consecutive days, and the FlexiPass allows a number of travel days within a set period of time. The cost (in U.S. dollars) of a BritRail Consecutive Pass adult ticket for 8 days is $359 standard and $535 first-class; for 15 days, $535 standard and $799 first-class. The cost of a BritRail FlexiPass adult ticket for 4 days' travel in two months is $315 standard and $465 first-class; for 8 days' travel in two months, $459 standard and $679 first-class. Prices drop by about 25% for off-peak travel passes between October and March. Passes for students, seniors, and ages 16 to 25 are discounted, too.

Many travelers assume that rail passes guarantee them seats or sleeping accommodations on the trains they wish to ride. Not so. You need to book seats ahead even if you are using a rail pass, especially on trains that may be crowded, particularly in summer on popular routes.

There are also some discount passes from different rail companies for travel within regions; you can call National Rail Enquiries.

Discount Passes ACP Rail International (☎ *866/938–7245* ⊕ *www.acprail.com).* **Bri-tRail** (☎ *877/677–1066* ⊕ *www.britrail.com).* **Flight Centre** (☎ *866/967–5351* ⊕ *www. flightcentre.com).* **Rail Europe** (☎ *888/382–7245* ⊕ *www.raileurope.com* ☎ *0870/584–8848 in U.K.).*

PAYING

Cash and credit cards are accepted by all train ticket offices; credit cards are accepted over the phone.

RESERVATIONS

Reserving your ticket in advance is always recommended. Even a reservation 24 hours in advance can provide a substantial discount. Look into cheap day returns if you plan to travel a round-trip in one day.

CHANNEL TUNNEL

Short of flying, taking the Eurostar through the Channel Tunnel is the fastest way to cross the English Channel. Travel time is 35 minutes from Folkestone to Calais, 60 minutes from motorway to motorway, or two hours and 15 minutes from London's St. Pancras Station to Paris's Gare du Nord. It takes two hours to reach Midi Station in Brussels from London.

Early risers can easily take a day trip to Paris or an overnight if time is short. Book ahead, though, as Eurostar tickets increase in price the closer you get to your day of travel. If purchased in advance, round-trip tickets from London to Belgium or France cost around £125.

Channel Tunnel Car Transport Eurotunnel (☎ *0870/535–3535 in U.K., 070/223210 in Belgium, 03–21–00–61–00 in France* ⊕ *www.eurotunnel.com*). **French Motorail/ Rail Europe** (☎ *0870/241–5415* ⊕ *www. raileurope.co.uk*).

Channel Tunnel Passenger Service Eurostar (☎ *0870/518–6186 in U.K.* ⊕ *www. eurostar.co.uk*). **Rail Europe** (☎ *888/382–7245 in U.S., 0870/584–8848 in U.K. for inquiries and credit-card bookings* ⊕ *www.raileurope.com*).

ESSENTIALS

▌ ACCOMMODATIONS

Hotels, bed-and-breakfasts, or small country houses—there's a style and price to suit most travelers. The lodgings listed are the best options we've found in each price category. Wherever you stay, make reservations well in advance: England is popular.

Properties are assigned price categories based on a range that includes the cost of the least expensive standard double room in high season (excluding holidays) and the most expensive. Lodgings are indicated in the text by 🏨. Unless otherwise noted, all lodgings listed have a private bathroom, air-conditioning, a room phone, and a television.

We always list the facilities that are available—but we don't specify whether they cost extra: when pricing accommodations, always ask what's included and what costs extra. Throughout Britain, lodging prices often include breakfast of some kind, but this is generally not the case in London.

CATEGORY	LONDON	ELSEWHERE
£	under £80	under £70
££	£80–£140	£70–£120
£££	£141–£200	£121–£160
££££	£201–£300	£161–£220
£££££	over £300	over £220

Prices are for two people in a standard double room in high season, including V.A.T., and are given in pounds.

▌TIP→ Assume that hotels operate on the European Plan (**EP**, no meals) unless we specify that they use the Breakfast Plan (**BP**, with full breakfast), Continental Plan (**CP**, continental breakfast), or Modified American Plan (**MAP**, breakfast and dinner).

APARTMENT AND HOUSE RENTALS

If you deal directly with local agents, get a recommendation from someone who has used the company. Unlike with hotels, there's no accredited system for apartment-rental standards. *Also see Chapter 2 for London rental resources.*

BED-AND-BREAKFASTS

B&Bs can be a good budget option, and will also help you meet the locals.

Reservation Services Bed & Breakfast.com (☎512/322–2710 or 800/462–2632 ⊕www.bedandbreakfast.com). **Bed & Breakfast (GB)** (☎800/454–8704, 0871/781–0834 in U.K. ⊕www.bedbreak.com). **Bulldog Club** (☎877/727–3004 in U.S. ⊕www.bulldogclub.com). **Host & Guest Service** (☎020/7385–9922 in U.K. ⊕www.host-guest.co.uk). **Wolsey Lodges** (☎01473/822058, 01473/827500 for brochure ⊕www.wolseylodges.com).

COTTAGES

Contacts Luxury Cottages Direct (☎029/2021–2491 ⊕www.luxury-cottages.co.uk). **National Trust** (☎0870/458–4422 ⊕www.nationaltrustcottages.co.uk). **Rural Retreats** (☎01386/701177 ⊕www.ruralretreats.co.uk). **VisitBritain** (⊕www.visitbritain.us).

FARMHOUSES

Contacts Farm Stay UK (☎024/7669–6909 ⊕www.farmstayuk.co.uk). **VisitBritain** (⊕www.visitbritain.us).

HISTORIC BUILDINGS

Contacts Celtic Castles (☎870/050–3232 ⊕www.celticcastles.com). **English Heritage** (☎870/333–1187 ⊕www.english-heritage.org.uk). **Landmark Trust** (☎01628/825925 ⊕www.landmarktrust.org.uk). **National Trust** (☎0870/458–4422 ⊕www.nationaltrustcottages.co.uk). **Portmeirion Cottages** (☎01766/770000 ⊕www.portmeirion-village.com). **Rural Retreats** (☎01386/701177 ⊕www.ruralretreats.co.uk). **Stately Holiday Homes** (☎01638/674756

Online Booking Resources

Contacts		
The Apartment Service	020/8944-1444	www.apartmentservice.com
At Home Abroad	212/421-9165	www.athomeabroadinc.com
Barclay International Group	516/364-0064 or 800/845-6636	www.barclayweb.com
English Country Cottages	0870/781100	www.english-country-cottages.co.uk
In the English Manner	01559/371600	www.english-manner.co.uk
Interhome	954/791-8282 or 800/882-6864	www.interhome.us
National Trust	0870/458-4422	www.nationaltrustcottages.co.uk
Suzanne B. Cohen & Associates	207/622-0743	www.villaeurope.com
Vacation Home Rentals Worldwide	201/767-9393 or 800/633-3284	www.vhrww.com
Villanet	206/417-3444 or 800/964-1891	www.rentavilla.com
Villas International	415/499-9490 or 800/221-2260	www.villasintl.com

⊕ www.statelyholidayhomes.co.uk). **Vivat Trust** (☏ 020/7336-8825 from U.S., 0845/090-0194 from U.K. ⊕ www.vivat.org.uk).

HOME EXCHANGES

With a direct home exchange you stay in someone else's home while they stay in yours. Some outfits also deal with vacation homes, so you're not actually staying in someone's full-time residence, just their vacant weekend place. There are several exchange clubs to choose from. Home Exchange.com offers a one-year membership for $99.95, HomeLink International costs $110 for an annual Web-only membership and $170 for the Web access plus two catalogs, and Intervac U.S. offers international membership for $95.

If you're interested in home exchange but don't feel like sharing, some home-exchange directories list rentals, too.

Exchange Clubs Home Exchange.com (☏ 800/877-8723 ⊕ www.homeexchange. com). **HomeLink International** (☏ 800/638-3841 ⊕ www.homelink.org). **Intervac U.S.** (☏ 800/756-4663 ⊕ www.intervacus.com).

HOTELS

Most hotels have rooms with "ensuite" bathrooms—as private bathrooms are called—although some older ones may have only washbasins; in this case, showers and bathtubs (and toilets) are usually just down the hall. When you book a room in the mid-to-lower price categories, it's best to confirm your request for a room with ensuite facilities. Especially in London, rooms and bathrooms may be smaller than what you find in the United States.

Besides familiar international chains, England has some local chains that are worth a look; they provide rooms from the less expensive (Premier Travel Inn is a good value) to the trendy (ABode, Hotel du Vin, Malmaison).

Local Chains ABode (⊕ www.abodehotels. co.uk). **Hotel du Vin** (⊕ www.hotelduvin. com). **Malmaison** (☏ 845/365-4247 ⊕ www.malmaison.com). **Premier Travel Inn** (☏ 0870/242-8000, 1582/567890 outside U.K. ⊕ www.premiertravelinn.com).

LOCAL DO'S AND TABOOS

CUSTOMS OF THE COUNTRY

In general, British and American rules of etiquette are much the same. Differences are subtle. British people find Americans' and Canadians' bluntness somewhat startling from time to time, but are charmed by their friendliness.

British people tend to take politeness extremely seriously. They say "thank you" at every stage of a financial transaction, but are less likely to offer a "God bless you" should a stranger sneeze.

The famous British stiff upper lip is more relaxed these days, but on social occasions the best option is to observe what the others do, and then go with the flow. If you're visiting a family home, a gift of flowers is welcome, as is a bottle of wine, or maybe some candy for the children—but not all three.

GREETINGS

British people will shake hands on greeting old friends or acquaintances; female friends may greet each other with a kiss on the cheek. In Britain, you can never say "please," "thank you," or "sorry" too often; to thank your host, a phone call or thank-you card does nicely.

SIGHTSEEING

As in the United States, in public places it is considered polite to give up your seat to an elderly person, to a pregnant woman, or to a parent struggling with children and bags. Sometimes if only a woman is standing, men will offer her their seats. Jaywalking is not illegal in England and everybody does it.

British people take waiting in line (called queuing) incredibly seriously. They highly value patience, and will turn on "queue jumpers" who try to cut in line. Complaining while waiting in line is considered wimpy. Enduring the wait with good humor is considered a sign of strong moral character.

The single thing you can do that will most mark you as a tourist—and an impolite one—is fail to observe the written and spoken rule that, on virtually all escalators but especially those in Tube stations, you stand on the right side of the escalator and leave room for people to walk past you on the left.

OUT ON THE TOWN

Etiquette in restaurants is much the same as in any major U.S. city. In restaurants you hail a waiter by saying, "Excuse me . . ." as one passes by, or by trying to catch their eye by politely signaling with subtle hand signals. It is common to have drinks before dinner, and wine with dinner. Friends and co-workers frequently gather in pubs, but you don't have to drink alcohol—many people in the pub drink juice or sodas. Nonetheless, drunkenness can be common in major cities after 10 PM; many people take taxis to avoid drunk travelers.

You're generally expected to dress "casually smart" for the theater (suits or nice jackets for men, skirts or nice slacks for women), and those going to nightclubs will dress just the same here as they would in New York or Chicago—the flashier the better. Pubs are very casual places, however.

Smoking is forbidden in all public places, including bars and restaurants.

DOING BUSINESS

Punctuality is of prime importance; if you anticipate a late arrival, call ahead. For business dinners, if you proffered the invitation, it's usually assumed that you will pick up the tab. If you're the visitor, however, it's good form for the host to pay the bill. Alternatively, play it safe and offer to split the check.

HOTEL GRADING SYSTEM

Hotels, guesthouses, inns, and B&Bs in the United Kingdom are all graded from one to five stars by the tourism board, VisitBritain. Basically, the more stars a property has, the more facilities it has, and the facilities will be of a higher standard. It's a fairly good reflection of lodging from small B&Bs up to palatial hotels. The most luxurious hotels will have five stars; a simple, clean, acceptable hostelry will have one star.

DISCOUNTS AND DEALS

Hotel rates in major cities tend to be cheapest on weekends, whereas rural hotels are cheapest on weeknights. The lowest occupancy is between November and April, so hotels lower their prices substantially during these months.

In larger cities and in some towns, certain universities offer their residence halls to paying vacationers between terms. The facilities available are usually compact single sleeping units that share bath facilities, and they can be rented on a nightly basis. You can check with local tourist boards for information.

Lastminute.com offers deals on hotel rooms all over the United Kingdom. VisitLondon.com, London's official Web site, has some good deals. LondonTown.com's London Visitor Information Centre provides free maps, tourist information, and last-minute hotel bookings in the city, with savings of up to 50%. Its kiosk in Leicester Square is open daily 8 AM–11 PM.

Choice Hotels Europe (Clarion, Comfort, and Quality brands) offers 10% off accommodation for people age 55 and over.

Local Resources Choice Hotels (☎ *800/ 645-6200* ⊕ *www.choicehotels.com*).
Lastminute.com (⊕ *www.lastminute.com*).
LondonTown.com's London Visitor Information Centre (✉ *Leicester Sq.* ☎ *020/7292– 2333* ⊕ *www.londoninformationcentre.com*).

▌ COMMUNICATIONS

INTERNET

If you're traveling with a laptop, carry a spare battery and adapter. If you are going to use dial-up, get a telephone cord that's compatible with a British phone jack; these are available in Britain at airports and electronics stores. Wi-Fi is increasingly available in hotels, and broadband coverage is widespread in cities. Generally speaking, the pricier the hotel, the more likely you are to find Wi-Fi there. Wireless access is still rare in cafés and coffee shops, but Starbucks is spreading the word, and so its popularity there is likely to grow.

Contacts Cybercafes (⊕ *www.cybercafes. com*).

PHONES

British Telecom runs the telephone service in Great Britain and is generally reliable. All calls (including local calls) made within the United Kingdom are charged according to the time of day. The standard rate applies weekdays 8 AM to 6 PM; a cheaper rate is in effect weekdays 6 PM to 8 AM and all day on weekends, when it's even cheaper. A local call before 6 PM costs 20p for three minutes; this doubles to 40p for the same from a pay phone. A daytime call to the United States will cost 24p a minute on a regular phone (weekends are cheaper), 80p on a pay phone.

A word of warning: 0870 numbers are *not* toll-free numbers in Britain; in fact, numbers beginning with this or the 0900 (premium rate) prefix cost extra to call. The amount varies—and is usually relatively small when dialed from within the country—but can be excessive when dialed from outside Britain.

CALLING ENGLAND

The country code for Great Britain (and thus England) is 44. When dialing an English number from abroad, drop the initial 0 from the local area code. For example, let's say you're calling Buckingham Palace—020/7839-1377—from the United States. First, dial 011 (the international access code), then 44 (Great Britain's country code), then 20 (London's center-city code—without its initial 0), then the remainder of the telephone number.

CALLING WITHIN ENGLAND

All calls within England (and Britain) are local calls. Dial the area code (which usually begins with 01, except in London), followed by the telephone number.

Cell phones are very popular, and there are three types of pay phones: those that accept (a) only coins, (b) only British Telecom (BT) phone cards, or (c) BT phone cards and credit cards. Most coin-operated phones take 10p, 20p, 50p, and £1 coins. Insert the coins *before* dialing (minimum charge is 20p). The indicator panel shows how much money is left; add more whenever you like. If there is no answer, replace the receiver and your money will be returned.

For pay and other phones, if you hear a repeated single tone after dialing, the line is busy; a continuous tone means the number didn't work.

There are several different directory-assistance providers. For information anywhere in Britain, try dialing 118–888 or 118–118; you'll need to know the town and the street (or at least the neighborhood) of the person or organization for which you're requesting information. For the operator, dial 100.

CALLING OUTSIDE ENGLAND

For direct overseas dialing from England, dial 00, then the country code, area code, and number. For the international operator, credit card, or collect calls, dial 155; for international directory assistance, dial 118505.

The country code for the United States is 1.

Access Codes AT&T Direct (☎ *In the U.K., there are AT&T access numbers to dial the U.S. using three different phone types: 0500/890011 Cable & Wireless, 0800/890011 British Telecom, 0800/013–0011 AT&T*). **MCI WorldPhone** (☎ *0800/279–5088 in the U.K. for the U.S. via MCI*). **Sprint International Access** (☎ *0800/890877*).

CALLING CARDS

Public card phones operate with special cards that you can buy from post offices or newsstands. Ideal for longer calls, the cards are composed of units of 10p, and come in values of £3, £5, £10, and more. To use a card phone, lift the receiver, insert your card, and dial the number. An indicator panel shows the number of units used. At the end of your call the card will be returned. Where credit cards are taken, slide the card through, as indicated.

MOBILE PHONES

Any cell phone can be used in Europe if it's tri-band, quad-band, or GSM. Travelers should ask their cell-phone company if their phone fits in this category and make sure it is activated for international calling before leaving their home country. Roaming fees can be steep, however: $1 a minute is considered reasonable. And overseas you normally pay the toll charges for incoming calls. It's almost always cheaper to send a text message than to make a call, since text messages have a low set fee (often less than 25¢).

If you just want to make local calls, consider buying a new SIM card once you're in England (note that your provider may have to unlock your phone for you to use a different SIM card) and a prepaid service plan in the destination. You'll then have a local number and can make local calls at local rates. If your trip is extensive, you could simply buy a new cell phone in your destination.

You can rent a cell phone from most major car-rental agencies in England. Some upscale hotels now provide loaner cell phones to their guests. Beware, however, of the per-minute rates charged.

Contacts Cellular Abroad (☎ 800/287-5072 ⊕ www.cellularabroad.com). **Mobal** (☎ 888/888-9162 ⊕ www.mobalrental.com). **Planet Fone** (☎ 888/988-4777 ⊕ www. planetfone.com). **Renta Mobile Phone** (☎ 020/7353-7705 ⊕ www.rent-mobile-phone.com).

▋ CUSTOMS AND DUTIES

You're always allowed to bring goods of a certain value back home without having to pay any duty or import tax. But there's a limit on the amount of tobacco and liquor you can bring back duty-free, and some countries have separate limits for perfumes; for exact figures, check with your customs department. The values of so-called "duty-free" goods are included in these amounts. When you shop abroad, save all your receipts, as customs inspectors may ask to see them as well as the items you purchased. If the total value of your goods is more than the duty-free limit, you'll have to pay a tax (most often a flat percentage) on the value of everything beyond that limit.

Fresh meats, plants and vegetables, controlled drugs, and firearms and ammunition may not be brought into the United Kingdom. Pets from the United States or Canada with the proper documentation may be brought into the country without quarantine under the U.K. Pet Travel Scheme (PETS). The process takes about six months to complete and involves detailed steps.

You will face no customs formalities if you enter Scotland or Wales from any other part of the United Kingdom.

Information in England HM Customs and Excise (☎ 0208/929-0152, 0845/010-9000 advice service ⊕ www.hmce.gov.uk). **Pet Travel Scheme** (☎ 0870/241-1710 ⊕ www. defra.gov.uk/animalh/quarantine/index.htm).

U.S. Information U.S. Customs and Border Protection (⊕ www.cbp.gov).

▋ EATING OUT

The stereotypical notion of English meals as parades of roast beef, overcooked vegetables, and stodgy puddings (desserts) is gradually being replaced—particularly in London and other major cities—with an evolving picture of the country as hot foodie territory. From trendy gastro-pubs to the see-and-be-seen dining shrines, England is shedding its tired image and becoming known for a global palate.

In general, restaurant prices are high. If you're watching your budget, seek out pubs and ethnic restaurants.

CATEGORY	LONDON	ELSEWHERE
£	under £10	under £10
££	£10–£16	£10–£14
£££	£17–£23	£15–£19
££££	£24–£32	£20–£25
£££££	over £32	over £25

All prices are per person in pounds for a main course at dinner.

DISCOUNTS AND DEALS

Eating out in England's big cities in particular can be expensive, but you can do it cheaply. Try local cafés, often called workers' cafés, where heaping plates of English comfort food (bacon sandwiches and stuffed baked potatoes, for example) are served. England has plenty of the big names in fast food, as well as smaller places selling sandwiches, fish-and-chips, burgers, falafel, kebabs, and the like. For a local touch, check out curry houses; Indian food is popular throughout the country. Marks & Spencer, Sainsbury's, Tesco, and Waitrose are chain supermarkets with outlets throughout the country. They're good choices for groceries, premade sandwiches, or picnic fixings.

MEALS AND MEALTIMES

Cafés serving the traditional English breakfast of eggs, bacon, beans, half a grilled tomato, and strong tea are often the cheapest—and most authentic—places for breakfast. For lighter morning fare (or for real brewed coffee), try the continental-style sandwich bars and coffee shops—the Pret-a-Manger chain being one of the largest—offering croissants and other pastries.

At lunch you can grab a sandwich between sights, pop into the local pub, or sit down in a restaurant. Dinner, too, has no set rules, but a three-course meal is standard in most mid-range or high-end restaurants. Pre- or post-theater menus, offering two or three courses for a set price, are usually a good value.

Note that most pubs do not have any waitstaff and that you are expected to go to the bar, order a beverage and your meal, and inform them of your table number. Also, in cities many pubs do not serve food after 3 PM, so they're usually a better lunch option than dinner.

On Sunday, for pure Englishness, a traditional roast beef, pork, or lamb dinner still tops the list. Its typical accompaniment is Yorkshire pudding—a savory soufflé-like batter of eggs, milk, and flour oven-baked until crisp, then topped with a rich, dark gravy. Shepherd's pie, a classic pub dish, is made with diced or minced lamb and a mashed-potato topping, and "bangers and mash" are English sausages with mashed potatoes and onion gravy. In the pubs, you'll also find a ploughman's lunch—crusty bread, English cheese (perhaps cheddar, blue Stilton, crumbly Cheshire, or smooth red Leicester), and pickles. And there's also fish-and-chips, usually made from cod or haddock deepfried in a crispy batter and served with thick french fries. Take time for afternoon tea—whether with scones (with cream and

jam, called a "cream tea") and pastries or just a hot cup of Assam—at least once on your stay; it's a civilized respite.

Breakfast is generally served between 7:30 and 9, lunch between noon and 2, dinner or supper between 7:30 and 9:30, sometimes earlier, seldom later except in large cities. These days tea is rarely a proper meal anymore (it was once served between 4:30 and 6), and tea shops are often open all day in touristy areas (they're not found at all in nontouristy places). So you can have a cup and pastry or sandwich whenever you feel you need it. Sunday roasts at pubs last from 11 AM or noon to 3 PM.

Smoking is banned in pubs, clubs, and restaurants throughout Britain.

PAYING

Credit cards are widely accepted in restaurants, but not in pubs, which generally still require cash (although a growing minority are taking plastic). Be sure that you don't double-pay a service charge. Many restaurants exclude service charges from the printed menu (which the law obliges them to display outside), and then add 10% to 15% to the check. Others will stamp SERVICE NOT INCLUDED along the bottom of the bill, in which case you should add 10% to 15%.

PUBS

A common misconception among visitors to England is that pubs are bars. Pubs are also gathering places, conversation zones, even restaurants. In many pubs alcohol is almost an afterthought. Pubs are, generally speaking, where people go to meet their friends and catch up on one another's lives. In small towns pubs act almost as town halls. Many people in a pub drink soft drinks, tea, or coffee, rather than beer, and hard liquor is usually in short supply. Even if you don't drink alcohol, go to a pub and have an orange juice or a soda, relax, and meet the locals. Traditionally pub hours are 11–11, with last orders called about 20 minutes before closing time, but pubs can choose to stay open until midnight or 1 AM, or later.

Most pubs tend to be child-friendly, but others have restricted hours for children. If a pub serves food, it will generally allow children in during the day with adults. Some pubs are stricter than others, though, and will not admit anyone younger than 18. Some will allow children in during the day, but only until 6 PM. If you're in doubt, ask the bartender. Family-friendly pubs tend to be packed with kids, parents, and all of their accoutrements, so you can just use your common sense. Some even have children's play areas with jungle gyms and toys.

RESERVATIONS AND DRESS

Regardless of where you are, it's a good idea to make a reservation if you can. We mention them specifically only when reservations are essential or when they are not accepted. For popular restaurants, book as far ahead as you can (often 30 days), and reconfirm as soon as you arrive. (Large parties should always call ahead to check the reservations policy.) We mention dress only when men are required to wear a jacket or a jacket and tie.

Online reservation services aren't as popular in England as in the United States, but Toptable has a fair number of listings in England.

Contact **Toptable** (⊕ *www.toptable.co.uk).*

WINES, BEER, AND SPIRITS

Although hundreds of varieties of beer are brewed around the country, the traditional brew is known as bitter and is not carbonated; it's usually served at room temperature. Fizzy American-style beer is called lager. There are also plenty of other potations: stouts like Guinness and Murphy's are thick, pitch-black brews you'll either love or hate; ciders, made from apples, are an alcoholic drink in Britain (Bulmer's and Strongbow are the names to remember); shandies (oddly) are a low-alcohol mix of lager and lemon soda. Real ales, which have a natural second fermentation in the cask, have a shorter shelf life (so many are brewed locally) but special flavor; these are worth seeking out. Generally the selection and quality of cocktails is higher in a wine bar or café than in a pub. The legal drinking age is 18.

▮ ECOTOURISM

Ecotourism is an emerging trend in the United Kingdom. The Shetland Environmental Agency Ltd. runs the Green Tourism Business Scheme (GTBS), a program that evaluates sites and lodgings in England, Scotland, and Wales and gives them a gold, silver, or bronze rating according to their sustainability. You can find a list of green hotels, B&Bs, apartments, and other properties on the GTBS Web site. Also check out the VisitBritain Web site, which has information and tips about green travel in Britain.

Contact **Green Tourism Business Scheme** (☎ *01738/632162* ⊕ *www.green-business. co.uk).* **VisitBritain** (⊕ *www.visitbritain.us).*

▮ ELECTRICITY

The electrical current in Great Britain is 220–240 volts (in line with the rest of Europe), 50 cycles alternating current (AC); wall outlets take three-pin plugs, and shaver sockets take two round, oversize prongs. Blackouts and brownouts are rare and are usually fixed in a few hours.

Consider making a small investment in a universal adapter, which has several types of plugs in one lightweight, compact unit. Most laptops and mobile phone chargers are dual voltage (i.e., they operate equally well on 110 and 220 volts), so require only an adapter. These days the same is true of small appliances such as hair dryers. Always check labels and manufacturer instructions. Don't use 110-volt outlets marked FOR SHAVERS ONLY for high-wattage appliances such as hair dryers.

Contacts Steve Kropla's Help for World Travelers (⊕ www.kropla.com). **Walkabout Travel Gear** (⊕ www.walkabouttravelgear.com).

▮ EMERGENCIES

If you need to report an emergency, dial 999 for police, fire, or ambulance. Be prepared to give the telephone number you're calling from. You can get 24-hour treatment in Accident and Emergency at British hospitals, although you should expect to wait hours for treatment. Prescriptions are valid only if made out by doctors registered in the United Kingdom.

Although England has a subsidized National Health Service, free at the point of service for British residents, foreign visitors are expected to pay for any treatment they receive. Expect to receive a bill after you return home. Check with your health-insurance company to make sure you're covered. Some British hospitals now require a credit card or other forms of payment before they'll offer treatment.

U.S. Embassies American Embassy (⊠ 24 Grosvenor Sq., London ☎ 020/7499–9000 ⊕ www.usembassy.org.uk). **U.S. Passport Unit** (⊠ 55 Upper Brook St., London ☎ 020/7499–9000).

General Emergency Contacts Ambulance, fire, police (☎ 999).

▮ HEALTH

SPECIFIC ISSUES IN ENGLAND

If you take prescription drugs, keep a supply in your carry-on luggage and make a list of all your prescriptions to keep on file

at home while you are abroad. You will not be able to renew a U.S. prescription at a pharmacy in Britain. Prescriptions are accepted only if issued by a U.K.-registered physician.

OVER-THE-COUNTER REMEDIES

Over-the-counter medications in England are similar to those in the United States, with a few significant differences. Medications are sold in boxes rather than bottles, and are sold in very small amounts—usually no more than 12 pills. There are also fewer brands. All headache medicine is usually filed under the "painkillers." You can buy generic ibuprofen or a popular European brand of ibuprofen, Nurofen. Tylenol is not sold in the United Kingdom, but its main ingredient, acetaminophen, is—although, confusingly, it's called paracetomol.

Among sinus and allergy medicines, Claritin is the main option here; it's the same brand sold in the United States. Some medicines are pretty much the same as brands sold in the United States—instead of Nyquil cold medicine, there's Night Nurse, and instead of Dayquil, there's Day Nurse. The most popular over-the-counter cough medicine is Benylin.

Drugstores are generally called pharmacies, but sometimes referred to as chemists' shops. The biggest drugstore chain in the country is Boots, which has outlets everywhere, except for the smallest towns. If you're in a rural area, look for shops marked with a sign of a green cross.

If you can't find what you're looking for, ask at the counter; many over-the-counter medicines are kept behind the cash register.

SHOTS AND MEDICATIONS

No special shots are required or suggested for England.

Health Warnings National Centers for Disease Control & Prevention (CDC ☎ 877/394–8747 international travelers' health line ⊕ wwwn.cdc.gov/travel). **World Health Organization** (WHO ⊕ www.who.int).

▌ HOURS OF OPERATION

Most banks are open weekdays from 9:30 until 3:30 or 4:30. Some have Thursday evening hours, and a few are open Saturday morning. Many offices are open weekdays 9:30–5:30.

The major national museums and galleries are open daily from 9 until 6, including lunchtime, but have shorter hours on Sunday. Regional museums are usually closed Monday and have shorter hours in winter. In London many museums are open late one evening a week.

Independently owned pharmacies are generally open Monday through Saturday 9:30 to 5:30, although in larger cities some stay open until 10 PM; local newspapers list which pharmacies are open late.

Usual business hours are Monday through Saturday 9 to 5:30, Sunday noon to 4. Outside the main centers most shops close at 1 PM once a week, often Wednesday or Thursday. In small villages many also close for lunch and do not open on Sunday at all. In large cities—especially London—department stores stay open late (usually until 7:30 or 8) one night a week, usually Thursday. On national holidays most stores are closed, and over the Christmas holidays most restaurants are closed as well.

HOLIDAYS

Holidays are January 1, New Year's Day; Good Friday and Easter Monday; May Day (first Monday in May); spring and summer bank holidays (last Monday in May and August, respectively); December 25, Christmas Day; and December 26, Boxing Day (day after Christmas). If any of these holidays falls on a weekend, then the holiday is observed on the following Monday. During the Christmas holidays many restaurants, as well as museums and other attractions, may close for at least a week—call to verify hours. Book hotels for Christmas travel well in advance, and check whether the hotel restaurant will be open.

▌ MAIL

Stamps can be bought from post offices (open weekdays 9 to 5:30, Saturday 9 to noon), from stamp machines outside post offices, and from news dealers' stores and newsstands. Mailboxes, known as post or letter boxes, are painted bright red. Allow 7 days for a letter to reach the United States and about 10 days to two weeks to Australia or New Zealand by airmail. Surface mail service can take up to four or five weeks. The useful Royal Mail Web site has information on everything from buying stamps to finding a post office.

Airmail letters up to 10 grams (0.35 ounce) to North America cost 70p; postcards cost 50p. Letters within Britain are 39p for first class, 28p for second class (these rates are subject to change).

Contact Royal Mail (⊕ *www.royalmail.com*).

SHIPPING PACKAGES

Most department stores and retail outlets can ship your goods home. You should check your insurance for coverage of possible damage. Private delivery companies such as Federal Express and DHL offer two-day delivery service to the United States, but you'll pay a considerable amount for the privilege.

Express Services DHL (☎ *0870/110–0300* ⊕ *www.dhl.co.uk*). **Federal Express** (☎ *0800/123800* ⊕ *www.fedex.com*). **Parcelforce** (☎ *0870/850–1150* ⊕ *www.parcelforce.co.uk*).

▌ MEDIA

NEWSPAPERS AND MAGAZINES

The main serious national newspapers in England are the *Times,* the *Telegraph,* the *Independent,* and the *Guardian* (the *Observer* is the *Guardian*'s Sunday paper). Each has a political viewpoint in both its news coverage and its opinion pages. The *Times* and *Telegraph* are more conservative, whereas the *Independent* and *Guardian* take a more left-wing approach. Tabloids, such as the *Sun,* the *Mirror,* and the *Daily Mail*, present a notably livelier version of the news, with an emphasis on celebrities, nudity, sports, and scandal. They, too, have political agendas: the *Sun* and *Daily Mail* are both conservative, whereas the *Mirror* is liberal. This is more significant to the English than it likely will be for you—English people may make sweeping generalizations about one another based upon which newspaper is tucked under one's arm.

For detailed information about what's going on in London, pick up a copy of *Time Out* magazine. For countrywide information about shops, restaurants, and art events, peruse the glossy monthly magazines: *Tatler, Country Living, Harpers & Queen, Vogue, Wallpaper, World of Interiors, House & Garden.*

TELEVISION

The main television channels are BBC1 and BBC2 from the British Broadcasting Corporation. BBC2 is considered the more eclectic and artsy, with a higher proportion of alternative humor, drama, and documentaries. The independent channels are ITV (Independent Television); Channel 4, which offers a mixture of mainstream and off-the-wall programming; and Channel 5, which has more sports and films. Cable channels increase the diet of entertainment.

▌ MONEY

No doubt about it, prices in England can seem high because of the exchange rate. The rate has improved during the ongoing recession, though: between this and the increased availability of deals, the country has become more affordable. London remains one of the most expensive cities in the world. However, for every yin there's a yang, and travelers can get breaks: staying in bed-and-breakfasts or renting a city apartment brings down lodging costs, and national museums are free. The chart below gives some ideas of the kinds of prices you can expect to pay for day-to-day life.

ITEM	AVERAGE COST
Cup of Coffee	£1.50–£3
Glass of Wine	£3.50 in a pub or wine bar, £5.50 or more in a restaurant
Glass of Beer	£2.70 or more
Sandwich	£3.50
One-Mile Taxi Ride in London	£5
Museum Admission	National museums free; others £5–£10

Prices throughout this guide are given for adults. Substantially reduced fees—generally referred to as "concessions" throughout Great Britain—are almost always available for children, students, and senior citizens.

▐ TIP➔ Banks never have every foreign currency on hand, and it may take as long as a week to order. If you're planning to exchange funds before leaving home, don't wait till the last minute.

ATMS AND BANKS

Make sure before leaving home that your credit and debit cards have been programmed for ATM use abroad—ATMs in England and Wales accept PINs of four or fewer digits only; if your PIN is longer, ask about changing it. If you know your PIN as a word, learn the numerical equivalent, since most keypads in England show numbers only, not letters. Most ATMs are on both the Cirrus and Plus networks. ATMs are available at most main-street banks, large supermarkets such as Sainsbury's and Tesco's, some Tube stops in London, and many rail stations. Major banks include Barclays, HSBC, and NatWest.

Your own bank will probably charge a fee for using ATMs abroad; the foreign bank you use may also charge a fee. Nevertheless, you'll usually get a better rate of exchange at an ATM than you will at a currency-exchange office or even when changing money in a bank. And extracting funds as you need them is a safer option than carrying around a large amount of cash.

CREDIT CARDS

Throughout this guide the following abbreviations are used: **AE**, American Express; **DC**, Diners Club; **MC**, Master-Card; and **V**, Visa.

The Discover card is not accepted throughout Britain. Other major credit cards are accepted virtually everywhere in Britain; however, you're expected to know and use your pin number for all transactions—even for credit cards, so it's a good idea to do some quick memorization for whichever card you intend to use in England.

Inform your credit-card company before you travel, especially if you're going abroad and don't travel internationally very often. Otherwise, the credit-card company might put a hold on your card owing to unusual activity. Record all your credit-card numbers in a safe place. Both MasterCard and Visa have general numbers you can call (collect if you're abroad) if your card is lost, but you're better off calling the number of your issuing bank, since MasterCard and Visa usually just transfer you to your bank; your bank's number is usually printed on your card.

If you plan to use your credit card for cash advances, you'll need to apply for a PIN at least two weeks before your trip. Although it's usually cheaper (and safer) to use a credit card abroad for large purchases (so you can cancel payments or be reimbursed if there's a problem), note that some credit-card companies *and* the banks that issue them add substantial percentages to all foreign transactions, whether they're in a foreign currency or not. Check on these fees before leaving home.

Reporting Lost Cards American Express (☎ 800/992–3404 in U.S., 336/393–1111 collect from abroad ⊕ www.americanexpress. com). **Diners Club** (☎ 800/234–6377 in U.S., 303/799–1504 collect from abroad ⊕ www. dinersclub.com). **MasterCard** (☎ 800/622–7747 in U.S., 636/722–7111 collect from abroad ⊕ www.mastercard.com). **Visa** (☎ 800/847–2911 in U.S., 410/581–9994 collect from abroad ⊕ www.visa.com).

CURRENCY AND EXCHANGE

The unit of currency in Great Britain is the pound sterling (£), divided into 100 pence (p). The bills (called notes in Britain) are 50, 20, 10, and 5 pounds. Coins are £2, £1, 50p, 20p, 10p, 5p, 2p, and 1p. If you are traveling beyond England and Wales, note that Scotland and the Channel Islands have their own bills, and the Channel Islands their own coins, too. Scottish bills are accepted in the rest of Britain, but you cannot use Channel Islands currency outside the islands.

At the time of this writing, the exchange rate was about U.S. $1.60 to £1.

British post offices exchange currency with no fee, and at decent rates.

■ TIP→ Even if a currency-exchange booth has a sign promising no commission, rest assured that there's some kind of huge, hidden fee. And as for rates, you're almost always better off getting foreign currency at an ATM or exchanging money at a bank.

Currency Conversion Google (⊕ www. google.com). **Oanda.com** (⊕ www.oanda.com). **XE.com** (⊕ www.xe.com).

■ PACKING

England can be cool, damp, and overcast, even in summer. You'll want a heavy coat for winter and a lightweight coat or warm jacket for summer. There's no time of year when a raincoat or umbrella won't come in handy. For the cities, pack as you would for an American city: coats and ties for expensive restaurants and nightspots, casual clothes elsewhere. Jeans are popular in England and are perfectly acceptable for sightseeing and informal dining. Casual blazers are popular here with men. For women, ordinary street dress is acceptable everywhere. If you plan to stay in budget hotels, take your own soap. It's also a good idea to take a washcloth.Pack insect repellent if you plan to hike.

▌ PASSPORTS

U.S. citizens need only a valid passport to enter Great Britain for stays of up to six months. Travelers should be prepared to show sufficient funds to support and accommodate themselves while in Britain (credit cards will usually suffice for this) and to show a return or onward ticket. If you're within six months of your passport's expiration date, renew it before you leave—nearly extinct passports are not strictly banned, but they make immigration officials anxious, and may cause you problems. Health certificates are not required.

▌ RESTROOMS

Public restrooms are sparse in England, although most big cities maintain public facilities that are clean and modern. If there is an attendant, which is rare, you are expected to pay admission (usually 30p). Train stations and department stores have public restrooms that occasionally charge a small fee, usually 30p. Most pubs, restaurants, and even fast-food chains reserve their bathrooms for customer use only. Hotels and museums are usually a good place to find clean, free facilities. On the road, gas-station facilities are usually clean and free.

Find a Loo The Bathroom Diaries (⊕ www.thebathroomdiaries.com).

▌ SAFETY

England has a low incidence of violent crime. However, petty crime is on the rise, and tourists can be the target, although this problem is limited almost exclusively to city centers such as London, Birmingham, and Liverpool.

Use common sense. When in a city center, if you're paying at a shop or a restaurant, never put your wallet down or let your bag out of your hand. When sitting on a chair in a public place, keep your purse on your lap or between your feet. Always use the bag hooks in public toilet stalls instead of putting your bag on the floor where it may be snatched.

Don't wear expensive jewelry or watches. Store your passport in the hotel safe; use your driver's license for identification, although you'll never be asked for it. Don't leave anything in your car.

In recent years there have been a few terrorist incidents in England, usually on public transportation. While traveling, don't leave any bags unattended, as they may be viewed as a security risk and taken away by the authorities. If bags are taken away, they will be destroyed. If you see an unattended bag on the train, bus, or Tube, find a worker and report it, but do not touch the bag yourself. Never hesitate to get off of a Tube, train, or bus if you feel unsafe.

Although scams do occur in Britain, they are not pervasive. Do, however, watch out for pickpockets, particularly in London. They often work in pairs, one distracting you in some way. Always take a licensed black taxi or call a car service (sometimes called minicabs) recommended by your hotel. Avoid using minicab services offered by drivers who approach you on the street. In most cases they will overcharge you. Always buy theater tickets from a reputable dealer. If you are driving in from a British port, beware of thieves posing as customs officials. The thieves stop travelers after they have followed them from the port. Then they flag them down and "confiscate illegal goods."

If you're getting money out of an ATM, beware of someone bumping into you to distract you. You may want to use ATMs inside banks rather than those outside them. In London scams are most common at ATMs on Oxford Street and around Piccadilly Circus.

▌TIP→ **Distribute your cash, credit cards, IDs, and other valuables between a deep front pocket, an inside jacket or vest pocket, and a hidden money pouch. Don't reach for the money pouch once you're in public.**

General Information and Warnings **Transportation Security Administration** (*TSA* ⊕ *www.tsa.gov*). **U.K. Foreign & Commonwealth Office** (⊕ *www.fco.gov.uk/travel*). **U.S. Department of State** (⊕ *www.travel.state. gov*).

▌ SIGHTSEEING PASSES

DISCOUNT PASSES

If you plan to visit castles, gardens, and historic houses during your stay in England and Wales, look into discount passes or organization memberships that can provide significant savings. Just be sure to match what the pass or membership offers against your itinerary to see if it's worthwhile.

The National Trust, English Heritage, and the Historic Houses Association each encompass hundreds of properties. English Heritage's Overseas Visitors Pass costs £19 for a 7-day pass and £23 for a 14-day pass for one adult. You can order it in advance by phone or online, or get the order form online and then submit it by fax or mail. If you are traveling within 21 days, you can purchase the pass at a participating property in England. The National Trust Touring Pass, for overseas visitors, must be purchased in advance of a visit; it is sold online or by phone but not at the properties. A 7-day pass is £20; a 14-day pass is £25.

VisitBritain's Great British Heritage Pass is £30 for 4 days, £44 for one week, and £59 for 15 days, and includes more than 500 properties belonging to English Heritage and the National Trust. The pass is sold online and at major tourist information centers in Britain. Family passes are available, too. Annual membership in the National Trust (through the Royal Oak Foundation, the U.S. affiliate) is $55 a year, versus £46 if you join in Britain. English Heritage membership is £40, and the Historic Houses Association is £36. Memberships entitle you to free entry to properties.

For London Pass information, Chapter 2. For passes specifically for Wales, Chapter 15.seesee

Information **English Heritage** (☎ *0870/ 333–1181* ⊕ *www.english-heritage.org. uk*). **Great British Heritage Pass** (⊕ *www. britishheritagepass.com*). **Historic Houses Association** (☎ *01464/896–688* ⊕ *www.hha. org.uk*). **National Trust** (☎ *0844/800–1895* ⊕ *www.nationaltrust.org.uk*). **Royal Oak Foundation** (☎ *212/480–2889 or 800/913–6565* ⊕ *www.royal-oak.org*).

▌ SPORTS AND THE OUTDOORS

In addition to the associations listed below, VisitBritain and local Tourist Information Centres can recommend places to enjoy your favorite sport.

BIKING

The national body promoting cycle touring is the Cyclists' Touring Club (CTC: £35 a year). Members get free advice and route information, a bed-and-breakfast handbook, and a magazine. The CTC and VisitBritain publish a free guide, "Britain for Cyclists." Both the CTC and VisitBritain provide lists of travel agencies specializing in cycling vacations.

Contacts **Cyclists' Touring Club** (☎ *01483/ 417217 or 0870/873–0061* ⊕ *www.ctc.org.uk*). **VisitBritain** (⊕ *www.visitbritain.us*).

BOATING

Boating can be a leisurely way to explore the countryside. For boat-rental operators along Britain's several hundred miles of historic canals and waterways, from the Norfolk Broads to the Lake District, contact the Association of Pleasure Craft Operators or Waterway Holidays UK. British Waterways has maps and other information. Waterway Holidays UK arranges boat accommodations of all kinds, from traditional narrow boats (small, slender barges) to motorboats and sailboats.

Contacts **Association of Pleasure Craft Operators** (☎ *01952/813572* ⊕ *www.apco.*

org.uk). **British Waterways** (☎ *01923/ 201120* ⊕ *www.waterscape.com*). **Waterway Holidays UK** (☎ *0870/241–5956* ⊕ *www. waterwaysholidaysuk.com*).

GOLF

Originally invented in Scotland, golf is a beloved pastime all over England. Some courses take advantage of spectacular natural settings, from the ocean to mountain backdrops. Most courses are reserved for club members and adhere to strict rules of protocol and dress. However, many famous courses can be used by visiting golfers if they reserve well in advance. Package tours with companies such as Golf International and Owenoak International Golf Travel allow visitors into usually exclusive clubs. For further information on courses, fees, and locations, try the Web site UK Golf Guide.

Contacts Golf International (☎ *212/ 986–9176, 800/833–1389 in U.S.* ⊕ *www. golfinternational.com*). **Owenoak International Golf Travel** (☎ *203/854–9000, 800/426–4498 in U.S.* ⊕ *www.owenoak.com*). **UK Golf Guide** (⊕ *www.uk-golfguide.com*).

WALKING

Walking and hiking, from the slowest ramble to a mountainside climb requiring technical equipment, are enormously popular in England. For information about stunning National Trails visit ⊕ *www. nationaltrail.co.uk*. The Ramblers' Association publishes a magazine and a yearbook full of resources, and a list of B&Bs within 2 mi of selected long-distance footpaths. Some of the best maps for walking are the Explorer Maps, published by the Ordnance Survey; check out ⊕ *www. ordnancesurvey.co.uk*.

Contacts Natural England (☎ *0845/600– 3078* ⊕ *www.naturalengland.gov.uk*). **Long Distance Walkers Association** (☎ *01753/866685* ⊕ *www.ldwa.org.uk*). **The Ramblers' Association** (☎ *020/7339–8500* ⊕ *www.ramblers.org.uk*).

▌ TAXES

An airport departure tax of £20 (£10 for travel within U.K. and EU countries) per person is included in the price of your ticket.

The British sales tax (V.A.T., Value Added Tax) is 17.5%. The tax is almost always included in quoted prices in shops, hotels, and restaurants. The most common exception is at high-end hotels, where prices often exclude V.A.T. Be sure to verify whether the room price includes V.A.T. Outside of hotels and rental-car agencies, which have specific additional taxes, there is no other sales tax in England.

Most travelers can get a V.A.T. refund by either the Retail Export or the more cumbersome Direct Export method. Refunds apply for V.A.T. only on goods being taken out of Britain, and purchases must exceed a minimum limit (check with the store—generally £50–£100). Many large stores provide V.A.T.-refund services, but only if you request them; they will handle the paperwork. For the Retail Export method, you must ask the store to complete Form V.A.T. 407 (you must have identification—passports are best), to be given to customs at your last port of departure. Have the form stamped like any customs form by customs officials when you leave the country or, if you're visiting several European Union countries, when you leave the EU. Be ready to show customs officials what you've bought; budget extra time at the airport for this. After you're through passport control, take the form to a refund-service counter for an on-the-spot refund (if the retailer has an agreement with the firm running the counter; ask the store when you make your purchase), or mail it back to the store or a refund service from the airport or after you arrive home. The refund will be forwarded to you in about eight weeks, minus a service charge, either in the form of a credit to your charge card or as a British check, which American banks charge you to convert.

With the Direct Export method, the goods are mailed directly to your home; you must have a Form V.A.T. 407 certified by customs, police, or a notary public when you get home and then sent back to the store, which will refund your money. For inquiries, call the local Customs & Excise office listed in the telephone directory. Remember, V.A.T. refunds can't be processed after you arrive back home.

Another option is a refund service, which processes refunds for most shops. Global Refund is a Europe-wide service with 225,000 affiliated stores and more than 700 refund counters at major airports and border crossings. Its refund form, called a Tax Free Check, is the most common across the European continent. The service issues refunds in the form of cash, check, or credit-card adjustment.

V.A.T. Refunds Global Refund (☎ *800/566–9828* ⊕ *www.globalrefund.com*). **Her Majesty's Revenue & Customs** (☎ *0845/010–9000 within U.K., 2920/501261 from outside U.K.* ⊕ *www.hmrc.gov.uk*).

▍ TIME

England sets its clocks by Greenwich Mean Time, five hours ahead of the U.S. East Coast. British summer time (GMT plus one hour) generally coincides with American daylight saving time adjustments.

Time Zones Timeanddate.com (⊕ *www.timeanddate.com/worldclock*).

▍ TIPPING

Tipping is done in Britain just as in the United States, but at a lower level than you would back home. Tipping more can look like you're showing off. Do not tip movie or theater ushers, elevator operators, or bar staff in pubs—although you can always offer to buy them a drink. There's no need to tip at clubs (it's acceptable at posher establishments, though) unless you're being served at your table.

TIPPING GUIDELINES FOR ENGLAND	
Bartender	£1–£2 per round of drinks, depending on the number of drinks, except in pubs where tipping is not the custom
Bellhop	£1 per bag, depending on the level of the hotel
Hotel Concierge	£5 or more, if he or she performs a service for you
Hotel Doorman	£1 if he helps you get a cab
Hotel Maid	It's extremely rare for hotel maids to be tipped; £1 or £2 would be generous.
Hotel Room-Service Waiter	Nothing, if a service charge is added to the bill
Porter at Airport or Train Station	£1 per bag
Skycap at Airport	£1 per bag checked
Taxi Driver	10%–15%, perhaps a little more for a short ride
Tour Guide	Tipping optional: £1 or £2 is generous.
Waiter	10%–15%, with 15% being the norm at high-end London restaurants; nothing additional if a service charge is added to the bill. Check your bill carefully, or ask.
Other	Restroom attendants in more expensive restaurants expect some small change or £1. Tip coat-check personnel £1 unless there is a fee, then nothing. Hairdresser and barbers get 10%–15%.

▍ TOURS

Visiting London on a fully escorted tour can feel a bit unnecessary because of its extensive public transport and wide network of taxicabs. There are ample tour companies offering day tours to the city's sights highlights, and getting around is fairly easy. However, there can be cost advantages to booking all-inclusive trips.

If you're planning to travel beyond London, packaged tours can be very useful, particularly for those who don't want to rent a car or take trains and strike out on their own. Because many sights are off the beaten track and not accessible by public transportation—particularly castles, great houses, and small villages—tour groups make the country accessible to all. There are a few downsides to escorted tours: rooms in castles and medieval houses tend to be small and can feel overrun when tour groups roll in.

Dozens of companies offer fully guided tours in Britain. Most of these are full packages including hotels, all food, and transportation costs in one flat fee. Because each tour company has different specialties, do a bit of research—either on your own or through a travel agent—before booking. You'll want to know about the hotels you'll be staying in, how big your group is likely to be, precisely how your days will be structured, and who the other people are likely to be.

Among the most reliable tour companies, two U.S.-based companies—Trafalgar Tours and Globus & Cosmos Tours—specialize in moderately priced trips that feature plenty of sights but not much in the way of five-star hotels. Both offer fairly comprehensive, two-week tours within Britain, as well as shorter, less wide-ranging trip options. Tauck is another well-established company. At the high end of the price scale is Abercrombie & Kent, known for luxurious tours that include everything from castle hotels to journeys on vintage railways.

Contacts Abercrombie & Kent (☎ *800/323–7308* ⊕ *www.abercrombiekent.com*). **Globus & Cosmos Tours** (☎ *800/338–7092* ⊕ *www. globusandcosmos.com*). **Tauck** (☎ *800/788–7885* ⊕ *www.tauck.com*). **Trafalgar Tours** (☎ *800/854–0103* ⊕ *www.trafalgartours.com*).

SPECIAL-INTEREST TOURS

CULINARY

Britain's foodie culture is increasingly rich and thriving. Gourmet on Tour, a U.S.-based tour company, offers vacations dominated by cooking, eating, and fine wine.

Contacts Gourmet on Tour (☎ *646/461–6088* ⊕ *www.gourmetontour.com*).

GARDENS

England is a land of garden lovers, and its gardens are varied and impressive. Tarka Garden tours offers small-group tours of gardens in Devon and Somerset. The American tour companies Coopersmiths and Lynott Tours offer tours of gardens around Britain. The Web site ⊕ *www. gardenvisit.com* is a useful reference site.

Contacts Adderley Travel Ltd. (☎ *01953/ 606906* ⊕ *www.adderleytravel.com*). **Coopersmiths** (☎ *415/669–1914* ⊕ *www. coopersmiths.com*). **Flora Garden Tours** (☎ *01366/328946* ⊕ *www.flora-garden-tours.co.uk*). **Lynott Tours** (☎ *800/221–2474* ⊕ *www.lynotttours.com*). **Tarka Garden Tours** (☎ *01271/375002* ⊕ *www.tarkagardentours. co.uk*).

HEALTH

You can relax with yoga and spa-based holidays throughout the United Kingdom. Lotus Journeys offers some good options.

Contact Lotus Journeys (☎ *0208/968–3666* ⊕ *www.lotusjourneys.com*).

HIKING AND WALKING

For those who prefer to spend their vacations on the move, Adventureline will keep you on your bike, on your feet, or swinging from hillsides. Country Walkers and England Lakeland Ramblers, based in the United States, have guided walks in Britain.

Contacts Adventureline (☎ *01209/820847* ⊕ *www.adventureline.co.uk*). **Country Walkers** (☎ *800/464–9255* ⊕ *www.countrywalkers. com*). **England Lakeland Ramblers** (☎ *800/ 724–8801* ⊕ *www.ramblers.com*).

▮ VISITOR INFORMATION

ONLINE TRAVEL TOOLS

ALL ABOUT ENGLAND AND WALES

Britain USA (⊕ *www.britainusa.com*) is Britain's official Web site for the United States. Enjoy England (⊕ *www. enjoyengland.com*), part of VisitBritain, includes a handy list of local Tourist Information Centres. VisitBritain (⊕ *www. visitbritain.us*), the official visitor Web site, focuses on information most helpful to England-bound U.S. travelers, from practical information to money-saving deals; you can even find out about movie locations. Visit London (⊕ *www.visitlondon. com*) is packed with information and can help you book your accommodation. VisitWales (⊕ *www.visitwales.com*) is the official site for Wales.

GARDENS

The National Gardens Scheme opens private gardens to the public.

Contact National Gardens Scheme (⊕ *www. ngs.org.uk*).

HISTORIC SITES

British Monarchy has an official Web site with practical information about visiting royal homes and more. English Heritage cares for historic properties; look into discount passes sold at properties or online. The Great Britain Heritage Pass, created by VisitBritain, offers free entry to more than 600 attractions. You can buy it online. The National Trust offers information about castles and stately homes. Check about National Trust membership and discount passes sold before your trip

Contacts British Monarchy (⊕ *www.royal. gov.uk*). **English Heritage** (⊕ *www.english-heritage.org.uk*). **Great Britain Heritage Pass** (⊕ *www.britishheritagepass.com*). **National Trust** (⊕ *www.nationaltrust.org.uk*).

MUSEUMS AND THE ARTS

The London Theatre Guide, created by the Society of London Theatre, presents what's on and sells tickets. Culture 24 is a nonprofit, partly government-funded site packed with information about publicly

funded museums (including special exhibits), art galleries, and historic sights.

Contacts London Theatre Guide (⊕ *www. officiallondontheatre.co.uk*). **Culture 24** (☎ *01273/623266* ⊕ *www.culture24.org.uk*).

VISITOR INFORMATION OFFICES

In many towns there are local and regional tourist information centers, and many have Web sites. The Britain and London Visitor Centre (open weekdays 9:30 to 6:30, weekends 10 to 4) provides details about travel, accommodations, and entertainment for London and the whole of Britain, but you need to visit the center in person to get information.

In London Britain and London Visitor Centre (✉ *1 Regent St., Piccadilly Circus* ☎ *No phone* ⊕ *www.visitbritain.com*).

In the U.S. VisitBritain (✉ *551 5th Ave., 7th fl., New York, NY* ☎ *212/986–2200 or 800/462–2748* ⊕ *www.visitbritain.us*).

INDEX

ABOUT OUR WRITERS

Longtime contributor Robert Andrews loves warm beer and soggy moors, but hates shopping malls and the sort of weather when you're not sure if it's raining—all of which he found in abundance while updating the South, West Country, and Bath and the Cotswolds chapters. He writes and revises other guidebooks and has penned his own guide to Devon and Cornwall.

Texan by birth and Anglophile at heart, Christi Daugherty has lived in (and written about) England for nearly a decade. Her Fodor's territory included Where to Stay in London, as well as Travel Smart England and chapters on areas from the Southeast to Yorkshire. She has written and edited guidebooks to Ireland and Paris.

Julius Honnor lives in London, but his Fodor's beat included rural spots in the Lake District, where he has observed chic new hotels and restaurants popping up alongside more traditional places. His work for other guidebooks has taken him around the globe.

Writer and editor Kate Hughes acquired a liking for the big city when she studied classical literature in Liverpool. Having since indulged her penchant for the country and landed gentry by getting a master's in garden history, she feels qualified to pass judgment on matters both urban and rural. She is responsible for the Thames Valley, Welsh Borders, and Lancashire and the Peaks chapters.

A Londoner since public transportation was cheap, Jack Jewers has directed films for the BBC and reviewed pubs for *Time Out;* he writes a popular blog called *The Red Pants of Justice.* He updated the East Anglia chapter as well as London neighborhoods including Kensington, Knightsbridge, and the South Bank.

Ellin Stein has written for publications on both sides of the Atlantic, including the *New York Times,* the *Times of London,* and *InStyle.* She has lived in London for 15 years and is married to a native. For this edition, Ellin updated the Westminster and Royal London, St. James's and Mayfair, Soho and Covent Garden, and Arts sections of the London chapter.

Always hoping to entertain—and surprise—his readers, Fodor's contributor Roger Thomas spends almost every minute tracking down the latest and the best of Wales. He has to: he's editor of *A View of Wales* magazine.

Christina Valhouli is the London-based editor of iTraveliShop.com. Her work has also appeared in the *New York Times, Forbes.com,* and *Town & Country.* She updated the London shopping section.

By day, Londoner and Shoalin kung fu enthusiast Alex Wijeratna works as a global hunger activist for ActionAid; by night he hunts down the capital's best food. With his English/Sri Lankan roots, Alex knows that the real flavor of London is found in its ethnic diversity. Alex updated the Where to Eat section of London.